Robert Kelly

Library of America, a nonprofit organization,
champions our nation's cultural heritage
by publishing America's greatest writing in
authoritative new editions and providing resources
for readers to explore this rich, living legacy.

PLYMOUTH COLONY

PLYMOUTH COLONY

*Narratives of English Settlement
and Native Resistance
from the* Mayflower *to King Philip's War*

Lisa Brooks and
Kelly Wisecup, *editors*

THE LIBRARY OF AMERICA

Published in the United States by Library of America.
Visit our website at www.loa.org.

*"Good News from New England" by Edward Winslow: A Scholarly
Edition.* Copyright © 2014 by the University of Massachusetts Press.
Reprinted by permission.

Experience Mayhew's Indian Converts: A Cultural Edition.
Copyright © 2008 by the University of Massachusetts Press. Selection
reprinted by permission.

Caleb Cheeshateaumuck letter to "Honoratissimi Benefactores,"
translation by Wolfgang Hochbruck and Beatrix Dudensing Reichel published
in *Early Native American Writing: New Critical Essays* copyright © 1996 by
Cambridge University Press. Translation by Lisa Brooks, Mark Schiefsky,
and Cassandra Hradril, published in *Our Beloved Kin: A New History of King
Philip's War* copyright © 2018 by Lisa Brooks.

"The Audacity of Assumption," by Linda Coombs copyright © 2021
by Linda Coombs.

Wôpanâak terms for leaders are used in the editorial matter of this volume
with the permission of the Wôpanâak Language Reclamation Project.

This paper exceeds the requirements of
ANSI/NISO Z39.48–1992 (Permanence of Paper).

Distributed to the trade in the United States
by Penguin Random House Inc.
and in Canada by Penguin Random House Canada Ltd.

Library of Congress Control Number: 2020941338

ISBN 978-1-59853-673-7

First Printing
The Library of America—337

Manufactured in the United States of America

Plymouth Colony:
Narratives of English Settlement and Native Resistance
from the Mayflower *to King Philip's War*
is published with support from

THE ACHELIS & BODMAN FOUNDATION

Contents

WRITINGS ABOUT THE BROADER WAMPANOAG AND MASSACHUSETT HOMELANDS

KING PHILIP'S WAR OR THE FIRST INDIAN WAR

WAMPANOAG CONTINUANCE

PLYMOUTH IN PATUXET:
A REORIENTATION

PATUXET, WAMPANOAG HOMELANDS

"Before there was Plymouth there was Patuxet," says Sôtyum Vernon Lopez of the Mashpee Wampanoag Tribe, the narrator of the *Our Story: 400 Years of Wampanoag History* multimedia exhibit. This traveling exhibit was created by Mashpee journalist and filmmaker Paula Peters in collaboration with other members of the Wampanoag nation for Plymouth 400. Plymouth is often mythologized as the origin place and origin story for the United States, and with the 2020 anniversary of the Plymouth colonists' settlement, these origin stories are once again being circulated and celebrated. However, as Sôtyum Lopez reminds us, Plymouth was "founded" in Patuxet, within the Wampanoag homelands, which included over sixty communities at the beginning of the seventeenth century.

The word "Wampanoag" refers to the land of the east, the place where the sun rises, and to the original people of this place, sometimes called "the Dawnland." This volume seeks to shift orientation, asking us to view transatlantic travel and colonization from the perspective of the Wampanoag coast and to reconsider the location(s) of where we are when we think of Plymouth, Massachusetts, and the United States. This means questioning the idea of providence, which the Plymouth settlers carried with them, and its relationship to a westward-moving "manifest destiny" for the United States as a nation. This process of understanding the complex history of Indigenous people and European colonization is ongoing; it is anything but settled. Like the Wampanoag traveling exhibit *Our Story*, this volume seeks to embed readers in that process of understanding, through deliberation and engagement with primary texts. The book includes a vast array of writings from multiple points of view, but also highlights Indigenous voices and perspectives, to give a multifaceted view of Plymouth

Colony *within* Wampanoag homelands, of New England as a place and concept constructed both in and in conflict with Native space.

The arrival of Plymouth settlers is but a small moment in the longer narrative of Wampanoag history and the history of the continent. Traditional stories contain knowledge of the glaciers that shaped this land, the great waters that flooded then receded, the lands that are now covered by ocean, and the great transformer beings, like Moshup and Squannit, who embody the forces that shaped them. Moshup taught Wampanoag people to hunt whales in their ocean home, to fish the oceans and rivers, to sustain themselves and the waters. Traditional ecological knowledge, geological knowledge, and collective historical memory are lodged in such stories, continuing in Wampanoag communities today. These narratives show that technological innovations like snowshoes and canoes enabled long-distance travel, on land, waterways, and sea, fostering trade and diplomacy. Indigenous stories also contain knowledge about the arrival of corn from the southwest, along with sustainable horticultural techniques and technologies.

Long before European settlers arrived, planting had been the domain of Indigenous women, and they derived power from their ability to feed their extended families and to sustain the fertility of the land over centuries. Oral traditions and annual ceremonies recognized the power of women and their relationships to the plants they cultivated as sacred. European voyagers, like Giovanni da Verrazzano, Samuel de Champlain, and John Smith, who traveled the Wampanoag coast in the sixteenth and early seventeenth centuries, testified to these abundant fields. They witnessed flourishing populations of diverse fish—including salmon, shad, sturgeon, striped bass, herring, and cod—in the ocean, tidal wetlands, and rivers, as well as shellfish, including lobster, so prevalent it could be scooped up by swimmers and used for bait as well as food. The voyagers also described open, parklike forests of oak, chestnut, and elm, which Indigenous men managed through selective cutting and controlled burns. This cultivated abundance, combined with a wide network of trade and distribution, enabled a balanced social and ecological environment. The arrival of English settlers brought more invasive agricultural technologies and techniques, such as plowing, monocrop planting, and animal husbandry, as well as logging of the massive indigenous oaks and pines. Combined with an economic system of commodification, colonization caused a major disruption of an agricultural and social system that had sustained communities for countless generations.

PLIMOTH PLANTATION

In his essay "Of Plantations" (1625), English philosopher and political leader Francis Bacon wrote, "I like a plantation in a pure soil; that is, where people are not displanted, to the end, to plant in others. For else it is rather an extirpation, than a plantation."* When a small group of English religious dissenters met with merchants in London and Southampton in 1619–20, they envisioned a plantation in "pure soil," where they would not face the taint of "popish corruption," of which they accused the Church of England. They also hoped to avoid corruption by a foreign culture, which they feared among the Dutch in Leiden, the Netherlands, where they had taken refuge.

The "plantation" these Englishmen envisioned held many connotations. The word itself transformed with the colonization of the Americas and the confiscation of lands in Ireland. When the group of dissenters (also called Separatists) and the "Adventurer" merchants who funded their expedition were granted a patent for a "plantation," the granters understood this to mean a colony, a settlement that would represent English dominion and domination, as well as a company of "planters" in a conquered place. The words "plantation" and "planters" also had religious connotations that the Separatists embraced. Just as they would use plows to sow seeds in the spring, God, in their view, would make them instruments of his will, cultivating a "pure" plantation in a place he had cleared. Planting a church and cultivating a community of planters was a major motivation for the Separatists who traveled to Patuxet, under the legal authorization of a patent for a "plantation" in "Virginia" and then "New England."

*Francis Bacon, *The Essays or Counsels Civil and Moral*, ed. Brian Vickers (New York: Oxford University Press, 1999), 78.

The Separatists' imagination of cleared ground in what John Smith called "New England" was only possible because by 1620, the Indigenous population had been devastated by epidemic disease. The dissenters knew of English voyager Thomas Dermer's recent report that the coastal land they were sailing toward, "not long since populous," was now "utterly void" of inhabitants. When Samuel de Champlain had traveled the Wampanoag coast, fifteen years before the English Separatists, his French sponsors were considering this area as a site for a trading settlement, noting the bounty of the land. However, witnessing the large Indigenous population, and noting the potential for conflict, Champlain and his sponsors decided that "Port St. Louis," their name for Patuxet, was not a suitable location. Only after the epidemics of 1616–19 did settlement seem possible. Although astounding numbers of Indigenous people died of the sweeping illnesses carried by European merchants, traders, and fishermen, many survivors moved inland, often joining other kin; however, these towns were unseen by European sailors, who stuck mainly to the shore. Thus, Dermer reported that the abundant fields, witnessed by Champlain and Smith, had been cleared, offering the possibility to his fellow Englishmen of planting in "pure soil."

The Separatists who arrived in Patuxet in November 1620 envisioned a plantation in the midst of this fertile, unobstructed ground, carrying domesticated animals and grains on their ship. Although they had originally planned to voyage farther south, they landed in Wampanoag territory, first at Nauset on Cape Cod, and then at the cove that John Smith had named "Plimouth," after a southern port in England. They arrived at a place of death and desolation, at the beginning of the winter season, and the majority of them remained aboard their ship through the first several months, barely touching ground. Wampanoag people who had survived the first epidemic waves observed them at a distance.

Many English writers attributed the survival of the settlers to God, and regarded the clearing of land by disease as divine intervention. Yet, the epidemic diseases that Native people faced originated in Europe, and many arose from and spread through close contact with domesticated animals and the conditions of densely settled urban spaces. Domestication itself arose from the need and desire to have greater control over animals as labor and food sources. Native people had not developed immunities to these diseases, because these diseases did not exist on the North American continent, and European carriers were largely asymptomatic, mildly symptomatic, or harbored disease in a dormant state. Native people had also not domesticated animals. While some historians argue that animals like deer and moose could not be domesticated, oral traditional narratives suggest that Native people chose not to contain beings they regarded as animate kin, with whom they shared reciprocal relationships. Thus, along with their poultry, pigs, and wheat, settlers also carried radical new ideas about both animals and plants, including the use of livestock, and a sense of divine purpose to their domestication of the land.

The settlers at Patuxet would never have been able to sustain a plantation or pay their debts to their English financial backers if they had not learned how, when, and where to plant unfamiliar crops from Wampanoag hosts. Native women cultivated extensive communal fields, wide mounds of corn, beans, squash, pumpkins, sunchokes, and sunflowers, companion plants known as mothers and sisters that nourished each other and the soil. Recognized also as givers of life, Native women practiced low till, shifting agriculture that enabled them to sustain soil health and productivity, thus giving back to the mother-land. The seemingly "pure" soil and abundant fields which impressed European voyagers were made possible by Indigenous women's knowledge and labor. English planters learned how to plant corn, seeded differently than their crops of wheat, rye, and barley, from Tisquantum, a Wampanoag man from Patuxet who had learned the English language and customs when he was captured and taken to Europe. By the time Tisquantum returned to his homeland in 1619, he faced the loss of his entire town from disease, but he retained his relationships to Wampanoags in other places. The Wampanoag leader Ousamequin of Pokanoket, known also by his title Massasoit ("great or supreme leader"), sent Tisquantum to serve as a translator, diplomat, and guide for the English people who landed at Patuxet. Without such guides and teachers, it is doubtful Plymouth's plantation would have survived.

Many of those Separatists who arrived in 1620 were yeoman

planters and artisans who benefitted from the dissolution of the feudal system and the development of the textile industry, and they carried a commitment to independence in their planting and property. During the first years of Plymouth plantation, the English settlers agreed to contribute their harvest to a communal holding, to be distributed among them, and held most of their livestock in common. This was very similar to the way that Indigenous communities gathered and distributed corn and other resources, ensuring that everyone was fed equally. However, within just a few years, according to William Bradford, some men, particularly those "yong-men" who "were most able and fitte for labour," lamented "that they should spend their time and streingth to worke for other mens wives and children, with out any recompense." They believed it was unjust that the strong man "had no more" in the "devission of victails and cloaths" than "he that was weake."* From the spring of 1623 onward, individual male-led households cultivated their own individual fields, on their own lots, and retained their harvest to consume and sell. Each man harnessed his own draught animal and plough to prepare and plant his field. Corn, by that time, was already being transformed from sacred sustenance to a commodity, which the Plymouth leaders carried as far as Wabanaki territory on the Kennebec to trade for furs, and in turn, enabled them to begin to distribute profits to the Adventurers who funded their plantation.

The colonial venture of Plymouth plantation arose from the merging of the interests of King James I, who sought to extend English dominion and increase his kingdom's wealth; the interests of merchant "Adventurers," including the Plymouth Company (and its successor, the Council of New England), who sought to profit from the extraction of resources like fish and furs; and the interests of the "planters," who sought both sustainable profits and a sustainable Separatist church. This, they believed, was not possible in England. The Separatists were part of a small, radical fringe of the English Protestant Reformation, "dissenters" who believed that the Church of England had failed to fully reform. They believed the Church was much too inclusive, allowing all Englishmen to take part in the

---

*William Bradford, *Of Plimoth Plantation*, p. 357 in this volume.

sacrament and to be members of the Church, and corrupted by "popish" idolatry, such as adornment in worship, prayer books, and signs of the cross.* As Calvinists, the Separatists believed that all people were born in sin, but that some were predestined to be saved by grace alone, as opposed to good works. God had seen all, and had spared a select few godly people from damnation. Salvation was not a course that a person could choose to follow. Nor could salvation be earned through good works or repentance from sin. Rather, a person could only try to discern, through prayer, reading the Bible, and communion with other saints, including the right ministers, whether they were among the spared "saints." Both England and the Netherlands, which was generally more tolerant of dissenters, were rife with heated, and sometimes violent and repressive, arguments about the most minute details of doctrine.

However, the Separatists were the "hotter sort of Protestant."† Rather than advocating further reformation, as most Puritan dissenters did, Separatists sought a separation from the Church of England, whose supreme governor was the king. Therefore, Separatists posed a special threat not only to the Church, but to royal dominion. When this particular group of Separatists sought to remove from their homes in Leiden, to emigrate to "Virginia," they had to pledge their loyalty to the King. Moreover, when they made an agreement with their Wampanoag hosts, they took it upon themselves to pledge their hosts' loyalty to the English king, as well. These were all strategic moves, on their part, to protect their vision of a plantation as a Separatist community, which would have liberty to practice a particular, precise form of Protestant Christianity, but would also have liberty to govern its affairs. The planters sought to separate themselves, to the extent possible and allowable under English law, from the religious, political, and cultural influence of their fellow Englishmen and Europeans, as well as from the Wampanoag people in whose country they landed. However, they also aspired to serve as a model for true

---

*John G. Turner, *They Knew They Were Pilgrims: Plymouth Colony and the Contest for American Liberty* (New Haven: Yale University Press, 2020), 137.
†Andrew Lipman, *The Saltwater Frontier: Indians and the Contest for the American Coast* (New Haven: Yale University Press, 2015), 50.

religious reformation. As historian Andrew Lipman has noted, "many of these 'hotter sort of Protestant' would take a special interest in colonial projects, seeing them as social laboratories where a select population could set a more godly example for their respective home countries."*

ENCOUNTER AND DIPLOMACY

Americans often associate Plymouth with diplomacy, noting the "friendship" between colonists and Native Americans, often evoked as "the first Thanksgiving." The popular myth of Plymouth as a founding place for the United States has its own origins in nineteenth-century nationalism, connected to anti-immigrant sentiments and the desire for union in the wake of the Civil War. After Abraham Lincoln declared a national day of Thanksgiving in 1863, this myth slowly aligned with Thanksgiving celebrations, with the association between Thanksgiving and "Pilgrim" imagery taking firm shape by the end of the nineteenth century. However, giving thanks has always been a crucial aspect of Wampanoag culture and Indigenous ceremony, and the exchange of food and gifts occurred throughout the year in seasonal festivals, including harvest. Sôtyumâak (male leaders), like Ousamequin, and Sôkushqâak (female leaders) were respected for their ability to gather and distribute the foods, like corn and beans, and carry the symbols of alliance and exchange, like wampum strings and belts, across communities. Ousamequin's role as a respected diplomat meant he was an apt leader for making the familiar trip to Patuxet to welcome and assess the newcomers who had arrived in their territory, and who, unlike the many Europeans who had come in the decades before, intended to stay.

Expanding our view from 1620, from Plymouth Colony, and from the colonists' predicaments allows us to see what might seem familiar moments of "encounter" between two groups as instead moments of diplomacy. Indigenous diplomats served as linguistic and cultural translators, and as speakers and messengers who transmitted settler statements and their own impressions back to their communities and within wide-ranging networks of kinship. A Wabanaki visitor to Wampanoag

*Lipman, *Saltwater Frontier*, 50.

country named Samoset was the first to initiate diplomacy with the settlers at Patuxet, greeting them with a "welcome," in English. He served as the first interpreter between them and Ousamequin and other Wampanoag counselors in the spring of 1621. Thus, this initial meeting arose from Wabanaki-Wampanoag diplomacy and relationships, as well as English-Wampanoag encounters.

In the interior, beyond the Separatists' fledgling coastal settlement, Indigenous people deliberated in councils, making decisions about how to incorporate these newcomers into their systems of trade and diplomacy, whether and how to allocate resources for struggling newcomers, and, over time, how to respond to colonists' violence, hunger, and desire to expand onto Native lands. Leaders made these decisions by using their knowledge of Europeans, gathered from long experience with European sailors who had traveled to fish and trade along the coast and by Indigenous people who had been captured and traveled to England, then returned.

TRANSATLANTIC TRAVELERS AND CAPTIVITY

Turning from Plymouth and 1620 as origin points in a story about America brings into view Wampanoag people as diplomats and transatlantic travelers already acquainted with Europeans. Numerous Wampanoag and Wabanaki men were captured and taken across the Atlantic Ocean well before the Separatists sailed west from England, while others, like Samoset, had been trading with European visitors to their homelands for decades. In comparison, only one *Mayflower* passenger had set foot on the North American continent: Stephen Hopkins, who had spent some time in Jamestown, in Virginia. Native men like Tisquantum had already been taken to Europe and returned home, negotiating what to say in response to colonists' questions about commodities in their homelands and considering what colonists' presence in the northeast might mean for Native communities.

Taken as captives by English sailors, these Native men lived in London and other port cities, usually near or in the homes of colonial promoters and speculators. Some did not survive the ocean voyage, while others never made it home, sold into slavery or dying of diseases to which they had no immunity. Their captivities lasted for periods of several months and in some cases several years, and survivors learned English and answered questions from speculators eager to imagine the northeast as a land rich in commodities for extraction, including fish, fur, timber, and land for settlement. In 1611, Epenow, a Sôtyum from Noepe (Martha's Vineyard), was taken to London as a captive of Captain Edward Harlow, where the colonial promoter and speculator Ferdinando Gorges hoped that Epenow would provide firsthand information about the northeast and the resources Gorges hoped to extract, as well as possible locations for settlement and trade. As Gorges proclaimed, "the Natives . . . must be acknowledged the meanes under God of . . . giving life to all our Plantations."* Gorges employed a Wabanaki captive, Sassacomoit, taken by Weymouth in 1605, to help teach Epenow English; they lived in Gorges's home with several other Wabanaki and Wampanoag captives. Gorges wrote that Epenow "learned so much *English* as to bid those that wondred at him, welcome, welcome."† Gorges sent Sassacomoit and several other Wabanaki men back to their homelands on English ships, where they provided the geographic and social knowledge that enabled English men to navigate unfamiliar places. The short-lived Popham Colony (1607–8) on the Kennebec River resulted in part from the application of this newfound knowledge. Indeed, the "Plymouth Company" (named for the English port that Gorges had commanded) was formed by men who sought to capitalize on the knowledge of Wabanaki captive-guides to build an English settlement on the Kennebec River, and later, after the capture of Epenow and his relations, on the Wampanoag coast. Tisquantum—now famous for acting as the Plymouth colonists' translator—does not enter the story in 1620 but rather in 1614, when he was captured, along with twenty other Wampanoag men. Colonial reports suggest that Tisquantum and the other Wampanoag men were taken to England after their captors failed to sell the men as slaves in Spain. Wampanoag people still remembered and grieved the loss of these family members when Plymouth

---

*Ferdinando Gorges, *A Briefe Narration of the Original Undertaking of the Advancement of Plantations into the Parts of America*, p. 96 in this volume.
†Ferdinando Gorges, *A Briefe Narration*, p. 103 in this volume.

colonists met them six or seven years later, for the colonists observed that a Wampanoag mother they met in the summer of 1621 in Cummaquid "could not behold us without breaking forth into great passion, weeping and crying excessively" at the memory of losing three sons to English captors.* While the Plymouth colonists attempted to assure her that they would not behave in a similar way, the Wampanoag mother's grief and the lasting memory of English violence created a precarious ground for diplomacy and settlement.

Tisquantum, Epenow, and the other Wampanoag men taken captive were not helpless victims, for they actively employed their bilingual knowledge to obtain information about colonists' motivations and to take that information home, where it informed Wampanoag leaders' decisions about how to interact with and establish diplomatic relations with Plymouth colonists. Epenow, for example, learned not just the English word "welcome" but enough words to understand Gorges's prospective plans for the northeast. Epenow informed Gorges of "commodities" the colonists might find, and after having convinced Gorges to send a ship back to Noepe, Epenow planned and executed his own escape, negotiating with Wampanoag men who returned the next day to attack the ship and free him. Epenow's escape plan, made on Gorges's ship and literally under the noses of English colonists, shows how English colonists' ignorance of the Wôpanâak language limited their understanding and ability to engage in diplomatic relations with Wampanoag people that would prove essential to Plymouth. It also shows Epenow's navigational knowledge of the ocean that was part of his homeland and his ability to strategically navigate social relationships in order to escape the holds that his captors placed upon him.

CONFLICT AND GOVERNANCE

Wabanaki oral tradition describes the arrival of European ships as initiating a fog throughout the land, so that people could not see beyond what lay immediately in front of them. This describes the state of obfuscation and confusion that came with

---

*A Relation or Journall of the beginning and proceedings of the English Plantation settled at Plimouth in New England, p. 161 in this volume.

colonization. Disease created unimaginable grief and loss, generating conflict. Samuel de Champlain famously introduced guns into Indigenous warfare, affecting not only intertribal diplomacy but relationships with animals that Native men hunted. Warfare in the Dawnland was traditionally small-scale and temporary, with swift strategic strikes. However, the disruptions caused by disease, the introduction of firearms, and the transformations of the fur trade fostered a kind of chaos that traditional diplomatic methods could not always resolve, particularly when communities lost many of their most effective political and spiritual leaders during the epidemics.

The voyages of Europeans thus initiated both diplomacy and conflict. Many voyagers described the welcomes and the gifts they received from Wabanaki and Wampanoag hosts, part of the common practice of Indigenous diplomacy and hospitality. Europeans did not always comprehend the vital role of reciprocal gift-giving in Indigenous networks and often sought, following common practices of a capitalist economic system, to retain individual property and/or gain trade goods and profit through deceptive schemes. Conflicts arose when visitors took more than had been offered, or complained that Native people "stole" goods that visitors carried with them. For example, Champlain reported a skirmish that occurred in Wampanoag territory when a Wampanoag man took a kettle that one of his sailors was using to gather water, resulting in the death of one of his men and a volley of shot sent out among the Wampanoag party. The Plymouth settlers experienced a similar conflict on their first arrival in Wampanoag territory on Cape Cod, where they took corn and violated graves, maintaining an armed defense, and then experienced their first taste of Indigenous guerilla warfare, a volley of arrows shot by a group of Wampanoag men, who retreated quickly into the trees.

To secure their safety and security, the Plymouth colonists maintained their arms, but they also pursued their own forms of diplomacy to ensure their settlement did not follow the course of the Popham Colony. In order to fulfill the demands of their merchant sponsors, they were compelled to accept "strangers" among them when they sailed from England, men who were not part of their Separatist congregation. This was already a source of conflict as they sailed toward the Wampanoag coast.

When they landed at Cape Cod, beyond the jurisdiction of Jamestown and the Virginia Company of London, they had no legal charter or patent that would direct their governance and no colonial government to oversee order among them. Because of their precarious situation and the urgent need for an agreement regarding administration, they created the Mayflower Compact on November 11, 1620, on board the ship. In it, they affirmed their fidelity to both King James and the Christian God, but they also formed what William Bradford called "a covenant" and "civil body politic" among themselves, with John Carver chosen as their first governor. This agreement empowered Separatist leaders, including Carver, Bradford, Edward Winslow and Isaac Allerton, to govern the colony. Before they left England, the Separatists had also recruited Miles Standish, a veteran of the Dutch wars, to serve as their military leader. Soon after, they would acquire a patent for their "plantation" that would provide the legal foundation for their formation of this "government" of their colony within the newly named "country of New England." This patent was granted by the authority of a newly formed joint stock company, the Council for New England, led by Ferdinando Gorges.

In the first winter, the settlers lost about half of their population to starvation and disease, including common ailments like pneumonia and scurvy, as they were isolated and both poorly equipped and adapted to this cold winter climate. Miles Standish advocated that they avoid contact with Native people, although they pilfered stored Indigenous food. Wampanoag people observed these newcomers at a distance until the spring of 1621, when Samoset and Tisquantum served as intermediaries to initiate diplomatic relations between Wampanoag leaders and the English newcomers. Ousamequin and his counselors sought to draw the settlers into Indigenous protocols, while the settlers sought terms that reflected an English treaty with a foreign nation. Their agreements created the terms of alliance, not only between the settlers at Patuxet and Ousamequin's community, but between Massasoit and the English king, who "would esteem of him as his friend and ally." Nathaniel Morton, Bradford's nephew, secretary of Plymouth Colony, and author of the colonial history *New England's Memorial*, would later claim that Massasoit thus "acknowledged himself content to become the Subject" of King James, but this is an unlikely scenario. It is likely true, however, that the two groups made an agreement to avoid conflict with each other, and that the colonists agreed to a form of alliance. This meant that Ousamequin would allow the colonists to remain at Patuxet and provide them with the knowledge necessary to survival, and it included a commitment to communication and diplomacy, which would be facilitated by Tisquantum and the Wampanoag diplomat Hobbomock, who remained among the settlers.

Through this agreement, the Wampanoags also acquired an ally that would bolster their defense against the neighboring Narragansetts, who had been largely spared by the epidemic diseases. In the midst of this chaos and loss, the political influence of the Narragansetts had expanded, and according to both English and Wampanoag sources, they posed a threat to the balance of power in the region. The early pact of mutual defense between Plymouth settlers and Wampanoag people also served to protect the colony, when it was most vulnerable, years before the arrival of other English colonists in places like Massachusetts Bay and Connecticut. This practice of alliance-making continued throughout the seventeenth century, as other colonies formed: the Mohegan leader Uncas sought military assistance from Connecticut Colony, which was organized in 1636, and joined forces with them against the neighboring Pequots, while some Nipmuc communities inland and Massachusett and Patucket leaders on the coast provided and sought protection from Massachusetts Bay Colony as its influence grew. The Narragansetts forged new alliances as they pursued trade with the Dutch colonies to the west and extended diplomacy to the colony of Rhode Island, in 1636, allowing settlements to be built in their territory by settlers, led by Roger Williams, who had been banished by Massachusetts Bay.

However, as Ousamequin would later make clear, the agreement with Plymouth Colony leaders did not give them the right to settle in other Wampanoag leaders' territories, including the homeland of Pocasset, led by the Sôtyum Conbitant, who was more distrustful of the newcomers. Ousamequin made agreements that allowed Plymouth colonists to build settlements within his territory of Pokanoket, but he also affirmed the authority of Conbitant's daughter and successor, Weetamoo, as

Sôkushqâ and the rightful leader in Pocasset, and recognized neighboring Sôtyumâak and Sôkushqâak, like Tuspaquin of Nemasket (who married Ousamequin's daughter Amie) and Awashonks of Sakonnet, as leaders in their territories. Indeed, as he affirmed, Ousamequin was also bound by agreements with them through kinship and alliance. Although the settlers wished to attribute to Massasoit the power of a king, he was one leader among many, responsible for maintaining secure, reciprocal relations with many communities.

Plymouth colonists demonstrated their understanding of Ousamequin's role as such a leader in the spring of 1623. Hearing news that Ousamequin was ill, they followed Wampanoag protocols by sending Edward Winslow to Ousamequin's town at Sowams to pay respects and affirm their relationship. Winslow explained that it was a "commendable manner of the Indians when any (especially of note) are dangerously sick, for all that profess friendship to them, to visit them in their extremity, either in their persons, or else to send some acceptable persons to them." When Winslow arrived at Sowams, he found so many people present to "profess friendship" that he had trouble finding space in Ousamaquin's house. Winslow also observed the diplomatic relations among Wampanoag communities as he traveled to Sowams. At Mattapoisett, he was hosted by a woman he describes only as a "squa sachem" (a corruption of Sôkushqâ) and Conbitant's wife—but who was a leader in her own right and the mother of Weetamoo and Wootonakanuske, who themselves would later form marriage alliances with Ousamequin's sons, Wamsutta and Metacom. Winslow also saw these relations in practice as he learned from Ousamequin that Massachusett emissaries were seeking to convince their relations in Wampanoag communities to the south to join them in a plan to address problems caused by the colonists at Wessagusset, the small colony established in 1622 and financed by the Plymouth colonists' investor Thomas Weston. Wessagusset colonists had been stealing Massachusett corn, and the colony's leaders refused to contain their men. When Ousamequin told Winslow and Hobbomock of the Massachusett plan, he was acting as a leader among multiple parties, seeking to maintain relations with Plymouth and with other related communities.

Winslow's observations reflect the responsibilities that Indigenous leaders had to provide for their communities and to use warfare carefully to resolve conflict. Sôtyumâak and Sôkushqâak (the titles of traditional male and female leaders), along with ahtasuhkawâak (counselors), held the responsibility of distributing resources, within their own communities and to neighboring nations, and ameliorating conflicts through diplomatic protocols, ceremonies, and councils. Wampanoag Sôtyumâak and Sôkushqâak also relied on pniesesak, who were counselor-warriors who could navigate the difficult terrain of conflict. Plymouth leader Edward Winslow acknowledged that "the *Pnieses* are men of great courage and wisdom," among the "*Sachims* Council," who would "endure most hardness, and yet are more discreet, courteous, and humane in their carriages than any amongst them." Warfare could be used as a strategic tool, waged to reset an imbalance in power or resources between communities or to address a great wrong. Or, it could come like a storm, a temporary state of conflict and chaos that would be resolved by diplomatic protocols.

In the case of the conflict at Wessagusset between Massachusett and English men, it is important to recognize that the violence was exacerbated by the language barrier and the great potential for miscommunication. For example, Miles Standish was valued by the colonists not only for his military experience but also because he was regarded by Winslow as "the best Linguist amongst us." Still, when the settlers tried to negotiate with the Massachusett on their own, Winslow noted that Standish "could not gather any thing" (because he could not understand the language). This was a dangerous circumstance that threatened diplomatic relations. Winslow recognized the importance of clear communication in Plymouth's alliance with Ousamequin, and when he traveled to meet with Ousamequin at Sowams, he traveled with a Wampanoag interpreter in order to consult with Ousamequin about their burgeoning conflict with the Massachusett people to the north.

PLYMOUTH COURT
AND THE UNITED COLONIES

Plymouth settlers adopted the form of a General Court early on to govern their colony, including an annual meeting in March

1623 to consider how to respond to the rumors involving Massachusett people to the north. At that court, their annual election, they re-elected William Bradford as governor—he had served in that role since the death of John Carver in 1621—and elected Isaac Allerton as first Assistant. At that time, eligible voters consisted of the male passengers who had arrived on the early ships like the *Mayflower* and who were shareholders in the joint-stock company on which the settlement rested. This included both the Separatists and the "Adventurers" who traveled with them. In 1636, the membership of the General Court solidified to include all the "freemen of the corporation"; sixty-eight men qualified as "freemen" in 1633, according to historian John Turner, who notes that "the percentage of men who were freemen declined as the years passed and the colony's population grew."*

As settlement expanded, however, towns began to select "deputies," freemen who attended the General Court as representatives of their towns. The freemen of the colony annually elected the governor and six or seven Assistants, nearly always elite Separatists like Edward Winslow, Isaac Allerton, and Thomas Prence. Although the freemen voted every year, they generally selected the same men to serve continually, with some variation in office. The settlers also tended to follow patrilineal inheritance, with the next generation of sons serving on the "Court of Assistants," including William Bradford, Jr., Constant Southworth (Bradford's stepson), and Josiah Winslow. The Court of Assistants resolved conflicts, decided disputes, disciplined violators, and granted land, while only the General Court as a whole could vote on laws and raise taxes. As was the case in England, women did not participate in the Court or in any form of governance. This is notable only because of the difference from Indigenous governance in the region. As the English captive Mary Rowlandson noted, both women and men participated in Indigenous councils, which she likened to the General Court, and both could hold leadership positions. Even Rowlandson was allowed to participate in council, when she lived among the Wampanoag, Nipmuc, Narragansett, and Sokoki people who gathered in the Connecticut River Valley

*Turner, *They Knew They Were Pilgrims*, 179–180.

and at Mount Wachusett in the spring of 1676. Women and men sometimes gathered separately, but they also joined together in council and could voice their experiences and insights. Native leaders were often responsible for bringing the voice of the whole to neighboring communities, including to the Plymouth Court.

Although the Court was established to govern settlers in the colony, it also became the place that Indigenous people were compelled to travel to in order to council with the settlers and to seek resolution of conflicts between the communities. Plymouth Colony leaders likewise used the Court to assert jurisdiction and rule over Wampanoag lands and people. Wampanoag people were often affected by decisions made in their absence by the Plymouth Court, including land grants to colonists. The complaints of Wampanoag leaders, including Wamsutta, Weetamoo, and Metacom, about encroachments by settlers and their cattle on Wampanoag communities' subsistence lands appear frequently in the records of the Plymouth Court.

English settlers allowed their cattle to range freely, and often sought fallow fields and marshes to graze their livestock. However, livestock interfered directly with the ability of Native women to plant their fields and gather both shellfish and wetland plants for food, medicine, ceremony, and material culture such as baskets, mats, bags, and other artistic and utilitarian materials. Pigs rooted out the clam banks and acted aggressively toward humans who tried to drive them off. Wandering cattle and hogs trampled corn and companion plants in women's fields. Wampanoag Sôtyumâak and Sôkushqâak advocated for the men on the Plymouth Court to rein in colonists and cattle who were encroaching on Wampanoag lands, as part of the diplomatic agreement between them. But the Court advised the Wampanoags to fence in their corn and report offending livestock rather than require settlers to contain their animals. As the settler population increased, the Court increasingly expanded its jurisdiction, including the imposition of colonial laws on Wampanoag people and the imposition of colonial land grants and agricultural practices on Indigenous places of sustenance. For many Indigenous people, the Court became a space of containment and dispossession rather than a place where they might seek conflict resolution.

As early as 1643, the neighboring Narragansett leader Mian-tonomi recognized the dire political and environmental chal-lenges that Indigenous people across the region faced. In a speech to the neighboring Montauks (on Long Island), he said:

For so are we all Indians as the English are, and say brother to one another; so must we be one as they are, otherwise we shall all gone shortly, for you know our fathers had plenty of deer and skins, our plains were full of deer, as also our woods, and of turkies, and our coves full of fish and fowl. But these English having gotten our land, they with scythes cut down the grass, and with axes fell the trees; their cows and horses eat the grass, and their hogs spoil our·clam banks, and we shall all be starved; therefore it is best for you to do as we, for we are all the Sachems from east to west, both Moquakues and Mohauks joining with us, and we are all resolved to fall upon them all, at one appointed day.*

This was the first recorded articulation, by an Indigenous leader in New England, of the idea of "Indian" unity. The con-tinent was diverse, composed of many different Native nations, who were connected to each other through kinship and trade, but not all the same. However, in the face of resource depletion from the Muhheakunuk or Hudson River to the Wampanoag coast, Miantonomi advocated for unity, the recognition of a shared identity, in relation to and in opposition to the English. His words would resonate for generations to come, even though his movement was short-lived. Hearing reports, from both Dutch settlers and fellow English colonists, of Miantonomi's attempt to build alliances, colonial leaders in New England feared the prospect of an Indian confederation and sought to contain the Narragansett leader. Miantonomi's organizing led to colonists' own unification. In the very first meeting of "the United Colonies" of New England, colonial governors called for an organized opposition against the Narragansett leader.

---

*"Lieft Lion Gardener, His Relation of the Pequot Warres," *Collections of the Massachusetts Historical Society*, 3rd ser., 3:154. Gardiner arrived in Con-necticut in 1633 or 1634, and built a fort at the mouth of Kwinitekw, the Connecticut River; he wrote this account in 1660 from his papers, for friends. The Massachusetts Historical Society was given the original manuscript along with a copy made by Connecticut governor Jonathan Trumbull.

Puritan settlers had arrived in Massachusetts Bay in 1630 with a solid English legal footing through their own charter. Connecticut Colony was formed out of several small settlements, following Dutch and English forts and posts, including a fur-trading post built by Plymouth colonists on the Connecticut River that was eventually abandoned. Massachusetts Bay Puritans also traveled to the Connecticut River, and were part of the body that formed the Connecticut Colony in 1636. One of their first acts was to declare war on the neighboring Pequots. Yet another group of Puritans formed the New Haven Colony in 1638. These four colonies then formed the United Colonies in 1643.

By that time, Connecticut had already forged an alliance with the Mohegan leader Uncas, who had broken with his Pequot relations to form a separate community. He gathered together his Mohegan kin and fiercely protected them, reclaiming their ancient name, as Wolf clan of the Lenape (Delaware) Nation. Although Miantonomi sought to draw Uncas into alliance, Uncas resisted, because of both his distrust of his rival and his commitment to the political relationship he had formed with the newcomers in the Connecticut Colony. While unifying themselves, the United Colonies stirred intertribal conflicts to their own benefit. When they captured Miantonomi, they insisted that Uncas be his executioner. Although the Wampanoags largely stayed out of this conflict, it bolstered the presence and power of the United Colonies in their homelands.

Rhode Island, a colony first established by Roger Williams and other Separatists who were banished from Massachusetts Bay, was not invited into the United Colonies. For some years, Rhode Island's existence rested on their diplomatic agreements with both the neighboring Wampanoags and the Narragansett leaders, in whose homelands they built their settlements. Many disputes arose between Plymouth and Rhode Island, as both sought to expand into Wampanoag territory. Likewise, many settlers in the United Colonies sought land in fertile Narragansett territory, not only to plant but to graze cattle for the expanding colonial economy. Rhode Island secured a royal charter in 1663, causing great concern to Plymouth Colony, which was not granted a charter when they requested one in 1665. Instead a Royal Commission, sent by the newly restored

King Charles II to New England in 1664–65, suggested sending a royal governor to oversee Plymouth, a solution that Plymouth men resisted.

Thus Plymouth's legal status, especially in relationship to
adjacent colonies, remained precarious through the second half
of the seventeenth century, even as it was bolstered through
membership in the United Colonies. The Separatists continued
to govern themselves through the Plymouth Court, but they
faced increasing challenges from other colonies, from newcomers who arrived from England, and from their mother country.
Following the English Civil Wars (1642–51) and the restoration
of the monarchy (and Anglican power in England) in 1660,
Charles II sought to resolve the burgeoning conflicts among
the New England colonies, in part so that they could better
serve royal interests. In the wake of the Royal Commission's
1665 visit, the Plymouth Separatists sought to bolster their
standing as a colony. They affirmed their preemptive right to
land in Wampanoag territory, based on their patent and their
original agreement with Ousamequin, and sought to confirm
their deeds and their rights of inheritance.

At this time, a new generation of "first born sons" came
into power on the Court of Assistants. Josiah Winslow became
governor in 1673, succeeding original settler Thomas Prence
who had served from 1657 until his death, but he was active in
colonial leadership and expansion long before he was governor.
The firstborn sons believed they had a right, as the sons of the
first English planters at Plymouth, to both land and power, as
their inheritance and divine appropriation. The legal bounds
of Plymouth's colonial claim rested on the geographic bounds
of the Wampanoag country. Wampanoag leaders faced new
colonial strategies to acquire land as this second generation of
English settlers came to power and immigrants continued to
arrive on their shores. These included the threat of imprisonment for debt and other English "crimes," such as damage to
livestock, even as subsistence was increasingly threatened by
deforestation, settler expansion, and livestock. In the 1660s,
the Plymouth men compelled Ousamequin's son and successor,
Metacom, or Philip, to sign a series of deeds confirming and
further extending their rights to numerous large tracts of land
in Wampanoag territory. These agreements took place after the

suspicious death of Metacom's brother, the Sôtyum Wamsutta, who was taken by force to Plymouth and died on the journey homeward.

Even as they confirmed and extended earlier deeds, Plymouth leaders also sought to expand their reach outward toward the west, north, and south, into Weetamoo's territory of Pocasset, Tuspaquin and Amie's territory of Nemasket, Awashonks's territory of Sakonnet, as well as expanding settlements on Cape Cod. In 1671, the Plymouth leaders called Metacom, and several other Wampanoag leaders, including Awashonks, to councils where they insisted, by threat of force, that they sign acts of submission, not only for themselves but for their people. Through these written forms, the Plymouth men sought to document their jurisdiction, not only over Wampanoag people and land, but also against other colonial competitors, such as Massachusetts Bay and Rhode Island settlers. Not surprisingly, this aggressive expansion created conflicts with numerous Wampanoag leaders and their communities, who, like Miantonomi, increasingly saw their English neighbors directly threatening their subsistence and their responsibility to sustain their kin. In the midst of this rising conflict, leaders like Metacom and Weetamoo continued to pursue diplomatic solutions, including seeking out the assistance of Rhode Island leader John Easton, the Quaker lieutenant governor, to serve as a mediator with Plymouth.

KING PHILIP'S WAR AND THE END OF PLYMOUTH COLONY

In the spring of 1675, Governor Josiah Winslow and the Plymouth Court once more demanded that Philip come to Court, after the controversial execution of three of his counselors for the crime of murder in the death of Massachusett interpreter and informant John Sassamon. Metacom did not oblige them, but instead gathered his relations to him. Rumors circulated that the Plymouth men sought to capture Metacom and, likewise, that the Wampanoags were conspiring against the English. Winslow authorized a considerable force, backed by Massachusetts Bay Colony militia, to march toward Metacom's stronghold of Montaup, one of the only remaining places in Pokanoket territory that had not been overtaken by colonial settlement. Winslow anticipated the swift capture or defeat of Philip and the acquisition of Montaup. He did not anticipate that Metacom and his kin would escape their grasp and take refuge with Weetamoo, who took them in and sheltered her relations deep in the cedar swamps of Pocasset. Winslow also did not anticipate that the quick strikes and ambushes of Wampanoag protectors would force Plymouth men to hole up in their garrisons before they could even attempt their planned capture of Metacom.

The "Indian War," later named "the First Indian War" and then "King Philip's War," spiraled into chaos in the summer and fall of 1675, with intense violence spreading throughout the land, from the Wampanoag and Wabanaki coast to the Connecticut River Valley, until a treaty finally ended the war in 1677. Plymouth called on the United Colonies for support, and Rhode Island colonists felt obliged to join with fellow Englishmen. Massachusetts Bay and Connecticut colonists called on their own alliances with neighboring Indigenous communities, recruiting Massachusett, Nipmuc, and Mohegan scouts. Other Nipmuc leaders provided sanctuary to Metacom, Weetamoo, and their relations, and struck at settlements that encroached upon their homelands in the interior. Leaders in Narragansett country and Wabanaki communities in the Connecticut River Valley and along the northeastern coast also provided refuge to Wampanoag kin and allies during the war, and led raids on colonial settlements in their territories. Some Wampanoag people survived by remaining in northern sanctuaries, but others returned to their homelands. Many Wampanoag people were killed, imprisoned, or sent into slavery in the summer of 1676 by United Colonies forces, who pursued total conquest. Although many Wampanoag and Narragansett leaders, including both Metacom and Weetamoo, were killed that summer, the resistance continued in Wabanaki territory to the north. The Treaty of Pemaquid, in 1677, was negotiated through the diplomacy of Wabanaki leaders on the Kennebec and New York Colony governor Edmund Andros. This was followed by the Treaty of Casco Bay in 1678, in which Wabanaki leaders required the pledge of an annual acknowledgment, or contribution from their harvest, from English settlers who wished to return to the northern coastal settlements they had abandoned during the war. Although Plymouth Colony claimed Metacom's Montaup, Weetamoo's Pocasset, and other Wampanoag homelands by conquest after the war, the conflict also devastated the structures of the colony. Massachusetts Bay gained power through the war and solidified its leadership role in the United Colonies. Josiah Winslow continued to advocate for a charter for Plymouth, but even his diplomacy with his English relations failed. When he tried to send trophies from the war, along with a narrative that advocated that the recent conflict with Philip was a just war, to King James II, his own brother-in-law intercepted the delivery, as they were in a conflict over inheritance. Following Josiah Winslow's death in 1680, the power of the colony dwindled, and it was absorbed into the Massachusetts Bay Colony by a new royal charter, granted by King William III and Queen Mary II in 1691.

WAMPANOAG CONTINUANCE

Wampanoag communities were devastated by the violence of the First Indian War, but they survived, remaining in crucial enclaves at places like Mashpee, on Cape Cod; Dartmouth, Assonet, Tiverton, and Fall River on the mainland; and the islands, including Noepe. The Plymouth settlers viewed themselves as a divinely placed people in a promised land, and as their population increased they also came to believe that "New England" and Plymouth plantation would replace the Wampanoag population. This belief provided moral support for increasingly aggressive claims on Wampanoag lands, first through compulsion and then through outright violence and war. The common American origin story of Plymouth colonists as the "first people" to "settle" in New England arose in part as a justification for the violent displacement of the original people in both New England and the United States, who nevertheless persisted and remained.

Through tremendous changes, Indigenous people adapted, as they always had, drawing sustenance from kinship networks and stories that sustained their ancestors through the most challenging times. Indeed, some of the later texts included in this volume, such as the writings of William Apess, in the 1830s, and Wamsutta Frank James, in 1970, demonstrate the power of resistance and renewal. William Apess, a Pequot minister and author, published an account of the Mashpee Revolt of 1833 and an Indigenous history of King Philip's War, in which he asked his white "brethren" in New England to reckon with the ways their ancestors' legacy of violence continued in contemporary legislation and policy. By the 1830s, when the Mashpee Wampanoag people "revolted" against neighboring settlers for stealing their wood, 90 percent of the state had been deforested. The Mashpee Indian town, built on reserved Wampanoag lands, was one of the only forested tracts left in Massachusetts. Mashpee people still held their land collectively and maintained the forest through Indigenous techniques, such as controlled burning. In 1833, Mashpee people rose up to protect their resources and their relationship to the land, as well as their right to self-government. The Mashpee Wampanoags pursued diplomacy through public writing, through nonviolent protest, including the "Mashpee Revolt" of July 4, 1833, and by addressing the Massachusetts legislature, just as their ancestors had attended the Plymouth Court. They successfully advocated for the recognition of their sovereignty, as they continue to do today, in the state of Massachusetts, in relation to the U.S. government, and on the international stage. As Apess witnessed in his writings, many of his contemporary New Englanders organized performances in which they collectively mourned the passing of Massasoit and other Indigenous leaders, propagating a myth of the "vanishing Indian," even as Wampanoag and related communities, including Nipmuc people, remained on ten reservations across the state.

Those nations remain today, with two federally recognized tribes, the Mashpee Wampanoag Tribe and the Wampanoag Tribe of Aquinnah, and several tribes recognized by the state Indian Commission (including the Nipmuc Nation and the Ponkapoag Massachusett, as well as other Wampanoag communities). Indeed, the commemoration of 2020 has served as an important platform for Wampanoag communities to address regional, national, and transnational audiences, creating new ways to reckon with this history. The *Our Story* exhibit is even now serving as a diplomatic intervention, traveling through both Native and non-Native communities and sharing not only the story of Patuxet but also of Wampanoag continuance. Moreover, reckoning with the legacies of 1620 has led to

new innovations and creations, from curriculum that reenvi-
sions the interactions between Wampanoag hosts and English
visitors to a community-crafted wampum belt that enables the
Wampanoag tribe to tell their own history, on their own terms,
using a traditional form of diplomacy to weave multiple stories
together.

Lisa Brooks and Kelly Wisecup

VOYAGES AND CAPTIVITIES

James Rosier:
A True Relation

*A True Relation of the most prosperous voyage made this present
yeere 1605, by Captaine George Waymouth, in the Discovery
of the Land of Virginia:*
*Where he discovered 60 miles up a most excellent River; together
with a most fertile land.*
*Written by James Rosier, a Gentleman employed in the voyage.
Londini, Impensis Geor. Bishop, 1605.*

TO THE READER

BEING employed in this Voyage by the right honourable
Thomas Arundell Baron of Warder, to take due notice, and
make true report of the discovery therein performed: I became
very diligent to observe (as much as I could) whatsoever was
materiall or of consequence in the businesse which I collected
into this briefe summe, intending upon our returne to publish
the same. But he soone changed the course of his intendments; and long before our arrivall in England had so farre
engaged himselfe with the Archduke, that he was constrained
to relinquish this action. But the commodities and profits of
the countrey, together with the fitnesse of plantation, being by
some honourable Gentlemen of good woorth and qualitie, and
Merchants of good sufficiency and judgment duly considered,
have at their owne charge (intending both their private and the
common benefit of their countrey) undertaken the transporting of a Colony for the plantation thereof; being much encouraged thereunto by the gracious favour of the KINGS MAJESTY
himselfe, and divers Lords of his Highnesse most Honourable
Privie Councell. After these purposed designes were concluded, I was animated to publish this briefe Relation, and not
before; because some forrein Nation (being fully assured of
the fruitfulnesse of the countrie) have hoped hereby to gaine
some knowledge of the place, seeing they could not allure our
Captaine or any speciall man of our Company to combine

3

with them for their direction, nor obtaine their purpose, in conveying away our Salvages, which was busily in practise. And this is the cause that I have neither written of the latitude or variation most exactly observed by our Captaine with sundrie instruments, which together with his perfect Geographicall Map of the countrey, he entendeth hereafter to set forth. I have likewise purposedly omitted here to adde a collection of many words in their language to the number of foure or five hundred, as also the names of divers of their governours, as well their friends as their enemies: being reserved to be made knowen for the benefit of those that shal goe in the next Voyage. But our particular proceedings in the whole Discoverie, the commodious situation of the River, the fertilitie of the land, with the profits there to be had, and here reported, I refer to be verified by the whole Company, as being eye-witnesses of my words, and most of them neere inhabitants upon the Thames. So with my prayers to God for the conversion of so ingenious and well-disposed people, and for the prosperous successive events of the noble intenders the prosecution thereof, I rest

Your friend   J. R.

A TRUE RELATION

of Captaine George Waymouth his Voyage, made this present yeere 1605; in the Discoverie of the North part of Virginia.

Upon Tuesday the 5 day of March, about ten a clocke afore noone, we set saile from Ratcliffe, and came to an anker that tide about two a clocke before Gravesend.

From thence the 10 of March being Sunday at night we ankered in the Downes: and there rode till the next day about three a clocke after noone, when with a scant winde we set saile; and by reason the winde continued Southwardly, we were beaten up and doune: but on Saturday the 16 day about foure a clocke after noon we put into Dartmouth Haven, where the continuance of the winde at South and Southwest constrained us to ride till the last of this moneth. There we shipped some of our men and supplied necessaries for our Ship and Voyage.

Upon Easter day, being the last of March, the winde comming at North-North-East, about five a clocke after noone we wayed anker, and put to sea, In the name of God, being

well victualled and furnished with munition and all necessaries:
Our whole Company being but 29 persons; of whom I may
boldly say, few voyages have beene manned forth with better
Sea-men generally in respect of our small number.

Munday the next day, being the first of Aprill, by sixe a
clocke in the morning we were sixe leagues South-South-East
from the Lizarde.

At two a clocke in the afternoone this day, the weather being
very faire, our Captaine for his owne experience and others
with him sounded, and had sixe and fiftie fathoms and a halfe.
The sounding was some small blacke perrie sand, some reddish sand, a match or two, with small shels called Saint James
his Shels.

The foureteenth of Aprill being Sunday, betweene nine and
ten of the clocke in the morning our Captaine descried the
Iland Cuervo: which bare South-west and by West, about seven
leagues from us: by eleven of the clocke we descried Flores
to the Southward of Cuervo, as it lieth: by foure a clocke in
the afternoone we brought Cuervo due South from us within
two leagues of the shore, but we touched not, because the
winde was faire, and we thought our selves sufficiently watered
and wooded.

Heere our Captaine observed the Sunne, and found himselfe
in the latitude of 40 degrees and 7 minutes: so he judged the
North part of Cuervo to be in 40 degrees. After we had kept
our course about a hundred leagues from the Ilands, by continuall Southerly windes we were forced and driven from the
Southward, whither we first intended. And when our Captaine
by long beating saw it was but in vaine to strive with windes,
not knowing Gods purposes heerein to our further blessing,
(which after by his especiall direction wee found) he thought
best to stand as nigh as he could by the winde to recover what
land we might first discover.

Munday, the 6 of May, being in the latitude of 39 and a halfe
about ten a clocke afore noone, we came to a riplin, which we
discerned a head our ship, which is a breach of water caused
either by a fall, or by some meeting of currents, which we
judged this to be; for the weather being very faire, and a small
gale of winde, we sounded and found no ground in a hundred
fathoms.

Munday, the 13 of May, about eleven a clocke afore noone, our Captaine, judging we were not farre from land, sounded, and had a soft oaze in a hundred and sixty fathomes. At fowre a clocke after noone we sounded againe, and had the same oaze in a hundred fathomes.

From ten a clocke that night till three a clocke in the morning, our Captaine tooke in all sailes and lay at hull, being desirous to fall with the land in the day time, because it was an unknowen coast, which it pleased God in his mercy to grant us, otherwise we had run our ship upon the hidden rockes and perished all. For when we set saile we sounded in 100 fathoms: and by eight a clock, having not made above five or six leagues, our Captaine upon a sudden change of water (supposing verily he saw the sand) presently sounded, and had but five fathoms. Much marvelling because we saw no land, he sent one to the top, who thence descried a whitish sandy cliffe, which bare West-North-West about six leagues off from us: but comming neerer within three or fowre leagues, we saw many breaches still neerer the land: at last we espied a great breach a head us al along the shore, into which before we should enter, our Captaine thought best to hoist out his ship boate and sound it. Which if he had not done, we had beene in great danger: for he bare up the ship, as neere as he durst after the boate: untill Thomas Cam, his mate, being in the boat, called to him to tacke about and stand off, for in this breach he had very showld water, two fathoms and lesse upon rockes, and sometime they supposed they saw the rocke within three or fowre foote, whereon the sea made a very strong breach: which we might discern (from the top) to run along as we sailed by it 6 or 7 leagues to the Southward. This was in the latitude of 41 degrees, 20 minuts: wherefore we were constrained to put backe againe from the land: and sounding, (the weather being very faire and a small winde) we found our selves embaied with continuall showldes and rockes in a most uncertaine ground, from five or sixe fathoms, at the next cast of the lead we should have 15 and 18 fathoms. Over many which we passed, and God so blessed us, that we had wind and weather as faire as poore men in this distresse could wish: whereby we both perfectly discerned every breach, and with the winde were able to turne, where we saw most hope of safest passage. Thus we parted from the land, which we had not so much before desired, and at the first sight rejoiced, as now we all joifully praised God, that it had pleased him to deliver us from so imminent danger.

Heere we found great store of excellent Cod fish, and saw many Whales, as we had done two or three daies before.

We stood off all that night, and the next day being Wednesday; but the wind still continuing between the points of South-South-West, and West-South-West: so as we could not make any way to the Southward, in regard of our great want of water and wood (which was now spent) we much desired land and therefore sought for it, where the wind would best suffer us to refresh our selves.

Thursday, the 16 of May, we stood in directly with the land, and much marvelled we descried it not, wherein we found our sea charts very false, putting land where none is.

Friday the 17 of May, about sixe a clocke at night we descried the land, which bare from us North-North-East; but because it blew a great gale of winde, the sea very high and neere night, not fit to come upon an unknowen coast, we stood off till two a clocke in the morning, being Saturday: then standing in with it againe, we descried it by eight a clocke in the morning, bearing North-East from us. It appeared a meane high land, as we after found it, being but an Iland of some six miles in compasse, but I hope the most fortunate ever yet discovred. About twelve a clocke that day, we came to an anker on the North side of this Iland, about a league from the shore. About two a clocke our Captaine with twelve men rowed in his ship boat to the shore, where we made no long stay, but laded our boat with dry wood of olde trees upon the shore side, and returned to our ship, where we rode that night.

This Iland is woody, grouen with Firre, Birch, Oke and Beech, as farre as we saw along the shore; and so likely to be within. On the verge grow Gooseberries, Strawberries, Wild pease, and Wild rose bushes. The water issued foorth downe the Rocky cliffes in many places: and much fowle of divers kinds breed upon the shore and rocks.

While we were at shore, our men aboord with a few hooks got above thirty great Cods and Hadocks, which gave us a taste

of the great plenty of fish which we found afterward whereso-
ever we went upon the coast.

From hence we might discerne the maine land from the
West-South-West to the East-North-East, and a great way (as
it then seemed, and as we after found it) up into the maine
we might discerne very high mountaines, though the maine
seemed but low land; which gave us a hope it would please
God to direct us to the discoverie of some good; although wee
were driven by winds farre from that place, whither (both by
our direction and desire) we ever intended to shape the course
of our voyage.

The next day being Whit-Sunday; because we rode too much
open to the sea and windes, we weyed anker about twelve a
clocke, and came along to the other Ilands more adjoyning to
the maine, and in the rode directly with the mountaines, about
three leagues from the first Iland where we had ankered.

When we came neere unto them (sounding all along in a
good depth) our Captaine manned his ship-boat and sent her
before with Thomas Cam one of his Mates, whom he knew
to be of good experience, to sound and search betweene the
Ilands for a place safe for our shippe to ride in; in the meane
while we kept aloofe at sea, having given them in the boat a
token to weffe in the ship, if he found a convenient Harbour;
which it pleased God to send us, farre beyond our expectation,
in a most safe birth defended from all windes, in an excellent
depth of water for ships of any burthen, in six, seven, eight,
nine and ten fathoms upon a clay oaze very tough.

We all with great joy praised God for his unspeakable
goodnesse, who had from so apparent danger delivered us,
and directed us upon this day into so secure an Harbour: in
remembrance whereof we named it Pentecost harbor, we arriving there that day out of our last Harbour in England, from
whence we set saile upon Easterday.

About foure a clocke, after we were ankered and well mored,
our Captaine with halfe a dozen of our Company went on shore
to seeke fresh watering, and a convenient place to set together
a pinnesse, which we brought in pieces out of England; both
which we found very fitting.

Upon this Iland, as also upon the former, we found (at our
first comming to shore) where fire had beene made: and about

the place were very great egge shelles bigger than goose egges, fish bones, and as we judged, the bones of some beast.

Here we espied Cranes stalking on the shore of a little Iland adjoyning; where we after saw they used to breed.

Whitsun-munday, the 20 day of May, very early in the morning, our Captaine caused the pieces of the pinnesse to be carried a shore, where while some were busied about her, others digged welles to receive the fresh water, which we found issuing downe out of the land in many places. Heere I cannot omit (for foolish feare of imputation of flattery) the painfull industry of our Captaine, who as at sea he is alwayes most carefull and vigilant, so at land he refuseth no paines; but his labour was ever as much or rather more than any mans: which not only encourageth others with better content, but also effecteth much with great expedition.

In digging we found excellent clay for bricke or tile.

The next day we finished a well of good and holesome cleere water in a great empty caske, which we left there. We cut yards, waste trees, and many necessaries for our ship, while our Carpenter and Cooper laboured to fit and furnish forth the shallop.

This day our boat went out about a mile from our ship, and in small time with two or three hooks was fished sufficiently for our whole Company three dayes, with great Cod, Haddocke, and Thornebacke.

And towards night we drew with a small net of twenty fathoms very nigh the shore: we got about thirty very good and great Lobsters, many Rockfish, some Plaise, and other small fishes, and fishes called Lumpes, verie pleasant to the taste: and we generally observed, that all the fish, of what kinde soever we tooke, were well fed, fat, and sweet in taste.

Wednesday, the 22 of May, we felled and cut wood for our ships use, cleansed and scoured our wels, and digged a plot of ground, wherein, amongst some garden seeds, we sowed peaze and barley, which in sixteen dayes grew eight inches above ground; and so continued growing every day halfe an inch, although this was but the crust of the ground, and much inferior to the mould we after found in the maine.

Friday, the 24 of May, after we had made an end of cutting wood, and carying water aboord our shippe, with fourteene

Shot and Pikes we marched about and thorow part of two of the Ilands; the bigger of which we judged to be foure or five miles in compasse, and a mile broad.

The profits and fruits which are naturally on these Ilands are these:

All along the shore and some space within, where the wood hindereth not, grow plentifully

Rasberries.
Gooseberries.
Strawberries.
Roses.
Currants.
Wild-Vines.
Angelica.

Within the Ilands growe wood of sundry sorts, some very great, and all tall:

Birch.
Beech.
Ash.
Maple.
Spruce.
Cherry-tree.
Yew.
Oke very great and good.
Firre-tree, out of which

issueth Turpentine in so marvellous plenty, and so sweet, as our Chirurgeon and others affirmed they never saw so good in England. We pulled off much Gumme congealed on the outside of the barke, which smelled like Frankincense. This would be a great benefit for making Tarre and Pitch.

We stayed the longer in this place, not only because of our good Harbour, (which is an excellent comfort) but because every day we did more and more discover the pleasant fruitfulnesse; insomuch as many of our Companie wished themselves setled heere, not expecting any further hopes, or better discovery to be made.

Heere our men found abundance of great muscels among the rocks; and in some of them many small Pearls: and in one muscell (which we drew up in our net) was found foureteene Pearles, whereof one of prety bignesse and orient; in another above fiftie small Pearles; and if we had had a Drag, no doubt we had found some of great valew, seeing these did certainly shew, that heere they were bred: the shels all glistering with mother of Pearle.

Wednesday, the 29 day, our shallop being now finished, and our Captaine and men furnished to depart with hir from the ship: we set up a crosse on the shore side upon the rockes.

Thursday, the 30 of May, about ten a clock afore noon, our Captaine with 13 men more, in the name of God, and with all our praiers for their prosperous discoverie, and safe returne, departed in the shallop; leaving the ship in a good harbour, which before I mentioned, well mored, and manned with 14 men.

This day, about five a clocke in the afternoone, we in the shippe espied three Canoas comming towards us, which went to the iland adjoining, where they went a shore, and very quickly had made a fire, about which they stood beholding our ships: to whom we made signes with our hands and hats, weffing unto them to come unto us, because we had not seene any of the people yet. They sent one Canoa with three men, one of which, when they came neere unto us, spake in his language very lowd and very boldly: seeming as though he would know why we were there, and by pointing with his oare towards the sea, we conjectured he ment we should be gone. But when we shewed them knives and their use, by cutting of stickes and other trifles, as combs and glasses, they came close aboard our ship, as desirous to entertaine our friendship. To these we gave such things as we perceived they liked, when wee shewed them the use: bracelets, rings, peacocke feathers, which they stucke in their haire, and Tabacco pipes. After their departure to their company on the shore, presently came foure other in another Canoa: to whom we gave as to the former, using them with as much kindnes as we could.

The shape of their body is very proportionable, they are wel countenanced, not very tal nor big, but in stature like to us: they paint their bodies with blacke, their faces, some with red, some with blacke, and some with blew.

Their clothing is Beavers skins, or Deares skins, cast over them like a mantle, and hanging downe to their knees, made fast together upon the shoulder with leather; some of them had sleeves, most had none; some had buskins of such leather tewed: they have besides a peece of Beavers skin betweene their legs, made fast about their waste, to cover their privities.

They suffer no haire to grow on their faces, but on their head very long and very blacke, which those that have wives, binde up behinde with a leather string, in a long round knot.

They seemed all very civill and merrie: shewing tokens of much thankefulnesse, for those things we gave them. We found them then (as after) a people of exceeding good invention, quicke understanding and readie capacitie.

Their Canoas are made without any iron, of the bark of a birch tree, strengthened within with ribs and hoops of wood, in so good fashion, with such excellent ingenious art, as they are able to beare seven or eight persons, far exceeding any in the Indies.

One of their Canoas came not to us, wherein we imagined their women were: of whom they are (as all Salvages) very jealous.

When I signed unto them they should goe sleepe, because it was night, they understood presently, and pointed that at the shore, right against our ship, they would stay all night: as they did.

The next morning very early, came one Canoa abord us againe with three Salvages, whom we easily then enticed into our ship, and under the decke: where we gave them porke, fish, bread and pease, all which they did eat; and this I noted, they would eat nothing raw, either fish or flesh. They marvelled much and much looked upon the making of our canne and kettle, so they did at a head-peece and at our guns, of which they are most fearefull, and would fall flat downe at the report of them. At their departure I signed unto them, that if they would bring me such skins as they ware I would give them knives, and such things as I saw they most liked, which the chiefe of them promised to do by that time the Sunne should be beyond the middest of the firmament; this I did to bring them to an understanding of exchange, and that they might conceive the intent of our comming to them to be for no other end.

About 10 a clocke this day we descried our Shallop returning toward us, which so soone as we espied, we certainly conjectured our Captaine had found some unexpected harbour, further up towards the maine to bring the ship into, or some river; knowing his determination and resolution, not so suddenly else to make returne: which when they came neerer they expressed by shooting volleies of shot; and when they were come within Musket shot, they gave us a volley and haled us, then we in the shippe gave them a great peece and haled them.

Thus we welcomed them; who gladded us exceedingly with their joifull relation of their happie discoverie, which shall appeare in the sequele. And we likewise gave them cause of mutuall joy with us, in discoursing of the kinde civility we found in a people, where we little expected any sparke of humanity.

Our Captaine had in this small time discovered up a great river, trending alongst into the maine about forty miles. The pleasantnesse whereof, with the safety of harbour for shipping, together with the fertility of ground and other fruits, which were generally by his whole company related, I omit, till I report of the whole discovery therein after performed. For by the breadth, depth and strong flood, imagining it to run far up into the land, he with speed returned, intending to flanke his light horsman for arrowes, least it might happen that the further part of the river should be narrow, and by that meanes subject to the volley of Salvages on either side out of the woods.

Untill his returne, our Captaine left on shore where he landed in a path (which seemed to be frequented) a pipe, a brooch and a knife, thereby to know if the Salvages had recourse that way, because they could at that time see none of them, but they were taken away before our returne thither.

I returne now to our Salvages, who according to their appointment about one a clocke, came with 4 Canoas to the shoare of the iland right over against us, where they had lodged the last night, and sent one Canoa to us with two of those Salvages, who had beene a bord, and another, who then seemed to have command of them; for though we perceived their willingnesse, yet he would not permit them to come abord; but he having viewed us and our ship, signed that he would go to the rest of the company and returne againe. Presently after their departure it began to raine, and continued all that afternoone, so as they could not come to us with their skins and furs, nor we go to them. But after an houre or there about, the three

which had beene with us before came againe, whom we had
to our fire and covered them with our gownes. Our Captaine
bestowed a shirt upon him, whom we thought to be their
chiefe, who seemed never to have seene any before; we gave
him a brooch to hang about his necke, a great knife, and lesser
knives to the two other, and to every one of them a combe and
glasse, the use whereof we shewed them: whereat they laughed
and tooke gladly; we victualled them, and gave them aqua vitæ,
which they tasted, but would by no meanes drinke; our bev-
eridge they liked well, we gave them Sugar Candy, which after
they had tasted they liked and desired more, and raisons which
were given them; and some of every thing they would reserve
to carry to their company. Wherefore we pittying their being
in the raine, and therefore not able to get themselves victuall
(as we thought) we gave them bread and fish.

Thus because we found the land a place answereable to the
intent of our discovery, viz. fit for any nation to inhabit, we
used the people with as great kindnes as we could devise, or
found them capable of.

The next day, being Saturday and the first of June, I traded
with the Salvages all the fore noone upon the shore, where
were eight and twenty of them: and because our ship rode
nigh, we were but five or sixe: where for knives, glasses, combes
and other trifles to the valew of foure or five shillings, we had
40 good Beavers skins, Otters skins, Sables, and other small
skins, which we knewe not how to call. Our trade being ended,
many of them came abord us, and did eat by our fire, and
would be verie merrie and bold, in regard of our kinde usage
of them. Towards night our Captaine went on shore, to have
a draught with the Sein or Net. And we carried two of them
with us, who marvelled to see us catch fish with a net. Most
of that we caught we gave them and their company. Then on
the shore I learned the names of divers things of them: and
when they perceived me to note them downe, they would of
themselves, fetch fishes, and fruit bushes, and stand by me to
see me write their names.

Our Captaine shewed them a strange thing which they
woondred at. His sword and mine having beene touched with
the Loadstone, tooke up a knife, and held it fast when they
plucked it away, made the knife turne, being laid on a blocke,

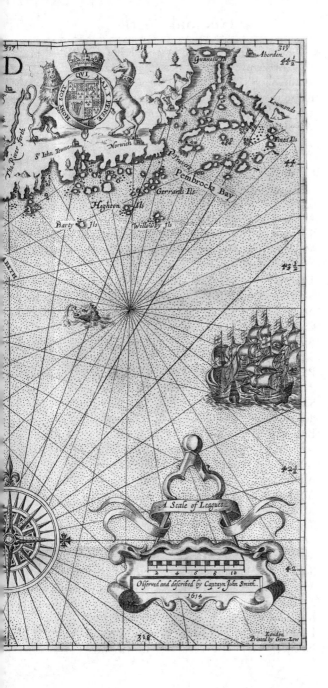

D

317   318   319

Aborden

44½

Gunnells Ili

Lowmonds

The River forth

St Iohn Towne

Norwich

Inas Ils

44

Prowen

Pembrocke Bay

Gerrards Ils

Heghton Ili

Barty Ile

Willowby Ili

43½

A Scale of Leagues

42½

Observed and described by Captayn Iohn Smith.

1614

2   4   6   8   10

42

London
Printed by Geor: Low

318

BECAUSE THE BOOKE WAS PRINTED ERE
the Prince his Highnesse had altered
the names, I intreate the Reader, peruse
this schedule; which will plainely shew him the
correspondence of the old names to the new.

The old names.	The new.
Cape Cod	Cape James
	Milford haven
Chawum	Barwick
Accomack	Plimouth
Sagoquas	Oxford
Massachusets Mount	Chevit hill
Massachusets River	Charles River
Totant	Fawmouth
A Country not discovered	Bristow
Naemkeck	Bastable
Cape Trabigzanda	Cape Anne
Aggawom	Southhampton
Smiths Iles	Smiths Iles
Passataquack	Hull
Accominticus	Boston
Sassanowes Mount	Snodon hill
Sowocatuck	Ipswitch
Bahana	Dartmouth
	Sandwich
Aucociscos Mount	Shooters hill
Aucocisco	The Base
Aumoughcawgen	Cambridge
Kinebeck	Edenborough
Sagadahock	Leeth
Pemmaquid	S. Johns towne
Monahigan	Barties Iles
Segocket	Norwich
Matinnack	Willowby's Iles
Metinnicut	Hoghton's Iles
Mecadacut	Dunbarton
Pennobscot	Aborden
Nusket	Lowmonds

TO THE HIGH
Hopeful Charles,
Prince of Great Britaine.

Sir:

So favourable was your most renowned and memorable Brother, Prince Henry, to all generous designes; that in my discovery of Virginia, I presumed to call two namelesse Headlands after my Soveraignes heires, Cape Henry, and Cape Charles. Since then, it beeing my chance to range some other parts of America, whereof I heere present your Highness the description in a Map; my humble sute is, you would please to change their Barbarous names, for such English, as Posterity may say, Prince Charles was their Godfather. What here in this relation I promise my Countrey, let mee live or die the slave of scorne and infamy, if (having meanes) I make it not apparent; please God to blesse me but from such accidents as are beyond my power and reason to prevent. For my labours, I desire but such conditions as were promised me out of the gaines; and that your Highnesse would daigne to grace this Work, by your Princely and favourable respect unto it, and know mee to be
Your Highnesse true and faithfull servant,
John Smith.

TO THE RIGHT HONOURABLE
and worthy Lords, Knights, and
Gentlemen, of his Majesties Councell,
for all Plantations and discoveries;
especially, of New England.

Seeing the deedes of the most just, and the writings of the most wise, not onely of men, but of God himselfe, have beene diversly traduced by variable judgements of the Times opinionists; what shall such an ignorant as I expect? Yet reposing my selfe on your favours, I present this rude discourse, to the worldes construction; though I am perswaded, that few do think there may be had from New England Staple commodities, well worth 3 or 400000 pound a yeare, with so small charge, and such facilitie, as this discourse will acquaint you. But, lest your Honours, that know mee not, should thinke

I goe by hearesay or affection; I intreat your pardons to say thus much of my selfe: Neere twice nine yeares, I have beene taught by lamentable experience, aswell in Europe and Asia, as Affrick, and America, such honest adventures as the chance of warre doth cast upon poore Souldiers. So that, if I bee not able to judge of what I have seene, contrived, and done; it is not the fault either of my eyes, or foure quarters. And these nine yeares, I have bent my endeavours to finde a sure foundation to begin these ensuing projects: which though I never so plainely and seriously propound; yet it resteth in God, and you, still to dispose of. Not doubting but your goodnesse will pardon my rudenesse, and ponder errours in the balance of good will; No more: but sacring all my best abilities to the good of my Prince, and Countrey, and submitting my selfe to the exquisit judgements of your renowned vertue, I ever rest

Your Honours, in all honest service,
J. S.

TO THE RIGHT WORSHIPFULL
Adventurers for the Countrey of
New England, in the Cities of
London, Bristow, Exceter, Plimouth,
Dartmouth, Bastable, Totneys, etc.
and in all other Cities and Ports,
in the Kingdome of England.

If the little Ant, and the sillie Bee seek by their diligence the good of their Commonwealth; much more ought Man. If they punish the drones and sting them steales their labour; then blame not Man. Little hony hath that hive, where there are more Drones then Bees: and miserable is that Land, where more are idle then well imployed. If the endeavours of those vermin be acceptable, I hope mine may be excuseable; Though I confesse it were more proper for mee, To be doing what I say, then writing what I knowe. Had I returned rich, I could not have erred: Now having onely such fish as came to my net, I must be taxed. But, I would my taxers were as ready to adventure their purses, as I, purse, life, and all I have: or as diligent to furnish the charge, as I know they are vigilant to crop the fruits of my labours. Then would I not doubt (did God please

I might safely arrive in New England, and safely returne) but to performe somewhat more then I have promised, and approve my words by deeds, according to proportion.

I am not the first hath beene betrayed by Pirats: And foure men of warre, provided as they were, had beene sufficient to have taken Sampson, Hercules, and Alexander the great, no other way furnisht then I was. I knowe not what assurance any have do passe the Seas, Not to bee subject to casualty as well as my selfe: but least this disaster may hinder my proceedings, or ill will (by rumour) the behoofefull worke I pretend; I have writ this little: which I did thinke to have concealed from any publike use, till I had made my returnes speake as much, as my pen now doth.

But because I speake so much of fishing, if any take mee for such a devote fisher, as I dreame of nought else, they mistake mee. I know a ring of golde from a graine of barley, aswell as a goldesmith: and nothing is there to bee had which fishing doth hinder, but furder us to obtaine. Now for that I have made knowne unto you a fit place for plantation, limited within the bounds of your Patent and Commission; having also received meanes, power, and authority by your directions, to plant there a Colony, and make further search, and discovery in those parts there yet unknowne: Considering, withall, first those of his Majesties Councell, then those Cities above named, and diverse others that have beene moved to lend their assistance to so great a worke, doe expect (especially the adventurers) the true relation or event of my proceedings which I heare are so abused; I am inforced for all these respects, rather to expose my imbecillitie to contempt, by the testimonie of these rude lines, then all should condemne me for so bad a Factor, as could neither give reason nor account of my actions and designes.

Yours to command,
John Smith.

IN THE DESERVED
Honour of the Author,
Captaine John Smith,
and his Worke.

Damn'd Envie is a sp'ite, that ever haunts
Beasts, mis-nam'd Men; Cowards, or Ignorants.
But, onely such shee followes, whose deere WORTH
(Maugre her malice) sets their glorie forth.
    If this faire Overture, then, take not; It
    Is Envie's *spight (dear friend) in men-of-wit;*
Or Feare, *lest morsels, which our mouthes possesse,*
Might fall from thence; or else, tis Sottishnesse.
    If either; (I hope neither) thee they raise;
    Thy* Letters are as Letters in thy praise;
Who, by their vice, improve *(when they* reproove*)*
Thy vertue; so, in hate, procure thee Love.
    Then, On firme Worth: this Monument I frame;
    Scorning for any Smith to forge *such* fame.
                  Jo: Davies, Heref:

*Hinderers.

TO HIS WORTHY
Captaine the Author.

That which wee call the subject of all Storie,
Is Truth: which in this Worke of thine gives glorie
To all that thou hast done. Then, scorne the spight
Of Envie; which doth no mans merits right.
    My sword may helpe the rest: my Pen no more
    Can doe, but this; I'ave said enough before.
               Your sometime souldier,
               J. Codrinton, now Templer.

TO MY WORTHY
friend and Cosen,
Captain John Smith.

It over-joyes my heart, when as thy Words
Of these designes, with deeds I doe compare.
Heere is a Booke, such worthy truth affords,
None should the due desert thereof impare;
Sith thou, the man, deserving of these Ages,
Much paine hast ta'en for this our Kingdoms good,
In Climes unknowne, Mongst Turks and Salvages,
T'inlarge our bounds; though with thy losse of blood.
  Hence damn'd Detraction: stand not in our way.
  Envie, it selfe, will not the Truth gainesay.

N. Smith.

TO THAT WORTHY
and generous Gentleman,
my verie good friend,
Captain Smith.

May Fate thy Project prosper, that thy name
May be eternised with living fame:
  Though foule Detraction Honour would pervert,
  And Envie ever waits upon desert:
In spight of Pelias, when his hate lies colde,
Returne as Jason with a fleece of Golde.
  Then after-ages shall record thy praise,
  That a New England to this Ile didst raise:
And when thou dy'st (as all that live must die)
Thy fame live heere; thou, with Eternitie.

R: Gunnell.

TO HIS FRIEND
Captaine Smith, upon his
description of New England.

Sir; your Relations I have read: which shewe,
Ther's reason I should honour, them and you:
And if their meaning I have understood,
I dare to censure, thus: Your Project's good;

And may (if follow'd) doubtlesse quit the paine,
With honour, pleasure and a trebble gaine;
Beside the benefit that shall arise
To make more happie our Posterities.
    For would we daigne to spare, though 'twere no more
Then what o're-filles, and surfets us in store,
To order Nature's fruitfulnesse a while
In that rude Garden, you New England stile;
With present good, ther's hope in after-daies
Thence to repaire what Time and Pride decaies
In this rich kingdome. And the spatious West
Beeing still more with English blood possest,
The Proud Iberians shall not rule those Seas,
To checke our ships from sayling where they please;
Nor future times make any forraine power
Become so great to force a bound to Our.
    Much good my minde fore tels would follow hence
With little labour, and with lesse expence.
Thrive therefore thy Designe, who ere envie:
England may joy in England's Colony,
Virginia seeke her Virgine sisters good,
Be blessed in such happie neighbourhood:
    Or, what-soere Fate pleaseth to permit,
    Be thou still honor'd for first mooving it.
                    George Wither, è societate Lincol.

MICHAEL PHETTIPLACE,
William Phettiplace, and Richard Wiffing,
Gentlemen, and Souldiers under
Captaine Smiths Command:
In his deserved honor for
his Worke, and worth.

Why may not we in this Worke have our Mite,
That had our share in each black day and night,
When thou Virginia foild'st, yet kept'st unstaind;
And held'st the King of Paspeheh enchaind.
Thou all alone this Salvage sterne didst take.

Pamunkes *king wee saw thee captive make.*
Among seaven hundred of his stoutest men,
To murther thee and us resolved; when
Fast by the hand thou ledst this Salvage grim,
Thy Pistoll at his breast to governe him:
Which did infuse such awe in all the rest
(Sith their drad Soveraigne thou had'st so distrest)
That thou and wee (poore sixteene) safe retir'd
Unto our helplesse ships. *Thou (thus admir'd)*
Didst make proud Powhatan, *his subjects send*
To James *his Towne, thy censure to attend:*
And all Virginia's *Lords, and pettie Kings,*
Aw'd by thy vertue, crouch, and Presents brings
To gaine thy grace; so dreaded thou hast beene:
And yet a heart more milde is seldome seene;
So, making Valour Vertue, really;
Who hast nought in thee counterfet, or slie;
If in the sleight bee not the truest art,
That makes men famoused for faire desert.

Who saith of thee, this savors of vaine-glorie,
Mistakes both thee and us, and this true storie.
If it bee ill in Thee, so well to doe;
Then, is it ill in Us, to praise thee too.
But, if the first bee well done; it is well,
To say it doth (if so it doth) excell!
Praise is the guerdon of each deere desert,
Making the praised act the praised part
With more alacritie: Honours *Spurre is* Praise;
Without which, it (regardlesse) soone decaies.

And for this paines of thine wee praise thee rather,
That future Times may know who was the father
Of this rare Worke (New Engand) *which may bring*
Praise to thy God, and profit to thy King.

A DESCRIPTION OF
New-England, by Captaine John Smith.

IN the moneth of Aprill, 1614. with two Ships from London, of a few Marchants, I chanced to arrive in New-England, a parte of Ameryca, at the Ile of Monahiggan, in 43½ of Northerly latitude: our plot was there to take Whales and make tryalls of a Myne of Gold and Copper. If those failed, Fish and Furres was then our refuge, to make our selves savers howsoever: we found this Whale-fishing a costly conclusion: we saw many, and spent much time in chasing them; but could not kill any: They beeing a kinde of Jubartes, and not the Whale that yeeldes Finnes and Oyle as wee expected. For our Golde, it was rather the Masters device to get a voyage that projected it, then any knowledge hee had at all of any such matter. Fish and Furres was now our guard: and by our late arrival, and long lingring about the Whale, the prime of both those seasons were past ere wee perceived it; we thinking that their seasons served at all times: but wee found it otherwise; for, by the midst of June, the fishing failed. Yet in July and August some was taken, but not sufficient to defray so great a charge as our stay required. Of dry fish we made about 40000. of Cor fish about 7000. Whilest the sailers fished, my selfe with eight or nine others of them might best bee spared; Ranging the coast in a small boat, wee got for trifles neer 1100 Bever skinnes, 100 Martins, and neer as many Otters; and the most of them within the distance of twenty leagues. We ranged the Coast both East and West much furder; but Eastwards our commodities were not esteemed, they were so neare the French who affords them better: and right against us in the Main was a Ship of Sir Frances Popphames, that had there such acquaintance, having many yeares used onely that porte, that the most parte there was had by him. And 40 leagues westwards were two French Ships, that had made there a great voyage by trade, during the time wee tryed those conclusions, not knowing the Coast, nor Salvages habitation. With these Furres, the Traine, and Corfish I returned for England in the Bark: where within six monthes after our departure from the Downes, we safe arrived back. The best of this fish was solde for five pound the hundreth, the rest by ill usage betwixt three pound and fifty

My first voyage to new-England.

shillings. The other Ship staied to fit herselfe for Spaine with the dry fish which was sould, by the Sailers reporte that returned, at forty ryalls the quintall, each hundred weighing two quintalls and a halfe.

The situation of New England.

New England is that part of America in the Ocean Sea opposite to Nova Albyon in the South Sea; discovered by the most memorable Sir Francis Drake in his voyage about the worlde. In regarde whereto this is stiled New England, beeing in the same latitude. New France, off it, is Northward: Southwardes is Virginia, and all the adjoyning Continent, with New Granado, New Spain, New Andolosia and the West Indies. Now because I have beene so oft asked such strange questions, of the goodnesse and greatnesse of those spatious Tracts of land, how they can bee thus long unknown, or not possessed by the Spaniard, and many such like demands; I intreat your pardons, if I chance to be too plaine, or tedious in relating my knowledge for plaine mens satisfaction.

Florida is the next adjoyning to the Indes, which unprosperously was attempted to bee planted by the French.

Notes of Florida.

A Country farre bigger then England, Scotland, France and Ireland, yet little knowne to any Christian, but by the wonderful endevours of Ferdinando de Soto a valiant Spaniard: whose writings in this age is the best guide knowne to search those parts.

Notes of Virginia.

Virginia is no Ile (as many doe imagine) but part of the Continent adjoyning to Florida; whose bounds may be stretched to the magnitude thereof without offence to any Christian inhabitant. For from the degrees of 30. to 45 his Majestie hath granted his Letters patents, the Coast extending South-west and North-east aboute 1500 miles; but to follow it aboard, the shore may well be 2000. at the least: of which, 20. miles is the most gives entrance into the Bay of Chisapeak, where is the London plantation: within which is a Country (as you may perceive by the description in a Booke and Map printed in my name of that little I there discovered) may well suffice 300000 people to inhabit. And Southward adjoyneth that part discovered at the charge of Sir Walter Rawley, by Sir Ralph Lane, and that learned Mathematician Master Thomas Heryot. Northward six or seaven degrees is the

River Sagadahock, where was planted the Westerne Colony, by that Honourable Patrone of vertue Sir John Poppham, Lord chief Justice of England. Ther is also a relation printed by Captaine Bartholomew Gosnould, of Elizabeths Iles: and an other by Captaine Waymoth, of Pemmaquid. From all these diligent observers, posterity may be bettered by the fruits of their labours. But for divers others that long before and since have ranged those parts, within a kenning sometimes of the shore, some touching in one place some in another, I must entreat them pardon me for omitting them; or if I offend in saying that their true descriptions are concealed, or never well observed, or died with the Authors: so that the Coast is yet still but even as a Coast unknowne and undiscovered. I have had six or seaven severall plots of those Northren parts, so unlike each to other, and most so differing from any true proportion, or resemblance of the Countrey, as they did mee no more good, then so much waste paper, though they cost me more. It may be it was not my chance to see the best; but least others may be deceived as I was, or throgh dangerous ignorance hazard themselves as I did, I have drawen a Map from Point to Point, Ile to Ile, and Harbour to Harbour, with the Soundings, Sands, Rocks, and Land-marks as I passed close aboard the Shore in a little Boat; although there be many things to bee observed which the haste of other affaires did cause me omit: for, being sent more to get present commodities, then knowledge by discoveries for any future good, I had not power to search as I would: yet it will serve to direct any shall goe that waies, to safe Harbours and the Salvages habitations: What marchandize and commodities for their labour they may finde, this following discourse shall plainely demonstrate.

Thus you may see, of this 2000. miles more then halfe is yet unknowne to any purpose: no not so much as the borders of the Sea are yet certainly discovered. As for the goodnes and true substances of the Land, wee are for most part yet altogether ignorant of them, unlesse it bee those parts about the Bay of Chisapeack and Sagadahock: but onely here and there wee touched or have seene a little the edges of those large dominions, which doe stretch themselves into the Maine, God doth know how many thousand miles; whereof we can yet no more judge, then a stranger that saileth betwixt England and

France can describe the Harbors and dangers by landing here or there in some River or Bay, tell thereby the goodnesse and substances of Spaine, Italy, Germany, Bohemia, Hungaria and the rest. By this you may perceive how much they erre, that think every one which hath bin at Virginia understandeth or knowes what Virginia is: Or that the Spaniards know one halfe quarter of those Territories they possesse; no, not so much as the true circumference of Terra Incognita, whose large dominions may equalize the greatnesse and goodnes of America, for any thing yet known. It is strange with what small power hee hath raigned in the East Indes; and few will understand the truth of his strength in America: where he having so much to keepe with such a pampered force, they neede not greatly feare his furie, in the Bermudas, Virginia, New France, or New England; beyond whose bounds America doth stretch many thousand miles: into the frozen partes whereof one Master Hutson an English Mariner did make the greatest discoverie of any Christian I knowe of, where he unfortunately died. For Affrica, had not the industrious Portugales ranged her unknowne parts, who would have sought for wealth among those fryed Regions of blacke brutish Negers, where notwithstanding all the wealth and admirable adventures and endeavours more then 140 yeares, they knowe not one third of those blacke habitations. But it is not a worke for every one, to manage such an affaire as makes a discoverie, and plants a Colony: It requires all the best parts of Art, Judgement, Courage, Honesty, Constancy, Diligence and Industrie, to doe but neere well. Some are more proper for one thing then another; and therein are to be imployed: and nothing breedes more confusion then misplacing and misimploying men in their undertakings. Columbus, Cortez, Pitzara, Soto, Magellanes, and the rest served more then a prentiship to learne how to begin their most memorable attempts in the West Indes: which to the wonder of all ages succesfully they effected, when many hundreds of others farre above them in the worlds opinion, beeing instructed but by relation, came to shame and confusion in actions of small moment, who doubtlesse in other matters, were both wise, discreet, generous, and couragious. I say not this to detract any thing from their incomparable merits, but to answer those questionlesse questions that keep us back from imitating the worthinesse of their brave spirits that advanced themselves from poore Souldiers to great Captaines, their posterity to great Lords, their King to be one of the greatest Potentates on earth, and the fruites of their labours, his greatest glory, power and renowne.

That part wee call New England is betwixt the degrees of 41. and 45: but that parte this discourse speaketh of, stretcheth but from Pennobscot to Cape Cod, some 75 leagues by a right line distant each from other: within which bounds I have seene at least 40. severall habitations upon the Sea Coast, and sounded about 25 excellent good Harbours; In many whereof there is ancorage for 500. sayle of ships of any burthen; in some of them for 5000: And more then 200 Iles overgrowne with good timber, of divers sorts of wood, which doe make so many harbours as requireth a longer time then I had, to be well discovered.

The principall habitation Northward we were at, was Pennobscot: Southward along the Coast and up the Rivers we found Mecadacut, Segocket, Pemmaquid, Nusconcus, Kenebeck, Sagadahock, and Aumoughcawgen; And to those Countries belong the people of Segotago, Paghhuntanuck, Pocopassum, Taughtanakagnet, Warbigganus, Nassaque, Masherosqueck, Wawrigweck, Moshoquen, Wakcogo, Passharanack, etc. To these are allied the Countries of Aucocisco, Accominticus, Passataquack, Aggawom, and Naemkeck: all these, I could perceive, differ little in language, fashion, or government: though most be Lords of themselves, yet they hold the Bashabes of Pennobscot, the chiefe and greatest amongst them.

The next I can remember by name are Mattahunts; two pleasant Iles of groves, gardens and corne fields a league in the Sea from the Mayne. Then Totant, Massachuset, Pocapawmet, Quonahassit, Sagoquas, Nahapassumkeck, Topeent, Seccasaw, Totheet, Nasnocomacack, Accomack, Chawum; Then Cape Cod by which is Pawmet and the Ile Nawset, of the language, and alliance of them of Chawum: The others are called Massachusets; of another language, humor and condition: For their trade and marchandize; to each of their habitations they have diverse Townes and people belonging; and by their relations and descriptions, more then 20 severall Habitations and Rivers

The description of New England.

The particular Countries or Governments

that stretch themselves farre up into the Countrey, even to the borders of diverse great Lakes, where they kill and take most of their Bevers and Otters. From Pennobscot to Sagadahock this Coast is all Mountainous and Iles of huge Rocks, but overgrowen with all sorts of excellent good woodes for building houses, boats, barks or shippes; with an incredible abundance of most sorts of fish, much fowle, and sundry sorts of good fruites for mans use.

The mixture of an excellent soyle. Betwixt Sagadahock and Sowocatuck there is but two or three sandy Bayes, but betwixt that and Cape Cod very many: especialy the Coast of the Massachusets is so indifferently mixed with high clayie or sandy cliffes in one place, and then tracts of large long ledges of divers sorts, and quarries of stones in other places so strangely divided with tinctured veines of divers colours: as, Free stone for building, Slate for tiling, smooth stone to make Fornaces and Forges for glasse or iron, and iron ore sufficient, conveniently to melt in them: but the most part so resembleth the Coast of Devonshire, I thinke most of the cliffes would make such lime-stone: If they be not of these qualities, they are so like, they may deceive a better judgement then mine; all which are so neere adjoyning to those other advantages I observed in these parts, that if the Ore prove as good iron and steele in those parts, as I know it is within the bounds of the Countrey, I dare engage my head (having but men skilfull to worke the simples there growing) to have all things belonging to the building and the rigging of shippes of any proportion, and good marchandize for the fraught, within a square of 10 or 14 leagues: and were it for a good rewarde, I would not feare to proove it in a lesse limitation.

A proofe of an excellent temper. And surely by reason of those sandy cliffes and cliffes of rocks, both which we saw so planted with Gardens and Corne fields, and so well inhabited with a goodly, strong and well proportioned people, besides the greatnesse of the Timber growing on them, the greatnesse of the fish and the moderate temper of the ayre (for of twentie five, not any was sicke, but two that were many *A proofe of health.* yeares diseased before they went, notwithstanding our bad lodging and accidentall diet) who can but approove this a most excellent place, both for health and fertility? And of all the foure parts of the world that I have yet seene not inhabited, could I have but meanes to transport a Colonie, I would rather live here then any where: and if it did not maintaine it selfe, were wee but once indifferently well fitted, let us starve.

Staple commodities present.

The maine Staple, from hence to bee extracted for the present to produce the rest, is fish; which however it may seeme a mean and a base com-moditie: yet who will but truely take the pains and consider the sequell, I thinke will allow it well worth the labour. It is strange to see what great adventures the hopes of setting forth men of war to rob the industrious innocent, would procure; or such massie promises in grosse: though more are choked then well fedde with such hastie hopes.

The Hollanders fishing.

But who doth not know that the poore Holland-ers, chiefly by fishing, at a great charge and labour in all weath-ers in the open Sea, are made a people so hardy, and industrious? and by the venting this poore commodity to the Easterlings for as meane, which is Wood, Flax, Pitch, Tarre, Rosin, Cord-age, and such like (which they exchange againe, to the French, Spaniards, Portugales, and English, etc. for what they want) are made so mighty, strong and rich, as no State but Venice, of twice their magnitude, is so well furnished with so many faire Cities, goodly Townes, strong Fortresses, and that aboundance of shipping and all sorts of marchandize, as well of Golde, Silver, Pearles, Diamonds, Pretious stones, Silkes, Velvets, and Cloth of golde; as Fish, Pitch, Wood, or such grosse commodities? What Voyages and Discoveries, East and West, North and South, yea about the world, make they? What an Army by Sea and Land, have they long maintained in despite of one of the greatest Princes of the world? And never could the Spaniard with all his Mynes of golde and Silver, pay his debts, his friends, and army, halfe so truly, as the Holland-ers stil have done by this contemptible trade of fish. Divers (I know) may alledge many other assistances: But this is their Myne; and the Sea the source of those silvered streames of all their vertue; which hath made them now the very miracle of industrie, the pattern of perfection for these affaires: and the benefit of fishing is that Primum mobile that turnes all their Spheres to this height of plentie, strength, honour and admiration.

Herring, Cod, and Ling, is that triplicitie that makes their wealth and shippings multiplicities, such as it is, and from which (few would thinke it) they yearly draw at least one million and a halfe of pounds starling; yet it is most certaine (if records be true): and in this faculty they are so naturalized, and of their vents so certainely acquainted, as there is no likelihood they will ever bee paralleld, having 2 or 3000 Busses, Flat bottomes, Sword pinks, Todes, and such like, that breedes them Saylers, Mariners, Souldiers and Marchants, never to be wrought out of that trade, and fit for any other. I will not deny but others may gaine as well as they, that will use it, though not so certainely, nor so much in quantity; for want of experience. And this Herring they take upon the Coast of Scotland and England; their Cod and Ling, upon the Coast of Izeland and in the North Seas.

Which is fifteen hundred thousand pound.

Hamborough, and the East Countries, for Sturgion and Caviare, gets many thousands of pounds from England, and the Straites: Portugale, the Biskaines, and the Spaniards, make 40 or 50 Saile yearely to Capeblank, to hooke for Porgos, Mullet, and make Puttargo: and New found Land, doth yearely fraught neere 800 sayle of Ships with a sillie leane skinny Poore-John, and Corfish, which at least yearely amounts to 3 or 400000 pound. If from all those parts such paines is taken for this poore gaines of fish, and by them hath neither meate, drinke, nor clothes, wood, iron, nor steele, pitch, tarre, nets, leades, salt, hookes, nor lines, for shipping, fishing, nor provision, but at the second, third, fourth, or fift hand, drawne from so many severall parts of the world ere they come together to be used in this voyage: If these I say can gaine, and the Saylers live going for shares, lesse then the third part of their labours, and yet spend as much time in going and comming, as in staying there, so short is the season of fishing; why should wee more doubt, then Holland, Portugale, Spaniard, French, or other, but to doe much better then they, where there is victuall to feede us, wood of all sorts, to build Boats, Ships, or Barks; the fish at our

Examples of the altitude comparatively.

doores, pitch, tarre, masts, yards, and most of other necessaries onely for making? And here are no hard Landlords to racke us with high rents, or extorted fines to consume us, no tedious pleas in law to consume us with their many years disputations for Justice: no multitudes to occasion such impediments to good orders, as in popular States. So freely hath God and his Majesty bestowed those blessings on them that will attempt to obtaine them, as here every man may be master and owner of his owne labour and land; or the greatest part in a small time. If hee have nothing but his hands, he may set up this trade; and by industrie quickly grow rich; spending but halfe that time wel, which in England we abuse in idlenes, worse or as ill. Here is ground also as good as any lyeth in the height of forty one, forty two, forty three, etc. which is as temperate and as fruitfull as any other paralell in the world. As for example, on this side the line West of it in the South Sea, is Nova Albion, discovered as is said, by Sir Francis Drake. East from it, is the most temperate part of Portugale, the ancient kingdomes of Galazia, Biskey, Navarre, Arragon, Catalonia, Castilia the olde, and the most moderatest of Castilia the new, and Valentia, which is the greatest part of Spain: which if the Spanish Histories bee true, in the Romanes time abounded no lesse with golde and silver Mines, then now the West Indies; the Romanes then using the Spaniards to work in those Mines, as now the Spaniard doth the Indians.

In France, the Provinces of Gasconie, Langadock, Avignon, Province, Dolphine, Pyamont, and Turyne, are in the same paralel: which are the best and richest parts of France. In Italy, the provinces of Genua, Lumbardy, and Verona, with a great part of the most famous State of Venice, the Dukedoms of Bononia, Mantua, Ferrara, Ravenna, Bolognia, Florence, Pisa, Sienna, Urbine, Ancona, and the ancient Citie and Countrey of Rome, with a great part of the great Kingdome of Naples. In Slavonia, Istrya, and Dalmatia, with the Kingdomes of Albania. In Grecia, that famous Kingdome of Macedonia, Bulgaria, Thessalia, Thracia, or Romania, where is seated the most pleasant and plentifull Citie in Europe, Constantinople. In Asia also, in the same latitude, are the temperatest parts of Natolia, Armenia, Persia, and China, besides divers other large Countries and Kingdomes in these most milde and temperate

Regions of Asia. Southward, in the same height, is the richest of golde Mynes, Chily and Baldivia, and the mouth of the great River of Plate, etc: for all the rest of the world in that height is yet unknown. Besides these reasons, mine owne eyes that have seene a great part of those Cities and their Kingdomes, as well as it, can finde no advantage they have in nature, but this, They are beautified by the long labour and diligence of industrious people and Art. This is onely as God made it, when he created the worlde. Therefore I conclude, if the heart and intralls of those Regions were sought: if their Land were cultured, planted and manured by men of industrie, judgement, and experience; what hope is there, or what neede they doubt, having those advantages of the Sea, but it might equalize any of those famous Kingdomes, in all commodities, pleasures, and conditions? seeing even the very edges doe naturally afford us such plenty, as no ship need returne away empty: and onely use but the season of the Sea, fish will returne an honest gaine, beside all other advantages; her treasures having yet never beene opened, nor her originalls wasted, consumed, nor abused.

And whereas it is said, the Hollanders serve the Easterlings themselves, and other parts that want, with Herring, Ling, and *The particular staple commodities that may be had.* wet Cod; the Easterlings, a great part of Europe, with Sturgion and Caviare; Cape-blanke, Spaine, Portugale, and the Levant, with Mullet, and Put-targo; New found Land, all Europe, with a thin Poore John: yet all is so overlaide with fishers, as the fishing decayeth, and many are constrained to returne with a small fraught. Norway, and Polonia, Pitch, Tar, Masts, and Yardes; Sweathland, and Russia, Iron, and Ropes; France, and Spaine, Canvas, Wine, Steele, Iron, and Oyle; Italy and Greece, Silks, and Fruites. I dare boldly say, because I have seen naturally growing, or breeding in those parts the same materialls that all those are made of, they may as well be had here, or the most part of them, within the distance of 70 leagues for some few ages, as from all those parts; using but the same meanes to have them that they doe, and with all those advantages.

The nature of ground approoved. First, the ground is so fertill, that questionless it is capable of producing any Grain, Fruits, or Seeds you will sow or plant, growing in the

Regions afore named: But it may be, not every kinde to that perfection of delicacy; or some tender plants may miscarie, because the Summer is not so hot, and the winter is more colde in those parts wee have yet tryed neere the Sea side, then we finde in the same height in Europe or Asia; Yet I made a Garden upon the top of a Rockie Ile in 43.½, 4 leagues from the Main, in May, that grew so well, as it served us for sallets in June and July. All sorts of cattell may here be bred and fed in the Iles, or Peninsulaes, securely for nothing. In the Interim till they encrease if need be (observing the seasons) I durst undertake to have corne enough from the Salvages for 300 men, for a few trifles; and if they should bee untoward (as it is most certaine they are) thirty or forty good men will be sufficient to bring them all in subjection, and make this provision; if they understand what they doe: 200 whereof may nine monethes in the yeare be imployed in making marchandable fish, till the rest provide other necessaries, fit to furnish us with other commodities.

In March, Aprill, May, and halfe June, here is Cod in abundance; in May, June, July, and August Mullet and Sturgion; whose roes doe make Caviare and Puttargo. Herring, if any desire them, I have taken many out of the bellies of Cods, some in nets; but the Salvages compare their store in the Sea, to the haires of their heads: and surely there are an incredible abundance upon this Coast. In the end of August, September, October, and November, you have Cod againe, to make Cor fish, or Poore John: and each hundred is as good as two or three hundred in the New-found Land. So that halfe the labour in hooking, splitting, and turning, is saved: and you may have your fish at what Market you will, before they can have any in New-found Land; where their fishing is chiefly but in June and July: whereas it is heere in March, Aprill, May, September, October, and November, as is said. So that by reason of this plantation, the Marchants may have fraught both out and home: which yeelds an advantage worth consideration.

The seasons for fishing approoved.

Your Cor-fish you may in like manner transport as you see cause, to serve the Ports in Portugale (as Lisbon, Avera, Porta port, and divers others, or what market you please) before your Ilanders returne: They being tyed to the season in the open

Sea; you having a double season, and fishing before your doors, may every night sleep quietly a shore with good cheare and what fires you will, or when you please with your wives and familie: they onely, their ships in the maine Ocean.

The Mullets heere are in that abundance, you may take them with nets, sometimes by hundreds, where at Cape blank they hooke them; yet those but one foot and a halfe in length; these two, three, or foure, as oft I have measured: much Salmon some have found up the Rivers, as they have passed: and heer the ayre is so temperate, as all these at any time may well be preserved.

Now, young boyes and girles Salvages, or any other, be they *Imployment for* never such idlers, may turne, carry, and return *poore people* fish, without either shame, or any great paine: hee *and fatherlesse* *children.* is very idle that is past twelve yeares of age and cannot doe so much: and she is very olde, that cannot spin a thred to make engines to catch them.

The facility of For their transportation, the ships that go there *the plantation.* to fish may transport the first: who for their passage will spare the charge of double manning their ships, which they must doe in the New-found Land, to get their fraught; but one third part of that companie are onely but proper to serve a stage, carry a barrow, and turne Poor John: notwithstanding, they must have meate, drinke, clothes, and passage, as well as the rest. Now all I desire, is but this; That those that voluntarily will send shipping, should make here the best choise they can, or accept such as are presented them, to serve them at that rate: and their ships returning leave such with me, with the value of that they should receive comming home, in such provisions and necessarie tooles, armes, bedding and apparell, salt, hookes, nets, lines, and such like as they spare of the remainings; who till the next returne may keepe their boates and doe them many other profitable offices: provided I have men of ability to teach them their functions, and a company fit for Souldiers to be ready upon an occasion; because of the abuses which have beene offered the poore Salvages, and the liberty both French, or any that will, hath to deale with them as they please: whose disorders will be hard to reforme; and the longer the worse. Now such order with facilitie might be taken, with every port Towne or Citie, to observe but this order, With free power to convert the benefits of their fraughts to what advantage they please, and increase their numbers as they see occasion; who ever as they are able to subsist of themselves, may beginne the new Townes in New England in memory of their olde: which freedome being confined but to the necessity of the generall good, the event (with Gods helpe) might produce an honest, a noble, and a profitable emulation.

Salt upon salt may assuredly he made; if not at the first in ponds, yet till they bee provided this may be used: then the Ships may transport Kine, Horse, Goates, course Cloath, and such commodities as we want; by whose arrivall may be made that provision of fish to fraught the Ships that they stay not: and then if the sailers goe for wages, it matters not. It is hard if this returne defray not the charge: but care must be had, they arrive in the Spring, or else provision be made for them against the Winter.

Present commodities.

Of certaine red berries called Alkermes which is worth ten shillings a pound, but of these hath been sould for thirty or forty shillings the pound, may yearely be gathered a good quantitie.

Of the Musk Rat may bee well raised gaines, well worth their labour, that will endevor to make tryall of their goodnesse.

Of Bevers, Otters, Martins, Blacke Foxes, and Furres of price, may yearely be had 6 or 7000: and if the trade of the French were prevented, many more: 25000 this yeare were brought from those Northren parts into France; of which trade we may have as good part as the French, if we take good courses.

Of Mynes of Golde and Silver, Copper, and probabilities of Lead, Christall and Allum, I could say much if relations were good assurances. It is true indeed, I made many trials according to those instructions I had, which doe perswade mee I need not despaire, but there are metalls in the Countrey: but I am no Alchymist, nor will promise more then I know: which is, Who will undertake the rectifying of an Iron forge, if those that buy meate, drinke, coals, ore, and all necessaries at a deer rate gaine; where all these things are to be had for the taking up, in my opinion cannot lose.

Of woods seeing there is such plenty of all sorts, if those that build ships and boates, buy wood at so great a price, as it is in

England, Spaine, France, Italy, and Holland, and all other provisions for the nourishing of mans life; live well by their trade: when labour is all required to take those necessaries without any other tax; what hazard will be here, but doe much better? And what commoditie in Europe doth more decay then wood? For the goodnesse of the ground, let us take it fertill, or barren, or as it is: seeing it is certaine it beares fruites, to nourish and feed man and beast, as well as England, and the Sea those severall sorts of fish I have related. Thus seeing all good provisions for mans sustenance, may with this facility be had, by a little extraordinarie labour, till that transported be increased; and all necessaries for shipping, onely for labour: to which may bee added the assistance of the Salvages, which may easily be had, if they be discreetly handled in their kindes; towards fishing, planting, and destroying woods. What gaines might be raised if this were followed (when there is but once men to fill your store houses, dwelling there, you may serve all Europe better and farre cheaper, then can the Izeland fishers, or the Hollanders, Cape blank, or New found Land: who must be at as much more charge, then you) may easily be conjectured by this example.

2000. pound will fit out a ship of 200. and 1 of a 100 tuns: If the dry fish they both make, fraught that of 200. and goe for Spaine, sell it but at ten shillings a quintall; but commonly it giveth fifteen, or twentie: especially when it commeth first, which amounts to 3 or 4000 pound: but say but tenne, which is the lowest, allowing the rest for waste, it amounts at that rate, to 2000 pound, which is the whole charge of your two ships, and their equipage: Then the returne of the money, and the fraught of the ship for the vintage, or any other voyage, is cleere gaine, with your shippe of a 100 tuns of Train oyle, besides the bevers, and other commodities; and that you may have at home within six monethes, if God please but to send an ordinarie passage. Then saving halfe this charge by the not staying of your ships, your victual, overplus of men and wages; with her fraught thither of things necessarie for the planters, the salt being there made: as also may the nets and lines, within a short time: if nothing were to bee expected but this, it might in time equalize your Hollanders gaines, if not exceed them: they returning

An example of the gains upon every yeare or six monethes returne.

but wood, pitch, tarre, and such grosse commodities; you wines, oyles, fruits, silkes, and such Straits commodities, as you please to provide by your Factors, against such times as your shippes arrive with them. This would so increase our shipping and sailers, and so employ and encourage a great part of our idlers and others that want imployments fitting their qualities at home, where they shame to doe that they would doe abroad; that could they but once taste the sweet fruites of their owne labours, doubtlesse many thousands would be advised by good discipline, to take more pleasure in honest industrie, then in their humours of dissolute idlenesse.

A description of the Countries in particular, and their situations. But, to returne a little more to the particulars of this Countrey, which I intermingle thus with my projects and reasons, not being so sufficiently yet acquainted in those parts, to write fully the estate of the Sea, the Ayre, the Land, the Fruites, the Rocks, the People, the Government, Religion, Territories, and Limitations, Friends, and Foes: but, as I gathered from the niggardly relations in a broken language to my understanding, during the time I ranged those Countries etc. The most Northren part I was at, was the Bay of Pennobscot, which is East and West, North and South, more then ten leagues: but such were my occasions, I was constrained to be satisfied of them I found in the Bay, that the River ranne farre up into the Land, and was well inhabited with many people, but they were from their habitations, either fishing among the Iles, or hunting the Lakes and Woods, for Deer and Bevers. The Bay is full of great Ilands, of one, two, six, eight, or ten miles in length, which divides it into many faire and excellent good harbours. On the East of it, are the Tarrantines, their mortall enemies, where inhabit the French, as they report that live with those people, as one nation or family. And Northwest of Pennobscot is Mecaddacut, at the foot of a high mountaine, a kinde of fortresse against the Tarrantines, adjoyning to the high mountaines of Pennobscot, against whose feet doth beat the Sea: But over all the Land, Iles, or other impediments, you may well see them sixteene or eighteene leagues from their situation. Segocket is the next; then Nusconcus, Pemmaquid, and Sagadahock. Up this River where was the Westerne plantation are Aumuckcawgen, Kinnebeck, and divers others, where there is planted some corne fields. Along this River 40 or 50 miles, I saw nothing but great high cliffes of barren Rocks, overgrowne with wood: but where the Salvages dwelt there the ground is exceeding fat and fertill. Westward of this River, is the Countrey of Aucocisco, in the bottome of a large deepe Bay, full of many great Iles, which divides it into many good harbours. Sowocotuck is the next, in the edge of a large sandy Bay, which hath many Rocks and Iles, but few good harbours, but for Barks, I yet know. But all this Coast to Pennobscot, and as farre I could see Eastward of it is nothing but such high craggy Cliffy Rocks and stony Iles that I wondered such great trees could growe upon so hard foundations. It is a Countrie rather to affright, then delight one. And how to describe a more plaine spectacle of desolation or more barren I knowe not. Yet the Sea there is the strangest fishpond I ever saw; and those barren Iles so furnished with good woods, springs, fruits, fish, and foule, that it makes mee thinke though the Coast be rockie, and thus affrightable; the Vallies, Plaines, and interior parts, may well (notwithstanding) be verie fertile. But there is no kingdome so fertile hath not some part barren: and New England is great enough, to make many Kingdomes and Countries, were it all inhabited. As you passe the Coast still Westward, Accominticus and Passataquack are two convenient harbors for small barks; and a good Countrie, within their craggie cliffs. Angoam is the next; This place might content a right curious judgement: but there are many sands at the entrance of the harbor: and the worst is, it is inbayed too farre from the deepe Sea. Heere are many rising hilles, and on their tops and descents many corne fields, and delightfull groves. On the East, is an Ile of two or three leagues in length; the one halfe, plaine morish grasse fit for pasture, with many faire high groves of mulberrie trees and gardens: and there is also Okes, Pines, and other woods to make this place an excellent habitation, beeing a good and safe harbor.

Naimkeck though it be more rockie ground (for Angoam is sandie) not much inferior; neither for the harbor, nor any thing I could perceive, but the multitude of people. From hence doth stretch into the Sea the faire headland Tragabigzanda, fronted with three Iles called the three Turks heads: to the North of this, doth enter a great Bay, where wee founde some habitations and corne fields: they report a great River, and at least

thirtie habitations, doo possesse this Countrie. But because
the French had got their Trade, I had no leasure to discover it.
The Iles of Mattahunts are on the West side of this Bay, where
are many Iles, and questionlesse good harbors: and then the
Countrie of the Massachusets, which is the Paradise of all those
parts: for, heere are many Iles all planted with corne; groves,
mulberries, salvage gardens, and good harbors: the Coast is for
the most part, high clayie sandie cliffs. The Sea Coast as you
passe, shewes you all along large corne fields, and great troupes
of well proportioned people: but the French having remained
heere neere sixe weekes, left nothing, for us to take occasion
to examine the inhabitants relations, viz. if there be neer three
thousand people upon these Iles; and that the River doth
pearce many daies journeies the intralles of that Countrey. We
found the people in those parts verie kinde; but in their furie
no lesse valiant. For, upon a quarrell wee had with one of them,
hee onely with three others crossed the harbor of Quonahassit
to certaine rocks whereby wee must passe; and there let flie
their arrowes for our shot, till we were out of danger.

Then come you to Accomack, an excellent good harbor,
good land; and no want of any thing, but industrious people.
After much kindnesse, upon a small occasion, wee fought also
with fortie or fiftie of those: though some were hurt, and some
slaine; yet within an houre after they became friendes. Cape
Cod is the next presents it selfe: which is onely a headland of
high hils of sand, overgrowne with shrubbie pines, hurts, and
such trash; but an excellent harbor for all weathers. This Cape
is made by the maine Sea on the one side, and a great Bay on
the other in forme of a sickle: on it doth inhabit the people of
Pawmet: and in the bottome of the Bay, the people of Chawum.
Towards the South and Southwest of this Cape, is found a long
and dangerous shoale of sands and rocks. But so farre as I
incircled it, I found thirtie fadom water aboard the shore, and
a strong current: which makes mee thinke there is a Channell
about this shoale; where is the best and greatest fish to be had,
Winter and Summer, in all that Countrie. But, the Salvages say
there is no Channell, but that the shoales beginne from the
maine at Pawmet, to the Ile of Nausit; and so extends beyond
their knowledge into the Sea. The next to this is Capawack,
and those abounding Countries of copper, corne, people, and

mineralls; which I went to discover this last yeare: but because I miscarried by the way, I will leave them, till God please I have better acquaintance with them.

The Massachusets, they report, sometimes have warres with the Bashabes of Pennobskot; and are not alwaies friends with them of Chawun and their alliants: but now they are all friends, and have each trade with other, so farre as they have societie, on each others frontiers. For they make no such voiages as from Pennobskot to Cape Cod; seldom to Massachewset. In the North (as I have said) they begunne to plant corne, whereof the South part hath such plentie, as they have what they will from them of the North; and in the Winter much more plenty of fish and foule: but both Winter and Summer hath it in the one part or other all the yeare; being the meane and most indifferent temper, betwixt heat and colde, of all the regions betwixt the Lyne and the Pole: but the furs Northward are much better, and in much more plentie, then Southward.

The remarkeablest Iles and mountains for Landmarkes are these; The highest Ile is Sorico, in the Bay of Pennobskot: but the three Iles and a rock of Matinnack are much furder in the Sea; Metinicus is also three plaine Iles and a rock, betwixt it and Monahigan: Monahigan is a rounde high Ile; and close by it Monanis, betwixt which is a small harbor where we ride. In Damerils Iles is such another: Sagadahock is knowne by Satquin, and foure or five Iles in the mouth. Smyths Iles are a heape together, none neere them, against Accominticus. The three Turks heads are three Iles seen far to Sea-ward in regard of the headland.

The cheefe headlands are onely Cape Tragabigzanda and Cape Cod.

The cheefe mountaines, them of Pennobscot; the twinkling mountaine of Aucocisco; the greate mountaine of Sasanou; and the high mountaine of Massachusit: each of which you shall

finde in the Mappe; their places, formes, and altitude. The waters are most pure, proceeding from the intrals of rockie mountaines; the hearbes and fruits are of many sorts and kindes: as alkermes, currans, or a fruit like currans, mulberries, vines, respices, goos-berries, plummes, walnuts, chesnuts, small nuts, etc. pumpions, gourds, strawberries, beans, pease, and mayze; a kinde or two of flax, wherewith they make nets, lines and ropes both small and great, verie strong for their quantities.

Woods. Oke, is the chiefe wood; of which there is great difference in regard of the soyle where it groweth. firre, pyne, walnut, chesnut, birch, ash, elme, cypresse, ceder, mulberrie, plumtree, hazell, saxefrage, and many other sorts.

Birds. Eagles, Gripes, diverse sorts of Haukes, Cranes, Geese, Brants, Cormorants, Ducks, Sheldrakes, Teale, Meawes, Guls, Turkies, Dive-doppers, and many other sorts, whose names I knowe not.

Fishes. Whales, Grampus, Porkpisces, Turbut, Sturgion, Cod, Hake, Haddock, Cole, Cusk, or small Ling, Shark, Mackerell, Herring, Mullet, Base, Pinacks, Cunners, Pearch, Eels, Crabs, Lobsters, Muskles, Wilkes, Oysters, and diverse others etc.

Beasts. Moos, a beast bigger then a Stagge; deere, red, and Fallow; Bevers, Wolves, Foxes, both blacke and other; Aroughconds, Wild-cats, Beares, Otters, Martins, Fitches, Musquassus, and diverse sorts of vermine, whose names I know not. All these and diverse other good things do heere, for want of use, still increase, and decrease with little diminution, whereby they growe to that abundance. You shall scarce finde any Baye, shallow shore, or Cove of sand, where you may not take many Clampes, or Lobsters, or both at your pleasure, and in many places lode your boat if you please; Nor Iles where you finde not fruits, birds, crabs, and muskles, or all of them, for taking, at a lowe water. And in the harbors we frequented, a little boye might take of Cunners, and Pinacks, and such delicate fish, at the ships sterne, more then sixe or tenne can eate in a daie; but with a casting-net, thousands when wee pleased: and scarce any place, but Cod, Cuske, Holybut, Mackerell, Scate, or such like, a man may take with a hooke or line what he will. And, in diverse sandy Baies, a man may draw with a net great store of Mullets, Bases, and diverse other sorts of such excellent fish, as many as his Net can drawe on shore: no River where there is not plentie of Sturgion, or Salmon, or both; all which are to be had in abundance observing but their seasons. But if a man will goe at Christmasse to gather Cherries in Kent, he may be deceived; though there be plentie in Summer: so, heere these plenties have each their seasons, as I have expressed. We for the most part had little but bread and vineger: and though the most part of July when the fishing decaied they wrought all day, laie abroade in the Iles all night, and lived on what they found; yet were not sicke: But I would wish none put himself long to such plunges; except necessitie constraine it: yet worthy is that person to starve that heere cannot live; if he have sense, strength and health: for, there is no such penury of these blessings in any place, but that a hundred men may, in one houre or two, make their provisions for a day: and hee that hath experience to mannage well these affaires, with fortie or thirtie honest industrious men, might well undertake (if they dwell in these parts) to subject the Salvages, and feed daily two or three hundred men, with as good corne, fish, and flesh, as the earth hath of those kindes, and yet make that labor but their pleasure: provided that they have engins, that be proper for their purposes.

Who can desire more content, that hath small

A note for men that have great spirits, and smal meanes.

meanes; or but only his merit to advance his fortune, then to tread, and plant that ground hee hath purchased by the hazard of his life? If he have but the taste of virtue, and magnanimitie, what to such a minde can bee more pleasant, then planting and building a foundation for his Posteritie, gotte from the rude earth, by Gods blessing and his owne industrie, without prejudice to any? If hee have any graine of faith or zeale in Religion, what can hee doe lesse hurtfull to any; or more agreeable to God, then to seeke to convert those poore Salvages to know Christ, and humanitie, whose labors with discretion will triple requite thy charge and paines? What so truely sutes with honour and honestie, as the discovering things unknowne? erecting Townes, peopling Countries, informing the ignorant, reforming things unjust, teaching virtue; and gaine to our Native mother-countrie a kingdom to attend her; finde imployment for those that are idle, because they know not what to doe: so farre from wronging any, as to cause Posteritie to remember thee; and remembring thee, ever honour that remembrance with praise? Consider: What were the beginnings and endings of the Monarkies of the Chaldeans, the Syrians, the Grecians, and Romanes, but this one rule; What was it they would not doe, for the good of the commonwealth, or their Mother-citie? For example: Rome, What made her such a Monarchesse, but onely the adventures of her youth, not in riots at home; but in dangers abroad? and the justice and judgement out of their experience, when they grewe aged. What was their ruine and hurt, but this; The excesse of idlenesse, the fondnesse of Parents, the want of experience in Magistrates, the admiration of their undeserved honours, the contempt of true merit, their unjust jealosies, their politicke incredulities, their hypocriticall seeming goodnesse, and their deeds of secret lewdnesse? finally, in fine, growing onely formall temporists, all that their predecessors got in many years, they lost in few daies. Those by their pains and vertues became Lords of the world; they by their ease and vices became slaves to their servants. This is the difference betwixt the use of Armes in the field, and on the monuments of stones; the golden age and the leaden age, prosperity and miserie, justice and corruption, substance and shadowes, words and deeds, experience and imagination, making Commonwealths and marring Commonwealths, the fruits of vertue and the conclusions of vice.

Then, who would live at home idly (or thinke in himselfe any worth to live) onely to eate, drink, and sleepe, and so die? Or by consuming that carelesly, his friends got worthily? Or by using that miserably, that maintained vertue honestly? Or, for being descended nobly, pine with the vaine vaunt of great kindred, in penurie? Or (to maintaine a silly shewe of bravery) toyle out thy heart, soule, and time, basely, by shifts, tricks, cards, and dice? Or by relating newes of others actions, sharke here or there for a dinner, or supper; deceive thy friends, by faire promises, and dissimulation, in borrowing where thou never intendest to pay; offend the lawes, surfeit with excesse, burden thy Country, abuse thy selfe, despaire in want, and then couzen thy kindred, yea even thine owne brother, and wish thy parents death (I will not say damnation) to have their estates? though thou seest what honours, and rewards, the world yet hath for them will seeke them and worthily deserve them.

I would be sory to offend, or that any should mistake my honest meaning: for I wish good to all, hurt to none. But rich men for the most part are growne to that dotage, through their pride in their wealth, as though there were no accident could end it, or their life. And what hellish care do such take to make it their owne miserie, and their Countries spoile, especially when there is most neede of their imployment? drawing by all manner of inventions, from the Prince and his honest subjects, even the vitall spirits of their powers and estates: as if their Bagges, or Bragges, were so powerfull a defence, the malicious could not assault them; when they are the onely baite, to cause us not to be onely assaulted; but betrayed and murdered in our owne security, ere we well perceive it.

An example of secure covetousness. May not the miserable ruine of Constantinople, their impregnable walles, riches, and pleasures last taken by the Turke (which are but a bit, in comparison of their now mightines) remember us, of the effects of private covetousness? at which time the good Emperour held himselfe rich enough, to have such rich subjects, so formall in all excesse of vanity, all kinde of delicacie, and prodigalitie. His povertie when the Turke besieged, the citizens (whose marchandizing thoughts were onely to get wealth, little conceiving the desperate resolution of a valiant expert enemy) left the Emperour so long to his conclusions, having spent all he had to pay his young, raw, discontented Souldiers; that sodainly he, they, and their citie were all a prey to the devouring Turke. And what they would not spare for the maintenance of them who adventured their lives to defend them, did serve onely their enemies to torment them, their friends, and countrey, and all Christendome to this present day. Let this lamentable example remember you that are rich (seeing there are such great theeves in the world to robbe you) not grudge to lend some proportion, to breed them that have little, yet willing to learne how to defend you: for, it is too late when the deede is a-doing. The Romanes estate hath beene worse then this: for, the meere covetousnesse and extortion of a few of them, so mooved the rest, that not having any imployment, but contemplation; their great judgements grew to so great malice, as themselves were sufficient to destroy themselves by faction: Let this moove you to embrace imployment, for those whose educations, spirits, and judgements, want but your purses; not onely to prevent such accustomed dangers, but also to gaine more thereby then you have. And you fathers that are either so foolishly fond, or so miserably covetous, or so willfully

ignorant, or so negligently carelesse, as that you will rather
maintaine your children in idle wantonness, till they growe
your masters; or become so basely unkinde, as they wish nothing but your deaths; so that both sorts growe dissolute: and
although you would wish them any where to escape the gallowes, and ease your cares; though they spend you here one,
two, or three hundred pound a yeer; you would grudge to give
halfe so much in adventure with them, to obtaine an estate,
which in a small time but with a little assistance of your providence, might bee better then your owne. But if an Angell
should tell you, that any place yet unknowne can afford such
fortunes; you would not beleeve him, no more then Columbus
was beleeved there was any such Land as is now the well knowne
abounding America; much lesse such large Regions as are yet
unknowne, as well in America, as in Affrica, and Asia, and
Terra incognita; where were courses for gentlemen (and them
that would be so reputed) more suiting their qualities, then
begging from their Princes generous disposition, the labours
of his subjects, and the very marrow of his maintenance.

I have not beene so ill bred, but I have tasted of
Plenty and Pleasure, as well as Want and Miserie:
nor doth necessity yet, or occasion of discontent,
force me to these endeavors: nor am I ignorant what small
thanke I shall have for my paines; or that many would have the
Worlde imagine them to be of great judgement, that can but
blemish these my designs, by their witty objections and detrac-
tions: yet (I hope) my reasons with my deeds, will so prevaile
with some, that I shall not want imployment in these affaires,
to make the most blinde see his owne senselesnesse, and incre-
dulity; Hoping that gaine will make them affect that, which
Religion, Charity, and the Common good cannot. It were but
a poore device in me, To deceive my selfe; much more the
King, and State, my Friends, and Countrey, with these inducements: which, seeing his Majestie hath given permission, I wish
all sorts of worthie, honest, industrious spirits, would understand: and if they desire any further satisfaction, I will doe my
best to give it: Not to perswade them to goe onely; but goe
with them: Not leave them there; but live with them there. I
will not say, but by ill providing and undue managing, such
courses may be taken, may make us miserable enough: But if I

The Authors conditions.

may have the execution of what I have projected; if they want to eate, let them eate or never digest Me. If I performe what I say, I desire but that reward out of the gaines may sute my paines, quality, and condition. And if I abuse you with my tongue, take my head for satisfaction. If any dislike at the yeares end, defraying their charge, by my consent they should freely returne. I feare not want of companie sufficient, were it but knowne what I know of those Countries; and by the proofe of that wealth I hope yearely to returne, if God please to blesse me from such accidents, as are beyond my power in reason to The planters prevent: For, I am not so simple, to thinke, that pleasures, and ever any other motive then wealth, will ever erect profits. there a Commonweale; or draw companie from their ease and humours at home, to stay in New England to effect my purposes. And lest any should thinke the toile might be insupportable, though these things may be had by labour, and diligence: I assure my selfe there are who delight extreamly in vaine pleasure, that take much more paines in England, to enjoy it, then I should doe heere to gaine wealth sufficient: and yet I thinke they should not have halfe such sweet content: for, our pleasure here is still gaines; in England charges and losse. Heer nature and liberty affords us that freely, which in England we want, or it costeth us dearely. What pleasure can be more, then (being tired with any occasion a-shore) in planting Vines, Fruits, or Hearbs, in contriving their owne Grounds, to the pleasure of their owne mindes, their Fields, Gardens, Orchards, Buildings, Ships, and other works, etc. to recreate themselves before their owne doores, in their owne boates upon the Sea, where man woman and childe, with a small hooke and line, by angling, may take diverse sorts of excellent fish, at their pleasures? And is it not pretty sport, to pull up two pence, six pence, and twelve pence, as fast as you can hale and veare a line? He is a very bad fisher, cannot kill in one day with his hooke and line, one, two, or three hundred Cods: which dressed and dryed, if they be sould there for ten shillings the hundred, though in England they will give more then twentie; may not both the servant, the master, and marchant, be well content with this gaine? If a man worke but three dayes in seaven, he may get more then hee can spend, unlesse he will be excessive. Now that Carpenter, Mason, Gardiner, Taylor, Smith, Sailer,

Forgers, or what other, may they not make this a pretty recreation though they fish but an houre in a day, to take more then they eate in a weeke: or if they will not eate it, because there is so much better choise; yet sell it, or change it, with the fisher men, or marchants, for any thing they want. And what sport doth yeeld a more pleasing content, and lesse hurt or charge then angling with a hooke, and crossing the sweete ayre from Ile to Ile, over the silent streames of a calme Sea? wherein the most curious may finde pleasure, profit, and content. Thus, though all men he not fishers: yet all men, whatsoever, may in other matters doe as well. For necessity doth in these cases so rule a Commonwealth, and each in their severall functions, as their labours in their qualities may be as profitable, because there is a necessary mutuall use of all.

For Gentlemen, what exercise should more delight them, then ranging dayly those unknowne parts, using fowling and fishing, for hunting and hauking? and yet you shall see the wilde haukes give you some pleasure, in seeing them stoope (six or seaven after one another) an houre or two together, at the skuls of fish in the faire harbours, as those a-shore at a foule; and never trouble nor torment your selves, with watching, mewing, feeding, and attending them: nor kill horse and man with running and crying, See you not a hauk? For hunting also: the woods, lakes, and rivers, affoord not onely chase sufficient, for any that delights in that kinde of toyle, or pleasure; but such beasts to hunt, that besides the delicacy of their bodies for food, their skins are so rich, as may well recompence thy dayly labour, with a Captains pay.

Imployments for gentlemen.

For labourers, if those that sowe hemp, rape, turnups, parsnips, carrats, cabidge, and such like; give 20, 30, 40, 50 shillings yearely for an acre of ground, and meat drinke and wages to use it, and yet grow rich: when better, or at least as good ground, may be had and cost nothing but labour; it seemes strange to me, any such should there grow poore.

Imployments for labourers.

My purpose is not to perswade children from their parents; men from their wives; nor servants from their masters: onely, such as with free consent may be spared: But that each parish, or village, in Citie, or Countrey, that will but apparell their

with these affaires, I have not learned there is a great difference, betwixt the directions and judgement of experimentall
knowledge, and the superficiall conjecture of variable relation:
wherein rumor, humor, or misprision have such power, that oft
times one is enough to beguile twentie, but twentie not sufficient to keep one from being deceived. Therefore I know no
reason but to beleeve my own eies, before any mans imagination, that is but wrested from the conceits of my owne projects,
and indeavours. But I honor, with all affection, the counsell
and instructions of judiciall directions, or any other honest
advertisement; so farre to observe, as they tie mee not to the
crueltie of unknowne events.

These are the inducements that thus drew me to neglect all
other imployments, and spend my time and best abilities in
these adventures. Wherein, though I have had many discouragements by the ingratitude of some, the malicious slanders of
others, the falsenesse of friendes, the trechery of cowards, and
slownesse of adventurers; but chiefly by one Hunt, who was
Master of the ship, with whom oft arguing these projects, for
a plantation, however hee seemed well in words to like it, yet
he practiced to have robbed mee of my plots, and observations,
and so to leave me alone in a desolate Ile, to the fury of famine,
and all other extreamities (lest I should have acquainted Sir
Thomas Smith, my Honourable good friend, and the Councell
of Virginia) to the end, he and his associates, might secretly
ingrosse it, ere it were knowne to the State: Yet that God that
alway hath kept me from the worst of such practices, delivered
me from the worst of his dissimulations. Notwithstanding after
my departure, hee abused the Salvages where hee came, and
betrayed twenty seaven of these poore innocent soules, which
he sould in Spaine for slaves, to moove their hate against our
Nation, as well as to cause my proceedings to be so much the
more difficult.

Now, returning in the Bark, in the fift of August, I arrived
at Plimouth: where imparting those my purposes to my honourable friende Sir Ferdinando Gorge, and some others; I was
so incouraged, and assured to have the managing their authoritie in those parts, during my life, that I ingaged my selfe to
undertake it for them. Arriving at London, I found also many
promise me such assistance, that I entertained Michaell Cooper

the Master, who returned with mee, and others of the company. How hee dealt with others, or others with him I know not: But my publike proceeding gave such incouragement, that it became so well apprehended by some fewe of the Southren Company, as these projects were liked, and he furnished from London with foure ships at Sea, before they at Plimouth had made any provision at all, but onely a ship cheefely set out by sir Ferdinando Gorge; which upon Hunts late trecherie among the Salvages, returned as shee went, and did little or nothing, but lost her time. I must confesse I was beholden to the setters forth of the foure ships that went with Cooper; in that they offered mee that imploiment if I would accept it: and I finde, my refusall hath incurred some of their displeasures, whose favor and love I exceedingly desire, if I may honestly injoy it. And though they doe censure me as opposite to their proceedings; they shall yet still in all my words and deedes finde, it is their error, not my fault, that occasions their dislike: for having ingaged my selfe in this husinesse to the West Countrie; I had beene verie dishonest to have broke my promise; nor will I spend more time in discoverie, or fishing, till I may goe with a companie for plantation: for, I know my grounds. Yet every one that reades this booke can not put it in practice; though it may helpe any that have seene those parts. And though they endeavour to worke me even out of my owne designes, I will not much envy their fortunes: but, I would bee sory, their intruding ignorance should, by their defailements, bring those certainties to douhtfulnesse: So that the businesse prosper, I have my desire; be it by Londoner, Scot, Welch, or English, that are true subjects to our King and Countrey: the good of my Countrey is that I seeke; and there is more then enough for all, if they could bee content but to proceed.

At last it pleased Sir Ferdinando Gorge, and Master Doctor Sutliffe, Deane of Exceter, to conceive so well of these projects, and my former imployments, as induced them to make a new adventure with me in those parts, whither they have so often sent to their continuall losse. By whose example, many inhabitants of the west Country, made promises of much more then was looked for, but their private emulations quickly qualified that heat in the greater number; so that the burden lay principally on them,

The occasion of my returne.

and some few Gentlemen my friends, in London. In the end I was furnished with a Ship of 200. and another of 50. But ere I had sayled 120 leagues, shee broke all her masts; pumping each watch 5 or 6000 strokes: onely her spret saile remayned to spoon before the wind, till we had re-accommodated a Jury mast, and the rest, to returne for Plimouth. My Vice-admirall beeing lost, not knowing of this, proceeded her voyage: Now with the remainder of those provisions, I got out again in a small Barke of 60 tuns with 30 men (for this of 200 and provision for 70) which were the 16 before named, and 14 other saylors for the ship. With those I set saile againe the 24 of June: where what befell me (because my actions and writings are so publicke to the world, envy still seeking to scandalize my indeavours, and seeing no power but death, can stop the chat of ill tongues, nor imagination of mens mindes) lest my owne relations of those hard events, might by some constructors, be made doubtfull, I have thought it best to insert the examinations of those proceedings, taken by Sir Lewis Stukley a worthie Knight, and Viceadmirall of Devonshire; which were as followeth.

My reimbark-
ment, in-
counters with
pyrats and
imprisonment
by the French.

Captaine Fry
his ship 140
tuns, 36 cast
peeces and
murderers, 80
men; of which
40, or 50.
were master
gunners.

The examination of Daniel Baker, late Steward to Captaine John Smith in the returne of Plimouth; taken before Sir Lewis Stukley, Knight, the eight of December 1615.

Who saith, being chased two dayes by one Fry, an English Pirate, that could not board us, by reason of foule weather, Edmund Chambers, the Master, John Minter, his mate, Thomas Digby the Pilot, and others importuned his saide Captaine to yeeld; houlding it umpossible hee should defend himselfe: and that the saide Captaine should send them his boate, in that they had none: which at last he concluded upon these conditions, That Fry the Pyrate should vow not to take any thing from Captaine Smith, that might overthrowe his voyage, nor send more Pirats into his ship then hee liked off; otherwaies, he would make sure of them he had, and defend himselfe against the rest as hee could.

More: he confesseth that the quarter-masters and Chambers received golde of those Pirats; but how much, he knoweth not: Nor would his Captain come out of his Caben to entertaine them; although a great many of them had beene his saylers, and for his love would have wafted us to the Iles of Flowers.

The one of 200, the other 20.

At Fyall, wee were chased by two French Pyrats, who commanded us Amaine. Chambers, Minter, Digby, and others, importuned againe the Captaine to yeeld; alledging they were Turks, and would make them all slaves: or Frenchmen, and would throw them all over board if they shot but a peece; and that they were entertained to fish, and not to fight: untill the Captaine vowed to fire the powder and split the ship, if they would not stand to their defence; whereby at last wee went cleere of them, for all their shot.

The Admirall 140 tuns, 12 peeces, 12 murderers, 90 men, with long pistols, pocket pistols, musket, sword and poniard, the Vice-admirall 100 tuns, the Rere-admiral 60, the other 80: all had 250 men most armed as is said.

At Flowers, wee were chased by foure French men of warre; all with their close fights afore and after. And this examinants Captaine having provided for our defence, Chambers, Minter, Digby, and some others, againe importuned him to yeeld to the favour of those, against whom there was nothing but ruine by fighting: But if he would goe aboard them, in that hee could speake French, by curtesie hee might goe cleere; seeing they offered him such faire quarter, and vowed they were Protestants, and all of Rochell, and had the Kings commission onely to take Spaniards, Portugales, and Pyrats; which at last hee did: but they kept this examinates Captaine and some other of his company with him. The next day the French men of warre went aboard us, and tooke what they listed, and divided the company into their severall ships, and manned this examinates ship with the Frenchmen; and chased with her all the shippes they saw: untill about five or six dayes after upon better consideration, they surrendered the ship, and victualls, with the most part of our provision, but not our weapons.

The gentlemen and souldiers were ever willing to fight.

More: he confesseth that his Captain exhorted them to performe their voyage, or goe for New found Land to returne fraughted with fish, where hee would finde meanes to proceed in his plantation: but Chambers and Minter grew upon tearms they would not; untill those that were Souldiers concluded with their Captaines resolution, they would; seeing they had clothes, victualls, salt, nets, and lines sufficient, and expected their armes: and such other things as they wanted, the French men promised to restore, which the Captaine the next day went to seeke, and sent them about loading of commodities, as powder, match, hookes, instruments, his sword and dagger, bedding, aqua vitæ, his commission, apparell, and many other things; the particulars he remembreth not: But, as for the cloath, canvas, and the Captaines cloathes, Chambers, and his associats divided it amongst themselves, and to whom they best liked; his Captaine not having any thing, to his knowledge, but his wastecoat and breeches. And in this manner going from ship to ship, to regaine our armes, and the rest; they seeing a sayle, gave chase untill night. The next day being very foule weather, this examinate came so neere with the ship unto the French men of warre, that they split the maine sayle on the others spret sayle yard. Chambers willed the Captaine come aboard, or hee would leave him: whereupon the Captaine commanded Chambers to send his boate for him. Chambers replyed shee was split (which was false) telling him hee might come if he would in the Admiralls boat. The Captaines answer was, he could not command her, nor come when hee would: so this examinate fell on sterne; and that night left his said Captaine alone amongst the French men, in this manner, by the command of Chambers, Minter, and others.

Daniel Cage, Edward Stalings, Gentlemen; Walter Chissell, David Cooper, Robert Miller, and John Partridge, beeing examined, doe acknowledge and confesse, that Daniel Baker his examination above writen is true.

Now the cause why the French detayned me againe, was the suspicion this Chambers and Minter gave them, that I would revenge my selfe, upon the Bank, or in New found Land, of all the French I could there incounter; and how I would have fired the ship, had they not overperswaded mee: and many other such like tricks to catch but opportunitie in this maner to leave me. And thus they returned to Plimouth; and perforce with the French I thus proceeded.

A double treachery.

Being a Fleet of eight or nine sayle, we watched for the West Indies fleet, till ill weather separated us from the other 8. Still we spent our time about the Iles neere Fyall: where to keepe my perplexed thoughts from too much meditation of my miserable estate, I writ this discourse; thinking to have sent it you of his Majesties Councell, by some ship or other: for I saw their purpose was to take all they could. At last we were chased by one Captain Barra, an English Pyrat, in a small ship, with some twelve peeces of ordinance, about thirty men, and neer all starved. They sought by curtesie releefe of us; who gave them such faire promises, as at last wee betrayed Captaine Wolliston (his Lieftenant) and foure or five of their men aboard us, and then provided to take the rest perforce. Now my part was to be prisoner in the gun-roum, and not to speake to any of them upon my life: yet had Barra knowledge what I was. Then Barra perceiving wel these French intents, made ready to fight, and Wolliston as resolutely regarded not their threats, which caused us demurre upon the matter longer, som sixteene houres; and then returned their prisoners, and some victualls also, upon a small composition. The next wee tooke was a small English man of Poole from New found Land. The great caben at this present, was my prison; from whence I could see them pillage those poore men of all that they had, and halfe their fish. When hee was gone, they sould his poore cloathes at the maine mast, by an outcry, which scarce gave each man seaven pence a peece. Not long after, wee tooke a Scot fraught from Saint Michaels to Bristow: hee had better fortune then the other. For, having but taken a boats loading of suger, marmelade, suckets, and such like, we discried foure sayle, after whom we stood; who forling their maine sayles attended us to fight. But our French spirits were content onely to perceive they were English red crosses. Within a very small time after, wee chased foure Spanish shippes came from the Indies: wee fought with them foure or five houres, tore their sayles and sides; yet not daring to board them, lost them. A poore Carvell of Brasile, was the next we chased: and after a small fight, thirteene or fourteene of her men being wounded, which was the better halfe, we tooke her, with 370 chests of sugar. The next was a West

A fleet of nine French men of war, and fights with the Spaniards.

A prize worth 1600 crowns.

A prize worth 200000 crownes.

Indies man, of 160 tuns, with 1200 hides, 50 chests of cutchanell, 14 coffers of wedges of silver, 8000 ryalls of 8, and six coffers of the King of Spaines treasure, besides the pillage and rich coffers of many rich passengers. Two monethes they kept me in this manner to manage their fights against the Spaniards, and be a prisoner when they tooke any English. Now though the Captaine had oft broke his promise, which was to put me a-shore on the Iles, or the next ship he tooke; yet at last, he was intreated I should goe for France in the Carvell of sugar: himselfe resolved still to keepe the Seas. Within two dayes after, we were haled by two West Indy men: but when they saw us wave them for the King of France, they gave us their broad sides, shot through our mayne mast and so left us. Having lived thus, neer three moneths among those French men of warre; with much adoe, we arrived at the Gulion, not far from Rochel; where in stead of the great promises they alwaies fed me with, of double satisfaction, and full content, they kept me five or six daies prisoner in the Carvell, accusing me to bee him that burnt their Colony in New France; to force mee give them a discharge before the Judge of the Admiralty, and so stand to their curtesie for satisfaction, or lie in prison, or a worse mischiefe. To prevent this choise, in the end of such

My escape from the French men.

a storme that beat them all under Hatches, I watched my opportunity to get a-shore in their boat; where-into, in the darke night, I secretly got: and with a halfe pike that lay by me, put a drift for Rat Ile: but the Current was so strong and the Sea so great, I went a drift to Sea; till it pleased God the winde so turned with the tide, that although I was all this fearefull night of gusts and raine, in the Sea, the space of 12 houres, when many ships were driven a shore, and diverse split (and being with sculling and bayling the water tired, I expected each minute would sinke mee) at last I arrived in an oazie Ile by Charowne; where certaine fowlers found mee neere drowned, and halfe dead, with water, colde, and hunger. By those, I found meanes to gette to Rochell; where I understood the man of warre which we left at Sea, and the rich prize was split, the Captaine drowned and halfe his companie the same night, within seaven leagues of that place, from whence I escaped alone, in the little boate, by the mercy of God; far beyond all mens reason, or my expectation. Arriving at Rochell, upon my complaint to the Judge of the Admiraltie, I founde many good words, and faire promises; and ere long many of them that escaped drowning, tolde mee the newes they heard of my owne death: these I arresting, their severall examinations did so confirme my complaint, it was held proofe sufficient. All which being performed according to the order of justice, from under the judges hand; I presented it to the English Ambassador then at Burdeaux, where it was my chance to see the arrivall of the Kings great mariage brought from Spaine. Of the wrack of the rich prize some 36000 crownes worth of goods came a shore and was saved with the Carvell, which I did my best to arrest: the Judge did promise me I shold have justice; what will bee the conclusion as yet, I know not. But under the colour to take Pirats and West-Indie men (because the Spanyards will not suffer the French trade in the West-Indies) any goods from thence, thogh they take them upon the Coast of Spaine, are lawfull prize; or from any of his territories out of the limits of Europe.

Sir Thomas Edmunds.

They betraied mee having the broad seale of England: and neere twentie sayle of English more, besides them concealed, in like maner were betrayed that year. My returne for England, 1615.

Leaving thus my businesse in France, I returned to Plimouth, to find them that had thus buried me amongst the French: and not onely buried mee, but with so much infamy, as such trecherous cowards could suggest to excuse their villanies: But my clothes, bookes, instruments, Armes, and what I had, they shared amongst them, and what they liked; fayning, the French had all was wanting; and had throwne them into the Sea, taken their ship, and all, had they not runne away and left me as they did. The cheeftaines of this mutinie that I could finde, I laied by the heeles; the rest, like themselves, confessed the truth as you have heard. Now how I have or could prevent these accidents, I rest at your censures. But to the matter.

The successe of my vice Admirall and the foure ships of London, from New England.

Newfound-land at the first, I have heard, was held as desperate a fishing, as this I project in New England. Placentia, and the Banke, were also as doubtfull to the French: But, for all the disasters happened mee, the businesse is the same it was: and the five ships (whereof one was reported more then three hundred tunnes) went forward; and found fish so much, that neither Izeland-man, nor Newfound-land-man, I could heare of hath beene there, will goe any more to either place, if they may goe thither. So, that upon the returne of my Viceadmirall that proceeded on her voyage when I spent my masts, from Plimouth this yeare are gone foure or five saile: and from London as many; onely to make voyages of profit: where the Englishmen have yet beene, all their returnes together (except Sir Francis Popphames) would scarce make one a saver of neere a douzen I could nominate; though there be fish sufficient, as I perswade my selfe, to fraught yearely foure or five hundred sayle, or as many as will goe. For, this fishing stretcheth along the Coast from Cape Cod to New-found-land, which is seaven or eight hundered miles at the least; and hath his course in the deepes, and by the shore, all the yeare long; keeping their hants and feedings as the beasts of the field, and the birds of the aire. But, all men are not such as they should bee, that have undertaken those voiages: and a man that hath but heard of an instrument, can hardly use it so well, as hee that by use hath contrived to make it. All the Romanes were not Scipioes: nor all the Geneweses, Columbuses: nor all Spanyards, Corteses: had they dived no deeper in the secrets of their discoveries, then wee, or stopped at such doubts and poore accidentall chances; they had never beene remembred as they are: yet had they no such certainties to begin as wee. But, to conclude, Adam and Eve did first beginne this innocent worke, To plant the earth to remaine to posteritie; but not without labour, trouble and industrie. Noe, and his family, beganne againe the second plantation; and their seede as it still increased, hath still planted new Countries, and one countrie another: and so the world to that estate it is. But not without much hazard, travell, discontents, and many disasters. Had those worthie Fathers and their memorable off-spring not beene more diligent for us now in these Ages, then wee are to plant that yet unplanted, for the after livers: Had the seede of Abraham, our Saviour Christ, and his Apostles, exposed themselves to no more daungers to teach the Gospell, and the will of God then wee; Even wee our selves, had at this present been as Salvage, and as miserable as the most barbarous Salvage yet uncivilized. The Hebrewes, and Lacedæmonians, the Goths, the Grecians, the Romanes, and the rest, what was it they would not undertake to inlarge their Territories, enrich their subjects, resist their enemies? Those that were the founders of those great Monarchies and their vertues, were no silvered idle golden Pharises, but industrious iron-steeled Publicans: They regarded more provisions, and necessaries for their people, then jewels, riches, ease, or delight for themselves. Riches were their servants, not their Maisters. They ruled (as Fathers, not as Tyrantes) their people as children, not as slaves: there was no disaster, could discourage them; and let none thinke they incountered not with all manner of incumbrances. And what have ever beene the workes of the greatest Princes of the earth, but planting of countries, and civilizing barbarous and inhumane Nations, to civilitie and humanitie? whose eternall actions, fill our histories. Lastly, the Portugales, and Spanyards: whose everliving actions, before our eyes will testifie with them our idlenesse, and ingratitude to all posterities, and the neglect of our duties in our pietie and religion we owe our God, our King, and Countrie; and want of charity to those poore salvages, whose Countrie wee challenge, use and possesse; except wee bee but made to use, and marre what our Fore-fathers made, or but onely tell what they did, or esteeme our selves too good to take the like paines. Was it vertue in them, to provide that doth maintaine us? and basenesse for us to doe the like for others? Surely no. Then seeing we are not borne for our selves, but each to helpe other, and our abilities are much alike at the houre of our birth, and the minute of our death: Seeing our good deedes, or our badde, by faith in Christs merits, is all we have to carrie our soules to heaven, or hell: Seeing honour is our lives ambition; and our ambition after death, to have an honourable memorie of our life: and seeing by noe meanes wee would bee abated of the dignities and glories of our Predecessors; let us imitate their vertues to bee worthily their successors.

FINIS.

To his worthy Captaine,
the Author.

Oft thou hast led, when I brought up the Rere
In bloodie wars, where thousands have bin slaine.
    Then give mee leave, in this some part to beare;
And as thy servant, heere to read my name.
    Tis true, long time thou host my Captaine beene
In the fierce wars of Transilvania:
    Long ere that thou America *hadst seene,*
Or led wast captived in Virginia;
    Thou that to passe the worlds foure parts dost deeme
No more, then t'were to goe to bed, or drinke,
    And all thou yet hast done, thou dost esteeme
As nothing. This doth cause mee thinke
    That thou I'ave seene so oft approv'd in dangers
(And thrice captiv'd, thy valor still hath freed)
    Art yet preserved, to convert those strangers:
By God thy guide, I trust it is decreed.
    For mee: I not commend, but much admire
    Thy England yet unknowne to passers by-her.
    For it will praise it selfe in spight of me;
    Thou it, it thou, to all posteritie.
                    Your true friend, and souldier,
                    Ed. Robinson.

To my honest Captaine,
the Author.

Malignant Times! What can be said or don,
But shall be censur'd and traduc't by some!
    This worthy Work, which thou hast bought so dear,
    Ne thou, nor it, Detractors neede to fear.
Thy words by deedes so long thou hast approv'd,
Of thousands knowe thee not thou art belov'd.
    And this great Plot will make thee ten times more
    Knowne and belov'd, than ere thou wert before.
I never knew a Warryer yet, but thee,
From wine, Tobacco, debts, dice, oaths, so free.
    I call thee Warrier: *and I make the bolder;*
    For, many a Captaine *now, was never Souldier*

Some such may swell at this: but (to their praise)
When they have don like thee, my Muse shall raise
Their due deserts to Worthies yet to come,
To live like thine (admir'd) till day of Doome.
                    Your true friend, somtimes your soldier,
                                        Tho. Carlton.

CAPTAIN JOHN SMITH:
A DESCRIPTION OF NEW ENGLAND

THE EDITORS' COMMENT

John Smith made a voyage to Wabanaki and Wampanoag homelands in 1614, noting the large number of "habitations," before the devastating epidemics struck. Although his narrative served as an advertisement for extraction and settlement, it also reveals a strong, thriving Indigenous populace. Upon his return to England, Smith quickly published his promotional tract, which highlighted the fertility of the soil and the abundance of resources in the place he called "New-England." This name reflected English claims, particularly against the French, who had established trade in Wabanaki territory. Smith used some local Indigenous place-names, such as Penobscot, Kennebec, Massachusett, and Nauset, but also took the liberty to rename waterways and landforms in honor of the English king, his prince, and other patrons. Of course, Smith's labels did not always reflect accurate names of Native places and people, but they did enable English navigation. When the Separatists arrived at Patuxet in 1620, they recognized the place as "Plimouth" because of Smith's map and description. Smith and his crew spent most of their time ranging the coast and fishing, so his descriptions are at a distance. He noted the extensive fields of corn, squash, and beans from the Kennebec River to Cape Cod, but did not describe the women who cultivated them. He described "overgrown" forests that could be transformed into "houses, boats, barks," and "shippes," but did not comprehend their Indigenous management through controlled burns. He expounded on the "abundance" of "furres" and fish and the ways in which these commodities could be harvested to support a colony. He created a portrait of "virgin land" from which resources could be extracted and even suggested that the Indigenous people could be harnessed as labor. Indeed, the French were already successfully recruiting Indigenous men into the fur trade in the north, introducing guns to both Indigenous hunting and warfare.

Thomas Dermer to Samuel Purchas

*To his Worshipfull Friend M. SAMUEL PURCHAS, Preacher of
the Word, at the Church a little within* Ludgate, London.

Sir,—It was the nineteenth of May, before I was fitted for
my discovery, when from Monahiggan I set sayle in an open
Pinnace of five tun, for the Iland I told you of. I passed alongst
the Coast where I found some antient Plantations, not long
since populous now utterly void; in other places a remnant
remaines, but not free of sicknesse. Their disease the Plague,
for wee might perceive the sores of some that had escaped, who
described the spots of such as usually die. When I arrived at
my savages native country (finding all dead) I travelled alongst
adaies journey Westward, to a place called Nummastaquyt,
where finding Inhabitants, I dispatched a Messenger a dayes
journey further West to Poconackit which bordereth on the
sea; whence came to see me two Kings, attended with a guard
of fiftie armed men, who being well satisfied with that my
Savage and I discoursed unto them (being desirous of noveltie)
gave mee content in whatsoever I demanded, where I found
that former relations were true. Here I redeemed a Frenchman,
and afterwards another at Mastachusit who three yeeres since
escaped shipwracke at the North-east of Cape Cod, I must
(amongst many things worthy observation) for want of leisure,
therefore hence I passe (not mentioning any place where we
touched in the way) to the Iland, which we discovered the
twelfth of June. Here we had good quarter with the Savages,
who likewise confirmed former reports. I found seven severall
places digged, sent home of the earth, with samples of other
commodities elsewhere found, founded the Coast, and the
time being farre spent bare up for Monnahiggan, arriving the
three and twentieth of June, where wee found our Ship ready
to depart. To this Ile are two other neere adjoyning, all which
I called by the name of King James his Iles, because from
thence I had the first motives to search, For that (now probable

passage) which may hereafter be both honourable and profitable to his Majestie.

When I had dispatched with the ships ready to depart, I thus
concluded for the accomplishing my businesse, In regard of the
fewnesse of my men, not being able to leave behind mee a competent number for defence, and yet sufficiently furnish myselfe,
I put most of my provisions aboord the *Sampson* of Cape Ward
ready bound for Virginia, from whence hee came, taking no
more into the Pinnace then I thought might serve our turnes,
determining with Gods helpe to search the Coast along, and
at Virginia to supply ourselves for a second discovery, if the
first failed. But as the best actions are commonly hardest in
effecting and are seldome without their crosses, so in this we
had our share, and met with many difficulties: for wee had not
sayled above forty leagues, but wee were taken with a Southerly
storme, which drave us to this strait; eyther we must weather a
rockie point of Land, or run into a broad Bay no lesse dangerous. Incidit in Syllam, &c. the Rockes wee could not weather,
though wee loosed till we recevied much water, but at last were
forced to beare up for the Bay, and run on ground a furlong off
the shoare, where we had beene beaten to pieces, had wee not
instantly throwne overboord our provisions to have our lives;
by which meanes we escaped and brought off our Pinnace the
next high water without hurt, having our Planke broken, and
a small leake or two which we easily mended. Being left in
this misery, having lost much bread, all our Beefe and Sider,
some Meale and Apparell, with other provisions and necessaries; having now little left besides hope to encourage us to
persist; Yet after a little deliberation we resolved to proceed
and departed with the next faire winde. We had not now that
faire quarter amongst the Savages as before, which I take it
was by reason of our Savages absence, who desired (in regard
of our long journey) to stay with some of our Savage friends
Sawahquatooke) for now almost everywhere, where they were
of any strength they fought to betray us. At Manamock (the
Southerne part of Cape Cod, now called Sutcliffe Inlets) I was
unawares taken prisoner, when they sought to kill my men,
which I left to man the Pinnace; but missing of their purpose,
they demanded a ransome, which had, I was as farre from

libertie as before: yet it pleased God at last, after a strange manner to deliver me, with three of them into my hands, and a little after the chiefe Sacheum himselfe; who seeing me weigh anchor, would have leaped over boord, but intercepted, craved pardon, and sent for the Hatchets given for ransome, excusing himselfe by laying the fault on his neighbours; and to be friends sent for a Canoas lading of Corne, which received we set him free. I am loth to omit the story, wherein you would finde cause to admire the great mercy of God even in our greatest misery, in giving us both freedome and reliefe at one time. Departing hence, the next place we arrived at was Capavek, an Iland formerly discovered by the English, where I met with Epinew, a Savage that had lived in England, and speakes indifferent good English, who foure yeeres since being carried home, was reported to have beene slaine, with divers of his Countrey-men, by Saylers which was false. With him I had much conference, who gave mee very good satisfaction in every thing almost I could demand. Time not permitting me to search here, which I should have done for sundry things of special moment: the wind faire, I stood away shaping my course as the Coast led mee, till I came to the most Westerly part where the Coast began to fall away Southerly. In my way I discovered Land about thirtie leagues in length, heretofore taken for Mayne, where I feared I had beene imbayed, but by the help of an Indian I got to the Sea againe, through many crooked and streight passages. I let passe many accidents in this journey occasioned by treacherie, where wee were compelled twice to goe together by the eares, once the Savages had great advantage of us in a streight, not above a Bowe shot, and where a multitude of Indians let flye at us from the banke, but it pleased God to make us victours; neere unto this wee found a most dangerous Catwrack amongst small rockie Ilands, occasioned by two unequall tydes, the one ebbing and flowing two houres before the other; here wee lost an Anchor by the strength of the current, but found it deepe enough; from hence were wee carried in a short space by the tydes swiftnesse into a great Bay (to us so appearing) but indeede is broken land, which gave us light of the Sea: here, as I said, the Land treadeth Southerly. In this place I talked with many Salvages, who told me of two sundry passages to the great Sea on the West, offered me Pilots, and one of them drew mee a Plot with Chalke upon a Chest, whereby I found it a great Iland, parted the two Seas; they report the one scarce passable for shoalds, perillous currents, the other no question to be made of. Having received these directions, I hasten to the place of greatest hope, where I purposed to make triall of Gods goodnesse towards us, and use my best endevour to bring the truth to light, but wee were but onely shewed the entrance, where in seeking to passe wee were forced backe with contrary and overblowing windes, hardly escaping both our lives. Being thus overcharged with weather, I stood alongst the coast to seeke harbours, to attend a favourable gale to recover the streight, but being a harbourlesse Coast for ought we could then perceive, wee found no succour, till wee arrived betwixt Cape Charles and the Maine on the East side the Bay Chestapeak, where in a wilde Roade wee anchored: and the next day (the eight of September) crossed the Bay to Kecoughtan, where the first newes strooke cold to our hearts, the generall sicknesse over the Land. Here I resolved with all possible speede to returne in pursuite of this businesse; so that after a little refreshing, wee recovered up the River to James Citie, and from thence to Cape Warde his Plantacon, where immediately wee fell to hewing of Boords for a close Decke, having found it a most desired course to attempt as before As wee were thus labouring to affect our purposes, it pleased almighty God (who only disposeth of the times and seasons, wherein all workes shall be accomplished) to visite us with his heavie hand, so that at one time there were but two of us able to helpe the rest, my selfe so sore shaken with a burning feaver, that I was brought even unto deaths doore; but at length by Gods assistance escaped, and have now with the rest almost recovered my former strength. The Winter having overtaken us (a time on these Coasts especially) subject to gusts and fearefull stormes, I have now resolved to choose a more temperate season, both for generall good and our own safeties. And thus I have sent you a broken discourse, though indeede very unwilling to have given any notice at all, till it had pleased God to have blessed mee with a thorow search, that our eyes might have witnessed the truth, I have drawne a Plot of the Coast, which I dare not yet part with for feare of danger, let this therefore serve for confirmation of your hopes, till I can better performe my promise and your desire; for what I have spoken I can produce at least mille testes; farre separate, of the Sea behinde them, and of Ships, which come many dayes journey from the West, and of the great extent of this Sea to the North and South, not knowing any bounds thereof Westward. I cease to trouble you till a better opportunity offer it selfe remembering my best love &c. I rest

Yours to command,
THO. DERMER.

From CAPTAINE MARTYN
his Plantation. 27 Decemb. 1619.

THE EDITORS' COMMENT

Thomas Dermer sailed several times to Wampanoag homelands, once with John Smith in 1614 and a second time in
the employment of colonial investor Ferdinando Gorges. He
wrote this letter in 1619, addressing it to the minister Samuel
Purchas, who collected information from Native men taken
as captives to England (including the Wabanaki men Rosier
captured) and from European sailors who had traveled to the
Americas. Purchas published their accounts as part of *Purchas
his Pilgrimes*, an encyclopedic collection of global travel narratives. Dermer's letter is one of the two firsthand European
reports of the illnesses that Native communities experienced
from 1616 to 1619. Dermer reported seeing formerly "populous" areas now "utterly void," perhaps comparing his observations of destitution along the coast in 1619 with the expansive
villages he observed in 1614. But while settlers would soon pick
up the language of "void," empty lands to describe their first
impressions of the northeastern coasts and imagine that no one
remained on the lands on which they settled, Dermer's letter
shows that Wampanoag people had not vanished but had with-
drawn inland, away from the epidemics' impacts. He described
meeting two Native "kings" from whom he learned the news of
the illnesses. And a Frenchman whom Dermer "redeemed" (or
rescued) from his Wampanoag hosts indicated that some European men were learning to live with Wampanoag people during
this period, even though traders also spread disease (it remains
difficult to pinpoint the origins of the 1616–19 epidemics, but
they are certainly linked to trading and diplomatic interactions). Indeed, disease was still prevalent during Dermer's visit,
for he described seeing people still suffering from illness.

Ferdinando Gorges: from
A Briefe Narration

A ND so it pleased our great God that there hapned to
come into the harbour of *Plymouth* (where I then commanded) one Captain *Waymouth* that had been imployed by
the Lord *Arundell* of *Warder* for the discovery of the North-
west passage.

But falling short of his Course, hapned into a River on the
Coast of *America*, called *Pemmaquid*, from whence he brought
five of the Natives, three of whose names were *Manida*,
Skettwarroes, and *Tasquantum*, whom I seized upon; they were
all of one Nation, but of severall parts, and severall Families;
This accident must be acknowledged the meanes under God
of putting on foote, and giving life to all our Plantations, as by
the ensuing discourse will manifestly appeare.

CHAPTER III.
Of the use I made of the Natives.

A FTER I had those people sometimes in my Custody, I
observed in them an inclination to follow the example of
the better sort; And in all their carriages manifest shewes of
great civility farre from the rudenesse of our common people;
And the longer I conversed with them, the better hope they
gave me of those parts where they did inhabit, as proper for
our uses, especially when I found what goodly Rivers, stately
Islands, and safe harbours those parts abounded with, being
the speciall marks I levelled at as the onely want our Nation
met with in all their Navigations along that Coast, and having
kept them full three yeares, I made them able to set me downe
what great Rivers ran up into the Land, what Men of note were
seated on them, what power they were of, how allyed, what
enemies they had, and the like of which in his proper place.

CHAPTER IV.
Captain Henry Challoung sent to make his
residence in the Countrey till supplyes came.

T HOSE credible informations the Natives had given me of
the condition and state of their Countrey, made me send
away a Ship furnished with Men and all necessaries, provisions convenient for the service intended under the command
of Captain *Henry Challoung*, a gentleman of a good Family,
industrious, and of fair condition, to whom I gave such directions and instructions for his better direction as I knew proper
for his use, and my satisfaction, being grounded upon the
information I had of the Natives, sending two of them with
him to aver the same, Binding both the Captain his Master,
and company strictly to follow it; Or to expect the miscarriage of the Voyage to be laid unto their Charge, Commanding
them by all meanes to keep the northerly gage, as high as Cape
Britton, till they had discovered the Maine, and then to beate
it up to the Southward, as the Coast tended, till they found
by the Natives they were neer the place they were assigned
unto; Though this were a direction contrary to the opinion
of our best Sea-men of these times; yet I knew many reasons
perswading me thereunto, as well as for that I understood the
Natives themselves to be exact Pilots for that Coast, having
been accustomed to frequent the same, both as Fishermen and
in passing along the shoare to seek their enemies, that dwelt
to the Northward of them; But it is not in the wit of Man to
prevent the providence of the most High.

For this Captain being some 100 leagues of the Island of
Canara, fell sick of a Feaver, and the windes being Westerly,
his company shaped their course for the *Indies*, and coming to
St. John De Porteriko, the Captain himselfe went a shoare for
the recovery of his health, whiles the Company took in water,
and such other provision as they had present use of, expend-
ing some time there, hunting after such things as best pleased
themselves; That ended, they set their course to fall with their
owne height they were directed unto; By which meanes they
met the *Spanish* Fleet that came from *Havana*, by whom they
were taken and carried into *Spaine*, where their Ship and goods

were confiscate, themselves made Prisoners, the voyage overthrowne, and both my Natives lost; This the gaine of their
breach of Order, which afterwards observed, brought all our
Shippes to their desired Ports; The affliction of the Captain and
his Company put the Lord Chief Justice *Popham* to charge, and
myselfe to trouble in procuring their liberties, which was not
suddainly obtained.

CHAPTER V.
The Lord Chief Justice dispatching Captaine Prin *from*
Bristoll *for the supply of Captaine* Challounge.

SHORTLY upon my sending away of Captaine *Challounge*,
it pleased the Lord Chiefe Justice according to his promise to dispatch Captain *Prin* from *Bristoll*, with hope to have
found Captaine *Challounge*, where by his instructions he was
assigned, who observing the same, happily arrived there, but
not hearing by any meanes what became of him, after he had
made a perfect discovery of all those Rivers and Harbours he
was informed of by his instructions, (the season of the yeare
requiring his return) brings with him the most exact discovery
of that Coast that ever came to my hands since, and indeed
he was the best able to performe it of any I met withall to this
present, which with his relation of the Country, wrought such
an impression in the Lord Chiefe Justice, and us all that were
his associates, that (notwithstanding our first disaster) we set
up our resolutions to follow it with effect, and that upon better
grounds, for as yet, our authority was but in motion.

CHAPTER VI.
Of his Lordships care in procuring his Majesties
Authority for setling two Colonies.

IN this Interim his Lordship failed not to interest many of the
Lords and others to be Petitioners to his MAJESTY for his
Royall Authority, for setling two Plantations upon the coasts
of *America*, by the names of the *First* and *Second* Colonie;
the first to be undertaken by certaine Noble Men, Knights,
Gentlemen, and Merchants in and about the City of *London*;
the second by certaine Knights, Gentlemen, and Merchants in

the western parts: This being obtained, theirs of *London* made a very hopefull entrance into their designe, sending away under the command of Sir *Thomas Gates*, Sir *George Summers*, and many other Gentlemen of quality, a very great and hopefull Plantation to repossesse the parts of *Virginia*, Sir *Thomas Gates* happily arrived in the Bay of *Jessepiock*, in which navigation Sir *George Summers* unhappily cast away his Ship upon the Islands of *Bermathaes*, since called the *Summer Islands*, in memory of him that deserved the honour for the great paines, care, and industry he used out of the carkasse of his wracked Ship, to build a New Barque sufficient for the transportation of himselfe, distressed company, and provision to finde out Sir *Thomas Gates* who timely arrived to the wonder of the rest of his consorts.

CHAPTER VII.
The dispatch of the first Plantation, for the second Colonie sent from Plymouth.

B Y the same Authority all things fully agreed upon between both the Colonies the Lord cheife justice his friends and associates of the West Country, sent from *Plymouth* Captain *Popham* as president for that imployment with Captain *Rawley Gilbert*, and divers other Gentlemen of note in three saile of ships with 100. land-men, for the seizing such a place as they were directed unto by the counsell of that Colonie, who departed from the coast of *England* the one and thirtieth day of *May*, *Anno* 1607. and arrived at their Rendezvouz the 8th of *August* following; as soone as the President had taken notice of the place, and given order for landing the provisions, he dispatcht away Captain *Gilbert* with *Skitwarres* his guide for the through discovery of the rivers and habitations of the Natives, by whom he was brought to severall of them where he found civill entertainment, and kind respects far from brutish or Savage natures, so as they suddainely became familiar friends, especially by the meanes of *Dehamda*, and *Skitwarrers*, who had been in *England*, *Dehamda* being sent by the Lord cheife Justice with Captain *Prin* and *Skitwarres* by me in company, so as the President was earnestly intreated by *Sassenow*, *Aberemet*, and others the principall *Sagamores* (as they call their great

Lords) to go to the *Bashabas*, who it seemes was their King, and held a State agreeable, expecting that all strangers should have their addresse to him, not he to them.

To whom the president would have gone after severall invitations, but was hindred by crosse winds and foul weather, so as he was forced to return back, without making good what he had promised, much to the greife of those *Sagamores*, that were to attend him, the *Bashabas* notwithstanding hearing of his misfortune, sent his own Son to visit him, and to beat a trade with him for furrs. How it succeded, I could not understand, for that the ships were to be dispatched away for *England*, the Winter being already come; for it was the 15. day of *December* before they set saile to return, who brought with them the successe of what had past in that imployment, which so soon as it came to the Lord cheife justice hands, he gave out order to the Councell for sending them back with supplies necessary.

CHAPTER VIII.
The sending supplies to the Colonie, and the unhappie death of the Lord cheife justice before their departure.

THE supplies being furnished and all things ready onely attending for a faire wind, which hapned not before the news of the chiefe justice death was posted to them to be transported to the discomfort of the poor Planters, but the ships arriving there in good time, was a great refreshing to those that had had their store-house and most of their provisions burnt the Winter before.

Besides that they were strangely perplexed with the great and unseasonable cold they suffered with that extremity, as the like hath not been heard of since, and it seemes, was universall, it being the same yeare, that our *Thames* were so lockt up that they built their boates upon it, and sould provisions of severall sorts to those that delighted in the Novelties of the times, but the miseries they had past, were nothing to that they suffered by the disasterous news they received of the death of the Lord cheif justice, that suddainely followed the death of their President, but the latter was not so strange, in that he was well stricken in years before he went, and had long been an infirme man. Howsoever heartned by hopes, willing he was to dye in acting something that might be serviceable to God, and honourable to his Country, but that of the death of the cheife justice was such a corrasive to all, as struck them with despaire of future remedy, and it was the more augmented, when they heard of the Sir *John Gilbert*, Elder brother of *Ralph Gilbert* that was then their President, a man worthy to be beloved of them all for his industry, and care for their well being; The President was to return to settle the state his Brother had left him, upon which all resolved to quit the place, and with one consent to away, by which means all our former hopes wer frozen to death, though Sir *Francis Popham* could not so give it over, but continued to send thither severall years after in hope of better fortunes, but found it fruitlesse, and was necessitated at last to sit down with the losse he had already undergone.

CHAPTER IX.
My resolution not to abandon the prosecution of the businesse, in my opinion so well grounded.

ALTHOUGH I were interested in all those misfortunes, and found it wholly given over by the body of the adventurers, aswell for that they had lost the principall support of the designe, as also that the Country it selfe was branded by the returne of the Plantation, as being over cold, and in respect of that, not habitable by our Nation.

Besides, they understood it to be a taske too great for perticular persons to undertake, though the Country it selfe, the Rivers, Havens, Harbours, upon that coast might in time prove profitable to us.

These last acknowledgements bound me confidently to prosecute my first resolution, not doubting but *G O D* would effect that which Man despaired of, as for those reasons, the causes of others discouragements, the first onely was given to me, in that I had lost so Noble a Friend, and my Nation so worthy a Subject. As for the coldnesse of the Clyme, I had had too much experience in the World to be frighted with such a blast, as knowing many great Kingdomes and large Territories more northerly seated, and by many degrees colder than the Clyme from whence they came, yet plentifully inhabited, and divers of them stored with no better commodities from Trade and Commerce than those parts afforded, if like Industry, Art, and Labour be used, for the last I had no reason greatly to despaire of meanes when *G O D* should be pleased by our ordinary frequenting that Country, to make it appeare, it would yeild both profit and content to as many as aimed thereat, these being truly (for the most part) the motives that all men labour, howsoever otherwise adjoyned with faire colours and goodly shadows.

CHAPTER X.
A resolution to put new life into that scattered and lacerated Body.

FINDING I could no longer be seconded by others, I became an owner of a Ship my selfe fit for that imployment, and under colour of fishing and trade, I got a Master and company for her, to which I sent *Vines* and others my owne servants with their provision for trade and discovery, appointing them to leave the Ship and Ships Company for to follow their businesse in the usuall place, (for I knew they would not be drawn to seek by any meanes) by these and the help of those Natives formerly sent over, I came to be truly informed of so much as gave me assurance that in time I should want no undertakers, though as yet I was forced to hire Men to stay there the Winter Quarter at extream rates, and not without danger, for that the War had consumed the Bashaba, and the most of the great Sagamores, with such Men of action as followed them, and those that remained were sore afflicted with the Plague, for that the Country was in a manner left void of Inhabitants; Notwithstanding, *Vines* and the rest with him that lay in the Cabbins with those People that dyed some more, some lesse, mightily, (blessed be *G O D* for it) not one of them ever felt their heads to ake while they stayed there; and this course I held some years together, but nothing to my private profit, for what I got one way I spent another, so that I began to grow weary of that businesse as not for my turne till better times.

CHAPTER XI.
Captain Harles *comming to me with a new proposition of other hopes.*

WHILE I was labouring by what meanes I might best continue life in my languishing hopes, there comes one Captain *Henry Harley* unto me, bringing with him a Native of the Island of *Capawick*, a place seated to the Southward of *Cape Codd* whose name was *Epenewe* a person of a goodly stature, strong and well proportioned, this man was taken upon the main with some twenty nine others by a ship of *London* that endeavoured to sell them for slaves in *Spaine*, but being understood that they were *Americans*, and found to be unapt for their uses, they would not meddle with them, this being one of them they refused, wherein they exprest more worth then those that brought them to the market, who could not but know that our Nation was at that time in travaile for setling of Christian Colonies upon that continent, it being an act much tending to our prejudice, when we came into that part of the Countries, as it shall further appeare; how Captaine *Harley* came to be possessed of this *Savage*, I know not, but I understood by others how he had been shewed in *London* for a wonder, it is true (as I have said) he was a goodly man of a brave aspect, stout and sober in his demeanor, and had learned so much *English* as to bid those that wondred at him, welcome, welcome, this being the last and best use they could make of him, that was now growne out of the peoples wonder, the Captain, falling further into his familiarity, found him to be of acquaintance and friendship with those subject to the *Bashaba*, whom the Captain well knew, being himselfe one of the Plantation, sent over by the Lord chiefe justice, and by that means understood much of his language, found out the place of his birth, nature of the Country, their severall kinds of commodities, and the like, by which he conceived great hope that good might be made of him, if meanes could be found for his imployment, but finding adventurers of that kind were worne out of date; after so many saylings, and so soone upon the return of our late Colony, but the Gentleman calling to mind my aptnesse to designes of that nature, lays up his rest to

discover his greatest secrets to me, by whom had hoped to rise
or fall in this action, after he had spoken with me, and that I
had seen his *Savage*, though I had some reason to beleive the
Gentleman in what he told me, yet I thought it not amisse to
take some time before I undertook a businesse (as I thought)
so improbable in some particulars, but yet I doubted not, my
resolution being such (as is said) I might make some use of
his service; And therefore wisht him to leave him with me,
giving him my word, that when I saw my time to send againe
to those parts, he should have notice of it, and I would be glad
to accept of his service, and that with as great kindnesse as he
freely offered it, in the meane time, he might be pleased to take
his owne course.

CHAPTER XII.
The reasons of my undertaking the imployment
for the Island of Capawick.

A T the time this new *Savage* came unto me, I had recovered *Assacumet*, one of the Natives I sent with Captain
Chalownes in his unhappy imployment, with whom I lodged
Epenaw, who at the first hardly understood one the others
speech, till after a while; I perceived the difference was no more
then that, as ours is betweene the Northern and Southerne
people, so that I was a little eased in the use I made of my old
servant whom I ingaged to give account of what he learned by
conference between themselves, and he as faithfully performed
it; Being fully satisfied of what he was able to say, and the time
of making ready, drawing on, following my pretended designes;
I thought it became me to acquaint the thrice honoured Lord
of *South-Hampton* with it, for that I knew the Captain had
some relation to his Lordship, and I not willing in those daies,
to undertake any matter extraordinary without his Lordships
advice, who approved of it so well that he adventured 100 *l.* in
that imployment, and his Lordship being at that time Commander of the Isle of *Wight*, where the Captain had his abiding
under his Lordship, who out of his noblenesse was pleased to
furnish me with some land Souldiers, and to commend to me
a grave Gentleman, one Captain *Hobson*, who was willing to
go that voyage, and to adventure 100 *l.* himselfe. To him I

gave the command of the Ship, all things being ready, and the company came together, attending but for a faire winde; they set saile in *June*, in *Anno* 1614. being fully instructed how to demeane themselves in every kind, carrying with them *Epenow*, *Assacomet*, and *Wanape*, another Native of those parts sent me out of the Isle of *Wight* for my better information in the parts of the Country of his knowledge, when as it pleased God that they were arrived upon the coast they were Pilotted from place to place, by the Natives themselves, as well as their hearts could desire; And comming to the Harbour where *Epenow* was to make good his undertaking, the principall inhabitants of the place came aboard, some of them being his Brothers, others his near Couzens, who after they had communed together and were kindly entertained by the Captain, departed in their Cannowes, promising the next morning to come aboard again, and bring some trade with them: But *Epenow* privately (as it appeared) had contracted with his friends, how he might make his escape without performing what he had undertaken, being in truth no more then he had told me he was to do though with losse of his life, for otherwise if it were found that he had discovered the secrets of his Country, he was sure to have his braines knockt out as soone as he came a shoar, for that cause I gave the Captaine strict charge to endeavour by all meanes to prevent his escapeing from them, and for the more surety, I gave order to have three Gentlemen of my owne kinred to be ever at hand with him, cloathing him with long garments, fitly to be laid hold on, if occasion should require; Notwithstanding all this, his friends being all come at the time appointed with twenty Cannows, and lying at a certaine distance with their Bows ready, the Captaine calles to them to come aboard, but they not moving, he speakes to *Epenow* to come unto him, where he was in the fore castle of the Ship, he being then in the wast of the Ship between two of the Gentlemen that had him in gard, start, suddainly from them, and comming to the Captaine, calls to his friends in *English* to come aboard, in the interim flips himselfe over board, and although he were taken hold of by one of the company, yet being a strong and heavy Man, could not be stayed, and was no sooner in the water, but the Natives sent such a showre of arrowes, and came withall desperately so neer the Ship, that they carryed him away in despight of all the Musquetteers aboard, who were for the number as good as our nation did afford; And thus were my hopes of that particular made void and frustrate, and they returned without doing more, though otherwise ordered how to have spent that summer to good purpose; but such are the fruits to be looked for, by imploying men Men more zealous of gain than frought with experience how to make it.

CHAPTER XIII.
Sir Richard Hakings *undertook by authority from the Councell of the second Colonie to trie what service he could do them as President for that yeare.*

HAVING received his Commission and Instructions, he departed in *October* 1615, and spent the time of his being in those parts in searching of the Country, and finding out the commodities thereof, but the war was at the height and the principall Natives almost destroyed, so that his observation could not be such as could give account of any new matter, more than formerly had been received, from thence he past along the coast to *Virginia*, & stay'd there some time, in expectation of what he could not be satisfied in, so took his next course for *Spain*, to make the best of such commodities he had got together, as he coasted from place to place having sent his Ship laden with Fish to the Market before, and this was all that was done by any of us that yeare.

CHAPTER XIV.
Of the sending of Captaine Rocraft *to meete with Captaine* Dermor *in* New-England.

ABOUT this time I received letters from Captaine *Dermor* out of *New-England*, giving me to understand that there was one of my Savages sent into those parts brought from *Malago* in a Ship of *Bristol*, acquainting me with the meanes I might recover him, which I followed and had him sent me, who was after imployed with others in the voyage with Captaine *Hobson* sent to *Capawike* as is abovesaid, by this Savage Captaine *Dermor* understood so much of the state of his Country, as drew his affections wholly to follow his hopes that way, to

which purpose he writes, that if I pleased to send a Commission to meete him in *New-England*, he would endeavour to
come from the *New-found Land* to receive it, and to observe
such other instructions as I pleased to give him, whereupon
the next season I sent Captaine *Rocraft* with a company I had
of purpose hired for the service. At his arrivall upon the coast
he met with a small Barque of *Deepe*, which he seized upon
according to such liberties as was granted unto him in such
cases, notwithstanding, the poore *French*-Man being of our
Religion, I was easily perswaded upon his petition to give content for his losse, although it proved much to dammage afterwards, for Captaine *Rocraft* being now shipped and furnished
with all things necessary, left the Coast contrary to my directions, and went to *Virginia*, where he had formerly dwelt, and
there falling into company with some of his old acquaintance,
a quarrell happened between him and another, so that before
he could get away he was slaine, by which accident the Barque
was left at random, (the most part of the company being on
shoar) a storme arising, she was cast away, and all her provisions
lost, something was saved but nothing ever came to my hands.

CHAPTER XV.
Of my imployment of Captain Dormer *after his saylings*
to come from the New-found *land to* New-England.

CAPTAIN *Dormer* being disappointed of his meanes to come
from *New-found-land*, to *New-England*, took shipping for
England; and came to me at *Plymouth* where I gave him an
account of what I had done, and he me, what his hopes were,
to be able to do me service (if I pleased) to imploy him, hereupon I conferred his informations, together with mine owne
I received by severall wayes, and found them to agree in Many
the particulars of highest consequence and best considerations,
whereupon I dispatched him away with the company he had
gotten together, as fast as my owne Ship could be made ready for
her ordinary imployment, sending with him what he thought
necessary, hopeing to have met Captaine *Rocraft*, where he
was assigned to attend till he received further directions from
me, but at the Ships arrivall they found Captain *Rocraft* gone
for *Virginia*, with all his company in the Barque he had taken,

of which before Captaine *Dormer* arriving, and seeing *Rocraft* gon, was much perplexed, yet so resolved he was, that he ceased not to follow his designe with the Men and Meanes which I had sent him, and so shaped his course from *Sagadahock* in 44 degrees to *Capawike* being in 41 and 36 minutes, sending me a journall of his proceeding, with the description of the Coast all along as he pas'd. Passing by *Capawike*, he continued his course along the coast from Harbour to Harbour till he came to *Virginia*, where he expected to meete with *Rocraft* (as afore) but finding him dead, and all lost that should have supply'd him, he was forced to shift as he could to make his returne, and comming to *Capawike* and *Nautican*, and going first to *Nautican* and from thence to *Capawike*, he set himselfe and some of his people on shoar, where he met with *Epenow* the *Savage*, who had escaped (of whom) before,: This *Savage* speaking some *English*, laughed at his owne escape, and reported the story of it, Mr. *Dormer* tould him he came from mee, and was one of my servants, and that I was much grieved he had beene so ill used, as to be forced to steale away; this *Savage* was so cunning, that after he had questioned him about me and all he knew belonged unto me, conceived he was come on purpose to betray him, and conspired with some of his fellowes to take the Captaine, thereupon they laid hands upon him, but he being a brave stoute Gentleman, drew his Sword and freed himselfe, but not without fourteen wounds, this disaster forced him to make all possible hast to *Virginia* to be cured of his wounds; at the second returne he had the misfortune to fall sick and die of the infirmity many of our Nation are subject unto at their first comming into those parts; the losse of this Man, I confesse, much troubled me, and had almost made me resolve never to intermeddle in any of those courses.

THE EDITORS' COMMENT

Like Rosier's and Smith's narratives, Gorges's *A Briefe Nar-ration of the Originall Undertakings of the Advancement of Plantations Into the parts of America* is a highly speculative, imaginative narrative, all the more so because Gorges himself never traveled to the Americas. Deeming his account an "abso-lute"—meaning essential or fundamental—narrative, Gorges uses the language of "plantation" (which in the early seven-teenth century had evolved to mean a settlement or colony in a place that had been conquered) as well as "discovery" to give English settlements a connotation of firstness and right-ful domination. Gorges imagined such future settlements by drawing on previously published texts, as well as information from men he sent to explore possible settlement sites and from captured Native people, including the five Wabanaki men and the Wampanoag man from Noepe (now Martha's Vineyard), Epenow. Captured in 1611 along with several other Wabanaki and Wampanoag men, Epenow was taken to England, where he, like the Wabanaki captives taken by Rosier and Waymouth, was interviewed by Gorges. Gorges reported that Epenow learned enough English to say "welcome, welcome," words that indicate both Native acquisition of English words impor-tant for diplomatic relations and the desire of English inves-tors like Gorges to train Native captives to potentially serve as guides and interpreters for colonists. Epenow's surprising (and to Gorges, disappointing) escape indicates that Epenow also pursued his own goals, which remained largely invisible to Gorges and other captors. The knowledge Epenow and, later, Tisquantum gleaned in their travels across the Atlantic proved valuable as both men later confronted decisions about how to interact with colonists who intended to make real, rather than imagined, settlements.

PLYMOUTH PLANTATION
IN PATUXET

Edward Winslow and William Bradford:
A Relation or Journall

A
RELATION OR
Journall of the beginning and proceedings
of the English Plantation settled at *Plimoth* in NEW
ENGLAND, by certaine English Adventurers both
Merchants and others.

With their difficult passage, their safe arival, their
joyfull building of, and comfortable planting themselves in the now well defended Towne
of NEW PLIMOTH.

AS ALSO A RELATION OF FOURE
severall discoveries since made by some of the
same English Planters there resident.

I. In a journey to PUCKANOKICK *the habitation of the Indians greatest King* Massasoyt: *as also their message, the answer
and entertainment they had of him.*

II. In a voyage made by ten of them to the Kingdome of
Nawset, *to seeke a boy that had lost himselfe in the woods: with
such accidents as befell them in that voyage.*

III. In their journey to the Kingdome of Namaschet, *in
defence of their greatest King* Massasoyt, *against the* Narrohig-
gonsets, *and to revenge the supposed death of their Interpreter*
Tisquantum.

IIII. Their voyage to the Massachusets, *and their entertainement there.*

With an answer to all such objections as are in any way made
against the lawfulnesse of English plantations
in those parts.

LONDON,
Printed for *John Bellamie*, and are to be sold at his shop at
the two Greyhounds in Cornhill neere the Royall Exchange.
1622.

To His Much Respected
Friend, Mr. *J. P.*

GOOD Friend: As wee cannot but account it an extraordinary blessing of God in directing our course for these
parts, after we came out of our native countrey, for that we had
the happinesse to be possessed of the comforts we receive by
the benefit of one of the most pleasant, most healthfull, and
most fruitfull parts of the world: So must wee acknowledge the
same blessing to bee multiplied upon our whole company, for
that we obtained the honour to receive allowance and approbation of our free possession, and enjoying thereof under the
authority of those thrice honoured Persons, the *President* and
Counsell for the affaires of *New-England*, by whose bounty
and grace, in that behalfe, all of us are tied to dedicate our
best service unto them, as those under his Majestie, that wee
owe it unto: whose noble endevours in these their actions the
God of heaven and earth multiply to his glory and their owne
eternall comforts.

As for this poore Relation, I pray you to accept it, as being
writ by the severall Actors themselves, after their plaine and
rude manner; therefore doubt nothing of the truth thereof: if
it be defective in any thing, it is their ignorance, that are better
acquainted with planting then writing. If it satisfie those that
are well affected to the businesse, it is all I care for. Sure I am
the place we are in, and the hopes that are apparent, cannot
but suffice any that will not desire more then enough, neither
is there want of ought among us but company to enjoy the
blessings so plentifully bestowed upon the inhabitants that are
here. While I was a writing this, I had almost forgot, that I had
but the recommendation of the relation it selfe, to your further
consideration, and therefore I will end without saying more,
save that I shall alwaies rest

From PLIMOTH in
New-England.

Yours in the way of
friendship, R. C.

To the Reader.

*Courteous Reader, be intreated to make a favorable construc-
tion of my forwardnes, in publishing these inseuing discourses,
the desire of carrying the Gospell of Christ into those forraigne
parts, amongst those people that as yet have had no knowledge,
nor tast of God, as also to procure unto themselves and others a
quiet and comfortable habytation: weare amongst other things
the inducements (unto these undertakers of the then hopefull, and
now experimentally knowne good enterprice for plantation, in*
New England, *to set afoote and prosecute the same & though it
fared with them, as it is common to the most actions of this nature,
that the first attemps prove diffecult, as the sequell more at large
expresseth, yet it hath pleased God, eve beyond our expectation in
so short a time, to give hope of letting some of them see (though some
he hath taken out of this vale of teares) some grounds of hope, of the
accomplishment of both those endes by them, at first propounded.*

*And as myselfe then much desired, and shortly hope to effect,
if the Lord will, the putting to of my shoulder iu this hopefull
business, and in the meane time, these relations comming to my
hand from my both known & faithful friends, on whose writings I do much rely, I thought it not a misse to make them more
generall, hoping of a cheerefull proceeding, both of Adventurers
and planters, intreating that the example of the hon:* Virginia
and Bermudas *Companies, incountering with so many disasters,
and that for divers yeares together, with an unwearied resolution, the good effects whereof are now eminent, may prevaile as a
spurre of preparation also touching this no lesse hopefull Country
though yet an infant, the extent & comodities whereof are as yet
not fully known, after time wil unfould more: such as desire to
take knowledge of things, may in forme themselves by this insuing
treatise, and if they please also by such as have bin there a first
and second time, my harty prayer to God is that the event of this
and all other honorable and honest undertakings, may be for
the furtherance of the kingdome of Christ, the inlarging of the
bounds of our Soveraigne Lord King* James, *& the good and
profit of those, who either by purse, or person, or both, are agents
in the same, so I take leave and rest*

Thy friend, G. MOURT.

CERTAINE USEFUL
ADVERTISEMENTS SENT
in a Letter written by a discreete friend unto
the Planters in *New England*, at their first setting
*saile from Southhampton, who earnestly desireth
the prosperitie of that their new
Plantation.*

L OVING and Christian friends, I doe heartily and in the
Lord salute you all, as being they with whom I am present in my best affection, and most earnest longings after you,
though I be constrained for a while to be bodily absent from
you, I say constrained, God knowing how willingly and much
rather then otherwise I would have have borne my part with
you in this first brunt, were I not by strong necessitie held backe
for the present. Make account of me in the meane while, as of
a man devided in my selfe with great paine, and as (naturall
bonds set aside) having my better part with you. And though
I doubt not but in your godly wisedomes you both forsee and
resolve upon that which concerneth your present state and condition both severally and joyntly, yet have I thought but my
dutie to adde some further spurre of provocation unto them
who run already, if not because you need it, yet because I owe
it in love and dutie.

And first, as we are daily to renew our repentance with our
God, speciall for our sinnes knowne, and generall for our
unknowne trespasses; so doth the Lord call us in a singular
maner upon occasions of such difficultie and danger as lieth
upon you, to a both more narrow search and carefull reformation of our wayes in his fight, lest he calling to remembrance
our sinnes forgotten by us or unrepented of, take advantage
against us, and in judgement leave us for the same to be swallowed up in one danger or other; whereas on the contrary, sin
being taken away by earnest repentance and the pardon thereof
from the Lord, sealed up unto a mans conscience by his Spirit,
great shall be his securitie and peace in all dangers, sweete his
comforts in all distresses, with happie deliverance from all evill,
whether in life or in death.

Now next after this heavenly peace with God and our owne consciences, we are carefully to provide for peace with all men what in us lieth, especially with our associates, and for that end watchfulnes must be had, that we neither at all in our selves do give, no nor easily take offence being given by others. Woe be unto the world for offences, for though it be necessary (considering the malice of Satan and mans corruption) that offences come, yet woe unto the man or woman either by whom the offence cometh, faith Christ, Math. 18. 7. And if offences in the unseasonable use of things in themselves indifferent, be more to be feared then death it selfe, as the Apostle teacheth, 1. Cor. 9. 15. how much more in things simply evill, in which neither honour of God nor love of man is thought worthy to be regarded.

Neither yet is it sufficient that we keep our selves by the grace of God from giving offence, except withall we be armed against the taking of them when they are given by others. For how unperfect and lame is the worke of grace in that person, who wants charitie to cover a multitude of offences, as the Scriptures speake. Neither are you to be exhorted to this grace onely upon the common grounds of Christianitie, which are, that persons ready to take offence, either want charitie to cover offences, or wisedome duly to weigh humane frailtie; or lastly are grosse, though close hypocrites, as Christ our Lord teacheth, Math. 7. 1, 2, 3. as indeed in mine owne experience, few or none have beene found which sooner give offence, then such as easily take it; neither have they ever proved found and profitable members in societies, which have nourished in themselves that touchey humour. But besides these there are divers spetiall motives provoking you above others to great care and conscience this way: As first, you are many of you strangers, as to the persons, so to the infirmities one of another, and so stand in need of more watchfulnesse this way, lest when such things fall out in men and women as you suspected not, you be inordinately affected with them; which doth require at your hands much wisedome and charitie for the covering and preventing of incident offences that way. And lastly your intended course of civill communitie wil minister continuall occasion of offence, and will be as fuell for that fire, except you diligently quench it with brotherly forbearance. And if taking of offence causlesly or easily at mens doings be so carefully to be avoided, how much more heed is to be taken that we take not offence at God himselfe, which yet we certainly do so oft, as we do murmure at his providence in our crosses, or beare impatiently such afflictions as wherewith he pleaseth to visit us. Store we up therefore patience against the evill day, without which we take offence at the Lord himselfe in his holy and just works.

A fourth thing there is carefully to be provided for, to wit, that with your common emploiments you joyne common affections truly bent upon the generall good, avoiding as a deadly plague of your both common and speciall comfort all retirednesse of minde for proper advantage, and all singularly affected any maner of way; let every man represse in himselfe and the whole bodie in each person, as so many rebels against the common good, all private respects of mens selves, not sorting with the generall conveniencie. And as men are carefull not to have a new house shaken with any violence before it be well settled and the parts firmly knit: so be you, I beseech you brethren, much more carefull, that the house of God which you are and are to be, be not shaken with unnecessary novelties or other oppositions at the first settling thereof.

Lastly, whereas you are to become a body politik, using amongst your selves civill government, and are not furnished with any persons of speciall eminencie above the rest, to be chosen by you into office of government: Let your wisedome and godlinesse appeare, not onely in chusing such persons as do entirely love, and will diligently promote the common good, but also in yeelding unto them all due honour and obedience in their lawfull administrations; not beholding in them the ordinarinesse of their persons, but God's ordinance for your good; nor being like unto the foolish multitude, who more honour the gay coate, then either the vertuous mind of the man, or glorious ordinance of the Lord. But you know better things, and that the image of the Lords power and authoritie which the Magistrate beareth, is honorable, in how meane persons soever. And this dutie you both may the more willingly, and ought the more conscionably to performe, because you are at least for the present to have onely them for your ordinary governours, which your selves shall make choise of for that worke.

Sundrie other things of importance I could put you in mind of, and of those before mentioned in more words, but I will not so far wrong your godly minds, as to thinke you heedlesse of these things, there being also divers among you so well able to admonish both themselves and others of what concerneth them. These few things therefore, and the same in few words I do earnestly commend unto your care and conscience, joyning therewith my daily incessant prayers unto the Lord, that he who hath made the heavens and the earth, the sea and all rivers of waters, and whose providence is over all his workes, espe-cially over all his deare children for good, would so guide and guard you in your wayes, as inwardly by his Spirit, so outwardly by the hand of his power, as that both you and we also, for and with you, may have after matter of praising his Name all the days of your and our lives. Fare you well in him in whom you trust, and in whom I rest

An unfained well-willer
of your happie successe
in this hopefull voyage,
J. R.

A RELATION OR
JOURNALL OF THE
PROCEEDINGS OF THE
Plantation Setled at *Plimoth* in
NEW ENGLAND.

WEDNESDAY the sixt of *September*, the Wind comming East North East, a fine small gale, we loosed from *Plimoth*, having beene kindly intertained and curteously used by divers friends there dwelling, and after many difficulties in boysterous stormes, at length by Gods providence upon the ninth of *November* following, by breake of the day we espied land which we deemed to be *Cape Cod*, and so afterward it proved. And the appearance of it much comforted us, especially, seeing so goodly a Land, and woodded to the brinke of the sea, it caused us to rejoyce together, and praise God that had given us once againe to see land. And thus wee made our course South South West, purposing to goe to a River ten leagues to the South of the Cape, but at night the winde being contrary, we put round againe for the Bay of *Cape Cod*: and upon the 11. of *November*, we came to an anchor in the Bay, which is a good harbour and pleasant Bay, circled round, except in the entrance, which is about foure miles over from land to land, compassed about to the very Sea with Okes, Pines, Juniper, Sassafras, and other sweet wood; it is a harbour wherein 1000. saile of Ships may safely ride, there we relieved our selves with wood and water, and refreshed our people, while our shallop was fitted to coast the Bay, to search for an habitation: there was the greatest store of fowle that ever we saw.

And every day we saw Whales playing hard by us, of which in that place, if we had instruments & meanes to take them, we might have made a very rich returne, which to our great griefe we wanted. Our master and his mate, and others experienced in fishing, professed, we might have made three or foure thousand pounds worth of Oyle; they preferred it before Greenland Whale-fishing, & purpose the next winter to fish for Whale here; for Cod we assayed, but found none, there is good store no doubt in their season. Neither got we any fish all the time we lay there, but some few little ones on the shore. We found great Mussles, and very fat and full of Sea pearle, but we could not eat them, for they made us all sicke that did eat, as well saylers as passengers; they caused to cast and scoure, but they were soone well againe. The bay is so round & circling, that before we could come to anchor, we went round all the points of the Compasse. We could not come neere the shore by three quarters of an English mile, because of shallow water, which was a great prejudice to us, for our people going on shore were forced to wade a bow shoot or two in going a-land, which caused many to get colds and coughs, for it was ny times freezing cold weather.

This day before we came to harbour, observing some not well affected to unitie and concord, but gave some appearance of faction, it was thought good there should be an associa-tion and agreement, that we should combine together in one body, and to submit to such government and governours, as we should by common consent agree to make and chose, and set our hands to this that followes word for word.

I N the name of God, Amen. We whose names are underwrit-ten, the loyall Subjects of our dread soveraigne Lord King JAMES, by the grace of God of Great *Britaine, France*, and *Ireland* King, Defender of the Faith, &c.

Having under-taken for the glory of God, and advancement of the Christian Faith, and honour of our King and Countrey, a Voyage to plant the first Colony in the Northerne parts of VIRGINIA, doe by these presents solemnly & mutually in the presence of *God* and one of another, covenant, and combine our selves together into a civill body politike, for our better order-ing and preservation, and furtherance of the ends aforesaid; and by vertue hereof to enact, constitute, and frame such just and equall Lawes, Ordinances, acts, constitutions, offices from time to time, as shall be thought most meet and convenient for the generall good of the Colony: unto which we promise all due submission and obedience. In witnesse whereof we have here-under subscribed our names, *Cape Cod* 11. of *November*, in the yeare of the raigne of our soveraigne Lord King JAMES, of *England, France*, and *Ireland* 18. and of *Scotland* 54. *Anna Domino* 1620.

The same day so soon as we could we set a-shore 15. or 16. men, well armed, with some to fetch wood, for we had none left; as also to see what the Land was, and what Inhabitants they could meet with, they found it to be a small neck of Land; on this side where we lay is the *Bay*, and the further side the Sea; the ground or earth, sand hils, much like the Downes in *Holland*, but much better; the crust of the earth a Spits depth, excellent blacke earth; all wooded with Okes, Pines, Sassafras, Juniper, Birch, Holly, Vines, some Ash, Walnut; the wood for the most part open and without under-wood, fit either to goe or ride in: at night our people returned, but found not any person, nor habitation, and laded their Boat with Juniper, which smelled very sweet & strong, and of which we burnt the most part of the time we lay there.

Munday the 13. of *November*, we unshipped our Shallop and drew her on land, to mend and repaire her, having bin forced to cut her downe in bestowing her betwixt the decks, and she was much opened with the peoples lying in her, which kept us long there, for it was 16. or 17. dayes before the Carpenter had finished her; our people went on shore to refresh themselves, and our women to wash, as they had great need; but whilest we lay thus still, hoping our Shallop would be ready in five or sixe dayes at the furthest, but our Carpenter made slow worke of it, so that some of our people impatient of delay, desired for our better furtherance to travaile by Land into the Countrey, which was not without appearance of danger, not having the Shallop with them, nor meanes to carry provision, but on their backes, to see whether it might be fit for us to seate in or no, and the rather because as we sayled into the Harbour, there seemed to be a river opening it selfe into the maine land; the willingnes of the persons was liked, but the thing it selfe, in regard of the danger was rather permitted then approved, and so with cautions, directions, and instructions, sixteene men were set out with every man his Musket, Sword, and Corslet, under the conduct of Captaine *Miles Standish*, unto whom was adjoyned for counsell and advise, *William Bradford*, *Stephen Hopkins*, and *Edward Tilley*.

Wednesday the 15. of *November*, they were set a shore, and when they had ordered themselves in the order of a single File, and marched about the space of a myle, by the Sea they espyed

five or sixe people, with a Dogge, comming towards them, who
were Savages, who when they saw them ran into the Wood and
whisled the Dogge after them, &c. First, they supposed them
to be master *Jones*, the Master and some of his men, for they
were a-shore, and knew of their comming, but after they knew
them to be *Indians* they marched after them into the Woods,
least other of the *Indians* should lie in Ambush; but when the
Indians saw our men following them, they ran away with might
and mayne, and our men turned out of the Wood after them,
for it was the way they intended to goe, but they could not
come neare them. They followed them that night about ten
miles by the trace of their footings, and saw how they had come
the same way they went, and at a turning perceived how they
run up an hill, to see whether they followed them. At length
night came upon them, and they were constrained to take up
their lodging, so they set forth three Sentinells, and the rest,
some kindled a fire, and others fetched wood, and there held
our Randevous that night. In the morning so soone as we
could see the trace, we proceeded on our journey, & had the
tracke untill we had compassed the head of a long creake, and
there they tooke into another wood, and we after them, supposing to finde some of their dwellings, but we marched
thorow boughes and bushes, and under hills and vallies, which
tore our very Armour in peeces, and yet could meete with none
of them, nor their houses, nor finde any fresh water, which we
greatly desired, and stood in need off, for we brought neither
Beere nor Water with us, and our victuals was onely Bisket and
Holland cheese, and a little Bottle of *aquavite*, so as we were
sore a thirst. About ten a clocke we came into a deepe Valley,
full of brush, wood-gaile, and long grasse, through which we
found little paths or tracts, and there we saw a Deere, and
found springs of fresh water, of which we were heartily glad,
and sat us downe and drunke our first *New-England* water with
as much delight as ever we drunke drinke in all our lives. When
we had refreshed our selves, we directed our course full South,
that we might come to the shore, which within a short while
after we did, and there made a fire, that they in the ship might
see where wee were (as we had direction) and so marched on
towards this supposed River; and as we went in another valley,
we found a fine cleere Pond of fresh water, being about a

Musket shot broad, and twise as long; there grew also many small vines, and Foule and Deere haunted there; there grew much Sasafras: from thence we went on & found much plaine ground, about fiftie Acres, fit for the Plow, and some signes where the *Indians* had formerly planted their corne; after this, some thought it best for nearenesse of the river to goe downe and travaile on the Sea sands, by which meanes some of our men were tyred, and lagged behind, so we stayed and gathered them up, and struck into the Land againe; where we found a little path to certaine heapes of sand, one whereof was covered with old Matts, and had a woodden thing like a morter whelmed on the top of it, and an earthen pot layd in a little hole at the end thereof; we musing what it might be, digged & found a Bow, and, as we thought, Arrowes, but they were rotten; We supposed there were many other things, but because we deemed them graves, we put in the Bow againe and made it up as it was, and left the rest untouched, because we thought it would be odious unto them to ransacke their Sepulchers. We went on further and found new stubble, of which they had gotten Corne this yeare, and many Wallnut trees full of Nuts, and great store of Strawberries, and some Vines; passing thus a field or two, which were not great, we came to another, which had also bin new gotten, and there we found where an house had beene, and foure or five old Plankes layed together; also we found a great Ketle, which had beene some Ships ketle and brought out of *Europe*; there was also an heape of sand, made like the former, but it was newly done, we might see how they had padled it with their hands, which we digged up, and in it we found a little old Basket full of faire *Indian* Corne, and digged further & found a fine great new Basket full of very faire corne of this yeare, with some 36. goodly eares of corne, some yellow, and some red, and others mixt with blew, which was a very goodly sight: the Basket was round, and narrow at the top, it held about three or foure Bushels, which was as much as two of us could lift up from the ground, and was very handsomely and cunningly made; But whilst wee were busie about these things, we set our men Sentinell in a round ring, all but two or three which digged up the corne. We were in suspence, what to doe with it, and the Ketle, and at length after much consultation, we concluded to take the Ketle, and as

much of the Corne as we could carry away with us; and when
our Shallop came, if we could find any of the people, and come
to parley with them, we would give them the Ketle againe, and
satisfie them for their Corne, so we tooke all the eares and put
a good deale of the loose Corne in the Ketle for two men to
bring away on a staffe; besides, they that could put any into
their Pockets filled the same; the rest wee buried againe, for we
were so laden with Armour that we could carry no more. Not
farre from this place we found the remainder of an old Fort, or
Palizide, which as we conceived had beene made by some
Christians, this was also hard by that place which we thought
had beene a river, unto which wee went and found it so to be,
devicing it selfe into two armes by an high banke, standing
right by the cut or mouth which came from the Sea, that which
was next unto us was the lesse, the other arme was more then
twise as big, and not unlike to be an harbour for ships; but
whether it be a fresh river, or onely an indraught of the Sea, we
had no time to discover; for wee had Commandement to be
out but two dayes. Here also we saw two Canoas, the one on
the one side, the other on the other side, wee could not beleeve
it was a Canoa, till we came neare it, so we returned leaving
the further discovery hereof to our Shallop, and came that
night backe againe to the fresh water pond, and there we made
our Randevous that night, making a great fire, and a Baricado
to windward of us, and kept good watch with three Sentinells
all night, every one standing when his turne came, while five
or sixe inches of Match was burning. It proved a very rainie
night. In the morning we tooke our Ketle and sunke it in the
pond, and trimmed our Muskets, for few of them would goe
off because of the wett, and so coasted the wood againe to
come home, in which we were shrewdly pus-led, and lost our
way, as we wandred we came to a tree, where a yong Spritt was
bowed downe over a bow, and some Acornes strewed underneath; *Stephen Hopkins* sayd, it had beene to catch some Deere,
so, as we were looking at it, *William Bradford* being in the
Reare, when he came looked also upon it, and as he went
about, it gave a sodaine jerk up, and he was immediately caught
by the leg; It was a very pretie devise, made with a Rope of their
owne making, and having a noose as artificially made, as any
Roper in *England* can make, and as like ours as can be, which

we brought away with us. In the end wee got out of the Wood, and were fallen about a myle too high above the creake, where we saw three Bucks, but we had rather have had one of them. Wee also did spring three couple of Partridges; and as we came along by the creake, wee saw great flockes of wild Geese and Duckes, but they were very fearfull of us. So we marched some while in the Woods, some while on the sands, and other while in the water up to the knees, till at length we came neare the Ship, and then we shot off our Peeces, and the long Boat came to fetch us; master *Jones*, and master *Carver* being on the shore, with many of our people, came to meete us. And thus wee came both weary and well-come home, and delivered in our Corne into the store, to be kept for seed, for wee knew not how to come by any, and therefore were very glad, purposing so soone as we could meete with any of the Inhabitants of that place, to make them large satisfaction. This was our first Discovery, whilst our Shallop was in repairing; our people did make things as fitting as they could, and time would, in seeking out wood, and helving of Tooles, and sawing of Tymber to build a new Shallop, but the discommodiousnes of the harbour did much hinder us, for we could neither goe to, nor come from the shore, but at high water, which was much to our hinderance and hurt, for oftentimes they waded to the midle of the thigh, and oft to the knees, to goe and come from land; some did it necessarily, and some for their owne pleasure, but it brought to the most, if not to all, coughes and colds, the weather proving sodainly cold and stormie, which afterward turned to the scurvey, whereof many dyed.

When our Shallop was fit indeed, before she was fully fitted, for there was two dayes worke after bestowed on her, there was appointed some 24. men of our owne, and armed, then to goe and make a more full discovery of the rivers before mentioned. Master *Jones* was desirous to goe with us, and tooke such of his saylers as he thought usefull for us, so as we were in all about 34. men; wee made master *Jones* our Leader, for we thought it best herein to gratifie his kindnes and forwardnes. When we were set forth, it proved rough weather and crosse windes, so as we were constrained, some in the Shallop, and others in the long Boate, to row to the neerest shore the wind would suffer them to goe unto, and then to wade out above the knees; the wind was so strong as the Shallop could not keepe the water, but was forced to harbour there that night, but we marched sixe or seaven miles further, and appointed the Shallop to come to us as soone as they could. It blowed and did snow all that day & night, and froze withall: some of our people that are dead tooke the originall of their death here. The next day about 11. a clocke our Shallop came to us, and wee shipped our selves, and the wind being good, we sayled to the river we formerly discovered, which we named, *Cold Harbour*, to which when wee came we found it not Navigable for Ships, yet we thought it might be a good harbour for Boats, for it flowes there 12. foote at high water. We landed our men betweene the two creekes, and marched some foure or five myles by the greater of them, and the Shallop followed us; at length night grew on, and our men were tired with marching up and downe the steepe hills, and deepe vallies, which lay halfe a foot thicke with snow: Master *Jones* wearied with marching, was desirous we should take up our lodging, though some of us would have marched further, so we made there our Randevous for that night, under a few Pine trees, and as it fell out, wee got three fat Geese, and six Ducks to our Supper, which we eate with Souldiers stomacks, for we had eaten little all that day; our resolution was next morning to goe up to the head of this river, for we supposed it would prove fresh water, but in the morning our resolution held not, because many liked not the hillinesse of the soyle, and badnesse of the harbour, so we turned towards the other creeke, that wee might goe over and looke for the rest of the Corne that we left behind when we were here before; when we came to the creeke, we saw the Canow lie on the dry ground, and a flocke of Geese in the river, at which one made a shot, and killed a couple of them, and we lanched the Canow & fetcht them, and when we had done, she carryed us over by seaven or eight at once. This done, we marched to the place where we had the corne formerly, which place we called *Corne-hill*; and digged and found the rest, of which we were very glad: we also digged in a place a little further off, and found a Botle of oyle; wee went to another place, which we had seene before, and digged, and found more corne, *viz.* two or three Baskets full of *Indian* Wheat, and a bag of Beanes, with a good many of faire Wheat-eares; whilst some of us were digging up this, some others found another heape of Corne, which they digged up also, so as we had in all about ten Bushels, which will serve us sufficiently for seed. And sure it was Gods good providence NOTE. that we found this Corne, for els wee know not how we should have done, for we knew not how we should find, or meete with any of the *Indians*, except it be to doe us a mischiefe. Also we had never in all likelihood seene a graine of it, if we had not made our first Journey; for the ground was now covered with snow, and so hard frozen, that we were faine with our Curtlaxes and short Swords, to hew and carve the ground a foot deepe, and then wrest it up with leavers, for we had forgot to bring other Tooles; whilst we were in this imployment, foule weather being towards, Master *Jones* was earnest to goe abourd, but sundry of us desired to make further discovery, and to find out the *Indians* habitations, so we sent home with him our weakest people, and some that were sicke, and all the Corne, and 18. of us stayed still, and lodged there that night, and desired that the Shallop might returne to us next day, and bring us some Mattocks and Spades with them.

The next morning we followed certaine beaten pathes and tracts of the *Indians* into the Woods, supposing they would have led us into some Towne, or houses; after wee had gone a while, we light upon a very broad beaten path, well nigh two foote broad, then we lighted all our Matches, and prepared our selves, concluding wee were neare their dwellings, but in the end we found it to be onely a path made to drive Deere in, when the *Indians* hunt, as wee supposed; when we had marched five or six myles into the Woods, and could find no signes of any people, we returned againe another way, and as we came into the plaine ground, wee found a place like a grave, but it was much bigger and longer then any we had yet seene. It was also covered with boords, so as we mused what it should be, and resolved to digge it up, where we found, first a Matt, and under that a fayre Bow, and there another Matt, and under that a boord about three quarters long, finely carved and paynted, with three tynes, or broches on the top, like a Crowne; also betweene the Matts we found Boules, Trayes, Dishes, and such like Trinkets; at length we came to a faire new Matt, and under that two Bundles, the one bigger, the other lesse, we opened the greater and found in it a great quantitie of fine and perfect red Powder, and in it the bones and skull of a man. The skull had fine yellow haire still on it, and some of the flesh unconsumed; there was bound up with it a knife, a pack-needle, and two or three old iron things. It was bound up in a Saylers canvas Casacke, and a payre of cloth breeches; the red Powder was a kind of Embaulment, and yeelded a strong, but no offensive smell; It was as fine as any flower. We opened the lesse bundle likewise, and found of the same Powder in it, and the bones and head of a little childe, about the leggs, and other parts of it was bound strings, and bracelets of fine white Beads; there was also by it a little Bow, about three quarters long, and some other odd knackes; we brought sundry of the pretiest things away with us, and covered the Corps up againe. After this, we digged in sundry like places, but found no more Corne, nor any things els but graves: There was varietie of opinions amongst us about the embalmed person; some thought it was an *Indian* Lord and King: others sayd, the *Indians* have all blacke hayre, and never any was seene with browne or yellow hayre; some thought, it was a Christian of some speciall note, which had dyed amongst them, and they thus buried him to honour him; others thought, they had killed him, and did it in triumph over him. Whilest we were thus ranging and searching, two of the Saylers, which were newly come on the shore,"' by chance espied two houses, which had beene lately dwelt in, but the people were gone. They having their peeces, and hearing no body entred the houses, and tooke out some things, and durst not stay but came againe and told us; so some seaven or eight of us went with them, and found how we had gone within a flight shot of them before. The houses were made with long yong Sapling trees, bended and both ends stucke into the ground; they were made round, like unto an Arbour, and covered downe to the ground with thicke and well wrought matts, and the doore was not over a yard high, made of a matt to open; the chimney was a wide open hole in the top, for which they had a matt to cover it close when they pleased; one might stand and goe upright in them, in the midst of them were foure little trunches knockt into the ground, and small stickes laid over, on which they hung their Pots, and what they had to seeth; round about the fire they lay on matts, which are their beds. The houses were double matted, for as they were matted without, so were they within, with newer & fairer matts. In the houses we found wooden Boules, Trayes & Dishes, Earthen Pots, Hand baskets made of Crab shells, wrought together; also an English Paile or Bucket, it wanted a bayle, but it had two Iron eares: there was also Baskets of sundry sorts, bigger and some lesser, finer and some courser: some were curiously wrought with blacke and white in pretie workes, and sundry other of their houshold stuffe: we found also two or three Deeres heads, one whereof had bin newly killed, for it was still fresh; there was also a company of Deeres feete, stuck up in the houses, Harts hornes, and Eagles clawes, and sundry such like things there was: also two or three Baskets full of parched Acornes, peeces of fish, and a peece of a broyled Hering. We found also a little silke grasse, and a little Tobacco seed, with some other seeds which wee knew not; without was sundry bundles of Flags, and Sedge, Bull-rushes, and other stuffe to make matts; there was thrust into an hollow tree, two or three peeces of Venison, but we thought it fitter for the Dogs then for us: some of the best things we tooke away with us, and left the houses standing still as they were, so it growing towards night, and the tyde almost spent, we hasted with our things downe to the Shallop, and got abourd that night, intending to have brought some Beades, and other things to have left in the houses, in signe of Peace, and that we meant to truk with them, but it was not done, by meanes of our hastie comming away from Cape Cod, but so soone as we can meete conveniently with them, we will give them full satisfaction. Thus much of our second Discovery.

Having thus discovered this place, it was controversall amongst us, what to doe touching our aboad and setling there; some thought it best for many reasons to abide there.

As first, that there was a convenient harbour for Boates, though not for Ships.

Secondly, Good Corne ground readie to our hands, as we saw by experience in the goodly corne it yeelded, which would againe agree with the ground, and be naturall seed for the same.

Thirdly, Cape Cod was like to be a place of good fishing, for we saw daily great Whales of the best kind for oyle and bone, come close aboord our Ship, and in fayre weather swim and play about us; there was once one when the Sun shone warme, came and lay above water, as if she had beene dead, for a good while together, within halfe a Musket shot of the Ship, at which two were prepared to shoote, to see whether she would stir or no, he that gave fire first, his Musket flew in peeces, both stocke and barrell, yet thankes be to God, neither he nor any man els was hurt with it, though many were there about, but when the Whale saw her time she gave a snuffe and away.

Fourthly, the place was likely to be healthfull, secure, and defensible.

But the last and especiall reason was, that now the heart of Winter and unseasonable weather was come upon us, so that we could not goe upon coasting and discovery, without danger of loosing men and Boat, upon which would follow the overthrow of all, especially considering what variable windes and sodaine storms doe there arise. Also cold and wett lodging had so taynted our people, for scarce any of us were free from vehement coughs, as if they should continue long in that estate, it would indanger the lives of many, and breed diseases and infection amongst us. Againe, we had yet some Beere, Butter, Flesh, and other such victuals left, which would quickly be all gone, and then we should have nothing to comfort us in the great labour and toyle we were like to under-goe at the first; It was also conceived, whilst we had competent victuals, that the Ship would stay with us, but when that grew low, they would be gone, and let us shift as we could.

Others againe, urged greatly the going to *Anguum* or *Angoum*, a place twentie leagues off to the Northwards, which they had heard to be an excellent harbour for ships; better ground and better fishing. Secondly, for any thing we knew, there might be hard by us a farre better seate, and it should be a great hindrance to seate where wee should remove againe. Thirdly, The water was but in ponds, and it was thought there would be none in Summer, or very little. Fourthly, the water there must be fetched up a steepe hill: but to omit many reasons and replies used heere abouts; It was in the ende concluded, to make some discovery within the Bay, but in no case so farre as *Angoum*: besides, *Robert Coppin* our Pilot, made relation of a great Navigable River and good harbour in the other head-land of this Bay, almost right over against *Cape Cod*, being a right line, not much above eight leagues distant, in which hee had beene once: and because that one of the wild men with whom they had some trucking, stole a harping Iron from them, they called it theevish harbour. And beyond that place they were enjoyned not to goe, whereupon, a Company was chosen to goe out uppon a third discovery: whilest some were imployed in this discovery, it pleased God that Mistris *White* was brought a bed of a Sonne, which was called *Peregrine*.

The fift day, we through Gods mercy escaped a great danger by the foolishnes of a Boy, one of *Francis Billingtons* Sonnes, who in his Fathers absence, had got Gun-powder, and had shot off a peice or two, and made squibs, and there being a fowling peice charged in his fathers Cabbin, shot her off in the Cabbin, there being a little barrell of powder halfe full, scattered in and about the Cabbin, the fire being within foure foote of the bed betweene the Deckes, and many flints and Iron things about the Cabbin, and many people about the fire, and yet by Gods mercy no harme done.

Wednesday, the sixt of December, it was resolved our discoverers should set forth, for the day before was too fowle weather, and so they did, though it was well ore the day ere all things could be readie: So ten of our men were appointed who were of themselves willing to undertake it, to wit, Captaine *Standish*, Maister *Carver*, *William Bradford*, *Edward Winsloe*, *John Tilley*, *Edward Tilley*, *John Houland*, and three of London, *Richard Warren*, *Steeven Hopkins*, and *Edward Dotte*, and two of our Sea-men, *John Alderton* and *Thomas English*, of the Ships Company there went two of the Masters Mates, Master *Clarke* and Master *Copin*, the Master Gunner, and three Saylers. The narration of which Discovery, followes, penned by one of the Company.

Wednesday the sixt of December wee set out, being very cold and hard weather, wee were a long while after we launched from the ship, before we could get cleare of a sandie poynt, which lay within lesse then a furlong of the same. In which time, two were very sicke, and *Edward Tilley* had like to have sounded with cold; the Gunner was also sicke unto Death, (but hope of truking made him to goe) and so remained all that day, and the next night; at length we got cleare of the sandy poynt,

and got up our sayles, and within an houre or two we got
under the weather shore, and then had smoother water and
better sayling, but it was very cold, for the water frose on our
clothes, and made them many times like coats of Iron: wee
sayled sixe or seaven leagues by the shore, but saw neither river
nor creeke, at length wee mett with a tongue of Land, being
flat off from the shore, with a sandy poynt, we bore up to gaine
the poynt, & found there a fayre income or rode, of a Bay,
being a league over at the narrowest, and some two or three in
length, but wee made right over to the land before us, and left
the discovery of this *Income* till the next day: as we drew neare
to the shore, wee espied some ten or twelve *Indians*, very busie
about a blacke thing, what it was we could not tell, till afterwards they saw us, and ran to and fro, as if they had beene
carrying some thing away, wee landed a league or two from
them, and had much adoe to put a shore any where, it lay so
full of flat sands, when we came to shore, we made us a Baricado, and got fire wood, and set out our Sentinells, and betooke
us to our lodging, such as it was; we saw the smoke of the fire
which the Savages made that night, about foure or five myles
from us, in the morning we devided our company, some eight
in the Shallop, and the rest on the shore went to discover this
place, but we found it onely to be a Bay, without either river or
creeke comming into it, yet we deemed it to be as good an
harbour as Cape Cod, for they that sounded it, found a ship
might ride in five fathom water, wee on the land found it to be
a levill soyle, but none of the fruitfullest; wee saw two beckes
of fresh water, which were the first running streames that we
saw in the Country, but one might stride over them: we found
also a great fish, called a *Grampus* dead on the sands, they in
the Shallop found two of them also in the bottome of the bay,
dead in like sort, they were cast up at high water, and could not
get off for the frost and ice; they were some five or sixe paces
long, and about two inches thicke of fat, and fleshed like a
Swine, they would have yeelded a great deale of oyle, if there
had beene time and meanes to have taken it, so we finding
nothing for our turne, both we and our Shallop returned. We
then directed our course along the Seasands, to the place where
we first saw the *Indians*, when we were there, we saw it was also
a *Grampus* which they were cutting up, they cut it into long

rands or peeces, about an ell long, and two handfull broad, wee found here and there a peece scattered by the way, as it seemed, for hast: this place the most were minded we should call, the *Grampus Bay*, because we found so many of them there: wee followed the tract of the *Indians* bare feete a good way on the sands, at length we saw where they strucke into the Woods by the side of a Pond, as wee went to view the place, one sayd, hee thought hee saw an *Indian*-house among the trees, so went up to see: and here we and the Shallop lost sight one of another till night, it being now about nine or ten a clocke, so we light on a path, but saw no house, and followed a great way into the woods, at length wee found where Corne had beene set, but not that yeare, anone we found a great burying place, one part whereof was incompassed with a large Palazado, like a Church-yard, with yong spires foure or five yards long, set as close one by another as they could two or three foot in the ground, within it was full of Graves, some bigger, and some lesse, some were also paled about, & others had like an *Indian*-house made over them, but not matted: those Graves were more sumptuous then those at *Corne-hill*, yet we digged none of them up, but onely viewed them, and went our way; without the Palazado were graves also, but not so costly: from this place we went and found more Corne ground, but not of this yeare. As we ranged we light on foure or five *Indian*-houses, which had beene lately dwelt in, but they were uncovered, and had no matts about them, els they were like those we found at *Corne-hill*, but had not beene so lately dwelt in, there was nothing left but two or three peeces of old matts, a little sedge, also a little further we found two Baskets full of parched Acorns hid in the ground, which we supposed had beene Corne when we beganne to dig the same, we cast earth thereon againe & went our way. All this while we saw no people, wee went ranging up and downe till the Sunne began to draw low, and then we hasted out of the woods, that we might come to our Shallop, which when we were out of the woods, we espied a great way off, and call'd them to come unto us, the which they did as soone as they could, for it was not yet high water, they were exceeding glad to see us, (for they feared because they had not seene us in so long a time) thinking we would have kept by the shoreside, so being both weary and faint, for we had eaten nothing all that

day, we fell to make our Randevous and get fire wood, which
always cost us a great deale of labour, by that time we had done,
& our Shallop come to us, it was within night, and we fed upon
such victualls as we had, and betooke us to our rest, after we
had set out our watch. About midnight we heard a great and
hideous cry, and our Sentinell called, *Arme, Arme.* So we
bestirred our selves and shot off a couple of Muskets, and noyse
ceased; we concluded, that it was a company of Wolves or
Foxes, for one told us, hee had heard such a noyse in *New-
found-land.* About five a clocke in the morning wee began to
be stirring, and two or three which doubted whether their
Peeces would goe off or no made tryall of them, and shot them
off, but thought nothing at all, after Prayer we prepared our
selves for brek-fast, and for a journey, and it being now the
twilight in the morning, it was thought meet to carry the
things downe to the Shallop: some sayd, it was not best to carry
the Armour downe, others sayd, they would be readier, two or
three sayd, they would not carry theirs, till they went themselves, but mistrusting nothing at all: as it fell out, the water
not being high enough, they layd the things downe upon the
shore, & came up to brek-fast. Anone, all upon a sudden, we
heard a great & strange cry, which we knew to be the same
voyces, though they varied their notes, one of our company
being abroad came running in, and cryed, *They are men, Indians, Indians*; and withall, their arrowes came flying amongst
us, our men ran out with all speed to recover their armes, as by
the good Providence of God they did. In the meane time,
Our first   Captaine *Miles Standish*, having a snaphance
Combat with   ready, made a shot, and after him another, after
the *Indians.*   they two had shot, other two of us were ready, but
he wisht us not to shoot, till we could take ayme, for we knew
not what need we should have, & there were foure only of us,
which had their armes there readie, and stood before the open
side of our Baricado, which was first assaulted, they thought it
best to defend it, least the enemie should take it and our stuffe,
and so have the more vantage against us, our care was no lesse
for the Shallop, but we hoped all the rest would defend it; we
called unto them to know how it was with them, and they
answered, Well, Well, every one, and be of good courage: wee
heard three of their Peeces goe off, and the rest called for a

fire-brand to light their matches, one tooke a log out of the fire on his shoulder and went and carried it unto them, which was thought did not a little discourage our enemies. The cry of our enemies was dreadfull, especially, when our men ran out to recover their Armes, their note was after this manner, *Woath woach ha ha hach woach*: our men were no sooner come to their Armes, but the enemy was ready to assault them.

There was a lustie man and no whit lesse valiant, who was thought to bee their Captaine, stood behind a tree within halfe a musket shot of us, and there let his arrowes fly at us; hee was seene to shoote three arrowes, which were all avoyded, for he at whom the first arrow was aymed, saw it, and stooped downe and it flew over him, the rest were avoyded also: he stood three shots of a Musket, at length one tooke as he sayd full ayme at him, after which he gave an extraordinary cry and away they went all, wee followed them about a quarter of a mile, but wee left sixe to keepe our Shallop, for we were carefull of our businesse: then wee shouted all together two severall times, and shot off a couple of muskets and so returned: this wee did that they might see wee were not afrayd of them nor discouraged. Thus it pleased God to vanquish our Enemies and give us deliverance, by their noyse we could not guesse that they were lesse then thirty or forty, though some thought that they were many more yet in the darke of the morning, wee could not so well discerne them among the trees, as they could see us by our fire side, we took up 18. of their arrowes which we have sent to *England* by Master *Jones*, some whereof were headed with brasse, others with Harts horne, & others with Eagles clawes many more no doubt were shot, for these we found, were almost covered with leaves: yet by the especiall providence of God, none of them either hit or hurt us, though many came close by us, and on every side of us, and some coates which hung up in our Baricado, were shot through and through. So after wee had given God thankes for our deliverance, wee tooke our Shallop and went on our Journey, and called this place, *The first Encounter*, from hence we intended to have sayled to the aforesayd theevish Harbour, if wee found no convenient Harbour by the way, having the wind good, we sayled all that day along the Coast about 15. leagues, but saw neither River nor Creeke to put into, after we had sayled an houre or two, it began to snow and raine, and to be bad weather; about the midst of the afternoone, the winde increased and the Seas began to be very rough, and the hinges of the rudder broke, so that we could steere no longer with it, but two men with much adoe were faine to serve with a couple of Oares, the Seas were growne so great, that we were much troubled and in great danger, and night grew on: Anon Master *Coppin* bad us be of good cheere he saw the Harbour, as we drew neare, the gale being stiffe, and we bearing great sayle to get in, split our Mast in 3. peices, and were like to have cast away our Shallop, yet by Gods mercy recovering our selves, wee had the floud with us, and struck into the Harbour.

Now he that thought that had beene the place was deceived, it being a place where not any of us had beene before, and comming into the Harbour, he that was our Pilot did beare up Northward, which if we had continued wee had beene cast away, yet still the Lord kept us, and we bare up for an Iland before us, and recovering of that Iland, being compassed about with many Rocks, and darke night growing upon us, it pleased the Divine providence that we fell upon a place of sandy ground, where our Shallop did ride safe and secure all that night, and comming upon a strange Iland kept our watch all night in the raine upon that Iland: and in the morning we marched about it, & found no Inhabitants at all, and here wee made our Randevous all that day, being Saturday, 10. of December, on the Sabboth day wee rested, and on Munday we sounded the Harbour, and found it a very good Harbour for our shipping, we marched also into the Land, and found divers corne fields, and little running brookes, a place very good for scituation, so we returned to our Ship againe with good newes to the rest of our people, which did much comfort their hearts.

On the fifteenth day, we waighed Anchor, to goe to the place we had discovered, and comming within two leagues of the Land, we could not fetch the Harbour, but were faine to put roome againe towards *Cape Cod*, our course lying West; and the wind was at North west, but it pleased God that the next day being Saturday the 16. day, the winde came faire, and wee put to Sea againe, and came safely into a safe Harbour; and within halfe an houre the winde changed, so as if we had beene

letted but a little, we had gone backe to *Cape Cod*. This Harbour is a Bay greater then *Cape Cod*, compassed with a goodly
Land, and in the Bay, 2. fine Ilands uninhabited, wherein are
nothing but wood, Okes, Pines, Walnut, Beech, Sasifras, Vines,
and other trees which wee know not; This Bay is a most hopefull place, innumerable store of fowle, and excellent good, and
cannot but bee of fish in their seasons: Skote, Cod, Turbot, and
Herring, wee have tasted of, abundance of Musles the greatest
& best that ever we saw; Crabs and Lobsters, in their time
infinite, It is in fashion like a Cikle or Fish-hooke.

Munday the 13. day, we went a land, manned with the Maister of the Ship, and 3. or 4. of the Saylers, we marched along
the coast in the woods, some 7. or 8. mile, but saw not an
Indian nor an *Indian* house, only we found where formerly,
had beene some Inhabitants, and where they had planted their
corne: we found not any Navigable River, but 4. or 5. small
running brookes of very sweet fresh water, that all run into the
Sea: The Land for the crust of the earth is a spits depth, excellent blacke mold and fat in some places, 2. or 3. great Oakes
but not very thicke, Pines, Wal-nuts Beech Ash, Birch, Hasell,
Holley, Asp, Sasifras, in abundance, & Vines every where,
Cherry trees, Plum-trees, and many other which we know not;
many kinds of hearbes, we found heere in Winter, as Strawberry leaves innumerable, Sorrell, Yarow, Carvell, Brook-lime,
Liver-wort, Water-cresses, great store of Leekes, and Onyons,
and an excellent strong kind of Flaxe, and Hempe; here is sand,
gravell, and excellent clay no better in the Worlde, excellent for
pots, and will wash like sope, and great store of stone, though
somewhat soft, and the best water that ever we drunke, and
the Brookes now begin to be full of fish; that night many being
weary with marching, wee went abourd againe.

The next morning being Tuesday the 19. of December, wee
went againe to discover further; some went on Land, and some
in the Shallop, the Land we found as the former day we did,
and we found a Creeke, and went up three English myles, a
very pleasant river at full Sea, a Barke of thirty tunne may
goe up, but at low water scarce our Shallop could passe: this
place we had a great liking to plant in, but that it was so farre
from our fishing our principall profit, and so incompassed with
woods, that we should bee in much danger of the Salvages, and

our number being so little, and so much ground to cleare, so as we thought good to quit and cleare that place, till we were of more strength; some of us having a good minde for safety to plant in the greater Ile, wee crossed the Bay which there is five or sixe myles over, and found the Ile about a myle and a halfe, or two myles about, all wooded, and no fresh water but 2. or 3. pits, that we doubted of fresh water in Summer, and so full of wood, as we could hardly cleare so much as to serve us for Corne, besides wee judged it colde for our Corne, and some part very rockie, yet divers thought of it as a place defensible, and of great securitie.

That night we returned againe a ship boord, with resolution the next morning to settle on some of those places, so in the morning, after we had called on God for direction, we came to this resolution, to goe presently ashore againe, and to take a better view of two places, which wee thought most fitting for us, for we could not now take time for further search or consideration, our victuals being much spent, especially, our Beere, and it being now the 19. of *December*. After our landing and viewing of the places, so well as we could we came to a conclusion, by most voyces, to set on the maine Land, on the first place, on an high ground, where there is a great deale of Land cleared, and hath beene planted with Corne three or four yeares agoe, and there is a very sweet brooke runnes under the hill side, and many delicate springs of as good water as can be drunke, and where we may harbour our Shallops and Boates exceeding well, and in this brooke much good fish in their seasons: on the further side of the river also much Corne ground cleared, in one field is a great hill, on which wee poynt to make a platforme, and plant our Ordinance, which will command all round about, from thence we may see into the *Bay*, and farre into the Sea, and we may see thence *Cap Cod*: our greatest labour will be fetching of our wood, which is halfe a quarter of an English myle, but there is enough so farre off; what people inhabite here we yet know not, for as yet we have seene none, so there we made our Randevous, and a place for some of our people about twentie, resolving in the morning to come all ashore, and to build houses, but the next morning being Thursday the 21. of *December*, it was stormie and wett, that we could not goe ashore, and those that remained there all night could doe nothing, but were wet, not having dai-light enough to make them a sufficient court of gard, to keepe them dry. All that night it blew and rayned extreamely; it was so tempestuous, that the Shallop could not goe on land so soone as was meet, for they had no victuals on land. About 11. a Clocke the Shallop went off with much adoe with provision, but could not returne it blew so strong, and was such foule weather, that we were forced to let fall our Anchor, and ride with three Anchors an head.

Friday the 22. the storme still continued, that we could not get a-land, nor they come to us aboord: this morning Good wife *Alderton* was delivered of a sonne, but dead borne.

Saturday the 23. so many of us as could, went on shore, felled and carried tymber, to provide themselves stuffe for building.

Sunday the 24. our people on shore heard a cry of some Savages (as they thought) which caused an Alarm, and to stand on their gard, expecting an assault, but all was quiet.

Munday the 25. day, we went on shore, some to fell tymber, some to saw, some to rive, and some to carry, so no man rested all that day, but towards night some as they were at worke, heard a noyse of some *Indians*, which caused us all to goe to our Muskets, but we heard no further, so we came aboord againe, and left some twentie to keepe the court of gard; that night we had a sore storme of winde and rayne.

Munday the 25. being Christmas day, we began to drinke water aboord, but at night the Master caused us to have some Beere, and so on boord we had diverse times now and then some Beere, but on shore none at all.

Tuesday the 26. it was foule weather, that we could not goe ashore.

Wednesday the 27. we went to worke againe.

Thursday the 28. of *December*, so many as could went to worke on the hill, where we purposed to build our platforme for our Ordinance, and which doth command all the plaine, and the *Bay*, and from whence we may see farre into the sea, and might be easier impayled, having two rowes of houses and a faire streete. So in the afternoone we went to measure out the grounds, and first, we tooke notice how many Families they were, willing all single men that had no wives to joyne with some Familie, as they thought fit, that so we might build fewer

houses, which was done, and we reduced them to 19. Families;
to greater Families we allotted larger plots, to every person
halfe a pole in breadth, and three in length, and so Lots were
cast where every man should lie, which was done, and staked
out; we thought this proportion was large enough at the first,
for houses and gardens, to impale them round, considering the
weaknes of our people, many of them growing ill with coldes,
for our former Discoveries in frost and stormes, and the wading
at Cape *Cod* had brought much weakenes amongst us, which
increased so every day more and more, and after was the cause
of many of their deaths.

Fryday and Saturday, we fitted our selves for our labour, but
our people on shore were much troubled and discouraged with
rayne and wett that day, being very stormie and cold; we saw
great smokes of fire made by the *Indians* about six or seaven
myles from us as we conjectured.

Munday the first of *January*, we went betimes to worke, we
were much hindred in lying so farre off from the Land, and
faine to goe as the tyde served, that we lost much time, for our
Ship drew so much water, that she lay a myle and almost a halfe
off, though a ship of seaventie or eightie tun at high water may
come to the shore.

Wednesday the third of *January*, some of our people being
abroad, to get and gather thatch, they saw great fires of the
Indians, and were at their Corne fields, yet saw none of the
Savages, nor had seene any of them since wee came to this
Bay.

Thursday the fourth of *January*, Captaine *Miles Standish*
with foure or five more, went to see if they could meet with
any of the Savages in that place where the fires were made, they
went to some of their houses, but not lately inhabited, yet could
they not meete with any; as they came home, they shot at an
Eagle and killed her, which was excellent meat; It was hardly
to be discerned from Mutton.

Fryday the fifth of *January*, one of the Saylers found alive
upon the shore an Hering, which the Master had to his supper,
which put us in hope of fish, but as yet we had got but one Cod;
we wanted small hookes.

Saturday the sixt of *January*, Master *Marten* was very sicke,
and to our judgement, no hope of life, so Master *Carver* was

sent for to come abourd to speake with him about his accompts, who came the next morning.

Munday the eight day of *January*, was a very fayre day, and we went betimes to worke, master *Jones* sent the Shallop as he had formerly done, to see where fish could be got, they had a greate storme at Sea, and were in some danger, at night they returned with three greate Seales, and an excellent good Cod, which did assure us that we thould have plentie of fish shortly.

This day, *Francis Billington,* having the weeke before seene from the top of a tree on an hie hill, a great sea as he thought, went with one of the Masters mates to see it, they went three myles, and then came to a great water, devided into two great Lakes, the bigger of them five or sixe myles in circuit, and in it an Ile of a Cable length square, the other three miles in compasse; in their estimation they are fine fresh water, full of fish, and foule; a brooke issues from it, it will be an excellent helpe for us in time. They found seaven or eight *Indian* houses, but not lately inhabited, when they saw the houses they were in some feare, for they were but two persons and one peece.

Tuesday the 9. January, was a reasonable faire day, and wee went to labour that day in the building of our Towne, in two rowes of houses for more safety: we devided by lott the plot of ground whereon to build our Towne: After the proportion formerly allotted, wee agreed that every man should build his owne house, thinking by that course, men would make more hast then working in common: the common house, in which for the first, we made our Rendevous, being neere finished wanted onely covering, it being about 20. foote square, some should make morter, and some gather thatch, so that in foure days halfe of it was thatched, frost and foule weather hindred us much, this time of the yeare seldome could wee worke halfe the weeke.

Thursday the eleventh, *William Bradford* being at worke, (for it was a faire day) was vehemently taken with a griefe and paine, and so shot to his huckle-bone; It was doubted that he would have instantly dyed, hee got colde in the former discoveries, especially the last, and felt some paine in his anckles by times, but he grew a little better towards night and in time through Gods mercie in the use of meanes recovered.

Friday the 12. we went to worke, but about noone, it began to raine, that it forced us to give over worke.

This day, two of our people put us in great sorrow and care, there was 4. sent to gather and cut thatch in the morning, and two of them, *John Goodman* and *Peter Browne*, having cut thatch all the fore-noone, went to a further place, and willed the other two, to binde up that which was cut and to follow them; so they did, being about a myle and a halfe from our Plantation: but when the two came after, they could not finde them, nor heare any thing of them at all, though they hallowed and shouted as loud as they could, so they returned to the Company and told them of it: whereupon Master *Leaver* & three or foure more went to seeke them, but could heare nothing of them, so they returning, sent more, but that night they could heare nothing at all of them: the next day they armed 10. or 12. men out, verily thinking the *Indians* had surprised them, they went seeking 7. or 8. myles, but could neither see nor heare any thing at all, so they returned with much discomfort to us all. These two that were missed, at dinner time tooke their meate in their hands, and would goe walke and refresh themselves, so going a litle off they finde a lake of water, and having a great Mastiffe bitch with them and a Spannell; by the water side they found a great Deere, the Dogs chased him, and they followed so farre as they lost themselves, and could not finde the way backe, they wandred all that after-noone being wett, and at night it did freeze and snow, they were slenderly apparelled and had no weapons but each one his Cicle, nor any victuals, they ranged up and downe and could finde none of the Salvages habitations; when it drew to night they were much perplexed, for they could finde neither harbour nor meate, but in frost and snow, were forced to make the earth their bed, and the Element their covering, and another thing did very much terrifie them, they heard as they thought two Lyons roaring exceedingly for a long time together, and a third, that they thought was very nere them, so not knowing what to do, they resolved to climbe up into a tree as their safest refuge, though that would prove an intollerable colde lodging; so they stoode at the trees roote, that when the Lyons came they might take their opportunitie of climbing up, the bitch they were faine to hold by the necke, for shee would have beene gone to the Lyon; but it pleased God so to dispose, that the wilde Beastes came not: so they walked up and downe under the Tree all night, it was an extreame colde night, so soone as it was light they travailed againe, passing by many lakes and brookes and woods, and in one place where the Salvages had burnt the space of 5. myles in length, which is a fine Champion Countrey, and even. In the after-noone, it pleased God from an high Hill they discovered the two Iles in the Bay, and so that night got to the Plantation, being ready to faint with travaile and want of victuals, and almost famished with colde, *John Goodman* was faine to have his shooes cut off his feete they were so swelled with colde, and it was a long while after ere he was able to goe; those on the shore were much comforted at their returne, but they on ship-boord were grieved as deeming them lost; but the next day being the 14. of January, in the morning about sixe of the clocke the winde being very great, they on ship-boord spied their great new Randevous on fire, which was to them a new discomfort, fearing because of the supposed losse of the men, that the Salvages had fiered them, neither could they presently goe to them for want of water, but after 3. quarters of an houre they went, as they had purposed the day before to keepe the Sabboth on shore, because now there was the greater number of people. At their landing they heard good tidings of the returne of the 2. men, and that the house was fiered occasionally by a sparke that flew into the thatch, which instantly burnt it all up, but the roofe stood and little hurt; the most losse was Maister *Carvers* and *William Bradfords*, who then lay sicke in bed, and if they had not risen with good speede, had been blowne up with powder: but through Gods mercy they had no harme, the house was as full of beds as they could lie one by another, and their Muskets charged, but blessed be God there was no harme done.

Munday the 15. day, it rayned much all day, that they on ship-boord could not goe on shore, nor they on shore doe any labour but were all wet.

Tuesday, wednesday, thursday, were very faire Sunshinie dayes, as if it had been in Aprill, and our people so many as were in health wrought chearefully.

The 19. day, we resolved to make a Shed, to put our common provision in, of which some were alreadie set on shore, but at noone it rayned, that we could not worke. This day in the evening, *John Goodman* went abroad to use his lame feete, that were pittifully ill with the cold he had got, having a little Spannell with him, a little way from the Plantation, two great Wolves ran after the Dog, the Dog ran to him and betwixt his leggs for succour, he had nothing in his hand but tooke up a sticke, and threw at one of them and hit him, and they presently ran both away, but came againe, he got a paile bord in his hand, and they sat both on their tayles, grinning at him, a good while, and went their way, and left him.

Saturday 20. we made up our Shed for our common goods.

Sunday the 21. we kept our meeting on Land.

Munday the 22. was a faire day, we wrought on our houses, and in the after-noone carried up our hogsheads of meale to our common store-house.

The rest of the weeke we followed our businesse likewise.

Munday the 29. in the morning cold frost and sleete, but after reasonable fayre; both the long Boate and the Shallop brought our common goods on shore.

Tuesday and wednesday 30. and 31. of *January*, cold frosty weather and sleete, that we could not worke: in the morning the Master and others saw two Savages, that had beene on the Iland nere our Ship, what they came for wee could not tell, they were going so farre backe againe before they were descried, that we could not speake with them.

Sunday the 4. of *February*, was very wett and rainie, with the greatest gusts of winde that ever we had since wee came forth, that though we rid in a very good harbour, yet we were in danger, because our Ship was light, the goods taken out, and she unballased; and it caused much daubing of our houses to fall downe.

Fryday the 9. still the cold weather continued, that wee could doe little worke. That after-noone our little house for our sicke people was set on fire by a sparke that kindled in the roofe, but no great harme was done. That evening the master going ashore, killed five Geese, which he friendly distributed among the sicke people; he found also a good Deere killed, the

Savages had cut off the hornes, and a Wolfe was eating of him, how he came there we could not conceive.

Friday the 16. day, was a faire day, but the northerly wind continued, which continued the frost, this day after-noone one of our people being a fouling, and having taken a stand by a creeke side in the Reeds, about a myle and an halfe from our Plantation, there came by him twelve *Indians*, marching towards our Plantation, & in the woods he heard the noyse of many more, he lay close till they were passed, and then with what speed he could he went home & gave the Alarm, so the people abroad in the woods returned & armed themselves, but saw none of them, onely toward the evening they made a great fire, about the place where they were first discovered: Captaine *Miles Standish*, and *Francis Cooke*, being at worke in the Woods, comming home, left their tooles behind them, but before they returned, their tooles were taken away by the Savages. This comming of the Savages gave us occasion to keepe more strict watch, and to make our peeces and furniture readie, which by the moysture and rayne were out of temper.

Saturday the 17 day, in the morning we called a meeting for the establishing of military Orders amongst our selves, and we chose *Miles Standish* our Captaine, and gave him authoritie of command in affayres: and as we were in consultation here abouts, two Savages presented themselves upon the top of an hill, over against our Plantation, about a quarter of a myle and lesse, and made signes unto us to come unto them; we likewise made signes unto them to come to us, whereupon we armed our selves, and stood readie, and sent two over the brooke towards them, to wit, Captaine *Standish* and *Steven Hopkins*, who went towards them, onely one of them had a Musket, which they layd downe on the ground in their sight, in signe of peace, and to parley with them, but the Savages would not tarry their comming: a noyse of a great many more was heard behind the hill, but no more came in sight. This caused us to plant our great Ordinances in places most convenient.

Wednesday the 21. of *February*, the master came on shore with many of his Saylers, and brought with him one of the great Peeces, called a *Minion*, and helped us to draw it up the hill, with another Peece that lay on shore, and mounted them, and a saller and two bases; he brought with him a very fat Goose to eate with us, and we had a fat Crane, and a Mallerd, and a dry'd neats-tongue, and so wee were kindly and friendly together.

Saturday the third of *March*, the winde was South, the morning mistie, but towards noone warme and fayre weather; the Birds sang in the Woods most pleasantly; at one of the Clocke it thundred, which was the first wee heard in that Countrey, it was strong and great claps, but short, but after an houre it rayned very sadly till midnight.

Wednesday the seaventh of *March*, the wind was full East, cold, but faire, that day Master *Carver* with five other went to the great Ponds, which seeme to be excellent fishing-places; all the way they went they found it exceedingly beaten and haunted with Deere, but they saw none; amongst other foule, they saw one a milke white foule, with a very blacke head: this day some garden seeds were sowen.

Fryday, the 16. a fayre warme day towards; this morning we determined to conclude of the military Orders, which we had began to consider of before, but were interrupted by the Savages, as we mentioned formerly; and whilst we were busied here about, we were interrupted againe, for there presented himself a *Savage*, which caused an Alarm, he very boldly came all alone and along the houses straight to the Randevous, where we intercepted him, not suffering him to goe in, as undoubtedly he would, out of his boldnesse, hee saluted us in English, and bad us well-come, for he had learned some broken English amongst the English men that came to fish at *Monchiggon*, and knew by name the most of the Captaines, Commanders, & Masters, that usually come, he was a man free in speech, so farre as he could expresse his minde, and of a seemely carriage, we questioned him of many things, he was the first *Savage* we could meete withall; he sayd he was not of these parts, but of *Morattiggon*, and one of the *Sagamores* or *Lords* thereof, and had beene 8. moneths in these parts, it lying hence a dayes sayle with a great wind, and five dayes by land; he discoursed of the whole Country, and of every Province, and of their *Sagamores*, and their number of men, and strength; the wind beginning to rise a little, we cast a horsemans coat about him, for he was starke naked, onely a leather about his wast, with a fringe about a span long, or little more; he had a bow & 2 arrowes, the one headed, and the other unheaded; he was a tall straight man, the haire of his head blacke, long behind, onely short before, none on his face at all; he asked some beere, but we gave him strong water, and bisket, and butter, and cheese, & pudding, and a peece of a mallerd, all which he liked well, and had bin acquainted with such amongst the English; he told us the place where we now live, is called, *Patuxet*, and that about foure yeares agoe, all the Inhabitants dyed of an extraordinary plague, and there is neither man, woman, nor childe remaining, as indeed we have found none, so as there is none to hinder our possession, or to lay claime unto it; all the after-noone we spent in communication with him, we would gladly have beene rid of him at night, but he was not willing to goe this night, then we thought to carry him on ship-boord, wherewith he was well content, and went into the Shallop, but the winde was high and water scant, that it could not returne backe: we lodged him that night at *Steven Hopkins* house, and watched him; the next day he went away backe to the *Masasoits*, from whence he sayd he came, who are our next bordering neighbours: they are sixtie strong, as he sayth: the *Nausites* are as neere South-east of them, and are a hundred strong, and those were they of whom our people were encountred, as we before related. They are much incensed and provoked against the English, and about eyght moneths agoe slew three English men, and two more hardly escaped by flight to *Monhiggon*; they were Sir *Ferdinando Gorge* his men, as this Savage told us, as he did likewise of the *Huggerie*, that is, *Fight*, that our discoverers had with the *Nausites*, & of our tooles that were taken out of the woods, which we willed him should be brought againe, otherwise, we would right our selves. These people are ill affected towards the English, by reason of one *Hunt*, a master of a ship, who deceived the people, and got them under colour of truking with them, twentie out of this very place where we inhabite, and seaven men from the *Nausites*, and carried them away, and sold them for slaves, like a wretched man (for 20. pound a man) that cares not what mischiefe he doth for his profit.

Saturday in the morning we dismissed the Salvage, and gave him a knife, a bracelet, and a ring; he promised within a night or two to come againe, and to bring with him some of the *Massasoyts* our neighbours, with such Bevers skins as they had to trucke with us.

Saturday and Sunday reasonable fayre dayes. On this day came againe the Savage, and brought with him five other tall proper men, they had every man a Deeres skin on him, and the principall of them had a wild Cats skin, or such like on the one arme; they had most of them long hosen up to their groynes, close made; and above their groynes to their wast another leather, they were altogether like the *Irish*-trouses; they are of complexion like our English Gipseys, no haire or very little on their faces, on their heads long haire to their shoulders, onely cut before some trussed up before with a feather, broad wise, like a fanne, another a fox tayle hanging out: these left (according to our charge given him before) their Bowes and Arrowes a quarter of a myle from our Towne, we gave them entertaynement as we thought was fitting them, they did eate liberally of our English victuals, they made semblance unto us of friendship and amitie; they song & danced after their maner like Anticks; they brought with them in a thing like a Bow-case (which the principall of them had about his wast) a little of their Corne pownded to Powder, which put to a little water they eate; he had a little Tobacco in a bag, but none of them drunke but when he lifted, some of them had their faces paynted black, from the forehead to the chin, foure or five fingers broad; others after other fashions, as they liked; they brought three or foure skins, but we would not trucke with them at all that day, but wished them to bring more, and we would trucke for all, which they promised within a night or two, and would leave these behind them, though we were not willing they should, and they brought us all our tooles againe which were taken in the Woods, in our mens absence, so because of the day we dismissed them so soone as we could. But *Samoset* our first acquaintance, eyther was sicke, or fayned himselfe so, and would not goe with them, and stayed with us till Wednesday morning: Then we sent him to them, to know the reason they came not according to their words, and we gave him an hat, a payre of stockings and shooes, a shirt, and a peece of cloth to tie about his wast.

The Sabboth day, when we sent them from us, wee gave every one of them some trifles, especially, the principall of them, we carried them along with our Armes to the place where they left their Bowes and Arrowes, whereat they were amazed, and two of them began to slinke away, but that the other called them, when they tooke their Arrowes, we bad them farewell, and they were glad, and so with many thankes given us they departed, with promise they would come againe.

Munday and tuesday proved fayre dayes, we digged our grounds, and sowed our garden seeds.

Wednesday a fine warme day, we sent away *Samoset.*

That day we had againe a meeting, to conclude of lawes and orders for our selves, and to confirme those Military Orders that were formerly propounded, and twise broken off by the Savages comming, but so we were againe the third time, for after we had beene an houre together, on the top of the hill over against us two or three Savages presented themselves, that made semblance of daring us, as we thought, so Captaine *Standish* with another, with their Muskets went over to them, with two of the masters mates that follows them without Armes, having two Muskets with them, they whetted and rubbed their Arrowes and Strings, and made shew of defiance, but when our men drew nere them, they ranne away. Thus we were againe interrupted by them; this day with much adoe we got our Carpenter that had beene long sicke of the scurvey, to fit our Shallop, to fetch all from aboord.

Thursday the 22. of *March*, was a very fayre warme day. About noone we met againe about our publique businesse, but we had scarce beene an houre together, but *Samoset* came againe, and *Squanto*, the onely native of *Patuxat*, where we now inhabite, who was one of the twentie Captives that by *Hunt* were carried away, and had beene in *England* & dwelt in *Cornehill* with master *John Slanie* a Marchant, and could speake a little English, with three others, and they brought with them some few skinnes to trucke, and some red Herrings newly taken and dryed, but not salted, and signified unto us, that their great Sagamore *Masasoyt* was hard by, with *Quadequina* his brother, and all their men. They could not well expresse in English what they would, but after an houre the King came to the top of an hill over against us, and had in his trayne sixtie men, that wee could well behold them, and they us: we were not willing to send our governour to them, and they unwilling to come to us, so *Squanto* went againe unto him, who brought word that wee should send one to parley with him, which we did, which was *Edward Winsloe*, to know his mind, and to signifie the mind and will of our governour, which was to have trading and peace with him. We sent to the King a payre of Knives, and a Copper Chayne, with a Jewell at it. To *Quadequina* we sent likewise a Knife and a Jewell to hang in his eare, and withall a Pot of strong water, a good quantitie of Bisket, and some butter, which were all willingly accepted: our Messenger made a speech unto him, that King JAMES saluted him with words of love and Peace, and did accept of him as his Friend and Alie, and that our Governour desired to see him and to trucke with him, and to confirme a Peace with him, as his next neighbour: he liked well of the speech and heard it attentively, though the Interpreters did not well expresse it; after he had eaten and drunke himselfe, and given the rest to his company, he looked upon our messengers sword and armour which he had on, with intimation of his desire to buy it, but on the other side, our messenger shewed his unwillingnes to part with it: In the end he left him in the custodie of *Quadequina* his brother, and came over the brooke, and some twentie men following him, leaving all their Bowes and Arrowes behind them. We kept six or seaven as hostages for our messenger; Captaine *Standish* and master *Williamson* met the King at the brooke, with halfe a dozen Musketiers, they saluted him and he them, so one going over, the one on the one side, and the other on the other, conducted him to an house then in building, where we placed a greene Rugge, and three or foure Cushions, then instantly came our Governour with Drumme and Trumpet after him, and some few Musketiers. After salutations, our Governour kissing his hand, the King kissed him, and so they sat downe. The Governour called for some strong water, and drunke to him, and he drunke a great draught that made him sweate all the while after, he called for a little fresh meate, which the King did eate willingly, and did give his followers. Then they treated of Peace, which was;

1. That neyther he nor any of his should injure or doe hurt to any of our people.

2. And if any of his did hurt to any of ours, he should send the offender, that we might punish him.

The agreements of peace betweene us and Massasoyt.

3. That if any of our Tooles were taken away when our people were at worke, he should cause them to be restored, and if ours did any harme to any of his, wee would doe the like to them.

4. If any did unjustly warre against him, we would ayde him; If any did warre against us, he should ayde us.

5. He should send to his neighbour Confederates, to certifie them of this, that they might not wrong us, but might be likewise comprised in the conditions of Peace.

6. That when their men came to us, they should leave their Bowes and Arrowes behind them, as wee should doe our Peeces when we came to them.

Lastly, that doing thus, King JAMES would esteeme of him as his friend and Alie: all which the King seemed to like well, and it was applauded of his followers, all the while he sat by the Governour he trembled for feare: In his person he is a very lustie man, in his best yeares, an able body, grave of countenance, and spare of speech: In his Attyre little or nothing differing from the rest of his followers, only in a great Chaine of white bone Beades about his necke, and at it behinde his necke, hangs a little bagg of Tobacco, which he dranke and gave us to drinke; his face was paynted with a sad red like murry, and oyled both head and face, that hee looked greasily: All his followers likewise, were in their faces, in part or in whole painted, some blacke, some red, some yellow, and some white, some with crosses, and other Antick workes, some had skins on them, and some naked, all strong, tall, all men in appearance: so after all was done, the Governour conducted him to the Brooke, and there they embraced each other and he departed: we diligently keeping our hostages, wee expected our messengers comming, but anon word was brought us, that *Quaddequina* was comming, and our messenger was stayed till his returne, who presently came and a troupe with him, so likewise wee entertained him, and convayed him to the place prepared; he was very fearefull of our peeces, and made signes of dislike, that they should be carried away, whereupon Commandement was given, they should be layd away. He was a very proper tall young man, of a very modest and seemely countenance, and he did kindely like of our entertainement, so we convayed him likewise as wee did the King, but divers of their people stayed still, when hee was returned, then they dismissed our messenger. Two of his people would have stayed all night, but wee would not suffer it: one thing I forgot, the King had in his bosome hanging in a string, a great long knife; hee marveiled much at our Trumpet, and some of his men would sound it as well as they could, *Samoset* and *Squanto*, they stayed al night with us, and the King and al his men lay all night in the woods, not above halfe an Englith myle from us, and all their wives and women with them, they sayd that within 8. or 9. dayes, they would come and set corne on the other side of the Brooke, and dwell there all Summer, which is hard by us: That night we kept good watch, but there was no appearance of danger; the next morning divers of their people came over to us, hoping to get some victuales as wee imagined, som of them told us the King would have some of us come see him; Captaine *Standish* and *Isaac Alderton* went venterously, who were welcommed of him after their manner: he gave them three or foure ground Nuts, and some Tobacco. Wee cannot yet conceive, but that he is willing to have peace with us, for they have seene our people sometimes alone two or three in the woods at worke and fowling, when as they offered them no harme as they might easily have done, and especially because hee hath a potent Adversary the *Narowhiganseis*, that are at warre with him, against whom hee thinks wee may be some strength to him, for our peeces are terrible unto them; this morning, they stayed till ten or eleven of the Clocke, and our Governour bid them send the Kings kettle, and filled it full of pease, which pleased them well, and so they went their way.

Fryday was a very faire day, *Samoset* and *Squanto* still remained with us, *Squanto* went at noone to fish for Eeles, at night he came home with as many as he could well lift in one hand, which our people were glad of, they were fat & sweet, he trod them out with his feete, and so caught them with his hands without any other Instrument.

This day we proceeded on with our common businesse, from which we had been so often hindred by the Salvages comming, and concluded both of Military orders, and of some Lawes and Orders as wee thought behoofefull for our present estate, and condition, and did likewise choose our Governour for this yeare, which was Master *John Carver* a man well approoved amongst us.

A JOURNEY TO *PACKANOKIK*,
The Habitation of the Great King
MASSASOYT.
As also our Message, the
Answere and intertainement
wee had of
HIM.

IT seemed good to the Company for many considerations to send some amongst them to *Massasoyt*, the greatest Commander amongst the Savages, bordering about us; partly to know where to find them, if occasion served, as also to see their strength, discover the Country, prevent abuses in their disorderly comming unto us, make satisfaction for some conceived injuries to be done on our parts, and to continue the league of Peace and Friendship betweene them and us. For these, and the like ends, it pleased the Governour to make choice of *Steven Hopkins*, & *Edward Winsloe* to goe unto him, and having a fit opportunitie, by reason of a Savage, called *Tisquantum* (that could speake English) comming unto us; with all expedition provided a Horse-mans coat, of red Cotton, and laced with a slight lace for a present, that both they and their message might be the more acceptable amongst them. The Message was as followeth; That forasmuch as his subjects came often and without feare, upon all occasions amongst us, so wee were now come unto him, and in witnesse of the love and good will the English beare unto him, the Governour hath sent him a coat, desiring that the Peace and Amitie that was betweene them and us might be continued, not that we feared them, but because we intended not to injure any, desiring to live peaceably: and as with all men, so especially with them our neerest neighbours. But whereas his people came very often, and very many together unto us, bringing for the most part their wives and children with them, they were well come; yet we being but strangers as yet at *Patuxet, alias New Plimmoth*, and not knowing how our Corne might prosper, we could no longer give them such entertainment as we had done, and as we desired still to doe: yet if he would be pleased to come himselfe, or any speciall friend of his desired to see us, comming from him they should be wellcome; and to the end wee might know them from others, our Governour had sent him a copper Chayne, desiring if any Messenger should come from him to us, we might know him by bringing it with him, and hearken and give credite to his Message accordingly. Also requesting him that such as have skins, should bring them to us, and that he would hinder the multitude from oppressing us with them. And whereas at our first arrivall at *Paomet* (called by us *Cape Cod*) we found there Corne buried in the ground, and finding no inhabitants but some graves of dead new buryed, tooke the Corne, resolving if ever we could heare of any that had right thereunto, to make satisfaction to the full for it, yet since we understand the owners thereof were fled for feare of us, our desire was either to pay them with the like quantitie of corne, English meale, or any other Commodities we had to pleasure them withall; requesting him that some one of his men might signifie so much unto them, and wee would content him for his paines. And last of all, our Governour requested one favour of him, which was, that he would exchange some of their Corne for seede with us, that we might make tryall which best agreed with the soyle where we live.

With these presents and message we set forward the tenth June, about 9. a clocke in the Morning, our guide resolving that night to rest at *Namaschet*, a Towne under *Massasoyt*, and conceived by us to bee very neere, because the Inhabitants flocked so thicke upon every slight occasion amongst us: but wee found it to bee some fifteene English myles. On the way we found some ten or twelve men women and children, which had pestered us, till wee were wearie of them, perceiving that (as the manner of them all is) where victuall is easiliest to be got, there they live, especially in the Summer: by reason whereof our Bay affording many Lobsters, they resort every spring tide thither: & now returned with us to *Namaschet*. Thither we came about 3. a clock after noone, the Inhabitants entertaining us with joy, in the best manner they could, giving us a kinde of bread called by them *Maizium*, and the spawne of Shads, which then they got in abundance, in so much as they gave us spoones to eate them, with these they boyled mustie Acorns, but of the Shads we eate heartily. After this they desired one of our men to shoote at a Crow, complaining what damage they sustained in their Corne by them, who shooting some fourescore off and killing, they much admired it, as other shots on other occasions. After this *Tisquantum* told us we should hardly in one day reach *Pakanokick*, moving us to goe some 8. myles further, where we should finde more store and better victuals then there: Being willing to haften our Journey we went, and came thither at Sunne setting, where we found many of the *Namascheucks* (they so calling the men of *Namaschet*) fishing uppon a Ware which they had made on a River which belonged to them, where they caught abundance of Basse. These welcommed us also, gave us of their fish, and we them of our victuals, not doubting but we should have enough where ere we came. There we lodged in the open fieldes: for houses they had none, though they spent the most of the Summer there. The head of this River is reported to bee not farre from the place of our abode, upon it are, and have beene many Townes, it being a good length. The ground is very good on both sides, it being for the most part cleered: Thousands of men have lived there, which dyed in a great plague not long since: and pitty it was and is to see, so many goodly fieldes, & so well seated, without men to dresse and manure the same. Uppon this River dwelleth *Massasoyt*: It commeth into the Sea at the *Narrohiganset* Bay, where the French men so much use. A shipp may goe many myles up it, as the Salvages report, and a shallop to the head of it: but so farre as wee saw, wee are sure a Shallop may.

But to returne to our Journey: The next morning wee brake our fast, tooke our leave and departed, being then accompanied with some sixe Salvages, having gone about six myles by the River side, at a knowne shole place, it beeing low water, they spake to us to put off our breeches, for wee must wade thorow. Heere let me not forget the vallour and courrage of some of the Salvages, on the opposite side of the river, for there were remaining alive only 2. men, both aged, especially the one being above threescore; These two espying a company of men entring the River, ran very swiftly & low in the grasse to meete us at the banck, where with shrill voyces and great courage standing charged uppon us with their bowes, they demaunded what we were, supposing us to be enemies, and thinking to take advantage on us in the water: but seeing we were friends, they welcommed us with such foode as they had, and we bestowed a small bracelet of Beades on them. Thus farre wee are sure the Tide ebs and flowes.

Having here againe refreshed our selves, we proceeded in our Journey, the weather being very hote for travell, yet the Country so well watered that a man could scarce be drie, but he should have a spring at hand to coole his thirst, beside smal Rivers in abundance: but the Salvages will not willingly drinke, but at a spring head. When wee came to any small Brooke where no bridge was, two of them desired to carry us through of their owne accords, also fearing wee were or would be weary, offered to carry our peeces, also if we would lay off any of our clothes, we should have them carried: and as the one of them had found more speciall kindnesse from one of the Messengers, and the other Salvage from the other so they shewed their thankefulnesse accordingly in affording us all helpe, and furtherance in the Journey.

As we passed along, we observed that there were few places by the River, but had beene inhabited, by reason whereof, much ground was cleare, save of weedes which grewe higher then our heads. There is much good Timber both Oake, Waltnut-tree, Firre, Beech, and exceeding great Chessnut-trees. The Country in respect of the lying of it, is both Champanie and hilly, like many places in England. In some places its very rockie both above ground and in it: And though the Countrey bee wilde and over-growne with woods, yet the trees stand not thicke, but a man may well ride a horse amongst them.

Passing on at length, one of the Company an *Indian* espied a man, and told the rest of it, we asked them if they feared any, they told us that if they were *Narrohigganset*, men they would not trust them, whereat, we called for our peeces and bid them not to feare; for though they were twenty, we two alone would not care for them: but they hayling him, hee prooved a friend, and had onely two women with him: their baskets were empty, but they fetched water in their bottels, so that we dranke with them and departed. After we met another man with other two women, which had beene at Randevow by the salt water, and their baskets were full of rosted Crab fishes, and other dryed shell fish, of which they gave us, and wee eate and dranke with them: and gave each of the women a string of Beades, and departed.

After wee came to a Towne of *Massasoyts*, where we eat Oysters and other fish. From thence we went to *Packanokick*, but *Massasoyt* was not at home, there we stayed, he being sent for: when newes was brought of his comming, our guide *Tisquantum* requested that at our meeting, wee would discharge our peeces, but one of us going about to charge his peece, the women and children through feare to see him take upp his peece, ran away, and could not bee pacified, till hee layd it downe againe, who afterward were better informed by our Interpreter.

Massasoyt being come, wee discharged our Peeces, and saluted him, who after their manner kindly well commed us, and tooke us into his house, and set us downe by him, where having delivered our foresayd Message, and Presents, and having put the Coat on his backe, and the Chayne about his necke, he was not a little proud to behold himselfe, and his men also to see their King so bravely attyred.

For answere to our Message, he told us we were well-come, and he would gladly continue that Peace and Friendship which was betweene him & us: and for his men they should no more pester us as they had done: Also, that he would send to *Paomet*, and would helpe us with Corne for seed, according to our request.

This being done, his men gathered neere to him, to whom he turned himselfe, and made a great Speech; they sometime interposing, and as it were, confirming and applauding him in that he sayd. The meaning whereof was (as farre as we could learne) thus; Was not he *Massasoyt* Commander of the Countrey about them? Was not such a Towne his and the people of it? and should they not bring their skins unto us? To which they answered, they were his & would be at peace with us, and bring their skins to us. After this manner, he named at least thirtie places, and their answere was as aforesayd to every one: so that as it was delightfull, it was tedious unto us.

This being ended, he lighted Tobacco for us, and fell to discoursing of *England*, & of the Kings Majestie, marvayling that he would live without a wife. Also he talked of the French-men, bidding us not to suffer them to come to *Narrohiganset*, for it was King JAMES his Countrey, and he also was King JAMES his man. Late it grew, but victualls he offered none; for indeed he had not any, being he came so newly home. So we desired to goe to rest: he layd us on the bed with himselfe and his wife, they at the one end and we at the other, it being onely plancks layd a foot from the ground, and a thin Mat upon them. Two more of his chiefe men for want of roome pressed by and upon us; so that we were worse weary of our lodging then of our journey.

The next day being Thursday, many of their Sachmis, or petty Governours came to see us, and many of their men also. There they went to their manner of Games for skins and knives. There we challenged them to shoote with them for skins: but they durst not: onely they desired to see one of us shoote at a marke, who shooting with Haile-shot, they wondred to see the marke so full of holes. About one a clocke, *Massasoyt* brought two fishes that he had shot, they were like Breame but three times so bigge, and better meate. These being boyled there were at lest fortie looked for share in them, the most eate of them: This meale onely we had in two nights and a day, and had not one of us bought a Partridge, we had taken our Journey fasting: Very importunate he was to have us stay with them longer: But wee desired to keepe the Sabboth at home: and feared we should either be light-headed for want of sleepe, for what with bad lodging, the Savages barbarous singing, (for they use to sing themselves asleepe) lice and fleas within doores, and Muskeetoes without, wee could hardly sleepe all the time of our being there; we much fearing, that if wee should stay any longer, we should not be able to recover home for want of strength. So that on the Fryday morning before Sun-rising, we tooke our leave and departed, *Massasoyt* being both grieved and ashamed, that he could no better entertaine us: and retaining *Tisquantum* to send from place to place to procure trucke for us: and appointing another, called *Tokamahamon* in his place, whom we had found faithfull before and after upon all occasions.

At this towne of *Massasoyts*, where we before eate, wee were againe refreshed with a little fish; and bought about a handfull of Meale of their parched Corne, which was very precious at that time of the yeere, and a small string of dryed shell-fish, as big as Oysters. The latter we gave to the sixe Savages that accompanied us, keeping the Meale for our selves, when we dranke we eate each a spoonefull of it with a Pipe of Tobacco,

in stead of other victuals; and of this also we could not but give
them, so long as it lasted. Five myles they led us to a house out
of the way in hope of victualls: but we found no body there,
and so were but worse able to returne home. That night we
reached to the wire where we lay before, but the *Namascheucks*
were returned: so that we had no hope of any thing there.
One of the Savages had shot a Shad in the water, and a small
Squirrill as big as a Rat, called a *Neuxis*, the one halfe of either
he gave us, and after went to the wire to fish. From hence we
wrote to *Plimouth*, and sent *Tokamahamon* before to *Namasket*, willing him from thence to send another, that he might
meet us with food at *Namasket*. Two men now onely remained
with us, and it pleased God to give them good store of fish, so
that we were well refreshed. After supper we went to rest, and
they to fishing againe: more they gat and fell to eating a-fresh,
and retayned sufficient readie rost for all our break-fasts. About
two a Clocke in the morning, arose a great storme of wind,
raine, lightning, and thunder, in such violent manner, that we
could not keepe in our fire; and had the Savages not rosted fish
when we were asleepe, we had set forward fasting: for the raine
still continued with great violence, even the whole day thorow,
till wee came within two myles of home.

Being wett and weary, at length we came to *Namaschet*, there
we refreshed our selves, giving gifts to all such as had shewed us
any kindnesse. Amongst others one of the sixe that came with
us from *Packanokik* having before this on the way unkindly
forsaken us, marvayled we gave him nothing, and told us what
he had done for us; we also told him of some discurtesies he
offered us, whereby he deserved nothing, yet we gave him a
small trifle: whereupon he offered us Tobacco: but the house
being full of people, we told them hee stole some by the way,
and if it were of that we would not take it: For we would not
receive that which was stolne upon any termes; if we did, our
God would be angry with us, and destroy us. This abashed
him, and gave the rest great content: but at our departure he
would needs carry him on his backe thorow a River, whom he
had formerly in some sort abused. Faine they would have had
us to lodge there all night: and wondered we would set forth
againe in such Weather: but GOD be praysed, wee came safe
home that night, though wett, weary, and surbated.

A VOYAGE MADE BY TEN
of Our Men to the Kingdome of
NAUSET, to seeke a Boy that had
lost himselfe in the WOODS;
With such Accidents as
befell us in that
VOYAGE.

THE 11th of *June* we set forth, the weather being very faire: but ere we had bin long at Sea, there arose a storme of wind and raine, with much lightning and thunder, in so much that a spout arose not far from us: but God be praysed, it dured not long, and we put in that night for Harbour at a place, called *Cummaquid*, where wee had some hope to finde the Boy. Two Savages were in the Boat with us, the one was *Tisquantum* our Interpreter, the other *Tokamahamon*, a speciall friend. It being night before we came in, we Anchored in the middest of the Bay, where we were drie at a low water. In the morning we espied Savages seeking Lobsters, and sent our two Interpreters to speake with them, the channell being betweene them; where they told them what we were, and for what we were come, willing them not at all to feare us, for we would not hurt them. Their answere was, that the Boy was well, but he was at *Nauset*; yet since wee were there they desired us to come ashore & eate with them: which as soone as our Boat floated we did: and went sixe ashore, having foure pledges for them in the Boate. They brought us to their Sachim or Governour, whom they call *Iya-nough*, a man not exceeding twentie-six yeeres of age, but very personable, gentle, courteous, and fayre conditioned, indeed not like a Savage, save for his attyre; his entertainement was answerable to his parts, and his cheare plentifull and various.

One thing was very grievous unto us at this place; There was an old woman, whom we judged to be no lesse then an hundred yeeres old, which came to see us because shee never saw English, yet could not behold us without breaking forth into great passion, weeping and crying excessively. We demaunding the reason of it, they told us, she had three sons, who when master *Hunt* was in these parts went aboord his Ship to trade with him, and he carried them Captives into Spaine (for *Tisquantum* at that time was carried away also) by which meanes shee was deprived of the comfort of her children in her old age. We told them we were sorry that any English man should give them that offence, that *Hunt* was a bad man, and that all the English that heard of it condemned him for the same: but for us we would not offer them any such injury, though it would gaine us all the skins in the Countrey. So we gave her some small trifles, which somewhat appeased her.

After dinner we tooke Boat for *Nauset*, *Iyanough* and two of his men accompanying us. Ere we came to *Nauset*, the day and tyde were almost spent, in so much as we could not goe in with our Shallop: but the Sachim or Governour of *Commaquid* went a shore and his men with him, we also sent *Tisquantum* to tell *Aspinet* the Sachim of *Nauset* wherefore we came. The Savages here came very thicke amongst us, and were earnest with us to bring in our Boate. But we neither well could, nor yet desired to doe it, because we had lest cause to trust them, being they onely had formerly made an Assault upon us in the same place, in time of our Winter Discovery for Habitation. And indeed it was no marvayle they did so, for howsoever through snow or otherwise wee saw no houses, yet wee were in the middest of them.

When our boat was a ground they came very thicke, but wee stood therein upon our guard, not suffering any to enter except two: the one being of *Maramoick*, and one of those, whose Corne we had formerly found, we promised him restitution, & desired him either to come to *Patuxet* for satisfaction, or else we would bring them so much corne againe, hee promised to come, wee used him very kindely for the present. Some few skins we gate there but not many.

After Sun-set, *Aspinet* came with a great traine, & brought the boy with him, one bearing him through the water: hee had not lesse then an hundred with him, the halfe whereof came to the Shallop side unarmed with him, the other stood aloofe with their bow and arrowes. There he delivered us the boy, behung with beades, and made peace with us, wee bestowing a knife on him, and likewise on another that first entertained the Boy and brought him thither. So they departed from us.

Here we understood, that the *Narrohigansets* had spoyled some of *Massasoyts* men, and taken him. This strucke some feare in us, because the Colony was so weakely guarded, the strength thereof being abroad: But we set foorth with resolution to make the best hast home wee could; yet the winde being contrary, having scarce any fresh water leaft, and at least, 16. leagues home, we put in againe for the shore. There we met againe with *Iyanough* the *Sachim* of *Cūmaquid*, and the most of his Towne, both men women & children with him. Hee being still willing to gratifie us, tooke a runlet and led our men in the darke a great way for water, but could finde none good: yet brought such as there was on his necke with them. In the meane time the women joyned hand in hand, singing and dancing before the Shallop, the men also shewing all the kindnes they could, *Iyanough* himselfe taking a bracelet from about his necke, and hanging it upon one of us.

Againe we set out but to small purpose: for wee gat but little homeward; Our water also was very brackish, and not to be drunke.

The next morning, *Iyanough* espied us againe and ran after us; we being resolved to goe to *Cummaquid* againe to water, tooke him into the Shallop, whose entertainement was not inferiour unto the former.

The soyle at *Nauset* and here is alike, even and sandy, not so good for corne as where wee are; Shipps may safely ride in eyther harbour. In the Summer, they abound with fish. Being now watered, we put forth againe, and by Gods providence, came safely home that night.

A JOURNEY TO THE
Kingdome of *NAMASCHET*
in defence of the Great King
MASSASOYT *against the*
Narrohiggansets,
and to revenge the
supposed Death of
our Interpreter
Tisquantum.

AT our returne from *Nauset*, we found it true, that *Massasoyt* was put from his Countrey by the *Narrohiggansets*. Word also was brought unto us, that one *Coubatant* a petty Sachim or Governour under *Massasoyt* (whom they ever feared to be too conversant with the *Narrohiggansets*) was at *Namaschet*, who fought to draw the hearts of *Massasoyts* subjects from him, speaking also disdainfully of us, storming at the Peace between *Nauset*, *Cummaquid*, and us, and at *Tisquantum* the worker of it; also at *Tokamahamon*, and one *Hobbamock* (two Indians or Lemes, one of which he would trecherously have murdered a little before, being a speciall and trusty man of *Massasoyts*) *Tokamahamon* went to him, but the other two would not; yet put their lives in their hands, privately went to see if they could heare of their King, and lodging at *Namaschet* were discovered to *Coubatant*, who set a guard to beset the house and tooke *Tisquantum* (for he had sayd, if he were dead, the English had lost their tongue) *Hobbamock* seeing that *Tisquantum* was taken and *Coubatant* held a knife at his breast, being a strong and stout man, brake from them and came to *New-Plimmouth*, full of feare and sorrow for *Tisquantum*, whom he thought to be slaine.

Upon this Newes the Company assembled together, and resolved on the morrow to send ten men armed to *Namaschet* and *Hobbamock*, for their guide, to revenge the supposed death of *Tisquantum* on *Coubatant* our bitter Enemy, and to retaine *Nepeof*, another Sachim or Governour, who was of this confederacy, till we heard, what was become of our friend *Massasoyt*.

On the morrow we set out ten men Armed, who tooke their journey as aforesayd, but the day proved very wett. When wee supposed we were within three or foure myles of *Namaschet*, we went out of the way and stayed there till night, because we would not be discovered. There we consulted what to doe, and thinking best to beset the house at mid-night, each was appointed his taske by the Captaine, all men incouraging one another, to the utmost of their power.

By night our guide lost his way, which much discouraged our men, being we were wet, and weary of our armes: but one of our men having beene before at *Namaschet* brought us into the way againe.

Before we came to the Towne we sat downe and ate such as our Knapsacke affoorded, that being done, wee threw them aside, and all such things as might hinder us, and so went on and beset the house, according to our last resolution. Those that entred, demaunded if *Coubatant* were not there: but feare had bereft the Savages of speech. We charged them not to stirre, for if *Coubatant* were not there, we would not meddle with them, if he were, we came principally for him, to be avenged on him for the supposed death of *Tisquantum*, and other matters: but howsoever wee would not at all hurt their women, or children. Notwithstanding some of them pressed out at a private doore and escaped, but with some wounds: At length perceiving our principall ends, they told us *Coubatant* was returned with all his traine, and that *Tisquantum* was yet living, and in the towne offering some Tobacco, other such as they had to eate. In this hurley burley we discharged two Peeces at randome, which much terrified all the Inhabitants, except *Tisquantum* and *Tokamahamon*, who though they knew not our end in comming, yet assured them of our honesty, that we would not hurt them. Those boyes that were in the house seeing our care of women, often cried *Neensquaes*, that is to say, I am a Woman: the Women also hanging upon *Hobbamock*, calling him *Towam*, that is, Friend. But to be short, we kept them we had, and made them make a fire that we might see to search the house. In the meane time, *Hobbamock* gat on the top of the house, and called *Tissquantum* and *Tokamahamon*, which came unto us accompanied with others, some armed and others naked. Those that had Bowes and Arrowes we tooke them away, promising them againe when it was day. The house we tooke for our better safegard: but released those we had taken, manifesting whom we came for and wherefore.

On the next morning we marched into the middest of the Towne, and went to the house of *Tisquantum* to breakfast. Thither came all whose hearts were upright towardes us, but all *Coubatants* faction were fled away. There in the middest of them we manifested againe our intendment, assuring them, that although *Coubatant* had now escaped us, yet there was no place should secure him and his from us if he continued his threatning us, and provoking others against us, who had kindly entertained him, and never intended evill towards him till he now so justly deserved it. Moreover, if *Massasoyt* did not returne in safetie from *Narrohigganset*, or if hereafter he should make any insurrection against him, or offer violence to *Tisquantum*, *Hobbamock*, or any of *Massasoyts* Subjects, we would revenge it upon him, to the overthrow of him and his. As for those were wounded, we were sorry for it, though themselves procured it in not staying in the house at our command: yet if they would returne home with us, our Surgeon should heale them.

At this offer, one man and a woman that were wounded went home with us, *Tisquantum* and many other knowne friends accompanying us, and offering all helpe that might be by carriage of any thing wee had to ease us. So that by Gods good Providence wee safely returned home the morrow night after we set forth.

A RELATION OF OUR
Voyage to the *MASSACHUSETS*,
And what happened there.

I T seemed good to the Company in generall, that though the *Massachusets* had often threatened us (as we were informed) yet we should goe amongst them, partly to see the Countrey, partly to make Peace with them, and partly to procure their trucke.

For these ends the Governours chose ten men, fit for the purpose, and sent *Tisquantum*, and two other Salvages to bring us to speech with the people, and interpret for us.

We set out about mid-night, the tyde then serving for us; we supposing it to be neerer then it is, thought to be there the next morning betimes: but it proved well neere twentie Leagues from *New Plimmouth*.

We came into the bottome of the Bay, but being late wee anchored and lay in the Shallop, not having seene any of the people. The next morning we put in for the shore. There we found many Lobsters that had beene gathered together by the Salvages, which we made ready under a cliffe. The Captaine set two Sentinels behind the cliffe to the landward to secure the Shallop, and taking a guide with him, and foure of our company, went to seeke the Inhabitants, where they met a woman comming for her Lobsters, they told her of them, and contented her for them. She told them where the people were; *Tisquantum* went to them, the rest returned, having direction which way to bring the Shallop to them.

The Sachim, or Governour of this place, is called *Obbatine-wat*, and though he live in the bottome of the *Massachuset* bay, yet he is under *Massasoyt*. He used us very kindly; he told us, he durst not then remaine in any setled place, for feare of the *Tarentines*. Also the *Squa Sachim*, or *Massachusets* Queene was an enemy to him.

We told him of divers Sachims that had acknowledged themselves to be King JAMES his men, and if he also would submit himselfe, we would be his safegard from his enemies; which he did, and went along with us to bring us to the *Squa Sachim*. Againe we crossed the Bay which is very large, and hath at lest fiftie Ilands in it: but the certaine number is not knowne to the Inhabitants. Night it was before wee came to that side of the Bay where this people were. On shore the Salvages went but found no body. That night also we rid at Anchor aboord the Shallop.

On the morrow we went ashore, all but two men, and marched in Armes up in the Countrey. Having gone three myles, we came to a place where Corne had beene newly gathered, a house pulled downe, and the people gone. A myle from hence, *Nanepashemet* their King in his life time had lived. His house was not like others, but a scaffold was largely built, with pools and plancks some six foote from ground, and the house upon that, being situated on the top of a hill.

Not farre from hence in a bottome, wee came to a Fort built by their deceased King, the manner thus; There were pools some thirtie or fortie foote long, stucke in the ground as thicke as they could be set one by another, and with these they inclosed a ring some forty or fifty foote over. A trench breast high was digged on each side; one way there was to goe into it with a bridge; in the midst of this Pallizado stood the frame of an house, wherein being dead he lay buryed.

About a myle from hence, we came to such another, but seated on the top of an hill: here *Nanepashemet* was killed, none dwelling in it since the time of his death. At this place we stayed, and sent two Salvages to looke the Inhabitants, and to informe them of our ends in comming, that they might not be fearefull of us: Within a myle of this place they found the women of the place together, with their Corne on heapes, whither we supposed them to be fled for feare of us, and the more, because in divers places they had newly pulled downe their houses, and for hast in one place had left some of their Corne covered with a Mat, and no body with it.

With much feare they entertained us at first, but seeing our gentle carriage towards them, they tooke heart and entertained us in the best manner they could, boyling Cod and such other things as they had for us. At length with much sending for came one of their men, shaking and trembling for feare. But when he saw we intended them no hurt, but came to trucke, he promised us his skins also. Of him we enquired for their

Queene, but it seemed shee was far from thence, at lest we could not see her.

Here *Tisquantum* would have had us rifled the Salvage women, and taken their skins, and all such things as might be serviceable for us; for (sayd he) they are a bad people, and have oft threatned you: But our answere was; Were they never so bad, we would not wrong them, or give them any just occasion against us: for their words we little weighed them, but if they once attempted any thing against us, then we would deale far worse then he desired.

Having well spent the day, we returned to the Shallop, almost all the Women accompanying us, to trucke, who sold their coats from their backes, and tyed boughes about them, but with great shamefastnesse (for indeed they are more modest then some of our English women are) we promised them to come againe to them, and they us, to keepe their skins.

Within this Bay, the Salvages say, there are two Rivers; the one whereof we saw, having a faire entrance, but we had no time to discover it. Better harbours for shipping cannot be then here are. At the entrance of the Bay are many Rockes; and in all likelihood very good fishing ground. Many, yea, most of the Ilands have beene inhabited, some being cleered from end to end, but the people are all dead, or removed.

Our victuall growing scarce, the Winde comming fayre, and having a light Moone, we set out at evening, and through the goodnesse of GOD, came safely home before noone the day following.

A LETTER SENT FROM
New-England to a friend in these parts,
setting forth a briefe and true Declaration
of the worth of that Plantation;
As also certaine usefull Directions
for such as intend a VOYAGE
into those parts.

L OVING, and old Friend, although I received no Letter from
you by this Ship, yet forasmuch as I know you expect the
performance of my promise, which was, to write unto you
truely and faithfully of all things, I have therefore at this time
sent unto you accordingly. Referring you for further satisfaction to our more large Relations You shall understand, that in
this little time, that a few of us have beene here, we have built
seaven dwelling houses, and foure for the use of the Plantation,
and have made preparation for divers others. We set the last
Spring some twentie Acres of *Indian* Corne, and sowed some
six Acres of Barly & Pease, and according to the manner of
the *Indians*, we manured our ground with Herings or rather
Shadds, which we have in great abundance, and take with great
ease at our doores. Our Corne did prove well, & God be praysed, we had a good increase of *Indian*-Corne, and our Barly
indifferent good, but our Pease not worth the gathering, for
we feared they were too late sowne, they came up very well,
and blossomed, but the Sunne parched them in the blossome;
our harvest being gotten in, our Governour sent foure men on
fowling, that so we might after a more speciall manner rejoyce
together, after we had gathered the fruit of our labours; they
foure in one day killed as much fowle, as with a little helpe
beside, served the Company almost a weeke, at which time
amongst other Recreations, we exercised our Armes, many of
the *Indians* coming amongst us, and amongst the rest their
greatest King *Massasoyt*, with some ninetie men, whom for
three dayes we entertained and feasted, and they went out
and killed five Deere, which they brought to the Plantation
and bestowed on our Governour, and upon the Captaine, and
others. And although it be not alwayes so plentifull, as it was at

this time with us, yet by the goodnesse of God, we are so farre from want, that we often with you partakers of our plentie. Wee have found the *Indians* very faithfull in their Covenant of Peace with us; very loving and readie to pleasure us: we often goe to them, and they come to us; some of us have bin fiftie myles by Land in the Country with them; the occasions and Relations whereof, you shall undestand by our generall and more full Declaration of such things as are worth the noting, yea, it hath pleased God so to possesse the *Indians* with a feare of us, and love unto us, that not onely the greatest King amongst them called *Massasoyt*, but also all the Princes and peoples round about us, have either made sute unto us, or beene glad of any occasion to make peace with us, so that seaven of them at once have sent their messengers to us to that end, yea, an Fle at sea, which we never saw hath also together with the former yeelded willingly to be under the protection, and subjects to our soveraigne Lord King JAMES, so that there is now great peace amongst the *Indians* themselves, which was not formerly, neither would have bin but for us; and we for our parts walke as peaceably and safely in the wood, as in the hie-wayes in *England*, we entertaine them familiarly in our houses, and they as friendly bestowing their Venison on us. They are a people without any Religion, or knowledge of any God, yet very trustie, quicke of apprehension, ripe witted, just, the men and women goe naked, onely a skin about their middles; for the temper of the ayre, here it agreeth well with that in *England*, and if there be any difference at all, this is somewhat hotter in Summer, some thinke it to be colder in Winter, but I cannot out of experience so say; the ayre is very cleere and not foggie, as hath beene reported. I never in my life remember a more seasonable yeare, then we have here enjoyed: and if we have once but Kine, Horses, and Sheepe, I make no question, but men might live as contented here, as in any part of the world. For fish and fowle, we have great abundance, fresh Codd in the Summer is but course meat with us, our Bay is full of Lobsters all the Summer, and affordeth varietie of other Fish; in September we can take a Hogshead of Eeles in a night, with small labour, & can dig them out of their beds, all the Winter we have Mussells and Othus at our doores: Oysters we have none neere, but we can have them brought by the *Indians* when we will; all the Spring time the earth sendeth forth naturally very good Sallet Herbs; here are Grapes, white and red, and very sweete and strong also. Strawberies, Goosberies, Raspas, &c. Plums of three sorts, with blacke and red, being almost as good as a Damsen: abundance of Roses, white, red, and damask: single, but very sweet indeed; the Countrey wanteth onely industrious men to imploy, for it would grieve your hearts (if as I) you had seene so many myles together by goodly Rivers uninhabited, and withall to consider those parts of the world wherein you live, to be even greatly burthened with abundance of people. These things I thought good to let you understand, being the truth of things as nere as I could experimentally take knowledge of, and that you might on our behalfe give God thankes who hath delt so favourably with us.

Our supply of men from you came the ninth of *November* 1621. putting in at Cape Cod, some eight or ten leagues from us, the *Indians* that dwell thereabout were they who were owners of the Corne which we found in Caves, for which we have given them full content, and are in great league with them, they sent us word there was a ship nere unto them, but thought it to be a French man, and indeede for our selves, we expected not a friend so soone. But when we perceived that she made for our Bay, the Governor commanded a great Peece to be shot off, to call home such as were abroad at worke; whereupon every man, yea, boy that could handle a Gun were readie, with full resolution, that if she were an Enemy, we would stand in our just defence, not fearing them, but God provided better for us then we supposed; these came all in health unto us, not any being sicke by the way (otherwise then by Sea sicknesse) and so continue at this time, by the blessing of God, the good-wife *Ford* was delivered of a sonne the first night shee landed, and both of them are very well. When it pleaseth God, we are setled and fitted for the fishing busines, and other trading, I doubt not but by the blessing of God, the gayne will give content to all; in the meane time, that we have gotten we have sent by this ship, and though it be not much, yet it will witnesse for us, that wee have not beene idle, considering the smallnesse of our number all this Summer. We hope the Marchants will accept of it, and be incouraged to furnish us with things needfull for further imployment, which will also incourage us to put forth

our selves to the uttermost. Now because I expect your comming unto us with other of our friends, whose companie we
much desire, I thought good to advertise you of a few things
needfull; be carefull to have a very good bread-roome to put
your Biskets in, let your Cask for Beere and Water be Iron-
bound for the first tyre if not more; let not your meat be drie
salted, none can better doe it then the Saylers; let your meale
be so hard trodd in your Cask that you shall need an Ads or
Hatchet to worke it out with: Trust not too much on us for
Corne at this time, for by reason of this last company that
came, depending wholy upon us, we shall have little enough till
harvest; be carefull to come by some of your meale to spend by
the way, it will much refresh you, build your Cabbins as open as
you can, and bring good store of clothes, and beding with you;
bring every man a Musket or fowling Peece, let your Peece be
long in the barrell, and feare not the waight of it, for most of
our shooting is from Stands; bring juyce of Lemons, and take
it fasting, it is of good use; for hot waters, Anni-feed water is
the best, but use it sparingly: if you bring any thing for comfort
in the Country, Butter or Sallet oyle, or both is very good; our
Indian Corne even the coursest, maketh as pleasant meat as
Rice, therefore spare that unlesse to spend by the way; bring
Paper, and Linced oyle for your Windowes, with Cotton yarne
for your Lamps; let your shott be most for bigge Fowles, and
bring store of Powder and shot: I forbeare further to write for
the present, hoping to see you by the next returne, so I take my
leave, commending you to the LORD for a safe conduct unto
us. Resting in him

Plimmouth in *New-England*
   this 11. of December.   *Your loving Friend*
   1621.   E. W.

Reasons & considerations touching the lawfulnesse of removing out of *England* into the parts of *America*.

FORASMUCH as many exceptions are daily made against the going into, and inhabiting of forraine desert places, to the hinderances of plantations abroad, and the increase of distractions at home: It is not amisse that some which have beene eare witnesses of the exceptions made, and are either Agents or Abettors of such removals and plantations, doe seeke to give content to the world, in all things that possibly they can.

The Preamble.

And although the most of the opposites are such as either dreame of raising their fortunes here, to that then which there is nothing more unlike, or such as affecting their home-borne countrey so vehemently, as that they had rather with all their friends begge, yea starve in it, then undergoe a little difficultie in seeking abroad; yet are there some who out of doubt in tendernesse of conscience, and feare to offend God by running before they be called, are straitned and doe straiten others, from going to forraine plantations.

For whose cause especially, I have beene drawne out of my good affection to them, to publish some reasons that might give them content and satisfaction, and also stay and stop the wilfull and wittie cauiller: and herein I trust I shall not be blamed of any godly wise, though thorow my slender judgement I should misse the marke, and not strike the naile on the head, considering it is the first attempt that hath beene made (that I know of) to defend those enterprises. Reason would therefore, that if any man of deeper reach and better judgement see further or otherwise, that he rather instruct me, then deride me.

And being studious for brevitie, we must first consider, that whereas God of old did call and summon our Fathers by predictions, dreames, visions, and certaine illuminations to goe from their countries, places and habitations, to reside and dwell here or there, and to wander up and downe from citie to citie, and Land to Land, according to his will and

Cautions, Gen.
12. 1, 2. & 35. 1.

Mat. 2. 19.
Psal. 105. 13.

pleasure. Now there is no such calling to be expected for any
Heb. 3. 5, 2.   matter whatsoever, neither must any so much as
imagine that there will now be any such thing.
God did once so traine up his people, but now he doth not,
but speakes in another manner, and so we must apply our selves
to Gods present dealing, and not to his wonted dealing: and as
Josh. 5. 12.   the miracle of giving *Manna* ceased, when the
fruits of the land became plentie, so God having
such a plentifull storehouse of directions in his holy word,
there must not now any extraordinarie revelations be expected.

But now the ordinarie examples and precepts of the Scriptures reasonably and rightly understood and applied, must be
the voice and word, that must call us, presse us, and direct us
in every action.

Neither is there any land or possession now, like unto the
Gen. 17. 8.   possession which the Jewes had in *Canaan*, being
legally holy and appropriated unto a holy people
the seed of *Abraham*, in which they dwelt securely, and had
their daies prolonged, it being by an immediate voice said,
that he (the Lord) gave it them as a land of rest after their
wearie travels, and a type of *Eternall* rest in heaven, but now
there is no land of that Sanctimonie, no land so appropriated;
none typicall: much lesse any that can be said to be given of
2 Cor. 5. 1, 2, 3.   God to any nation as was *Canaan*, which they
and their seed must dwell in, till God sendeth
upon them sword or captivitie: but now we are in all places
strangers and Pilgrims, travellers and sojourners, most prop-
So were the   erly, having no dwelling but in this earthen Tab-
Jewes, but yet   ernacle; our dwelling is but a wandring, and our
their temporall
blessings and   abiding but as a fleeting, and in a word our home
inheritances   is no where, but in the heavens: in that house not
were more   made with hands, whose maker and builder is
large then ours.
God, and to which all ascend that love the comming of our Lord Jesus.

Though then, there may be reasons to perswade a man to
live in this or that land, yet there cannot be the same reasons
which the Jewes had, but now as naturall, civill and Religious
bands tie men, so they must be bound, and as good reasons for
Object.   things terrene and heavenly appeare, so they must
be led. And so here falleth in our question, how a

man that is here borne and bred, and hath lived some yeares, may remove himselfe into another countrie.

Answ.

1
What persons may hence remove.

I answer, a man must not respect only to live, and doe good to himselfe, but he should see where he can live to doe most good to others: for as one faith, *He whose living is but for himselfe, it is time he were dead.* Some men there are who of necessitie must here live, as being tied to duties either to Church, Common-wealth, houshold, kindred, &c. but others, and that many, who doe no good in none of those nor can doe none, as being not able, or not in favour, or as wanting opportunitie, and live as outcasts: no bodies, eie-sores, eating but for themselves, teaching but themselves, and doing good to none, either in soule or body, and so passe over daies, yeares, and moneths, yea so live and so die. Now such should lift up their eies and see whether there be not some other place and countrie to which they may goe

2
Why they should remove.

to doe good and have use towards others of that knowledge, wisdome, humanitie, reason, strength, skill, facultie, &c. which God hath given them for the service of others and his owne glory.

But not to passe the bounds of modestie so far as to name any, though I confesse I know many, who sit here still with

Luk. 19. 20.

their talent in a napkin, having notable endow-ments both of body and minde, and might doe great good if they were in some places, which here doe none, nor can doe none, and yet through fleshly feare, nicenesse, straitnesse of heart, &c. sit still and looke on, and will not

Reas. 1.

hazard a dram of health, nor a day of pleasure, nor an houre of rest to further the knowledge and salvation of the sons of *Adam* in that *New world*, where a drop

Object.

of the knowledge of Christ is most precious, which is here not set by. Now what shall we say to such a profession of Christ, to which is joyned no more deniall of a mans selfe? But some will say, what right have I to goe live in the heathens countrie?

Answ.

Letting passe the ancient discoveries, contracts and agreements which our English men have long since made in those parts, together with the acknowledgement of the histories and Chronicles of other nations, who professe the land of *America* from the Cape *De Florida* unto the Bay of *Canado* (which is South and North 300. leagues and upwards; and East and West, further then yet hath beene discovered) is proper to the King of England, yet letting that passe, lest I be thought to meddle further then it concerns me, or further then I have discerning: I will mention such things as are within my reach, knowledge, fight and practise, since I have travailed in these affaires.

Reas. 2.

And first seeing we daily pray for the conversion of the heathens, we must consider whether there be not some ordinary meanes, and course for us to take to convert them, or whether praier for them be only referred to Gods extraordinarie worke from heaven. Now it seemeth unto me that we ought also to endevour and use the meanes to convert them, and the meanes cannot be used unlesse we goe to them or they come to us: to us they cannot come, our land is full: to them we may goe, their land is emptie.

Reas. 3.

This then is a sufficient reason to prove our going thither to live, lawfull: their land is spatious and void, & there are few and doe but run over the grasse, as doe also the Foxes and wilde beasts: they are not industrious, neither have art, science, skill or facultie to use either the land or the commodities of it, but all spoiles, rots, and is marred for want of manuring, gathering, ordering, &c. As the ancient Patriarkes therefore removed from straiter places into more roomthy, where the Land lay idle and waste, and none used it, though there dwelt inhabitants by them, as *Gen.* 13. 6. 11. 12. and 34. 21. and 41. 20. so is it lawfull now to take a land which none useth, and make use of it.

Reas. 4.
This is to be considered as respecting new *England*, and the territories about the plantation.

And as it is a common land or unused, & undressed countrey; so we have it by common consent, composition and agreement, which agreement is double: First the Imperial Governor *Massasoit*, whose circuits in likelihood are larger then *England* and *Scotland*, hath acknowledged the Kings Majestie of *England* to be his Master and Commander, and that once in my hearing, yea and in writing, under his hand to Captaine *Standish*, both he and many other Kings which are under him, as *Pamet, Nauset, Cummaquid,*

Narrowhiggonset, *Namaschet*, *&c.*, with divers others that
dwell about the baies of *Patuxet*, and *Massachuset*:
neither hath this beene accomplished by threats
and blowes, or shaking of sword, and sound of
trumpet, for as our facultie that way is small, and our strength
lesse: so our warring with them is after another manner, namely
by friendly usage, love, peace, honest and just cariages, good
counsell, *&c.*, that so we and they may not only live in peace
in that land, and they yeeld subjection to an earthly Prince, but
that as voluntaries they may be perswaded at length to embrace
the Prince of peace Christ Jesus, and rest in peace with him for
ever.

Psal. 110. 3. &
48. 3.

Secondly, this composition is also more particular and appli-
catorie as touching our selves there inhabiting: the Emperour
by a joynt content, hath promised and appointed us to live at
peace, where we will in all his dominions, taking what place we
will, and as much land as we will, and bringing as many people
as we will, and that for these two causes. First, because we are
the servants of *James* King of *England*, whose the land (as he
confesseth) is, 2. because he hath found us just, honest, kinde
and peaceable, and so loves our company; yea, and that in
these things there is no dissimulation on his part, nor feare of
breach (except our securitie ingender in them some unthought
of trecherie, or our uncivilitie provoke them to anger) is most
plaine in other Relations, which shew that the things they did
were more out of love then out of feare.

It being then first a vast and emptie *Chaos*: Secondly acknowledged the right of our Soveraigne King: Thirdly, by a peaceable
composition in part possessed of divers of his loving subjects,
I see not who can doubt or call in question the lawfulnesse of
inhabiting or dwelling there, but that it may be as lawfull for
such as are not tied upon some speciall occasion here, to live
there as well as here, yea, and as the enterprise is weightie and
difficult, so the honour is more worthy, to plant a rude wildernesse, to enlarge the honour and fame of our dread Soveraigne,
but chiefly to displaie the efficacie & power of the Gospell both
in zealous preaching, professing, and wise walking under it,
before the faces of these poore blinde Infidels.

As for such as object the tediousnesse of the
voyage thither, the danger of Pirats robberie, of

Prov. 22. 13.

the savages treacherie, &c. these are but Lyons in the way, and it were well for such men if they were in heaven, for who can shew them a place in this world where iniquitie shall not compasse them at the heeles, and where they shall have a day without griefe, or a lease of life for a moment; and who *Psal.* 49. 5. can tell but God, what dangers may lie at our *Mat.* 6. 34. doores, even in our native countrie, or what plots may be abroad, or when God will cause our sunne to goe downe at noone daies, and in the midst of our peace and *Amos* 8. 9. securitie, lay upon us some lasting scourge for our so long neglect and contempt of his most glorious Gospell.

Ob. But we have here great peace, plentie of the Gospell, and many sweet delights and varietie of comforts.

Answ. True indeed, and farre be it from us to denie and diminish the least of these mercies, but have we rendered unto God thankfull obedience for this long peace, whilst other peoples have beene at wars? have we *2 Chron.* 32. 25. not rather murmured, repined, and fallen at jars amongst our selves, whilst our peace hath lasted with forraigne power? was there ever more suits in law, more enuie, contempt and reproch then now adaies? *Abraham* and *Gen.* 13.9, 10. *Lot* departed asunder when there fell a breach betwixt them, which was occasioned by the straightnesse of the land: and surely I am perswaded, that howsoever the frailties of men are principall in all contentions, yet the straitnes of the place is such, as each man is faine to plucke his meanes as it were out of his neighbours throat, there is such pressing and oppressing in towne and countrie, about Farmes, trades, traffique, &c. so as a man can hardly any where set up a trade but he shall pull downe two of his neighbours.

The Townes abound with young trades-men, and the Hospitals are full of the Auncient, the country is replenished with new Farmers, and the Almes-houses are filled with old Labourers, many there are who get their living with bearing burdens, but moe are faine to burden the land with their whole bodies: multitudes get their meanes of life by prating, and so doe numbers more by begging. Neither come these straits upon men alwaies through intemperancy, ill husbandry, indiscretion, &c.

as some thinke, but even the most wise, sober, and discreet men, goe often to the wall, when they have done their best, wherein as God's providence swaieth all, so it is easie to see, that the straitnesse of the place having in it so many strait hearts, cannot but produce such effects more and more, so as every indifferent minded man should be ready to say with Father *Abraham, Take thou the right hand, and I will take the left*: Let us not thus oppresse, straiten, and afflict one another, but seeing there is a spatious Land, the way to which is thorow the sea, wee will end this difference in a day.

That I speake nothing about the bitter contention that hath beene about Religion, by writing, disputing, and inveighing earnestly one against another, the heat of which zeale if it were turned against the rude barbarisme of the Heathens, it might doe more good in a day, then it hath done here in many yeares. Neither of the little love to the Gospell, and profit which is made by the Preachers in most places, which might easily drive the zealous to the Heathens who no doubt if they had but a drop of that knowledge which here flieth about the streetes, would be filled with exceeding great joy and gladnesse, as that they would even plucke the kingdome of heaven by violence, and take it as it were by force.

The greatest let that is yet behinde is the sweet fellowship of friends, and the satietie of bodily delights.

The last let.   But can there be two neerer friends almost then *Abraham* and *Lot*, or then *Paul* and *Barnabas*, and yet upon as little occasions as we have heere, they departed asunder, two of them being Patriarches of the Church of old; the other the Apostles of the Church which is new, and their covenants were such as it seemeth might binde as much as any covenant betweene men at this day, and yet to avoid greater inconveniences they departed asunder.

Neither must men take so much thought for the flesh, as not to be pleased except they can pamper their bodies with varietie of dainties. Nature is content with little, and health is much endangered, by mixtures upon the stomach: The delights of the palate doe often inflame the vitall parts: as the tongue

James 3. 6.   setteth a fire the whole body. Secondly, varieties here are not common to all, but many good men are glad to snap at a crust. The rent taker lives on sweet morsels, but the rent payer eats a drie crust often with watery eies: and it is nothing to say what some one of a hundreth hath, but what the bulke, body and cominalty hath, which I warrant you is short enough.

And they also which now live so sweetly, hardly will their children attaine to that priviledge, but some circumventor or other will outstrip them, and make them sit in the dust, to which men are brought in one age, but cannot get out of it againe in 7. generations.

To conclude, without all partialitie, the present consumption which groweth upon us here, whilst the land groaneth under so many close-fisted and unmercifull men, being compared with the easinesse, plainenesse and plentifulnesse in living in those remote places, may quickly perswade any man to a liking of this course, and to practise a removal, which being done by honest, godly and industrious men, they shall there be right hartily welcome, but for other of dissolute and prophane life, their roomes are better then their companies; for if here where the Gospell hath beene so long and plentifully taught, they are yet frequent in such vices as the Heathen would shame to speake of, what will they be when there is lesse restraint in word and deed? My onely sute to all men is, that whether they live there or here, they would learne to use this world as they used it not, keeping faith and a good conscience, both with God and men, that when the day of account shall come, they may come forth as good and fruitfull servants, and freely be received, and enter into the joy of their master.

R. C.

FINIS.

EDWARD WINSLOW AND WILLIAM BRADFORD:
A Relation or Journall

THE EDITORS' COMMENT

A Relation or Journall (also known as *Mourt's Relation*) is a collection of letters written by Plymouth settlers William Bradford and Edward Winslow to friends and supporters in England. When they wrote in the early 1620s, the Plymouth colonists were still learning how to survive in an unfamiliar political world and natural environment. Discussing experiences of the first few seasons at Plymouth, the letters convey the settlers' sense of uncertainty about the colony's future, their concern at losing half of the colonists to disease and starvation in their first winter, and their reliance on Wampanoag peoples' diplomacy and generosity to find food and to trade with Massachusett and Wampanoag people. The letters in *Mourt's Relation* reflect these experiences: in their tentative tone, concern with supplies, and detailed descriptions of Wampanoag people, the letters differ from the often exaggerated, positive descriptions in promotional texts like John Smith's *Description of New England* and from the sense of inevitability present in William Bradford's *Of Plimoth Plantation*. *Mourt's Relation* thus represents the colonists' concerns about survival, initial uncertainty about interacting with Wampanoag people, and reliance on Native diplomacy, long before they were certain the colony would be permanent.

Edward Winslow:
Good News from New England

GOOD
NEWS
FROM NEW ENGLAND:

OR

A true Relation of things very remarkable
at the Plantation of *Plimoth*
in NEW-ENGLAND.

Shewing the wondrous providence and goodness
of GOD, in their preservation and continuance,
*being delivered from many apparent
deaths and dangers.*

Together with a Relation of such religious and
civil Laws and Customs, as are in practise amongst
the *Indians*, adjoining to them at this day. As also
*what Commodities are there to be raised for the
maintenance of that and other Plantations
in the said Country.*

Written by *E.W.* who hath borne a part in the
fore-named troubles, and there lived since
their first Arrival.

LONDON

Printed by *J.D.* for *William Bladen* and *John Bellamie*, and
are to be sold at their Shops, at the *Bible* in *Pauls*-Church-yard,
and at the three Golden Lions in Corn-hill,
near the *Royall Exchange.* 1624.

TO
ALL WELL-WILLERS
AND FURTHERERS OF
Plantations in *New England*: especially
to such as ever have or desire to assist, the
people of Plimoth *in their just
proceedings, Grace, and Peace, be
multiplied.*

R IGHT Honourable and Worshipful Gentlemen, or whatsoever: Since it hath pleased God to stir you up to be
instruments of his glory, in so honourable an enterprise as the
enlarging of his Majesties Dominions, by planting his loyal
subjects in so healthful and hopeful a Country as *New-England* is; where the Church of God being seated in sincerity,
there is no less hope of convincing the Heathen of their evil
ways, and converting them to the true knowledge and worship
of the living God, and so consequently the salvation of their
souls by the merits of Jesus Christ, than else-where though it
be much talked on, & lightly or lamely prosecuted. I therefore think it but my duty to offer the view of our proceedings
to your worthy considerations, having to that end composed
them together thus briefly as you see; wherein to your great
encouragement, you may behold the good providence of God
working with you in our preservation from so many dangerous
plots and treacheries, as have been intended against us; as also
in giving his blessing so powerfully upon the weak means we
had, enabling us with health and ability beyond expectation,
in our greatest scarcities, and possessing the hearts of the Savages with astonishment and fear of us, whereas if God had let
them loose, they might easily have swallowed us up, scarce
being an handful in comparison of those forces they might
have gathered together against us, which now by Gods blessing
will be more hard and difficult, in regard our number of men is
increased, our town better fortified, and our store better victualed. Blessed therefore be his name, that hath done so great
things for us, & hath wrought so great a change amongst us.

Accept I pray you my weak endeavours, pardon my unskillfulness, and bear with my plainness in the things I have handled. Be not discouraged by our former necessities, but rather encouraged with us, hoping that as God hath wrought with us in our beginning of this worthy Work, undertaken in his name and fear; so he will by us accomplish the same to his glory and our comfort, if we neglect not the means. I confess, it hath not been much less chargeable to some of you, than hard and difficult to us, that have endured the brunt of the battle, and yet small profits returned; only by Gods mercy we are safely seated, housed, and fortified, by which means a great step is made unto gain, and a more direct course taken for the same, than if at first we had rashly and covetously fallen upon it.

Indeed, three things are the overthrow and bane (as I may term it) of Plantations.

1. The vain expectation of present profit, which too commonly taketh a principal seat in the heart and affection; though Gods glory, &c. is preferred before it in the mouth with protestation.

2. Ambition in their Governours and Commanders, seeking only to make themselves great, and slaves of all that are under them, to maintain a transitory base honour in themselves, which God oft punisheth with contempt.

3. The carelessness of those that send over supplies of men unto them, not caring how they be qualified: so that oft times they are rather the Image of men endued with bestial, yea, diabolical affections, than the Image of God, endued with reason, understanding, and holiness. I praise God I speak not these things experimentally, by way of complaint of our own condition, but having great cause on the contrary part to be thankful to God for his mercies towards us: but rather, if there be any too desirous of gain, to entreat them to moderate their affections, and consider that no man expecteth fruit before the tree be grown; advising all men, that as they tender their own well-fare, so to make choice of such to manage and govern their affairs, as are approved not to be seekers of themselves, but the common good of all for whom they are employed; and beseeching such as have the care of transporting men for the supply and furnishing of Plantations, to be truly careful

in sending such as may further and not hinder so good an action. There is no godly honest man, but will be helpful in his kind, and adorn his profession with an upright life and conversation, which Doctrine of manners ought first to be Preached by giving good example to the poor Savage Heathens amongst whom they live. On the contrary part, what great offense hath been given by many profane men, who being but seeming Christians, have made Christ and Christianity stink in the nostrils of the poor Infidels, and so laid a stumbling block before them: *but woe be to them by whom such offenses come.*

These things I offer to your Christian considerations, beseeching you to make a good construction of my simple meaning, and take in good part this ensuing Relation, dedicating my self and it evermore unto your service; beseeching God to crown our Christian and faithful endeavours with his blessings temporal and eternal.

Yours in this service, ever to be commanded:
E.W.

To the Reader.

Good Reader, when I first penned this discourse, I intended it chiefly for the satisfaction of my private friends, but since that time have been persuaded to publish the same: And the rather, because of a disorderly Colony that are dispersed, and most of them returned, to the great prejudice and damage of him that set them forth; who as they were a stain to old England *that bred them, in respect of their lives and manners amongst the* Indians: *So it is to be feared, will be no less to* New-England *in their vile and clamorous reports, because she would not foster them in their desired idle courses. I would not be understood to think there were no well-deserving persons amongst them: for of mine own knowledge it was a grief to some that they were so yoked; whose deserts as they were then suitable to their honest protestations, so I desire still may be, in respect of their just and true Relations.*

Peradventure thou wilt rather marvel that I deal so plainly, than any way doubt of the truth of this my Relation, yea it may be tax me therewith, as seeming rather to discourage men, than any way to further so noble an action? If any honest mind be discouraged, I am sorry, sure I am, I have given no just cause; and am so far from being discouraged my self, as I purpose to return forthwith. And for other light and vain persons, if they stumble hereat I have my desire, accounting it better for them and us that they keep where they are, as being unfit and unable to perform so great a task.

Some faults have escaped because I could not attend on the Press, which I pray thee correct as thou findest, and I shall account it as a favour unto me.

Thine E. W.

GOOD NEWS FROM New-England.

The Good Ship called the *Fortune*, which in the Month of *Novemb.* 1621. (blessed be God) brought us a new supply of 35. persons, was not long departed our Coast, ere the Great People of *Nanohigganset,* which are reported to be many thousands strong, began to breathe forth many threats against us, not withstanding their desired and obtained peace with us in the fore-going summer. Insomuch as the common talk of our neighbor *Indians* on all sides was of the preparation they made to come against us. In reason a man would think they should have now more cause to fear us than before our supply came: but though none of them were present, yet understanding by others that they neither brought Arms nor other provisions with them, but wholly relied on us, it occasioned them to sleight and brave us with so many threats as they did. At length came one of them to us, who was sent by *Conanacus* their chief *Sachim* or King, accompanied with one *Tokamahamon* a friendly *Indian.* This messenger inquired for *Tisquantum* our Interpreter, who not being at home seemed rather to be glad than sorry, and leaving for him a bundle of new arrows lapped in a rattle Snakes skin, desired to depart with all expedition. But our Governours not knowing what to make of this strange carriage, and comparing it with that we had formerly heard, committed him to the custody of Captain *Standish*, hoping now to know some certainty of that we so often heard, either by his own relation to us, or to *Tisquantum* at his return, desiring my self, having special familiarity with the other forenamed *Indian*, to see if I could learn any thing from him, whose answer was sparingly to this effect; that he could not certainly tell, but thought they were enemies to us. That night

Captain *Standish* gave me and another charge of him, and gave us order to use him kindly, and that he should not want any thing he desired, and to take all occasions to talk and inquire of the reasons of those reports we heard, and withal to signify that upon his true relation he should be sure of his own freedom. At first fear so possessed him, that he could scarce say any thing: but in the end became more familiar, and told us that the messenger which his Master sent in Summer to treat of peace, at his return persuaded him rather to war; and to the end he might provoke him thereunto, (as appeared to him by our reports) detained many of the things were sent him by our Governour, scorning the meanness of them both in respect of what himself had formerly sent, & also of the greatness of his own person; so that he much blamed the former Messenger, saying, that upon the knowledge of this his false carriage, it would cost him his life; but assured us that upon his relation of our speech then with him to his Master, he would be friends with us. Of this we informed the Governour and his Assistant, and Captain *Standish*, who after consultation considered him howsoever but in the state of a messenger, and it being as well against the Law of Arms amongst them as us in *Europe*, to lay violent hands on any such, set him at liberty, the Governour giving him order to certify his Master that he had heard of his large and many threatenings, at which he was much offended, daring him in those respects to the utmost, if he would not be reconciled to live peaceably as other his neighbors; manifesting withal (as ever) his desire of peace; but his fearless resolution, if he could not so live amongst them. After which he caused meat to be offered him, but he refused to eat, making all speed to return, and giving many thanks for his liberty. But requesting the other *Indian* again to return, the weather being violent, he used many words to persuade him to stay longer, but could not. Whereupon he left him, and said he was with his friends, and would not take a journey in such extremity.

After this when *Tisquantum* returned, and the arrows were delivered, and the manner of the messengers carriage related, he signified to the Governour, that to send the rattle Snakes skin in that manner, imported enmity, and that it was no better than a challenge. Here-upon after some deliberation, the Governour stuffed the skin with powder and shot, and sent it back, returning no less defiance to *Conanacus*, assuring him if he had shipping now present thereby to send his men to *Nanohigganset* (the place of his abode) they should not need to come so far by land to us: yet withal shewing that they should never come unwelcome or unlooked for. This message was sent by an *Indian*, and delivered in such sort, as it was no small terrour to this savage King, insomuch as he would not once touch the powder and shot, or suffer it to stay in his house or Country. Whereupon the Messenger refusing it, another took it up, and having been posted from place to place a long time, at length came whole back again.

In the mean time, knowing our own weakness, notwithstanding our high words and lofty looks towards them, and still lying open to all casualty, having as yet (under God) no other defense than our Arms, we thought it most needful to impale our Town, which with all expedition we accomplished in the month of February and some few days, taking in the top of the Hill under which our Town is seated, making four bulwarks or jetties without the ordinary circuit of the pale, from whence we could defend the whole Town: In three whereof are gates, and the fourth in time to be. This being done, Captain *Standish* divided our strength into four squadrons or companies, appointing whom he thought most fit to have command of each; And at a general Muster or Training, appointed each his place, gave each his Company, giving them charge upon every alarm to resort to their Leaders to their appointed place, and in his absence, to be commanded and directed by them. That done according to his order, each drew his Company to his appointed place for defense, and there together discharged their muskets. After which they brought their new Commanders to their houses, where again they graced them with their shot, and so departed.

Fearing also lest the enemy at any time should take any advantage by firing our houses, Captain *Standish* appointed a certain Company, that whensoever they saw or heard fire to be cried in the Town, should only betake themselves to their Arms, and should enclose the house or place so endangered, and stand aloof on their guard, with their backs towards the fire, to prevent treachery, if any were in that kind intended. If the fire were in any of the houses of this guard, they were then freed from it, but not otherwise, without special command.

Long before this time we promised the people of *Massachuset* in the beginning of March to come unto them, and trade for their Furs, which being then come, we began to make preparation for that voyage. In the mean time, an *Indian* called *Hobbamock*, who still lived in the Town, told us, that he feared the *Massachusets* or *Massachuseucks* (for they so called the people of that place) were joined in confederacy with the *Nanohigganneucks*, or people of *Nanohigganset*, and that they therefore would take this opportunity to cut off Captain *Standish* and his company abroad: but howsoever in the mean time, it was to be feared that the *Nanohigganeuks* would assault the Town at home, giving many reasons for his jealousy, as also that *Tisquantum* was in the confederacy, who we should find would use many persuasions to draw us from our shallops to the *Indians* houses for their better advantage. To confirm this his jealousy he told us of many secret passages that passed between him and others, having their meetings ordinarily abroad in the woods: but if at home howsoever he was excluded from their secrecy, saying it was the manner of the *Indians* when they meant plainly to deal openly: but in this his practise there was no shew of honesty.

Hereupon the Governour, together with his Assistant and Captain *Standish*, called together such, as by them were thought most meet for advice in so weighty a business, who after consideration hereof came to this resolution; That as hitherto upon all occasions between them and us, we had ever manifested undaunted courage and resolution, so it would not now stand with our safety to mew up our selves in our new-enclosed town, partly because our Store was almost empty, and therefore must seek out for our daily food, without which we could not long subsist; but especially for that thereby they would see us dismayed, & be encouraged to prosecute their malicious purposes, with more eagerness than ever they intended: whereas on the contrary, by the blessing of God, our fearless carriage might be a means to discourage and weaken their proceedings. And therefore thought best to proceed in our trading voyage, making this use of that we heard, to go the better provided, and use the more carefulness both at home and abroad, leaving the event to the disposing of the Almighty, whose providence as it had hitherto been over us for good, so we had now no cause (save our sins) to despair of his mercy in our preservation and continuance, where we desired rather to be instruments of good to the Heathens about us, than to give them the least measure of just offense.

All things being now in readiness, the forenamed Captain with ten men, accompanied with *Tisquantum* and *Hobbamock*, set forwards for the *Massachusets*: but we had no sooner turned the point of the harbour called the *Gurnets nose* (where being becalmed we let fall our grapnel, to set things to rights, and prepare to row) but there came an Indian of *Tisquantums* family, running to certain of our people that were from home with all eagerness, having his face wounded, and the blood still fresh on the same, calling to them to repair home, oft looking behind him, as if some others had him in chase, saying that at *Namaschet* (a town some fifteen miles from us) there were many of the *Nanohiggansets*, *Massassowat* our supposed friend, and *Conbatant* our feared enemy, with many others, with a resolution to take advantage on the present opportunity, to assault the town in the Captains absence, affirming that he received the wound in his face for speaking in our behalf, and by sleight escaped, looking oft backward, as if he suspected them to be at hand. This he affirmed again to the Governour, whereupon he gave command that three piece of Ordnance should be made ready and discharged, to the end that if we were not out of hearing, we might return thereat. Which we no sooner heard, but we repaired homeward with all convenient speed, arming our selves, and making all in readiness to fight. When we entered the harbour, we saw the Town likewise on their guard, whither we hasted with all convenient speed. The news being made known unto us, *Hobbamock* said flatly that it was false, assuring us of *Massassowats* faithfulness; howsoever he presumed he would never have undertaken any such act without his privity, himself being a Pniese, that is, one of his chiefest champions or men of valour, it being the manner amongst them not to undertake such enterprises without the advice and furtherance of men of that rank. To this the Governour answered, he should be sorry that any just and necessary occasions of war should arise between him and any of the Savages, but especially *Massassowat*, not that he feared him more than the rest, but because his love more exceeded towards him than any. Whereunto *Hobbamock* replied; There was no cause wherefore he should distrust him, and therefore should do well to continue his affections.

But to the end things might be made more manifest, the Governour caused *Hobbamock* to send his wife with all privacy to *Puckanokick* the chief place of *Massassowats* residence, (pretending other occasions) there to inform herself, and so us, of the right state of things. When she came thither, and saw all things quiet, and that no such matter was or had been intended, told *Massassowat* what had happened at *Plimoth*, (by them called *Patuxet*) which when he understood, he was much offended at the carriage of *Tisquantum*, returning many thanks to the Governour for his good thoughts of him; and assuring him that according to their first Articles of peace, he would send word and give warning when any such business was towards.

Thus by degrees we began to discover *Tisquantum*, whose ends were only to make himself great in the eyes of this Country-men, by means of his nearness and favour with us, not caring who fell so he stood. In the general, his course was to persuade them he could lead us to peace or war at his pleasure, and would oft threaten the *Indians*, sending them word in a private manner, we were intended shortly to kill them, that thereby he might get gifts to himself to work their peace, insomuch as they had him in greater esteem than many of their *Sachims*; yea they themselves sought to him, who promised them peace in respect of us; yea and protection also, so as they would resort to him. So that whereas diverse were wont to rely on *Massassowat* for protection, and resort to his abode, now they began to leave him, and seek after *Tisquantum*. Now though he could not make good these his large promises, especially because of the continued peace between *Massassowat* and us, he therefore raised this false alarm, hoping whilst things were hot in the heat of blood, to provoke us to march into his Country against him, whereby he hoped to kindle such a flame as would not easily be quenched, and hoping if that block were once removed, there were no other between him and honour;

which he loved as his life, and preferred before his peace. For these and the like abuses, the Governour sharply reproved him, yet was he so necessary and profitable an instrument, as at that time we could not miss him. But when we understood his dealings, we certified all the *Indians* of our ignorance and innocence therein, assuring them till they begun with us, they should have no cause to fear. And if any hereafter should raise any such reports, they should punish them as liars and seekers of their and our disturbance, which gave the *Indians* good satisfaction on all sides.

After this we proceeded in our voyage to the *Massachusets*, where we had good store of Trade, and (blessed be God) returned in safety, though driven from before our Town in great danger and extremity of weather.

At our return, we found *Massassowat* at the Plantation, who made his seeming just Apology for all former matters of accusation, being much offended and enraged against *Tisquantum*, whom the Governour pacified as much as he could for the present. But not long after his departure, he sent a messenger to the Governour, entreating him to give way to the death of *Tisquantum*, who had so much abused him. But the Governour answered; Although he had deserved to die both in respect of him and us; yet for our sakes he desired he would spare him, and the rather because without him he knew not well how to understand himself, or any other the *Indians*. With this answer the messenger returned, but came again not long after, accompanied with diverse others, demanding him from *Massassowat* their Master, as being one of his subjects, whom by our first Articles of peace we could not retain: yet because he would not willingly do it without the Governours approbation, offered him many Beavers skins for his consent thereto, saying, that according to their manner, their *Sachim* had sent his own knife, and them therewith, to cut off his head and hands, and bring them to him. To which the Governour answered; It was not the manner of the *English* to sell mens lives at a price, but when they had deserved justly to die, to give them their reward, and therefore refused their Beavers as a gift: but sent for *Tisquantum*, who though he knew their intent, yet offered not to fly, but came and accused *Hobbamock* as the author and worker of his overthrow; yielding himself to the Governour to be sent or not according as he thought meet. But at the instant, when our Governour was ready to deliver him into the hands of his Executioners, a Boat was seen at Sea to cross before our Town, and fall behind a head-land not far off: whereupon, having heard many rumors of the *French*, and not knowing whether there were any combination between the Savages and them, the Governour told the *Indians*, he would first know what Boat that was ere he would deliver him into their custody. But being mad with rage, and impatient at delay, they departed in great heat.

Here let me not omit one notable (though wicked) practise of this *Tisquantum*, who to the end he might possess his Countrymen with the greater fear of us, and so consequently of himself, told them we had the plague buried in our store-house, which at our pleasure we could send forth to what place or people we would, and destroy them therewith, though we stirred not from home. Being upon the fore-named brabbles sent for by the Governour to this place, where *Hobbamock* was and some other of us, the ground being broke in the mid-dest of the house, (whereunder certain barrels of powder were buried, though unknown to him) *Hobbamock* asked him what it meant? To whom he readily answered; That was the place wherein the plague was buried, whereof he formerly told him and others. After this *Hobbamock* asked one of our people, whether such a thing were, and whether we had such command of it? Who answered no; But the God of the English had it in store, and could send it at his pleasure to the destruction of his and our enemies.

This was, as I take it, about the end of May 1622. At which time our store of victuals was wholly spent, having lived long before with a bare and short allowance: The reason was, that supply of men before mentioned, which came so unprovided, not landing so much as a barrel of bread or meal for their whole company, but contrariwise received from us for their ships store homeward. Neither were the setters forth thereof altogether to be blamed therein, but rather certain amongst our selves, who were too prodigal in their writing and reporting of that plenty we enjoyed. But that I may return.

This Boat proved to be a Shallop that belonged to a fishing ship, called the Sparrow, set forth by Master *Thomas Weston*, late Merchant and Citizen of London, which brought six or seven passengers at his charge, that should before have been landed at our Plantation, who also brought no more provision for the present than served the Boats gang for their return to the ship, which made her voyage at a place called *Damarins Cove* near *Munhiggen* some forty leagues from us North-eastward; about which place there fished above thirty sail of ships, and whither my self was employed by our Governour, with orders to take up such victuals as the ships could spare, where I found kind entertainment and good respect, with a willingness to supply our wants: But being not able to spare that quantity I required, by reason of the necessity of some amongst themselves, whom they supplied before my coming, would not take any Bills for the same, but did what they could freely, wishing their store had been such as they might in greater measure have expressed their own love, and supplied our necessities, for which they sorrowed, provoking one another to the utmost of their abilities: which although it were not much amongst so many people as were at the Plantation, yet through the provident and discreet care of the Governours, recovered and preserved strength till our own crop on the ground was ready.

Having dispatched there, I returned home with all speed convenient, where I found the state of the Colony much weaker than when I left it: for till now we were never without some bread, the want whereof much abated the strength and flesh of some, and swelled others. But here it may be said, if the Country abound with Fish and Fowl in such measure as is reported, how could men undergo such measure of hardness, except through their own negligence? I answer; Every thing must be expected in its proper season. No man, as one saith, will go into an Orchard in the Winter to gather Cherries: so he that looks for Fowl there in the Summer, will be deceived in his expectation. The time they continue in plenty with us, is from the beginning of October to the end of March: but these extremities befell us in May and June. I confess that as the Fowl decrease, so Fish increase. And indeed their exceeding abundance was a great cause of increasing our wants. For though our Bay and Creeks were full of Bass, and other fish, yet for want of fit and strong Saynes, and other netting, they for the most part break through and carried all away before them. And though the Sea were full of Cod, yet we had neither tackling nor harseis for our Shallops. And indeed had we not been in a place where diverse sorts of shell-fish are that may be taken with the hand, we must have perished, unless God had raised some unknown or extraordinary means for our preservation.

In the time of these straits (indeed before my going to *Munhiggen*) the *Indians* began again to cast forth many insulting speeches, glorying in our weakness, and giving out how easy it would be ere long to cut us off. Now also *Massassowat* seemed to frown on us, and neither came or sent to us as formerly. These things occasioned further thoughts of Fortification: And whereas we have a Hill called the Mount, enclosed within our pale, under which our Town is seated, we resolved to erect a Fort thereon, from whence a few might easily secure the Town from any assault the *Indians* can make, whilst the rest might be employed as occasion served. This work was begun with great eagerness, and with the approbation of all men, hoping that this being once finished, and a continual guard there kept, it would utterly discourage the Savages from having any hopes or thoughts of rising against us. And though it took the greatest part of our strength from dressing our corn, yet (life being continued) we hoped God would raise some means in stead thereof for our further preservation.

In the end of June, or beginning of July, came into our harbour two ships of Master *Westons* aforesaid, the one called the *Charitie*, the other the *Swan*, having in them some fifty or sixty men sent over at his own charge to plant for him. These we received into our Town, affording them whatsoever courtesy our mean condition could afford. There the *Charitie*, being the bigger ship, left them, having many passengers which she was to land in *Virginia*. In the mean time, the body of them refreshed themselves at *Plimoth*, whilst some most fit sought out a place for them. That little store of corn we had, was exceedingly wasted by the unjust and dishonest walking of these strangers, who though they would sometimes seem to help us in our labour about our corn, yet spared not day and night to steal the same, it being then eatable, and pleasant to taste, though green and unprofitable. And though they received much kindness, set light both by it and us; not sparing to requite the love we shewed them, with secret backbitings, revilings, &c. the chief of them being forestalled and made against us, before they came, as after appeared: Nevertheless for their Masters sake, who formerly had deserved well from us, we continued to do them whatsoever good or furtherance we could, attributing these things to the want of conscience and discretion, expecting each day, when God in his providence would disburden us of them, sorrowing that their Over-seers were not of more ability and fitness for their places, and much fearing what would be the issue of such raw and unconscionable beginnings.

At length their Coasters returned, having found in their judgment a place fit for plantation, within the Bay of the *Massachusets*, at a place called by the Indians *Wichaguscusset*. To which place the body of them went with all convenient speed, leaving still with us such as were sick and lame, by the Governours permission, though on their parts undeserved, whom our Surgeon by the help of God recovered gratis for them, and they fetched home, as occasion served.

They had not been long from us, ere the Indians filled our ears with clamours against them, for stealing their corn, and other abuses conceived by them. At which we grieved the more, because the same men, in mine own hearing, had been earnest in persuading Captain *Standish*, before their coming to solicit our Governour to send some of his men to plant by them, alleging many reasons how it might be commodious for us. But we knew no means to redress those abuses, save reproof, and advising them to better walking, as occasion served.

In the end of *August* came other two ships into our harbour, the one (as I take it) was called the *Discoverie*, Captain *Jones* having the command thereof, the other was that ship of Mr. *Westons* called the *Sparrow*, which had now made her voyage of fish, and was consorted with the other, being both bound for *Virginia*. Of Captain *Jones* we furnished our selves of such provisions as we most needed, and he could best spare, who as he used us kindly, so made us pay largely for the things we had. And had not the Almighty, in his All-ordering Providence, directed him to us, it would have gone worse with us, than ever it had been, or after was: for, as we had now but small store of corn for the year following: so for want of supply, we were worn out of all manner of trucking stuff, not having any means left to help our selves by trade; but, through Gods good mercy towards us, he had wherewith, and did supply our wants on that kind competently.

In the end of *September*, or beginning of *October*, Mr. *Westons* biggest ship called the *Charitie*, returned for *England*, and left their Colony sufficiently victualed, as some of most credit amongst them reported. The lesser, called the *Swan*, remained with his Colony for their further help. At which time they desired to join in partnership with us to trade for corn; to which our Governour and his Assistant agreed upon such equal conditions, as were drawn and confirmed between them and us. The chief places aimed at were to the Southward of *Cape Cod*, and the more because *Tisquantum*, whose peace before this time was wrought with *Massassowat*, undertook to discover unto us that supposed, and still hoped passage within the Sholes.

Both Colonies being thus agreed, and their companies fitted and joined together, we resolved to set forward, but were oft crossed in our purposes; as first Master *Richard Greene*, brother in Law to Master *Weston*, who from him had a charge in the oversight and government of his Colony, died suddenly at our Plantation, to whom we gave burial befitting his place, in the best manner we could. Afterward, having further order to pro- ceed by letter from their other Governour at the *Massachusets*, twice Captain *Standish* set forth with them, but were driven in again by cross and violent winds: himself the second time being sick of a violent fever. By reason whereof (our own wants being like to be now greater than formerly; partly, because we were enforced to neglect our corn, and spend much time in fortification, but especially because such havoc was made of that little we had, through the unjust and dishonest carriage of those people before mentioned, at our first entertainment of them) our Governour in his own person supplied the Captains place, and in the month of *November* again set forth, having *Tisquantum* for his Interpreter and Pilot, who affirmed he had twice passed within the Sholes of *Cape Cod*, both with *English* and *French*. Nevertheless, they went so far with him, as the Master of the ship saw no hope of passage: but being (as he thought) in danger, bear up, and according to *Tisquan- tums* directions, made for an harbour not far from them, at a place called *Manamoycke*, which they found, and sounding it with their shallop found the channel, though but narrow and crooked, where at length they harboured the ship. Here they perceived that the tide set in and out with more violence at some other place more Southerly, which they had not seen nor could discover, by reason of the violence of the season all the time of their abode there. Some judged the entrance thereof might be beyond the Sholes, but there is no certainty thereof as yet known. That night the Governour accompanied with others, having *Tisquantum* for his Interpreter went ashore; At first the Inhabitants played least in sight, because none of our people had ever been there before; but understanding the ends of their coming, at length came to them, welcoming our Governour according to their Savage manner, refreshing them very well with store of venison and other victuals, which they brought them in great abundance, promising to trade with them, with a seeming gladness of the occasion: yet their joy was mixed with much jealousy, as appeared by their after practises: for at first they were loath their dwellings should be known, but when they saw our Governours resolution to stay on the shore all night, they brought him to their houses, having first conveyed all their stuff to a remote place, not far from the same, which one of our men walking forth occasionally espied; whereupon, on the sudden, neither it nor them could be found, and so many times after upon conceived occasions, they would be all gone, bag and baggage: But being afterwards (by *Tisquantums* means) better persuaded, they left their jealousy and traded with them; where they got eight hogsheads of corn and beans, though the people were but few. This gave our Governour and the company good encouragement. *Tisquantum* being still confident in the passage, and the Inhabitants affirming, they had seen ships of good burden pass within the Sholes aforesaid. But here, though they had determined to make a second assay, yet God had otherways disposed, who struck *Tisquantum* with sickness, in so much as he there died, which crossed their Southward trading, and the more because the Masters sufficiency was much doubted, and the season very tempestuous, and not fit to go upon discovery, having no guide to direct them.

From thence they departed, and the wind being fair for the *Massachusets* went thither, and the rather because the Savages upon our motion had planted much corn for us, which they promised not long before that time. When they came thither, they found a great sickness to be amongst the *Indians*, not unlike the plague, if not the same. They renewed their complaints to our Governour, against that other plantation seated by them, for their injurious walking. But indeed the trade both for Furs and corn was overthrown in that place, they giving as much for a quart of corn, as we used to do for a Beavers skin; so that little good could be there done. From thence they returned into the bottom of the Bay of Cape Cod, to a place called *Nauset*, where the *Sachim* used the Governour very kindly, and where they bought eight or ten hogsheads of corn and beans. Also at a place called *Mattachiest*, where they had like kind entertainment and corn also. During the time of their trade in these places, there were so great and violent storms, as the ship was much endangered, and our shallop cast away, so that they had now no means to carry the corn aboard that they had bought, the ship riding by their report well near two leagues from the same, her own Boat being small, and so leaky, (having no Carpenter with them) as they durst scarce fetch wood or water in her. Hereupon the Governour caused the corn to be made in a round stack, and bought mats, and cut sedge to cover it, and gave charge to the *Indians* not to meddle with it, promising him that dwelt next to it a reward, if he would keep vermin also from it, which he undertook, and the *Sachim* promised to make good. In the mean time, according to the Governours request, the *Sachim* sent men to seek the shallop, which they found buried almost in sand at a high-water mark, having many things remaining in her, but unserviceable for the present; whereof the Governour gave the *Sachim* special charge that it should not be further broken, promising ere long to fetch both it and the corn; assuring them, if neither were diminished, he would take it as a sign of their honest and true friendship, which they so much made shew of, but if they were, they should certainly smart for their unjust and dishonest dealing, and further make good whatsoever they had so taken. So he did likewise at *Mattachiest*, and took leave of them, being resolved to leave the ship, and take his journey home by land with our own company, sending word to the ship, that they should take their first opportunity to go for *Plimoth*, where he determined, by the permission of God, to meet them. And having procured a Guide, it being no less than fifty miles to our Plantation, set forward, receiving all respect that could be from the *Indians* in his journey, and came safely home, though weary and surbated, whither some three days after the ship also came. The corn being divided which they had got, Master *Westons* company went to their own Plantation, it being further agreed, that they should return with all convenient speed, and bring their Carpenter, that they might fetch the rest of the corn, and save the shallop.

At their return, Captain *Standish* being recovered and in health, took another shallop, and went with them to the corn, which they found in safety as they left it: also they mended the other shallop, and got all their corn aboard the ship. This was in January, as I take it, it being very cold and stormy, insomuch as (the harbour being none of the best) they were constrained to cut both the shallops from the ships stern, and so lost them both a second time. But the storm being over, and seeking out, they found them both, not having received any great hurt. Whilst they were at *Nauset*, having occasion to lie on the shore, laying their shallop in a Creek not far from them, an *Indian* came into the same, and stole certain Beads, Cissers, and other trifles out of the same, which when the Captain missed, he took certain of his company with him, and went to the *Sachim*, telling him what had happened, and requiring the same again, or the party that stole them, (who was known to certain of the *Indians*) or else he would revenge it on them before his departure, and so took leave for that night being late, refusing whatsoever kindness they offered. On the morrow, the *Sachim* came to their rendezvous, accompanied with many men, in a stately manner, who saluting the Captain in this wise; He thrust out his tongue, that one might see the root thereof, and therewith licked his hand from the wrist to the fingers end, withal bowing the knee, striving to imitate the English gesture, being instructed therein formerly by *Tisquantum*: his men did the like, but in so rude and savage a manner, as our men could scarce forbear to break out in open laughter. After salutation, he delivered the Beads, & other things, to the Captain, saying, he had much beaten the party for doing it, causing the women to make bread, and bring them, according to their desire, seeming to be very sorry for the fact, but glad to be reconciled. So they departed, and came home in safety; where the corn was equally divided, as before.

After this the Governour went to two other inland Towns, with another company, and bought corn likewise of them, the one is called *Namasket*, the other *Manomet*. That from *Namasket* was brought home partly by *Indian* women; but a great sickness arising amongst them, our own men were enforced to fetch home the rest. That at *Manomet* the Governour left in the *Sachims* custody: this Town lieth from us South well near twenty miles, and stands upon a fresh river, which runneth into the Bay of *Nanohigganset*, and cannot be less than sixty miles from thence. It will bear a boat of eight or ten ton to this place. Hither the Dutch or French, or both use to come. It is from hence to the Bay of Cape Cod about eight miles; out of which Bay it floweth into a Creek some six miles almost direct towards the Town. The heads of the River, and this Creek are not far distant. This River yieldeth thus high, Oysters, Mussels, Clams, and other shell-fish, one in shape like a bean, another like a Clam, both good meat, and great abundance at all times; besides it aboundeth with diverse sorts of fresh fish in their seasons. The Governour or *Sachim* of this place, was called *Canacum*, who had formerly, as well as many others, (yea all with whom as yet we had to do) acknowledged themselves the subjects of our Sovereign Lord the King. This *Sachim* used the Governour very kindly, and it seemed was of good respect and authority amongst the *Indians*. For whilst the Governour was there within night in bitter weather, came two men from *Manamoick* before spoken of, and having set aside their bows and quivers, according to their manner, sat down by the fire, and took a pipe of Tobacco, not using any words in that time, nor any other to them, but all remained silent, expecting when they would speak: At length they looked toward *Canacum*, and one of them made a short speech, and delivered a present to him from his *Sachim*, which was a basket of Tobacco, and many Beads, which the other received thankfully. After which he made a long speech to him, the contents hereof was related to us by *Hobbamock* (who then accompanied the Governour for his Guide) to be as followeth; It happened that two of their men fell out as they were in game (for they use gaming

as much as any where, and will play away all, even their skin
from their backs, yea and for their wives skins also, though it
may be they are many miles distant from them, as my self have
seen) and growing to great heat, the one killed the other. The
actor of this fact was a *Powah*, one of special note amongst
them, and such an one as they could not well miss, yet another
people greater than themselves threatened them with war, if
they would not put him to death. The party offending was
in hold, neither would their *Sachim* do one way or other till
their return, resting upon him for advice and furtherance in
so weighty a matter. After this there was silence a short time;
at length men gave their judgment what they thought best.
Amongst others, he asked *Hobbamock* what he thought? Who
answered, he was but a stranger to them, but thought it was
better that one should die than many, since he had deserved it,
and the rest were innocent; whereupon he passed the sentence
of death upon him.

Not long after (having no great quantity of corn left) Captain *Standish* went again with a shallop to *Mattachiest*, meeting
also with the like extremity of weather, both of wind, snow,
and frost, insomuch as they were frozen in the harbour the first
night they entered the same. Here they pretended their wonted
love, and spared them a good quantity of corn to confirm the
same: Strangers also came to this place, pretending only to
see him and his company, whom they never saw before that
time, but intending to join with the rest to kill them, as after
appeared. But being forced through extremity to lodge in their
houses, which they much pressed, God possessed the heart of
the Captain with just jealousy, giving straight command, that
as one part of his company slept, the rest should wake, declaring some things to them which he understood, whereof he
could make no good construction. Some of the *Indians* spying
a fit opportunity, stole some beads also from him, which he no
sooner perceived, having not above six men with him, drew
them all from the Boat, and set them on their guard about the
Sachims house, where the most of the people were, threatening to fall upon them without further delay, if they would not
forthwith restore them, signifying to the *Sachim* especially, and
so to them all, that as he would not offer the least injury; so
he would not receive any at their hands, which should escape

without punishment or due satisfaction. Hereupon the *Sachim*
bestirred him to find out the party, which when he had done,
caused him to return them again to the shallop, and came to
the Captain, desiring him to search whether they were not
about the Boat, who suspecting their knavery, sent one, who
found them lying openly upon the Boats cuddy; yet to appease
his anger, they brought corn afresh to trade, insomuch as he
laded his shallop, and so departed. This accident so daunted
their courage, as they durst not attempt any thing against him.
So that through the good mercy and providence of God they
returned in safety. At this place the *Indians* get abundance of
Bass both summer and winter: for it being now February they
abounded with them.

In the beginning of March, having refreshed himself, he
took a shallop, and went to *Manomet*, to fetch home that which
the Governour had formerly bought, hoping also to get more
from them, but was deceived in his expectation, not finding
that entertainment he found else-where, and the Governour
had there received. The reason whereof, and of the treachery
intended in the place before spoken of, was not then known
unto us, but afterwards: wherein may be observed the abundant mercies of God working with his providence for our
good. Captain *Standish* being now far from the Boat, and not
above two or three of our men with him, and as many with
the shallop, was not long at *Canacum* the *Sachims* house, but
in came two of the *Massachuset* men, the chief of them was
called *Wituwamat*, a notable insulting villain, one who had
formerly imbrued his hands in the blood of *English* and *French*,
and had oft boasted of his own valour, and derided their weakness, especially because (as he said) they died crying, making
sour faces, more like children than men. This villain took a
dagger from about his neck, (which he had gotten of Master
Westons people) and presented it to the *Sachim*, and after made
a long speech in an audacious manner, framing it in such sort,
as the Captain (though he be the best Linguist amongst us)
could not gather any thing from it. The end of it was afterward discovered to be as followeth: The *Massacheuseucks* had
formerly concluded to ruinate Master *Westons* Colony, and
thought themselves, being about thirty or forty men strong,
enough to execute the same: yet they durst not attempt it, till

such time as they had gathered more strength to themselves
to make their party good against us at *Plimoth*, concluding,
that if we remained, (though they had no other Arguments
to use against us) yet we would never leave the death of our
Countrymen unrevenged, and therefore their safety could not
be without the overthrow of both Plantations. To this end
they had formerly solicited this *Sachim*, as also the other called
Ianough at *Mattachiest*, and many others to assist them, and
now again came to prosecute the same; and since there was
so fair an opportunity offered by the Captains presence, they
thought best to make sure him and his company. After this his
message was delivered, his entertainment much exceeded the
Captains, insomuch as he scorned at their behaviour, and told
them of it: after which they would have persuaded him, because
the weather was cold, to have sent to the Boat for the rest of
his company, but he would not, desiring according to promise,
that the corn might be carried down, and he would content
the women for their labour, which they did. At the same time
there was a lusty *Indian* of *Paomet* or *Cape Cod* then present,
who had ever demeaned himself well towards us, being in his
general carriage, very affable, courteous, and loving, especially
towards the Captain. This Savage was now entered into confederacy with the rest, yet to avoid suspicion, made many signs
of his continued affections, and would needs bestow a kettle
of some six or seven gallons on him, and would not accept of
any thing in lieu thereof, saying, he was rich, and could afford
to bestow such favours on his friends whom he loved: also
he would freely help to carry some of the corn, affirming he
had never done the like in his life before, and the wind being
bad would needs lodge with him at their Rendezvous, having
indeed undertaken to kill him before they parted, which done
they intended to fall upon the rest. The night proved exceeding cold, insomuch as the Captain could not take any rest, but
either walked or turned himself to and fro at the fire: This
the other observed, and asked wherefore he did not sleep as at
other times, who answered he knew not well, but had no desire
at all to rest. So that he then missed his opportunity. The wind
serving on the next day, they returned home, accompanied
with the other *Indian*, who used many arguments to persuade
them to go to *Paomet*, where himself had much corn, and many

other, the most whereof he would procure for us, seeming to sorrow for our wants. Once the Captain put forth with him, and was forced back by contrary wind; which wind serving for the *Massachuset*, was fitted to go thither. But on a sudden it altered again.

During the time that the Captain was at *Manomet*, news came to *Plimoth*, that *Massassowat* was like to die, and that at the same time there was a Dutch ship driven so high on the shore by stress of weather, right before his dwelling, that till the tides increased, she could not be got off. Now it being a commendable manner of the Indians, when any (especially of note) are dangerously sick, for all that profess friendship to them, to visit them in their extremity, either in their persons, or else to send some acceptable persons to them, therefore it was thought meet (being a good and warrantable action) that as we had ever professed friendship, so we should now maintain the same, by observing this their laudable custom: and the rather, because we desired to have some conference with the Dutch, not knowing when we should have so fit an opportunity. To that end my self having formerly been there, and understanding in some measure the Dutch tongue, the Governour again laid this service upon my self, and fitted me with some cordials to administer to him, having one Master *John Hamden* a Gentleman of *London* (who then wintered with us, and desired much to see the Country) for my Consort, and *Hobbamock* for our guide. So we set forward, and lodged the first night at *Namasket*, where we had friendly entertainment. The next day about one of the clock, we came to a ferry in *Conbatants* Country, where upon discharge of my piece, diverse Indians came to us from a house not far off. There they told us, that *Massassowat* was dead, and that day buried, and that the Dutch would be gone before we could get thither, having hove off their ship already. This news struck us blank: but especially *Hobbamock*, who desired we might return with all speed. I told him I would first think of it, considering now that he being dead, *Conbatant* was the most like to succeed him, and that we were not above three miles from *Mattapuyst* his dwelling place, although he were but a hollow-hearted friend towards us, I thought no time so fit as this, to enter into more friendly terms with him, and the rest of the *Sachims* thereabout, hoping (through the blessing of God) it would be a means in that unsettled state, to settle their affections towards us, and though it were somewhat dangerous, in respect of our personal safety, because my self and *Hobbamock* had been employed upon a service against him, which he might now fitly revenge, yet esteeming it the best means, leaving the event to God in his mercy, I resolved to put it in practise, if Master *Hamden* and *Hobbamock* durst attempt it with me, whom I found willing to that or any other course might tend to the general good. So we went towards *Mattapuyst*. In the way, *Hobbamock* manifesting a troubled spirit, broke forth into these speeches, *Neen womasu Sagimus, neen womasu Sagimus*, &c. My loving *Sachim*, my loving *Sachim*. Many have I known, but never any like thee: And turning him to me said; Whilst I lived, I should never see his like amongst the *Indians*, saying, he was no liar, he was not bloody and cruel like other *Indians*; In anger and passion he was soon reclaimed, easy to be reconciled towards such as had offended him, ruled by reason in such measure, as he would not scorn the advice of mean men, and that he governed his men better with few strokes than others did with many; truly loving where he loved; yea he feared we had not a faithful friend left among the *Indians*, shewing how he oft-times restrained their malice, &c. continuing a long speech with such signs of lamentation and unfeigned sorrow, as it would have made the hardest heart relent. At length we came to *Mattapuyst*, and went to the *Sachimo Comaco* (for so they call the *Sachims* place, though they call an ordinary house *Witeo*) but *Conbatant* the *Sachim* was not at home, but at *Puckanokick*, which was some five or six miles off; the *Squa-sachim* (for so they call the *Sachims* wife) gave us friendly entertainment. Here we inquired again concerning *Massassowat*, they thought him dead, but knew no certainty; whereupon I hired one to go with all expedition to *Puckanokick* that we might know the certainty thereof, and withal to acquaint *Conbatant* with our there being. About half an hour before Sunsetting, the messenger returned, and told us that he was not yet dead, though there was no hope we should find him living. Upon this we were much revived, and set forward with all speed, though it was late within night ere we got thither. About two of the clock that afternoon the Dutchmen departed, so that in that respect our journey was frustrate. When we came thither, we found the house so full of men, as we could scarce get in, though they used their best diligence to make way for us. There were they in the middest of their charms for him, making such a hellish noise, as it distempered us that were well, and therefore unlike to ease him that was sick. About him were six or eight women, who chafed his arms, legs, and thighs, to keep heat in him; when they had made an end of their charming, one told him that his friends the *English* were come to see him; (having understanding left, but his sight was wholly gone) he asked who was come, they told him *Winsnow* (for they cannot pronounce the letter l, but ordinarily n in the place thereof) he desired to speak with me; when I came to him, and they told him of it, he put forth his hand to me, which I took; then he said twice, though very inwardly, *keen Winsnow*, which is to say, Art though *Winslow?* I answered, *ahhe* that is, yes; Then he doubled these words, *Matta neen wonckanet namen Winsnow*; that is to say, *O Winslow I shall never see thee again.* Then I called *Hobbamock* and desired him to tell *Massassowat*, that the Governour hearing of his sickness was sorry for the same, and though by reason of many businesses he could not come himself, yet he sent me with such things for him as he thought most likely to do him good in this his extremity, and whereof if he pleased to take, I would presently give him; which he desired, and having a confection of many comfortable conserves, &c. on the point of my knife, I gave him some, which I could scarce get through his teeth; when it was dissolved in his mouth, he swallowed the juice of it, whereat those that were about him much rejoiced, saying, he had not swallowed any thing in two days before. Then I desired to see his mouth, which was exceedingly furred, and his tongue swelled in such manner, as it was not possible for him to eat such meat as they had, his passage being stopped up: then I washed his mouth, and scraped his tongue, and got abundance of corruption out of the same. After which, I gave him more of the confection, which he swallowed with more readiness; then he desiring to drink, I dissolved some of it in water, and gave him thereof: within half an hour this wrought a great alteration in him in the eyes of all that beheld him; presently after his sight began to come to him, which gave him and us good encouragement.

In the mean time I inquired how he slept, and when he went to the stool? They said he slept not in two days before, and had not had a stool in five; then I gave him more, and told him of a mishap we had by the way in breaking a bottle of drink, which the Governour also sent him, saying, if he would send any of his men to *Patuxet*, I would send for more of the same, also for chickens to make him broth, and for other things which I knew were good for him, and would stay the return of the messenger if he desired. This he took marvelous kindly, and appointed some who were ready to go by two of the clock in the morning, against which time I made ready a letter, declaring therein our good success, the state of his body, &c. desiring to send me such things as I sent for, and such physic as the Surgeon durst administer to him. He requested me that the day following, I would take my Piece, and kill him some Fowl, and make him some English pottage, such as he had eaten at *Plimoth*, which I promised: after his stomach coming to him, I must needs make him some without Fowl, before I went abroad, which somewhat troubled me, being unaccustomed and unacquainted in such businesses, especially having nothing to make it comfortable, my Consort being as ignorant as my self; but being we must do somewhat, I caused a woman to bruise some corn, and take the flower from it, and set over the grut or broken corn in a pipkin (for they have earthen pots of all sizes.) When the day broke, we went out (it being now March) to seek herbs, but could not find any but strawberry leaves, of which I gathered a handful and put into the same, and because I had nothing to relish it, I went forth again, and pulled up a Saxafras root, and sliced a piece thereof, and boiled it till it had a good relish, and then took it out again. The broth being boiled, I strained it through my handkerchief, and gave him at least a pint, which he drank, and liked it very well. After this his sight mended more and more, also he had three moderate stools, and took some rest. Insomuch as we with admiration blessed God for giving his blessing to such raw and ignorant means, making no doubt of his recovery, himself and all of them acknowledging us the instruments of his preservation. That morning he caused me to spend in going from one to another amongst those that were sick in the Town, requesting me to wash their mouths also, and give to each of them some of the same I gave him, saying, they were good folk. This pains I took with willingness, though it were much offensive to me, not being accustomed with such poisonous savours. After dinner he desired me to get him a Goose or Duck, and make him some pottage therewith, with as much speed as I could: so I took a man with me, and made a shot at a couple of Ducks, some six score paces off, and killed one, at which he wondered: so we returned forthwith, and dressed it, making more broth therewith, which he much desired; never did I see a man so low brought, recover in that measure in so short a time. The Fowl being extraordinary fat, I told *Hobbamock* I must take off the top thereof, saying it would make him very sick again if he did eat it; this he acquainted *Massassowat* therewith, who would not be persuaded to it, though I pressed it very much, shewing the strength thereof, and the weakness of his stomach, which could not possibly bear it. Notwithstanding he made a gross meal of it, and ate as much as would well have satisfied a man in health. About an hour after he began to be very sick, and straining very much, cast up the broth again, and in over-straining himself, began to bleed at the nose, and so continued the space of four hours; then they all wished he had been ruled, concluding now he would die, which we much feared also. They asked me what I thought of him; I answered, his case was desperate, yet it might be it would save his life: for if it ceased in time, he would forthwith sleep and take rest, which was the principal thing he wanted. Not long after his blood stayed, and he slept at least six or eight hours; when he awaked I washed his face, and bathed and suppled his beard and nose with a linen cloth: but on a sudden he chopped his nose in the water, and drew up some therein, and sent it forth again with such violence, as he began to bleed afresh, then they thought there was no hope, but we perceived it was but the tenderness of his nostril, and therefore told them I thought it would stay presently, as indeed it did.

The messengers were now returned, but finding his stomach come to him, he would not have the chickens killed, but kept them for breed. Neither durst we give him any physic which was then sent, because his body was so much altered since our instructions, neither saw we any need, not doubting now of his recovery, if he were careful. Many whilst we were there came to see him, some by their report from a place not less than an hundred miles. To all that came one of his chief men related the manner of his sickness, how near he was spent, how amongst others his friends the *English* came to see him, and how suddenly they recovered him to this strength they saw, he being now able to sit upright of himself.

The day before our coming, another *Sachim* being there, told him, that now he might see how hollow-hearted the *English* were, saying if we had been such friends in deed, as we were in shew, we would have visited him in this his sickness, using many arguments to withdraw his affections, and to persuade him to give way to some things against us, which were motioned to him not long before: but upon this his recovery, he broke forth into these speeches; Now I see the *English* are my friends and love me, and whilst I live I will never forget this kindness they have shewed me. Whilst we were there, our entertainment exceeded all other strangers. Diverse other things were worthy the noting, but I fear I have been too tedious.

At our coming away, he called *Hobbamock* to him, & privately (none hearing save two or three other of his *Pnieses*, who are of his Council) revealed the plot of the *Massacheuseucks* before spoken of, against Master *Westons* Colony, and so against us, saying that the people of *Nauset, Paomet, Succonet Mattachiest, Manomet Agowaywam*, and the Ile of *Capawack* were joined with them; himself also in his sickness was earnestly solicited, but he would neither join therein, nor give way to any of his. Therefore as we respected the lives of our Countrymen, and our own after-safety, he advised us to kill the men of *Massachuset*, who were the authors of this intended mischief. And whereas we were wont to say, we would not strike a stroke till they first begun; if said he upon this intelligence, they make that answer, tell them, when their Countrymen at *Wichaguscusset* are killed, they being not able to defend themselves, that then it will be too late to recover their lives, nay through the multitude of adversaries they shall with great difficulty preserve their own, and therefore he counseled without delay to take away the principals, and then the plot would cease. With this he charged him thoroughly to acquaint me by the way, that I might inform the Governour thereof at my first coming home. Being fitted for our return, we took our leave of him, who returned many thanks to our Governour, and also to our selves for our labour and love: the like did all that were about him. So we departed.

That night through the earnest request of *Conbatant*, who til now remained at *Sawaams* or *Puckanokick*, we lodged with him at *Mattapuyst*. By the way I had much conference with him; so likewise at his house, he being a notable politician, yet full of merry jests & squibs, & never better pleased than when the like are returned again upon him. Amongst other things he asked me, If in case he were thus dangerously sick, as *Massassowat* had been, and should send word thereof to *Patuxet* for *Maskiet*, that is, Physic, whether then Mr Governour would send it? & if he would, whether I would come therewith to him? To both which I answered yea, whereat he gave me many joyful thanks. After that, being at his house he demanded further, how we durst being but two come so far into the Country? I answered, where was true love there was no fear, and my heart was so upright towards them that for mine own part I was fearless to come amongst them. But, said he, if your love be such, and it bring forth such fruits, how commeth it to pass, that when we come to *Patuxet*, you stand upon your guard, with the mouths of your Pieces presented towards us? Whereunto I answered, it was the most honourable and respective entertainment we could give them; it being an order amongst us so to receive our best respected friends: and as it was used on the Land, so the ships observed it also at Sea, which *Hobbamock* knew, and had seen observed. But shaking the head he answered, that he liked not such salutations.

Further, observing us to crave a blessing on our meat before we did eat, and after to give thanks for the same, he asked us what was the meaning of that ordinary custom? Hereupon I took occasion to tell them of Gods works of Creation, and Preservation, of his Laws and Ordinances, especially of the ten Commandments, all which they hearkened unto with great attention, and liked well of: only the seventh Commandment they excepted against, thinking there were many inconveniences in it, that a man should be tied to one woman: about which we reasoned a good time. Also I told them that whatsoever good things we had, we received from God, as the Author and giver thereof, and therefore craved his blessing upon that we had, and were about to eat, that it might nourish and strengthen our bodies, and having eaten sufficient, being satisfied therewith, we again returned thanks to the same our God for that our refreshing, &c. This all of them concluded to be very well, and said, they believed almost all the same things, and that the same power that we called God, they called *Kietitan*. Much profitable conference was occasioned hereby, which would be too tedious to relate, yet was no less delightful to them, than comfortable to us. Here we remained only that night, but never had better entertainment amongst any of them.

The day following, in our journey, *Hobbamock* told me of the private conference he had with *Massassowat*, and how he charged him perfectly to acquaint me therewith (as I shewed before) which having done, he used many arguments himself to move us thereunto; That night we lodged at *Namasket*, and the day following about the mid way between it and home, we met two *Indians*, who told us that Captain *Standish* was that day gone to the *Massachusets*: but contrary winds again drive him back, so that we found him at home; where the *Indian* of *Paomet* still was, being very importunate that the Captain should take the first opportunity of a fair wind to go with him, but their secret and villainous purposes being through Gods mercy now made known, the Governour caused Captain *Standish* to send him away without any distaste or manifestation of anger, that we might the better effect and bring to pass that which should be thought most necessary.

Before this journey we heard many complaints both by the *Indians* and some others of best desert amongst Master *Westons* Colony, how exceedingly their Company abased themselves by undirect means, to get victuals from the *Indians*, who dwelt not far from them, fetching them wood and water, &c. and all for a meals meat, whereas in the mean time, they might with diligence have gotten enough to have served them three or four times. Other by night broke the earth, and robbed the *Indians* store, for which they had been publicly stocked and whipped, and yet was there small amendment. This was about the end of February, at which time they had spent all their bread and corn, not leaving any for seed, neither would the *Indians* lend or sell them any more upon any terms. Hereupon they had thoughts to take it by violence, and to that spiked up every entrance into

their Town (being well impaled) save one, with a full resolution to proceed. But some more honestly minded, advised *John
Sanders* their Over-seer first to write to *Plimoth*, and if the
Governour advised him thereunto, he might the better do it.
This course was well liked, and an *Indian* was sent with all
speed with a letter to our Governour, the contents whereof
were to this effect; That being in great want, and their people
daily falling down, he intended to go to *Munhiggen*, where
was a Plantation of Sir *Ferdi: Gorges*, to buy bread from the
Ships that came thither a fishing, with the first opportunity of
wind; but knew not how the Colony would be preserved till his
return: he had used all means both to buy and borrow of *Indians* whom he knew to be stored, and he thought maliciously
with held it, and therefore was resolved to take it by violence,
and only waited the return of the Messenger, which he desired
should be hastened, craving his advice therein, promising also
to make restitution afterward. The Governour upon the receipt
hereof, asked the Messenger what store of corn they had, as
if he had intended to buy of them; who answered very little
more than that they reserved for seed, having already spared
all they could. Forth-with the Governour and his Assistant sent
for many of us to advise with them herein, who after serious
consideration, no way approving of this intended course, the
Governour answered his Letter, and caused many of us to set
our hands thereto, the contents whereof were to this purpose;
We altogether disliked their intendment, as being against the
law of God and Nature, shewing how it would cross the worthy
ends and proceedings of the Kings Majesty, and his honourable
Council for this place, both in respect of the peaceable enlarging of his Majesties Dominions, and also of the propagation
of the knowledge and Law of God, and the glad tidings of
salvation, which we and they were bound to seek, and were
not to use such means as would breed a distaste in the Savages against our persons and professions, assuring them their
Master would incur much blame hereby, neither could they
answer the same; For our own parts our case was almost the
same with theirs, having but a small quantity of Corn left,
and were enforced to live on ground nuts, clams, mussels, and
such other things as naturally the Country afforded, and which
did and would maintain strength, and were easy to be gotten,

all which things they had in great abundance, yea, Oysters also which we wanted, and therefore necessity could not be said to constrain them thereunto. Moreover, that they should consider, if they proceeded therein, all they could so get would maintain them but a small time, and then they must perforce seek their food abroad, which having made the *Indians* their enemies, would be very difficult for them, and therefore much better to begin a little the sooner, and so continue their peace, upon which course they might with good conscience desire and expect the blessing of God, whereas on the contrary they could not.

Also that they should consider their own weakness, being most swelled, and diseased in their bodies, and therefore the more unlikely to make their party good against them, and that they should not expect help from us in that or any the like unlawful actions. Lastly, that howsoever some of them might escape, yet the principal Agents should expect no better than the Galhouse, whensoever any special Officer should be sent over by his Majesty, or his Council for *New England*, which we expected, and who would undoubtedly call them to account for the same. These were the contents of our Answer, which was directed to their whole Colony. Another particular Letter our Governour sent to *John Sanders*, shewing how dangerous it would be for him above all others, being he was their leader and commander; and therefore in friendly manner advised him to desist.

With these Letters we dispatched the Messenger; Upon the receipt whereof they altered their determination, resolving to shift as they could, till the return of *John Sanders* from *Munhiggen*, who first coming to *Plimoth*, notwithstanding our own necessities, the Governour spared him some Corn to carry them to *Munhiggen*. But not having sufficient for the Ships store, he took a Shallop and leaving others with instructions to over-see things till his return, set forward about the end of February, so that he knew not of this conspiracy of the *Indians* before his going; neither was it known to any of us till our return from *Sawaams* or *Puckanokick*: At which time also another *Sachim* called *Wassapinewat*, brother to *Obtakiest* the *Sachim* of the *Massachusets*, who had formerly smarted for partaking with *Conbatant*, and fearing the like again, to purge himself revealed the same thing.

The three and twentieth of March being now come, which is a yearly Court day, the Governour having a double testimony, and many circumstances agreeing with the truth thereof, not being to undertake war without the consent of the body of the Company; made known the same in public Court, offering it to the consideration of the Company, it being high time to come to resolution, how sudden soever it seemed to them, fearing it would be put in execution before we could give any intelligence thereof. This business was no less troublesome than grievous, and the more, because it is so ordinary in these times for men to measure things by the events thereof: but especially for that we knew no means to deliver our Countrymen and preserve our selves, than by returning their malicious and cruel purposes upon their own heads, and causing them to fall into the same pit they had digged for others, though it much grieved us to shed the blood of those whose good we ever intended and aimed at, as a principal in all our proceedings. But in the end we came to this public conclusion, that because it was a matter of such weight as every man was not of sufficiency to judge, nor fitness to know because of many other *Indians* which daily as occasion serveth converse with us; therefore the Governour, his Assistant, and the Captain, should take such to themselves as they thought most meet, and conclude thereof; which done we came to this conclusion, That Captain *Standish* should take so many men as he thought sufficient to make his party good against all the *Indians* in the *Massachuset-bay*; and because (as all men know that have had to do in that kind) it is impossible to deal with them upon open defiance, but to take them in such traps as they lay for others; therefore he should pretend trade as at other times: but first go to the *English* and acquaint them with the plot, and the end of his own coming, that comparing it with their carriages towards them he might the better judge of the certainty of it, and more fitly take opportunity to revenge the same: but should forbear if it were possible till such time as he could make sure *Wituwamat*, that bloody and bold villain before spoken of, whose head he had order to bring with him, that he might be a warning and terrour to all of that disposition. Upon this Captain *Standish* made choice of eight men, and would not take more because he would prevent jealousy, knowing their guilty consciences would soon be provoked thereunto: but on the next day before he could go, came one of Mr. *Westons* Company by land unto us, with his pack at his back, who made a pitiful narration of their lamentable and weak estate, and of the *Indians* carriages, whose boldness increased abundantly, insomuch as the victuals they got they would take it out of their pots and eat before their faces, yea if any thing they gain-said them, they were ready to hold a knife at their breasts; that to give them content, since *John Sanders* went to *Munhiggen*, they had hanged one of them that stole their corn, and yet they regarded it not; that another of their Company was turned Savage, that their people had most forsaken the town, and made their rendezvous where they got their victuals, because they would not take pains to bring it home; that they had sold their clothes for corn, and were ready to starve both with cold and hunger also, because they could not endure to get victuals by reason of their nakedness; and that they were dispersed into three Companies scarce having any powder and shot left. What would be the event of these things (he said) he much feared; and therefore not daring to stay any longer among them, though he knew not the way yet adventured to come to us, partly to make known their weak and dangerous estate, as he conceived, and partly to desire he might there remain till things were better settled at the other plantation. As this relation was grievous to us, so it gave us good encouragement to proceed in our intendments, for which Captain *Standish* was now fitted, and the wind coming fair, the next day set forth for the *Massachusets*.

The *Indians* at the *Massachusets* missed this man, and suspecting his coming, to us as we conceive, sent one after him and gave out there that he would never come to *Patuxet*, but that some Wolves or Bears would eat him: but we know both by our own experience and the report of others, that though they find a man sleeping, yet so soon as there is life discerned they fear and shun him. This *Indian* missed him but very little, and missing him passed by the town and went to *Manomet*, whom we hoped to take at his return, as afterward we did. Now was our Fort made fit for service and some Ordnance mounted; and though it may seem long work it being ten months since it begun, yet we must note, that where so great a work is begun with such small means, a little time cannot bring to perfection: beside those works which tend to the preservation of man, the enemy of mankind will hinder what in him lieth, sometimes blinding the judgment and causing reasonable men to reason against their own safety, as amongst us diverse seeing the work prove tedious, would have dissuaded from proceeding, flattering themselves with peace and security, and accounting it rather a work of superfluity and vain-glory, than simple necessity. But God (whose providence hath waked and as I may say, watched for us whilst we slept) having determined to preserve us from these intended treacheries, undoubtedly ordained this as a special means to advantage us and discourage our adversaries, and therefore so stirred up the hearts of the Governours and other forward instruments, as the work was just made serviceable against this needful and dangerous time, though we ignorant of the same. But that I may proceed, the *Indian* last mentioned in his return from *Manomet*, came through the town pretending still friendship and in love to see us, but as formerly others, so his end was to see whether we continued still in health and strength, or fell into weakness like their neighbors, which they hoped and looked for (though God in mercy provided better for us) and he knew would be glad tidings to his Country men. But here the Governour stayed him, and sending for him to the Fort, there gave the Guard charge of him as their prisoner, where he told him he must be contented to remain till the return of Captain *Standish* from the *Massachusets*, so he was locked in a chain to a staple in the Court of guard, and there kept. Thus was our Fort hanselled, this being the first day as I take it, that ever any watch was there kept.

The Captain being now come to the *Massachusets*, went first to the ship, but found neither man, or so much as a dog therein: upon the discharge of a Musket the Master and some others of the plantation shewed themselves, who were on the shore gathering ground-nuts, and getting other food. After salutation Captain *Standish* asked them how they durst so leave the ship and live in such security, who answered like men senseless of their own misery, they feared not the *Indians*, but lived and suffered them to lodge with them, not having sword, or gun, or needing the same. To which the Captain answered, if there were no cause he was the gladder, but upon further inquiry, understanding that those in whom *John Sanders* had received most special confidence and left in his stead to govern the rest were at the Plantation, thither he went, and to be brief, made known the *Indians* purpose and the end of his own coming, as also (which formerly I omitted) that if afterward they durst not there stay, it was the intendment of the Governours and people of *Plimoth* there to receive them till they could be better provided: but if they conceived of any other course that might be more likely for their good, that himself should further them therein to the uttermost of his power. These men comparing other circumstances with that they now heard, answered, they could expect no better, and it was Gods mercy that they were not killed before his coming, desiring therefore that he would neglect no opportunity to proceed: Hereupon he advised them to secrecy, yet withal to send special command to one third of their Company that were farthest off to come home, and there enjoin them on pain of death to keep the town, himself allowing them a pint of *Indian* corn to a man for a day (though that store he had was spared out of our seed.) The weather proving very wet and stormy, it was the longer before he could do any thing.

In the mean time an *Indian* came to him and brought some furs, but rather to gather what he could from the Captains, than coming then for trade; and though the Captain carried things as smoothly as possibly he could, yet at his return he reported he saw by his eyes that he was angry in his heart, and therefore began to suspect themselves discovered. This caused one *Pecksuot* who was a *Pniese*, being a man of notable spirit to come to *Hobbamock* who was then with them, and told him he understood that the Captain was come to kill himself and the rest of the Savages there, tell him said he we know it, but fear him not, neither will we shun him; but let him begin when he dare, he shall not take us at unawares: many times after diverse of them severally, or few together, came to the Plantation to him, where they would whet and sharpen the points of their knives before his face, and use many other insulting gestures and speeches. Amongst the rest, *Wituwamat* bragged of the excellency of his knife; on the end of the handle there was pictured a womans face, but said he, I have another at home wherewith I have killed both *French* and *English*, and that hath a mans face on it, and by and by these two must marry: Further he said of that knife he there had; *Hinnaim namen, hinnaim michen, matta cuts*: that is to say, By and by it should see, and by and by it should eat, but not speak. Also *Pecksuot* being a man of greater stature than the Captain, told him though he were a great Captain, yet he was but a little man: and said he, though I be no Sachim, yet I am a man of great strength and courage. These things the Captain observed, yet bare with patience for the present. On the next day, seeing he could not get many of them together at once, and this *Pecksuot* and *Wituwamat* both together, with another man, and a youth of some eighteen years of age, which was brother to *Wituwamat*, and villain-like trod in his steps, daily putting many tricks upon the weaker sort of men, and having about as many of his own Company in a room with them, gave the word to his men, and the door being fast shut began himself with *Pecksuot*, and snatching his own knife from his neck though with much struggling killed him therewith, the point whereof he had made as sharp as a needle, and ground the back also to an edge: *Wituwamat* and the other man, the rest killed, and took the youth, whom the Cap. caused to be hanged; but it is incredible how many wounds these two Pnieses received before they died, not making any fearful noise, but catching at their weapons and striving to the last. *Hobbamock* stood by all this time as a spectator and meddled not, observing how our men demeaned themselves in this action; all being here ended, smiling he broke forth into these speeches to the Captain, Yester-day *Pecksuot* bragging of his own strength and stature, said, though you were a great Captain yet you were but a little man; but to day I see you are big enough to lay him on the ground. But to proceed, there being some women at the same time, Captain *Standish* left them in the custody of Mr. *Westons* people at the town, and sent word to another Company that had intelligence of things to kill those *Indian* men that were amongst them, these killed two more: himself also with some of his own men went to another place, where they killed another, and through the negligence of one man an *Indian* escaped, who discovered and crossed their proceedings.

Not long before this execution, three of Mr. *Westons* men which more regarded their bellies than any command or Commander, having formerly fared well with the *Indians* for making them Canoes, went again to the *Sachim* to offer their service, and had entertainment. The first night they came thither within night late came a Messenger with all speed, and delivered a sad and short message: Whereupon all the men gathered together, put on their boots and breeches, trusled up themselves, and took their bows and arrows and went forth, telling them they went a hunting, and that at their return they should have venison enough. Being now gone, one being more ancient and wise than the rest, calling former things to mind, especially the Captains presence, and the straight charge that on pain of death none should go a Musket-shot from the plantation, and comparing this sudden departure of theirs there with, began to dislike and wish himself at home again, which was further off than diverse other dwelt: Hereupon he moved his fellows to return but could not persuade them: so there being none but women left and the other that was turned savage, about midnight came away, forsaking the paths lest he should be pursued, and by this means saved his life.

Captain *Standish* took the one half of his men, and one or two of Mr. *Westons*, and *Hobbamock*, still seeking to make spoil of them and theirs. At length they espied a file of *Indians* which made towards them amain, and there being a small advantage in the ground by reason of a hill near them, both Companies strove for it, Captain *Standish* got it, whereupon they retreated and took each man his tree, letting fly their arrows amain, especially at himself and *Hobbamock*, whereupon *Hobbamock* cast off his coat, and being a known Pniese, (theirs being now killed) chased them so fast as our people were not able to hold way with him, insomuch as our men could have but one certain mark and then but the arm and half face of a notable villain as he drew at Captain *Standish*, who together with another both discharged at once at him, and broke his arm; whereupon they fled into a swamp, when they were in the thicket they parleyed, but to small purpose, getting nothing but foul language. So our Captain dared the Sachim to come out and fight like a man, shewing how base and woman-like he was in tonguing it as he did: but he refused and fled. So the captain returned to the Plantation, where he released the women and would not take their beaver coats from them, nor suffer the least discourtesy to be offered them. Now were Mr. *Westons* people resolved to leave their Plantation and go for *Munhiggen*, hoping to get passage and return with the fishing ships. The Captain told them, that for his own part he durst there live with fewer men than they were, yet since they were otherways minded, according to his order from the Governours and people of *Plimoth* he would help them with corn competent for their provision by the way, which he did, scarce leaving himself more than brought them home. Some of them disliked the choice of the body to go to *Munhiggen*, and therefore desiring to go with him to *Plimoth*, he took them into the shallop: and seeing them set sail and clear of the *Massachuset bay*, he took leave and returned to *Plimoth*, whither he came in safety (blessed be God) and brought the head of *Wituwamat* with him.

Amongst the rest there was an *Indian* youth that was ever of a courteous and loving disposition towards us, he notwithstanding the death of his Countrymen came to the Captain without fear, saying his good conscience and love towards us emboldened him so to do. This youth confessed that the *Indians* intended to kill Mr. *Westons* people, and not to delay any longer than till they had two more Canoes or Boats, which Mr. *Westons* men would have finished by this time (having made them three already) had not the Captain prevented them, and the end of stay for those Boats, was to take their Ship therewith.

Now was the Captain returned and received with joy, the head being brought to the fort and there set up, the Governours and Captains with diverse others went up the same further, to examine the prisoner, who looked piteously on the head, being asked whether he knew it, he answered, yea: Then he confessed the plot, and that all the people provoked *Obtakiest* their *Sachim* thereunto, being drawn to it by their importunity: Five there were (he said) that prosecuted it with more eagerness than the rest, the two principal were killed, being *Pecksuot* and *Wituwamat*, whose head was there, the other three were *Powahs*, being yet living, and known unto us, though one of them was wounded, as aforesaid. For himself he would not acknowledge that he had any hand therein, begging earnestly for his life, saying, he was not a *Massachuset* man, but as a stranger lived with them. *Hobbamock* also gave a good report of him, and besought for him, but was bribed so to do: Nevertheless, that we might shew mercy as well as extremity, the Governour released him, and the rather because we desired he might carry a message to *Obtakiest* his Master. No sooner were the irons from his legs, but he would have been gone, but the Governour bid him stay and fear not, for he should receive no hurt, and by *Hobbamock* commanded him to deliver this message to his Master; That for our parts, it never entered into our hearts to take such a course with them, till their own treachery enforced us thereunto, and therefore might thank themselves for their own over-throw, yet since he had begun, if again by any the like courses he did provoke him, his Country should not hold him, for he would never suffer him or his to rest in peace, till he had utterly consumed them, and therefore should take this as a warning. Further, that he should send to *Patuxet* the three Englishmen he had and not kill them; also that he should not spoil the pale and houses at *Wichaguscusset*, and that this Messenger should either bring the English, or an answer, or both, promising his safe return.

This message was delivered, and the party would have returned with answer, but was at first dissuaded by them, whom afterward they would but could not persuade to come to us. At length (though long) a Woman came and told us that *Obtakiest* was sorry that the English were killed before he heard from the Governour, otherwise he would have sent them. Also she said, he would fain make his peace again with us, but none of his men durst come to treat about it, having forsaken his dwelling, and daily removed from place to place, expecting when we would take further vengeance on him.

Concerning those other people that intended to join with the *Massachuseucks* against us, though we never went against any of them, yet this sudden and unexpected execution, together with the just judgment of God upon their guilty consciences, hath so terrified and amazed them, as in like manner they forsook their houses, running to and fro like men distracted, living in swamps and other desert places, and so brought manifold diseases amongst themselves, whereof very many are dead, as *Canacum* the *Sachim* of *Manomet*, *Aspinet*, the *Sachim* of *Nauset*, and *Ianowh*, *Sachim* of *Mattachuest*. This *Sachim* in his life, in the middest of these distractions, said the God of the English was offended with them, and would destroy them in his anger, and certainly it is strange to hear how many of late have, and still daily die amongst them, neither is there any likelihood it will easily cease, because through fear they set little or no Corn, which is the staff of life, and without which they cannot long preserve health and strength. From one of these places a boat was sent with presents to the Governour, hoping thereby to work their peace, but the boat was cast away, and three of the persons drowned, not far from our plantation, only one escaped, who durst not come to us, but returned, so as none of them dare come amongst us.

I fear I have been too tedious both in this and other things, yet when I considered how necessary a thing it is that the truth and grounds of this action, especially should be made known, and the several dispositions of that dissolved Colony, whose reports undoubtedly will be as various, I could not but enlarge my self where I thought to be most brief; neither durst I be too brief, least I should eclipse and rob God of that honour, glory, and praise, which belongeth to him for preserving us from falling when we were at the pits brim, and yet feared nor knew not that we were in danger.

The month of April being now come, on all hands we began to prepare for Corn. And because there was no Corn left before this time, save that was preserved for seed, being also hopeless of relief by supply, we thought best to leave off all other works, and prosecute that as most necessary. And because there was no small hope of doing good in that common course of labour that formerly we were in, for that the Governours that followed men to their labours, had nothing to give men for their necessities, and therefore could not so well exercise that command over them therein as formerly they had done, especially considering that self-love wherewith every man (in a measure more or less) loveth and preferreth his own good before his neighbors, and also the base disposition of some drones, that as at other times so now especially would be most burdenous to the rest; It was therefore thought best that every man should use the best diligence he could for his own preservation, both in respect of the time present, and to prepare his own Corn for the year following: and bring in a competent portion for the maintenance of public Officers, Fishermen, &c. which could not be freed from their calling without greater inconveniences. This course was to continue till harvest, and then the Governours to gather in the appointed portion, for the maintenance of themselves and such others as necessity constrained to exempt from this condition. Only if occasion served upon any special service they might employ such as they thought most fit to execute the same, during this appointed time, and at the end thereof all men to be employed by them in such service as they thought most necessary for the general good. And because there is great difference in the ground, that therefore a set quantity should be set down for a person, and each man to have his fall by lot, as being most just and equal, and against which no man could except.

At a general meeting of the Company, many courses were propounded, but this approved and followed, as being the most likely for the present and future good of the Company; and therefore before this month began to prepare our ground against seed-time. In the middest of April we began to set, the weather being then seasonable, which much encouraged us, giving us good hopes of after plenty: the setting season is good till the latter end of May. But it pleased God for our further chastisement, to send a great drowth, insomuch, as in six weeks after the latter setting there scarce fell any rain, so that the stalk of that was first set began to send forth the ear before it came to half growth, and that which was later, not like to yield any at all, both blade and stalk hanging the head, and changing the color in such manner, as we judged it utterly dead: our Beans also ran not up according to their wonted manner, but stood at a stay, many being parched away, as though they had been scorched before the fire. Now were our hopes overthrown, and we discouraged, our joy being turned into mourning.

To add also to this sorrowful estate in which we were, we heard of a supply that was sent unto us many months since, which having two repulses before, was a third time in company of another ship three hundred Leagues at Sea, and now in three months time heard no further of her, only the signs of a wreck were seen on the coast, which could not be judged to be any other than the same. So that at once God seemed to deprive us of all future hopes. The most courageous were now discouraged, because God which hitherto had been our only Shield and Supporter, now seemed in his anger to arm himself against us; and who can withstand the fierceness of his wrath.

These, and the like considerations moved not only every good man privately to enter into examination with his own estate between God and his conscience, and so to humiliation before him: but also more solemnly to humble our selves together before the Lord by fasting and prayer. To that end a day was appointed by public authority, and set a-part from all other employments, hoping that the same God which had stirred us up hereunto, would be moved hereby in mercy to look down upon us, & grant the request of our dejected souls, if our continuance there might any way stand with his glory and our good. But oh the mercy of our God! Who was as ready to hear as we to ask: For though in the morning when we assembled together, the heavens were as clear and the drought as like to continue as ever it was: yet (our exercise continuing some eight or nine hours) before our departure the weather was over-cast, the clouds gathered together on all sides, and on the next morning distilled such soft, sweet, and moderate showers of rain, continuing some fourteen days, and mixed with such seasonable weather, as it was hard to say whether our withered Corn, or drooping affections were most quickened or revived. Such was the bounty and goodness of our God. Of this the *Indians* by means of *Hobbamock* took notice: who being then in the Town, and this exercise in the midst of the week, said, it was but three days since Sunday, and therefore demanded of a boy what was the reason thereof? Which when he knew and saw what effects followed thereupon, he and all of them admired the goodness of our God towards us, that wrought so great a change in so short a time, shewing the difference between their conjuration, and our invocation on the name of God for rain; theirs being mixed with such storms and tempests, as sometimes in stead of doing them good, it layeth the Corn flat on the ground, to their prejudice: but ours in so gentle and seasonable a manner, as they never observed the like.

At the same time Captain *Standish* being formerly employed by the Governour to buy provisions for the refreshing of the Colony, returned with the same, accompanied with one Mr *David Tomson*, a Scotchman, who also that Spring began a Plantation twenty five leagues northeast from us, near *Smiths* Iles, at a place called *Pascatoquack*, where he liketh well. Now also heard we of the third repulse that our supply had, of their safe though dangerous return into *England*, and of their preparation to come to us. So that having these many signs of Gods favour and acceptation, we thought it would be great ingratitude, if secretly we should smother up the same, or content our selves with private thanksgiving for that which by private prayer could not be obtained. And therefore another solemn day was set a-part and appointed for that end, wherein we returned glory, honour, and praise, with all thankfulness to our good God, which dealt so graciously with us, whose name for these and all other his mercies towards his Church and chosen ones, by them be blessed and praised now and evermore, Amen.

In the latter end of July and the beginning of August, came two Ships with supply unto us, who brought all their passengers, except one, in health, who recovered in short time, who also notwithstanding, all our wants and hardship (blessed be God) found not any one sick person amongst us at the Plantation. The bigger Ship called the *Anne* was hired, and there again freighted back, from whence we set sail the tenth of September. The lesser called the little *James*, was built for the company at their charge. She was now also fitted for Trade and discovery to the South-ward of Cape *Cod*, and almost ready to set sail, whom I pray God to bless in her good and lawful proceedings.

Thus have I made a true and full Narration of the state of our Plantation, and such things as were most remarkable therein since Decemb. 1621. If I have omitted any thing, it is either through weakness of memory, or because I judged it not material: I confess my style rude, and unskillfulness in the task I undertook, being urged thereunto by opportunity, which I knew to be wanting in others, and but for which I would not have undertaken the same; yet as it is rude so it is plain, and

therefore the easier to be understood; wherein others may see
that which we are bound to acknowledge, *viz*. That if ever any
people in these later ages were upheld by the providence of God
after a more special manner than others, then we: and therefore
are the more bound to celebrate the memory of his goodness,
with everlasting thankfulness. For in these forenamed straits,
such was our state, as in the morning we had often our food to
seek for the day, and yet performed the duties of our Callings, I
mean other daily labours, to provide for after time: and though
at some times in some seasons at noon I have seen men stagger
by reason of faintness for want of food, yet ere night by the
good providence and blessing of God, we have enjoyed such
plenty as though the windows of heaven had been opened unto
us. How few, weak, and raw were we at our first beginning, and
there settling, and in the middest of barbarous enemies? yet
God wrought our peace for us. How often have we been at the
pits brim, and in danger to be swallowed up, yea, not knowing, till afterward that we were in peril? and yet God preserved
us: yea, and from how many that we yet know not of, he that
knoweth all things can best tell: So that when I seriously consider of things, I cannot but think that God hath a purpose to
give that Land as an inheritance to our Nation, and great pity it
were that it should long lie in so desolate a state, considering it
agreeth so well with the constitution of our bodies, being both
fertile, and so temperate for heat and cold, as in that respect one
can scarce distinguish *New-England* from *Old*.

A few things I thought meet to add hereunto, which I have
observed amongst the *Indians*, both touching their Religion,
and sundry other Customs amongst them. And first, whereas
my self and others, in former Letters (which came to the Press
against my will and knowledge) wrote, that the *Indians* about
us are a people without any Religion, or knowledge of any
God, therein I erred, though we could then gather no better:
For as they conceive of many divine powers, so of one whom
they call *Kiehtan*, to be the principal and maker of all the rest,
and to be made by none: He (they say) created the heavens,
earth, sea, and all creatures contained therein. Also that he
made one man and one woman, of whom they and we and
all mankind came: but how they became so far dispersed that
know they not. At first they say, there was no *Sachim*, or *King*,

but *Kiehtan*,* who dwelleth above in the Heavens, whither all good men go when they die, to see their friends, and have their fill of all things: This his habitation lieth far West-ward in the heavens, they say; thither the bad men go also, and knock at his door, but he bids them *Quatchet*, that is to say, Walk abroad, for there is no place for such; so that they wander in restless want and penury: Never man saw this *Kiehtan*; only old men tell them of him, and bid them tell their children, yea, to charge them to teach their posterities the same, and lay the like charge upon them. This power they acknowledge to be good, and when they would obtain any great matter, meet together, and cry unto him, and so likewise for plenty, victory, &c. sing, dance, feast, give thanks, and hang up Garlands and other things in memory of the same.

Another power they worship, whom they call *Hobbamock*, and to the Norward of us *Hobbamoqui*; this as far as we can conceive is the Devil, him they call upon to cure their wounds and diseases. When they are curable, he persuades them he sends the same for some conceived anger against them, but upon their calling upon him can and doth help them: But when they are mortal, and not curable in nature, then he persuades them *Kiehtan* is angry and sends them, whom none can cure: in so much, as in that respect only they somewhat doubt whether he be simply good, and therefore in sickness never call upon him.

This *Hobbamock* appears in sundry forms unto them, as in the shape of a Man, a Deer, a Fawn, an Eagle, &c. but most ordinarily a Snake: He appears not to all but the chiefest and most judicious amongst them, though all of them strive to attain to that hellish height of honour.

He appeareth most ordinary and is most conversant with three sorts of people, one I confess I neither know by name nor office directly: Of these they have few but esteem highly of them, and think that no weapon can kill them: another they call by the name of *Powah*, and the third *Pniese*.

The office and duty of the *Powah* is to be exercised principally in calling upon the Devil, and curing diseases of the sick

*The meaning of the word *Kiehtan*, I think hath reference to Antiquity, for *Chise* is an old man, and *Kiehchise*, a man that exceedeth in age.

or wounded. The common people join with him in the exercise
of invocation, but do only assent, or as we term it, say *Amen*
to that he saith, yet sometime break out into a short musical
note with him. The *Powah* is eager and free in speech, fierce in
countenance, and joineth many antic and labourious gestures
with the same over the party diseased. If the party be wounded
he will also seem to suck the wound, but if they be curable (as
they say) he toucheth it not, but a Skooke, that is the Snake, or
Wobsacuck, that is the Eagle, sitteth on his shoulder and licks
the same. This none see but the *Powah*, who tells them he doth
it himself. If the party be otherwise diseased, it is accounted
sufficient if in any shape he but come into the house, taking it
for an undoubted sign of recovery.

And as in former ages *Apollo* had his temple at *Delphos*, and
Diana at *Ephesus*; so have I heard them call upon some as if
they had their residence in some certain places, or because they
appeared in those forms in the same. In the *Powahs* speech he
promiseth to sacrifice many skins of beasts, kettles, hatchets,
beads, knives, and other the best things they have to the fiend,
if he will come to help the party diseased: But whether they
perform it I know not. The other practises I have seen, being
necessarily called at some times to be with their sick, and have
used the best arguments I could make them understand against
the same: They have told me I should see the Devil at those
times come to the party, but I assured my self and them of
the contrary, which so proved: yea, themselves have confessed
they never saw him when any of us were present. In desperate
and extraordinary hard travail in child-birth, when the party
cannot be delivered by the ordinary means, they send for this
Powah, though ordinarily their travail is not so extreme as in
our parts of the world, they being of a more hardy nature; for
on the third day after child-birth I have seen the mother with
the infant upon a small occasion in cold weather in a boat upon
the Sea.

Many sacrifices the *Indians* use, and in some cases kill children. It seemeth they are various in their religious worship in a
little distance, and grow more and more cold in their worship
to *Kiehtan*; saying in their memory he was much more called
upon. The *Nanohiggansets* exceed in their blind devotion, and
have a great spacious house wherein only some few (that are

as we may term them Priests) come: thither at certain known times resort all their people, and offer almost all the riches they have to their gods, as kettles, skins, hatchets, beads, knives, &c. all which are cast by the Priests into a great fire that they make in the midst of the house, and there consumed to ashes. To this offering every man bringeth freely, and the more he is known to bring, hath the better esteem of all men. This the other *Indians* about us approve of as good, and wish their *Sachims* would appoint the like: and because the plague hath not reigned at *Nanohigganset* as at other places about them, they attribute to this custom there used.

The *Pnieses* are men of great courage and wisdom, and to these also the Devil appeareth more familiarly than to others, and as we conceive maketh covenant with them to preserve them from death, by wounds, with arrows, knives, hatchets, &c. or at least both themselves and especially the people think themselves to be freed from the same. And though against their battles all of them by painting disfigure themselves, yet they are known by their courage and boldness, by reason whereof one of them will chase almost an hundred men, for they account it death for whomsoever stand in their way. These are highly esteemed of all sorts of people, and are of the *Sachims* Council, without whom they will not war or undertake any weighty business. In war their *Sachims* for their more safety go in the midst of them. They are commonly men of the greatest stature & strength, and such as will endure most hardness, and yet are more discreet, courteous, and humane in their carriages than any amongst them, scorning theft, lying, and the like base dealings, and stand as much upon their reputation as any men.

And to the end they may have store of these, they train up the most forward and likeliest boys from their childhood in great hardness, and make them abstain from dainty meat, observing diverse orders prescribed, to the end that when they are of age the Devil may appear to them, causing to drink the juice of Sentry and other bitter herbs till they cast, which they must disgorge into the platter, and drink again, and again, till at length through extraordinary oppressing of nature it will seem to be all blood, and this the boys will do with eagerness at the first, and so continue till by reason of faintness they can

scarce stand on their legs, and then must go forth into the
cold: also they beat their shins with sticks, and cause them
to run through bushes, stumps, and brambles, to make them
hardy and acceptable to the Devil, that in time he may appear
unto them.

Their *Sachims* cannot be all called Kings, but only some
few of them, to whom the rest resort for protection, and pay
homage unto them, neither may they war with-out their knowledge and approbation, yet to be commanded by the greater as
occasion serveth. Of this sort is *Massassowat* our friend, and
Conanacus of *Nanohiggenset* our supposed enemy.

Every *Sachim* taketh care for the widow and fatherless, also
for such as are aged, and any way maimed, if their friends be
dead or not able to provide for them.

A *Sachim* will not take any to wife but such an one as is
equal to him in birth, otherwise they say their seed would in
time become ignoble, and though they have many other wives,
yet are they no other than concubines or servants, and yield a
kind of obedience to the principal, who ordereth the family,
and them in it. The like their men observe also, and will adhere
to the first during their lives; but put away the other at their
pleasure.

This government is successive and not by choice. If the father
die before the son or daughter be of age, then the child is
committed to the protection and tuition of some one amongst
them, who ruleth in his stead till he be of age, but when that
is I know not.

Every *Sachim* knoweth how far the bounds and limits of his
own Country extendeth, and that is his own proper inheritance, out of that if any of his men desire land to set their
corn, he giveth them as much as they can use, and sets them
their bounds. In this circuit whosoever hunteth, if they kill any
venison, bring him his fee, which is the fore parts of the same,
if it be killed on the land, but if in the water, then the skin
thereof: The great *Sachims* or Kings, know their own bounds
or limits of land, as well as the rest.

All travelers or strangers for the most part lodge at the
Sachims, when they come they tell them how long they will
stay, and to what place they go, during which time they receive
entertainment according to their persons, but want not.

Once a year the *Pnieses* use to provoke the people to bestow much corn on the *Sachim*. To that end they appoint a certain time and place near the *Sachims* dwelling, where the people bring many baskets of corn, and make a great stack thereof. There the *Pnieses* stand ready to give thanks to the people on the *Sachims* behalf, and after acquainteth the *Sachim* therewith, who fetcheth the same, and is no less thankful, bestowing many gifts on them.

When any are visited with sickness, their friends resort unto them for their comfort, and continue with them ofttimes till their death or recovery. If they die they stay a certain time to mourn for them. Night and morning they perform this duty many days after the burial in a most doleful manner, insomuch as though it be ordinary and the note musical, which they take one from another, and all together, yet it will draw tears from their eyes, & almost from ours also. But if they recover then because their sickness was chargeable, they send corn and other gifts unto them at a certain appointed time, whereat they feast and dance, which they call *Commoco*.

When they bury the dead they sew up the corpse in a mat and so put it in the earth. If the party be a *Sachim* they cover him with many curious mats, and bury all his riches with him, and enclose the grave with a pale. If it be a child the father will also put his own most special jewels and ornaments in the earth with it, also will cut his hair and disfigure himself very much in token of sorrow. If it be the man or woman of the house, they will pull down the mats and leave the frame standing, and bury them in or near the same, and either remove their dwelling or give over house-keeping.

The men employ themselves wholly in hunting, and other exercises of the bow, except at some times they take some pains in fishing.

The women live a most slavish life, they carry all their burdens, set and dress their corn, gather it in, seek out for much of their food, beat and make ready the corn to eat, and have all household care lying upon them.

The younger sort reverence the elder, and do all mean offices whilst they are together, although they be strangers. Boys and girls may not wear their hair like men and women, but are distinguished thereby.

A man is not accounted a man till he do some notable act, or shew forth such courage and resolution as becometh his place. The men take much tobacco, but for boys so to do they account it odious.

All their names are significant and variable, for when they come to the state of men and women, they alter them according to their deeds or dispositions.

When a maid is taken in marriage she first cutteth her hair, and after weareth a covering on her head till her hair be grown out. Their women are diversely disposed, some as modest as they will scarce talk one with another in the company of men, being very chaste also: yet other some light, lascivious and wanton.

If a woman have a bad husband, or cannot affect him, and there be war or opposition between that and any other people, she will run away from him to the contrary party and there live, where they never come unwelcome: for where are most women, there is greatest plenty.

When a woman hath her monthly terms she separateth her self from all other company, and liveth certain days in a house alone: after which she washeth her self and all that she hath touched or used, and is again received to her husbands bed or family.

For adultery the husband will beat his wife and put her away, if he please. Some common strumpets there are as well as in other places, but they are such as either never married, or widows, or put away for adultery: for no man will keep such an one to wife.

In matters of unjust and dis-honest dealing the *Sachim* examineth and punisheth the same. In case of thefts, for the first offence he is disgracefully rebuked, for the second beaten by the *Sachim* with a cudgel on the naked back, for the third he is beaten with many strokes, and hath his nose slit upward, that thereby all men may both know and shun him. If any man kill another, he must likewise die for the same. The *Sachim* not only passeth the sentence upon malefactors, but executeth the same with his own hands, if the party be then present; if not, sendeth his own knife in case of death, in the hands of others to perform the same. But if the offender be to receive other punishment, he will not receive the same but from the *Sachim* himself, before whom being naked he kneeleth, and will not offer to run away though he beat him never so much, it being a greater disparagement for a man to cry during the time of his correction, than is his offence and punishment.

As for their apparel they wear breeches and stockings in one like some *Irish*, which is made of Deer skins, and have shoes of the same leather. They wear also a Deers skin loose about them like a cloak, which they will turn to the weather side. In this habit they travel, but when they are at home or come to their journeys end, presently they pull off their breeches, stockings, and shoes, wring out the water if they be wet, and dry them, and rub or chafe the same. Though these be off, yet have they another small garment that covereth their secrets. The men wear also when they go abroad in cold weather an Otter or Fox skin on their right arm, but only their bracer on the left. Women and all of that sex wear strings about their legs, which the men never do.

The people are very ingenious and observative, they keep account of time by the moon, and winters or summers; they know diverse of the stars by name, in particular, they know the North-star and call it maske, which is to say the bear. Also they have many names for the winds. They will guess very well at the wind and weather before hand, by observations in the heavens. They report also, that some of them can cause the wind to blow in what part they list, can raise storms and tempests which they usually do when they intend the death or destruction of other people, that by reason of the unseasonable weather they may take advantage of their enemies in their houses. At such times they perform their greatest exploits, and in such seasons when they are at enmity with any, they keep more careful watch than at other times.

As for the language it is very copious, large, and difficult, as yet we cannot attain to any great measure thereof; but can understand them, and explain our selves to their understanding, by the help of those that daily converse with us. And though there be difference in an hundred miles distance of place, both in language and manners, yet not so much but that they very well understand each other. And thus much of their lives and manners.

Instead of Records and Chronicles, they take this course,

where any remarkable act is done, in memory of it, either in the place, or by some path-way near adjoining, they make a round hole in the ground about a foot deep, and as much over, which when others passing by behold, they enquire the cause and occasion of the same, which being once known, they are careful to acquaint all men, as occasion serveth therewith. And lest such holes should be filled, or grown up by any accident, as men pass by they will oft renew the same: By which means many things of great Antiquity are fresh in memory. So that as a man travelleth, if he can understand his guide, his journey will be the less tedious, by reason of the many historical Discourses will be related unto him.

In all this it may be said, I have neither praised nor dispraised the Country: and since I lived so long therein, my judgment thereof will give no less satisfaction to them that know me, than the Relation of our proceedings. To which I answer, that as in one so of the other, I will speak as sparingly as I can, yet will make known what I conceive thereof.

And first for that Continent, on which we are called *New England*, although it hath ever been conceived by the English to be part of that main Land adjoining to *Virginia*, yet by relation of the *Indians* it should appear to be otherwise: for they affirm confidently, that it is an Island, and that either the *Dutch* or *French* pass through from Sea to Sea, between us and *Virginia*, and drive a great Trade in the same. The name of that inlet of the Sea they call *Mohegon*, which I take to be the same which we call *Hudsons*-River, up which Master *Hudson* went many Leagues, and for want of means (as I hear) left it undiscovered. For confirmation of this, their opinion is thus much; Though *Virginia* be not above an hundred and fifty Leagues from us, yet they never heard of *Powhatan*, or knew that any English were planted in his Country, save only by us and *Tisquantum*, who went in an English Ship thither: And therefore it is the more probable, because the water is not passable for them, who are very adventurous in their Boats.

Then for the temperature of the air, in almost three years experience, I can scarce distinguish *New-England* from *Old England*, in respect of heat, and cold, frost, snow, rain, winds, &c. Some object, because our Plantation lieth in the Latitude of 42. it must needs be much hotter. I confess, I cannot give the reason of the contrary; only experience teacheth us, that if it do exceed *England*, it is so little as must require better judgments to discern it. And for the Winter, I rather think (if there be difference) it is both sharper and longer in *New England* than *Old*; and yet the want of those comforts in the one which I have enjoyed in the other, may deceive my judgment also. But in my best observation, comparing our own condition with the Relations of other parts of America, I cannot conceive of any to agree better with the constitution of the English, not being oppressed with extremity of heat, nor nipped with biting cold, by which means, blessed be God, we enjoy our health, notwithstanding, those difficulties we have under-gone, in such a measure as would have been admired, if we had lived in *England* with the like means.

The day is two hours longer than here when it is at the shortest, and as much shorter there, when it is at the longest.

The soil is variable, in some places mould, in some clay, others, a mixed sand, &c. The chiefest grain is the *Indian* Mays, or *Ginny*-Wheat; the seed-time beginneth in midst of April, and continueth good till the midst of May. Our harvest beginneth with September. This corn increaseth in great measure, but is inferiour in quantity to the same in *Virginia*, the reason I conceive, is because *Virginia* is far hotter than it is with us, it requiring great heat to ripen; but whereas it is objected against *New-England*, that Corn will not there grow, except the ground be manured with fish? I answer, That where men set with fish (as with us) it is more easy so to do than to clear ground and set without some five or six years, and so begin anew, as in *Virginia* and else-where. Not but that in some places, where they cannot be taken with ease in such abundance, the *Indians* set four years together without, and have as good Corn or better than we have that set with them, though indeed I think if we had Cattle to till the ground, it would be more profitable and better agreeable to the soil, to sow Wheat, Rye, Barley, Peas, and Oats, than to set Mays, which our *Indians* call *Ewachim*: for we have had experience that they like and thrive well; and the other will not be procured without good labour and diligence, especially at seed-time, when it must also be watched by night to keep the Wolves from the fish, till it be rotten, which will be in fourteen days; yet men agreeing together, and taking their turns it is not much.

Much might be spoken of the benefit that may come to such as shall here plant by Trade with the *Indians* for Furs, if men take a right course for obtaining the same, for I dare presume upon that small experience I have had, to affirm, that the *English*, *Dutch*, and *French*, return yearly many thousand pounds profits by Trade only from that *Island*, on which we are seated.

Tobacco may be there planted, but not with that profit as in some other places, neither were it profitable there to follow it, though the increase were equal, because fish is a better and richer Commodity, and more necessary, which may be and are there had in as great abundance as in any other part of the world; Witness the West-country Merchants of *England*, which return incredible gains yearly from thence. And if they can so do which here buy their salt at a great charge, and transport more Company to make their voyage, than will sail their Ships, what may the planters expect when once they are seated, and make the most of their salt there, and employ themselves at least eight months in fishing, whereas the other fish but four, and have their ship lie dead in the harbour all the time, whereas such shipping as belong to plantations, may take freight of passengers or cattle thither, and have their lading provided against they come. I confess, we have come so far short of the means to raise such returns, as with great difficulty we have preserved our lives; insomuch, as when I look back upon our condition, and weak means to preserve the same, I rather admire at Gods mercy and providence in our preservation, than that no greater things have been effected by us. But though our beginning have been thus raw, small, and difficult, as thou hast seen, yet the same God that hath hitherto led us through the former, I hope will raise means to accomplish the latter. Not that we altogether, or principally propound profit to be the main end of that we have undertaken, but the glory of God, and the honour of our Country, in the enlarging of his Majesties Dominions, yet wanting outward means, to set things in that forwardness we desire, and to further the latter by the former, I thought meet to offer both to consideration, hoping that where Religion and profit jump together (which is rare) in so honourable an action, it will encourage every honest man, either in person or purse, to set forward the same, or at least-wise to commend the well-fare thereof in his daily prayers to the blessing of the blessed God.

I will not again speak of the abundance of fowl, store of Venison, and variety of Fish, in their seasons, which might encourage many to go in their persons, only I advise all such before hand to consider, that as they hear of Countries that abound with the good creatures of God, so means must be used for the taking of every one in his kind, and therefore not only to content themselves that there is sufficient, but to foresee how they shall be able to obtain the same, otherwise, as he that walketh *London* streets, though he be in the middest of plenty, yet if he want means, is not the better but hath rather his sorrow increased by the sight of that he wanteth, and cannot enjoy it: so also there, if thou want art and other necessaries thereunto belonging, thou mayest see that thou wantest, and thy heart desireth, and yet be never the better for the same. Therefore if thou see thine own insufficiency of thy self, then join to some others, where thou mayest in some measure enjoy the same, otherwise assure thy self, thou art better where thou art. Some there be that thinking altogether of their present wants they enjoy here, and not dreaming of any there, through indiscretion plunge themselves into a deeper sea of misery. As for example, it may be here, rent and firing are so chargeable, as without great difficulty a man cannot accomplish the same; never considering, that as he shall have no rent to pay, so he must build his house before he have it, and peradventure may with more ease pay for his fuel here, than cut and fetch it home, if he have not cattle to draw it there; though there is no scarcity but rather too great plenty.

I write not these things to dissuade any that shall seriously upon due examination set themselves to further the glory of God, and the honour of our Country, in so worthy an Enterprise, but rather to discourage such as with too great lightness undertake such courses, who peradventure strain themselves and their friends for their passage thither, and are no sooner there, than seeing their foolish imagination made void, are at their wits end, and would give ten times so much for their return, if they could procure it, and out of such discontented passions and humors, spare not to lay that imputation upon the Country, and others, which themselves deserve.

As for example, I have heard some complain of others for their large reports of *New-England*, and yet because they must drink water and want many delicates they here enjoyed, could presently return with their mouths full of clamours. And can any be so simple as to conceive that the fountains should stream forth Wine, or Beer, or the woods and rivers be like Butchers-shops, or Fish-mongers stalls, where they might have things taken to their hands. If thou canst not live without such things, and hast no means to procure the one, and wilt not take pains for the other, nor hast ability to employ others for thee, rest where thou art: for as a proud heart, a dainty tooth, a beggars purse, and an idle hand, be here intolerable, so that person that hath these qualities there, is much more abominable. If therefore God hath given thee a heart to undertake such courses, upon such grounds as bear thee out in all difficulties, *viz.* his glory as a principal, and all other outward good things but as accessories, which peradventure thou shalt enjoy, and it may be not: then thou wilt with true comfort and thankfulness receive the least of his mercies; whereas on the contrary, men deprive themselves of much happiness, being senseless of greater blessings, and through prejudice smother up the love and bounty of God, whose name be ever glorified in us, and by us, now and evermore. *Amen.*

FINIS.

A Postscript.

If any man desire a more ample relation of the State of this Country, before such time as this present relation taketh place, I refer them to the two former printed books: The one published by the President *and* Council *for* New-England, *and the other gathered by the Inhabitants of this Present Plantation at* Plimoth *in* New-England: *Both which books are to be sold by* John Bellamy, *at his shop at the three golden Lions in Corne-hill near the* Royal Exchange.

A brief Relation of a credible intelligence of the present
estate of VIRGINIA.

At the earnest entreaty of some of my much respected friends,
I have added to the former Discourse, a Relation of such things
as were credibly reported at *Plimoth* in *New-England* in *September* last past, concerning the present estate of *Virginia*. And
because men may doubt how we should have intelligence of
their Affairs, being we are so far distant, I will therefore satisfy
the doubtful therein. Captain *Francis West* being in *New-England* about the latter end of *May* past, sailed from thence to
Virginia, and returned in *August*: In *September* the same Ship
and Company being discharged by him at *Damarins*-Cove,
came to *New-Plimoth*, where upon our earnest enquiry after
the state of *Virginia* since that bloody slaughter committed
by the *Indians* upon our friends and Country-men, the whole
ships Company agreed in this; *Viz.* That upon all occasions
they chased the *Indians* to and fro, insomuch, as they sued
daily unto the *English* for peace, who for the present would
not admit of any; That Sr *George Early*, &c. was at that present employed upon service against them; That amongst many
others, *Opachancano* the chief Emperour was supposed to be
slain, his son also was killed at the same time. And though by
reason of these fore-named broils in the fore-part of the year,
the *English* had under-gone great want of food, yet through
Gods mercy there was never more shew of plenty, having as
much and as good Corn on the ground as ever they had; neither was the hopes of their *Tobacco*-crop inferiour to that of
their Corn: so that the Planters were never more full of encouragement, which I pray God long to continue, and so to direct
both them and us, as his glory may be the principal aim and
end of all our Actions, and that for his mercies sake,

AMEN.

FINIS.

THE EDITORS' COMMENT

Edward Winslow followed his contributions to *A Relation or Journall* with *Good News from New England*, which takes up the narrative of Plymouth Colony in 1621, with the settlers' anxieties about running out of supplies and their rumor-fueled fears that Narragansett, Massachusett, and Wampanoag people were preparing to attack the colony. In contrast to *Of Plimoth Plantation*, which was published long after the events Bradford discussed, Winslow had *Good News* published while he was briefly in England in 1624, immediately after the incidents it relates. Winslow's narrative was written from the perspective of a man who was learning how to conduct himself on Wampanoag lands: he described his travels in Wampanoag and Narragansett country, his reliance on Native guides like Tisquantum and Hobbomock, and his growing awareness of the Wampanoag diplomatic protocols necessary to the settlers' survival. Winslow paid careful attention to these details, locating places and people not in imagined maps of colonial claims (like Champlain's) or places made familiar by English place-names (as in Smith's *Description of New England*) but in Indigenous homelands where understanding territorial boundaries and how to approach Native leaders was critical. Yet Winslow's *Relation* also shows how Plymouth's diplomacy with its Indigenous neighbors could be precarious: in April 1623, Plymouth military leader Miles Standish and several other colonists killed seven Massachusett men they suspected of harboring a plot to attack Plymouth and a neighboring colony at Wessagusset (now Weymouth). As conflict and rumors overtook diplomacy that spring, the violence spread, as the Massachusett leader Obtaki-est killed three Wessagusset colonists before a belated message arrived from Plymouth attempting to make peace. Writing in the aftermath, Winslow attempted to convince the settlers' minister John Robinson and other supporters in England that they had not abandoned their charge to be examples of charity but acted in justifiable self-defense. *Good News* aimed to convince readers that what Winslow had to convey from Plymouth was indeed "good news," and the narrative represented Winslow's observations of Wampanoag people and homelands to assure readers of Plymouth's good relations with the Wampanoags, despite the colonists' use of preemptive violence against a neighboring Indigenous community.

Phenehas Pratt:
A Declaration of the Affairs

A DECLIRATION OF THE AFAIRES OF THE EINGLISH PEOPLE THAT FIRST INHABITED NEW EINGLAND.

In the Time of Sperituall darkness, when the State Eclei-sasti [   ] Roome Ruled & over Ruled most of the Nations of Urope, it plea [   ] to give wisdom to many, kings and people, in breaking that sperituall yo [   ]; yet, not with standing, there Arose great strif Among such people that ar knowne by the name of prodastonce, in many Cases Concerning the worship of God; but the greatest & strongest number of men Comonly pualed Against the smaller and lesor Number. At this time the honored States of Holland gave moore Liberty in Casses of Relidgon then could be injoyed in some other places. Upon wich divers good Cristians Removed the [   ] dwellings into the Low Cuntrys.

Then on Company that Dwelt in the Sitty of Laydon, being not well Able outwardly to subsist, tooke Counsell & Agred to Remove into Amerika, into some port Northward of Verginia. The Duch people ofored them divers Condishons to suply them with things Nesasary if thay would Live undor the Goverment of thayr State, but thay Refused it. This thay did that all men might know the Intier Love thay bore to thayr King & Cuntry; for in them ther was never found any lack of Lifill obedience. Thay sent to thayr freinds in Eingland to Let them Understand what thay intended to doe. Then divers fr[   ] Disbursed some monys for the ferthering of soe good a work.

It is f [   ] to be understod that, in the yeare 1618, ther apeared a blasing star over Garmany that maed the wiss men of Urope astonished thayr [   ].

Spedily after, near about that time, these people begun to propoes Removall. Thay Agred that thayr strongest & Ablest men should goe [   ] to provid for thayr Wiffs & children. Then Coming into Eingland, they sett forward in to ships, but thayr Leser ship sprung a leak & reterned [   ] Eingland; the biger ship Arived att Cape Codd, 1620 it being winter, then Caled new Eingland but formerly Caled Canidy. They sent forth thayr boat upon discovery. Thayr boat being Reterned to theyr Shipp, thay Removed into the bay of Plimoth & begun theyr planta [   ] by the River of Petuxet. Thayr Shipp being reterned & safly Arived in Eingland, those Gentlemen & Marchents, that had undertaken to suply them with things nesasary, understanding that many of them weare sick & some ded, maed hast to send a ship with many things nesasery; but som Indescret men, hoping to incoridg thayr freinds to Come to them, writ Letters Conserning the great plenty of fish fowle and deare, not considering that the wild Salvages weare many times hungrye, that have a better scill to catch such things then Einglish men have. The Adventurers, willing to saf thayr Monys, sent them weekly provided of vicktûalls, as Many moor after them did the lyke; & that was the great Cause of famine.

At the same time, Mr. Thomas Westorne, a Merchent of good credit in London, that was then thayr treshurer, that had disberst much of his Mony for the good of New Eingland, sent forth a ship for the settleing a plantation in the Massachusetts Bay, but wanting a pilote we Arived att Damoralls Cove. The men that belong to the ship, ther fishing, had newly set up a may pole & weare very mery. We maed hast to prepare a boat fit for costing. Then said Mr. Rodgers, Master of our ship, "heare ar Many ships & at Munhigin, but no man that does undertake to be your pilate; for they say that an Indian Caled Rumhigin undertook to pilot a boat to Plimoth, but thay all lost thayr Lives." Then said Mr. Gibbs, Mastrs Mate of our ship, "I will uenter my Live with them." At this Time of our discovery, we first Arived att Smithe's Ilands, first soe Caled by Capt. Smith, att the Time of his discovery of New Eingland, [   ] fterwards Caled Ilands of Sholes; from thence to Cape Ann [   ] so Caled by Capt Mason; from thence to the Mathechusits Bay. Ther we continued 4 or 5 days.

Then we pseaued, that on the south part of the Bay, weare fewest of the natives of the Cuntry Dwelling ther. We thought best to begine our plantation, but fearing A great Company of Salvages, we being but 10 men, thought it best to see if our friends weare Living at Plimoth. Then sayling Along the Cost, not knowing the harber, thay shot of a peece of Ardinance, and at our coming Ashore, thay entertaned us with 3 vally of shotts. Theyr seckond ship was Reterned for Eingland before we Came to them. We asked them wheare the Rest of our freinds weare that came in the first ship. Thay said that God had taken them Away by deth, & that before thayr seckond ship came, thay weare soe destresed with sicknes that thay, feareing the salvages should know it, had sett up thayr sick men with thayr muscits upon thayr Rests & thayr backs Leaning Aganst trees. At this Time, on or two of them went with us in our vesill to the place of fishing to bye vicktualls. 8 or 9 weeks after this, to of our ships Arived att Plimoth—the leser of our 3 ships continued in the Cuntry with us. Then we maed hast to settle our plantation in the Masachusets bay—our Number being neare sixty men. Att the same time ther was a great plag Among the salvagis, &, as them selfs told us, half thayr people died thereof. The Nativs caled the place of our plantation Wesaguscasit. Neare unto it is a towne of Later Time Caled Weymoth.

The Salvagis seemed to be good freinds with us while they feared us, but when they see famin prevall, they begun to insult, as apeareth by the seaquell; for on of thayr Pennesses or Chef men, Caled Pexsouth, implyed himself to Learne to speek Einglish, obsarving all things for his blody ends. He told me he Loved Einglish men very well, but he Loved me best of all. Then he said, "you say french men doe not love you, but I will tell you what wee have don to them. Ther was a ship broken by a storm. Thay saved most of theyr goods & hid it in the Ground. We maed them tell us whear it was. Then we maed them our sarvants. Thay weept much. When we parted them, we gave them such meat as our dogs eate. On of them had a Booke he would ofen Reed in. We Asked him "what his Booke said." He answered, "It saith, ther will a people, lick French men, com into this Cuntry and drive you all a way, & now we thincke you ar thay. We took Away thayr Clothes. Thay lived but a little while. On of them Lived Longer than the Rest, for he had a good master & gave him a wiff. He is now ded, but hath a sonn Alive. An other Ship Came into the bay with much goods to Trucke, then I said to the Sacham, I will tell you how you shall have all for nothing. Bring all our Canows & all our Beaver & a great many men, but no bow nor Arow Clubs,

nor Hachits, but knives under the scins that About our Lines.
Throw up much Beaver upon thayr Deck; sell it very Cheep &
when I give the word, thrust your knives in the French mens
Bellys. Thus we killed them all. But Mounsear Finch, Master
of thayr ship, being wounded, Leped into the hold. We bidd
him com up, but he would not. Then we cutt thayr Cable & the
ship went Ashore & lay upon her sid & slept ther. Finch Came
up & we killed him. Then our Sachem devided thayr goods
& fiered theyr Ship & it maed a very great fier." Som of our
Company Asked them "how long it was Agow sinc thay first see
ships?" Thay said thay could not tell, but thay had heard men
say the first ship that thay see, seemed to be a floting Iland, as
thay suposed broken of from the maine Land, wrapt together
with the roats of Trees, with some trees upon it. Thay went to
it with thayr Canows, but seeing men & hearing guns, thay
maed hast to be gon.

But after this, when thay saw famin prevale, Peckworth said,
"why doe your men & your dogs dy?" I said, "I had Corn for a
Time of need. Then I filed a Chest, but not with Corne & spred
Corn on [   ] him Com opened the Cover and when I was
shure he see it, I put dow [   ] as if I would not have him see
it." Then he said "No Indian Soe [   ] You have much Corne
& Einglish men dye for want." Then thay h [   ] intent to
make warr thay Removed some of thayr howses to th[   ] a
great swamp neare to the pale of our plantation. After this yer
[   ] a morning I see a man goeing into on of thayr howses,
weary with trafelling & Galded on his feet. Then I said to Mr.
Salsbery, our Chirurgeon, shurly thayr Sacham hath implyed
him for som intent to make war upon us. Then I took a Bagg
with gunpowder and putt it in my pockitt, with the Top of
the bagg hanging out, & went to the house whear the man
was laid upon a matt. The woman of the howse took hold of
the bagg, saying, what is this soe bigg? I said it is good for
Salvagis to eat, and strock hur on the Arm as hard as I could.
Then she said, Matchet powder Einglish men, much Matchit.
By and by Abordicis bring Mouch Mans, Mouch Sannups, &
kill you & all Einglish men att Wessaguscus & Patuckset. The
man that lay upon the mats, seeing this, was Angry and in a
great Rage, and the woman seemed to be sore afraid. Then I
went out of the howse, and said to a young man that could best

understand thayr Langwig, goe Aske the woman, but not in the man's hearing, why the man was Agry, & shee Afraid? Our interpreter, Coming to me, said, "these are the words of the woman—the man will [   ] Abordicis what I said & he & all Indians will be angry with me [   ]" This Peexworth said, "I love you." I said "I love you." I said "I love you as well as you Love me." Then he said, in broken Einglish, "me heare you can make the Lickness of men & of women, dogs & dears, in wood & stone. Can you make [   ]" I said, "I can see a knive in your hand, with an Ill favored fase upon the haft." Then he gave it into my hand to see his workmanship, & said, "this knive cannot see, it Can not heare, it Can not spek, but by & by it can eat. I have Another knive at home with a fase upon the haft as lick a man as this is lick a woman. That knive Can not see, it Can not heare, it Can not speke, but it can eat. It hath killed much, french men, & by & by this knive & that knive shall mary & you shall be thear[   ] knive at home he had kep for a moniment, from the tim they had killed Mounsear Finch;" but as the word went out of his mouth, I had a good will to thrust it in his belly. He said, "I see you ar much angry." I said, "Guns ar Longer then knivs."

Som tim after this thar Sacham Cam sudingly upon us with a great numbor of Armed men; but thayr spys seeing us in a Redines, he & some of his Chif men, terned into on of thar howses a quartor of An our. Then wee met them wthout the pale of our plantation & brought them in. Then said I to a yong man that could best speke thayr Langwig, "Aske Pexworth whi thay com thus Armed." He Answered, "our Sacham is angry with you." I said, "Tell him if he be Angry with us, wee be Angry with him." Then said thayr Sachem, "Einglish men, when you Com into the Cuntry, we gave you gifts and you gave us gifts; we bought and sold with you and we weare freinds; and now tell me if I or any of my men have don you Rong." We answered, "First tell us if we have don you Any Rong." He answered, "Some of you steele our Corne & I have sent you word times wthout number & yet our Corne is stole. I come to see what you will doe." We answered, "It is on man wich hath don it. Your men have seen us whip him divers times, besids other manor of punishments, & now heare he is Bound. We give him unto you to doe with him what you please." He answered, "that is not just dealeing. If my men wrong my nabur sacham, or his men, he sends me word & I beat or kill my men, acording to the ofenc. If his men wrong me or my men, I send him word & he beats or kills his men Acording to the ofence. All Sachams do Justis by thayr own men. If not we say they ar all Agreed & then we fite, & now I say you all steele my Corne."

At this Time som of them, seeing som of our men upon our forte, begun to start, saying, "Machit Pesconk," that is nawty Guns. Then Looking Round about them went a way in a great Rage. Att this Time we strenthened our wach untell we had no food left. In thes times the Salvagis ofentime did Crep upon the snow, starting behind Boushes & trees to see whether we kepe wach or not [   ] times I haveing Rounded our plantation untell I had no longer [   ] nth; then in the night, goeing into our Corte of Gard, I see on man ded before me & Another at my writ hand & An other att my left for want of food. O all the people in New Eingland that shall heare of these times of our week beginning, Consider what was the strenth of the Arm of flesh or the witt of man; therfor in the times of your greatest distres put your trust in God.

The ofendor being bound, we lett him louse, because we had no food to give him, Charging him to gather Ground Nutts, Clams, & Musells, as other men did, & steel no more. On or two days after this, the salvagis brot him, leading him by the armes, saying "Heare is the Corne. Com see the plase wheare he stole it." Then we kep him bound som few days. After this, to of our Company said "we have bin at the Sachem's howse & thay have near finished thayr last Canoe that thay may incounter with our ship. Thayr greatest Care is how to send thayr Army's to Plimoth because of the snow. Then we prepared to meet them there. On of our Company said "thay have killed on of our hogs." An other said, "on of them striked (?) at me with his knife;" & others say "they threw dust in our fases." Then said Pexworth to me, "give me powder & Gunns & I will give you much corne." I said, "by & by men bring ships & vittls." But when we understod that their plot was to kill all Einglish people in on day when the snow was gon, I would have sent a man to Plimoth, but non weare willing to goe. Then I said if Plimoth men know not of this Trecherous plot, they & we are all ded men; Therefore if God willing, to morrow I will goe. That night a yong man, wanting witt, towld Pexworth yearly in the Morning. Pexworth came to me & said in Einglish, "Me heare you goe to Patuxit; you will loose your self; the bears and the wolfs will eate you; but because I Love you I will send my boy Nahamit with you; & I will give you vicktualls to eat by the way & to be mery with your freinds when you Com there." I said; "Who towld you soe great a Lye that I may kill him." He said, "it is noe lye, you shall not know." Then he went whom to his howse. Then Came 5 men Armed. We said, "Why Com you thus Armed." They said, "we are freinds; you cary Guns wheare we dwell & we cary bowe & Arows wheare you dwell." Thes Atended me 7 or 8 days & nights. Then thay suposeing it was a lye, wheare Carlis of thayr wach near two ours on the morning. Then said I to our Company, "now is the Time to Run to Plimoth. Is ther any Compas to be found." Thay said, "non but them that belong to the ship." I said "thay are to Bigg. I have born no armes of Defence this 7 or 8 days. Now if I take my armes thay will mistrust me." Then thay said "The salvages will pshue after you & kill you & we shall never see you Agayne." Thus with other words of great Lamentation, we parted. Then I took a how & went to the Long Swamp neare by thayr howses & diged on the ege thereof as if I had bin looking for ground nutts, but seeing no man I went in & Run through it. Then Looking Round a bout me, I Run Southward tell 3 of the Clock, but the snow being in many places, I was the more distresed becaus of my foot steps. The sonn being beclouded, I wandered, not knowing my way; but att the Goeing down of the sonn, it apeared Red; then hearing a great howling of wolfs, I came to a River; the water being depe & cold & many Rocks, I pased through with much adoe. Then was I in great distres—fant for want of food, weary with Running, fearing to make a fier because of them that pshued me. Then I came to a depe dell or hole, ther being much wood falen into it. Then I said in my thoughts, this is God's providence that heare I may make a fier. Then haveing maed a fier, the stars began to a pear and I saw Ursa Magor & the [   ] pole yet fearing [   ] beclouded. The day following I began to trafell [   ] but being unable, I went back to the fier the day fall [   ] sonn shined & about

three of the clock I came to that part [   ] Plimoth bay wher
ther is a Town of Later Time [   ] Duxbery. Then passing by
the water on my left hand [   ] cam to a brock & ther was a
path. Haveing but a short Time to Consider [   ] fearing to
goe beyond the plantation, I kept Running in the path; then
passing through James Ryver I said in my thoughts, now am
I as a deare Chased [   ] the wolfs. If I perish, what will be
the Condish [   ] of distresed Einglish men. Then finding
a peec of a [   ] I took it up & Caried it in my hand. Then
finding a [   ] of a Jurkin, I Caried them under my arme.
Then said I in my [   ] God hath given me these two tookens
for my Comfort; that now he will give me my live for a pray.
Then Running down a hill J [   ] an Einglish man Coming
in the path before me. Then I sat down on a tree & Rising up
to salute him said, "Mr. Hamdin, I am Glad to see you alive."
He said "I am Glad & full of wonder to see you alive: lett us
sitt downe, I see you are weary." I said, "Let [   ] eate som
parched corne." Then he said "I know the Caus [   ] Come.
Masasoit hath sent word to the Governor to let him (   ) that
Aberdikees & his Confederates have contrived a plot hopeing
[   ] all Einglish people in on day heare as men hard by (ma)
king Canoe [   ] stay & we will goe with you. The next day
a yong [   ] named Hugh Stacye went forth to fell a tree
& see two [   ] rising from the Ground. They said Aberdikees had sent [   ] the Governor that he might send men
to trucke for much Beaver, but thay would not goe, but said,
"Was not ther An Einglish [   ] Come from Wesaguscus."
He Answered "he came" [   ] Thay said he was thayr friend,
and said come and see who [   ] But they Terned another
way. He said, "You come to let us [   ]" Providence to us was
great in those times as apeareth [   ] after the time of the
Arivall of the first ship at pl [   ] fornamed Masasoit Came to
Plimoth & thayr maed a co [   ] peace, for an Indian Caled
Tisquantom Came to them & spek Einglish [   ] Thay Asked
him, how he learned to speeke Einglish? He said that An Ein-
glishman Caled Capt Hunt Came into the Harbor pretending
to trade for beaver & stoole 24 men & thayr beavr & Caried
& Sould them in Spaine. & from thence with much adoe he
went into Eingland & from Eingland with much adoe he gott
into his owne Cuntry. This man tould Masasoit what wonders

he had seen in Eingland & that if he Could make Einglish his freinds then [   ] Enemies that weare to strong for him would be Constrained to bowe to him; but being prevented by some that Came in the first ship that [   ] Recorded that wich Conserned them I leave it.

Two or 3 days after my Coming to Plimoth, 10 or 11 men went in a boat to our plantation, but I being fanted was not able to goe with them. They first gave warning to the master of the ship & then Contrived how to make sure of the Lives of to of thayr Cheef men, Wittiwomitt, of whom they bosted no Gun would kill, and Pexworth, a suttle man. These being slaine they fell opon others wheare thay could find them. Then Abordikees, hearing that some of his men weare killed, Came to try his manwhod, but as thay weare starting behind bushes & trees, on of them was shott in the Arme. At this time An Indian caled Hobermack, that formerly had fleed for his live from his Sacham to Plimoth, aproved himself a valient man in fiting & pshuing after them. Two of our men were killed that thay took in thayr howses att An Advantage [   ] this Time pl [   ] weare instruments in the [   ] nds of God for [   ] thayr own lives and ours. Thay tooke the head of [   ] & sett it on thayr fort att Plimoth att [   ] 9 (?) of our men weare ded with famine and on died in the ship before thay Came to the place whear at that Time of yeare ships Came to fish—it being in March. At this Time ships began to fish at the Islands of Sholes and I haveing Recovered a Little of my [   ]th went to my Company near about this Time [   ] the first planta-tion att Pascataqua the [   ] thereof was Mr. David Tomson at the time of my arivall (?) att Pascataqua. To of Abordikees men Came thither & seeing me said, "when we killed your men thay cried and maed Il favored fases." I said, "when we killed your men, we did not Torment them to make ourself(?) mery." Then we went with our ship into the bay & took from them two Shalops Loading of Corne & of thayr men prisoners ther as a Towne of Later Time Caled Dorchester. The third and last time was in the bay of Agawam. At this Time they took for thayr casell a thick swamp. At this time on of our ablest men was shot in the sholder. Wether Any of them wear killed or wounded we could not tell. Ther is a Town of Later time, neare unto that place Caled Ipswich. Thus [   ] plantation being deserted, Capt. Robert Gore cam [   ] the Cuntry with six gentlemen Atending him & divers men to doe his Labor & other men with thayr familys. Thay took possession of our plantation, but thayr ship suply from Eingland Came to late. Thus was famine thayr final oforthrow. Most of them that lived Reterned for Eingland. The oforseers of the third plantation in the bay was Capt. Wooliston & Mr. Rosdell. Thes seeing the Ruing of the former plantation, said, we will not pich our Tents heare, least we should doe as thay have Done. Notwithstanding these Gentlemen wear wiss men, thay seemed to blame the oforseeors of the formur Companies not Considering that God plants & pull up Bilds & pulls down & terns the wisdom of wiss men into foolishness. These Caled the name of thayr place Mountwooliston. They Continued neare a yeare as others had don before them; but famin was thayr finall aforthrow. Neare unto that place is a Town of Lator Time Caled Brantry. Not long after the oferthrow of the first plantation in the bay, Capt. Louit Cam to your Cuntry. At the Time of his being at Pascataway a Sacham or Sagamor Gave two of his men, on to Capt. Louit & An other to Mr. Tomson, but on that was ther said, "How can you trust these Salvagis. Cale the nam of on Watt Tylor, & the other Jack Straw, after the names of the two greatest Rebills that ever weare in Eingland." Watt Tylor said "when he was a boy Capt. Dormer found him upon an Island in great distress."

THE EDITORS' COMMENT

Pratt first presented *A Declaration of the Affairs of the English People that First Inhabited New England* as a manuscript to the Massachusetts Bay General Court in 1662, as an appeal for land and financial assistance. However, Pratt described events in the spring of 1623, when he had traveled to Massachusett homelands as part of a settlement funded by Thomas Weston, one of the merchant "Adventurers" who funded Plymouth Colony in exchange for an expected return on his investment. In 1622, Weston sent indentured servants to settle land at Wessagusset (now Weymouth), but the new settlement struggled from the beginning, quickly running out of food and relying on Plymouth, which begrudgingly shared its meager stores. Some Wessagusset settlers also left the settlement and lived with Massachusett people, finding more opportunities for food and shelter. But other Wessagusset settlers stole corn from Massachusett people, leading Massachusett leaders to bring complaints against this behavior to Plymouth. Some Wessagusset and Plymouth colonists feared that the theft would be met with violent retribution from the Massachusett, and the settlers interpreted actions by other Native leaders and rumors conveyed by Tisquantum as signs of an impending attack on the settlements. Pratt's *Declaration* describes the days leading up to Plymouth's preemptive attack on the Massachusett and his terrifying journey from Wessagusset to warn Plymouth that he believed the Massachusett were planning to attack.

William Bradford:
Of Plimoth Plantation

Of Plimmoth Plantation

And first of the occasion and Indusments ther unto; the which that I may truly unfould, I must begine at the very roote and rise of the same. The which I shall endevor to manefest in a plaine stile; with singuler regard unto the simple trueth in all things, at least as near as my slender Judgmente can attaine the same.

·1· CHAPTER

IT is well knowne unto the godly and judicious, how ever since the first breaking out of the lighte of the gospell, in our Honourable Nation of England (which was the first of nations, whom the Lord adorned ther with, affter that grosse darknes of popery which had covered, and overspred the christian worled) what warrs, and oppossissions ever since Satan hath raised, maintained, and continued against the Saincts, from time, to time, in one sorte, or other. Some times by bloody death and cruell torments, other whiles Imprisonments, banishments, and other hard usages. As being loath his kingdom should goe downe, the trueth prevaile; and the churches of God reverte to their anciente puritie; and recover their primative order, libertie, and bewtie. But when he could not prevaile by these means, against the maine trueths of the gospell, but that they began to take rootting in many places; being watered with the blooud of the martires, and blessed from heaven with a gracious encrease; He then begane to take him to his anciente strategemes, used of old against the first christians. That when by the bloody, and barbarous persecutions of the Heathen Emperours, he could not stoppe, and subverte the course of the Gospell; but that it speedily overspred, with a wounderfull celeritie, the then best known parts, of the world; He then begane to sow errours, heresies, and wounderfull dissentions amongst the proffessours them selves (working upon their pride, and ambition, with other corrupte passions, incidente to all mortall men; yea to the saints them selves in some measure.) By which wofull effects followed; as not only bitter contentions, and hartburnings, schismes, with other horrible confusions. But Satan tooke occasion and advantage therby to foyst in a number of vile ceremoneys, with many unproffitable Cannons, and decrees which have since been as snares, to many poore and peaceable souls, even to this day. So as in the anciente times, the persecutiaons by the heathen, and their Emperours, was not greater then of the christians one against other. The Arians, and other their complices, against the orthodoxe and true christians. As witneseth Socrates in his ·2· booke. His words are these; *the violence truly (saith he) was no less then that of ould, practised towards the christians when they were compelled, and drawne to sacrifice to Idoles; for many endured sundrie kinds of tormente, often rackings, and dismembering of their joynts; confiscating of ther goods; some bereaved of their native soyle; others departed this life under the hands of the tormentor, and some died in banishmente, and never saw ther cuntrie again &c.*

The like methode Satan hath seemed to hold in these later times, since the trueth begane to springe and spread after the great defection made by Antichrist that man of sinne.

For to let pass the infinite examples in sundrie nations, and severall places of the world, and instance in our owne. When as that old Serpente could not prevaile by those firie flames and other his cruell Tragedies which he (by his instruments) put in ure, every wher in the days of queene Mary, and before. He then begane an other kind of warre, and went more closely to worke, not only to oppuggen, but even to ruinate and destroy the kingdom of christ, by more secrete and subtile means, by kindling the flames of contention, and sowing the seeds of discorde, and bitter enmitie amongst the proffessors (and seeming reformed) them selves. For when he could not prevaile (by the former means) against the principall doctrines of faith; he bente his force against the holy disipline, and outward regimente of the kingdom of christ, by which those holy doctrines should be conserved, and true pietie maintained amongest the saints, and people of God.

Mr. Foxe recordeth, how that besides those worthy martires and conffessors which were burned in queene Marys days and otherwise tormented,* *many (both studients, and others) fled out of the land, to the number of ·800. And became severall congregations. At Wesell, Frankford, Bassill, Emden, Markpurge, Strausborugh, and Geneva, &c.* Amongst whom (but especialy those at Frankford) begane that bitter warr of contention and persecution aboute the ceremonies, and servise-booke, and other popish and antichristian stuffe, the plague of England to this day, which are like the highplases in Israell, which the prophets cried out against, and were their ruine; Which the better parte sought, (according to the puritie of the gospell,) to roote out, and utterly to abandon. And the other parte (under veiled pretences) for their ouwn ends, and advancments, sought as stifly, to continue, maintaine, and defend. As appeareth by the discourse therof published in printe, Anno: 1575· (a booke that deserves better to be knowne, and considred.)

The one side laboured to have the right worship of God, and discipline of christ, established in the church, according to the simplisitie of the Gospell; without the mixture of mens inventions. And to have and to be ruled by the laws of Gods word; dispensed in those offices, and by those officers of pastors, Teachers, and Elders, &c., according to the Scriptures. The other partie, (though under many colours, and pretences) endevored to have the Episcopal dignitie (affter the popish maner) with their large power, and jurisdiction, still retained; with all those courts, cannons, and ceremonies, togeather with all shuch livings, revenues, and subordinate officers, with other shuch means, as formerly upheld their antichristian greatnes. And enabled them with lordly, and tyranous power to persecute the poore servants of God. This contention was so great, as neither the honour of God, the commone persecution, nor the mediation of Mr. Calvin, and other worthies of the Lord, in those places, could prevaile with those thus Episcopally minded, but they proceeded by all means to disturbe the peace of this poor persecuted church. Even so farr as to charge (very unjustly, and ungodlily; yet prelate-like) some of their cheefe

*Acts and Mon: pag. 1587. editi: 2.

opposers, with rebellion, and high treason against the Emperour, and other shuch crimes.

And this contention dyed not with queene Mary; nor was left beyonde the seas, but at her death these people returning into England under gracious queene Elizabeth, many of them being preferred to bishopriks, and other promotions, according to their aimes and desires. That inveterate hatered against the holy discipline of christ in his church hath continued to this day. In somuch that for fear it should preveile, all plotts, and devices have been used to keepe it out, incensing the queene, and state against it as dangerous for the common wealth; And that it was most needfull that the fundamentall poynts of Religion should be preached in those ignorante, and superstitious times; And to wine the weake and ignorante they might retaine divers harmles ceremoneis, and though it were to be wished that diverse things were reformed, yet this was not a season for it. And many the like to stop the mouthes of the more godly. To bring them over to yeeld to one ceremonei after another; and one corruption after another; by these wyles begyleing some, and corrupting others till at length they begane to persecute all the zealous proffessors in the land (though they knew little what this discipline mente) both by word, and deed, if they would not submitte to their ceremonies, and become slaves to them, and their popish trash, which have no ground in the word of God, but are relikes of that man of sine. And the more the light of the gospell grew, the more they urged their subscriptions to these corruptions. So as (notwithstanding all their former pretences, and fair colures) they whose eyes God had not justly blinded might easily see wherto these things tended. And to cast contempte the more upon the sincere servants of God; they opprobriously and most injuriously, gave unto, and imposed upon them, that name of Puritans; which it is said the Novatians (out of prid) did assume and take unto themselves.* And lamentable it is to see the effects which have followed; Religion hath been disgraced, the godly greeved, afflicted, persecuted, and many exiled, sundrie have lost their lives in prisones, and otherways. On the other hand, sin hath been countenanced; ignorance, profannes, and

*Eus: lib: 6. Chap. 42.

Atheisme increased, and the papists encouraged to hope againe for a day.

This made that holy man Mr. Perkins* crie out in his exhortation to repentance, upon Zeph. 2. Religion (saith he) hath been amongst us this ·35· years; but the more it is published, the more it is contemned, and reproached of many, &c. Thus not prophanes nor wickedness; but Religion it selfe is a byword, a moking-stock, and a matter of reproach; so that in England at this day, the man or woman that begines to profes Religion, and to serve God, must resolve with him selfe to sustaine mocks and injueries even as though he lived amongst the enimies of Religion. And this commone experience hath confirmed, and made too apparente.

A late observation, as it were by the way, worthy to be noted.

Full litle did I thinke, that the downfall of the Bishops, with their courts, cannons, and ceremonies, &c. had been so neare, when I first begane these scribled writings (which was aboute the year 1630, and so peeced up at times of leasure afterward) or that I should have lived, to have seene, or heard of the same; but it is the lords doing, and ought to be marvelous in our eyes! Every plante which mine heavenly father hath not planted, (saith our saviour) shall be rooted up. Mat: 15. 13. I have snared the, and thou art taken, O Babell [Bishops] and thou wast not aware; thou art found, and also caught, because thou hast striven against the Lord. Jer. 50. 24. But will they needs strive? against the truth, against the servants of God, what, and against the Lord him selfe? Doe they provoke the Lord to anger? Are they stronger than he? 1. Cor: 10. 22. No, no, they have mete with their match. Behold, I come unto the, O proud man, saith the Lord god of hosts; for thy day is come, even the time that I will visite the. Jer: 50. 31. May not the people of God now say, (and these pore people among the rest), the lord, hath brought forth our righteousnes; come let us declare in Sion the work of the lord our god. Jer: 51. 10. Let all flesh be still before the lord; for he is raised up out of his holy place. Zach: 2. 13.

In this case, these poore people may say (among the thousands of Israll) *when the lord brougt againe the captivite of Zion, we were like them that dreame. Psa:* 126. 1. *The lord hath done greate things for us, wherof we rejoyce. v.* 3. *They that sow in teares, shall reap in joye. They wente weeping, and carried precious seede, but they shall returne with joye, and bring their sheaves. v.* 5. 6.

*Pag. 421.

Doe you not now see the fruits of your labours, O all yee servants of the lord? that have suffered for his truth, and have been faithfull witneses of the same, and yee litle handfull amongst the rest, the least amongest the thousands of Israll? You have not only had a seede time, but many of you have seene the joyefull Harvest. Should you not then rejoyse? yea, and againe rejoyce, and say Hallelu-iah, salvation, and glorie, and honour, and power, be to the lord our God; for true, and righteous are his Judgments. Rev. 19. 1, 2.

But thou wilte aske what is the mater, what is done? Why, art thou a stranger, in Israll, that thou shouldest not know what is done? Are not those Jebusites overcome, that have vexed the people of Israll so long, even holding Jerusalem till David's days, and been as thorns in their sides, so many ages; and now begane to scorne that any David should meadle with them; they begane to fortifie their tower, as that of the old babelonians; but those proud Anakimes are throwne downe, and their glory laid in the dust. The tiranous bishops are ejected, their courts disolved, their cannons forceless, their servise casheired, their ceremonies uselese and despised; their plots for popery prevented, and all their superstitions discarded, and returned to Roome from whence they came, and the monuments of idolatrie rooted out of the land. And the proud and profane suporters, and cruell defenders of these, (as bloody papists and wicked Atheists, and their malignante consorts) marvelously over throwne. And are not these greate things? Who can deney it?

But who hath done it? Who, even he that siteth on the white horse, who is caled faithfull, and true, and judgeth, and fighteth righteously. Rev: 19. 11. Whose garments are dipte in blood, and his name was caled the word of God. v. 13. For he shall rule them with a rode of Iron; for it is he that treadeth the winepress of the feircenes, and wrath of god almighty! And he hath upon his garmente, and upon his thigh, a name writen, The King of Kings, and Lord of Lords. v. 15, 16.

HALLELU-IAH.

Anno Dom: 1646.

But that I may come more near my Intendmente; when as by the travell, and diligence of some godly, and zealous preachers, and Gods blessing on their labours; as in other places of the land, so in the North parts, many became inlightened by the word of God; and had their ignorance and sins discovered unto them, and begane by his grace to reforme their lives, and make conscience of their wayes. The worke of God was no sooner manifest in them; but presently they were both scoffed and scorned by the prophane multitude, and the ministers urged

with the yoak of subscription, or els must be silenced; and
the poore people were so vexed with apparators, and pursu-
ants, and the comissarie courts, as truly their affliction was not
smale; which notwithstanding they bore sundrie years with
much patience, till they were occasioned (by the continuance,
and encrease of these troubles, and other means which the
Lord raised up in those days) to see further into things by the
light of the word of God. How not only these base and beggerly ceremoneis were unlawfull; but also that the lordly and
tiranous power of the prelates, ought not to be submitted unto;
which thus (contrary to the freedome of the gospell,) would
load and burden mens consciences; and by their compulsive
power make a prophane mixture of persons, and things in the
worship of God. And that their offices and calings; courts and
cannons &c. were unlawfull and Antichristian; being shuch as
have no warrante in the word of God; but the same that were
used in poperie, and still retained. Of which a famous author
thus writeth in his dutch commentaries.* At the coming of
king James into England; *The new king* (*saith he*) *found their
established the reformed Religion, according to the reformed religion of king Edward the ·6· Retaining, or keeping still the spirituall state of the Bishops, &c. after the ould maner, much varying
and differing from the reformed churches, in Scotland, France,
and the Neatherlands, Embden, Geneva, &c. whose Reformation
is cut, or shapen much nerer the first Christian churches, as it was
used in the Apostles times.*†

So many therfore (of these proffessors) as saw the evill of
these things (in thes parts,) and whose harts the Lord had
touched with heavenly zeale for his trueth; they shooke of this
yoake of Antichristian bondage. And as the Lords free people,
joyned them selves (by a covenant of the Lord) into a church
estate, in the felowship of the Gospell, to walke in all his wayes,
made known, or to be made known unto them (according to
their best endeavours) whatsoever it should cost them, the

---

*Em: meter: lib: 25. fol. 119.

†The reformed churches shapen much neerer the primitive patterne *then
England*, for they cashered the Bishops with al their courts, cannons, and
ceremoneis, at the first; and left them amongst the popishtrash to which they
pertained.

Lord assisting them. And that it cost them something this ensewing historie will declare.

These people became ·2· distincte bodys or churches; and in regarde of distance of place did congregate severally; for they were of sundrie townes and vilages, some in Notingamshire, some of Lincollinshire, and some of Yorkshire, wher they border nearest togeather. In one of these churches (besides others of note) was Mr. John Smith, a man of able gifts, and a good preacher; who afterwards was chosen their pastor. But these afterwards falling into some errours in the Low Countries, ther (for the most part) buried themselves, and their names.

But in this other church (which must be the subjecte of our discourse) besides other worthy men, was Mr. Richard Clifton, a grave and reverend preacher, who by his paines and dilligens had done much good, and under god had ben a means of the conversion of many. And also that famous and worthy man Mr. John Robinson, who affterwards was their pastor for many years, till the Lord tooke him away by death. Also Mr. William Brewster a reverent man, who afterwards was chosen an Elder of the church and lived with them till old age.

But after these things; they could not long continue in any peaceable condition; but were hunted and persecuted on every side, so as their former afflictions were but as flea-bitings in comparison of these which now came upon them. For some were taken and clapt up in prison, others had their houses besett and watcht night and day, and hardly escaped their hands; and the most were faine to flie and leave their howses and habitations, and the means of their livelehood. Yet these and many other sharper things which affterward befell them, were no other then they looked for, and therfore were the better prepared to bear them by the assistance of Gods grace and spirite; yet seeing them selves thus molested, and that ther was no hope of their continuance ther, by a joynte consente they resolved to goe into the Low-Countries, wher they heard was freedome of Religion for all men; as also how sundrie from London, and other parts of the land had been exiled and persecuted for the same cause, and were gone thither; and lived at Amsterdam, and in other places of the land. So affter they had continued togeither aboute a year, and kept their meetings every Saboth, in one place, or other, exercising the worship of God amongst them selves, notwithstanding all the dilligence and malice of their adverssaries, they seeing they could no longer continue in that condition, they resolved to get over into Holland as they could. Which was in the year ·1607· and ·1608· of which more at large in the next chapter.

·2· CHAPTER
Of their departure into Holland and their troubles ther aboute, with some of the many difficulties they found and mete withall.
Anno 1608.

B EING thus constrained to leave their native soyle and coun- trie, their lands and livings, and all their freinds, and famil- lier aquaintance, it was much; and thought marvelous by many. But to goe into a countrie they knew not (but by hearsay) wher they must learne a new language, and get their livings they knew not how, it being a dear place, and subjecte to the misseries of warr, it was by many thought an adventure almost desperate, a case intolerable, and a misserie worse then death. Espetially seeing they were not aquainted with trades nor traf- fique (by which that countrie doth subsiste) but had only been used to a plaine countrie life, and the inocente trade of hus- bandrey. But these things did not dismay them (though they did some times trouble them) for their desires were sett on the ways of god, and to injoye his ordinances; but they rested on his providence, and knew whom they had beleeved. Yet this was not all, for though they could not stay, yet were they not suf- fered to goe, but the ports, and havens were shut against them, so as they were faine to seeke secrete means of conveance, and to bribe and fee the mariners, and give exterordinarie rates for their passages. And yet were they often times betrayed (many of them) and both they and their goods intercepted and sur- prised, and therby put to great trouble, and charge, of which I will give an instance or tow, and omitte the rest.

Ther was a large companie of them purposed to get passage at Boston in Lincolin-shire, and for that end, had hired a shipe wholy to them selves; and made agreement with the maister to be ready at a certaine day, and take them, and their goods in, at a conveniente place, wher they accordingly would all attende in readines. So after long waiting, and large expences (though he kepte not day with them) yet he came at length and tooke them in, in the night; But when he had them and their goods abord, he betrayed them, haveing before hand complotted with the serchers, and other officers so to doe. Who tooke them, and put them into open boats, and ther rifled and ransaked them, searching them to their shirts for money, yea even the women furder then became modestie; and then caried them back into the towne, and made them a spectackle, and wonder to the multitude, which came flocking on all sides to behould them. Being thus first, by the chatchpoule officers, rifled, and stripte of their money, books, and much other goods; they were presented to the majestrates, and messengers sente to informe the lords of the Counsell of them; and so they were commited to ward. Indeed the majestrats used them courteously, and shewed them what favour they could; but could not deliver them, till order came from the Counsell-table. But the issue was that after a months imprisonmente, the greatest parte were dismiste, and sent to the places from whence they came; but ·7· of the principall were still kept in prison, and bound over to the Assises.

The nexte spring after, ther was another attempte made by some of these and others; to get over at an other place. And it so fell out, that they light of a Dutchman at Hull, having a ship of his owne belonging to Zealand; they made agreemente with him, and aquainted him with their condition, hoping to find more faithfullness in him, then in the former of their owne nation; he bad them not fear, for he would doe well enough. He was (by appointment) to take them in betweene Grimsbe, and Hull, wher was a large commone a good way distante from any towne. Now against the prefixed time, the women and children, with the goods, were sent to the place in a small barke, which they had hired for that end; and the men were to meete them by land. But it so fell out, that they were ther a day before the shipe came, and the sea being rough, and the women very sicke, prevailed with the seamen to put into a creeke hardby, where they lay on ground at low-water. The nexte morning the shipe came, but they were fast, and could not stir, till aboute noone; In the mean time (the shipe maister,

perceiveing how the matter was) sente his boate to be getting
the men abord whom he saw ready, walking aboute the shore.
But after the first boat full was gott abord, and she was ready
to goe for more, the mr. espied a greate company (both horse,
and foote) with bills, and gunes, and other weapons (for the
countrie was raised to take them). The Dutch-man seeing that,
swore (his countries oath), sacremente; and having the wind
faire, waiged his Ancor, hoysed sayles, and away. But the poore-
men which were gott abord, were in great distress for their
wives, and children, which they saw thus to be taken, and were
left destitute of their helps; and them selves also, not having a
cloath to shifte them with, more then they had on their baks,
and some scarce a peney aboute them, all they had being abord
the barke. It drew tears from their eyes, and any thing they
had they would have given to have been a shore againe; but all
in vaine, ther was no remedy; they must thus sadly part. And
afterward endured a fearfull storme at sea, being ·14· days or
more before they arived at their porte, in ·7· wherof they neither saw son, moone, nor stars, and were driven near the coast
of Norway; the mariners them selves often despairing of life;
and once with shriks and cries gave over all, as if the ship had
been foundred in the sea, and they sinking without recoverie.
But when mans hope, and helpe wholy failed, the lords power
and mercie appeared in ther recoverie; for the ship rose againe,
and gave the mariners courage againe to manage here. And if
modestie would suffer me, I might declare with what fervente
prayres they cried unto the lord in this great distres, (espetialy
some of them) even without any great distraction when the
water rane into their mouthes and ears; and the mariners cried
out we sinke, we sinke; they cried (if not with mirakelous, yet
with a great hight or degree of devine faith) yet Lord thou canst
save; yet Lord thou canst save; with shuch other expressions as
I will forbeare. Upon which the ship did not only recover, but
shortly after the violence of the storme begane to abate; and
the lord filed their afflicted minds with shuch comforts as every
one cannot understand. And in the end brought them to their
desired Haven, wher the people came flockeing admiring their
deliverance, the storme having ben so Ionge and sore, in which
much hurt had been don, as the masters freinds related unto
him in their congrattulations.

But to returne to the others wher we left. The rest of the men that were in greatest danger, made shift to escape away before the troope could surprise them; those only staying that best might, to be assistante unto the women. But pitifull it was to see the heavie case of these poore women in this distress; what weeping and crying on every side, some for their husbands, that were caried away in the ship as is before related. Others not knowing what should become of them, and their litle ones; others againe melted in teares, seeing their poore litle ones hanging aboute them, crying for feare, and quaking with could. Being thus aprehended, they were hurried from one place to another, and from one justice to another, till in the ende they knew not what to doe with them; for to imprison so many women and innocent children for no other cause (many of them) but that they must goe with their husbands; semed to be unreasonable, and all would crie out of them; and to send them home againe was as difficult, for they aledged (as the trueth was) they had no homes to goe to, for they had either sould, or otherwise disposed of their houses, and livings. To be shorte, after they had been thus turmoyled a good while, and conveyed from one constable to another, they were glad to be ridd of them in the end upon any termes; for all were wearied and tired with them. Though in the mean time, they (poore soules) indured miserie enough; and thus in the end necessitie forste a way for them.

But that I be not tedious in these things, I will omitte the rest, though I might relate many other notable passages, and troubles which they endured, and underwente in these their wanderings, and travells both at land, and sea; but I hast to other things. Yet I may not omitte the fruite that came heerby, for by these so publick troubles; in so many eminente places, their cause became famouss, and occasioned many to looke into the same; and their godly cariage and christian behaviour was shuch as left a deep Impression in the minds of many. And though some few shrunk, at these first conflicts, and sharp beginings (as it was no marvell) yet many more came on, with fresh courage, and greatly animated others. And in the end, notwithstanding all these stormes of oppossicion, they all gat over at length, some at one time, and some at an other, and some in one place, and some in an other, And mete togeather againe according to their desires, with no small rejoycing.

*Of their setling in Holand, and their maner of living,
and entertainmente ther.*

BEING now come into the Low countries, they saw many goodly and fortified cities, strongly walled and garded with tropes of armed men. Also they heard a strange, and uncouth language, and beheld the differente manners, and custumes of the people, with their strange fashons, and attires; all so farre differing from that of their plaine countrie villages (wherin they were bred, and had so longe lived) as it seemed they were come into a new world. But these were not the things, they much looked on, or long tooke up their thoughts; for they had other work in hand, and an other kind of warr to wage, and maintaine. For though they saw faire, and bewtifull cities, flowing with abundance of all sorts of welth and riches, yet it was not longe before they saw the grimme and grisly face of povertie coming upon them like an armed man; with whom they must bukle, and incounter, and from whom they could not flye; but they were armed with faith, and patience against him, and all his encounters; and though they were sometimes foyled, yet by Gods assistance they prevailed, and got the victorie.

Now when Mr. Robinson, Mr. Brewster, and other principall members were come over (for they were of the last and stayed to help the weakest over before them) shuch things were thought on as were necessarie for their setling, and best ordering of the church affairs. And when they had lived at Amsterdam aboute a year, Mr. Robinson (their pastor) and some others of best discerning, seeing how Mr. John Smith and his companie, was allready fallen in to contention with the church that was ther before them, and no means they could use, would doe any good to cure the same, and also that the flames of contention were like to breake out in that anciente church it selfe (as affterwards lamentably came to pass) which things they prudently foreseeing, thought it was best to remove, before they were any way engaged with the same. Though they well knew it would

be much to the prejudice of their outward estates, both at presente and in licklyhood in the future; as indeed it proved to be.

Their remoovall to Leyden.

For these and some other reasons they removed to Leyden,
a fair and bewtifull citie, and of a sweete situation, but made
more famous by the universitie wherwith it is adorned, in
which (of late) had been so many learned men. But wanting
that traffike by sea which Amsterdam injoyes, it was not so
beneficiall for their outward means of living and estates. But
being now hear pitched they fell to shuch trades and imployments as they best could; valewing peace, and their spirituall
comforte above any other riches what soever. And at lenght
they came to raise a competente and comforteable living, but
with hard, and continuall labore.

Being thus setled (after many difficulties) they continued
many years, in a comfortable condition; injoying much sweete
and delightefull societie and spirituall comforte togeather in
the wayes of God; under the able ministrie, and prudente governmente of Mr. John Robinson, and Mr. William Brewster,
who was an assistante unto him, in the place of an Elder, unto
which he was now called, and chosen by the church. So as they
grew in knowledge and other gifts and graces of the spirite
of God; and lived togeather in peace, and love, and holines;
and many came unto them from diverse parts of England, so
as they grew a great congregation. And if at any time, any
differences arose, or offences broak out (as it cannot be, but
some time ther will, even amongst the best of men) they were
ever so mete with, and nipt in the head betimes, or otherwise so well composed, as still love, peace, and communion
was continued; or els the church purged of those that were
incurable and incorrigible, when, after much patience used,
no other means would serve, which seldom came to pass. Yea
shuch was the mutuall love, and reciprocall respecte that this
worthy man had to his flocke, and his flocke to him; that it
might be said of them as it once was of that famouse Emperour Marcus Aurelious,* and the people of Rome, that it was
hard to judge wheather he delighted more in haveing shuch a

*Goulden booke, &c.

people, or they in haveing shuch a pastor. His love was greate towards them, and his care was all ways bente for their best good, both for soule and body; for besides his singuler abilities in devine things (wherin he excelled) he was also very able to give directions in civill affaires, and to foresee dangers and inconveniences; by which means he was very helpfull to their outward estates, and so was every way as a commone father unto them. And none did more offend him then those that were close, and cleaving to them selves, and retired from the commone good; as also shuch as would be stiffe, and riged in matters of outward order, and invey against the evills of others, and yet be remisse in them selves, and not so carefull to express a vertuous conversation. They in like maner had ever a reverente regard unto him, and had him in precious estimation, as his worth and wisdom did deserve; and though they esteemed him highly whilst he lived and laboured amongst them; yet much more after his death, when they came to feele the wante of his help, and saw (by woefull experience) what a treasure they had lost, to the greefe of their harts, and wounding of their sowls; yea shuch a loss as they saw could not be repaired; for it was as hard for them to find shuch another leader and feeder in all respects, as for the Taborits to find another Ziska. And though they did not call them selves orphans, as the other did (after his death), yet they had cause as much to lamente (in another regard) their present condition, and after usage. But to returne; I know not but it may be spoken, to the honour of God, and without prejudice to any; that shuch was the true pietie, the humble zeale, the fervent love, of this people (whilst they thus lived together) towards God, and his waies, and the single hartednes and sinceir affection one towards another, that they came as near the primative patterne of the first churches, as any other church of these later times have done, according to their ranke and qualitie.

But seeing it is not my porpose to treat of the severall passages that befell this people whilst they thus lived in the Low countries, (which might worthily require a large treatise of it selfe) but to make way to shew the begining of this plantation, which is that I aime at; yet because some of their adversaries did, (upon the rumore of their removall) cast out slanders against them, as if that state had been wearie of them, and had rather driven them out (as the heathen historians did faine of moyses and the Isralites when they went out of Egipte) then that it was their owne free choyse and motion, I will therfore mention a perticuler or too, to shew the contrary, and the good acceptation they had in the place wher they lived. And first though many of them weer poore, yet ther was none so poore but if they were known to be of that congregation, the *Dutch* (either bakers or others) would trust them in any reasonable matter when they wanted money. Because they had found by experience how carfull they were to keep their word, and saw them so painfull, and dilligente in their callings; yea, they would strive to gett their custome, and to imploy them above others, in their worke, for their honestie and diligence.

Againe; the magistrates of the citie, aboute the time of their coming away, or a litle before, in the publick place of justice, gave this comendable testemoney of them (in the reproofe of the Wallons, who were of the french church in that citie). These English (said they) have lived amongst us now these ·12· years, and yet we never had any sute, or accusation came against any of them; but your strifes, and quarels are continuall, etc. In these times allso were the great troubles raised by the Arminians, who as they greatly mollested the whole state, so this citie in perticuler (in which was the cheefe universitie) so as ther were dayly and hotte disputes in the schooles ther aboute, and as the students and other lerned were devided in their oppinions hearin, so were the ·2· proffessors or devinitie readers them selves; the one daly teaching for it, the other against it. Which grue to that pass, that few of the disciples of the one would hear the other teach. But Mr. Robinson, though he taught thrise a weeke him selfe, and write sundrie books, besides his manyfould pains otherwise, yet he went constantly to hear ther readings, and heard the one as well as the other; by which means he was so well grounded in the controversie, and saw the force of all their arguments, and knew the shifts of the adversarie. And being him selfe very able; none was fitter to buckle with them then him selfe. As appered by sundrie disputes, so as he begane to be terrible to the Arminians; which made Episcopius (the Arminian professor) to put forth his best stringth, and set forth sundrie Thesies, which by publick dispute he would defend against all men. Now Poliander the

other proffessor, and the cheefe preachers of the citie, desired
Mr. Robinson to dispute against him; but he was loath, being
a stranger; yet the other did importune him, and tould him
that shuch was the abilitie and nimblenes of the adversarie;
that the truth would suffer, if he did not help them. So as he
condescended, and prepared him selfe against the time, and
when the day came, the lord did so help him to defend the
truth, and foyle this adversarie, as he put him to an apparent
nonplus, in this great and publike audiance. And the like he
did a ·2· or ·3· time, upon such like occasions. The which as
it caused many to praise God, that the trueth had so famous
victory, so it procured him much honour and respecte from
those lerned men, and others which loved the trueth. Yea, so
farr were they from being weary of him, and his people, or
desiring their absence; as it was said by some (of no mean note)
that were it not for giveing offence to the state of England;
they would have preferd him otherwise if he would, and alowd
them some publike favour. Yea when ther was speech of their
remoovall into these parts, sundrie of note, and eminencie of
that nation would have had them come under them, and for
that end made them large offers. Now though I might aledg
many other perticulers, and examples of the like kinde, to shew
the untruth and unlicklyhode of this slander, yet these shall
suffice, seeing it was beleeved of few; being only raised by the
malice of some, who laboured their disgrace.

THE ·4· CHAPTER
Shouting the reasons, and causes of their remoovall.

AFTER they had lived in this citie about some ·11· or ·12·
years, (which is the more observable being the whole time
of that famose truce between that state and the Spaniards,) and
sundrie of them were taken away by death; and many others
begane to be well striken in years (the grave mistris Experience
haveing taught them many things) those prudent governours,
with sundrie of the sagest members begane both deeply to
apprehend their present dangers, and wisely to foresee the
future; and thinke of timly remedy. In the agitation of their
thoughts, and much discours of things hear aboute, at length
they began to incline to this conclusion, of remoovall to some

other place. Not out of any new fanglednes, or other shuch like giddie humor, by which men are oftentimes transported to their great hurt, and danger. But for sundrie weightie and solid reasons; some of the cheefe of which I will hear breefly touch. And first, they saw and found by experience the hardnes of the place and countrie to be shuch, as few in comparison would come to them; and fewer that would bide it out, and continew with them. For many that came to them, and many more that desired to be with them; could not endure that great labor and hard fare, with other inconveniences which they underwent and were contented with. But though they loved their persons, approved their cause, and honoured their sufferings, yet they left them, as it weer weeping, as Orpah did her mother in law Naomie; or as those Romans did Cato in Utica, who desired to be excused, and borne with, though they could not all be Catoes. For many, though they desired to injoye the ordinances of God in their puritie, and the libertie of the gospell with them, yet (alass) they admitted of bondage—with deanger of conscience, rather then to indure these hardships; yea, some preferred, and chose the prisons in England, rather then this libertie in Holland, with these afflictions. But it was thought that if a better, and easier place of living, could be had, it would draw many, and take away these discouragments. Yea, their pastor would often say, that many of those that both wrate, and preached now against them, if they were in a place, wher they might have libertie and live comfortably, they would then practise as they did.

2ly. They saw, that though the people generally, bore all these difficulties very cherfully, and with a resolute courage, being in the best, and strength of their years, yet old age began to steale on many of them, (and their great and continuall labours, with other crosses, and sorrows, hastened it before the time) so as it was not only probably thought, but apparently seen, that within a few years more, they would be in danger to scatter (by necessities pressing them) or sinke under their burdens, or both. And therfore according to the devine proverb, that a wise man seeth the plague when it cometh, and hideth him selfe, Pro. 22. 3. so they like skillfull and beaten souldiers were fearfull, either to be intrapped or surrounded by their enimies, so as they should neither be able to fight nor flie. And therfor thought it better to dislodge betimes to some place of better advantage and less danger, if any shuch could be found.

3ly. Thirdly; As necessitie was a taskmaster over them, so they were forced to be shuch, not only to their servants (but in a sorte) to their dearest chilldren; the which as it did not a litle wound the tender harts of many a loving father, and mother; so it produced likwise sundrie sad and sorowfull effects. For many of their children, that were of best dispositions, and gracious Inclinations; (haveing lernde to bear the yoake in their youth) and willing to bear parte of their parents burden, were (often times) so oppressed with their hevie labours, that though their minds were free and willing, yet their bodies bowed under the weight of the same, and became decreped in their early youth; the vigor of nature being consumed in the very budd as it were. But that which was more lamentable, and of all sorowes most heavie to be borne, was that many of their children, by these occasions, and the great licentiousnes of youth in that countrie, and the manifold temptations of the place, were drawne away by evill examples into extravagante and dangerous courses, getting the raines off their neks, and departing from their parents. Some became souldiers, others tooke upon them farr viages by sea; and other some worse courses, tending to dissolutnes, and the danger of their soules, to the great greefe of their parents and dishonour of God. So that they saw their posteritie would be in danger to degenerate and be corrupted.

Lastly, (and which was not least) a great hope, and inward zeall they had of laying some good foundation, (or at least to make some way therunto) for the propagating, and advancing the gospell of the kingdom of Christ in those remote parts of the world; yea, though they should be but even as steppingstones, unto others for the performing of so great a work.

These, and some other like reasons, moved them to undertake this resolution of their removall; the which they afterward prosecuted with so great difficulties, as by the sequell will appeare.

The place they had thoughts on, was some of those vast, and unpeopled countries of America, which are frutfull, and fitt for habitation; being devoyd of all civill inhabitants; wher ther are only salvage, and brutish men, which range up and downe, litle otherwise then the wild beasts of the same. This proposition being made publike, and coming to the scaning of all; it raised many variable opinions amongst men, and caused many fears, and doubts amongst them selves. Some from their reasons, and hopes conceived, laboured to stirr up and incourage the rest to undertake, and prosecute the same; others againe out of their fears, objected against it, and sought to diverte from it; aledging many things, and those neither unreasonable, nor unprobable. As that it was a great designe, and subjecte to many unconceivable perills, and dangers; as, besides the casualties of the seas (which none can be freed from) the length of the vioage was shuch, as the weake bodys of women, and other persons worne out with age, and travaille (as many of them were) could never be able to endure. And yet if they should, the miseries of the land, which they should be exposed unto, would be to hard to be borne; and lickly, some, or all of them togeither, to consume, and utterly to ruinate them. For ther they should be liable to famine, and nakednes, and the wante in a maner of all things. The chang of aire, diate, and drinking of water, would infecte their bodies with sore sickneses, and greevous diseases. And also those which should escape or overcome these difficulties, should yett be in continuall danger of the salvage people; who are cruell, barbarous, and most trecherous, being most furious in their rage, and merciles wher they overcome; not being contente only to kill, and take away life, but delight to tormente men in the most bloodie manner that may be; fleaing some alive with the shells of fishes, cutting of the members, and joynts of others by peesmeale; and broiling on the coles, eate the collops of their flesh in their sight whilst they live, with other cruelties horrible to be related. And surely it could not be thought but the very hearing of these things, could not but move the very bowels of men to grate within them, and make the weake to quake, and tremble. It was furder objected, that it would require greater summes of money to furnish shuch a voiage (and to fitt them with neccessaries) then their consumed estates would amounte too; and yett they must as well looke to be seconded with supplies, as presently to be transported. Also many presidents of ill success, and lamentable misseries befalne others, in the like designes, were easie to be found, and not forgotten to be aledged. Besides their owne experience, in their former troubles, and hardships, in their removall into

Holand; and how hard a thing it was for them to live in that strange place, though it was a neighbour countrie, and a civill and rich comone wealth.

It was answered, that all great, and honourable actions, are accompanied with great difficulties; and must be, both enterprised, and overcome with answerable courages. It was granted the dangers were great, but not desperate; the difficulties were many, but not invincible. For though their were many of them likly, yet they were not certaine; it might be sundrie of the things feared, might never befale; others by providente care and the use of good means, might in a great measure be prevented; and all of them (through the help of God) by fortitude, and patience, might either be borne, or overcome. True it was, that shuch atempts were not to be made and undertaken without good ground, and reason; not rashly, or lightly as many have done for curiositie, or hope of gaine, etc. But their condition was not ordinarie; their ends were good and honourable; their calling lawfull, and urgente; and therfore they might expecte the blessing of God in their proceding. Yea though they should loose their lives in this action, yet might they have comforte in the same, and their endeavors would be honourable. They lived hear but as men in exile, and in a poore condition; and as great miseries might possiblie befale them in this place; for the ·12· years of truce were now out, and ther was nothing but beating of drumes, and preparing for warr, the events wherof are allway uncertaine. The Spaniard might prove as cruell as the salvages of America; and the famine and pestelence as sore hear as ther; and their libertie less to looke out for remedie. After many other perticuler things answered, and aledged on both sides, it was fully concluded by the major parte, to put this designe in execution; and to prosecute it by the best means they could.

THE ·5· CHAPTER
Shewing what means they used for preparation to this waightie vioag.

AND first, after thir humble praiers unto God, for his direction, and assistance, and a generall confferrence held hear aboute, they consulted what perticuler place to pitch upon, and prepare for. Some (and none of the meanest) had thoughts, and were ernest for Guiana, or some of those fertill places in those hott climates; others were for some parts of Virginia, wher the English had all ready made enterance, and begining. Those for Guiana aledged that the countrie was rich, fruitfull, and blessed with a perpetuall spring, and a florishing greenes; where vigorous nature brought forth all things in abundance, and plentie without any great labour, or art of man. So as it must needs make the inhabitants rich; seing less provissions of clothing and other things, would serve, then in more coulder, and less fruitfull countries must be had. As also that the Spaniards (haveing much more then they could possess) had not yet planted there, nor any wher very near the same. But to this it was answered, that out of question, the countrie was both frutfull, and pleasante; and might yeeld riches, and maintenance to the possessors, more easily then the other; yet, other things considered, it would not be so fitt for them. And first that shuch hott countries are subject to greevos diseases, and many noysome Impediments, which other more temperate places are freer from and would not so well agree with our English bodys. Againe if they should ther live, and doe well, the jealous Spaniard would never suffer them long; but would displante, or overthrow them. As he did the French in Florida; who were seated furder from his richest countries; and the sooner because they should have none to protect them; and their owne strength, would be too smale to resiste so potente an enemie, and so neare a neighbor.

On the other hand, for Virginia, it was objected; that if they lived among the English which wear ther planted, or so near them as to be under their goverment; they should be in as great danger to be troubled, and persecuted for the cause of religion, as if they lived in England, and it might be worse. And if they lived too farr of, they should neither have succour, nor defence frome them.

But at length the conclusion was, to live as a distincte body by them selves, under the generall Goverment of Virginia; and by their freinds to sue to his majestie that he would be pleased to grant them freedome of Religion; and that this might be obtained, they weer putt in good hope (by some great persons, of good ranke and qualitie) that were made their freinds. Whereupon ·2· were chosen and sent in to England (at the charge of the rest) to sollicite this matter; who found

the Virginia Company very desirous to have them goe thither.
And willing to grante them a patent, with as ample priviliges
as they had, or could grant to any, and to give them the best
furderance they could. And some of the cheefe of that company douted not to obtaine their suite of the king for liberty
in Religion, and to have it confirmed under the kings broad
seale, according to their desires. But it prooved a harder peece
of worke then they tooke it for; for though many means were
used to bring it aboute, yet it could not be effected; for ther
were diverse of good worth laboured with the king to obtaine
it (amongst whom was one of his cheefe secretaries)* and some
other wrought with the archbishop to give way therunto, but
it proved all in vaine. Yet thus farr they prevailed, in sounding
his majesties mind, that he would connive at them, and not
molest them (provided they carried them selves peacably). But
to allow, or tollerate them by his publick authoritie, under his
seale, they found it would not be. And this was all (the cheefe
of the Virginia companie) or any other of their best freinds
could doe in the case. Yet they perswaded them to goe on,
for they presumed they should not be troubled. And with this
answer the messengers returned, and signified what diligence
had bene used and to what issue things were come.

But this made a dampe in the bussines, and caused some
distraction, for many were afraid that if they should unsetle
them selves, and put of their estates, and goe upon these hopes,
it might prove dangerous, and but a sandie foundation. Yea,
it was thought they might better have presumed hear upon
without makeing any suite at all, then, haveing made it, to be
thus rejected. But some of the cheefest thought other wise, and
that they might well proceede hereupon, and that the kings
majestie was willing enough to suffer them without molestation; though for other reasons he would not confirme it by
any publick acte. And furdermore, if ther was no securitie in
this promise intimated, ther would be no great certainty in a
furder confirmation of the same; for if after wards ther should
be a purpose or desire to wrong them, though they had a seale
as broad as the house flore, it would not serve the turne; for
ther would be means enew found to recall or reverse it. Seeing

*Sir Robart Nanton.

therfore the course was probable, they must rest herein on Gods providence, as they had done in other things.

Upon this resolution, other messengers wear dispatched, to end with the Virginia Company as well as they could. And to procure a patent with as good and ample conditions as they might by any good means obtaine. As also to treate and con-dude with shuch marchants and other freinds as had manifested their forwardnes to provoke too and adventure in this vioage. For which end they had instructions given them upon what conditions they should procceed with them, or els to conclude nothing without further advice. And here it will be requisite to inserte a letter or too that may give light to these proceedings.

A coppie of leter from Sir Edwin Sands, directed to Mr. John Robinson and Mr. William Brewster.

After my hartie salutations. The agents of your congregation, Robert Cushman and John Carver, have been in communication with diverse selecte gentlemen of his Majesties Counsell for Virginia; and by the writing of ·7· Articles subscribed with your names, have given them that good degree of satisfaction, which hath caried them on with a resolution to sett forward your desire in the best sorte that may be, for your owne and the publick good. Divers perticulers wherof we leave to their faithfull reporte; having carried them selves heere with that good discretion, as is both to their owne and their credite from whence they came. And wheras being to treate for a multitude of people, they have requested further time to conferr with them that are to be interested in this action, aboute the severall particularities which in the prosecution therof will fall out considerable, it hath been very willingly assented too. And so they doe now returne unto you. If therfore it may please God so to directe your desires as that on your parts ther fall out no just impediments, I trust by the same direction it shall likewise appear, that on our parte, all forwardnes to set you forward shall be found in the best sorte which with reason may be expected. And so I betake you with this designe (which I hope verily is the worke of God), to the gracious protection and blessing of the Highest.

London, November 12.   Your very loving freind
Ano: 1617.   EDWIN SANDYS.

Their answer was as foloweth

RIGHTE WORSHIPFULL:

Our humble duties remembred, in our owne, our messengers, and our churches name, with all thankfull acknowledgmente of your singuler love, expressing itselfe, as otherwise, so more spetially in your great care and earnest endeavor of our good in this weightie bussines aboute Virginia, which the less able we are to requite, we shall thinke our selves the more bound to commend in our prayers unto God for recompence; whom, as for the presente you rightly behould in our indeavors, so shall we not be wanting on our parts (the same God assisting us) to returne all answerable fruite, and respecte unto the laboure of your love bestowed upon us. We have, with the best speed and consideration withall that we could, sett downe our requests in writing, subscribed, as you willed, with the hands of the greatest parte of our congregation, and have sente the same unto the Counsell by our agente, and a deacon of our church, John Carver, unto whom we have also requested a gentleman of our company to adyone him selfe; to the care and discretion of which two, we doe refferr the prosecuting of the bussines. Now we perswade our selves Right Worships that we need not provoke your godly and loving minde to any further or more tender care of us, since you have pleased so farr to interest us in your selfe, that, under God, above all persons and things in the world, we relye upon you, expecting the care of your love, counsell of your wisdome, and the help and countenance of your authority. Notwithstanding, for your encouragmente in the worke, so farr as probabilities may leade, we will not forbeare to mention these instances of indusmente.

1. We veryly beleeve and trust the Lord is with us, unto whom and whose service we have given our selves in many trialls; and that he will graciously prosper our indeavours according to the simplicitie of our harts therin.

2ly. We are well weaned from the dellicate milke of our mother countrie, and enured to the difficulties of a strange and hard land, which yet in a great parte we have by patience overcome.

3ly. The people are for the body of them, industrious, and frugall, we thinke we may safly say, as any company of people in the world.

4ly. We are knite togeather as a body in a most stricte and sacred bond and covenante of the Lord, of the violation* wherof we make

---

*O sacred bond, whilst inviollably preserved! how sweete and precious were the fruits that flowed from the same! but when this fidelity decayed, then their ruine approached. O that these anciente members had not dyed, or been dissipated, (if it had been the will of God) or els that this holy care and constante faithfullnes had still lived, and remained with those that survived, and were in times afterwards added unto them. But (alass) that subtill serpente hath slylie wound in him selfe under faire pretences of necessitie and the like, to untwiste these sacred bonds and tyes, and as it were insensibly by degrees to dissolve, or in a great measure to weaken, the same. I have been happy, in my first times, to see, and with much comforte to injoye, the blessed fruits of this great conscience, and by vertue wherof we doe hould our selves straitly tied to all care of each others good, and of the whole by every one and so mutually.

5. Lastly, it is not with us as with other men, whom small things can discourage, or small discontentments cause to wish them selves at home againe. We knowe our entertainmente in England, and in Holand; we shall much prejudice both our arts and means by removall; who, if we should be driven to returne, we should not hope to recover our present helps and comforts, neither indeed looke ever, for our selves, to attaine unto the like in any other place during our lives, which are now drawing towards their periods.

These motives we have been bould to tender unto you, which you in your wisdome may also imparte to any other our worshipps freinds of the Counsell with you; of all whose godly dispossition and loving towards our despised persons, we are most glad, and shall not faile by all good means to continue and increase the same. We will not be further troublesome, but doe, with the renewed remembrance of our humble duties to your Worshipps and (so farr as in modestie we may be bould) to any other of our wellwillers of the Counsell with you, we take our leaves, commiting your persons and counsels to the guidance and direction of the Allmighty.

Yours much bounden in all duty,

Leyden, Desem: 15. JOHN ROBINSON,
Ano: 1617. WILLIAM BREWSTER.

For further light in these proceedings see some other letters and notes as followeth.

The coppy of a letter sent to Sir John Worssenham.

RIGHT WORSHIPFULL: With due acknowledgmente of our thankfullnes for your singular care and pains in the bussines of Virginia, for our, and, we hope, the commone good, we doe remember our humble dutys unto you, and have sent inclosed, as is required, a further explanation of our judgments in the ·3· points specified by some of his majesties Honorable Privie Counsell; and though it be greevious unto us that shuch unjust insinuations are made against us, yet we are most glad of the occasion of making our just purgation unto

---

sweete communion, but it is now a parte of my miserie in old age, to find and feele the decay and wante therof (in a great measure), and with greefe and sorrow of hart to lamente and bewaile the same. And for others warning and admonnition, and my owne humiliation, doe I hear note the same.

so honourable personages. The declarations we have sent inclosed, the one more breefe and generall, which we thinke the fitter to be presented; the other something more large, and in which we express some smale accidentall differances, which if it seeme good unto you and other of our worshipful freinds, you may send in stead of the former. Our prayers unto God is, that your Worshipps may see the frute of your worthy endeavours, which on our parts we shall not faile to furder by all good means in us. And so praing that you would please with the convenientest speed that may be, to give us knowledge of the success of the bussines with his majesties Privie Counsell, and accordingly what your further pleasure is, either for our direction or furtherance in the same, so we rest

Your Worships in all duty,
JOHN ROBINSON,
WILLIAM BREWSTER.

Leyden, Jan: 27.
Ano: 1617. old stile.

The first breefe note was this.

Touching the Ecclesiasticall ministrie, namly of pastores for teaching, elders for ruling, and deacons for distributing the churches contribution, as allso for the too Sacraments, baptisme, and the Lords supper, we doe wholy and in all points agree with the French reformed churches, according to their publick confession of faith.

The oath of Supremacie we shall willingly take if it be required of us, and that conveniente satisfaction be not given by our taking the oath of Alleagence.

JOHN ROB:
WILLIAM BREWSTER.

The ·2· was this.

Touching the Ecclesiasticall ministrie, etc. as in the former, we agree in all things with the French reformed churches, according to their publick confession of faith; though some small differences be to be found in our practises, not at all in the substance of the things, but only in some accidentall circumstances.

1. As first, their ministers doe pray with their heads covered; ours uncovered.

2. We chose none for Governing Elders but shuch as are able to teach; which abilitie they doe not require.

3. Their elders and deacons are annuall, or at most for ·2· or ·3· years; ours perpetuall.

4. Our elders doe administer their office in admonitions and excommunications for publick scandals, publickly and before the congregation; theirs more privatly, and in their consistories.

5. We doe administer baptisme only to shuch infants as wherof the one parente, at the least, is of some church, which some of ther churches doe not observe; though in it our practice accords with their publick confession and the judgmente of the most larned amongst them.

Other differences, worthy mentioning, we know none in these points. Then aboute the oath, as in the former.

Subscribed,   JOHN R.
W. B.

Part of another letter from him that delivered these.

London. Feb: 14. 1617.

Your letter to Sir John Worstenholme I delivered allmost as soone as I had it, to his owne hands, and staid with him the opening and reading. Ther were ·2· papers inclosed, he read them to him selfe, as also the letter, and in the reading he spake to me and said, Who shall make them, viz. the ministers; I answered his Worship that the power of making was in the church, to be ordained by the imposition of hands, by the fittest instruments they had. It must either be in the church or from the pope, and the pope is Antichrist. Ho! said Sir John, what the pope houlds good, (as in the Trinitie,) that we doe well to assente too; but, said he, we will not enter into dispute now. And as for your letters he would not show them at any hand, least he should spoyle all. He expected you should have been of the Archbishop's minde for the calling of ministers, but it seems you differed. I could have wished to have known the contents of your tow inclosed, at which he stuck so much, espetially the larger. I asked his Worship what good news he had for me to write to morrow. He tould me very good news, for both the kings majestie and the bishops have consented. He said he would goe to Mr. Chancelor, Sir Fulk Grivell, as this day, and nexte weeke I should know more. I mett Sir Edw: Sands on Wedensday night; he wished me to be at the Virginia Courte the nexte Wedensday, wher I purpose to be. Thus loath to be troublsome at present, I hope to have somewhate nexte week of certentie concerning you. I committe you to the Lord. Yours,

S. B.

These things being long in agitation, and messengers passing too and againe aboute them, after all their hopes they were long delayed by many rubs that fell in the way; for at the returne of these messengers into England they found things farr otherwise then they expected. For the Virginia Counsell was now so disturbed with factions and quarrels amongst them selves, as no bussines could well goe forward. The which may the better appear in one of the messengers letters as followeth.

TO HIS LOVING FREINDS, etc.

I had thought long since to have write unto you, but could not effecte that which I aimed at, neither can yet sett things as I wished; yet, not withstanding, I doubt not but Mr. B. hath writen to Mr. Robinson. But I thinke my selfe bound also to doe something, least I be thought to neglecte you. The maine hinderance of our proseed-ings in the Virginia bussines, is the dissentions and factions, as they terme it, amongs the Counsell and Company of Virginia; which are shuch, as that ever since we came up no bussines could by them be dispatched. The occasion of this trouble amongst them is, for that a while since Sir Thomas Smith, repining at his many offices and troubles, wished the Company of Virginia to ease him of his office in being Treasurer and Governour of the Virginia Company. Wereupon the Company tooke occasion to dismisse him, and chose Sir Edwin Sands Treasurer and Governour of the Company. He having ·60· voyces, Sir John Worstenholme ·16· voices, and Alderman Johnsone ·24· But Sir Thomas Smith, when he saw some parte of his honour lost, was very angrie, and raised a faction to cavill and contend aboute the election, and sought to taxe Sir Edwin with many things that might both disgrace him, and allso put him by his office of Gover-nour. In which contentions they yet stick, and are not fit nor readie to intermedle in any bussines; and what issue things will come to we are not yet certaine. It is most like Sir Edwin will carrie it away, and if he doe, things will goe well in Virginia; if other wise, they will goe ill enough. Always we hope in some ·2· or ·3· Courtsdays things will setle. Mean space I thinke to goe downe into Kente, and come up againe aboute ·14· days, or ·3· weeks hence; except either by these afforesaid contentions, or by the ille tidings from Virginia, we be wholy discouraged, of which tidings I am now to speake.

Captaine Argoll is come home this weeke (he upon notice of the intente of the Counsell, came away before Sir Georg Yeardley came ther, and so ther is no small dissention). But his tidings are ill, though his person be wellcome. He saith Mr. Blackwells shipe came not ther till March, but going towards winter, they had still norwest winds, which carried them to the southward beyond their course. And the master of the ship and some ·6· of the mariners dieing, it seemed they could not find the bay, till after long seeking and beating aboute. Mr. Blackwell is dead, and Mr. Maggner, the Captain; yea, ther are dead, he saith, ·130· persons, one and other in that ship; it is said ther was in all an ·180· persons in the ship, so as they were packed togeather like herings. They had amongst them the fluxe, and allso wante of fresh water; so as it is hear rather wondred at that so many are alive, then that so many are dead. The marchants hear say it was Mr. Blackwells faulte to pack so many in the ship; yea, and ther were great mutterings and repinings amongst them, and upbraiding of Mr. Blackwell, for his dealing and dispossing of them, when they saw how he had dispossed of them, and how he insulted over them. Yea, the streets at Gravsend runge of their extreame quarrelings, crying out one of another, Thou hast brought me to this, and, I may thanke the for this. Heavie newes it is, and I would be glad to heare how farr it will discourage. I see none hear discouraged much, but rather desire to larne to beware by other mens harmes, and to amend that wherin they have failed. As we desire to serve one another in love, so take heed of being inthraled by any imperious persone, especially if they be discerned to have an eye to them selves. It doth often trouble me to thinke that in this bussines we are all to learne and none to teach; but better so, then to depend upon shuch teachers as Mr. Blackwell was. Shuch a stratageme he once made for Mr. Johnson and his people at Emden, which was their subversion. But though he ther clenlily (yet unhonestly) plucked his neck out of the collar, yet at last his foote is caught. Hear are no letters come, the ship Captain Argole came in is yet in the west parts; all that we hear is but his reporte; it seemeth he came away secretly. The ship that Mr. Blackwell went in will be hear shortly. It is as Mr. Robinson once said; he thought we should hear no good of them.

Mr. B. is not well at this time; whether he will come back to you or goe into the north, I yet know not. For my selfe, I hope to see an end of this bussines ere I come, though I am sorie to be thus from you; if things had gone roundly forward, I should have been with you within these ·14· days. I pray God directe us, and give us that spirite which is fitting for shuch a bussines. Thus having summarily pointed at things which Mr. Brewster (I thinke) hath more largly write of to Mr. Robinson, I leave you to the Lords protection.

Yours in all readines, &c.
ROBART CUSHMAN.

London, May 8. Ano: 1619.

A word or tow by way of digression touching this Mr. Blackwell; he was an elder of the church at Amsterdam, a man well known of most of them. He declined from the trueth with Mr. Johnson and the rest, and went with him when they parted assunder in that wofull maner, which brought so great dishonour to God, scandall to the trueth, and outward ruine to them selves in this world. But I hope, notwithstanding, through the mercies of the Lord, their souls are now at rest with him in the heavens, and that they are arrived in the Haven of hapines; though some of their bodies were thus buried in the terrable seas, and others sunke under the burthen of bitter afflictions. He with some others had prepared for to goe to Virginia. And he, with sundrie godly citizens, being at a private meeting (I take it a fast) in London, being discovered, many of them were apprehended, wherof Mr. Blakwell was one; but he so glossed with the bishops, and either dissembled or flatly deneyed the trueth which formerly he had maintained; and not only so, but very unworthily betrayed and accused another godly man who had escaped, that so he might slip his own neck out of the collar, and to obtaine his owne freedome brought others into bonds. Wherupon he so wone the bishops favour (but lost the Lord's) as he was not only dismiste, but in oppen courte the Archbishop gave him great applause and his sollemne blessing to proseed in his vioage. But if shuch events follow the bishops blessing, happie are they that misse the same; it is much better to keepe a good conscience and have the Lords blessing, whether in life or death.

But see how the man thus apprehended by Mr. Blackwells means, writes to a freind of his.

RIGHT DEAR FREIND AND CHRISTIAN BROTHER, *Mr. Carver*, I salute you and yours in the Lord, etc. As for my owne presente condition, I doubt not but you well understand it ere this by our brother Maistersone, who should have tasted of the same cupp, had his place of residence and his person been as well knowne as my selfe. Some what I have written to *Mr. Cushman* how the matter *still continues*. I have petitioned *twise* to Mr. Sherives, and *once* to my Lord Cooke, and have used such reasons to move them to pittie, that if they were not overruled by some others, I suppose I should soon gaine my libertie; as that I was a yonge man living by my credite, indebted to diverse in our citie, living at more then ordinarie charges in a close and tedious prison; besides great rents abroad, all my bussines lying still, my only servante lying lame in the countrie, my wife being also great with child. And yet no answer till the lords of his majesties Counsell gave consente. Howbeit, Mr. Blackwell, a man as deepe in this action as I, was delivered at a cheaper rate, with a great deale less adoe; yea, with an addition of the Archbishop blessing. I am sorie for Mr. Blackwels weaknes, I wish it may prove no worse. But yet he and some others of them, *before their going*, were not sorie, but thought it was for the best that I was nominated, not because the Lord sanctifies evill to good, but that the action was good, yea for the best. One reason I well remember he used was, because this trouble would encrease the Virginia plantation, in that now people begane to be more generally inclined to goe; and if he had not nomminated some shuch as I, he had not bene free, being it was knowne that diverse citizens besides them selves were ther. I expecte an answer shortly what they intend conscerning me; I purpose to write to some others of you, by whom you shall know the certaintie. Thus not haveing further at present to aquaint you withall, commending my selfe to your prairs, I cease, and committe you and us all to the Lord.

> From my chamber in Wodstreete Compter.
> Your freind, and brother in bonds,
> SABIN STARESMORE.

September: 4. Anno: 1618.

But thus much by the way, which may be of instruction and good use.

But at last, after all these things, and their long attendance, they had a patent granted them, and confirmed under the Companies seale; but these devissions and distractions had shaken of many of ther pretended freinds, and disappointed them of much of their hoped for and proffered means. By the advise of some freinds this pattente was not taken in the name of any of their owne, but in the name of Mr. John Wincob (a religious gentleman then belonging to the Countess of Lincoline), who intended to goe with them. But God so disposed as he never went, nor they ever made use of this patente, which had cost them so much labour and charge, as by the sequell will appeare. This patente being sente over for them to veiw and consider, as also the passages aboute the propossitions between them and shuch marchants and freinds as should either goe or adventure with them, and espetially with those* on whom they did cheefly depend for shipping and means, whose proffers had been large, they were requested to fitt and prepare them selves with all speed. A right emblime, it may be, of the uncertine things of this world; that when men have toyld them selves for them, they vanish into smoke.

*Mr. Tho: Weston, etc.

THE ·6· CHAPTER

Conscerning the agreements and artickles between them,
and shuch marchants and others as adventured moneys; with
other things falling out aboute making their provissions.

UPON the receite of these things by one of their messengers, they had a sollemne meeting and a day of humilliation to seeke the Lord for his direction; and their pastor tooke this texte, ·1· *Sam.* 23. 3, 4. *And David's men said unto him, see, we be afraid hear in Judah, how much more if we come to Keilah against the host of the Philistimes? Then David asked counsell of the Lord again, etc.* From which texte he taught many things very aptly, and befitting ther presente occasion and condition, strengthing them against their fears and perplexities, and incouraging them in their resolutions.

After which they concluded both what number and what persons should prepare them selves to goe with the first; for all that were willing to have gone could not gett ready for their other affairs in so shorte a time; neither if all could have been ready, had ther been means to have transported them allto-geather. Those that staied being the greater number required the pastor to stay with them; and indeede for other reasons he could not then well goe, and so it was the more easilie yeelded unto. The other then desired the elder, Mr. Brewster, to goe with them, which was also condescended unto. It was also agreed on by mutuall consente and covenante, that those that went should be an absolute church of them selves, as well as those that staid; seing in shuch a dangerus vioage, and a removall to shuch a distance, it might come to pass they should (for the body of them) never meete againe in this world; yet with this proviso, that as any of the rest came over to them, or of the other returned upon occasion, they should be reputed as members without any further dismission or testimoniall. It was allso promised to those that wente first, by the body of the rest, that if the Lord gave them life, and means, and opportunitie, they would come to them as soone as they could.

Aboute this time, whilst they were perplexed with the pros-seeddings of the Virginia Company, and the ill news from thence aboute Mr. Blackwell and his company, and making inquirey about the hiring and buying of shiping for their vioage, some Dutchmen made them faire offers aboute goeing with them.

Also one Mr. Thomas Weston, a marchant of London, came
to Leyden aboute the same time, (who was well aquainted with
some of them, and a furtherer of them in their former proseed-
ings,) haveing much conferance with Mr. Robinson and other
of the cheefe of them, perswaded them to goe on (as it seems)
and not to medle with the Dutch, or too much to depend on
the Virginia Company; for if that failed, if they came to resolution, he and shuch marchants as were his freinds (togeather
with their owne means) would sett them forth; and they should
make ready, and neither feare wante of shipping nor money;
for what they wanted should be provided. And, not so much
for him selfe as for the satisfing of shuch freinds as he should
procure to adventure in this bussines, they were to draw shuch
articles of agreemente, and make such propossitions, as might
the better induce his freinds to venture. Upon which (after the
formere conclusion) articles were drawne and agreed unto, and
were showne unto him, and approved by him; and afterwards
by their messenger (Mr. John Carver) sent into England, who,
togeather with Robart Cushman, were to receive the moneys
and make provissione both for shiping and other things for the
vioage; with this charge, not to exseede their commission, but
to proceed according to the former articles. Also some were
chossen to doe the like for shuch things as were to be prepared
there; so those that were to goe, prepared them selves with all
speed, and sould of their estates and (shuch as were able) put
in their moneys into the commone stock, which was disposed
by those appointed, for the making of generall provissions.
Aboute this time also they had heard, both by Mr. Weston
and others, that sundrie Honourable Lords had obtained a
large grante from the king, for the more northerly parts of
that countrie, derived out of the Virginia patente, and wholy
secluded from their Govermente, and to be called by another
name, viz. New-England. Unto which Mr. Weston, and the
cheefe of them, begane to incline it was best for them to goe,
as for other reasons, so cheefly for the hope of present profite
to be made by the fishing that was found in that countrie.

But as in all bussineses the acting parte is most difficulte,
espetially wher the worke of many agents must concurr, so
was it found in this; for some of those that should have gone
in England, fell of and would not goe; other marchants and

friends that had offered to adventure their moneys withdrew, and pretended many excuses. Some disliking they wente not to Guiana; others againe would adventure nothing excepte they wente to Virginia. Some againe (and those that were most relied on) fell in utter dislike with Virginia, and would doe nothing if they wente thither. In the midds of these distractions, they of Leyden, who had put of their estates, and laid out their moneys, were brought into a greate streight, fearing what issue these things would come too; but at length the generalitie was swaid to this latter opinion.

But now another difficultie arose, for Mr. Weston and some other that were for this course, either for their better advantage, or rather for the drawing on of others, as they pretended, would have some of those conditions altered that were first agreed on at Leyden. To which the ·2· agents sent from Leyden (or at least one of them who is most charged with it) did consente; seeing els that all was like to be dashte, and the opportunitie lost, and that they which had put of their estates and paid in their moneys were in hazard to be undon. They presumed to conclude with the marchants on those termes, in some things contrary to their order and commission, and without giving them notice of the same; yea, it was conceled, least it should make any furder delay; which was the cause afterward of much trouble and contention.

It will be meete I here inserte these conditions, which are as foloweth.

Anno, 1620. July 1.

1. The adventurers and planters doe agree, that every person that goeth being aged ·16· years and upward, be rated at ·10*li*· and ten pounds to be accounted a single share.

2. That he that goeth in person, and furnisheth him selfe out with ·10*li*· either in money or other provissions, be accounted as haveing ·20*li*· in stock, and in the devission shall receive a doble share.

3. The persons transported and the adventurers shall continue their joynt stock and partnership togeather, the space of ·7· years, (excepte some unexpected impedimente doe cause the whole company to agree otherwise,) during which time, all profits and benifits that are gotte by trade, traffick, trucking, working, fishing, or any other means of any person or persons, remaine still in the commone stock untill the division.

4. That at their comming ther, they chose out shuch a number of fitt persons, as may furnish their ships and boats for fishing upon the sea; imploying the rest in their severall faculties upon the land; as building houses, tilling, and planting the ground, and makeing shuch commodities as shall be most usefull for the collonie.

5. That at the end of the ·7· years, the capitall and profits, viz. the houses, lands, goods and chatles, be equally devided betwixte the adventurers, and planters; which done, every man shall be free from other of them of any debt or detrimente concerning this adventure.

6. Whosoever cometh to the colonie herafter, or putteth any into the stock, shall at the ende of the ·7· years be alowed proportionably to the time of his so doing.

7. He that shall carie his wife and children, or servants, shall be alowed for everie person now aged ·16· years and upward, a single share in the devision, or if he provid them necessaries, a duble share, or if they be between ·10· year old and ·16· then ·2· of them to be reconed for a person, both in transportation and devision.

8. That shuch children as now goe, and are under the age of ten years, have noe other shar in the devission, but ·50· acers of unmanured land.

9. That shuch persons as die before the ·7· years be expired, their executors to have their parte or share at the devission, proportionably to the time of their life in the collonie.

10. That all such persons as are of this collonie, are to have their meate, drink, apparell, and all provissions out of the common stock and goods of the said collonie.

The cheefe and principall differences betwene these and the former conditions, stood in those ·2· points; that the houses, and lands improved, espetialy gardens and home lotts should remaine undevided wholy to the planters at the ·7· years end. 2ly, that they should have had ·2· days in a weeke for their owne private imploymente, for the more comforte of them selves and their families, espetialy shuch as had families. But because letters are by some wise men counted the best parte of histories, I shall shew their greevances hereaboute by their owne letters, in which the passages of things will be more truly discerned.

A letter of Mr. Robinsons to John Carver.

June 14. 1620. N. stile.
MY DEAR FREIND AND BROTHER, whom with yours I alwaise remember in my best affection, and whose wellfare I shall never cease to commend to God by my best and most earnest praires. You doe throwly understand by our generall letters the estate of things hear,

which indeed is very pitifull; espetialy by wante of shiping, and not
seeing means lickly, much less certaine, of having it provided; though
withall ther be great want of money and means to doe needfull
things. Mr. Pickering, you know before this, will not defray a peny
hear; though Robart Cushman presumed of I know not how many
·100*li*· from him, and I know not whom. Yet it seems strange that we
should be put to him to receive both his and his partners adventer,
and yet Mr. Weston write unto him, that in regard of it, he hath
drawne upon him a ·100*li*· more. But ther is in this some misterie, as
indeed it seems ther is in the whole course. Besides, wheras diverse
are to pay in some parts of their moneys yet behinde, they refuse to
doe it, till they see shiping provided, or a course taken for it. Neither
doe I thinke is ther a man hear would pay any thing, if he had againe
his money in his purse. You know right well we depended on Mr.
Weston alone, and upon shuch means as he would procure for this
commone bussines; and when we had in hand another course with the
Dutchmen, broke it of at his motion, and upon the conditions by him
shortly after propounded. He did this in his love I know, but things
appeare not answerable from him hitherto. That he should have first
have put in his moneys, is thought by many to have been but fitt, but
that I can well excuse, he being a marchante and haveing use of it to
his benefite; wheras others, if it had been in their hands, would have
consumed it. But that he should not but have had either shipping
ready before this time, or at least certaine means, and course, and the
same knowne to us for it, or have taken other order otherwise, cannot
in my conscience be excused. I have heard that when he hath been
moved in the bussines, he hath put it of from him selfe, and referred
it to the others; and would come to Georg Morton, and enquire news
of him aboute things, as if he had scarce been some accessarie unto it.
Wether he hath failed of some helps from others which he expected,
and so be not well able to goe through with things, or whether he
hath feared least you should be ready too soone and so encrease the
charge of shiping above that is meete; or whether he have thought by
withhoulding to put us upon straits, thinking that therby Mr. Brewer
and Mr. Pickering would be drawne by importunitie to doe more,
or what other misterie is in it, we know not; but sure we are that
things are not answerable to shuch an occasion. Mr. Weston makes
himselfe mery with our endeavors about buying a ship, but we have
done nothing in this but with good reason, as I am perswaded, nor
yet that I know in any thing els, save in those tow; the one, that we
imployed Robart Cushman, who is known (though a good man, and
of spetiall abilities in his kind, yet) most unfitte to deale for other
men, by reason of his singularitie, and too great indifferancie for any
conditions, and for (to speak truly) that we have had nothing from

him but termes and presumptions. The other, that we have so much relyed, by implicite faith as it were, upon generalities, without seeing the perticuler course and means for so waghtie an affaire set down unto us. For shiping, Mr. Weston, it should seeme, is set upon hireing, which yet I wish he may presently effecte; but I see litle hope of help from hence if so it be. Of Mr. Brewer you know what to expecte. I doe not thinke Mr. Pickering will ingage, excepte in the course of buying, in former letters specified. Aboute the conditions, you have our reasons for our judgments of what is agreed. And let this spetially be borne in minde, that the greatest parte of the Collonie is like to be imployed constantly, not upon dressing ther perticuler land and building houses, but upon fishing, trading, etc. So as the land and house will be but a trifell for advantage to the adventurers, and yet the devission of it a great discouragemente to the planters, who would with singuler care make it comfortable with borowed houres from their sleep. The same consideration of commone imploymente constantly by the most is a good reason not to have the ·2· daies in a weeke deneyed the few planters for private use, which yet is subordinate to commone good. Consider also how much unfite that you and your likes must serve a new prentishipe of ·7· years, and not a daies freedome from taske. Send me word what persons are to goe, who of usefull faculties, and how many and perticulerly of every thing. I know you wante not a minde. I am sorie you have not been at London all this while, but the provissions could not wante you. Time will suffer me to write no more; fare you and yours well allways in the Lord, in whom I rest,

Yours to use,
JOHN ROBINSON.

An other letter from sundrie of them at the same time.

To their loving friends John Carver and Robart Cushman, these, etc.

GOOD BRETHEREN, after salutations, etc. We received diverse letters at the coming of Mr. Nash and our pilott, which is a great incouragmente unto us, and for whom we hope after times will minister occasion of praising God; and indeed had you not sente him, many would have been ready to fainte and goe backe. Partly in respecte of the new conditions which have bene taken up by you, which all men are against, and partly in regard of our owne inabillitie to doe any one of those many waightie bussineses you referr to us here. For the former wherof, wheras Robart Cushman desires reasons for our dislike, promising therupon to alter the same, or els saing we should thinke he hath no brains, we desire him to exercise them therin, refering him to our pastors former reasons, and them to the censure of the godly wise. But our desires are that you will not entangle your selves and us in any shuch unreasonable courses as those are, viz. that the marchants should have the halfe of mens houses and lands at the dividente; and that persons should be deprived of the ·2· days in a weeke agreed upon, yea every momente of time for their owne perticuler; by reason wherof we cannot conceive why any should carie servants for their own help and comfort; for that we can require no more of them then all men one of another. This we have only by relation from Mr. Nash, and not from any writing of your owne, and therfore hope you have not proceeded farr in so great a thing without us. But requiring you not to exseed the bounds of your com-mission, which was to proceed upon the things or conditions agred upon and expressed in writing (at your going over about it), we leave it, not without marveling, that your selfe, as you write, knowing how smale a thing troubleth our consultations, and how few, as you fear, understands the busines aright, should trouble us with shuch matters as these are, etc.

Salute Mr. Weston from us, in whom we hope we are not deceived; we pray you make known our estate unto him, and if you thinke good shew him our letters, at least tell him (that under God) we much relie upon him and put our confidence in him; and, as your selves well know, that if he had not been an adventurer with us, we had not taken it in hand; presuming that if he had not seene means to accomplish it, he would not have begune it; so we hope in our extremitie he will so farr help us as our expectation be no way made frustrate concern-ing him. Since therfore, good brethren, we have plainly opened the state of things with us in this matter, you will, etc. Thus beseeching the Allmightie, who is allsufficiente to raise us out of this depth of dificulties, to assiste us herein; raising shuch means by his providence and fatherly care for us, his pore children and servants, as we may with comforte behould the hand of our God for good towards us in this our bussines, which we undertake in his name and fear, we take leave and remaine

	Your perplexed, yet hopfull
June 10. New Stille,	bretheren,
Anno: 1620.	S. F. E. W. W. B. I. A.

A letter of Robart Cushman's to them.

BRETHERN, I understand by letters and passages that have come to me, that ther are great discontents, and dislikes of my proceedings amongst you. Sorie I am to hear it, yet contente to beare it, as not doubting but that partly by writing, and more principally by word when we shall come togeather, I shall satisfie any reasonable man. I have been perswaded by some, espetialy this bearer, to come and clear things unto you; but as things now stand I cannot be absente one day, excepte I should hazard all the viage. Neither conceive I any great good would come of it. Take then, brethern, this as a step to give you contente. First, for your dislike of the alteration of one clause in the conditions, if you conceive it right, ther can be no blame lye on me at all. For the articles first brought over by John Carver were never seene of any of the adventurers hear, excepte Mr. Weston, neither did any of them like them because of that clause; nor Mr. Weston himselfe, after he had well considered it. But as at the first ther was ·500*li*. withdrawne by Sir Georg Farrer and his brother upon that dislike, so all the rest would have withdrawne (Mr. Weston excepted) if we had not altered that clause. Now whilst we at Leyden conclude upon points, as we did, we reckoned without our host, which was not my falte. Besides, I shewed you by a letter the equitie of that condition, and our inconveniences, which might be sett against all Mr. Robinson's inconveniences, that without the alteration of that clause, we could neither have means to gett thither, nor supplie wherby to subsiste when we were ther. Yet notwithstanding all those reasons, which were not mine, but other mens wiser then my self, without answer to any one of them, here cometh over many quirimonies, and complaints against me, of lording it over my brethern, and making conditions fitter for theeves and bond-slaves then honest men, and that of my owne head I did what I list. And at last a paper of reasons, framed against that clause in the conditions, which as they were delivered me open, so my answer is open to you all. And first, as they are no other but inconveniences, shuch as a man might frame ·20· as great on the other side, and yet prove nor disprove nothing by them, so they misse and mistake both the very ground of the article and nature of the project. For, first, it is said, that if ther had been no divission of houses and lands, it had been better for the poore. True, and that showeth the inequalitie of the conditions; we should more respecte him that ventureth both his money and his person, then him that ventureth but his person only.

2. Consider wheraboute we are, not giveing almes, but furnishing a store house; no one shall be porer then another for ·7· years, and if any be rich, none can be pore. At the least, we must not in shuch bussines crie, pore, pore, mercie, mercie. Charitie hath it life in wraks, not in ventures; you are by this most in a hopefull pitie of makeing, therfore complaine not before you have need.

3. This will hinder the building of good and faire houses, contrarie to the advise of pollitiks. A. So we would have it; our purpose is to build for the presente shuch houses as, if need be, we may with litle greefe set a fire, and rune away by the lighte; our riches shall not be in

pompe, but in strenght; if God send us riches, we will imploye them to provid more men, ships, munition, etc. You may see it amongst the best pollitiks, that a common wele is readier to ebe then to flow, when once fine houses and gay cloaths come up.

4. The Government may prevente excess in building. A. But if it be on all men beforehand resolved on, to build mean houses, the Governor's laboure is spared.

5. All men are not of one condition. A. If by condition you mean wealth, you are mistaken; if you mean by condition, qualities, then I say he that is not contente his neighbour shall have as good a house, fare, means, etc. as him selfe, is not of a good qualitie. 2ly. Shuch retired, persons, as have an eie only to them selves, are fitter to come wher catching is, then closing; and are fitter to live alone, then in any societie, either civill or religious.

6. It will be of litle value, scarce worth ·5*li*. A. True, it may be not worth halfe 5*li*. If then so smale a thing will content them, why strive we thus aboute it, and give them occasion to suspecte us to be worldly and covetous? I will not say what I have heard since these complaints came first over.

7. Our freinds with us that adventure mind not their owne profite, as did the old adventurers. A. Then they are better then we, who for a litle matter of profite are readie to draw back, and it is more apparente brethern looke too it, that make profite your maine end; repente of this, els goe not least you be like Jonas to Tarshis. 2ly. Though some of them mind not their profite, yet others doe mind it; and why not as well as we? ventures are made by all sorts of men, and we must labour to give them all contente, if we can.

8. It will break the course of communitie, as may be showed by many reasons. A. That is but said, and I say againe, it will best foster comunion, as may be showed by many reasons.

9. Great profite is like to be made by trucking, fishing, etc. A. As it is better for them, so for us; for halfe is ours, besides our living still upon it, and if such profite in that way come, our labour shall be the less on the land, and our houses and lands must and will be of less value.

10. Our hazard is greater then theirs. A. True, but doe they put us upon it? doe they urge or egg us? hath not the motion and resolution been always in our selves? doe they any more then in seeing us resolute if we had means, help us to means upon equall termes and conditions? If we will not goe, they are content to keep their moneys. Thus I have pointed at a way to loose those knots, which I hope you will consider seriously, and let me have no more stirre about them.

Now furder, I hear a noise of slavish conditions by me made; but surly this is all that I have altered, and reasons I have sent you. If you mean it of the ·2· days in a week for perticuler, as some insinuate, you are deceived; you may have ·3· days in a week for me if you will. And when I have spoken to the adventurers of times of working, they have said they hope we are men of discretion and conscience, and so fitte to be trusted our selves with that. But indeed the ground of our proceedings at Leyden was mistaken, and so here is nothing but tottering every day, etc.

As for them of Amsterdam I had thought they would as soone have gone to Rome as with us; for our libertie is to them as ratts bane, and their riggour as bad to us as the Spanish Inquisition. If any practise of mine discourage them, let them yet draw back; I will undertake they shall have their money againe presently paid hear. Or if the company thinke me to be the Jonas, let them cast me of before we goe; I shall be content to stay with good will, having but the cloaths on my back; only let us have quietnes, and no more of these clamors; full litle did I expecte these things which are now come to pass, etc.

Yours,   R. CUSHMAN.

But whether this letter of his ever came to their hands at Leyden I well know not; I rather thinke it was staied by Mr. Carver and keept by him, for giving offence. But this which follows was ther received; both which I thought pertenent to recite.

Another of his to the foresaid.

June II. 1620.

Salutations, etc. I received your letter yesterday, by John Turner, with another the same day from Amsterdam by Mr. W. savouring of the place whenc it came. And indeed the many discouragements I find hear, togeather with the demurrs and retirings ther, had made me to say, I would give up my accounts to John Carver, and at his comeing acquainte him fully with all courses, and so leave it quite, with only the pore cloaths on my back. But gathering up my selfe by further consideration, I resolved yet to make one triall more, and to acquainte Mr. Weston with the fainted state of our bussines; and though he hath been much discontented at some thing amongst us of late, which hath made him often say, that save for his promise, he would not meadle at all with the bussines any more, yet considering how farr we were plunged into maters, and how it stood both on our credits and undoing, at the last he gathered up him selfe a litle more, and coming to me ·2· hours after, he tould me he would not yet leave it. And so advising togeather we resolved to hire a ship, and have tooke liking of one till Monday, about ·60· laste, for a greater we cannot gett, excepte it be tow great; but a fine ship it is. And seeing our neer freinds ther are so streite lased, we hope to assure her without troubling them any further; and if the ship fale too small, it fitteth well that shuch as stumble at strawes allready, may rest them ther a while, least worse blocks come in the way ere ·7· years be ended. If you had beaten this bussines so throuly a month agoe, and write to us as now you doe, we could thus have done much more conveniently. But it is as it is; I hope our freinds ther, if they be quitted of the ship hire, will be indusced to venture the more. All that I now require is that salt and netts may ther be boughte, and for all the rest we will here provid it; yet if that will not be, let them but stand for it a month or tow, and we will take order to pay it all. Let Mr. *Reinholds* tarie ther, and bring the ship to Southampton. We have hired another pilote here, one Mr. *Clarke*, who went last year to Virginia with a ship of kine.

You shall here distinctly by John Turner, who I thinke shall come hence on Tewsday night. I had thought to have come with him, to have answerd to my complaints; but I shal lerne to pass litle for their censures; and if I had more minde to goe and dispute and expostulate with them, then I have care of this waightie bussines, I were like them who live by clamours and jangling. But neither my mind nor my body is at libertie to doe much, for I am fettered with bussines, and had rather study to be quiet, then to make answer to their exceptions. If men be set on it, let them beat the eair; I hope shuch as are my sinceire freinds will not thinke but I can give some reason of my actions. But of your mistaking aboute the mater, and other things tending to this bussines, I shall nexte informe you more distinctly. Mean space entreate our freinds not to be too bussie in answering matters, before they know them. If I doe shuch things as I cannot give reasons for, it is like you have sett a foole aboute your bussines, and so turne the reproofe to your selves, and send an other, and let me come againe to my Combes. But setting a side my naturall infirmities, I refuse not to have my cause judged, both of God, and all indifferent men; and when we come togeather I shall give accounte of my actions hear. The Lord, who judgeth justly without respect of persons, see into the equitie of my cause, and give us quiet, peacable, and patient minds, in all these turmoiles, and sanctifie unto us all crosses whatsoever. And so I take my leave of you all, in all love and affection.

I hope we shall gett all hear ready in ·14· days.

Your pore brother,
ROBART CUSHMAN.

June 11. 1620.

Besides these things, ther fell out a differance amongs those ·3· that received the moneys and made the provissions in

England; for besides these tow formerly mentioned sent from Leyden for this end, viz. Mr. Carver and Robart Cushman, ther was one chosen in England to be joyned with them, to make the provisions for the vioage; his name was Mr. Martin, he came from Billirike in Essexe, from which parts came sundrie others to goe with them, as also from London and other places; and therfore it was thought meete and conveniente by them in Holand that these strangers that were to goe with them, should apointe one thus to be joyned with them, not so much for any great need of their help, as to avoyd all susspition, or jelosie of any partiallitie. And indeed their care for giving offence, both in this and other things after ward, turned to great inconvenience unto them, as in the sequell will apeare; but however it shewed their equall and honest minds. The provissions were for the most parte made at Southhamton, contrarie to Mr. Westons and Robert Cushmans mind (whose counsells did most concure in all things). A touch of which things I shall give in a letter of his to Mr. Carver, and more will appear afterward.

To his loving freind Mr. John Carver, these, etc.

LOVING FREIND, I have received from you some letters, full of affection and complaints, and what it is you would have of me I know not; for your crieing out, negligence, negligence, negligence, I marvell why so negligente a man was used in the bussines. Yet know you that all that I have power to doe hear, shall not be one hower behind, I warent you. You have reference to Mr. Weston to help us with money, more then his adventure; when he protesteth but for his promise, he would not have done any thing. He saith we take a heady course, and is offended that our provissions are made so farr of; as also that he was not made acquainted with our quantitie of things; and saith that in now being in ·3· places, so farr remote, we will, with going up and downe, and wrangling and expostulating, pass over the sommer before we will goe. And to speake the trueth, ther is fallen already amongst us a flatt schisme; and we are redier to goe to dispute, then to sett forwarde a voiage. I have received from Leyden since you wente ·3· or ·4· letters directed to you, though they only conscerne me. I will not trouble you with them. I always feared the event of the Amsterdamers striking in with us. I trow you must excommunicate me, or els you must goe without their companie, or we shall wante no quareling; but let them pass. We have reckoned, it should seeme, without our host; and, counting upon a ·150· persons, ther cannot be founde above 1200*li.* and odd moneys of all the ventures you can reckone, besides some cloath, stockings, and shoes, which are not counted; so we shall come shorte at least ·3· or ·400*li.* I would have had some thing shortened at first of beare and other provissions in hope of other adventures, and now we could have, both in Amsterdam and Kente, beere inough to serve our turne, but now we cannot accept it without prejudice. You fear we have begune to build and shall not be able to make an end; indeed, our courses were never established by counsell, we may therfore justly fear their standing. Yea, ther was a schisme amongst us ·3· at the first. You wrote to Mr. Martin, to prevente the making of the provissions in Kente, which he did, and sett downe his resolution how much he would have of every thing, without respecte to any counsell or exception. Surely he that is in a societie and yet regards not counsell, may better be a king then a consorte. To be shorte, if ther be not some other dispossition setled unto then yet is, we that should be partners of humilitie and peace, shall be examples of jangling and insulting. Yet your money which you ther must have, we will get provided for you instantly. 500*li* you say will serve; for the rest which hear and in Holand is to be used, we may goe scratch for it. For Mr. Crabe,* of whom you write, he hath promised to goe with us, yet I tell you I shall not be without feare till I see him shipped, for he is much opposed, yet I hope he will not faile. Thinke the best of all, and bear with patience what is wanting, and the Lord guid us all.

Your loving freind,

London, June 10.   ROBART CUSHMAN.
Anno: 1620.

I have bene the larger in these things, and so shall crave leave in some like passages following, (thoug in other things I shal labour to be more contracte,) that their children may see with what difficulties their fathers wrastled in going throug these things in their first beginnings, and how God brought them along notwithstanding all their weaknesses and infirmities. As allso that some use may be made hereof in after times by others in shuch like waightie imployments; and herewith I will end this chapter.

---

*He was a minister.

THE ·7· CHAPTER

Of their departure from Leyden, and other things ther
aboute, with their arivall at Southhamton, were they
all mete togeather, and tooke in ther provissions.

A T length, after much travell and these debates, all things
were got ready and provided. A smale ship* was bought,
and fitted in Holand, which was intended as to serve to help
to transport them, so to stay in the cuntrie and atend upon
fishing and shuch other affairs as might be for the good and
benefite of the colonie when they came ther. Another was hired
at London, of burden about ·9· score; and all other things
gott in readines. So being ready to departe, they had a day of
solleme humiliation, their pastor taking his texte from Ezra ·8·
21. *And ther at the river, by Ahava, I proclaimed a fast, that we*
might humble our selves before our God, and seeke of him a right
way for us, and for our children, and for all our substance. Upon
which he spente a good parte of the day very profitably, and
suitable to their presente occasion. The rest of the time was
spente in powering out prairs to the Lord with great fervencie,
mixed with abundance of tears. And the time being come that
they must departe, they were accompanied with most of their
brethren out of the citie, unto a towne sundrie miles of called
Delfes-Haven, wher the ship lay ready to receive them. So they
lefte the goodly and pleasante citie, which had been ther resting place near ·12· years; but they knew they were pilgrimes,†
and looked not much on those things, but lift up their eyes
to the heavens, their dearest cuntrie, and quieted their spirits.
When they came to the place they found the ship and all things
ready; and shuch of their freinds as could not come with them
followed after them, and sundrie also came from Amsterdame
to see them shipte and to take their leave of them. That night
was spent with litle sleepe by the most, but with freindly entertainmente and christian discourse and other reall expressions
of true christian love. The next day, the wind being faire, they
wente aborde, and their freinds with them, where truly dolfull
was the sight of that sadd and mournfull parting; to see what

*Of some ·60· tune.
†Heb. 11.

sighs and sobbs and praires did sound amongst them, what tears did gush from every eye, and pithy speeches peirst each harte; that sundry of the Dutch strangers that stood on the key as spectators, could not refraine from tears. Yet comfortable and sweete it was to see shuch lively and true expressions of dear and unfained love. But the tide (which stays for no man) caling them away that were thus loath to departe, their Reverend pastor falling downe on his knees, (and they all with him,) with watrie cheeks commended them with most fervente praiers to the Lord and his blessing. And then with mutuall imbrases and many tears, they tooke their leaves one of an other; which proved to be the last leave to many of them.

Thus hoysing saile,* with a prosperus winde they came in short time to Southhamton, wher they found the bigger ship come from London, lying ready, with all the rest of their company. After a joyfull wellcome, and mutuall congratulations, with other frendly entertainements, they fell to parley aboute their bussines, how to dispatch with the best expedition; as allso with their agents, aboute the alteration of the conditions. Mr. Carver pleaded he was imployed hear at Hamton, and knew not well what the other had don at London. Mr. Cushman answered, he had done nothing but what he was urged too, partly by the grounds of equity, and more espetialy by necessitie, other wise all had bene dasht and many undon. And in the begining he aquainted his felow agents here with, who consented unto him, and left it to him to execute, and to receive the money at London and send it downe to them at Hamton, wher they made the provissions; the which he accordingly did, though it was against his minde, and some of the marchants, that they were their made. And for giveing them notise at Leyden of this change, he could not well in regarde of the shortnes of the time; againe, he knew it would trouble them and hinder the bussines, which was already delayed overlong in regard of the season of the year, which he feared they would find to their cost. But these things gave not contente at presente. Mr. Weston, likewise, came up from London to see them dispatcht and to have the conditions confirmed; but they refused, and answered him, that he knew right well that

*This was about ·22· of July.

these were not according to the first agreemente, neither could they yeeld to them without the consente of the rest that were behind. And indeed they had spetiall charge when they came away, from the cheefe of those that were behind, not to doe it. At which he was much offended, and tould them, they must then looke to stand on their owne leggs. So he returned in displeasure, and this was the first ground of discontent betweene them. And wheras ther wanted well near 100*li.* to clear things at their going away, he would not take order to disburse a penie, but let them shift as they could. So they were forst to selle of some of their provissions to stop this gape, which was some ·3· or ·4· score firkins of butter, which comoditie they might best spare, haveing provided to large a quantitie of that kind. Then they write a leter to the marchants and adventurers aboute the diferances concerning the conditions, as foloweth.

Aug. 3. Anno: 1620.

BELOVED FREINDS, Sory we are that ther should be occasion of writing at all unto you, partly because we ever expected to see the most of you hear, but espetially because ther should any differance at all be conceived betweene us. But seing it faleth out that we cannot conferr togeather, we thinke it meete (though brefly) to show you the just cause and reason of our differing from those articles last made by Robart Cushman, without our comission or knowledg. And though he might propound good ends to him selfe, yet it no way justifies his doing it. Our maine diference is in the ·5· and ·9· article, concerning the deviding or holding of house and lands; the injoying wherof some of your selves well know, was one spetiall motive, amongst many other, to provoke us to goe. This was thought so reasonable, that when the greatest of you in adventure (whom we have much cause to respecte), when he propounded conditions to us freely of his owne accorde, he set this downe for one; a coppy wherof we have sent unto you, with some additions then added by us; which being liked on both sides, and a day set for the paimente of moneys, those of Holland paid in theirs. After that, Robart Cushman, Mr. Peirce, and Mr. Martine, brought them into a better forme, and write them in a booke now extante; and upon Robarts shewing them and delivering Mr. Mullins a coppy therof under his hand (which we have), he payd in his money. And we of Holland had never seen other before our coming to Hamton, but only as one got for him selfe a private coppy of them; upon sight wherof we manyfested uter dislike, but had put of our estates and were ready to come, and therfore was too late to rejecte the vioage. Judge therfore we beseech you indiferently of things, and if a faulte have bene commited, lay it wher it is, and not upon us, who have more cause to stand for the one, then you have for the other. We never gave Robart Cushman comission to make any one article for us, but only sent him to receive moneys upon articles before agreed on, and to further the provissions till John Carver came, and to assiste him in it. Yet since you conceive your selves wronged as well as we, we thought meete to add a branch to the end of our ·9· article, as will allmost heale that wound of it selfe, which you conceive to be in it. But that it may appeare to all men that we are not lovers of our selves only, but desire also the good and inriching of our freinds who have adventured your moneys with our persons, we have added our last article to the rest, promising you againe by leters in the behalfe of the whole company, that if large profits should not arise within the ·7· years, that we will continue togeather longer with you, if the Lord give a blesing.* This we hope is sufficente to satisfie any in this case, espetialy freinds, since we are asured that if the whole charge was devided into ·4· parts, ·3· of them will not stand upon it, netheir doe regarde it, etc. We are in shuch a streate at presente, as we are forced to sell away ·60*li.* worth of our provissions to cleare the Haven, and withall put our selves upon great extremities, scarce haveing any butter, no oyle, not a sole to mend a shoe, nor every man a sword to his side, wanting many muskets, much armoure, etc. And yet we are willing to expose our selves to shuch eminente dangers as are like to insue, and trust to the good providence of God, rather then his name and truth should be evill spoken of for us. Thus saluting all of you in love, and beseeching the Lord to give a blesing to our endeavore, and keepe all our harts in the bonds of peace and love, we take leave and rest,

Yours, etc.

August 3. 1620.

It was subscribed with many names of the cheefest of the company.

At their parting Mr. Robinson write a leter to the whole company, which though it hath already bene printed, yet I thought good here likwise to inserte it; as also a breefe leter writ at the same time to Mr. Carver, in which the tender love and godly care of a true pastor appears.

MY DEAR BROTHER, I received inclosed in your last leter the note of information, which I shall carefuly keepe and make use of as ther

---

*It was well for them that this was not accepted.

shall be occasion. I have a true feeling of your perplexitie of mind and toyle of body, but I hope that you who have allways been able so plentifully to administer comforte unto others in their trials, are so well furnished for your selfe as that farr greater difficulties then you have yet undergone (though I conceive them to have been great enough) cannot opprese you, though they press you, as the Apostle speaks. The spirite of a man (sustained by the spirite of God) will sustaine his infirmitie, I dout not so will yours. And the beter much when you shall injoye the presence and help of so many godly and wise bretheren, for the bearing of part of your burthen, who also will not admitte into their harts the least thought of suspition of any the least negligence, at least presumption, to have been in you, what so ever they thinke in others. Now what shall I say or write unto you and your goodwife my loving sister? even only this, I desire (and allways shall) unto you from the Lord, as unto my owne soule; and assure your selfe that my harte is with you, and that I will not forslowe my bodily coming at the first oppertunitie. I have writen a large leter to the whole, and am sorie I shall not rather speak then write to them; and the more, considering the wante of a preacher, which I shall also make sume spurr to my hastening after you. I doe ever commend my best affection unto you, which if I thought you made any doubte of, I would express in more, and the same more, ample and full words. And the Lord in whom you trust and whom you serve ever in this bussines and journey, guid you with his hand, protecte you with his winge, and shew you and us his salvation in the end, and bring us in the mean while togeather in the place desired, if shuch be his good will, for his Christs sake. Amen.

Yours, etc.
Jo: R.

July 27, 1620.

This was the last letter that Mr. Carver lived to see from him. The other follows.

LOVINGE CHRISTIAN FRIENDS, I doe hartily and in the Lord salute you all, as being they with whom I am presente in my best affection, and most ernest longings after you, though I be constrained for a while to be bodily absente from you. I say constrained, God knowing how willingly, and much rather then other wise, I would have borne my part with you in this first brunt, were I not by strong necessitie held back for the present. Make accounte of me in the mean while, as of a man devided in my selfe with great paine, and as (naturall bonds set a side) having my beter parte with you. And though I doubt not but in your godly wisdoms, you both foresee and resolve upon that which concerneth your presente state and condition, both severally and joyntly, yet have I thought it but my duty to add some furder spurr of provocation unto them, who rune allready, if not because you need it, yet because I owe it in love and dutie. And first, as we are daly to renew our repentance with our God, espetially for our sines known, and generally for our unknowne trespasses, so doth the Lord call us in a singuler maner upon occasions of shuch difficultie and danger as lieth upon you, to a both more narrow search and careful reformation of your ways in his sight; least he, calling to remembrance our sines forgotten by us or unrepented of, take advantage against us, and in judgmente leave us for the same to be swalowed up in one danger or other; wheras, on the contrary, sine being taken away by ernest repentance and the pardon therof from the Lord sealed up unto a mans conscience by his spirite, great shall be his securitie and peace in all dangers, sweete his comforts in all distresses, with hapie deliverance from all evill, whether in life or in death.

Now next after this heavenly peace with God and our owne consciences, we are carefully to provide for peace with all men what in us lieth, espetially with our associates, and for that watchfullnes must be had, that we neither at all in our selves doe give, no nor easily take offence being given by others. Woe be unto the world for offences, for though it be necessarie (considering the malice of Satan and mans corruption) that offences come, yet woe unto the man or woman either by whom the offence cometh, saith Christ, Mat. 18. 7. And if offences in the unseasonable use of things in them selves indifferent, be more to be feared then death it selfe, as the Apostle teacheth, 1. Cor. 9. 15. how much more in things simply evill, in which neither honour of God nor love of man is thought worthy to be regarded. Neither yet is it sufficiente that we keepe our selves by the grace of God from giveing offence, exepte withall we be armed against the taking of them when they be given by others. For how unperfect and lame is the work of grace in that person, who wants charritie to cover a multitude of offences, as the scriptures speaks. Neither are you to be exhorted to this grace only upon the commone grounds of Christianitie, which are, that persons ready to take offence, either wante charitie, to cover offences, or wisdome duly to waigh humane frailtie; or lastly, are grosse, though close hipocrites, as Christ our Lord teacheth, Mat. ·7· 1, 2, 3, as indeed in my owne experience, few or none have bene found which sooner give offence, then shuch as easily take it; neither have they ever proved sound and profitable members in societies, which have nurished this touchey humor. But besides these, ther are diverse motives provoking you above others to great care and conscience this way: As first, you are many of you strangers, as to the persons, so to the infirmities one of another, and so stand in neede of more watchfullnes this way, least when shuch things fall out in men and women as you suspected not, you be inordinatly affected with them; which doth require at your hands much wisdome and charitie for the covering and preventing of incident offences that way. And lastly, your intended course of civill comunitie will minister continuall occasion of offence, and will be as fuell for that fire, excepte you dilligently quench it with brotherly forbearance. And if taking of offence causlesly or easilie at mens doings be so carefuly to be avoyded, how much more heed is to be taken that we take not offence at God him selfe, which yet we certainly doe so ofte as we doe murmure at his providence in our crosses, or beare impatiently shuch afflictions as wherwith he pleaseth to visite us. Store up therfore patience against the evill day, without which we take offence at the Lord him selfe in his holy and just works.

A ·4· thing ther is carfully to be provided for, to witte, that with your commone imployments you joyne commone affections truly bente upon the generall good, avoyding as a deadly plague of your both commone and spetiall comfort all retirednes of minde for proper advantage, and all singularly affected any maner of way; let every man represe in him selfe and the whol body in each person, as so many rebels against the commone good, all private respects of mens selves, not sorting with the generall conveniencie. And as men are carfull not to have a new house shaken with any violence before it be well setled and the parts firmly knite, so be you, I besheech you, brethren, much more carfull, that the house of God which you are, and are to be, be not shaken with unnecessarie novelties or other oppositions at the first setling therof.

Lastly, wheras you are become a body politik, using amongst your selves civill goverments, and are not furnished with any persons of spetiall eminencie above the rest, to be chosen by you into office of goverment, let your wisdome and godlines appeare, not only in chusing shuch persons as doe entirely love and will promote the commone good, but also in yeelding unto them all due honour and obedience in their lawfull administrations; not behoulding in them the ordinarinesse of their persons, but Gods ordinance for your good, not being like the foolish multitud who more honour the gay coate, then either the vertuous minde of the man, or glorious ordinance of the Lord. But you know better things, and that the image of the Lords power and authoritie which the magistrate beareth, is honourable, in how meane persons soever. And this dutie you both may the more willingly and ought the more conscionably to performe, because you

are at least for the present to have only them for your ordinarie governours, which your selves shall make choyse of for that worke.

Sundrie other things of importance I could put you in minde
of, and of those before mentioned, in more words, but I will not
so farr wrong your godly minds as to thinke you heedless of these
things, ther being also diverce among you so well able to admonish
both them selves and others of what concerneth them. These few
things therfore, and the same in few words, I doe ernestly commend
unto your care and conscience, joyning therwith my daily incessante
prayers unto the Lord, that he who hath made the heavens and the
earth, the sea and all rivers of waters, and whose providence is over
all his workes, espetially over all his dear children for good, would
so guide and gard you in your wayes, as inwardly by his Spirite, so
outwardly by the hand of his power, as that both you and we allso,
for and with you, may have after matter of praising his name all the
days of your and our lives. Fare you well in him in whom you trust,
and in whom I rest.

> An unfained wellwiller of your hapie
> success in this hopefull voyage,
> JOHN ROBINSON.

This letter, though large, yet being so frutfull in it selfe, and
suitable to their occation, I thought meete to inserte in this
place.

All things being now ready, and every bussines dispatched,
the company was caled togeather, and this letter read amongst
them, which had good acceptation with all, and after fruit
with many. Then they ordered and distributed their company
for either shipe, as they conceived for the best. And chose a
Governour and ·2· or ·3· assistants for each shipe, to order
the people by the way, and see to the dispossing of there provissions, and shuch like affairs. All which was not only with
the liking of the maisters of the ships, but according to their
desires. Which being done, they sett sayle from thence aboute
the ·5· of August; but what befell them further upon the coast
of England will appeare in the nexte chapter.

THE ·8· CHAPTER
Off the troubles that befell them on the coaste, and at
sea, being forced, after much trouble, to leave one of
ther ships and some of their companie behind them.

BEING thus put to sea they had not gone farr, but Mr.
Reinolds the master of the leser ship complained that he
found his ship so leak as he durst not put further to sea till
she was mended. So the master of the biger ship (caled Mr.
Joans) being consulted with, they both resolved to put into
Dartmouth and have her ther searched and mended, which
accordingly was done, to their great charg and losse of time
and a faire winde. She was hear thorowly searcht from steme
to sterne, some leaks were found and mended, and now it was
conceived by the workmen and all, that she was sufficiente, and
they might proceede without either fear or danger. So with
good hopes from hence, they put to sea againe, conceiving they
should goe comfortably on, not looking for any more lets of
this kind; but it fell out otherwise, for after they were gone to
sea againe above ·100· leagues without the Lands End, hould-
ing company togeather all this while, the master of the small
ship complained his ship was so leake as he must beare up or
sinke at sea, for they could scarce free her with much pumping.
So they came to consultation againe, and resolved both ships
to bear up backe againe and put into Plimmoth, which accordingly was done. But no spetiall leake could be founde, but it
was judged to be the generall weaknes of the shipe, and that
shee would not prove sufficiente for the voiage. Upon which
it was resolved to dismise her and parte of the companie, and
proceede with the other shipe. The which (though it was greeveous, and caused great discouragmente) was put in execution.
So after they had tooke out shuch provission as the other ship
could well stow, and concluded both what number and what
persons to send bak, they made another sad parting, the one
ship going backe for London, and the other was to proceede
on her viage. Those that went bak were for the most parte
shuch as were willing so to doe, either out of some discontente,
or feare they conceived of the ill success of the vioage, seeing
so many croses befale, and the year time so farr spente; but

others, in regarde of their owne weaknes, and charge of many
yonge children, were thought least usefull, and most unfite to
bear the brunte of this hard adventure; unto which worke of
God, and judgmente of their brethern, they were contented
to submite. And thus, like Gedions armie, this small number
was devided, as if the Lord by this worke of his providence
thought these few to many for the great worke he had to doe.
But here by the way let me show, how afterward it was found
that the leaknes of this ship was partly by being overmasted,
and too much pressed with sayles; for after she was sould and
put into her old trime, she made many viages and performed
her service very sufficently, to the great profite of her owners.
But more espetially, by the cuning and deceite of the master
and his company, who were hired to stay a whole year in the
cuntrie, and now fancying dislike and fearing wante of victeles,
they ploted this stratagem to free them selves; as afterwards
was knowne, and by some of them confessed. For they apprehended that the greater ship, being of force, and in whom most
of the provissions were stowed, she would retayne enough for
her selfe, what soever became of them or the passengers; and
indeed shuch speeches had bene cast out by some of them; and
yet, besides other incouragments, the cheefe of them that came
from Leyden wente in this shipe to give the master contente.
But so strong was self love and his fears, as he forgott all duty
and former kindnesses, and delt thus falsly with them, though
he pretended otherwise. Amongest those that returned was
Mr. Cushman and his familie, whose hart and courage was
gone from them before, as it seems, though his body was with
them till now he departed; as may appear by a passionate letter
he write to a freind in London from Dartmouth, whilst the
ship lay ther a mending; the which, besides the expressions of
his owne fears, it shows much of the providence of God working for their good beyonde mans expectation, and other things
concerning their condition in these streats. I will hear relate it.
And though it discover some infirmities in him (as who under
temtation is free), yet after this he continued to be a spetiall
instrumente for their good, and to doe the offices of a loving
freind and faithfull brother unto them, and pertaker of much
comforte with them.

The letter is as followth.

To his loving friend Ed: S at Henige House in the Dukes
Place, these, &c.

Dartmouth, Aug. 17.

LOVING FRIEND, My most kind remembrance to you and your
wife, with loving E. M. etc. whom in this world I never looke to see
againe. For besides the eminente dangers of this viage, which are no
less then deadly, an infirmitie of body hath ceased me, which will not
in all liclyhoode leave me till death. What to call it I know not, but it
is a bundle of lead, as it were, crushing my harte more and more these
·14· days, as that allthough I doe the acctions of a liveing man, yet I
am but as dead; but the will of God be done. Our pinass will not cease
leaking, els I thinke, we had been halfe way at Virginia, our viage
hither hath been as full of crosses, as our selves have been of crok-
ednes. We put in hear to trimme her, and I thinke, as others also, if
we had stayed at sea but ·3· or ·4· howers more, shee would have sunke
right downe. And though she was twise trimmed at Hamton, yet now
shee is as open and leakie as a seive; and ther was a borde, a man might
have puld of with his fingers, ·2· foote longe, wher the water came in
as at a mole hole. We lay at Hamton ·7· days, in fair weather, waiting
for her, and now we lye hear waiting for her in as faire a wind as can
blowe, and so have done these ·4· days, and are like to lye ·4· more,
and by that time the wind will happily turne as it did at Hampton.
Our victualls will be halfe eaten up, I thinke, before we goe from
the coaste of England, and if our viage last longe, we shall not have
a months victialls when we come in the countrie. Neare ·700*li.* hath
bene bestowed at Hampton, upon what I know not. Mr. Martin saith
he neither can nor will give any accounte of it, and if he be called upon
for accounts he crieth out of unthankfullnes for his paines and care,
that we are susspitious of him, and flings away, and will end nothing. Also he so insulteth over our poore people, with shuch scorne
and contempte, as if they were not good enough to wipe his shoes.
It would break your hart to see his dealing,* and the mourning of
our people. They complaine to me, and alass! I can doe nothing for
them; if I speake to him, he flies in my face, as mutinous, and saith no
complaints shall be heard or received but by him selfe, and saith they
are forwarde, and waspish, discontented people, and I doe ill to hear
them. Ther are others that would lose all they have put in, or make
satisfaction for what they have had, that they might departe; but he
will not hear them, nor suffer them to goe ashore, least they should
rune away. The sailors also are so offended at his ignorante bouldnes,

---

*He was governour in the biger ship, and Mr. Cushman assistante.

in medling and controuling in things he knows not what belongs too, as that some threaten to misscheefe him, others say they will leave the shipe and goe their way. But at the best this cometh of it, that he makes him selfe a scorne and laughing stock unto them. As for Mr. Weston, excepte grace doe greatly swaye with him, he will hate us ten times more then ever he loved us, for not confirming the conditions. But now, since some pinches have taken them, they begine to reveile the trueth, and say Mr. Robinson was in the falte who charged them never to consente to those conditions, nor chuse me into office, but indeede apointed them to chose them they did chose.* But he and they will rue too late, they may now see, and all be ashamed when it is too late, that they were so ignorante, yea, and so inordinate in their courses. I am sure as they were resolved not to seale those conditions, I was not so resolute at Hampton to have left the whole bussines, excepte they would seale them, and better the vioage to have bene broken of then, then to have brought shuch miserie to our selves, dishonour to God, and detrimente to our loving freinds, as now it is like to doe ·4· or ·5· of the cheefe of them which came from Leyden, came resolved never to goe on those conditions. And Mr. Martine, he said he never received no money on those conditions, he was not beholden to the marchants for a pine, they were bloudsuckers, and I know not what. Simple man, he indeed never made any conditions with the marchants, nor ever spake with them. But did all that money flie to Hampton, or was it his owne? Who will goe and lay out money so rashly and lavishly as he did, and never know how he comes by it, or on what conditions? 2ly. I tould him of the alteration longe agoe, and he was contente; but now he dominires, and said I had betrayed them into the hands of shaves; he is not beholden to them, he can set out ·2· ships him self to a viage. When, good man? He hath but ·50li· in, and if he should give up his accounts he would not have a penie left him, as I am persuaded,† etc. Freind, if ever we make a plantation, God works a mirakle; espetially considering how scante we shall be of victualls, and most of all ununited amongst our selves, and devoyd of good tutors and regimente. Violence will break all. Wher is the meek and humble spirite of Moyses? and of Nehemiah who reedified the wals of Jerusalem, and the state of Israell? Is not the sound of Rehoboams braggs daly hear amongst us? Have not the philosiphers and all wise men observed that, even in setled commone welths, violente governours bring either them selves, or people, or boath, to ruine; how much more in the raising of commone wealths, when the morter is yet scarce tempered that should bind the wales. If

---

*I thinke he was deceived in these things.
†This was found true afterward.

I should write to you of all things which promiscuously forerune our ruine, I should over charge my weake head and greeve your tender hart; only this, I pray you prepare for evill tidings of us every day. But pray for us instantly, it may be the Lord will be yet entreated one way or other to make for us. I see not in reason how we shall escape even the gasping of hunger starved persons; but God can doe much, and his will be done. It is better for me to dye, then now for me to bear it, which I doe daly, and expecte it howerly; haveing received the sentance of death, both within me and without me. Poore William Ring and my selfe doe strive who shall be meate first for the fishes; but we looke for a glorious resurrection, knowing Christ Jesus after the flesh no more, but looking unto the joye that is before us, we shall endure all these things and accounte them light in comparison of that joye we hope for. Remember me in all love to our freinds as if I named them, whose praiers I desire ernestly, and wish againe to see, but not till I can with more comforte looke them in the face. The Lord give us that true comforte which none can take from us. I had a desire to make a breefe relation of our estate to some freind. I doubte not but your wisdome will teach you seasonably to utter things as here after you shall be called to it. That which I have writen is treue, and many things more which I have forborne. I write it as upon my life, and last confession in England. What is of use to be spoken of presently, you may speake of it, and what is fitt to conceile, conceall. Pass by my weake maner, for my head is weake, and my body feeble, the Lord make me strong in him, and keepe both you and yours.

Your loving freind,-
ROBART CUSHMAN.

Dartmouth, August 17. 1620.

These being his conceptions and fears at Dartmouth, they must needs be much stronger now at Plimoth.

THE ·9· CHAPTER
Of their vioage, and how they passed the sea, and of their safe arrivall at Cape Codd.

SEPTEMBER: 6. These troubles being blowne over, and now all being compacte togeather in one shipe, they put to sea againe with a prosperus winde, which continued diverse days togeather, which was some incouragmente unto them; yet according to the usuall maner many were afflicted with sea-sicknes. And I may not omite hear a spetiall worke of Gods providence. Ther was a proud and very profane yonge man, one of the sea-men, of a lustie, able body, which made him the more hauty; he would allway be contemning the poore people in their sicknes, and cursing them dayly with greevous execrations, and did not let to tell them, that he hoped to help to cast halfe of them over board before they came to their jurneys end, and to make mery with what they had; and if he were by any gently reproved, he would curse and swear most bitterly. But it pleased God before they came halfe seas over, to smite this yong man with a greeveous disease, of which he dyed in a desperate maner, and so was him selfe the first that was thrown overbord. Thus his curses light on his owne head; and it was an astonishmente to all his fellows, for they noted it to be the just hand of God upon him.

After they had injoyed faire winds and weather for a season, they were incountred many times with crosse winds, and mette with many feirce stormes, with which the shipe was shroudly shaken, and her upper works made very leakie; and one of the maine beames in the midd ships was bowed and craked, which put them in some fear that the shipe could not be able to performe the vioage. So some of the cheefe of the company, perceiveing the mariners to feare the suffisiencie of the shipe, as appeared by their mutterings, they entred into serious consulltation with the master and other officers of the ship, to consider in time of the danger; and rather to returne then to cast them selves into a desperate and inevitable perill. And truly ther was great distraction and differance of oppinion amongst the mariners them selves; faine would they doe what could be done for their wages sake, (being now halfe the seas over,) and on the other hand they were loath to hazard their lives too desperatly. But in examening of all oppinions, the master and others affirmed they knew the ship to be stronge and firme underwater; and for the buckling of the maine beame, ther was a great iron scrue the passengers brought out of Holland, which would raise the beame into his place; the which being done, the carpenter and master affirmed that with a post put under it, set firme in the lower deck, and otherways bounde, he would make it sufficiente. And as for the decks and uper workes they would calke them as well as they could, and though with the workeing of the ship they would not longe keepe stanch, yet ther would otherwise be no great danger, if they did not overpress her with sails. So they commited them selves to the will of God, and resolved to proseede. In sundrie of these stormes the winds were so feirce, and the seas so high, as they could not beare a knote of saile, but were forced to hull, for diverce days togither. And in one of them, as they thus lay at hull, in a mighty storme, a lustie yonge man (called John Howland) coming upon some occasion above the grattings, was, with a seele of the shipe throwne into the sea; but it pleased God that he caught hould of the top-saile halliards, which hunge over board, and rane out at length; yet he held his hould (though he was sundrie fadomes under water) till he was hald up by the same rope to the brime of the water, and then with a boathooke and other means got into the shipe againe, and his life saved; and though he was something ill with it, yet he lived many years after, and became a profitable member both in church and commone wealthe. In all this viage ther died but one of the passengers, which was William Butten, a youth, servant to Samuell Fuller, when they drew near the coast. But to omite other things, (that I may be breefe,) after longe beating at sea they fell with that land which is called Cape Cod; the which being made and certainly knowne to be it, they were not a litle joyfull. After some deliberation had amongst them selves and with the master of the ship, they tacked aboute and resolved to stande for the southward (the wind and weather being faire) to finde some place aboute Hudsons river for their habitation. But after they had sailed that course aboute halfe the day, they fell amongst deangerous shoulds and roring breakers, and they were so farr intangled ther with as they conceived them selves in great danger; and the wind shrinking upon them withall, they resolved to bear up againe for the Cape, and thought them selves hapy to gett out of those dangers before night overtooke them, as by Gods good providence they did. And the next day they gott into the Cape-harbor wher they ridd in saftie. A word or too by the way of this cape; it was thus first named by Capten Gosnole and his company,* Anno: 1602, and after by Capten Smith was caled Cape James; but it retains the former name amongst sea-men. Also that pointe which first shewed those dangerous shoulds unto them, they called Pointe Care, and Tuckers Terrour; but the French and Dutch to this

*Because they tooke much of that fishe ther.

day call it Malabarr, by reason of those perilous shoulds, and the losses they have suffered their.

Being thus arived in a good harbor and brought safe to land, they fell upon their knees and blessed the God of heaven, who had brought them over the vast and furious ocean, and delivered them from all the periles and miseries therof, againe to set their feete on the firme and stable earth, their proper elemente. And no marvell if they were thus joyefull, seeing wise Seneca was so affected with sailing a few miles on the coast of his owne Italy; as he affirmed,* that he had rather remaine twentie years on his way by land, then pass by sea to any place in a short time; so tedious and dreadfull was the same unto him.

But hear I cannot but stay and make a pause, and stand half amazed at this poore peoples presente condition; and so I thinke will the reader too, when he well considers the same. Being thus passed the vast ocean, and a sea of troubles before in their preparation (as may be remembred by that which wente before), they had now no freinds to wellcome them, nor inns to entertaine or refresh their weatherbeaten bodys, no houses or much less townes to repaire too, to seeke for succoure. It is recorded in scripture† as a mercie to the apostle and his shipwraked company, that the barbarians shewed them no smale kindnes in refreshing them, but these savage barbarians, when they mette with them (as after will appeare) were readier to fill their sides full of arrows then other wise. And for the season it was winter, and they that know the winters of that cuntrie know them to be sharp and violent, and subjecte to cruell and feirce stormes, deangerous to travill to known places, much more to serch an unknown coast. Besides, what could they see but a hidious and desolate wildernes, full of wild beasts and willd men? and what multitudes ther might be of them they knew not. Nether could they, as it were, goe up to the tope of Pisgah, to vew from this willdernes a more goodly cuntrie to feed their hopes; for which way soever they turnd their eyes (save upward to the heavens) they could have litle solace or content in respecte of any outward objects. For summer being done, all things stand upon them with a wetherbeaten face; and

*Epist: 53.
†Act. 28.

the whole countrie, full of woods and thickets, represented a wild and savage heiw. If they looked behind them, ther was the mighty ocean which they had passed, and was now as a maine barr and goulfe to seperate them from all the civill parts of the world. If it be said they had a ship to sucour them, it is trew; but what heard they daly from the master and company? but that with speede they should looke out a place with their shallop, wher they would be at some near distance; for the season was shuch as he would not stirr from thence till a safe harbor was discovered by them wher they would be, and he might goe without danger; and that victells consumed apace, but he must and would keepe sufficient for them selves and their returne. Yea, it was muttered by some, that if they gott not a place in time, they would turne them and their goods a shore and leave them. Let it also be considred what weake hopes of supply and succoure they left behinde them, that might bear up their minds in this sade condition and trialls they were under; and they could not but be very smale. It is true, indeed, the affections and love of their brethren at Leyden was cordiall and entire towards them, but they had litle power to help them, or them selves; and how the case stoode betweene them and the marchants at their coming away, hath allready been declared. What could now sustaine them but the spirite of God and his grace? May not and ought not the children of these fathers rightly say: *Our faithers were English men which came over this great ocean, and were ready to perish in this willdernes,* but they cried unto the Lord, and he heard their voyce, and looked on their adversitie, etc. Let them therfore praise the Lord, because he is good, and his mercies endure for ever.† Yea, let them which have been redeemed of the Lord, shew how he hath delivered them from the hand of the oppressour. When they wandered in the deserte and willdernes out of the way, and found no citie to dwell in, both hungrie, and thirstie, their sowle was overwhelmed in them. Let them confess before the Lord his loving kindnes, and his wonderfull works before the sons of men.*

*Deu: 26. 5, 7.
†107 Psa: v. 1, 2, 4, 5, 8.

THE ·10· CHAPTER
Showing how they sought out a place of habitation,
and what befell them theraboute.

BEING thus arrived at Cap-Cod the ·11· of November, and necessitie calling them to looke out a place for habitation, (as well as the maisters and mariners importunitie,) they having brought a large shalop with them out of England, stowed in quarters in the ship, they now gott her out and sett their carpenters to worke to trime her up; but being much brused and shatered in the shipe with foule weather, they saw she would be longe in mending. Wherupon a few of them tendered them selves to goe by land and discovere those nearest places, whilst the shallop was in mending; and the rather because as they wente into that harbor ther seemed to be an opening some ·2· or ·3· leagues of, which the maister judged to be a river. It was conceived ther might be some danger in the attempte, yet seeing them resolute, they were permited to goe, being ·16· of them well armed, under the conduct of Captein Standish, having shuch instructions given them as was thought meete. They sett forth the ·15· of November: and when they had marched aboute the space of a mile by the sea side, they espied ·5· or ·6· persons with a dogg coming towards them, who were salvages; but they fled from them, and ranne up into the woods, and the English followed them, partly to see if they could speake with them, and partly to discover if ther might not be more of them lying in ambush. But the Indeans seeing them selves thus followed, they againe forsooke the woods, and rane away on the sands as hard as they could, so as they could not come near them, but followed them by the tracte of their feet sundrie miles, and saw that they had come the same way. So, night coming on, they made their randevous and set out their sentinels, and rested in quiete *that night*, and the next morning followed their tracte till they had headed a great creeke, and so left the sands, and turned an other way into the woods. But they still followed them by geuss, hoping to find their dwellings; but they soone lost both them and them selves, falling into shuch thickets as were ready to tear their cloaths and armore in peeces, but were most distressed for wante of drinke. But at length they found water and refreshed them selves, being the first New-England water they drunke of, and was now in thir great thirste as pleasante unto them as wine or bear had been in for-times. Afterwards they directed their course to come to the other shore, for they knew it was a necke of land they were to crosse over, and so at length gott to the sea-side, and marched to this supposed river, and by the way found a pond of clear fresh water, and shortly after a good quantitie of clear ground wher the Indeans had formerly set corne, and some of their graves. And proceeding furder they saw new-stuble wher corne had been set the same year, also they found wher latly a house had been, wher some planks and a great ketle was remaining, and heaps of sand newly padled with their hands, which they, digging up, found in them diverce faire Indean baskets filled with corne, and some in eares, faire and good, of diverce collours, which seemed to them a very goodly sight, (haveing never seen any shuch before). This was near the place of that supposed river they came to seeck; unto which they wente and found it to open it selfe into ·2· armes with a high cliffe of sand in the enterance, but more like to be crikes of salte water then any fresh, for ought they saw; and that ther was good harborige for their shalope; leaving it further to be discovered by their shalop when she was ready. So their time limeted them being expired, they returned to the ship, least they should be in fear of their saftie, and tooke with them parte of the corne, and buried up the rest, and so like the men from Eshcoll carried with them of the fruits of the land, and showed their breethren; of which, and their returne, they were marvelusly glad, and their harts incouraged.

After this, the shalop being got ready, they set out againe for the better discovery of this place, and the master of the ship desired to goe him selfe, so ther went some ·30· men, but found it to be no harbor for ships but only for boats; ther was allso found ·2· of their houses covered with matts, and sundrie of their implements in them, but the people were rune away and could not be seen; also ther was found more of their corne, and of their beans of various collours. The corne and beans they brought away, purposing to give them full satisfaction when they should meete with any of them (as about some ·6· months afterward they did, to their good contente). And here is to be noted a spetiall providence of God, and a great mercie to this

poore people, that hear they gott seed to plant them corne the
next yeare, or els they might have starved, for they had none,
nor any liklyhood to get any till the season had beene past (as
the sequell did manyfest). Neither is it lickly they had had this,
if the first viage had not been made, for the ground was now
all covered with snow, and hard frosen. But the Lord is never
wanting unto his in their greatest needs; let his holy name have
all the praise.

The month of November being spente in these affairs, and
much foule weather falling in, the ·6· of *Desember* they sente
out their shallop againe with ·10· of their principall men, and
some sea men, upon further discovery, intending to circulate
that deepe bay of Cap-Codd. The weather was very could, and
it frose so hard as the sprea of the sea lighting on their coats,
they were as if they had been glased; yet *that night* betimes they
gott downe into the botome of the bay, and as they drue nere
the shore they saw some ·10· or ·12· Indeans very busie aboute
some thing. They landed aboute a league or ·2· from them, and
had much a doe to put a shore any wher, it lay so full of flats.
Being landed, it grew late, and they made them selves a barricado with loggs and bowes as well as they could in the time,
and set out their sentenill and betooke them to rest, and saw
the smoake of the fire the savages made that night. When
morning was come they devided their company, some to coast
along the shore in the boate, and the rest marched throw the
woods to see the land, if any fit place might be for their dwelling. They came allso to the place wher they saw the Indians the
night before, and found they had been cuting up a great fish
like a grampus, being some ·2· inches thike of fate like a hogg,
some peeces wher of they had left by the way; and the shallop
found ·2· more of these fishes dead on the sands, a thing usuall
after storms in that place, by reason of the great flats of sand
that lye of. So they ranged up and doune all that day, but found
no people, nor any place they liked. When the sune grue low,
they hasted out of the woods to meete with their shallop, to
whom they made signes to come to them into a *creeke* hardby,
the which they did at high-water; of which they were very glad,
for they had not seen each other all that day, since the morning.
So they made them a barricado (as usually they did every night)
with loggs, stakes, and thike pine bowes, the height of a man,

leaving it open to leeward, partly to shelter them from the could and wind (making their fire in the midle, and lying round aboute it), and partly to defend them from any sudden assaults of the savages, if they should surround them. So being very weary, they betooke them to rest. But aboute *midnight*, they heard a hideous and great crie, and their sentinell caled, Arme, arme; so they bestired them and stood to their armes, and shote of a cupple of moskets, and then the noys seased. They concluded it was a companie of wolves, or such like willd beasts; for one of the sea men tould them he had often heard shuch a noyse in New-found land. So they rested till about ·5· of the clock in the *morning*; for the tide, and ther purpose to goe from thence, made them be stiring betimes. So after praier they prepared for breakfast, and it being day dawning, it was thought best to be carring things downe to the boate. But some said it was not best to carrie the armes downe, others said they would be the readier, for they had laped them up in their coats from the dew. But some ·3· or ·4· would not cary theirs till they wente them selves, yet as it fell out, the water being not high enough, they layed them downe on the banke side, and came up to breakfast. But presently, all on the sudain, they heard a great and strange crie, which they knew to be the same voyces they heard in the night, though they varied their notes, and one of their company being abroad came runing in, and cried, Men, Indeans, Indeans; and withall, their arowes came flying amongst them. Their men rane with all speed to recover their armes, as by the good providence of God they did. In the mean time, of those that were ther ready, tow muskets were discharged at them, and ·2· more stood ready in the enterance of ther randevoue, but were comanded not to shoote till they could take full aime at them; and the other ·2· charged againe with all speed, for ther were only ·4· had armes ther, and defended the baricado which was first assalted. The crie of the Indeans was dreadfull, espetially when they saw ther men rune out of the randevoue towourds the shallop, to recover ther armes the Indeans wheeling aboute upon them. But some running out with coats of malle on, and cutlashess in their hands, they soone got their armes, and let flye amongs them, and quickly stopped their violence. Yet ther was a lustie man, and no less valiante, stood behind a tree within halfe a musket shot, and let his arrows flie at them. He was seen shoot ·3· arrowes, which were all avoyded. He stood ·3· shot of a musket, till one taking full aime at him, and made the barke or splinters of the tree fly about his ears, after which he gave an extraordinary shrike, and away they wente all of them. They left some to keep the shalop, and followed them aboute a quarter of a mille, and shouted once or twise, and shot of ·2· or ·3· peces, and so returned. This they did, that they might conceive that they were not affrade of them or any way discouraged. Thus it pleased God to vanquish their enimies, and give them deliverance; and by his spetiall providence so to dispose that not any one of them were either hurte, or hitt, though their arrows came close by them, and on every side of them, and sundry of their coats, which hunge up in the barricado, were shot throw and throw. Aterwards they gave God sollemne thanks and praise for their deliverance, and gathered up a bundle of their arrows, and sente them into England afterward by the master of the ship, and called that place the first encounter. From hence they departed, and costed all along, but discerned no place likly for harbor; and therfore hasted to a place that their pillote, (one Mr. Coppin who had bine in the cuntrie before) did assure them was a good harbor, which he had been in, and they might fetch it before night; of which they were glad, for it begane to be foule weather. After some houres sailing, it begane to snow and raine, and about the midle of the afternoone, the wind increased, and the sea became very rough, and they broake their rudder, and it was as much as ·2· men could doe to steere her with a cupple of oares. But their pillott bad them be of good cheere, for he saw the harbor; but the storme increasing, and night drawing on, they bore what saile they could to gett in, while they could see. But herwith they broake their mast in ·3· peeces, and their saill fell over bord, in a very grown sea, so as they had like to have been cast away; yet by Gods mercie they recovered them selves, and having the floud with them, struck into the harbore. But when it came too, the pillott was deceived in the place, and said, the Lord be mercifull unto them, for his eyes never saw that place before; and he and the master mate would have rune her a shore, in a cove full of breakers, before the winde. But a lusty seaman which steered, bad those which rowed, if they were men, about with her, or ells they were all cast away; the which they did with speed. So he bid them be of good cheere and row lustly, for ther was a faire sound before them, and he doubted not but they should find one place or other wher they might ride in saftie. And though it was *very darke*, and rained sore, yet in the end they gott under the lee of a smalle iland, and remained ther all *that night* in saftie. But they knew not this to be an iland till morning, but were devided in their minds; some would keepe the boate for fear they might be amongst the Indians; others were so weake and could, they could not endure, but got a shore, and with much adoe got fire, (all things being so wett,) and the rest were glad to come to them; for after midnight the wind shifted to the north-west, and it frose hard. But though this had been a day and night of much trouble and danger unto them, yet God gave them a *morning* of comforte and refreshing (as usually he doth to his children), for the next day was a faire sunshininge day, and they found them sellves to be on an iland secure from the Indeans, wher they might drie their stufe, fixe their peeces, and rest them selves, and gave God thanks for his mercies, in their manifould deliverances. And this being the *last day of the weeke*, they prepared ther to keepe the *Sabath*. On *Munday* they sounded the harbor, and founde it fitt for shipping; and marched into the land, and found diverse corn-feilds, and litle runing brooks, a place (as they supposed) fitt for situation; at least it was the best they could find, and the season, and their presente necessitie, made them glad to accepte of it. So they returned to their shipp againe with this news to the rest of their people, which did much comforte their harts.

On the ·15· *of Desember*: they wayed anchor to goe to the place they had discovered, and came within ·2· leagues of it, but were faine to bear up againe; but the ·16· *day* the winde came faire, and they arrived safe in this harbor. And after wards tooke better view of the place, and resolved wher to pitch their dwelling; and the ·25· *day* begane to erecte the first house for commone use to receive them and their goods.

The ·2· Booke

The rest of this history (if God give me life, and opportunitie) I shall, for brevitis sake, handle by way of annalls, noteing only the heads of principall things, and passages as they fell in order of time, and may seeme to be profitable to know, or to make use of. And this may be as the ·2· Booke.

The remainder of Anno 1620.

I SHALL a litle returne backe and begine with a combination made by them before they came a shore, being the first foundation of their govermente in this place; occasioned partly by the discontented and mutinous speeches that some of the strangers amongst them had let fall from them in the ship; That when they came a shore they would use their owne libertie; for none had power to command them, the patente they had being for Virginia, and not for New England, which belonged to an other Goverment, with which the Virginia Company had nothing to doe. And partly that shuch an acte by them done (this their condition considered) might be as firme as any patent, and in some respects more sure.

The forme was as followeth.

In the name of God, Amen. We whose names are underwriten, the loyall subjects of our dread soveraigne Lord, King James, by the grace of God, of Great Britaine, Franc, and Ireland king, defender of the faith, etc.

Haveing undertaken, for the glorie of God, and advancemente of the Christian faith, and honour of our king and countrie, a voyage to plant the first colonie in the Northerne parts of Virginia, doe by these presents solemnly and mutualy in the presence of God, and one of another, covenant and combine our selves togeather into a civill body politick, for our better ordering and preservation and furtherance of the ends aforesaid; and by vertue hearof to enacte, constitute, and frame shuch just and equall lawes, ordinances, acts, constitutions, and offices, from time to time, as shall be thought most meete and convenient for the generall good of the Colonie, unto which we promise all due submission and obedience. In witnes wherof we have hereunder subscribed our names at Cap-Codd the ·11· of November, in the year of the raigne of our soveraigne lord, King James, of England, France, and Ireland, the eighteenth, and of Scotland the fiftie fourth. Anno Dom. 1620.

After this they chose, or rather confirmed, Mr. John Carver (a man godly and well approved amongst them) their Governour for that year. And after they had provided a place for their goods, or comone store, (which were long in unlading for want of boats, foulnes of the winter weather, and sicknes of diverce,) and begune some small cottages for their habitation, as time would admitte, they mette and consulted of lawes and orders, both for their civill and military Govermente, as the necessitie of their condition did require, still adding therunto as urgent occasion in severall times, and as cases did require.

In these hard and difficulte beginings they found some discontents and murmurings arise amongst some, and mutinous speeches and carriages in other; but they were soone quelled and overcome by the wisdome, patience, and just and equall carrage of things by the Governor and better part, which clave faithfully togeather in the maine. But that which was most sadd and lamaentable was, that in ·2· or ·3· moneths time halfe of their company dyed, espetialy in Jan: and February, being the depth of winter, and wanting houses and other comforts; being infected with the scurvie and other diseases, which this long voiage and their inacomodate condition had brought upon them; so as ther dyed some times ·2· or ·3· of a day, in the aforesaid time; that of ·100· and odd persons, scarce ·50· remained. And of these in the time of most distres, ther was but ·6· or ·7· sound persons, who, to their great comendations be it spoken, spared no pains, night nor day, but with abundance of toyle and hazard of their owne health, fetched them woode, made them fires, drest them meat, made their beads, washed their lothsome cloaths, cloathed and uncloathed them; in a word, did all the homly and necessarie offices for them which dainty and quesie stomacks cannot endure to hear named; and all this willingly and cherfully, without any grudging in the least, shewing herein their true love unto their freinds and bretheren. A rare example and worthy to be remembred. Tow of these ·7· were Mr. William Brewster, ther reverend Elder, and Myles Standish, ther Captein and military comander, unto whom my selfe, and many others, were much beholden in our low and sicke condition. And yet the Lord so upheld these persons, as in this generall calamity they were not at all infected either with sicknes, or lamnes. And what I have said of these, I may say of

many others who dyed in this generall vissitation, and others
yet living, that whilst they had health, yea, or any strength
continuing, they were not wanting to any that had need of
them. And I doute not but their recompence is with the Lord.

But I may not hear pass by an other remarkable passage not
to be forgotten. As this calamitie fell among the passengers
that were to be left here to plant, and were hasted a shore and
made to drinke water, that the sea-men might have the more
bear, and one in his sicknes desiring but a small cann of beere,*
it was answered, that if he were their owne father he should
have none; the disease begane to fall amongst them also, so
as allmost halfe of their company dyed before they went away,
and many of their officers and lustyest men, as the boatson,
gunner, ·3· quartermaisters, the cooke, and others. At which
the master was something strucken and sent to the sick a shore
and tould the Governor he should send for beer for them that
had need of it, though he drunke water homward bound. But
now amongst his company ther was farr another kind of carriage in this miserie then amongst the passengers; for they that
before had been boone companions in drinking and joyllity in
the time of their health and wellfare, begane now to deserte
one another in this calamitie saing, they would not hasard ther
lives for them, they should be infected by coming to help them
in their cabins, and so, after they came to lye by it, would doe
litle or nothing for them, but if they dyed let them dye. But
shuch of the passengers as were yet abord shewed them what
mercy they could, which made some of their harts relente, as
the boatson (and some others), who was a prowd yonge man,
and would often curse and scofe at the passengers; but when
he grew weak, they had compasion on him, and helped him;
then he confessed he did not deserve it at their hands, he had
abused them in word and deed. O! saith he, you, I now see,
shew your love like Christians indeed one to another, but we
let one another lye and dye like doggs. Another lay cursing
his wife, saing if it had not ben for her he had never come this
unlucky viage, and anone cursing his felows, saing he had done
this and that, for some of them, he had spente so much, and so
much, amongst them, and they were now weary of him, and

*Which was this auther him selfe.

did not help him, having need. Another gave his companion all he had, if he died, to help him in his weaknes; he went and got a litle spise and made him a mess of meat once or twise, and because he dyed not so soone as he expected, he went amongst his fellows, and swore the rogue would cousen him, he would see him chooked before he made him any more meate; and yet the pore fellow dyed before morning.

All this while the Indians came skulking about them, and would sometimes show them selves aloofe of, but when any aproached near them, they would rune away. And once they stoale away their tools wher they had been at worke, and were gone to diner. But about the *·16· of March* a certaine Indian came bouldly amongst them, and spoke to them in broken English, which they could well understand, but marvelled at it. At length they understood by discourse with him, that he was not of these parts, but belonged to the eastrene parts, wher some English-ships came to fhish, with whom he was aquainted, and could name sundrie of them by their names, amongst whom he had gott his language. He became profitable to them in aquainting them with many things concerning the state of the cuntry in the east-parts wher he lived, which was afterwards profitable unto them; as also of the people hear, of their names, number, and strength; of their situation and distance from this place, and who was cheefe amongst them. His name was *Samasett*; he tould them also of another Indian whose name was *Squanto*, a native of this place, who had been in England and could speake better English then him selfe. Being, after some time of entertainmente and gifts, dismist, a while after he came againe, and ·5· more with him, and they brought againe all the tooles that were stolen away before, and made way for the coming of their great Sachem, called *Massasoyt*; who, about ·4· or ·5· *days after*, came with the cheefe of his freinds and other attendance, with the aforesaid *Squanto*. With whom, after frendly entertainment, and some gifts given him, they made a peace with him (which hath now continued this ·24· years) in these terms.

·I· That neither he nor any of his, should injurie or doe hurte to any of their people.

·2· That if any of his did any hurte to any of theirs, he should send the offender, that they might punish him.

·3· That if any thing were taken away from any of theirs, he should cause it to be restored; and they should doe the like to his.

·4· If any did unjustly warr against him, they would aide him; if any did warr against them, he should aide them.

·5· He should send to his neighbours confederates, to certifie them of this, that they might not wrong them, but might be likewise comprised in the conditions of peace.

·6· That when ther men came to them, they should leave their bows and arrows behind them.

After these things he returned to his place caled *Sowams*, some ·40· *mile* from this place, but *Squanto* continued with them, and was their interpreter, and was a spetiall instrument sent of God for their good beyond their expectation. He directed them how to set their corne, wher to take fish, and to procure other comodities, and was also their pilott to bring them to unknowne places for their profitt, and never left them till he dyed. He was a *native of this place*, and scarce any left alive besides him selfe. He was caried away with diverce others by one *Hunt*, a master of a ship, who thought to sell them for slaves in Spaine; but he got away for England, and was entertained by a marchante in London, and imployed to New-found-land and other parts, and lastly brought hither into these parts by one Mr. *Dermer*, a gentle-man imployed by Sir Ferdinando Gorges and others, for discovery, and other designes in these parts. Of whom I shall say some thing, because it is mentioned in a booke set forth Anno: 1622. by the Presidente and Counsell for New-England,* that he made the peace betweene the salvages of these parts and the English; of which this plantation, as it is intimated, had the benefite. But what a peace it was, may apeare by what befell him and his men.

This Mr. Dermer was hear the same year that these people came, as apears by a relation written by him, and given me by a freind, bearing date *June* ·30· Anno: 1620. And they came in November following, so ther was but ·4· months differance. In which relation to his honored freind, he hath these pasages of this very place.

*Page 17.

I will first begine (saith he) with that place from whence *Squanto,
or Tisquantem*, was taken away; which in Cap: *Smiths mape* is called
Plimoth; and I would that Plimoth had the like comodities. I would
that the first plantation might hear be seated, if ther come to the
number of ·50· persons, or upward. Otherwise at Charlton, because
ther the savages are lese to be feared. The *Pocanawkits*, which live to
the *west* of *Plimoth*, bear an invetrate malice to the English, and are
of more streingth then all the savages from thence to Penobscote.
Their desire of revenge was occasioned by an English man, who
having many of them on bord, made a great slaughter with their
murderers and smale shot, when as (they say) they offered no injurie
on their parts. Whether they were English or no, it may be douted;
yet they beleeve they were, for the Frenche have so possest them; for

Note   which cause *Squanto* cannot deney but they would have
              kild me when I was at *Namasket*, had he not entreated
hard for me. The soyle of the borders of this great bay, may be compared to most of the plantations which I have seene in Virginia. The
land is of diverce sorts; for *Patuxite* is a hardy but strong soyle, *Nawset*
and *Saughtughtett* are for the most part a blakish and deep mould,
much like that wher groweth the best tobaco in Virginia. In the
botume of the great bay is store of codd and basse, or mulett, etc. But
above all he comends *Pacanawkite* for the richest soyle, and much
open ground fitt for English graine, etc. *Massachusets* is about ·9·
leagues from *Plimoth*, and situate in the mids betweene both, is full
of ilands and peninsules very fertill for the most part.

With sundrie shuch relations which I forbear to transcribe,
being now better knowne then they were to him.

He was taken prisoner by the Indeans at *Manamoiak* (a place
not farr from hence, now well knowne). He gave them what
they demanded for his liberty, but when they had gott what
they desired, they kept him still and indevored to kill his men;
but he was freed by seasing on some of them, and kept them
bound till they gave him a cannows load of corne. Of which,
see Purch: lib. ·9· fol. 1778. But this was Anno: 1619.

After the writing of the former relation he came to the Ile of
Capawack (which lyes *south* of *this place* in the way to Virginia),
and the foresaid *Squanto* with him, wher he going a shore
amongst the Indeans to trad, as he used to doe, was betrayed
and assaulted by them, and *all his men slain, but one that kept
the boat*; but him selfe gott abord very sore wounded, and they
had cut of his head upon the cudy of his boat, had not the

man reskued him with a sword. And so they got away, and made shift to gett into Virginia, wher he dyed; whether of his wounds or the diseases of the cuntrie, or both togeather, is uncertaine. By all which it may appear how farr these people were from peace, and with what danger this plantation was begune, save as the powerfull hand of the Lord did protect them. These things were partly the reason why they kept aloofe and were so long before they came to the English. An other reason (as after them selves made known) was how aboute ·3· *years before*, a French-ship was cast away at *Cap-Codd*, but the men gott ashore, and saved their lives, and much of their vic-tails, and other goods; but after the Indeans heard of it, they geathered togeather from these parts, and never left watching and dogging them till they got advantage, and *kild them all but* ·3· *or* ·4· which they kept, and sent from one Sachem to another, to make sporte with, and used them worse then slaves; (of which the foresaid Mr. Dermer redemed ·2· of them;) and they conceived this ship was now come to revenge it.

Also, (as after was made knowne,) before they came to the English to make freindship, they gott all the *Powachs* of the cuntrie, for ·3· days togeather, in a horid and divellish maner to curse and execrate them with their cunjurations, which asembly and service they held in a darke and dismale swampe.

But to returne. The spring now approaching, it pleased God the mortalitie begane to cease amongst them, and the sick and lame recovered apace, which put as it were new life into them; though they had borne their sadd affliction with much patience and contentednes, as I thinke any people could doe. But it was the Lord which upheld them, and had beforehand prepared them; many having long borne the yoake, yea from their youth. Many other smaler maters I omite, sundrie of them having been allready published in a Jurnall made by one of the company; and some other passages of jurneys and relations allredy published, to which I referr those that are willing to know them more perticulerly. And being now come to the ·25· of March I shall begine the year 1621.

ANNO ·1621·

THEY now begane to dispatch the ship away which brought them over, which lay tille aboute this time, or the begining of Aprill. The reason on their parts why she stayed so long, was the necessitie and danger that lay upon them, for it was well towards the ende of Desember before she could land any thing hear, or they able to receive any thing a shore. Afterwards, the ·14· of January the house which they had made for a generall randevoze by casualty fell afire, and some were faine to retire abord for shilter. Then the sicknes begane to fall sore amongst them, and the weather so bad as they could not make much sooner any dispatch. Againe, the Governor and cheefe of them, seeing so many dye, and fall downe sick dayly, thought it no wisdom to send away the ship, their condition considered, and the danger they stood in from the Indeans, till they could procure some shelter; and therfore thought it better to draw some more charge upon them selves and freinds, then hazard all. The master and seamen likewise, though before they hasted the passengers a shore to be goone, now many of their men being dead, and of the ablest of them, (as is before noted,) and of the rest many lay sick and weake, the master durst not put to sea, till he saw his men begine to recover, and the hart of winter over.

Afterwards they (as many as were able) began to plant ther corne, in which servise Squanto stood them in great stead, showing them both the maner how to set it, and after how to dress and tend it. Also he tould them excepte they gott fish and set with it (in these old grounds) it would come to nothing, and he showed them that in the midle of Aprill they should have store enough come up the brooke, by which they begane to build, and taught them how to take it, and wher to get other provisions necessary for them; all which they found true by triall and experience. Some English seed they sew, as wheat and pease, but it came not to good, eather by the badnes of the seed, or latenes of the season, or both, or some other defecte. In this month of *Aprill* whilst they were bussie about their seed, their Governor (Mr. John Carver) came out of the feild very sick, it being a hott day; he complained greatly of his head, and lay downe, and within a few howers his sences failed, so as he never spake more till he dyed, which was within a few days after. Whoss death was much lamented, and caused great heavines amongst them, as ther was cause. He was buried in the best maner they could, with some vollies of shott by all that bore armes; and his wife, being a weak woman, dyed within ·5· or ·6· weeks after him.

Shortly after William Bradford was chosen Governor in his stead, and being not yet recoverd of his ilnes, in which he had been near the point of death, Isaack Allerton was chosen to be an Asistante unto him, who, by renewed election every year, continued sundry years togeather, which I hear note once for all.

May ·12· was the first mariage in this place, which, according to the laudable custome of the Low-cuntries, in which they had lived, was thought most requisite to be performed by the magistrate, as being a civill thing, upon which many questions aboute inheritances doe depende, with other things most proper to their cognizans, and most consonante to the scriptures, Ruth ·4· and no wher found in the gospell to be layed on the ministers as a part of their office. "This decree or law about mariage was publisht by the States of the Low-countries Anno: 1590. That those of any religion, after lawfull and open publication, coming before the magistrates, in the Town or Stat-house, were to be orderly (by them) maried one to another." Petets Hist. fol: 1029. And this practiss hath continued amongst, not only them, but hath been followed by all the famous churches of Christ in these parts to this time, Anno: 1646.

Haveing in some sorte ordered their bussines at home, it was thought meete to send some abroad to see their new freind Massasoyet, and to bestow upon him some gratuitie to bind him the faster unto them; as also that hearby they might veiw the countrie, and see in what maner he lived, what strength he had aboute him, and how the ways were to his place, if at any time they should have occasion. So the ·2· *of July* they sente Mr. Edward Winslow and Mr. Hopkins, with the fore said Squanto for ther guid, who gave him a suite of cloaths, and a horse-mans coat; with some other small things, which were kindly accepted; but they found but short commons, and came both weary and hungrie home. For the Indeans used then to have nothing so much corne as they have since the English have stored them with their hows, and seene their industrie in breaking up new-grounds therwith. *They found his place to be* ·40· *myles from hence*, the soyle good, and the people not many, being dead and abundantly wasted in the late great mortalitie which fell in all these parts aboute *three years* before the coming of the English, wherin thousands of them dyed; they not being able to burie one another, ther sculs and bones were found in many places lying still above ground, where their houses and dwellings had been; a very sad spectackle to behould. But they brought word that the Narighansets lived but on the other side of that great bay, and were a strong people, and many in number, living compacte togeather, and had not been at all touched with this wasting plague.

About the *later end of this month*, one John Billington lost him selfe in the woods, and wandered up and downe some ·5· days, living on beries and what he could find. At length he light on an Indean plantation, ·20· miles south of this place, called *Manamet*. They conveid him furder of, to *Nawssett*, among those people that had before set upon the English when they were costing, whilest the ship lay at the Cape, as is before noted. But the Governor caused him to be enquired for among the Indeans, and at length Massassoyt sent word wher he was, and the Governor sent a shalop for him, and had him delivered. Those people also came and made their peace; and they gave full satisfaction to those whose corne they had found and taken when they were at Cap-Codd.

Thus ther peace and aquaintance was prety well establisht with the natives aboute them; and ther was an other Indean called *Hobamack* come to live amongst them, a proper lustie man, and a man of accounte for his vallour and parts amongst the Indeans, and continued very faithfull and constant to the English till he dyed. He and Squanto being gone upon bussines amonge the Indeans, at their returne (whether it was out of envie to them or malice to the English) ther was a Sachem called Corbitant, alyed to Massassoyte, but never any good freind to the English to this day, mett with them at an Indean towne caled Namassakett ·14· miles to the west of this place, and begane to quarell with them, and offered to stabe Hobamack; but being a lusty man, he cleared him selfe of him, and came running away all sweating and tould the Governor what had befalne him, and he feared they had killed Squanto, for they threatened them both, and for no other cause but because they were freinds to the English, and servisable unto them. Upon this the Governor taking counsell, it was conceivd not fitt to be borne; for if they should suffer their freinds and messengers thus to be wronged, they should have none would cleave to them, or give them any inteligence, or doe them serviss afterwards; but nexte they would fall upon them selves. Where upon it was resolved to send the Captaine and ·14· men well armed, and to goe and fall upon them in the night; and if they found that Squanto was kild, to cut of Corbitants head, but not to hurt any but those that had a hand in it. Hobamack was asked if he would goe and be their guid, and bring them ther before day. He said he would, and bring them to the house wher the man lay, and show them which was he. So they set forth the ·14· of August, and beset the house round; the Captin giving charg to let none pass out, entred the house to search for him. But he was goone away that day, so they mist him; but understood that Squanto was alive, and that he had only threatened to kill him, and made an offer to stabe him but did not. So they withheld and did no more hurte, and the people came trembling, and brought them the best provissions they had, after they were aquainted by Hobamack what was only intended. Ther was ·3· sore wounded which broak out of the house, and asaid to pass through the garde. These they brought home with them, and they had their wounds drest and cured, and sente home. After this they had many gratulations from diverce sachims, and much firmer peace; yea, those of the Iles of Capawack sent to make frendship; and this Corbitant him selfe used the mediation of Massassoyte to make his peace, but was shie to come neare them a longe while after.

After this, the ·18· of September they sente out ther shalop to the Massachusets, with ·10· men, and Squanto for their guid and interpreter, to discover and view that bay, and trade with the natives; the which they performed, and found kind entertainement. The people were much affraid of the Tarentins, a people to the eastward which used to come in harvest time and take away their corne, and many times kill their persons. They returned in saftie, and brought home a good quantity of beaver, and made reporte of the place, wishing they had been ther seated; (but it seems the Lord, who assignes to all men the bounds of their habitations, had apoynted it for an other use). And thus they found the Lord to be with them in all their ways, and to blesse their outgoings and incommings, for which let his holy name have the praise for ever, to all posteritie.

They begane now to gather in the small harvest they had, and to fitte up their houses and dwellings against winter, being all well recovered in health and strenght, and had all things in good plenty; for as some were thus imployed in affairs abroad, others were excersised in fishing, aboute codd, and bass, and other fish, of which they tooke good store, of which every family had their portion. All the sommer ther was no wante. And now begane to come in store of foule, as winter aproached, of which this place did abound when they came first (but afterward decreased by degrees). And besides water foule, ther was great store of wild Turkies, of which they tooke many, besides venison, etc. Besides they had aboute a peck a meale a weeke to a person, or now since harvest, Indean corne to that proportion. Which made many afterwards write so largely of their plenty hear to their freinds in England, which were not fained, but true reports.

In November, about that time twelfe month that them selves came, ther came in a small ship to them unexpected or loked for,* in which came Mr. Cushman (so much spoken of before) and with him ·35· persons to remaine and live in the plantation; which did not a litle rejoyce them. And they when they came a shore and found all well, and saw plenty of vitails in every house, were no less glade. For most of them were lusty yong men, and many of them wild enough, who litle considered whither or aboute what they wente, till they came into the harbore at Cap-Codd, and ther saw nothing but a naked and barren place. They then begane to thinke what should become of them, if the people here were dead or cut of by the Indeans. They begane to consulte (upon some speeches that some of the sea-men had cast out) to take the sayls from the yeard least the ship should gett away and leave them ther. But the master hereing of it, gave them good words, and tould them if any

*She came the ·9· to the Cap.

thing but well should have befallne the people hear, he hoped he had vitails enough to cary them to Virginia, and whilst he had a bitt they should have their parte; which gave them good satisfaction. So they were all landed; but ther was not so much as bisket-cake or any other* victialls for them, neither had they any beding, but some sory things they had in their cabins, nor pot, nor pan, to drese any meate in; nor over many cloaths, for many of them had brusht away their coats and cloaks at Plimouth as they came. But ther was sent over some burching-lane suits in the ship, out of which they were supplied. The plantation was glad of this addition of strenght, but could have wished that many of them had been of beter condition, and all of them beter furnished with provissions; but that could not now be helpte.

In this ship Mr. Weston sent a large leter to Mr. Carver, the late Governor, now deseased, full of complaints and expostulations aboute former passagess at Hampton; and the keeping the shipe so long in the country, and returning her without lading, etc., which for brevitie I omite. The rest is as followeth.

Part of Mr. Weston's letter.

I durst never aquainte the adventurers with the alterations of the conditions first agreed on betweene us, which I have since been very glad of, for I am well assured had they knowne as much as I doe, they would not have adventured a halfe-peny of what was necesary for this ship. That you sent no lading in the ship is wonderfull, and worthily distasted. I know your weaknes was the cause of it, and I beleeve more weaknes of judgmente, then weaknes of hands. A quarter of the time you spente in discoursing, arguing, and consulting, would have done much more; but that is past, etc. If you mean, bona fide, to performe the conditions agreed upon, doe us the favore to coppy them out faire, and subscribe them with the principall of your names. And likwise give us accounte as perticulerly as you can how our moneys were laid out. And then I shall be able to give them some satisfaction, whom I am now forsed with good words to shift of. And consider that the life of the bussines depends on the lading of this ship, which, if you doe to any good purpose, that I may be freed from the great *sums I have disbursed for the former, and must doe for the later, I promise you I will never quit the bussines, though all the other adventurers should.*

---

*Nay, they were faine to spare the shipe some to carry her home.

We have procured you a Charter, the best we could, which is beter then your former, and with less limitation. For any thing that is els worth writting, Mr. Cushman can informe you. I pray write instantly for Mr. Robinson to come to you. And so praying God to blesse you with all graces nessessary both for this life and that to come, I rest

Your very loving frend,
THO. WESTON.

London, July 6. 1621.

This ship (caled the Fortune) was speedily dispacht away, being laden with good clapbord as full as she could stowe, and ·2· hoggsheads of beaver and otter skins, which they gott with a few trifling comodities brought with them at first, being all to geether unprovided for trade; neither was ther any amongst them that ever saw a beaver skin till they came hear, and were informed by Squanto. The fraight was estimated to be worth near 500*li*. Mr. Cushman returned backe also with this ship, for so Mr. Weston and the rest had apoynted him, for their better information. And he doubted not, nor them selves neither, but they should have a speedy supply; considering allso how by Mr. Cushmans perswation, and letters received from Leyden, wherin they willed them so to doe, they yeelded to the afforesaid conditions, and subscribed them with their hands. But it proved other wise, for Mr. Weston, who had made that large promise in his leter, (as is before noted,) that if all the rest should fall of, yet he would never quit the bussines, but stick to them, if they yeelded to the conditions, and sente some lading in the ship; and of this Mr. Cushman was confident, and confirmed the same from his mouth, and serious protestations to him selfe before he came. But all proved but wind, for he was the first and only man that forsooke them, and that before he so much as heard of the returne of this ship, or knew what was done; (so vaine is the confidence in man.) But of this more in its place.

A leter in answer to his write to Mr. Carver, was sente to him from the Governor, of which so much as is pertenente to the thing in hand I shall hear inserte.

SIR, Your large letter writen to Mr. Carver, and dated the ·6· of July, 1621, I have received the ·10· of November, wherin (after the apologie made for your selfe) you lay many heavie imputations upon him and us all. Touching him, he is departed this life, and now is at rest in the Lord from all those troubles and incoumbrances with which we are yet to strive. He needs not my appologie; for his care and pains was so great for the commone good, both ours and yours, as that therwith (it is thought) he oppressed him selfe and shortened his days; of whose loss we cannot sufficiently complaine. At great charges in this adventure, I confess you have beene, and many losses may sustaine; but the loss of his and many other honest and industrious mens lives, cannot be vallewed at any prise. Of the one, ther may be hope of recovery, but the other no recompence can make good. But I will not insiste in generalls, but come more perticulerly to the things them selves. You greatly blame us for keping the ship so long in the countrie, and then to send her away emptie. She lay ·5· weks at Cap-Codd whilst with many a weary step (after a long journey) and the indurance of many a hard brunte, we sought out in the foule winter a place of habitation. Then we went in so tedious a time to make provission to sheelter us and our goods, aboute which labour, many of our armes and leggs can tell us to this day we were not necligent. But it pleased God to vissite us then, with death dayly, and with so generall a disease, that the living were scarce able to burie the dead; and the well not in any measure sufficente to tend the sick. And now to be so greatly blamed, for not fraighting the ship, doth indeed goe near us, and much discourage us. But you say, you know we will pretend weaknes; and doe you think we had not cause? Yes, you tell us you beleeve it, but it was more weaknes of judgmente, then of hands. Our weaknes herin is great we confess, therfore we will bear this check patiently amongst the rest, till God send us wiser men. But they which tould you we spent so much time in discoursing and consulting, etc., their harts can tell their toungs, they lye. They cared not, so they might salve their owne sores, how they wounded others. Indeede, it is our callamitie that we are (beyound expectation) yoked with some ill conditioned people, who will never doe good, but corrupte and abuse others, etc.

The rest of the letter declared how they had subscribed those conditions according to his desire, and sente him the former accounts very perticulerly; also how the ship was laden, and in what condition their affairs stood; that the coming of these people would bring famine upon them unavoydably, if they had not supply in time (as Mr. Cushman could more fully informe him and the rest of the adventurers). Also that seeing he was now satisfied in all his demands, that offences would be forgoten, and he remember his promise, etc.

After the departure of this ship, (which stayed not above ·14· days,) the Governor and his assistante haveing disposed these late commers into severall families, as they best could, tooke an exacte accounte of all their provissions in store, and proportioned the same to the number of persons, and found that it would not hould out above ·6· months at halfe alowance, and hardly that. And they could not well give less this winter time till fish came in againe. So they were presently put to half alowance, one as well as an other, which begane to be hard, but they bore it patiently under hope of supply.

Sone after this ships departure, the great people of the Narigansets, in a braving maner, sente a messenger unto them with a bundle of arrows tyed aboute with a great sneak-skine; which their interpretours tould them was a threatening and a chaleng. Upon which the Governor, with the advice of others, sente them a round answere, that if they had rather have warre then peace, they might begine when they would; they had done them no wrong, neither did they fear them, or should they find them unprovided. And by another messenger sente the sneake skine back with bulits in it; but they would not receive it, but sent it back againe. But these things I doe but mention, because they are more at large allready put forth in printe, by Mr. Winslow, at the requeste of some freinds. And it is like the reason was their owne ambition, who, (since the death of so many of the Indeans,) thought to dominire and lord it over the rest, and conceived the English would be a barr in their way, and saw that Massasoyt took sheilter allready under their wings.

But this made them the more carefully to looke to them selves, so as they agreed to inclose their dwellings with a good strong pale, and make flankers in convenient places, with gates to shute, which were every night locked, and a watch kept, and when neede required ther was also warding in the day time. And the company was by the Captaine and the Governor advise, devided into ·4· squadrons, and every one had ther quarter apoynted them, unto which they were to repaire upon any suddane alarme. And if ther should be any crie of fire, a company were appointed for a gard, with muskets, whilst others quenchet the same, to prevent Indean treachery. This was accomplished very cherfully, and the towne impayled

round by the begining of March, in which evry family had
a prety garden plote secured. And herewith I shall end this
year. Only I shall remember one passage more, rather of mirth
then of waight. One the day called Chrismas-day, the Governor
caled them out to worke, (as was used,) but the most of this
new-company excused them selves and said it wente against
their consciences to work on that day. So the Governor tould
them that if they made it mater of conscience, he would spare
them till they were better informed. So he led-away the rest
and left them; but when they came home at noone from their
worke, he found them in the streete at play, openly; some pitching the barr, and some at stoole-ball, and shuch like sports. So
he went to them, and tooke away their implements, and tould
them that was against his conscience, that they should play and
others worke. If they made the keeping of it mater of devotion,
let them kepe their houses, but ther should be no gameing or
revelling in the streets. Since which time nothing hath been
atempted that way, at least openly.

ANNO ·1622·

A T the spring of the year they had apointed the Massachusets to come againe and trade with them, and begane
now to prepare for that vioag about the later end of March.
But upon some rumors heard, Hobamak, their Indean, tould
them upon some jealocies he had, he feared they were joyned
with the Narighansets and might betray them if they were
not carefull. He intimated also some jealocie of Squanto, by
what he gathered from some private whisperings betweene
him and other Indeans. But they resolved to proseede, and
sente out their shalop with ·10· of their cheefe men aboute the
begining of Aprill, and both Squanto and Hobamake with
them, in regarde of the jelocie betweene them. But they had
not bene gone longe, but an Indean belonging to Squantos
family came runing in seeming great fear, and tould them that
many of the Narihgansets, with Corbytant, and he thought
also Massasoyte, were coming against them; and he gott away
to tell them, not without danger. And being examined by the
Governor, he made as if they were at hand, and would still
be looking back, as if they were at his heels. At which the

Governor caused them to take armes and stand on their garde, and supposing the boat to be still within hearing (by reason it was calme) caused a warning peece or ·2· to be shote of, the which they heard and came in. But no Indeans apeared; watch was kepte all night, but nothing was seene. Hobamak was confidente for Massasoyt, and thought all was false; yet the Governor caused him to send his wife privatly, to see what she could observe (pretending other occasions), but ther was nothing found, but all was quiet. After this they proseeded on their vioge to the Massachusets, and had good trade, and returned in saftie, blessed be God.

But by the former passages, and other things of like nature, they begane to see that Squanto sought his owne ends, and plaid his owne game, by putting the Indians in fear, and drawing gifts from them to enrich him selfe; making them beleeve he could stir up warr against whom he would, and make peace for whom he would. Yea, he made them beleeve they kept the plague buried in the ground, and could send it amongs whom they would, which did much terrifie the Indeans, and made them depend more on him, and seeke more to him then to Massasoyte, which proucured him envie, and had like to have cost him his life. For after the discovery of his practises, Massosoyt sought it both privatly and openly; which caused him to stick close to the English, and never durst goe from them till he dyed. They also made good use of the emulation that grue betweene Hobamack and him, which made them cary more squarely. And the Governor seemed to countenance the one, and the Captaine the other, by which they had better intelligence, and made them both more diligente.

Now in a maner their provissions were wholy spent, and they looked hard for supply, but none came. But about the *later end of May*, they spied *a boat* at sea, which at first they thought had beene some French-man; but it proved a shalop which came from a ship which Mr. Weston and an other had set out a fishing, at a place called Damarins-cove, ·40· leagues to the eastward of them, wher were that year many more ships come a fishing. This boat brought ·7· passengers and some letters; but no vitails, nor any hope of any. Some part of which I shall set downe.

MR. CARVER, In my last leters by the Fortune, in whom Mr. Cushman wente, and who I hope is with you, for we daly expecte the
shipe back againe. She departed hence, the begining of July, with ·35·
persons, though not over well provided with necesaries, by reason of
the parsemonie of the adventurers. I have solisited them to send you a
supply of men and provissions before shee come. They all answer they
will doe great maters, when they hear good news. Nothing before;
so faithfull, constant, and carefull of your good, are your olde and
honest freinds, that if they hear not from them, they are like to send
you no supplie, etc. I am now to relate the occasion of sending *this
ship*, hoping if you give credite to my words, you will have a more
favourable opinion of it, then some hear, wherof Pickering is one,
who taxed me to mind my owne ends, which is in part true, etc. *Mr.
Beachamp and my selfe* bought *this litle ship*, and have set her out,
partly, if it may be, to uphold* the plantation, as well to doe others
good as our selves; and partly to gett up what we are formerly out;
though we are otherwise censured, etc. This is the occasion we have
sent *this ship* and these passengers, on our owne accounte; whom we
desire you will frendly entertaine and supply with shuch necesaries
as you cane spare, and they wante, etc. And among other things we
pray you lend or sell them some seed corne, and if you have the salt
remaining of the last year, that you will let them have it for their
presente use, and we will either pay you for it, or give you more when
we have set our salt-pan to worke, which we desire may be set up in
one of the litle ilands in your bay, etc. And because we intende, if God
plase, (and the generallitie doe it not,) *to send within a month another
shipe*, who, having discharged her passengers, *shal goe to Virginia*,
etc. And it may be we shall send a *small ship to abide with you* on the
coast, which I conceive may be a great help to the plantation. To the
end our desire may be effected, which, I assure my selfe, will be also
for your good, we pray you give them entertainmente in your houses
the time they shall be with you, that they may lose no time, but may
presently goe in hand to fell trees and cleave them, to the end lading
may be ready and our ship stay not.

Some of the adventurers have sent you hearwith all some directions
for your furtherance in the commone bussines, who are like those
St. James speaks of, that bid their brother eat, and warme him, but
give him nothing; so they bid you make salt, and uphold the plantation, but send you no means wherwithall to doe it, etc. By *the next*
we purpose *to send more people on our owne accounte*, and *to take a*

---

*I know not which way.

patente; that if your people should be as unhumane as some of the adventurers, not to admite us to dwell with them, which were extreme barbarisme, and which will never enter into my head to thinke you have any shuch Pickerings amongst you. Yet to satisfie our passengers I must of force doe it; and for some other reasons not necessary to be writen, etc.

I find the generall so backward, and your freinds at Leyden so could, that I fear you must stand on your leggs, and trust (as they say) to God and your selves.

Subscribed,
your loving freind,
THO: WESTON.

Jan: 12. 1621.

Sundry other things I pass over, being tedious and impertinent.

All this was but could comfort to fill their hungrie bellies, and a slender performance of his former late promiss; and as litle did it either fill or warme them, as those the Apostle James spake of, by him before mentioned. And well might it make them remember what the psalmist saith, *Psa.* 118. 8. *It is better to trust in the Lord, then to have confidence in man. And Psa.* 146. *Put not your trust in princes* (much less in marchants) *nor in the sone of man, for ther is no help in them. v. 5. Blesed is he that hath the God of Jacob for his help, whose hope is in the Lord his God.* And as they were now fayled of suply by him and others in this their greatest neede and wants, which was caused by him and the rest, who put so great a company of men upon them, as the former company were, without any food, and came at shuch a time as they must live almost a whole year before any could be raised, excepte they had sente some; so, upon the pointe they never had any supply of vitales more afterwards (but what the Lord gave them otherwise); for all the company sent at any time was allways too short for those people that came with it.

Ther came allso *by the same ship* other leters, but of later date; one from Mr. Weston, an other from a parte of the adventurers, as foloweth.

MR. CARVER, Since my last, to the end we might the more readily proceed to help the generall, at a meeting of some of the principall adventurers, a proposition was put forth, and alowed by all presente (save Pickering), to adventure each man the third parte of what he formerly had done. And ther are some other that folow his example, and will adventure no furder. In regard wherof the greater part of the adventurers being willing to uphold the bussines, finding it no reason that those that are willing should uphold the bussines of those that are unwilling, whose backwardnes doth discourage those that are forward, and hinder other new-adventurers from coming in, we having well considered therof, have resolved, according to an article in the agreemente, (*that it may be lawfull by a generall consente of the adventurers and planters, upon just occasion, to break of their joynte stock,*) to breake it of; and doe pray you to ratifie, and confirme the same on your parts. Which being done, we shall the more willingly goe forward for the upholding of you with all things necesarie. But in any case you must agree to the artickles, and send it by the first under your hands and seals. So I end

Your loving freind,
THO: WESTON.

Jan: 17. 1621.

Another leter was write from part of the company of the adventurers to the same purpose, and subscribed with ·9· of their names, wherof Mr. Westons and Mr. Beachamphs were tow. These things seemed strange unto them, seeing this unconstancie and shufling; it made them to thinke ther was some misterie in the matter. And therfore the Governor concealed these letters from the publick, only imparted them to some trustie freinds for advice, who concluded with him, that this tended to disband and scater them (in regard of their straits); and if Mr. Weston and others, who seemed to rune in a perticuler way, should come over with shiping so provided as his letters did intimate, they most would fall to him, to the prejudice of them selves and the rest of the adventurers, their freinds, from whom as yet they heard nothing. And it was doubted whether he had not sente over shuch a company in the former ship, for shuch an end. Yet they tooke compassion of those ·7· men which *this ship, which fished to the eastward, had kept till planting time was over,* and so could set no corne; and allso wanting vitals, (for they turned them off without any, and indeed wanted for them selves,) neither was their salt-pan come, so as they could not performe any of those things which

Mr. Weston had apointed, and might have starved if the plantation had not succoured them; who, in their wants, gave them
as good as any of their owne. *The ship wente to Virginia*, wher
they sould both ship and fish, of which (it was conceived) Mr.
Weston had a very slender accounte.

After this came another of his ships, and brought letters dated
the ·10· of Aprill, from Mr. Weston, as followeth.

Mr. Bradford, these, etc. *The Fortune* is arived, of whose good
news touching your estate and proceedings, I am very glad to hear.
And how soever he was robed on the way by the French-men, yet I
hope your loss will not be great, for the conceite of so great a returne
doth much animate the adventurers, so that I hope some matter of
importance will be done by them, etc. As for my selfe, I have sould
my adventure and debts unto them, so as I am quite* of you, and you
of me, for that matter, etc. Now though I have nothing to pretend
as an adventurer amongst you, yet I will advise you a litle for your
good, if you can apprehend it. I perceive and know as well as another,
the dispossitions of *your adventurers*, whom the hope of gaine hath
drawne on to this they have done; and yet I fear that hope will not
draw them much furder. Besides, *most of them are against the sending
of them of Leyden, for whose cause this bussines was first begune*, and
some of the most religious (as Mr. Greene by name) excepts against
them. So that my advice is (you may follow it if you please) that you
forthwith break of your joynte stock, which you have warente to doe,
both in law and conscience, for the most parte of the adventurers have
given way unto it by a former letter. And the means you have ther,
which I hope will be to some purpose by the trade of this spring, may,
with the help of some freinds hear, bear the charge of transporting
those of Leyden; and when they are with you I make no question,
but by Gods help you will be able to subsist of your selves. But I shall
leave you to your discretion.

I desired diverce of the adventurers, as Mr. Peirce, Mr. Greene,
and others, if they had any thing to send you, either vitails or leters,
to send them *by these ships*; and marvelling they sent not so much as
a letter, I asked our passengers what leters they had, and with some
dificultie one of them tould me he had one, which was delivered him
with great charge of secrecie; and for more securitie, to buy a paire
of new-shoes, and sow it betweene the soles for fear of intercepting.
I, taking the leter, wondering what mistrie might be in it, broke it

---

*See how his promise is fulfild.

open, and found this treacherous leter subscribed by the hands of Mr. Pickering and Mr. Greene. Wich leter had it come to your hands without answer, might have caused the hurt, if not the ruine of us all. For assuredly if you had followed their instructions, and shewed us that unkindness which they advise you unto, to hold us in distruste as enimise, etc., it might have been an occasion to have set us togeather by the ears, to the distruction of us all. For I doe beleeve that in shuch a case, they knowing what bussines hath been betweene us, not only my brother, but others also, would have been violent, and heady against you, etc. I mente to have setled the people I before and now send, with or near you, as well for their as your more securitie and defence, as help on all occasions. But I find the adventurers so jealous and suspitious, that I have altered my resolution, and given order to my brother and those with him, to doe as they and him selfe shall find fitte. Thus, etc.

Your loving freind,
THO: WESTON.

Aprill 10, 1621.

Some part of Mr. Pickerings letter before mentioned.

To Mr. BRADFORD and Mr. BREWSTER, etc.

My dear love remembred unto you all, etc. The company hath bought out Mr. Weston, and are very glad they are freed of him, he being judged a man that thought him selfe above the generall, and not expresing so much the fear of God as was meete in a man, to whom shuch trust should have been reposed in a matter of so great importance. I am sparing to be so plaine as indeed is clear against him; but a few words to the wise.

Mr. Weston will not permitte leters to be sent in *his ships*, nor any thing for your good or ours, of which ther is some reason in respecte of him selfe, etc. His brother Andrew, whom he doth send as principall *in one of these ships*, is a heady yong man, and violente, and set against you ther, and the company hear; ploting with Mr. Weston their owne ends, which tend to your and our undooing in respecte of our estates ther, and prevention of our good ends. For by credible testimoney we are informed his purpose is to come to your colonie, pretending he comes for and from the adventurers, and will seeke to gett what you have in readynes into *his ships*, as if they came from the company, and possessing all, will be so much profite to him selfe. And further to informe them selves what speciall places or things you have discovered, to the end that they may supres and deprive you, etc.

The Lord, who is the watchman of Israll and slepeth not, preserve you and deliver you from unreasonable men. I am sorie that ther is cause to admonish you of these things concerning this man; so I leave you to God, who bless and multiply you into thousands, to the advancemente of the glorious gospell of our Lord Jesus. Amen. Fare well.

> Your loving freinds,
> EDWARD PICKERING.
> WILLIAM GREENE.

I pray conceale both the writing and deliverie of this leter, but make the best use of it. *We hope to sete forth a ship our selves with in this month.*

The heads of his answer.

Mr. BRADFORD, This is the leter that I wrote unto you of, which to answer in every perticuler is needles and tedious. My owne conscience and all our people can and I thinke will testifie, that my end in sending *the ship Sparrow* was your good, etc. Now I will not deney but ther are many of our people rude fellows, as these men terme them; yet I presume they will be governed by shuch as I set over them. And I hope not only to be able to reclaime them from that profanenes that may scandalise the vioage, but by degrees to draw them to God, etc. I am so farr from sending rude fellows to deprive you either by fraude or violence of what is yours, as I have charged the master of the *ship Sparrow*, not only to leave with you 2000. of bread, but also a good quantitie of fish,* etc. But I will leave it to you to consider what evill this leter would or might have done, had it come to your hands and taken the effecte the other desired.

Now if you be of the mind that these men are, deale plainly with us, and we will seeke our residence els-wher. If you are as freindly as we have thought you to be, give us the entertainment of freinds, and we will take nothing from you, neither meat, drinke, nor lodging, but what we will, in one kind or other, pay you for, etc. I shall leave in the countrie *a litle ship* (if God send her safe thither) with mariners and fisher-men to stay ther, who shall coast, and trad with the savages, and the old plantation. It may be we shall be as helpfull to you, as you will be to us. I thinke I shall see you the next spring, and so I comend you to the protection of God, who ever keep you.

> Your loving freind,
> THO: WESTON.

Thus all ther hopes in regard of Mr. Weston were layed in the dust, and all his promised helpe turned into an empttie advice,

---

*But ye he left not his own men a bite of bread.

which they apprehended was nether lawfull nor profitable for
them to follow. And they were not only thus left destitute of
help in their extreme wants, haveing neither vitails, nor any
thing to trade with, but others prepared and ready to glean up
what the cuntrie might have afforded for their releefe.

As for those harsh censures and susspitions intimated in the
former and following leters, they desired to judg as charitably and wisly of them as they could, waighing them in the
ballance of love and reason; and though they (in parte) came
from godly and loveing freinds, yet they conceived many things
might arise from over deepe jealocie and fear, togeather with
unmeete provocations, though they well saw Mr. Weston pursued his owne ends, and was inbittered in spirite. For after the
receit of the former leters, the Governor received one from Mr.
Cushman, who went home in the ship, and was allway intimate
with Mr. Weston, (as former passages declare), and it was much
marveled that nothing was heard from him, all this while. But
it should seeme it was the difficulty of sending, for this leter
was directed as the leter of a wife to her husband, who was
here, and brought by him to the Governor. It was as followeth.

BELOVED SIR, I hartily salute you, with trust of your health, and
many thanks for your love. By Gods providence we got well home the
·17· of Feb. Being robbed by the French-men by the way, and carried
by them into France, and were kepte ther ·15· days, and lost all that
we had that was worth taking; but thanks be to God, we escaped
with our lives and ship. I see not that it worketh any discouragment
hear. I purpose by Gods grace to see you shortly, I hope in June nexte,
or before. In the mean space know these things, and I pray you be
advertised a litle. Mr. Weston hath quite broken of from our company,
through some discontents that arose betwext him and some of our
adventurers, and hath sould all his adventures, and hath now sent ·3·
smale ships for his perticuler plantation. The greatest wherof, being
·100· tune, Mr. Reynolds goeth master and he with the rest purposeth
to come him selfe; for what end I know not.

The people which they cary are no men for us, wherfore I pray
you entertaine them not, neither exchainge man for man with them,
excepte it be some of your worst. He hath taken a patente for him
selfe. If they offerr to buy any thing of you, let it be shuch as you can
spare, and let them give the worth of it. If they borrow any thing
of you, let them leave a good pawne, etc. It is like he will plant to
the southward of the Cape, for William Trevore, hath lavishly tould

but what he knew or imagined of Capewack, Mohiggen, and the Narigansets. I fear these people will hardly deale so well with the savages as they should. I pray you therfore signifie to Squanto, that they are a distincte body from us, and we have nothing to doe with them, neither must be blamed for their falts, much less can warrente their fidelitie. We are aboute to recover our losses in France. Our freinds at Leyden are well, and will come to you as many as can *this time.* I hope all will turne to the best, wherfore I pray you be not discouraged, but gather up your selfe to goe thorow these dificulties cherfully and with courage in that place wherin God hath sett you, untill the day of refreshing come. And the Lord God of sea and land bring us comfortably togeather againe, if it may stand with his glorie.

Yours,

ROBART CUSHMAN.

On the other sid of the leafe, in the same leter, came these few lines from Mr. John Peirce, in whose name the patente was taken, and of whom more will follow, to be spoken in its place.

WORTHY SIR, I desire you to take into consideration that which is writen on the other side, and not any way to damnifie your owne collony, whos strength is but weaknes, and may therby be more infeebled. And for the leters of association, by the next ship we send, I hope you shall receive satisfaction; in the mean time whom you admite I will approve. But as for Mr. Weston's company, I thinke them so base in condition (for the most parte) as in all apearance not fitt for an honest mans company. I wish they prove other wise. My purpose is not to enlarge my selfe, but cease in these few lines, and so rest

Your loving freind,

JOHN PEIRCE.

All these things they pondred and well considered, yet concluded to give his men frendly entertainmente; partly in regard of Mr. Weston him selfe, considering what he had been unto them, and done for them, and to some, more espetially; and partly in compassion to the people, who were now come into a willdernes, (as them selves were,) and were by *the ship* to be presently put a shore, (for she was *to cary other passengers* to *Virginia*, who lay at great charge;) and they were alltogeather unacquainted and knew not what to doe. So as they had received his former companyof ·7· *men*, and vitailed them as their owne hitherto, so they also received *these* (being *aboute ·60· lusty men*), and gave housing for them selves and their goods; and many being sicke, they had the best means the place could aford them. They stayed hear the most parte of the sommer till *the ship came back againe from Virginia.* Then, by his direction, or those whom he set over them, they removed into the Massachusset Bay, he having got a patente for some part ther, (by light of ther former discovery in leters sent home). Yet they left all ther sicke folke hear till they were setled and housed. But of ther victails they had not any, though they were in great wante, nor any thing els in recompence of any courtecie done them; neither did they desire it, for they saw they were an unruly company, and had no good govermente over them, and by disorder would soone fall into wants if Mr. Weston came not the sooner amongst them; and therfore, to prevente all after occasion, would have nothing of them.

Amids these streigths, and the desertion of those from whom they had hoped for supply, and when famine begane now to pinch them sore, they not knowing what to doe, the Lord, (who never fails his,) presents them with an occasion, beyond all expectation. This boat which came from the eastward brought them a letter from a stranger, of whose name they had never heard before, being a captaine of a ship come ther a fishing. This leter was as followeth. Being thus inscribed.

To ALL HIS GOOD FREINDS AT PLIMOTH, these, etc.

FRIENDS, CUNTRIMEN, AND NEIGHBOURS: I salute you, and wish you all health and hapines in the Lord. I make bould with these few lines to trouble you, because unless I were unhumane, I can doe no less. Bad news doth spread it selfe too farr; yet I will so farr informe you that my selfe, with many good freinds in the south-collonie of Virginia, have received shuch a blow, that ·400· persons large will not make good our losses. Therfore I doe intreat you (allthough not knowing you) that the old rule which I learned when I went to schoole, may be sufficente. That is, Hapie is he whom other mens harmes doth make to beware. And now againe and againe, wishing all those that willingly would serve the Lord, all health and happines in this world, and everlasting peace in the world to come. And so I rest,

Yours,
JOHN HUDLESTON.

By this boat the Governor returned a thankfull answer, as was meete, and sent a boate of their owne with them, which was piloted by them, in which Mr. Winslow was sente to procure what provissions he could of the ships, who was kindly received by the foresaid gentill-man, who not only spared what he could, but writ to others to doe the like. By which means he gott some good quantitie and returned in saftie, by which the plantation had a duble benefite, first, a present refreshing by the food brought, and secondly, they knew the way to those parts for their benefite hearafter. But what was gott, and this small boat brought, being devided among so many, came but to a litle, yet by Gods blesing it upheld them till harvest. It arose but to a quarter of a pound of bread a day to each person; and the Governor caused it to be dayly given them, otherwise, had it been in their owne custody, they would have eate it up and then starved. But thus, with what els they could get, they made pretie shift till corne was ripe.

This sommer they builte a fort with good timber, both strong and comly, which was of good defence, made with a flate rofe and batllements, on which their ordnance were mounted, and wher they kepte constante watch, espetially in time of danger. It served them allso for a meeting house, and was fitted accordingly for that use. It was a great worke for them in this weaknes and time of wants; but the deanger of the time required it, and both the continuall rumors of the fears from the Indeans hear, espetially the Narigansets, and also the hearing of that great massacre in Virginia, made all hands willing to despatch the same.

Now the wellcome time of harvest aproached, in which all had their hungrie bellies filled. But it arose but to a litle, in comparison of a full years supplie; partly by reason they were not yet well aquainted with the manner of Indean corne, (and they had no other,) allso their many other imployments, but cheefly their weaknes for wante of food, to tend it as they should have done. Also much was stolne both by night and day, before it became scarce eatable, and much more afterward. And though many were well whipt (when they were taken) for a few ears of corne, yet hunger made others (whom conscience did not restraines) to venture. So as it well appeared that famine must still insue the next year allso, if not some way prevented, or supplie should faile, to which they durst not trust. Markets ther was non to goe too, but only the Indeans, and they had no trading comodities. Behold now another providence of God; a ship comes into the harbor, one Captain Jones being cheefe ther in. They were set out by some marchants to discovere all the harbors betweene this and Virginia, and the shoulds of Cap-Cod, and to trade along the coast wher they could. This ship had store of English-beads (which were then good trade) and some knives, but would sell none but at dear rates, and also a good quantie togeather. Yet they weere glad of the occasion, and faine to buy at any rate; they were faine to give after the rate of cento per cento, if not more, and yet pay away coat-beaver at 3*s*. per *li.*, which in a few years after yeelded 20*s*. By this means they were fitted againe to trade for beaver and other things, and intended to buy what corne they could.

But I will hear take liberty to make a litle digression. Ther was in *this ship* a gentle-man by name Mr. John Poory; he had been secretarie in Virginia, and was now going home passenger *in this ship*. After his departure he write a leter to the Governor in the postscrite whereof he hath these lines.

To your selfe and Mr. Brewster, I must acknowledg my selfe many ways indebted, whose books I would have you thinke very well bestowed on him, who esteemeth them shuch juells. My hast would not suffer me to remember (much less to begg) Mr. Ainsworths elaborate worke upon the ·5· books of Moyses. Both his and Mr. Robinsons doe highly comend the authors, as being most conversante in the scriptures of all others. And what good (who knows) it may please God to worke by them, through my hands, (though most unworthy,) who finds shuch high contente in them. God have you all in his keeping.

Your unfained and firme freind,

Aug. 28. 1622.   JOHN PORY.

These things I hear inserte for honour sake of the authores memorie, which this gentle-man doth thus ingeniusly acknowledg; and him selfe after his returne did this poore-plantation much credite amongst those of no mean ranck. But to returne.

Shortly after harvest Mr. Westons people who were now seated at the Massachusets, and by disorder (as it seems) had made havock of their provissions, begane now to perceive that

want would come upon them. And hearing that they hear had
bought trading comodities and intended to trade for corne,
they write to the Governor and desired they might joyne with
them, and they would imploy their small ship in the servise;
and furder requested either to lend or sell them so much of
their trading comodities as their part might come to, and they
would undertake to make paymente when Mr. Weston, or their
supply, should come. The Governor condesended upon equall
terms of agreemente, thinkeing to goe aboute the Cap to the
southward with the ship, wher some store of corne might be
got. Althings being provided, Captain Standish was apointed
to goe with them, and Squanto for a guid and interpreter,
about the *latter end of September*; but the winds put them in
againe, and putting out the ·2· time, he fell sick of a feavor, so
the Governor wente him selfe. But they could not get aboute
the should of Cap-Cod, for flats and breakers, neither could
Squanto directe them better, nor the master durst venture
any further, so they put into Manamoyack Bay and got what
they could ther. In this place Squanto fell sick of an Indean
feavor, bleeding much at the nose (which the Indeans take
for a simptome of death), and within a few days dyed ther;
desiring the Governor to pray for him, that he might goe to
the Englishmens God in heaven, and bequeathed sundrie of
his things to sundry of his English freinds, as remembrances
of his love; of whom they had a great loss. They got in this
vioage, in one place and other, about ·26· or ·28· hogsheads of
corne and beans, which was more then the Indeans could well
spare in these parts, for they set but a litle till they got English
hows. And so were faine to returne, being sory they could not
gett about the Cap, to have been better laden. After ward the
Governor tooke a few men and wente to the inland places, to
get what he could, and to fetch it home at the spring, which
did help them something.

After these things, in *February*, a messenger came from John
Sanders, who was left cheefe over Mr. Westons men in the
bay of Massachusets, who brought a letter shewing the great
wants they were falen into; and he would have borrowed a hh
of corne of the Indeans, but they would lend him none. He
desired advice whether he might not take it from them by force
to succore his men till he came from the eastward, whither

he was going. The Governor and rest deswaded him by all means from it, for it might so exasperate the Indeans as might endanger their saftie, and all of us might smart for it; for they had already heard how they had so wronged the Indeans by stealing their corne, etc., as they were much incensed against them. Yea, so base were some of their own company, as they wente and tould the Indeans that their Governor was purposed to come and take their corne by force. The which with other things made them enter into a conspiracie against the English, of which more in the nexte. Hear with I end this year.

ANNO DOM: ·1623·

IT may be thought strang that these people should fall to these extremities in so short a time, being left competently provided when the ship left them, and had an addition by that moyetie of corn that was got by trade, besides much they gott of the Indeans wher they lived, by one means and other. It must needs be their great disorder, for they spent excesseivly whilst they had, or could get it; and, it may be, wasted parte away among the Indeans (for he that was their cheef was taxed by some amongst them for keeping Indean women, how truly I know not). And after they begane to come into wants, many sould away their cloathes and bed coverings; others (so base were they) became servants to the Indeans, and would cutt them woode and fetch them water, for a cap full of corne; others fell to plaine stealing, both night and day, from the Indeans, of which they greevosly complained. In the end, they came to that misery, that some starved and dyed with could and hunger. One in geathering shell-fish was so weake as he stuck fast in the mudd, and was found dead in the place. At last most of them left their dwellings and scatered up and downe in the woods, and by the water sides, wher they could find ground nuts and clames, hear ·6· and ther ten. By which their cariages they became contemned and scorned of the Indeans, and they begane greatly to insulte over them in a most insolente maner; insomuch, many times as they lay thus scatered abrod, and had set on a pot with ground nuts or shell-fish, when it was ready the Indeans would come and eate it up; and when night came, wheras some of them had a sorie blanket, or shuch like, to lappe them selves in, the Indeans would take it and let the other lye all nighte in the could; so as their condition was very lamentable. Yea, in the end they were faine to hange one of their men, whom they could not reclaime from stealing, to give the Indeans contente.

Whilst things wente in this maner with them, the Governor and people hear had notice that Massasoyte ther freind was sick and near unto death. They sent to vissete him, and with all sente him shuch comfortable things as gave him great contente, and was a means of his recovery; upon which occasion he discovers the conspiracie of these Indeans, how they were resolved to cutt of Mr. Westons people, for the continuall injuries they did them, and would now take opportunitie of their weaknes to doe it; and for that end had conspired with other Indeans their neighbours their aboute. And thinking the people hear would revenge their death, they therfore thought to doe the like by them, and had solisited him to joyne with them. He advised them therfore to prevent it, and that speedly by taking of some of the cheefe of them, before it was to late, for he asured them of the truth hereof.

This did much trouble them, and they tooke it in to serious delibration, and found upon examenation other evidence to give light hear unto, to longe hear to relate. In the mean time, came one of them from the Massachucets, with a small pack at his back; and though he knew not a foote of the way, yet he got safe hither, but lost his way, which was well for him, for he was pursued, and so was mist. He tould them hear how all things stood amongst them, and that he durst stay no longer, he apprehended they (by what he observed) would be all knokt in the head shortly. This made them make the more hast, and dispatched a boate away with Capten Standish and some men, who found them in a miserable condition, out of which he rescued them, and helped them to some releef, cut of some few of the cheefe conspirators, and, according to his order, offered to bring them all hither if they thought good; and they should fare no worse then them selves, till Mr. Weston or some supplie came to them. Or, if any other course liked them better, he was to doe them any helpfullnes he could. They thanked him and the rest. But most of them desired he would help them with some corne, and they would goe with their smale ship to the

eastward, wher hapily they might here of Mr. Weston, or some
supply from him, seing the time of the year was for fishing ships
to be in the land. If not, they would worke among the fisher-
men for their liveing, and get ther passage into England, if they
heard nothing from Mr. Weston in time. So they shipped what
they had of any worth, and he got them all the corne he could
(scarce leaving to bring him home), and saw them well out of
the bay, under saile at sea, and so came home, not takeing the
worth of a peny of any thing that was theirs. I have but touched
these things breefly, because they have allready been published
in printe more at large.

This was the end of these that some time bosted of their
strength, (being all able lustie men,) and what they would doe
and bring to pass, in comparison of the people hear, who had
many women and children and weak ones amongst them; and
said at their first arivall, when they saw the wants hear, that
they would take an other course, and not fall into shuch a
condition, as this simple people were come too. But a mans way
is not in his owne power; God can make the weake to stand;
let him also that standeth take heed least he fall.

Shortly after, Mr. Weston came over with some of the fisher-
men, under another name, and the disguise of a blacke-smith,
where he heard of the ruine and disolution of his colony. He
got a boat and with a man or ·2· came to see how things were.
But by the way, for wante of skill, in a storme, he cast away his
shalop in the botome of the bay between Meremek river and
Pascataquack, and hardly escaped with life, and afterwards fell
into the hands of the Indeans, who pillaged him of all he saved
from the sea, and striped him out of all his cloaths to his shirte.
At last he got to Pascataquack, and borrowed a suite of cloaths,
and got means to come to Plimoth. A strang alteration ther
was in him to shuch as had seen and known him in his former
florishing condition; so uncertaine are the mutable things of
this unstable world. And yet men set their harts upon them,
though they dayly see the vanity therof.

After many passages, and much discourse, (former things
boyling in his mind, but bit in as was discernd,) so he desired
to borrow some beaver of them; and tould them he had hope of
a ship and good supply to come to him, and then they should
have any thing for it they stood in neede of. They gave litle

credite to his supplie, but pitied his case, and remembered
former curtesies. They tould him he saw their wants, and they
knew not when they should have any supply; also how the case
stood betweene them and their adventurers, he well knew; they
had not much bever, and if they should let him have it, it were
enoughe to make a mutinie among the people, seeing ther was
no other means to procure them foode which they so much
wanted, and cloaths allso. Yet they tould him they would help
him, considering his necessitie, but must doe it secretly for
the former reasons. So they let him have ·100· beaver-skins,
which waighed 170 *li.* odd pounds. Thus they helpt him when
all the world faild him, and with this means he went againe
to the ships, and stayed his small ship and some of his men,
and bought provissions and fited him selfe; and it was the only
foundation of his after course. But he requited them ill, for he
proved after a bitter enimie unto them upon all occasions, and
never repayed them any thing for it, to this day, but reproches
and evill words. Yea, he divolged it to some that were none of
their best freinds, whilst he yet had the beaver in his boat; that
he could now set them alltogeather by the ears, because they
had done more then they could answer, in letting him have
this beaver, and he did not spare to doe what he could. But his
malice could not prevaile.

All this whille no supply was heard of, neither knew they
when they might expecte any. So they begane to thinke how
they might raise as much corne as they could, and obtaine a
beter crope then they had done, that they might not still thus
languish in miserie. At length, after much debate of things,
the Governor (with the advise of the cheefest amongest them)
gave way that they should set corne every man for his owne
perticuler, and in that regard trust to them selves; in all other
things to goe on in the generall way as before. And so assigned
to every family a parcell of land, according to the proportion
of their number for that end, only for present use (but made
no devission for inheritance), and ranged all boys and youth
under some familie. This had very good success; for it made
all hands very industrious, so as much more corne was planted
then other waise would have bene by any means the Governor
or any other could use, and saved him a great deall of trouble,
and gave farr better contente. The women now wente willingly

into the feild, and tooke their litle-ones with them to set corne, which before would aledg weaknes, and inabilitie; whom to have compelled would have bene thought great tiranie and oppression.

The experience that was had in this commone course and condition, tried sundrie years, and that amongst godly and sober men, may well evince the vanitie of that conceite of Platos and other ancients, applauded by some of later times; that the taking away of propertie, and bringing in communitie into a comone wealth, would make them happy and florishing; as if they were wiser then God. For this comunitie (so farr as it was) was found to breed much confusion and discontent, and retard much imployment that would have been to their benefite and comforte. For the yong-men that were most able and fitte for labour and service did repine that they should spend their time and streingth to worke for other mens wives and children, with out any recompence. The strong, or man of parts, had no more in devission of victails and cloaths, then he that was weake and not able to doe a quarter the other could; this was thought injuestice. The aged and graver men to be ranked and equal-ised in labours, and victails, cloaths, etc., with the meaner and yonger sorte, thought it some indignite and disrespect unto them. And for mens wives to be commanded to doe servise for other men, as dresing their meate, washing their cloaths, etc., they deemd it a kind of slaverie, neither could many husbands well brooke it. Upon the poynte all being to have alike, and all to doe alike, they thought them selves in the like condition, and one as good as another; and so, if it did not cut of those relations that God hath set amongest men, yet it did at least much diminish and take of the mutuall respects that should be preserved amongst them. And would have bene worse if they had been men of another condition. Let none objecte this is men's corruption, and nothing to the course it selfe. I answer, seeing all men have this corruption in them, God in his wisdome saw another course fiter for them.

But to returne. After this course setled, and by that their corne was planted, all ther victails were spente, and they were only to rest on Gods providence; at night not many times knowing wher to have a bitt of any thing the next day. And so, as one well observed, had need to pray that God would give them their dayly brade, above all people in the world. Yet they bore these wants with great patience and allacritie of spirite, and that for so long a time as for the most parte of ·2· years; which makes me remember what Peter Martire writes, (in magnifying the Spaniards) in his ·5· Decade, pag. 208. *"They* (saith he) *led a miserable life for ·5· days togeather, with the parched graine of maize only, and that not to saturitie;* and then concludes, *that shuch pains, shuch labours, and shuch hunger, he thought none living which is not a Spaniard could have endured."* But alass! these, when they had maize (that is, Indean corne) they thought it as good as a feast, and wanted not only for ·5· days togeather, but some time ·2· or ·3· months togeather, and neither had bread nor any kind of corne. Indeed, in an other place, in his ·2· Decade, page 94, he mentions how others of them were worse put to it, wher they were faine to eate doggs, toads, and dead men, and so dyed almost all. From these extremities the Lord in his goodnes kept these his people, and in their great wants preserved both their lives and healthes; let his name have the praise. Yet let me hear make use of his conclusion, which in some sorte may be applied to this people: *"That with their miseries they oppened a way to these new-lands; and after these stormes, with what ease other men came to inhabite in them, in respecte of the calamities these men suffered; so as they seeme to goe to a bride feaste wher all things are provided for them."*

They haveing but one boat left and she not over well fitted, they were devided into severall companies, ·6· or ·7· to a gangg or company, and so wente out with a nett they had bought, to take bass and shuch like fish, by course, every company knowing their turne. No sooner was the boate discharged of what she brought, but the next company tooke her and wente out with her. Neither did they returne till they had cauight something, though it were ·5· or ·6· days before, for they knew ther was nothing at home, and to goe home emptie would be a great discouragemente to the rest. Yea, they strive who would doe best. If she stayed longe or got litle, then all wente to seeking of shelfish, which at low-water they digged out of the sands. And this was their living in the sommer time, till God sente them beter; and in winter they were helped with groundnuts and foule. Also in the sommer they gott now and then a dear; for one or ·2· of the fitest was apoynted to range the woods for that end, and what was gott that way was devided amongst them.

At length they received some leters from the adventurers, too long and tedious hear to record, by which they heard of their further crosses and frustrations; begining in this maner.

LOVING FREINDS, As your sorrows and afflictions have bin great, so our croses and interceptions in our proceedings hear, have not been small. For after we had with much trouble and charge sente the *Parragon* away to sea, and thought all the paine past, within ·14· days after she came againe hither, being dangerously leaked, and brused with tempestious stormes, so as shee was faine to be had into the docke, and an 100 *li.* bestowed upon her. All the passengers lying upon our charg or ·6· or ·7· weeks, and much discontent and distemper was occasioned hereby, so as some dangerous evente had like to insewed. But we trust all shall be well and worke for the best and your benefite, if yet with patience you can waite, and but have strength to hold in life. Whilst these things were doing, Mr. Westons ship came and brought diverce leters from you, etc. It rejoyseth us much to hear of those good reports that diverce have brought home from you, etc.

These letters were dated Des. 21: 1622.

So farr of this leter.

This ship was bought by Mr. John Peirce, and set out at his owne charge, upon hope of great maters. These passengers, and the goods the company sent in her, he tooke in for fraught, for which they agreed with him to be delivered hear. This was he in whose name their *first patente* was taken, by reason of aquaintance and some aliance that some of their freinds had with him. But his name was only used in trust. But when he saw they were hear hopfully thus seated, and by the success God gave them had obtained the favour of the Counsell of New-England, he goes and sues to them for *another patent* of much larger extente (in their names), which was easily obtained. But he mente to keep it to him selfe and alow them what he pleased, to hold of him as tenants, and sue to his courts as cheefe Lord, as will appear by that which follows. But the Lord marvelously crost him; for after this first returne, and the charge above mentioned, when shee was againe fitted he pesters him selfe and takes in more passengers, and those not very good to help to bear his losses, and sets out the ·2· time. But what the event was will appear from another leter from one of the cheefe of the company, dated the ·9· of Aprill, 1623. writ to the Governor hear, as followeth.

LOVING FREIND, When I write my last leter, I hoped to have received one from you well-nigh by this time. But when I write in Descember I litle thought to have seen Mr. John Peirce till he had brought some good tidings from you. But it pleased God, he brought us the wofull tidings of his returne when he was half way over, by extraime tempest, werin the goodnes and mercie of God appeared in sparing their lives, being ·109· souls. The loss is so great to Mr. Peirce, etc., and the companie put upon so great charge, as veryly, etc.

Now with great trouble and loss, we have got Mr. John Peirce to assigne over the grand patente to the companie, which he had taken in his owne name, and made quite voyd our former grante. I am sorie to writ how many hear thinke that the hand of God was justly against him, both the first and ·2· time of his returne; in regard he, whom you and we so confidently trusted, but only to use his name for the company, should aspire to be lord over us all, and so make you and us tenants at his will and pleasure, our assurance or patente being quite voyd and disanuled by his means. I desire to judg charitably of him. But his unwillingnes to part with his royall Lordship, and the high-rate he set it at, which was 500*li.* which cost him but 50*li.*, makes many speake and judg hardly of him. The company are out for goods in his ship, with charge aboute the passengers, 640*li.*, etc.

We have agreed with ·2· marchants for a ship of ·140· tunes, caled the *Anne*, which is to be ready the last of this month, to bring ·60· passengers and ·60· tune of goods, etc.

This was dated Aprill ·9· 1623.

These were ther owne words and judgmente of this mans dealing and proceedings; for I thought it more meete to render them in theirs then my owne words. And yet though ther was never got other recompence then the resignation of this patente, and the shares he had in adventure, for all the former great sumes, he was never quiet, but sued them in most of the cheefe courts in England, and when he was still cast, brought it to the Parlemente. But he is now dead, and I will leave him to the Lord.

This ship suffered the greatest extreemitie at sea at her ·2· returne, that one shall lightly hear of, to be saved; as I have been informed by Mr. William Peirce who was then master of her, and many others that were passengers in her. It was aboute the *midle of February*. The storme was for the most parte of ·14· days, but for ·2· or ·3· days and nights togeather in most violent extremitie. After they had cut downe their mast, the storme beat of their round house and all their uper works; ·3· men had worke enough at the helme, and he that cund the ship before the sea, was faine to be bound fast for washing away; the seas did so over-rake them, as many times those upon the decke knew not whether they were within bord or withoute; and once she was so foundered in the sea as they all thought she would never rise againe. But yet the Lord preserved them, and brought them at last safe to *Ports-mouth*, to the wonder of all men that saw in what a case she was in, and heard what they had endured.

About the later end of *June* came in a ship, with Captaine Francis West, who had a comission to be admirall of New-England, to restraine interlopers, and shuch fishing ships as came to fish and trade without a licence from the Counsell of New-England, for which they should pay a round sume of money. But he could doe no good of them, for they were to stronge for him, and he found the fisher men to be stuberne fellows. And their owners, upon complainte made to the Parlemente, procured an order that fishing should be free. He tould the Governor they spooke with a ship at sea, and were abord her, that was coming for this plantation, in which were sundrie passengers, and they marvelled she was not arrived, fearing some miscariage; for they lost her in a storme that fell shortly after they had been abord. Which relation filled them full of fear, yet mixed with hope. The master of this ship had some ·2· hh of pease to sell, but seeing their wants, held them at 9*li.* sterling a hoggshead, and under 8*li.* he would not take, and yet would have beaver at an under rate. But they tould him they had lived so long with out, and would doe still, rather then give so unreasonably. So they went from hence to Virginia.

About ·14· days after came in this ship, caled the *Anne*, wherof Mr. William Peirce was master, and aboute a weeke or ·10· days after came in the pinass which in foule weather they lost at sea, a fine new vessell of about ·44· tune, which the company had builte to stay in the cuntrie. They brought about ·60· persons for the generall, some of them being very usefull persons, and became good members to the body, and some were the wives and children of shuch as were hear allready. And some were so bad, as they were faine to be at charge to send them home againe the next year. Also, besides these ther came a company, that did not belong to the generall body, but came on their perticuler, and were to have lands assigned them, and be for them selves, yet to be subjecte to the generall Goverment; which caused some diferance and disturbance amongst them, as will after apeare. I shall hear againe take libertie to inserte a few things out of shuch leters as came in this shipe, desiring rather to manefest things in ther words and apprehentions, then in my owne, as much as may be, without tediousness.

BELOVED FREINDS, I kindly salute you all, with trust of your healths and wellfare, being right sorie that no supplie hath been made to you all this while; for defence wher of, I must referr you to our generall leters. Naither indeed have we now sent you many things, which we should and would, for want of money. But persons, more then inough, (though not all we should,) for people come flying in upon us, but monys come creeping in to us. Some few of your old freinds are come, as, etc. So they come droping to you, and by degrees, I hope ere long you shall enjoye them all. And because people press so hard upon us to goe, and often shuch as are none of the fitest, I pray you write ernestly to the Treasurer and directe what persons should be sente. It greeveth me to see so weake a company sent you, and yet had I not been hear they had been weaker. You must still call upon the company hear to see that honest men be sente you, and threaten to send them back if any other come, etc. We are not any way so much in danger, as by corrupte and noughty persons. Shuch, and shuch, came without my consente; but the importunite of their freinds got promise of our Treasurer in my absence. Neither is ther need we should take any lewd men, for we may have honest men enew, etc.

Your assured freind,
R C

The following was from the genrall.

LOVING FREINDS, we most hartily salute you in all love and harty affection; being yet in hope that the same God which hath hithertoo preserved you in a marvelous maner, doth yet continue your lives and health, to his owne praise and all our comforts. Being right sory that you have not been sent unto all this time, etc. We have in this ship sent shuch women, as were willing and ready to goe to their husbands and freinds, with their children, etc. We would not have you discontente, because we have not sent you more of your old freinds, and in spetiall, him* on whom you most depend. Farr be it from us to neclecte you, or contemne him. But as the intente was at first, so the evente at last shall shew it, that we will deal fairly, and squarly answer your expectations to the full. Ther are also come unto you, some honest men to plant upon their perticulers besides you. A thing which if we should not give way unto, we should wrong both them and you. Them, by puting them on things more inconveniente, and you, for that being honest men, they will be a strengthening to the place, and good neighbours unto you. Tow things we would advise you of, which we have likwise signified them hear. First, the trade for skins to be retained for the generall till the devidente; 2ly. that their setling by you, be with shuch distance of place as is neither inconvenient for the lying of your lands, nor hurtfull to your speedy and easie assembling togeather.

We have sente you diverse fisher men, with salte, etc. Diverse other provissions we have sente you, as will appear in your bill of lading, and though we have not sent all we would (because our cash is small), yet it is that we could, etc.

And allthough it seemeth you have discovered many more rivers and fertill grounds then that wher you are, yet seeing by Gods provi-dence that place fell to your lote, let it be accounted as your portion; and rather fixe your eyes upon that which may be done ther, then languish in hopes after things els-wher. If your place be not the best, it is better, you shall be the less envied and encroached upon; and shuch as are earthly minded, will not setle too near your border.† If the land afford you bread, and the sea yeeld you fish, rest you a while contented, God will one day afford you better fare. And all men shall know you are neither fugetives nor discontents. But can, if God so order it, take the worst to your selves, with content, and leave the best to your neighbours, with cherfullnes.

Let it not be greeveous unto you that you have been instruments to breake the ise for others who come after with less dificulty; the honour shall be yours to the worlds end, etc.

We bear you always in our brests, and our harty affection is towards you all, as are the harts of hundreds more which never saw your faces, who doubtles pray for your saftie as their owne, as we our selves both doe and ever shall, that the same God which hath so marvelously

*John Robinson.
†This proved rather, a propheti, then advice.

preserved you from seas, foes, and famine, will still preserve you from all future dangers, and make you honourable amongst men, and glorious in blise at the last day. And so the Lord be with you all and send us joyfull news from you, and inable us with one shoulder so to accomplish and perfecte this worke, as much glorie may come to Him that confoundeth the mighty by the weak, and maketh small thinges great. To whose greatnes, be all glorie for ever and ever.

This leter was subscribed with ·13· of their names.

These passengers, when they saw their low and poore condition a shore, were much danted and dismayed, and according to their diverse humores were diversly affected; some wished them selves in England againe; others fell a weeping, fancying their own miserie in what they saw now in others; other some pitying the distress they saw their freinds had been long in, and still were under; in a word, all were full of sadnes. Only some of their old freinds rejoysed to see them, and that it was no worse with them, for they could not expecte it should be better, and now hoped they should injoye better days togeather. And truly it was no marvell they should be thus affected, for they were in a very low condition, many were ragged in aparell, and some litle beter then halfe naked; though some that were well stord before, were well enough in this regard. But for food they were all alike, save some that had got a few pease of the ship that was last hear. The best dish they could presente their freinds with was a lobster, or a peece of fish, without bread or any thing els but a cupp of fair spring water. And the long continuance of this diate, and their labours abroad, had something abated the freshnes of their former complexion. But God gave them health and strength in *a good measure; and shewed them by experience the truth of that word, Deut.* ·8· 3. *That man liveth not by bread only, but by every word that proceedeth out of the mouth of the Lord doth a man live.*

When I think how sadly the scripture speaks of the famine in Jaakobs time, when he said to his sonns, Goe buy us food, that we may live and not dye. Gen.: ·42· 2. and ·43· 1, that the famine was great, or heavie in the land; and yet they had shuch great heirds, and store of catle of sundrie kinds, which, besides flesh, must needs produse other food, as milke, butter and cheese, etc., and yet it was counted a sore affliction; theirs hear must needs be very great, therfore, who not only wanted the staffe of bread, but all these things, and had no Egipte to goe too. But God fedd them out of the sea for the most parte, so wonderfull is his providence over his in all ages; for his mercie endureth for ever.

On the other hand the old planters were affraid that their corne, when it was ripe, should be imparted to the new-commers, whose provissions which they brought with them they feared would fall short before the year wente aboute (as indeed it did). They came to the Governor and besought him that as it was before agreed that they should set corne for their perticuler, and accordingly they had taken extraordinary pains ther aboute, that they might freely injoye the same, and they would not have a bitte of the victails now come, but waite till harvest for their owne, and let the new-commers injoye what they had brought; they would have none of it, excepte they could purchase any of it of them by bargaine or exchainge. Their requeste was granted them, for it gave both sides good contente; for the new-commers were as much afraid that the hungrie planters would have eat up the provissions brought, and they should have fallen into the like condition.

This ship was in a shorte time laden with clapbord, by the help of many hands. Also they sente in her all the beaver and other furrs they had, and Mr. Winslow was sent over with her, to informe of all things, and procure shuch things as were thought needfull for their presente condition. By this time harvest was come, and in stead of famine, now God gave them plentie, and the face of things was changed, to the rejoysing of the harts of many, for which they blessed God. And the effect of their particuler planting was well seene, for all had, one way and other, pretty well to bring the year aboute, and some of the abler sorte and more industrious had to spare, and sell to others, so as any generall wante or famine hath not been amongst them since to this day.

I may not here omite how, notwithstanding all their great paines and industrie, and the great hopes of a large cropp, the Lord seemed to blast, and take away the same, and to threaten further and more sore famine unto them, by a great drought which continued from the ·3· weeke in May, till about the midle of July, without any raine, and with great heat (for the most parte), insomuch as the corne begane to wither away, though it was set with fishe, the moysture whereof helped it much. Yet at length it begane to languish sore, and some of the drier grounds were partched like withered hay, part whereof was never recovered. Upon which they sett a parte a solemne day of humilliation, to seek the Lord by humble and fervente prayer, in this great distrese. And he was pleased to give them a gracious and speedy answer, both to their owne, and the Indeans admiration, that lived amongest them. For all the morning, and greatest part of the day, it was clear weather and very hotte, and not a cloud or any signe of raine to be seen, yet toward evening it begane to overcast and shortly after to raine, with shuch sweete and gentle showers, as gave them cause of rejoyceing, and blessing God. It came, without either wind, or thunder, or any violence, and by degreese in that abundance, as that the earth was thorowly wete and soked therwith. Which did so apparently revive and quicken the decayed corne and other fruits, as was wonderfull to see, and made the Indeans astonished to behold; and after wards the Lord sent them shuch seasonable showers, with enterchange of faire warme weather, as, through his blessing, caused a fruitfull and liberall harvest, to their no small comforte and rejoycing. For which mercie (in time conveniente) they also sett aparte a day of thanksgiveing. This being overslipt in its place, I thought meet here to inserte the same.

Those that came on their perticuler looked for greater matters then they found or could attaine unto, aboute building great houses, and shuch pleasant situations for them, as them selves had fancied; as if they would be great men and rich, all of a sudaine; but they proved castels in the aire. These were the conditions agreed on betweene the colony and them.

First, that the Governor, in the name and with the consente of the company, doth in all love and frendship receive and imbrace them; and is to allote them competente places for habitations within the towne. And promiseth to shew them all shuch other curtesies as shall be reasonable for them to desire, or us to performe.

·2· That they, on their parts, be subjecte to all shuch laws and orders as are already made, or hear after shall be, for the publick good.

·3· That they be freed and exempte from the generall imployments of the said company, (which their presente condition of
comunitie requireth,) excepte commune defence, and shuch
other imployments as tend to the perpetuall good of the
collony.

·4ly· Towards the maintenance of Government, and publick
officers of the said collony, every male above the age of ·16·
years shall pay a bushell of Indean wheat, or the worth of it,
into the commone store.

·5ly· That (according to the agreemente, the marchants made
with them before they came) they are to be wholy debarred
from all trade with the Indeans for all sorts of furrs, and shuch
like commodities, till the time of the comunallitie be ended.

About the midle of September arrived Captaine Robart
Gorges in the Bay of the Massachusets, with sundrie passengers and families, intending their to begine a plantation; and
pitched upon the place Mr. Weston's people had forsaken. He
had a commission from the Counsell of New-England, to be
generall Governor of the cuntrie, and they appoynted for his
counsell and assistance, Captaine Francis West, the aforesaid
admirall, Christopher Levite, Esquire, and the Governor of Plimoth for the time beeing, etc. Allso, they gave him authoritie
to chuse shuch other as he should find fit. Allso, they gave (by
their commission) full power to him and his assistants, or any
·3· of them, wherof him selfe was all way to be one, to doe and
execute what to them should seeme good, in all cases, Capitall,
Criminall, and Civill, etc., with diverce other instructions. Of
which, and his comission, it pleased him to suffer the Governor
hear to take a coppy.

He gave them notice of his arivall by letter, but before they
could visite him he went to the eastward with the ship he came
in; but a storme arising, (and they wanting a good pilot to
harbor them in those parts,) they bore up for this harbor. He
and his men were hear kindly entertained; he stayed hear ·14·
days. In the mean time came in Mr. Weston with his small ship,
which he had now recovered. Captaine Gorges tooke hold of
the opportunite, and acquainted the Governor hear, that one
occasion of his going to the eastward was to meete with Mr.
Weston, and call him to accounte for some abuses he had to
lay to his charge. Wherupon he called him before him, and

some other of his assistants, with the Governor of this place; and charged him, first, with the ille carriage of his men at the Massachusets; by which means the peace of the cuntrie was disturbed, and him selfe and the people which he had brought over to plante in that bay were therby much prejudised. To this Mr. Weston easily answered, that what was that way done, was in his absence, and might have befalen any man; he left them sufficiently provided, and conceived they would have been well governed; and for any errour committed he had sufficiently smarted. This particuler was passed by. A 2d. was, for an abuse done to his father, Sir Ferdenando Gorges, and to the State. The thing was this; he used him and others of the Counsell of New-England, to procure him a licence for the transporting of many peeces of great ordnance for New-England, pretending great fortification hear in the countrie, and I know not what shipping. The which when he had obtained, he went and sould them beyond seas for his private profite; for which (he said) the State was much offended, and his father suffered a shrowd check, and he had order to apprehend him for it. Mr. Weston excused it as well as he could, but could not deney it; it being one maine thing (as was said) for which he with-drew him self. But after many passages, by the mediation of the Governor and some other freinds hear, he was inclined to gentlnes (though he aprehended the abuse of his father deeply); which, when Mr. Weston saw, he grew more presumptuous, and gave shuch provocking and cutting speches, as made him rise up in great indignation and distemper, and vowed that he would either curb him, or send him home for England. At which Mr. Weston was something danted, and came privatly to the Governor hear, to know whether they would suffer Captaine Gorges to apprehend him. He was tould they could not hinder him, but much blamed him, that after they had pacified things, he should thus breake out, by his owne folly and rashnes, to bring trouble upon him selfe and them too. He confest it was his passion, and prayd the Governor to entreat for him, and pacifie him if he could. The which at last he did, with much adoe; so he was called againe, and the Governor was contente to take his owne bond to be ready to make further answer, when either he or the lords should send for him. And at last he tooke only his word, and ther was a freindly parting on all hands.

But after he was gone, Mr. Weston in lue of thanks to the Governor and his freinds hear, gave them this quib (behind their baks) for all their pains. That though they were but yonge justices, yet they wear good beggers. Thus they parted at this time, and shortly after the Governor tooke his leave and went to the Massachusets by land, being very thankfull for his kind entertainemente. The ship stayed hear, and fitted her selfe to goe for Virginia, having some passengers ther to deliver; and with her returned sundrie of those from hence which came over on their perticuler, some out of discontente and dislike of the cuntrie; others by reason of a fire that broke out, and burnt the houses they lived in, and all their provissions so as they were necessitated therunto. This fire was occasioned by some of the sea-men that were roystering in a house wher it first begane, makeing a great fire in very could weather, which broke out of the chimney into the thatch, and burnte downe ·3· or ·4· houses, and consumed all the goods and provissions in them. The house in which it begane was right against their store-house, which they had much adoe to save, in which were their commone store and all their provissions; the which if it had been lost, the plantation had been overthrowne. But through Gods mercie it was saved by the great dilligence of the people, and care of the Governor and some aboute him. Some would have had the goods throwne out; but if they had, ther would much have been stolne by the rude company that belonged to these ·2· ships, which were all most all ashore. But a trusty company was plased within, as well as those that with wet-cloath and other means kept of the fire without, that if necessitie required they might have them out with all speed. For they suspected some malicious dealling, if not plaine treacherie, and whether it was only suspition or no, God knows; but this is certaine, that when the tumulte was greatest, there was a voice heard (but from whom it was not knowne) that bid them looke well aboute them, for all were not freinds that were near them. And shortly after, when the vehemencie of the fire was over, smoke was seen to arise within a shed that was joynd to the end of the store-house, which was watled up with bowes, in the withered leaves wherof the fire was kindled, which some, runing to quench, found a longe fire brand of an ell longe, lying under the wale on the inside, which could not possibly come their by casualtie, but must be laid ther by some hand, in the judgmente of all that saw it. But God kept them from this deanger, what ever was intended.

Shortly after Captaine Gorges, the generall Governor, was come home to the Massachusets, he sends a warrante to arrest Mr. Weston and his ship, and sends a master to bring her away thither, and one Captain Hanson (that belonged to him) to conducte him along. The Governor and others hear were very sory to see him take this course, and tooke exception at the warrante, as not legall nor sufficiente; and withall write to him to disswade him from this course, shewing him that he would but entangle and burthen him selfe in doing this; for he could not doe Mr. Weston a better turne, (as things stood with him); for he had a great many men that belonged to him in this barke, and was deeply ingaged to them for wages, and was in a manner out of victails (*and now winter*); all which would light upon him, if he did arrest his barke. In the time mean Mr. Weston had notice to shift for him selfe; but it was conceived he either knew not whither to goe, or how to mend him selfe, but was rather glad of the occasion, and so stirred not. But the Governor would not be perswaded, but sent a very formall warrente under his hand and seall, with strict charge as they would answere it to the state; he also write that he had better considered of things since he was hear, and he could not answer it to let him goe so; besides other things that were come to his knowledg since, which he must answer too. So he was suffered to proceede, but he found in the end that to be true that was tould him; for when an inventorie was taken of what was in the ship, ther was not vitailes found for above ·14· days, at a bare allowance, and not much else of any great worth, and the men did so crie out of him for wages and diate, in the mean time, as made him soone weary. So as in conclusion it turned to his loss, and the expence of his owne provisions; and *towards the spring* they came to agreement, (after they had bene to the eastward,) and the Governor restord him his vessell againe, and made him satisfaction, in bisket, meal, and shuch like provissions, for what he had made use of that was his, or what his men had any way wasted or consumed. So Mr. Weston came hither againe, and afterward shaped his course for Virginie, and so for present

I shall leave him. He dyed afterwards at Bristoll, in the time of the warrs, of the sicknes in that place.

The Governor and some that depended upon him returned for England, haveing scarcely saluted the cuntrie in his Governmente, not finding the state of things hear to answer his quallitie and condition. The people dispersed them selves, some went for England, others for Virginia, some few remained, and were helped with supplies from hence. The Governor brought over a minister with him, one Mr. Morell, who, about a year after the Governor returned, tooke shipping from hence. He had I know not what power and authority of superintendancie over other churches granted him, and sundrie instructions for that end; but he never shewed it, or made any use of it; (it should seeme he saw it was in vaine;) he only speake of it to some hear at his going away. This was in effect the end of a ·2· plantation in that place.

Ther were allso this year some scatering beginings made in other places, as at Paskataway, by Mr. David Thomson, at Monhigen, and some other places by sundrie others.

It rests now that I speake a word aboute the pinnass spoken of before, which was sent by the adventurers to be imployed in the cuntrie. She was a fine vessell, and bravely set out,* and I fear the adventurers did over pride them selves in her, for she had ill success. How ever, they erred grosly in tow things aboute her; first, though she had a sufficiente maister, yet she was rudly manned, and all her men were upon shares, and none was to have any wages but the master. 2ly, wheras they mainly lookt at trade, they had sent nothing of any value to trade with. When the men came hear, and mette with ill counsell from Mr. Weston and his crue, with others of the same stampe, neither master nor Governor could scarce rule them, for they exclaimed that they were abused and deceived, for they were tould they should goe for a man of warr, and take I know not whom, French and Spaniards, etc. They would neither trade nor fish, excepte they had wages; in fine, they would obey no command of the maisters; so as it was apprehended they would either rune away with the vessell, or get away with the ships,

*With her flages, and streamers, pendents, and wast cloaths, etc.

and leave here; so as Mr. Peirce and others of their freinds perswaded the Governor to chaing their condition, and give them wages; which was accordingly done. And she was sente about the Cape to the Narigansets to trade, but they made but a poore vioage of it. Some corne and beaver they got, but the Dutch used to furnish them with cloath and better commodities, they haveing only a few beads and knives, which were not ther much esteemed. Allso, in her returne home, at the very entrance into ther owne harbore, she had like to have been cast away in a storme, and was forced to cut her maine mast by the bord, to save herselfe from driving on the flats that lye without, caled Browns Ilands, the force of the wind being so great as made her anchors give way and she drive right upon them; but her mast and takling being gone, they held her till the wind shifted.

ANNO DOM: ·1624·

THE time of new election of ther officers for this year being come, and the number of their people increased, and their troubles and occasions therwith, the Governor desired them to chainge the persons, as well as renew the election; and also to adde more Assistans to the Governor for help and counsell, and the better carrying on of affairs. Showing that it was necessarie it should be so. If it was any honour or benefite, it was fitte others should be made pertakers of it; if it was a burthen, (as doubtles it was,) it was but equall others should help to bear it; and that this was the end of Annuall Elections. The issue was, that as before ther was but one Assistante, they now chose ·5· giving the Governor a duble voyce; and afterwards they increased them to ·7· which course hath continued to this day.

They having with some truble and charge new-masted and rigged their pinass, in the begining of March they sent her well vitaled to the eastward on fishing. She arrived safly at a place near Damarins cove, and was there well harbored in a place wher ships used to ride, ther being also some ships allready arived out of England. But shortly after ther arose shuch a violent and extraordinarie storme, as the seas broak over shuch places in the harbor as was never seene before, and drive her against great roks, which beat shuch a hole in her bulke, as a horse and carte might have gone in, and after drive her into deep-water, wher she lay sunke. The master was drowned, the rest of the men, all save one, saved their lives, with much a doe; all her provision, salt, and what els was in her, was lost. And here I must leave her to lye till afterward.

Some of those that still remained hear on their perticuler, begane privatly to nurish a faction, and being privie to a strong faction that was among the adventurers in England, on whom sundry of them did depend, by their private whispering they drew some of the weaker sorte of the company to their side, and so filld them with discontente, as nothing would satisfie them excepte they might be suffered to be in their perticuler allsoe; and made great offers, so they might be freed from the generall. The Governor consulting with the ablest of the generall body what was best to be done hear in, it was resolved to permitte them so to doe, upon equall conditions. The conditions were the same in effect with the former before related. Only some more added, as that they should be bound here to remaine till the generall partnership was ended. And also that they should pay into the store, the on halfe of all shuch goods and comodities as they should any waise raise above their food, in consideration of what charg had been layed out for them, with some shuch like things. This liberty granted, soone stopt this gape, for ther was but a few that undertooke this course when it came too; and they were as sone weary of it. For the other had perswaded them, and Mr. Weston togeather, that ther would never come more supply to the generall body; but the perticulers had shuch freinds as would carry all, and doe for them I know not what.

Shortly after, Mr. Winslow came over, and brought a prety good supply, and the ship came on fishing, a thing fatall to this plantation. He brought ·3· heifers and a bull, the first begining of any catle of that kind in the land, with some cloathing and other necessaries, as will further appear; but withall the reporte of a strong faction amongst the adventurers against them, and espetially against the coming of the rest from Leyden, and with what difficulty this supply was procured, and how, by their strong and long opposision, bussines was so retarded as not only they were now falne too late for the fishing season, but the best men were taken up of the fishermen in the west

countrie, and he was forct to take shuch a master and company
for that imployment as he could procure upon the present.
Some letters from thence shall beter declare these things, being
as followeth.

MOST WORTHY AND LOVING FREINDS, Your kind and loving leters
I have received, and render you many thanks, etc. It hath plased God
to stirre up the harts of our adventurers to raise a new stock for the
seting forth of this shipe, caled the Charitie, with men and necessaries, both for the plantation and the fishing, though accomplished
with very great difficulty; in regard we have some amongst us which
undoubtedly aime more at their owne private ends, and the thwart-
ing and opposing of some hear, and other worthy instruments* of
Gods glory elswher, then at the generall good and furtherance of
this noble and laudable action. Yet againe we have many other, and
I hope the greatest parte, very honest Christian men, which I am
perswaded their ends and intents are wholy for the glory of our Lord
Jesus Christ, in the propagation of his gospell, and hope of gaining
those poore salvages to the knowledg of God. But, as we have a
proverbe, One scabed sheep may marr a whole flock, so these male
contented persons, and turbulente spirits, doe what in them lyeth to
withdraw mens harts from you and your freinds, yea, even from the
generall bussines; and yet under show and pretence of godlynes and
furtherance of the plantation. Wheras the quite contrary doth plainly
appeare; as some of the honester harted men (though of late of their
faction) did make manifest at our late meeting. But what should I
trouble you or my selfe with these restles opposers of all goodnes,
and I doubte will be continuall disturbers of our frendly meetings and
love. On Thurs-day the ·8· of January we had a meeting aboute the
artickles betweene you and us; wher they would rejecte that, which
we in our late leters prest you to grante, (an addition to the time of
our joynt stock). And their reason which they would make known to
us was, it trobled their conscience to exacte longer time of you then
was agreed upon at the first. But that night they were so followed
and crost of their perverse courses, as they were even wearied, and
offered to sell their adventures; and some were willing to buy. But I,
doubting they would raise more scandale and false reports, and so
diverse waise doe us more hurt, by going of in shuch a furie, then
they could or can by continuing adventurers amongst us, would not
suffer them. But on the ·12· of January, we had another meting, but in

*He means Mr. Robinson.

the interime diverse of us had talked with most of them privatly, and had great combats and reasoning, pro and con. But at night when we mete to read the generall letter, we had the loveingest and frendlyest meeting that ever I knew* and our greatest enemise offered to lend us 50*li*. So I sent for a potle of wine, (I would you could† doe the like,) which we dranke freindly together. Thus God can turne the harts of men when it pleaseth him, etc. Thus loving freinds, I hartily salute you all in the Lord, hoping ever to rest.

Yours to my power,
JAMES SHERLEY.

Jan: 25. 1623–24.

Another leter.

BELOVED SIR, etc. We have now sent you, we hope, men and means, to setle these ·3· things, viz. fishing, salt making, and boat making; if you can bring them to pass to some perfection, your wants may be supplyed. I pray you bend your selfe what you can to setle these bussinesses. Let the ship be fraught away as soone as you can, and sent to Bilbow. You must send some discreete man for factore, whom, once more, you must also authorise to confirme the conditions. If Mr. Winslow could be spared, I could wish he came againe.

This ship carpenter is thought to be the fittest man for you in the land, and will no doubte doe you much good. Let him have an absolute comand over his servants and shuch as you put to him. Let him build you ·2· catches, a lighter, and some ·6· or ·7· shalops, as soone as you can. The salt-man is a skillfull and industrious man, put some to him, that may quickly apprehende the misterie of it. The preacher we have sent is (we hope) an honest plaine man, though none of the most eminente and rare. Aboute chusing him into office use your owne liberty and discretion; he knows he is no officer amongst you, though perhaps custome and universalitie may make him forget him selfe. Mr. Winslow and my selfe gave way to his going, to give

---

*But this lasted not long, they had now provided Lyford and others to send over.

†It is worthy to be observed, how the Lord doth chaing times and things; for what is now more plentifull then wine? and that of the best, coming from Malago, the Cannaries, and other places, sundry ships lading in a year. So as ther is now more cause to complaine of the excess and the abuse of wine (through mens corruption) even to drunkennes, then of any defecte or wante of the same. Witnes this year 1646. The good Lord lay not the sins and unthankfullnes of men to their charge in this perticuler.

contente to some hear, and we see no hurt in it, but only his great charge of children.

We have tooke a patente for Cap Anne, etc. I am sory ther is no more discretion used by some in their leters hither. Some say you are starved in body and soule; others, that you eate piggs and doggs, that dye alone; others, that the things hear spoaken of, the goodnes of the cuntry, are gross and palpable lyes; that ther is scarce a foule to be seene, or a fish to be taken, and many shuch like.* I would shuch discontented men were hear againe, for it is a miserie when the whole state of a plantation shall be thus exposed to the passionate humors of some discontented men. And for my selfe I shall hinder for hearafter some that would goe, and have not better composed their affections; mean space it is all our crosses, and we must bear them.

I am sorie we have not sent you more and other things, but in truth we have rune into so much charge, to victaile the ship, provide salte and other fishing implements, etc. as we could not provid other comfortable things, as buter, suger, etc. I hope the returne of this ship, and the James, will put us in cash againe. The Lord make you full of courage in this troublesome bussines, which now must be stuck unto, till God give us rest from our labours. Fare well in all harty affection.

Your assured freind,

Jan: 24. 1623.   R C

With the former letter write by Mr. Sherley, there were sente sundrie objections concerning which he thus writeth. "These are the cheefe objections which they that are now returned make against you and the countrie. I pray you consider them, and answer them by the first conveniencie." These objections were made by some of those that came over on their perticuler and were returned home, as is before mentioned, and were of the same suite with those that this other letter mentions.

I shall here set them downe, with the answers then made unto them, and sent over at the returne of this ship; which did so confound the objectors, as some confessed their falte, and others deneyed what they had said, and eate their words, and some others of them have since come over againe and heere lived to convince them selves sufficiently, both in their owne and other mens judgments.

---

*This was John Oldome and his like.

1. obj. was diversitie aboute Religion. Ans: We know no shuch matter, for here was never any controversie or opposition, either publicke or private, (to our knowledg,) since we came.

2. ob: Neglecte of familie duties, on the Lords day.

Ans. We allow no such thing, but blame it in our selves and others; and they that thus reporte it, should have shewed their Christian love the more if they had in love tould the offenders of it, rather then thus to reproach them behind their baks. But (to say no more) we wish them selves had given better example.

3. ob: Wante of both the sacrements.

Ans. The more is our greefe, that our pastor is kept from us, by whom we might injoye them; for we used to have the Lords Supper every Saboth, and baptisme as often as ther was occasion of children to baptise.

4. ob: Children not catechised nor taught to read.

Ans: Neither is true; for diverse take pains with their owne as they can; indeede, we have no commone schoole for want of a fitt person, or hithertoo means to maintaine one; though we desire now to begine.

5. ob: Many of the perticuler members of the plantation will not work for the generall.

Ans: This allso is not wholy true; for though some doe it not willingly, and other not honestly, yet all doe it; and he that doth worst gets his owne foode and something besides. But we will not excuse them, but labour to reforme them the best we cane, or else to quitte the plantation of them.

6. ob: The water is not wholsome.

Ans: If they mean, not so wholsome as the good beere and wine in London, (which they so dearly love,) we will not dispute with them; but els, for water, it is as good as any in the world, (for ought we knowe,) and it is wholsome enough to us that can be contente therwith.

7. ob: The ground is barren and doth bear no grasse.

Ans: It is hear (as in all places) some better and some worse; and if they well consider their woods, in England they shall not find shuch grasse in them, as in their feelds and meadows. The catle find grasse, for they are as fatt as need be; we wish we had but one for every hundred that here is grase to keep. Indeed, this objection, as some other, are ridiculous to all here which see and know the contrary.

8. ob: The fish will not take salt to keepe sweete.

Ans: This is as true as that which was written, that ther is scarce a foule to be seene or a fish to be taken. Things likly to be true in a cuntrie wher so many sayle of ships come yearly a fishing; they might as well say, there can no aile or beere in London be kept from sowering.

9. ob: Many of them are theevish and steale on from an other. Ans: Would London had been free from that crime, then we should not have been trobled with these here; it is well knowne sundrie have smarted well for it, and so are the rest like to doe, if they be taken.

10. ob: The countrie is anoyed with foxes and woules.

Ans: So are many other good cuntries too; but poyson, traps, and other shuch means will help to destroy them.

11. ob: The Dutch are planted nere Hudsons Bay, and are likely to over throw the trade.

Ans: They will come and plante in these parts, also, if we and others doe not, but goe home and leave it to them. We rather commend them, then condemne them for it.

12. ob: The people are much anoyed with muskeetoes.

Ans: They are too delicate and unfitte to begin new-plantations and collonies, that cannot enduer the biting of a muskeeto; we would wish shuch to keepe at home till at least they be muskeeto proofe. Yet this place is as free as any, and experience teacheth that the more the land is tild, and the woods cut downe, the fewer ther will be, and in the end scarse any at all.

Having thus dispatcht these things, that I may handle things togeather, I shall here inserte ·2· other letters from Mr. Robinson their pastor; the one to the Governor, the other to Mr. Brewster their Elder, which will give much light to the former things, and express the tender love and care of a true pastor over them.

His leter to the Governor.

MY LOVING AND MUCH BELOVED FREIND, whom God hath hithertoo preserved, preserve and keepe you still to his glorie, and the good of many; that his blessing may make your godly and wise endeavours answerable to the valuation which they ther have, and set upon the same. Of your love too and care for us here, we never doubted; so are we glad to take knowledg of it in that fullnes we doe. Our love and care too and for you, is mutuall, though our hopes of coming unto you be small, and weaker then ever. But of this at large in Mr. Brewsters letter, with whom you, and he with you, mutualy, I know, comunicate your letters, as I desire you may doe these, etc.

Concerning the killing of those poor Indeans, of which we heard at first by reporte, and since by more certaine relation, oh! how happy a thing had it been, if you had converted some, before you had killed any; besides, wher bloud is once begune to be shed, it is seldome stanched of a long time after. You will say they deserved it. I grant it; but upon what provocations and invitments by those heathenish Christians?* Besides, you, being no magistrates over them, were to consider, not what they deserved, but what you were by necessitie constrained to inflicte. Necessitie of this, espetially of killing so many, (and many more, it seems, they would, if they could,) I see not. Me thinks on or tow principals should have been full enough, according to that approved rule, The punishmente to a few, and the fear to many. Upon this occasion let me be bould to exhorte you seriously to consider of the dispossition of your Captaine, whom I love, and am perswaded the Lord in great mercie and for much good hath sent you him, if you use him aright. He is a man humble and meek amongst you, and towards all in ordinarie course. But now if this be meerly from an humane spirite, ther is cause to fear that by occasion, espetially of provocation, ther may be wanting that tendernes of the life of man (made after Gods image) which is meete. It is also a thing more glorious in mens eyes, then pleasing in Gods, or conveniente for Christians, to be a terrour to poore barbarous people; and indeed I am afraid least, by these occasions, others should be drawne to affecte a kind of rufling course in the world. I doubt not but you will take in good part these things which I write, and as ther is cause make use of them. It were to us more comfortable and convenient, that we comunicated our mutuall helps in presence, but seeing that canot be done, we shall always long after you, and love you, and waite Gods apoynted time. The adventurers it seems have neither money nor any great mind of us, for the most parte. They deney it to be any part of the covenants betwixte us, that they should transporte us, neither doe I looke for any further help from them, till means come from you. We hear are strangers in effecte to the whole course, and so both we and you (save as your owne wisdoms and worths have intressed you further) of principals intended in this bussines, are scarce accessaries,

*Mr. Westons men.

etc. My wife, with me, resalutes you and yours. Unto him who is the same to his in all places, and nere to them which are farr from one an other, I comend you and all with you, resting,

Yours truly loving,
JOHN ROBINSON.

Leyden, Des: 19. 1623.

His to Mr. Brewster.

LOVING AND DEAR FREIND AND BROTHER: That which I most desired of God in regard of you, namly, the continuance of your life and health, and the safe coming of these sent unto you, that I most gladly hear of, and praise God for the same. And I hope Mrs. Brewsters weake and decayed state of body, will have some reparing by the coming of her daughters, and the provissions in this and former ships, I hear is made for you; which makes us with more patience bear our languishing state, and the deferring of our desired transportation; which I call desired, rather than hoped for, whatsoever you are borne in hand by any others. For first, ther is no hope at all, that I know, or can conceive of, of any new stock to be raised for that end; so that all must depend upon returns from you, in which are so many uncertainties, as that nothing with any certaintie can thence be concluded. Besides, howsoever for the presente the adventurers aledg nothing but want of money, which is an invincible difculty, yet if that be taken away by you, others without doubte will be found. For the beter clearing of this, we must dispose the adventurers into ·3· parts; and of them some ·5· or ·6· (as I conceive) are absolutly bent for us, above any others. Other ·5· or ·6· are our bitter profesed adversaries. The rest, being the body, I conceive to be honestly minded, and loveingly also towards us; yet shuch as have others (namly the forward preachers) nerer unto them, then us, and whose course so farr as ther is any difference, they would rather advance then ours. Now what a hanck these men have over the professors, you know. And I perswade my selfe, that for me, they of all others are unwilling I should be transported, espetially shuch of them as have an eye that way them selves; as thinking if I come ther, ther market will be mard in many regards. And for these adversaries, if they have but halfe the witte to their malice, they will stope my course when they see it intended, for which this delaying serveth them very opportunly. And as one restie jade can hinder, by hanging back, more then two or ·3· can (or will at least, if they be not very free) draw forward, so will it be in this case. A notable experimente of this, they gave in your messengers presence, constraining the company to promise that none of the money now gathered should be expended or imployed to the help of any of us towards you. Now touching the question propounded by you, I judg it not lawfull for you, being a ruling Elder, as Rom. 12. 7. 8. and 1. Tim. 5. 17. opposed to the Elders that teach and exhorte and labore in the word and doctrine, to which the sacraments are annexed, to administer them, nor convenient if it were lawfull. Whether any larned man will come unto you or not, I know not; if any doe, you must *Consilium capere in arena.* Be you mostly hartily saluted, and your wife with you, both from me and mine. Your God and ours, and the God of all his, bring us together if it be his will, and keep us in the mean while, and all ways to his glory, and make us servisable to his majestie, and faithfull to the end. Amen.

Your very loving brother,
JOHN ROBINSON.

Leyden, Des: 20. 1623.

These things premised, I shall now prosecute the procedings and afairs here. And before I come to other things I must speak a word of their planting this year; they having found the benifite of their last years harvest, and setting corne for their particuler, having therby with a great deale of patience overcome hunger and famine. Which makes me remember a saing of Senecas, *Epis*: 123. *That a great parte of libertie is a well governed belly, and to be patiente in all wants.* They begane now highly to prise corne as more pretious then silver, and those that had some to spare begane to trade one with another for smale things, by the quarte, potle, and peck, etc.; for money they had none, and if any had, corne was prefered before it. That they might therfore encrease their tillage to better advantage, they made suite to the Governor to have some portion of land given them for continuance, and not by yearly lotte, for by that means, that which the more industrious had brought into good culture (by much pains) one year, came to leave it the nexte, and often another might injoye it; so as the dressing of their lands were the more sleighted over, and to lese profite. Which being well considered, their request was granted. And to every person was given only one acrre of land, to them and theirs, as nere the towne as might be, and they had no more till the ·7· years were expired. The reason was, that they might be kept close together, both for more saftie and defence, and the better improvement of the generall imployments. Which condition of theirs did make me often thinke, of what I had read in Plinie* of the Romans first beginings in Romulus time. *How every man contented him selfe with ·2· acres of land, and had no more assigned them. And chap. ·3· It was thought a great reward, to receive at the hands of the people of Rome a pinte of corne. And long after, the greatest presente given to a Captaine that had gotte a victory over their enemise, was as much ground as they could till in one day. And he was not counted a good, but a dangerous man, that would not contente him selfe with ·7· Acres of land. As also how they did pound their corne in morters, as these people were forcte to doe many years before they could get a mille.*

The ship which brought this supply, was speedily discharged, and with her master and company sente to Cap-Anne (of which place they had gott a patente, as before is shewed) on fishing, and because the season was so farr spente some of the planters were sent to help to built their stage, to their owne hinderance. But partly by the latenes of the year, and more espetialy by the basnes of the master, one Baker, they made a poore viage of it. He proved a very drunken beast, and did nothing (in a maner) but drink, and gusle, and consume away the time and his victails; and most of his company followed his example; and though Mr. William Peirce was to over see the busines, and to be master of the ship home, yet he could doe no good amongst them, so as the loss was great, and would have bene more to them, but that they kept one a trading ther, which in those times got some store of skins, which was some help unto them.

The ship-carpenter that was sent them, was an honest and very industrious man, and followed his labour very dilligently, and made all that were imployed with him doe the like; he quickly builte them ·2· very good and strong shalops (which after did them greate service), and a great and strong lighter, and had hewne timber for ·2· catches; but that was lost, for he fell into a feaver in the hote season of the year, and though he had the best means the place could aforde, yet he dyed; of whom they had a very great loss, and were very sorie for his death. But he whom they sent to make salte was an ignorante, foolish, self-willd fellow; he bore them in hand he could doe

*Plin: lib: 18. chap. 2.

great matters in making salt-works, so he was sente to seeke out fitte ground for his purpose; and after some serch he tould the Governor that he had found a sufficente place, with a good botome to hold water, and otherwise very conveniente, which he doubted not but in a short time to bring to good perfection, and to yeeld them great profite; but he must have ·8· or ten men to be constantly imployed. He was wisht to be sure that the ground was good, and other things answerable, and that he could bring it to perfection; otherwise he would bring upon them a great charge by imploying him selfe and so many men. But he was, after some triall, so confidente, as he caused them to send carpenters to rear a great frame for a large house, to receive the salte and such other uses. But in the end all proved vaine. Then he layed fault of the ground, in which he was deceived; but if he might have the lighter to cary clay, he was sure then he could doe it. Now though the Governor and some other foresaw that this would come to litle, yet they had so many malignant spirits amongst them, that would have laid it upon them, in their letters of complainte to the adventurers, as to be their falte that would not suffer him to goe on to bring his work to perfection; for as he by his bould confidence and large promises deceived them in England that sente him, so had he wound him selfe in to these mens high esteeme hear, so as they were faine to let him goe on till all men saw his vanity. For he could not doe any thing but boyle salt in pans, and yet would make them that were joynd with him beleeve ther was so grat a misterie in it as was not easie to be attained, and made them doe many unnecessary things to blind their eyes, till they discerned his sutletie. The next yere he was sente to Cap-Anne, and the pans were set up ther wher the fishing was; but before sommer was out, he burnte the house, and the fire was so vehemente as it spoyld the pans, at least some of them, and this was the end of that chargable bussines.

The 3d. eminente person (which the letters before mention) was the minister which they sent over, by name Mr. John Lyford, of whom and whose doings I must be more large, though I shall abridg things as much as I can. When this man first came a shore, he saluted them with that reverence and humilitie as is seldome to be seen, and indeed made them ashamed, he so bowed and cringed unto them, and would have kissed their hands if they would have suffered him;* yea, he wept and shed many tears, blessing God that had brought him to see their faces; and admiring the things they had done in their wants, etc. as if he had been made all of love, and the humblest person in the world. And all the while (if we may judg by his after cariages) he was but like him mentioned in Psa: 10. 10. That croucheth and boweth, that heaps of poore may fall by his might. Or like to that dissembling Ishmaell,† who, when he had slaine Gedelia, went out weeping and mette them that were coming to offer incence in the house of the Lord; saing, Come to Gedelia, when he ment to slay them. They gave him the best entertainment they could, (in all simplisitie,) and a larger alowans of food out of the store then any other had, and as the Governor had used in all waightie affairs to consulte with their Elder, Mr. Brewster, (togeither with his assistants), so now he caled Mr. Liford also to counsell with them in their waightiest bussineses. After some short time he desired to joyne him selfe a member to the church hear, and was accordingly received. He made a large confession of his faith, and an acknowledgemente of his former disorderly walking, and his being intangled with many corruptions, which had been a burthen to his conscience, and blessed God for this opportunitie of freedom and libertie to injoye the ordinances of God in puritie among his people, with many more shuch like expressions. I must hear speake a word also of Mr. John Oldom, who was a copartner with him in his after courses. He had bene a cheefe sticler in the former faction among the perticulers, and an intelligencer to those in England. But now, since the coming of this ship and he saw the supply that came, he tooke occasion to open his minde to some of the cheefe amongst them heere, and confessed he had done them wrong both by word and deed, and writing into England; but he now saw the eminente hand of God to be with them, and his blesing upon them, which made his hart smite him, neither should those in England ever use him as an instrumente any longer against them in any thing; he also desired former things might be forgotten, and that they would

---

*Of which were many witneses.
†Jer. 41. 6.

looke upon him as one that desired to close with them in all things, with shuch like expressions. Now whether this was in hipocrisie, or out of some sudden pange of conviction (which I rather thinke), God only knows. Upon it they shew all readynes to imbrace his love, and carry towards him in all frendlynes, and called him to counsell with them in all cheefe affairs, as the other, without any distrust at all.

Thus all things seemed to goe very comfortably and smothly on amongst them, at which they did much rejoyce; but this lasted not long, for both Oldom and he grew very perverse, and shewed a spirite of great malignancie, drawing as many into faction as they could; were they never so vile or profane, they did nourish and back them in all their doings; so they would but cleave to them and speak against the church hear; so as ther was nothing but private meetings and whisperings amongst them; they feeding themselves and others with what they should bring to pass in England by the faction of their friends their, which brought others as well as them selves into a fools paradise. Yet they could not cary so closly but much of both their doings and sayings were discovered, yet outwardly they still set a faire face of things.

At lenght when the ship was ready to goe, it was observed Liford was long in writing, and sente many letters, and could not forbear to comunicate to his intimates shuch things as made them laugh in their sleeves, and thought he had done ther errand sufficiently. The Governor and some other of his freinds knowing how things stood in England, and what hurt these things might doe, tooke a shalop and wente out with the ship a league or ·2· to sea, and caled for all Lifords and Oldums letters. Mr. William Peirce being master of the ship, (and knew well their evill dealing both in England and here,) afforded him all the assistance he could. He found above ·20· of Lyfords letters, many of them larg, and full of slanders, and false accusations, tending not only to their prejudice, but to their ruine and utter subversion. Most of the letters they let pas, only tooke copys of them, but some of the most materiall they sent true copyes of them, and kept the originalls, least he should deney them, and that they might produce his owne hand against him. Amongst his letters they found the coppyes of tow letters which he sent inclosed in a leter of his to Mr. John

Pemberton, a minster, and a great opposite of theirs. These ·2· letters of which he tooke the coppyes were one of them write by a gentle-man in England to Mr. Brewster here, the other by Mr. Winslow to Mr. Robinson, in Holand, at his coming away, as the ship lay at Gravsend. They lying sealed in the great cabin, (whilst Mr. Winslow was bussie aboute the affairs of the ship,) this slye marchante takes and opens them, takes these coppys, and seals them up againe; and not only sends the coppyes of them thus to his friend and their adversarie, but adds thertoo in the margente many scurrilous and flouting annotations. This ship went out *towards evening*, and *in the night* the Governor returned. They were somwaht blanke at it, but after some weeks, when they heard nothing, they then were as briske as ever, thinking nothing had been knowne, but all was gone currente, and that the Governor went but to dispatch his owne letters. The reason why the Governor and rest concealed these things the longer, was to let things ripen, that they might the better discover their intents and see who were their adherents. And the rather because amongst the rest they found a letter of one of their confederates, in which was writen that Mr. Oldame and Mr. Lyford intended a reformation in church and commone wealth; and, as soone as the ship was gone, they intended to joyne togeather, and have the sacrements, etc.

For Oldame, few of his leters were found, (for he was so bad a scribe as his hand was scarce legable,) yet he was as deepe in the mischeefe as the other. And thinking they were now strong enough, they begane to pick quarells at every thing. Oldame being called to watch (according to order) refused to come, fell out with the Capten, caled him raskell, and begerly raskell, and resisted him, drew his knife at him; though he offered him no wrong, nor gave him no ille termes, but with all fairnes required him to doe his duty. The Governor, hearing the tumulte, sent to quiet it, but he ramped more like a furious beast then a man, and cald them all treatours, and rebells, and other shuch foule language as I am ashamed to remember; but after he was clapt up a while, he came to him selfe, and with some slight punishmente was let goe upon his behaviour for further censure.

But to cutt things shorte, at length it grew to this esseue, that Lyford with his complicies, without ever speaking one word either to the Governor, Church, or Elder, withdrewe them selves and set up a publick meeting aparte, on the Lord's day; with sundry shuch insolente cariages, too long here to relate, begining now publikly to acte what privatly they had been long plotting.

It was now thought high time (to prevent further mischeefe) to calle them to accounte; so the Governor called a courte and summoned the whole company to appeare. And then charged Lyford and Oldam with shuch things as they were guilty of. But they were stiffe, and stood resolutly upon the deneyall of most things, and required proofe. They first alledged what was write to them out of England, compared with their doings and practises hear; that it was evident they joyned in plotting against them, and disturbing their peace, both in respecte of their civill and church state, which was most injurious; for both they and all the world knew they came hither to injoye the libertie of their conscience and the free use of Gods ordinances; and for that end had ventured their lives and passed throwgh so much hard shipe hithertoo, and they and their freinds had borne the charg of these beginings, which was not small. And that Lyford for his parte was sent over on this charge, and that both he and his great family was maintained on the same, and also was joyned to the church, and a member of them; and for him to plote against them and seek their ruine, was most unjust and perfidious. And for Oldam or any other that came over at their owne charge, and were on ther perticuler, seeing they were received in curtesie by the plantation, when they came only to seeke shelter and protection under their wings, not being able to stand alone, that they, (according to the fable,) like the hedghogg whom the conny in a stormy day in pittie received into her borrow, would not be content to take part with her, but in the end with her sharp pricks forst the poore conny to forsake her owne borrow; so these men with the like injustice indevored to doe the same to thos that entertained them.

Lyford denyed that he had any thing to doe with them in England or knew of their courses, and made other things as strange that he was charged with. Then his letters were prodused and some of them read, at which he was struck mute. But Oldam begane to rage furiously, because they had intercepted and opened his letters, threatening them in very high language, and in a most audacious and mutinous maner stood up and caled upon the people, saying, My maisters, wher is your harts? now shew your courage, you have oft complained to me so and so; now is the time, if you will doe any thing, I will stand by you, etc. Thinking that every one (knowing his humor) that had soothed and flattered him, or other wise in their discontente uttered any thing unto him, would now side with him in open rebellion. But he was deceived, for not a man opened his mouth, but all were silent, being strucken with the injustice of the thing. Then the Governor turned his speech to Mr. Lyford, and asked him if he thought they had done evill to open his letters; but he was silente, and would not say a word, well knowing what they might reply. Then the Governor shewed the people he did it as a magistrate, and was bound to it by his place, to prevent the mischeefe and ruine that this conspiracie and plots of theirs would bring on this poor colony. But he, besides his evill dealing hear, had delte trecherusly with his freinds that trusted him, and stole their letters and opened them, and sent coppies of them, with disgracefull annotations, to his freinds in England. And then the Governor produced them and his other letters under his owne hand, (which he could not deney,) and caused them to be read before all the people; at which all his freinds were blanke, and had not a word to say.

It would be too long and tedious here to inserte his letters (which would almost fill a volume), though I have them by me. I shall only note a few of the cheefe things collected out of them, with the answers to them as they were then given; and but a few of those many, only for instance, by which the rest may be judged of.

1. First, he saith, the church would have none to live hear but them selves. 2ly. Neither are any willing so to doe if they had company to live els-wher.

Ans: Their answer was, that this was false, in both the parts of it; for they were willing and desirous that any honest men may live with them, that will cary them selves peaceably, and seek the commone good, or at least doe them no hurte. And againe, ther are many that will not live els wher so long as they may live with them.

2. That if ther come over any honest men that are not of the seperation, they will quickly distast them, etc.

A. Ther answer was as before, that it was a false callumniation, for they had many amongst them that they liked well of, and were glad of their company; and should be of any shuch like that should come amongst them.

3. That they excepted against him for these ·2· doctrines raised from ·2· Sam.: 12. 7. First, that ministers must sume times perticulerly apply their doctrine to spetiall persons; 2ly, that great men may be reproved as well as meaner.

A. Their answer was, that both these were without either truth or colour of the same (as was proved to his face), and that they had taught and beleeved these things long before they knew Mr. Liford.

4. That they utterly sought the ruine of the perticulers; as appeareth by this, that they would not suffer any of the generall either to buy or sell with them, or to exchaing one commoditie for another.

Ans: This was a most malicious slander and voyd of all truth, as was evidently proved to him before all men; for any of them did both buy, sell, or exchaing with them as often as they had any occation. Yea, and allso both lend and give to them when they wanted; and this the perticuler persons them selves could not deney, but freely confest in open court. But the ground from whence this arose made it much worse, for he was in counsell with them. When one was called before them, and questioned for receiving powder and bisket from the gunner of the small ship, which was the companys, and had it put in at his window in the night, and allso for buying salt of one, that had no right to it, he not only stood to back him (being one of these perticulers) by excusing and extenuating his falte, as long as he could, but upon this builds this mischeevous and most false slander: That because they would not suffer them to buy stolne goods, ergo, they sought their utter ruine. Bad logick for a devine.

5. Next he writes, that he chocked them with this; that they turned men into their perticuler, and then sought to starve them, and deprive them of all means of subsistance.

A. To this was answered, he did them manifest wrong, for

they turned none into their perticuler; it was their owne importunitie and ernest desire that moved them, yea, constrained
them to doe it. And they apealed to the persons them selves
for the truth hereof. And they testified the same against him
before all present, as allso that they had no cause to complaine
of any either hard or unkind usage.

6. He accuseth them with unjust distribution, and writeth,
that it was a strange difference, that some have bene alowed
16*li.* of meale by the weeke, and others but 4*li.* And then
(floutingly) saith, it seems some mens mouths and bellies are
very litle and slender over others.

Ans: This might seeme strange indeed to those to whom
he write his leters in England, which knew not the reason of
it; but to him and others hear, it could not be strange, who
knew how things stood. For the first commers had none at all,
but lived on their corne. Those which *came in the Anne, the
August before,* and were to live ·13· months of the provissions
they brought, had as good alowance in meal and pease as it
would extend too, the most part of the year; but a litle before
harvest, when thay had not only fish, but other fruits began to
come in, they had but 4*li.* having their libertie to make their
owne provissions. But some of these which came last, as the
ship carpenter, and sawiers, the salte-men and others that were
to follow constante imployments and had not an howers time,
from their hard labours, to looke for any thing above their
alowance; they had at first, 16*li* alowed them, and after wards as
fish, and other food could be gott, they had abatemente, to ·14·
and ·12· yea some of them to ·8· as the times and occasions did
vary. And yet those which followed planting and their owne
occasions, and had but 4*li.* of meall a week, lived better then
the other, as was well knowne to all. And yet it must be remembered that Lyford and his had allwais the highest alowance.

Many other things (in his letters) he accused them of, with
many aggravations; as that he saw exseeding great wast of tools
and vesseles; and this, when it came to be examened, all the
instance he could give was, that he had seen an old hogshed
or too fallen to peeces, and a broken how or tow lefte car-
lesly in the feilds by some. Though he also knew that a godly,
honest man was appointed to looke to these things. But these
things and shuch like was write of by him, to cast disgrace and

prejudice upon them; as thinking what came from a minister would pass for currente. Then he tells them that Winslow should say, that ther was not above ·7· of the adventurers that souight the good of the collony. That Mr. Oldam and him selfe had had much to doe with them, and that the faction here might match the Jesuits for politie. With many the like greevious complaints and accusations.

1. Then, in the next place, he comes to give his freinds counsell and directtion. And first, that the Leyden company (Mr. Robinson and the rest) must still be kepte back, or els all will be spoyled. And least any of them should be taken in privatly somewher on the coast of England, (as it was feared might be done,) they must chaing the master of the ship (Mr. William Peirce), and put another allso in Winslows stead, for marchante, or els it would not be prevented.

2. Then he would have shuch a number provided as might oversway them hear. And that the perticulers should have voyces in all courts and elections, and be free to bear any office. And that every perticuler should come over as an adventurer, if he but be a servante; some other venturing 10*li.*, the bill may be taken out in the servants name, and then assigned to the party whose money it was, and good covenants drawn betweene them for the clearing of the matter; and this (saith he) would be a means to strengthen this side the more.

3. Then he tells them that if that capten they spoake of should come over hither as a generall, he was perswaded he would be chosen capten; for this Captaine Standish looks like a silly boy, and is in utter contempte.

4. Then he shows that if by the formentioned means they cannot be sterngthened to cary and over-bear things, it will be best for them to plant els wher by them selves; and would have it artickled by them that they might make choyse of any place that they liked best within ·3· or ·4· myls distance, shewing ther were farr better places for plantation then this.

5. And lastly he concludes, that if some number came not over to bear them up here, then ther would be no abiding for them, but by joyning with these hear. Then he adds: Since I begane to write, ther are letters come from your company, wherin they would give sole authoritie in diverce things unto the Governor here; which, if it take place, then, *Ve nobis.* But

I hope you will be more vigilante hereafter, that nothing may pass in shuch a manner, I suppose (saith he) Mr. Oldame will write to you further of these things. I pray you conceall me in the discovery of these things, etc.

Thus I have breefly touched some cheefe things in his leters, and shall now returne to their procceeding with him. After the reading of his leters before the whole company, he was demanded what he could say to these things. But all the answer he made was, that Billington and some others had informed him of many things, and made sundrie complaints, which they now deneyed. He was againe asked if that was a sufficiente ground for him thus to accuse and traduse them by his letters, and never say word to them, considering the many bonds betweene them. And so they went on from poynte to poynte; and wisht him, or any of his freinds and confederates, not to spare them in any thing; if he or they had any proofe or witnes of any corrupte or evill dealing of theirs, his or their evidence must needs be ther presente, for ther was the whole company and sundery strangers. He said he had been abused by others in their informations, (as he now well saw,) and so had abused them. And this was all the answer they could have, for none would take his parte in any thing; but Billington, and any whom he named, deneyed the things, and protested he wronged them, and would have drawne them to shuch and shuch things which they could not consente too, though they were sometimes drawne to his meetings. Then they delte with him aboute his dissembling with them aboute the church, and that he professed to concur with them in all things, and what a large confession he made at his admittance, and that he held not him selfe a minister till he had a new calling, etc. And yet now he contested against them, and drew a company aparte, and sequestred him selfe; and would goe minister the sacrements (by his Episcopall caling) without ever speaking a word unto them, either as magistrates or bretheren. In conclusion, he was fully convicted, and burst out into tears, and "confest he feared he was a reprobate, his sinns were so great that he doubted God would not pardon them, he was unsavorie salte, etc.; and that he had so wronged them as he could never make them amends, confessing all he had write against them was false and nought, both for matter and manner." And all this he did with as much fullnes as words and tears could express.

After ther triall and conviction, the court censured them to be expeld the place; Oldame presently, though his wife and family had liberty to stay all winter, or longer, till he could make provission to remove them comfortably. Lyford had liberty to stay ·6· months. It was, indeede, with some eye to his release, if he caried him selfe well in the meane time, and that his repentance proved sound. Lyford acknowledged his censure was farr less then he deserved.

Afterwards, he confest his sin publikly in the church, with tears more largly then before. I shall here put it downe as I find it recorded by some who tooke it from his owne words, as him selfe utered them. Acknowledging "That he had don very evill, and slanderously abused them; and thinking most of the people would take parte with him, he thought to cary all by violence and strong hand against them. And that God might justly lay innocente blood to his charge, for he knew not what hurt might have come of these his writings, and blest God they were stayed. And that he spared not to take knowledg from any, of any evill that was spoaken, but shut his eyes and ears against all the good; and if God should make him a vacabund in the earth, as was Caine, it was but just, for he had sined in envie and malice against his brethren as he did. And he confessed ·3· things to be the ground and causes of these his doings: pride, vaine glorie, and selfe love." Amplifying these heads with many other sade expressions, in the perticulers of them.

So as they begane againe to conceive good thoughts of him upon this his repentance, and admited him to teach amongst them as before; and Samuell Fuller (a deacon amongst them), and some other tender harted men amongst them were so taken with his signes of sorrow and repentance, as they professed they would fall upon their knees to have his censure released.

But that which made them all stand amased in the end, and may doe all others that shall come to hear the same, (for a rarer president can scarse be showne,) was, that after a month or ·2· notwithstanding all his former conffessions, convictions, and publick acknowledgments, both in the face of the church and whole company, with so many tears and sadde censures of him selfe before God and men, he should goe againe to justifie what he had done.

For secretly he write a 2d. leter to the adventurers in England, in which he justified all his former writings, (save in some things which tended to their damage,) the which, because it is brefer then the former, I shall here inserte.

WORTHY SIRS: Though the filth of mine owne doings may justly be cast in my face, and with blushing cause my perpetuall silence, yet that the truth may not herby be injuried, your selves any longer deluded, nor injurious dealing caried out still, with bould out facings, I have adventured once more to write unto you. Firest, I doe freely confess I delte very indiscreetly in some of my perticuler leters which I wrote to private freinds, for the courses in coming hither and the like; which I doe in no sorte seeke to justifie, though stired up ther unto in the beholding the indirecte courses held by others, both hear, and ther with you, for effecting their designes. But am hartily sory for it, and doe to the glory of God and mine owne shame acknowledg it. Which leters being intercepted by the Governor, I have for the same undergone the censure of banishmente. And had it not been for the respecte I have unto you, and some other matters of private regard, I had returned againe at this time by the pinass for England; for hear I purpose not to abide, unless I receive better incouragmente from you, then from the church (as they call them selves) here I doe receive. I purposed before I came, to undergoe hardnes, therfore I shall I hope cherfully bear the conditions of the place, though very mean; and they have chainged my wages ten times allready. I suppose my letters, or at least the coppies of them, are come to your hands, for so they hear reporte; which, if it be so, I pray you take notice of this, that I have writen nothing but what is certainly true, and I could make so apeare planly to any indifferente men, whatsoever colours be cast to darken the truth, and some ther are very audatious this way; besides many other matters which are farre out of order hear. My mind was not to enlarge my selfe any further, but in respecte of diverse poore souls heere, the care of whom in parte belongs to you, being here destitute of the means of salvation. For how so ever the church are provided for, to their contente, who are the smalest number in the collony, and doe so apropriate the ministrie to them selves, hould-ing this principle, that the Lord hath not appointed any ordinary ministrie for the conversion of those that are without, so that some of the poor souls have with tears complained of this to me, and I was taxed for preaching to all in generall. Though in truth they have had no ministrie here since they came, but shuch as may be performed by any of you, by their owne possition, what soever great pretences they make; but herin they equivocate, as in many other things they doe. But I exceede the bounds I set my selfe, therfore resting thus, untill I hear further from you, so it be within the time limited me. I rest, etc.,

Remaining yours ever,

JOHN LYFORD, Exille.

Dated Aug: 22. Ano: 1624.

They made a breefe answer to some things in this leter, but referred cheefly to their former. The effecte was to this purpose: That if God in his providence had not brought these things to their hands (both the former and later), they might have been thus abused, tradused, and calumniated, overthrowne, and undone; and never have knowne by whom, nor for what. They desired but this equall favoure, that they would be pleased to hear their just defence, as well as his accusations, and waigh them in the balance of justice and reason, and then censure as they pleased. They had write breefly to the heads of things before, and should be ready to give further answer as any occasion should require; craving leave to adde a word or tow to this last.

1. And first, they desired to examene what filth that was that he acknowledgeth might justly be throwne in his face, and might cause blushing and perpetuall silence; some great mater sure! But if it be looked into, it amounts to no more than a poynte of indiscretion, and thats all; and yet he licks of that too with this excuse, that he was stired up therunto by beholding the indirecte course here. But this point never troubled him here, it was counted a light matter both by him and his freinds, and put of with this,—that any man might doe so, to advise his private freinds to come over for their best advantage. All his sorrow and tears here was for the wrong and hurt he had done us, and not at all for this he pretends to be done to you: it was not counted so much as indiscretion.

2. Having thus payed you full satisfaction, he thinks he may lay load of us here. And first complains that we have changed his wages ten times. We never agreed with him for any wages, nor made any bargen at all with him, neither know of any that you have made. You sent him over to teach amongst us, and desired he might be kindly used; and more then this we know

not. That he hath beene kindly used, (and farr beter then he deserves from us,) he shall be judged first of his owne mouth. If you please to looke upon that writing of his, that was sent you amongst his leters, which he cals a generall relation, in which, though he doth otherwise traduse us, yet in this he him selfe clears us. In the latter end therof he hath these words. *I speak not this* (saith he) *out of any ill affection to the men, for I have found them very kind and loving to me.* You may ther see these to be his owne words under his owne hand. 2ly. It will appere by this that he hath ever had a larger alowance of food out of the store for him and his then any, and clothing as his neede hath required; a dwelling in one of our best houses, and a man wholy at his owne command to tend his private affairs. What cause he hath therfore to complaine, judge ye; and what he means in his speech we know not, except he aludes to that of Jaacob and Laban. If you have promised him more or other wise, you may doe it when you please.

3. Then with an impudente face he would have you take notice, that (in his leters) he hath write nothing but what is certainly true, yea, and he could make it so appeare plainly to any indifferente men. This indeed doth astonish us and causeth us to tremble at the deceitfullnes and desperate wickednes of mans harte. This is to devoure holy things, and after voues to enquire. It is admirable that after shuch publick confession, and acknowledgmente in court, in church, before God, and men, with shuch sadd expressions as he used, and with shuch melting into teares, that after all this he shoud now justifie all againe. If things had bene done in a corner, it had been some thinge to deney them; but being done in the open view of the cuntrie and before all men, it is more then strange now to avow to make them plainly appear to any indifferente men; and here wher things were done, and all the evidence that could be were presente, and yet could make nothing appear, but even his freinds condemnd him and gave their voyce to his censure, so grose were they; we leave your selves to judge herein. Yet least this man should triumph in his wikednes, we shall be ready to answer him, when, or wher you will, to any thing he shall lay to our charg, though we have done it sufficently allready.

4. Then he saith he would not inlarge, but for some poore souls here who are destitute of the means of salvation, etc.

But all his soothing is but that you would use means, that his censure might be released that he might here continue; and under you (at least) be sheltered, till he sees what his freinds (on whom he depends) can bring about and effecte. For shuch men pretend much for poor souls, but they will looke to their wages and conditions; if that be not to their content, let poor souls doe what they will, they will shift for them selves, and seek poore souls some wher els among richer bodys.

5. Next he fals upon the church, that indeed is the burthensome stone that troubles him. First, he saith they hold this principle, that the Lord hath not apointed any ordinarie ministrie for the converssion of those without. The church needs not be ashamed of what she houlds in this, haveing Gods word for her warrante; that ordinarie officers are bound cheefly to their flocks, Acts 20. 28. and are not to be extravagants, to goe, come, and leave them at their pleasures to shift for them selves, or to be devoured of wolves. But he perverts the truth in this as in other things, for the Lord hath as well appoynted them to converte, as to feede in their severall charges; and he wrongs the church to say other wise. Againe, he saith he was taxed for preaching to all in generall. This is a meere untruth, for this dissembler knows that every Lords day some are appointed to visite suspected places, and if any be found idling and neglecte the hearing of the word, (through idlnes or profanes,) they are punished for the same. Now to procure all to come to hear, and then to blame him for preaching to all, were to play the madd men.

6. Next (he saith) they have had no ministrie since they came, what soever pretences they make, etc. We answer, the more is our wrong, that our pastor is kept from us by these mens means, and then reproach for it us when they have done. Yet have we not been wholy distitute of the means of salvation, as this man would make the world beleeve; for our reverend Elder hath laboured diligently in dispencing the word of God unto us, before he came; and since hath taken equalle pains with him selfe in preaching the same; and, be it spoaken without ostentation, he is not inferriour to Mr. Lyford (and some of his betters) either in gifts or lerning, though he would never be perswaded to take higher office upon him. Nor ever was more pretended in this matter. For equivocating, he may take

it to him selfe; what the church houlds, they have manifested to the world, in all plaines, both in open confession, doctrine, and writing.

This was the sume of ther answer, and hear I will let them rest for the presente. I have bene longer in these things then I desired, and yet not so long as the things might require, for I pass many things in silence, and many more deserve to have been more largly handled. But I will returne to other things, and leave the rest to its place.

The pinass that was left sunck and cast away near Damarin-scove, as is before showed, some of the fishing maisters said it was pitie so fine a vessell should be lost, and sent them word that, if they would be at the cost, they would both directe them how to waygh her, and let them have their carpenters to mend her. They thanked them, and sente men aboute it, and beaver to defray the charge, (without which all had been in vaine). So they gott coopers to trime, I know not how many tune of cask, and being made tight and fastened to her at low-water, they boyed her up; and then with many hands hald her on shore in a conveniente place wher she might be wrought upon; and then hired sundrie carpenters to work upon her, and other to saw planks, and at last fitted her and got her home. But she cost a great deale of money, in thus recovering her, and buying riging and seails for her, both now and when before she lost her mast; so as she proved a chargable vessell to the poor plantation. So they sent her home, and with her Lyford sent his last letter, in great secrecie; but the party intrusted with it gave it the Governor.

The winter was passed over in ther ordinarie affairs, without any spetiall mater worth noteing; saveing that many who before stood something of from the church, now seeing Lyfords unrighteous dealing, and malignitie against the church, now tendered them selves to the church, and were joyned to the same; proffessing that it was not out of the dislike of any thing that they had stood of so long, but a desire to fitte them selves beter for shuch a state, and they saw now the Lord cald for their help. And so these troubles prodused a quite contrary effecte in sundrie hear, then these adversaries hoped for. Which was looked at as a great worke of God, to draw on men by unlickly means; and that in reason which might rather have set them further of. And thus I shall end this year.

ANNO DOM: ·1625·

A T the spring of the year, about the time of their Election Court, Oldam came againe amongst them; and though it was a part of his censure for his former mutinye and miscariage, not to returne without leave first obtained, yet in his dareing spirite, he presumed without any leave at all, being also set on and hardend by the ill counsell of others. And not only so, but suffered his unruly passion to rune beyond the limits of all reason and modestie; in so much that some strangers which came with him were ashamed of his outrage, and rebuked him; but all reprofes were but as oyle to the fire, and made the flame of his coller greater. He caled them all to nought, in this his madd furie, and a hundred rebells and traytors, and I know not what. But in conclusion they commited him till he was tamer, and then apointed a gard of musketers which he was to pass throw, and ever one was ordered to give him a thump on the brich, with the but end of his musket, and then was conveied to the water side, wher a boat was ready to cary him away. Then they bid him goe and mende his maners.

Whilst this was in doing, Mr. William Peirce and Mr. Winslow came up from the water side, being come from England; but they were so busie with Oldam, as they never saw them till they came thus upon them. They bid them not spare either him or Liford, for they had played the vilanes with them. But that I may hear make an end with him, I shall hear once for all relate what befell concerning him in the future, and that breefly. After the removall of his familie from hence, he fell in to some straits, (as some others did,) and aboute a year or more afterwards, towards winter, he intended a vioage for Virginia; but it so pleased God that the barke that caried him, and many other passengers, was in that danger, as they dispaired of life; so as many of them, as they fell to prayer, so also did they begine to examine their consciences and confess shuch sins as did most burthen them. And Mr. Ouldame did make a free and large confession of the wrongs and hurt he had done to

the people and church here, in many perticulers, that as he
had sought their ruine, so God had now mette with him and
might destroy him; yea, he feared they all fared the worce for
his sake; he prayed God to forgive him, and made vowes that,
if the Lord spard his life, he would become otherwise, and the
like. This I had from some of good credite, yet living in the
Bay, and were them selves partners in the same dangers on the
shoulds of Cap-Codd, and heard it from his owne mouth. It
pleased God to spare their lives, though they lost their viage;
and in time after wards, Ouldam caried him selfe fairly towards
them, and acknowledged the hand of God to be with them,
and seemed to have an honourable respecte of them; and so
farr made his peace with them, as he in after time had libertie
to goe and come, and converse with them, at his pleasure. He
went after this to Virginia, and had ther a great sicknes, but
recovered and came back againe to his familie in the Bay, and
ther lived till some store of people came over. At lenght going a
trading in a smale vessell among the Indians, and being weakly
mand, upon some quarell they knockt him on the head with a
hatched, so as he fell downe dead, and never spake word more.
·2· litle boys that were his kinsmen were saved, but had some
hurte, and the vessell was strangly recovered from the Indeans
by another that belonged to the Bay of Massachusets; and this
his death was one ground of the Pequente warr which followed.

	I am now come to Mr. Lyford. His time being now expired,
his censure was to take place. He was so farr from answering their hopes by amendmente in the time, as he had dubled
his evill, as is before noted. But first behold the hand of God
conceirning him, wherin that of the Psalmist is verified. Psa: 7.
15. He hath made a pitte, and digged it, and is fallen into the
pitte he made. He thought to bring shame and disgrace upon
them, but in stead therof opens his owne to all the world. For
when he was delte with all aboute his second letter, his wife
was so affected with his doings, as she could no longer conceaill
her greefe and sorrow of minde, but opens the same to one of
their deacons and some other of her freinds, and after uttered
the same to Mr. Peirce upon his arrivall. Which was to this
purpose, that she feared some great judgment of God would
fall upon them, and upon her, for her husbands cause; now that
they were to remove, she feared to fall into the Indeans hands,

and to be defiled by them, as he had defiled other women; or some shuch like judgmente, as God had threatened David, 2. Sam. 12. 11. I will raise up evill against ye, and will take thy wives and give them, etc. And upon it showed how he had wronged her, as first he had a bastard by another before they were maried, and she having some inkling of some ill cariage that way, when he was a suitor to her, she tould him what she heard, and deneyd him; but she not certainly knowing the thing, other wise then by some darke and secrete mutterings, he not only stifly denied it, but to satisfie her tooke a solemne oath ther was no shuch matter. Upon which she gave consente, and maried with him; but afterwards it was found true, and the bastard brought home to them. She then charged him with his oath, but he prayed pardon, and said he should els not have had her. And yet afterwards she could keep no maids but he would be medling with them, and some time she hath taken him in the maner, as they lay at their beds feete, with shuch other circumstances as I am ashamed to relate. The woman being a grave matron, and of good cariage all the while she was hear, and spoake these things out of the sorrow of her harte, sparingly, and yet with some further intimations. And that which did most seeme to affecte her (as they conceived) was, to see his former cariage in his repentance, not only hear with the church, but formerly about these things; sheding tears, and using great and sade expressions, and yet eftsone fall into the like things.

Another thing of the same nature did strangly concurr herewith. When Mr. Winslow and Mr. Peirce were come over, Mr. Winslow informed them that they had had the like bickering with Lyfords freinds in England, as they had with him selfe and his freinds hear, aboute his letters and accusations in them. And many meetings and much clamour was made by his freinds thereaboute crying out, a minister, a man so godly, to be so esteemed and taxed they held a great skandale, and threated to prosecute law against them for it. But things being referred to a further meeting of most of the adventurers, to heare the case and decide the matters, they agreed to chose ·2· eminente men for moderators in the bussines. Lyfords faction chose Mr. White, a councelor at law, the other parte chose Reverend Mr. Hooker, the minister, and many freinds on both sides were brought in, so as ther was a great assemblie. In the mean time, God in his providence had detected Lyford's evill cariage in Ireland to some freinds amongst the company, who made it knowne to Mr. Winslow; and directed him to ·2· godly and grave witnesses, who would testifie the same (if caled therunto) upon their oath. The thing was this; he being gott into Ireland, had wound him selfe into the esteeme of sundry goodly and zelous professours in those parts, who, having been burthened with the ceremonies in England, found ther some more liberty to their consciences; amongst whom were these ·2· men, which gave this evidence. Amongst the rest of his hearers, ther was a godly yonge man that intended to marie, and cast his affection on a maide which lived their aboute; but desiring to chose in the Lord, and preferred the fear of God before all other things, before he suffered his affection to rune too farr, he resolved to take Mr. Lyfords advise and judgmente of this maide, (being the minister of the place,) and so broak the matter unto him; and he promised faithfully to informe him, but would first take better knowledg of her, and have private conferance with her; and so had sundry times; and in conclusion commended her highly to the yong man as a very fitte wife for him. So they were maried togeather; but some time after mariage the woman was much troubled in mind, and afflicted in conscience, and did nothing but weepe and mourne, and long it was before her husband could get of her what was the cause. But at length she discovered the thing, and prayed him to forgive her, for Lyford had overcome her, and defiled her body before marriage, after he had comended him unto her for a husband, and she resolved to have him, when he came to her in that private way. The circumstances I forbear, for they would offend chast ears to hear them related, (for though he satisfied his lust on her, yet he indeavoured to hinder conception.) These things being thus discovered, the womans husband tooke some godly freinds with him, to deale with Liford for this evill. At length he confest it, with a great deale of seeming sorrow and repentance, but was forct to leave Irland upon it, partly for shame, and partly for fear of further punishmente, for the godly withdrew them selves from him upon it; and so comming into England unhapily he was light upon and sente hither.

But in this great assembly, and before the moderators, in handling the former matters aboute the letters, upon provocation, in some heate of replie to some of Lyfords defenders, Mr. Winslow let fall these words, That he had delte knavishly; upon which on of his freinds tooke hold, and caled for witneses, that he cald a minister of the gospell knave, and would prosecute law upon it, which made a great tumulte, upon which (to be shorte) this matter broke out, and the witnes were prodused, whose persons were so grave, and evidence so plaine, and the facte so foule, yet delivered in shuch modest and chast terms, and with shuch circumstances, as strucke all his freinds mute, and made them all ashamed; insomuch as the moderators with great gravitie declared that the former matters gave them cause enough to refuse him and to deal with him as they had done, but these made him unmeete for ever to bear ministrie any more, what repentance soever he should pretend; with much more to like effecte, and so wisht his freinds to rest quiete. Thus was this mater ended.

From hence Lyford wente to Natasco, in the Bay of the Massachusets, with some other of his freinds with him, wher Oldom allso lived. From thence he removed to Namkeke, since called Salem; but after ther came some people over, wheather for hope of greater profite, or what ends els I know not, he left his freinds that followed him, and went from thence to Virginia, wher he shortly after dyed, and so I leave him to the Lord. His wife afterwards returned againe to this cuntry, and thus much of this matter.

This storme being thus blowne over, yet sundrie sad effects followed the same; for the Company of Adventurers broake in peeces here upon, and the greatest parte wholy deserted the colony in regarde of any further supply, or care of their subsistance. And not only so, but some of Lyfords and Oldoms freinds, and their adherents, set out a shipe on fishing, on their owne accounte, and getting the starte of the ships that came to the plantation, they tooke away their stage, and other necessary provisions that they had made for fishing at Cap-Anne the yeare before, at their great charge, and would not restore the same, excepte they would fight for it. But the Governor sent some of the planters to help the fisher men to build a new one, and so let them keepe it. This shipe also brought them some small supply, of little value; but they made so pore a bussines of their fishing, (neither could these men make them any returne for the supply sente,) so as, after this year, they never looked more after them.

Also by this ship, they, some of them, sent (in the name of the rest) certaine reasons of their breaking of from the plantation, and some tenders, upon certaine conditions, of reuniting againe. The which because they are longe and tedious, and most of them aboute the former things allready touched, I shall omite them; only giving an instance in one, or tow. 1. reason, they charged them for dissembling with his majestie in their petition, and with the adventurers about the French discipline, etc. 2ly, for receiveing a man* into their church, that in his conffession renownced all, universall, nationall, and diocessan churches, etc., by which (say they) it appears, that though they deney the name of Brownists, yet they practiss the same, etc. And therfore they should sinne against God in building up shuch a people.

1. Then they adde: Our dislikes thus laid downe, that we may goe on in trade with better contente and credite, our desires are as followeth. First, that as we are partners in trade, so we may be in Government ther, as the patente doth give us power, etc.

2. That the French discipline may be practised in the plantation, as well in the circumstances theirof, as in the substance; wherby the scandallous name of the Brownists, and other church differences, may be taken away.

3. Lastly, that Mr. Robinson and his company may not goe over to our plantation, unless he and they will reconcile them selves to our church by a recantation under their hands, etc.

Their answer in part to these things was then as foloweth.

Whereas you taxe us for dissembling with his majestie and the adventurers aboute the French discipline, you doe us wrong, for we both hold and practice the discipline of the French and other reformed churches, (as they have published the same in the Harmony of Confessions,) according to our means, in effecte and substance. But wheras you would tye us

*This was Lyford himselfe.

to the French discipline in every circumstance, you derogate from the libertie we have in Christ Jesus. The Apostle Paule would have none to follow him in any thing but wherin he follows Christ, much less ought any Christian or church in the world to doe it. The French may erre, we may erre, and other churches may erre, and doubtless doe in many circumstances. That honour therfore belongs only to the infallible word of God, and pure Testamente of Christ, to be propounded and followed as the only rule and pattern for direction herin to all churches and Christians. And it is too great arrogancie for any man, or church to thinke that he or they have so sounded the word of God to the bottome, as precislie to sett downe the churches discipline, without error in substance or circum-stance, as that no other without blame may digress or differ in any thing from the same. And it is not difficulte to shew, that the reformed churches differ in many circumstances amongest them selves.

The rest I omitte, for brevities sake, and so leave to prosecute these men or their doings any further, but shall returne to the rest of their freinds of the company, which stuck to them.

And I shall first inserte some part of their letters as followeth; for I thinke it best to render their minds in ther owne words.

To our loving freinds, etc.

Though the thing we feared be come upon us, and the evill we strove against have overtaken us, yet we cannot forgett you, nor our freindship and fellowship which togeather we have had some years; wherin though our expressions have been small, yet our harty affec-tions towards you (unknown by face) have been no less then to our nearest freinds, yea, to our owne selves. And though this your freind Mr. Winslow can tell you the state of things hear, yet least we should seeme to neglecte you, to whom, by a wonderfull providence of God, we are so nearly united, we have thought good once more to write unto you, to let you know what is here befallen, and the resons of it; as also our purposes and desires toward you for hereafter.

The former course for the generalitie here is wholy dissolved from what it was; and wheras you and we were formerly sharers and part-ners, in all viages and deallings, this way is now no more, but you and we are left to bethinke our sellves what course to take in the future, that your lives and our monies be not lost.

The reasons and causes of this allteration have been these. First and mainly, the many losses and crosses at sea, and abuses of sea-men, which have caused us to rune into so much charge, debts, and ingagementes, as our estates and means were not able to goe on without impoverishing our selves, except our estates had been greater, and our associates cloven beter unto us. 2ly, as here hath been a faction and siding amongst us now more then ·2· years, so now there is an utter breach and sequestration amongst us, and in tow parts of us full dissertion and forsaking of you, without any intente or purpose of medling more with you. And though we are perswaded the maine cause of this their doing is wante of money, (for neede wherof men use to make many excuses,) yet other things are pretended, as that you are Brownists, etc.

Now what use you or we ought to make of these things, it remaineth to be considered, for we know the hand of God to be in all these things, and no doubt he would admonish some thing therby, and to looke what is amise. And allthough it be now too late for us or you to prevent and stay these things, yet is it not to late to exercise patience, wisdom, and conscience in bearing them, and in carrying our selves in and under them for the time to come.

And as we our selves stand ready to imbrace all occasions that may tend to the furthrance of so hopefull a work, rather admiring of what is, then grudging for what is not; so it must rest in you to make all good againe. And if in nothing else you can be approved, yet let your honestie and conscience be still approved, and lose not one jote of your innocencie, amids your crosses and afflictions. And surly if you upon this allteration behave your selves wisly, and goe on fairly, as men whose hope is not in this life, you shall need no other weapon to wound your adversaries; for when your righteousnes is revealled as the light, they shall cover their faces with shame, that causlesly have sought your overthrow.

Now we thinke it but reason, that all shuch things as these apertaine to the generall, be kept and preserved togeather, and rather increased dayly, then any way be dispersed or imbeseled away for any private ends or intents whatsoever. And after your necessities are served, you gather togeather such commodities as the cuntrie yeelds, and send them over to pay debts and clear ingagements hear, which are not less then 1400*li*. And we hope you will doe your best to free our ingagements, etc. Let us all indeavor to keep a faire and honest course, and see what time will bring forth, and how God in his providence will worke for us. We still are perswaded you are the people that must make a plantation in those remote places when all others faile and returne. And your experience of Gods providence and preservation of you is shuch as we hope your harts will not faile you, though your freinds should forsake you (which we our selves shall not doe whilst we live, so long as your honestie so well appereth). Yet surly help would arise from some other place whilst you waite on God, with uprightnes, though we should leave you allso.

And lastly be you all intreated to walke circumspectly, and carry your selves so uprightly in all your ways, as that no man may make just exceptions against you. And more espetially that the favor and countenance of God may be so toward you, as that you may find abundante joye and peace even amids tribulations, that you may say with David, Though my father and mother should forsake me, yet the Lord would take me up.

We have sent you hear some catle, cloath, hose, shoes, leather, etc., but in another nature then formerly, as it stood us in hand to doe; we have committed them to the charge and custody of Mr. Allerton and Mr. Winslow, as our factours, at whose discretion they are to be sould, and commodities to be taken for them, as is fitting. And by how much the more they will be chargable unto you, the better they had need to be husbanded, etc. Goe on, good freinds, comfortably, pluck up your spirits, and quitte your selves like men in all your difficulties, that not withstanding all displeasure and threats of men, yet the work may goe on you are aboute, and not be neglected. Which is so much for the glorie of God, and the furthrance of our countrie-men, as that a man may with more comforte spend his life in it, then live the life of Methusala, in wasting the plentie of a tilled land, or eating the fruite of a growne tree. Thus with harty salutations to you all, and harty prayers for you all, we lovingly take our leaves, this ·18· of Des: 1624.

Your assured freinds to our powers,
J. S.   W. C.   T. F.   R. H. etc.

By this leter it appears in what state the affairs of the planta-tion stood at this time. These goods they bought, but they were at deare rates, for they put ·40· in the hundred upon them, for profite and adventure, outward bound; and because of the venture of the paiment homeward, they would have ·30·*li** in the ·100· more, which was in all ·70· per cent; a thing thought unreasonable by some, and too great an oppression upon the poore people, as their case stood. The catle were the best goods, for the other being ventured ware, were neither

---

*If I mistake not, it was not much less.

at the best (some of them) nor at the best prises. Sundrie of their freinds disliked these high rates, but comming from many hands, they could not help it.

They sent over also ·2· ships on fishing on their owne acounte; the one was the pinass that was cast away the last year hear in the cuntrie, and recovered by the planters, (as was before related,) who, after she came home, was attached by one of the company for his perticuler debte, and now sent againe on this accounte. The other was a great ship, who was well fitted with an experienced master and company of fisher-men, to make a viage, and to goe to Bilbo or Sabastians with her fish; the lesser, her order was to load with cor-fish, and to bring the beaver home for England, that should be received for the goods sould to the plantation. This bigger ship made a great viage of good drie fish, the which, if they had gone to a market with, would have yeelded them (as such fish was sould that season) 1800*li.* which would have enriched them. But because ther was a bruite of warr with France, the master neglected (through timerousnes) his order, and put first into Plimoth, and after into Portsmouth, and so lost their opportunitie, and came by the loss. The lesser ship had as ill success, though she was as hopfull as the other for the marchants profite; for they had fild her with goodly cor-fish taken upon the banke, as full as she could swime; and besides she had some 800*li.* weaight of beaver, besides other furrs to a good value from the plantation. The master seeing so much goods come, put it abord the biger ship, for more saftie; but Mr. Winslow (their factor in this busines) was bound in a bond of 500*li.* to send it to London in the smale ship; ther was some contending between the master and him aboute it. But he tould the master he would follow his order aboute it; if he would take it out afterward, it should be at his perill. So it went in the smale ship, and he sent bills of lading in both. The master was so carfull being both so well laden, as they went joyfully home togeather, for he towed the leser ship at his sterne all the way over bound, and they had shuch fayr weather as he never cast her of till they were shott deep in to the English Chanell, almost within the sight of Plimoth; and yet ther she was unhaply taken by a Turks man of warr, and carried into Saly, wher the master and men were made slaves, and many of the beaver skins were sould for 4*d.* a peece.

Thus was all their hopes dasht, and the joyfull news they ment to cary home turned to heavie tidings. Some thought this a hand of God for their too great exaction of the poore plantation, but Gods judgments are unscerchable, neither dare I be bould therwith; but however it shows us the uncertainty of all humane things, and what litle cause ther is of joying in them or trusting to them.

In the bigger of these ships was sent over Captine Standish from the plantation, with leters and instructions, both to their freinds of the company which still clave to them, and also to the Honourable Counsell of New England. To the company to desire that seeing that they ment only to let them have goods upon sale, that they might have them upon easier termes, for they should never be able to bear shuch high intrest, or to allow so much per cent; also that what they would doe in that way that it might be disburst in money, or shuch goods as were fitte and needfull for them, and bought at best hand; and to acquainte them with the contents of his leters to the Counsell above said, which was to this purpose, to desire their favour and help; that shuch of the adventurers as had thus forsaken and deserted them, might be brought to some order, and not to keepe them bound, and them selves be free. But that they might either stand to ther former covenants, or ells come to some faire end, by dividente, or composition. But he came in a very bad time, for the Stat was full of trouble, and the plague very hote in London, so as no bussiness could be done; yet he spake with some of the Honourd Counsell, who promised all helpfullnes to the plantation which lay in them. And sundrie of their freinds the adventurers were so weakened with their losses the last year, by the losse of the ship taken by the Turks, and the loss of their fish, which by reason of the warrs they were forcte to land at Portsmouth, and so came to litle; so as, though their wills were good, yet theyr power was litle. And thir dyed shuch multitudes weekly of the plague, as all trade was dead, and litle money stirring. Yet with much adooe he tooke up 150*li.* (and spent a good deal of it in expences) at ·50· per cent. which he bestowed in trading goods and such other most needfull comodities as he knew requiset for their use; and so returned passenger in a fhishing ship, haveing prepared a good way for the compossition that was afterward made.

In the mean time it pleased the Lord to give the plantation peace and health and contented minds, and so to blese ther labours, as they had corne sufficient, (and some to spare to others,) with other foode; neither ever had they any supply of foode but what they first brought with them. After harvest this year, they sende out a boats load of corne ·40· or ·50· leagues to the eastward, up a river called Kenibeck; it being one of those ·2· shalops which their carpenter had built them the year before; for bigger vessell had they none. They had laid a litle deck over her midships to keepe the corne drie, but the men were faine to stand it out all weathers without shealter, and that time of the year begins to growe tempestious. But God preserved them, and gave them good success, for they brought home 700*li.* of beaver, besides some other furrs, having litle or nothing els but this corne, which themselves had raised out of the earth. This viage was made by Mr. Winslow and some of the old standards, for seamen they had none.

ANNO DOM: ·1626·

ABOUT the begining of Aprill they heard of Captain Standish his arrivall, and sent a boat to fetch him home, and the things he had brought. Welcome he was, but the news he broughte was sadd in many regards; not only in regarde of the former losses, before related, which their freinds had suffered, by which some in a maner were undon, others much disabled from doing any further help, and some dead of the plague, but also that Mr. Robinson, their pastor, was dead, which struck them with much sorrow and sadnes, as they had cause. His and their adversaries had been long and continually plotting how they might hinder his coming hither, but the Lord had appointed him a better place; concerning whose death and the maner therof, it will appere by these few lines write to the Governor and Mr. Brewster.

LOVING AND KIND FRINDS, etc. I know not whether this will ever come to your hands, or miscarie, as other my letters have done; yet in regard of the Lords dealing with us hear, I have had a great desire to write unto you, knowing your desire to bear a parte with us, both in our joyes, and sorrows, as we doe with you. These are therfore to give you to understand, that it hath pleased the Lord to take out of this vaell of tears, your and our loving and faithfull pastor, and my dear and Reverend brother, Mr. John Robinson, who was sick some ·8· days. He begane to be sick on Saturday in the morning, yet the next day (being the Lords day) he taught us twise. And so the weeke after grew weaker, every day more then other; yet he felt no paine but weaknes all the time of his sicknes. The phisick he tooke wrought kindly in mans judgmente, but he grew weaker every day, feeling litle or no paine, and sensible to the very last. He fell sicke the ·22· of February, and departed this life the ·1· of March. He had a continuall inwarde ague, but free from infection, so that all his freinds came freely to him. And if either prayers, tears, or means, would have saved his life, he had not gone hence. But he having faithfully finished his course, and performed his worke which the Lord had appointed him here to doe, he now resteth with the Lord in eternall hapines. We wanting him and all Church Governors yet we still (by the mercie of God) continue and hould close togeather, in peace and quietnes; and so hope we shall doe, though we be very weake. Wishing (if shuch were the will of God) that you and we were againe united togeather in one, either ther or here; but seeing it is the will of the Lord thus to dispose of things, we must labour with patience to rest contented, till it please the Lord otherwise to dispose. For news, is here not much; only as in England we have lost our old king James, who departed this life aboute a month agoe, so here they have lost the old prince, Grave Maurise; who both departed this life since my brother Robinson. And as in England we have a new king Charles, of whom ther is great hope, so hear they have made prince Hendrick Generall in his brothers place, etc. Thus with my love remembred, I take leave and rest,

Your assured loving freind,
ROGER WHITE.

Leyden, April 28. Anno: 1625.

Thus these too great princes, and their pastor, left this world near aboute one time. Death makes no difference.

He further brought them notice of the death of their anciente freind, Mr. Cush-man, whom the Lord tooke away allso this year, and aboute this time, who was as their right hand with their freinds the adventurers, and for diverce years had done and agitated all their bussines with them to ther great advantage. He had write to the Governor but some few months before, of the sore sicknes of Mr. James Sherley, who was a cheefe freind to the plantation, and lay at the pointe of death, declaring his love and helpfullnes, in all things; and much bemoned the loss they should have of him, if God should now take him away, as being the stay and life of the whole bussines. As allso his owne purpos this year to come over, and spend his days with them. But he that thus write of anothers sicknes, knew not that his owne death was so near. It shows allso that a mans ways are not in his owne power, but in his hands, who hath the issues of life and death. Man may purpose, but God doth dispose.

Their other freinds from Leyden writ many leters to them full of sad laments for ther heavie loss; and though their wills were good to come to them, yet they saw no probabilitie of means, how it might be effected, but concluded (as it were) that all their hopes were cutt of; and many, being aged, begane to drop away by death.

All which things (before related) being well weighed and laied togither, it could not but strick them with great perplexitie; and to looke humanly on the state of things as they presented them selves at this time, it is a marvell it did not wholy discourage them, and sinck them. But they gathered up their spirits, and the Lord so helped them, whose worke they had in hand, as now when they were at lowest they begane to rise againe, and being striped (in a maner) of all humane helps and hopes, he brought things aboute other wise, in his devine providence, as they were not only upheld and sustained, but their proceedings both honoured and imitated by others; as by the sequell will more appeare, if the Lord spare me life and time to declare the same.

Note

Haveing now no fishing bussines, or other things to intend, but only their trading and planting, they sett them selves to follow the same with the best industrie they could. The planters finding their corne, what they could spare from ther necessities, to be a commoditie, (for they sould it at 6s. a bushell,) used great dilligence in planting the same. And the Governor and shuch as were designed to manage the trade, (for it was retained for the generall good, and none were to trade in particuler,) they followed it to the best advantage they could; and wanting trading goods, they understoode that a plantation which was at Monhigen, and belonged to some marchants of Plimoth was to breake up, and diverse usefull goods was ther to be sould; the Governor and Mr. Winslow tooke a boat and some hands and went thither. But Mr. David Thomson, who lived at Pascataway, understanding their purpose, tooke oppertunitie to goe with them, which was some hinderance to them both; for they, perceiveing their joynt desires to buy, held their goods at higher rates; and not only so, but would not sell a parcell of their trading goods, excepte they sould all. So, lest they should further prejudice one an other, they agreed to buy all, and devid them equally betweene them. They bought allso a parcell of goats, which they distributed at home as they saw neede and occasion, and tooke corne for them of the people, which gave them good content. Their moyety of the goods came to above 400*li*. starling. Ther was allso that spring a French ship cast away at Sacadahock, in which were many Biscaie ruggs and other commodities, which were falen into these mens hands, and some other fisher men at Damerins-cove, which were allso bought in partnership, and made their parte arise to above 500*li*. This they made shift to pay for, for the most part, with the beaver and comodities they had gott the winter before, and what they had gathered up that somer. Mr. Thomson having some thing overcharged him selfe, desired they would take some of his, but they refused except he would let them have his French goods only; and the marchant (who was one of Bristol) would take their bill for to be paid the next year. They were both willing, so they became ingaged for them and tooke them. By which means they became very well furnished for trade; and tooke of therby some other ingagments which lay upon them, as the money taken up by Captaine Standish, and the remains of former debts. With these goods, and their corne after harvest, they gott good store of trade, so as they were enabled to pay their ingagments against the time, and to get some cloathing for the people, and had some comodities before hand. But now they begane to be envied, and others wente and fild the Indeans with corne, and beat downe the prise, giveing them twise as much as they had done, and under traded them in other comodities allso.

This year they sent Mr. Allerton into England, and gave him order to make a composition with the adventurers, upon as good termes as he could (unto which some way had ben made the year before by Captaine Standish); but yet injoyned him not to conclud absolutly till they knew the termes, and had well considered of them; but to drive it to as good an issew as he could, and referr the conclusion to them. Also they gave him a commission under their hands and seals to take up some money, provided it exseeded not shuch a summe specified, for which they engaged them selves, and gave him order how to lay out the same for the use of the plantation.

And finding they ranne a great hazard to goe so long viages in a smale open boat, espetialy the winter season, they begane to thinke how they might gett a small pinass; as for the reason afforesaid, so also because others had raised the prise with the Indeans above the halfe of what they had formerly given, so as in shuch a boat they could not carry a quantity sufficent to answer their ends. They had no ship-carpenter amongst them, neither knew how to get one at presente; but they having an ingenious man that was a house carpenter, who also had wrought with the ship carpenter (that was dead) when he built their boats, at their request he put forth him selfe to make a triall that way of his skill; and tooke one of the bigest of ther shalops and sawed her in the midle, and so lenthened her some ·5· or ·6· feete, and strengthened her with timbers, and so builte her up, and laid a deck on her; and so made her a conveniente and wholsome vessell, very fitt and comfortable for their use, which did them servise ·7· years after; and they gott her finished, and fitted with sayles and anchors, the insuing year. And thus passed the affairs of this year.

ANNO DOM: ·1627·

A T the usuall season of the coming of ships Mr. Allerton returned, and brought some usfull goods with him, according to the order given him. For upon his commission he tooke up 200*li.* which he now gott at ·30· per cent. The which goods they gott safly home, and well conditioned, which was much to the comfort and contente of the plantation. He declared unto them, allso, how, with much adoe and no small trouble, he had made a composition with the adventurers, by the help of sundrie of their faithfull freinds ther, who had allso taken much pains their about. The agreement or bargen he had brought a draught of, with a list of ther names ther too annexed, drawne by the best counsell of law they could get, to make it firme. The heads wherof I shall here inserte.

To all Christian people, greeting, etc. Wheras at a meeting the ·26· of October last past, diverse and sundrie persons, whose names to the one part of these presents are subscribed in a schedule hereunto annexed, Adventurers to New-Plimoth in New-England in America, were contented and agreed, in consideration of the sume of one thousand and eight hundred pounds sterling to be paid, (in maner and forme following,) to sell, and make sale of all and every the stocks, shares, lands, marchandise, and chatles, what soever, to the said adventurers, and other ther fellow adventurers to New Plimoth aforesaid, any way accruing, or belonging to the generalitie of the said adventurers afforesaid; as well by reason of any sume or sumes of money, or marchandise, at any times heretofore adventured or disbursed by them, or other wise howsoever; for the better expression and setting forth of which said agreemente, the parties to these presents subscribing, doe for them selves severally, and as much as in them is, grant, bargain, alien, sell, and transfere all and every the said shares, goods, lands, marchandice, and chatles to them belonging as afforesaid, unto Isaack Alerton, one of the planters resident at Plimoth afforesaid, assigned, and sent over as agente for the rest of the planters ther, and to shuch other planters at Plimoth afforesaid as the said Isack, his heirs, or assignes, at his or ther arrivall, shall by writing or otherwise thinke fitte to joyne or partake in the premisses, their heirs, and assignes, in as large, ample, and beneficiall maner and forme, to all intents and purposes, as the said subscribing adventurers here could or may doe, or performe. All which stocks, shares, lands, etc. to the said adventurers in severallitie alloted, apportioned, or any way belonging, the said adventurers doe warrant and defend unto the said Isaack Allerton, his heirs and assignes, against them, their heirs and assignes, by these presents. And therfore the said Isaack Allerton doth, for him, his heirs and assigns, covenant, promise, and grant too and with the adventurers whose names are here unto subscribed, ther heirs, etc. well and truly to pay, or cause to be payed, unto the said adventurers or ·5· of them which were, at that meeting afforsaid, nominated and deputed, viz. *John Pocock, John Beauchamp, Robart Keane, Edward Base*, and *James Sherley*, marchants, their heirs, etc. too and for the use of the generallitie of them, the sume of 1800*li.* of law full money of England, at the place appoynted for the receipts of money, on the west side of the Royall Exchaing in London, by 200*li.*

yearly, and every year, on the feast of St. Migchell, the first paiment
to be made Anno: 1628. etc. Allso the said Isaack is to indeavor to
procure and obtaine from the planters of New Plimoth aforesaid,
securitie, by severall obligations, or writings obligatory, to make
paiment of the said sume of 1800*li.* in forme afforsaid, according
to the true meaning of these presents. In testimonie wherof to this
part of these presents remaining with the said Isaack Allerton, the
said subscribing adventurers; have sett to their names, etc. And to
the other part remaining with the said adventurers; the said Isaack
Allerton hath subscribed his name, the ·15· *November Anno.* 1626. *in
the ·2· year of his Majesties raigne.*

This agreemente was very well liked of, and approved by all
the plantation, and consented unto; though they knew not well
how to raise the payment, and discharge their other ingagements, and supply the yearly wants of the plantation, seeing
they were forced for their necessities to take up money or goods
at so high intrests. Yet they undertooke it, and ·7· or ·8· of the
cheefe of the place became joyntly bound for the paimente of
this 1800*li.* (in the behalfe of the rest) at the severall days. In
which they rane a great adventure, as their present state stood,
having many other heavie burthens allready upon them, and
all things in an uncertaine condition amongst them. So the
next returne it was absolutly confirmed on both sides, and the
bargen fairly ingrossed in partchmente and in many things put
into better forme, by the advice of the learnedest counsell they
could gett; and least any forfeiture should fall on the whole for
none paimente at any of the days, it rane thus: to forfite 30*s.* a
weeke if they missed the time; and was concluded under their
hands and seals, as may be seen at large by the deed it selfe.

Now though they had some untowarde persons mixed
amongst them from the first, which came out of England,
and more afterwards by some of the adventurers, as freindship or other affections led them,—though sundrie were gone,
some for Virginia, and some to other places,—yet diverse were
still mingled amongst them, about whom the Governor and
counsell with other of their cheefe freinds had serious consideration, how to setle things in regard of this new bargen or
purchas made, in respecte of the distribution of things both
for the presente and future. For the present, excepte peace and

union were preserved, they should be able to doe nothing, but indanger to over throw all, now that other tyes and bonds were taken away. Therfore they resolved, for sundrie reasons, to take in all amongst them, that were either heads of families, or single yonge men, that were of ability, and free, (and able to governe them selves with meete descretion, and their affairs, so as to be helpfull in the comone-welth,) into this partnership or purchass. First, they considered that they had need of men and strength both for defence and carrying on of bussinesses. 2ly, most of them had borne ther parts in former miseries and wants with them, and therfore (in some sort) but equall to partake in a better condition, if the Lord be pleased to give it. But cheefly they saw not how peace would be preserved without so doing, but danger and great disturbance might grow to their great hurte and prejudice other wise. Yet they resolved to keep shuch a mean in distribution of lands, and other courses, as should not hinder their growth in others coming to them.

So they caled the company togeather, and conferred with them, and came to this conclusion, that the trade should be managed as before, to help to pay the debts; and all shuch persons as were above named should be reputed and inrouled for purchasers; single free men to have a single share, and every father of a familie to be alowed to purchass so many shares as he had persons in his family; that is to say, one for him selfe, and one for his wife, and for every child that he had living with him, one. As for servants, they had none, but what either their maisters should give them out of theirs, or their deservings should obtaine from the company afterwards. Thus all were to be cast into single shares according to the order abovesaid; and so every one was to pay his part according to his proportion towards the purchass, and all other debts, what the profite of the trade would not reach too; viz. a single man for a single share, a maister of a famalie for so many as he had. This gave all good contente. And first accordingly the few catle which they had were devided, which arose to this proportion; a cowe to ·6· persons or shares, and ·2· to goats the same, which were first equalised for age and goodnes, and then lotted for; single persons consorting with others, as they thought good, and smaler familys likwise; and swine though more in number, yet by the same rule. Then they agreed that every person or share should have ·20· acres of land devided unto them, besides the single acres they had allready; and they appoynted were to begin first on the one side of the towne, and how farr to goe; and then on the other side in like maner; and so to devide it by lotte; and appointed sundrie by name to doe it, and tyed them to certaine rules to proceed by; as that they should only lay out settable or tillable land, at least shuch of it as should butt on the water side, (as the most they were to lay out did,) and pass by the rest as refuse and commone; and what they judged fitte should be so taken. And they were first to agree of the goodnes and fitnes of it before the lott was drawne, and so it might as well prove some of ther owne, as an other mans; and this course they were to hould throwout. But yet seeking to keepe the people togither, as much as might be, they allso agreed upon this order, by mutuall consente, before any lots were cast: that whose lotts soever should fall next the towne, or most conveninte for nearnes, they should take to them a neigboure or tow, whom they best liked; and should suffer them to plant corne with them for ·4· years, and afterwards they might use as much of theirs for as long time, if they would. Allso every share or ·20· acres was to be laid out ·5· acres in breadth by the water side, and ·4· acres in lenght, excepting nooks and corners, which were to be measured as they would bear to best advantage. But no meadows were to be laid out at all, nor were not of many years after, because they were but streight of meadow grounds; and if they had bene now given out, it would have hindred all addition to them afterwards; but every season all were appoynted wher they should mowe, according to the proportion of catle they had. This distribution gave generally good contente, and setled mens minds. Also they gave the Governor and ·4· or ·5· of the spetiall men amongst them, the houses they lived in; the rest were valued and equalised at an indiferent rate, and so every man kept his owne, and he that had a better alowed some thing to him that had a worse, as the valuation wente.

Ther is one thing that fell out in the begining of the winter before, which I have resserved to this place, that I may handle the whole matter togeither. Ther was a ship, with many passengers in her and sundrie goods, bound for Virginia. They had lost them selves at sea, either by the insufficiencie of the maister, or his ilnes; for he was sick and lame of the scurvie, so that he could but lye in the cabin dore, and give direction; and it should seeme was badly assisted either with mate or mariners; or else the fear and unrulines of the passengers were shuch, as they made them stear a course betwene the southwest and the norwest, that they might fall with some land, what soever it was they cared not. For they had been ·6· weeks at sea, and had no water, nor beere, nor any woode left, but had burnt up all their emptie caske; only one of the company had a hogshead of wine or ·2· which was allso allmost spente, so as they feared they should be starved at sea, or consumed with diseases, which made them rune this desperate course. But it plased God that though they came so neare the shoulds of Cap-Codd or else ran stumbling over them in the night, they knew not how, they came right before a small blind harbore, that lyes about the midle of Manamoyake Bay, to the southward of Cap-Codd, with a small gale of wind; and about highwater toucht upon a barr of sand that lyes before it, but had no hurte, the sea being smoth; so they laid out an anchore. But towards the evening the wind sprunge up at sea, and was so rough, as broake their cable, and beat them over the barr into the harbor, wher they saved their lives and goods, though much were hurte with salt water; for with beating they had sprung the but end of a planke or too, and beat out ther occome; but they were soone over, and ran on a drie flate within the harbor, close by a beach; so at low water they gatt out their goods on drie shore, and dried those that were wette, and saved most of their things without any great loss; neither was the ship much hurt, but shee might be mended, and made servisable againe. But though they were not a litle glad that they had thus saved their lives, yet when they had a litle refreshed them selves, and begane to thinke on their condition, not knowing wher they were, nor what they should doe, they begane to be strucken with sadnes. But shortly after they saw some Indians come to them in canows, which made them stand upon their gard. But when they heard some of the Indeans speake English unto them, they were not a litle revived, especially when they heard them demand if they were the Governor of Plimoths men, or freinds; and that they would bring them to the English houses, or carry their letters.

They feasted these Indeans, and gave them many giftes; and
sente ·2· men and a letter with them to the Governor, and did
intreat him to send a boat unto them, with some pitch, and
occume, and spikes, with divers other necessaries for the mending of ther ship (which was recoverable). Allso they besought
him to help them with some corne and sundrie other things
they wanted, to enable them to make their viage to Virginia;
and they should be much bound to him, and would make satisfaction for any thing they had, in any comodities they had
abord. After the Governor was well informed by the messengers of their condition, he caused a boate to be made ready,
and shuch things to be provided as they write for; and because
others were abroad upon trading, and shuch other affairs, as
had been fitte to send unto them, he went him selfe, and allso
carried some trading comodities, to buy them corne of the
Indeans. It was no season of the year to goe withoute the Cape,
but understanding wher the ship lay, he went into the bottom
of the bay, on the inside, and put into a crick called Naumska-
chett, wher it is not much above ·2· mile over land to the bay
wher they were, wher he had the Indeans ready to cary over any
thing to them. Of his arrivall they were very glad, and received
the things to mend ther ship, and other necessaries. Allso he
bought them as much corne as they would have; and wheras
some of their sea-men were rune away amonge the Indeans,
he procured their returne to the ship, and so left them well
furnished and contented, being very thankfull for the curtesies
they receaved. But after the Governor thus left them, he went
into some other harbors ther aboute and loaded his boat with
corne, which he traded, and so went home. But he had not
been at home many days, but he had notice from them, that
by the violence of a great storme, and the bad morring of their
ship (after she was mended) she was put a shore, and so beatten
and shaken as she was now wholy unfitte to goe to sea. And
so their request was that they might have leave to repaire to
them, and soujourne with them, till they could have means
to convey them selves to Virginia; and that they might have
means to transport their goods, and they would pay for the
same, or any thing els wher with the plantation should releeve
them. Considering their distres, their requests were granted,

and all helpfullnes done unto them; their goods transported, and them selves and goods sheltered in their houses as well as they could.

The cheefe amongst these people was one Mr. Fells and Mr. Sibsie, which had many servants belonging unto them, many of them being Irish. Some others ther were that had a servante or ·2· a peece; but the most were servants, and shuch as were ingaged to the former persons, who allso had the most goods. Affter they were hither come, and some thing setled, the maist-ers desired some ground to imploye ther servants upon; seing it was like to be the latter end of the year before they could have passage for Virginia, and they had now the winter before them; they might clear some ground, and plant a crope (seeing they had tools, and necessaries for the same) to help to bear their charge, and keep their servants in imployment; and if they had oppertunitie to departe before the same was ripe, they would sell it on the ground. So they had ground appointed them in convenient places, and Fells and some other of them raised a great deall of corne, which they sould at their departure. This Fells, amongst his other servants, had a maid servante which kept his house and did his household affairs, and by the intimation of some that belonged unto him, he was susspected to keep her, as his concubine; and both of them were examined ther upon, but nothing could be proved, and they stood upon their justification; so with admonition they were dismiste. But afterward it appeard she was with child, so he gott a small boat, and ran away with her, for fear of punishmente. First he went to Cap-Anne, and after into the bay of the Massachus-sets, but could get no passage, and had like to have been cast away; and was forst to come againe and submite him selfe; but they pact him away and those that belonged unto him by the first oppertunitie, and dismiste all the rest as soone as could, being many untoward people amongst them; though ther were allso some that caried them selves very orderly all the time they stayed. And the plantation had some benefite by them, in selling them corne and other provissions of food for cloathing; for they had of diverse kinds, as cloath, perpetuanes, and other stuffs, besides hose, and shoes, and such like commodities as the planters stood in need of. So they both did good, and received good one from another; and a cuple of barks caried them away at the later end of sommer. And sundrie of them have acknowledged their thankfullnes since from Virginia.

That they might the better take all convenient opportunitie to follow their trade, both to maintaine them selves, and to disingage them of those great sumes which they stood charged with, and bound for, they resoloved to build a smale pinass at Manamet, a place ·20· mile from the plantation, standing on the sea to the south ward of them, unto which, by an other creeke on this side, they could cary their goods, within ·4· or ·5· miles, and then transport them over land to their vessell; and so avoyd the compasing of Cap-Codd, and those deangerous shoulds, and so make any vioage to the southward in much shorter time, and with farr less danger. Also for the saftie of their vessell and goods, they builte a house theire, and kept some servants, who also planted corne, and reared some swine, and were allwayes ready to goe out with the barke when ther was occasion. All which tooke good effecte, and turned to their profite.

They now sent (with the returne of the ships) Mr. Allerton againe into England, giveing him full power, under their hands and seals, to conclude the former bargaine with the adventurers; and sent ther bonds for the paimente of the money. Allso they sent what beaver they could spare to pay some of their ingagementes, and to defray his charges; for those deepe interests still kepte them low. Also he had order to procure a patente for a fitt trading place in the river of Kenebeck; for being emulated both by the planters at Pascataway and other places to the eastward of them, and allso by the fishing ships, which used to draw much profite from the Indeans of those parts, they threatened to procure a grante, and shutte them out from thence; espetially after they saw them so well furnished with commodities, as to carie the trade from them. They thought it but needfull to prevente shuch a thing, at least that they might not be excluded from free trade ther, wher them selves had first begune and discovered the same, and brought it to so good effecte. This year allso they had letters, and messengers from the Dutch-plantation, sent unto them from the Governor ther, writen both in Dutch and French. The Dutch had traded in these southerne parts, diverse years before they came; but they begane no plantation hear till ·4· or ·5· years after their coming, and here begining. Ther letters were as followeth. It being their maner to be full of complementall titles.

Eedele, Eerenfeste Wyse Voorsinnige Heeren, den Goveerneur, ende Raeden in Nieu-Pliemuen residerende; onse seer Goede vrinden.

Den directeur ende Raed van Nieu-Nederlande, wensen vue Ede: eerenfesten, ende wijse voorsinnige geluck salichitt [gelukzaligheid?], In Christi Jesu onsen Heere; met goede voorspoet, ende gesonthijt, naer siele, ende lichaem. Amen.

The rest I shall render in English, leaving out the repetition of superfluous titles.

We have often before this wished for an opportunitie or an occasion to congratulate you, and your prosperous and praise-worthy undertakeings, and Goverment of your colony ther. And the more, in that we also have made a good begining to pitch the foundation of a collonie hear; and seeing our native countrie lyes not farr from yours, and our forefathers (diverse hundred years agoe) have made and held frendship and alliance with your ancestours, as sufficently appears by the old contractes and entercourses, confirmed under the hands of kings and princes, in the pointe of warr and trafick; as may be seene and, read by all the world in the old chronakles. The which are not only by the king now reigning confirmed, but it hath pleased his majesty, upon mature deliberation, to make a new covenante, (and to take up armes,) with the States Generall of our dear native country, against our commone enemie the Spaniards, who seeke nothing else but to usurpe and overcome other Christian kings and princes lands, that so he might obtaine and possess his pretended monarchie over all Christendom; and so to rule and command, after his owne pleasure, over the consciences of so many hundred thousand sowles, which God forbid.

And also seeing it hath some time since been reported unto us, by some of our people, that by occasion came so farr northward with their shalop, and met with sundry of the Indeans, who tould them that they were within halfe a days journey of your plantation, and offered ther service to cary letters unto you; therfore we could not forbear to salute you with these few lines, with presentation of our good will and servise unto you, in all frendly kindnes and neighbourhood. And if it so fall out that any goods that comes to our hands from our native countrie, may be serviceable unto you, we shall take

ourselves bound to help and accommodate you ther with; either for
beaver or any other wares or merchandise that you should be pleased
to deale for. And if in case we have no commodity at present that may
give you contente, if you please to sell us any beaver, or otter, or shuch
like comodities as may be usefull for us, for ready money, and let us
understand therof by this bearer in writing, (whom we have apoynted
to stay ·3· or ·4· days for your answer,) when we understand your
minds therin, we shall depute one to deale with you, at shuch place
as you shall appointe. In the mean time we pray the Lord to take you,
our honoured good freinds and neighbours, into his holy protection.

By the appointment of the Governor and Counsell, etc.

ISAAK DE RASIERE, Secrectaris.

From the Manhatas, in the fort Amsterdam,
    March ·9·Anno, 1627.

To this they returned answer as followeth, on the other side.

TO THE HONOURED, etc.

The Governor and Counsell of New-Plimouth wisheth, etc. We
have received your leters, etc. wherin appeareth your good wills and
frendship towards us; but is expresed with over high titles, more then
belongs to us, or is meete for us to receive. But for your good will,
and congratulations of our prosperitie in these smale beginings of
our poore colonie, we are much bound unto you, and with many
thanks doe acknowledge the same; taking it both for a great honour
done unto us, and for a certaine testimoney of your love and good
neighbourhood.

Now these are further to give your Worshipps to understand, that
it is to us no smale joye to hear, that his majestie hath not only bene
pleased to confirme that ancient amitie, aliance, and frendship, and
other contracts, formerly made and ratified by his predecessors of
famous memorie, but hath him selfe (as you say) strengthened the
same with a new-union the better to resist the pride of that commone
enemy the Spaniard, from whose cruelty the Lord keep us both, and
our native countries. Now forasmuch as this is sufficiente to unite us
to geather in love and good neighbourhood, in all our dealings, yet
are many of us further obliged, by the good and curteous entreaty
which we have found in your countrie; haveing lived ther many years,
with freedome, and good contente, as also many of our freinds doe
to this day; for which we, and our children after us, are bound to be
thankfull to your Nation, and shall never forgett the same, but shall
hartily desire your good and prosperity, as our owne, for ever.

Likewise for your freindly tender, and offer to accommodate and help us with any comodities or marchandise you have, or shall come to you, either for beaver, otters, or other wares, it is to us very acceptable, and we doubte not but in short time we may have profitable commerce and trade togeather. But for this year we are fully supplyed with all necessaries, both for cloathing and other things; but hereafter it is like we shall deale with you, if your rates be reasonable. And therfore when you please to send to us againe by any of yours, we desire to know how you will take beaver, by the pounde, and otters, by the skine; and how you will deal per cent: for other comodities, and what you can furnishe us with. As likwise what other commodities from us may be acceptable unto you, as tobaco, fish, corne, or other things, and what prises you will give, etc.

Thus hoping that you will pardon and excuse us for our rude and imperfecte writing in your language, and take it in good parte, because for wante of use we cannot so well express that we understand, nor hapily understand every thing so fully as we should. And so we humbly pray the Lord for his mercie sake, that he will take both us and you into his keeping and gratious protection.

By the Governor and Counsell of New-Plimoth,

Your Worshipps very good freinds and neigbours, etc.

New-Plimouth: March 19.

After this ther was many passages between them both by letters and other entercourse; and they had some profitable commerce togither for diverce years, till other occasions interrupted the same, as may happily appear afterwards, more at large.

Before they sent Mr. Allerton away for England this year, the Governor and some of their cheefe freinds had serious consideration, not only how they might discharge those great ingagements which lay so heavily upon them, as is affore mentioned, but also how they might (if possiblie they could) devise means to help some of their freinds and breethren of Leyden over unto them, who desired so much to come to them, and they desired as much their company. To effecte which, they resolved to rune a high course, and of great adventure, not knowing otherwise how to bring it aboute. Which was to hire the trade of the company for certaine years, and in that time to undertake to pay that 1800*li*. and all the rest of the debts that then lay upon the plantation, which was aboute some 600*li*. more; and so to set them free, and returne the trade to the generalitie againe at the end of the terme. Upon which resolution they called the company togeither, and made it clearly appear unto all what their debts were, and upon what terms they would undertake to pay them all in shuch a time, and sett them clear. But their other ends they were faine to keepe secrete, haveing only privatly acquaynted some of their trusty freinds therwith; which were glad of the same, but doubted how they would be able to performe it. So after some agitation of the thing with the company, it was yeelded unto, and the agreemente made upon the conditions following.

Articles of agreemente betweene the collony of New-Plimmoth of the one partie, and William Bradford, Captein Myles Standish, Isaack Allerton, etc. one the other partie; and shuch others as they shall thinke good to take as partners and undertakers with them, concerning the trade for beaver and other furrs and comodities, etc.; made July, 1627.

First, it is agreed and covenanted betweexte the said parties, that the afforsaid William Bradford, Captain Myles Standish, and Isaack Allerton, etc., have undertaken, and doe by these presents, covenante and agree to pay, discharge, and acquite the said collony of all the debtes both due for the purchass, or any other belonging to them, at the day of the date of these presents.

Secondly, the above-said parties are to have and freely injoye the pinass latly builte, the boat at Manamett, and the shalop, called the Bass-boat, with all other implements to them belonging, that is in the store of the said company; with all the whole stock of furrs, fells, beads, corne, wampampeak, hatchets, knives, etc. that is now in the storre, or any way due unto the same uppon accounte.

3ly. That the above said parties have the whole trade to them selves their heires and assignes, with all the privileges therof, as the said collonie doth now, or may use the same, for ·6· full years, to begine the last of September next insuing.

4ly. In furder consideration of the discharge of the said debtes, every severall purchaser doth promise and covenante yearly to pay, or cause to be payed, to the above said parties, during the full terme of the said ·6· years, ·3· bushells of corne, or 6*li.* of tobaco, at the undertakers choyse.

5ly. The said undertakers shall dureing the afforesaid terme bestow 50*li.* per annum, in hose and shoese, to be brought over for the collonies use, to be sould unto them for corne at 6*s.* per bushell.

6ly. That at the end of the said terme of ·6· years, the whole trade shall returne to the use and benefite of the said collonie, as before.

Lastly, if the afforesaid undertakers, after they have aquainted their freinds in England with these covenants, doe (upon the first returne) resolve to performe them, and undertake to discharge the debtes of the said collony, according to the true meaning and intente of these presents, then they are (upon shuch notice given) to stand in full force; otherwise all things to remaine as formerly they were, and a true accounte to be given to the said collonie, of the disposing of all things according to the former order.

Mr. Allerton carried a coppy of this agreemente with him into England, and amongst other his instructions had order given him to deale with some of their speciall freinds, to joyne with them in this trade upon the above recited conditions; as allso to imparte their further ends that moved them to take this course, namly, the helping over of some their freinds from Leyden, as they should be able; in which if any of them would joyne with them they should thankfully accepte of their love and partnership herein. And with all (by their letters) gave them some grounds of their hopes of the accomplishmente of these things with some advantage.

ANNO DOM: ·1628·

AFTER Mr. Alertons arivall in England, he aquainted them with his comission and full power to conclude the forementioned bargan and purchas; upon the veiw wherof, and the delivery of the bonds for the paymente of the money yearly, (as is before mentioned,) it was fully concluded, and a *deede** fairly ingrossed in partchmente was delivered him, under their hands and seals confirming the same. Morover he delte with them aboute other things according to his instructions. As to admitte some of these their good freinds into this purchass if they pleased, and to deal with them for moneys at better rates, etc. Touching which I shall hear inserte a letter of Mr. Sherleys, giving light to what followed thereof, writ to the Governor as followeth.

---

*Nov. 6, 1627, Page 238.

SIR: I have received yours of the ·26· of May by Mr. *Gibs*, and Mr. *Goffe*, with the barrell of otter skins, according to the contents; for which I got a bill of store, and so tooke them up, and sould them togeather at 78*li*. 12*s*. sterling; and since, Mr. Allerton hath received the money, as will apear by the accounte. It is true (as you write) that your ingagments are great, not only the purchass, but you are yet necessitated to take up the stock you work upon; and that not at ·6· or ·8· per cent. as it is here let out, but at ·30· ·40· yea, and some at ·50· per cent. which, were not your gaines great, and Gods blessing on your honest indeavours more then ordinarie, it could not be that you should longe subsiste in the maintaining of, and upholding of your worldly affaires. And this your honest and discreete agente, Mr. Allerton, hath seriously considered, and deeply laid to mind, how to ease you of it. He tould me you were contented to accepte of me and some few others, to joyne with you in the purchass, as partners; for which I kindly thanke you and all the rest, and doe willingly accepte of it. And though absente, shall willingly be at shuch charge as you and the rest shall thinke meete; and this year am contented to forbear my former 50*li*. and ·2· years increase for the venture, both which now makes it 80*li*. without any bargaine or condition for the profite, you (I mean the generalitie) stand to the adventure, outward, and homeward. I have perswaded Mr. Andrews and Mr. Beachamp to doe the like, so as you are eased of the high rate, you were at the other ·2· yeares; I say we leave it freely to your selves to alow us what you please, and as God shall blesse. What course I rune, Mr. Beachamp desireth to doe the same; and though he have been or seemed somwhat harsh heretofore, yet now you shall find he is new moulded. I allso see by your letter, you desire I should be your agente or factore hear. I have ever found you so faithfull, honest, and upright men, as I have even resolved with my selfe (God assisting me) to doe you all the good lyeth in my power; and therfore if you please to make choyse of so weak a man, both for abillities and body, to performe your bussines, I promise (the Lord enabling me) to doe the best I can according to those abillities he hath given me; and wherin I faile, blame your selves, that you made no better choyce. Now, because I am sickly, and we are all mortall, I have advised Mr. Allerton to joyne Mr. Beachamp with me in your deputation, which I conceive to be very necessary and good for you; your charge shall be no more, for it is not your salarie makes me undertake your bussines. Thus comending you and yours, and all Gods people, unto the guidance and protection of the Allmightie, I ever rest,

Your faithfull loving freind,
London, November 17. 1628.				JAMES SHERLEY.

Another letter of his, that should have bene placed before.

We cannot but take notice how the Lord hath been pleased to crosse our proseedings, and caused many disasters to befale us therin. I conceive the only reason to be, we, or many of us, aimed at other ends then Gods glorie; but now I hope that cause is taken away; the bargen being fully concluded, as farr as our powers will reach, and confirmed under our hands and seals, to Mr. Allerton and the rest of his and your copartners. But for my owne parte, I confess as I was loath to hinder the full confirming of it, being the first propounder ther of at our meeting; so on the other side, I was as unwilling to set my hand to the sale, being the receiver of most part of the adventures, and a second causer of much of the ingagments; and one more threatened, being most envied and aimed at (if they could find any stepe to ground their malice on) then any other whosoever. I profess I know no just cause they ever had, or have, so to doe; neither shall it ever be proved that I have wronged them or any of the adventurers, wittingly or willingly, one peny in the disbursing of so many pounds in those ·2· years trouble. No, the sole cause why they maligne me (as I and others conceived) was that I would not side with them against you, and the going over of the Leyden people. But as I then card not, so now I litle fear what they can doe; yet charge and trouble I know they may cause me to be at. And for these reasons, I would gladly have perswaded the other ·4· to have sealed to this bargaine, and left me out, but they would not; so rather then it should faile, Mr. Alerton having taken so much pains, I have sealed with the rest; with this proviso and promise of his, that if any trouble arise hear, you are to bear halfe the charge. Wherfore now I doubt not but you will give your generallitie good contente, and setle peace amongst your selves, and peace with the natives; and then no doubt but the God of Peace will blesse your going out and your returning, and cause all that you sett your hands unto to prosper; the which I shall ever pray the Lord to grante if it be his blessed will. Asuredly unless the Lord be mercifull unto us and the whole land in generall, our estate and condition is farr worse then yours. Wherfore if the Lord should send persecution or trouble hear, (which is much to be feared,) and so should put into our minds to flye for refuge, I know no place safer then to come to you, (for all Europ is at varience one with another, but cheefly with us,) not doubting but to find shuch frendly entertainmente as shall be honest and conscionable, notwithstanding what hath latly passed. For I profess in the word of an honest man, had it not been to procure your peace and quiet from some turbulent spirites hear, I would not have sealed to this last deed; though you would have given me all my adventure and debte ready downe. Thus desiring the Lord to blesse and prosper you, I cease ever resting,

Your faithfull and loving freind,

to my power,

JAMES SHERLEY.

Des: 27.

With this leter they sent a draught of a formall deputation to be hear sealed and sent back unto them, to authorise them as their agents, according to what is mentioned in the above said letter; and because some inconvenience grue therby afterward I shall here inserte it.

TO ALL TO WHOM THESE PRESENTS SHALL COME greeting; Know yee that we, William Bradford, Governor of Plimoth, in N. E. in America, Isaak Allerton, Myles Standish, William Brewster, and Ed: Winslow, of Plimoth aforesaid, merchants, doe by these presents for us and in our names, make, substitute, and appointe James Sherley, Goldsmith, and John Beachamp, Salter, citizens of London, our true and lawfull agents, factors, substitutes, and assignes; as well to take and receive all shuch goods, wares, and marchandise what soever as to our said substitutes or either of them, or to the citie of London, or other place of the Relme of Engl: shall be sente, transported, or come from us or any of us, as allso to vend, sell, barter, or exchaing the said goods, wares, and marchandise so from time to time to be sent to shuch person or persons upon credite, or other wise in shuch maner as to our said agents and factors joyently, or to either of them severally shall seeme meete. And further we doe make and ordain our said substitutes and assignes joyntly and severally for us, and to our uses, and accounts, to buy and consigne for and to us into New-Engl: aforesaid, shuch goods and marchandise to be provided here, and to be returned hence, as by our said assignes, or either of them, shall be thought fitt. And to recover, receive, and demand for us and in our names all shuch debtes and sumes of money, as now are or hereafter shall be due, incidente, accruing or belonging to us, or any of us, by any wayes or means; and to acquite, discharge, or compound for any debte or sume of money, which now or hereafter shall be due or oweing by any person or persons to us, or any of us. And generally for us and in our names to doe, performe, and execute every acte and thing which to our said assignes, or either of them, shall seeme meete to be done in or aboute the premissies, as fully and effectually, to all intents and purposes, as if we or any of us were in person presente. And whatsoever our said agents and factors joyntly or severally shall doe, or cause to be done, in or aboute the premisses, we will and doe, and every of us doth ratife, alow, and confirme, by these presents. In wittnes wherof we have here unto put our hands and seals. Dated 18. November, 1628.

This was accordingly confirmed by the above named, and ·4· more of the cheefe of them under their hands and seals, and delivered unto them. Also Mr. Allerton formerly had authoritie under their hands and seals for the transacting of the former bussines, and taking up of moneys, etc. which still he retained whilst he was imployed in these affaires; they mistrusting neither him nor any of their freinds faithfullnes, which made them more remisse in looking to shuch acts as had passed under their hands, as necessarie for the time; but letting them rune on to long unminded or recaled, it turned to their harme afterwards, as will appere in its place.

Mr. Allerton having setled all things thus in a good and hopfull way, he made hast to returne in the first of the spring to be hear with their supply for trade, (for the fishermen with whom he came used to sett forth in winter and be here betimes.) He brought a reasonable supply of goods for the plantation, and without those great interests as before is noted; and brought an accounte of the beaver sould, and how the money was disposed for goods, and the paymente of other debtes, having paid all debts abroad to others, save to Mr. Sherley, Mr. Beachamp, and Mr. Andrews; from whom likwise he brought an accounte which to them all amounted not to above 400*li*. for which he had passed bonds. Allso he had payed the first paymente for the purchass, being due for this year, viz. 200*li*. and brought them the bonde for the same canselled; so as they now had no more foreine debtes but the abovesaid 400*li*. and odde pownds, and the rest of the yearly purchass monie. Some other debtes they had in the cuntrie, but they were without any intrest, and they had wherwith to discharge them when they were due. To this pass the Lord had brought things for them. Also he brought them further notice that their freinds, the abovenamed, and some others that would joyne with them in the trade and purchass, did intend for to send over to Leyden, for a competente number of them, to be hear the next year without fayle, if the Lord pleased to blesse their journey. He allso brought them a patente for Kenebeck, but it was so straite and ill bounded, as they were faine to renew and inlarge it the next year, as allso that which they had at home, to their great charge, as will after appeare. Hithertoo Mr. Allerton did them good and faithfull service; and well had it been if he had so continued, or els they had now ceased for employing him any longer thus into England. But of this more afterwards.

Having procured a patente (as is above said) for *Kenebeck*, they *now erected a house* up above in the river in the most convenientest place for trade, as they conceived, and furnished the same with commodities for the end, both winter and sommer, not only with corne, but also with shuch other commodities as the fishermen had traded with them, as coats, shirts, ruggs, and blankets, biskett, pease, prunes, etc.; and what they could not have out of England, they bought of the fishing ships, and so carried on their bussines as well as they could.

This year the Dutch sent againe unto them from their plantation, both kind leterss, and also diverse comodities, as sugar, linen cloth, Holand finer and courser stufes, etc. They came up with their barke to Manamete, to their house ther, in which came their Secretarie Rasier; who was accompanied with a noyse of trumpeters, and some other attendants; and desired that they would send a boat for him, for he could not travill so farr over land. So they sent a boat to Manonscussett, and brought him to the plantation, with the cheefe of his company. And after some few days entertainmente, he returned to his barke, and some of them wente with him, and bought sundry of his goods; after which begining thus made, they sente often times to the same place, and had entercourse togeather for diverce years; and amongst other comodities, they vended much tobaco for linen cloath, stuffs, etc., which was a good benefite to the people, till the Virginians found out their plantation. But that which turned most to their profite, in time, was an entrance into the trade of Wampampeake; for they now bought aboute 50*li.* worth of it of them; and they tould them how vendable it was at their forte Orania; and did perswade them they would find it so at Kenebeck; and so it came to pass in time, though at first it stuck, and it was ·2· years before they could put of this small quantity, till the inland people knew of it; and afterwards they could scarce ever gett enough for them, for many years togeather. And so this, with

their other provissions, cutt of their trade quite from the fisher-
men, and in great part from other of the stragling planters.
And strange it was to see the great allteration it made in a few
years amonge the Indeans them selves; for all the Indeans of
these parts, and the Massachussets, had none or very litle of
it,* but the sachems and some spetiall persons that wore a
litle of it for ornamente. Only it was made and kepte amonge
the Nariganssets, and Pequents, which grew rich and potent
by it, and these people were poore and begerly, and had no
use of it. Neither did the English of this plantation, or any
other in the land, till now that they had knowledg of it from
the Dutch, so much as know what it was, much less that it
was a commoditie of that worth and valew. But after it grue
thus to be a comoditie in these parts, these Indeans fell into
it allso, and to learne how to make it; for the Narigansets doe
geather the shells of which they make it from their shores.
And it hath now continued a current comoditie aboute this
·20· years, and it may prove a drugg in time. In the mean time
it makes the Indeans of these parts rich and power full and
also prowd therby; and fills them with peeces, powder, and
shote, which no laws can restraine, by reason of the bassnes of
sundry unworthy persons, both English, Dutch, and French,
which may turne to the ruine of many. Hithertoo the Indeans
of these parts had no peeces nor other armes but their bowes
and arrowes, nor of many years after; nether durst they scarce
handle a gune, so much were they affraid of them; and the very
sight of one (though out of kilter) was a terrour unto them.
But those Indeans to the east parts, which had commerce with
the French, got peces of them, and they in the end made a
commone trade of it; and in time our English fisher-men, led
with the like covetoussnes, followed their example, for their
owne gaine; but upon complainte against them, it pleased the
kings majestie to prohibite the same by a stricte proclaimation,
commanding that no sorte of armes, or munition, should by
any of his subjects be traded with them.

Aboute some ·3· or ·4· years before this time, ther came over
one Captaine Wolastone, (a man of pretie parts,) and with him
·3· or ·4· more of some eminencie, who brought with them a

*Peag.

great many servants, with provissions and other implements for to begine a plantation; and pitched them selves in a place within the Massachusets, which they called, after their captains name, Mount-Wollaston. Amongst whom was one Mr. Morton, who, it should seeme, had some small adventure (of his owne or other mens) amongst them; but had litle respecte amongst them, and was sleghted by the meanest servants. Haveing continued ther some time, and not finding things to answer their expectations, nor profite to arise as they looked for, Captaine Wollaston takes a great part of the sarvants, and transports them to Virginia, wher he puts them of at good rates, selling their time to other men; and writes back to one Mr. Rassdall, one of his cheefe partners, and accounted their marchant, to bring another parte of them to Verginia likewise, intending to put them of ther as he had done the rest. And he, with the consente of the said Rasdall, appoynted one Fitcher to be his Liuetenante, and governe the remaines of the plantation, till he or Rasdall returned to take further order theraboute. But this Morton abovesaid, haveing more craft then honestie, (who had been a kind of petie-fogger, of Furneffells Inne,) in the others absence, watches an oppertunitie, (and commons being but hard amongst them), and gott some strong drinck and other junkats, and made them a feast; and after they were merie, he begane to tell them, he would give them good counsell. You see (saith he) that many of your fellows are carried to Virginia; and if you stay till this Rasdall returne, you will also be carried away and sould for slaves with the rest. Therfore I would advise you to thruste out this Lieutenant Fitcher; and I, having a parte in the plantation, will receive you as my partners and consociates; so may you be free from service, and we will converse, trade, plante, and live togeather as equalls, and supporte and protecte one another, or to like effecte. This counsell was easily received; so they tooke oppertunitie, and thrust Leuetenante Fitcher out a dores, and would suffer him to come no more amongst them, but forct him to seeke bread to eate, and other releefe from his neigbours, till he could gett passages for England. After this they fell to great licenciousnes, and led a dissolute life, powering out them selves into all profanenes. And Morton became lord of misrule, and maintained (as it were) a schoole of Athisme. And after they had gott some goods into their hands, and gott much by trading with the Indeans, they spent it as vainly, in quaffing and drinking both wine and strong waters in great exsess, and, as some reported, 10*lis.* worth in a morning. They allso set up a May-pole, drinking and dancing aboute it many days togeather, inviting the Indean women, for their consorts, dancing and frisking togither, (like so many fairies, or furies rather,) and worse practises. As if they had anew revived and celebrated the feasts of the Roman Goddes Flora, or the beasly practieses of the madd Bacchinalians. Morton likwise (to shew his poetrie) composed sundry rimes and verses, some tending to lasciviousnes, and others to the detraction and scandall of some persons, which he affixed to this idle or idoll May-polle. They chainged allso the name of their place, and in stead of calling it Mounte Wollaston, they call it Meriemounte, as if this joylity would have lasted ever. But this continued not long, for after Morton was sent for England, (as folows to be declared,) shortly after came over that worthy gentleman, Mr. John Indecott, who brought over a patent under the broad seall, for the govermente of the Massachusets, who visiting those parts caused that May-polle to be cutt downe, and rebuked them for their profannes, and admonished them to looke ther should be better walking; so they now, or others, changed the name of their place againe, and called it Mounte-Dagon.

Now to maintaine this riotous prodigallitie and profuse excess, Morton, thinking him selfe lawless, and hearing what gaine the French and fisher-men made by trading of peeces, powder, and shotte to the Indeans, he, as the head of this consortship, begane the practise of the same in these parts; and first he taught them how to use them, to charge, and discharge, and what proportion of powder to give the peece, according to the sise or bignes of the same; and what shotte to use for foule, and what for deare. And having thus instructed them, he imployed some of them to hunte and fowle for him, so as they became farr more active in that imploymente then any of the English, by reason of ther swiftnes of foote, and nimblenes of body, being also quicksighted, and by continuall exercise well knowing the hants of all sorts of game. So as when they saw the execution that a peece would doe, and the benefite that might come by the same, they became madd, as it were, after them, and would not stick to give any prise they could attaine too for them; accounting their bowes and arrowes but bables in comparison of them.

And here I may take occasion to bewaile the mischefe that this wicked man began in these parts, and which since base covetousnes prevailing in men that should know better, hathe now at length gott the upper hand, and made this thing commone, notwithstanding any laws to the contrary; so as the Indeans are full of peeces all over, both fouling peeces, muskets, pistols, etc. They have also their moulds to make shotte, of all sorts, as muskett bulletts, pistoll bullets, swan and gose shote, and of smaler sorts; yea, some have seen them have their scruplates to make scrupins them selves, when they wante them, with sundery other implements, wherwith they are ordinarily better fited and furnished then the English them selves. Yea, it is well knowne that they will have powder and shot, when the English want it, nor cannot gett it; and that in a time of warr or danger, as experience hath manifested, that when lead hath been scarce, and men for their owne defence would gladly have given a groat a li, which is deare enoughe, yet hath it bene bought up and sent to other places, and sould to shuch as trade it with the Indeans, at ·12· pence the li.; and it is like they give ·3· or ·4· s. the pound, for they will have it at any rate. And these things have been done in the same times, when some of their neigbours and freinds are daly killed by the Indeans, or are in deanger therof, and live but at the Indeans mercie. Yea, some (as they have aquainted them with all other things) have tould them how gunpowder is made, and all the materialls in it, and that they are to be had in their owne land; and I am confidente, could they attaine to make salt-peter, they would teach them to make powder. O the horiblenes of this vilanie! how many both Dutch and English have been latly slaine by those Indeans, thus furnished; and no remedie provided, nay, the evill more increased, and the blood of their brethren sould for gaine, as is to be feared; and in what danger all these colonies are in is too well known. Oh! that princes and parlements would take some timly order to prevente this mischeefe, and at length to suppress it, by some exemplerie punishmente upon some of these gaine thirstie murderers, (for they deserve no better title,) before their collonies in these parts be over throwne by these barbarous savages, thus armed with their owne weapons, by these evill instruments, and traytors to their neigbors and cuntrie.

But I have forgott my selfe, and have been to longe in this digression; but now to returne. This Morton having thus taught them the use of peeces, he sould them all he could spare; and he and his consorts detirmined to send for many out of England, and had by some of the ships sente for above a score. The which being knowne, and his neigbours meeting the Indeans in the woods armed with guns in this sorte, it was a terrour unto them, who lived straglingly, and were of no strenght in any place. And other places (though more remote) saw this mischeefe would quiclly spread over all, if not prevented. Besides, they saw they should keep no servants, for Morton would entertaine any, how vile soever, and all the scume of the countrie, or any discontents, would flock to him from all places, if this nest was not broken; and they should stand in more fear of their lives and goods (in short time) from this wicked and deboste crue, then from the salvages them selves.

So sundrie of the cheefe of the stragling plantations, meeting togither, agreed by mutuall consente to sollissite those of Plimoth (who were then of more strength then them all) to joyne with them, to prevente the further grouth of this mischeefe, and suppress Morton and his consorts before they grewe to further head and strength. Those that joyned in this action (and after contributed to the charge of sending him for England) were from Pascataway, Namkeake, Winisimett, Weesagascusett, Natasco, and other places wher any English were seated. Those of Plimoth being thus sought too by their messengers and letters, and waying both their reasons, and the commone danger, were willing to afford them their help; though them selves had least cause of fear or hurte. So, to be short, they first resolved joyntly to write to him, and in a freindly and neigborly way to admonish him to forbear those courses, and sent a messenger with their letters to bring his answer. But he was so highe as he scorned all advise, and asked who had to doe with him; he had and would trade peeces with the Indeans in dispite of all, with many other scurillous termes full of disdaine. They sente to him a second time, and bad him be better advised, and more temperate in his termes, for the countrie could not beare the injure he did; it was against their comone saftie, and against the king's proclamation. He answerd in high terms as before, and that the kings proclaimation was no law; demanding what penaltie was upon it. It was answered, more then he could bear, his majesties displeasure. But insolently he persisted, and said the king was dead and his displeasure with him, and many the like things; and threatened withall that if any came to molest him, let them looke to them selves, for he would prepare for them. Upon which they saw ther was no way but to take him by force; and having so farr proceeded, now to give over would make him farr more hautie and insolente. So they mutually resolved to proceed, and obtained of the Governor of Plimoth to send Captaine Standish, and some other aide with him, to take Morton by force. The which accordingly was done; but they found him to stand stifly in his defence, having made fast his dors, armed his consorts, set diverse dishes of powder and bullets ready on the table; and if they had not been over armed with drinke, more hurt might have been done. They sommaned him to yeeld, but he kept his house, and they could gett nothing but scofes and scorns from him; but at length, fearing they would doe some violence to the house, he and some of his crue came out, but not to yeeld, but to shoote; but they were so steeld with drinke as their peeces were to heavie for them; him selfe with a carbine (over charged and allmost halfe fild with powder and shote, as was after found) had thought to have shot Captaine Standish; but he stept to him, and put by his peece, and tooke him. Neither was ther any hurte done to any of either side, save that one was so drunke that he rane his owne nose upon the pointe of a sword that one held before him as he entred the house; but he lost but a litle of his hott blood. Morton they brought away to Plimoth, wher he was kepte, till a ship went from the Ile of Shols for England, with which he was sente to the Counsell of New-England; and letters writen to give them information of his course and cariage; and also one was sent at their comone charge to informe their Honors more perticulerly, and to prosecute against him. But he foold of the messenger, after he was gone from hence, and though he wente for England, yet nothing was done to him, not so much as rebukte, for ought was heard; but returned the nexte year. Some of the worst of the company were disperst, and some of the more modest kepte the house till he should be heard from. But I have been too long aboute so unworthy a person, and bad a cause.

This year Mr. Allerton brought over a yonge man for a minister to the people hear, wheather upon his owne head, or at the motion of some freinds ther, I well know not, but it was without the churches sending; for they had bene so bitten by Mr. Lyford, as they desired to know the person well whom they should invite amongst them. His name was Mr. Rogers; but they perceived, upon some triall, that he was crased in his braine; so they were faine to be at further charge to send him back againe the nexte year, and loose all the charge that was expended in his hither bringing, which was not smalle by Mr. Allerton's accounte, in provissions, aparell, bedding, etc. After his returne he grue quite distracted, and Mr. Allerton was much blamed that he would bring shuch a man over, they having charge enough otherwise.

Mr. Allerton, in the years before, had brought over some small quantitie of goods, upon his owne perticuler, and sould them for his owne private benefite; which was more then any man had yet hithertoo attempted. But because he had other wise done them good service, and also he sould them among the people at the plantation, by which their wants were supplied, and he aledged it was the love of Mr. Sherley and some other freinds that would needs trust him with some goods, conceiveing it might doe him some good, and none hurte, it was not much lookt at, but past over. But this year he brought over a greater quantitie, and they were so intermixte with the goods of the generall, as they knew not which were theirs, and which was his, being pact up together; so as they well saw that, if any casualty had beefalne at sea, he might have laid the whole on them, if he would; for ther was no distinction. Allso what was most vendible, and would yeeld presente pay, usualy that was his; and he now begane allso to sell abroad to others of forine places, which, considering their commone course, they began to dislike. Yet because love thinkes no evill, nor is susspitious, they tooke his faire words for excuse, and resolved to send him againe this year for England; considering how well he had done the former bussines, and what good acceptation

he had with their freinds ther; as also seeing sundry of their
freinds from Leyden were sente for, which would or might be
much furthered by his means. Againe, seeing the patente for
Kenebeck must be inlarged, by reason of the former mistakes
in the bounding of it, and it was conceived, in a maner, the
same charge would serve to inlarge this at home with it, and
he that had begane the former the last year would be the fittest
to effecte this; so they gave him instructions and *sente him for
England this year againe.* And in his instructions bound him to
bring over no goods on their accounte, but 50 *li.* in hose and
shoes, and some linen cloth, (as they were bound by covenante
when they tooke the trade;) also some trading goods to shuch
a value; and in no case to exseed his instructions, nor rune
them into any further charge; he well knowing how their state
stood. Also that he should so provide that their trading goods
came over betimes, and what so ever was sent on their accounte
should be pact up by it selfe, marked with their marke, and no
other goods to be mixed with theirs. For so he prayed them to
give him shuch instructions as they saw good, and he would
folow them, to prevente any jellocie or farther offence, upon
the former forementioned dislikes. And thus they conceived
they had well provided for all things.

ANNO DOM: ·1629·

M R. ALLERTON safly ariveing in England, and delivering
his leters to their freinds their, and aquainting them
with his instructions, found good acceptation with them,
and they were very forward and willing to joyne with them
in the partnership of trade, and in the charge to send over
the *Leyden people; a company wherof were allready come out of
Holand, and prepared to come over, and so were sent away before
Mr. Allerton could be ready to come. They had passage with the
ships that came to Salem, that brought over many godly persons
to begine the plantations and churches of Christ ther, and in
the Bay of the Massachussets*; so their long stay and keeping
back was recompensed by the Lord to ther freinds here with a
duble blessing, in that they not only injoyed them now beyond
ther late expectation, (when all their hopes seemed to be cutt
of,) but, with them, many more godly freinds and Christian

breethren, as the begining of a larger harvest unto the Lord, in the increase of his churches and people in these parts, to the admiration of many, and allmost wonder of the world; that of so small beginings so great things should insue, as time after manifested; and that here should be a resting place for so many of the Lords people, when so sharp a scourge came upon their owne nation. But it was the Lords doing, and it ought to be marvellous in our eyes.

But I shall hear inserte some of their freinds letters, which doe best expresse their owne minds in these thir proceedings.

A leter of Mr. Sherleys to the Governor.

May 25, 1629.

SIR: etc. *Here are many of your and our freinds from Leyden* coming over, who, though for the most parte be but a weak company, yet herein, is a good parte of that end obtained which was aimed at, and which hath been so strongly opposed by some of our former adventurers. But God hath his working in these things, which man cannot frustrate. With them we have allso sent some servants in the ship called the Talbut, that wente hence lately; but these come in the *Mayflower*. Mr. Beachamp and my selfe, with Mr. Andrews and Mr. Hatherly, are, with your love and liking, joyned partners with you, &c. Your deputation we have received, and the goods have been taken up and sould by your freind and agente, Mr. Allerton, my selfe having bine nere ·3· months in Holland, at Amsterdam and other parts in the Low-Countries. I see further the agreemente you have made with the generallitie, in which I cannot understand but you have done very well, both for them and you, and also for your freinds at Leyden. Mr. Beachamp, Mr. Andrews, Mr. Hatherley, and my selfe, doe so like and approve of it, as we are willing to joyne with you, and, God directing and inabling us, will be assisting and helpfull to you, the best that possiblie we can. Nay, had you not taken this course, I doe not see how you should accomplish *the end you first aimed at, and some others indevoured these years past.* We know it must keep us from the profite, which otherwise by the blessing of God and your indeavours, might be gained; for most of *those that came in may,* and *these now sente,* though I hope honest and good people, yet not like to be helpfull to raise profite, but rather, ney, certaine must, some while, be chargable to you and us; at which it is lickly, had not this wise and discreete course been taken, many of your generalitie would have grudged. Againe, you say well in your letter, and I make no doubte but you will performe it, that now being but a few, on whom the burthen must be, you will both menage it the beter, and sett too it more cherfully, haveing no discontents nor contradiction, but so lovingly to joyne togeither, in affection and counsell, as God no doubte will blesse and prosper your honest labours and indeavors. And therfore in all respects I doe not see but *you have done marvelously discreetly, and advisedly*, and no doubt but it gives all parties good contente; I mean that are reasonable and honest men, shuch as make conscience of giving the best satisfaction they be able for their debts, and that regard not their owne perticuler so much as the accomplishing of *that good end for which this bussines was first intended*, etc. Thus desiring the Lord to blese and prosper you, and all yours, and all our honest endeavors, I rest

Your unfained and ever loving freind,
JAMES SHERLEY.

London: March 8. 1629.

That I may handle things togeather, I have put these ·2· companies that came from Leyden in this place; though they came at ·2· severall times, yet they both came out of England *this year*. The former company, being ·35· persons, were shiped in *May*, and arived here aboute *August*. The later were shiped in the begining of *March*, and arived hear the later end of *May, 1630*. Mr. Sherleys ·2· letters, the effect whereof I have before related, (as much of them as is pertinente,) mentions both. Their charge, as Mr. Allerton brought it in afterwards on accounte, came to above 550*li*. besides ther fetching hither from *Salem* and the *Bay*, wher they and their goods were landed; viz. their transportation from Holland to England, and their charges lying ther, and passages hither, with clothing provided for them. For I find by accounte for the one company, ·125· yeards of karsey, ·127· ellons of linen cloath, shoes, 66 pairs, with many other perticulers. The charge of the other company is reckoned on the severall families, some ·50*li*·, some ·40*li*·, some ·30*li*·, and so more or less, as their number and expencess were. And besides all this charg, their freinds and bretheren here were to provid corne and other provissions for them, till they could reap a crope which was long before. Those that came in May were thus maintained upward of ·16· or ·18· months, before they had any harvest of their owne, and the other by proportion. And all they could doe in the mean time was to gett them some housing, and prepare them grounds to plant on, against the season. And this charg of maintaining them all this while was litle less then the former sume. These things I note more perticulerly, for sundry regards. First, to shew a rare example herein of brotherly love, and Christian care in performing their promises and covenants to their bretheren, too, and in a sorte beyonde their power; that they should venture so desperatly to ingage themselves to accomplish this thing, and bear it so cheerfully; for they never demanded, much less had, any repaymente of all these great sumes thus disbursed. 2ly. It must needs be that ther was more then of man in these acheevements, that should thus readily stire up the harts of shuch able frinds to joyne in partnership with them in shuch a case, and cleave so faithfullie to them as these did, in so great adventures; and the more because the most of them never saw their faces to this day; ther being neither kindred, aliance, or other acquaintance or relations betweene any of them, then hath been before mentioned; it must needs be therfore the spetiall worke and hand of God. 3ly. That these poore people here in a willderness should, notwithstanding, be inabled in time to repay all these ingagments, and many more unjustly brought upon them through the unfaithfullnes of some, and many other great losses which they sustained, which will be made manifest, if the Lord be pleased to give life and time. In the mean time, I cannot but admire his ways and workes towards his servants, and humbly desire to blesse his holy name for his great mercies hither-too.

The Leyden people being thus come over, and sundry of the generalitie seeing and hearing how great the charge was like to be that was that way to be expended, they begane to murmure and repine at it, notwithstanding the burden lay on other mens shoulders; espetially at the paying of the ·3· bushells of corne a year, according to the former agreemente, when the trade was lett for the ·6· years aforesaid. But to give them contente herein allso, it was promised them, that if they could doe it in the time without it, they would never demand it of them; which gave them good contente. And indeed it never was paid, as will appeare by the sequell.

Concerning Mr. Allertons procceedings about the inlarging and confirming of their patent, both that at home and Kenebeck, will best appere by *another leter of Mr. Sherleys*; for though much time and money was expended aboute it, yet he left it unaccomplisht this year, and came withoute it. See Mr. Sherleys letter.

MOST WORTHY AND LOVING FREINDS, etc.

Some of your letters I received in July, and some since by Mr. Peirce, but till our maine bussines, the patent, was granted, I could not setle my mind nor pen to writing. Mr. Allerton was so turmoyled about it, as verily I would not nor could not have undergone it, if I might have had a thousand pounds; but the Lord so blessed his labours (even beyond expectation in these evill days) as he obtained the love and favore of great men in repute and place. He got granted from the *Earle of Warwick and Sr. Ferdinando Gorge* all that Mr. Winslow desired in his letters to me, and more allso, which I leave to him to relate. Then he sued to the king to confirme their grante, and to make you a corporation, and so to inable you to make and execute lawes, in shuch large and ample maner as the Massachusett plantation hath it; which the king graciously granted, referring it to the Lord Keeper to give order to the solisiter to draw it up, if ther were a presidente for it. So the Lord Keeper furthered it all he could, and allso the solissiter; but as Festus said to Paule, With no small sume of money obtained I this freedom; for by the way many ridells must be resolved, and many locks must be opened with the silver, ney, the golden key. Then it was to come to the Lord Treasurer, to have his warrente for freeing the custume for a certaine time; but he would not doe it, but refferd it to the Counsell table. And ther Mr. Allerton atended day by day, when they sate, but could not gett his petition read. And by reason of Mr. *Peirce his staying with all the passengers at Bristoll,* he was *forct to leave* the further prosecuting of it to a solissiter. But ther is no fear nor doubte but it will be granted, for he hath the cheefe of them to freind; yet it will be marvelously *needfull for him to returne by the first ship that comes from thence;* for if you had this confirmed, then were you compleate, and might bear shuch sway and goverment as were fitt for your ranke and place that God hath called you unto; and stope the moueths of base and scurrulous fellowes, that are ready to question and threaten you in every action you doe. And besides, if you have the custume free for ·7· years inward, and ·21· outward, the charge of the patent will be soone recovered, and ther is no fear of recovering [obtaining] it. But shuch things must work by degrees; men cannot hasten it as they would; werefore we (I write in the behalfe of all our partners here) *desire you to be ernest with Mr. Allerton to come,* and his wife to spare him this one year more, to finish this great and waighty bussines, which we conceive will be much for your good, and I hope for your posteritie, and for many generations to come.

Thus much of this letter. It was dated the March 19, 1629.

By which it appears what progress was made herein, and in part what charge it was, and how left unfinished, and some reason of the same; but in truth (as was afterwards appre- hended) the meaine reason was Mr. Allerton's policie, to have an opportunitie to be sent over againe, for other regards; and for that end procured them thus to write. For it might then well enough have been finished, if not with that clause aboute the custumes, which was Mr. Allertons and Mr. Sherleys device, and not at all thought on by the colony here, nor much regarded, yet it might have been done without it, without all question, *having passed the kings hand*; nay it was conceived it might then have beene done with it, if he had pleased; but covetousnes never brings ought home, as the proverb is, for this oppertunytie being lost, it was never accomplished, but a great deale of money veainly and lavishly cast away aboute it, as doth appear upon their accounts. But of this more in its place.

Mr. Alerton gave them great and just ofence in this (which I had omited and almost forgotten),—in bringing over this year, for base gaine, that unworthy man, and instrumente of mischeefe, *Morton*, who was sent home but the year before for his misdemenors. He not only brought him over, but to the towne (as it were to nose them), and lodged him at his owne house, and for a while used him as a scribe to doe his bussines, till he was caused to pack him away. So he wente to his old nest in the Massachusets, wher it was not long but by his miscariage he gave them just occation to lay hands on him; and he was by them againe sent prisoner into England, wher he lay a good while in Exeter Jeole. For besides his miscariage here, he was vehemently suspected for the murder of a man that had adventured moneys with him, when he came first into New-England. And a warrente was sente from the Lord Cheefe Justice to apprehend him, by vertue whereof he was by the Governor of the Massachusets sent into England; and for other his misdemenors amongst them, they demolisht his house, that it might be no longer a roost for shuch unclaine birds to nestle

in. Yet he got free againe, and write an infamouse and scurillous booke against many godly and cheefe men of the cuntrie;
full of lyes and slanders, and fraight with profane callumnies
against their names and persons, and the ways of God. After
sundry years, when the warrs were hott in England, he came
againe into the cuntrie, and was imprisoned at Boston for this
booke and other things, being grown old in wickednes.

Concerning the rest of Mr. Allertons instructions, in which
they strictly injoyned him not to exceed above that 50*li.* in the
goods before mentioned, not to bring any but trading commodities, he followed them not at all, but did the quite contrarie; bringing over many other sorts of retaile goods, selling
what he could by the way on his owne accounte, and delivering
the rest, which he said to be theirs, into the store; and for trading goods brought but litle in comparison; excusing the matter,
they *had laid out much aboute the Laiden people, and patent,*
etc. And for other goods, they had much of them of ther owne
dealings, without present disbursemente, and to like effect.
And as for passing his bounds and instructions, he laid it on
Mr. Sherley, etc., who, he said, they might see his mind in his
leters; also *that they had sett out Ashley at great charg;* but *next
year they should have what trading goods they would send for,* if
things were now well setled, etc. And thus were they put off;
indeed Mr. *Sherley* write things tending this way, but it is like
he was overruled by Mr. Allerton, and harkened more to him
then to their letters from hence.

Thus he *further writes in the former leter.*

I see what you write in your leters concerning the overcomming
and paying of our debts, which I confess are great, and had need be
carfully looked unto; yet no doubt but we, joyning in love, may soone
over-come them; but we must follow it roundly and to purpose, for
if we pedle out the time of our trade, others will step in and nose us.
But we know that you have that aquaintance and experience in the
countrie, as none have the like; wherfore, freinds and partners, be no
way discouraged with the greatnes of the debt, etc., but let us not
fullfill the proverbe, to bestow 12*d.* on a purse, and put 6*d.* in it; but as
you and we have been at great charg, and undergone much for setling
you ther, and to gaine experience, so as God shall enable us, let us
make use of it. And think not with 50*li.* pound a yeare sent you over,
to rayse shuch means as to pay our debts. We see a possibillitie of good

if you be well supplied, and fully furnished; and cheefly if you lovingly agree. *I know I write to godly and wise men*, shuch as have lerned to bear one an others infirmities, and rejoyce at any ones prosperities; and if I were able I would press this more, because it is hoped by some of your enimies, that you will fall out one with another, and so over throw *your hopfull bussines.* Nay, I have heard it crediblie reported, that some have said, that till you be disjoynted by discontents and fractions amongst your sellves, it bootes not any to goe over, in hope of getting or doing good in those parts. But we hope beter things of you, and that you will not only bear one with another, but banish shuch thoughts, and not suffer them to lodg in your brests. God grant you may disappointe the hopes of your foes, and procure the hartie desire of your selves and friends in this perticuler.

By this it appears that ther was a kind of concurrance betweene Mr. Allerton and them in these things, and that they gave more regard to his way and course in these things, then to the advise from hence; which made him bould to presume above his instructions, and to rune on in the course he did, to ther greater hurt after wards, as will appear. These things did much trouble them hear, but they well knew not how to help it, being loath to make any breach or contention hear aboute; being so premonished as before in the leter above recited. An other more secrete cause was herewith concurrente; Mr. Allerton had maried the daughter of *their Reverend Elder, Mr. Brewster (a man beloved and honoured amongst them, and who tooke great paines in teaching and dispenceing the word of God unto them)*, whom they were loath to greeve or any way offend, so as they bore with much in that respecte. And with all Mr. Allerton carried so faire with him, and procured shuch leters from Mr. Sherley to him, with shuch applause of Mr. Allertons wisdom, care, and faithfullnes, in the bussines; and as things stood none were so fitte to send aboute them as he; and if any should suggest other wise, it was reather out of envie, or some other sinister respecte then other wise. Besides, though private gaine, I doe perswade my selfe, was some cause to lead Mr. Allerton aside in these beginings, yet I thinke, or at least charitie caries me to hope, that he intended to deale faithfully with them in the maine, and had shuch an opinion of his owne abillitie, and some experience of the benefite that he had made in this singuler way, as he conceived he might both raise him selfe an estate, and allso be a means to bring in shuch profite to Mr. Sherley, (and it may be the rest,) as might be as lickly to bring in their moneys againe with advantage, and it may be sooner then from the generall way; or at least it was looked upon by some of them to be a good help ther unto; and that neither he nor any other did intend to charge the generall accounte with any thing that rane in perticuler; or that Mr. Sherley or any other did purposs but that the generall should be first and fully supplyed. I say charitie makes me thus conceive; though things fell out other wise, and they missed of their aimes, and the generall suffered abundantly hereby, as will afterwards apear.

Togeither herewith sorted an other bussines contrived by Mr. Allerton and them ther, without any knowledg of the partners, and so farr proceeded in as they were constrained to allow therof, and joyne in the same, though they had no great liking of it, but feared what might be the evente of the same. I shall relate it in a *further part of Mr. Sherley's leter* as followeth.

I am to aquainte you that we have thought good to joyne with one *Edward Ashley* (a man I thinke that some of you know); but it is only of *that place wherof he hath a patente in Mr. Beauchamps name*; and to that end have furnished him with large provissions, etc. Now if you please to be partners with us in this, we are willing you shall; for after we heard how forward Bristoll men (and as I hear some able men of his owne kindrid) have been to stock and supply him, hoping of profite, we thought it fitter for us to lay hould of such an opportunitie, and to keep a kind of running plantation, then others who have not borne the burthen of setling a plantation, as we have done. And he, on the other side, like an understanding *yonge man*, thought it better to joyne with those that had means by a plantation to supply and back him ther, rather then strangers, that looke but only after profite. Now it is not knowne that you are partners with him; but only we ·4·, Mr. *Andrews*, Mr. *Beachamp*, my *selfe*, and Mr. *Hatherley*, who *desired to have the patente*, in consideration of our great loss we have allready sustained in setling the first plantation ther; so we *agreed togeather to take it in our names*. And now, as I said before, if you please to joyne with us, we are willing you should. Mr. Allerton had no power from you to make this new contracte, neither was he willing to doe any thing therin without your consente and approbation. Mr. *William Peirce* is joyned with us in this, for we thought it very conveniente, *because of landing Ashley* and his goods ther, if God please; and he *will bend his course accordingly.* He hath *a new boate* with him, and *boards to make another*, with ·4· or ·5· lustie fellowes, wherof one is a carpenter. Now in the case you are not willing in this perticuler to joyne with us, fearing the charge and doubting the success, yet thus much we intreate of you, to afford him all the help you can, either by men, commodities, or boats; yet not but that we will pay you for any thing he hath. And we desire you to keep the accounts apart, though you joyne with us; becase ther is, as you see, other partners in this then the other; so, for all mens wages, boats-hire, or comodities, which we shall have of you, make him debtore for it; and what you shall have of him, make the plantation or your selves debtors for it to him, and so ther will need no mingling of the accounts.

And now, loving freinds and partners, if you joyne in Ashles patent and bussines, though we have laid out the money and taken up much to stock this bussines and the other, yet I thinke it conscionable and reasonable that you should beare your shares and proportion of the stock, if not by present money, yet by securing us for so much as it shall come too; for it is not barly the interest that is to be alowed and considered of, but allso the adventure; though I hope in God, by his blessing and your honest indeavors, it may soon be payed; yet the years that this partnership holds is not long, nor many; let all therfore lay it to harte, and make the best use of the time that possiblie we cann, and let every man put too his shoulder, and the burthen will be the lighter. I know you are so honest and conscionable men, as you will consider hereof, and returne shuch an answer as may give good satisfaction. Ther is none of us that would venture as we have done, were it not to strengthen and setle you more then our owne perticuler profite.

Ther is no liclyhood of doing any good in buying the debte for the purchas. I know some will not abate the interest, and therfore let it rune its course; they are to be paied yearly, and so I hope they shall, according to agreemente. The Lord grante that our loves and affections may still be united, and knit togeither; and so we rest your ever loving freinds,

JAMES SHERLEY.
TIMOTHY HATHERLEY.

Bristoll, March 19. 1629

This mater of the buying the debts of the purchass was parte of Mr. Allertons instructions, and in many of them it might have been done to good profite for ready pay (as some were); but Mr. Sherley had no mind to it. But this bussines aboute Ashley did not a litle trouble them; for though he had wite and abillitie enough to menage the bussines, yet some of them knew him to be a very profane yonge man; and he had for some time lived amonge the Indeans as a savage, and wente naked amongst them, and used their maners (in which time he got their language), so they feared he might still rune into evill courses (though he promised better), and God would not prosper his ways. *As soone as he was landed at the place intended, caled Penobscote, some ·4· score leagues from this place, he write (and afterwards came)* for to desire *to be supplyed with Wampampeake, corne* AGAINST WINTER, and other things. They considered these were of their cheefe commodities, and would be continually needed by him, and it would much prejudice their owne trade at Kenebeck if they did not joyne with him in the ordering of things, if thus they should supply him; and on the other hand, if they refused to joyne with him, and allso to afford any supply unto him, they should greatly offend their above named friends, and might hapily lose them hereby; and he and Mr. Allerton, laying their craftie wits togither, might gett supplies of these things els wher; besides, they considered that if they joyned not in the bussines, they knew Mr. Allerton would be with them in it, and so would swime, as it were, betweene both, to the prejudice of boath, but of them selves espetially. For they had reason to thinke this bussines was cheefly of his contriving, and Ashley was a man fitte for his turne and dealings. So they, to prevente a worse mischeefe, resolved to joyne in the bussines, and gave him supplies in what they could, and overlooked his procceedings as well as they could; the which they did the better, by joyning an honest yonge man,* that came from Leyden, with him as his fellow (in some sorte), and not merely as a servante. Which yonge man being discreete, and one whom they could trust, they so instructed as keept Ashley in some good mesure within bounds. And so they *returned their answer to their freinds in England, that they accepted of their motion,* and *joyned with them in Ashleys bussines;* and yet withall tould them what their fears were concerning him.

But when they came to have full notice of all the goods brought them that year, they saw they fell very short of trading

---

*Thomas Willett.

goods, and Ashley farr better suppleyed then them selves; so as they were *forced to buy of the fisher men* to furnish them selves, *yea*, and cottens and carseys and other shuch like cloath (for want of trading cloath) *of Mr. Allerton him selfe*, and so to put away a great parte of their beaver, at under rate, in the countrie, which they should have sente home, to help to discharge their great ingagementes; which was to their great vexation; but Mr. Allerton prayed them to be contente, and *the nexte yere they* might have what they would write for. And *their ingagmentes of this year* were great indeed when they came to know them, (which was not wholy *till ·2· years after*); and that which made them the more, Mr. *Allerton had taken up some large summes at Bristoll at ·50li· per cent. againe*, which he excused, that he was forcte too it, because other wise he could *at the spring of year* get no goods transported, shuch were their envie against their trade. But wheither this was any more then an excuse, some of them doubted; but however, the burden did lye on their backs, and they must bear it, as they did many heavie loads more in the end.

This paying of 50*li* per cent. and dificulty of having their goods transported by the fishing ships at the first of the year, (as was beleeved,) which was the cheefe season for trade, put them upon another projecte. Mr. *Allerton, after the fishing season was over*, light of a bargan of salte, at a good fishing place, and bought it; which came to aboute 113*li*; and shortly after he might have had 30*li*. cleare profite for it, without any more trouble aboute it. But Mr. *Winslow coming that way from Kenebeck*, and some other of ther partners with him in the barke, they mett with Mr. Allerton, and falling into discourse with him, they stayed him from selling the salte; and resolved, if it might please the rest, to keep it for them selves, and to *hire a ship in the west cuntrie to come on fishing for them, on shares, according to the coustome*; and seeing she might have her salte here ready, and a stage ready builte and fitted wher the salt lay safely landed and housed. In stead of bringing salte, they might stowe her full of trading goods, as bread, pease, cloth, etc., and so they might have a full supply of goods without paing fraight, and in due season, which might turne greatly to their advantage. Coming home, this was propounded, and considered on, and approved by all but *the Governor, who had no mind* *to it, seeing they had allway lost by fishing*; but the rest were so ernest, as thinkeing that they might gaine well by the fishing in this way; and if they should but save, yea, or lose some thing by it, the other benefite would be advantage inough; so, seeing their ernestnes, he gave way, and it was referd to their freinds in England to alow, or disalow it. Of which more in its place.

Upon the consideration of the bussines about *the patent*, and in what state it was left, as is before remembred, and Mr. *Sherleys ernest pressing to have Mr. Allerton to come over againe to finish it*, and perfect the accounts, etc., it was *concluded to send him over this year againe*; though it was with some fear and jeolocie; yet he gave them fair words and promises of well performing all their bussinesses according to their directions, and to mend his former errors. So he was accordingly sent with full instructions for all things, *with large letters to Mr. Sherley and the rest, both aboute Ashleys bussines and their owne suply with trading comodities, and how much it did concerne them to be furnished therwith, and what they had suffered for wante therof; and of what litle use other goods were in comparison therof*; and so likewise aboute *this fishing ship, to be thus hired*, and *fraught with trading goods*, which might *both supply them and Ashley*, and *the benefite therof*; which was left to their consideration to hire and set her out, or not; *but in no case not to send any, excepte she was thus fraighte with trading goods.* But what these things came too will appere in the next years passages.

I had like to have omited an other passage that fell out the *begining of this year*. Ther was one Mr. *Ralfe Smith*, and his wife and familie, that came over into the Bay of the Massachusets, and sojourned at presente with some stragling people that lived at Natascoe; here being a boat of this place putting in ther on some occasion, he ernestly desired that they would give him and his, passage for Plimoth, and some shuch things as they could well carrie; having before heard that ther was liklyhood he might procure house rome for some time, till he should resolve to setle ther, if he might, or els-wher as God should disposs; for he was werie of being in that uncoth place, and in a poore house that would neither keep him nor his goods drie. So, seeing him to be a grave man, and understood he had been a minister, though they had no order for any shuch thing, yet they presumed and brought him. He was here accordingly kindly entertained and housed, and had the rest of his goods and servants sente for, and exercised his gifts amongst them, and afterwards was chosen into the ministrie, and so remained for sundrie years.

It was before noted that sundry of those that came from *Leyden*, came over in the ships that came to *Salem*, wher Mr. Endecott had cheefe command; and by infection that grue amonge the passengers at sea, it spread also among them a shore, of which many dyed, some of the scurvie, other of an infectious feavore, which continued some time amongst them (though our people, through Gods goodnes, escaped it). Upon which occasion he write hither for some help, understanding here was one that had some skill that way, and had cured diverse of the scurvie, and others of other diseases, by letting blood, and other means. Upon which his request the Governor hear sent him unto them, and also write to him, from whom he received an answere; the which, because it is breefe, and shows the begining of their aquaintance, and closing in the truth and ways of God, I thought it not unmeete, nor without use, hear to inserte it; and an other showing the begining of their fellowship and church estate ther.

Being as followeth.

RIGHT WORTHY SIR:

It is a thing not usuall, that servants to one master and of the same houshold should be strangers; I assure you I desire it not, nay, to speake more plainly, I cannot be so to you. Gods people are all marked with one and the same marke, and sealed with one and the same seale, and have for the maine, one and the same harte, guided by one and the same spirite of truth; and wher this is, ther can be no discorde, nay, here must needs be sweete harmonie. And the same request (with you) I make unto the Lord, that we may, as Christian breethren, be united by a heavenly and unfained love; bending all our harts and forces in furthering a worke beyond our strength, with reverence and fear, fastening our eyes allways on him that only is able to directe and prosper all our ways. I acknowledge my selfe much bound to you for your kind love and care in sending Mr. Fuller among us, and rejoyce much that I am by him satisfied touching your judgments of the outward forme of Gods worshipe. It is, as farr as I can yet gather, no other then is warrented by the evidence of truth, and the same which I have proffessed and maintained ever since the Lord in mercie revealed him selfe unto me; being farr from the commone reporte that hath been spread of you touching that perticuler. But Gods children must not looke for less here below, and it is the great mercie of God, that he strengthens them to goe through with it. I shall not neede at this time to be tedious unto you, for, God willing, I purpose to see your face shortly. In the mean time, I humbly take my leave of you, commiting you to the Lords blessed protection, and rest,

> Your assured loving friend,
> JO: ENDECOTT.

Naumkeak, May 11. Anno. 1629.

This second leter sheweth ther proceedings in their church affaires at Salem, which was the ·2· church erected in these parts; and afterwards the Lord established many more in sundrie places.

SIR: I make bould to trouble you with a few lines, for to certifie you how it hath pleased God to deale with us, since you heard from us. How, notwithstanding all opposition that hath been hear, and els wher, it hath pleased God to lay a foundation, the which I hope is agreeable to his word in every thing. The ·20· of July, it pleased the Lord to move the hart of our Governor to set it aparte for a sollemne day of humilliation for the choyce of a pastor and teacher. The former parte of the day being spente in praier and teaching, the later parte aboute the election, which was after this maner. The persons thought on (who had been ministers in England) were demanded concerning their callings; they acknowledged ther was a towfould calling, the one an inward calling, when the Lord moved the harte of a man to take that calling upon him, and fitted him with guiftes for the same; the second was an outward calling, which was from the people, when a company of beleevers are joyned togither in covenante, to walke togither in all the ways of God, and every member (being men) are to have a free voyce in the choyce of their officers, etc. Now, we being perswaded that these ·2· men were so quallified, as the apostle speaks to Timothy, wher he saith, A bishop must be blamles, sober, apte to teach, etc., I think I may say, as the eunuch said unto Philip, What should let from being baptised, seeing ther was water, and he beleeved? So these ·2· servants of God, clearing all things by their answers, (and being thus fitted,) we saw noe reason but we might freely give our voyces for their election, after this triall. So Mr. Skelton was chosen pastor, and Mr. Higginson to be teacher; and they accepting the choyce, Mr. Higginson, with ·3· or ·4· of the gravest members of the church, laid their hands on Mr. Skellton, using prayer therwith. This being done, ther was imposission of hands on Mr. Higginson also. And since that time, Thursday (being, as I take it, the ·6· of August) is appoynted for another day of humilliation, for the choyce of elders and deacons, and ordaining of them.

And now, good Sir, I hope that you and the rest of Gods people (who are aquainted with the ways of God) with you, will say that hear was a right foundation layed, and that these ·2· blessed servants of the Lord came in at the dore, and not at the window. Thus I have made bould to trouble you with these few lines, desiring you to remember us, etc. And so rest,

At your service in what I may,
CHARLES GOTT.

Salem, July 30. 1629.

ANNO DOM: ·1630·

ASHLEY, being well supplyed, had quickly gathered a good parcell of beaver, and like a crafty pate he sent it all home, and would not pay for the goods he had had of the plantation hear, but lett them stand still on the score, and tooke up still more. Now though they well enough knew his aime, yet they let him goe one, and write of it into England. But partly the beaver they received, and sould, (of which they weer sencible,) and partly by Mr. Allertons extolling of him, they cast more how to supplie him then the plantation, and something to upbraid them, with it. They were forct to buy him *a barke* allso, and to furnish her with a master and men, to transporte his corne and provissions (of which he put of much); for the Indeans of those parts have no corne growing, and *at harvest*, after corne is ready, the weather grows foule, and the seas dangerous, so as he could doe litle good with his shallope for that purposs.

They looked ernestly for a timely supply *this spring*, by the *fishing ship* which they expected, and had been at charg to keepe *a stage* for her; but none came, nor any supply heard of for them. *At length they heard sume supply was sent to Ashley by a fishing ship*, at which they something marvelled, and the more that they had no letters either from Mr. Allerton or Mr. Sherley; so they went on in their bussines as well as they could. *At last they heard of Mr. Peirce his arivall in the Bay of the Massachusetts*, who brought passengers and goods thither. They presently sent a shallop, conceiving they should have some thing by him. But he tould them he had none; and *a ship was sett out on fishing*, but after ·11· weekes beating at sea, she mett with shuch foull weather as she was forcte back againe for England, and, the season being over, gave off the vioage. Neither did he hear of much goods in her for the plantation, or that she did belong to them, for he had heard some thing from Mr. Allerton tending that way. But Mr. *Allerton had bought another ship*, and *was to come in her*, and was *to fish for bass to the eastward*, and to bring goods, etc. These things did much trouble them, and half astonish them. *Mr. Winslow haveing been to the eastward*, brought nuese of the like things, with some more perticulers, and *that it was like Mr. Allerton would be late before he came*. At length they, *having an oppertunitie*, resolved to *send Mr. Winslow*, with what beaver they had ready, into England, *to see how the squares wente*, being very jeolouse of these things, and Mr. Allertons courses; and writ shuch leters, and gave him shuch instructions, as they thought meet; and if he found things not well, *to discharge Mr. Allerton for being any longer agent* for them, or to deal any more in the bussines, and *to see how the accounts stood*, etc.

Aboute the *midle of sommer* arrives Mr. *Hatherley in the Bay of the Massachusetts*, (being one of the partners,) and came over *in the same ship that was set out on fhishing* (called *the Frendship*). They presently sent to him, making no question but now they had goods come, and should know how all things stood. But they found the former news true, how this ship had been so long at sea, and spente and spoyled her provissions, and overthrowne the viage. And he being sent over by the rest of the partners, to see how things wente hear, *being at Bristoll with Mr. Allerton, in the shipe bought* (called *the White-Angell*), *ready to set sayle*, over night came a messenger from Bastable to Mr. Allerton, and tould him of the returne of the ship, and what had befallen. And he not knowing what to doe, having a great chareg under hand, the ship lying at his rates, and now ready to set sayle, *got him to goe and discharg the ship*, and take order for the goods. To be short, they found Mr. Hatherley some thing reserved, and troubled in him selfe, (Mr. Allerton not being ther,) not knowing how to dispose of the goods till he came; but he *heard he was arived with the other ship to the eastward*, and expected his coming. But he tould them ther was not much for them in this ship, only ·2· packs of Bastable ruggs, and ·2· hoggsheads of meatheglin, drawne out in wooden flackets (but when these flackets came to be received, ther was left but ·6· gallons of the ·2· hogsheads, it being drunke up under the name leackage, and so lost). But *the ship was filled with goods for sundrie gentle men, and others, that were come to plant in the Massachusetts*, for which they payed fraight by the tunn. And this was all the satisfaction they could have at presente, so they brought this small parcell of goods and *returned with this nues, and a letter as obscure*; which made them much to marvell therat. The letter was as followeth.

GENTLE-MEN, PARTNERS, AND LOVING FRIENDS, etc.

Breefly thus: wee have this year set forth a *fishing ship*, and a *trading ship, which later we have bought*; and so have disbursed a great deale of money, as may and will appeare by the accounts. And because *this ship* (*called the White Angell*) is to acte ·2· parts, (as I may say,) *fishing for bass*, and *trading*; and that while Mr. Allerton was imployed aboute the trading, the fishing might suffer by carlesnes or neglecte of the sailors, *we have entreated your and our loving friend, Mr. Hatherley, to goe over with him*, knowing he will be a comforte to Mr. *Allerton*, a joye to you, to see a carfull and loving friend, and a great stay to the bussines; and so great contente to us, that if it should please God the one should faile, (as God forbid,) yet the other would keepe both recconings, and things uprighte. For we are now out great sumes of money, as they will acquainte you withall, etc. When we were out but ·4· or ·5· hundred pounds a peece, we looked not much after it, but left it to you, and *your agente, (who, without flaterie, deserveth infinite thanks and comendations, both of you and us, for his pains*, etc.); but now we are out double, nay, treble a peece, some of us, etc.; which makes us both write, and send over our friend, Mr. Hatherley, whom we pray you to entertaine kindly, of which we doubte not of. The main end of sending him is to see the state and accountes of all the bussines, of all which we pray you informe him fully, though the ship and bussines wayte for it and him. For we should take it very unkindly that we should intreat him to take shuch a journey, and that, when it pleaseth God he returnes, he could not give us contente and satisfaction in this perticuler, through defaulte of any of you. But we hope you will so order bussines, as neither he nor we shall have cause to complaine, but to doe as we ever have done, thinke well of you all, etc. I will not promise, but shall indeaour and hope to effecte the full desire and grant of your patente, and that ere it be longe. I would not have you take any thing unkindly. I have not write out of jeoloucie of any unjuste dealing. Be you all kindly saluted in the Lord, so I rest,

> Yours in what I may,
> JAMES SHERLEY.

March 25, 1630.

It needs not be thought strange, that these things should amase and trouble them; first, that *this fishing ship* should be set out, and *fraight with other mens goods, and scarce any of theirs*; seeing their maine end was (as is before remembred) to bring them a full supply, and their speatiall order not to sett out any excepte this was done. And now a ship to come on their accounte, clear contrary to their both end and order, was a misterie they could not understand; and so much the worse, seeing she had shuch ill success as *to lose both her vioage and provissions.* The ·2· thing, that *another ship should be bought* and *sente out on new designes,* a thing not so much as once thought on by any here, much less, not a word intimated or spoaken of by any here, either by word or leter, neither could they imagine why this should be. *Bass fishing was never lookt at by them, but as soone as ever they heard on it, they looked at it as a vaine thing, that would certainly turne to loss.* And for Mr. Allerton to follow any trade for them, it was never in their thoughts. And 3ly, that their friends should complaine of disbursements, and yet rune into shuch great things, and charge of shiping and new projects of their owne heads, not only without, but against, all order and advice, was to them very strange. And 4ly, that all these matters of so great charg and imployments should be thus wrapped up in a breefe and obscure letter, they knew not what to make of it. But *amids all their doubts they must have patience till Mr. Allerton and Mr. Hatherley should come.* In the mean time *Mr. Winslow was gone for England*; and others of them were forst to folow their imployments with the best means they had, till they could hear of better.

At length Mr. Hatherley and Mr. Allerton came unto them, (*after they had delivered their goods,*) and finding them strucken with some sadnes aboute these things, Mr. *Allerton* tould them that the ship *Whit-Angele* did not belong to them, nor their accounte, neither neede they have any thing to doe with her,

excepte they would. And Mr. *Hatherley* confirmed the same,
and said that they would have had him to have had a parte,
but he refused; but he made question whether they would not
turne her upon the generall accounte, if ther came loss (as he
now saw was like), seeing Mr. *Allerton* laid downe this course,
and put them on this projecte. But for *the fishing ship*, he
tould them they need not be so much troubled, for he had her
accounts here, and showed them that her *first setting* out came
not much to exceed 600*li.* as they might see by the accounte,
which he showed them; and for *this later viage*, it would arrise
to profite by the *fraight* of the goods, and the salle of some
katle which he shiped and had allready sould, and was to be
paid for partly here and partly by bills into England, so as they
should not have this put on their acounte at all, except they
would. And for *the former*, he had sould so much goods out
of her in England, and imployed the money in *this ·2· viage*, as
it, togeither with shuch goods and implements as *Mr. Allerton
must need aboute his fishing*, would rise to a good parte of the
money; for he must have the sallt and nets, allso spikes, nails,
etc.; all which would rise to nere 400*li.*; so, with the bearing
of their parts of the rest of the loses (which would not be much
above 200*li.*), they would clear them of this whole accounte.
Of which motion they were glad, not being willing to have any
accounts lye upon them; but aboute *their trade*, which made
them willing to harken therunto, and demand of Mr. *Hatherley*
how he could make these good, if they should agree their unto,
he tould them *he was sent over as their agente* and had this order
from them, that whatsoever *he* and Mr. *Allerton* did togeather,
they would stand to it; but they would not alow of what Mr.
Allerton did alone, except they liked it; but if he did it alone,
they would not gaine say it. Upon which they sould to *him* and
Mr. *Allerton* all the rest of the goods, and gave them present
possession of them; and a *writing* was made, and confirmed
under both Mr. *Hatherleys* and Mr. *Allertons* hands, to the
effecte afforesaide. And Mr. *Allertone*, being best aquainted
with the people, sould away presenly all shuch goods as he had
no need of for the fishing, as ·9· shallop sails, made of good
new canvas, and the roads for them being all new, with sundry
shuch usefull goods, for ready beaver, by Mr. *Hatherleys* allowance. And thus they thought they had well provided for them

selves. Yet they rebuked Mr. Allerton very much for runing into these courses, fearing the success of them.

Mr. *Allerton* and Mr. *Hatherley* brought to *the towne with them* (after he had sould what he could abroad) a great quantity of other goods besides trading comodities; as linen cloath, bedticks, stockings, tape, pins, ruggs, etc., and tould them they were to have them, if they would; but they tould Mr. *Allerton* that they had forbid him before for bringing any shuch on their accounte; it would hinder their trade and returnes. But *he* and Mr. *Hatherley* said, if they would not have them, they would sell them, them selves, and take corne for what they could not otherwise sell. They tould them they might, if they had order for it. The goods of one sorte and other came to upward of 500*li*.

After these things, Mr. Allerton wente to the ship aboute his bass fishing; and Mr. Hatherley, (according to his order,) after he tooke knowledg how things stood at the plantation, (of all which they informed him fully,) he then *desired a boate of them to goe and visite the trading houeses, both Kenebeck, and Ashley at Penobscote*; for so they in England had injoyned him. They accordingly furnished him with a boate and men for the viage, and aquainted him plainly and thorowly with all things; by which he had good contente and satisfaction, and saw plainly that Mr. *Allerton* plaid his owne game, and rane a course not only to the great wrong and detrimente of the plantation, who imployed and trusted him, but abused them in England also, in possessing them with prejudice against the plantation; as that they would never be able to repaye their moneys (in regard of their great charge), but if they would follow his advice and projects, *he* and *Ashley* (being well supplyed) would quickly bring in their moneys with good advantage. Mr. *Hatherley* disclosed also a further projecte aboute the setting out of this ship, the *White angell*; how, she being well fitted with good ordnance, and known to have made a great fight at sea (when she belonged to Bristoll) and caried away the victory, they had agreed (by Mr. *Allerton's* means) that, after she had brought a fraight of goods here into the countrie, and fraight her selfe with fish, she should goe from hence to *Port of porte*, and ther be sould, both ship, goods, and ordenance; and had, for this end, had speech with a factore of those parts, before hand, to whom she should have been consigned. But this was prevented at this time, (after it was known,) partly by the contrary advice given by their freinds hear to Mr. *Allerton* and Mr. *Hatherley*, showing how it might insnare their friends in England, (being men of estate,) if it should come to be knowne; and for the plantation, they did and would disalow it, and protest against it; and partly by their bad viage, for they *both came too late to doe any good for fishing*, and allso had *shuch a wicked and drunken company* as neither Mr. *Allerton* nor any else could rule; as Mr. *Hatherley*, to his great greefe and shame, saw, and beheld, and all others that came nere them.

Ashley likwise was taken in a trape, (before Mr. Hatherley returned), for trading powder and shote with the Indeans; and was ceased upon by some in authoritie, who allso would have confiscated above a thousand weight of beaver; but the goods were freed, for the Governor here made it appere, by a bond under Ashleys hand, wherin he was bound to them in 500*li.* not to trade any munition with the Indeans, or other wise to abuse him selfe; it was allso manifest against him that he had commited uncleannes with Indean women, (things that they feared at his first implyment, which made them take this strict course with him in the begining); so, to be shorte, they gott their goods freed, but he was sent home prisoner. And that I may make an end concerning him, after some time of imprisonmente in the Fleet, by the means of friends he was set at liberty, and intended to come over againe, but the Lord prevented it; for he had a motion made to him, by some marchants, to goe into Russia, because he had shuch good skill in the beaver trade, the which he accepted of, and in his returne home was cast away at sea; this was his end.

Mr. *Hatherley*, fully understanding the state of all things, had good satisfaction, and could well informe them how all things stood between Mr. *Allerton* and the plantation. Yea, he found that Mr. *Allerton* had gott within him, and got all the goods into his owne hands, for which Mr. *Hatherley* stood joyntly ingaged to them hear, aboute the ship-*Freindship*, as also most of the fraigte money, besides some of his owne perticuler estate; about which more will appear here after. So *he returned into England, and they sente a good quantity of beaver with him to the rest of the partners*; so both he and it was very wellcome unto them.

Mr. Allerton followed his affaires, and returned with his White Angell, being no more imployed by the plantation; but these bussinesses were not ended till many years after, nor well understood of a longe time, but foulded up in obscuritie, and kepte in the clouds, to the great loss and vexation of the plantation, who in the end were (for peace sake) forced to bear the unjust burthen of them, to their allmost undoing, as will appear, if God give life to finish this history.

They sent their letters also by Mr. Hatherley to the partners ther, to show them how Mr. Hatherley and Mr. Allerton had discharged them of the Friendships accounte, and that they boath affirmed that the White-Angell did not at all belong to them; and therfore desired that their accounte might not be charged therwith. Also they write to Mr. Winslow, their agente, that he in like maner should (in their names) protest against it, if any shuch thing should be intended, for they would never yeeld to the same. As allso to signifie to them that they renounsed Mr. Allerton wholy, for being their agente, or to have any thing to doe in any of their bussines.

This year John Billinton the elder (one that came over with the first) was arrained, and both by grand and petie jurie found guilty of willfull murder, by plaine and notorious evidence. And was for the same accordingly executed. This, as it was the first execution amongst them, so was it a mater of great sadnes unto them. They used all due means about his triall, and tooke the advice of Mr. Winthrop and other the ablest gentle-men in the Bay of the Massachusets, that were then new-ly come over, who concured with them that he ought to dye, and the land to be purged from blood. He and some of his had been often punished for miscariages before, being one of the profanest families amongst them. They came from London, and I know not by what freinds shufled into their company. His facte, was, that he way-laid a yong-man, one John New-comin, (about a former quarell,) and shote him with a gune, wherof he dyed.

Having by a providence a letter or to that came to my hands concerning the proceedings of their Reverend freinds in the Bay of the Massachusets, who were latly come over, I thought it not amise here to inserte them, (so farr as is pertenente, and may be usefull for after times,) before I conclude this year.

SIR: Being at Salem the 25 of July, being the saboath, after the evening exercise, Mr. Johnson received a letter from the Governor, Mr. John Winthrop, manifesting the hand of God to be upon them, and against them, at Charles-towne, in visiting them with sicknes, and taking diverse from amongst them, not sparing the righteous, but partaking with the wicked in these bodily judgments. It was therfore by his desire taken into the Godly consideration of the best hear, what was to be done to pacifie the Lords wrath, etc. When it was concluded, that the Lord was to be sought in righteousnes; and to that end, the ·6· day (being Friday) of this present weeke, is set aparte, that they may humble them selves before God, and seeke him in his ordenances; and that then also shuch godly persons that are amongst them, and known each to other, may publickly, at the end of their exercise, make known their Godly desire, and practise the same, viz. solemnly to enter into covenante with the Lord to walke in his ways. And since they are so disposed of in their outward estates, as to live in three distinct places, each having men of abilitie amongst them, ther to observe the day, and become ·3· distincte bodys; not then intending rashly to proceed to the choyce of officers, or the admitting of any other to their societie then a few, to witte, shuch as are well knowne unto them; promising after to receive in shuch by confession of faith, as shall appeare to be fitly qualified for that estate. They doe ernestly entreate that the church of Plimoth would set apparte the same day, for the same ends, beseeching the Lord, as to withdraw his hand of correction from them, so also to establish and direct them in his wayes. And though the time be shorte, we pray you be provocked to this godly worke, seing the causes are so urgente; wherin God will be honoured, and they and we undoubtedly have sweete comforte. Be you all kindly saluted, etc.

Your brethren in Christ, etc.
Salem, July 26. 1630.

SIR, etc. The sadd news here is, that many are sicke, and many are dead; the Lord in mercie looke upon them. Some are here entered into church covenante, the first were ·4· namly, the Governor, Mr. John Winthrop, Mr. Johnson, Mr. Dudley, and Mr. Willson; since that ·5· more are joyned unto them, and others, it is like, will adde them selves to them dayly; the Lord increase them, both in number and in holines for his mercie sake. Here is a gentleman, one Mr. Cottington, (a Boston Man,) who tould me, that Mr. Cottons charge at

Hamton was, that they should take advise of them at Plimoth, and should doe nothing to offend them. Here are diverce honest Christians that are desirous to see us, some out of love which they bear to us, and the good perswasion they have of us; others to see whether we be so ill as they have heard of us. We have a name of holines, and love to God and his saincts; the Lord make us more and more answerable, and that it may be more then a name, or els it will doe us no good. Be you lovingly saluted, and all the rest of our friends. The Lord Jesus blese us, and the whole Israll of God. Amen.

Your loving brother, etc.

Charles-towne, Aug. 2. 1630.

Thus out of smalle beginings greater things have been produced by his hand that made all things of nothing, and gives being to all things that are; and as one small candle may light a thousand, so the light here kindled hath shone to many, yea in some sorte to our whole nation; let the glorious name of Jehova have all the praise.

ANNO DOM: ·1631·

A SHLEY being thus by the hand of God taken away, and Mr. *Allerton discharged of his imploymente for them*, their bussines began againe to rune in one chanell, and them selves better able to guide the same, Penobscote being wholy now at their disposing. And though Mr. *William* Peirce had a parte ther as is before noted, yet now, as things stood, he was glad to have his money repayed him, and stand out. Mr. *Winslow*, whom they had sent over, sent them over some supply as soone as he could; and afterwards when he came, which was something longe by reason of bussines, he brought a large supply of suitable goods with him, by which ther trading was well carried on. But by no means either he, or the letters they write, could take off Mr. *Sherley* and the rest from putting both the *Friendship* and *Whit-Angell* on the generall accounte; which caused continuall contention betweene them, as will more appeare.

I shall inserte a leter of Mr. *Winslow's* about these things, being as foloweth.

SIR: It fell out by Gods providence, that I received and brought *your leters per Mr. Allerton from Bristoll, to London*; and doe much feare what will be the event of things. Mr. *Allerton* intended to prepare the ship againe, to set forth upon *fishing*. Mr. *Sherley*, Mr. *Beachamp*, and Mr. *Andrews*, they renounce all perticulers, protesting but for us they would never have adventured one penie into those parts; Mr. *Hatherley* stands inclinable to either. And wheras *you write* that *he* and Mr. *Allerton* have taken the *Whit-Angell* upon them, for their partners here, they professe they neiver gave any shuch order, nor will make it good; if them selves will cleare the accounte and doe it, all shall be well. What the evente of these things will be, I know not. The Lord so directe and assiste us, as he may not be dishonoured by our divissions. I hear (per a freind) that I was much blamed for speaking *what I heard in the spring of the year*, concerning the buying and setting forth of *that ship*;* sure, if I should not have tould you what I heard so peremptorily reported (which report I offered now to prove at Bristoll), I should have been unworthy my imploymente. And concerning the *commission* so long since given to Mr. *Allerton*, the truth is, the thing we feared is come upon us; for Mr. *Sherley* and the rest have it, and will not deliver it, that being the ground of our agents credite to procure shuch great sumes. But I looke for bitter words, hard thoughts, and sower looks, from sundrie, as well for writing this, as reporting the former. I would I had a more thankfull imploymente; but I hope a good conscience shall make it comefortable, etc.

Thus farr he. Dated *November* 16. 1631.

The *comission* above said was given by them under their hand and seale, when Mr. *Allerton* was *first imployed* by them, and *redemanded of him in the year ·29· when they begane to suspecte his course*. He tould them it was amongst his papers, but he would seeke it out and give it them before he wente. But he being ready to goe, it was demanded againe. He said he could not find it, but it was amongst his papers, which he must take with him, and *he would send it by the boat from the eastward*; but ther it could not be had neither, but he would seeke it up at sea. But whether Mr. *Sherly* had it before or after, it is not certaine; but having it, he would not let it goe, but keeps it to this day. Wherfore, even amongst freinds, men had need be carfull whom they trust, and not lett things of this nature lye long unrecaled.

---

*This was about the selling the ship in Spaine.

*Some parts of Mr. Sherley's letters aboute these
things, in which the truth is best manifested.*

SIR: *Yours I have received by our loving friends, Mr. Allerton and
Mr. Hatherley,* who, blesed be God, *after a long and dangerous passage
with the ship Angell,* are safely come to Bristoll. Mr. *Hatherley is come
up,* but Mr. *Allerton I have not yet seen.* We thanke you, and *are very
glad you have disswaded him from his Spanish viage,* and that he did not
goe on in those designes he intended; for we did all uterly dislick of
that course, as allso of the *fishing* that the *Freindship* should have performed; for we wished him to sell the salte, and were unwilling to have
him undertake so much bussines, partly for the ill success we formerly
had in those affairs, and partly being loath to disburse so much money.
But he perswaded us this must be one way that must repay us, for the
plantation would be long in doing of it; ney, to my rememberance,
he doubted you could not be able, with the trade ther, to maintaine
your charge and pay us. And for this very cause he brought us on that
bussines with *Ed. Ashley,* for he was a stranger to us, etc.

For the *fishing ship,* we are sorie it proves so heavie, and will be
willing to bear our parts. What Mr. *Hatherley* and Mr. *Allerton* have
done, no doubt but them selves will make good; we gave them no
order to make any composition, to seperate you and us in this or any
other. And I thinke you have no cause to forsake us, for we put you
upon no new thing, but what your agent perswaded us to, and you
by your letters desired. If he exceede your order, I hope you will not
blame us, much less cast us of, when our moneys be layed out, etc.
But I fear neither you nor we have been well delt withall, for sure,
as you write, halfe 4000*li.*, nay, a quarter, in fitting comodities, and
in seasonable time, would have furnished you beter then you were.
And yet for all this, and much more I might write, *I dare not but
thinke him honest, and that his desire and intente was good;* but the
wisest may faile. Well, now that it hath pleased God to give us hope
of meeting, doubte not but we will all indeavore to perfecte these
accounts just and right, as soone as possibly we can. And I suppose
you sente over Mr. Winslow, and *we Mr. Hatherley,* to certifie each
other how the state of things stood. *We have received some contente
upon Mr. Hatherley's returne,* and I *hope you will receive good contente
upon Mr. Winslow's returne.* Now I should come to answer more
perticulerly your letter, but herin I shall be very breefe. The coming
of the *White Angele* on your accounte could not be more strang to
you, then the *buying of her* was to us; for you gave him commission*

---

*This commission is abused; he never had any for shuch end, as they well
knew, nether had they any to pay this money, nor would have paid a peny, if
they had not pleased for some other respecte.

that what he did you would stand too; we gave him none, and yet for his credite, and your sakes, payed what bills he charged on us, etc. For that I write she *was to acte tow parts, fishing and trade*; beleeve me, I never so much as thought of any perticuler trade, nor will side with any that doth, if I conceive it may wrong you; for I ever was against it, useing these words: They will eate up and destroy the generall.

Other things I omite as tedious, and not very pertenente. This was dated *November* 19. 1631.

They were too shorte in resting on Mr. *Hatherley's* honest word, for his order to discharge them from the *Friendship's* accounte, when he and Mr. *Allerton* made the bargane with them, and they delivered them the rest of the goods; and therby gave them oppertunitie also to receive all the fraight of boath viages, without seeing an order (to have shuch power) under their hands in writing, which they never doubted of, seeing he affirmed he had power; and they both knew his honestie, and that he was spetially imployed for their agente at this time. And he was as shorte in resting on a verball order from them; which was now denyed, when it came to a perticuler of loss; but he still affirmed the same. But they were both now taught how to deale in the world, espetially with marchants, in shuch cases. But in the end this light upon these here also, for Mr. *Allerton* had gott all into his owne hand, and Mr. *Hatherley* was not able to pay it, except they would have uterlie undon him, as the sequell will manifest.

In an other leter bearing date the ·24· *of this month*, being an answer to the generall leter, he hath these words:

For the *White Angell*, against which you write so ernestly, and say we thrust her upon you, contrary to the intente of the buyer, herin we say you forgett your selves, and doe us wrong. We will not take uppon us to devine what the thougts or intents of the buyer was, but what he spack we heard, and that we will affirme, and make good against any that oppose it; which, is that *unles shee were bought, and shuch a course taken, Ashley could not be supplyed*; and againe, *if he weer not supplyed, we could not be satisfied what we were out for you.* And further, *you were not able to doe it*; and he gave some reasons which we spare to relate, unless by your unreasonable refusall you will force us, and so hasten that fire which is a kindling too fast allready, etc.

Out of another of his, bearing date January 2. 1631

We purpose to keep the Freindship and the Whit Angell, for the last year viages, on the generall accounte, hoping togeither they will rather produse profite then loss, and breed less confution in our accounts, and less disturbance in our affections. As for the *White Angell,* though we layed out the money, and tooke bills of salle in our owne names, yet none of us had so much as a thought (I dare say) of devideing from you in any thing *this year,* because we would not have the world (I may say *Bristoll*) take notice of any breach betwixte Mr. *Allerton* and you, and he and us; and so disgrace him in his proceedings or in his intended viage. We have now let him the ship at 30*li.* per month, by charterpartie, and bound him in a bond of a 1000*li.* to performe covenants, and bring her to *London* (if God please). And what he brings in her for you, shall be marked with your marke, and bils of laden taken, and sent in *Mr. Winslows letter, who is this day riding to Bristoll about it.* So in this viage, we deale and are with him as strangers. He hath brought in ·3· books of acounts, one for the *company,* an other for *Ashley's* bussines, and the third for the *Whit-Angell* and *Freindship.* The books, or coppies, we purpose to send you, for you may discover the errours in them better than we. We can make it appear how much money he hath had of us, and you can charg him with all the beaver he hath had of you. The totall sume, as he hath put it, is 7103. 17. 1. Of this he hath expended, and given to Mr. *Vines* and others, aboute 543*li.* ode money, and then by your books you will find whether you had shuch, and so much goods, as he chargeth you with all; and this is all that I can say at presente concerning these accounts. He thought to dispatch them in a few howers, but he and *Straton* and *Fogge* were above a month aboute them; but *he could not stay till we had examined them, for losing his fishing viage, which I fear he hath allready done,* etc.

We blese God, who put both you and us in mind to send each to other, for verily had he rune on in that desperate and chargable course one year more, we had not been able to suport him; nay, both he and we must have lyen in the ditch, and sunck under the burthen, etc. *Had ther been an orderly course taken, and your bussines better managed, assuredly (by the blessing of God) you had been the ablest plantation that, as we think, or know, hath been undertaken by English-men, etc.*

Thus farr of these letters of Mr. Sherley.

A few observations from the former letters, and then I shall set downe the simple truth of the things (thus in controversie betweene them), at least as farr as by any good evidence it could be made to appeare; and so laboure to be breefe in so tedious and intricate a bussines, which hunge in expostulation betweene them many years before the same was ended. That though ther will be often occasion to touch these things about other passages, yet I shall not neede to be large therin; doing it hear once for all.

I. First, it seemes to appere clearly that *Ashley's* bussines, and the buying of *this ship*, and the courses framed ther upon, were first contrived and proposed by Mr. *Allerton*, as also that the pleaes and pretences which he made, of the inabilitie of the plantation to re-paye their moneys, etc., and the hopes he gave them of doing it with profite, was more beleeved and rested on by them (at least some of them) then any thing the plantation did or said.

2. It is like, though Mr. *Allerton* might thinke not to wrong the plantation in the maine, yet his owne gaine and private ends led him a side in these things; for it came to be knowne, and I have it in a letter under Mr. *Sherley's* hand, that in the first ·2· or ·3· years of his imploymente, he had cleared up 400*li*. and put it into a brew-house of Mr. *Colliers* in *London*, at first under Mr. *Sherley's* name, etc.; besides what he might have other wise. Againe, Mr. *Sherley* and he had perticuler dealings in some things; for he bought up the beaver that sea-men and other passengers brought over to *Bristoll*, and at other places, and charged the bills to *London*, which Mr. *Sherley* payed; and they got some time 50*li*. a peece in a bargen, as was made knowne by Mr. *Hatherley* and others, besides what might be other wise; which might make Mr. *Sherley* harken unto him in many things; and yet I beleeve, as he in his forementioned leter write, he never would side in any perticuler trade which he conceived would wrong the plantation, and eate up and destroy the generall.

3ly. It may be perceived that, seeing they had done so much for the plantation, both in former adventures and late disburse-ments, and allso that Mr. *Allerton* was the first occasioner of bringing them upon these new designes, which at first seemed faire and profitable unto them, and unto which they agreed; but now, seeing them to turne to loss, and decline to greater intanglements, they thought it more meete for the plantation to bear them, then them selves, who had bourne much in other things allready, and so tooke advantage of shuch *comission* and power as Mr. *Allerton* had formerly had as their agente, to devolve these things upon them.

4ly. *With pitie and compassion (touching Mr. Allerton) I may say with the apostle* to Timothy, 1. Tim. 6. 9. *They that will be rich fall into many temtations and snares, etc., and pearce them selves throw with many sorrows, etc.; for the love of money is the roote of all evill,* v. 10. God give him to see the evill in his failings, that he may find mercie by repentance for the wrongs he hath done to any, and this pore plantation in spetiall. They that doe shuch things doe not only bring them selves into snares, and sorrows, but many with them, (though in an other kind,) as lamentable experience shows; and is too manifest in this bussines.

Now about these ships and their setting forth, the truth, as farr as could be learned, is this. The motion aboute setting forth the *fishing ship* (caled the *Frindship*) came first from the plantation, and the reasons of it, as is before remembered; but wholy left to them selves to doe or not to doe, as they saw cause. But when it fell into consideration, and the designe was held to be profitable and hopefull, it was propounded by some of them, why might not they doe it of them selves, seeing they must disburse all the money, and what need they have any refference to the plantation in that; they might take the profite them selves, towards other losses, and need not let the plantation share therin; and if their ends were other wise answered for their supplyes to come too them in time, it would be well enough. So they hired her, and set her out, and fraighted her as full as she could carry with passengers goods that belonged to the Massachussets, which rise to a good sume of money; intending to send the plantations supply in the other ship. The effecte of this Mr. *Hatherley* not only declared afterward upon occasion, but affirmed upon othe, taken before the Governor and Deputy Governor of the Massachusets, Mr. *Winthrop* and Mr. *Dudley*: That this ship—*Freindship*—was not sett out nor intended for the joynt partnership of the plantations, but for the perticuler accounte of Mr. *James Sherley*, Mr. *Beachampe*, Mr. *Andrews*, Mr. *Allerton*, and *him selfe*. This deposition was taken at *Boston* the *29. of August*, 1639. as is to be seen under their hands; besides some other concurente testimonies declared at severall times to sundrie of them.

About the *Whit-Angell*, though she was first bought, or at least the price beaten, by Mr. *Allerton* (at *Bristoll*), yet that had been nothing if Mr. *Sherley* had not liked it, and disbursed the money. And that she was not intended for the plantation appears by sundrie evidences; as, first, the bills of sale, or charterparties, were taken in their owne names, without any mention or refference to the plantation at all; viz. Mr. *Sherley*, Mr. *Beachampe*, Mr. *Andrews*, Mr. *Denison*, and Mr. *Allerton*; for Mr. *Hatherley* fell off, and would not joyne with them in this. That she was not bought for their accounte, Mr. *Hatherley* tooke his oath before the parties afforesaid, the day and year above writen.

About the *Whit-Angell* they all mette at a certaine taverne in London, wher they had a diner prepared, and had conference with a factore aboute selling of her in Spaine, or at Port a porte, as hath been before mentioned; as Mr. Hatherley manifested, and Mr. Allerton could not deney.

Mr. Allerton tooke his oath to like effecte concerning this ship, the *Whit-Angell*, before the Governor and Deputie, the ·7· *of September*, 1639. and likewise deposed, the same time, that Mr. *Hatherley* and *him selfe* did, in the behalfe of them selves and the said Mr. *Sherley*, Mr. *Andrews*, and Mr. *Beachamp*, agree and under take to discharge, and save harmles, all the rest of the partners and purchasers, of and from the said losses of the *Freindship* for 200*li.*, which was to be discounted therupon; as by ther depossitions (which are in writing) may appeare more at large, and some other depositions and other testemonies by Mr. *Winslow*, etc. But I suppose these may be sufficente to evince the truth in these things, against all pretences to the contrary. And yet the burthen lay still upon the plantation; or, to speake more truly and rightly, upon those few that were ingaged for all, for they were faine to wade through these things without any help from any.

Mr. Winslow deposed, the same time, before the Governor afore said, etc. that when he came into England, and the partners inquired of the success of the *Whit-Angell*, which should have been laden with bass and so sent for Port, of Portinggall, and their ship and goods to be sould; having informed them that they were like to faile in their lading of bass, that then Mr. James Sherly used these termes: Feck, we must make one accounte of all; and ther upon presed him, as agente for the partners in New-England, to accepte the said ship *Whit-Angell*, and her accounte, into the joynte partner-ship; which he refused, for many reasons; and after received instructions from New-England to refuse her if she should be offered, which instructions he shewed them; and wheras he was often pressed to accept her, he ever refused her, etc.

Concerning Mr. *Allerton's* accounts, they were so large and intrecate, as they could not well understand them, much less examine and correcte them, without a great deale of time and help, and his owne presence, which was now hard to gett amongst them; and it was ·2· or ·3· years before they could bring them to any good pass, but never make them perfecte. I know not how it came to pass, or what misterie was in it, for he tooke upon him to make up all accounts till this time, though Mr. *Sherley* was their agente to buy and sell their goods, and did more then he therin; yet he past in accounts in a maner for all disbursments, both concerning goods bought, which he never saw, but were done when he was hear in the cuntrie or at sea; and all the expences of the *Leyden people*, done by others in his absence; the charges aboute the *patente*, etc. In all which he made them debtore to him above 300*li.* and demanded paimente of it. But when things came to scaning, he was found above 2000*li.* debtore to them, (this wherin Mr. *Hatherley* and he being joyntly ingaged, which he only had, being included,) besides I know not how much that could never be cleared; and interest moneys which ate them up, which he never accounted. Also they were faine to alow shuch large bills of charges as were intolerable; *the charges of the patent came to above 500li.* and *yet nothing done in it but what was done at first without any confirmation*; 30*li.* given at a clape, and 50*li.* spent in a journey. No marvell therfore if Mr. *Sherley* said in his leter, if their bussines had been better managed, they might have been the richest plantation of any English at that time. Yea, he scrued up *his poore old father in laws* accounte to *above 200li.* and brought it on the generall accounte, and to befreind him made most of it to arise out of those goods taken up by him at *Bristoll*, at 50*li.* per cent., because he knew they would never let it lye on the old man, when, alass! he, poore man, never dreamte of any shuch thing, nor that what he had could arise nere that valew; but thought that many of them had been freely bestowed on him and his children by Mr. *Allerton*. Nither in truth did they come nere the valew in worth, but that sume was blowne up by interest and high prises, which the company did for the most parte bear, (*he deserving farr more*,) being most sory that he should have a name to have much, when he had in effecte litle.

This year also Mr. *Sherley* sent over an accounte, which was in a maner but a cash-accounte what Mr. *Allerton* had had of them, and disbursed, for which he referd to his accounts; besides an account of *beaver* sould, which Mr. *Winslow* and *some others* had carried over, and *a large supply of goods which Mr. Winslow had sent and brought over*, all which was comprised in that accounte, and all the disbursments aboute the *Freind-ship* and *Whit-Angell*, and what concerned their accounts from first to last; or any thing else he could charge the partners with. So they were made debtor in the foote of that accounte *4770li. 19. 2.* besides *1000li. still due for the purchase* yet unpayed; notwithstanding all the *beaver*, and *returnes* that both *Ashley* and *they* had made, which were not small.

So as a while before, wheras their great care was how to pay the purchase, and those other few debts which were upon them, now it was with them as it was some times with *Saule's-father*, who left careing for the Asses, and sorrowed for his sonn. 1. Sam. 10. 2. So that which before they looked at as a heavie burthen, they now esteeme but a small thing and a light mater, in comparison of what was now upon them. And thus the Lord oftentimes deals with his people to teach them, and humble them, that he may doe them good in the later end.

In these accounts of Mr. *Sherley's* some things were obscure, and some things twise charged, as a ·100· of Bastable ruggs which came in the *Freindship*, and cost 75*li.*, charged before by Mr. *Allerton*, and now by him againe, with other perticulers of like nature doubtfull, to be twise or thrise charged; as also a sume of *600li.* which Mr. *Allerton* deneyed, and they could never understand for what it was. They sent a note of these and shuch like things afterward to Mr. *Sherley* by Mr. *Winslow*; but (I know not how it came to pass) could never have them explained.

Into these deepe sumes had Mr. Allerton rune them in *tow years*, for *in the later end of the year ·1628· all their debts did not amounte to much above 400li.*, as was then noted; and now come to so *many thousands.* And wheras *in the year 1629. Mr. Sherley and Mr. Hatherley being at Bristoll, and write a large letter from thence*, in which they had given an account of the debts, and what sumes were then disbursed, Mr. *Allerton* never left begging and intreating of them till they had put it out. So they bloted out ·2· lines in that leter in which the sumes were contained, and write upon it so as not a word could be perceived; as since by them was confessed, and by the leters may be seene. And thus were they kept hoodwinckte, till now they were so deeply ingaged. And wheras *Mr. Sherley did so ernestly press that Mr. Allerton might be sent over to finish the great bussines aboute the patente, as may be seen in his letter write 1629.* as is before recorded, and that they should be ernest with his wife to suffer him to goe, etc., he hath since confessed by a letter under my hands, that it was Mr. *Allerton's* owne doings, and not his, and he made him write his words, and not his owne. The patent was but a pretence, and not the thing. Thus were they abused in their simplicitie, and no beter than bought and sould, as it may seeme.

And to mend the matter, *Mr. Allerton* doth in a sorte *wholy now deserte them*; having brought them into the briers, he leaves them to gett out as they can. But God crost him mightily, for he *having hired the ship of Mr. Sherly at 30li. a month, he set forth againe* with a *most wicked and drunken crue*, and for covetousnes sake did so over lade her, not only filling her hould, but so stufed her betweene decks, as she was walte, and could not bear sayle, and they had like to have been cast away at sea, and were forced to put for Millford Havene, and new-stow her, and put some of ther ordnance and more heavie goods in the botome; which lost them time, and made them *come late into the countrie, lose ther season, and made a worse viage* then the year before. But being come into the countrie, he sells trading comodities to any that will buy, to the great prejudice of the plantation here; but that which is worse, what he could not sell, he trustes; and *sets up a company of base felows and makes them traders, to rune into every hole, and into the river of Kenebeck*, to gleane away the trade from the house ther, aboute

the patente and priviledge wherof he had dasht away so much
money of theirs here; and now what in him lay went aboute to
take away the benefite therof, and to overthrow them. Yea, not
only this, but he furnishes a company, and joyns with some
consorts, (being now deprived of Ashley at Penobscote,) and
sets up a trading house beyoned Penobscote, to cute of the trade
from thence also. But the *French* perceiving that that would be
greatly to their damage *allso,* they came *in their begining before
they were well setled, and displanted them,* slue ·2· of their men,
and tooke all their goods to a good valew, the loss being most,
if not all, Mr. *Allerton's*; for though some of them should have
been his partners, yet he trusted them for their partes; the rest
of the men were sent into *France,* and this was the end of that
projecte. The rest of those he trusted, being lose and drunken
fellows, did for the most parte but coussen and cheate him of
all they got into their hands; that howsoever he did his friends
some hurte hereby for the presente, yet he gate litle good, but
wente by the loss by Gods just hand. *After* in time, when he
came to *Plimmoth,* the church caled him to accounte for these,
and other his grosse miscarrages; he confessed his faulte, and
promised better walking, and that he would wind him selfe out
of these courses as soone as he could, etc.

This year their house at *Penobscott* was robed by the *French,*
and all their goods of any worth they carried away, to the value
of 400. or 500*li.* as the cost first peny worth; in beaver 300*li.*
waight; and the rest in trading goods, as coats, ruggs, blankett,
biskett, etc. It was in this maner. The master of the house, and
parte of the company with him, were come with their vessell
to the westward to fecth a supply of goods which was brought
over for them. In the mean time comes a smale French ship
into the harbore (and amongst the company was a false Scott);
they pretended they were nuly come from the sea, and knew
not wher they were, and that their vesell was very leake, and
desired they might hale her a shore and stop their leaks. And
many French complements they used, and congeess they made;
and in the ende, seeing but ·3· or ·4· simple men, that were servants, and by this Scoth-man understanding that the maister
and the rest of the company were gone from home, they fell
of comending their gunes and muskets, that lay upon racks by
the wall side, and tooke them downe to looke on them, asking

if they were charged. And when they were possest of them, one presents a peece ready charged against the servants, and another a pistoll; and bid them not sturr, but quietly deliver them their goods, and carries some of the men aborde, and made the other help to carry away the goods. And when they had tooke what they pleased, they sett them at liberty, and wente their way, with this mock, biding them tell their master when he came, that some of the *Ile of Rey* gentlemen had been ther.

This year also Mr. Sherley would needs send them over a new-acountante; he had made mention of shuch a thing the year before, but they write him word, that their charge was great allready, and they neede not increase it, as this would; but if they were well delte with, and had their goods well sent over, they could keep their accounts hear them sellves. Yet he now sente one, which they did not refuse, being *a yonger brother of Mr. Winslows*, whom they had been at charge to instructe at *London* before he came. He *came over in the White Angell with Mr. Allerton*, and ther begane his first imploymente; for though *Mr. Sherley had so farr befreinded Mr. Allerton, as to couson Mr. Winslow to ship the supply sente to the partners here in his ship, and give him 4li. per tune, wheras others carried for* ·3· and he made them pay their fraight ready downe, before the ship wente out of the harbore, wheras others payed upon certificate of the goods being delivered, and their fraight came to upward of ·6· score pounds, yet they had much adoe to have their goods delivered, for some of them were chainged, as bread and pease; they were forced to take worse for better, neither could they even gett all. And if *Josias Winslow* had not been ther, it had been worse; for he had the invoyce, and order to send them to the trading houses.

This year, on Sir Christopher Gardener, being, as him selfe said, discended of that house that the Bishop of Winchester came of (who was so great a persecutor of Gods saincts in Queene Maries days), and being a great traveler, received his first honour of knighthood at Jerusalem, being made Knight of the Sepulcher ther. He came into these parts under pretence of forsaking the world, and to live a private life, in a godly course, not unwilling to put him selfe upon any meane imployments, and take any paines for his living; and some time offered him

selfe to joyne the churchs in sundry places. He brought over
with him a servante or ·2· and a comly yonge woman, whom
he caled his cousin, but it was suspected, she (after the Italian maner) was his concubine. Living at the Massachusets, for
some miscariages which he should have answered, he fled away
from authority, and gott amonge the Indeans of these parts;
they sent after him, but could not gett him, and promissed
some reward to those that should find him. The Indeans came
to the Governor here, and tould wher he was, and asked if they
might kill him; he tould them no, by no means, but if they
could take him and bring him hither, they should be payed
for their paines. They said he had a gune, and a rapier, and he
would kill them if they wente aboute it; and the Massachuset
Indeans said they might kille him. But the Governor tould
them no, they should not kill him, but watch their opportunitie, and take him. And so they did, for when they light of
him by a river side, he got into a canowe to get from them,
and when they came nere him, whilst he presented his peece at
them to keep them of, the streame carried the canow against
a rock, and tumbled both him and his peece and rapire into
the water; yet he got out, and having a litle dagger by his
side, they durst not close with him, but getting longe poles
they soone beat his dagger out of his hand, so he was glad to
yeeld; and they brought him to the Governor. But his hands
and armes were swolen and very sore with the blowes they had
given him. So he used him kindly, and sent him to a lodging
wher his armes were bathed and anoynted, and he was quickly
well againe, and blamed the Indeans for beating him so much.
They said that they did but a litle whip him with sticks. In his
lodging, those that made his bed found a litle note booke that
by accidente had slipt out of his pockett, or some private place,
in which was a memoriall what day he was reconciled to the
pope and church of Rome, and in what universitie he tooke his
scapula, and shuch and shuch degrees. It being brought to the
Governor, he kept it, and sent to the Governor of the Massachusets word of his taking, who sent for him. So the Governor
sent him and these notes to the Governor ther, who tooke it
very thankfuly; but after he gott for England, he shewed his
malice, but God prevented him. See the Governor's leter on
the other side.

SIR: It hath pleased God to bring Sir Christopher Gardener safe to us, with thos that came with him. And howsoever I never intended any hard measure to him, but to respecte and use him according to his qualitie, yet I let him know your care of him, and that he shall speed the better for your mediation. It was a spetiall providence of God to bring those notes of his to our hands; I desire that you will please to speake to all that are privie to them, not to discovere them to any one, for that may frustrate the means of any further use to be made of them. The good Lord our God who hath allways ordered things for the good of his poore churches here, directe us in this arighte, and dispose it to a good issue. I am sorie we put you to so much trouble about this gentleman, espetialy at this time of great imploymente, but I know not how to avoyed it. I must againe intreate you, to let me knew what charge and troble any of your people have been at aboute him, that it may be recompenced. So with the true affection of a frind, desiring all happines to your selfe and yours, and to all my worthy friends with you (whom I love in the Lord), I comende you to his grace and good providence, and rest

Your most assured friend,
JOHN WINTHROP.

Boston, May 5. 1631.

By occation herof I will take a litle libertie to declare what fell out by this mans means and malice, complying with others. And though I doubt not but it will be more fully done by my honourd friends, whom it did more directly concerne, and have more perticuler knowledg of the matter, yet I will here give a hinte of the same, and Gods providence in preventing the hurte that might have come by the same. The intelligence I had by a letter from my much honoured and beloved freind, Mr. John Winthrop, Governor of the Massachusets.

SIR: Upon a petition exhibited by Sir Christo: Gardner, Sir Ferd: Gorges, Captaine Masson, etc., against you and us, the cause was heard before the lords of the Privie Counsell, and after reported to the king, the success wherof makes it evident to all, that the Lord hath care of his people hear. The passages are admirable, and too long to write. I hartily wish an opportunitie to imparte them unto you, being many sheets of paper. But the conclusion was (against all mens expectation) an order for our incouragmente, and much blame and disgrace upon the adversaries, which calls for much thankfullnes from us all, which we purpose (the Lord willing) to express in a day of thanks-giving to our mercifull God, (I doubt not but you will consider, if it be not fitt for you to joyne in it,) who, as he hath humbled us by his late correction, so he hath lifted us up, by an abundante rejoysing, in our deliverance out of so desperate a danger; so as that which our enemies builte their hopes upon to ruine us by, He hath mercifully disposed to our great advantage, as I shall further aquainte you, when occasion shall serve.*

The coppy of the order follows.

At the COURTE at WHIT-HALL the 19. January: 1632.

PRESENT

Sigillum	Lord Privie Seale	Lord Cottinton
	Ea: of Dorsett	Mr. Treasurer
	Lo: Vi: Falkland	Mr. Vic Chamberlain
	Lo: Bp: of London	Mr. Sec: Cooke
	Maister Sec: Windebanck	

Wheras his Majestie hath latly been informed of great distraction and much disorder in that plantation in the parts of America called New-England, which, if they be true, and suffered to rune on, would tende to the great dishonour of this kingdome, and utter ruine of that plantation. For prevention wherof, and for the orderly settling of government, according to the intention of those patents which have been granted by his Majestie and from his late royall father king James, it hath pleased his Majestie that the lords and others of his most honourable Privie Counsell, should take the same into consideration. Their lordships in the first place thought fitt to make a comitie of this bord, to take examination of the matters informed; which committies having called diverse of the principall adventurers in that plantation, and heard those that are complanants against them, most of the things informed being deneyed, and resting to be proved by parties that must be called from that place, which required a long expence of time; and at presente their lordships finding the adventurers were upon dispatch of men, victles, and marchandice for that place, all which would be at a stand, if the adventurers should have discouragmente, or take suspition that the state hear had no good opinion of that plantation; their lordships, not laying the faulte

*See the other side.

or fancies (if any be) of some perticuler men upon the generall govermente, or principall adventurers, (which in due time is further to be inquired into,) have thought fitt in the meane time to declare, that the appearences were so faire, and hopes so greate, that the countrie would prove both beneficiall to this kingdom, and profitable to the perticuler adventurers, as that the adventurers had cause to goe on cherfully with their undertakings, and rest assured, if things were carried as was pretended when the patents were granted, and accordingly as by the patentes it is appointed his Majestie would not only maintaine the liberties and privileges heretofore granted, but supply any thing further that might tend to the good govermente, prosperitie, and comforte of his people ther of that place, etc.

WILLIAM TRUMBALL.

ANNO DOM: ·1632·

MR. ALLERTON, returning for *England*, litle regarded his bound of a 1000*li.* to performe covenants; for wheras he was bound by the same to bring the ship to *London*, and to pay 30*li.* per month for her hire, he did neither of boath, for he carried her to *Bristoll* againe, from whence he *intended to sett her out againe, and so did the ·3· time, into these parts* (as after will appear); and though she had been months upon the former viage, at 30*li.* per month, yet he never payed peney for hire. It should seeme he knew well enough how to deale with Mr. *Sherley.* And Mr. *Sherley*, though he would needs tye her and her accounte upon the generall, yet he would dispose of her as him selfe pleased; for though Mr. *Winslow* had in their names protested against the receiving her on that accounte, or if ever they should hope to preveile in shuch a thing, yet never to suffer Mr. *Allerton* to have any more to doe in her, yet he *the last year* let her wholy unto him, and injoyned them to send all their supplye in her to their prejudice, as is before noted. And now, though he broke his bonds, kepte no covenante, paid no hire, nor was ever like to keep covenants, yet now he goes and *sells him all, both ship, and all her accounts*, from first to last (and in effecte he might as well have given him the same); and not only this, but he doth as good as provide a sanctuary for him, for he gives him one years time to prepare his accounte, and then to give up the same to them here; and then another year for him to make paymente of what should be

due upon that accounte. And in the mean time writes ernestly
to them not to interupte or hinder him from his bussines, or
stay him aboute clearing accounts, etc.; so as he in the mean
time gathers up all monies due for fraighte, and any other
debtes belonging either to her, or the *Frindship's* accounts, as
his owne perticuler; and after, sells ship, and ordnans, fish, and
what he had raised, in *Spane*, according to the first designe, in
effecte; and who had, or what became of the money, he best
knows. In the mean time their hands were bound, and could
doe nothing but looke on, till he had made all away into other
mens hands (save a few catle and a litle land and some small
maters he had here at *Plimoth*), and so in the end removed,
as he had allready his person, so all his from hence. This will
better appere by Mr. *Sherley's* leter.

SIR: These few lines are further to give you to understand, that
seeing you and we, that never differed yet but aboute the *White-
Angell*, which some what troubleth us, as I perceive it doth you.
And now Mr. *Allerton* beeing here, we have had some confferance
with him about her, and find him very willing to give you and us all
contente that possiblie he can, though he burthen him selfe. He is
contente to take the *White-Angell* wholy on him selfe, notwithstanding he mett with *pirates* neer the coast of *Ierland*, which tooke away
his best sayles and other provissions from her; so as verily if we should
now sell her, she would yeeld but a small price, besides her ordnance.
And to set her forth againe with fresh money we would not, she being
now at *Bristoll.* Wherfore we thought it best, both for you and us,
Mr. *Allerton* being willing to take her, to accepte of his bond of *tow
thousand pounds*, to give you a true and perfecte accounte, and take
the whole charge of the *Whit-Angell* wholy to him selfe, from the
first to the last. The accounte he is to make and perfecte within ·12·
months from the date of this letter, and then to pay you at ·6· and
·6· months after, what soever shall be due unto you and us upon the
foote of that accounte. And verily, notwithstanding all the disasters
he hath had, I am perswaded he hath enough to pay all men here and
ther. Only they must have patience till he can gather in what is due
to him their. I doe not write this slightly, but upon some ground of
what I have seen (and perhaps you know not of) under the hands and
seals of some, etc. I rest

Your assured friend,
JAMES SHERLEY.

Desember: 6. 1632.

But heres not a word of the breach of former bonds and covenants, or paimente of the ships hire; this is passt by as if no shuch thing had been; besides what bonds or obligments so ever they had of him, ther never came any to the hands or sight of the partners here. And for this that Mr. *Sherley* seems to intimate (as a secrete) of his abilitie, under the hands and seals of some, it was but a trick, having gathered up an accounte of what was owing from shuch base fellows as he had made traders for him, and other debts; and then got Mr. *Mahue*, and some others, to affirme under their hand and seale, that they had seen shuch accounts that were due to him.

Mr. *Hatherley* came over againe this year, but upon his owne occasions, and begane to make preparation to plant and dwell in the countrie. He with his former dealings had wound in what money he had in the partnership into his owne hands, and so gave off all partnership (excepte in name), as was found in the issue of things; neither did he medle, or take any care aboute the same; only he was troubled about his ingagmente aboute the *Friendship*, as will after appeare. And now partly aboute that accounte, in some reconings betweene Mr. *Allerton* and *him*, and some debts that Mr. *Allerton* otherwise owed him upon dealing between them in perticuler, he drue up an accounte of above 2000*li.*, and would faine have ingaged the partners here with it, because Mr. *Allerton* had been their *agent*. But they tould him they had been fool'd longe enough with shuch things, and shewed him that it no way belonged to them; but tould him he must looke to make good his ingagment for the *Freindship*, which caused some trouble betweene Mr. *Allerton* and *him*.

Mr. *William Peirce* did the like, Mr. *Allerton* being wound into his debte also upon particuler dealings; as if they had been bound to make good all mens debts. But they easily shooke off these things. But Mr. *Allerton* herby rane into much trouble and vexation, as well as he had troubled others, for Mr. *Denison* sued him for the money he had disbursed for the ·6· part of the *Whit-Angell*, and recovered the same with damages.

Though the partners were thus plunged into great ingagments, and oppresed with unjust debts, yet the Lord prospered their trading, that they made yearly large returnes, and had soone wound them selves out of all, if yet they had otherwise been well delt with all; as will more appear here after. Also the people of the plantation begane to grow in their owtward estates, by reason of the flowing of many people into the cuntrie, espetially into the Bay of the Massachusets; by which means corne and catle rose to a great prise, by which many were much inriched, and commodities grue plentifull; and yet in other regards this benefite turned to their hurte, and this accession of strength to their weaknes. For now as their stocks increased, and the increse vendible, ther was no longer any holding them togeather, but now they must of necessitie goe to their great lots; they could not other wise keep their katle; and having oxen growne, they must have land for plowing and tillage. And no man now thought he could live, except he had catle and a great deale of ground to keep them; all striving to increase their stocks. By which means they were scatered all over the bay, quickly, and the towne, in which they lived compactly till now, was left very thine, and in a short time allmost desolate. And if this had been all, it had been less, thoug to much; but the church must also be devided, and those that had lived so long togeather in Christian and comfortable fellowship must now part and suffer many divissions. First, those that lived on their lots on the other side of the bay (called Duxberie) they could not long bring their wives and children to the publick worship and church meetings here, but with shuch burthen, as, growing to some competente number, they sued to be dismissed and become a body of them selves; and so they were dismiste (about this time), though very unwillingly. But to touch this sadd matter, and handle things together that fell out afterwards. To prevent any further scatering from this place, and weakning of the same, it was thought best to give out some good faroms to spetiall persons, that would promise to live at Plimoth, and lickly to be helpfull to the church or comone-welth, and so tye the lands to Plimoth as farmes for the same; and ther they might keepe their catle and tillage by some servants, and retaine their dwellings here. And so some spetiall lands were granted at a place generall, called Greens Harbor, wher no allotments had been in the former divission, a plase very weell meadowed, and fitt to keep and rear catle, good store. But alass! this remedy proved worse then the dis-ease; for *within a few years* those that had thus gott footing

ther rente them selves away, partly by force, and partly wearing
the rest with importunitie and pleas of necessitie, so as they
must either suffer them to goe, or live in continuall opposition
and contention. And others still, as they conceived them selves
straitened, or to want accommodation, broak away under one
pretence or other, thinking their owne conceived necessitie,
and the example of others, a warrente sufficente for them. And
this, I fear, will be the ruine of New-England, at least of the
churches of God ther, and will provock the Lords displeasure
against them.

This year, Mr.William Perce came into the cuntry, and
brought goods and passenger, in a ship caled the Lyon, which
belonged cheefly to Mr. Sherley, and the rest of the London
partners, but these hear had nothing to doe with her. In this
ship (besides beaver which they had sent home before) they
sent *upward of 800li. in her*, and *some otter skines*; and also the
coppies of Mr. Allertons accounts, desiring that they would
also peruse and examene them, and rectifie shuch things as
they should find amise in them; and the rather because they
were better acquaynted with the goods bought ther, and the
disbursments made, then they could bee here; yea, a great part
were done by them selves, though Mr. Allerton brougt in the
accounte, and sundry things seemed to them obscure and
had need of clearing. Also they sente a booke of exceptions
against his accounts, in shuch things as they could manifest,
and doubted not but they might adde more therunto. And
also shewed them how much Mr. Allerton was debtor to the
accounte; and desired, seeing they had now put the ship White-
Angell, and all, wholy into his power, and tyed their hands
here, that they could not call him to accounte for any thinge,
till the time was expired which they had given him, and by
that time other men would get their debts of him, (as sume
had done already by suing him,) and he would make all away
here quickly out of their reach; and therfore prayed them to
looke to things, and gett paymente of him ther, as it was all
the reason they should, seeing they keept all the bonds and
covenants they made with him in their owne hands; and here
they could doe nothing by the course they had taken, nor had
any thing to show if they should goe aboute it. But it pleased
God, this ship, being first to goe to Verginia before she wente

home, was cast away on that coast, not farr from Virginia, and their beaver was all lost (which was *the first loss they sustained in that kind*); but Mr. Peirce and the men saved their lives, and also their leters, and gott into Virginia, and so safly home. The accounts were now sent from hence againe to them. And thus much of the passages of this year.

A part of Mr. Peirce his leter from Virginia.

It was dated in Desember: 25. 1632. and came to their hand the ·7· of Aprill, before they heard any thing from England.

DEAR FREINDS, etc. The bruit of this fatall stroke that the Lord hath brought both on me and you all will come to your ears before this commeth to your hands, (it is like,) and therfore I shall not need to inlarg in perticulers, etc. My whole estate (for the most parte) is taken away; and so yours, in a great measure, by this and your former, losses [he means by the French and Mr. Allerton]. It is time to looke aboute us, before the wrath of the Lord breake forth to utter destruction. The good Lord give us all grace to search our harts and trie our ways, and turne unto the Lord, and humble our selves under his mightie hand, and seeke atonemente, etc. Dear freinds, you may know that all your beaver, and the books of your accounts, are swallowed up in the sea; your letters remaine with me, and shall be delivered, if God bring me home. But what should I more say? Have we lost our outward estates? yet a hapy loss if our soules may gaine; ther is yet more in the Lord Jehova then ever we had yet in the world. Oh that our foolish harts could yet be wained from the things here below, which are vanity and vexation of spirite; and yet we fooles catch after shadows, that flye away, and are gone in a momente, etc. Thus with my continuall remembrance of you in my poore desires to the throne of grace, beseeching God to renew his love and favoure towards you all, in and through the Lord Jesus Christ, both in spirituall and temporall good things, as may be most to the glory and praise of his name, and your everlasting good. So I rest,

Your afflicted brother in Christ,
WILLIAM PEIRCE.

Virginia, Desember 25. 1632.

ANNO DOM: ·1633·

THIS year Mr. Ed: Winslow was chosen Governor. By the first returne this year, they had leters from Mr. Sherley of Mr. Allerton's further ill success, and the loss by

Mr. Peirce, with many sadd complaints; but litle hope of any thinge to be gott of Mr. Allerton, or how their accounts might be either eased, or any way rectified by them ther; but now saw plainly that the burthen of all would be cast on their backs. The spetiall passages of his letters I shall here inserte, as shall be pertinente to these things; for though I am weary of this tedious and uncomfortable subjecte, yet for the clearing of the truth I am compelled to be more large in the opening of these matters, upon which so much trouble hath insued, and so many hard censures have passed on both sides. I would not be partiall to either, but deliver the truth in all, and, as nere as I can, in their owne words and passages, and so leave it to the impartiall judgment of any that shall come to read, or veiw these things. His leters are as folow, dated June 24. 1633.

LOVING FREINDS, my last* was sente *in the Mary and John, by Mr. William Collier*, etc. I then certified of you the great, and uncomfortable, and unseasonable loss you and we had, in the loss of Mr. Peirce his ship, the Lyon; but the Lords holy name be blessed, who gives and takes as it pleaseth him; his will be done, Amen. I then related unto you that fearfull accidente, or rather judgmente, the Lord pleased to lay on London Bridge, by fire, and therin gave you a touch of my great loss; the Lord, I hope, will give me patience to bear it, and faith to trust in him, and not in these slipery and uncertaine things of this world.

I hope Mr. Allerton is nere upon sayle with you by this; but he had many disasters here before he could gett away; yet the last was a heavie one; his ship, going out of the harbor at Bristoll, by stormie weather was so farr driven on the shore, as it cost him above 100*li.* before shee could be gott off againe. Verily his case was so lamentable as I could not but afford him some help therin (and so did some mere strangers to him); besides, your goods were in her, and if he had not been supported, he must have broke off his viage, and so loss could not have been avoyded on all sides. When he first bought her, I thinke he had made a saving match, if he had then sunck her, and never set her forth. I hope he sees the Lords hand against him, and will leave of these vioages. I thinke we did well in parting with her; she would have been but a clogge to the accounte from time to time, and now though we shall not gett much by way of satisfaction, yet we shall lose no more. And now, as before I have writte, I pray you finish all

*March 22.

the accounts and reconings with him there; for here he hath nothing, but many debtes that he stands ingaged to many men for. Besides, here is not a man that will spend a day, or scarce an hower, aboute the accounts but my selfe, and the bussines will require more time and help then I can afford. I shall not need to say any more; I hope you will doe that which shall be best and just, to which adde mercie, and consider his intente, though he failed in many perticulers, which now cannot be helped, etc.

To morrow, or next day at furthest, we are to pay 300*li*. and Mr. Beachamp is out of the towne, yet the bussines I must doe. Oh the greefe and trouble that man, Mr. Allerton, hath brought upon you and us! I cannot forgett it, and to thinke on it drawes many a sigh from my harte, and teares from my eyes. And now the Lord hath visited me with an other great loss, yet I can undergoe it with more patience. But this I have follishly pulled upon my selfe, etc. [*And in another he hath this passage*:] By Mr. Allertons faire propossitions and large promises, I have over rune my selfe; verily, at this time greefe hinders me to write, and tears will not suffer me to see; wherfore, *as you love those that ever loved you, and that plantation, thinke upon us.* Oh what shall I say of that man, who hath abused your trust and wronged our loves; but now to complaine is too late, nither can I complaine of your backwardnes, for I am perswaded it lys as heavie on your harts, as it doth on our purses or credites. And had the Lord sent Mr. Peirce safe home, we had eased both you and us of some of those debts; the Lord I hope will give us patience to bear these crosses; and that great God, whose care and providence is every where, and spetially over all those that desire truly to fear and serve him, direct, guid, prosper, and blesse you so as that you may be able (as I perswade my selfe you are willing) to discharge and take off this great and heavie burthen which now lyes upon me for your sakes; and I hope in the ende for the good of you, and many thousands more; for *had not you and we joyned and continued togeather, New-England might yet have been scarce knowne, I am perswaded, not so replenished and inhabited with honest English people, as now it is.* The Lord increase and blesse them, etc. So, with my continuall praiers for you all, I rest

Your assured loving friend,
JAMES SHERLEY.

June 24. 1633.

By this it apperes when Mr. Sherly sould him the ship and all her accounts, it was more for Mr. Allertons advantage then theirs; and if they could get any there, well and good, for they were like to have nothing here. And what course was held to hinder them there, hath all ready beene manifested. And though Mr. Sherley became more sinsible of his owne condition, by these losses, and therby more sadly and plainly to complaine of Mr. Allerton, yet no course was taken to help them here, but all left unto them selves; not so much as to examene and rectifie the accounts, by which (it is like) some hundereds of pounds might have been taken off. But very probable it is, the more they saw was taken off, the less might come unto them selves. But I leave these maters, and come to other things.

Mr. Roger Williams (a man godly and zealous, having many precious parts, but very unsettled in judgmente) came over first to the Massachusets, but upon some discontente left that place, and came hither, (wher he was friendly entertained, according to their poore abilitie,) and exercised his gifts amongst them, and after some time was admitted a member of the church; and his teaching well approoved, for the benefite wherof I still blese God, and am thankfull to him, even for his sharpest admonitions and reproufs, so farr as they agreed with truth. He this year begane to fall into some strang opinions, and from opinion to practise; which caused some controversie betweene the church and him, and in the end some discontente on his parte, by occasion wherof he left them some thing abruptly. Yet after wards sued for his dismission to the church of Salem, which was granted, with some caution to them concerning him, and what care they ought to have of him. But he soone fell into more things ther, both to their and the goverments troble and disturbance. I shall not need to name perticulers, they are too well knowen now to all, though for a time the church here wente under some hard scensure by his occassion, from some that afterwards smarted them selves. But he is to be pitied, and prayed for, and so I shall leave the matter, and desire the Lord to shew him his errors, and reduce him into the way of truth, and give him a setled judgment and constancie in the same; for I hope he belongs to the Lord, and that he will shew him mercie.

Having had formerly converse and familiarity with the Dutch, (as is before remembred,) they, seeing them seated here in a barren quarter, tould them of a river called by them the Fresh River, but now is known by the name of Conightecute-River, which they often comended unto them for a fine place both for plantation and trade, and wished them to make use of it. But their hands being full otherwise, they let it pass. But afterwards ther coming a company of banishte Indeans into these parts, that were drivene out from thence by the potencie of the Pequents, which usurped upon them, and drive them from thence, they often sollicited them to goe thither, and they should have much trade, espetially if they would keep a house ther. And having now good store of comodities, and allso need to looke out wher they could advantage them selves to help them out of their great ingagments, they now begane to send that way to discover the same, and trade with the natives. They found it to be a fine place, but had no great store of trade; but the Indeans excused the same in regard of the season, and the fear the Indeans were in of their enemise. So they tried diverce times, not with out profite, but saw the most certainty would be by keeping a house ther, to receive the trad when it came down out of the inland. These Indeans, not seeing them very forward to build ther, solisited them of the Massachusets in like sorte (for their end was to be restored to their countrie againe); but they in the Bay being but latly come, were not fitte for the same; but some of their cheefe made a motion to joyne with the partners here, to trade joyntly with them in that river, the which they were willing to imbrace, and so they should have builte, and put in equall stock togeather. A time of meeting was appointed at the Massachusets, and some of the cheefe here was appointed to treat with them, and went accordingly; but they cast many fears of deanger and loss and the like, which was perceived to be the maine obstacles, though they alledged they were not provided of trading goods. But those hear offered at presente to put in sufficente for both, provided they would become ingaged for the halfe, and prepare against the nexte year. They conffessed more could not be offered, but thanked them, and tould them they had no mind to it. They then answered, they hoped it would be no offence unto them, if them selves wente on without them, if they saw it meete. They said there was no reason they should; and thus this treaty broake of, and those here tooke conveniente time to make a begining ther; and were the first English that both discovered that place, and built in the same, though they were litle better then thrust out of it afterward as may appeare.

But the Dutch begane now to repente, and hearing of their purpose and preparation, indevoured to prevente them, and gott in a litle before them, and made a slight forte, and planted ·2· peeces of ordnance, thretening to stopp their passage. But they having made a smale frame of a house ready, and haveing a great new-barke, they stowed their frame in her hold, and bords to cover and finishe it, having nayles and all other provisions fitting for their use. This they did the rather that they might have a presente defence against the Indeans, who weare much offended that they brought home and restored the right Sachem of the place (called Natawanute); so as they were to incounter with a duble danger in this attempte, both the Dutch and the Indeans. When they came up the river, the Dutch demanded what they intended, and whither they would goe; they answered, up the river to trade (now their order was to goe and seat above them). They bid them strike, and stay, or els they would shoote them; and stood by ther ordnance ready fitted. They answered they had commission from the Governor of Plimoth to goe up the river to shuch a place, and if they did shoote, they must obey their order and proceede; they would not molest them, but would goe one. So they passed along, and though the Dutch threatened them hard, yet they shoot not. Comming to their place, they clapt up their house quickly, and landed their provissions, and left the companie appoynted, and sent the barke home; and afterwards palisadoed their house aboute, and fortified them selves better. The Dutch sent word home to the Monhatas what was done; and in proces of time, they sent a band of aboute ·70· men, in warrlike maner, with collours displayed, to assaulte them; but seeing them strengthened, and that it would cost blood, they came to parley, and returned in peace. And this was their enterance ther, who deserved to have held it, and not by freinds to have been thrust out, as in a sorte they were, as will after appere. They did the Dutch no wrong, for they took not a foote of any land they bought, but went to the place above them, and bought that tracte of land which belonged to these Indeans which they carried with them, and their friends, with whom the Dutch had nothing to doe. But of these matters more in another place.

It pleased the Lord to visite them this year with an infectious fevoure, of which many fell very sicke, and upward of ·20· persons dyed, men and women, besides children, and sundry of them of their anciente friends which had lived in Holand; as Thomas Blossome, Richard Masterson, with sundry others, and in the end (after he had much helped others) Samuell Fuller, who was their surgeon and phisition, and had been a great help and comforte unto them; as in his facultie, so otherwise, being a deacon of the church, a man godly, and forward to doe good, being much missed after his death; and he and the rest of their brethren much lamented by them, and caused much sadnes and mourning amongst them; which caused them to humble them selves, and seeke the Lord; and towards winter it pleased the Lord the sicknes ceased. This disease allso swept away many of the Indeans from all the places near adjoyning; and the spring before, espetially all the *month of May*, ther was shuch a quantitie of a great sorte of flies, like (for bignes) to wasps, or bumble-bees, which came out of holes in the ground, and replenished all the woods, and eate the green-things, and made shuch a constante yelling noyes, as made all the woods ring of them, and ready to deafe the hearers. They have not by the English been heard or seen before or since. But the Indeans tould them that sicknes would follow, and so it did in *June, July, August*, and the cheefe heat of sommer.

It pleased the Lord to inable them this year to send home a great quantity of beaver, besides paing all their charges, and debts at home, which good returne did much incourage their freinds in England. They sent in beaver 3366*li.* waight, and much of it coat beaver, which yeeled 20*s.* per pound, and some of it above; and of otter-skines ·346· sould also at a good prise.*
And thus much of the affaires of this year.

ANNO DOM: ·1634·

THIS year Mr. Thomas Prence was chosen Governor. Mr. Sherleys letters were very breefe in answer of theirs this year. I will forbear to coppy any part therof, only name a head

*The skin was sold at ·14*s.* and ·15*s.* the pound.

or ·2· therin. First, he desires they will take nothing ill in what
he formerly write, professing his good affection towards them
as before, etc. 2ly. For Mr. Allertons accounts, he is perswaded
they must suffer, and that in no small summes; and that they
have cause enough to complaine, but it was now too late. And
that he had failed them ther, those here, and him selfe in his
owne aimes. And that now, having thus left them here, he
feared God had left or would leave him, and it would not be
strange, but a wonder if he fell not into worse things, etc. 3ly.
He blesseth God and is thankfull to them for the good returne
made this year. This is the effecte of his letters, other things
being of more private nature.

I am now to enter upon one of the sadest things that befell
them since they came; but before I begine, it will be needfull
to premise shuch parte of their patente as gives them right and
priviledge at Kenebeck; as followeth;

The said Counsell hath further given, granted, bargaued, sold,
infeoffed, alloted, assigned, and sett over, and by these presents doe
clearly and absolutely give, grante, bargane, sell, alliene, enffeofe,
allote, assigne, and confirme unto the said William Bradford, his
heires, associates, and assignes, etc. All that tracte of land or part of
New-England in America afforesaid, which lyeth within or betweene,
and extendeth it selfe from the utmost limits of Cobiseconte, which
adjoyneth to the river of Kenebeck, towards the westerne ocean, and
a place called the falls of Nequamkick in America, aforsaid; and the
space of ·15· English myles on each side of the said river, commonly
called Kenebeck River, and all the said river called Kenebeck that
lyeth within the said limits and bounds, eastward, westward, northward, and southward, last above mentioned; and all lands, grounds,
soyles, rivers, waters, fishing, etc. And by vertue of the authority to us
derived by his said late Majestis Letters patents, to take, apprehend,
seise, and make prise of all shuch persons, their ships and goods, as
shall attempte to inhabite or trade with the savage people of that
countrie within the severall precincts and limits of his and their severall plantations, etc.

Now it so fell out, that one Hocking, belonging to the plantation of Pascataway, wente with a barke and commodities to
trade in that river, and would needs press into their limites;
and not only so, but would needs goe up the river above their
house, (towards the falls of the river,) and intercept the trade

that should come to them. He that was cheefe of the place
forbad them, and prayed him that he would not offer them that
injurie, nor goe aboute to infringe their liberties, which had
cost them so dear. But he answered he would goe up and trade
ther in dispite of them, and lye ther as longe as he pleased. The
other tould him he must then be forced to remove him from
thence, or make seasure of him if he could. He bid him doe his
worste, and so wente up, and anchored ther. The other tooke
a boat and some men and went up to him, when he saw his
time, and againe entreated him to departe by what perswasion
he could. But all in vaine: he could gett nothing of him but ill
words. So he considred that now was the season for trade to
come downe, and if he should suffer him to lye, and take it from
them, all ther former charge would be lost, and they had better
throw up all. So, consulting with his men, (who were willing
thertoe,) he resolved to put him from his anchores, and let
him drive downe the river with the streame; but commanded
the men that none should shoote a shote upon any occasion,
except he commanded them. He spoake to him againe, but all
in vaine; then he sente a cuple in a canow to cutte his cable,
the which one of them performes; but Hocking takes up a
pece which he had layed ready, and as the barke shered by the
canow, he shote him close under her side, in the head, (as I
take it,) so he fell downe dead instantly. One of his fellows
(that loved him well) could not hold, but with a muskett shot
Hocking, who fell downe dead and never speake word. This
was the truth of the thing. The rest of the men carried home
the vessell and the sad tidings of these things. Now the Lord
Saye and the Lord Brooke, with some other great persons, had
a hand in this plantation; they write home to them, as much
as they could to exasperate them in the matter, leaveing out all
the circumstances, as if he had been kild without any offence
of his parte, conceling that he had kild another first, and the
just occasion that he had given in offering shuch wrong; at
which their Lordships were much offended, till they were truly
informed of the mater.

   The bruite of this was quickly carried all aboute, (and that
in the worst manner,) and came into the Bay to their neighbours their. Their owne barke comming home, and bringing
a true relation of the matter, sundry were sadly affected with

the thing, as they had cause. It was not long before they had occasion to send their vessell into the Bay of the Massachusetts; but they were so prepossest with this matter, and affected with the same, as they commited Mr. Alden to prison, who was in the bark, and had been at Kenebeck, but was no actore in the bussines, but wente to carie them supply. They dismist the barke aboute her bussines, but kept him for some time. This was thought strange here, and they sente Capten Standish to give them true information, (togeather with their letters,) and the best satisfaction they could, and to procure Mr. Alden's release. I shall recite a letter or ·2· which will show the passages of these things, as folloeth.

Good Sir:

I have received your letter by Captaine Standish, and am unfainedly glad of Gods mercie towards you in the recovery of your health, or some way thertoo. For the bussines you write of, I thought meete to answer a word or ·2· to your selfe, leaving the answer of your Governor's letter to our courte, to whom the same, together with my selfe is directed. I conceive (till I hear new matter to the contrary) that your patente may warrante your resistance of any English from trading at Kenebeck, and that blood of Hocking, and the partie he slue, will be required at his hands. Yet doe I with your selfe and others sorrow for their deaths. I thinke likewise that your generall letters will satisfie our courte, and make them cease from any further inter medling in the mater. I have upon the same letter sett Mr. Allden at liberty, and his sureties, and yet, least I should seeme to neglecte the opinion of our court and the frequente speeches of others with us, I have bound Captaine Standish to appeare the ·3· of June at our nexte courte, to make affidavid for the coppie of the patente, and to manifest the circumstances of Hockins provocations; both which will tend to the clearing of your innocencie. If any unkindnes hath ben taken from what we have done, let it be further and better considred of, I pray you; and I hope the more you thinke of it, the lease blame you will impute to us. At least you ought to be just in differencing them, whose opinions concurr with your owne, from others who were opposites; and yet I may truly say, I have spoken with no man in the bussines who taxed you most, but they are shuch as have many wayes heretofore declared ther good affections towards your plantation. I further referr my selfe to the reporte of Captaine Standish and Mr. Allden; leaving you for this presente to Gods blessing, wishing unto you perfecte recovery of health, and the long continuance of it. I desire to be lovingly remembred to Mr. Prence, your Governor, Mr. Winslow, Mr. Brewster, whom I would see if I knew how. The Lord keepe you all. Amen.

Your very loving freind in our Lord Jesus,

THO: DUDLEY.

New-towne, the 22. of May, 1634.

Another of his about these Things as followeth.

SIR: I am right sorrie for the news that Captaine Standish and other of your neighbours and my beloved freinds will bring now to Plimoth, wherin I suffer with you, by reason of my opinion, which differeth from others, who are godly and wise, amongst us here, the reverence of whose judgments causeth me to suspecte myne owne ignorance; yet must I remaine in it untill I be convinced therof. I thought not to have shewed your letter written to me, but to have done my best to have reconciled differences in the best season and maner I could; but Captaine Standish requiring an answer therof publickly in the courte, I was forced to produce it, and that made the breach soe wide as he can tell you. I propounded to the courte, to answer Mr. Prences letter, your Governor, but our courte said it required no answer, it selfe being an answer to a former letter of ours. I pray you certifie Mr. Prence so much, and others whom it concerneth, that no neglecte or ill manners be imputed to me theraboute. The late letters I received from England wrought in me diverse fears of some trials which are shortly like to fall upon us; and this unhappie contention betweene you and us, and between you and Pascattaway, will hasten them, if God with an extraordinarie hand doe not help us. To reconcile this for the presente will be very difficulte, but time cooleth distempers, and a comone danger to us boath approaching, will necessitate our uniting againe. I pray you therfore, Sir, set your wisdom and patience a worke, and exhorte others to the same, that things may not proceede from bad to worse, so making our contentions like the barrs of a pallace, but that a way of peace may be kepte open, wherat the God of peace may have enterance in his owne time. If you suffer wrong, it shall be your honour to bear it patiently; but I goe to farr in needles putting you in mind of these things. God hath done great things for you, and I desire his blessings may be multiplied upon you more and more. I will commite no more to writing, but comending my selfe to your prayers, doe rest,

Your truly loving freind in our Lord Jesus,

THO: DUDLEY.

June 4. 1634.

Ther was cause enough of these feares, which arise by the underworking of some enemies to the churches here, by which this Commission following was procured from his Majestie.

Commission for Regulating Plantations.

Charles by the grace of God king of England, Scotland, France, and Ireland, Defender of the Faith, etc.

To the most Reverend father in Christ, our wellbeloved and faithfull counselour, William, by devine providence Archbishop of Counterbery, of all England Primate and Metropolitan; Thomas Lord Coventry, Keeper of our Great Seale of England; the most Reverente father in Christ our well-beloved and most faithful Counselour, Richard, by devine providence Archbishop of Yorke, Primate and Metropolitan; our well-beloved and most faithfull coussens and Counselours, Richard, Earle of Portland, our High Treasurer of England; Henery, Earle of Manchester, Keeper of our Privie Seals; Thomas, Earle of Arundalle and Surry, Earle Marshall of England; Edward, Earle of Dorsett, Chamberline of our most dear consorte, the Queene; and our beloved and faithfull Counselours, Francis Lord Cottington, Counseler, and Undertreasurour of our Eschequour; Sir Thomas Edmonds, knight, Treasurer of our houshould; Sir Henery Vane, Knight, controuler of the same houshould; Sir John Cooke, Knight, one of our Privie Secretaries; and Francis Windebanck, Knight, another of our Privie Secretaries, Greeting.

Wheras very many of our subjects, and of our late fathers of beloved memory, our sovereigne lord James, late king of England, by means of lycence royall, not only with desire of inlarging the teritories of our empire, but cheefly out of a pious and religious affection, and desire of propagating the gospell of our Lord Jesus Christ, with great industrie and expenses have caused to be planted large Collonies of the English nation, in diverse parts of the world alltogether unmanured, and voyd of inhabitants, or occupied of the barbarous people that have no knowledge of divine worship. We being willing to provide a remedy for the tranquillity and quietnes of those people, and being very confidente of your faith and wisdom, justice and providente circomspection, have constituted you the aforesaid Archbishop of Counterburie, Lord Keeper of the Great Seale of England, the Archbishop of Yorke, etc. and any ·5· or more, of you, our Comissioners; and to you, and any ·5· or more of you, we doe give and commite power for the governmente and safftie of the said collonies, drawen, or which, out of the English nation into those parts hereafter, shall be drawne, to make lawes, constitutions, and

ordinances, pertaining ether to the publick state of these collonies, or
the private profite of them; and concerning the lands, goods, debts,
and succession in those parts, and how they shall demeane them
selves, towards foraigne princes, and their people, or how they shall
bear them selves towards us, and our subjects, as well in any foraine
parts whatsoever, or on the seas in those parts, or in their returne
sayling home; or which may pertaine to the clargie govermente, or to
the cure of soules, among the people ther living, and exercising trade
in those parts; by designing out congruente porcions arising in tithes,
oblations, and other things ther, according to your sound discretions,
in politicall and civill causes; and by haveing the advise of ·2· or ·3·
bishops, for the setling, making, and ordering of the bussines, for the
designeing of necessary ecclesiasticall, and clargie porcions, which
you shall cause to be called, and taken to you. And to make provission
against the violation of those laws, constitutions, and ordinances, by
imposing penealties and mulcts, imprisonmente if ther be cause, and
the quality of the offence doe require it, by deprivation of member,
or life, to be inflicted. With power allso (our assente being had) to
remove, and displace the governours or rulers of those collonies, for
causes which to you shall seeme lawfull, and others in their stead to
constitute; and require an accounte of their rule and govermente, and
whom you shall finde culpable, either by deprivation from their place,
or by impossition of a mulcte upon the goods of them in those parts
to be levied, or banishmente from those provinces in which they have
been governor or otherwise to cashier according to the quantity of
the offence. And to constitute judges, and magistrates politicall and
civill, for civill causes and under the power and forme, which to you
·5· or more of you shall seeme expediente. And judges and magistrates
and dignities, to causes ecclesiasticall, and under the power and forme
which to you ·5· or more of you, with the bishops vicegerents (provided by the Archbishop of Counterbure for the time being), shall
seeme expediente; and to ordaine courts, pretoriane and tribunall,
as well ecclesiasticall, as civill, of judgmentes; to detirmine of the
formes and maner of procceedings in the same; and of appealing from
them in matters and causes as well criminall, as civill, personall, reale,
and mixte, and to their seats of justice, what may be equall and well
ordered, and what crimes, faults, or excessess, of contracts or injuries
ought to belonge to the Ecclesiasticall courte, and what to the civill
courte, and seate of justice.

Provided never the less, that the laws, ordinances, and constitutions of this kinde, shall not be put in execution, before our assent
be had therunto in writing under our signet, signed at least, and this
assente being had, and the same publikly proclaimed in the provinces

in which they are to be executed, we will and command that those lawes, ordinances, and constitutions more fully to obtaine strength and be observed and shall be inviolably of all men whom they shall concerne.

Notwithstanding it shall be for you, or any ·5· or more of you, (as is afforsaid,) allthough those lawes, constitutions, and ordinances shalbe proclaimed with our royall assente, to chainge, revocke, and abrogate them, and other new ones, in forme afforsaid, from time to time frame and make as afforesaid; and to new evills arissing, or new dangers, to apply new remedyes as is fitting, so often as to you it shall seeme expediente. Furthermore you shall understand that we have constituted you, and every ·5· or more of you, the afforesaid Archbishop of Counterburie, Thomas Lord Coventrie, Keeper of the Great Seale of England, Richard, Bishop of Yorke, Richard, Earle of Portland, Henery, Earle of Manchester, Thomas, Earle of Arundale and Surry, Edward, Earell of Dorsett, Francis Lord Cottinton, Sir Thomas Edwards, knighte, Sir Henry Vane, knight, Sir Francis Windebanke, knight, our comissioners to hear, and determine, according to your sound discretions, all maner of complaints either against those collonies, or their rulers, govenours, at the instance of the parties greeved, or at their accusation brought concerning injuries from hence, or from thence, betweene them, and their members to be moved, and to call the parties before you; and to the parties or to their procurators, from hence, or from thence being heard the full complemente of justice to be exhibited. Giving unto you, or any ·5· or more of you power, that if you shall find any of the colonies afforesaid, or any of the cheefe rulers upon the jurisdictions of others by unjust possession, or usurpation, or one against another making greevance, or in rebelion against us, or withdrawing from our alegiance, or our comandaments, not obeying, consultation first with us in that case had, to cause those colonies, or the rulers of them, for the causes afforesaid, or for other just causes, either to returne to England, or to comand them to other places designed, even as according to your sounde discretions it shall seeme to stand with equitie, and justice, or necessitie. Moreover we doe give unto you, and any ·5· or more of you, power and spetiall command over all the charters, leters patents, and rescripts royall, of the regions, provinces, ilands, or lands in foraigne parts, granted for raising colonies, to cause them to be brought before you, and the same being received, if any thing surrepticiously or unduly have been obtained, or that by the same priviledges, liberties, and prerogatives hurtfull to us, or to our crowne, or to foraigne princes, have been prejudicially suffered, or granted; the same being better made knowne unto you ·5· or more of you, to command them according to the laws and customs of England to be revoked, and to doe shuch other things, which to the profite and safgard of the aforesaid collonies, and of our subjects residente in the same, shall be necessary. And therfore we doe command you that aboute the premisses at days and times, which for these things you shall make provission, that you be diligente in attendance, as it becometh you; giveing in precepte also, and firmly injoyning, we doe give command to all and singuler cheefe rulers of provinces into which the colonies afforesaid have been drawne, or shall be drawne, and concerning the collonies themselves, and concerning others, that have been interest therin, that they give atendance upon you, and be observante and obediente unto your warrants in those affaires, as often as, and even as in our name they shall be required, at their perill. In testimoney whereof, we have caused these our letters to be made pattente. Wittnes our selfe at Westminster the ·28· day of Aprill, in the tenth year of our Raigne.

By write from the privie seale,
WILLIES.

Anno Dom: 1634.

By these things it appears what troubles rise herupon, and how hard they were to be reconciled; for though they hear were hartily sorrie for what was fallen out, yet they conceived they were unjustly injuried, and provoked to what was done; and that their neigbours (haveing no jurisdiction over them) did more then was mete, thus to imprison one of theirs, and bind them to their courte. But yet being assured of their Christian love, and perswaded what was done was out of godly zeale, that religion might not suffer, nor sinne any way covered or borne with, espetially the guilte of blood, of which all should be very consciencious in any whom soever, they did indeavore to appease and satisfie them the best they could; first, by inform- ing them the truth in all circomstances aboute the matter; 2*ly*, in being willing to refferr the case to any indifferante and equall hearing and judgmente of the thing hear, and to answere it els wher when they should be duly called therunto; and further they craved Mr. Winthrops, and other of the reverend magis- trates ther, their advice and direction herein. This did mollifie their minds, and bring things to a good and comfortable issue in the end.

For they had this advice given them by Mr. Winthrop, and others concurring with him, that from their courte, they should write to the neigboure plantations, and espetially that of the lords, at Pascataway, and theirs of the Massachusets, to appointe some to give them meeting at some fitt place, to consulte and determine in this matter, so as the parties meeting might have full power to order and bind, etc. And that nothing be done to the infringing or prejudice of the liberties of any place. And for the clearing of conscience, the law of God is, that the preist's lips must be consulted with, and therfore it was desired that the ministers of every plantation might be presente to give their advice in pointe of conscience. Though this course seemed dangerous to some, yet they were so well assured of the justice of their cause, and the equitie of their freinds, as they put them selves upon it, and appointed a time, of which they gave notice to the severall places a month before hand; viz. Massachusets, Salem, and Pascataway, or any other that they would give notice too, and disired them to produce any evidence they could in the case. The place for meeting was at Boston. But when the day and time came none appered, but some of the magistrates and ministers of the Massachusets, and their owne. Seeing none of Passcataway or other places came, (haveing been thus desired, and conveniente time given them for that end,) Mr. Winthrop and the rest said they could doe no more then they had done thus to requeste them, the blame must rest on them. So they fell into a fair debating of things them selves; and after all things had been fully opened and discussed, and the oppinione of each one demanded, both magistrates, and ministers, though they all could have wished these things had never been, yet they could not but lay the blame and guilt on Hockins owne head; and with all gave them shuch grave and godly exhortations and advice, as they thought meete, both for the presente and future; which they allso imbraced with love and thankfullnes, promising to indeavor to follow the same. And thus was this matter ended, and ther love and concord renewed; and also Mr. Winthrop and Mr. Dudley write in their behalfes to the Lord Say and other gentle-men that were interesed in that plantation, very effectually, with which, togeather with their owne leters, and

Mr. Winslows furder declaration of things unto them, they rested well satisfied.

Mr. Winslow was sente by them this year into England, partly to informe and satisfie the Lord Say and others, in the former matter, as also to make answer and their just defence for the same, if any thing should by any be prosecuted against them at Counsell-table, or els wher; but this matter tooke end, without any further trouble, as is before noted. And partly to signifie unto the partners in England, that the terme of their trade with the company here was out, and therfore he was sente to finishe the accounts with them, and to bring them notice how much debtore they should remaine on that accounte, and that they might know what further course would be best to hold. But the issue of these things will appear in the next years passages. They now sente over by him a great returne, which was very acceptable unto them; which was in beaver 3738*li.* waight, (a great part of it, being coat-beaver, sould at 20*s.* per pound,) and ·234· otter skines;* which alltogeather rise to a great sume of money.

This year (in the foreparte of the same) they sente forth a barke to trade at the Dutch-Plantation; and they mette ther with on Captaine Stone, that had lived in Christophers, one of the West-Ende Ilands, and now had been some time in Virginia, and came from thence into these parts. He kept company with the Dutch Governor, and, I know not in what drunken fitt, he gott leave of the Governor to cease on their barke, when they were ready to come away, and had done their markett, haveing the valew of 500*li.* worth of goods abord her; having no occasion at all, or any collour of ground for shuch a thing, but having made the Governor drunck, so as he could scarce speake a right word; and when he urged him hear aboute, he answered him, *Als't u beleeft.* So he gat abord, (the cheefe of their men and marchant being ashore,) and with some of his owne men, made the rest of theirs waigh anchor, sett sayle, and carry her away towards Virginia. But diverse of the Dutch sea-men, which had bene often at Plimoth, and kindly entertayned ther, said one to another, Shall we suffer our freinds to

*And the skin at 14*s.*

be thus abused, and have their goods carried away, before our faces, whilst our Governor is drunke? They vowed they would never suffer it; and so gott a vessell or ·2· and pursued him, and brought him in againe, and delivered them their barke and goods againe.

After wards Stone came into the Massachusets, and they sent and commensed suite against him for this facte; but by mediation of freinds it was taken up, and the suite lett fall. And in the company of some other gentle-men Stone came afterwards to Plimoth, and had freindly and civill entertainmente amongst them, with the rest; but revenge boyled within his brest, (though concelled,) for some conceived he had a purpose (at one time) to have stapted the Governor, and put his hand to his dagger for that end, but by Gods providence and the vigilance of some was prevented. He afterward returned to Virginia, in a pinass, with one Captaine Norton and some others; and, I know not for what occasion, they would needs goe up Coonigtecutt River; and how they carried themselves I know not, but the Indeans knoct him in the head, as he lay in his cabine, and had thrown the covering over his face (whether out of fear or desperation is uncertaine); this was his end. They likewise killed all the rest, but Captaine Norton defended him selfe a long time against them all in the cooke-roome, till by accidente the gunpowder tooke fire, which (for readynes) he had sett in an open thing before him, which did so burne, and scald him, and blind his eyes, as he could make no longer resistance, but was slaine also by them, though they much comended his vallour. And having killed the men, they made a pray of what they had, and chafered away some of their things to the Dutch that lived their. But it was not longe before a quarell fell betweene the Dutch and them, and they would have cutt of their bark; but they slue the cheef sachem with the shott of a murderer.

I am now to relate some strange and remarkable passages. Ther was a company of people lived in the country, up above in the river of Conigtecut, a great way from their trading house ther, and were enimise to those Indeans which lived aboute them, and of whom they stood in some fear (being a stout people). About a thousand of them had inclosed them selves in a forte, which they had strongly palissadoed about. ·3· or

·4· Dutch men went up *in the begining of winter* to live with them, to gett their trade, and prevente them for bringing it to the English, or to fall into amitie with them; but *at spring* to bring all downe to their place. But their enterprise failed, for it pleased God to visite these Indeans with a great sicknes, and shuch a mortalitie that of a ·1000· above ·900· and a halfe of them dyed, and many of them did rott above ground for want of buriall, and the Dutch men allmost starved before they could gett away, for ise and snow. But about February, they got with much difficultie to their trading house; whom they kindly releeved, being allmost spente with hunger and could. Being thus refreshed by them diverce days, they got to their owne place, and the Dutch were very thankfull for this kindnes.

This spring, also, those Indeans that lived aboute their trading house there fell sick of the small poxe, and dyed most miserably; for a sorer disease cannot befall them; they fear it more then the plague; for usualy they that have this disease have them in abundance, and for wante of bedding and linning and other helps, they fall into a lamentable condition, as they lye on their hard matts, the poxe breaking and mattering, and runing one into another, their skin cleaving (by reason therof) to the matts they lye on; when they turne them, a whole side will flea of at once, (as it were,) and they will be all of a gore blood, most fearfull to behold; and then being very sore, what with could and other distempers, they dye like rotten sheep. The condition of this people was so lamentable, and they fell downe so generally of this diseas, as they were (in the end) not able to help on another; no, not to make a fire, nor to fetch a litle water to drinke, nor any to burie the dead; but would strivie as long as they could, and when they could procure no other means to make fire, they would burne the woden trayes and dishes they ate their meate in, and their very bowes and arrowes; and some would crawle out on all foure to gett a litle water, and some times dye by the way, and not be able to gett in againe. But those of the English house, (though at first they were afraid of the infection,) yet seeing their woefull and sadd condition, and hearing their pitifull cries and lamentations, they had compastion of them, and dayly fetched them wood and water, and made them fires, gott them victualls whilst they lived, and buried them when they dyed. For very few of them escaped, notwithstanding they did what they could for them, to the haszard of them selves. The cheefe Sachem him selfe now dyed, and allmost all his freinds and kinred. But by the marvelous goodnes and providens of God not one of the English was so much as sicke, or in the least measure tainted with this disease, though they dayly did these offices for them for many weeks togeather. And this mercie which they shewed them was kindly taken, and thankfully acknowledged of all the Indeans that knew or heard of the same; and their masters here did much comend and reward them for the same.

ANNO DOM: ·1635·

MR. WINSLOW was very wellcome to them in England, and the more in regard of the large returne he brought with him, which came all safe to their hands, and was well sould. And he was borne in hand, (at least he so apprehended,) that all accounts should be cleared before his returne, and all former differences ther aboute well setled. And so he writ over to them hear, that he hoped to cleare the accounts, and bring them over with him; and that the accounte of the White Angele would be taken of, and all things fairly ended. But it came to pass that, being occasioned to answer some complaints made against the countrie at Counsell bord, more cheefly concerning their neigbours in the Bay then them selves hear, the which he did to good effecte, and further prosecuting shuch things as might tend to the good of the whole, as well them selves as others, aboute the wrongs and incrochments that the French and other strangers both had and were like further to doe unto them, if not prevented, he prefered this petition following to their Honours that were deputed Commissioners for the Plantations.

To the right honorable the Lords Comissioners for the Plantations in America.

The humble petition of Edw: Winslow, on the behalfe of the plantations in New-England,

Humbly sheweth unto your Lordships, that wheras your petitioners have planted them selves in New England under his Majesties most gratious protection; now so it is, right Honorables, that the French and Dutch doe indeaouer to devide the land betweene them;

for which purpose the French have, on the east side, entered and seased upon one of our houses, and carried away the goods, slew ·2· of the men in another place, and tooke the rest prisoners with their goods. And the Dutch, on the west, have also made entrie upon Conigtecute River, within the limits of his Majesties letters patent, where they have raised a forte, and threaten to expell your petitioners thence, who are also planted upon the same river, maintaining possession for his Majestie to their great charge, and hazard both of lives and goods.

In tender consideration hereof your petitioners humbly pray that your Lordshipps will either procure their peace with those foraine states, or else to give spetiall warrante unto your petitioners and the English Collonies, to right and defend them selves against all foraigne enimies. And your petitioners shall pray, etc.

This petition found good acceptation with most of them, and Mr. Winslow was heard sundry times by them, and appointed further to attend for an answer from their Lordshipps, espetially, having upon conference with them laid downe a way how this might be doone without any either charge or trouble to the state; only by furnishing some of the cheefe of the cuntry hear with authoritie, who would undertake it at their owne charge, and in shuch a way as should be without any publick disturbance. But this crossed both Sir Ferdinandoe Gorges' and Cap: Masons designe, and the archbishop of Counterberies by them; for Sir Ferd: Gorges (by the arch-bishopps favore) was to have been sent over generall Governor into the countrie, and to have had means from the state for that end, and was now upon dispatch and conclude of the bussines. And the arch-bishops purposs and intente was, by his means, and some he should send with him, (to be furnished with Episcopall power,) to disturbe the peace of the churches here, and to overthrow their proceedings and further growth, which was the thing he aimed at. But it so fell out (by Gods providence) that though he in the end crost this petition from taking any further effecte in this kind, yet by this as a cheefe means the plotte and whole bussines of his and Sir Ferdinandos fell to the ground, and came to nothing. When Mr. Winslow should have had his suit granted, (as indeed upon the pointe it was,) and should have been confirmed, the arch-bishop put a stop upon it, and Mr. Winslow, thinking to gett it freed, went to the bord againe; but the bishop, Sir Ferd: and Captine Masson, had, as it seemes, procured Morton (of whom mention is made before, and his base carriage) to complaine; to whose complaints Mr. Winslow made answer, to the good satisfaction of the borde, who checked Morton and rebuked him sharply, and allso blamed Sir Fer'd Gorges, and Masson, for countenancing him. But the bishop had a further end and use of his presence, for he now begane to question Mr. Winslow of many things; as of teaching in the church publickly, of which Morton accused him, and gave evidence that he had seen and heard him doe it; to which Mr. Winslow answered, that some time (wanting a minster) he did exercise his gifte to help the edification of his breethren, when they wanted better means, which was not often. Then aboute mariage, the which he also confessed, that, haveing been called to place of magistracie, he had sometimes maried some. And further tould their lordships that mariage was a civille thinge, and he found no wher in the word of God that it was tyed to ministrie. Again, they were necessitated so to doe, having for a long time togeather at first no minister; besides, it was no new-thing, for he had been so maried him selfe in Holand, by the magistrates in their Statt-house. But in the end (to be short), for these things, the bishop, by vehemente importunity, gott the bord at last to consente to his comittemente; so he was commited to the Fleete, and lay ther ·17· weeks, or ther aboute, before he could gett to be released. And this was the end of this petition, and this bussines; only the others designe was also frustrated hereby, with other things concurring, which was no smalle blessing to the people here.

But the charge fell heavie on them hear, not only in Mr. Winslows expences, (which could not be smale,) but by the hinderance of their bussines both ther and hear, by his personall imploymente. For though this was as much or more for others then for them hear, and by them cheefly he was put on this bussines, (for the plantation knewe nothing of it till they heard of his imprisonmente,) yet the whole charge lay on them.

Now for their owne bussines; whatsoever Mr. Sherleys mind was before, (or Mr. Winslow apprehension of the same,) he now declared him selfe plainly, that he would neither take of the White-Angell from the accounte, nor give any further accounte, till he had received more into his hands; only a prety good supply of goods were sent over, but of the most, no note of their prises, or so orderly an invoyce as formerly; which Mr. Winslow said he could not help, because of his restrainte. Only now Mr. Sherley and Mr. Beachamp and Mr. Andrews sent over a letter of atturney under their hands and seals, to recovere what they could of Mr. Allerton for the Angells accounte; but sent them neither the bonds, nor covenants, or shuch other evidence or accounts, as they had aboute these matters. I shall here inserte a few passages out of Mr. Sherleys letters aboute these things.

Your leter of the ·22· of July, 1634, by your trustie and our loving friend Mr. Winslow, I have received, and your large parcell of beaver and otter skines. Blessed be our God, both he and it came safly to us, and we have sould it in tow parcells; the skin at ·14s. a li. and some at ·16·; the coate at 20s. the pound. The accounts I have not sent you them this year, I will refferr you to Mr. Winslow to tell you the reason of it; yet be assured that none of you shall suffer by the not having of them, if God spare me life. And wheras you say the ·6· years are expired that the people put the trad into your and our hands for, for the discharge of that great debte which Mr. Allerton needlesly and unadvisedly ran you and us into; yet it was promised it should continue till our disbursments and ingagements were satisfied. You conceive it is done; we feele and know other wise, etc. I doubt not but we shall lovingly agree, notwithstanding all that hath been writen, on boath sides, aboute the Whit-Angell. We have now sent you a letter of atturney, therby giving you power in our names (and to shadow it the more we say for our uses) to obtaine what may be of Mr. Allerton towards the satisfying of that great charge of the White Angell. And sure he hath bound him selfe, (though at present I cannot find it,) but he hath often affirmed, with great protestations, that neither you nor we should lose a peny by him, and I hope you shall find enough to discharge it, so as we shall have no more contesting aboute it. Yet, notwithstanding his unnaturall and unkind dealing with you, in the midest of justice remember mercie, and doe not all you may doe, etc. Set us out of debte, and then let us recone and reason togeither, etc. Mr. Winslow hath undergone an unkind imprisonment, but I am perswaded it will turne much to all your good. I leave him to relate perticuleres, etc.

Your loving freind,
JAMES SHERLEY.

London, September 7. 1635.

This year they sustained an other great loss from the French. Monsier de Aulnay coming into the harbore of Penobscote, and having before gott some of the cheefe that belonged to the house abord his vessell, by sutlety coming upon them in their shalop, he gott them to pilote him in; and after getting the rest into his power, he tooke possession of the house in the name of the king of France; and partly by threatening, and other wise, made Mr. Willett (their agente ther) to approve of the sale of the goods their unto him, of which he sett the price him selfe in effecte, and made an inventory thereof, (yett leaving out sundry things,) but made no paymente for them; but tould them in convenient time he would doe it if they came for it. For the house and fortification, etc. he would not alow, nor accounte any thing, saing that they which build on another mans ground doe forfite the same. So thus turning them out of all, (with a great deale of complemente, and many fine words,) he let them have their shalop and some victualls to bring them home. Coming home and relating all the passages, they here were much troubled at it, haveing had this house robbed by the French once before, and lost then above 500 *li.* (as is before remembred), and now to loose house and all, did much move them. So as they resolved to consulte with their freinds in the Bay, and if they approved of it, (ther being now many ships ther,) intended to hire a ship of force, and seeke to beat out the Frenche, and recover it againe. Ther course was well approved on, if them selves could bear the charge; so they hired a fair ship of above ·300· tune, well fitted with ordnance, and agreed with the master (one Girling) to this effect: that he and his company should deliver them the house, (after they had driven out, or surprised the French,) and give them peaceable possession therof, and of all shuch trading comodities as should ther be found; and give the French fair quarter and usage, if they would yeeld. In consideration wherof he was to have 700 *li.* of beaver, to be delivered him ther, when he had done the thing; but if he did not accomplish it, he was to loose his labour, and have nothing. With him they also sent their owne bark, and about ·20· men, with Captaine Standish, to aide him (if neede weer), and to order things, if the house was regained; and then to pay him the beaver, which they keept abord their owne barke. So they with their bark piloted him thither, and brought him safe into the harbor. But he was so rash and heady as he would take no advice, nor would suffer Captaine Standish to have time to summone them, (who had commission and order so to doe,) neither would doe it him selfe; the which, it was like, if it had been done, and they come to a faire parley, seeing their force, they would have yeelded. Neither would he have patience to bring his ship wher she might doe execution, but begane to shoot at distance like a madd man, and did them no hurte at all; the which when those of the plantation saw, they were much greeved, and went to him and tould him he would doe no good if he did not lay his ship beter to pass (for she might lye within pistoll shott of the house). At last, when he saw his owne folly, he was perswaded, and layed her well, and bestowed a few shott to good purposs. But now, when he was in a way to doe some good, his powder was goone; for though he had . . . peece of ordnance, it did now appeare he had but a barrell of powder, and a peece; so he could doe no good, but was faine to draw of againe; by which means the enterprise was made frustrate, and the French incouraged; for all the while that he shot so unadvisedly, they lay close under a worke of earth, and let him consume him selfe. He advised with the Captaine how he might be supplyed with powder, for he had not to carie him home; so he tould him he would goe to the next plantation, and doe his indevour to procure him some, and so did; but understanding, by intelligence, that he intended to ceiase on the barke, and surprise the beaver, he sent him the powder, and brought the barke and beaver home. But Girling never assualted the place more, (seeing him selfe disapoyented,) but went his way; and this was the end of this bussines.

Upon the ill success of this bussines, the Governor and Assistants here by their leters certified their freinds in the Bay, how by this ship they had been abused and disapoynted, and that the French partly had, and were now likly to fortifie them selves more strongly, and likly to become ill neigbours to the English. Upon this they thus writ to them as folloeth:—

WORTHY SIRS: Upon the reading of your leters, and consideration of the waightines of the cause therin mentioned, the courte hath joyntly expressed their willingnes to assist you with men and munition, for the accomplishing of your desires upon the French. But because here are none of yours that have authority to conclude of any thing herein, nothing can be done by us for the presente. We desire, therfore, that you would with all conveniente speed send some man of trust, furnished with instructions from your selves, to make shuch agreemente with us about this bussines as may be usefull for you, and equall for us. So in hast we commite you to God, and remaine

Your assured loving freinds,
JOHN HAYNES, Governor.
RI: BELLINGHAM, Dep.
JO: WINTHROP.
THO: DUDLEY.
JO: HUMFRAY.
WM. CODDINGTON.
WM. PINCHON.
ATHERTON HOUGHE.
INCREAS NOWELL.
RIC: DUMER.
SIMON BRADSTRETE.

New-towne, October 9. 1635.

Upon the receite of the above mentioned, they presently deputed ·2· of theirs to treate with them, giving them full power to conclude, according to the instructions they gave them, being to this purposs: that if they would afford shuch assistance as, togeather with their owne, was like to effecte the thing, and allso bear a considerable parte of the charge, they would goe on; if not, they (having lost so much allready) should not be able, but must desiste, and waite further opportunitie as God should give, to help them selves. But this came to nothing, for when it came to the issue, they would be at no charge, but sente them this letter, and referd them more at large to their owne messengers.

SIR: Having, upon the consideration of your letter, with the message you sente, had some serious consultations aboute the great importance of your bussines with the French, we gave our answer to those whom you deputed to conferr with us aboute the viage to Penobscote. We shewed our willingnes to help, but withall we declared our presente condition, and in what state we were, for our abilitie to help; which we for our parts shall be willing to improve, to procure you sufficiente supply of men and munition. But for matter of moneys we have no authority at all to promise, and if we should, we should rather disapoynte you, then incourage you by that help, which we are not able to performe. We likwise thought it fitt to take the help of other Esterne plantations; but those things we leave to your owne wisdoms. And for other things we refer you to your owne committies, who are able to relate all the passages more at large. We salute you, and wish you all good success in the Lord.

Your faithfull and loving friend,

Ri: Bellingham, Dep:

In the name of the rest of the Comities.

Boston, October 16. 1635.

This thing did not only thus breake of, but some of their marchants shortly after sent to trade with them, and furnished them both with provissions, and poweder and shott; and so have continued to doe till this day, as they have seen opportunitie for their profite. So as in truth the English them selves have been the cheefest supporters of these French; for besides these, the plantation at Pemaquid (which lyes near unto them) doth not only supply them with what they wante, but gives them continuall intelligence of all things that passes among the English, (espetially some of them,) so as it is no marvell though they still grow, and incroach more and more upon the English, and fill the Indeans with gunes and munition, to the great deanger of the English, who lye oppen and unfortified, living upon husbandrie; and the other closed up in their forts, well fortified, and live upon trade, in good securitie. If these things be not looked too, and remeady provided in time, it may easily be conjectured what they may come toe; but I leave them.

This year, the ·14· or ·15· of August (being Saturday) was shuch a mighty storme of wind and raine, as none living in these parts, either English or Indeans, ever saw. Being like (for the time it continued) to those Hauricanes and Tuffons that writers make mention of in the Indeas. It began in the morning, a litle before day, and grue not by degrees, but came with violence in the begining, to the great amasmente of many. It blew downe sundry houses, and uncovered others; diverce vessells were lost at sea, and many more in extreme danger. It caused the sea to swell (to the southward of this place) above ·20· foote, right up and downe, and made many of the Indeans to clime into trees for their saftie; it tooke of the borded roofe of a house which belonged to this plantation at Manamet, and floted it to another place, the posts still standing in the ground; and if it had continued long without the shifting of the wind, it is like it would have drouned some parte of the cuntrie. It blew downe many hundered thowsands of trees, turning up the stronger by the roots, and breaking the hiegher pine trees of in the midle, and the tall yonge oaks and walnut trees of good biggnes were wound like a withe, very strange and fearfull to behould. It begane in the southeast, and parted toward the south and east, and vered sundry ways; but the greatest force of it here was from the former quarters. It continued not (in the extremitie) above ·5· or ·6· houers, but the violence begane to abate. The signes and marks of it will remaine this ·100· years in these parts wher it was sorest. The moone suffered a great eclipse the ·2· night after it.

Some of their neighbours in the Bay, hereing of the fame of Conightecute River, had a hankering mind after it, (as was before noted,) and now understanding that the Indeans were swepte away with the late great mortalitie, the fear of whom was an obstacle unto them before, which being now taken away, they begane now to prosecute it with great egernes. The greatest differances fell betweene those of Dorchester planta-tion and them hear; for they set their minde on that place, which they had not only purchased of the Indeans, but whey they had builte; intending only (if they could not remove them) that they should have but a smale moyety left to the house, as to a single family; whose doings and procceedings were con-ceived to be very injurious, to attempte not only to intrude them selves into the rights and possessions of others, but in effect to thrust them out of all. Many were the leters and pas-sages that went betweene them hear aboute, which would be to long here to relate.

I shall here first inserte a few lines that was write by their own agente from thence.

SIR, etc.: The Massachuset men are coming almost dayly, some by water, and some by land, who are not yet determined wher to setle, though some have a great mind to the place we are upon, and which was last bought. Many of them look at that which this river will not afford, excepte it be at this place which we have, namly, to be a great towne, and have comodious dwellings for many togeather. So as what they will doe I cannot yet resolve you; for this place ther is none of them say any thing to me, but what I hear from their servants (by whom I perceive their minds), I shall doe what I can to withstand them. I hope they will hear reason; as that we were here first, and entred with much difficulty and danger, both in regard of the Dutch and Indeans, and bought the land, (to your great charge, allready disbursed,) and have since held here a chargable possession, and kept the Dutch from further incroaching, which would els long before this day have possessed all, and kept out all others, etc. I hope these and shuch like arguments will stoppe them. It was your will we should use their persons and messengers kindly, and so we have done, and doe dayly, to your great charge; for the first company had well nie starved had it not been for this house, for want of victuals; I being forced to supply ·12· men for ·9· days togeather; and those which came last, I entertained the best we could, helping both them (and the other) with canows, and guides. They gott me to goe with them to the Dutch, to see if I could procure some of them to have quiet setling nere them; but they did peremtorily withstand them. But this later company did not once speak therof, etc. Also I gave their goods house roome according to their ernest request, and Mr. Pinchons letter in their behalfe (which I thought good to send you, here inclosed). And what trouble and charge I shall be further at I know not; for they are coming dayly, and I expecte these back againe from below, whither they are gone to veiw the countrie. All which trouble and charge we under goe for their occasion, may give us just cause (in the judgmente of all wise and understanding men) to hold and keep that we are setled upon. Thus with my duty remembred, etc. I rest

Yours to be comanded
JOHNNATHAN BREWSTER.

Matianuck, July ·6· 1635.

Amongst the many agitations that pased betweene them, I shal note a few out of their last letters, and for the present omitte the rest, except upon other occasion I may have fitter opportunity. After their thorrow veiw of the place, they began to pitch them selves upon their land and near their house; which occasioned much expostulation betweene them. Some of which are shuch as follow.

BRETHREN, having latly sent ·2· of our body unto you, to agitate and bring to an issue some maters in difference betweene us, about some lands at Conightecutt, unto which you lay challeng; upon which

God by his providence cast us, and as we conceive in a faire way of providence tendered it to us, as a meete place to receive our body, now upon removall.

We shall not need to answer all the passages of your large letter, etc. But wheras you say God in his providence cast you, etc., we tould you before, and (upon this occasion) must now tell you still, that our mind is other wise, and that you cast rather a partiall, if not a covetous eye, upon that which is your neigbours, and not yours; and in so doing, your way could not be faire unto it. Looke that you abuse not Gods providence in shuch allegations.

Theirs.

Now allbeite we at first judged the place so free that we might with Gods good leave take and use it, without just offence to any man, it being the Lords wast, and for the presente altogeather voyd of inhab-itants, that indeede minded the imploymente therof, to the right ends for which land was created, Gen: 1. 28. and for future intentions of any, and uncertaine possibilities of this or that to be done by any, we judging them (in shuch a case as ours espetialy) not meete to be equalled with presente actions (shuch as ours was) much less worthy to be prefered before them; and therfore did we make some weake beginings in that good worke, in the place afforesaid.

Ans: Their answer was to this effecte. That if it was the Lords wast, it was them selves that found it so, and not they; and have since bought it of the right oweners, and maintained a chargable possession upon it al this while, as them selves could not but know. And because they could not presently remove them selves tow it, because of present ingagments and other hinderances which lay at presente upon them, must it therfore be lawfull for them to goe and take it from them? It was well known that they are upon a barren place, wher they were by necessitie cast; and neither they nor theirs could longe continue upon the same; and why should they (because they were more ready, and more able at presente) goe and deprive them of that which they had with charge and hazard provided, and intended to remove to, as soone as they could and were able?

They had another passage in their letter; they had rather have to doe with the lords in England, to whom (as they heard it reported) some of them should say that they had rather give up their right to them, (if they must part with it,) then to the church of Dorchester, etc. And that they should be less fearfull to offend the lords, then they were them.

Ans: Their answer was, that what soever they had heard, (more then was true,) yet the case was not so with them that they had need to give away their rights and adventures, either to the lords, or them; yet, if they might measure their fear of offence by their practise, they had rather (in that poynte) they should deal with the lords, who were beter able to bear it, or help them selves, then they were.

But least I should be teadious, I will forbear other things, and come to the conclusion that was made in the endd. To make any forcible resistance was farr from their thoughts, (they had enough of that about Kenebeck,) and to live in continuall contention with their freinds and brethren would be uncomfortable, and too heavie a burthen to bear. Therfore for peace sake (though they conceived they suffered much in this thing) they thought it better to let them have it upon as good termes as they could gett; and so they fell to treaty. The first thing that (because they had made so many and long disputes aboute it) they would have them to grante was, that they had right too it, or ells they would never treat aboute it. They which being acknowledged, and yeelded unto by them, this was the conclusion they came unto in the end after much adoe: that they should retaine their house, and have the ·16· parte of all they had bought of the Indeans; and the other should have all the rest of the land; leaveing such a moyety to those of New-towne, as they reserved for them. This ·16· part was to be taken in too places; one towards the house, the other towards New-townes proportion. Also they were to pay according to proportion, what had been disbursed to the Indeans for the purchass. Thus was the controversie ended, but the unkindnes not so soone forgotten. They of New-towne delt more fairly, desireing only what they could conveniently spare, from a competancie reserved for a plantation, for them selves; which made them the more carfull to procure a moyety for them, in this agreement and distribution.

Amongst the other bussinesses that Mr. Winslow had to doe in England, he had order from the church to provide and bring over some able and fitt man for to be their minister. And accordingly he had procured a godly and a worthy man, one Mr. Glover; but it pleased God when he was prepared for the viage, he fell sick of a feaver and dyed. After wards, when he was ready to come away, he became acquainted with Mr. Norton, who was willing to come over, but would not ingage him selfe to this place, otherwise then he should see occasion when he came hear; and if he liked better else wher, to repay the charge laid out for him, (which came to aboute 70*li*.) and to be at his liberty. He stayed aboute a year with them, after he came over, and was well liked of them, and much desired by them; but he was invited to Ipswich, wher were many rich and able men, and sundry of his aquaintance; so he wente to them, and is their minister. Aboute half of the charg was repayed, the rest he had for the pains he tooke amongst them.

ANNO DOM: ·1636·

Mr. ED: WINSLOW was chosen Governor this year.
In the former year, because they perceived by Mr. Winslows later leters that no accounts would be sente, they resolved to keep the beaver, and send no more, till they had them, or came to some further agreemente. At least they would forbear till Mr. Winslow came over, that by more full conferance with him they might better understand what was meete to be done. But when he came, though he brought no accounts, yet he perswaded them to send the beaver, and was confident upon the receite of that beaver, and his letters, they should have accounts the nexte year; and though they thought his grounds but weake, that gave him this hope, and made him so confidente, yet by his importunitie they yeelded, and sente the same, ther being a ship at the latter end of year, by whom they sente 1150 *li*. waight of beaver, and ·200· otter skins, besides sundrie small furrs, as ·55· minks, ·2· black foxe skins, etc. And this year, in the spring, came in a Dutch man, who thought to have traded at the Dutch forte; but they would not suffer him. He, having good store of trading goods, came to this place, and tendred them to sell; of whom they bought a good quantitie, they being very good and fitte for their turne, as Dutch roll, ketles, etc., which goods amounted to the valew

of 500*li*., for the paymente of which they passed bills to Mr. Sherley in England, having before sente the forementioned parcell of beaver. And now this year (by another ship) sente an other good round parcell that might come to his hands, and be sould before any of these bills should be due. The quantity of beaver now sent was 1809*li*. waight, and of otters ·10· skins, and shortly after (the same year) was sent by another ship (Mr. Langrume maister), in beaver 0719*li*. waight, and of otter skins ·199· concerning which Mr. Sherley thus writes.

Your leters I have received, with ·8· hoggsheads of beaver by Ed: Wilkinson, master of the Falcon. Blessed be God for the safe coming of it. I have also seen and acceped ·3· bills of exchainge, etc. But I must now acquainte you how the Lords heavie hand is upon this kingdom in many places, but cheefly in this cittie, with his judgmente of the plague. The last weeks bill was ·1200· and odd, I fear this will be more; and it is much feared it will be a winter sicknes. By reason wherof it is incredible the number of people that are gone into the cuntry and left the citie. I am perswaded many more then wente out the last great sicknes; so as here is no trading, carriors from most places put downe; nor no receiving of any money, though long due. Mr. Hall ows us more then would pay these bills, but he, his wife, and all, are in the cuntrie, ·60· miles from London. I write to him, he came up, but could not pay us. I am perswaded if I should offer to sell the beaver at 8*s*. per pound, it would not yeeld money; but when the Lord shall please to cease his hand, I hope we shall have better and quicker markets; so it shall lye by. Before I accepted the bills, I acquainted Mr. Beachamp and Mr. Andrews with them, and how ther could be no money made nor received; and that it would be a great discredite to you, which never yet had any turned back, and a shame to us, haveing 1800 *li*. of beaver lying by us, and more oweing then the bills come too, etc. But all was nothing; neither of them both will put too their finger to help. I offered to supply my ·3· parte, but they gave me their answer they neither would nor could, etc. How ever, your bils shall be satisfied to the parties good contente; but I would not have thought they would have left either you or me at this time, etc. You will and may expect I should write more, and answer your leters, but I am not a day in the weeke at home at towne, but carry my books and all to Clapham; for here is the miserablest time that I thinke hath been known in many ages. I have known ·3· great sickneses, but none like this. And that which should be a means to pacifie the Lord, and help us, that is taken away, preaching put downe in many places, not a sermone in Westminster on the saboth, nor in many townes aboute us; the Lord in mercie looke uppon us. In the begining of the year was a great drought, and no raine for many weeks togeather, so as all was burnte up, haye, at 5*li*. a load; and now all raine, so as much sommer corne and later haye is spoyled. Thus the Lord sends judgmente after judgmente, and yet we cannot see, nor humble our selves; and therfore may justly fear heavier judgments, unless we speedyly repente, and returne unto him, which the Lord give us grace to doe, if it be his blessed will. Thus desiring you to remember us in your prayers, I ever rest

Your loving friend,
JAMES SHERLEY.

September 14. 1636.

This was all the answer they had from Mr. Sherley, by which Mr. Winslow saw his hopes failed him. So they now resoloved to send no more beaver in that way which they had done, till they came to some issue or other aboute these things. But now came over letters from Mr. Andrews and Mr. Beachamp full of complaints, that they marveled that nothing was sent over, by which any of their moneys should be payed in; for it did appear by the accounte sente in Anno 1631. that they were each of them out, aboute a leven hundred pounds a peece, and all this while had not received one penie towards the same. But now Mr. Sherley sought to draw more money from them, and was offended because they deneyed him; and blamed them hear very much that all was sent to Mr. Sherley, and nothing to them. They marvelled much at this, for they conceived that much of their moneis had been paid in, and that yearly each of them had received a proportionable quantity out of the large returnes sent home. For they had sente home since that accounte was received in Anno 1631. (in which all and more then all their debts, with that years supply, was charged upon them) these sumes following.

Novbr. 18.	Ano 1631.	By Mr. Peirce	0400*li*.	waight of beaver, and otters	20.
July 13.	Ano 1632.	By Mr. Griffin	1348*li*.	beaver, and otters . .	147.
	Ano 1633.	By Mr. Graves	3366*li*.	beaver, and otters . .	346.
	Ano 1634.	By Mr. Andrews	3738*li*.	beaver, and otters . .	234.
	Ano 1635.	By Mr. Babb	1150*li*.	beaver, and otters . .	200.
June 24.	Ano 1636.	By Mr. Willkinson	1809*li*.	beaver, and otters . .	010.
	Ibidem.	By Mr. Langrume	0719*li*.	beaver, and otters . .	199.
			12150*li*.		1156

All these sumes were safly received and well sould, as appears by leters. The coat beaver usualy at ·20s. per pound, and some at ·24s.; the skin at ·15· and sometimes ·16· I doe not remember any under ·14· It may be the last year might be something lower, so also ther were some small furrs that are not recconed in this accounte, and some black beaver at higher rates, to make up the defects. It was conceived that the former parcells of beaver came to litle less then 10000*li.* sterling, and the otter skins would pay all the charge, and they with other furrs make up besides if any thing wanted of the former sume. When the former accounte was passed, all their debts (those of White-Angelle and Frendship included) came but to 4770*li.* And they could not estimate that all the supplies since sent them, and bills payed for them, could come to above 2000*li.* so as they conceived their debts had been payed, with advantage or intrest. But it may be objected, how comes it that they could not as well exactly sett downe their receits, as their returnes, but thus estimate it. I answer, ·2· things were the cause of it; the first and principall was, that the new accountante, which they in England would needs presse upon them, did wholy faile them, and could never give them any accounte; but trusting to his memorie, and lose papers, let things rune into shuch confusion, that neither he, nor any with him, could bring things to rights. But being often called upon to perfecte his accounts, he desired to have shuch a time, and shuch a time of leasure, and he would doe it. In the intrime he fell into a great sicknes, and in conclusion it fell out he could make no accounte at all. His books were after a litle good begining left altogeather unperfect; and his papers, some were lost, and others so confused, as he knew not what to make of them him selfe, when they came to be searched and examined. This was not unknowne to Mr. Sherley; and they came to smarte for it to purposs, (though it was not their faulte,) both thus in England, and also here; for they conceived they lost some hundreds of pounds for goods trusted out in the place, which were lost for want of clear accounts to call them in. Another reason of this mischeefe was, that after Mr. *Winslow* was sente into England to demand accounts, and to excepte against the *Whit-Angell*, they never had any price sent with their goods, nor any certain invoyce of them; but all things stood in confusion, and they were faine to guesse at the prises of them.

They write back to Mr. Andrews and Mr. Beachamp, and tould them they marveled they should write they had sent nothing home since the last accounts; for they had sente a great deale; and it might rather be marvelled how they could be able to send so much, besides defraying all charge at home, and what they had lost by the French, and so much cast away at sea, when Mr. Peirce lost his ship on the coast of Virginia. What they had sente was to them all, and to them selves as well as Mr. Sherley, and if they did not looke after it, it was their owne falts; they must referr them to Mr. Sherley, who had received it, to demand it of him. They allso write to Mr. Sherley to the same purpos, and what the others complaintes were.

This year ·2· shallops going to Coonigtecutt with goods from the Massachusetts of shuch as removed theither to plante, were in an easterly storme cast away in coming into this harbore in the night; the boats men were lost, and the goods were driven all alonge the shore, and strowed up and downe at highwater marke. But the Governor caused them to be gathered up, and drawn togeather, and appointed some to take an inventory of them, and others to wash and drie shuch things as had neede therof; by which means most of the goods were saved, and restored to the owners. Afterwards anotheir boate of theirs (going thither likwise) was cast away near unto Manoanscusett, and shuch goods as came a shore were preserved for them. Shuch crosses they mette with in their beginings; which some imputed as a correction from God for their intrution (to the wrong of others) into that place. But I dare not be bould with Gods judgments in this kind.

In the year 1634, the Pequents (a stoute and warlike people,) who had made warrs with sundry of their neigbours, and puft up with many victories, grue now at varience with the Narigansets, a great people bordering upon them. These Narigansets held correspondance and termes of freindship with the English of the Massachusetts. Now the Pequents, being conscious of the guilte of Captain-Stones death, whom they knew to be an-English man, as also those that were with him, and being fallen out with the Dutch, least they should have over many enemies at once, sought to make friendship with the English of the Massachusetts; and for that end sent both messengers and gifts unto them, as appears by some letters sent from the Governor hither.

DEAR AND WORTHY SIR: ETC. To let you know somwhat of our affairs, you may understand that the Pequents have sent some of theirs to us, to desire our freindship, and offered much wampam and beaver, etc. The first messengers were dismissed without answer; with the next we had diverce dayes conferance, and taking the advice of some of our ministers, and seeking the Lord in it, we concluded a peace and freindship with them, upon these conditions: that they should deliver up to us those men who were guilty of Stones death, etc. And if we desired to plant in Conightecute, they should give up their right to us, and so we would send to trade with them as our freinds (which was the cheefe thing we aimed at, being now in warr with the Dutch and the rest of their neigbours). To this they readily agreed; and that we should meadiate a peace betweene them and the Narigansetts; for which end they were contente we should give the Narigansets parte of that presente, they would bestow on us (for they stood so much on their honour, as they would not be seen to give any thing of them selves). As for Captein Stone, they tould us ther were but ·2· left of those who had any hand in his death; and that they killed him in a just quarell, for (say they) he surprised ·2· of our men, and bound them, to make them by force to shew him the way up the river;* and he with ·2· other coming on shore, ·9· Indeans watched him, and when they were a sleepe in the night, they kiled them, to deliver their owne men; and some of them going afterwards to the pinass, it was suddainly blowne up. We are now preparing to send a pinass unto them, etc.

In an other of his, dated the 12. of the first month, he hath this:

Our pinass is latly returned from the Pequents; they put of but litle comoditie, and found them a very false people, so as they mean to have no more to doe with them. I have diverce other things to write unto you, etc.

Yours ever assured,
JO: WINTHROP.

Boston, 12. of the 1. month, 1634.

*Ther is litle trust to be given to their relations in these things.

After these things, and, as I take, this year, John Oldom, (of whom much is spoken before,) being now an inhabitant of the Massachusetts, went with a small vessell, and slenderly mand, a trading into these south parts, and upon a quarell betweene him and the Indeans was cutt of by them (as hath been before noted), at an iland called by the Indeans Munisses but since by the English Block Iland. This, with the former about the death of Stone, and the baffoylling of the Pequents with the English of the Massachusetts, moved them to set out some to take revenge, and require satisfaction for these wrongs; but it was done so superfitially, and without their acquainting of those of Conightecute and other neighbours with the same, as they did little good. But their neigbours had more hurt done, for some of the murderers of Oldome fled to the Pequents, and though the English went to the Pequents, and had some parley with them, yet they did but delude them, and the English returned without doing any thing to purpose, being frustrate of their oppertunitie by the others deceite. After the English were returned, the Pequents tooke their time and oppertunitie to cut of some of the English as they passed in boats, and went on fouling, and assaulted them the next spring at ther habytations, as will appear in its place. I doe but touch these things, because I make no question they will be more fully and distinctly handled by them selves, who had more exacte knowledg of them, and whom they did more properly concerne.

This year Mr. Smith layed downe his place of ministrie, partly by his owne willingnes, as thinking it too heavie a burthen, and partly at the desire, and by the perswasion, of others; and the church sought out for some other, having often been disappointed in their hopes and desires heretofore. And it pleased the Lord to send them an able and a godly man,* and of a meeke and humble spirite, sound in the truth, and every way unreproveable in his life and conversation; whom, after some time of triall, they chose for their teacher, the fruits of whose labours they injoyed many years with much comforte, in peace, and good agreemente.

*Mr. John Reinor.

ANNO DOM: ·1637·

IN the fore parte of this year, the Pequents fell openly upon the English at Conightecute, in the lower parts of the river, and slew sundry of them, (as they were at work in the feilds,) both men and women, to the great terrour of the rest; and wente away in great pride and triumph, with many high threats. They allso assalted a fort at the rivers mouth, though strong and well defended; and though they did not their prevaile, yet it struck them with much fear and astonishmente to see their bould attempts in the face of danger; which made them in all places to stand upon their gard, and to prepare for resistance, and ernestly to solissite their freinds and confedrates in the Bay of Massachusets to send them speedy aide, for they looked for more forcible assaults. Mr. Vane, being then Governor, write from their Generall Courte to them hear, to joyne with them in this warr; to which they were cordially willing, but tooke opportunitie to write to them aboute some former things, as well as presente, considerable hereaboute. The which will best appear in the Governor's answer which he returned to the same, which I shall here inserte.

SIR: The Lord having so disposed, as that your letters to our late Governor is fallen to my lott to make answer unto, I could have wished I might have been at more freedome of time and thoughts also, that I might have done it more to your and my owne satisfaction. But what shall be wanting now may be supplyed hearafter. For the matters which from your selfe and counsell were propounded and objected to us, we thought not fitte to make them so publicke as the cognizance of our Generall Courte. But as they have been considered by those of our counsell, this answer we thinke fitt to returne unto you (1) Wereas you signifie your willingnes to joyne with us in this warr against the Pequents, though you cannot ingage your selves without the consente of your Generall Courte, we acknowledg your good affection towards us, (which we never had cause to doubt of,) and are willing to attend your full resolution, when it may most seasonably be ripened. (2ly.) Wheras you make this warr to be our peoples, and not to conceirne your selves, otherwise then by consequence, we do in parte consente to you therin; yet we suppose, that, in case of perill, you will not stand upon shuch terms, as we hope we should not doe towards you;

and withall we conceive that you looke at the Pequents, and all other Indeans, as a commone enimie, who, though he may take occasion of the begining of his rage, from some one parte of the English, yet if he prevaile, will surly pursue his advantage, to the rooting out of the whole nation. Therfore when we desired your help, we did it not without respecte to your owne saftie, as ours. (3ly.) Wheras you desire we should be ingaged to aide you, upon all like occasions; we are perswaded you doe not doubte of it; yet as we now deale with you as a free people, and at libertie, so as we cannot draw you into this warr with us, otherwise then as reason may guid and provock you; so we desire we may be at the like freedome, when any occasion may call for help from us. And wheras it is objected to us, that we refused to aide you against the French; we conceive the case was not alicke; yet we cannot wholy excuse our failing in that matter.

(4ly.) Weras you objecte that we began the warr without your privitie, and managed it contrary to your advise; the truth is, that our first intentions being only against Block Island, and the interprice seeming of small difficultie, we did not so much as consider of taking advice, or looking out for aide abroad. And when we had resolved upon the Pequents, we sent presently, or not long after, to you about it; but the answer received, it was not seasonable for us to chaing our counsells, excepte we had seen and waighed your grounds, which might have out wayed our owne.

(5ly.) For our peoples trading at Kenebeck, we assure you (to our knowledge) it hath not been by any allowance from us; and what we have provided in this and like cases, at our last Courte, Mr. E. Winslow can certifie you.

And (6ly.); wheras you objecte to us that we should hold trade and correspondencie with the French, your enemise; we answer, you are misinformed, for, besides some letters which hath passed betweene our late Governor and them, to which we were privie, we have neither sente nor incouraged ours to trade with them; only one vessell or tow, for the better conveance of our letters, had licens from our Governor to sayle thither.*

Diverce other things have been privatly objected to us, by our worthy freind, wherunto he received some answer; but most of them concerning the apprehentions of perticuler discurteseis, or injueries from some perticuler persons amongst us. It concernes us not to give any other answer to them then this; that, if the offenders shall be brought forth in a right way, we shall be ready to doe justice as the

---

*But by this means they did furnish them, and have still continued to doe.

case shall require. In the meane time, we desire you to rest assured, that shuch things are without our privity, and not a litle greeveous to us.

Now for the joyning with us in this warr, which indeed concerns us no other wise then it may your selves, viz.: the releeving of our freinds and Christian breethren, who are now first in the danger; though you may thinke us able to make it good without you, (as, if the Lord please to be with us, we may,) yet ·3· things we offer to your consideration, which (we conceive) may have some waight with you. (First) that if we should sinck under this burden, your opportunitie of seasonable help would be lost in ·3· respects. 1. You cannot recover us, or secure your selves ther, with ·3· times the charge and hazard which now you may. 2ly. The sorrowes which we should lye under (if through your neglect) would much abate of the acceptablenes of your help afterwards. 3ly. Those of yours, who are now full of courage and forwardnes, would be much damped, and so less able to undergoe so great a burden. The (2) thing is this, that it concernes us much to hasten this warr to an end before the end of this sommer, other wise the newes of it will discourage both your and our freinds from coming to us next year; with what further hazard and losse it may expose us unto, your selves may judge.

The (3) thing is this, that if the Lord shall please to blesse our endeavours, so as we end the warr, or put it in a hopefull way without you, it may breed shuch ill thoughts in our people towards yours, as will be hard to entertaine shuch opinione of your good will towards us, as were fitt to be nurished among shuch neigbours and brethren as we are. And what ill consequences may follow, on both sides, wise men may fear, and would rather prevente then hope to redress. So with my harty salutations to you selfe, and all your counsell, and other our good freinds with you, I rest

Yours most assured in the Lord,
JO: WINTHROP.

Boston, the ·20· of the ·3· month, 1637.

In the mean time, the Pequents, espetially in the *winter before*, sought to make peace with the Narigansets, and used very pernicious arguments to move them therunto: as that the English were strangers and begane to overspred their countrie, and would deprive them thereof in time, if they were suffered to grow and increse; and if the Narigansets did assist the English to subdue them, they did but make way for their owne overthrow, for if they were rooted out, the English would soone take occasion to subjugate them; and if they would harken to them, they should not neede to fear the strength of the English; for they would not come to open battle with them, but fire their houses, kill their katle, and lye in ambush for them as they went abroad upon their occasions; and all this they might easily doe without any or litle danger to them selves. The which course being held, they well saw the English could not long subsiste, but they would either be starved with hunger, or be forced to forsake the countrie; with many the like things; insomuch that the Narigansets were once wavering, and were halfe minded to have made peace with them, and joyned against the English. But againe when they considered, how much wrong they had received from the Pequents, and what an oppertunitie they now had by the help of the English to right them selves, revenge was so sweete unto them, as it prevailed above all the rest; so as they resolved to joyne with the English against them, and did. The Court here agreed forthwith to send ·50· men at their owne charge; and with as much speed as possiblie they could, gott them armed, and had made them ready under sufficiente leaders, and provided a barke to carrie them provisions and tend upon them for all occasions; but when they were ready to march (with a supply from the Bay) they had word to stay, for the enimy was as good as vanquished, and their would be no neede.

I shall not take upon me exactly to describe their proceedings in these things, because I expecte it will be fully done by them selves, who best know the carrage and circumstances of things; I shall therfore but touch them in generall. From Connightecute (who were most sencible of the hurt sustained, and the present danger), they sett out a partie of men, and an other partie mett them from the Bay, at the Narigansets, who were to joyne with them. The Narigansets were ernest to be gone before the English were well rested and refreshte, espetially some of them which came last. It should seeme their desire was to come upon the enemie sudenly, and undiscovered. Ther was a barke of this place, newly put in ther, which was come from Conightecutte, who did incourage them to lay hold of the Indeans forwardnes, and to shew as great forwardnes as they, for it would incorage them, and expedition might prove to their great advantage. So they wente on, and so ordered their march, as the Indeans brought them to a forte of the enimies (in which most of their cheefe men were) before day. They aproached the same with great silence, and surrounded it both with English and Indeans, that they might not breake out; and so assualted them with great courage, shooting amongst them, and entered the forte with all speed; and those that first entered found sharp resistance from the enimie, who both shott at and grapled with them; others rane into their howses, and brought out fire, and sett them one fire, which some tooke in their matts, and standing close togeather, with the wind, all was quickly on a flame, and therby more were burnte to death then was otherwise slain; it burnte their bowstrings, and made them unservisable. Those that scaped the fire were slaine with the sword; some hewed to peeces, others rune throw with their rapiers, so as they were quickly dispatchte, and very few escaped. It was conceived they thus destroyed about ·400· at this time. It was a fearfull sight to see them thus frying in the fyer, and the streams of blood quenching the same, and horrible was the stinck and sente ther of; but the victory seemed a sweete sacrifice, and they gave the prays therof to God, who had wrought so wonderfuly for them, thus to inclose their enimise in their hands, and give them so speedy a victory over so proud and insulting an enimie. The Narigansett Indeans, all this while, stood round aboute, but aloofe from all danger, and left the whole execution to the English, exept it were the stoping of any that broke away, insulting over their enimies in this their ruine and miserie, when they saw them dancing in the flames, calling them by a word in their owne language, signifing, O brave Pequents! which they used familierly among them selves in their own prayes, in songs of triumph after their victories. After this servis was thus happily accomplished, they marcht to the water side, wher they mett with some of their vesells, by which they had refreshing with victualls and other necessaries. But in their march the rest of the Pequents drew into a body, and acoasted them, thinking to have some advantage against them by reason of a neck of land; but when they saw the English prepare for them, they kept aloofe, so as they neither did hurt, nor could receive any. After their refreshing and repair to geather for further counsell and directions, they resolved to pursue their victory, and follow the warr against the rest, but the Narigansett Indeans most of them forsooke them, and shuch of them as they had with them for guides, or other wise, they found them very could and backward in the bussines, etheir out of envie, or that they saw the English would make more profite of the victorie then they were willing they should, or els deprive them of such advantage as them selves desired by having them become tributaries unto them, or the like.

For the rest of this bussines, I shall only relate the same as it is in a leter which came from Mr. Winthrop to the Governor hear, as followeth.

WORTHY SIR: I received your loving letter, and am much provocked to express my affections towards you, but straitnes of time forbids me; for my desire is to acquainte you with the Lords greate mercies towards us, in our prevailing against his and our enimies; that you may rejoyce and praise his name with us. About ·80· of our men, haveing costed along towards the Dutch plantation, (some times by water, but most by land,) mett hear and ther with some Pequents, whom they slew or tooke prisoners. ·2· sachems they tooke, and beheaded; and not hearing of Sassacous, (the cheefe sachem,) they gave a prisoner his life, to goe and find him out. He wente and brought them word wher he was, but Sassacouse, suspecting him to be a spie, after he was gone, fled away with some ·20· more to the Mowakes, so our men missed of him. Yet, devideing them selves, and ranging up and downe, as the providence of God guided them (for the Indeans were all gone, save ·3· or ·4· and they knew not whither to guide them, or els would not), upon the ·13· *of this month*, they light upon a great company of them, viz. 80. strong men, and ·200· women and children, in a small Indean towne, fast by a hideous swamp, which they all slipped into before our men could gett to them. Our captains were not then come togeither, but ther was Mr. Ludlow and Captaine Masson, with some ·10· of their men, and Captaine Patrick with some ·20· or more of his, who, shooting at the Indeans, Captaine Trask with ·50· more came soone in at the noyse. Then they gave order to surround the swampe, it being aboute a mile aboute; but Levetenante Davenporte and some ·12· more, not hearing that command, fell into the swampe among the Indeans. The swampe was so thicke with shrubwoode, and so boggie with all, that some of them stuck fast, and received many shott. Levetenant Davenport was dangerously wounded aboute his armehole, and another shott in the head, so as, fainting, they were in great danger to have been taken by the Indeans. But Sargante

Rigges, and Jeffery, and ·2· or ·3· more, rescued them, and slew diverse of the Indeans with their swords. After they were drawne out, the Indeans desired parley, and were offered (by Thomas Stanton, our interpretour) that, if they would come out, and yeeld them selves, they should have their lives, all that had not their hands in the English blood. Wherupon the sachem of the place came forth, and an old man or ·2· and their wives and chilldren, and after that some other women and children, and so they spake ·2· howers, till it was night. Then Thomas Stanton was sente into them againe, to call them forth; but they said they would selle their lives their, and so shott at him so thicke as, if he had not cried out, and been presently rescued, they had slaine him. Then our men cutt of a place of the swampe with their swords, and cooped the Indeans into so narrow a compass, as they could easier kill them throw the thikets. So they continued all the night, standing aboute ·12· foote one from an other, and the Indeans, coming close up to our men, shot their arrows so thicke, as they pierced their hatte brimes, and their sleeves, and stockins, and other parts of their cloaths, yet so miraculously did the Lord preserve them as not one of them was wounded, save those ·3· who rashly went into the swampe. When it was nere day, it grue very darke, so as those of them which were left dropt away betweene our men, though they stood but ·12· or ·14· foote assunder; but were presenly discovered, and some killed in the pursute. Upon searching of the swampe, the next morning, they found ·9· slaine, and some they pulled up, whom the Indeans had buried in the mire, so as they doe thinke that, of all this company, not ·20· did escape, for they after found some who dyed in their flight of their wounds received. The prisoners were devided, some to those of the river, and the rest to us. Of these we send the male children to Bermuda,* by Mr. William Peirce, and the women and maid children are disposed aboute in the townes. Ther have been now slaine and taken, in all, aboute ·700· The rest are dispersed, and the Indeans in all quarters so terrified as all their friends are affraid to receive them. 2. of the sachems of Long Iland came to Mr. Stoughton and tendered them selves to be tributaries under our protection. And ·2· of the Neepnett sachems have been with me to seeke our frendship. Amonge the prisoners we have the wife and children of Mononotto, a woman of a very modest countenance and behaviour. It was by her mediation that the ·2· English maids were spared from death, and were kindly used by her; so that I have taken charge of her. One of her first requests was, that the English would not abuse her body, and that her children might not be taken from her. Those which were

*But they were carried to the West-Indeas.

wounded were fetched of soone by John Galopp, who came with his shalop in a happie houre, to bring them victuals, and to carrie their wounded men to the pinnass, wher our cheefe surgeon was, with Mr. Willson, being aboute ·8· leagues off. Our people are all in health, (the Lord be praised,) and allthough they had marched in their armes all the day, and had been in fight all the night, yet they professed they found them selves so fresh as they could willingly have gone to shuch another bussines.

This is the substance of that which I received, though I am forced to omite many considerable circomstances. So, being in much straitnes of time, (the ships being to departe within this ·4· days, and in them the Lord Lee and Mr. Vane,) I hear breake of, and with harty salutes to, etc., I rest

Yours assured,
JO: WINTHROP.

The ·28· of the ·5· month 1637.

The captains reporte we have slaine ·13· sachems; but Sassacouse and Monotto are yet living.

That I may make an end of this matter: this Sassacouse (the Pequents cheefe sachem) being fled to the Mowhakes, they cutt of his head, with some other of the cheefe of them, whether to satisfie the English, or rather the Narigansets, (who, as I have since heard, hired them to doe it,) or for their owne advantage, I well know not; but thus this warr tooke end. The rest of the Pequents were wholy driven from their place, and some of them submitted them selves to the Narigansets, and lived under them; others of them betooke them selves to the Monhiggs, under Uncass, their sachem, with the approbation of the English of Conightecutt, under whose protection Uncass lived, and he and his men had been faithfull to them in this warr, and done them very good service. But this did so vexe the Narrigansetts, that they had not the whole sweay over them, as they have never ceased plotting and contriving how to bring them under, and because they cannot attaine their ends, because of the English who have protected them, they have sought to raise a generall conspiracie against the English, as will appear in an other place.

They had now letters againe out of England from Mr. Andrews and Mr. Beachamp, that Mr. Sherley neither had nor

would pay them any money, or give them any accounte, and so
with much discontent desired them hear to send them some,
much blaming them still, that they had sent all to Mr. Sherley,
and none to them selves. Now, though they might have justly
referred them to their former answer, and insisted ther upon,
and some wise men counselled them so to doe, yet because
they beleeved that they were realy out round sumes of money,
(espetialy Mr. Andrews,) and they had some in their hands,
they resolved to send them what bever they had.* Mr. Sherleys
letters were to this purpose: that, as they had left him in the
paiment of the former bills, so he had tould them he would
leave them in this, and beleeve it, they should find it true. And
he was as good as his word, for they could never gett peney from
him, nor bring him to any accounte, though Mr. Beachamp
sued him in the Chancerie. But they all of them turned their
complaints against them here, wher ther was least cause, and
who had suffered most unjustly; first from Mr. Allerton and
them, in being charged with so much of that which they never
had, nor drunke for; and now in paying all, and more then all
(as they conceived), and yet still thus more demanded, and that
with many heavie charges. They now discharged Mr. Sherley
from his agencie, and forbad him to buy or send over any more
goods for them, and prest him to come to some end about
these things.

ANNO DOM: ·1638·

THIS year Mr. Thomas Prence was chosen Governor.
Amongst other enormities that fell out amongst them,
this year ·3· men were (after due triall) executed for robery and
murder which they had committed; their names were these,
Arthur Peach, Thomas Jackson, and Richard Stinnings; ther
was a ·4·, Daniel Crose, who was also guilty, but he escaped
away, and could not be found. This Arthur Peach was the
cheefe of them, and the ring leader of all the rest. He was a
lustie and a desperate yonge man, and had been one of the
souldiers in the Pequente warr, and had done as good servise
as the most ther, and one of the forwardest in any attempte.

*But staid it till the next year.

And being now out of means, and loath to worke, and falling to idle courses and company, he intended to goe to the
Dutch plantation; and had alured these ·3·, being other mens
servants and apprentices, to goe with him. But another cause
ther was allso of his secret going away in this maner; he was
not only rune into debte, but he had gott a maid with child,
(which was not known till after his death,) a mans servante in
the towne, and fear of punishmente made him gett away. The
other ·3· complotting with him, ranne away from their maisters
in the night, and could not be heard of, for they went not the
ordinarie way, but shaped shuch a course as they thought to
avoyd the pursute of any. But falling into the way that lyeth
betweene the Bay of Massachusetts and the Narrigansets, and
being disposed to rest them selves, struck fire, and took tobaco,
a litle out of the way, by the way side. At length ther came an
Narigansett Indean by, who had been in the Bay a trading, and
had both cloth and beads aboute him. (They had meett him
the day before, and he was now returning.) Peach called him
to drinke tobaco with them, and he came and sate downe with
them. Peach tould the other he would kill him, and take what
he had from him. But they were some thing afraid; but he said,
Hang him, rogue, he had killed many of them. So they let him
alone to doe as he would; and when he saw his time, he tooke a
rapier and rane him through the body once or twise, and tooke
from him ·5· fathume of wampam, and ·3· coats of cloath, and
wente their way, leaving him for dead. But he scrabled away,
when they were gone, and made shift to gett home, (but dyed
within a few days after,) by which means they were discovered;
and by subtilty the Indeans tooke them. For they desiring a
canow to sett them over a water, (not thinking their facte had
been known,) by the sachems command they were carried to
Aquidnett Iland, and ther accused of the murder, and were
examined and comitted upon it by the English ther. The Indeans sent for Mr. Williams, and made a greevous complainte;
his freinds and kinred were ready to rise in armes, and provock
the rest therunto, some conceiving they should now find the
Pequents words trew: that the English would fall upon them.
But Mr. Williams pacified them, and tould them they should
see justice done upon the offenders; and wente to the man, and
tooke Mr. James, a phisition, with him. The man tould him

who did it, and in what maner it was done; but the phisition found his wounds mortall, and that he could not live, (as he after testified upon othe, before the jurie in oppen courte,) and so he dyed shortly after, as both Mr. Williams, Mr. James, and some Indeans testified in courte. The Government in the Bay were aquented with it, but refferrd it hither, because it was done in this jurissdiction;* but pressed by all means that justice might be done in it; or els the countrie must rise and see justice done, otherwise it would raise a warr. Yet some of the rude and ignorante sorte murmured that any English should be put to death for the Indeans. So at last they of the iland brought them hither, and being often examened, and the evidence prodused, they all in the end freely confessed in effect all that the Indean accused them of, and that they had done it, in the maner afforesaid; and so, upon the forementioned evidence, were cast by the jurie, and condemned, and executed for the same. September 4. And some of the Narigansett Indeans, and of the parties freinds, were presente when it was done, which gave them and all the countrie good satisfaction. But it was a matter of much sadnes to them hear, and was the ·2· execution which they had since they came; being both for willfull murder, as hath bene before related. Thus much of this mater.

They received this year more letters from England full of reneued complaints, one the one side, that they could gett no money nor accounte from Mr. Sherley; and he againe, that he was pressed therto, saying he was to accounte with those hear, and not with them, etc. So, as was before resolved, if nothing came of their last letters, they would now send them what they could, as supposing, when some good parte was payed them, that Mr. Sherley and they would more easily agree aboute the remainder.

So they sent to Mr. Andrews and Mr. Beachamp, by Mr. Joseph Yonge, in the Mary and Anne, 1325*li*. waight of beaver, devided betweene them. Mr. Beachamp returned an accounte of his moyety, that he made 400*li*. starling of it, fraight and all charges paid. But Mr. Andrews, though he had the more and beter parte, yet he made not so much of his, through his

---

*And yet afterwards they laid claime to those parts in this controversie about Seacunk.

owne indiscretion; and yet turned the loss* upon them hear, but without cause.

They sent them more by bills and other paimente, which was received and acknowledged by them, in money† and the like; which was for katle sould of Mr. Allertons, and the price of a bark sold, which belonged to the stock, and made over to them in money, 434*li*. sterling. The whole sume was 1234*li*. sterling, save what Mr. Andrews lost in the beaver, which was otherwise made good. But yet this did not stay their clamors, as will apeare here after more at large.

It pleased God, in these times, so to blesse the cuntry with shuch access and confluance of people into it, as it was therby much inriched, and catle of all kinds stood at a high rate for diverce years togeather. Kine were sould at 20*li*. and some at 25*li*. a peece, yea, some times at 28*li*. A cow-calfe usually at 10*li*. A milch goate at 3*li*. and some at 4*li*. And femall kids at 30*s*. and often at 40*s*. a peece. By which means the anciente planters which had any stock begane to grow in their estates. Corne also wente at a round rate, viz. 6*s*. a bushell. So as other trading begane to be neglected; and the old partners (having now forbidden Mr. Sherley to send them any more goods) broke of their trade at Kenebeck, and, as things stood, would follow it no longer. But some of them, (with other they joyned with,) being loath it should be lost by discontinuance, agreed with the company for it, and gave them aboute the ·6· parte of their gaines for it; with the first fruits of which they builte a house for a prison; and the trade ther hath been since continued, to the great benefite of the place; for some well foresawe that these high prises of corne and catle would not long continue, and that then the commodities ther raised would be much missed.

This year, aboute the ·1· or ·2· of June, was a great and fearfull earthquake; it was in this place heard before it was felte. It came with a rumbling noyse, or low murmure, like unto remoate thunder; it came from the norward, and pased southward. As the noyse aproched nerer, they earth begane to shake, and came at length with that violence as caused platters, dishes, and shuch like things as stoode upon shelves, to clatter and fall

---

*Being about 40 *li*.
†And devided betweene them.

downe; yea, persons were afraid of the houses them selves. It so fell oute that at the same time diverse of the cheefe of this towne were mett together at one house, conferring with some of their freinds that were upon their removall from the place, (as if the Lord would herby shew the signes of his displeasure, in their shaking a peeces and removalls one from an other.) How ever it was very terrible for the time, and as the men were set talking in the house, some women and others were without the dores, and the earth shooke with that violence as they could not stand without catching hould of the posts and pails that stood next them; but the violence lasted not long. And about halfe an hower, or less, came an other noyse and shaking, but nether so loud nor strong as the former, but quickly passed over; and so it ceased. It was not only on the sea coast, but the Indeans felt it within land; and some ships that were upon coast were shaken by it. So powerfull is the mighty hand of the Lord, as to make both the earth and sea to shake, and the mountaines to tremble before him, when he pleases; and who can stay his hand? It was observed that the sommers, for divers years togeather after this earthquake, were not so hotte and seasonable for the ripning of corne and other fruits as formerly; but more could and moyst, and subjecte to erly and untimly frosts, by which, many times, much Indean corne came not to maturitie; but whether this was any cause, I leave it to naturallists to judge.

ANNO DOM: ·1639· *AND* ANNO DOM: ·1640

THESE ·2· years I joyne togeather, because in them fell not out many things more then the ordinary passages of their commone affaires, which are not needfull to be touched. Those of this plantation having at sundrie times granted lands for severall townships, and amongst the rest to the inhabitants of Sityate, some wherof issewed from them selves, and allso a large tracte of land was given to their ·4· London partners in that place, viz. Mr. Sherley, Mr. Beacham, Mr. Andrews, and Mr. Hatherley. At Mr. Hatherley's request and choys it was by him taken for him selfe and them in that place; for the other ·3· had invested him with power and trust to chose for them. And this tracte of land extended to their utmost limets

that way, and bordered on their neigbours of the Massachusets, who had some years after seated a towne (called Hingam)
on their lands next to these parts. So as now ther grue great
difference betweene these ·2· townships, about their bounds,
and some meadow grownds that lay between them. They of
Hingam presumed to alotte parte of them to their people, and
measure and stack them out. The other pulled up their stacks,
and threw them. So it grew to a controversie betweene the
·2· goverments, and many letters and passages were betweene
them aboute it; and it hunge some ·2· years in suspense. The
Courte of Massachusets appointed some to range their line
according to the bounds of their patente, and (as they wente
to worke) they made it to take in all Sityate, and I know not
how much more. Againe, on the other hand, according to the
line of the patente of this place, it would take in Hingame and
much more within their bounds.

In the end boath Courts agreed to chose ·2· comissioners of
each side, and to give them full and absolute power to agree
and setle the bounds betwene them; and what they should
doe in the case should stand irrevocably. One meeting they
had at Hingam, but could not conclude; for their comissioners
stoode stiffly on a clawes in their graunte, that from Charles-
river, or any branch or parte therof, they were to extend their
limits, and ·3· myles further to the southward; or from the most
southward parte of the Massachusets Bay, and ·3· mile further.
But they chose to stand on the former termes, for they had
found a smale river, or brooke rather, that a great way with in
land trended southward, and issued into some part of that river
taken to be Charles-river, and from the most southerly part of
this, and ·3· mile more southward of the same, they would rune
a line east to the sea, aboute ·20· mile; which will (say they)
take in a part of Plimoth it selfe. Now it is to be knowne that
though this patente and plantation were much the ancienter,
yet this inlargemente of the same (in which Sityate stood) was
granted after theirs, and so theirs were first to take place, before
this inlargmente. Now their answer was, first, that, however
according to their owne plan, they could noway come upon
any part of their ancieante grante. 2*ly*. They could never prove
that to be a parte of Charles-river, for they knew not which
was Charles-river, but as the people of this place, which came
first, imposed shuch a name upon that river, upon which, since,

Charles-towne is builte (supposing that was it, which Captaine Smith in his mapp so named). Now they that first named it have best reason to know it, and to explaine which is it. But they only tooke it to be Charles river, as fare as it was by them navigated, and that was as farr as a boate could goe. But that every runlett or small brooke, that should, farr within land, come into it, or mixe their stremes with it, and were by the natives called by other and differente names from it, should now by them be made Charels-river, or parts of it, they saw no reason for it. And gave instance in Humber, in Old England, which had the Trente, Ouse, and many others of lesser note fell into it, and yet were not counted parts of it; and many smaler rivers and broks fell into the Trente, and Ouse, and no parts of them, but had names aparte, and divissions and nominations of them selves. Againe, it was pleaded that they had no east line in their patente, but were to begine at the sea, and goe west by a line, etc. At this meeting no conclution was made, but things discussed and well prepared for an issue. The *next year* the same commissioners had their power continued or renewed, and mett at Sityate, and concluded the mater, as followeth.

The agreemente of the bounds betwixte Plimoth and Massachusetts.

Wheras ther were tow comissiones granted by the ·2· jurisdictions, the one of Massachusets Govermente, granted unto John Endecott, gent: and Israell Stoughton, gent: the other of New-Plimoth Govermente, to William Bradford, Governor, and Edward Winslow, gent: and both these for the setting out, setling, and determining of the bounds and limitts of the lands betweene the said jurisdictions, wherby not only this presente age, but the posteritie to come may live peaceably and quietly in that behalfe. And for as much as the said comissioners on both sides have full power so to doe, as appeareth by the records of both jurisdictions; we therfore, the said comissioners above named, doe hearby with one consente and agreemente conclude, detirmine, and by these presents declare, that all the marshes at Conahasett that lye of the one side of the river next to Hingam, shall belong to the jurisdiction of Massachusetts Plantation; and all the marshes that lye on the other side of the river next to Sityate, shall be long to the jurisdiction of New-Plimoth; excepting ·60· acers of marsh at the mouth of the river, on Sityate side next to the sea, which we doe herby agree, conclude, and detirmine shall belong to the jurisdiction of the Massachusetts. And further, we doe hearby agree, determine, and conclude, that the bounds of the limites betweene both the said jurisdictions are as followeth, viz. from the mouth of the brook that runeth into Chonahasett marches (which we call by the name of Bound-brooke) with a stright and directe line to the midle of a great ponde, that lyeth on the right hand of the uper path, or commone way, that leadeth betweene Waimoth and Plimoth, close to the path as we goe alonge, which was formerly named (and still we desire may be caled) *Accord pond*, lying aboute five or ·6· myles from Weimoth southerley; and from thence with a straight line to the souther-most part of Charles-river,* and ·3· miles southerly, inward into the countrie, according as is expresed in the patente granted by his Majestie to the Company of the Massachusetts Plantation. Provided allways and never the less concluded and determined by mutuall agreemente betweene the said comissioners, that if it fall out that the said line from Accord-pond to the sothermost parte of Charles-river, and ·3· myles southerly as is before expresed, straiten or hinder any parte of any plantation begune by the Government of New-Plimoth, or hereafter to be begune within ·10· years after the date of these presents, that then, notwithstanding the said line, it shall be lawfull for the said Government of New-Plimoth to assume on the northerly side of the said line, wher it shall so intrench as afforesaid, so much land as will make up the quantity of eight miles square, to belong to every shuch plantation begune, or to begune as afforesaid; which we agree, determine, and conclude to appertaine and belong to the said Government of New-Plimoth. And wheras the said line, from the said brooke which runeth into Chonahassett salt-marshes, called by us Bound-brooke, and the pond called Accord-pond, lyeth nere the lands belonging to the tounships of Sityate and Hingam, we doe therfore hereby determine and conclude, that if any devissions allready made and recorded, by either the said townships, doe crose the said line, that then it shall stand, and be of force according to the former intents and purposes of the said townes granting them (the marshes formerly agreed on exepted). And that no towne in either jurisdiction shall hereafter exceede, but containe them selves within the said lines expressed. In witnes wherof we, the comissioners of both jurisdictions, doe by these presents indented set our hands and seales the ninth day of the ·4· month in ·16· year of our soveraine lord, king Charles; and in the year of our Lord, 1640.

WILLIAM BRADFORD, Govr.   JO: ENDECOTT.
ED: WINSLOW.   ISRAELL STOUGHTON.

*Which is Charles River may still be questioned.

Wheras the patente was taken in the name of William Bradford, (as in trust,) and rane in these termes: To him, his heires, and associates and assignes; and now the noumber of freemen being much increased, and diverce tounships established and setled in severall quarters of the govermente, as *Plimoth, Duxberie, Sityate, Tanton, Sandwich, Yarmouth, Barnstable, Marchfeeld*, and not longe after, *Seacunke* (called afterward, at the desire of the inhabitants, *Rehoboth*) and *Nawsett*, it was by the Courte desired that William Bradford should make a surrender of the same into their hands. The which he willingly did, in this maner following.

Wheras William Bradford, and diverce others the first instruments of God in the beginning of this great work of plantation, togeather with such as the allordering hand of God in his providence soone added unto them, have been at very great charges to procure the lands, priviledges, and freedoms from all intanglements, as may appeare by diverse and sundrie deeds, inlargments of grants, purchases, and payments of debts, etc., by reason wherof the title to the day of these presents remaineth in the said William Bradford, his heires, associates, and assignes: now, for the better setling of the estate of the said lands (contained in the grant or pattente), the said William Bradford, and those first instruments termed and called in sondry orders upon publick recorde, The Purchasers, or Old comers; witnes ·2· in espetiall, the one bearing date the ·3· of March, 1639. the other in Desember: the I. Anno 1640. wherunto these presents have spetiall relation and agreemente, and wherby they are distinguished from others the freemen and inhabitants of the said corporation. Be it knowne unto all men, therfore, by these presents, that the said William Bradford, for him selfe, his heires, together with the said purchassers, doe only reserve unto them selves, their heires, and assignes those ·3· tractes of land mentioned in the said resolution, order, and agreemente, bearing date the first of Desember, 1640. viz. first, from the bounds of Yarmouth ·3· miles to the eastward of Naemschatet, and from sea to sea, crose the neck of land. The ·2· of a place called Acoughcouss, which lyeth in the botome of the bay adjoyning to the west-side of Pointe Perill, and ·2· myles to the westerne side of the said river, to an other place called Acushente river, which entereth at the westerne end of Nacata, and ·2· miles to the eastward therof, and to extend ·8· myles up into the countrie. The ·3· place, from Sowamsett river to Patucket river, (with Cawsumsett neck, which is the cheefe habitation of the Indeans, and reserved for them to dwell upon,) extending into the land ·8· myles through the whole breadth therof. Togeather with shuch other small parcells of lands as they or any of them are personally possessed of or intressed in, by vertue of any former titles or grantes whatsoever. And the said William Bradford doth, by the free and full consente, approbation, and agreemente of the said old-planters, or purchasers, together with the liking, approbation, and acceptation of the other parte of the said corporation, surrender into the hands of the whole courte, consisting of the free-men of this corporation of New-Plimoth, all that other right and title, power, authority, priviledges, immunities, and freedomes granted in the said letters patents by the said right Hon'ble Counsell for New-England; reserveing his and their personall right of free-men, together with the said old planters afforesaid, excepte the said lands before excepted, declaring the freemen of this corporation togeather with all shuch as shal be legally admitted into the same, his associates. And the said William Bradford, for him, his heiers, and assignes, doe hereby further promise and grant to doe and performe whatsoever further thing or things, acte or acres, which in him lyeth, which shall be needfull and expediente for the better confirming and establishing the said premises, as by counsell lerned in the lawes shall be reasonably advised and devised, when he shall be ther unto required. In witness wherof, the said William Bradford hath in publick courte surrendered the said letters patents actually into the hands and power of the said courte, binding him selfe, his heires, executors, administrators, and assignes to deliver up whatsoever spetialties are in his hands that doe or may concerne the same.

In these ·2· years they had sundry letters out of England to send one over to end the buissines and accounte with Mr. Sherley; who now proffesed he could not make up his accounts without the help of some from hence, espetially Mr. Winslows. They had serious thoughts of it, and the most parte of the partners hear thought it best to send; but they had formerly written shuch bitter and threatening letters as Mr. Winslow was neither willing to goe, nor that any other of the partners should; for he was perswaded, if any of them wente, they should be arested, and an action of shuch summe layed upon them as they should not procure baele, but must lye in prison, and then they would bring them to what they liste; or other wise they might be brought into trouble by the archbishops means, as the times then stood. But notwithstanding, they weer much inclined to send, and Captaine Standish was willing to goe, but they

resolved, seeing they could not all agree in this thing, and that
it was waighty, and the consequence might prove dangerous, to
take Mr. Winthrops advise in the thing, and the rather, because
Mr. Andrews had by many letters acquaynted him with the differences betweene them, and appoynted him for his assigne to
receive his parte of the debte. (And though they deneyed to pay
him any as a debte, till the controversie was ended, yet they had
depossited 110*li.* in money in his hands for Mr. Andrews, to pay
to him in parte as soone as he would come to any agreement
with the rest.) But Mr. Winthrop was of Mr. Winslows minde,
and disswaded them from sending; so they broak of their resolution from sending, and returned this answer: that the times
were dangerous as things stood with them, for they knew how
Mr. Winslow had suffered formerley, and for a small matter was
clapte up in the Fleete, and it was long before he could gett out,
to both his and their great loss and damage; and times were not
better, but worse, in that respecte. Yet, that their equall and
honest minds might appeare to all men, they made them this
tender: to refferr the case to some gentle-men and marchants in
the Bay of the Massachusetts, shuch as they should chuse, and
were well knowne unto them selves, (as they perceived their
wer many of their aquaintance and freinds ther, better knowne
to them then the partners hear,) and let them be informed in
the case by both sides, and have all the evidence that could be
prodused, in writing, or other wise; and they would be bound
to stand to their determination, and make good their award,
though it should cost them all they had in the world. But this
did not please them, but they were offended at it, without
any great reasone for ought I know, (seeing nether side could
give in clear accountes, the partners here could not, by reason
they (to their smarte) were failed by the accountante they sent
them, and Mr. Sherley pretended he could not allso,) save as
they conceived it a disparagmente to yeeld to their inferiours
in respecte of the place and other concurring circomstances.
So this came to nothing; and afterward Mr. Sherley write, that
if Mr. Winslow would met him in France, the Low-Countries,
or Scotland, let the place be knowne, and he come to him
ther. But in regard of the troubles that now begane to arise in
our owne nation, and other reasons, this did not come to any
effecte. That which made them so desirous to bring things to

an end was partly to stope the clamours and aspertions raised and cast upon them hereaboute; though they conceived them selves to sustaine the greatest wrong, and had most cause of complainte; and partly because they feared the fall of catle, in which most parte of their estates lay. And this was not a vaine feare; for they fell indeede before they came to a conclusion, and that so souddenly, as a cowe, that but a month before was worth 20*li.*, and would so have passed in any paymente, fell now to ·5*li*· and would yeeld no more; and a goate that wente at ·3*li*· or ·50*s*· would now yeeld but ·8· or ·10*s*· at most. All men feard a fall of catle, but it was thought it would be by degrees; and not be from the highest pitch at once to the lowest, as it did, which was greatly to the damage of many, and the undoing of some. An other reason was, they many of them grew aged, (and indeed a rare thing it was that so many partners should all live together so many years as these did,) and saw many changes were like to befall; so as they were loath to leave these intanglements upon their children and posteritie, who might be driven to remove places, as they had done; yea, them selves might doe it yet before they deyed. But this bussines must yet rest; the next year gave it more ripnes, though it rendred them less able to pay, for the reasons afforesaid.

ANNO DOM: ·1641·

M R. SHERLEY being weary of this controversie, and desirous of an end, (as well as them selves,) write to Mr. John Atwode and Mr. William Collier, ·2· of the inhabitants of this place, and of his speatiall aquaintance, and desired them to be a means to bring this bussines to an end, by advising and counselling the partners hear, by some way to bring it to a composition, by mutuall agreemente. And he write to them selves allso to that end, as by his letter may apear; so much therof as concernse the same I shall hear relate.

SIR: My love remembered, etc. I have writte so much concerning the ending of accounts betweexte us, as I profess I know not what more to write, etc. If you desire an end, as you seeme to doe, ther is (as I conceive) but ·2· waise; that is, to parfecte all accounts, from the first to the last, etc. Now if we find this difficulte, and tedious,

haveing not been so stricte and carefull as we should and oughte to
have done, as for my owne parte I doe confess I have been somewhat
to remisse, and doe verily thinke so are you, etc. I fear you can never
make a perfecte accounte of all your pety viages, out, and home too
and againe, etc.* So then the second way must be, by biding, or
compounding; and this way, first or last, we must fall upon, etc. If we
must warr at law for it, doe not you expecte from me, nether will I
from you, but to cleave the heare, and then I dare say the lawyers will
be most gainers, etc. Thus let us set to the worke, one way or other,
and end, that I may not allways suffer in my name and estate. And you
are not free; nay, the gospell suffers by your delaying, and causeth the
professors of it to be hardly spoken of, that you, being many, and now
able, should combine and joyne togeather to oppress and burden me,
etc. Fear not to make a faire and reasonable offer; beleeve me, I will
never take any advantage to plead it against you, or to wrong you; or
else let Mr. Winslow come over, and let him have shuch full power
and authority as we may ende by compounding; or else, the accounts
so well and fully made up, as we may end by reconing. Now, blesed
be God, the times be much changed here, I hope to see many of you
returne to your native countrie againe, and have shuch freedome and
libertie as the word of God prescribes. Our bishops were never so near
a downfall as now; God hath miraculously confounded them, and
turned all their popish and Machavillian plots and projects on their
owne heads, etc. Thus you see what is fitt to be done concerning our
perticulere greevances. I pray you take it seriously into consideration;
let each give way a litle that we may meete, etc. Be you and all yours
kindly saluted, etc. So I ever rest,

Your loving friend,
JAMES SHERLEY.

Clapham, May 18, 1641.

Being thus by this leter, and allso by Mr. Atwodes and Mr.
Colliers mediation urged to bring things to an end, (and the
continuall clamors from the rest,) and by none more urged
then by their own desires, they tooke this course (because many
scandals had been raised upon them). They apoynted these ·2·
men before mentioned to meet on a certaine day, and called
some other freinds on both sides, and Mr. *Free-man, brother
in law to Mr. Beachamp*; and having drawne up a collection

---

*This was but to pretend advantage, for it could not be done, neither did it
need.

of all the remains of the stock, in what soever it was, as housing, boats, bark, and all implements belonging to the same, as
they were used in the time of the trade, were they better or
worce, with the remaines of all commodities, as beads, knives,
hatchetts, cloth, or any thing els, as well the refuse as the more
vendible, with all debts, as well those that were desperate as
others more hopefull; and having spent diverce days to bring
this to pass, having the helpe of all bookes and papers, which
either any of them selves had, or Josias Winslow, who was their
accountante; and they found the sume in all to arise (as the
things were valued) to aboute 1400*li*. And they all of them
tooke a voluntary but a sollem oath, in the presence one of an
other, and of all their frends, the persons abovesaid that were
now presente, that this was all that any of them knew of, or
could remember; and Josias Winslow did the like for his parte.
But the truth is they wrongd them selves much in the valuation, for they reconed some catle as they were taken of Mr.
Allerton, as for instance a cowe in the hands of one cost 25*li*.
and so she was valued in this accounte; but when she came to
be past away in parte of paymente, after the agreemente, she
would be accepted but at 4*li*. 15*s*. Also, being tender of their
oaths, they brought in all they knew owing to the stock; but
they had not made the like diligente search what the stocke
might owe to any, so as many scattering debts fell upon afterwards more then now they knew of.

Upon this they drew certaine articles of agreemente betweene
Mr. Atwode, on Mr. Sherleys behalfe, and them selves. The
effecte is as folloeth.

Articles of agreemente made and concluded upon the
15. day of October, 1641. etc.

Imprimis: Wheras ther was a partnership for diverce years agreed
upon betweene James Sherley, John Beacham, and Richard Andrews,
of London, marchants, and William Bradford, Edward Winslow,
Thomas Prence, Myles Standish, William Brewster, John Alden,
and John Howland, with Isaack Allerton, in a trade of beaver skines
and other furrs arising in New England; the terme of which said
partnership being expired, and diverse summes of money in goods
adventured into New-England by the said James Sherley, John
Beachamp, and Richard Andrews, and many large returnes made
from New-England by the said William Bradford, Ed: Winslow, etc.;

and differance arising aboute the charge of ·2· ships, the one called
the White Angele, of Bristow, and the other the Frindship, of Barnstable, and a viage intended in her, etc.; which said ships and their
viages, the said William Bradford, Ed: W. etc. conceive doe not at all
appertaine to their accounts of partnership; and weras the accounts
of the said partnership are found to be confused, and cannot orderley
appeare (through the defaulte of Josias Winslow, the booke keeper);
and weras the said W. B. etc. have received all their goods for the said
trade from the foresaid James Sherley, and have made most of their
returnes to him, by consente of the said John Beachamp and Richard
Andrews; and wheras also the said James Sherley hath given power
and authoritie to Mr. John Atwode, with the advice and consente of
William Collier, of Duxborow, for and on his behalfe, to put shuch
an absolute end to the said partnership, with all and every accounts,
reconings, dues, claimes, demands, whatsoever, to the said James
Sherley, John Beacham, and Richard Andrews, from the said W. B.
etc. for and concerning the said beaver trade, and also the charge
the said ·2· ships, and their viages made or pretended, whether just
or unjuste, from the worlds begining to this presente, as also for the
paimente of a purchas of 1800*li.* made by Isaack Allerton, for and
on the behalfe of the said W. B., Ed: W., etc., and of the joynt stock,
shares, lands, and adventures, what soever in New-England aforesaid,
as apeareth by a deede bearing date the *6. Nov'br 1627*; and also for
and from shuch sume and sumes of money or goods as are received
by William Bradford, Tho: Prence, and Myles Standish, for the recovery of dues, by accounts betwexte them, the said James Sherly, John
Beachamp, and Richard Andrews, and Isaack Allerton, for the ship
caled the White Angell. Now the said John Attwode, with advice
and counsell of the said William Collier, having had much comunica-
tion and spente diverse days in agitation of all the said differances
and accounts with the said W. B., E. W., etc.; and the said W. B.,
E. W., etc. have also, with the said book-keeper spente much time
in collecting and gathering togeither the remainder of the stock of
partnership for the said trade, and what soever hath beene received,
or is due by the said attorneyship before expresed, and all, and all
manner of goods, debts, and dues therunto belonging, as well those
debts that are weake and doubtfull and desperate, as those that are
more secure, which in all doe amounte to the sume of 1400*li.* or ther
aboute; and for more full satisfaction of the said James Sherley, John
Beachamp, and Richard Andrews, the said W. B. and all the rest of the
abovesaid partners, togeither with Josias Winslow the booke-keeper,
have taken a voluntarie oath, that within the said sume of 1400*li.*
or theraboute, is contained what soever they know, to the utmost of
their rememberance.

In consideration of all which matters and things before expressed, and to the end that a full, absolute, and finall end may be now made, and all suits in law may be avoyded, and love and peace continued, it is therfore agreed and concluded betweene the said John Attwode, with the advice and consent of the said William Colier, for and on the behalfe of the said James Sherley, to and with the said W. B., etc. in maner and forme following: viz. that the said John Attwode shall procure a sufficiente release and discharge, under the hands and seals of the said James Sherley, John Beachamp, and Richard Andrews, to be delivered fayer and unconcealed unto the said William Bradford, etc., at or before the last day of August, next insuing the date hereof, whereby the said William Bradford, etc., their heires, executors, and administrators, and every of them shall be fully and absolutly aquited and discharged of all actions, suits, reconings, accounts, claimes, and demands whatsoever concerning the generall stock of beaver trade, paymente of the said 1800*li.* for the purchass, and all demands, reckonings, and accounts, just or unjuste, concerning the tow ships Whit-Angell and Frendship aforesaid, togeather with what soever hath been received by the said William Bradford, of the goods or estate of Isack Allerton, for satisfaction of the accounts of the said ship called the Whit Angele, by vertue of a letter of attourney to him, Thomas Prence, and Myles Standish, directed from the said James Sherley, John Beachamp, and Richard Andrews, for that purpose as afforesaid.

It is also agreed and concluded upon betweene the said parties to these presents, that the said W. B., E. W., etc. shall now be bound in 2400*li.* for paymente of 1200*li.* in full satisfaction of all demands as afforesaid; to be payed in maner and forme following; that is to say, 400*li.* within ·2· months next after the receite of the aforesaid releases and discharges, one hundred and ten pounds wherof is allready in the hands of John Winthrop senior of Boston, Esquire, by the means of Mr. Richard Andrews afforesaid, and 80*li.* waight of beaver now deposited into the hands of the said John Attwode, to be both in part of paimente of the said 400*li.* and the other 800*li.* to be payed by 200*li.* per annume, to shuch assignes as shall be appointed, inhabiting either in Plimoth or Massachusetts Bay, in shuch goods and comodities, and at shuch rates, as the countrie shall afford at the time of delivery and paymente; and in the mean time the said bond of 2400*li.* to be deposited into the hands of the said John Attwode. And it is agreed upon by and betweene the said parties to these presents, that if the said John Attwode shall not or cannot procure shuch said releases and discharges as afforesaid from the said James Sherley, John Beachamp, and Richard Andrews, at or before the last day of August next insuing the date hear of, that then the said John Attwode shall, at the said day precisely, redeliver, or cause to be delivered unto

the said W. B., E. W., etc. their said bond of 2400*li.* and the said
80*li.* waight of beaver, or the due valew therof, without any fraud or
further delay; and for performance of all and singuler the covenants
and agreements hearin contained and expressed, which on the one
parte and behalfe of the said James Sherley are to be observed and
performed, shall become bound in the summe of 2400*li.* to them,
the said William Bradford, Edward Winslow, Thomas Prence, Myles
Standish, William Brewster, John Allden, and John Howland. And
it is lastly agreed upon betweene the said parties, that these presents
shall be left in trust, to be kepte for boath parties, in the hands of
Mr. John Reanour, teacher of Plimoth. In witnes wherof, all the said
parties have hereunto severally sett their hands, the day and year first
above writen.

	JOHN ATTWODE,
In the presence of	WILLIAM BRADFORD,
EDMOND FREEMAN,	EDWARD WINSLOW, etc.
WILLIAM THOMAS,	
WILLIAM PADY,	
NATHANIELL SOUTHER.	

The nexte year this long and tedious bussines came to some
issue, as will then appeare, though not to a finall ende with all
the parties; but this much for the presente.

I had forgoten to inserte in its place how the church here had
invited and sent for Mr. Charles Chansey,* a reverend, godly,
and very larned man, intending upon triall to chose him pastor
of the church hear, for the more comfortable performance of
the ministrie with Mr. John Reinor, the teacher of the same.
But ther fell out some differance aboute baptising, he holding it
ought only to be by diping, and putting the whole body under
water, and that sprinkling was unlawfull. The church yeelded
that imersion, or dipping, was lawfull, but in this could countrie not so conveniente. But they could not nor durst not yeeld
to him in this, that sprinkling (which all the churches of Christ
doe for the most parte use at this day) was unlawfull, and an
humane invention, as the same was prest; but they were willing
to yeeld to him as farr as they could, and to the utmost; and
were contented to suffer him to practise as he was perswaded;
and when he came to minister that ordnance, he might so

---

*Mr. Chancey came to them in the year 1638, and staid till the later part of
this year 1641.

doe it to any that did desire it in that way, provided he could peacably suffer Mr. Reinor, and shuch as desired to have theirs other wise baptised by him, by sprinkling or powering on of water upon them; so as ther might be no disturbance in the church hereaboute. But he said he could not yeeld therunto. Upon which the church procured some other ministers to dispute the pointe with him publikly; as Mr. Ralfe Partrich, of Duxberie, who did it sundrie times, very ablie and sufficently, as allso some other ministers within this govermente. But he was not satisfied; so the church sent to many other churches to crave their help and advise in this mater, and, with his will and consente, sent them his arguments writen under his owne hand. They sente them to the church at Boston in the Bay of Massachusets, to be comunicated with other churches ther. Also they sent the same to the churches of Conightecutt and New-Haven, with sundrie others; and received very able and sufficent answers, as they conceived, from them and their larned ministers, who all concluded against him. But him selfe was not satisfied therwith. Their answers are too large hear to relate. They conceived the church had done what was meete in the thing, so Mr. Chansey, having been the most parte of ·3· years here, removed him selfe to Sityate, wher he now remaines a minister to the church ther. Also about these times, now that catle and other things begane greatly to fall from their former rates, and persons begane to fall into more straits, and many being allready gone from them, (as is noted before,) both to Duxberie, Marshfeeld, and other places, and those of the cheefe sorte, as Mr. Winslow, Captaine Standish, Mr. Allden, and many other, and stille some dropping away daly, and some at this time, and many more unsetled, it did greatly weaken the place, and by reason of the straitnes and barrennes of the place, it sett the thoughts of many upon removeall; as will appere more hereafter.

ANNO DOM: ·1642·

Marvilous it may be to see and consider how some kind of wickednes did grow and breake forth here, in a land wher the same was so much witnesed against, and so narrowly looked unto, and severly punished when it was knowne; as in no place more, or so much, that I have known or heard of; insomuch as they have been somewhat censured, even by moderate and good men, for their severitie in punishments. And yet all this could not suppress the breaking out of sundrie notorious sins, (as this year, besides other, gives us too many sad presidents and instances,) espetially drunkennes and unclainnes; not only incontinencie betweene persons unmaried, for which many both men and women have been punished sharply enough, but some maried persons allso. But that which is worse, even sodomie and bugerie, (things fearfull to name,) have broak forth in this land, oftener then once. I say it may justly be marveled at, and cause us to fear and tremble at the consideration of our corrupte natures, which are so hardly bridled, subdued, and mortified; nay, cannot by any other means but the powerful worke and grace of Gods spirite. But (besides this) one reason may be, that the Divell may carrie a greater spite against the churches of Christ and the gospell hear, by how much the more they indeavour to preserve holynes and puritie amongst them, and strictly punisheth the contrary when it ariseth either in church or comone wealth; that he might cast a blemishe and staine upon them in the eyes of the world, who use to be rash in judgmente. I would rather thinke thus, then that Satane hath more power in these heathen lands, as som have thought, then in more Christian nations, espetially over Gods servants in them.

2. An other reason may be, that it may be in this case as it is with waters when their streames are stopped or dammed up, when they gett passage they flow with more violence, and make more noys and disturbance, then when they are suffered to rune quietly in their owne chanels. So wikednes being here more stopped by strict laws, and the same more nerly looked unto, so as it cannot rune in a comone road of liberty as it would, and is inclined, it searches every wher, and at last breaks out wher it getts vente.

3. A third reason may be, hear (as I am verily perswaded) is not more evills in this kind, nor nothing nere so many by proportion, as in other places; but they are here more discoverd and seen, and made publick by due serch, inquisision, and due

punishment; for the churches looke narrowly to their members, and the magistrates over all, more strictly then in other places. Besides, here the people are but few in comparison of other places, which are full and populous, and lye hid, as it were, in a wood or thickett, and many horrible evills by that means are never seen nor knowne; wheras hear, they are, as it were, brought into the light, and set in the plaine feeld, or rather on a hill, made conspicuous to the veiw of all.

But to proceede; ther came a letter from the Governor in the Bay to them here, touching matters of the fore-mentioned nature, which because it may be usefull I shall hear relate it, and the passages ther aboute.

SIR: Having an opportunitie to signifie the desires of our Generall Court in tow things of spetiall importance, I willingly take this occasion to imparte them to you, that you may imparte them to the rest of your magistrates, and also to your Elders, for counsell; and give us your advise in them. The first is concerning heinous offences in point of uncleannes; the perticuler cases, with the circomstances, and the questions ther upon, you have hear inclosed. The ·2· thing is concerning the Islanders at Aquidnett; that seeing the cheefest of them are gone from us, in offences, either to churches, or commone welth, or both; others are dependants on them, and the best sorte are shuch as close with them in all their rejections of us. Neither is it only in a faction that they are devided from us, but in very deed they rend them selves from all the true churches of Christ, and, many of them, from all the powers of majestracie. We have had some experience hereof by some of their underworkers, or emissaries, who have latly come amongst us, and have made publick defiance against magistracie, ministrie, churches, and church covenants, etc. as anti-christian; secretly also sowing the seeds of Familisme, and Anabaptistrie, to the infection of some, and danger of others; so that we are not willing to joyne with them in any league or confederacie at all, but rather that you would consider and advise with us how we may avoyd them, and keep ours from being infected by them. Another thing I should mention to you, for the maintenance of the trade of beaver; if ther be not a company to order it in every jurisdition among the English, which companies should agree in generall of their way in trade, I supose that the trade will be overthrowne, and the Indeans will abuse us. For this cause we have latly put it into order amongst us, hoping of incouragmente from you (as we have had) that we may continue the same. Thus not further to trouble you, I rest, with my loving remembrance to your selfe, etc.

Your loving friend,
Ri: Bellingham.

Boston, 28 (i.), 1642.

The note inclosed follows on the other side.

Worthy and beloved Sir:

Your letter (with the questions inclosed) I have comunicated with our Assistants, and we have refered the answer of them to shuch Reverend Elders as are amongst us, some of whose answers thertoo we have here sent you inclosed, under their owne hands; from the rest we have not yet received any. Our farr distance hath bene the reason of this long delay, as also that they could not conferr their counsells togeather.

For our selves, (you know our breedings and abillities,) we rather desire light from your selves, and others, whom God hath better inabled, then to presume to give our judgments in cases so difficulte and of so high a nature. Yet under correction, and submission to better judgments, we propose this one thing to your prudent considerations. As it seems to us, in the case even of willfull murder, that though a man did smite or wound an other, with a full pourpose or desire to kill him, (which is murder in a high degree, before God,) yet if he did not dye, the magistrate was not to take away the others life.* So by proportion in other grosse and foule sines, though high attempts and nere approaches to the same be made, and shuch as in the sight and account of God may be as ill as the accomplishmente of the foulest acts of that sine, yet we doute whether it may be safe for the magistrate to proceed to death; we thinke, upon the former grounds, rather he may not. As, for instance, in the case of adultrie, (if it be admitted that it is to be punished with death, which to some of us is not cleare,) if the body be not actually defiled, then death is not to be inflicted. So in sodomie, and beastialitie, if ther be not penetration. Yet we confess foulnes of circomstances, and frequencie in the same, doth make us remaine in the darke, and desire further light from you, or any, as God shall give.

As for the ·2· thing, concerning the Ilanders? we have no conversing with them, nor desire to have, furder then necessitie or humanity may require.

---

*Exod: 21. 22. Deu: 19. 11. Num: 35. 16. 18.

And as for trade? we have as farr as we could ever therin held an orderly course, and have been sory to see the spoyle therof by others, and fear it will hardly be recovered. But in these, or any other things which may concerne the commone good, we shall be willing to advise and concure with you in what we may. Thus with my love remembered to your selfe, and the rest of our worthy friends, your Assistants, I take leave, and rest,

Your loving friend,
W. B.

Plim: 17 ·3· month, 1642.

Now follows the ministers answers. And first Mr. Reynors.

Qest: What sodomiticall acts are to be punished with death, and what very facte (ipso facto) is worthy of death, or, if the fact it selfe be not capitall, what circomstances concurring may make it capitall?

Ans: In the judiciall law (the moralitie wherof concerneth us) it is manyfest that carnall knowledg of man, or lying with man, as with woman, cum penetratione corporis, was sodomie, to be punished with death; what els can be understood by Levit: 18. 22. and 20. 13. and Gen: 19. 5? 2ly. It seems allso that this foule sine might be capitall, though ther was not penitratio corporis, but only contactus et fricatio usque ad effusionem seminis, for these reasons: 1. Because it was sin to be punished with death, Levit. 20. 13. in the man who was lyen withall, as well as in him that lyeth with him; now his sin is not mitigated wher ther is not penitration, nor augmented wher it is, wheras its charged upon the women, that they were guilty of this unnaturall sine, as well as men, Rom. 1. 26. 27. the same thing doth furder apeare.

2. because of that proportion betwexte this sin and beastialitie, wherin if a woman did stand before, or aproach to, a beast, for that end, to lye downe therto, (whether penetration was or not,) it was capitall, Levit: 18. 23. and 20. 16.

3ly. Because something els might be equivalent to penetration wher it had not been, viz. the fore mentioned acts with frequencie and long continuance with a high hand, utterly extinguishing all light of nature; besides, full intention and bould attempting of the foulest acts may seeme to have been capitall here, as well as coming presumtu-ously to slay with guile was capitall. Exod: 21. 14.

Yet it is not so manyfest that the same acts were to be punished with death in some other sines of uncleannes, which yet by the law of God were capitall crimes; besides other reasons, (1.) because sodomie, and also bestialitie, is more against the light of nature then some other capitall crimes of unclainnes, which reason is to be attended unto, as that which most of all made this sin capitall; (2.) because it might be commited with more secrecie and less suspition, and therfore needed the more to be restrained and suppresed by the law; (3ly) because ther was not the like reason and degree of sinning against family and posteritie in this sin as in some other capitall sines of uncleannes.

2. Quest: How farr a magistrate may extracte a confession from a delinquente, to acuse him selfe of a capitall crime, seeing Nemo tenetur prodere seipsum.

Ans: A majestrate cannot without sin neglecte diligente inquisition into the cause brought before him. Job 29. 16. Pro: 24. 11. 12. and 25. 2. (2ly.) If it be manifest that a capitall crime is committed, and the comone reporte, or probabilitie, suspition, or some complainte, (or the like,) be of this or that person, a magistrate ought to require, and by all due means to procure from the person (so farr allready bewrayed) a naked confession of the fact, as apears by that which is morall and of perpetuall equitie, both in the case of uncertaine murder, Deut: 21. 1. 9 and slander, Deut: 22. 13. 21; for though nemo tenetur prodere seipsum, yet by that which may be known to the magistrate by the forenamed means, he is bound thus to doe, or els he may betray his countrie and people to the heavie displeasure of God, Levit: 18. 24. 25. Jos: 22. 18. Psa: 106. 30; shuch as are innocente to the sinfull, base, cruell lusts of the profane, and shuch as are delinquents, and others with them, into the hands of the stronger temptations, and more bouldness, and hardnes of harte, to commite more and worse villany, besides all the guilt and hurt he will bring upon him selfe. (3ly.) To inflicte some punishmente meerly for this reason, to extracte a conffession of a capitall crime, is contrary to the nature of vindictive justice, which always hath respecte to a known crime committed by the person punished; and it will therfore, for any thing which can before be knowne, be the provocking and forcing of wrath, compared to the wringing of the nose, Pro: 30. 33. which is as well forbiden the fathers of the countrie as of the family, Ephe. 6. 4. as produsing many sad and dangerous effects. That an oath (ex officio) for shuch a purpose is no due means, hath been abundantly proved by the godly learned, and is well known.

Q. 3. In what cases of capitall crimes one witnes with other circomstances shall be sufficiente to convince? or is ther no conviction without ·2· witneses?

Ans: In taking away the life of man, one witnes alone will not suffice, ther must be tow, or that which is instare; the texts are manifest, Numb: 35. 30. Deut: 17. 6. and 19. 15. 2ly. Ther may be conviction by one witnes, and some thing that hath the force of another, as the evidencie of the fact done by shuch an one, and not an otther; unforced confession when ther was no fear or danger of suffering for the fact, hand writings acknowledged and confessed.

JOHN REYNOR.

Mr. Partrich his writing, in answer to the questions.

What is that sodomiticall acte which is to be punished with death?

Though I conceive probable that a voluntary effusion of seed per modum concubitus of man with man, as of a man with woman, though in concubitu ther be not penetratio corporis, is that sin which is forbiden, Levit: 18. 22. and adjudged to be punished with death, Levit: 20. 13. because, though ther be not penetratio corporis, yet ther may be similitudo concubitus muliebris, which is that the law specifieth; yet I dar not be con- (1.) because, Gen: 19. 5. the intended acte of the Sodomites (who were the first noted maisters of this unnaturall art of more then brutish filthines) is expressed by carnall copulation of man with woman: Bring them out unto us, that we may know them; (2ly.) because it is observed among the nations wher this unnaturall unclainnes is commited, it is with penetration of the body; (3ly.) because, in the judiciall proceedings of the judges in England, the indictments so rune (as I have been informed).

Q. How farr may a magistrate extracte a confession of a capitall crime from a suspected and an accused person?

Ans. I conceive that a magistrate is bound, by carfull examenation of circomstances and waighing of probabilities, to sifte the accused, and by force of argumente to draw him to an acknowledgment of the truth; but he may not extracte a confession of a capitall crime from a suspected person by any violent means, whether it be by an oath imposed, or by any punishmente inflicted or threatened to be inflicted, for so he may draw forth an acknowledgmente of a crime from a fearfull innocente; if guilty, he shall be compelled to be his owne accuser, when no other can, which is against the rule of justice.

Q. In what cases of capitall crimes one witnes with other circomstances shall be sufficente to convicte; or is ther no conviction without two witnesses?

Ans: I conceive that, in the case of capitall crimes, ther can be no safe proceedings unto judgmente without too witnesses, as Numb: 35. 30. Deut: 19. 15. excepte ther can some evidence be prodused as aveilable and firme to prove the facte as a witnes is, then one witnes may suffice; for therin the end and equitie of the law is attained. But to proceede unto sentence of death upon presumptions, wher probably ther may subesse falsum, though ther be the testimony of one wittnes, I supose it cannot be a safe way; better for shuch a one to be held in safe custodie for further triall, I conceive.

RALPH PARTRICH.

The Answer of Mr. Charles Chancy.

An contactus et fricatio usque ad seminis effusionem sine penetratione corporis sit sodomia morte plectenda?

Q. The question is what sodomiticall acts are to be punished with death, and what very facte committed, (ipso facto,) is worthy of death, or if the facte it selfe be not capitall, what circomstances concuring may make it capital. The same question may be asked of rape, inceste, beastialitie, unnaturall sins, presumtuous sins? These be the words of the first question.

Ans: The answer unto this I will lay downe (as God shall directe by his word and spirite) in these following conclusions: (1.) That the judicials of Moyses, that are appendances to the morall law, and grounded on the law of nature, or the decalogue, are immutable, and perpetuall, which all orthodox devines acknowledge; see the authors following. Luther, Tom. 1. Whitenberge: fol. 435. and fol. 7. Melancthon, in loc: com loco deconjugio. Calvin, l. 4. Institu. c. 4. sect. 15. Junious de politia Moyses, thes. 29. and 30. Hen: Bulin: Decad. 3. sermo. 8. Wolf: Muscu. loc: com: in ·6· precepti explicaci: Bucer de regno Christi, l. ·2· c. ·17· Theo: Beza, vol: 1. de hereti: puniendis, fol. 154. Zanch: in 3. precept: Ursin: Pt. 4. explicat. contra John. Piscat: in Aphorismi loc. de lege dei aphorism ·17· And more might be added. I forbear, for brevities sake, to set downe their very words; this being the constante and generall oppinion of the best devines, I will rest in this as undoubtedly true, though much more might be said to confirme it.

2. That all the sinnes mentioned in the question were punished with death by the judiciall law of Moyses, as adultry, Levit: 20. 10. Deut: 22. 22. Ecech: 16. 38. Jhon. 8. 5. which is to be understood not only of double adultrie, when as both parties are maried, (as some conceive,) but whosoever (besides her husband) lyes with a married woman, whether the man be maried or not, as in the place, Deut: 22. 22. or whosoever, being a maried man, lyeth with another woman (besides his wife), as P. Martire saith, loc: com: which in diverce respects makes the sine worse on the maried mans parte; for the Lord in this law hath respect as well to publick honesty, (the sin being so prejudicall to the church and state,) as the private wrongs (saith Junious). So incest is to be punished with death, Levit: 20. 11. 21. Beastiality likwise, Lev: 20. 15. Exod: 22. 19. Rapes in like maner,

Deut: 22. 25. Sodomie in like sort, Levit: 18. 22. and 20. 13. And all presumptuous sins, Numb: 15. 30. 31.

3. That the punishmente of these foule sines with death is grounded on the law of nature, and is agreable to the morall law. (1.) Because the reasons annexed shew them to be perpetuall. Deut. 22. 22. So shalt thou put away evill. Incest, beastiality, are caled confusion, and wickednes. (2.) Infamie to the whole humane nature, Levit: 20. 12. Levit: 18. 23. Rapes are as murder, Deut: 22. 25. Sodomie is an abomination, Levit: 22 18 ·22· No holier and juster laws can be devised by any man or angele then have been by the Judge of all the world, the wisdome of the Father, by whom kings doe raigne, etc. (3.) Because, before the giving of the Law, this punishmente was anciently practised, Gen: 26. 11. 38. 29 ·39· 20. and even by the heathen, by the very light of nature, as P. Martire shews. (4ly.) Because the land is defiled by shuch sins, and spews out the inhabitants, Levit: 18. 24, 25. and that in regard of those nations that were not acquainted with the law of Moyses. 5. All the devines above specified consent in this, that the unclean acts punishable with death by the law of God are not only the grose acts of uncleannes by way of carnall copulation, but all the evidente attempts therof, which may appeare by those severall words that are used by the spirite of God, expressing the sins to be punished with death; as the discovering of nakednes, Levit: 18. 20. which is retegere pudenda, as parts per euphemismum (saith Junius), or detegere ad cubandum (saith Willett), to uncover the shamefull parts of the body (saith Ainsworth), which, though it reaches to the grose acts, yet it is plaine it doth comprehend the other foregoing immodest attempts, as contactum, fricationem, etc.; likwise the phrase of lying with, so often used, doth not only signifie carnall copulation, but other obscure acts, preceding the same, is implyed in Pauls word ἀρσενοκοῖται, 1. Cor: 6. 9. and men lying with men, 1. Tim: 1. 10. men defiling them selves with mankind, men burning with lust towards men, Rom: 1. 26. and Levit: 18. 22. sodomy and sin going after strange flesh, Jud: v. 7. 8. and lying with mankind as with a woman, Levit: 18. 22. Abulentis says that it signifies omnes modos quibus masculus masculo abutatur, changing the naturall use into that which is against nature, Rom: 1. 26. arogare sibi cubare, as Junius well translates Levit: 20. 15. to give consente to lye withall, so approaching to a beast, and lying downe therto, Levit: 20. 16. ob solum contiē (saith Willett) or for going about to doe it. Add to this a notable speech of Zepperus de legibus (who hath enough to end controversies of this nature). L. 1. he saith: In crimine adulterii voluntas (understanding manifeste) sine effectu subsecuto de jure attenditur; and he proves it out of good laws, in these words: solicitations

alienum nuptiam itemque matrimonium interpellatores, etsi effectu sceleris potiri non possunt, propter voluntatem tamen perniciosæ libidinis extra ordinem puniuntur; nam generale est quidem effectum sine effectu [non] puniri, sed contrarium observatur in atrocioribus et horum similibus.

5. In concluding punishments from the judiciall law of Moyses that is perpetuall, we must often proceed by analogicall proportion and interpretation, as a paribus similibus, minore ad majus, etc.; for ther will still fall out some cases, in every commone-wealth, which are not in so many words extante in holy write, yet the substance of the matter in every kind (I conceive under correction) may be drawne and concluded out of the scripture by good consequence of an equevalent nature; as, for example, ther is no express law against destroying conception in the wombe by potions, yet by anologie with Exod: 21. 22, 23. we may reason that life is to be given for life. Againe, the question, An contactus et fricatio, etc., and methinks that place Gen: 38. 9. in the punishmente of Onans sin, may give some cleare light to it; it was (saith Pareus) beluina crudelitas quam Deus pari loco cum parricidio habuit, nam semen corrumpere, quid fuit aliud quam hominem ex semine generandum occidere? Propterea juste a Deo occisus est. Observe his words. And againe, Discamus quanto-pere Deus abominetur omnem seminis genitalis abusum, illicitam effusionem, et corruptionem, etc., very pertinente to this case. That allso is considerable, Deut: 25. 11, 12. God comanded that, if any wife drue nigh to deliver her husband out of the hand of him that smiteth him, etc., her hand should be cutt off. Yet shuch a woman in that case might say much for her selfe, that what she did was in trouble and perplexitie of her minde, and in her husbands defence; yet her hand must be cutt of for shuch impuritie (and this is morall, as I conceive). Then we may reason from the less to the greater, what greevous sin in the sight of God it is, by the instigation of burning lusts, set on fire of hell, to proceede to contactum and fricationem ad emissionem seminis, etc., and that contra naturam, or to attempte the grosse acts of unnaturall filthines. Againe, if that unnaturall lusts of men with men, or woman with woman, or either with beasts, be to be punished with death, then a pari naturall lusts of men towards children under age are so to be punished.

6. Circumstantiæ variant vis e actuines, (saith the lawiers,) and circomstances in these cases cannot possibly be all reckoned up; but God hath given laws for those causes and cases that are of great-est momente, by which others are to be judged of, as in the differ-ance betwixte chance medley, and willfull murder; so in the sins of uncleannes, it is one thing to doe an acte of uncleannes by sudden

temptation, and another to lye in waite for it, yea, to make a commune practise of it; this mightily augments and multiplies the sin. Againe, some sinnes of this nature are simple, others compound, as that is simple adultrie, or inceste, or simple sodomie; but when ther is a mixture of diverce kinds of lust, as when adultery and sodomie and perditio seminis goe togeather in the same acte of uncleannes, this is capitall, double, and trible. Againe, when adultrie or sodomie is commited by professors or church members, I fear it comes too near the sine of the preists daughters, forbidden, and comanded to be punished, Levit: 21. 9. besides the presumption of the sinnes of shuch. Againe, when uncleannes is comited with those whose chastity they are bound to preserve, this comes very nere the incestious copulation, I feare; but I must hasten to the other questions.

2. Question the second, upon the pointe of examination, how farr a magistrate may extracte a confession from a delinquente to accuse him selfe in a capitall crime, seeing Nemo tenetur prodere seipsum.

Ans: The words of the question may be understood of extracting a confession from a delinquente either by oath or bodily tormente. If it be mente of extracting by requiring an oath, (ex officio, as some call it,) and that in capitall crimes, I fear it is not safe, nor warented by Gods word, to extracte a confession from a delinquente by an oath in matters of life and death. (1.) Because the practise in the Scriptures is other wise, as in the case of Achan, Jos: 7. 19. Give, I pray you, glorie to the Lord God of Israll, and make a confession to him, and tell me how thou hast done. He did not compell him to sweare. So when as Johnathans life was indangered, 1. Sam. 14. 43. Saule said unto Johnathan, Tell me what thou hast done; he did not require an oath. And notable is that, Jer: 38. 14. Jeremiah was charged by Zedechias, who said, I will aske the a thing, hide it not from me; and Jeremiah said, If I declare it unto ye, wilt thou not surely put me to death? implying that, in case of death, he would have refused to answer him. (2.) Reason shews it, and experience; Job: 2. 4. Skin for skin, etc. It is to be feared that those words (what soever a man hath) will comprehend also the conscience of an oath, and the fear of God, and all care of religion; therfore for laying a snare before the guiltie, I think it ought not to be donn. But now, if the question be mente of inflicting bodyly torments to extracte a confession from a mallefactor, I conceive that in maters of higest consequence, shuch as doe conceirne the saftie or ruine of states or countries, magistrates may proceede so farr to bodily torments, as racks, hote-irons, etc., to extracte a conffession, espetially wher presumptions are strounge; but otherwise by no means. God sometimes hides a sinner till his wickednes is filled up.

Question 3. In what cases of capitall crimes, one witnes with other circumstances shall be sufficente to convicte, or is ther no conviction without ·2· witneses?

Ans: Deut: 19. 15. God hath given an express rule that in no case one witness shall arise in judgmente, espetially not in capitall cases God would not put our lives into the power of any one tounge. Besides, by the examination of more wittneses agreeing or disagreeing, any falshood ordenarilly may be discovered; but this is to be understood of one witnes of another; but if a man witnes against him selfe, his owne testimony is sufficente, as in the case of the Amalakite, 2. Sam: 1. 16. Againe, when ther are sure and certaine signes and evidences by circumstances, ther needs no witnes in this case, as in the bussines of Adoniah desiring Abishage the Shunamite to wife, that therby he might make way for him selfe unto the kingdome, 1. King: 2. 23, 24. Againe, probably by many concurring circumstances, if probabillity may have the strength of a witnes, somthing may be this way gathered, me thinks, from Sallomons judging betweexte the true mother, and the harlote, 1. King. 3. 25. Lastly, I see no cause why in waighty matters, in defecte of witneses and other proofes, we may not have recourse to a lott, as in the case of Achan, Josu: 7. 16. which is a clearer way in shuch doubtfull cases (it being solemnely and religiously performed) then any other that I know, if it be made the last refuge. But all this under correction.

The Lord in mercie directe and prosper the desires of his servants that desire to walk before him in truth and righteousnes in the administration of justice, and give them wisdome and largnes of harte.

CHARLES CHAUNCY.

Besides the occation before mentioned in these writings concerning the abuse of those ·2· children, they had aboute the same time a case of buggerie fell out amongst them, which occasioned these questions, to which these answers have been made.

And after the time of the writing of these things befell a very sadd accidente of the like foule nature in this govermente, this very year, which I shall now relate. Ther was a youth whose name was Thomas Granger; he was servant to an honest man of Duxbery, being aboute ·16· or ·17· years of age. (His father and mother lived at the same time at Sityate.) He was this year detected of buggery (and indicted for the same) with a mare, a cowe, tow goats, five sheep, ·2· calves, and a turkey. Horrible it is to mention, but the truth of the historie requires it. He was first discovered by one that accidentally saw his lewd practise towards the mare. (I forbear perticulers.) Being upon it examined and committed, in the end he not only confest the fact with that beast at that time, but sundrie times before, and at severall times with all the rest of the forenamed in his indictmente; and this his free-confession was not only in private to the magistrates, (though at first he strived to deney it,) but to sundrie, both ministers and others, and afterwards, upon his indictemente, to the whole court and jury; and confirmed it at his execution. And wheras some of the sheep could not so well be knowne by his description of them, others with them were brought before him, and he declared which were they, and which were not. And accordingly he was cast by the jury, and condemned, and after executed about the ·8· of September, 1642. A very sade spectakle it was; for first the mare, and then the cowe, and the rest of the lesser catle, were kild before his face, according to the law, Levit: 20. 15. and then he him selfe was executed. The catle were all cast into a great and large pitte that was digged of purposs for them, and no use made of any part of them.

Upon the examenation of this person, and also of a former that had made some sodomiticall attempts upon another, it being demanded of them how they came first to the knowledge and practice of shuch wickednes, the one confessed he had long used it in old England; and this youth last spoaken of said he was taught it by an other that had heard of shuch things from some in England when he was ther, and they kept catle togeather. By which it appears how one wicked person may infecte many; and what care all ought to have what servants they bring into their families.

But it may be demanded how came it to pass that so many wicked persons and profane people should so quickly come over into this land, and mixe them selves amongst them? seeing it was religious men that begane the work, and they came for religions sake. I confess this may be marveilled at, at least in time to come, when the reasons therof should not be knowne; and the more because here was so many hardships and wants mett withall. I shall therfore indeavor to give some answer hereunto. 1. And first, according to that in the gospell, it is ever to be remembred that wher the Lord begins to sow good seed, ther the envious man will endeavore to sow tares. 2. Men being to come over into a wildernes, in which much labour and servise was to be done aboute building and planting, etc., shuch as wanted help in that respecte, when they could not have shuch as they would, were glad to take shuch as they could; and so, many untoward servants, sundry of them proved, that were thus brought over, both men and women kind; who, when their times were expired, became families of them selves, which gave increase hereunto. 3. An other and a maine reason hearof was, that men, finding so many godly disposed persons willing to come into these parts, some begane to make a trade of it, to transeport passengers and their goods, and hired ships for that end; and then, to make up their fraight and advance their profite, cared not who the persons were, so they had money to pay them. And by this means the cuntrie became pestered with many unworthy persons, who, being come over, crept into one place or other. 4. Againe, the Lords blesing usually following his people, as well in outward as spirituall things, (though afflictions be mixed withall,) doe make many to adhear to the people of God, as many followed Christ, for the loaves sake, John 6. 26. and a mixed multitud came into the willdernes with the people of God out of Eagipte of old, Exod. 12. 38. 5. So allso many were sente by their freinds some under hope that they would be made better; others that they might be eased of shuch burthens, and they kept from shame at home that would necessarily follow their dissolute courses. And thus, by one means or other, in ·20· years time, it is a question whether the greater part be not growne the worser?

I am now come to the conclusion of that long and tedious bussines betweene the partners hear, and them in England, the which I shall manifest by their owne letters as followeth, in shuch parts of them as are pertinente to the same.

Mr. Sherleys to Mr. Attwood.

Mr. Attwood, my approved loving freind: Your letter of the 18. of October last I have received, wherin I find you have taken a great deall of paines and care aboute that troublesome bussines betwixte our Plimoth partners and freinds, and us hear, and have deeply ingaged your selfe, for which complements and words are no reall satisfaction, etc.

For the agreemente you have made with Mr. Bradford, Mr. Winslow, and the rest of the partners ther, considering how honestly and justly I am perswaded they have brought in an accounte of the remaining stock, for my owne parte I am well satisfied, and so I thinke is Mr. Andrewes, and I supose will be Mr. Beachampe, if most of it might acrew to him, to whom the least is due, etc. And now for peace sake, and to conclude as we began, lovingly and freindly, and to pass by all failings of all, the conclude is accepted of; I say this agreemente that you have made is condesended unto, and Mr. Andrews hath sent his release to Mr. Winthrop, with shuch directions as he conceives fitt; and I have made bould to trouble you with mine, and we have both sealed in the presence of *Mr. Weld*, and *Mr. Peeters*, and some others, and I have also sente you an other, for the partners ther, to seale to me; for you must not deliver mine to them, excepte they seale and deliver one to me; this is fitt and equall, etc. Yours to command in what I may or can,

JAMES SHERLEY.

June 14. 1642.

His to the partners as followeth.

LOVING FREINDS,

Mr. Bradford, Mr. Winslow, Mr. Prence, Captaine Standish, Mr. Brewster, Mr. Alden, and Mr. Howland, give me leave to joyne you all in one letter, concerning the finall end and conclude of that tedious and troublesome bussines, and I thinke I may truly say uncomfurtable and unprofitable to all, etc. It hath pleased God now to put us upon a way to sease all suits, and disquieting of our spirites, and to conclude with peace and love, as we began. I am contented to yeeld and make good what Mr. Attwood and you have agreed upon; and for that end have sente to my loving freind, Mr. Attwood, an absolute and generall release unto you all, and if ther wante any thing to make it more full, write it your selves, and it shall be done, provided that all you, either joyntly or severally, seale the like discharge to me. And for that end I have drawne one joyntly, and sent it to Mr. Attwood, with that I have sealed to you. Mr. Andrews hath sealed an aquitance also, and sent it to Mr. Winthrop, whith shuch directions as he conceived fitt, and, as I hear, hath given his debte, which he makes 544*li*. unto the gentlemen of the Bay. Indeed, Mr. *Welld*, Mr. *Peters*, and Mr. *Hibbens* have taken a great deale of paines with Mr. Andrews, Mr. Beachamp, and my selfe, to bring us to agree, and to that end we have had many meetings and spent much time aboute it. But as they are very religious and honest gentle-men, yet they had an end that they drove at and laboured to accomplish (I meane not any private end, but for the generall good of their patente). It had been very well you had sent one over. Mr. Andrew wished you might have one ·3· parte of the 1200*li*. and the Bay ·2· thirds; but then we ·3· must have agreed togeather, which were a hard mater now. But Mr. Weld, Mr. Peters, and Mr. Hibbens, and I, have agreed, they giving you bond (so to compose with Mr. Beachamp, as) to procure his generall release, and free you from all trouble and charge that he may put you too; which indeed is nothing, for I am perswaded Mr. Weld will in time gaine him to give them all that is dew to him, which in some sorte is granted allready; for though his demands be great, yet Mr. Andrewes hath taken some paines in it, and makes it appear to be less then I thinke he will consente to give them for so good an use; so you neede not fear, that for taking bond ther to save you harmles, you be safe and well. Now our accord is, that you must pay to the gentle-men of the Bay 900*li*.; they are to bear all charges that may any way arise concerning the free and absolute clearing of you from us three. And you to have the other 300*li*. etc.

Upon the receiving of my release from you, I will send you your bonds for the purchass money. I would have sent them now, but I would have Mr. Beachamp release as well as I, because you are bound to him in them. Now I know if a man be bound to ·10· men, if one release, it is as if all released, and my discharge doth cutt them of; wherfore doubte you not but you shall have them, and your commission, or any thing els that is fitt. Now you know ther is two years of the purchass money, that I would not owne, for I have formerley certified you that I would but pay 7. years; but now you are discharged of all, etc.

Your loving and kind friend in what I may or can,
JAMES SHERLEY.

June 14. 1642.

The coppy of his release is as followeth.

Wheras diverce questions, differences, and demands have arisen and depended betweene William Bradford, Edward Winslow, Thomas Prence, Mylest Standish, William Brewster, John Allden, and John Howland, gent: now or latly inhabitants or resident at New-Plimoth, in New-England, on the one party, and James Sherley of London, marchante, and others, in th' other parte, for and concerning a stocke and partable trade of beaver and other comodities, and fraighting of ships, as the White Angell, Frindship, or others, and the goods of Isaack Allerton which were seazed upon by vertue of a leter of atturney made by the said James Sherley and John Beachamp and Richard

Andrews, or any other maters concerning the said trade, either hear in Old-England or ther in New-England or else wher, all which differences are since by mediation of freinds composed, compremissed, and all the said parties agreed. Now know all men by these presents, that I, the said James Sherley, in performance of the said compremise and agreemente, have remised, released, and quite claimed, and doe by these presents remise, release, and for me, myne heires, executors, and Administrators, and for every of us, for ever quite claime unto the said William Bradford, Edward Winslow, Thomas Prence, Myles Standish, William Brewster, John Alden, and John Howland, and every of them, their and every of their heires, executors, and administrators, all and all maner of actions, suits, debts, accounts, rekonings, comissions, bonds, bills, specialties, judgments, executions, claimes, challinges, differences, and demands what soever, with or against the said William Bradford, Edward Winslow, Thomas Prence, Myles Standish, William Brewster, John Alden, and John Howland, or any of them, ever I had, now have, or in time to come can, shall, or may have, for any mater, cause, or thing whatsoever from the begining of the world untill the day of the date of these presents. In witnes wherof I have hereunto put my hand and seale, given the second day of June, 1642, and in the eighteenth year of the raigne of our soveraigne lord, king Charles, etc.

JAMES SHERLEY.

Sealed and delivered in the presence of
    THOMAS WELD,
    HUGH PETERS,
    WILLIAM HIBBINS.
    ARTHUR TIRREY, Scr.
    THO: STURGES, his servante.

Mr. Andrews his discharge was to the same effecte; he was by agreemente to have 500*li.* of the money, the which he gave to them in the Bay, who brought his discharge and demanded the money. And they tooke in his release and paid the money according to agreemente, viz. one third of the 500*li.* they paid downe in hand, and the rest in 4. equall payments, to be paid yearly, for which they gave their bonds. And wheras 44*li.* was more demanded, they conceived they could take it of with Mr. Andrews, and therfore it was not in the bonde. But Mr. Beachamp would not parte with any of his, but demanded 400*li.* of the partners here, and sent a release to a friend, to deliver it to them upon the receite of the money. But his relese was not perfecte, for he had left out some of the partners names, with some other defects; and besides, the other gave them to understand he had not near so much due. So no end was made with him till 4. years after; of which in its plase. And in that regard, that them selves did not agree, I shall inserte some part of Mr. Andrews leter, by which he conceives the partners here were wronged, as followeth. This letter of his was write to Mr. *Edmond Freeman, brother in law* to Mr. *Beachamp.*

MR. FREEMAN,

My love remembred unto you, etc. I then certified the partners how I found Mr. Beachamp and Mr. Sherley, in their perticuler demands, which was according to mens principles, of getting what they could; allthough the one will not shew any accounte, and the other a very unfaire and unjust one; and both of them discouraged me from sending the partners my accounte, Mr. Beachamp espetially. Their reason, I have cause to conceive, was, that allthough I doe not, nor ever intended to, wrong the partners or the bussines, yet, if I gave no accounte, I might be esteemed as guiltie as they, in some degree at least; and they might seeme to be the more free from taxation in not delivering their accounts, who have both of them charged the accounte with much intrest they have payed forth, and one of them would likwise for much intrest he hath not paid forth, as appeareth by his accounte, etc. And seeing the partners have now made it appear that ther is 1200*li.* remaining due between us all, and that it may appear by my accounte I have not charged the bussines with any intrest, but doe forgive it unto the partners, above 200*li.* if Mr. Sherley and Mr. Beachamp, who have betweene them wronged the business so many 100*li.* both in principall and intrest likwise, and have therin wronged me as well and as much as any of the partners; yet if they will not make and deliver faire and true accounts of the same, nor be contente to take what by computation is more then can be justly due to either, that is, to Mr. Beachamp 150*li.* as by Mr. Allertons accounte, and Mr. Sherleys accounte, on oath in chancerie; and though ther might be nothing due to Mr. Sherley, yet he requires 100*li.*, etc. I conceive, seing the partners have delivered on their oaths the summe remaining in their hands, that they may justly detaine the 650*li.* which may remain in theire hands, after I am satisfied, untill Mr. Sherley and Mr. Beachamp will be more fair and just in their ending, etc. And as I intend, if the partners fayrly end with me, in satisfying in parte and ingaging them selves for the rest of my said 544*li.* to returne back for the poore my parte of the land at Sityate, so likwise I intend to relinquish my right and intrest in their dear patente, on which much of our money was laid forth, and also my right and intrest in the cheap purchass, the which may have cost me first and last 350*li*.* But I doubte whether other men have not charged or taken on accounte what they have disbursed in the like case, which I have not charged, neither did I conceive any other durst so doe, untill I saw the accounte of the one and heard the words of the other; the which gives me just cause to suspecte both their accounts to be unfaire; for it seemeth they cunsulted one with another aboute some perticulers therin. Therfore I conceive the partners ought the rather to require just accounts from each of them before they parte with any money to either of them. For marchants understand how to give an acounte; if they mean fairley, they will not deney to give an accounte, for they keep memorialls to helpe them to give exacte acounts in all perticulers, and memoriall cannot forget his charge, if the man will remember.

I desire not to wrong Mr. Beachamp or Mr. Sherley, nor may be silente in shuch apparente probabilities of their wronging the partners, and me likwise, either in deneying to deliver or shew any accounte, or in delivering one very unjuste in some perticulers, and very suspitious in many more; either of which, being from understanding marchants, cannot be from weaknes or simplisitie, and therfore the more unfaire. So comending you and yours, and all the Lord's people, unto the gratious protection and blessing of the Lord, and rest your loving friend,

RICHARD ANDREWES.

Aprill 7. 1643.

This leter was write the year after the agreement, as doth appear; and what his judgmente was herein, the contents doth manifest, and so I leave it to the equall judgmente of any to consider, as they see cause.

Only I shall adde what Mr. Sherley furder write in a leter of his, about the same time, and so leave this bussines. His is as followeth on the other side.

LOVING FREINDS, Mr. BRADFORD, Mr. WINSLOW, Cap: STANDISH, Mr. PRENCE, and the rest of the partners with you; I shall write this generall leter to you all, hoping it will be a good conclude of a generall, but a costly and tedious bussines I thinke to all, I am sure to me, etc.

---

*This he means of the first adventures, all which were lost, as hath before been shown; and what he here writes is probable at least.

I received from Mr. Winslow a letter of the 28. of September last, and so much as concernes the generall bussines I shall answer in this, not knowing whether I shall have opportunitie to write perticuler letters, etc. I expected more letters from you all, as some perticuler writes, but it seemeth no fitt opportunity was offered. And now, though the bussines for the maine may stand, yet some perticulers is alltered; I say my former agreemente with Mr. Weld and Mr. Peters, before they could conclude or gett any grante of Mr. Andrews, they sought to have my release; and ther upon they sealed me a bond for a 110*li*. So I sente my acquittance, for they said without mine ther would be no end made (and ther was good reason for it). Now they hoped, if they ended with me, to gaine Mr. Andrews parte, as they did holy, to a pound, (at which I should wonder, but that I observe some passages,) and they also hoped to have gotten Mr. Beachamps part, and I did thinke he would have given it them. But if he did well understand him selfe, and that acounte, he would give it; for his demands make a great sound.* But it seemeth he would not parte with it, supposing it too greate a sume, and that he might easily gaine it from you. Once he would have given them 40*li*. but now they say he will not doe that, or rather I suppose they will not take it; for if they doe, and have Mr. Andrewses, then they must pay me their bond of 110*li* ·3· months hence. Now it will fall out farr better for you, that they deal not with Mr. Beachamp, and also for me, if you be as kind to me as I have been and will be to you; and that thus, if you pay Mr. Andrews, or the Bay men, by his order, 544*li*. which is his full demande; but if looked into, perhaps might be less. The man is honest, and in my conscience would not wittingly doe wronge, yett he may forgett as well as other men; and Mr. Winslow may call to minde wherin he forgetts; (but some times it is good to buy peace.) The gentle-men of the Bay may abate 100*li*. and so both sides have more right and justice then if they exacte all, etc. Now if you send me a 150*li*. then say Mr. Andrews full sume, and this, it is nere 700*li*. Mr. Beachamp he demands 400*li*. and we all know that, if a man demands money, he must shew wherfore, and make proofe of his debte; which I know he can never make good proafe of one hunderd pound dew unto him as principall money; so till he can, you have good reason to keep the 500*li*. etc. This I proteste I write not in malice against Mr. Beachamp, for it is a reall truth. You may partly see it by Mr. Andrews making up his accounte, and I think you are all perswaded I can say more then Mr. Andrews concerning that accounte. I wish I

---

*This was a misterie to them, for they heard nothing hereof from any side the last year, till now the conclution was past, and bonds given.

could make up my owne as plaine and easily, but because of former discontents, I will be sparing till I be called; and you may injoye the 500*li*. quietly till he begine; for let him take his course hear or ther, it shall be all one, I will doe him no wronge; and if he have not on peney more, he is less loser then either Mr. Andrews or I. This I conceive to be just and honest; the having or not having of his release matters not; let him make shuch proafe of his debte as you cannot disprove, and according to your first agreemente you will pay it, etc.

Your truly affectioned freind,

JAMES SHERLEY.

London, Aprill 27. 1643.

ANNO DOM: ·1643·

I AM to begine this year whith that which was a mater of great saddnes and mourning unto them all. Aboute the 18· of Aprill dyed their Reverend Elder, and my dear and loving friend, Mr. William Brewster; a man that had done and suffered much for the Lord Jesus and the gospells sake, and had bore his parte in well and woe with this poore persecuted church above ·36· years in England, Holand, and in this wildernes, and done the Lord and them faithfull service in his place and calling. And notwithstanding the many troubles and sorrows he passed throw, the Lord upheld him to a great age. He was nere fourskore years of age (if not all out) when he dyed. He had this blesing added by the Lord to all the rest, to dye in his bed, in peace, amongst the mids of his freinds who mourned and wepte over him, and ministered what help and comforte they could unto him, and he againe recomforted them whilst he could. His sicknes was not long, and till the last day therof he did not wholy keepe his bed. His speech continued till somewhat more then halfe a day, and then failed him; and aboute ·9· or ·10· a clock that evening he dyed, without any pangs at all. A few howers before, he drew his breath shorte, and some few minutes before his last, he drew his breath long, as a man falen into a sound slepe, without any pangs or gaspings, and so sweetly departed this life unto a better.

I would now demand of any, what he was the worse for any former sufferings? What doe I say, worse? Nay, sure he was the better, and they now added to his honour. *It is a manifest token* (saith the Apostle, 2. Thes: 5, 6, 7.) *of the righteous judgmente*

of God that ye may be counted worthy of the kingdome of God,
for which ye allso suffer; seing it is a righteous thing with God to
recompence tribulation to them that trouble you: and to you who
are troubled, rest with us, when the Lord Jesus shall be revealed
from heaven, with his mighty angels. 1. Pet. 4. 14. *If you be*
reproached for the name of Christ, hapy are ye, for the spirite
of glory and of God resteth upon you. What though he wanted
the riches and pleasures of the world in his life, and pompious
monuments at his funurall? yet the memoriall of the just shall
be blessed, when the name of the wicked shall rott (with their
marble monuments). Pro: 10. 7.

I should say something of his life, if to say a litle were not
worse then to be silent. But I cannot wholy forbear, though
hapily more may be done hereafter. After he had attained some
learning, viz. the knowledg of the Latine tongue, and some
insight in the Greeke, and spent some small time at Cambridge,
and then being first seasoned with the seeds of grace and
vertue, he went to the Courte, and served that religious and
godly gentlman, Mr. Davison, diverce years, when he was Secretary of State; who found him so discreete and faithfull as he
trusted him above all other that were aboute him, and only
imployed him in all matters of greatest trust and secrecie. He
esteemed him rather as a sonne then a servante, and for his
wisdom and godlines (in private) he would converse with him
more like a freind and familier then a maister. He attended his
master when he was sente in ambassage by the Queene into the
Low-Countries, in the Earle of Leicesters time, as for other
waighty affaires of state, so to receive possession of the caution-
ary townes, and in token and signe therof the keyes of Flushing
being delivered to him, in her majesties name, he kepte them
some time, and committed them to this his servante, who kept
them under his pillow, on which he slepte the first night. And,
at his returne, the States honoured him with a gould chaine,
and his maister committed it to him, and commanded him to
wear it when they arrived in England, as they ridd thorrow the
country, till they came to the Courte. He afterwards remained
with him till his troubles, that he was put from his place aboute
the death of the Queene of Scots; and some good time after,
doeing him manie faithfull offices of servise in the time of his
troubles. Afterwards he wente and lived in the country, in good

esteeme amongst his freinds and the gentle-men of those parts,
espetially the godly and religious. He did much good in the
countrie wher he lived, in promoting and furthering religion,
not only by his practiss and example, and provocking and
incouraging of others, but by procuring of good preachers to
the places theraboute, and drawing on of others to assiste and
help forward in shuch a worke; he him selfe most comonly
deepest in the charge, and some times above his abillitie. And
in this state he continued many years, doeing the best good he
could, and walking according to the light he saw, till the Lord
reveiled further unto him. And in the end, by the tirrany of the
bishops against godly preachers and people, in silenceing the
one and persecuting the other, he and many more of those
times begane to looke further into things, and to see into the
unlawfullnes of their callings, and the burthen of many antichristian corruptions, which both he and they endeavored to
cast of; as they allso did, as in the begining of this treatis is to
be seene. After they were joyned togither in comunion, he was
a spetiall stay and help unto them. They ordinarily mett at his
house on the Lords day, (which was a manor of the bishops,)
and with great love he entertained them when they came,
making provission for them to his great charge, and continued
so to doe, whilst they could stay in England. And when they
were to remove out of the cuntrie he was one of the first in all
adventures, and forwardest in any charge. He was the cheefe of
those that were taken at Boston, and suffered the greatest loss;
and of the seven that were kept longest in prison, and after
bound over to the assises. Affter he came into Holland he suffered much hardship, after he had spente the most of his means,
haveing a great charge, and many children; and, in regard of
his former breeding and course of life, not so fitt for many
imployments as others were, espetially shuch as were toylesume
and laborious. But yet he ever bore his condition with much
cherfullnes and contentation. Towards the later parte of those
·12· years spente in Holland, his outward condition was
mended, and he lived well and plentifully; for he fell into a way
(by reason he had the Latine tongue) to teach many students,
who had a disire to lerne the English tongue, to teach them
English; and by his method they quickly attained it with great
facilitie; for he drew rules to lerne it by, after the Latine maner;

and many gentlemen, both Danes and Germans, resorted to
him, as they had time from other studies, some of them being
great mens sonnes. He also had means to set up printing, (by
the help of some freinds,) and so had imploymente inoughg,
and by reason of many books which would not be alowed to
be printed in England, they might have had more then they
could doe. But now removeing into this countrie, all these
things were laid aside againe, and a new course of living must
be framed unto; in which he was no way unwilling to take his
parte, and to bear his burthen with the rest, living many times
without bread, or corne, many months together, having many
times nothing but fish, and often wanting that also; and drunke
nothing but water for many years togeather, yea, till within ·5·
or ·6· years of his death. And yet he lived (by the blessing of
God) in health till very old age. And besides that, he would
labour with his hands in the feilds as long as he was able; yet
when the church had no other minister, he taught twise every
Saboth, and that both powerfully and profitably, to the great
contentment of the hearers, and their comfortable edification;
yea, many were brought to God by his ministrie. He did more
in this behalfe in a year, then many that have their hundreds a
year doe in all their lives. For his personall abilities, he was
qualified above many; he was wise and discreete and well
spoken, having a grave and deliberate utterance, of a very cher-
full spirite, very sociable and pleasante amongst his freinds, of
an humble and modest mind, of a peaceable disposition, under
vallewing him self and his owne abilities, and some time over
valewing others; inoffencive and innocente in his life and conversation, which gained him the love of those without, as well
as those within; yet he would tell them plainely of their faults
and evills, both publickly and privatly, but in shuch a maner as
usually was well taken from him. He was tender harted, and
compassionate of shuch as were in miserie, but espetialy of
shuch as had been of good estate and ranke, and were fallen
unto want and poverty, either for goodnes and religions sake,
or by the injury and oppression of others; he would say, of all
men these deserved to be pitied most. And none did more
offend and displease him then shuch as would hautily and
proudly carry and lift up themselves, being rise from nothing,
and haveing litle els in them to comend them but a few fine

cloaths, or a litle riches more then others. In teaching, he was very moving and staring of affections, also very plaine and distincte in what he taught; by which means he became the more profitable to the hearers. He had a singuler good gift in prayer, both publick and private, in ripping up the hart and conscience before God, in the humble confession of sinne, and begging the mercies of God in Christ for the pardon of the same. He always thought it were better for ministers to pray oftener, and devide their preyars, then be longe and tedious in the same (excepte upon sollemne and spetiall occations, as in days of humiliation and the like). His reason was, that the harte and spirits of all, espetialy the weake, could hardly continue and stand bente (as it were) so long towards God, as they ought to doe in that duty, without flagging and falling of. For the govermente of the church, (which was most proper to his office,) he was carfull to preserve good order in the same, and to preserve puritie, both in the doctrine and comunion of the same; and to supress any errour or contention that might begine to rise up amongst them; and accordingly God gave good success to his indeavors herein all his days, and he saw the fruite of his labours in that behalfe. But I must breake of, having only thus touched a few, as it were, heads of things.

I cannot but here take occasion, not only to mention, but greatly to admire the marvelous providence of God, that notwithstanding the many changes and hardships that these people wente throwgh, and the many enemies they had and difficulties they mette with all, that so many of them should live to very olde age! It was not only this reverend mans condition, (for one swallow makes no summer, as they say,) but many more of them did the like, some dying aboute and before this time, and many still living, who attained to ·60· years of age, and to ·65· diverse to ·70· and above, and some nere ·80· as he did. It must needs be more then ordinarie, and above naturall reason, that so it should be; for it is found in experience, that chaing of aeir, famine, or unholsome foode, much drinking of water, sorrows and troubles, etc., all of them are enimies to health, causes of many diseaces, consumers of naturall vigoure and the bodys of men, and shortners of life. And yet of all these things they had a large parte, and suffered deeply in the same. They wente from England to Holand, wher they found both worse air and dyet then that they came from; from thence (induring a long imprisonmente, as it were, in the ships at sea) into New-England; and how it hath been with them hear hath allready beene showne; and what crosses, troubles, fears, wants, and sorrowes they have been lyable unto, is easie to conjecture; so as in some sorte they may say with the Apostle, ·2· Cor: II. 26, 27. *They were in journeyings often, in perils of waters, in perills of robers, in perills of their owne nation, in perils among the heathen, in perills in the willdernes, in perills in the sea, in perills among false breethern; in wearines and painfullnes, in watching often, in hunger and thirst, in fasting often, in could and nakednes.* What was it then that upheld them? It was Gods vissitation that preserved their spirits. Job ·10· 12. Thou hast given me life and grace, and thy vissitation hath preserved my spirite. He that upheld the Apostle upheld them. *They were persecuted, but not forsaken, cast downe, but perished not.* 2. Cor: 4. 9. *As unknowen, and yet knowen; as dying, and behold we live; as chastened, and yett not kiled.* 2. Cor: 6. 9. God, it seems, would have all men to behold and observe such mercies and works of his providence as these are towards his people, that they in like cases might be incouraged to depend upon God in their trials, and also blese his name when they see his goodnes towards others. Man lives not by bread only, Deut: 8. 3. It is not by good and dainty fare, by peace, and rest, and harts ease, in injoying the contentments and good things of this world only, that preserves health and prolongs life. God in shuch examples would have the world see and behold that he can doe it without them; and if the world will shut ther eyes, and take no notice therof, yet he would have his people to see and consider it. Daniell could be better liking with pulse then others were with the kings dainties. Jaacob, though he wente forom one nation to another people, and passed thorow famine, fears, and many afflictions, yet he lived till old age, and dyed sweetly, and rested in the Lord, as infinite others of Gods servants have done, and still shall doe, (through Gods goodnes,) notwithstanding all the malice of their enemies; *when the branch of the wicked shall be cut of before his day,* Job. 15. 32. *and the bloody and deceitfull men shall not live* [out] *halfe their days.* Psa: 55. 23.

By reason of the plottings of the Narigansets, (ever since the Pequents warr,) the Indeans were drawne into a generall conspiracie against the English in all parts, as was in part discovered the yeare before; and now made more plaine and evidente by many discoveries and free-conffessions of sundrie Indeans (upon severall occasions) from diverse places, concuring in one; with shuch other concuring circomstances as gave them suffissently to understand the trueth therof, and to thinke of means how to prevente the same, and secure them selves. Which made them enter into this more nere union and confederation following.

Articles of Conffederation betweene the Plantations under the Govermente of Massachusets, the Plantations under the Govermente of New-Plimoth, the Plantations under the Govermente of Conightecute, and the Govermente of New-Haven, with the Plantations in combination therwith.

Wheras we all came into these parts of America with one and the same end and aime, namly, to advance the kingdome of our Lord Jesus Christ, and to injoye the liberties of the Gospell in puritie with peace; and wheras in our setling (by a wise providence of God) we are further disperced upon the sea coasts and rivers then was at first intended, so that we cannot, according to our desires, with conveniencie comunicate in one govermente and jurisdiction; and wheras we live encompassed with people of severall nations and strange languages, which hereafter may prove injurious to us and our posteritie; and for as much as the natives have formerly committed sundrie insolencies and outrages upon severall plantations of the English, and have of late combined them selves against us; and seeing, by reason of those [sad] distractions in England (which they have heard of) and by which they know we are hindered from that humble way of seeking advice or reaping those comfurtable fruits of protection which at other times we might well expecte; we therfore doe conceive it our bounden duty, without delay, to enter into a presente consociation amongst our selves, for mutuall help and strength in all our future concernments. That as in nation and religion, so in other respects, we be and continue one, according to the tenor and true meaning of the insuing articles. (1) Wherfore it is fully agreed and concluded by and betweene the parties or jurisdictions above named, and they joyntly and severally doe by these presents agree and conclude, that they all be and henceforth be called by the name of THE UNITED COLONIES OF NEW-ENGLAND.

2. The said United Collonies, for them selves and their posterities, doe joyntly and severally hereby enter into a firme and perpetuall league of frendship and amitie, for offence and defence, mutuall advice and succore upon all just occasions, both for preserving and propagating the truth of the Gospell, and for their owne mutuall saftie and wellfare.

3. It is further agreed that the plantations which at presente are or hereafter shall be setled with the limites of the Massachusets shall be for ever under the Massachusets, and shall have peculier jurisdiction amonge them selves in all cases, as an intire body. And that Plimoth, Conightecutt, and New-Haven shall each of them have like peculier jurisdition and govermente within their limites and in refference to the plantations which allready are setled, or shall hereafter be erected, or shall setle within their limites, respectively; provided that no other jurisdition shall hereafter be taken in, as a distincte head or member of this confederation, nor shall any other plantation or jurisdiction in presente being, and not allready in combination or under the jurisdiction of any of these confederates, be received by any of them; nor shall any tow of the confederates joyne in one jurisdiction, without consente of the rest, which consente to be interpreted as is expresed in the sixte article ensewing.

4. It is by these conffederates agreed, that the charge of all just warrs, whether offencive or defencive, upon what parte or member of this confederation soever they fall, shall, both in men, provissions, and all other disbursments, be borne by all the parts of this confederation, in differente proportions, according to their differente abillities, in maner following: namely, that the comissioners for each jurisdiction, from time to time, as ther shall be occasion, bring a true accounte and number of all their males in every plantation, or any way belonging too or under their severall jurisdictions, of what qualitie or condition soever they be, from ·16· years old to ·60· being inhabitants ther; and that according to the differente numbers which from time to time shall be found in each jurisdiction upon a true and just accounte, the service of men and all charges of the warr be borne by the pole; each jurisdiction or plantation being left to their owne just course and custome of rating them selves and people according to their differente estates, with due respects to their qualities and exemptions amongst them selves, though the confederates take no notice of any shuch priviledg. And that according to their differente charge of each jurisdiction and plantation, the whole advantage of the warr, (if it please God to blesse their indeaours,) whether it be in lands, goods, or persons, shall be proportionably devided amonge the said confederates.

5. It is further agreed, that if these jurisdictions, or any plantation under or in combynacion with them, be invaded by any enemie
whomsoever, upon notice and requeste of any ·3· magistrates of that
jurisdiction so invaded, the rest of the confederates, without any
further meeting or expostulation, shall forthwith send ayd to the
confederate in danger, but in differente proportion; namely, the Massachusets an hundred men sufficently armed and provided for shuch
a service and journey, and each of the rest forty five so armed and
provided, or any lesser number, if less be required according to this
proportion. But if shuch confederate in danger may be supplyed by
their nexte confederates, not exceeding the number hereby agreed,
they may crave help ther, and seeke no further for the presente; the
charge to be borne as in this article is exprest, and at the returne to
be victuled and suplyed with powder and shote for their jurney (if ther
be need) by that jurisdiction which imployed or sent for them. But
none of the jurisdictions to exceede these numbers till, by a meeting
of the commissioners for this confederation, a greater aide appear
nessessarie. And this proportion to continue till upon knowlege of
greater numbers in each jurisdiction, which shall be brought to the
nexte meeting, and some other proportion be ordered. But in shuch
case of sending men for presente aide, whether before or after shuch
order or alteration, it is agreed that at the meeting of the comissioners
for this confederation, that the cause of shuch warr or invasion be
duly considered; and if it appeare that the falte lay in the parties so
invaded, that then that jurisdiction or plantation make just satisfaction both to the invaders whom they have injured, and beare all the
charges of the warr them selves, without requiring any allowance
from the rest of the confederates towards the same. And further, that
if any jurisdiction see any danger of any invasion approaching, and
ther be time for a meeting, that in shuch a case ·3· magistrates of that
jurisdiction may summone a meeting, at shuch conveniente place as
them selves shall thinke meete, to consider and provid against the
threatened danger, provided when they are mett, they may remove
to what place they please; only, whilst any of these foure confederates
have but ·3· magistrates in their jurisdiction, their requeste, or sum-
mons, from any ·2· of them shall be accounted of equall force with
the ·3· mentioned in both the clauses of this article, till ther be an
increase of majestrates ther.

6. It is also agreed that, for the managing and concluding of all
affairs propper, and concerning the whole confederation, two comissioners shall be chosen by and out of each of these ·4· jurisdictions;
namly, ·2· for the Massachusets, ·2· for Plimoth, ·2· for Conightecutt,
and ·2· for New-Haven, being all in church fellowship with us, which

shall bring full power from their severall Generall Courts respectively
to hear, examene, waigh, and detirmine all affairs of warr, or peace,
leagues, aids, charges, and numbers of men for warr, divissions of
spoyles, and whatsoever is gotten by conquest; receiving of more confederates, or plantations into combination with any of the confederates, and all things of like nature, which are the proper concomitants
or consequences of shuch a confederation, for amitie, offence, and
defence; not intermedling with the govermente of any of the jurisdictions, which by the ·3· article is preserved entirely to them selves. But
if these ·8· comissioners when they meete shall not all agree, yet it
concluded that any ·6· of the ·8· agreeing shall have power to setle
and determine the bussines in question. But if ·6· doe not agree, that
then shuch propositions, with their reasons, so farr as they have been
debated, be sente, and referred to the ·4· Generall Courts, viz. the
Massachusets, Plimoth, Conightecutt, and New-haven; and if at all
the said Generall Courts the bussines so referred be concluded, then
to be prosecuted by the confederates, and all their members. It was
further agreed that these ·8· comisioners shal meete once every year,
besides extraordinarie meetings, (according to the fifte article,) to
consider, treate, and conclude of all affaires belonging to this confederation, which meeting shall ever be the first Thursday in September.
And that the next meeting after the date of these presents, which shall
be accounted the second meeting, shall be at Boston in the Massachusets, the ·3· at Hartford, the ·4· at New-Haven, the ·5· at Plimoth,
and so in course successively, if in the meane time some midle place
be not found out and agreed on, which may be comodious for all the
jurisdictions.

7. It is further agreed, that at each meeting of these ·8· comissioners, whether ordinarie, or extraordinary, they all ·6· of them agreeing
as before, may chuse a presidente out of them selves, whose office and
work shall be to take care and directe for order, and a comly carrying
on of all proceedings in the present meeting; but he shall be invested
with no shuch power or, respecte, as by which he shall hinder the
propounding or progrese of any bussines, or any way cast the scailes
otherwise then in the precedente article is agreed.

8. It is also agreed, that the comissioners for this confederation
hereafter at their meetings, whether ordinarie or extraordinary, as
they may have comission or opportunitie, doe indeaover to frame and
establish agreements and orders in generall cases of a civill nature,
wherin all the plantations are interested, for the preserving of peace
amongst them selves, and preventing as much as may be all occasions
of warr or difference with others; as aboute the free and speedy passage of justice, in every jurisdiction, to all the confederates equally as

to their owne; not receiving those that remove from one plantation to another without due certificate; how all the jurisdictions may carry towards the Indeans, that they neither growe insolente, nor be injured without due satisfaction, least warr breake in upon the confederates through such miscarriages. It is also agreed, that if any servante rune away from his maister into another of these confederated jurisdictions, that in shuch case, upon the certificate of one magistrate in the jurisdiction out of which the said servante fledd, or upon other due proofe, the said servante shall be delivered, either to his maister, or any other that pursues and brings such certificate or proofe. And that upon the escape of any prisoner whatsoever, or fugitive for any criminall cause, whether breaking prison, or getting from the officer, or otherwise escaping, upon the certificate of ·2· magistrates of the jurisdiction out of which the escape is made, that he was a prisoner, or such an offender at the time of the escape, the magistrates, or sume of them of that jurisdiction wher for the presente the said prisoner or fugitive abideth, shall forthwith grante shuch a warrante as the case will beare, for the apprehending of any shuch person, and the delivering of him into the hands of the officer, or other person who pursues him. And if ther be help required, for the safe returning of any shuch offender, then it shall be granted to him that craves the same, he paying the charges therof.

9. And for that the justest warrs may be of dangerous consequence, espetially to the smaler plantations in these United Collonies, it is agreed that neither the Massachusets, Plimoth, Conightecutt, nor New-Haven, nor any member of any of them, shall at any time hear after begine, undertake, or ingage them selves, or this confederation, or any parte therof, in any warr whatsoever, (sudden exegents, with the necessary consequents therof excepted which are also to be moderated as much as the case will permitte,) without the consente and agreemente of the forementioned ·8· comissioners, or at the least ·6· of them, as in the sixt article is provided. And that no charge be required of any of they [the] confederates, in case of a defensive warr, till the said comissioners have mett, and approved the justice of the warr, and have agreed upon the summe of money to be levied, which sume is then to be paid by the severall confederates in proportion according to the fourth article.

10. That in extraordinary occasions, when meetings are sumoned by three magistrates of any jurisdiction, or ·2· as in the ·5· article, if any of the comissioners come not, due warning being given or sente, it is agreed that ·4· of the comissioners shall have power, to directe a warr which cannot be delayed, and to send for due proportions of men out of each jurisdiction, as well as ·6· might doe if all mett; but not less then ·6· shall determine the justice of the warr, or alow the

demands or bills of charges, or cause any levies to be made for the same.

11. It is further agreed, that if any of the confederates shall hereafter breake any of these presente articles, or be any other ways injurious to any one of the other jurisdictions, such breach of agreemente or injurie shall be duly considered and ordered by the comissioners for the other jurisdictions; that both peace and this presente confederation may be intirly preserved without violation.

12. Lastly, this perpetuall confederation, and the severall articles therof being read, and seriously considered, both by the Generall Courte for the Massachusets, and by the comissioners for Plimoth, Conigtecute, and New-Haven, were fully alowed and confirmed by ·3· of the forenamed confederates, namly, the Massachusets, Conightecutt, and New-Haven; only the comissioners for Plimoth haveing no commission to conclude, desired respite till they might advise with their Generall Courte; wher upon it was agreed and concluded by the said Courte of the Massachusets, and the comissioners for the other tow confederates, that, if Plimoth consente, then the whole treaty as it stands in these present articles is, and shall continue, firme and stable without alteration. But if Plimoth come not in, yet the other three confederates doe by these presents confeirme the whole confederation, and the articles therof; only in September nexte, when the second meeting of the commissioners is to be at Boston, new consideration may be taken of the ·6· article, which concerns numbers of comissioners for meeting and concluding they [the] affaires of this confederation, to the satisfaction of the Courte of the Massachusets, and the comissioners for the other ·2· confederates, but the rest to stand unquestioned. In the testimonie wherof, the Generall Courte of the Massachusets, by ther Secretary, and the comissioners for Conightecutt and New-Haven, have subscribed these presente articles this ·19· of the third month, comonly called May, Anno Dom: 1643.

At a meeting of the comissioners for the confederation held at Boston the ·7· of September, it appearing that the Generall Courte of New-Plimoth, and the severall towneshipes therof, have read and considered and approved these articles of confederation, as appeareth by commission from their Generall Courte bearing date the ·29· of August, 1643. to Mr. Edward Winslow and Mr. William Collier, to ratifie and confirme the same on their behalfes. We, therfore, the Comissioners for the Massachusets, Conightecutt, and New Haven, doe also, for our severall goverments, subscribe unto them.

> JOHN WINTHROP, Governor of the Massachusest.
>
> THO: DUDLEY.   THEOPH: EATON.
> GEO: FENWICK.   EDWA: HOPKINS.
>   THOMAS GREGSON.

These were the articles of agreemente in the union and confederation which they now first entered into; and in this their first meeting, held at Boston the day and year abovesaid, amongst other things they had this matter of great consequence to considere on: the Narigansets, after the subduing of the Pequents, thought to have ruled over all the Indeans aboute them; but the English, espetially those of Conightecutt holding correspondence and frenship with Uncass, sachem of the Monhigg Indeans which lived nere them, (as the Massachusets had done with the Narigansets,) and he had been faithfull to them in the Pequente warr, they were ingaged to supporte him in his just liberties, and were contented that such of the surviving Pequents as had submited to him should remaine with him and quietly under his protection. This did much increase his power and augmente his greatnes, which the Narigansets could not indure to see. But Myantinomo, their cheefe sachem, (an ambitious and politick man,) sought privatly and by trearchery (according to the Indean maner) to make him away, by hiring some to kill him. Sometime they assayed to poyson him; that not takeing, then in the night time to knock him on the head in his house, or secretly to shoot him, and shuch like attempts. But none of these taking effecte, he made open warr upon him (though it was against the covenants both betweene the English and them, as also betweene them selves, and a plaine breach of the same). He came suddanly upon him with ·900· or ·1000· men (never denouncing any warr before). The others power at that presente was not aboute halfe so many; but it pleased God to give Uncass the victory, and he slew many of his men, and wounded many more; but the cheefe of all was, he tooke Miantinomo prisoner. And seeing he was a greate man, and the Narigansets a potente people and would seeke revenge, he would doe nothing in the case without the advise of the English; so he (by the help and direction of those of Conightecutt) kept him prisoner till this meeting of the comissioners. The comissioners weighed the cause and passages, as they were clearly represented and sufficiently evidenced betwixte Uncass and Myantinomo; and the things being duly considered, the comissioners apparently saw that Uncass could not be safe whilst Miantynomo lived, but, either by secrete trechery or open force, his life would be still in danger. Wherfore they thought he might justly put shuch a false and bloud-thirstie enimie to death; but in his owne jurisdiction, not in the English plantations. And they advised, in the maner of his death all mercy and moderation should be showed, contrary to the practise of the Indeans, who exercise tortures and cruelty. And, Uncass having hitherto shewed him selfe a freind to the English, and in this craving their advise, if the Narigansett Indeans or others shall unjustly assaulte Uncass for this execution, upon notice and request, the English promise to assiste and protecte him as farr as they may againste shuch violence.

This was the issue of this bussines. The reasons and passages hereof are more at large to be seene in the acts and records of this meeting of the comissioners. And Uncass followed this advise, and accordingly executed him, in a very faire maner, acording as they advised, with due respecte to his honour and greatnes. But what followed on the Narigansets parte will appear heare after.

ANNO DOM: ·1644·

M R. EDWARD WINSLOW was chosen Governor this year. Many having left this place (as is before noted) by reason of the straightnes and barrennes of the same, and their finding of better accomodations elsewher, more suitable to their ends and minds; and sundrie others still upon every occasion desiring their dismissions, the church begane seriously to thinke whether it were not better joyntly to remove to some other place, then to be thus weakened, and as it were insensibly dissolved. Many meetings and much consultation was held hearaboute, and diverse were mens minds and oppinions. Some were still for staying togeather in this place, alledging men might hear live, if they would be contente with their condition; and that it was not for wante or necessitie so much that they removed, as for the enriching of them selves. Others were resolute upon removall, and so signified that hear they could not stay; but if the church did not remove, they must; insomuch as many were swayed, rather then ther should be a dissolution, to condescend to a removall, if a fitt place could be found, that might more conveniently and comfortablie receive the whole, with shuch accession of others as might come to them, for their better strength and subsistence; and some shuch like cautions and limitations. So as, with the afforesaide provissos, the greater parte consented to a removall to a place called Nawsett, which had been superficially viewed and the good will of the purchassers (to whom it belonged) obtained, with some addition thertoo from the Courte. But now they begane to see their errour, that they had given away already the best and most commodious places to others, and now wanted them selves; for this place was about ·50· myles from hence, and at an outside of the countrie, remote from all society; also, that it would prove so straite, as it would not be competente to receive the whole body, much less be capable of any addition or increase; so as (at least in a shorte time) they should be worse ther then they are now hear. The which, with sundery other like considerations and inconveniences, made them chang their resolutions; but shuch as were before resoloved upon removall tooke advantage of this agreemente, and wente on nonwithstanding, neither could the rest hinder them, they haveing made some beginning. And thus was this poore church left, like an anciente mother, growne olde, and forsaken of her children, (though not in their affections,) yett in regarde of their bodily presence and personall helpfullnes. Her anciente members being most of them worne away by death; and these of later time being like children translated into other families, and she like a widow left only to trust in God. Thus she that had made many rich became her selfe poore.

Some things handled, and pacified by the commissioners this year.

Wheras, by a wise providence of God, tow of the jurisdictions in the westerne parts, viz. Conightecutt and New-haven, have beene latly exercised by sundrie insolencies and outrages from the Indeans; as, first, an Englishman, runing from his master out of the Massachusets, was murdered in the woods, in or nere the limites of Conightecute jurisdiction; and aboute ·6· weeks after, upon discovery by an Indean, the Indean Sagamores in these parts promised to deliver the murderer to the English, bound; and having accordingly brought him within the sight of Uncaway, by their joynte consente, as it is informed, he was ther unbound, and left to shifte for him selfe; wherupon ·10· Englishmen forthwith coming to the place, being sente by Mr. Ludlow, at the Indeans desire, to receive the murderer, who seeing him escaped, layed hold of ·8· of the Indeans ther presente, amongst whom ther was a sagamore or ·2· and kept them in hold ·2· days, till ·4· sagamors ingaged themselves within one month to deliver the prisoner. And about a weeke after this agreemente, an Indean came presumtuously and with guile, in the day time, and murtherously assalted an English woman in her house at Stamford, and by ·3· wounds, supposed mortall, left her for dead, after he had robbed the house. By which passages the English were provoaked, and called to a due consideration of their owne saftie; and the Indeans generally in those parts arose in an hostile manner, refused to come to the English to carry on treaties of peace, departed from their wigwames, left their corne unweeded, and shewed them selves tumultuously about some of the English plantations, and shott of peeces within hearing of the towne; and some Indeans came to the English and tould them the Indeans would fall upon them. So that most of the English thought it unsafe to travell in those parts by land, and some of the plantations were put upon strong watches and ward, night and day, and could not attend their private occasions, and yet distrusted their owne strength for their defence. Wherupon Hartford and New-Haven were sent unto for aide, and saw cause both to send into the weaker parts of their owne jurisdiction thus in danger, and New-Haven, for conveniencie of situation, sente aide to Uncaway, though belonging to Conightecutt. Of all which passages they presently acquainted the comissioners in the Bay, and had the allowance and approbation from the Generall Courte ther, with directions neither to hasten a warr nor to bear shuch insolencies too longe. Which courses, though chargable to them selves, yet through Gods blessing they hope the fruite is, and will be, sweete and wholsome to all the collonies; the murderers are since delivered to justice, the publick peace preserved for the presente, and probabillitie it may be better secured for the future.

Thus this mischeefe was prevented, and the fear of a warr hereby diverted. But now an other broyle was begune by the Narigansets; though they unjustly had made warr upon Uncass, (as is before declared,) and had, the winter before this, ernestly presed the Governor of the Massachusets that they might still make warr upon them to revenge the death of their sagamore, which being taken prisoner, was by them put to death, (as before was noted,) pretending that they had first received and accepted his ransome, and then put him to death. But the Governor refused their presents, and tould them that it was them selves had done the wronge, and broaken the conditions of peace; and he nor the English neither could nor would allow them to make any further warr upon him, but if they did, must assiste him, and oppose them; but if it did appeare, upon good proofe, that he had received a ransome for his life, before he put him to death, when the comissioners mett, they should have a fair hearing, and they would cause Uncass to returne the same. But notwithstanding, at the spring of the year they gathered a great power, and fell upon Uncass, and slue sundrie of his men, and wounded more, and also had some loss them selves. Uncass cald for aide from the English; they tould him what the Narigansets objected, he deneyed the same; they tould him it must come to triall, and if he was inocente, if the Narigansets would not desiste, they would aide and assiste him. So at this meeting they sent both to Uncass and the Narrigansets, and required their sagamors to come or send to the comissioners now mete at Hartford, and they should have a faire and inpartiall hearing in all their greevances, and would endeavor that all wrongs should be rectified wher they should be found; and they promised that they should safly come and returne without any danger or molestation; and sundry the like things, as appears more at large in the messengers instructions. Upon which the Narigansets sent one sagamore and some other deputies, with full power to doe in the case as should be meete. Uncass came in person, accompanyed with some cheefe aboute him. After the agitation of the bussines, the issue was this. The comissioners declared to the Narigansett deputies as followeth:

1. That they did not find any proofe of any ransome agreed on.

2. It appeared not that any wampam had been paied as a ransome, or any parte of a ransome, for Myantinomos life.

3. That if they had in any measure proved their charge against Uncass, the comissioners would have required him to have made answerable satisfaction.

4. That if hereafter they can make satisfying profe, the English will consider the same, and proceed accordingly.

5. The comissioners did require that neither them selves nor the Nyanticks make any warr or injurious assaulte upon Unquass or any of his company untill they make profe of the ransume charged, and that due satisfaction be deneyed, unless he first assaulte them.

6. That if they assaulte Uncass, the English are engaged to assist him.

Hearupon the Narigansette sachim, advising with the other deputies, ingaged him selfe in the behalfe of the Narigansets and Nyanticks
that no hostile acts should be comitted upon Uncass, or any of his,
untill after the next planting of corne; and that after that, before they
begine any warr, they will give ·30· days warning to the Governor of
the Massachusets or Conightecutt. The comissioners approving of
this offer, and taking their ingagmente under their hands, required
Uncass, as he expected the continuance of the favour of the English,
to observe the same termes of peace with the Narigansets and theirs.

These foregoing conclusions were subscribed by the comissioners,
for the severall jurisdictions, the ·19· of Sept: 1644.

> EDWA: HOPKINS, Presidente.
> SIMON BRADSTREETE.
> WILLM. HATHORNE.
> EDW: WINSLOW.
> JOHN BROWNE.
> GEOR: FENWICK.
> THEOPH: EATON.
> THO: GREGSON.

The forenamed Narigansets deputies did further promise, that if,
contrary to this agreemente, any of the Nyantick Pequents should
make any assaulte upon Uncass, or any of his, they would deliver them
up to the English, to be punished according to their demerits; and
that they would not use any means to procure the Mowacks to come
against Uncass during this truce.

These were their names subscribed with their marks.

> WEETOWISH.   CHINNOUGH.
> PAMPIAMETT.   PUMMUNISH.

ANNO DOM: ·1645·

THE comissioners this year were caled to meete together
at Boston, before their ordinarie time; partly in regard
of some differances falen betweene the French and the govermente of the Massachusets, about their aiding of Munseire
Latore against Munsseire de Aulney, and partly aboute the
Indeans, who had broaken the former agreements aboute the
peace concluded the last year. This meeting was held at Boston,
the 28. of July.

Besides some underhand assualts made on both sides, the
Narigansets gathered a great power, and fell upon Uncass, and
slew many of his men, and wounded more, by reason that they

farr exseeded him in number, and had gott store of peeces, with which they did him most hurte. And as they did this withoute the knowledg and consente of the English, (contrary to former agreemente,) so they were resolved to prosecute the same, notwithstanding any thing the English said or should doe against them. So, being incouraged by ther late victorie, and promise of assistance from the Mowacks, (being a strong, warlike, and desperate people,) they had allready devoured Uncass and his, in their hopes; and surly they had done it in deed, if the English had not timly sett in for his aide. For those of Conightecute sent him ·40· men, who were a garison to him, till the comissioners could meete and take further order.

Being thus mett, they forthwith sente ·3· messengers, viz. Sargent John Davis, Benedicte Arnold, and Francis Smith, with full and ample instructions, both to the Narigansets and Uncass; to require them that they should either come in person or send sufficiente men fully instructed to deale in the bussines; and if they refused or delayed, to let them know (according to former agreements) that the English are engaged to assiste against these hostile invasions, and that they have sente their men to defend Uncass, and to know of the Narigansets whether they will stand to the former peace, or they will assaulte the English also, that they may provide accordingly.

But the messengers returned, not only with a sleighting, but a threatening answer from the Narigansets (as will more appear hereafter). Also they brought a letter from Mr. Roger Williams, wherin he assures them that the warr would presenly breake forth, and the whole country would be all of a flame. And that the sachems of the Narigansets had concluded a newtrality with the English of Providence and those of Aquidnett Iland. Wherupon the comissioners, considering the great danger and provocations offered, and the necessitie we should be put unto of making war with the Narigansets, and being also carfull, in a matter of so great waight and generall concernmente, to see the way cleared, and to give satisfaction to all the colonies, did thinke fitte to advise with such of the magistrates, and elders of the Massachusets as were then at hand, and also with some of the cheefe millitary comanders ther; who being assembled, it was then agreed,

First, that our ingagmente bound us to aide and defend
Uncass. 2. That this ayde could not be intended only to defend
him and his forte, or habitation, but (according to the comone
acceptation of shuch covenants, or ingagments, considered with
the grounds or occasion therof) so to ayde him as he might be
preserved in his liberty and estate. 3ly. That this ayde must be
speedy, least he might be swalowed up in the mean time, and so
come to late. 4ly. The justice of this warr being cleared to our
selves and the rest then presente, it was thought meete that the
case should be stated, and the reasons and grounds of the warr
declared and published. 5ly. That a day of humilliation should
be apoynted, which was the ·5· day of the weeke following. 6ly.
It was then allso agreed by the comissioners that the whole
number of men to be raised in all the colonies should be ·300·
Whereof from the Massachusets a ·190· Plimoth, ·40· Conightecute, ·40· New-Haven, ·30· And considering that Uncass was
in present danger, ·40· men of this number were forthwith
sente from the Massachusets for his sucoure; and it was but
neede, for the other ·40· from Conightecutt had order to stay
but a month, and their time being out, they returned; and the
Narigansets, hearing therof, tooke the advantage, and came
suddanly upon him, and gave him another blow, to his further
loss, and were ready to doe the like againe; but these ·40· men
being arrived, they returned, and did nothing.

The declarations which they sett forth I shall not transcribe,
it being very large, and put forth in printe, to which I referr
those that would see the same, in which all passages are layed
open from the first. I shall only note their prowd carriage, and
answers to the ·3· messengers sent from the comissioners. They
received them with scorne and contempte, and tould them they
resoloved to have no peace without Uncass his head; also they
gave them this further answer: that it mattered not who begane
the warr, they were resolved to follow it, and that the English
should withdraw their garison from Uncass, or they would
procure the Mowakes against them; and withall gave them
this threatening answer: that they would lay the English catle
on heaps, as high as their houses, and that no English-man
should sturr out of his dore to pisse, but he should be kild.
And wheras they required guides to pass throw their countrie,

to deliver their message to Uncass from the comissioners, they deneyed them, but at length (in way of scorne) offered them an old Pequente woman. Besides allso they conceived them selves in danger, for whilst the interpretoure was speakeing with them about the answer he should returne, ·3· men came and stood behind him with ther hatchets, according to their murderous maner; but one of his fellows gave him notice of it, so they broak of and came away; with sundry shuch like affrontes, which made those Indeans they carryed with them to rune away for fear, and leave them to goe home as they could.

Thus whilst the comissioners in care of the publick peace sought to quench the fire kindled amongst the Indeans, these children of strife breath out threatenings, provocations, and warr against the English them selves. So that, unless they should dishonour and provoak God, by violating a just ingagmente, and expose the colonies to contempte and danger from the barbarians, they cannot but exerciese force, when no other means will prevaile to reduse the Narigansets and their confederates to a more just and sober temper.

So as here upon they went on to hasten the preparations, according to the former agreemente, and sent to Plimoth to send forth their ·40· men with all speed, to lye at Seacunke, least any deanger should befalle it, before the rest were ready, it lying next the enemie, and ther to stay till the Massachusetts should joyne with them. Allso Conigtecute and Newhaven forces were to joyne togeather, and march with all speed, and the Indean confederates of those parts with them. All which was done accordingly; and the souldiers of this place were at Seacunk, the place of their rendevouze, ·8· or ·10· days before the rest were ready; they were well armed all with snaphance peeces, and wente under the camand of Captain Standish. Those from other places were led likwise by able comanders, as Captaine Mason for Conigtecute, etc.; and Majore Gibons was made generall over the whole, with shuch comissions and instructions as was meete.

Upon the suden dispatch of these souldiears, (the present necessitie requiring it,) the deputies of the Massachusetts Courte (being now assembled immediatly after the setting forth of their ·40· men) made a question whether it was legally done, without their comission. It was answered, that howsoever

it did properly belong to the authority of the severall jurisdictions (after the warr was agreed upon by the comissioners, and
the number of men) to provid the men and means to carry
on the warr; yet in this presente case, the proceeding of the
comissioners and the comission given was as sufficiente as if it
had been done by the Generall Courte.

1. First, it was a case of shuch presente and urgente necessitie, as
could not stay the calling of the Courte or Counsell. 2ly. In the Articles of Confederation, power is given to the comissioners to consult,
order, and determine all affaires of warr, etc. And the word *determine*
comprehends all acts of authority belonging therunto.

3ly. The comissioners are the judges of the necessitie of the
expedition.

4ly. The Generall Courte have made their owne comissioners their
sole counsell for these affaires.

5ly. These counsels could not have had their due effecte excepte
they had power to proceede in this case, as they have done; which
were to make the comissioners power, and the maine end of the confederation, to be frustrate, and that mearly for observing a ceremony.

6ly. The comissioners haveing sole power to manage the warr for
number of men, for time, place, etc., they only know their owne
counsells, and *determinations*, and therefore none can grante commission to acte according to these but them selves.

All things being thus in readines, and some of the souldiers gone forth, and the rest ready to march, the comissioners
thought it meete before any hostile acte was performed, to
cause a presente to be returned, which had been sente to the
Governor of the Massachusetts from the Narigansett sachems,
but not by him received, but layed up to be accepted or refused
as they should carry them selves, and observe the covenants.
Therfore they violating the same, and standing out thus to a
warr, it was againe returned, by ·2· messengers and an interpretour. And further to let know that their men already sent to
Uncass (and other wher sent forth) have hitherto had express
order only to stand upon his and their owne defence, and not
to attempte any invasion of the Narigansetts country; and yet
if they may have due reperation for what is past, and good
securitie for the future, it shall appear they are as desirous
of peace, and shall be as tender of the Narigansets blood as

ever. If therefore Pessecuss, Innemo, with other sachemes, will (without further delay) come along with you to Boston, the comissioners doe promise and assure them, they shall have free liberty to come, and retourne without molestation or any just greevance from the English. But deputies will not now serve, nor may the preparations in hand be now stayed, or the directions given recalled, till the forementioned sagamores come, and some further order be taken. But if they will have nothing but warr, the English are providing, and will proceede accordingly.

Pessecouss, Mixano, and Witowash, ·3· principall sachems of the Narigansett Indeans, and Amasequen, deputie for the Nyanticks, with a large traine of men, within a few days after came to Boston.

And to omitte all other circomstances and debates that past betweene them and the comissioners, they came to this conclusion following.

1. It was agreed betwixte the comissioners of the United Collonies, and the forementioned sagamores, and Niantick deputie, that the said Narigansets and Niantick sagamores should pay or cause to be payed at Boston, to the Massachusets comissioners, the full sume of ·2000· fathome of good white wampame, or a third parte of black wampampeage, in ·4· payments; namely, ·500· fathome within ·20· days, ·500· fathome within ·4· months, ·500· fathome at or before next planting time, and ·500· fathome within ·2· years next after the date of these presents; which ·2000 fathome the comissioners accepte for satisfaction of former charges expended.

2. The foresaid sagamores and deputie (on the behalfe of the Narigansett and Niantick Indeans) hereby promise and covenante that they upon demand and profe satisfie and restore unto Uncass, the Mohigan sagamore, all shuch captives, whether men, or women, or children, and all shuch canoowes, as they or any of their men have taken, or as many of their owne canowes in the roome of them, full as good as they were, with full satisfaction for all shuch corne as they or any of theire men have spoyled or destroyed, of his or his mens, since last planting time; and the English comissioners hereby promise that Uncass shall doe the like.

3. Wheras ther are sundry differences and greevances betwixte Narigansett and Niantick Indeans, and Uncass and his men, (which in Uncass his absence cannot now be detirmined,) it is hearby agreed that Nariganset and Niantick sagamores either come them selves, or

send their deputies to the next meeting of the commissioners for the collonies, either at New-Haven in September, 1646, or sooner (upon conveniente warning, if the said comissioners doe meete sooner), fully instructed to declare and make due proofe of their injuries, and to submite to the judgmente of the comissioners, in giving or receiving satisfaction; and the said comissioners (not doubting but Uncass will either come him selfe, or send his deputies, in like maner furnished) promising to give a full hearing to both parties with equall justice, without any partiall respects, according to their allegations and profse.

4. The said Narigansett and Niantick sagamores and deputies doe hearby promise and covenante to keep and maintaine a firme and perpetuall peace, both with all the English United Colonies and their successors, and with Uncass, the Monhegan sachem, and his men; with Ossamequine, Pumham, Sokananoke, Cutshamakin, Shoanan, Passaconaway, and all other Indean sagamores, and their companies, who are in freindship with or subjecte to any of the English; hearby ingaging them selves, that they will not at any time hearafter disturbe the peace of the cuntry, by any assaults, hostile attempts, invasions, or other injuries, to any of the Unnited Collonies, or their successors; or to the afforesaid Indeans; either in their persons, buildings, catle, or goods, directly or indirectly; nor will they confederate with any other against them; and if they know of any Indeans or others that conspire or intend hurt against the said English, or any Indeans subjecte to or in freindship with them, they will without delay acquainte and give notice thereof to the English Commissioners, or some of them.

Or if any questions or differences shall at any time hereafter arise or grow betwext them and Uncass, or any Endeans before mentioned, they will, according to former ingagments (which they hearby confirme and ratifie) first acquainte the English, and crave their judgments and advice therin; and will not attempte or begine any warr, or hostille invasion, till they have liberty and alowance from the comissioners of the United Collonies so to doe.

5. The said Narigansets and Niantick sagamores and deputies doe hearby promise that they will forthwith deliver and restore all such Indean fugitives, or captives which have at any time fled from any of the English, and are now living or abiding amongst them, or give due satisfaction for them to the comissioners for the Massachusets; and further, that they will (without more delays) pay, or cause to be payed, a yearly tribute, a month before harvest, every year after this, at Boston, to the English Colonies, for all shuch Pequents as live amongst them, according to the former treaty and agreemente, made at Hartford, ·1638· namly, one fathome of white wampam for every Pequente man, and halfe a fathume for each Pequente youth, and one hand length for each mal-child. And if Weequashcooke refuse

to pay this tribute for any Pequents with him, the Narigansetts saga-mores promise to assiste the English against him. And they further covenante that they will resigne and yeeld up the whole Pequente cuntrie, and every parte of it, to the English collonies, as due to them by conquest.

6. The said Narigansett and Niantick sagamores and deputie doe hereby promise and covenante that within ·14· days they will bring and deliver to the Massachusetts comissioners on the behalfe of the collonies, foure of their children, viz. Pessecous his eldest sonn, the sone Tassaquanawite, brother to Pessecouss, Awashawe his sone, and Ewangsos sone, a Niantick, to be kepte (as hostages and pledges) by the English, till both the forementioned ·2000· fathome of wampam be payed at the times appoynted, and the differences betweexte them-selves and Uncass be heard and ordered, and till these artickles be under writen at Boston, by Ienemo and Wipetock. And further they hereby promise and covenante, that if at any time hearafter any of the said children shall make escape, or be conveyed away from the English, before the premisses be fully accomplished, they will either bring back and deliver to the Massachusett comissioners the same children, or, if they be not to be founde, shuch and so many other children, to be chosen by the comissioners for the United Collonies, or their assignes, and that within ·20· days after demand, and in the mean time, untill the said ·4· children be delivered as hostages, the Narigansett and Niantick sagamores and deputy doe, freely and of their owne accorde, leave with the Massachusett comissioners, as pledges for presente securitie, ·4· Indeans, namely, Witowash, Puma-nise, Jawashoe, Waughwamino, who allso freely consente, and offer them selves to stay as pledges, till the said children be brought and delivered as abovesaid.

7. The comissioners for the United Collonies doe hereby promise and agree that, at the charge of the United Collonies, the ·4· Indeans now left as pledges shall be provided for, and that the ·4· children to be brought and delivered as hostages shall be kepte and maintained at the same charge; that they will require Uncass and his men, with all other Indean sagamores before named, to forbear all acts of hos-tilitie againste the Narigansetts and Niantick Indeans for the future. And further, all the premises being duly observed and kept by the Narigansett and Niantick Indians and their company, they will at the end of ·2· years restore the said children delivered as hostiages, and retaine a firme peace with the Narigansets and Nianticke Indeans and their successours.

8. It is fully agreed by and betwixte the said parties, that if any hostile attempte be made while this treaty is in hand, or before notice of this agreemente (to stay further preparations and directions) can

be given, shuch attempts and the consequenets therof shall on neither parte be accounted a violation of this treaty, nor a breach of the peace hear made and concluded.

9. The Narigansets and Niantick sagamores and deputie hereby agree and covenante to and with the comissioners of the United Collonies, that henceforth they will neither give, grante, sell, or in any maner alienate, any parte of their countrie, nor any parcell of land therin, either to any of the English or others, without consente or allowance of the commissioners.

10. Lastly, they promise that, if any Pequente or other be found and discovered amongst them who hath in time of peace murdered any of the English, he or they shall be delivered to just punishmente.

In witness wherof the parties above named have interchaingablie subscribed these presents, the day and year above writen.

JOHN WINTHROP, President.   PESSECOUSS his mark
HERBERT PELHAM.   MEEKESANO his mark
THO: PRENCE.   WITOWASH his mark
JOHN BROWNE.   AUMSEQUEN his mark
GEO: FENWICK.   *the Niantick deputy.*
EDWA: HOPKINS.   ABDAS his mark
THEOPH: EATON.   PUMMASH his mark
STEVEN GOODYEARE.   CUTCHAMAKIN his mark

This treaty and agreemente betwixte the comissioners of the United Collonies and the sagamores and deputy of Narrigansets and Niantick Indeans was made and concluded, Benedicte Arnold being interpretour upon his oath; Sergante Callicate and an Indean, his man, being presente, and Josias and Cutshamakin, tow Indeans aquainted with the English language, assisting therin; who opened and cleared the whole treaty, and every article, to the sagamores and deputie there presente.

And thus was the warr at this time stayed and prevented.

ANNO DOM: ·1646·

A BOUT the midle of May, this year, came in ·3· ships into this harbor, in warrlike order; they were found to be men of warr. The captains name was Crumwell, who had taken sundrie prizes from the Spaniards in the West Indies. He had a comission from the Earle of Warwick. He had abord his vessels about ·80· lustie men, (but very unruly,) who, after they came ashore, did so distemper them selves with drinke as they

became like madd-men; and though some of them were punished and imprisoned, yet could they hardly be restrained; yet
in the ende they became more moderate and orderly. They
continued here aboute a month or ·6· weeks, and then went
to the Massachusets; in which time they spente and scattered
a great deale of money among the people, and yet more sine
(I fear) then money, notwithstanding all the care and watchfullnes that was used towards them, to prevente what might be.

In which time one sadd accidente fell out. A desperate fellow
of the company fell a quareling with some of his company. His
captine commanded him to be quiet and surcease his qua-
relling; but he would not, but reviled his captaine with base
language, and in the end halfe drew his rapier, and intended
to rune at his captien; but he closed with him, and wrasted
his rapier from him, and gave him a boxe on the earr; but he
would not give over, but still assaulted his captaine. Wherupon
he tooke the same rapier as it was in the scaberd, and gave him
a blow with the hilts; but it light on his head, and the smal end
of the bar of the rapier hilts peirct his scull, and he dyed a few
days after. But the captaine was cleared by a counsell of warr.
This fellow was so desperate a quareller as the captaine was
faine many times to chaine him under hatches from hurting
his fellows, as the company did testifie; and this was his end.

This captaine Thomas Cormuell sett forth another vioage to
the Westindeas, from the Bay of the Massachusets, well maned
and victuled; and was out ·3· years, and tooke sundry prises,
and returned rich unto the Massachusets, and ther dyed the
same somere, having gott a fall from his horse, in which fall
he fell on his rapeir hilts, and so brused his body as he shortly
after dyed therof, with some other distempers, which brought
him into a feavor. Some observed that ther might be somthing
of the hand of God herein; that as the forenamed man dyed of
the blow he gave him with the rapeir hilts, so his owne death
was occationed by a like means.

This year Mr. Edward Winslow went into England, upon this
occation: some discontented persons under the govermente of
the Massachusets sought to trouble their peace, and disturbe, if
not innovate, their govermente, by laying many scandals upon
them; and intended to prosecute against them in England, by
petitioning and complaining to the Parlemente. Allso Samuell

Gorton and his company made complaints against them; so as they made choyse of Mr. Winslow to be their agente, to make their defence, and gave him comission and instructions for that end; in which he so carried him selfe as did well answer their ends, and cleared them from any blame or dishonour, to the shame of their adversaries. But by reason of the great alterations in the State, he was detained longer then was expected; and afterwards fell into other imployments their, so as he hath now bene absente this ·4· years, which hath been much to the weakning of this govermente, without whose consente he tooke these imployments upon him.

ANNO ·1647· AND ANNO ·1648·

The names of those which came over first, in the year ·1620· and were by the blessing of God the first beginers and (in a sort) the foundation of all the Plantations and Colonies in New England; and their families.

·8·   Mr. John Carver; Kathrine, his wife; Desire Minter; and ·2· man-servants, John Howland, Roger Wilder; William Latham, a boy; and a maid servant, and a child that was put to him, called Jasper More.

·6·   Mr. William Brewster; Mary, his wife; with ·2· sons, whose names were Love and Wrasling; and a boy was put to him called Richard More; and another of his brothers. The rest of his children were left behind, and came over afterwards.

·5·   Mr. Edward Winslow; Elizabeth, his wife; and ·2· men servants, caled Georg Sowle and Elias Story; also a litle girle was put to him, caled Ellen, the sister of Richard More.

·2·   William Bradford, and Dorothy, his wife; having but one child, a sone, left behind, who came afterward.

·6·   Mr. Isaack Allerton, and Mary, his wife; with ·3· children, Bartholomew, Remember, and Mary; and a servant boy, John Hooke.

·2·   Mr. Samuell Fuller, and a servant, caled William Butten. His wife was behind, and a child, which came afterwards.

·2·   John Crakston, and his sone, John Crakston.

·2·   Captin Myles Standish, and Rose, his wife.

·4·   Mr. Christopher Martin, and his wife, and ·2· servants, Salamon Prower and John Langemore.

·5·   Mr. William Mullines, and his wife, and ·2· children, Joseph and Priscila; and a servant, Robart Carter.

·6·   Mr. William White, and Susana, his wife, and one sone, caled Resolved, and one borne a ship-bord, caled Peregriene; and ·2· servants, named William Holbeck and Edward Thomson.

·8·   Mr. Steven Hopkins, and Elizabeth, his wife, and ·2· children, caled Giles, and Constanta, a doughter, both by a former wife; and ·2· more by this wife, caled Damaris and Oceanus; the last was borne at sea; and ·2· servants, called Edward Doty and Edward Litster.

·1·   Mr. Richard Warren; but his wife and children were lefte behind, and came afterwards.

·4·   John Billinton, and Elen, his wife; and ·2· sones, John and Francis.

·4· Edward Tillie, and Ann, his wife; and ·2· childeren that were their cossens, Henery Samson and Humillity Coper.

·3· John Tillie, and his wife; and Eelizabeth, their doughter.

·2· Francis Cooke, and his sone John. But his wife and other children came afterwards.

·2· Thomas Rogers, and Joseph, his sone. His other children came afterwards.

·3· Thomas Tinker, and his wife, and a sone.

·2· John Rigdale, and Alice, his wife.

·3· James Chilton, and his wife, and Mary, their dougter. They had an other doughter, that was maried, came afterward.

·3· Edward Fuller, and his wife, and Samuell, their sonne.

·3· John Turner, and ·2· sones. He had a doughter came some years after to Salem, wher she is now living.

·3· Francis Eaton, and Sarah, his wife, and Samuell, their sone, a yong child.

·10· Moyses Fletcher, John Goodman, Thomas Williams, Digerie Preist, Edmond Margeson, Peter Browne, Richard Britterige, Richard Clarke, Richard Gardenar, Gilbart Winslow.

·1· John Alden was hired for a cooper, at South-Hampton, wher the ship victuled; and being a hopefull yong man, was much desired, but left to his owne liking to go or stay when he came here; but he stayed, and maryed here.

·2· John Allerton and Thomas Enlish were both hired, the later to goe master of a shalop here, and the other was reputed as one of the company, but was to go back (being a seaman) for the help of others behind. But they both dyed here, before the shipe returned.

·2· There were allso other ·2· seamen hired to stay a year here in the country, William Trevore, and one Ely. But when their time was out, they both returned.

These, bening aboute a hundred sowls, came over in this first ship; and began this worke, which God of his goodnes hath hithertoo blesed; let his holy name have the praise.

And seeing it hath pleased him to give me to see ·30· years compleated since these beginings; and that the great works of his providence are to be observed, I have thought it not unworthy my paines to take a view of the decreasings and increasings of these persons, and such changes as hath pased over them and theirs, in this thirty years. It may be of some use to such as come after; but, however, I shall rest in my owne benefite.

I will therfore take them in order as they lye.

Mr. Carver and his wife dyed the first year; he in the spring, she in the sommer; also, his man Roger, and the litle boy Jasper dyed before either of them, of the commone infection. Desire Minter returned to her freinds, and proved not very well, and dyed in England. His servant boy Latham, after more then ·20· years stay in the country, went into England, and from thence to the Bahamy Ilands in the West ·15· Indies, and ther, with some others, was starved for want of food. His maid servant maried, and dyed a year or tow after, here in this place. His servant, John Howland, maried the doughter of John Tillie, Elizabeth, and they are both now living, and have ·10· children, now all living; and their eldest daughter hath ·4· children. And ther ·2· daughter, one, all living; and other of their children mariagable. So ·15· are come of them.

Mr. Brewster lived to very old age; about ·80· years he was when he dyed, having lived some ·23· or ·24· years here in the countrie; and though his wife dyed long before, yet she dyed ·4· aged. His sone Wrastle dyed a yonge man unmaried; his sone Love lived till this year ·1650· and dyed, and left ·4· children, now living. His doughters which came over after him are dead, but have left sundry children alive; his eldest sone is ·2· still liveing, and hath ·9· or ·10· children; one maried, who hath a child or ·2·

Richard More his brother dyed the first winter; but he is ·4· maried, and hath ·4· or ·5· children, all living.

Mr. Ed: Winslow his wife dyed the first winter; and he maried with the widow of Mr. White, and hath ·2· children ·2· living by her marigable, besides sundry that are dead.

One of his servants dyed, as also the litle girle, soone after ·8· the ships arivall. But his man, Georg Sowle, is still living, and hath ·8· children.

William Bradford his wife dyed soone after their arivall; ·4· and he maried againe; and hath ·4· children, ·3· wherof are maried.

Mr. Allerton his wife dyed with the first, and his servant, John Hooke. His sone Bartle is maried in England, but I know not how many children he hath. His doughter Remember is maried at Salem, and hath ·3· or ·4· children living. And ·8· his doughter Mary is maried here, and hath ·4· children. Him selfe maried againe with the doughter of Mr. Brewster, and hath one sone living by her, but she is long since dead. And he maried againe, and hath left this place long agoe. So I account his increase to be ·8· besides his sons in England.

·2· Mr. Fuller his servant dyed at sea; and after his wife came over, he had tow children by her, which are living and growne up to years; but he dyed some ·15· years agoe.

John Crakston dyed in the first mortality; and about some ·5· or ·6· years after, his sone dyed; having lost him selfe in the wodes, his feet became frosen, which put him into a feavor, of which he dyed.

·4· Captain Standish his wife dyed in the first sicknes, and he maried againe, and hath ·4· sones liveing, and some are dead.

Mr. Martin, he and all his, dyed in the first infection; not long after the arivall.

·15· Mr. Molines, and his wife, his sone, and his servant, dyed the first winter. Only his dougter Priscila survied, and maried with John Alden, who are both living, and have ·11· children. And their eldest daughter is maried, and hath five children. See N. E. Memorial, p. 22.

·7· Mr. White and his ·2· servants dyed soone after ther landing. His wife maried with Mr. Winslow (as is before noted). His ·2· sons are maried, and Resolved hath ·5· children, Peregrine tow, all living. So their increase are ·7·

·5· Mr. Hopkins and his wife are now both dead, but they lived above ·20· years in this place, and had one sone and ·4· doughters borne here. Ther sone became a seaman, and dyed at Barbadoes; one daughter dyed here, and ·2· are maried; one of them hath ·2· children; and one is yet to mary. So their ·4· increase which still survive are ·5· But his sone Giles is maried, and hath ·4· children.

·12· His doughter Constanta is also maried, and hath ·12· children, all of them living, and one of them maried.

Mr. Richard Warren lived some ·4· or ·5· years, and had his wife come over to him, by whom he had ·2· sons before [he] ·4· dyed; and one of them is maryed, and hath ·2· children. So his increase is ·4· But he had ·5· doughters more came over with his wife, who are all maried, and living, and have many children.

·8· John Billinton, after he had bene here ·10· yers, was executed for killing a man; and his eldest sone dyed before him; but his ·2· sone is alive, and maried, and hath ·8· children.

·7· Edward Tillie and his wife both dyed soon after their arivall; and the girle Humility, their cousen, was sent for into England, and dyed ther. But the youth Henery Samson is still liveing, and is maried, and hath ·7· children.

John Tillie and his wife both dyed a litle after they came ashore; and their daughter Elizabeth maried with John Howland, and hath isue as is before noted.

Francis Cooke is still living, a very olde man, and hath seene his childrens children have childen; after his wife came ·8· over, (with other of his children,) he hath ·3· still living by her, all maried, and have ·5· children; so their encrease is ·8· And ·4· his sone John, which came over with him, is maried, and hath ·4· chilldren living.

Thomas Rogers dyed in the first sicknes, but his sone Joseph is still living, and is maried, and hath ·6· children. ·6· The rest of Thomas Rogers came over, and are maried, and have many children.

Thomas Tinker, and his wife and sone, all dyed in the first sicknes.

And so did John Rigdale, and his wife.

James Chilton and his wife also dyed in the first infection. But their daughter Mary is still living, and hath ·9· children; ·10· and one daughter is maried, and hath a child; so their increase is ·10·

Edward Fuller and his wife dyed soon after they came ·4· ashore; but their sone Samuell is living, and maried, and hath ·4· children or more.

John Turner and his ·2· sones all dyed in the first siknes. But he hath a daugter still living at Salem, well maried, and approved of.

Francis Eeaton his first wife dyed in the generall sicknes; and he maried againe, and his ·2· wife dyed, and he maried ·4· the ·3· and had by her ·3· children. One of them is maried, and hath a child; the other are living, but one of them is an ideote. He dyed about ·16· years agoe.

His sone Samuell, who came over a sucking child, is allso ·1· maried, and hath a child.

Moyses Fletcher, Thomas Williams, Digerie Preist, John Goodman, Edmond Margeson, Richard Britterige, Richard Clarke. All these dyed sone after their arivall, in the generall sicknes that befell. But Digerie Preist had his wife and chil- dren sent hither afterwards, she being Mr. Allertons sister. But the rest left no posteritie here.

Richard Gardinar became a seaman, and died in England, or at sea.

Gilbert Winslow, after diverse years abboad here, returned into England, and dyed ther.

Peter Browne maried twise. By his first wife he had ·2· children, who are living, and both of them maried, and the ·6· one of them hath ·2· children; by his second wife he had ·2· more. He dyed about ·16· years since.

Thomas English and John Allerton dyed in the generall siknes.

John Alden maried with Priscila, Mr. Mollines his doughter, and had issue by her as is before related.

Edward Doty and Edward Litster, the servants of Mr. Hopins. Litster, after he was at liberty, went to Virginia, and ther dyed. But Edward Doty by a second wife hath ·7· children, and both he and they are living.

Of these ·100· persons which came first over in this first ship together, the greater halfe dyed in the generall mortality; and most of them in ·2· or three monthes time. And for those which survived, though some were ancient and past procreation, and others left the place and cuntrie, yet of those few remaining are sprunge up above ·160· persons, in this ·30· years, and are now living in this presente year, ·1650· besides many of their children which are dead, and come not within this account.

And of the old stock (of one and other) ther are yet living this present year, ·1650· nere ·30· persons. Let the Lord have the praise, who is the High Preserver of men.

Of Plimoth Plantation is the text most frequently associated with Plymouth Colony, and most often cited in histories of the northeast and New England. This ubiquity is relatively recent: *Of Plimoth Plantation* was not published until 1856, at a moment when nineteenth-century antiquarians were collecting and publishing documents related to the northeast's early colonial history in order to claim that history for the story of the United States' founding. Before 1856, Bradford's history circulated as a manuscript among his sons, other family members, and colonial leaders, who used it as a source for their own histories. Bradford gave the manuscript to his son William Bradford, Jr., and his nephew Nathaniel Morton used it as a source for his history *New-England's Memorial* (1669). Similarly, Puritan ministers Increase and Cotton Mather consulted Bradford's text for their histories of New England. The manuscript's circulation among family members and colonial religious leaders highlights the personal and religious networks that produced a history for Plymouth Colony, as well as these men's desire to bequeath both this history and land to their sons. The story of how Bradford's text was created and transmitted illuminates as well that he wrote for a different audience than the English readers of early published texts, such as *Good News from New England* and *Mourt's Relation*. In the early 1620s, Bradford and Winslow were still uncertain of the outcomes of their plan to establish a colony separate from both the religious influence of the Church of England and the Dutch cultural influences they had encountered while living in Leiden. Bradford participated in this endeavor as an economic investor, a colonist, and, starting in 1621, governor of Plymouth Colony for thirty-three years. By the time he wrote *Of Plimouth Plantation*, from 1630 to 1651, the Plymouth colonists had learned how to survive the harsh northeastern winters and attained an understanding of local food sources and trading networks. Bradford placed Plymouth's history within a religious narrative in which the colonists were chosen people, protected and aided through difficulties by divine aid. In this narrative, North America was the wilderness in which they established a settlement distinguished by its religious and cultural practices both from other Europeans and from Native people.

TRANSNATIONAL DIPLOMACY

COUNCILS AND DEEDS BETWEEN
INDIGENOUS LEADERS AND
SETTLERS FROM PLYMOUTH COLONY

Seekonk Deed, 1642

At a Court of Assistances held at Plymouth aforesaid, the first
Day of November, in the xviiith Yeare of the now Raigne
of our Soveraigne Lord, Charles, by the Grace of God King
of England, &c.

BEFORE William Bradford, gentleman, Governor,
                                    William Collyer,
          Edward Winslow,   John Browne, &
          Thomas Prence,   Edmond Freeman,
                    Gentlemen, Assistantes, &c.

JOHN HASSELL affirmeth that Ussamequine chose out x fathome of beads at Mr Williams, and put them in a baskett, and affirmed that he was fully satisfyed therewith for his landes at Seacunck, but he stood upon it that he would have a coat more, & left the beades with Mr Williams, & willed him to keepe them untill Mr Hubberd came up.

He affirmed the boundes were to Redstone Hill, viii miles into the land, & to Annawamscoate, vii miles down the water.

John Hassell doth acknowledge himself to owe the King,
    to be levyed of his landes, goodes, & cattels, &c, if he   } xxli.
    fayle in the condicion following, &c,

The condicion, that if the said John Hassell shall either take the oath of allegiance to the King, & fidelitie to the government, betwixt this and March Court next, or else remove his dwelling from Seacunck; that then, &c.

607

THE EDITORS' COMMENT

This deed and the two that follow show Plymouth settlers' attempts to expand further into Wampanoag territory, beyond Patuxet and the Cape. This 1642 document recorded testimony about a council that purportedly took place in 1641 between Ousamequin, representing the Wampanoags of Pokanoket, and John Brown and Edward Winslow, representing the English of Plymouth, at Roger Williams's home of Mooshausick, on the Seekonk River. It is one of the earliest records that documents the oral agreement between Ousamequin and the Plymouth men, which allowed the colonists to expand their settlement into Seekonk, later renamed Rehoboth. Seekonk was on the western edge of the Wampanoag country, near its intersection with Narragansett territory and Rhode Island Colony. Later deeds expanded "Rehoboth" from the original "ten miles square" to more than eight times the size of the initial settlement. Some of the early agreements between the Plymouth settlers and Wampanoag leaders were not written down as formal deeds, but rested on Indigenous protocols, including oral exchange accompanied by the gifting of wampum—which represented the bonds of relationships and pledges of mutual support—and coats—which symbolized acknowledgment of leadership, in this case continuing Wampanoag leadership in this place. After the death of Ousamequin (and his son Wamsutta), Plymouth sought his son Philip's consent and confirmation of this earlier deed for Rehoboth, in 1668, and its expansion, as part of a series of confirmation deeds that solidified Plymouth's claims to land against competing colonies, like Rhode Island and Massachusetts Bay.

Bridgewater Deed, 1649

DEED OF ANCIENT AND ORIGINAL BRIDGEWATER.

Witness these presents that I Ousamequin Sachem of the country of Poconocket have given, granted, enfeofed, and sold unto Miles Standish, of Duxbury, Samuel Nash and Constant Southworth, of Duxbury, aforesaid, in behalf of all the townsmen of Duxbury, aforesaid, a tract of land usually called Satucket, extending in the length and breadth thereof as followeth, that is to say from the wear at Satucket, seven miles due east, and from the said wear, seven miles due west, and from the said wear, seven miles due north, and from the said wear, seven miles due south; the which tract the said Ousamequin hath given, granted, enfeofed, and sold unto the said Miles Standish, Samuel Nash and Constant Southworth, in the behalf of all the townsmen of Duxbury, as aforesaid, with all the immunities, privileges and profits, whatsoever belonging to the said tract of land with all and singular, all woods, underwoods, lands, meadows, rivers, brooks, rivulets, &c., to have and to hold to the said Miles Standish, Samuel Nash and Constant Southworth, in behalf of all the townsmen of the town of Duxbury, to them and their heirs forever.

In witness whereof I, the said Ousamequin, have hereunto set my hand the 23d of March, 1649.

John Bradford   Witness the
Wm. Otway (alias) Parker   mark of   Ousamequin.

In consideration of the aforesaid bargain and sale, we the said Miles Standish, Samuel Nash and Constant Southworth do bind ourselves to pay unto the said Ousamequin for and in consideration of the said tract of land as followeth:

7 Coats, a yard and a half
in a coat
9 Hatchets
8 Hoes
29 Knives
4 Moose Skins
10 Yards and a half of Cotton

MILES STANDISH,

SAMUEL NASH,

CONSTANT SOUTHWORTH.

THE EDITORS' COMMENT

Unlike the previous document, the deed for the Bridgewater settlement originated not with a council, but with a grant by the Plymouth General Court. The court was composed of and created by Plymouth men to govern the colony, enforce local authority and retain control over the expanding settlement. In 1645, the court had granted settlers at Duxbury the right to a tract of land at Saquatucket for a plantation. The deed is centered on the weir that was on a bend of the river (now Town River) at Saquatucket, a Wampanoag waterway and fishing place. The written deed located the settlement within Wampanoag territory but also documented Ousamequin's consent for the colonists to build a plantation there, represented by his "mark." Although like many deeds this agreement may have also involved an oral council, the language is transactional, with the Plymouth men pledging to pay Ousamequin with goods in exchange for the land. It is one of the first deeds in which Constant Southworth, Bradford's stepson, appeared, along with military leader Miles Standish and John Nash, representing the Plymouth Court. This deed was later celebrated during the town's bicentennial commemoration in June 1856, as a symbol of legitimate inheritance of the land, with Bridgewater residents mourning in verse the passing of Ousamequin's "race." Ironically, as historian Jean O'Brien has pointed out, only five years later, Massachusetts commissioner John Milton Earle published his report on "the Indians of the Commonwealth," which included documentation of hundreds of Native people, many of them Wampanoag, living in the area at the time of the commemoration.

Nonaquaket Deed, 1651

Be it knowen unto all men by these Presents that we whous Names are here under writen beinge of the blood and kindred and Nabor Sachims or princis bordringe upon the Confines and in heritance of our beloved cosin wequequinequa and Nummampaum sachim and Squa Sachim the treu heire aparent unto a tract of land buttinge upon the East side of the East harbor Cominge in to Rood Eyland and for as much as our Cozins have sould unto captin Richard morris his heires executors Adminestrators and assines for Ever a Neck of land cauled Nunequoquit or Pogasek Neck with som othar parcilles Nere there unto we do here by Renownce and disclaime for our selves our heires Executors Adminestrators and assines for ever all claime of Right title or Intrest in any kind what so ever in or to the afore said land or any part or parcill there of with all the profits there unto appurtaining or any wais belonginge and do by these presents give unto captin Richard morris our free approbation and full consent unto the purches of the afore said land and do further here by testifie that this act and ded of saile from our cozins unto captin Richard morris is Just and with out all controvarcie sould out of there own propar Inheritanc no waies dependinge upon us or any othar Sachim confininge Ner these Inheritanc And for as much as I Osamekin chefe Sachim of a great tract of land confining upon the Inheritanc of this my brothars dafter have put my land under plimoth govrment these are to testifie that I Nevar did nor intendid to put undar plimoth any of my kinswomans land but my owne inheritanc and there fore I do disalow of any pretended claime to this land sould by my Cosin wequequinequa and Nummampaum to captin Richard morris Eathar by plimoth or the inhabitants of porchmoth one Rood Eyland by vartew of any grant from me or any through my mens in testimony here of

we do set to our markes and seales this twentie sixt day of July
one thousand six hundred fiftie and one 1651

          X The marke of OSAMEKINS
                chefe Sachim
          X The marke of WAMSUTTA
          X The marke of TASOMOCKON

Witnis here unto
   JAMES J. S. SANDS
     his marke
   RICHARD BULLGAR

THE EDITORS' COMMENT

The original manuscript of this 1651 "Indian deed" is held by the Massachusetts Historical Society, which published a version in 1915. Nonaquaket was a place of planting, fishing, and gathering within the Pocasset homeland, in western Wampanoag territory, adjacent to Narragansett country and Rhode Island. Plymouth men desired land in this fertile area, which they called "Pocasset neck." The colony's territorial claim was tied to their agreement with Ousamequin and to the perceived bounds of his territory. However, as Ousamequin here made clear, he had not by that agreement given the Plymouth colonists permission to claim land in other Wampanoag homelands, including Pocasset, which was under the jurisdiction of his "kinswoman" Namumpum, or Weetamoo. In this "deed," "neighboring sachems" recognized Weetamoo's rights in writing, including the right to choose which settlers—in this case a Rhode Island colonist—were permitted usury privileges in her territory. Even as Wampanoag communities held the rights to land collectively, Sôtyumâak and Sôkushqâak bore a vital symbolic and diplomatic responsibility in representing their communities in councils where rights and resources were negotiated and distributed, with the goal of balancing social relationships. Multiple Wampanoag leaders, all kin, are named here, including Tuspaquin of Nemasket, who was married to Ousamequin's daughter Amie, and Wamsutta, Ousamequin's son, who would later marry Weetamoo. This document represents an Indigenous council, including acknowledgment of Weetamoo's leadership, held during the summer, a season of bounty and exchange. Many of the early deeds represent councils where Indigenous people sought to draw Europeans into these diplomatic protocols. This deed also demonstrates that although the Plymouth Court granted settlers the right to pursue land in places like Pocasset, they did not always successfully acquire Native consent.

"Old Comers" Deeds, 1639–1652
Old Dartmouth Deed, 1652
Sowams Deed, 1653

"Old Comers" Deeds

Whereas upon a proposition made by the Grand Inquest at the generall Court held the fift day of March 1638 by what vertue & power the Governor and Assistants do give & dispose of lands either to particuler persons or Towneshipps and Plantacions whereupon ever since there hath beene a Cessacion of the graunt of lands to any persons by the Goverment: And now upon heareing and debateing the controversies matters and differences about & concerning the same in the Publike Court And whereas there was a larg summe of money disbursed by those that held the trade viz. Mr Bradford Mr Prence Captaine Standish & the rest of their partners for th enlargment of the Patent of New Plymouth in New England, In consideration that all controversies & differences about the same may hereafter cease and determine, whether betwixt the Purchsers, old Commers, freemen, or others about the same. The court hath by mutuall assent & consent of all as well purchasers Old Commers as freemen enacted & concluded that there shalbe three hundred pounds sterling (or so much as shalbe required not exceeding the said sume of three hunfred pounds) payd to those that held the trade viz. Mr Bradford Mr Prence Capt. Standish and the rest of the partners towards the charges of thenlargement of the said Patent if the same shalbe required out of the personall estats of the said Mr Bradford Mr Prence Capt. Standish & the rest of the partners which said three hundred pounds or lesser summe shalbe levyed upon the plantacions by such equall way as shalbe thought meete. And that they Purchasers or old Commers shall make choyce of two or three places for themselves & their heires before the next December Court & that after such choyce made and established All the residue of the lands not formerly graunted forth either to plantacions or particuler persons shalbe assigned & surrendred into the hands of the whole Body of the freemen

to be disposed of either by the whole Body or by such persons
as shalbe by the whole Body of freemen assigned & authorised
And that all lands already graunted either to plantacions or particuler persons shall stand & remayne firme to thim their heires
& assignes for ever to whom they are so given & graunted Provided that all lands shalbe now free to graunt to such persons
as stand in neede in the Plantacions now made save that there
shalbe no more Plantacions erected untill the Purchasers have
made their choyce as aforesd. And whatsoever shalbe further
materiall & requisite in law for the confirmeing & establishing
this act and order It shalbe donn by Counsell to the intents &
purposes herein contained & expressed if neede require.

It is also enacted by the whole Body of the Court That the
Governor and Assistants shall graunt lands to particuler persons within the Townes of Plymouth & Duxborrow as they
have donn formerly untill December next.

March 5, 1639

Whereas by the act of the Generall Court held the third day
of March 1639, it was agreed upon that the purchasers, or
old comers, shall make choyce of two or three plantacions
for themselves & their heires by this December Court—now
the said purchasers, or old comers, do signifie unto the Court
that accordingly they have made choyce of these three places,
viz.: First, from the bounds of Yarmouth, three miles to the
eastward of Naemskeckett, and from sea to sea crosse the neck
of land. The second place, of a place called Acconquesse, alias
Acokcus, which lyeth in the bottom of the bay, adjoyneing to
the west side of Pynt Perrill, and two miles to the westerne
side of the said river, to another place, called Acquissent River,
which entreth at the westerne end of Nickatay, and two miles
to the eastward thereof, and to extend eight miles up into the
countrey. The third place, from Sowamset River to Patuckquett
River, with Causumpsit Neck, which is the cheefe habitacion
of the Indians, & reserved for them to dwell upon, extending
into the land eight miles through the whole breadth thereof,
the which choyce beinge made as aforesaid, and allowed in the
Court, Mr William Bradford, for himself and his associates,

doth tenter a surrender to the body of freemen of all the rest
of the lands within the patents, (which are not graunted to
plantacions in generall, or persons in particuler.) And the said
William Bradford is ready further to confirme the same, on the
parte and behalf of himself & his associats, to the body of the
freemen, when he shalbe required.

December 1, 1640

Whereas divers and sondry treaties have beene in the publike
& Generall Courts of New Plymouth, his majestie, our dread
soveraigne, Charles, by the grace of God King of England,
Scotland, France, and Ireland &c, concerning the proper right
and title of the lands within the bounds and limmitts of his
said majesties lettres patents, graunted by the right honorable
and his majesties counsell for New England, ratifyed by their
common seale, and signed by the hand of the Right Honorable Earle of Warwick, then president of the said counsell,
to William Bradford, his heires, associats, and assignes, beareing date, &c; and whereas the said William Bradford and
divers others, the first instruments of God in the beginninge
of this greate work of plantacion, together with such as the
alorderinge hand of God, in his providence, soone added unto
them, have beene at very greate charges to procure the said
lands, priviledges & freedomes, from all entanglements, as may
appeare by divers and sundry deeds, enlargements of graunts,
purchases, payments of debts, &c, by reason whereof the title
to the day of this present, remayneth in the said William, his
heires, associats, and assignes—now, for the better setling of
the state of the said lands aforesaid, the said William Bradford,
and those first instruments termed and called in sondry orders
upon publike record, the purchasers, or old comers, witnes
two in especiall, thone beareing date the third of March,
1639, thother in December the first, 1640, whereunto these
presents have speciall relacion & agreement, and whereby
they are distinguished from others the freemen and inhabitants of the said corporation—be it knowne unto all men,
therefore, by these presents, that the said William Bradford,
for himself, his heires, together with the said purchasers, do
onely reserve unto themselves, their heires and assignes, those

three tracts of lands mencioned in the said resolucion, order, & agreement, beareing date the first day of December, 1640, viz., first, from the bounds of Yarmouth, three miles to the eastward of Naemskeckett, and from sea to sea, crosse the said neck of land; the second, of a place called Acconquesse, alias Acockcus, which lyeth in the bottom of the bay adjoyneing to the west side of Poynt Perrill, and two miles to the westerne side of the said river, to another place, called Acquessent River, which entreth at the westerne end of Nickatay, and two miles to the eastward thereof, and to extend eight miles up into the countrey; the third place from Sowamsett River to Patucquett River, with Causumpsit Neck, which is the cheef habitacion of the Indians, and reserved for them to dwell upon, extending into the land eight miles through the whole breadth thereof, together with such other smale percells of lands as they or any of them are personally possessed of or interested in by vertue of any former titles or graunts whatsoever. And the said William Bradford doth, by the free and full consent, approbacion, and agreement of the said old planters of purchasers, together with the likeing, approbacion, & acceptacion of the other part of the said corporacion, surrender into the hands of the whole Court, consistinge of the freemen of this corporacion of New Plymouth all that ther right & title, power, authorytie, priviledges, immunities, & freedomes granted in the said lettres patents by the said right honorable counsell for New England, reserveing his & their personall right of freemen, together with the said old planters aforesaid, except the said lands before excepted, declareing the freemen of this present corporacion, together with all such as shalbe legally admitted into the same, his associats. And the said William Bradford, for him, his heires and assignes, doe further hereby promise and graunt to doe & performe whatsoever further thinge or thinges, act or acts, which in him lyeth, which shalbe needfull and expedient for the better confirmeing & establisheinge the said premisses as by counsell learned in the lawes shalbe reasonably advised and devised, when he shalbe therunto required. In witnes wherof, the said William Bradford hath in publike Court surrendred the said lettres patents actually into the hands and power of the said Court, byding himself, his heires, executors, administrators, and assignes, to deliver up whatsoever specialties are in his hands that do or may concerne the same.

Memorand: that the said surrender was made by the said William Bradford, in publick Court, to Nathaniell Sowther, especially authorized by the whole Court to receive the same, together with the said lettres patents, in the name and for the use of the whole body of freemen.

It is ordered by the Court, that Mr William Bradford shall have the keepeing of the said lettres patents, which were afterwards delivered unto him by the said Nathaniell Sowther in the publike Court.

March 2, 1641

The bounds of Yarmouth on the easterly side are from the towne to a certaine brooke called by the Indians Shuckquam, but by the English Bound-brooke, with all that neck of land northward called by the Indians Atquiod, alias, Aquiatt, with all the uplands and marsh meddow which lye on the westerly side of the said broke, to the townewards unto the mouth of the said brooke; and from a marked tree at the payth over the said Bound Brooke by a straight line south and by east to the south sea, so it extend not in length above eight miles, excepting and reserveing unto Massatanpaine, the sachem, the lands from Nobscussetpann westerly, from a marked tree there unto another marked tree at a swamp extending westerly, and from thence to another marked trey northerly by a straight line to the sea, and from the northerly end of the said Nobscusset pan to the sea by a line from the westerly side of the said pan.

The bounds betwixt Yarmouth & Barnestable are as followeth, viz.: that the river of Stoney Cove shalbe the bounds from the sea as farr as it runneth to the landwards, and from thence from the upward parte thereof to begin at the easterly side of the lott of Andrew Hellot, at a knowne marked tree, by the heigh way leading betwixt Barnestable and Yarmouth aforesaid, and from the easterly side of the upward part of the said lot to runn upon the south southwest poynt of the compasse to the south sea, provided alwayes that the meddow land that was allotted and appoynted to the said Mr Hellotts farme be still reserved unto the said farme, according to the former intent & graunt thereof; excepting & reserveing unto Nepaiton & Twacommacus, & their heirs and assignes, if they shall dwell upon yt, all that percell of playne land bordering to the seawards from a pond to a tree by the wood side, marked by Mr Winslow, Capt. Standish, & Mr Freeman, and from thence easterly by the wood side to another marked tree, & from thence northerly to the sea, provided that if the said Nepaiton shall at any tyme sell the same, he shall sell it to the inhabitants of Barnestable before any other.

The Agreement betwixt Nepaiton & Twacommacus & their Heires and the Inhabitants of Barnestable

In consideracion besides what the said Nepaiton hath had already of the said inhabitants of Barnestable, that they shall build the said Nepaiton one dwelling house, with a chamber flored with bords, with a chimney and an oven therein, the said Nepaiton hath given and graunted unto the said inhabitants of Barnestable all the rest of his lands lying about Barnestable aforesaid, which were his & his owne proper inheritance, excepting & reserveing unto the said Nepaiton and Twacommacus & their heires & assignes forever, if they shall dwell upon it, all that percell of playne lands bordering upon the sea, from a pond to a tree by the wood side marked by Mr Winslow, Capt. Standish, and Mr Freeman, & from thence easterly by the wood side to another marked tree, and from thence northerly to the sea; provided alwayes, that if the said Nepaiton shall at any time sell the said lands, he shall sell them to the inhabitants of Barnestable before any other, and shall from tyme to tyme give leave for a draught to come through his ground when they shall desire it; and lastly, that they shall have liberty to gett wood for fenceing a fyer out of the woods there, and enjoy and reap the corne this yeare which they have set out of the foresaid bounds, and in winter to live where he pleaseth

June 17, 1641

The 29th of June *1652*) Bradford Governor

It was ordered by the Court and the Authoritie therof That wheras the Purchasers or and old Comers were graunted formerly two or three tractes of land for them and theire heires as by former actes of Court doe appeer which they never yett for divers causes enjoyed and some of which said tractes have bin graunted to other plantations

This Court now grauntes and gives libertie unto the said Purchasers and old Comers that all or whoseover amongst them will: shall have libertie to looke out and make choise of such place or places as they can find within this Goverment or Jurisdiction not graunted alreddy unto any provided they exceed not theire former proportions to accomodate them and theire heires withall and they have heerby libertie graunted them to purchase the said land of the natives by the approbation of the Court and soe many as shalbe thuse accomodated to Relinquish all theire Rightes Interest and title in former specify places made choise of by them and the Rest of the old comers and purchasers to take up theire particular proportions of land within the precinctes of the three former specifyed places all which to be performed by all the purchasers and old comers within fourteen month next ensueing this present Court;

And alsoe It is further graunted by this present Court That all those as were att the Courts graunt of the abovemencioned two or three places: Inhabitants alowed and now are freemen, shall have the like libertie to looke out and make Choise of some place or places for themselves and theire heires as may affoard them a sufficient accomodation for their Comfortable Exsistance within fourteen monthes after that if they Can find it;

June 29, 1652

Old Dartmouth Deed

1654   Bradford Governor   109
A deed appointed to bee Recorded
New Plymouth November the 29th 1652)

Know all men by these presents that I Wosamequen and Wamsutta my sonne have sould unto Mr William Bradford captaine Standish Thomas Southworth John Winslow John Cooke and theire associates the Purchasers or ouldcomers all the Tract or

Tracts of land lying three miles Eastward from a River called Cusheningg to a certaine harbour called Acoaksett to a flatt Rocke on the west ward side of the said harbour; And wheras the said harbour devideth it selfe into severall branches; the westermost arme to bee the bound; and all the Tract or tracts of land from the said westermost arme to the said River of Cushenigg three miles Eastward of the same; with all the profitts and benifitts within the said Tract with all the Rivers creekes Meddows Neckes and Islands that lye In or before the same; And from the sea upward to goe soe high that the English may not bee annoyed by the hunting of the Indians in any sort of theire Cattle; And I Wosamequen and Wamsutta doe promise to Remove all the Indians within a yeare from the date heerof That doe live in the said Tract And wee the said Wosamequen and Wamsutta have fully barganed and sold unto the aforsaid Mr William Bradford captaine Standish Thomas Southwort John Winslow John Cooke and the Rest of theire associates the Purchasers or oldcomers To have and to hold for them and theire heires and assignes for ever; and in consideration heerof wee the abovmencioned; are to pay to the said Wosamequen and Wamsutta as followeth thirty yards of cloth eight moose skins fifteen axes fifteen hoes fifteen paire of breeches eight blankets two kittles a cloake 2 in Wampam eight paire of stokens eight paire of shoes an Iron pott and ten shilling in another comoditie; And In Witnesse heerof Wee have Interchangably sett to our hands the day and yeare above written

Wamsutta   his Marke
In the presence of Jonathan Shaw   Samuell Eedy
John Winslow   John Cooke

November 29, 1652

Sowams Deeds

1653   Bradford Governor   78
A deed appointed to bee Recorded
To all people to whom these presents shall come Ousamequin Sachem and Wamsitto his eldest sonne sendeth greet &c

Know yea that wee the said Ousamequin and Wamsitto for and in consideracion of thirty five pounds sterlin to us the said Ousamequin and Wamsitto in hand paied per Thomas Prence Gentleman and Thomas Willett Gent. Myles Standish Gent. Josiah Winslow Gent.; for and in the behalf of themselves and divers others of the Inhabitants of Plymouth Jurisdiction whose names are heerafter specifyed with which said summe wee the said ousamequin and Wamsitto doe acknowlidge our selves fully satisfyed content and paied have freely and abso-lutly bargained and sold infeofed and confeirmed and per these presents doe bargaine sell infeofe & confeirme from us the said ousamequin and Wamsitto and our and every of our heires unto Thomas Prence Thomas Willett Myles Standish Josiah Winslow agents for themselves and William Bradford senior Gent. Thomas Clarke John Winslow Thomas Cushin and William White John Addams and Experience Michell; To them and every of them theire and every of theire heires and assignes for ever All those severall percells and Neckes of upland Swamps and meddowes lying and beinge on the southerly side of the Sinckuncke alias Rehoboth bounds and is bounded from a Little brooke of water called by the Indians Mosskituash Westerly and soe Ranging by a dead Swamp Eastward and so by marked trees as Ousamequin and Wamsitto diverted; unto the great River with all the Meddow in and about the sides of both the branches of the great River with all the creekes and brookes that are in or upon any the said Meddow as alsoe all the Mersh meddow lying and being without the bounds before Mencioned in or about the necke called by the Indians Chachacust; Alsoe all the Meddow of any kind lying and being att or about Papasquash Necke as alsoe all the meddow lying from the bay to Keecomewett on both sides or any way Joyn-ing to it or the Bay on eich side To have and to holde all the aforsaid upland Swampe Mershes creekes and Rivers with all theire appurtenances unto the aforsaid Thomas Prence Thomas Willett Myles Standish Josiah Winslow and the Rest of the parteners aforsaid To them and every of them theire and every of their heires exequitors and assignes for ever; And the said Ousamequin and Wamsitto doe alsoe covenant promise and graunt that whensoever the Indians shall Remove from the Necke that then and from thence forth The aforsaid Thomas

Prence Thomas Willett Myles Standish and Josiah Winslow
etc. shall enter upon the same by the same agreement as theire
proper Right and enterest to them and their heires for ever
To and for the true performance of all and every one of the
aforsaid severall particulares Wee the said Ousamequin and
Wamsitoo bind us and every of us our and every of our heirs
exequitors adminestrators and assignes feirmly per these presents In Witnesse wherof wee have heerunto sett our hands and
seales this twentyninth day of March Anno dom. 1653
the Mark of Ousamequin seale
the Marke of Wamsitto seale
Signed Sealed and delivered in the presence of John Browne
James Browne Richard Garrett

Mr James Browne one of the witnesses to this Instrument made
oath that hee did see Osamequin and Wamsitta his son Signe
seal and deliver it as theire acte and deed and that Mr John
Browne his father and Mr Richard Garrett were then alsoe
present as Witnesses to the same Taken upon oath this 28th
day of October 1681 Before Mee Thomas Hinkley Governor

March 29, 1653

THE EDITORS' COMMENT

Through a series of grants, the Plymouth Court sought to solidify the rights of the "Old Comers," the first group of proprietors at Patuxet, as the colony expanded into Wampanoag territory and the number of settlers from England increased. As the previous deeds demonstrate, not all English newcomers acquired land through Plymouth's court; some sought to negotiate with Native leaders directly or to purchase land from other colonists. Indeed, Plymouth's patent was less secure than neighboring Massachusetts Bay's charter, and Plymouth competed with Rhode Island for jurisdiction as both colonies began to expand. Plymouth sought to solidify not only the rights granted through the patent, but also what they regarded as preemptive rights to Wampanoag lands. Thus their own claims also depended on recognition of Wampanoag territory. As early as 1639, the Old Comers selected three loosely defined tracts in the Wampanoag country to reserve for themselves and their heirs, including land in Ousamequin's territory of Sowams, land on Cape Cod between Yarmouth and Namskaket, and land on the coast between Acoaxet and Acushnet. However, as they acknowledged, the Plymouth men first had to secure these lands by "purchase" of "the said land of the natives," that is, the recognized Wampanoag leaders in those places.

Wamsutta's Mortgage

A Deed apointed to bee Recorded
These presents witnesseth That wheras Capt: James Cudworth
Mr Josias Winslow senior Constant Southworth and John
Barnes have bine with mee Wamsutta to buy a persell of land
which they say is graunted by the Court of Plymouth unto
themselves with some others and I Wamsutta am not willinge
att present to sell all they doe desire yett of this att present I
Wamsutta doe tender and proffer unto Capt. Cudworth josias
Winslow John Barnes and Constant Southworth if they please
upon the viewing and Considering for to accept of; I the said
Wamsutta bind my selfe my heires executors and assignes to
make good; That is to say all the upland and meddow from
Quequetham unto Assonett necke except the land that
Sabadecauson hath in present use and all the meddow land
on the westerly side of the River from Taunton bounds unto
the head of Wepoisett River in all Creeks coves and Rivers and
Inland meddow not lying above four miles from the flowing
of the side The former mentioned land from Quequetham to
Assonett necke is to extend four miles from the River into the
woods; all the aforementioned Lands I Wamsutta doe bargane
and sell enfeofe and confeirme from mee and my heires unto
Capt: Cudworth Josias Winslow Constant Southworth and
John Barnes they and theire heires for ever; They yeilding and
paying unto mee the said Wamsutta Twenty Coates two Rugg
two Iron potts two kettles and one little kettle eight paire of
shoes six paire of stockings one dozen of hoe one dozen of
hatchetts two yards of broadcloth; and to satisfy unto John
Barnes for those thinges I the said Wamsutta tooke up of him
Alsoe I the said Wamsutta doe Covenant promise and agree
with Capt: Cudworth Josias Winslow Constant Southworth
and John Barnes never to sell nor give away any parte or persell
of the upland from Taunton bounds unto Wepoisett River unto

any other person or persons But when I the said Wamsutta am willing to sell or dispose of any or all the said land I doe by these presents promise to sell the same unto Capt: Cudworth Josias Winslow Constant Southworth and John barnes or theire heires or assignes and in and for the true performance wherof I Wamsutta doe by these presents bind mee my heires and assignes in Witnes wherof I have heerunto sett my hand this 24th of december 1657)

The marke   of Wamsutta

Witnessed by us John Tisdall

John Sasamon

The marke   of Capt. uskowantoson

December 24, 1657

Freemen's Deeds

A Deed appointed to bee Recorded

Know all men by these presents that wee Ussamequen Wamsutta Tatapanum Natives Inhabiting and liveing within the Goverment of New Plymouth in New England in America have bargained and sold enfeofed and Confeirmed unto Captaine James Cudworth Josias Winslow senior Constant Southworth John Barnes John Tisdall Humphery Turner Walter Hatch Samuel House Samuell Jackson John Daman Mr. Timothy Hatherley Timothy Foster Thomas Southworth Gorg Watson Nathaniell Morton Richard More Edmond Chandeler Samuell Nash Henery Howland Mr. Ralph Partrich Love Brewster Willam Paybody Christopher Wadsworth Kenelme Winslow Thomas Bourne John Waterman the son of Robert Waterman. and doe by these presents bargaine sell enfeof and Confeirme from us and our heires unto James Cudworth Josias Winslow John Tisdall &c: and they and theire heires all the tract of upland and meddow lying on the easterly side of Taunton River begining or bounded towards the south with the River called the falls or Quequeteand. and soe extending it selfe Northerly untill it comes to a little brooke called by the English by the name of Stacyes Creeke which brooke Issues out of the woods in to the marshes and bay of Assonett Close by the narrowing of Assonett necke; and from a marked tree neare the said brooke at the head of the marsh to extend itselfe into the woods on a North norwest point four miles and from the head of the said four miles on a straight line southerly untill it meets with the head of the four mile line att Quequeteand or the falls aforsaid; Including all meddows neckes or Ilands lying and being betwixt Assonett necke and the falls aforsaid; (except the land that Tebadecauson hath in present use) and all the meddow upon Assonett necke on the south side of the said necke and all the meddow on the westerly side of Taunton River from Taunton upland bounds Round untill it comes to the head of Wepoisett River; in al Creekes Coves Rivers with inland meddowes not lying above four miles from the flowing of the tide in and for the Consideration of Twenty Coates two Ruggs two Iron potts two kettles and one kittle eight paire of shooes six paire of stockens one dozen of howes one dozen of hatchetts two peeces of broadcloth and a debt satisfyed to John Barnes which was due from Wamsutta unto John Barnes before the twenty fourth of december 1657) all being unto us in hand payed wherwith wee the said Ussamequen Wamsutta Tatapanum are fully satisfyed Contented and payed; and doe by these presents exownerate acquitt and discharge James Cudworth Josias Winslow senior: Constant Southworth John Barnes John Tisdall Humphery Turner Walter Hatch Samuell House Samuell Jackson John Daman Mr Timothy Hatherly Timothy Foster Mr Thomas Southworth Gorge Watson Nathaniell Morton Richard More Edmond Chandeler Samuell Nash Henery Howland Mr Ralph Partrich Love Brewster Willam Paybody Christopher Wadsworth Kenelme Winslow Thomas Bourne John Waterman they and every of them and every of theire heires for ever; Warranting the sale heerof from all persons from by or under us as laying any Claime unto the premises from by or under us as claiming any Right and title therunto or ento any parte or persell therof; The said James Cudworth Josais Winslow Constant Southworth John Barnes &c.: To have and to hold to them and theire heires for ever all the abovesaid upland and meddow as is before expressed with all the appurtenances therunto belonging from us Ussamequin Wamsutta Tatapanum and every of us our heires and every of them for ever unto them they theire heires and exequitors adminnestrators and assignes for ever according to the tenure

of East greenwich in free soccage and not in Capite nor by
Knightes service Alsoe the said Ussamequin Wamsutta and
Tatapanum doe Covenant and graunt that it may bee lawfull
for the said James Cudwort &c: to enter this said deed in the
Court of Plymouth or in any other Court of Records provided
for in such Cases; In and for the true performance wherof Wee
Ussamequin Wamsutta and Tatapanum have heerunto sett our
hands and seales this second day of Aprill 1659)

Wamussuta his marke seale

Tatapanum her marke seale

Signed sealed and delivered in the presence of us

Thomas Cooke Jonathan Briggs John Sasamon

June the 9th 1659) Wamsutta did acknowlidg this to bee his
free act and deed and did make full Resignation to the parties
abovesaid of all and singulare the tracts of land above mensioned before us

Josias Winslow   Willam Bradford   assistants

June the 9th 1659 this Woman Tatapanum did acknowlidge
this to bee her free acte and deed and did make her full Resignation of her whole Interest in all or any tract or tracts of land
in this deed specifyed before us

Josias Winslow   William Bradford Assistants

April 2–June 9, 1659

Wamsutta's Protests Over Cattle

Wheras the Indians, viz., Wamsitta and others, have lately
bine att the Court, and complaine still of great damage by the
horses of the inhabitants of Rehoboth, the Court ordereth,
that the townsmen of Rehoboth take some speedy course that
theire horses doe not in-damage the Indians, and in speciall
such as had horses goeing on Causumsett Necke; and that
when Captaine Willett is att home the Indians which for the
futuer shalbee soe treaspased are to repaire to him, and hee is
authorised heerby to take such order therin as shalbee by him
thought meet.

June 7, 1659

In answare to the complaint of Wamsitta, about damage done by the swine of some of the inhabitants of Rehoboth in theire corne, the Court ordereth, that the Indians on the neckes called Annawamscutt and Kekamewett shall make a sufficient pound to impound swine in the convenientest place they can, and have libertie to impound such swine as treaspas them att any time in theire corn; and they shall repaire to the towne clarke of Rehoboth, and desire hime to give publicke notice therof, that the owners may take course to release the swine by satisfying the damage, which shalbee judged and levied by some indifferent man of the English, chosen by the Indians treaspased; and alsoe that then, with all convenient speed, the owners of the swine shall remove them of from the said neckes to some other place att some considerable distance, soe as they may not bee likely to doe the like damage againe.

In answare to Wamsitta, and an other Indian, called Willam, about a parcell of land layed claime unto by them, as alsoe by a Narragansett sachem, and by the said sachem sold, to the great offence of the said Wamsitta and William, they affeirming that the said sachem hath nor never had noe enterest in it, and desired direction of the Court what to doe in the case; the answare of the Court is, that they will request Captaine Willett to enquire into the case, and will doe therin as they shall see cause by further intelligence about the same.

In answare to the request of Wamsitta, requesting libertie to purchase a smale parcell of powder for the use of him and his brother, the Court have ordered the Treasurer to bestow on him as a smale gratuitee *have* a dozen pound of powder, but will not permitt him to purchase the same any.

Att the ernest request of Wamsitta, desiring that in regard his father is lately deceased, and hee being desirouse, according to the custome of the natives, to change his name, that the Court would confer an English name upon him, which accordingly they did, and therfore ordered, that for the future hee shalbee called by the name of Allexander Pokanokett; and desireing the same in the behalfe of his brother, they have named him Phillip.

June 13, 1660

THE EDITORS' COMMENT

The next generation of Plymouth leaders, known as the "first born sons", expressed a sense of entitlement to land in the colony as their rightful inheritance, even against Wampanoag people. This generation marked a change in diplomacy between the Plymouth settlers and the Wampanoags, with younger men like Constant Southworth and Josiah Winslow taking a more aggressive stance than their fathers toward Wampanoag people, based in part on English notions of racial superiority. The Plymouth Court increasingly asserted jurisdiction over Wampanoag people, as inhabitants of Plymouth Colony, even as they continued to exert a preemptive right against other settlers, both those from other colonies and English newcomers to Wampanoag lands. The preceding deeds represent more deceitful approaches to acquiring Indigenous consent, including debt and liquor, as well as attempts to enforce English couverture laws, whereby land belonging to a woman through inheritance would become her husband's property upon marriage.

In the first document, Southworth, Winslow, and James Cudworth used debt at a local tavern to gain the consent of Wamsutta, Ousamequin's son and the Pokanoket sachem, for their purchase of land at Pocasset, which remained under Weetamoo's jurisdiction by Wampanoag custom, even after her marriage to Wamsutta. This led to the Freemen's deeds, through which Plymouth Court members sought to acquire a great tract of Pocasset land to allot, settle, and sell. These records were only entered in the Plymouth Court in 1666, when the lands were set to be surveyed and allotted, after the dates of 1657 and 1659 that appear on the deeds. The consent of the Indigenous signers appeared by way of settler testimony. Wampanoag leaders also frequently appeared in the Plymouth Court records protesting encroachment. The complaint above is one of many that addressed the impact of cows, horses, and hogs on subsistence and sovereignty, and the failure of the court to reign in settlers and their livestock.

Metacom to Governor Thomas Prence
and
Exchange Between Awashonks and Governor Thomas Prence

Metacom to Governor Thomas Prence

KING Philip desire to let you understand that he could not come to the Court, for Tom, his interpreter, has a pain in his back, that he could not travil so far, and Philip sister is very sik.

Philip would intreat that favor of you, and aney of the majestrats, if aney English or Engians speak about aney land, he preay you to give them no answewer at all. This last sumer he maid that promis with you, that he would not sell no land in 7 years time, for that he would have no English trouble him before that time, he has not forgot that you promis him.

He will come a sune as posible he can to speak with you, and so I rest, your verey loveing friend, Philip, dwelling at mount hope nek.

To the much honered
  Governer, Mr. Thomas Prince,
    dwelling at Plimoth.

date unknown

Exchange Between Awashonks and Governor Thomas Prence

August 11, 1671.

HONORED SIR,

I HAVE received a very great favour from your Honor, in your's of the 7th instant; and as you are pleased to signify, that if I continue faithful to the agreement made with yourselves at Plymouth, I may expect all just favours from your Honor; I am fully resolved, while I live, with all fidelity to stand to my engagement, and in a peaceable submission to your commands, according to the best of my poor ability. It is true, and I am very sensible thereof, that there are some Indians who do seek an advantage against me, for my submitting to his majesty's authority in your jurisdiction; but being conscious to myself of my integrity and real intentions of peace, I doubt not but you will afford me all due encouragement and protection. I had resolved to send in all my guns, being six in number, according to the intimation of my letter; but two of them were so large, the messengers were not able to carry them; I since proffered to leave them with Mr. Barker, but he not having any order to receive, told me he conceived I might do well to send them to Mr. Almy, who is a person concerned in the jurisdiction, which I resolved to do; but since then an Indian, known by the name of broad faced Will, stole one of them out of the wigwam in the night, and is run away with it to Mount Hope; the other I think to send in to Mr. Almy. A list of those that are obedient to me, and, I hope and am persuaded, faithful to you, is here inclosed. Honored Sir, I shall not trouble you further; but desiring your peace and prosperity, in which I look at my own to be included, I remain,

> your unfeigned servant,
>
> † AWASUNCKS.

Mr. Barker presents his humble services to yourself and the honored magistrates.

Plymouth, October 20, 1671.

FRIEND Awasuncks, be you and your husband kindly saluted. I received by Mr. H. and Mr. Southworth, August the last, a list of the names of such of your men, as also your husband's that do freely submit to his majesty's authority here, and likewise own your government and engagement with us. And be well assured, we shall be ready, upon all just occasions, to carry friendly to you and them. But I see they fall much short of your persuasions and hopes, and indeed of my expectations by your last to me. Though I fault not you, with any failing to endeavour, only to notice your good persuasions of them outwent their deserts, for ought yet appeareth. I could have wished they had been wiser for themselves, especially your two sons, that may probably succeed you in your government, and your brother also, who is so nearly tied unto you by nature. Do they think themselves so great as to disregard and affront his majesty's interest and authority here, and the amity of the Enlish? Certainly if they do, I think they did much disservice, and wish they would yet show themselves wiser, before it be too late; but let them take their course till they be convinced of their folly. I think you may do well to send some of yours to the next court, to desire your arms that are here, that you may have the use of them in this season. Let me hear from you or your husband. Nothing else at present, but prosperity to you and your people.

Your loving friend,

THOMAS PRINCE.

EXCHANGE BETWEEN AWASHONKS AND
GOVERNOR THOMAS PRENCE, 1671

THE EDITORS' COMMENT

The preceding letters reflect rising conflict between Wampanoag people and Plymouth settlers, colonial attempts to extend jurisdiction over Wampanoag leaders, and Wampanoag people's use of writing as a tool of diplomacy. Plymouth's tense councils with Metacom in 1671 are fairly well known, but Plymouth also asserted control over neighboring leaders, including the Wampanoag sôkushqâ Awashonks, through the threat of military force and confiscation of arms. In July 1671, Plymouth recruited one hundred men to march upon Sakonnet and capture Awashonks. She responded to the threat with diplomacy, including an act of "submission," but continued to assert her responsibility as a leader to sustain her community and homeland.

The correspondence between Awashonks and Governor Thomas Prence demonstrates that Plymouth men were forced by Wampanoag political practice to negotiate with female leaders, although they hoped that males, in this case Awashonks's sons, would succeed them. At the same time, Prence and others expressed concern that Wampanoag leaders could only assert limited authority over their relations. Likewise, Awashonks would only agree to limited colonial authority, submitting to the English king's authority in Plymouth Colony, but not to the authority of Plymouth Colony over all of her people.

The "councils" of 1671 were orchestrated during a time when Plymouth's patent was fragile in relation to the royal charters of Massachusetts Bay and Rhode Island, which had recently been affirmed by the restored King Charles II. Even as settlers used deeds and treaties to demonstrate their rightful claims, Native leaders like Awashonks, Weetamoo, and Metacom began to adopt writing, often drawing on relations trained by missionaries, to communicate more nuanced understandings of those agreements or to counter them entirely. In Philip's letter to Prence he reminded the governor of his pledge that he would not sell any more land for seven years' time. Given Plymouth's precarious legal standing, the growing disaffection of Wampanoag leaders was a major threat to the colony's continuance. Likewise, the awareness that both Philip and Awashonks demonstrated about the growing threat to their homelands presages the resistance known as King Philip's War.

WRITINGS ABOUT THE
BROADER WAMPANOAG AND
MASSACHUSETT HOMELANDS

William Wood:
from *New England's Prospect*

CHAP. V.
Of the Hearbes, Fruites, Woods, Waters and Mineralls.

THE ground affoards very good kitchin Gardens, for Turneps, Parsnips, Carrots, Radishes, and Pumpions, Muskmillions, Isquouterquashes, Coucumbers, Onyons, and whatsoever growes well in *England*, growes as well there, many things being better and larger: there is likewise growing all manner of Hearbes for meate, and medicine, and that not onely in planted Gardens, but in the Woods, without eyther the art or the helpe of man, as sweet Marjoran, Purselane, Sorrell, Peneriall, Yarrow, Mirtle, Saxisarilla, Bayes, &c. There is likewise Strawberries in abundance, very large ones, some being two inches about; one may gather halfe a bushell in a forenoone: In other seasons there bee Gooseberries, Bilberies, Resberies, Treackleberies, Hurtleberries, Currants; which being dryed in the Sunne are little inferiour to those that our Grocers sell in *England*: This land likewise affoards Hempe and Flax, some naturally, and some planted by the *English*, with Rapes if they bee well managed. For such commodities as lie underground, I cannot out of mine owne experience or knowledge say much, having taken no great notice of such things; but it is certainely reported that there is Iron, stone; and the *Indians* informe us that they can leade us to the mountaines of blacke Lead, and have showne us lead ore, if our small judgement in such things doe not deceive us: and though no body dare confidently conclude, yet dare they not utterly deny, but that the *Spaniards* blisse may lye hid in the barren Mountaines, such as have coasted the countrey affirme that they know where to fetch Seacole if wood were scant; there is plenty of stone both rough and smooth, usefull for many things, with quarries of Slate, out of which they get covering for houses, with good clay, whereof they make Tiles and Brickes, and pavements for their necessary uses.

For the Countrey it is as well watered as any land under the Sunne, every family, or every two families having a spring of sweet waters betwixt them, which is farre different from the waters of *England*, being not so sharpe, but of a fatter substance, and of a more jetty colour; it is thought there can be no better water in the world, yet dare I not preferre it before good Beere, as some have done, but any man will choose it before bad Beere, Wheay, or Buttermilke. Those that drinke it be as healthfull, fresh, and lustie, as they that drinke beere; These springs be not onely within land, but likewise bordering upon the Sea coasts, so that some times the tides overflow some of them, which is accounted rare in the most parts of *England*. No man hitherto hath beene constrained to digge deepe for his water, or to fetch it farre, or to fetch of severall waters for severall uses; one kind of water serving for washing, and brewing and other things. Now besides these springs, there be divers spacious ponds in many places of the Countrey, out of which runne many sweet streames, which are constant in their course both winter and summer, whereat the Cattle quench their thirst, and upon which may be built water mills, as the plantation encreases.

The next commoditie the land affords, is good store of Woods, & that not onely such as may be needfull for fewell, but likewise for the building of Ships, and houses, & Mils, and all manner of water-worke about which Wood is needefull. The Timber of the Countrey growes straight, and tall, some trees being twenty, some thirty foot high, before they spread forth their branches; generally the Trees be not very thicke, though there be many that will serve for Mill posts, some beeing three foote and a halfe o're. And whereas it is generally conceived, that the woods grow so thicke, that there is no more cleare ground than is hewed out by labour of man; it is nothing so; in many places, divers Acres being cleare, so that one may ride a hunting in most places of the land, if he will venture himselfe for being soft: there is no underwood saving in swamps, and low grounds that are wet, in which the *English* get Osiers, and Hasles, and such small wood as is for their use. Of these swamps, some be ten, some twenty, some thirty miles long, being preserved by the wetnesse of the soile wherein they grow; for it being the custome of the *Indians* to burne the wood in *November*, when the grasse is withered, and leaves dryed, it consumes all the underwood, and rubbish, which otherwise would over grow the Country, making it unpassable, and spoile their much affected hunting: so that by this meanes in those places where the *Indians* inhabit, there is scarce a bush or bramble, or any combersome underwood to bee seene in the more champion ground. Small wood growing in these places where the fire could not come, is preserved. In some places where the *Indians* dyed of the Plague some foureteene yeares agoe, is much underwood, as in the mid way betwixt *Wessaguscus* and *Plimouth*, because it hath not beene burned; certaine Rivers stopping the fire from comming to cleare that place of the countrey, hath made it unusefull and troublesome to travell thorow, in so much that it is called ragged plaine, because it teares and rents the cloathes of them that passe. Now because it may be necessary for mechanicall artificers to know what Timber, and wood of use is in the Countrey, I will recite the most usefull as followeth.

> *Trees both in hills and plaines, in plenty be,*
> *The long liv'd Oake, and mournefull Cypris tree,*
> *Skie towring pines, and Chesnuts coated rough,*
> *The lasting Cedar, with the Walnut tough:*
> *The rozin dropping Firre for masts in use,*
> *The boatmen seeke for Oares light, neate growne sprewse,*
> *The brittle Ash, the ever trembling Aspes,*
> *The broad-spread Elme, whose concave harbours waspes,*
> *The water spungie Alder good for nought,*
> *Small Elderne by th'* Indian *Fletchers fought,*
> *The knottie Maple, pallid Birtch, Hawthornes,*
> *The Horne bound tree that to be cloven scornes;*
> *Which from the tender Vine oft takes his spouse,*
> *Who twinds imbracing armes about his boughes.*
> *Within this* Indian *Orchard fruites be some,*
> *The ruddie Cherrie, and the jettie Plumbe,*
> *Snake murthering Hazell, with sweet Saxaphrage,*
> *Whose spurnes in beere allayes hot fevers rage.*
> *The Diars Shumach, with more trees there be,*
> *That are both good to use, and rare to see.*

Though many of these trees may seeme to have epithites contrary to the nature of them as they grow in *England*, yet are they agreeable with the Trees of that Countrie. The chiefe and common Timber for ordinary use is Oake, and Walnut: Of Oakes there be three kindes, the red Oake, white, and blacke; as these are different in kinde, so are they chosen for such uses as they are most fit for, one kind being more fit for clappboard, others for sawne board, some fitter for shipping, others for houses. These Trees affoard much Mast for Hogges, especially every third yeare, bearing a bigger Acorne than our *English* Oake. The Wallnut tree is something different from the *English* Wallnut, being a great deale more tough, and more serviceable, and altogether as heavie: and whereas our Gunnes that are stocked with *English* Wallnut, are soone broaken and cracked in frost, beeing a brittle Wood; we are driven to stocke them new with the Country Wallnut, which will indure all blowes, and weather; lasting time out of minde. These trees beare a very good Nut, something smaller, but nothing inferiour in sweetnesse and goodnesse to the *English* Nut, having no bitter pill. There is likewise a tree in some part of the Countrey, that beares a Nut as bigge as a small peare. The Cedar tree is a tree of no great growth, not bearing above a foot and a halfe square at the most, neither is it very high. I suppose they be much inferiour to the Cedars of *Lebanon* so much commended in holy writ. This wood is more desired for ornament than substance, being of colour red and white like Eugh, smelling as sweete as Juniper; it is commonly used for seeling of houses, and making of Chests, boxes, and staves. The Firre and Pine bee trees that grow in many places, shooting up exceeding high, especially the Pine: they doe afford good masts, good board, Rozin and Turpentine. Out of these Pines is gotten the candlewood that is so much spoken of, which may serve for a shift amongst poore folkes; but I cannot commend it for singular good, because it is something sluttish, dropping a pitchie kinde of substance where it stands. Here no doubt might be good done with saw mils; for I have seene of these stately highgrowne trees, ten miles together close by the River side, from whence by shipping they might be conveyed to any desired Port. Likewise it is not improbable that Pitch and Tarre may be forced from these trees, which beare no other kinde of fruite. For that countrey

Ash, it is much different from the Ash of *England*, being brittle and good for little, so that Wallnut is used for it. The Horne-bound tree is a tough kind of Wood, that requires so much paines in riving as is almost incredible, being the best for to make bolles and dishes, not being subject to cracke or leake. This tree growing with broad spread Armes, the vines winde their curling branches about them; which vines affoard great store of grapes, which are very big both for the grape and Cluster, sweet and good: These be of two sorts, red and white, there is likewise a smaller kind of grape, which groweth in the Islands which is sooner ripe and more delectable; so that there is no knowne reason why as good wine may not be made in those parts, as well as in *Burdeuax* in *France*; being under the same degree. It is great pittie no man sets upon such a venture, whereby he might in small time inrich himselfe, and benefit the Countrie, I know nothing which doth hinder but want of skilfull men to manage such an imployment: For the countrey is hot enough, the ground good enough, and many convenient hills which lye toward the south Sunne, as if they were there placed for the purpose. The Cherrie trees yeeld great store of Cherries, which grow on clusters like grapes; they be much smaller than our *English* Cherrie, nothing neare so good if they be not very ripe: they so furre the mouth that the tongue will cleave to the roofe, and the throate wax horse with swallowing those red Bullies (as I may call them,) being little better in taste. *English* ordering may bring them to be an *English* Cherrie, but yet they are as wilde as the *Indians.* The Plummes of the Countrey be better for Plummes than the Cherries be for Cherries, they be blacke and yellow about the bignesse of a Damson, of a reasonable good taste. The white thorne affords hawes as bigge as an *English* Cherrie, which is esteemed above a Cherrie for his goodnesse and pleasantnesse to the taste.

CHAP. VII.

Of their dispositions and good qualifications, as
friendship, constancy, truth, and affability.

To enter into a serious discourse concerning the naturall conditions of these *Indians*, might procure admiration from the people of any civilized Nations, in regard of their civility and good natures. If a Tree may be judged by his fruite, and dispositions calculared by exteriour actions; then may it be concluded, that these *Indians* are of affable, courteous, and well disposed natures, ready to communicate the best of their wealth to the mutuall good of one another; and the lesse abundance they have, to manifest their entire friendship; so much the more perspicuous is their love, in that they are as willing to part with their Mite in poverty, as treasure in plenty. As he that kills a Deere, sends for his friends, and eates it merrily: So he that receives but a piece of bread from an *English* hand, parts it equally betweene himselfe and his comerades, and eates it lovingly. In a word, a friend can command his friend, his house, and whatsoever is his, (saving his Wife) and have it freely: And as they are love-linked thus in common courtesie, so are they no way sooner dis-joynted than by ingratitude; accounting an ungratefull person a double robber of a man, not onely of his courtesie, but of his thankes which he might receive of another for the same proffered, or received kindnesse. Such is their love to one another, that they cannot endure to see their Countrey-men wronged, but will stand stiffely in their defence: plead strongly in their behalfe, and justifie one anothers integrities in any warrantable action. If it were possible to recount the courtesies they have shewed the *English*, since their first arrivall in those parts, it would not onely steddy beleefe, that they are a loving people, but also winne the love of those that never saw them, and wipe off that needelesse feare that is too deeply rooted in the conceits of many, who thinke them envious, and of such rankerous and inhumane dispositions, that they will one day make an end of their *English* inmates. The worst indeede may be surmised, but the *English* hitherto have had little cause to suspect them, but rather to be convinced of their trustinesse, seeing they have as yet beene the disclosers of all such treacheries as have bin practised by other *Indians*.

And whereas once there was a proffer of an universall League amongst all the *Indians* in those parts, to the intent that they might all joyne in one united force, to extirpiate the *English*, our *Indians* refused the motion, replying, they had rather be servants to the *English*, of whom they were confident to receive no harme, and from whom they had received so many favours, and assured good testimonies of their love, than equals with them, who would cut their throates upon the least offence, and make them the shambles of their cruelty. Furthermore, if any roaving ships be upon the coasts, and chance to harbour either East-ward, North-ward, or South-ward in any unusuall Port, they will give us certaine intelligence of her burthen and forces, describing their men either by language or features; which is a great priviledge and no small advantage. Many wayes hath their advice and endeavour beene advantagious unto us; they being our first instructers for the planting of their *Indian* Corne, by teaching us to cull out the finest seede, to observe the fittest season, to keepe distance for holes, and fit measure for hills, to worme it, and weede it; to prune it, and dresse it as occasion shall require.

These *Indians* be very hospitable, insomuch that when the *English* have travelled forty, fifty, or threescore miles into the Countrey, they have entertained them into their houses, quartered them by themselves in the best roomes, providing the best victuals they could, expressing their welcome in as good termes as could be expected from their slender breeding; shewing more love than complement, not grumbling for a fort-nights or three weekes tarrying; but rather caring to provide accommodation, correspondent to their *English* custome. The doubtfull traveller hath oftentimes beene much beholding to them for their guidance thorow the unbeaten Wildernesse: my selfe in this particular can doe no lesse in the due acknowl-edgment of their love, than speake their commendations, who with two more of my associates bending our course to new *Plimouth*, lost our way, being deluded by a misleading path which we still followed, being as we thought too broad for an *Indian* path (which seldome is broader than a Cart's rutte) but that the dayly concourse of *Indians* from the *Naragansets* who traded for shooes, wearing them homewards had made this *Indian* tract like an *English* walke, and had rear'd up great stickes against the trees, and marked the rest with their hatchets in the *English* fashion, which begat in us a security of our wrong way to be right, when indeed there was nothing lesse: The day being gloomy and our compasses at home, we travelled hard till night to lesse purpose than if we had sat still, not gaining an inch of our journey for a dayes travell: but happily wee arrived at an *Indian Wigwamme*, where we were informed of our misprision, and invited to a homely lodging, feasted with the haunch of a fat Beere, and the ensuing morning the son of my naked hoast, for a peece of Tobacco, and a foure penny whittle, tooke the clew of his traveling experience, conducting us through the strange labyrinth of unbeaten bushy wayes in the woody wildernesse twentie miles to our desired harbour.

A second demonstration of their love in this kind may appeare in a passage of the same nature. An unexperienced wood man ranging in the woods for Deere, traveled so farre beyond his knowledge, till he could not tell how to get out of the wood for trees, but the more he sought to direct himselfe out, the more he ranne himselfe in, from the home he most desired; the night came upon him preventing his walking, and the extremitie of cold feasing upon his right foote for want of warming motion, deprived him of the use thereof, so that he could not remoove farther than his snowie bed, but had there ended his dayes, had not sixe commiserating *Indians*, who heard of his wandering, found him out by diligent search, being almost dead with despaire and cold: but after they had conquered his despaire with the assurance of his safe conduction to his habitation, and expelled the cold by the infusion of strong waters which they brought for the same purpose; they framed a thing like a hand barrow and carryed this selfe-helpelesse person on their bare shoulders twelve miles to his residence: many other wandring benighted coasters have beene kindly entertained into their habitations, where they have rested and reposed themselves more securely than if they had beene in some blind obscure old *Englands* Inne, being the next day directed in their right way: many lazie boyes that have runne away from their masters, have beene brought home by these ranging foresters, who are as welacquainted with the craggy mountaines, and the pleasant vales, the stately woods, and swampie groves, the spacious ponds, and swift running rivers, and can distinguish them by their names as perfectly, and finde them as presently, as the experienced Citizen knows how to finde out Cheape-side crosse, or *London* stone. Such is the wisedome and pollicie of these poore men, that they will be sure to keepe correspondence with our *English* Magistrates, expressing their love in the execution of any service they command them, so far as lyes in their powre, as may appeare in this one particular. A certaine man having layd himselfe open to the Kings lawes, fearing atachment, conviction, and consequently execution: sequestred himself from the honest societie of his neighbours, betaking himselfe unto the obscure thickets of the wildernesse, where hee lived for a time undiscovered, till the *Indians* who leave no place unsearched for Deere, found out his haunt, and having taken notice by diverse discourses concerning him, how that it was the governers desire to know where he was; they thought it a part of their service to certifie him where he kept his rendevouze, who thereupon desired if they could to direct men to him for his attachment, but he had shifted his dwelling, and could not be found for the present, yet he was after seene by other *Indians*, but being double pistold, and well sworded, they feared to approach so neere him as to grapple with him: wherefore they let him alone till his owne necessary businesse cast him upon them; for having occasion to crosse a river, he came to the side thereof, where was an *Indian Cannow*, in which the *Indians* were to crosse the river themselves, hee vauntingly commanded wastage; which they willingly graunted, but withall plotting how they might take him prisoner, which they thus effected; having placed him in the midship of their ticklish wherrie, they lanched forth into the deepe, causing the capering *Cannow* to cast out her combersome ballast into the liquid water; which swomme like a stone, and now the water having dank't his pistoles, and lost his *Spanish* progge in the bottome, the *Indians* swomme him out by the chinne to the shore, where having dropt himselfe a little dry, he began to bluster out a storme of rebellious resistance, till they becalmed his pelting chafe with their pelting of pibles at him, afterward leading him as they lift to the governour. These people be of a kinde and affable disposition, yet are they very warie with whom they strike hands in friendshippe: nothing is more hatefull to them than a churlish disposition, so likewise is dissimulation: he that speakes seldome, and opportunely, being as good as his word, is the onely man they love. The *Spaniard* they say is all one *Aramouse* (*viz*. all one as a dog) the *Frenchman* hath a good tongue, but a false heart: The *English* man all one speake, all one heart; wherefore they more approve of them than of any Nation: garrulitie is much condemmed of them, for they utter not many words, speake seldome, and then with such gravitie as is pleasing to the eare: such as understand them not, desire yet to heare their emphaticall expressions, and lively action; such is the milde temper of their spirits that they cannot endure objurgations, or scoldings. An *Indian Sagomore* once hearing an *English* woman scold with her husband, her quicke utterance exceeding his apprehension, her active lungs thundering in his eares, expelled him the house; from whence he went to the next neighbour, where he related the unseemelinesse of her behaviour; her language being strange to him, hee expressed it as strangely, telling them how she cryed Nannana Nannana Nannana Nan, saying he was a great foole to give her the audience, and no correction for usurping his charter, and abusing him by her tongue. I have beene amongst diverse of them, yet did I never see any falling out amongst them, not so much as crosse words, or reviling speeches, which might provoke to blowes. And whereas it is the custome of many people in their games, if they see the dice runne crosse or their cards not answere their expectations: what cursing and swearing, what imprecations, and raylings, fightings and stabbings oftentimes proceede from their testy spleene. How doe their blustering passions, make the place troublesome to themselves and others? But I have knowne when foure of these milder spirits have sit downe staking their treasures, where they have plaied foure and twentie houres, neither eating drinking or sleeping in the Interim; nay which is most to be wondered at, not quarreling, but as they came thither in peace so they depart in peace: when he that had lost all his *wampompeage*, his house, his kettle, his beaver, his hatchet, his knife, yea all his little all, having nothing left but his naked selfe, was as merry as they that won it: so in sports of activitie at footeball though they play never so fiercely to outward appearance, yet angrerboyling blood never streames in their cooler veines, if any man be throwne he laughes out his soyle, there is no seeking of revenge, no quarreling, no bloody noses, scratched faces, blacke eyes, broken shinnes, no brused members, or crushed ribs, the lamentables effects of rage; but the goale being wonne, the goods on the one side lost; friends they were at the footeball, and friends they must meete at the kettle. I never heard yet of that *Indian* that was his neighbours homicide or vexation by his malepart, saucy, or uncivill tongue: laughter in them is not common, seldome exceeding a smile, never breaking out into such a lowd laughter, as doe many of our *English*. Of all things they love not to be laught at upon any occasion; if a man be in trade with them and the bargaine be almost strucke, if they perceive you laugh, they will scarce proceed, supposing you laugh because you have cheated them: the *Crocodiles* teares may sooner deceive them, than the *Hienas* smiles: although they be not much addicted to laughter, yet are they not of a dumpish sad nature, but rather naturally chearefull: As I never saw a gigling *Democrite*, so I never saw a teare dropping *Heraclite*; no disaster being so prevalent as to open the flood-gate of their eyes, saving the death of friends, for whom they lament most exceedingly.

CHAP. XX.
Of their women, their dispositions, employments, usage by their husbands, their apparell, and modesty.

To satisfie the curious eye of women-readers, who otherwise might thinke their sex forgotten, or not worthy a record, let them peruse these few lines, wherein they may see their owne happinesse, if weighed in the womans ballance of these ruder *Indians*, who scorne the tuterings of their wives, or to admit them as their equals, though their qualities and industrious deservings may justly claime the preheminence, and command better usage and more conjugall esteeme, their persons and features being every way correspondent, their qualifications more excellent, being more loving, pittifull, and modest, milde, provident, and laborious than their lazie husbands. Their employments be many: First their building of houses, whose frames are formed like our garden-arbours, something more round, very strong and handsome, covered with close-wrought mats of their owne weaving, which deny entrance to any drop of raine, though it come both fierce and long, neither can the piercing North winde finde a crannie, through which he can conveigh his cooling breath, they be warmer than our *English* houses; at the top is a square hole for the smoakes evacuation, which in rainy weather is covered with a pluver; these bee such smoakie dwellings, that when there is good fires, they are not able to stand upright, but lie all along under the smoake, never using any stooles or chaires, it being as rare to see an *Indian* sit on a stoole at home, as it is strange to see an *English* man sit on his heeles abroad. Their houses are smaller in the Summer, when their families be dispersed, by reason of heate and occasions. In Winter they make some fiftie or threescore foote long, fortie or fiftie men being inmates under one roofe; and as is their husbands occasion these poore tectonists are often troubled like snailes, to carrie their houses on their backs sometime to fishing-places, other times to hunting-places, after that to a planting place, where it abides the longest: an other work is their planting of corne, wherein they exceede our *English* husband-men, keeping it so cleare with their Clamme shell-hooes, as if it were a garden rather than a corne-field, not suffering a choaking weede to advance his audacious head above their infant corne, or an undermining worme to spoile his spurnes. Their corne being ripe, they gather it, and drying it hard in the Sunne, conveigh it to their barnes, which be great holes digged in the ground in forme of a brasse pot, seeled with rinds of trees, wherein they put their corne, covering it from the inquisitive search of their gurmandizing husbands, who would eate up both their allowed portion, and reserved feede, if they knew where to finde it. But our hogges having found a way to unhindge their barne doores, and robbe their garners, they are glad to implore their husbands helpe to roule the bodies of trees over their holes, to prevent those pioners, whose theeverie they as much hate as their flesh. An other of their employments is their Summer processions to get Lobsters for their husbands, wherewith they baite their hookes when they goe a fishing for Basse or Codfish. This is an every dayes walke, be the weather cold or hot, the waters rough or calme, they must dive sometimes over head and eares for a Lobster, which often shakes them by their hands with a churlish nippe, and bids them adiew. The tide being spent, they trudge home two or three miles, with a hundred weight of Lobsters at their backs, and if none, a hundred scoules meete them at home, and a hungry belly for two dayes after. Their husbands having caught any fish, they bring it in their boates as farre as they can by water, and there leave it; as it was their care to catch it, so it must be their wives paines to fetch it home, or fast: which done, they must dresse it and cooke it, dish it, and present it, see it eaten over their shoulders; and their loggerships having filled their paunches, their sweete lullabies scramble for their scrappes. In the Summer these *Indian* women when Lobsters be in their plenty and prime, they drie them to keepe for Winter, erecting scaffolds in the hot sun-shine, making fires likewise underneath them, by whose smoake the flies are expelled, till the substance remain hard and drie. In this manner they drie Basse and other fishes without salt, cutting them very thinne to dry suddainely, before the flies spoile them, or the raine moist them, having a speciall care to hang them in their smoakie houses, in the night and dankish weather.

In Summer they gather flagges, of which they make Matts for houses, and Hempe and Rushes, with dying stuffe of which they make curious baskets with intermixed colours and protractures of antique Imagerie: these baskets be of all sizes from a quart to a quarter, in which they carry their luggage. In winter time they are their husbands Caterers, trudging to the Clamm bankes for their belly timber, and their Porters to lugge home their Venison which their lazinesse exposes to the Woolves till they impose it upon their wives shoulders. They likewise sew their husbands shooes, and weave coates of Turkie feathers, besides all their ordinary household drudgerie which daily lies upon them, so that a bigge bellie hinders no businesse, nor a childebirth takes much time, but the young Infant being greased and footed, wrapt in a Beaver skin, bound to his good behaviour with his feete up to his bumme, upon a board two foote long and one foot broade, his face exposed to all nipping weather; this little *Pappouse* travells about with his bare footed mother to paddle in the Icie Clammbankes after three or foure dayes of age have sealed his passeboard and his mothers recoverie. For their carriage it is very civill, smiles being the greatest grace of their mirth; their musick is lullabies to quiet their children, who generally are as quiet as if they had neither spleene or lungs. To heare one of these *Indians* unseene, a good eare might easily mistake their untaught voyce for the warbling of a well tuned instrument. Such command have they of their voices. These womens modesty drives them to weare more cloathes than their men, having alwayes a coate of cloath or skinnes wrapt like a blanket about their loynes, reaching downe to their hammes which they never put off in company. If a husband have a minde to sell his wives Beaver, petticote, as sometimes he doth, shee will not put it off untill shee have another to put on: commendable is their milde carriage and obedience to their husbands, notwithstanding all this their customarie churlishnesse and salvage inhumanitie, not seeming to delight in frownes or offering to word it with their lords, not presuming to proclaime their female superiority to the usurping of the least title of their husbands charter, but rest themselves content under their helplesse condition, counting it the womans portion: since the *English* arrivall comparison hath made them miserable, for seeing the kind usage of the *English* to their wives, they doe as much condemne their husbands for unkindnesse, and commend the *English* for their love. As their husbands commending themselves for their wit in keeping their wives industrious, doe condemne the *English* for their folly in spoyling good working creatures. These women resort often to the *English* houses, where *pares cum paribus congregatæ*, in Sex I meane, they do somewhat ease their miserie by complaining and seldome part without a releefe: If her husband come to seeke for his *Squaw* and beginne to bluster, the *English* woman betakes her to her armes which are the warlike Ladle, and the scalding liquors, threatning blistering to the naked runnaway, who is soone expelled by such liquid comminations. In a word to conclude this womans historie, their love to the *English* hath deserved no small esteeme, ever presenting them some thing that is either rare or desired, as Strawberries, Hurtleberries, Rasberries, Gooseberries, Cherries, Plummes, Fish, and other such gifts as their poore treasury yeelds them. But now it may be, that this relation of the churlish and inhumane behaviour of these ruder *Indians* towards their patient wives, may confirme some in the beliefe of an aspersion, which I have often heard men cast upon the *English* there, as if they should learne of the *Indians* to use their wives in the like manner, and to bring them to the same subjection, as to sit on the lower hand, and to carrie water, and the like drudgerie: but if my owne experience may out-ballance an ill-grounded scandalous rumour, I doe assure you, upon my credit and reputation, that there is no such matter, but the women finde there as much love, respect, and ease, as here in old *England*. I will not deny, but that some poore people may carrie their owne water, and doe not the poorer sort in *England* doe the same, witnesse your *London* Tankerd-bearers, and your countrie-cottagers? But this may well be knowne to be nothing, but the rancorous venome of some that beare no good will to the plantation. For what neede they carrie water, seeing every one hath a Spring at his doore, or the Sea by his house? Thus much for the satisfaction of women, touching this entrenchment upon their prerogative, as also concerning the relation of these *Indian* Squawes.

THE EDITORS' COMMENT

New England's Prospect relayed observations William Wood gathered as the Massachusetts Bay Colony was being established in the early 1630s. Wood's chapters describe the region's geography and catalogue the items he imagined would be useful as commodities or supplies. His promotional text acted as an orienting device for readers who had never traveled to the region and a reassuring publicity campaign intended for investors and prospective settlers. Wood's detailed descriptions of abundant fields and forests present those lands as resources that settlers could easily transform into commodities. Wood sometimes recognized that Wampanoag peoples' labor shaped fields and forests with planting and controlled burning, such as when he observed that Wampanoag agricultural practices produced yields in excess of English planting. He also hinted at the importance of diplomacy in the Wôpanâak language by including an "Indian vocabulary (not printed in this volume)," even as he presented the word lists as entertaining for readers who had no plans to leave England but found an "unknown" language to be of interest. Wood maintained this balance between giving practical advice based on careful observations and narratively packaging the lands and people he observed to align with English preconceptions. For example, while acknowledging Wampanoag women's agricultural labor, Wood painted the lands as naturally abundant and ready for English settlers, and he made sweeping proclamations about Indigenous peoples, departing from detailed accounts of Native individuals by settlers like Edward Winslow to describe Wampanoag people within cultural and racial types familiar to English readers. He likely drew these depictions from his readings of existing colonial literatures rather than from his own experiences. In these cases, *New England's Prospect*, like the narratives by Smith, Champlain, and Gorges, does not offer a documentary account but transformed observations into descriptions capable of convincing skeptical readers of the many "prospects" settlers might find in Massachusetts Bay.

Thomas Morton:
New English Canaan

NEW ENGLISH CANAAN
OR
NEW CANAAN.

Containing an Abstract of New England,

Composed in three Bookes.

The first Booke setting forth the originall of the
Natives, their Manners and Customes, together with
their tractable Nature and Love towards the English.

The second Booke setting forth the naturall
Indowments of the Country, and what staple
Commodities it yealdeth.

The third Booke setting forth, what people are planted
there, their prosperity, what remarkable accidents have
happened since the first planting of it, together with
their Tenents and practice of their Church.

Written by Thomas Morton of Cliffords Inne gent,
*upon tenne yeares knowledge and experiment
of the Country.*

Printed at AMSTERDAM,
*By JACOB FREDERICK STAM.
In the Yeare* 1637.

To the right honorable, the Lords and others of his Majesties most honorable privy Councell, Commissioners for the Government of all his Majesties forraigne Provinces.

Right honorable,

THE wise zeale which I beare to the advancement of the glory of God, the honor of his Majesty, and the good of the weale publike hath incouraged mee to compose this abstract, being the modell of a Rich, hopefull and very beautifull Country worthy the Title of Natures Masterpeece, and may be lost by too much sufferance. It is but a widowes mite, yet all the wrong and rapine hath left mee to bring from thence, where I have indevoured my best, bound by my allegeance, to doe his Majesty service. This in all humility I present as an offering, wherewith I prostrate my selfe at your honorable footstoole. If you please to vouchsafe it may receave a blessing from the Luster of your gracious Beames, you shall make your vassaile happy, in that hee yet doth live to shew how ready hee is, and always hath bin, to sacrifice hi dearest blood, as becomth a loyall subject, for the honor of his native Country. Being

Your honors humble vassaile
THOMAS MORTON.

The Epistle to the Reader.

GENTLE READER,

I Present to the publike view an abstract of New England, which I have undertaken to compose by the incouragment of such genious spirits as have been studious of the inlargment of his Majesties Territories; being not formerly satisfied by the relations of such as, through haste, have taken but a superficiall survey thereof: which thing time hath enabled mee to performe more punctually to the life, and to give a more exact accompt of what hath been required. I have therefore beene willing to doe my indevoure to communicat the knowledge which I have gained and collected together, by mine owne observation in the time of my many yeares residence in those parts, to my loving Country men: For the better information of all such as are desirous to be made partakers of the blessings of God in that fertile Soyle, as well as those that, out of Curiosity onely, have bin inquisitive after novelties. And the rather for that I have observed how divers persons (not so well affected to the weale publike in mine opinion), out of respect to their owne private ends, have laboured to keepe both the practise of the people there, and the Reall worth of that eminent Country concealed from publike knowledge; both which I have abundantly in this discourse layd open: yet if it be well accepted, I shall esteeme my selfe sufficiently rewardded for my undertaking, and rest,

Your Wellwisher.

THOMAS MORTON.

In laudem Authoris.

T' *Excuse the Author ere the worke be shewne*
   Is accusation in it selfe alone;
And to commend him might seeme oversight;
So divers are th' opinions of this age,
So quick and apt, to taxe the moderne stage,
That hard his taske is that must please in all:
Example have wee from great Cæsars fall.
But is the sonne to be dislik'd and blam'd,
Because the mole is of his face asham'd?
The fault is in the beast, not in the sonne;
Give sicke mouthes sweete meates, fy! they relish none.
But to the sound in censure, he commends
His love unto his Country; his true ends,
To modell out a Land of so much worth
As untill now noe traveller setteth forth;
Faire Canaans second selfe, second to none,
Natures rich Magazine till now unknowne.
Then here survay what nature hath in store,
And graunt him love for this. He craves no more.

                                      R. O. Gen.

Sir Christoffer Gardiner, Knight.

In laudem Authoris.

T*his worke a matchles mirror is, that shewes
The Humors of the seperatiste, and those*
*So truely personated by thy pen.
I was amaz'd to see't; herein all men
May plainely see, as in an inter-lude,
Each actor figure; and the scene well view'd
In Comick, Tragick, and in a pastorall strife,
For tyth of mint and Cummin, shewes their life
Nothing but opposition gainst the right
Of sacred Majestie: men full of spight,
Goodnes abuseing, turning vertue out
Of Dores, to whipping, stocking, and full bent
To plotting mischeife gainst the innocent,
Burning their houses, as if ordained by fate,
In spight of Lawe, to be made ruinate.
This taske is well perform'd, and patience be
Thy present comfort, and thy constancy
Thine honor; and this glasse, where it shall come,
Shall sing thy praises till the day of doome.*

Sir C. G.

In laudem Authoris.

B UT *that I rather pitty, I confesse,*
The practise of their Church, I could expresse
Myselfe a Satyrist, whose smarting fanges
Should strike it with a palsy, and the panges
Beget a feare to tempt the Majesty
Of those, or mortall Gods. Will they defie
The Thundring Jove? Like children they desire,
Such is their zeale, to sport themselves with fire:
So have I seene an angry Fly presume
To strike a burning taper, and consume
His feeble wings. Why, in an aire so milde,
Are they so monstrous growne up, and so vilde,
That Salvages can of themselves espy
Their errors, brand their names with infamy?
What! is their zeale for blood like Cyrus thirst?
Will they be over head and eares a curst?
A cruell way to found a Church on! noe,
T'is not their zeale but fury blinds them soe,
And pricks their malice on like fier to joyne,
And offer up the sacrifice of Kain.
Jonas, thou hast done well to call these men
Home to repentance, with thy painefull pen.

F. C. Armiger.

NEW ENGLISH CANAAN,
OR
NEW CANAAN.

The Authors Prologue.

IF art and industry should doe as much
As Nature hath for Canaan, not such
Another place, for benefit and rest,
In all the universe can be possest.
The more we proove it by discovery,
The more delight each object to the eye
Procures; as if the elements had here
Bin reconcil'd, and pleas'd it should appeare
Like a faire virgin, longing to be sped
And meete her lover in a Nuptiall bed,
Deck'd in rich ornaments t' advaunce her state
And excellence, being most fortunate
When most enjoy'd: so would our Canaan be
If well imploy'd by art and industry;
Whose offspring now, shewes that her fruitfull wombe,
Not being enjoy'd, is like a glorious tombe,
Admired things producing which there dye,
And ly fast bound in darck obscurity:
The worth of which, in each particuler,
Who list to know, this abstract will declare.

NEW ENGLISH CANAAN,
OR
NEW CANAAN.

The first Booke.

Containing the originall of the Natives, their
manners & Customes, with their tractable
nature and love towards the English.

CHAP. I.
*Prooving New England the principall part of all America,
and most commodious and fitt for habitation.*

THE wise Creator of the universall Globe hath placed a
golden meane betwixt two extreames; I meane the temperate Zones, betwixt the hote and cold; and every Creature, that
participates of Heavens blessings with in the Compasse of that
golden meane, is made most apt and fit for man to use, who
likewise by that wisedome is ordained to be the Lord of all.
This globe may be his glasse, to teach him how to use moderation and discretion, both in his actions and intentions, The
wise man sayes, give mee neither riches nor poverty; why?
Riches might make him proud like Nebuchadne-
Use of zar, and poverty despaire like Jobs wife; but a
vegetatives. meane betweene both. So it is likewise in the use
of Vegetatives, that which hath too much Heate
or too much Colde, is said to be venenum: so in the use of
sensitives, all those Animals, of what genus or species soever
they be, if they participate of heate or cold in the superlative
are said to be *Inimica naturæ*, as in some Fishes about the Isle
of Sall, and those Ilandes adjoyninge between the Tropickes;
Fish poysonous their participatinge of heate and cold, in the
about the Isle of superlative, is made most manifest, one of which
Sall. poysoned a whole Ships company that eate of it.
And so it is in Vipers, Toades, and Snakes, that have heate or
cold in the superlative degree.

Therefore the Creatures that participate of heate and cold in
a meane, are best and holsomest: And so it is in the choyse of
love, the middell Zone betweene the two extreames is best, and

662

it is therefore called *Zona temperata*, and is in the golden
meane; and all those landes lying under that Zone, most requisite and fitt for habitation. In Cosmography, the
two extreames are called, the one *Torrida Zona*,
lying betweene the Tropickes, the other *Frigida
Zona*, lying neare the poles: all the landes lying under either of
these Zones, by reason they doe participate too much of heate
or cold, are very inconvenient, and are accompanied with many
evils. And allthough I am not of opinion with Aristotle, that
the landes under *Torrida Zona* are alltogether uninhabited, I
my selfe having beene so neare the equinoctiall line that I have
had the Sunn for my Zenith and seene proofe to the contrary,
yet cannot I deny but that it is accompanied with many inconveniences, as that Fish and Flesh both will taint in those partes,
notwithstanding the use of Salt which cannot be wanting
there, ordained by natures hande-worke; And that
is a great hinderance to the setting forth and
supply of navigation, the very Sinewes of a florishing Commonwealth. Then barrennesse, caused through want
of raines, for in most of those partes of the world it is seldome
accustomed to raine untill the time of the Tornathees (as the
Portingals phrase is, who lived there) and then it will raine
about 40. dayes together, which moisture serveth
to fructify the earth for all the yeare after, duringe
which time is seene no raine at all: the heate and
cold, and length of day and night, being much
alike, with little difference. And these raines are
caused by the turning of the windes, which else betweene the
Tropickes doe blow Trade, that is allwayes one way. For next
the Tropicke of Cancer it is constantly North-East, and next
the Tropicke of Capricorne it is Southwest; so that the windes
comming from the Poles, do keepe the aire in those partes
coole, and make it temperate and the partes habitable, were it
not for those and other inconveniences.

This *Torrida Zona* is good for Grashoppers: and *Zona Temperata* for the Ant and Bee. But *Frigida Zona* is good for neither, as by lamentable experience of Captaine
Davis fate is manifest, who in his inquest of the
Northwest passage for the East India trade was
frozen to death. And therefore, for *Frigida Zona*, I agree with

*Zona
temperata, the
Golden meane.*

*Salt aboundeth
under the
Tropicks.*

Raine 40.
*dayes about
August
betweene
Cancer and the
Line.*

*Capt. Davis
froze to death.*

Aristotle that it is unfit for habitation: and I know by the
Groene Land Course of the cælestiall globe that in Groeneland,
too cold for many Degrees short of the Pole Articke, the place
habitation. is too cold, by reason of the Sunns absence almost
six monethes, and the land under the continuall power of the
frost; which thinge many more Navigators have prooved with
pittifull experience of their wintringe there, as appeareth by
the history. I thinke they will not venture to winter there
againe for an India mine.

And as it is found by our Nation under the Pole Articke, so
it is likewise to be found under the Antarticke Pole; yet what
hazard will not an industrious minde and couragious spirit
undergoe, according to that of the Poet: *Impiger extremos
currit Mercator ad Indos per mare pauperiem fugiens, per saxa,
per ignes.* And all to gett and hord up like the Ant and the Bee;
and yet, as Salomon saith, he cannot tell whether a foole or a
wise man shall enjoy it. Therefore let us leave these two
extreames, with their inconveniences, and indeavour to finde
out this golden meane, so free from any one of them. Behold
the secret wisedome of allmighty God, and love unto our Salomon, to raise a man of a lardge hart, full of worthy abilities, to
be the Index or Loadstarre, that doth point out unto the
Sir Ferdinando English Nation with ease and comfort how to
Gorges the finde it out. And this the noble minded Gentle-
originall cause man, Sir Ferdinando Gorges, Knight, zealous for
of plantinge the glory of God, the honor of his Majesty and the
New England. benefit of the weale publicke, hath done a great worke for the
good of his Country.

And herein this, the wondrous wisedome and love of God,
The Salvages is shewne, by sending to the place his Minister, to
dyed of the sweepe away by heapes the Salvages; and also
plague. giving him length of dayes to see the same performed after his enterprise was begunne, for the propagation
of the Church of Christ.

This judicious Gentleman hath found this goulden meane to
be scituated about the middle of those two extreames, and for
directions you may proove it thus: Counting the space betweene
the Line and either of the Poles, in true proportion, you shall
finde it to be 90. Degrees: then must we finde the meane to be
neare unto the Center of 90. and that is about 45. Degrees, and

then incline unto the Sotherne side of that Center, properly for the benefit of heate, remembringe that *Sol & Homo generàt hominem*; and then keepe us on that same side, and see what Land is to be found there, and we shall easily discerne that new England is on the South side of that Center.

New Engl. is placed in the golden meane. For that Country doth beginne her boundes at 40. Degrees of Northerne latitude, and endes at 45. Degrees of the same latitude, and doth participate of heate and cold indifferently, but is oppressed with neither: and therefore may be truly sayd to be within the compasse of that golden meane, most apt and fit for habitation and generation, being placed by Allmighty God, the great Creator, under that Zone called *Zona temperata*; and is therefore most fitt for the generation and habitation of our English nation, of all other, who are more neere neighbours to the Northerne Pole, whose Land lyeth betweene 50. and 54. Degrees of the selfesame latitude: now this new England, though it be nearer *New England 10. Degrees neerer the line then old England.* to the line then that old England by 10. Degrees of latitude, yet doth not this exceede that other in heate or cold, by reason of the cituation of it; for as the Coast lyeth, being circularly Northeast and Southwest, opposite towards the Sunnes risinge, which makes his course over the Ocean, it can have litle or no reflecting heat of the Sunbeames, by reason of the continuall motion of the waters makinge the aire there the cooler and the constanter; so that for the temperature of the Climent, sweetnesse of the aire, fertility of the Soile, and small number of the Salvages (which might seeme a rubb in the way off an effeminate minde,) this Country of new England is by all judicious men accounted the principall part of all America for habitation and the commodiousnesse of the Sea, Ships there not being subject to wormes as in Virginea and other places, and not to be paraleld in all Christendome. The Massachussets being the middell part thereof, is a very beautifull Land, not mountany nor inclininge *The Massachussets in the middel of New England.* to mountany, lyeth in 42. Degrees, and 30. minutes, and hath as yet the greatest number of inhabitants; and hath a very large bay to it divided by Islands into 4 great bayes, where shippinge may safely ride, all windes and weathers, the windes in those partes being not so violent as in England by many Degrees: for there are no

The Windes not shrubbs seene to leane from the windes, as by the
so violent in Sea Coast of England I have seene them leane,
New England. and the groundage is a sandy sleech, free from
rockes to gaule Cables, but is good for anchorage: the rest of
the Planters are disperst among the Coasts betweene 41. and
44. Degrees of Latitude, and as yet, have made very little way
into the inland. The riches of which Country I have set forth
in this abstract as in a Landskipp, for the better information of
the Travellers; which hee may peruse and plainely perceave by
the demonstration of it, that it is nothing inferior to Canaan
of Israel, but a kind of paralell to it in all points.

CHAP. II.
Of the originall of the Natives.

In the yeare since the incarnation of Christ, 1622, it was my
chance to be landed in the parts of New England, where I
found two sortes of people, the one Christians, the other Infidels; these I found most full of humanity, and more friendly
then the other: as shall hereafter be made apparant in Dew-
Course by their severall actions from time to time, whilest I
lived among them. After my arrivall in those partes, I endeavoured by all the wayes and meanes that I could to find out from
what people, or nation, the Natives of New England might be
conjectured originlly to proceede; and by continuance and
conversation amongst them, I attaned to so much of their language, as by all probable conjecture may make the same mani-
The Natives fest: for it hath been found by divers, and those of
have a mixed good judgement, that the Natives of this Country
language. doe use very many wordes, both of Greeke and
Latine, to the same signification that the Latins and Greekes
have done; as *en animia*, when an Indian expresseth that hee
doth anything with a good will; and *Pascopan*
Pasco Pan signifieth gredy gut, this being the name of an
greedy gutt. Indian that was so called of a Child, through the
greedinesse of his minde and much eating, for *Pasco* in Latine
signifieth to feede, and *Pan* in Greeke signifieth all; and *Pasco*
Mona an *nantum, quasi pasco nondum*, halfe starved, or not
Island. eating, as yet; *Equa coge*, set it upright; *Mona* is an

Island in their language, *quasi Monon*, that is alone, for an Island is a peece or plott of ground standing alone, and devided from the mane Land by force of water.

Cos a Whetstone. *Cos* is a Whetstone with them. *Hame* an instrument to take fish. Many places doe retaine the name of *Pan*, as Pantneket and *Matta pan*, so that it may be thought that these people heretofore have had the name of *Pan* in great reverence and estimation, and it may bee *Pan the Shepheards God.* have worshipped *Pan* the great God of the Heathens: Howsoever they doe use no manner of worship at all now: and it is most likely that the Natives of this Country are descended from people bred upon that part of the world which is towards the Tropicke of Cancer, for they doe still retaine the memory of some of the Starres one that part of the Cælestiall Globe, as the North-starre, which with them is called Maske, for Maske in their Language signifieth a Beare: and they doe divide the windes into eight partes, and it seemes originally have had some litterature amongst them, which time hath Cancelled and worne out of use.

And whereas it hath beene the opinion of some men, which shall be nameles, that the Natives of New-England may pro- *Not to proceede from the Tartars.* ceede from the race of the Tartars, and come from Tartaria into those partes, over the frozen Sea, I see no probality for any such Conjecture; for as much as a people once setled must be remooved by compulsion, or else tempted thereunto in hope of better fortunes, upon commendations of the place unto which they should be drawne to remoove: and if it may be thought that these people came over the frozen Sea, then would it be by compulsion? if so, then by whome, or when? or what part of this mane continent may *No part of America knowne to be neare Tartary.* be thought to border upon the Country of the Tartars, it is yet unknowne: and it is not like, that a people well enough at ease will of their one accord undertake to travayle over a Sea of Ice, considering how many difficulties they shall encounter with; as first, whether there be any Land at the end of their unknowne way, no Land beinge in view; then want of Food to sustane life in the meane time upon that Sea of Ice; or how should they doe for Fuell, to keepe them at night from freezing to death, which will not bee had in such a place. But it may perhaps be granted that the

Natives of this Country might originally come of the scattred
Trojans: For after that Brutus, who was the forth
Why Brutus left Latium. from Aneas, left Latium upon the conflict had
with the Latines, (where although hee gave them
a great overthrow, to the Slaughter of their grand Captaine and
many other of the Heroes of Latium, yet hee held it more safety
to depart unto some other place and people, then by staying to
runne the hazard of an unquiet life or doubtfull Conquest,
which as history maketh mention hee performed,) this people
were dispersed: there is no question but the people that lived
with him, by reason of their conversation with the Græcians and
Latines, had a mixed language that participated of both, whatsoever was that which was proper to their owne nation at first I
know not: for this is commonly seene where 2. nations traffique
together, the one indevouring to understand the others meaning makes them both many times speak a mixed
Two nations meetinge make a mixt language. language, as is approved by the Natives of New
England, through the coveteous desire they have
to commerce with our nation and wee with them.

And when Brutus did depart from Latium, we doe not finde
that his whole number went with him at once, or arrived at one
place; and being put to Sea might encounter with a storme that
would carry them out of sight of Land, and then they might
sayle God knoweth whether, and so might be put upon this
Coast, as well as any other. Compasse I beleeve they had none
Dædalus the first that used Sayles. in those dayes; Sayles they might have, (which
Dædalus the first inventor thereof left to after
ages, having taught his Sonne Icarus the use of it,
who to this Cost found how dangerous it is for a Sonne not to
Icarus the second that used Sayles. observe the precepts of a wise Father, so that the
Icarian Sea now retaines the memory of it to this
day,) and Victuals they might have good store,
and many other things fittinge; oares without all question they
would store themselves with, in such a case; but for the use of
Troy destroyed about Sauls time. Compasse, there is no mention made of it at that
time (which was much about Sauls time, the first
that was made King of Israell.) Yet it is thought
The Loadstone in Salomons time. (and that not without good reason for it) that the
use of the Loadstone and Compasse was knowne
in Salomons time, for as much as hee sent Shippes

to fetch of the gould of Ophir, to adorne and bewtify that magnificent Temple of Hierusalem by him built for the glory of Almighty God, and by his speciall appointment: and it is held by Cosmographers to be 3. yeares voyage from Hierusalem to Ophir, and it is conceaved that such a voyage could not have beene performed, without the helpe of the Loadstone and Compasse.

And why should any man thinke the Natives of New England to be the gleanings of all Nations, onely because by the pronunciation and termination their words seeme to trench upon severall languages, when time hath not furnished him with the interpretation thereof. The thinge that must induce a man of reasonable capacity to any maner of conjecture of their originall, must be the sence and signification of the words, principally to frame this argument by, when hee shall drawe to any conclusion thereupon: otherwise hee shall but runne rounde about a maze (as some of the fantasticall tribe use to do about the tythe of mint and comin.) Therefore, since I have had the approbation of Sir Christopher Gardiner, Knight, an able gentl. that lived amongst them, and of David Tompson, a Scottish gentl. that likewise was conversant with those people, both Scollers and Travellers that were diligent in taking notice of these things, as men of good judgement, and that have bin in those parts any time, besides others of lesse, now I am bold to conclude that the originall of the Natives of New England may be well conjectured to be from the scattered Trojans, after such time as Brutus departed from Latium.

CHAP. III.
Of a great mortality that happened amongst the Natives of New England, neere about the time that the English came there to plant.

It fortuned some few yeares before the English came to inhabit at new Plimmouth, in New England, that upon some distast given in the Massachussets bay by Frenchmen, then trading there with the Natives for beaver, they set upon the men at such advantage that they killed manie of them, burned their shipp, then riding at Anchor by an Island there, now called Peddocks Island, in memory of Leonard Peddock that landed there, (where many wilde Anckies haunted that time, which hee thought had bin tame,) distributing them unto 5. Sachems, which were Lords of the severall territories adjoyninge: they did keepe them so longe as they lived, onely to sport themselves *Five Frenchmen* at them, and made these five Frenchmen fetch *kept by the* them wood and water, which is the generall worke *Salvages.* that they require of a servant. One of these five men, out livinge the rest, had learned so much of their language as to rebuke them for their bloudy deede, saying that God would be angry with them for it, and that hee would in his displeasure destroy them; but the Salvages (it seemes boasting of their strenght,) replyed and sayd, that they were so many that God could not kill them.

But contrary wise, in short time after the hand *The Plague fell* of God fell heavily upon them, with such a mortall *on the Indians.* stroake that they died on heapes as they lay in their houses; and the living, that were able to shift for themselves, would runne away and let them dy, and let there Carkases ly above the ground without buriall. For in a place where many inhabited, there hath been but one left a live to tell what *The livinge not* became of the rest; the livinge being (as it seemes) *able to bury the* not able to bury the dead, they were left for *dead.* Crowes, Kites and vermin to pray upon. And the bones and skulls upon the severall places of their habitations made such a spectacle after my comming into those partes, that, as I travailed in that Forrest nere the Massachussets, it seemed to mee a new found Golgatha.

But otherwise, it is the custome of those Indian people to bury their dead ceremoniously and carefully, and then to abandon that place, because they have no desire the place should put them in minde of mortality: and this mortality was not ended when the Brownists of new Plimmouth were setled at Patuxet in New England: and by all likelyhood the sicknesse that these Indians died of was the Plague, as by conference with them since my arrivall and habitation in those partes, I have learned. And by this meanes there is as yet but a small number of Salvages in New England, to that which hath beene in former time, and the place is made so much the more fitt for the English Nation to inhabit in, and erect in it *2 Sam.* 24. Temples to the glory of God.

CHAP. IV.
Of their Houses and Habitations.

THE Natives of New England are accustomed to build them houses much like the wild Irish; they gather Poles in the woodes and put the great end of them in the ground, placinge them in forme of a circle or circumference, and, bendinge the topps of them in forme of an Arch, they bind them together with the Barke of Walnut trees, which is wondrous tuffe, so that they make the same round on the Topp for the smooke of their fire to assend and passe through; these they cover with matts, some made of reeds and some of longe flagges, or sedge, finely sowed together with needles made of the splinter bones of a Cranes legge, with threeds made of their Indian hempe, which their groueth naturally, leaving severall places for dores, which are covered with mats, which may be rowled up and let downe againe at their pleasures, making use of the severall dores, according as the winde fitts. The fire is alwayes made in the middest of the house, with winde fals commonly: yet some times they fell a tree that groweth neere the house, and, by drawing in the end thereof, maintaine the fire on both sids, burning the tree by Degrees shorter and shorter, untill it be all consumed; for it burneth night and day. Their lodging is made in three places of the house about the fire; they lye upon plankes, commonly about a foote or 18. inches above the ground, raised upon railes that are borne up upon forks; they lay mats under them, and Coats of Deares skinnes, otters, beavers, Racownes, and of Beares hides, all which they have dressed and converted into good lether, with the haire on, for their coverings: and in this manner they lye as warme as they desire. In the night they take their rest; in the day time, either the kettle is on with fish or flesh, by no allowance, or else the fire is imployed in roasting of fishes, which they delight in. The aire doeth beget good stomacks, and they feede continually, and are no niggards of their vittels; for they are willing that any one shall eate with them. Nay, if any one that shall come into their houses and there fall a sleepe, when they see him disposed to lye downe, they will spreade a matt for him of their owne accord, and lay a roule of skinnes for a boulster, and let him lye. If hee sleepe untill their meate be dished up, they will set a wooden boule of meate by him that sleepeth, and wake him saying, Cattup keene Meckin: That is, If you be hungry, there is meat for you, where if you will eate you may. Such is their Humanity.

Likewise, when they are minded to remoove, they carry away the mats with them; other materiales the place adjoyning will yeald. They use not to winter and summer in one place, for that would be a reason to make fuell scarse; but, after the manner of the gentry of Civilized natives, remoove for their pleasures; some times to their hunting places, where they remaine keeping good hospitality for that season; and sometimes to their fishing places, where they abide for that season likewise: and at the spring, when fish comes in plentifully, they have meetinges from severall places, where they exercise themselves in gaminge and playing of juglinge trickes and all manner of Revelles, which they are deligted in; so that it is admirable to behould what pastime they use of severall kindes, every one striving to surpasse each other. After this manner they spend their time.

CHAP. V.
Of their Religion.

It has bin a common receaved opinion from Cicero, that there is no people so barbarous but have some worshipp or other. In this particular, I am not of opinion therein with Tully; and, surely, if hee had bin amongst those people so longe as I have bin, and converted so much with them touching this matter of Religion, hee would have changed his opinion. Neither should we have found this error, amongst the rest, by the helpe of that wodden prospect, if it had not been so unadvisedly built upon such highe land as that Coast. (all mens judgements in generall,) doth not yeeld, had hee but taken the judiciall councell of Sir William Alexander, that setts this thing forth in an exact and conclusive sentence; if hee be not too obstinate? hee would graunt that worthy writer, that these people are *sine fide*, *sine lege*, & *sine rege*, and hee hath exemplified this thinge by a familiar demonstration, which I have by longe experience observed to be true.

And, me thinks, it is absurd to say they have a kinde of worship, and not able to demonstrate whome or what it is they are accustomed to worship. For my part I am more willing to beleeve that the Elephants (which are reported to be the most intelligible of all beasts) doe worship the moone, for the reasons given by the author of this report, as Mr. Thomas May, the minion of the Muses dos recite it in his continuation of Lucans historicall poem, rather then this man: to that I must bee constrained, to conclude against him, and Cicero, that the Natives of New England have no worship nor religion at all; and I am sure it has been so observed by those that neede not the helpe of a wodden prospect for the matter.

CHAP. VI.
Of the Indians apparrell.

THE Indians in these parts do make their apparrell of the skinnes of severall sortes of beastes, and commonly of those that doe frequent those partes where they doe live; yet some of them, for variety, will have the skinnes of such beasts that frequent the partes of their neighbors, which they purchase of them by Commerce and Trade.

The Indians make good lether. These skinnes they convert into very good lether, making the same plume and soft. Some of these skinnes they dresse with the haire on, and some with the haire off; the hairy side in winter time they weare next their bodies, and in warme weather they weare the haire outwardes: they make likewise some Coates of the Feathers of Turkies, which they weave together with twine of their owne makinge, very prittily: these garments they weare like mantels knit over their shoulders, and put under their arme: they have likewise another sort of mantels, made of Mose skinnes, which beast is a great large Deere so bigge as a horse; these skinnes they commonly dresse bare, and make them wondrous white, and stripe them with size round about the borders, in forme like lace set on by a Taylor, and *Indians ingenious workemen for their garments.* some they stripe with size in workes of severall fashions very curious, according to the severall fantasies of the workemen, wherein they strive to excell one another: And Mantels made of Beares skinnes is an usuall wearinge, among the Natives that live where the Beares doe haunt: they make shooes of Mose skinnes, which is the principall leather used to that purpose; and for want of such lether (which is the strongest) they make shooes of Deeres skinnes, very handsomly and commodious; and, of such deeres skinnes as they dresse bare, they make stockinges that comes within their shooes, like a stirrop stockinge, and is fastned above at their belt, which is about their middell; Every male, *The modesty* after hee attaines unto the age which they call *of the Indian* Pubes, wereth a belt about his middell, and a *men.* broad peece of lether that goeth betweene his leggs and is tuckt up both before and behinde under that belt; and this they weare to hide their secreats of nature, which by no meanes they will suffer to be seene, so much modesty they use in that particular; those garments they allwayes put on, when they goe a huntinge, to keepe their skinnes from the brush of the Shrubbs: and when they have their Apparrell one they looke like Irish in their trouses, the Stockinges joyne so to their breeches. A good well growne deere skin is of great account with them, and it must have the tale on, or else they account it defaced; the tale being three times as long as the tales of our English Deere, yea foure times so longe, this when they travell is raped round about their body, and, with a girdle *Indians* of their making, bound round about their mid- *travaile with* dles, to which girdle is fastned a bagg, in which *materials to* *strike fire at all* his instruments be with which hee can strike fire *times.* upon any occasion.

Thus with their bow in their left hand, and their quiver of Arrowes at their back, hanging one their left shoulder with the lower end of it in their right hand, they will runne away a dogg trot untill they come to their journey end; and, in this kinde of ornament, they doe seeme to me to be hansomer then when they are in English apparrell, their gesture being answerable to their one habit and not unto ours.

Their women have shooes and stockinges to weare likewise when they please, such as the men have, but the mantle they use to cover their nakednesse with is much longer then that which the men use; for, as the men have one Deeres skinn, the women have two soed together at the full lenght, and it is so lardge that it trailes after them like a great Ladies trane; and in time I thinke they may have their Pages to beare them up; and where the men use but one Beares skin for a Mantle, the women have two soed together; and if any of their women would at any time shift one, they take that which they intend to make use of, and cast it over them round, before they shifte away the other, for modesty, being unwilling to be seene to discover their nakednesse; and the one being so cast over, they flip the other from under them in a decent manner, which is to be noted in people uncivilized; therein they seeme to have as much modesty as civilized people, and deserve to be applauded for it.

The Indians ashamed of their nakednesse.

CHAP. VII.
Of their Child-bearing, and delivery, and what manner of persons they are.

THE women of this Country are not suffered to be used for procreation untill the ripenesse of their age, at which time they weare a redd cap made of lether, in forme like to our flat caps, and this they weare for the space of 12 moneths, for all men to take notice of them that have any minde to a wife; and then it is the custome of some of their Sachems or Lords of the territories, to have the first say or maidenhead of the females. Very apt they are to be with childe, and very laborious when they beare children; yea, when they are as great as they can be: yet in that case they neither forbeare labour, nor travaile; I have seene them in that plight with burthens at their backs enough to load a horse; yet doe they not miscarry, but have a faire delivery, and a quick: their women are very good midwifes, and the women very lusty after delivery, and in a day or two will travell or trudge about. Their infants are borne with haire on their heads, and are of complexion white as our nation; but their mothers in their infancy make a bath of Wallnut leaves, huskes of Walnuts, and such things as will staine their skinne for ever, wherein they dip and washe them to make them tawny; the coloure of their haire is black, and their eyes black. These infants are carried at their mothers backs by the help of a cradle made of a board forket at both ends, whereon the childe is fast bound and wrapped in furres; his knees thrust up towards his bellie, because they may be the more usefull for them when he sitteth, which is as a dogge does

The women big with child very laborious.

Children bathed to staine the skinne.

on his bumme: and this cradle surely preserves them better
then the cradles of our nation, for as much as we finde them
well proportioned, not any of them crooked backed or wry
legged: and to give their charracter in a worde, they are as
proper men and women for feature and limbes as can be found,
for flesh and bloud as active: longe handed they are, (I never
sawe a clunchfisted Salvadg amongst them all in my time.) The
colour of their eies being so generally black made a Salvage,
that had a younge infant whose eies were gray, shewed him to
us, and said they were English mens eies; I tould the Father
that his sonne was *nan weeteo*, which is a bastard; hee replied
titta Cheshetue squaa, which is, hee could not tell, his wife
might play the whore; and this childe the father desired might
have an English name, because of the litenesse of his eies,
which his father had in admiration because of novelty amongst
their nation.

CHAP. VIII.
Of their Reverence, and respect to age.

I⊤ is a thing to be admired, and indeede made a president, that
Age honoured   a Nation yet uncivilizied should more respect age
among the   then some nations civilized, since there are so
Indians.   many precepts both of divine and humane writers
extant to instruct more Civill Nations: in that particular,
wherein they excell, the younger are allwayes obedient unto the
elder people, and at their commaunds in every respect without
grummbling; in all councels, (as therein they are circumspect
to do their acciones by advise and councell, and not rashly or
inconsiderately,) the younger mens opinion shall be heard, but
the old mens opinion and councell imbraced and followed:
besides, as the elder feede and provide for the younger in
infancy, so doe the younger, after being growne to yeares of
manhood, provide for those that be aged: and in distribution
of Acctes the elder men are first served by their dispensator;
and their counsels (especially if they be powahs) are esteemed
as oracles amongst the younger Natives.

The consideration of these things, mee thinkes, should
reduce some of our irregular young people of civilized Nations,

when this story shall come to their knowledge, to better manners, and make them ashamed of their former error in this
kinde, and to become hereafter more duetyfull; which I, as a
friend, (by observation having found,) have herein recorded
for that purpose.

CHAP. IX.
Of their pretty conjuring tricks.

Iғ we doe not judge amisse of these Salvages in accounting
them witches, yet out of all question we may be bould to
conclude them to be but weake witches, such of them as wee
call by the names of Powahs: some correspondency they have
with the Devil out of al doubt, as by some of their accions, in
which they glory, is manifested. Papasiquineo, that Sachem or
Sagamore, is a Powah of greate estimation amongst all kinde
of Salvages there: hee is at their Revels (which is the time when
a great company of Salvages meete from severall parts of the
Country, in amity with their neighbours) hath advaunced his
honor in his feats or jugling tricks (as I may right tearme them)
to the admiration of the spectators, whome hee endevoured to
perswade that he would goe under water to the further side
of a river, to broade for any man to undertake with a breath,
which thing hee performed by swimming over, and deluding
the company with casting a mist before their eies that see him
enter in and come out, but no part of the way hee has bin seene:
likewise by our English, in the heat of all summer to make Ice
appeare in a bowle of faire water; first, having the water set
before him, hee hath begunne his incantation according to
their usuall accustome, and before the same has bin ended a
thick Clowde has darkned the aire and, on a sodane, a thunder
clap hath bin heard that has amazed the natives; in an instant
hee hath shewed a firme peece of Ice to flote in the middest of
the bowle in the presence of the vulgar people, which doubtles
was done by the agility of Satan, his consort.

And by meanes of these sleights, and such like trivial things
as these, they gaine such estimation amongst the rest of the
Salvages that it is thought a very impious matter for any man
to derogate from the words of these Powahs. In so much as hee

that should slight them, is thought to commit a crime no lesse hainous amongst them as sacriledge is with us, as may appeare by this one passage, which I wil set forth for an instance.

A Salvage entertained a factor. A neighbour of mine that had entertain'd a Salvage into his service, to be his factor for the beaver trade amongst his countrymen, delivered unto him divers parcells of commodities fit for them to trade with; amongst the rest there was one coate of more esteeme then any of the other, and with this his new entertained marchant man travels amonst his countrymen to truck them away for beaver: as our custome hath bin, the Salvage went up into the Country amongst his neighbours for beaver, and returned with some, but not enough answerable to his Masteers expectation, but being called to an accompt, and especially for that one Coate of speciall note, made answer that he had given that coate to Tantoquineo, a Powah: to which his master in a rage cryed, what have I to doe with Tantoquineo? The Salvage, very angry at the matter, cryed, what you speake? you are not a very good man; wil you not give Tantoq. a coat? whats this? as if he had offered *Tantoquineo* the greatest indignity that could be devised: so great is the estimation and reverence that these people have of these Jugling Powahs, who are usually sent for when any person is sicke and ill at ease to recover them, for *An Englishman cured of a swelling.* which they receive rewards as doe our Chirgeons and Phisitions; and they doe make a trade of it, and boast of their skill where they come: One amongst the rest did undertake to cure an Englishman of a swelling of his hand for a parcell of biskett, which being delivered him hee tooke the party greived into the woods aside from company, and with the helpe of the devill, (as may be conjectured,) quickly recovered him of that swelling, and sent him about his worke againe.

CHAP. X.
Of their duels, and the honourable estimation of victory obtained thereby.

THESE Salvages are not apt to quarrell one with another: yet such hath bin the occasion that a difference hath happened which hath growne to that height that it has not bin reconciled otherwise then by combat, which hath bin performed in this manner: the two champions prepared for the fight, with their bowes in hand and a quiver full of arrowes at their backs, they *How the* have entered into the field; the Challenger and *Salvages* challenged have chosen two trees, standing within *performe theire* a little distance of each other; they have cast lotts *duells.* for the cheife of the trees, then either champion setting himselfe behinde his tree watches an advantage to let fly his shafts, and to gall his enemy; there they continue shooting at each other; if by chaunce they espie any part open, they endeavour to gall the combatant in that part, and use much agility in the performance of the taske they have in hand. Resolute they are in the execution of their vengeance, when once they have begunne; and will in no wise be daunted, or seeme to shrinck though they doe catch a clap with an arrow, but fight it out in this manner untill one or both be slaine.

I have bin shewed the places where such duels have bin performed, and have fuond the trees marked for a memoriall of *Trees marked* the Combat, where that champion hath stood that *where they* had the hap to be slaine in the duell: and they *performe a* count it the greatest honor that can be to the ser- *duell.* viving Cumbatant, to shew the scares of the wounds received in this kinde of Conflict, and if it happen to be on the arme, as those parts are most in danger in these cases, they will alwayes weare a bracelet upon that place of the arme, as a trophy of honor to their dying day.

CHAP. XI.
Of the maintaining of their Reputation.

REPUTATION is such a thing that it keepes many men in awe, even amongst Civilized nations, and is very much stood upon: it is (as one hath very well noted) the awe of great men and of Kings. And, since I have observed it to be maintained amongst Salvage people, I cannot chuse but give an instance thereof in this treatise, to confirme the common received opinion thereof.

The Sachem or Sagamore of Sagus made choise, when hee came to mans estate, of a Lady of noble discent, Daughter to Papasiquineo, the Sachem or Sagamore of the territories neare

Merrimack River, a man of the best note and estimation in all
those parts, and (as my Countryman Mr. Wood

A marriage.

declares in his prospect) a great Nigromancer; this
Lady the younge Sachem with the consent and good liking of
her father marries, and takes for his wife. Great entertainement
hee and his receaved in those parts at her fathers hands, where
they weare fested in the best manner that might be expected,
according to the Custome of their nation, with reveling and
such other solemnities as is usuall amongst them. The solemnity being ended, Papasiquineo causes a selected number of his
men to waite upon his Daughter home into those parts that did
properly belong to her Lord and husband; where the attendants
had entertainment by the Sachem of Sagus and his Countrymen: the solemnity being ended, the attendants were
gratified.

Not long after the new married Lady had a great desire to
see her father and her native country, from whence shee came;
her Lord willing to pleasure her and not deny her request,
amongst them thought to be reasonable, commanded a selected
number of his owne men to conduct his Lady to her Father,
wher, with great respect, they brought her; and, having feasted
there a while, returned to their owne country againe, leaving
the Lady to continue there at her owne pleasure, amongst her
friends and old acquaintance; where shee passed away the time
for a while, and in the end desired to returne to her Lord

An ambassage   againe. Her father, the old Papasiquineo, having
sent from   notice of her intent, sent some of his men on
Papasiquineo
to his sonne in ambassage to the younge Sachem, his sonne in
law, a Sachem. law, to let him understand that his daughter was
not willing to absent her selfe from his company any longer,
and therfore, as the messengers had in charge, desired the
younge Lord to send a convoy for her; but hee, standing upon
tearmes of honor, and the maintaining of his reputation,
returned to his father in law this answere, that, when she
departed from him, hee caused his men to waite upon her to
her fathers territories, as it did become him; but, now shee had
an intent to returne, it did become her father to send her back
with a convoy of his own people; and that it stood not with his
reputation to make himself or his men so servile, to fetch her

againe. The old Sachem Papasiquineo, having this message returned, was inraged to think that his young son in law did not esteeme him at a higher rate then to capitulate with him about the matter, and returned him this sharpe reply; that his daughters bloud and birth deserved more respect then to be so slighted; and, therefore, if he would have her company, hee were best to send or come for her.

The younge Sachem, not willing to under value himselfe and being a man of a stout spirit, did not stick to say that hee should either send her by his owne Convey, or keepe her; for hee was determined not to stoope so lowe.

So much these two Sachems stood upon tearmes of reputation with each other, the one would not send her, and the other would not send for her, least it should be any diminishing of honor on his part that should seeme to comply, that the Lady (when I came out of the Country) remained still with her father; which is a thinge worth the noting, that Salvage people should seeke to maintaine their reputation so much as they doe.

CHAP. XII.
Of their trafficke and trade one with another.

ALTHOUGH these people have not the use of navigation, whereby they may trafficke as other nations, that are civilized, use to doe, yet doe they barter for such commodi-

Beads instead of Money. ties as they have, and have a kinde of beads, insteede of money, to buy withall such things as they want, which they call Wampampeak: and it is of two sorts, the one is white, the other is of a violet coloure. These are made of the shells of fishe. The white with them is as silver with us; the other as our gould: and for these beads they buy and sell, not onely amongst themselves, but even with us.

The name of their beads Wampampeak. We have used to sell them any of our commodities for this Wampampeak, because we know we can have beaver againe of them for it: and these beads are currant in all the parts of New England, from one end of the Coast to the other.

And although some have indevoured by example to have the

like made of the same kinde of shels, yet none hath ever, as yet, attained to any perfection in the composure of them, but that the Salvages have found a great difference to be in the one and the other; and have knowne the counterfett beads from those of their owne making; and have, and doe slight them.

The skinnes of beasts are sould and bartered, to such people as have none of the same kinde in the parts where they live.

Likewise they have earthen potts of divers sizes, from a quarte to a gallon, 2. or 3. to boyle their vitels in; very stronge, though they be thin like our Iron potts.

They have dainty wooden bowles of maple, of highe price amongst them; and these are dispersed by bartering one with the other, and are but in certaine parts of the Country made, where the severall trades are appropriated to the inhabitants of those parts onely.

So likewise (at the season of the yeare) the Salvages that live by the Sea side for trade with the inlanders for fresh water, reles curious silver reles, which are bought up of such as have them not frequent in other places: chestnuts, and such like usefull things as one place affordeth, are sould to the inhabitants of another, where they are a novelty accompted amongst the natives of the land. And there is no such thing to barter withall, as is their Whampampeake.

CHAP. XIII.
Of their Magazines or Storehowses.

THESE people are not without providence, though they be uncivilized, but are carefull to preserve foede in store against winter; which is the corne that they laboure and dresse in the summer. And, although they eate freely of it, whiles it is growinge, yet have they a care to keepe a convenient portion thereof to releeve them in the dead of winter, (like to the Ant and the Bee,) which they put under ground.

What care they take to lay up corne for winter.

Their barnes are holes made in the earth, that will hold a Hogshead of corne a peece in them. In these (when their corne is out of the huske and well dried) they lay their store in greate baskets (which they make of Sparke) with matts under, about the sides, and on the top; and putting it into the place made for

it, they cover it with earth: and in this manner it is preserved
from destruction or putrifaction; to be used in case of necessity,
and not else.

And I am perswaded, that if they knew the benefit of Salte
(as they may in time,) and the meanes to make salte meate fresh
againe, they would endeaver to preserve fishe for winter, as well
as corne; and that if any thinge bring them to civility, it will be
the use of Salte, to have foode in store, which is a cheife benefit
in a civilized Commonwealth.

They begg Salte
of the English.

These people have begunne already to incline
to the use of Salte. Many of them would begge
Salte of mee for to carry home with them, that
had frequented our howses and had been acquainted with our
Salte meats: and Salte I willingly gave them, although I sould
them all things else, onely because they should be delighted
with the use there of, and thinke it a commodity of no value
in it selfe, allthough the benefit was great that might be had
by the use of it.

CHAP. XIV.
Of theire Subtilety.

THESE people are not, as some have thought, a dull, or slender
witted people, but very ingenious, and very subtile. I could
give maine instances to maintaine mine opinion of them in
this; but I will onely relate one, which is a passage worthy to
be observed.

In the Massachussets bay lived Cheecatawback the Sachem
or Sagamore of those territories, who had large dominions
which hee did appropriate to himselfe.

Into those parts came a greate company of Salvages from the
territories of Narohiganset, to the number of 100. persons; and
in this Sachems Dominions they intended to winter.

When they went a hunting for turkies they spreade over such
a greate scope of ground that a Turkie could hardily escape
them: Deare they killed up in greate abundance, and feasted
their bodies very plentifully: Beavers they killed
by no allowance; the skinnes of those they traded
away at Wassaguscus with my neighboures for
corne, and such other commodities as they had neede of; and

They trade
away beavers
skinnes for
corne.

my neighboures had a wonderfull great benefit by their being
in those parts. Yea, sometimes (like genious fellowes) they
would present their Marchant with a fatt beaver skinne, alwayes
the tayle was not diminished, but presented full
and whole; although the tayle is a present for a
Sachem, and is of such masculaine vertue that if
some of our Ladies knew the benefit thereof they
would desire to have ships sent of purpose to trade for the tayle
alone: it is such a rarity, as is not more esteemed of then reason
doth require.

A beaver skinne with his tayle on of great estimacion.

But the Sachem Cheecatawbak, (on whose possessions they
usurped, and converted the commodities thereof to their owne
use, contrary to his likeing,) not being of power
to resist them, practised to doe it by a subtile
stratagem. And to that end gave it out amongst us,
that the cause why these other Salvages of the Narohigansets
came into these parts, was to see what strength we were of, and
to watch an opportunity to cut us off, and take that which they
found in our custody usefull for them; And added further, they
would burne our howses, and that they had caught one of his
men, named Meshebro, and compelled him to discover to them
where their barnes, Magazines, or storehowses were, and had
taken away his corne; and seemed to be in a pittifull perplexity
about the matter.

A subtile plot of a Sachem.

And, the more to adde reputation to this tale, desires that
his wifes and children might be harbered in one of our houses.
This was graunted; and my neighbours put on corslets, head-
peeces, and weapons defensive and offensive.

This thing being knowne to Cheecatawback, hee caused
some of his men to bring the Narohigansets to trade, that they
might see the preparation. The Salvage, that was a stranger to
the plott, simply comming to trade, and findding his merchants
lookes like lobsters, all cladd in harnesse, was in a maze to
thinke what would be the end of it. Haste hee made to trade
away his furres, and tooke anything for them, wishing himselfe
well rid of them and of the company in the howse.

But (as the manner has bin) hee must eate some
furmety before hee goe: downe hee sits and eats,
and withall had an eie on every side; and now
and then saw a sword or a dagger layd a thwart a head peece,

A Salvage scared.

which hee wondered at, and asked his giude whether the company were not angry. The guide, (that was privy to his Lords plot) answered in his language that hee could not tell. But the harmelesse Salvage, before hee had halfe filled his belly, started up on a sodayne, and ranne out of the howse in such hast that hee left his furmety there, and stayed not to looke behinde him who came after: Glad hee was that he had escaped so.

The subtile Sachem, hee playd the tragedian, and fained a feare of being surprised; and sent to see whether the enemies (as the Messenger termed them) were not in the howse; and comes in a by way with his wifes and children, and stopps the chinkes of the out howse, for feare the fire might be seene in the night, and be a meanes to direct his enemies where to finde them.

And, in the meane time, hee prepared for his Ambassador to his enemies a Salvage, that had lived 12. moneths in England, to the end it might adde reputation to his ambassage. This man *A Salvage* hee fends to those intruding Narohigansets, to *that had lived* tell them that they did very great injury to his *12. Moneths* *in England* Lord, to trench upon his prerogatives: and advised *sent for an* them to put up their pipes, and begon in time: if *Ambassador.* they would not, that his Lord would come upon them, and in his ayd his freinds the English, who were up in armes already to take his part, and compell them by force to be gone, if they refused to depart by faire meanes.

This message, comming on the neck of that which doubtlesse the fearefull Salvage had before related of his escape, and what hee had observed, caused all those hundred Narohigansets (that meant us no hurt) to be gone with bagg, and baggage. And my neighboures were gulled by the subtilety of this *A good* Sachem, and lost the best trade of beaver that ever *opportunity of* they had for the time; and in the end found theire *traffick lost by* error in this kinde of credulity when it was too *the subtility of a* late. *Sachem.*

CHAP. XV.
Of their admirable perfection, in the use of the sences.

THIS is a thinge not onely observed by mee and diverse of the Salvages of New England, but, also, by the French men in Nova

Francia, and therefore I am the more incouraged to publish in this Treatice my observation of them in the use of theire sences: which is a thinge that I should not easily have bin induced to beleeve, if I my selfe had not bin an eie witnesse of what I shall relate.

The Salvages have the sence of seeinge better then the English. I have observed that the Salvages have the sence of seeing so farre beyond any of our Nation, that one would allmost beleeve they had intelligence of the Devill sometimes, when they have tould us of a shipp at Sea, which they have seene soener by one hower, yea, two howers sayle, then any English man that stood by of purpose to looke out, their sight is so excellent.

Their eies indeede are black as jett; and that coler is accounted the strongest for sight. And as they excell us in this particular so much noted, so I thinke they excell us in all the rest.

This I am sure I have well observed, that in the sence of smelling they have very great perfection; which is confirmed by the opinion of the French that are planted about Canada, who *Salvages that will distinguish a Spaniard from a frenchman by the smell of the hand.* have made relation that they are so perfect in the use of that sence, that they will distinguish between a Spaniard and a Frenchman by the sent of the hand onely. And I am perswaded that the Author of this Relation has seene very probable reasons that have induced him to be of that opinion; and I am the more willing to give credit thereunto, because I have observed in them so much as that comes to.

I have seene a Deare passe by me upon a neck of Land, and a Salvage that has pursued him by the view. I have accompanied him in this pursuite; and the Salvage, pricking the Deare, *A Deare pursued by the view of the foote, hee was found and killed.* comes where hee findes the view of two deares together, leading several wayes. One, hee was sure, was fresh, but which (by the sence of seeing) hee could not judge; therefore, with his knife, hee diggs up the earth of one; and, by smelling, says, that was not of the fresh Deare: then diggs hee up the other; and viewing and smelling to that, concludes it to be the view of the fresh Deare, which hee had pursued; and thereby followes the chase, and killes that Deare, and I did eate part of it with him: such is their perfection in these two sences.

CHAP. XVI.
Of their acknowledgment of the Creation, and immortality of the Soule.

ALTHOUGH these Salvages are found to be without Religion, Law, and King (as Sir William Alexander hath well observed,) yet are they not altogether without the knowledge of God (historically); for they have it amongst them by tradition that God made one man and one woman, and bad them live together and get children, kill deare, beasts, birds, fish and fowle, and what they would at their pleasure; and that their posterity was full of evill, and made God so angry that hee let in the Sea upon them, and drowned the greatest part of them, that were naughty men, (the Lord destroyed so;) and they went to Sanaconquam, who feeds upon them (pointing to the Center of the Earth, where they imagine is the habitation of the Devill:) the other, (which were not destroyed,) increased the world, and when they died (because they were good) went to the howse of Kytan, pointing to the setting of the sonne; where they eate all manner of dainties, and never take paines (as now) to provide it.

The beleefe of the Salvages.

Kytan makes provision (they say) and saves them that laboure; and there they shall live with him forever, voyd of care. And they are perswaded that Kytan is hee that makes corne growe, trees growe, and all manner of fruits.

The Sonne called Kytan.

And that wee that use the booke of Common prayer doo it to declare to them, that cannot reade, what Kytan has commaunded us, and that wee doe pray to him with the helpe of that booke; and doe make so much accompt of it, that a Salvage (who had lived in my howse before hee had taken a wife, by whome hee had children) made this request to mee, (knowing that I allwayes used him with much more respect than others,) that I would let his sonne be brought up in my howse, that hee might be taught to reade in that booke: which request of his I granted; and hee was a very joyfull man to thinke that his sonne should thereby (as hee said) become an Englishman; and then hee would be a good man.

A Salvage desired to have his sonn brought up to learne the book of common prayer.

I asked him who was a good man; his answere was, hee that would not lye, nor steale.

These, with them, are all the capitall crimes that can be imagined; all other are nothing in respect of those; and hee that is free from these must live with Kytan for ever, in all manner of pleasure.

CHAP. XVII.
Of their Annals and funerals.

THESE people, that have by tradition some touch of the immortality of the soule, have likewise a custome *Their custom in burryinge.* to make some monuments over the place where the corps is interred: But they put a greate difference betwene persons of noble, and of ignoble, or obscure, or inferior discent. For, indeed, in the grave of the more noble they put a planck in the bottom for the corps to be layed upon, and on each side a plancke, and a plancke upon the *Their manner of Monuments.* top in forme of a chest, before they cover the place with earth. This done, they erect some thing over the grave in forme of a hearse cloath, as was that of Cheeka-tawbacks mother, which the Plimmouth planters defaced because they accounted it an act of superstition; which did breede a brawle as hath bin before related; for they hold impious and inhumane to deface the monuments of the dead. They themselves esteeme of it as piaculum; and have a custome amongst them to keepe their annals and come at certaine times to lament and bewaile the losse of their freind; and use to black *At burrials, they black their faces.* their faces, which they so weare, instead of a mourning ornament, for a longer or a shorter time according to the dignity of the person: so is their annals kept and observed with their accustomed solemnity. Afterwards they absolutely abandon the place, because they suppose the sight thereof will but renew their sorrow.

It was a thing very offensive to them, at our first comming into those parts, to aske of them for any one that had bin dead; but of later times it is not so offensively taken to renew the memory of any deseased person, because by our example (which they are apt to followe) it is made more familiare unto them; and they marvell to see no monuments over our dead, and therefore thinke no great Sachem is yet come into those parts, or not as yet deade; because they see the graves all alike.

CHAP. XVIII.
Of their Custome in burning the
Country, and the reason thereof.

THE Salvages are accustomed to set fire of the Country in all places where they come, and to burne it twize a yeare, viz: at the Spring, and the fall of the leafe. The reason that mooves *The Salvages* them to doe so, is because it would other wise *fire the Country* be so overgrowne with underweedes that it would *twice a yeare.* be all a coppice wood, and the people would not be able in any wise to passe through the Country out of a beaten path.

The meanes that they do it with, is with certaine minerall stones, that they carry about them in baggs made for that purpose of the skinnes of little beastes, which they convert into good lether, carrying in the same a peece of touch wood, very excellent for that purpose, of their owne making. These minerall stones they have from the Piquenteenes, (which is to the Southward of all the plantations in New England,) by trade and trafficke with those people.

The burning of the grasse destroyes the underwoods, and so scorcheth the elder trees that it shrinkes them, and hinders their growth very much: so that hee that will looke to finde large trees and good tymber, must not depend upon the help of a woodden prospect to finde them on the upland ground; but must seeke for them, (as I and others have done,) in the lower grounds, where the grounds are wett, when the Country is fired, by reason of the snow water that remaines there for a time, untill the Sunne by continuance of that hath exhaled the vapoures of the earth, and dried up those places where the fire, (by reason of the moisture,) can have no power to doe them any hurt: and if he would endevoure to finde out any goodly Cedars, hee must not seeke for them on the higher grounds, but make his inquest for them in the vallies, for the Salvages, by this custome of theirs, have spoiled all the rest: for this custome hath bin continued from the beginnings.

And least their firing of the Country in this manner should be an occasion of damnifying us, and indaingering our habitations, wee our selves have used carefully about the same times to observe the winds, and fire the grounds about our owne habitations; to prevent the Dammage that might happen by any neglect thereof, if the fire should come neere those howses in our absence.

For, when the fire is once kindled, it dilates and spreads it selfe as well against, as with the winde; burning continually night and day, untill a shower of raine falls to quench it.

And this custome of firing the Country is the meanes to make it passable; and by that meanes the trees growe here and there as in our parks: and makes the Country very beautifull and commodious.

CHAP. XIX.
Of their inclination to Drunkennesse.

ALTHOUGH Drunkennesse be justly termed a vice which the Salvages are ignorant of, yet the benefit is very great that comes to the planters by the sale of strong liquor to the Salvages, who are much taken with the delight of it; for they will pawne their wits, to purchase the acquaintance of it. Yet in al the commerce that I had with them, I never proffered them any such thing; nay, I would hardly let any of them have a drame, unles hee were a Sachem, or a Winnaytue, that is a rich man, or a man of estimation next in degree to a Sachem or Sagamore. I alwayes tould them it was amongst us the Sachems drinke. But they say if I come to the Northerne parts of the Country I shall have no trade, if I will not supply them with lusty liquors: it is the life of the trade in all those parts: for it so happened that thus a Salvage desperately killed himselfe; when hee was drunke, a gunne being charged and the cock up, hee sets the mouth to his brest, and, putting back the tricker with his foote, shot himselfe dead.

CHAP. XX.
That the Salvages live a contended life.

A GENTLEMAN and a traveller, that had bin in the parts of New England for a time, when hee retorned againe, in his discourse of the Country, wondered, (as hee said,) that the natives of the land lived so poorely in so rich a Country, like to our Beggers in England. Surely that Gentleman had not time or leasure whiles hee was there truely to informe himselfe of the state of that Country, and the happy life the Salvages would leade weare they once brought to Christianity.

The Salvages want the art of navigation. I must confesse they want the use and benefit of Navigation, (which is the very sinnus of a flourishing Commonwealth,) yet are they supplied with all manner of needefull things for the maintenance of life and lifelyhood. Foode and rayment are the cheife of all that we make true use of; and of these they finde no want, but have, and may have, them in a most plentifull manner.

If our beggers of England should, with so much ease as they, furnish themselves with foode at all seasons, there would not be so many starved in the streets, neither would so many gaoles be stuffed, or gallouses furnished with poore wretches, as I have seene them.

But they of this sort of our owne nation, that are fitt to goe to this Canaan, are not able to transport themselves; and most of them unwilling to goe from the good ale tap, which is the very loadstone of the lande by which our English beggers steere theire Course; it is the Northpole to which the flowre-de-luce of their compasse points. The more is the pitty that the Commonalty of oure Land are of such leaden capacities as to neglect so brave a Country, that doth so plentifully feede maine lusty and a brave, able men, women and children, that have not the meanes that a Civilized Nation hath to purchase foode and rayment; which that Country with a little industry will yeeld a man in a very comfortable measure, without overmuch carking.

I cannot deny but a civilized Nation hath the preheminence of an uncivilized, by meanes of those instruments that are found to be common amongst civile people, and the uncivile want the use of, to make themselves masters of those ornaments that make such a glorious shew, that will give a man occasion to cry, *sic transit gloria Mundi.*

Now since it is but foode and rayment that men that live needeth, (though not all alike,) why should not the Natives of New England be sayd to live richly, having no want of either? Cloaths are the badge of sinne; and the more variety of fashions is but the greater abuse of the Creature: the beasts of the forrest there doe serve to furnish them at any time when they please: fish and flesh they have in greate abundance, which they both roast and boyle.

They are indeed not served in dishes of plate with variety of Sauces to procure appetite; that needs not there. The rarity of the aire, begot by the medicinable quality of the sweete herbes of the Country, alwayes procures good stomakes to the inhabitants.

I must needs commend them in this particular, that, though they buy many commodities of our Nation, yet they keepe but fewe, and those of speciall use.

They love not to bee cumbered with many utensilles, and although every proprietor knowes his owne, yet all things, (so long as they will last), are used in common amongst them: A bisket cake given to one, that one breakes it equally into so many parts as there be persons in his company, and distributes it. Platoes Commonwealth is so much practised by these people.

They leade a happy life, being voyd of care. According to humane reason, guided onely by the light of nature, these people leades the more happy and freer life, being voyde of care, which torments the mindes of so many Christians: They are not delighted in baubles, but in usefull things.

Their naturall drinke is of the Cristall fountaine, and this they take up in their hands, by joyning them close together. They take up a great quantity at a time, and drinke at the wrists. It was the sight of such a feate which made Diogenes hurle away his dishe, and, like one that would have this princi-pall confirmed, *Natura paucis contentat*, used a dish no more.

I have observed that they will not be troubled with superflu-ous commodities. Such things as they finde they are taught by necessity to make use of, they will make choise of, and seeke to purchase with industry. So that, in respect that their life is so voyd of care, and they are so loving also that they make use of those things they enjoy, (the wife onely excepted,) as common goods, and are therein so compassionate that, rather than one should starve through want, they would starve all. Thus doe they passe awaye the time merrily, not regarding our pompe, (which they see dayly before their faces,) but are better content with their owne, which some men esteeme so meanely of.

They make use of ordinary things, one of anothers as common.

They may be rather accompted to live richly, wanting nothing that is needefull; and to be commended for leading a contented life, the younger being ruled by the Elder, and the Elder ruled by the Powahs, and the Powahs are ruled by the Devill; and then you may imagin what good rule is like to be amongst them.

FINIS.

NEW ENGLISH CANAAN,
OR
NEW CANAAN.

The Second Booke.

Containing a description of the bewty of the Country with
her naturall indowements, both in the Land and Sea;
with the great Lake of Erocoise.

CHAP. I.
The generall Survey of the Country.

IN the Moneth of June, Anno Salutis 1622, it was my chaunce
to arrive in the parts of New England with 30. Servants, and
provision of all sorts fit for a plantation: and whiles our howses
were building, I did indeavour to take a survey of
the Country: The more I looked, the more I liked
it. And when I had more seriously considered of
the bewty of the place, with all her faire indowments, I did not
thinke that in all the knowne world it could be paralel'd, for so
many goodly groves of trees, dainty fine round
rising hillucks, delicate faire large plaines, sweete
cristall fountaines, and cleare running streames
that twine in fine meanders through the meads,
making so sweete a murmering noise to heare as would even
lull the sences with delight a sleepe, so pleasantly doe they glide
upon the pebble stones, jetting most jocundly where they doe
meete and hand in hand runne downe to Neptunes Court, to
pay the yearely tribute which they owe to him as soveraigne
Lord of all the springs. Contained within the
volume of the Land, are Fowles in abundance,
Fish in multitude; and I discovered, besides, Millions of Turtledoves one the greene boughes, which sate peck-
ing of the full ripe pleasant grapes that were supported by the
lusty trees, whose fruitfull loade did cause the armes to bend:
among which here and there dispersed, you might see Lillies
and of the Daphnean-tree: which made the Land to mee seeme
paradice: for in mine eie t'was Natures Masterpeece; Her

*A famous
Country.*

*Their
fountaines are
as cleare as
Cristall.*

*Greate store of
fowles, fish and
turtledoves.*

694

cheifest Magazine of all where lives her store: if this Land be not rich, then is the whole world poore.

What I had resolved on, I have really performed; and I have endeavoured to use this abstract as an instrument, to bee the meanes to communicate the knowledge which I have gathered, by my many yeares residence in those parts, unto my Country-men: to the end that they may the better perceive their error, who cannot imagine that there is any Country in the universall world which may be compared unto our native soyle. I will now discover unto them a Country whose indowments are by learned men allowed to stand in a parallel with the Israelites Canaan, which none will deny to be a land farre more excellent then Old England, in her proper nature.

This I consider I am bound in duety (as becommeth a Christian man) to performe for the glory of God, in the first place; next, (according to Cicero,) to acknowledge that, *Non nobis solum nati sumus, sed partim patria, partim parentes, partim amici vindicant.*

For which cause I must approove of the indeavoures of my Country men, that have bin studious to inlarge the territories of his Majesties empire by planting Colonies in America.

And of all other, I must applaude the judgement of those that have made choise of this part, (whereof I now treat,) being of all other most absolute, as I will make it appeare hereafter by way of paralell. Among those that have setled themselvs in new England, some have gone for their conscience sake, (as they professe,) and I wish that they may plant the Gospel of Jesus Christ, as becommeth them, sincerely and without satisme or faction, whatsoever their former or present practises are, which I intend not to justifie: howsoever, they have deserved (in mine opinion) some commendationes, in that they have furnished the Country so commodiously in so short a time; although it hath bin but for their owne profit, yet posterity will taste the sweetnes of it, and that very sodainly.

And since my taske, in this part of mine abstract, is to intreat of the naturall indowments of the Country, I will make a breife demonstration of them in order, severally, according to their severall qualities: and shew you what they are, and what profitable use may be made of them by industry.

CHAP. II.
What trees are there and how commodious.

OAKES are there of two sorts, white and redd; excellent tymber

1. *Oake.* for the building both of howses and shipping: and they are found to be a tymber that is more tough then the oak of England. They are excellent for pipe-staves, and such like vessels; and pipe-staves at the Canary Ilands are a prime commodity. I have knowne them there at 35. p. the 1000, and will purchase a fraight of wines there before any commodity in England, their onely wood being pine, of which they are enforced also to build shippinge; of oackes there is great abundance in the parts of New England, and they may have a prime place in the Catalogue of commodities.

2. *Ashe.* Ashe there is store, and very good for staves, oares or pikes; and may have a place in the same Catalogue.

3. *Elme.* Elme: of this sort of trees there are some; but there hath not as yet bin found any quantity to speake of.

4. *Beech.* Beech there is of two sorts, redd and white; very excellent for trenchers or chaires, and also for oares; and may be accompted for a commodity.

5. *Walnutt.* Wallnutt: of this sorte of wood there is infinite store, and there are 4 sorts: it is an excellent wood, for many uses approoved; the younger trees are imployed for hoopes, and are the best for that imployement of all other stuffe whatsoever. The Nutts serve when they fall to feede our swine, which make them the delicatest bacon of all other foode: and is therein a cheife commodity.

6. *Chestnuts.* Chestnutt: of this sorte there is very greate plenty, the tymber whereof is excellent for building; and is a very good commodity, especially in respect of the fruit, both for man and beast.

7. *Pine.* Pine: of this sorte there is infinite store in some parts of the Country. I have travelled 10. miles together where is little or no other wood growing. And of these may be made rosin, pitch and tarre, which are such usefull commodities that if wee had them not from other Countries in Amity with England, our Navigation would decline.

Then how great the commodity of it will be to our Nation, to have it of our owne, let any man judge.

8. *Cedar.* Cedar: of this sorte there is abundaunce; and this wood was such as Salomon used for the building of that glorious Temple at Hierusalem; and there are of these Cedars, firre trees and other materialls necessary for the building of many faire Temples, if there were any Salomons to be at the Cost of them: and if any man be desirous to finde out in what part of the Country the best Cedars are, he must get into the bottom grounds, and in vallies that are wet at the spring of the yeare, where the moisture preserves them from the fire in spring time, and not in a woodden prospect. This wood cutts red, and is good for bedsteads, tables and chests; and may be placed in the Catalogue of Commodities.

9. *Cypres.* Cypres: of this there is great plenty; and vulgarly this tree hath bin taken for another sort of Cedar; but workemen put a difference betweene this Cypres, and the Cedar, especially in the colour; for this is white and that redd white: and likewise in the finenes of the leafe and the smoothnes of the barque. This wood is also sweeter then Cedar, and, (as it is in Garrets herball,) a more bewtifull tree; it is of all other, to my minde, most bewtifull, and cannot be denied to passe for a commodity.

10. *Spruce.* Spruce: of these there are infinite store, especially in the Northerne parts of the Country; and they have bin approoved by workemen in England to be more tough then those that they have out of the east country: from whence wee have them for masts and yards of shippes.

The Spruce of this Country are found to be 3. and 4. fadum about: The Spruce of this country are found to be 3. and 4. fadum about: and are reputed able, single, to make masts for the biggest ship that sayles on the maine Ocean, without peesing; which is more than the East country can afford. And seeing that Navigation is the very sinneus of a flourishing Commonwealth, it is fitting to allow the Spruce tree a principall place in the Catalogue of commodities.

11. *Alder.* Alder: of this sorte there is plenty by rivers sides, good for turners.

12. *Birch.* Birch: of this there is plenty in divers parts of the Country. Of the barck of these the Salvages of

the Northerne parts make them delicate Canowes, so light that two men will transport one of them over Land whither they list; and yet one of them will transporte tenne or twelffe Salvages by water at a time.

13. *Maple.*   Mayple: of those trees there is greate abundance; and these are very excellent for bowles. The Indians use of it to that purpose; and is to be accompted a good commodity.

14. *Elderne.*   Elderne: there is plenty in that Country; of this the Salvages make their Arrowes, and it hath no strong unsavery sent like our Eldern in England.

15. *Hawthorne.*   Hawthorne: of this there is two sorts, one of which beares a well tasting berry as bigg as ones thumbe, and lookes like little Queene apples.

16. *Vines.*   Vines: of this kinde of trees there are that beare grapes of three colours: that is to say, white, black and red.

The Country is so apt for vines, that, but for the fire at the spring of the yeare, the vines would so over spreade the land that one should not be able to passe for them; the fruit is as bigg, of some, as a musket bullet, and is excellent in taste.

17. *Plummes.*   Plumtrees: of this kinde there are many; some that beare fruit as bigg as our ordinary bullis: others there be that doe beare fruite much bigger than peare plummes; their colour redd, and their stones flat; very delitious in taste.

18. *Cherries.*   Cheritrees there are abundance; but the fruit is as small as our sloes; but if any of them were replanted and grafted, in an orchard, they would soone be raised by meanes of such; and the like fruits.

19. *Roses.*   There is greate abundance of Muske Roses in divers places: the water distilled excelleth our Rosewater of England.

20. *Sassafras* *and* 21. *Sarsaperilla.*   There is abundance of Saffafras and Sarsaperilla, growing in divers places of the land; whose budds at the spring doe perfume the aire.

Other trees there are not greatly materiall to be recited in this abstract, as goose berries, rasberies, and other beries.

There is Hempe that naturally groweth, finer then our Hempe of England.

CHAP. III.
Potthearbes and other herbes for Sallets.

THE Country there naturally affordeth very good potherbes

Potmarioram,
Tyme,
Alexander,
Angellica,
Pursland,
Violets, and
Anniseeds.

and sallet herbes, and those of a more maskuline vertue then any of the same species in England; as Potmarioram, Tyme, Alexander, Angellica, Pursland, Violets, and Anniseeds, in very great abundance: and for the pott I gathered in summer, dried and crumbled into a bagg to preserve for winter store.

Hunnisuckles
and Balme.

Hunnisuckles, balme, and divers other good herbes are there, that grow without the industry of man, that are used when occasion serveth very commodiously.

CHAP. IV.
Of Birds, and fethered fowles.

NOw that I have breifly shewed the Commodity of the trees, herbes, and fruits, I will shew you a description of the fowles of the aire; as most proper in ordinary course.

Swannes.

And first of the Swanne, because shee is the biggest of all the fowles of that Country. There are of them in Merrimack River, and in other parts of the country, greate store at the seasons of the yeare.

The flesh is not much desired of the inhabitants, but the skinnes may be accompted a commodity fitt for divers uses, both for fethers and quiles.

Geese, pide,
white, and gray.

There are Geese of three sorts, vize: brant Geese which are pide, and white Geese which are bigger, and gray Geese which are as bigg and bigger then the tame Geese of England, with black legges, black bills, heads and necks black; the flesh farre more excellent then the Geese of England, wild or tame; yet the purity of the aire is such that the biggest is accompted but an indifferent meale for a couple of men. There is of them great abundance.

Fethers pay for
powther and
shott.

I have had often 1000. before the mouth of my gunne. I never saw any in England, for my part, so fatt as I have killed there in those parts; the fethers of them makes a bedd softer then any down bed that I have lyen on, and is there a very good commodity; the fethers of the Geese, that I have killed in a short time, have paid for all the powther and shott I have spent in a yeare, and I have fed my doggs with as fatt Geese there as I have ever fed upon my selfe in England.

Ducks pide, gray, & black. Ducks there are of three kindes, pide Ducks, gray Ducks, and black Ducks in greate abundance: the most about my habitation were black Ducks: and it was a noted Custome at my howse, to have every mans Duck upon a trencher; and then you will thinke a man was not hardly used: they are bigger boddied then the tame Ducks of England: very fatt and dainty flesh.

The common doggs fees were the gibletts, unlesse they were boyled now and than for to make broath.

Teales, greene and blew. Teales there are of two sorts, greene winged, and blew winged: but a dainty bird. I have bin much delighted with a rost of these for a second course. I had plenty in the rivers and ponds about my howse.

Widggens. Widggens there are, and abundance of other water foule, some such as I have seene, and some such as I have not seene else where before I came into those parts, which are little regarded.

Simpes. Simpes there are like our Simpes in all respects, with very litle difference. I have shot at them onely to see what difference I could finde betweene them and those of my native Country, and more I did not regard them.

Sanderlings. Sanderlings are a dainty bird, more full boddied than a Snipe; and I was much delighted to feede on them because they were fatt and easie to come by, because I went but a stepp or to for them: and I have killed betweene foure and five dozen at a shoot, which would loade me home.

Their foode is at ebbing water on the sands, of small seeds that grows on weeds there, and are very good pastime in August.

Cranes. Cranes there are greate store, that ever more came there at S. Davids day, and not before: that day they never would misse.

These sometimes eate our corne, and doe pay for their presumption well enough; and serveth there in powther, with
turnips, to supply the place of powthered beefe, and is a goodly
bird in a dishe, and no discommodity.

Turkies. Turkies there are, which divers times in great
flocks have sallied by our doores; and then a
gunne, being commonly in a redinesse, salutes them with such
a courtesie, as makes them take a turne in the Cooke roome.
They daunce by the doore so well.

Of these there hath bin killed that have weighed forty eight
pound a peece.

They are by mainy degrees sweeter then the tame Turkies of
England, feede them how you can.

I had a Salvage who hath taken out his boy in a morning, and
they have brought home their loades about noone.

I have asked them what number they found in the woods,
who have answered Neent Metawna, which is a thosand that
day; the plenty of them is such in those parts. They are easily
killed at rooste, because, the one being killed, the other sit fast
neverthelesse; and this is no bad commodity.

Pheisants. There are a kinde of fowles which are commonly
called Pheisants, but whether they be pheysants or
no, I will not take upon mee to determine. They are in forme
like our pheisant henne of England. Both the male and the
female are alike; but they are rough footed, and have stareing
fethers about the head and neck; the body is as bigg as the
pheysant henne of England; and are excellent white flesh, and
delicate white meate, yet we seldome bestowe a shoote at them.

Partridges there are, much like our Partridges of England;
they are of the same plumes, but bigger in body.
Partridges
bigger in body They have not the signe of the horseshoe on the
as those of brest, as the Partridges of England; nor are they
England. coloured about the heads as those are. They sit on
the trees, for I have seene 40. in one tree at a time: yet at night
they fall on the ground, and sit untill morning so together; and
are dainty flesh.

Quailes bigger There are quailes also, but bigger then the
in body as those quailes in England. They take trees also: for I have
in England. numbered 60. upon a tree at a time. The cocks

doe call at the time of the yeare, but with a different note from
the cock quailes of England.

*The Larkes
sing not.*

The Larkes there are like our Larkes of England
in all respects: saving that they do not use to sing
at all.

Owles.

There are Owles of divers kindes: but I did
never heare any of them whop as ours doe.

*The Crowes
smell & tast
of Muske in
summer, but
not in winter.*

There are Crowes, kights and rooks that doe
differ in some respects from those of England.
The Crowes, which I have much admired what
should be the cause, both smell and taste of Muske
in summer, but not in winter.

*Hawkes of five
sorts.*

There are Hawkes in New England of 5. sorts;
and these of all other fether fowles I must not
omitt to speake of, nor neede I to make any Apology for my selfe concerning any trespasse that I am like to
make upon my judgement, concerning the nature of them,
having bin bred in so genious a way that I had the common use
of them in England: and at my first arrivall in those parts prac-

A Lannaret.

tised to take a Lannaret, which I reclaimed,
trained and made flying in a fortnight, the same
being a passinger at Michuelmas. I found that these are most
excellent Mettell, rank winged, well conditioned, and not tick-
leish footed; and, having whoods, bels, luers, and all things
fitting, was desirous to make experiment of that kinde of
Hawke before any other.

And I am perswaded that Nature hath ordained them to be
of a farre better kinde then any that have bin used in England.
They have neither dorre nor worm to feed upon, (as in other
parts of the world,) the Country affording none; the use
whereof in other parts makes the Lannars there more bussardly
then they be in New England.

Fawcons.

There are likewise Fawcons and tassell gentles,
admirable well shaped birds; and they will tower
up when they purpose to pray, and, on a sodaine when they
esspie their game, they will make such a cancellere that one
would admire to behold them. Some there are more black then
any that have bin used in England.

The Tassell gent, (but of the least size,) is an ornament for a
person of estimation among the Indians to weare in the knot of

his lock, with the traine upright, the body dried and stretched out. They take a great pride in the wearing of such an ornament, and give to one of us, that shall kill them one for that purpose, so much beaver as is worth three pounds sterling, very willingly.

These doe us but little trespas, because they pray on such birds as are by the Sea side, and not on our Chickens. Goshawkes there are, and Tassels.

Goshawkes well shaped. The Tassels are short trussed bussards; but the Goshawkes are well shaped, but they are small; some of white male, and some redd male, I have seene one with 8. barres in the traine. These fall on our bigger poultry: the lesser chicken, I thinke they scorne to make their pray of; for commonly the Cocke goes to wrack. Of these I have seene many; and if they come to trespasse me, I lay the law to them with the gunne, and take them dammage fesant.

Marlins small and greate. There are very many Marlins; some very small, and some so large as is the Barbary Tassell.

I have often beheld these pretty birds, how they have scoured after the black bird, which is a small sized Choffe that eateth the Indian maisze.

Sparhawkes. Sparhawkes there are also, the fairest and best shaped birds that I have ever beheld of that kinde those that are litle, no use is made of any of them, neither are they regarded. I onely tried conclusions with a Lannaret at first comming; and, when I found what was in that bird, I turned him going: but, for so much as I have observed of those birds, they may be a fitt present for a prince, and for goodnesse too be preferred before the Barbary, or any other used in Christendome; and especially the Lannars and Lannarets.

A Hunning bird, is as small as a Beetle. His bill as sharp as a needle point, and his fethers like silke. There is a curious bird to see to, called a hunning bird, no bigger then a great Beetle; that out of question lives upon the Bee, which hee eateth and catcheth amongst Flowers: For it is his Custome to frequent those places. Flowers hee cannot feed upon by reason of his sharp bill, which is like the poynt of a Spannish needle, but shorte. His fethers have a glosse like silke, and, as hee stirres, they shew to be of a chaingable coloure: and has bin, and is, admired for shape, coloure and size.

CHAP. V.
Of the Beasts of the forrest.

Now that I have made a rehearsall of the birds and fethered Fowles, which participate most of aire, I will give you a description of the beasts; and shew you what beasts are bred in those parts, and what my experience hath gathered by observation of their kinde and nature. I begin with the most usefull and most beneficiall beast which is bredd in those parts, which is the Deare.

Deare of 3. kindes. There are in this Country three kindes of Deare, of which there are greate plenty, and those are very usefull.

Mose or red deare. First, therefore, I will speake of the Elke, which the Salvages call a Mose: it is a very large Deare, with a very faire head, and a broade palme, like the palme of a fallow Deares horne, but much bigger, and is 6. footewide betweene the tipps, which grow curbing downwards: Hee is of the bignesse of a great horse.

Mose or deare greater than a horse, the height of them 18. hand fulles. There have bin of them seene that has bin 18. handfulls highe: hee hath a bunch of haire under his jawes: hee is not swifte, but stronge and large in body, and longe legged; in somuch that hee doth use to kneele, when hee feedeth on grasse.

They bringe forth three faunes at one time. Hee bringeth forth three faunes, or younge ones, at a time; and, being made tame, would be good for draught, and more usefull (by reason of their strength) then the Elke of Raushea. These are found very frequent in the northerne parts of New England: their flesh is very good foode, and much better then our redd Deare of England.

They make good lether of the hides of Deare. Their hids are by the Salvages converted into very good lether, and dressed as white as milke.

Of this lether the Salvages make the best shooes; and use to barter away the skinnes to other Salvages that have none of that kinde of bests in the parts where they live. Very good busse may be made of the hids. I have seene a hide as large as any horse hide that can be found. There is such abundance of them that the Salvages, at hunting time, have killed of them so many, that they have bestowed six or seaven at a time upon one English man whome they have borne affection to.

There is a second sort of Deare (lesse then the redd Deare of England, but much bigger then the English fallow Deare) *The midling* swift of foote, but of a more darke coloure; with *Deare or fallow* some griseld heares, when his coate is full growne *Deare.* in the summer season: his hornes grow curving, with a croked beame, resembling our redd Deare, not with a palme like the fallow Deare.

These bringe 3. fawnes at a time, spotted like our fallow Deares fawnes; the Salvages say, foure; I speake of what I know to be true, for I have killed in February a doe with three fawnes in her belly, all heared, and ready to fall; for these Deare fall their fawnes 2. moneths sooner then the fallow Deare of England. There is such abundance of them that an hundred have bin found at the spring of the yeare, within the compasse of a mile.

The Salvages take these in trappes made of their naturall Hempe, which they place in the earth where they fell a tree for browse; and when hee rounds the tree for the browse, if hee *Trappes to catch* tread on the trapp hee is horsed up by the legg, by *the Deare.* meanes of a pole that starts up and catcheth him.

Their hides the Salvages use for cloathing, and will give for one hide killed in season, 2. 3. or 4. beaver skinnes, which will yeild pounds a peece in that Country: so much is the Deares hide prised with them above the beaver. I have made good merchandize of these. The flesh is farre sweeter then the venison of England: and hee feedeth fatt and leane together, as a swine or mutton, where as our Deare of England feede fatt on the out side: they doe not croake at rutting time, nor spendle shafte, nor is their flesh discoloured at rutting. Hee, that will impale ground fitting, may be brought once in the yeare where with bats and men hee may take so many to put into that parke, as the hides will pay the chardge of impaleinge. If all these things be well considered, the Deare, as well as the Mose, may have a principall place in the catalogue of commodities.

I for my part may be bould to tell you, that my howse was not without the flesh of this sort of Deare winter *The Humbles* nor summer: the humbles was ever my dogges fee, *was the dogges* *fee.* which by the wesell was hanged on the barre in the chimney, for his diet only: for hee has brought to my stand a brace in a morning, one after the other before sunne rising, which I have killed.

Roe bucks or Rayne Deare. There is likewise a third sorte of deare, lesse then the other, (which are a kinde of rayne deare,) to the southward of all the English plantations: they are excellent good flesh. And these also bring three fawnes at a time; and in this particular the Deare of those parts excell all the knowne Deare of the whole world.

Wolfes pray upon Deare. On all these the Wolfes doe pray continually. The best meanes they have to escape the wolfes is by swimming to Islands, or necks of land, whereby they escape: for the wolfe will not presume to follow them untill they see them over a river; then, being landed, (they wayting on the shore,) undertake the water, and so follow with fresh suite.

Beaver. The next in mine opinion fit to be spoaken of, is the Beaver; which is a Beast ordained for land and water both, and hath fore feete like a cunny, her hinder feete like a goese, mouthed like a cunny, but short eared like a Serat. He feeds on fishe in summer, and wood in winter; which hee conveyes to his howse built on the water, wherein hee sitts with his tayle hanging in the water, which else would over heate and rot off.

The Beavers cut downe trees, with his fore teeth. Hee cuts the bodies of trees downe with his fore-teeth, which are so long as a boares tuskes, and with the help of other beavers, (which hold by each others tayles like a teeme of horses, the hindmost with the logg on his shoulder stayed by one of his fore feete against his head,) they draw the logg to the habitation appoynted, placing the loggs in a square; and so, by pyling one uppon another, they build up a howse, which with boghes is covered very strongly, and placed in some pond, to which they make a damme of brush wood, like a hedge, so stronge that I have gone on the top of it crosse the current of that pond. The flesh of this beast is excellent foode. The fleece is a very choise furre, which, (before the Salvages had commerce with Christians,) they burned of the tayle: this beast is of a masculine vertue for the advancement of Priapus, and is preserved for a dish for the

Sachems, or Sagamores; who are the princes of the people, but not Kings, (as is fondly supposed.)

Beaver at 10.
shil. a pound.

The skinnes are the best marchantable commodity that can be found, to cause ready money to be brought into the land, now that they are raised to 10. shillings a pound.

In 5 yeares
one man gott
together 1000
p. in good gold.

A servant of mine in 5. yeares was thought to have a 1000. p. in ready gold gotten by beaver when hee dyed; whatsoever became of it. And this beast may challenge preheminence in the Catalogue.

The Otter in
winter hath a
furre as black
as Jett.

The Otter of those parts, in winter season, hath a furre so black as jett; and is a furre of very highe price: a good black skinne is worth 3. or 4. Angels of gold. The Flesh is eaten by the Salvages: but how good it is I cannot shew, because it is not eaten by our Nation. Yet is this a beast that ought to be placed in the number amongst the Commodities of the Country.

The Luseran
as bigg as a
hound.

The Luseran, or Luseret, is a beast like a Catt, but so bigg as a great hound: with a tayle shorter then a Catt. His clawes are like a Catts. Hee will make a pray of the Deare. His Flesh is dainty meat, like a lambe: his hide is a choise furre, and accompted a good commodity.

The Martin
is about the
bignesse of a
Fox.

The Martin is a beast about the bignes of a Foxe. His furre is chestnutt coloure: and of those there are greate store in the Northerne parts of the Country, and is a good commodity.

Racowne.

The Racowne is a beast as bigg, full out, as a Foxe, with a Bushtayle. His Flesh excellent foode: his oyle precious for the Syattica: his furre course, but the skinnes serve the Salvages for coats, and is with those people of more esteeme then a coate of beaver, because of the tayles that (hanging round in their order) doe adorne the garment, and is therefore so much esteemed of them. His fore feete are like the feete of an ape; and by the print thereof, in the time of snow, he is followed to his hole, which is commonly in a hollow tree; from whence hee is fiered out, and so taken.

The Foxes red
and gray.

The Foxes are of two coloures; the one redd, the other gray: these feede on fish, and are good furre:

they doe not stinke, as the Foxes of England, but their condition for their pray is as the Foxes of England.

The Wolfes of diverse coloures.   The Wolfes are of divers coloures; some sandy coloured, some griselled, and some black: their foode is fish, which they catch when they passe up the rivers into the ponds to spawne, at the spring time. The Deare are also their pray, and at summer, when they have whelpes, the bitch will fetch a puppy dogg from our dores to feede their whelpes with. They are fearefull Curres, and will runne away from a man, (that meeteth them by chaunce at a banke end,) as fast as any fearefull dogge. These pray upon the Deare very much. The skinnes are used by the Salvages, espe-cially the skinne of the black wolfe, which is esteemed a present for a prince there.

The skin of a black wolfe a present for a prince.   When there ariseth any difference betweene prince and prince, the prince that desires to be reconciled to his neighbouring prince does endeavour to purchase it by sending him a black wolfes skinne for a present, and the acceptance of such a present is an assur-ance of reconciliation betweene them; and the Salvages will willingly give 40. beaver skinnes for the purchase of one of these black Wolfes skinnes: and allthough the beast himselfe be a discommodity, which other Countries of Christendome are subject unto, yet is the skinne of the black wolfe worthy the title of a commodity, in that respect that hath bin declared.

The Beares afraid of a man.   If I should not speake something of the beare, I might happily leave a scruple in the mindes of some effeminate persone who conceaved of more dainger in them then there is cause. Therefore, to incour-age them against all Feare and Fortifie their mindes against needles danger, I will relate what experience hath taught mee concerning them: they are beasts that doe no harme in those parts; they feede upon Hurtleburies, Nuts and Fish, especially shell-fish.

The Beare is a tyrant at a Lobster, and at low water will downe to the Rocks and groape after them with great diligence.

The Salvages seeing a beare chase him like a dogg and kill him.   Hee will runne away from a man as fast as a litle dogge. If a couple of Salvages chaunce to espie him at his banquet, his running away will not serve his turne, for they will coate him, and chase him betweene them home to theire howses, where they kill him, to save a laboure in carrying him farre. His Flesh is esteemed venison, and of a better taste then beefe.

His hide is used by the Salvages for garments, and is more commodious then discommodious; and may passe, (with some allowance,) with the rest.

Muskewashe.   The Muskewashe is a beast that frequenteth the ponds. What hee eats I cannot finde. Hee is but a small beast, lesse then a Cunny, and is indeede in those parts no other then a water Ratte; for I have seene the suckers of them digged out of a banke, and at that age they neither differed in shape, coloure, nor size, from one of our greate Ratts. When hee is ould, hee is of the Beavers coloure; and hath passed in waite with our Chapmen for Beaver.

The Male of them have stones, which the Salvages, in uncaseing of them, leave to the skinne, which is a most delicate perfume, and may compare with any perfume that I know for goodnesse: Then may not this be excluded the Catalogue.

Porcupines.   This Country, in the North parts thereof, hath many Porcupines, but I doe not finde the beast any way usefull or hurtfull.

Hedghoggs.   There are in those Northerne parts many Hedgehoggs, of the like nature to our English Hedghoggs.

Conyes of severall sorts.   Here are greate store of Conyes in those parts, of divers coloures; some white, some black, and some gray. Those towards the Southerne parts are very small, but those to the North are as bigg as the English Cony: their eares are very short. For meate the small rabbit is as good as any that I have eaten of else where.

Squirils of three sorts.   There are Squirils of three sorts, very different in shape and condition; one is gray, and hee is as bigg as the lesser Cony, and keepeth the woods, feeding upon nutts.

Another is red, and hee haunts our howses and will rob us of our Corne; but the Catt many times payes him the price of his presumption.

A Flying Squirill.   The third is a little flying Squirill, with batlike winges, which hee spreads when hee jumpes from tree to tree, and does no harme.

Snakes.   Now because I am upon a treaty of the beasts, I will place this creature, the snake, amongst the beasts, having my warrant from the holy Bible; who, (though his posture in his passage be so different from all other, being of a more subtile and aidry nature, that hee can make his way without feete, and lifte himselfe above the superficies of the earth, as hee glids along,) yet may hee not bee ranked with any but the beasts, notwithstanding hee frequents the water, as well as the land.

There are of Snakes divers and of severall kindes, as be with us in England; but that Country hath not so many as in England have bin knowne.

The generall Salvage name of them is Ascowke.

The rattle Snakes.   There is one creeping beast or longe creeple, (as the name is in Devonshire,) that hath a rattle at his tayle that does discover his age; for so many yeares as hee hath lived, so many joynts are in that rattle, which soundeth (when it is in motion,) like pease in a bladder; and this beast is called a rattle Snake; but the Salvages give him the name of Sesick, which some take to be the Adder; and it may well be so, for the Salvages are significiant in their denomination of any thing, and it is no lesse hurtfull than the Adder of England, nor no more. I have had my dogge venomed with troubling one of these, and so swelled that I had thought it would have bin his death: but with one Saucer of Salet oyle powred downe his throate he has recovered, and the swelling asswaged by the next day. The like experiment hath bin made upon a boy that hath by chaunce troad upon one of these, and the boy never the worse. Therefore it is simplicity in any one that shall tell a bugbeare tale of horrible, or terrible Serpents, that are in that land.

Mise.   Mise there are good store, and my Lady Wood-bees black gray-malkin may have pastime enough there: but for Rats, the Country by Nature is troubled with none.

Lyons alwaies in hot Clymats, not in cold.   Lyons there are none in New England: it is contrary to the Nature of the beast to frequent places accustomed to snow; being like the Catt, that will hazard the burning of her tayle rather than abide from the fire.

CHAP. VI.
Of Stones and Minerals.

Now, (for as much as I have in a breife abstract shewed you the Creatures whose specificall Natures doe simpathise with the elements of fire and aire,) I will come to speake of the Creatures that participate of earth more then the other two, which is stones.

Marble.
And first of the Marble for building; whereof there is much in those parts, in so much there is one bay in the land that beareth the name of Marble harber, because of the plenty of Marble there: and these are usefull for building of Sumpteous Pallaces.

Limestone.
And because no good building can be made permanent, or durable, without Lime, I will let you understand that there is good Limestone neere to the river of Monatoquinte, at Uttaquatock, to my knowledge; and we hope other places too, (that I have not taken so much notice of,) may have the like, or better: and those stones are very convenient for building.

Chalk.
Chalke stones there are neere Squantos Chappell, shewed me by a Salvage.

Slate.
There is abundance of excellent Slate in divers places of the Country; and the best that ever I beheld for covering of howses: and the inhabitants have made good use of these materials for building.

Whetstones.
There is a very usefull Stone in the Land, and as yet there is found out but one place where they may be had, in the whole Country: Ould Woodman, (that was choaked at Plimmouth after hee had played the unhappy Markes man when hee was pursued by a carelesse fellow that was new come into the Land,) they say laboured to get a patent of it to himselfe. Hee was beloved of many, and had many sonnes that had a minde to engrosse that commodity. And I cannot spie any mention made of it in the woodden prospect.

Therefore I begin to suspect his aime, that it was for himselfe; and therefore will I not discover it: it is the Stone so much commended by *Ovid*, because love delighteth to make his habitation in a building of those materials, where hee advises those that seeke for love to doe it, *Duris in Cotibus illum.*

This stone the Salvages doe call *Cos*; and of these, (on the North end of Richmond Iland,) are store, and those are very excellent good for edg'd tooles. I envy not his happinesse. I have bin there: viewed the place: liked the commodity: but will not plant so Northerly for that, nor any other commodity that is there to be had.

Loadstones.   There are Loadestones also in the Northerne parts of the land: and those which were found are very good, and are a commodity worth the noteing.

Ironstones.   Iron stones there are abundance: and severall sorts of them knowne.

Lead.   Lead ore is there likewise, and hath bin found by the breaking of the earth, which the Frost hath made mellow.

Blacklead.   Black Leade I have likewise found very good, which the Salvages use to paint their faces with.

Read lead.   Red Leade is there likewise in great abundance.

Boll.   There is very excellent Boll Armoniack.

Vermilion.   There is most excellent Vermilion. All these things the Salvages make some litle use of, and doe finde them on the circumference of the Earth.

Brimstone.   Brimstone mines there are likewise.

Tinne.   Mines of Tinne are likewise knowne to be in those parts: which will in short time be made use of: and this cannot be accompted a meane commodity.

Copper.   Copper mines are there found likewise, that will enrich the Inhabitants. But untill theire younge Cattell be growne hardy labourers in the yoake, that the Plough and the Wheate may be seene more plentifully, it is a worke must be forborne.

Silver.   They say there is a Silver, and a gold mine found by Captaine Littleworth: if hee get a patent of it to himselfe hee will surely change his name.

CHAP. VII.
Of the Fishes, and what commodity they proove.

AMONG Fishes, first I will begin with the Codd, because it is the most commodious of all fish, as may appeare by the use which is made of them in forraigne parts.

Codd.   The Codd fishing is much used in America, (whereof New England is a part,) in so much as 300. Sayle of shipps, from divers parts, have used to be imployed yearely in that trade.

        I have seene in one Harboure, next Richmond *15. Shipps at one time for Codd.* Iland, 15. Sayle of shipps at one time, that have taken in them dryied Codds for Spaine and the Straights, and it has bin found that the Saylers have made 15. 18. 20. 22. p. share for a common man.

Oyle mayd of the livers of the Codd.   The Coast aboundeth with such multitudes of Codd that the inhabitants of New England doe dunge their grounds with Codd; and it is a commodity better than the golden mines of the Spanish Indies; for without dried Codd the Spaniard, Portingal and Italian would not be able to vittel of a shipp for the Sea; and I am sure at the Canaries it is the principall commodity: which place lyeth neere New England, very convenient for the vending of this commodity, one hundred of these being at the price of 300. of New found land Codds: greate store of traine oyle is mayd of the livers of the Codd, and is a commodity that without question will enrich the inhabitants of New England quicly; and is therefore a principall commodity.

A 100 Basse sould for 5. p.   The Basse is an excellent Fish, both fresh and Salte; one hundred whereof salted, (at a market,) have yeilded 5. p. They are so large, the head of one will give a good eater a dinner; and for daintinesse of diet they excell the Marybones of Beefe. There are such multitudes, that I have seene stopped into the river close adjoyning to my howse, with a sand at one tide, so many as will loade a ship of a 100. Tonnes.

Other places have greater quantities, in so much as wagers have bin layed that one should not throw a stone in the water but that hee should hit a fish.

I my selfe, at the turning of the tyde, have seene such multitudes passe out of a pound, that it seemed to mee that one might goe over their backs drishod.

These follow the bayte up the rivers, and sometimes are followed for bayte and chased into the bayes, and shallow waters, by the grand pise: and these may have also a prime place in the Catalogue of Commodities.

Mackarell are baite for Basse. The Mackarels are the baite for the Basse, and these have bin chased into the shallow waters where so many thousands have shott themselves a shore with the surfe of the Sea, that whole hogges-heads have bin taken up on the Sands; and for length, they excell any of other parts: they have bin measured 18. and 19. inches in length and seaven in breadth: and are taken with a drayle, (as boats use to passe to and froe at Sea on businesse,) in very greate quantities all alonge the Coaste.

The Fish is good, salted, for store against the winter, as well as fresh; and to be accounted a good Commodity.

Sturgeon. This Sturgeon in England is *regalis piscis*; every man in New England may catch what hee will: there are multitudes of them, and they are much fatter then those that are brought into England from other parts, in so much as by reason of their fatnesse they doe not looke white, but yellow, which made a Cooke presume they were not so good as them of Roushea: silly fellow that could not understand that it is the nature of fish salted, or pickelled, the fatter the yellower being best to preserve.

For the taste, I have warrant of Ladies of worth, with choise pallats for the commendations, who liked the taste so well that they esteemed it beyond the Sturgeon of other parts, and sayd they were deceaved in the lookes: therefore let the Sturgeon passe for a Commodity.

Salmon. Of Salmons there is greate abundance: and these may be allowed for a Commodity, and placed in the Catallogue.

Herrings. Of Herrings there is greate store, fat and faire: and, (to my minde,) as good as any I have seene; and these may be preserved, and made a good commodity at the Canaries.

Of Eeles there is abundance, both in the Saltwaters and in the fresh: and the fresh water Eele there, (if I may take the judgement of a London Fishmonger,) is the best *Great plenty of Eeles.* that hee hath found in his life time. I have with 2. eele potts found my howsehold, (being nine persons, besides doggs,) with them, taking them every tide, (for 4. moneths space,) and preserving of them for winter store: and these may proove a good commodity.

Smelts.   Of Smelts there is such abundance that the Salvages doe take them up in the rivers with baskets, like sives.

Shadds or Allizes taken to dunge ground.   There is a Fish, (by some called shadds, by some allizes,) that at the spring of the yeare passe up the rivers to spaune in the ponds; and are taken in such multitudes in every river, that hath a pond at the end, that the Inhabitants doung their ground with them. You may see in one towneship a hundred acres together set with these Fish, every acre taking 1000. of them: and an acre thus dressed will produce and yeald so much corne as 3. acres without fish: and, least any Virginea man would inferre hereupon that the ground of New England is barren, because they use no fish in setting their corne, I desire them to be remembred the cause is plaine, in Virginea they have it not to sett. But this practise is onely for the Indian Maize, (which must be set by hands,) not for English graine: and this is therefore a commodity there.

Turbut or Hallibut.   There is a large sized fish called Hallibut, or Turbut: some are taken so bigg that two men have much a doe to hale them into the boate; but there is such plenty, that the fisher men onely eate the heads and finnes, and throw away the bodies: such in Paris would yeeld 5. or 6. crownes a peece: and this is no discommodity.

Plaice.   There are excellent Plaice, and easily taken. They, (at flowing water,) do almost come ashore, so that one may stepp but halfe a foote deepe and prick them up on the sands and this may passe with some allowance.

Hake.   Hake is a dainty white fish, and excellent vittell fresh; and may passe with other commodities, because there are multitudes.

Pilchers.   There are greate store of Pilchers: at Michelmas, in many places, I have seene the Cormorants in length 3. miles feedinge upon the Sent.

Lobsters.   Lobsters are there infinite in store in all the parts of the land, and very excellent. The most use that I made of them, in 5. yeares after I came there, was but to baite my Hooke for to catch Basse; I had bin so cloyed with them the first day I went a shore.

This being knowne, they shall passe for a commodity to the inhabitants; for the Salvages will meete 500, or 1000. at a place where Lobsters come in with the tyde, to eate, and save dried for store; abiding in that place, feasting and sporting, a moneth or 6. weekes together.

Oysters. There are greate store of Oysters in the entrance of all Rivers: they are not round as those of England, but excellent fat, and all good. I have seene an Oyster banke a mile at length.

Mustles. Mustles there are infinite store; I have often gon to Wassaguscus, where were excellent Mustles, to eate for variety, the fish is so fat and large.

Clames. Clames is a shellfish, which I have seene sold in Westminster for 12. pe. the skore. These our swine feede upon, and of them there is no want; every shore is full; it makes the swine proove exceedingly, they will not faile at low water to be with them. The Salvages are much taken with the delight of this fishe, and are not cloyed, notwithstanding the plenty: for our swine we finde it a good commodity.

Raser fish. Raser fishes there are.

Freele. Freeles there are, Cockles and Scallopes; and divers other sorts of Shellfishe, very good foode.

Now that I have shewed you what commodities are there to be had in the Sea, for a Market; I will shew what is in the Land, also, for the comfort of the inhabitants, wherein it doth abound. And because my taske is an abstract, I will discover to them the commodity thereof.

Fresh fish, There are in the rivers, and ponds, very excellent
Trouts, Carpes, Trouts, Carpes, Breames, Pikes, Roches, Perches,
Breames, Pikes,
Roches, Perches, Tenches, Eeles, and other fishes such as England
Tenches, and doth afford, and as good for variety; yea, many of
Eeles. them much better; and the Natives of the inland parts doe buy hookes of us, to catch them with: and I have knowne the time that a Trouts hooke hath yeelded a beaver skinne, which hath bin a good commodity to those that have bartered them away.

These things I offer to your consideration, (curteous Reader,) and require you to shew mee the like in any part of the knowne world, if you can.

CHAP. VIII.
Of the goodnes of the Country and the Waters.

Now since it is a Country so infinitely blest with foode, and
Foode and Fire.   fire, to roast or boyle our Flesh and Fish, why
should any man feare for cold there, in a Country
warmer in the winter than some parts of France, and neerer the
Sunne: unles hee be one of those that Salomon bids goe to the
Ant and the Bee.

Noe Boggs.   There is no boggy ground knowne in all the
Country, from whence the Sunne may exhale
unwholsom vapors: But there are divers arematicall herbes and
plants, as Sassafras, Muske Roses, Violets, Balm, Lawrell, Hunnisuckles, and the like, that with their vapors perfume the aire;
Perfumed aire   and it has bin a thing much observed that shipps
with sweet   have come from Virginea where there have bin
herbes.   scarce five men able to hale a rope, untill they have
come within 40. Degrees of latitude and smell the sweet aire
of the shore, where they have suddainly recovered.

Of Waters.   And for the water, therein it excelleth Canaan
by much; for the Land is so apt for Fountaines, a
man cannot digg amisse: therefore if the Abrahams and Lots of
our times come thether, there needs be no contention for wells.

Besides there are waters of most excellent vertues, worthy
admiration.

The Cure of   At Ma-re-Mount there was a water, (by mee
mellancolly at   discovered,) that is most excellent for the cure of
Maremount.   Melancolly probatum.

The cure of   At Weenasemute is a water, the vertue whereof
Barrennesse.   is to cure barrennesse. The place taketh his name
of that Fountaine which signifieth quick spring,
or quickning spring probatum.

Water   Neere Squantos Chappell, (a place so by us
procuring a   called,) is a Fountaine that causeth a dead sleepe
dead sleepe.   for 48. howres to those that drinke 24. ounces at
New Engl.   a draught, and so proportionably. The Salvages,
excels Canaan   that are Powahs, at set times use it, and reveale
in fountaines.   strang things to the vulgar people by meanes of it.
So that in the delicacy of waters, and the conveniency of them,
Canaan came not neere this Country.

As for the Milke and Hony, which that Canaan
*Milke and
Hony supplied.* flowed with, it is supplyed by the plenty of birds, beasts and Fish; whereof Canaan could not boast her selfe.

Yet never the lesse, (since the Milke came by the industry of the first Inhabitants,) let the cattell be chereshed *A plain paralell to Canaan.* that are at this time in New England, and forborne but a litle, I will aske no long time, no more but untill the Brethren have converted one Salvage and made him a good Christian, and I may be bold to say Butter and cheese will be cheaper there then ever it was in Canaan. It is cheaper there then in old England at this present; for there are store of Cowes, considering the people, which, (as my intelligence gives,) is 12000. persons: and in gods name let the people have their desire, who write to their freinds to come out of Sodome to the land of Canaan, a land that flowes with Milke and Hony. *The Request for the Nomination of New Canaan.* And I appeale to any man of judgement, whether it be not a Land that for her excellent indowments of Nature may passe for a plaine paralell to Canaan of Israell, being in a more temporat Climat, this being in 40. Degrees and that in 30.

CHAP. IX.
A Perspective to view the Country by.

As for the Soyle, I may be bould to commend the fertility thereof, and preferre it before the Soyle of Eng- *The Soyle.* land, (our Native Country); and I neede not to produce more then one argument for proffe thereof, because it is so infallible.

Hempe is a thing by Husband men in generall *The grouth of Hempe.* ageed upon to prosper best in the most fertile Soyle: and experience hath taught this rule, that Hempe seede prospers so well in New England that it shewteth up to be tenne foote high and tenne foote and a halfe, which is twice so high as the ground in old England produceth it; which argues New England the more fertile of the two.

As for the aire, I will produce but one proffe for *The aire.* the maintenance of the excellency thereof; which is so generall, as I assure myselfe it will suffice.

No cold cough or murre. No man living there was ever knowne to be troubled with a cold, a cough, or a murre; but many men, comming sick out of Virginea to New Canaan have instantly recovered with the helpe of the purity of that aire; no man ever surfeited himselfe either by eating or drinking.

As for the plenty of that Land, it is well knowne that no part of Asia, Affrica or Europe affordeth deare that doe *The plenty of the Land.* bring forth any more then one single faune; and in New Canaan the Deare are accustomed to bring forth 2. and 3. faunes at a time.

Besides, there are such infinite flocks of Fowle and Multitudes of fish, both in the fresh waters and also on the Coast, that the like hath not else where bin discovered by any traveller.

Windes. The windes there are not so violent as in England; which is prooved by the trees that grow in the face of the winde by the Sea Coast; for there they doe not leane from the winde as they doe in England: as we have heard before.

Raine. The Raine is there more moderate then in England; which thing I have noted in all the time of my residence to be so.

The Coast. The Coast is low Land, and not high Land: and hee is of a weake capacity that conceaveth otherwise of it, because it cannot be denied but that boats may come a ground in all places along the Coast, and especially within the Compas of the Massachusets patent, where the prospect is fixed.

Harboures. The Harboures are not to be bettered for safety and goodnesse of ground, for ancorage, and, (which is worthy observation,) shipping will not there be furred; neither are they subject to wormes, as in Virginea and other places.

Scituation. Let the Scituation also of the Country be considered, (together with the rest which is discovered in the front of this abstract,) and then I hope no man will hold this land unworthy to be intituled by the name of the second Canaan.

The Nomination. And, since the Seperatists are desirous to have the denomination thereof, I am become an humble Suter on their behalfe for your consents, (courteous Readers,) to it, before I doe shew you what Revels they have kept in New Canaan.

CHAP. X.
Of the Great Lake of Erocoise in New England, and the commodities thereof.

WESTWARDS from the Massachusetts bay, (which lyeth in 42. Degrees and 30. Minutes of Northerne latitude,) is scituated a very spacious Lake, (called of the Natives the Lake of Erocoise,) which is farre more excellent then the Lake of Genezereth, in the Country of Palestina, both in respect of the greatnes and properties thereof, and likewise of the manifould commodities

Fowle innumerable. it yealdeth: the circumference of which Lake is reputed to be 240. miles at the least: and it is distant from the Massachussetts bay 300. miles, or there abouts: wherein are very many faire Islands, where innumerable flocks of severall sorts of Fowle doe breede, Swannes, Geese, Ducks, Widgines, Teales, and other water Fowle.

There are also more abundance of Beavers, Deare and Tur-

Multitudes of Fish. kies breed about the parts of that lake then in any place in all the Country of New England; and also such multitudes of fish, (which is a great part of the foode that the Beavers live upon,) that it is a thing to be

The prime place of New Canaan. admired at: So that about this Lake is the princi-pallst place for a plantation in all New Canaan, both for pleasure and proffit.

Here may very many brave Townes and Citties be erected, which may have intercourse one with another by water, very commodiously: and it is of many men of good judgement accounted the prime seate for the Metropolis of New Canaan. From this Lake, Northwards, is derived the famous River of

Canada, so named of Monsier de Cane. Canada, (so named of Monsier de Cane, a French Lord that first planted a Colony of French in America, there called Nova Francia,) from whence Captaine Kerke of late, by taking that plantation, brought home in one shipp, (as a Seaman of his Company reported in my hearing,) 25000. Beaver skinnes.

And from this Lake, Southwards, trends that goodly River,
called of the Natives Patomack, which dis-

Patomack.

chardgeth herselfe in the parts of Virginea; from
whence it is navigable by shipping of great Burthen up to the
Falls, (which lieth in 41. Degrees and a halfe of North latitude,)
and from the Lake downe to the Falls by a faire current. This
River is navigable for vessels of good Burthen; and thus much
hath often bin related by the Natives, and is of late found to be
certaine.

They have also made description of great heards of well
growne beasts, that live about the parts of this Lake, such as

Great heards of
Beasts as bigg
as Cowes.

the Christian world, (untill this discovery,) hath
not bin made acquainted with. These beasts are
of the bignesse of a Cowe; their Flesh being very
good foode, their hides good lether, their fleeces
very usefull, being a kinde of wolle as fine almost as the wolle
of the Beaver; and the Salvages doe make garments thereof.

It is tenne yeares since first the relation of these things came
to the eares of the English: at which time wee were but slender
proficients in the language of the Natives, and they, (which
now have attained to more perfection of English,) could not
then make us rightly apprehend their meaninge.

Wee supposed, when they spake of Beasts thereabouts as
high as men, they have made report of men all over hairy like
Beavers, in so much as we questioned them whether they eate
of the Beavers, to which they replyed Matta, (noe) saying they
were almost Beavers Brothers. This relation at that time wee
concluded to be fruitles, which, since, time hath made more
apparent.

About the parts of this Lake may be made a very greate
Commodity by the trade of furres, to inrich those that shall
plant there; a more compleat discovery of those parts is, (to my
knowleadge,) undertaken by Henry Joseline, Esquier, sonne of
Sir Thomas Joseline of Kent, Knight, by the approbation and

Henry Joseline
imployed for
discovery.

appointement of that Heroick and very good
Common wealths man, Captaine John Mason,
Esquier, a true foster Father and lover of vertue,
(who at his owne chardge,) hath fitted Master Joseline and
imployed him to that purpose; who no doubt will performe as
much as is expected, if the Dutch, (by gettinge into those parts

before him,) doe not frustrate his so hopefull and laudable designes.

It is well knowne they aime at that place, and have a possibility to attaine unto the end of their desires therein, by meanes of the River of Mohegan, which of the English is named Hudsons River, where the Dutch have setled two well fortified plantations already. If that River be derived from the Lake, as our Country man in his prospect affirmes it to be, and if they get and fortifie this place also, they will gleane away the best of the Beaver both from the French and the English, who have hitherto lived wholely by it; and very many old planters have gained good estates out of small beginnings by meanes thereof.

The Dutch have a great trade of Beaver in the Hudsons River. And it is well knowne to some of our Nation that have lived in the Dutch plantation that the Dutch have gained by Beaver 20000. pound a yeare.

The Salvages make report of 3. great Rivers that issue out of this Lake, 2. of which are to us knowne, the one to be Patomack, the other Canada: and why may not the third be found there likewise, which they describe to trend westward, which is conceaved to discharge herselfe into the South Sea? The Salvages affirme that they have seene shipps in this Lake with 4. Masts, which have taken from thence for their ladinge earth, that is conjectured to be some minerall stuffe.

There is probability enough for this; and it may well be thought that so great a confluxe of waters as are there gathered together, must be vented by some great Rivers; and that if the third River, (which they have made mention of,) proove to be true, as the other two have done, there is no doubt but that the passage to the East India may be obtained without any such daingerous and fruitlesse inquest by the *The passage to the East-Indies.* Norwest, as hetherto hath bin endeavoured: And there is no Traveller of any resonable capacity but will graunt that about this Lake must be innumerable springes, and by that meanes many fruitfull and pleasant pastures all about it. It hath bin observed that the inland part, (witnes Neepnet,) are more pleasant and fertile then the borders of the Sea coaste. And the *The country of Erocois as fertile as Delta in Ægypt.* Country about Erocoise is, (not without good cause,) compared to Delta, the most fertile parte in all Ægypt, that aboundeth with Rivers and

Rivalets derived from Nilus fruitfull channell, like vaines from the liver; so in each respect is this famous Lake of Erocoise.

And, therefore, it would be adjudged an irreparable oversight to protract time, and suffer the Dutch, (who are but intruders upon his Majesties most hopefull Country of New England,) to possesse themselves of that so plesant and commodious Country of Erocoise before us: being, (as appeareth,) the principall part of all New Canaan for plantation, and not elsewhere to be paralelld in all the knowne world.

NEW CANAANS GENIUS.

EPILOGUS.

THOU *that art by Fates degree,*
  Or Providence, ordain'd to see
Natures wonder, her rich store
Ne'-r discovered before,
Th' admired Lake of Erocoise
And fertile Borders, now rejoyce.
See what multitudes of fish
Shee presents to fitt thy dish.
If rich furres thou dost adore,
And of Beaver Fleeces store,
See the Lake where they abound,
And what pleasures els are found.
There chast Leda, free from fire,
Does enjoy her hearts desire;
Mongst the flowry bancks at ease
Live the sporting Naiades,
Bigg lim'd Druides, whose browes
Bewtified with greenebowes.
See the Nimphes, how they doe make
Fine Meanders from the Lake,
Twining in and out, as they
Through the pleasant groves make way,
Weaving by the shady trees
Curious Anastomases,
Where the harmeles Turtles breede,
And such usefull Beasts doe feede
As no Traveller can tell
Els where how to paralell.
Colcos golden Fleece reject;
This deserveth best respect.
In sweete Peans let thy voyce,
Sing the praise of Erocoise,
Peans to advaunce her name,
New Canaans everlasting fame.

NEW ENGLISH CANAAN,
OR
NEW CANAAN.

The Third Booke.

Containing a description of the People that are planted there,
what remarkable Accidents have happened there since
they were setled, what Tenents they hould, together with
the practise of their Church.

CHAP. I.

*Of a great League made with the Plimmouth Planters
after their arrivall, by the Sachem of those Territories.*

THE Sachem of the Territories where the Planters of New
England are setled, that are the first of the now Inhabitants of New Canaan, not knowing what they were, or whether
they would be freindes or foes, and being desirous to purchase
their freindship that hee might have the better Assurance of
quiet tradinge with them, (which hee conceived would be very
advantagious to him,) was desirous to prepare an ambassador,
A Salvage sent with commission to treat on his behalfe, to that
an Ambassador purpose; and having one that had beene in Eng-
to the English land (taken by a worthlesse man out of other
at their first partes, and after left there by accident,) this Sal-
comminge. vage hee instructed how to behave himselfe in the treaty of
peace; and the more to give him incouragement to adventure
his person amongst these new come inhabitants, which was a
thinge hee durst not himselfe attempt without security or hostage, promised that Salvage freedome, who had beene detained
there as theire Captive: which offer hee accepted, and accordingly came to the Planters, salutinge them with wellcome in
the English phrase, which was of them admired to heare a
Salvage there speake in their owne language, and used him
great courtesie: to whome hee declared the cause of his comminge, and contrived the businesse so that hee brought the
Sachem and the English together, betweene whome was a firme
league concluded, which yet continueth. After which league
the Sachem, being in company with the other whome hee had

freed and suffered to live with the English, espiinge a place
where a hole had been made in the grounde, where was their
store of powder layed to be preserved from danger of fire,
(under ground,) demaunded of the Salvage what the English
had hid there under ground; who answered the plague; at
which hee starteled, because of the great mortality lately happened by meanes of the plague, (as it is conceaved,) and the
The Sachem   Salvage, the more to encrease his feare, told the
feared the   Sachem if he should give offence to the English
Plague.   party they would let out the plague to destroy
them all, which kept him in great awe. Not longe after, being
at varience with another Sachem borderinge upon his Territories, he came in solemne manner and intreated the governour
that he would let out the plague to destroy the Sachem and his
men who were his enemies, promising that he himselfe and all
his posterity would be their everlasting freindes, so great an
opinion he had of the English.

CHAP. II.
*Of the entertainement of Mr. Westons people
sent to settle a plantation there.*

MASTER Thomas Weston, a Merchant of London that had
been at some cost to further the Brethren of new Plimmouth
in their designes for these partes, shipped a company of Servants, fitted with provition of all sorts, for the undertaking of
a Plantation to be setled there; with an intent to follow after
Court holy   them in person. These servants at first arived at
bread at   new Plimmouth, where they were entertained
Plimmouth.   with court holy bread by the Brethren: they were
made very wellcome, in shew at least: there these servants
goodes were landed, with promises to be assisted in the choise
of a convenient place; and still the good cheare went forward,
and the strong liquors walked. In the meane time the Brethren
were in consultation what was best for their advantage, singing
the songe, *Frustra sapit, qui sibi non sapit.*

This plantation would hinder the present practice and future
profit; and Master Weston, an able man, would want for no
supplies upon the returne of Beaver, and so might be a plantation that might keepe them under, who had a Hope to be
the greatest: besides his people were no chosen Seperatists, but

men made choice of at all adventures, fit to have served for the
furtherance of Master Westons undertakinges: and that was as
much as hee neede to care for: ayminge at Beaver principally for
the better effecting of his purpose. Now when the Plimmouth
men began to finde that Master Westons mens store of provition grew short with feasting, then they hasted them to a place
called Wessaguscus, in a weake case, and there left them fasting.

CHAP. III.
Of a Battle fought at the Massachussets,
betweene the English and the French.

THE Planters of Plimmouth, at their last being in those parts,
having defaced the monument of the ded at Pasonagessit, (by
taking away the herse Cloath, which was two greate Beares
skinnes sowed together at full length, and propped up over the
grave of Chuatawbacks mother,) the Sachem of those territo-

The Sachems Oration. ries, being inraged at the same, stirred up his men
in his bee halfe to take revenge: and, having gath-
ered his men together, hee begins to make an
oration in this manner. When last the glorious light of all the
skey was underneath this globe, and Birds grew silent, I began

A spirit mooving the Sachem to Warre. to settle, (as my custome is,) to take repose; before
mine eies were fast closed, mee thought I saw a
vision, (at which my spirit was much troubled,)
and, trembling at that dolefull sight, a spirit cried aloude
behold, my sonne, whom I have cherisht, see the papps that
gave thee suck, the hands that lappd thee warme and fed thee
oft, canst thou forget to take revenge of those vild people that
hath my monument defaced in despitefull manner, disdaining
our ancient antiquities and honourable Customes? See now the
Sachems grave lies like unto the common people of ignoble
race, defaced; thy mother doth complaine, implores thy aide
against this theevish people new come hether; if this be suffered I shall not rest in quiet within my everlasting habitation.
This said, the spirit vanished; and I, all in a sweat, not able
scarce to speake, began to gett some strength, and recollect my
spirits that were fled: all which I thought to let you understand,

The grand Captaine makes a speech. to have your Councell, and your aide likewise; this
being spoken, straight way arose the grand Cap-
taine and cried aloud, come, let us to Armes, it

doth concerne us all, let us bid them Battaile; so to Armes they
went, and laid weight for the Plimmouth boate; and, forceinge
them to forsake their landinge place, they seeke another best
for their convenience; thither the Salvages repaire,
in hope to have the like successe; but all in vaine,
for the English Captaine warily foresaw, and, per-
ceavinge their plot, knew the better how to order his men fit
for Battaile in that place; hee, bouldly leading his men on,
rainged about the feild to and fro, and, taking his best advantage, lets fly, and makes the Salvages give ground: the English
followed them fiercely on, and made them take trees for their
shelter, (as their custome is,) from whence their Captaine let
flie a maine; yet no man was hurt; at last, lifting up his right
arm to draw a fatall shaft, (as hee then thought to end this
difference), received a shott upon his elbow, and straight way
fled; by whose example all the army followed the same way, and
yealded up the honor of the day to the English party; who were
such a terror to them after that the Salvages durst
never make to a head against them any more.

The maine Battaile.

The feild wonne by the English.

CHAP. IV.
Of a Parliament held at Wessaguscus, and the Actes.

MASTER Westons Plantation beinge setled at Wessaguscus, his
Servants, many of them lazy persons that would
use no endeavour to take the benefit of the Country, some of them fell sicke and died.

Some lazy people.

One amongst the rest, an able bodied man that
ranged the woodes to see what it would afford,
lighted by accident on an Indian barne, and from thence did
take a capp full of corne; the Salvage owner of it, finding by the
foote some English had bin there, came to the Plantation, and
made complaint after this manner.

A lusty fellow.

The cheife Commander of the Company one
this occation called a Parliament of all his people,
but those that were sicke and ill at ease. And
wisely now they must consult upon this huge
complaint, that a privy knife or stringe of beades
would well enough have qualified; and Edward Johnson was a

A poore complaint. Edward Johnson a cheife Judge. Maide a hainous fact.

spetiall judge of this businesse; the fact was there in repetition; construction made that it was fellony, and by the Lawes of England punished with death; and this in execution must be put for an example, and likewise to appease the Salvage: when straight wayes one arose, mooved as it were with some compassion, and said hee could not well gaine say the former sentence, yet hee had conceaved within the compasse of his braine an Embrion that was of spetiall consequence to be delivered and cherished; hee said that it would most aptly serve to pacifie the Salvages complaint, and save the life of one that might, (if neede should be,) stand them in some good steede, being younge and stronge, fit for resistance against an enemy, which might come unexpected for any thinge they knew. The Oration made was liked of every one, and hee intreated to proceede to

A fine device.   shew the meanes how this may be performed: sayes hee, you all agree that one must die, and one *A wise* shall die; this younge mans cloathes we will take *Sentence.*   of, and put upon one that is old and impotent, a sickly person that cannot escape death, such is the disease one him confirmed that die hee must; put the younge *To hange a sick* mans cloathes on this man, and let the sick person *man in the* be hanged in the others steede: Amen sayes one; *others steede.*   and so sayes many more.

And this had like to have prooved their finall sentence, and, being there confirmed by Act of Parliament, to after ages for a President: But that one with a ravenus voyce begunne to croake and bellow for revenge; and put by that conclusive motion, alledging such deceipts might be a meanes hereafter to exasperate the mindes of the complaininge Salvages, and that by his *Very fit Justice.*   death the Salvages should see their zeale to Justice; and therefore hee should die: this was concluded; yet neverthelesse a scruple was made; now to countermaund this act, did represent itselfe unto their mindes, which was, how they should doe to get the mans good wil? this *A dangerous* was indeede a spetiall obstacle: for without that, *Attempt.*   they all agreed it would be dangerous for any man to attempt the execution of it, lest mischeife should befall them every man; hee was a person that in his wrath did seeme to be a second Sampson, able to beate out

their branes with the jawbone of an Asse: therefore they called
the man, and by perswation got him fast bound in jest; and
then hanged him up hard by in good earnest, who with a
weapon, and at liberty, would have put all those
Jesting turned wise judges of this Parliament to a pittifull *non*
to earnest. *plus*, (as it hath beene credibly reported,) and
made the cheife Judge of them all buckell to him.

CHAP. V.
Of a Massacre made upon the Salvages at Wessaguscus.

Aᴛᴇʀ the end of that Parliament, some of the plantation
there, about three persons, went to live with Checatawback and
Good quarters his company; and had very good quarter, for all
with the the former quarrell with the Plimmouth planters:
Salvages. they are not like Will Sommers, to take one for
another. There they purposed to stay untill Master Westons
arrivall: but the Plimmouth men, intendinge no good to him,
(as appered by the consequence,) came in the meane time to
Wessaguscus, and there pretended to feast the
A plott from Salvages of those partes, bringing with them
Plimmouth. Porke and thinges for the purpose, which they sett
before the Salvages. They eate thereof without suspition of any
mischeife, who were taken upon a watchword given, and with
Salvages killed their owne knives, (hanging about their neckes,)
with their one were by the Plimmouth planters stabd and slaine:
weapons. one of which were hanged up there, after the
slaughter.

In the meane time the Sachem had knowledge of this accident, by one that ranne to his Countrymen, at the
News carried. Massachussets, and gave them intelligence of the
newes; after which time the Salvages there, consultinge of the
matter, in the night, (when the other English fearles of danger
were a sleepe,) knockt them all in the head, in revenge of the
death of their Countrymen: but if the Plimmouth
A revenge. Planters had really intended good to Master
Weston, or those men, why had they not kept the Salvages alive
in Custody, untill they had secured the other English? Who,
by meanes of this evill mannaginge of the businesse, lost their
lives, and the whole plantation was dissolved thereupon; as was

likely, for feare of a revenge to follow, as a relatione to this cruell antecedent; and when Master Weston came over hee found thinges at an evill exigent, by meanes thereof: But could not tell how it was brought about.

The Salvages of the Massachussets, that could not imagine from whence these men should come, or to what end, seeing them performe such unexpected actions; neither could tell by what name properly to distinguish them; did from that time

The Salvages call the English cutthroats. afterwards call the English Planters Wotawquenange, which in their language signifieth stabbers, or Cutthroates: and this name was received by those that came there after for good, being then unacquainted with the signification of it, for many yeares following; untill, from a Southerly Indian that understood English well, I was by demonstration made to conceave the interpretation of it, and rebucked these other that it was not forborne: The other callinge us by the name of Wotoquansawge, what that doth signifie, hee said, hee was not able by any demonstration to expresse; and my neighbours durst no more, in my hearinge, call us by the name formerly used, for feare of my displeasure.

CHAP. VI.
Of the surprizinge of a Merchants Shipp in Plimmouth harbour.

THIS Merchant, a man of worth, arrivinge in the parts of New

The Merchant with Supply. Canaan and findinge that his Plantation was dissolved, some of his men slaine, some dead with sicknes, and the rest at Plimmouth, hee was perplexed in his minde about the matter; comminge as hee did with supply, and meanes to have rased their fortunes and his one exceedingly: and seeinge what had happened resolved to make some stay in the Plimmouth harbour. And this suted to their purpose; wherefore the Brethren did congratulate with him at his safe arrivall, and their best of entertainement for a

A glosse upon the false text. swetning cast, deploring the disaster of his Plantation, and glozing upon the text, alledging the mischeivous intent of the Salvages there, which by freindly intelligence of their neighbours was discovered before it came to be full summed: so that they lost not all, allthough they saved not all: and this they pretended to proceede from the Fountaine of love and zeale to him and Christianity, and to chastise the insolency of the Salvages, of which that part had some dangerous persons. And this, as an article of the new creede of Canaan, would they have received of every new commer there to inhabit, that the Salvages are a dangerous people, subtill, secreat and mischeivous; and that it is dangerous to live seperated, but rather together: and so be under their Lee, that none might trade for Beaver, but at their pleasure, as none doe or shall doe there: nay they will not be reduced to any other song yet of the Salvages to the southward of Plimmouth, because they would have none come there, sayinge that hee that will sit downe there must come stronge: but I have found the Massachussets Indian more full of humanity then the Christians; and have had much better quarter with them; yet I observed not their humors, but they mine; althoug my *Where two* great number that I landed were dissolved, and *nations meet* my Company as few as might be: for I know that *one must rule* this falls out infallibly where two Nations meete, *the other must* *be ruled or no* one must rule and the other be ruled, before a *quietnes.* peace can be hoped for: and for a Christian to submit to the rule of a Salvage, you will say, is both shame and dishonor: at least it is my opinion, and my practise was accordingly, and I have the better quarter by the meanes thereof. The more Salvages the better quarter, the more Christians the worser quarter, I found; as all the indifferent minded Planters can testifie. Now, whiles the Merchant was ruminatinge on this mishapp, the Plimmouth Planters perceivinge that hee had furnished himselfe with excellent Commodities, fit for the Merchandise of the Country, (and holding it good *A Machivell* to fish in trobled waters, and so get a snatch *plot.* unseene,) practised in secret with some other in the land, whom they thought apt to imbrace the benefit of such *The Vaile.* a cheat, and it was concluded and resolved upon that all this shipp and goodes should be confiscated, for businesse done by him, the Lord knowes when, or where: a letter must be framed to them, and handes unto it, to be there warrant; this should shadow them. That is the first *Shippe* practise; they will insane a man, and then pretend *and goodes* that Justice must be done. They cause the Mer- *confiscated.* chant (secure) to come a shore, and then take him in hold, shewing they are compelled unto it legally, and enter strait abord, peruse the Cargazowne, and then deliver up the Charge of her to their Confederates: and how much lesse this is then Piraty, let any practise in the Admiralty be judge. The Merchant, his shipp and goodes confiscated, himselfe a prisoner and threatned so to be sent and conveyed to England, there to receave the somme of all that did belonge to him a *When every* malefactor, (and a great one to); this hee, good *Conspirator* man, indured with patience longe time, untill the *had his share* *the shipp* best of all his goodes were quite dispersed, and *delivered* every actor had his proportion; the Merchant was *againe.* then inlarged; his shipp, a burthen to the owner now, his undertakinges in these partes beinge quite over- *Bonds taken not* thrown, was redelivered, and bondes of him were *to prosecute.* taken not to prosecute: hee, being greived hereat, betakes him to drive a trade betweene that and Virginea many yeares. The brethren, (sharpe witted,) had it spread by and by amongst his freinds in England, that the man *Report Mr.* was mad. So thought his wife, so thought his *Weston was* other freindes that had it from a Planter of the *mad in New* *England.* Towne. So was it thought of those, that did not know the Brethren could dissemble: why, thus they are all of them honest men in their particular, and every man, beinge bound to seeke anothers good, shall in the gen- *Honest men in* erall doe the best hee can to effect it, and so they *particular.* may be excused I thinke.

CHAP. VII.
Of Thomas Mortons entertainement at Plimmouth, *and castinge away upon an Island.*

THIS man arrived in those parts, and, hearing newes of a Towne that was much praised, he was desirous to goe thither, *Brave* and see how thinges stood; where his entertaine- *entertainement* ment was their best, I dare be bould to say: for, *in a wildernes.* although they had but 3. Cowes in all, yet had they fresh butter and a sallet of egges in dainty wise, a dish not common in a wildernes. There hee bestowed some time in the survey of this plantation. His new come servants, in the meane time, were tane to taske, to have their zeale appeare, and questioned what preacher was among their company; and finding

none, did seeme to condole their estate as if undone, because
no man among them had the guilt to be in Jonas
steade, nor they the meanes to keepe them in that
path so hard to keepe.

The meanes.

Our Master, say they, reades the Bible and the word of God,
and useth the booke of common prayer: but this is not the
meanes, the answere is: the meanes, they crie, alas, poore
Soules where is the meanes? you seeme as if betrayed, to be
without the meanes: how can you be stayed from fallinge headlonge to perdition? *Facilis descensus averni*: the booke of
common prayer, sayd they, what poore thinge is that, for a man
to reade in a booke? No, no, good sirs, I would you were neere
us, you might receave comfort by instruction: give me a man
hath the guiftes of the spirit, not a booke in hand.
I doe professe says one, to live without the meanes
is dangerous, the Lord doth know.

*Booke learning
despised.*

By these insinuations, like the Serpent, they did creepe and
winde into the good opinion of the illiterate multitude, that
were desirous to be freed and gone to them, no doubdt, (which
some of them after confessed); and little good was to be done
one them after this charme was used: now plotts and factions
how they might get loose: and here was some 35. stout knaves;
and some plotted how to steale Master Westons
barque, others, exasperated knavishly to worke,
would practise how to gett theire Master to an
Island, and there leave him; which hee had notice of, and fitted
him to try what would be done; and steps aborde his shallop
bound for Cape Anne, to the Massachussets, with an Hogshead of Wine; Sugar hee tooke along, the Sailes hoist up, and
one of the Conspirators aboard to steere; who in the mid way
pretended foule weather at the harboure mouth, and therefore,
for a time, hee would put in to an Island neere, and make some
stay where hee thought to tempt his Master to walke the
woods, and so be gone: but their Master to prevent them caused the sales and oares to be brought
a shore, to make a tilt if neede should be, and
kindled fire, broched that Hogshed, and caused
them fill the can with lusty liqour, Claret spar-
klinge neate; which was not suffered to grow pale
and flatt, but tipled of with quick dexterity: the Master makes

*Villanous plots
of knaves.*

*Prevented by
discretion.*

*And discovered
in drinke.*

a shew of keepinge round, but with close lipps did seeme to make longe draughts, knowinge the wine would make them Protestants; and so the plot was then at large disclosed and discovered, and they made drowsie; and the inconstant windes shiftinge at night did force the kellecke home, and billedge the boat, that they were forced to leave her so, and cut downe trees that grew by the shore, to make Casses: two of them went over by help of a fore saile almost a mile to the maine; the other two stayed five dayes after, till the windes would serve to fill the sailes. The first two went to cape Ann by land, and had fowle enough, and fowle wether by the way; the Islanders had fish enough, shel-fish and fire to roast, and they could not perish for lacke of foode, and wine they had to be sure; and by this you see they were not then in any want: the wine and goodes brought thence; the boat left there so billedgd that it was not worth the labor to be mended.

The Shallop billedged.

Two men of the Company cast away swim to shore upon trees.

CHAP. VIII.
Of the Banishment of Master John Layford, and John Oldam from Plimmouth.

MASTER Layford was at the Merchants chardge sent to Plimmouth plantation to be their Pastor: But the Brethren, before they would allow of it, would have him first renounce his calling to the office of the Ministery, received in England, as hereticall and Papisticall, (so hee confest,) and then to receive a new callinge from them, after their fantasticall invention: which hee refused, alledging and maintaining that his calling as it stood was lawfull, and that hee would not renounce it; and so John Oldam, his opinion was one the affirmative; and both together did maintaine the Church of England to be a true Church, although in some particulars, (they said,) defective; concludinge so against the Tenents there: and by this meanes cancelled theire good opinion amonst the number of the Seperatists, that stay they must not, lest they should be spies: and to fall fowle on this occation the Brethren thought it would betray their cause, and make it fall under censure, therefore against Master Layford they had found out some scandall

A Minister required to renounce his callinge.

to be laid on his former corse of life, to blemish that; and so, to conclude, hee was a spotted beast, and not to be allowed where they ordained to have the Passover kept so zealously: as for John Oldam, they could see hee would be passionate and moody, and proove himselfe a mad Jack in his mood, and as soone mooved to be moody, and this impatience would Minister advantage to them to be ridd of him.

Hanniball when hee had to doe with Fabius was kept in awe *Impatience confuted by example.* more by the patience of that one enemy, then by the resolution of the whole army: A well tempered enemy is a terrible enemy to incounter. They injoyne him to come to their needeles watch howse in person, *New Plimmouth presse money.* and for refusinge give him a cracked Crowne for presse money, and make the blood run downe about his eares; a poore trick, yet a good vaile, though Luscus may see thorough it; and, for his further behaviour in the Case, proceed to sentence him with banishment, which was performed after a solemne invention in this manner: *The Solemnity of banishment.* A lane of Musketiers was made, and hee compelled in scorne to passe along betweene, and to receave a bob upon the bumme be every musketier; and then a board a shallop, and so convayed to Wessaguscus shoare, and staid at Massachussets: to whome John Layford and some few more did resort; where Master Layford freely executed his office and preached every Lords day, and yet maintained his wife and children foure or five upon his industry there, with the blessing of God and the plenty of the Land, without the helpe of his auditory, in an honest and laudable manner; till hee was wearied and made to leave the Country.

CHAP. IX.
Of a barren doe of Virginea growne fruithfull in New Canaan.

CHILDREN, and the fruit of the Wombe, are said in holy writt to be an inheritance that commeth of the Lord; then they must be coupled in Gods name first, and not as this, and some other, *A great happines comes by propagation.* have done.

They are as arrowes in the hand of a Gyant; and happy, saith David, is the man that hath his quiver full of them; and by that rule, happy is that Land, and blessed to, that is apt and fit for increase of children.

I have shewed you before, in the second part of the discourse, how apt it is for the increase of Minerals, Vegetables, and sensible Creatures.

Now I will shew you how apt New Canaan is likewise for the increase of the reasonable Creatures; Children, of all riches, being the principall: and I give you this for an instance.

This Country of New Canaan in seaven yeares time could show more Children livinge, that have beene borne there, then in 27. yeares could be shewen in Virginea; yet here are but a handful of weomen landed, to that of Virginea.

More Children in New Canaan in 7. yeares, then in Virginea in 27. The Country doth afford such plenty of Lobsters and other delicate shellfish, and Venus is said to be borne of the Sea; or else it was some sallet herbe proper to the Climate, or the fountaine at Weenaseemute made her become teeming here that had tried a campe royall in other partes where shee had been; and yet never the neere, till shee came in to New Canaan.

Shee was delivered, (in a voyage to Virginea,) about Bussardes bay, to west of Cape Cod, where shee had a Sonne borne, *Delivered neare Bussards bay.* but died without baptisme and was buried; and being a thinge remarkable, had this Epitaph fol- *Dead and buried.* lowinge made of purpose to memorize the worth of the persons.

EPITAPH.

Time, that bringes all thinges to light,
Doth hide this thinge out of sight:
Yet fame hath left behinde a story,
A hopefull race to shew the glory:
For underneath this heape of stones
Lieth a percell of small bones;
What hope at last can such impes have,
That from the wombe goes to the grave.

CHAP. X.

*Of a man indued with many speciall guifts
sent over to be Master of the Ceremonies.*

THIS was a man approoved of the Brethren, both for his zeale and guiftes, yet but a Bubble, and at the publike Chardge con-

Stenography one guift.

veyed to New England, I thinke to be Master of the Ceremonies betweene the Natives, and the Planters: for hee applied himselfe cheifly to pen the language downe in Stenography: But there for want of use, which hee rightly understood not, all was losse of labor; somethinge it was when next it came to view, but what hee could not tell.

This man, Master Bubble, was in the time of John Oldams absence made the howse Chaplaine there, and every night hee

Oratory another guift.

made use of his guifts, whose oratory luld his auditory fast a sleepe, as Mercuries pipes did Argus eies: for, when hee was in, they sayd hee could not tell how to get out; nay, hee would hardly out till hee were fired out, his zeale was such: (one fire they say drives out

A great Merchant a third guift.

another): hee would become a great Merchant, and by any thinge that was to be sold so as hee might have day and be trusted never so litle time: the price it seemed hee stood not much upon, but the day: for to his freind hee shewed commodities, so priced as caused him to blame the buyer, till the man this Bubble did declare that it was tane up at day, and did rejoyce in the bargaine, insistinge on the day; the day, yea, marry, quoth his friend, if you have doomesday for payment you are then well to passe. But if he had not, it were as good hee had; they were payed all alike.

His day made a common proverbe.

And now this Bubbles day is become a common proverbe. Hee obtained howse roome at Passonagessit and removed thether, because it stood convenient for the Beaver trade: and the rather because the owner of Passonagessit had no Corne left, and this man seemed a bigg boned man, and therefore thought to be a good laborer, and to have store of corne; but, contrary wise, hee had none at

Trophies of honor.

all, and hoped upon this freind his host: thithere were brought the trophies of this Master Bubbles honor, his water tankard and his Porters basket,

but no provision; so that one gunne did serve to helpe them
both to meat; and now the time for fowle was almost past.

His long grace   This man and his host at dinner, Bubble begins
made the meat   to say grace; yea, and a long one to, till all the
cold.   meate was cold; hee would not give his host leave
to say grace: belike, hee thought mine host past grace, and
further learned as many other Schollers are: but in the usage
and custome of this blinde oratory his host tooke himselfe
abused, and the whiles fell to and had halfe done before this
man Bubble would open his eies to see what stood afore him,
which made him more cautius, and learned that *brevis oratio
penetrat Cælum.* Together Bubbles and hee goes in the Canaw
to Nut Island for brants, and there his host makes a shotte and
breakes the winges of many: Bubble, in hast and single handed,
paddels out like a Cow in a cage: his host cals back to rowe
two handed like to a pare of oares; and, before this could be
performed, the fowle had time to swimme to other flockes, and
so to escape: the best part of the pray being lost mayd his host
to mutter at him, and so to parte for that time discontended.

CHAP. XI.

*Of a Composition made by the Sachem for a Theft committed
by some of his men, shewinge their honest meaninge.*

THE owner of Passonagessit, to have the benefit of company,
left his habitation in the Winter and reposed at Wessaguscus,
(to his cost): meane time, in the Depth of Winter, the neigh-
The Salvages   bour Salvages, accustomed to buy foode, came to
betake the howse the howse, (for that intent perhaps,) and peepinge
& take the
Corne.   in all the windowes, (then unglased,) espied corne,
but no body to sell the same; and having company and helpe
at hand did make a shift to get into the howse, and, take out
corne to serve but for the present, left enough behinde: the
Sachem having knowledge of the facte, and being advertised
likewise of the displeasure that had ben conceaved by the Proprietor thereof at this offence, prepares a Messenger, the Salvage that had lived in England, and sends him with commission
for the trespasse of his men, who had tenne skinnes perposed
for it to bee payd by a day certaine: The Sachem, at the time
appointed, brings the Beaver to Wessaguscus where the owner

lived, but just then was gone abroade: meane time the skinnes were by the Wessaguscus men gelded, and the better halfe by them juggled away before the owner came; and hee by the Actors perswaded to bee contended with the rest who not so pleased did draw the Sachem then to make a new agreement, and so to pay his remnant left in hand, and tenne skinnes more by a new day asigned, and then to bringe them to Passonagessit; but the Wessaguscus men went the day before to the Salvages with this sayinge, that they were sent to call upon him there for payement; and received tenne skinnes, and tooke a Salvage there to justifie that at their howse the owner stayed the while; hee verified this, because hee saw the man before at Wessaguscus: the Sachem did beleive the tale, and at that time delivered up tenne skinnes on that behalfe, in full dischardge of all demandes against the trespasse and the trespassers, to them; who consented to him, and them, to the owner, and kept nine to themselves, and made the Salvage take the tenth, and give the owner all that yet was to bee had, themselves confessinge their demaunds for him, and that there was but onely one as yet prepared: so that by this you may easily perceive the uncivilized people are more just than the civilized.

A dishonest tricke.

A consenting tricke. The Heathen more just, then the Christians.

CHAP. XII.

Of a voyadge made by the Master of the Ceremonies of New Canaan to Neepenett, from whence hee came away; and of the manifold dangers hee escaped.

THIS woorthy member Master Bubble, a new Master of the Ceremonies, having a conceipt in his head that hee had hatched a new device for the purchase of Beaver, beyond Imagination, packes up a sacke full of odde implements, and without any company but a couple of Indians for guides, (and therefore you may, if you please, beeleive they are so dangerous as the Brethren of Plimmouth give it out,) hee betakes him to his progresse into the Inlande for Beaver, with his carriadge on his shoulders like Milo: his guides and hee in processe of time come to the place appointed, which was about Neepenett, thereabouts being

Two Salvage guides conduct John, to Neepenett alone.

more Beavers to be had then this Milo could carry, and both his journey men: glad hee was good man, and his guides were willing to pleasure him: there the Salvages stay: night came on, but, before they were inclined to sleepe, this good man Master Bubble had an evation crept into his head, by misapplying the Salvages actions, that hee must needs be gone in all hast, yea and without his errand: hee purposed to doe it so cunningely that his flight should not be suspected: hee leaves his shooes in the howse, with all his other implements, and flies: as hee was on his way, to increase his feare, suggestinge himselfe that hee was pressed by a company of Indians and that there shafts were let fly as thick as haile at him, hee puts of his breeches and puts them one his head, for to save him from the shafts that flew after him so thick that no man could perceave them, and cry-inge out, avoyd Satan, what have yee to doe with mee! thus running one his way without his breeches hee was pittifully scratched with the brush of the underwoods, as hee wandred up and downe in unknowne wayes: The Salvages in the meane time put up all his implements in the sack hee left behinde and brought them to Wessaguscus, where they thought to have found him; but, understanding hee was not returned, were ferefull what to doe, and what would be conceaved of the English was become of this mazed man, the Master of the Ceremonies; and were in consultation of the matter. One of the Salvages was of opinion the English would suppose him to be made away; fearefull hee was to come in sight. The other, better acquainted with the English, (having lived some time in England,) was more confident, and hee perswaded his fellow that the English would be satisfied with relation of the truth, as having had testimony of his fidelity. So they boldly adven-

They take a note of what was in the sack. tured to shew what they had brougt and how the matter stood. The English, (when the sack was opened,) did take a note in writing of all the par-ticulers that were in the sack; and heard what was by the Sal-vages related of the accidents: but, when his shoes were showne, it was thought hee would not have departed without his shoes;

Mr. Bubble must be found againe or else they shall be destroyed. and therefore they did conceave that Master Bubble was made away by some sinister practise of the Salvages, who unadvisedly had bin culpable of a crime which now they sought to excuse; and straightly chardged the Salvages to finde him out againe, and bring him dead, or alive, else their wifes and children should be destroyed. The poore Salvages, being in a pittifull perplexity, caused their Countrymen to seeke out for this maz'd man; who, being in short time found, was brought to Wessaguscus; where hee made a discourse of his travels, and of the perrillous passages, which did seeme to be no lesse dangerous then these of that worthy Knight Errant, Don Quixote, and how miraculously hee had bin preserved; and, in conclusion, lamented the greate losse of his goods, whereby hee thought himselfe undone.

The perticuler whereof being demaunded, it appeared that the Salvages had not diminished any part of them; no, not so much as one bit of bread: the number being knowne, and the fragments laid together, it appeared all the bisket was preserved, and not any diminished at all: whereby the Master of the Ceremonies was overjoyed, and the whole Company made themselves merry at his discourse of all his perrillous adventures.

Not any thing diminished.

And by this you may observe whether the Salvage people are not full of humanity, or whether they are a dangerous people, as Master Bubble and the rest of his tribe would perswade you.

CHAP. XIII.

Of a lamentable fit of Mellancolly that the Barren doe fell into, (after the death of her infant, seeing herselfe despised of her Sweete hart,) whereof shee was cured.

WHETHER this goodly creature of incontinency went to worke upon even termes like Phillis, or noe, it does not appeare by any Indenture of covenants then extant; whereby shee might legally challenge the performance of any compleate Marriage at his hands that had bin tradeing with her, as Demopheon here to fore had bin with his ostis.

Neverthelesse, (for his future advantage,) shee indeavoured, (like Phillis,) to gaine this Demopheon all to herselfe; who, (as it seemes,) did meane nothing lesse by leaving her for the next commer, that had any minde to coole his courage by that meanes; the whipping post, (as it seemes,) at that time not being in publike use for such kinde of Cony katchers; but

seeing herselfe rejected, shee grew into such a passion of Mellancolly, on a sodaine, that it was thought shee would exhibit
a petition for redresse to grim Pluto, who had set her a worke;

Shee cannot and knowing that the howse of fate has many
one the sodaine entrances, shee was pusseld to finde the neerest
resolve which
dore to goe in way. Shee could not resolve on a sodaine which
att. doore would soonest bring her to his presence
handsomely.

If shee should make way with a knife, shee thought shee
might spoyle her drinking in after ages; if by poyson, shee
thought it might prolonge her passage thether; if by drowning,
shee thought Caron might come the while with his boate, and
waft her out of sight; if shee should tie up her complaint in
a halter, shee thought the Ropmakers would take exceptions
against her good speede. And in this manner shee debated
with herselfe, and demurred upon the matter: So that shee
did appeare willing enough, but a woman of small resolution.

Which thing when it was publikely knowne, made many come
to comfort her. One amongst the rest was by hir requested, on
her behalfe, to write to her late unkinde Demopheon. The
Gentleman, being merrily disposed, in steed of writing an
heroicall Epistle composed this Elegi, for a memoriall of some
mirth upon the Circumstance of the matter, to be sent unto
hir, as followeth:

CARMEN ELEGIACUM.

Melpomene, (at whose mischeifous love
The screech owles voyce is heard the mandraks grove,)
Commands my pen in an Iambick vaine
To tell a dismall tale, that may constraine
The hart of him to bleede, that shall discerne
How much this foule amisse does him concerne.
Alecto (grim Alecto,) light thy tortch
To thy beloved sister next the porch
That leads unto the mansion howse of fate,
Whose farewell makes her freind more fortunate.
A Great Squa Sachem can shee poynt to goe
Before grim Minos; and yet no man know
That knives and halters, ponds, and poysonous things

> *Are alwayes ready, when the Divell once brings*
> *Such deadly sinners to a deepe remorse*
> *Of conscience selfe accusing, that will force*
> *Them to dispaire, like wicked Kain, whiles death*
> *Stands ready with all these to stopp their breath.*
> *The beare comes by that oft hath bayted ben*
> *By many a Satyres whelp; unlesse you can*
> *Commaund your eies to drop huge milstones forth,*
> *In lamentation of this losse on earth*
> *Of her, of whome so much prayse wee may finde,*
> *Goe when shee will, shee'l leave none like behinde;*
> *Shee was too good for earth, too bad for heaven.*
> *Why then for hell the match is somewhat even.*

After this, the water of the fountaine at Ma-re Mount was thought fit to be applyed unto her for a remedy, shee willingly used according to the quality thereof.

And when this Elegy came to be divulged, shee was so conscious of her crime that shee put up her pipes, and with the next shipp shee packt away to Virginea, (her former habitation,) quite cured of her mellancolly, with the helpe of the water of the fountaine at Ma-re Mount.

CHAP. XIV.
Of the Revells of New Canaan.

THE Inhabitants of Pasonagessit, (having translated the name of their habitation from that ancient Salvage name to Ma-re Mount, and being resolved to have the new name confirmed for a memorial to after ages,) did devise amongst themselves to have it performed in a solemne manner, with Revels and merriment after the old English cuftome; they prepared to sett up *A Maypole.* a Maypole upon the festivall day of Philip and Jacob, and therefore brewed a barrell of excellent beare and provided a case of bottles, to be spent, with other good cheare, for all commers of that day. And because they would have it in a compleat forme, they had prepared a song fitting to the time and present occasion. And upon Mayday they brought the Maypole to the place appointed, with drumes, gunnes, pistols and other fitting instruments, for that purpose;

and there erected it with the help of Salvages, that came thether
of purpose to see the manner of our Revels. A goodly pine tree
of 80. foote longe was reared up, with a peare of buckshorns
nayled one somewhat neare unto the top of it: where it stood,
as a faire sea marke for directions how to finde out the way to
mine Hoste of Ma-re Mount.

And because it should more fully appeare to what end it was
placed there, they had a poem in readines made, which was
fixed to the Maypole, to shew the new name confirmed upon
that plantation; which, allthough it were made according to
the occurrents of the time, it, being Enigmattically composed, pusselled the Seperatists most pittifully to expound
it, which, (for the better information of the reader,) I have
here inserted.

THE POEM.

> Rise Oedipeus, and, if thou canst, unfould
> What meanes Caribdis underneath the mould,
> When Scilla sollitary on the ground
> (Sitting in forme of Niobe,) was found,
> Till Amphitrites Darling did acquaint
> Grim Neptune with the Tenor of her plaint,
> And causd him send forth Triton with the sound
> Of Trumpet lowd, at which the Seas were found
> So full of Protean formes that the bold shore
> Presented Scilla a new parramore
> So stronge as Sampson and so patient
> As Job himselfe, directed thus, by fate,
> To comfort Scilla so unfortunate.
> I doe professe, by Cupids beautious mother,
> Heres Scogans choise for Scilla, and none other;
> Though Scilla's sick with greife, because no signe
> Can there be found of vertue masculine.
> Esculapius come; I know right well
> His laboure's lost when you may ring her Knell.
> The fatall sisters doome none can withstand,
> Nor Cithareas powre, who poynts to land
> With proclamation that the first of May
> At Ma-re Mount shall be kept hollyday.

The man who brought her over was named Samson Job.

The setting up of this Maypole was a lamentable spectacle to the precise seperatists, that lived at new Plimmouth. They *The Maypole called an Idoll the Calfe of Horeb.* termed it an Idoll; yea, they called it the Calfe of Horeb, and stood at defiance with the place, naming it Mount Dagon; threatning to make it a woefull mount and not a merry mount.

The Riddle, for want of Oedipus, they could not expound; onely they made some explication of part of it, and sayd it was meant by Sampson Job, the carpenter of the shipp that brought over a woman to her husband, that had bin there longe before and thrived so well that hee sent for her and her children to come to him; where shortly after hee died: having no reason, but because of the sound of those two words; when as, (the truth is,) the man they applyed it to was altogether unknowne to the Author.

There was likewise a merry song made, which, (to make their Revells more fashionable,) was sung with a Corus, every man bearing his part; which they performed in a daunce, hand in hand about the Maypole, whiles one of the Company sung and filled out the good liquor, like gammedes and Jupiter.

THE SONGE.

Cor.

> *Drinke and be merry, merry, merry boyes;*
> *Let all your delight be in the Hymens joyes;*
> *Jô to Hymen, now the day is come,*
> *About the merry Maypole take a Roome.*
> > *Make greene garlons, bring bottles out*
> > *And fill sweet Nectar freely about.*
> > *Uncover thy head and feare no harme,*
> > *For hers good liquor to keepe it warme.*
> *Then drinke and be merry, &c.*
> *Jô to Hymen, &c.*
> > *Nectar is a thing assign'd*
> > *By the Deities owne minde*
> > *To cure the hart opprest with greife,*
> > *And of good liquors is the cheife.*
> *Then drinke, &c.*

Jô to Hymen, &c.
>   Give to the Mellancolly man
>   A cup or two of 't now and than;
>   This physick will soone revive his bloud,
>   And make him be of a merrier moode.
Then drinke, &c.
Jô to Hymen, &c.
>   Give to the Nymphe thats free from scorne
>   No Irish stuff nor Scotch over worne.
>   Lasses in beaver coats come away,
>   Yee shall be welcome to us night and day.
To drinke and be merry &c.
Jô to Hymen, &c.

This harmeles mirth made by younge men, (that lived in hope to have wifes brought over to them, that would save them a laboure to make a voyage to fetch any over,) was much distasted of the precise Seperatists, that keepe much a doe about the tyth of Muit and Cummin, troubling their braines more then reason would require about things that are indifferent: and from that time sought occasion against my honest Host of Ma-re Mount, to overthrow his ondertakings and to destroy his plantation quite and cleane. But because they presumed with their imaginary gifts, (which they have out of Phaos box,) they could expound hidden misteries, to convince them of blindnes, as well in this as in other matters of more consequence, I will illustrate the poem, according to the true intent of the authors of these Revells, so much distasted by those Moles.

Oedipus is generally receaved for the absolute reader of riddles, who is invoaked: Silla and Caribdis are two dangerous places for seamen to incounter, neere unto Vennice; and have bin by poets formerly resembled to man and wife. The like licence the author challenged for a paire of his nomination, the one lamenting for the losse of the other as Niobe for her children. Amphitrite is an arme of the Sea, by which the newes was carried up and downe of a rich widow, now to be tane up or laid downe. By Triton is the same spread that caused the Suters to muster, (as it had bin to Penellope of Greece;) and, the Coast lying circuler, all our passage to and froe is made more convenient by Sea then Land. Many aimed at this marke; but hee that played Proteus best and could comply with her humor must be the man that would carry her; and hee had need have Sampsons strenght to deale with a Dallila, and as much patience as Job that should come there, for a thing that I did observe in the life-time of the former.

But marriage and hanging, (they say,) comes by desteny and Scogans choise tis better than none at all. Hee that playd Proteus, (with the helpe of Priapus,) put their noses out of joynt, as the Proverbe is.

And this the whole company of the Revellers at Ma-re Mount knew to be the true sence and exposition of the riddle that was fixed to the Maypole, which the Seperatists were at defiance with. Some of them affirmed that the first institution thereof was in memory of a whore; not knowing that it was a Trophe erected at first in honor of Maja, the Lady of learning which they despise, vilifying the two universities with uncivile termes, accounting what is there obtained by studdy is but unnecessary learning; not considering that learninge does inable mens mindes to converse with eliments of a higher nature then is to be found within the habitation of the Mole.

CHAP. XV.
Of a great Monster supposed to be at Ma-re-Mount; and the preparation made to destroy it.

THE Seperatists, envying the prosperity and hope of the Plantation at Ma-re Mount, (which they perceaved beganne to come forward, and to be in a good way for gaine in the Beaver trade,) conspired together against mine Host especially, (who was the owner of that Plantation,) and made up a party against him; and mustred up what aide they could, accounting of him as of a great Monster.

Many threatening speeches were given out both against his person and his Habitation, which they divulged should be consumed with fire: And taking advantage of the time when his company, (which seemed little to regard theire threats,) were gone up into the Inlands to trade with the Salvages for Beaver, they set upon my honest host at a place called Wessaguscus, where, by accident, they found him. The inhabitants there were in good hope of the subvertion of the plantation at Mare Mount, (which they principally aymed at;) and the rather because mine host was a man that indeavoured to advaunce the dignity of the Church of England; which they, (on the contrary part,) would laboure to vilifie with uncivile termes: enveying against the sacred booke of common prayer, and mine host that used it in a laudable manner amongst his family, as a practise of piety.

There hee would be a meanes to bringe sacks to their mill, (such is the thirst after Beaver,) and helped the conspiratores to surprise mine host, (who was there all alone;) and they chardged him, (because they would seeme to have some reasonable cause against him to sett a glosse upon their mallice,) with criminall things; which indeede had beene done by such a person, but was of their conspiracy; mine host demaunded of the conspirators who it was that was author of that information, that seemed to be their ground for what they now intended. And because they answered they would not tell him, hee as peremptorily replyed, that hee would not say whether he had, or he had not done as they had bin informed.

The answere made no matter, (as it seemed,) whether it had bin negatively or affirmatively made; for they had resolved what hee should suffer, because, (as they boasted,) they were now become the greater number: they had shaked of their shackles of servitude, and were become Masters, and masterles people.

It appeares they were like beares whelpes in former time, when mine hosts plantation was of as much strength as theirs, but now, (theirs being stronger,) they, (like overgrowne beares,) seemed monsterous. In breife, mine host must indure to be their prisoner untill they could contrive it so that they might send him for England, (as they said,) there to suffer according to the merit of the fact which they intended to father upon him; supposing, (belike,) it would proove a hainous crime.

Much rejoycing was made that they had gotten their cappitall enemy, (as they concluded him;) whome they purposed to hamper in such sort that hee should not be able to uphold his plantation at Ma-re Mount.

The Conspirators sported themselves at my honest host, that meant them no hurt, and were so joccund that they feasted their bodies, and fell to tippeling as if they had obtained a great prize; like the Trojans when they had the custody of Hippeus pinetree horse.

Mine host fained greefe, and could not be perswaded either to eate or drinke; because hee knew emptines would be a meanes to make him as watchfull as the Geese kept in the Roman Cappitall: whereon, the contrary part, the conspirators would be so drowsy that hee might have an opportunity to give them a slip, insteade of a tester. Six persons of the conspiracy were set to watch him at Wessaguscus: But hee kept waking; and in the dead of night, (one lying on the bed for further suerty,) up gets mine Host and got to the second dore that hee was to passe, which, notwithstanding the lock, hee got open, and shut it after him with such violence that it affrighted some of the conspirators.

Mine Host got out of prison.

The word, which was given with an alarme, was, ô he 's gon, he 's gon, what shall wee doe, he 's gon! The rest, (halfe a sleepe,) start up in a maze, and, like rames, ran theire heads one at another full butt in the darke.

Theire grande leader, Captaine Shrimp, tooke on most furiously and tore his clothes for anger, to see the empty nest, and their bird gone.

The Captaine tore his clothes.

The rest were eager to have torne theire haire from theire heads; but it was so short that it would give them no hold. Now Captaine Shrimp thought in the losse of this prize, (which hee accoumpted his Master peece,) all his honor would be lost for ever.

In the meane time mine Host was got home to Ma-re Mount through the woods, eight miles round about the head of the river Monatoquit that parted the two Plantations, finding his way by the helpe of the lightening, (for it thundred as hee went terribly;) and there hee prepared powther, three pounds dried, for his present imployement, and foure good gunnes for him and the two assistants left at his howse, with bullets of severall sizes, three hounderd or thereabouts, to be used if the conspirators should pursue him thether: and these two persons promised theire aides in the quarrell, and confirmed that promise with health in good rosa solis.

Mine host got home to ma-re mount.

Hee provides for his enemies.

Now Captaine Shrimp, the first Captaine in the Land, (as hee supposed,) must doe some new act to repaire this losse, and, to vindicate his reputation, who had sustained blemish by this oversight, begins now to study, how to repaire or survive his honor: in this manner, callinge of Councell, they conclude.

Hee takes eight persons more to him, and, (like the nine Worthies of New Canaan,) they imbarque with preparation against Ma-re-Mount, where this Monster of a man, as theire phrase was, had his denne; the whole number, had the rest not bin from home, being but seaven, would have given Captaine Shrimpe, (a quondam Drummer,) such a wellcome as would have made him wish for a Drume as bigg as Diogenes tubb, that hee might have crept into it out of sight.

Now the nine Worthies are approached, and mine Host prepared: having intelligence by a Salvage, that hastened in love from Wessaguscus to give him notice of their intent.

One of mine Hosts men prooved a craven: the other had prooved his wits to purchase a little valoure, before mine Host had observed his posture.

The nine worthies comming before the Denne of this supposed Monster, (this seaven headed hydra, as they termed him,) *A Parly.* and began, like Don Quixote against the Windmill, to beate a parly, and to offer quarter, if mine Host would yeald; for they resolved to send him for England; and bad him lay by his armes.

But hee, (who was the Sonne of a Souldier,) having taken up armes in his just defence, replyed that hee would not lay by those armes, because they were so needefull at Sea, if hee should be sent over. Yet, to save the effusion of so much worty bloud, as would have issued out of the vaynes of these 9. worthies of New Canaan, if mine Host should have played upon them out at his port holes, (for they came within danger like a flocke of wild geese, as if they had bin tayled one to another, as coults to be sold at a faier,) mine Host was content to yeelde upon quarter; and did capitulate with them in what manner it should be for more certainety, because hee knew what Captaine Shrimpe was.

Captaine
Shrimpe   Hee expressed that no violence should be
promiseth that   offered to his person, none to his goods, nor any
no violence   of his Howsehold: but that hee should have his
should be offered
to his person.   armes, and what els was requisit for the voyage:

which theire Herald retornes, it was agreed upon, and should
be performed.

But mine Host no sooner had set open the dore, and issued
out, but instantly Captaine Shrimpe and the rest of the worties
stepped to him, layd hold of his armes, and had him downe:
and so eagerly was every man bent against him, (not regarding
any agreement made with such a carnall man,) that they fell
upon him as if they would have eaten him: some of them were
so violent that they would have a slice with scabbert, and all for
The Worthies haste; untill an old Souldier, (of the Queenes, as
rebuked for the Proverbe is,) that was there by accident, clapt
their unworthy his gunne under the weapons, and sharply rebuked
practises. these worthies for their unworthy practises. So the matter was
taken into more deliberate consideration.

Captaine Shrimpe, and the rest of the nine worthies, made
themselves, (by this outragious riot,) Masters of mine Hoste of
Ma-re Mount, and disposed of what hee had at his plantation.

This they knew, (in the eye of the Salvages,) would add to
their glory, and diminish the reputation of mine honest Host;
whome they practised to be ridd of upon any termes, as willingly as if hee had bin the very Hidra of the time.

CHAP. XVI.
*How the 9. worthies put mine Host of Ma-re-Mount into the
inchaunted Castle at Plimmouth, and terrified him with
the Monster Briareus.*

THE nine worthies of New Canaan having now the Law in
their owne hands, (there being no generall Governour in the
Land; nor none of the Seperation that regarded the duety
they owe their Soveraigne, whose naturall borne Subjects they
were, though translated out of Holland, from whence they
had learned to worke all to their owne ends, and make a great
shewe of Religion, but no humanity,) for they were now to sit
in Counsell on the cause.

And much it stood mine honest Host upon to be very circumspect, and to take Eacus to taske; for that his voyce was
more allowed of then both the other: and had not mine Host
confounded all the arguments that Eacus could make in their
defence, and confuted him that swaied the rest, they would

have made him unable to drinke in such manner of merriment any more. So that following this private counsell, given him by one that knew who ruled the rost, the Hiracano ceased that els would split his pinace.

A conclusion was made and sentence given that mine Host should be sent to England a prisoner. But when hee was brought to the shipps for that purpose, no man durst be so *Mine host* foole hardy as to undertake carry him. So these *set upon an* Worthies set mine Host upon an Island, without *Island without* gunne, powther, or shot or dogge or so much as *anything,* a knife to get any thinge to feede upon, or any *to shift for* *himselfe.* other cloathes to shelter him with at winter then a thinne suite which hee had one at that time. Home hee could not get to Ma-re-Mount. Upon this Island hee stayed a moneth at least, and was releeved by Salvages that tooke notice that mine Host was a Sachem of Passonagessit, and would bringe bottles of strong liquor to him, and unite themselves into a league of brother hood with mine Host; so full of humanity are these infidels before those Christians.

From this place for England failed mine Host in a Plimmouth shipp, (that came into the Land to fish upon the Coast,) that landed him safe in England at Plimmouth: and hee stayed in England untill the ordinary time for shipping to set forth for these parts, and then retorned: Noe man being able to taxe him of any thinge.

But the Worthies, (in the meane time,) hoped they had bin ridd of him.

CHAP. XVII.
Of the Baccanall Triumphe of the nine *worthies of New Canaan.*

THE Seperatists were not so contended, (when mine Host of Ma-re-Mount was gone,) but they were as much discontended when hee was retorned againe: and the rather because theire passages about him, and the businesse, were so much derided and in songes exemplified: which, (for better satisfaction of such as are in that kinde affected,) I have set forth, as it was then in use by the name of the *Baccanall Triumphe*, as followeth:

THE POEM.

Master
Ben:
Johnson.

I sing th' adventures of nine worthy wights,
And pitty 't is I cannot call them Knights,
Since they had brawne and braine, and were right able
To be installed of Prince Arthures table;
Yet all of them were Squires of low degree,
As did appeare by rules of heraldry.
The Magi tould of a prodigeous birth
That shortly should be found upon the earth,
By Archimedes art, which they misconster
Unto their Land would proove a hiddeous monster;
Seaven heades it had, and twice so many feete,
Arguing the body to be wondrous greate,
Besides a forked taile heav'd up on highe
As if it threaten'd battell to the skie.
The Rumor of this fearefull prodigy
Did cause th' effeminate multitude to cry
For want of great Alcides aide, and stood
Like People that have seene Medusas head.
Great was the greife of hart, great was the mone,
And great the feare conceaved by every one
Of Hydras hiddeous forme and dreadfull powre,
Doubting in time this Monster would devoure
All their best flocks, whose dainty wolle consorts
It selfe with Scarlet in all Princes Courts.
Not Jason nor the adventerous youths of Greece
Did bring from Colcos any richer Fleece.
In Emulation of the Gretian force
These Worthies nine prepar'd a woodden horse,
And, prick'd with pride of like successe, divise
How they may purchase glory by this prize;
And, if they give to Hidreas head the fall,
It will remaine a plat forme unto all
Theire brave atchivements, and in time to comme,
Per fas aut nefas, they'l erect a throne.
Cloubs are turn'd trumps: so now the lott is cast:
With fire and sword to Hidras den they haste,
Mars in th' assendant, Soll in Cancer now,
And Lerna Lake to Plutos court must bow.

What though they be rebuk'd by thundering Jove,
Tis neither Gods nor men that can remove
Their mindes from making this a dismall day.
These nine will now be actors in this play,
And Sumon Hidra to appeare anon
Before their witles Combination:
But his undaunted spirit, nursd with meate
Such as the Cecrops gave their babes to eate,
Scorn'd their base accons; for with Cecrops charme
Hee knew he could defend himselfe from harme
Of Minos, Eacus, and Radamand,
Princes of Limbo; who must out of hand
Consult bout Hidra, what must now be done:
Who, having sate in Counsell, one by one
Retorne this answere to the Stiggean feinds;
And first grim Minos spake: most loving freinds,
Hidra prognosticks ruine to our state
And that our Kingdome will grow desolate;
But if one head from thence be tane away
The Body and the members will decay.
To take in hand, quoth Eacus, this taske,
Is such as harebraind Phaeton did aske
Of Phebus, to begird the world about;
Which graunted put the Netherlands to rout;
Presumptious fooles learne wit at too much cost,
For life and laboure both at once hee lost.
Sterne Radamantus, being last to speake,
Made a great hum and thus did silence breake:
What if, with ratling chaines or Iron bands,
Hidra be bound either by feete or hands,
And after, being lashd with smarting rodds,
Hee be conveyd by Stix unto the godds
To be accused on the upper ground
Of Lesæ Majestatis, this crime found
T'will be unpossible from thence, I trowe,
Hidra shall come to trouble us belowe.
This sentence pleasd the friends exceedingly,
That up they tost their bonnets, and did cry,
Long live our Court in great prosperity.
The Sessions ended, some did straight devise

Court Revells, antiques and a world of joyes,
Brave Christmas gambols: there was open hall
Kept to the full, and sport, the Divell and all:
Laboure's despised, the loomes are laid away,
And this proclaim'd the Stigean Holliday.
In came grim Mino, with his motly beard,
And brought a distillation well prepar'd;
And Eacus, who is as suer as text,
Came in with his preparatives the next;
Then Radamantus, last and principall,
Feasted the Worthies in his sumptuous hall.
There Charon Cerberous and the rout of feinds
Had lap enough: and so their pastims ends.

THE ILLUSTRATIONS.

Now to illustrate this Poem, and make the sence more plaine, it is to be considered that the Persons at Ma-re-Mount were seaven, and they had seaven heads and 14. feete; these were accounted Hidra with the seaven heads: and the Maypole, with the Hornes nailed neere the topp, was the forked tayle of this supposed Monster, which they (for want of skill) imposed: yet feared in time, (if they hindred not mine Host), hee would hinder the benefit of their Beaver trade, as hee had done, (by meanes of this helpe,) in Kynyback river finely, ere they were awares; who, comming too late, were much dismaide to finde that mine Host his boate had gleaned away all before they came; which Beaver is a fitt companion for Scarlett: and I beleeve that Jasons golden Fleece was either the same, or some other Fleece not of so much value.

This action bred a kinde of hart burning in the Plimmouth Planters, who after sought occasion against mine Host to over-throwe his undertakings and to destroy his Plantation; whome they accoumpted a maine enemy to theire Church and State.

Now when they had begunne with him, they thought best to proceede: forasmuch as they thought themselves farre enough from any controule of Justice, and therefore resolved to be their owne carvers: (and the rather because they presumed upon some incouragement they had from the favourites of their Sect in England:) and with fire and sword, nine in number, pursued mine Host, who had escaped theire hands, in scorne of what they intended, and betooke him to his habitation in a night of great thunder and lightening, when they durst not follow him, as hardy as these nine worthies seemed to be.

It was in the Moneth of June that these Marshallists had appointed to goe about this mischeifous project, and deale so crabbidly with mine Host.

After a parly, hee capitulated with them about the quarter they proffered him, if hee would consent to goe for England, there to answere, (as they pretended,) some thing they could object against him principall to the generall: But what it would be hee cared not, neither was it any thing materiall.

Yet when quarter was agreed upon, they, contrary wise, abused him, and carried him to theire towne of Plimmouth, where, (if they had thought hee durst have gone to England,) rather then they would have bin any more affronted by him they would have dispatched him, as Captaine Shrimp in a rage profest that hee would doe with his Pistoll, as mine Host should set his foote into the boate. Howsoever, the cheife Elders voyce in that place was more powerfull than any of the rest, who concluded to send mine Host without any other thing to be done to him. And this being the finall agreement, (contrary to Shrimpe and others,) the nine Worthies had a great Feast made, and the furmity pott was provided for the boats gang by no allowance: and all manner of pastime.

Captaine Shrimpe was so overjoyed in the performance of this exployt, that they had, at that time, extraordinary merriment, (a thing not usuall amongst those presisians); and when the winde served they tooke mine Host into their Shallop, hoysed Saile, and carried him to the Northern parts; where they left him upon a Island.

CHAP. XVIII.
Of a Doctor made at a Commencement in New Canaan.

THE Church of Plimmouth, having due regard to the weale publike and the Brethren that were to come over, and knowing that they would be busily imployed to make provision for the cure of Soules, and therefore might neglect the body for that time, did hold themselves to be in duety bound to make search for a fitting man, that might be able, (if so neede requir'd,) to take the chardge upon him in that place of imployment: and therefore called a Counsell of the whole Synagoge: amongst which company, they chose out a man that long time had bin nurst up in the tender bosome of the Church: one that had speciall gifts: hee could wright and reade; nay, more: hee had tane the oath of abjuration, which is a speciall stepp, yea, and a maine degree unto perferment. Him they weane, and out of Phaos boxe fitt him with speciall guifts of no lesse worth: they stile him Doctor, and forth they send him to gaine imployement and opinion.

A Councell called.

What luck is it I cannot hit on his name: but I will give you him by a periphrasis, that you may know him when you meete him next.

Hee was borne at Wrington, in the County of Somerset, where hee was bred a Butcher. Hee weares a longe beard, and a Garment like the Greeke that beggd in Pauls Church. This new made Doctor, comes to Salem to congratulate: where hee findes some are newly come from Sea, and ill at ease.

He takes the patient, and the urinall: eies the State there; findes the Crasis Syptomes, and the attomi natantes: and tells the patient that his disease was winde, which hee had tane by gapeing feasting over board at Sea; but hee would quickly ease him of that greife, and quite expell the winde. And this hee did performe, with his gifts hee had: and then hee handled the patient so handsomely, that hee eased him of all the winde hee had in an instant.

And yet I hope this man may be forgiven, if hee were made a fitting Plant for Heaven.

How hee went to worke with his gifts is a question; yet hee did a great cure for Captaine Littleworth, hee cured him of a disease called a wife: and yet I hope this man may be forgiven, if shee were made a fitting plant for heaven.

By this meanes hee was allowed 4. p. a moneth, and the chirgeon's chest, and made Phisition generall of Salem: where hee exercised his gifts so well, that of full 42. that there hee tooke to cure, there is not one has more cause to complaine, or can say black 's his eie. This saved Captaine Littleworths credit, that had truck'd away the vittels: though it brought forth a scandall on the Country by it: and then I hope this man may be forgiven, if they were all made fitting plants for Heaven.

But in mine opinion, hee deserves to be set upon a palfrey and lead up and downe in triumph throw new Canaan, with a collar of Jurdans about his neck, as was one of like desert in Richard the seconds time through the streets of London, that men might know where to finde a Quacksalver.

CHAP. XIX.
Of the silencing of a Minister in new Canaan.

A silenced Minister, out of coveteousnesse, came over into new Canaan to play the spie: Hee pretended, out of a zealous intent to doe the Salvages good, and to teach them. Hee brought a great Bundell of Horne books with him, and carefull hee was, (good man,) to blott out all the crosses of them, for feare least the people of the land should become Idolaters. Hee was in hope, with his gifts, to prepare a great auditory against greate Josua should arive there.

Hee applyed himselfe on the weeke dayes to the trade of Beaver, but it was, (as might seeme,) to purchase the principall benefite of the Lande, when the time should come; for hee had a hope to be the Caiphas of the Country: and well hee might, for hee was higher by the head than any of his tribe that came after him.

This man, it seemes, played the spie very handsomely; for in the exercise of his guifts on the Lords day at Weenasimute, hee espied a Salvage come in with a good Beaver coate, and tooke occasion to reproove the covetous desire of his auditory to trade for Beaver on those dayes; which made them all use so much modesty about the matter for the present, that hee found opportunity, the same day, to take the Salvage a side into a corner, where (with the helpe of his Wampampeack hee had in his pocket for that purpose in a readinesse,) hee made a shifte to get that Beaver coate, which their mouthes watered at; and so deceaved them all.

This Caiphas that condemneth Covetousnesse, and committeth it himselfe.

But shortly after, when Josua came into the Land, hee had soone spied out Caiphas practise, and put him to silence; and either hee must put up his pipes and be packing, or forsake Jonas posture, and play Demas part alltogether.

CHAP. XX.
Of the Practise of the Seperatists to gett a snare to hamper mine Host of Ma-re-Mount.

ALTHOUGH the nine Worthies had left mine Hoste upon an Island, in such an inhumane manner as yee heard before; yet when they understood that hee had got shipping and was gone to England of his owne accord, they dispatched letters of advise to an Agent they had there: and by the next shipp sent after to have a snare made, that might hamper mine Host so as hee might not any more trouble theire conscience: and to that end made a generall collection of Beaver to defray the chardge, and hee was not thought a good Christian that would not lay much out for that imployment.

The generall collection made.

Some contributed three pounds, some foure, some five pounds; and procured a pretty quantity by that Devise, which should be given to a cunning man that could make a snare to hamper him.

The Agent, (according to his directions,) does his endeavoure, (in the best manner hee could,) to have this instrument made: and used no little diligence to have it effected. His reputation stood upon the taske imposed upon him against mine Host, the onely enemy (accounted) of their Church and State.

Noe cost spared for the getting of a skillfull man.

Much inquiry was made in London, and about, for a skillfull man that would worke the feate. Noe cost was spared, for gold hee had good store: first hee inquires of one, and then another: at the last hee heard newes of a very famous man, one that was excellent at making subtile instruments, such as that age had never bin acquainted with.

Hee was well knowne to be the man, that had wit and wondrous skill to make a cunning instrument where with to save himselfe and his whole family, if all the world besides should be drown'd; and this the best; yea, and the best cheap too, for, no good done, the man would nothing take.

To him this agent goes, and praies his aide: Declares his

cause, and tells the substance of his greivance, all at large, and
laid before his eies a heape of gold.

The heape of gold. When all was shewd, that could be she'd, and
said, what could be said, and all too little for
to have it done, the agent then did see his gold
refused, his cause despised, and thought himselfe disgraced
to leave the worke undone: so that hee was much dismaid, yet
importun'd the cunning man, who found no reason to take
the taske in hand.

Hee thought, perhaps, mine Host, (that had the slight to
escape from the nine Worthies, to chaine Argus eies, and by
inchauntment make the doores of the watch tower fly open at
an instant,) would not be hampered, but with much a doe: and
so hee was unwilling to be troubled with that taske.

The agent wondring to see that his gold would doe no good,
did aske the cunning man if hee could give him no advise? who
Mine Host arrived againe in Plimmouth. said, hee would: and what was that, thinke you?
To let mine Host alone. Who, being ship'd againe
for the parts of New Canaan, was put in at Plimmouth in the very faces of them, to their terrible amazement
to see him at liberty: and told him hee had not yet fully
answered the matter they could object against him. Hee onely
made this modest reply, that hee did perceave they were willfull
people, that would never be answered: and derided them for
their practises and losse of laboure.

CHAP. XXI.
Of Captaine Littleworth his new devise
for the purchase of Beaver.

In the meane time, whiles these former passages were, there
was a great swelling fellow, of Littleworth, crept over to Salem,
Charter party Tresorer. (by the helpe of Master Charter party, the
Tresorer, and Master Ananias Increase, the Col-
lector for the Company of Seperatists,) to take
upon him their imployments for a time.

Hee, resolving to make hay whiles the Sonne did shine, first
pretended himselfe to be sent over as cheife Justice of the Massachussets Bay and Salem, forsoth, and tooke unto him a councell; and a worthy one no doubt, for the Cowkeeper of Salem

was a prime man in those imployments; and to ad a Majesty, (as hee thought,) to his new assumed dignity, hee caused the Patent of the Massachussets, (new brought into the Land,) to be carried where hee went in his progresse to and froe, as an embleme of his authority: which the vulgar people, not acquainted with, thought it to be some instrument of Musick locked up in that covered case, and thought, (for so some said,) this man of littleworth had bin a fidler, and the rather because hee had put into the mouthes of poore silly things, that were sent alonge with him, what skill hee had in Engines, and in things of quaint devise: all which prooved in conclusion to be but impostury.

This man, thinking none so worthy as himselfe, tooke upon him infinitely: and made warrants in his owne name, (without *Warrants* relation to his Majesties authority in that place,) *made by Capt.* and summoned a generall apparance at the wor-*Littleworth in* *his name.* shipfull towne of Salem: there in open assembly was tendered certaine Articles, devised betweene him and theire new Pastor Master Eager, (that had renounced his old calling to the Ministry receaved in England, by warrant of Gods word, and taken a new one there, by their fantasticall way imposed, and conferred upon him with some speciall guifts had out of Phaos boxe.)

To these Articles every Planter, old and new, must signe, or be expelled from any manner of aboade within the Compas of the Land contained within that graunt then shewed: which was so large it would suffice for Elbow roome for more then were in all the Land by 700000. such an army might have planted them a Colony with in that cirquit which hee challenged, and not contend for roome for their Cattell. But for all that, hee that should refuse to subscribe, must pack.

The tenor of the *Articles* were these: *That in all causes, as well Ecclesiasticall as Politicall, wee should follow the rule of Gods word.*

This made a shew of a good intent, and all the assembly, (onely mine Host replyed,) did subscribe: hee would not, *Mine Host* unlesse they would ad this Caution: *So as nothing* *subscribed not.* *be done contrary or repugnant to the Lawes of the* *Kingdome of England.* These words hee knew, by former experience, were necessary, and without these the same would proove a very mousetrapp to catch some body by his owne consent, (which the rest nothing suspected,) for the construction of the worde would be made by them of the Seperation to serve their owne turnes: and if any man should, in such a case, be accused of a crime, (though in it selfe it were petty,) they might set it on the tenter hookes of their imaginary gifts, and stretch it to make it seeme cappitall; which was the reason why mine Host refused to subscribe.

The Patent.   It was then agreed upon that there should be one generall trade used within that Patent, (as hee said,) and a generall stock: and every man to put in a parte: and every man, for his person, to have shares alike: and for their stock, according to the ratable proportion was put in: and this to continue for 12. moneths, and then to call an accompt.

All were united, but mine Host refused: two truckmasters were chosen; wages prefixed; onely mine Host put *All consented but mine Host.* in a Caviat that the wages might be paid out of the cleare proffit, which there in black and white was plainely put downe.

But before the end of 6. moneths, the partners in this stock, (handled by the Truckmasters,) would have an accoumpt: some of them had perceaved that Wampambeacke could be pocketted up, and the underlings, (that went in the boats alonge,) would bee neere the Wiser for any thinge, but what was trucked for Beaver onely.

Insteed of proffit disproffit.   The accoumpt being made betweene Captaine Littleworth, and the two Truckmasters, it was found that instead of increasing the proffit, they had decreased it; for the principall stock, by this imployment, was freetted so, that there was a great hole to be seene in the very middle of it, which cost the partners afterwards one hundred markes to stopp and make good to Captaine Littleworth.

But mine Host, that sturred not his foote at all for the matter, did not onely save his stock from such a Cancar, but gained sixe and seaven for one: in the meane time hee derided the Contributers for being catch'd in that snare.

CHAP. XXII.
Of a Sequestration made in New Canaan.

CAPTAINE Littleworth, (that had an akeing tooth at mine Host of Ma-re-Mount,) devised how hee might put a trick upon him, by colour of a Sequestration; and got some persons to pretend that hee had corne and other goods of theirs in possession; and the rather because mine Host had store of corne and hee had improvidently truckt his store for the present gaine of Beaver; in so much that his people under his chardge were put to short allowance, which caused some of them to sicken with conceipt of such useage, and some of them by the practise of the new entertained Doctor Noddy, with his Imaginary gifts. They sent therefore to exhibit a petition to grim Minos, Eacus and Radamant, where they wished to have the author of their greife to be convented: and they had procured it quickly, if curses would have caused it: for good prayers would be of no validity, (as they supposed,) in this extremity.

Commission for corne. Now in this extremity Capt. Littleworth gave commission to such as hee had found ready for such imployments to enter in the howse at Ma-re-Mount, and, with a shallop, to bring from thence such corne and other utensilles as in their commission hee had specified. But mine Host, wary to prevent eminent mischeife, had conveyed his powther and shott, (and such other things as stood him in most steed for his present condition,) into the woods for safety: and, whiles this was put in practise by him, the shallop was landed and the Commissioners entred the howse, and willfully bent against mine honest Host, that loved good hospitality. After they had feasted their bodies with that they *Mine Hosts corne & goods carried away by violence.* found there, they carried all his corne away, with some other of his goods, contrary to the Lawes of hospitality: a smale parcell of refuse corne onely excepted, which they left mine Host to keepe Christmas with.

But when they were gone, mine Host fell to make use of his gunne, (as one that had a good faculty in the use of that instrument,) and feasted his body neverthelesse with fowle and venison, which hee purchased with the helpe of that instrument, the plenty of the Country and the commodiousnes of the place affording meanes, by the blessing of God; and hee did but deride Captaine Littleworth, that made his servants snap shorte in a Country so much abounding with plenty of foode for an industrious man, with greate variety.

CHAP. XXIII.

Of a great Bonfire made for joy of the arrivall of great Josua, surnamed Temperwell, into the Land of Canaan.

SEAVEN shipps set forth at once, and altogether arrived in the Land of Canaan, to take a full possession thereof: What are all the 12. Tribes of new Israell come? No, none but the tribe of Issacar, and some few scattered Levites of the remnant of those that were descended of old Elies howse.

And here comes their Josua too among them; and they make it a more miraculous thing for these seaven shipps to set forth together, and arrive at New Canaan together, then it was for the Israelites to goe over Jordan drishod: perhaps it was, because they had a wall on the right hand and a wall on the left hand.

These Seperatists suppose there was no more difficulty in the matter then for a man to finde the way to the Counter at noone dayes, betweene a Sergeant and his yeoman: Now you may thinke mine Host will be hamperd or never.

Men that come to ridd the land of pollution. These are the men that come prepared to ridd the Land of all pollution. These are more subtile then the Cunning, that did refuse a goodly heap of gold. These men have brought a very snare indeed; and now mine Host must suffer. The book of Common Prayer, which hee used, to be despised: and hee must not be spared.

Now they are come, his doome before hand was concluded on: they have a warrant now: A cheife one too: and now mine Host must know hee is the subject of their hatred: the Snare must now be used; this instrument must not be brought by Josua in vaine.

A Courte called about mine Host. A Court is called of purpose for mine host: hee there convented, and must heare his doome before hee goe: nor will they admit him to capitulate, and know wherefore they are so violent to put such things in practise against a man they never saw before: nor will they allow of it, though hee decline their Jurisdiction.

A divellish sentence against him. There they all with one assent put him to silence, crying out, heare the Governour, heare the Govern: who gave this sentence against mine Host at first sight: that he should be first put in the Billbowes, his goods should be all confiscated, his Plantation should be burned downe to the ground, because the habitation of the wicked should no more appeare in Israell, and his person banished from those territories; and this put in execution with all speede.

The harmeles Salvages, (his neighboures,) came the while, (greived, poore silly lambes, to see what they went about,) and *The Salvages reproove them.* did reproove these Eliphants of witt for their inhumane deede: the Lord above did open their mouthes like Balams Asse, and made them speake in his behalfe sentences of unexpected divinity, besides morrallity; and tould them that god would not love them that burned this good mans howse; and plainely sayed that they who were new come would finde the want of such a howses in the winter: so much themselves to him confest.

Epictetus summa totius Philosophiæ. The smoake that did assend appeared to be the very Sacrifice of Kain. Mine Host, (that a farre of abourd a ship did there behold this wofull spectacle,) knew not what hee should doe in this extremity but beare and forbeare, as Epictetus sayes: it was bootelesse to exclaime.

Hee did consider then these transitory things are but *ludibria fortunæ*, as Cicero calls them. All was burnt downe to the ground, and nothing did remaine but the bare ashes as an embleme of their cruelty: and unles it could, (like to the Phenix,) rise out of these ashes and be new againe, (to the immortall glory and renowne of this fertile Canaan the new,) the stumpes and postes in their black liveries will mourne; and piety it selfe will add a voyce to the bare remnant of that Monument, and make it cry for recompence, (or else revenge,) against the Sect of cruell Schismaticks.

CHAP. XXIV.
Of the digrading and creating gentry in New Canaan.

THERE was a zealous Professor in the Land of Canaan, (growne a great Merchant in the Beaver trade,) that came over for his conscience sake, (as other men have done,) and the meanes, (as the phrase is,) who in his minority had bin prentice to a tombe maker; who, comming to more ripenes of yeares, (though lesse discretion,) found a kinde of scruple in his conscience that the trade was in parte against the second commandement: and therefore left it off wholely, and betooke himselfe to some other imployments.

In the end hee settled upon this course, where hee had hope of preferrement, and become one of those things that any Judas might hange himselfe upon, that is an Elder.

An Elder. Hee had bin a man of some recconing in his time, (as himselfe would boast,) for hee was an officer, just under the Exchequer at Westminster, in a place called Phlegeton: there hee was comptroller, and conversed with noe plebeians, I tell you, but such as have angels or their attendance, (I meane some Lawyers with appertenances, that is, Clarks,) with whome a Jugg of Beare and a crusty rolle in the terme is as currant as a three penny scute at Hall time.

There is another place thereby, called sticks: these are two daingerous places, by which the infernall gods doe sweare: but this of Sticks is the more daingerous of the two, because there, (if a man be once in,) hee cannot tell how to get out againe handsomely.

I knew an under sheriff was in unawaires, and hee laboured to be free of it: yet hee broake his back before he got so farre as quietus est: There is no such danger in Phlegeton, where this man of so much recconing was comptroller.

Josua displeased. Hee being here, waited an opportunity to be made a gentl. and now it fell out that a gentl. newly come into the land of Canaan, (before hee knew what ground hee stood upon,) had incurred the displeasure of great Josua so highly that hee must therefore be digraded.

No reconciliation could be had for him: all hopes were past for that matter: Where upon this man of much recconing (pretending a graunt of the approach in avoydance,) helpes the lame dogge over the stile, and was as jocund on the matter as a Magpie over a Mutton.

Wherefore the Heralls, with Drums, and Trumpets, proclaiming in a very solemne manner that it was the pleasure of great Josua, (for divers and sundry very good causes and considerations, Master Temperwell thereunto especially mooving,) to take away the title, prerogative and preheminence of the Delinquent, so unworthy of it, and to place

Master Temperwell.

the same upon a Professor of more recconing: so that it was made a penall thing for any man after to lifte the same man againe on the top of that stile, but that hee should stand perpetually digraded from that prerogative. And the place by this meanes being voyde, this man, of so much more reckoning, was receaved in like a Cypher to fill up a roome, and was made a Gentleman of the first head; and his Coate of Armes, blazon'd and tricked out fit for that purpose, in this Poem following.

THE POEM.

> What ailes Pigmalion? Is it Lunacy;
> Or Doteage on his owne Imagery?
> Let him remember how hee came from Hell,
> That after ages by record may tell
> The compleate story to posterity.
> Blazon his Coate in forme of Heraldry.

Put it this way.

> Hee beareth argent alwaies at commaund,
> A barre betweene three crusty rolls at hand,
> And, for his crest, with froth, there does appeare
> Dextra Paw Elevant a Jugg of beare.

Now, that it may the more easily be understood, I have here endeavoured to set it forth in these illustrations following: Pigmalion was an Image maker, who, doteing on his owne perfection in making the Image of Venus, grew to be a mazed man, like our Gentleman here of the first head: and by the figure Antonomasia is hee herein exemplified.

Hee was translated from a tombe maker to be the tapster at hell, (which is in Westminster, under the Ex-Chequer office,) for benefit of the meanes hee translated himselfe into New England, where, by the help of Beaver and the commaund of a servant or two, hee was advaunced to the title of a gentleman; where I left him to the exercise of his guifts.

CHAP. XXV.

Of the manner how the Seperatists doe pay debts to them that
are without.

THERE was an honest man, one Mr. Innocence Fairecloath, by Mr. Mathias Charterparty sent over into New Canaan, to raise a very good marchantable commodity for his benefit; for, whiles the man was bound by covenant to stay for a time, and to imploy such servants as did there belong to Mr. Charterparty, hee disdained the tenents of the Seperatists: and they also, (finding him to be none,) disdained to be imployed by a carnall man, (as they termed him,) and sought occasion against him, to doe him a mischeife. Intelligence was conveyed to Mr. Charterparty that this man was a member of the Church of England, and therefore, (in their account,) an enemy to their Church and state. And, (to the end they might have some coloure against him,) some of them practised to get into his debte, which hee, not mistrusting, suffered, and gave credit for such Commodity as hee had sold at a price. When the day of payment came, insteede of monyes, hee, being at that time sick and weake and stood in neede of the Beaver hee had contracted for, hee had an Epistle full of zealous exhortations to provide for the soule; and not to minde these transitory things that perished with the body, and to bethinke himselfe whether his conscience would be so prompt to demaund so greate a somme of Beaver as had bin contracted for. Hee was further exhorted therein to consider hee was but a steward for a time, and by all likely hood was going to give up an accompt of his stewardship: and therfore perswaded the creditor not to load his conscience with such a burthen, which hee was bound by the Gospell to ease him of (if it were possible;) and for that cause hee had framed this Epistle in such a freindly maner to put him in minde of it. The perusall of this, (lap'd in the paper,) was as bad as a potion to the creditor, to see his debtor Master Subtilety (a zealous professor as hee thought) to deride him in this extremity, that hee could not chuse, (in admiration of the deceipt,) but cast out these words:

Goode
Payement.

Are these youre members? if they be all like these, I beleeve the Divell was the setter of their Church.

This was called in question when Mr. Fairecloath least thought of it. Capt. Littleworth must be the man must presse it against him, for blasphemy against the Church of Salem: and

Blasphemy an example for carnall men. to greate Josua Temperwell hee goes with a bitter accusation, to have Master Innocence made an example for all carnall men to presume to speake the least word that might tend to the dishonor of the Church of Salem; yea, the mother Church of all that holy Land.

And hee convented was before their Synagoge, where no defence would serve his turne; yet was there none to be seene to accuse him, save the Court alone.

The time of his sicknes, nor the urgent cause, were not allowed to be urg'd for him; but whatsoever could be thought upon against him was urged, seeing hee was a carnall man, of them that are without. So that it seemes, by those proceedings there, the matter was adjudged before he came: Hee onely brought to heare his sentence in publicke: which was, to have his tongue bored through; his nose slit; his face branded; his eares cut; his body to be whip'd in every severall plantation of their Jurisdiction; and a fine of forty pounds impos'd, with perpetuall banishment: and, (to execute this vengeance,) Shackles, (the Deacon of Charles Towne,) was as ready as Mephostophiles, when Doctor Faustus was bent upon mischeife.

Hee is the purser generall of New Canaan, who, (with his whipp, with knotts most terrible,) takes this man unto the Counting howse: there capitulates with him why hee should be so hasty for payment, when Gods deare children must pay as they are able: and hee weepes, and sobbes, and his handkercher walkes as a signe of his sorrow for Master Fairecloaths sinne, that hee should beare no better affection to the Church and the Saints of New Canaan: and strips Innocence the while, and comforts him.

Though hee be made to stay for payment, hee should not thinke it longe; the payment would be sure when it did come, and hee should have his due to a doite; hee should not wish for

Notable Pay. a token more; And then tould it him downe in such manner that hee made Fairecloaths Innocent back like the picture of Rawhead and blowdy bones, and his shirte like a pudding wifes aperon. In this imployment Shackles takes a greate felicity, and glories in the practise of it. This cruell sentence was stoped in part by Sir Christopher Gardiner, (then present at the execution,) by expostulating with Master Temperwell: who was content, (with that whipping and the cutting of parte of his eares,) to send Innocence going, with the losse of all his goods, to pay the fine imposed, and perpetuall banishment out of their Lands of New Canaan, in terrorem populi.

Loe this is the payment you shall get, if you be one of them they terme, without.

CHAP. XXVI.
Of the Charity of the Seperatists.

Charity is sayd to be the darling of Religion, and is indeed the Marke of a good Christian: But where we doe finde a Commission for ministring to the necessity of the Saints, we doe not finde any prohibition against casting our bread upon the waters, where the unsanctified, as well as the sanctified, are in possibility to make use of it.

I cannot perceave that the Seperatists doe allowe of helping our poore, though they magnify their practise in contributing to the nourishment of their Saints; For as much as some that are of the number of those whom they terme without, (though it were in case of sicknesse,) upon theire landing, when a little fresh victuals would have recovered their healths, yet could they not finde any charitable assistance from them. Nay, mine Host of Ma-re-Mount, (if hee might have had the use of his *Lame charity.* gunne, powther and shott, and his dogg, which were denied,) hee doubtles would have preserved such poore helples wretches as were neglected by those that brought them over; which was so apparent, (as it seemed,) that one of their owne tribe said, the death of them would be required at some bodies hands one day, (meaning Master Temperwell.)

But such good must not come from a carnall man: if it come from a member, then it is a sanctified worke; if otherwise, it is rejected as unsanctified.

But when Shackles wife, and such as had husbands, parents or freinds, happened to bee sick, mine Hosts helpe was used, and instruments provided for him to kill fresh vittell with, (wherein hee was industrious,) and the persons, having fresh vittell, lived.

So doubtles might many others have bin preserved, but they were of the number left without; neither will those precise people admit a carnall man into their howses, though they have made use of his in the like case; they are such antagonists to those that doe not comply with them, and seeke to be admitted to be of their Church, that in scorne they say, you may see what it is to be without.

CHAP. XXVII.
Of the practise of their Church.

THE Church of the Seperatists is governed by Pastors, Elders and Deacons, and there is not any of these, though hee be but a Cow keeper, but is allowed to exercise his guifts in the publik assembly on the Lords day, so as hee doe not make use of any notes for the helpe of his memory: for such things, they say, smell of Lampe oyle, and there must be no such unsavery perfume admitted to come into the congregation.

These are all publike preachers. There is amongst these people a Deakonesse, made of the sisters, that uses her guifts at home in an assembly of her sexe, by way of repetition or exhortation: such is their practise.

The Pastor, (before hee is allowed of,) must disclaime his former calling to the Ministry, as hereticall; and take a new calling after their fantasticall inventions: and then hee is admitted to bee their Pastor.

The manner of disclaimeing is, to renounce his calling with bitter execrations, for the time that hee hath heretofore lived in it: and after his new election, there is great joy conceaved at his commission.

And theire Pastors have this preheminence above the Civile Magistrate: Hee must first consider of the complaint made against a member: and if hee be disposed to give the partie complained of an admonition, there is no more to be said: if not; Hee delivers him over to the Magistrate to deale with him in a course of Justice, according to theire practise in cases of that nature.

Of these pastors I have not knowne many: some I have observed together with theire carriage in New Canaan, and can informe you what opinion hath bin conceaved of theire conditions in the perticuler. There is one who, (as they give it out there that thinke they speake it to advaunce his worth,) has bin expected to exercise his gifts in an assembly that stayed his comming, in the middest of his Jorney falls into a fitt, (which they terme a zealous meditation,) and was 4. miles past the place appointed before hee came to himselfe, or did remember where abouts hee went. And how much these things are different from the actions of mazed men, I leave to any indifferent man to judge; and if I should say they are all much alike, they that have seene and heard what I have done, will not condemne mee altogether.

Now, for as much as by the practise of theire Church every Elder or Deacon may preach, it is not amisse to discover their practise in that perticuler, before I part with them.

It has bin an old saying, and a true, what is bred in the bone will not out of the flesh, nor the stepping into the pulpit that can make the person fitt for the imployment. The unfitnes of *Lewes the* II. the person undertaking to be the Messenger has *sent a Barber* brought a blemish upon the message, as in the *Embassador.* time of Lewes the Eleventh, King of France, who, (having advaunced his Barber to place of Honor, and graced him with eminent titles), made him so presumptuous to undertake an Embassage to treat with forraine princes of Civile affaires.

But what was the issue? Hee behaved himselfe so unworthily, (yet as well as his breeding would give him leave,) that both *The Embassage* the Messenger and the message were despised; *despised.* and had not hee, (being discovered,) conveyed himselfe out of their territories, they had made him pay for his barbarous presumption.

Socrates sayes, *loquere ut te videam.* If a man observe these people in the exercise of their gifts, hee may thereby discerne the tincture of their proper calling, the asses eares will peepe through the lyons hide. I am sorry they cannot discerne their owne infirmities. I will deale fairely with them, for I will draw their pictures cap a pe, that you may discerne them plainely from head to foote in their postures, that so much bewitch, (as

I may speake with modesty,) these illiterate people to be so fantasticall, to take Jonas taske upon them without sufficient warrant.

One steps up like the Minister of Justice with the ballance onely, not the sword for feare of affrighting his auditory. Hee poynts at a text, and handles it as evenly as hee *A Grocer.* can; and teaches the auditory, that the thing hee has to deliver must be well waied, for it is a very pretious thing, yes, much more pretious then gold or pearle: and hee will teach them the meanes how to way things of that excellent worth; that a man would suppose hee and his auditory were to part stakes by the scale; and the like distribution they have used about a bag pudding.

A Taylor. Another, (of a more cutting disposition,) steps in his steed; and hee takes a text, which hee divides into many parts: (to speake truly) as many as hee list. The fag end of it hee pares away, as a superfluous remnant.

Hee puts his auditory in comfort, that hee will make a garment for them, and teach them how they shall put it on; and incourages them to be in love with it, for it is of such a fashion as doth best become a Christian man. Hee will assuer them that it shall be armor of proffe against all assaults of Satan. This garment, (sayes hee,) is not composed as the garments made by a carnall man, that are sowed with a hot needle and a burning thread; but it is a garment that shall out last all the garments: and, if they will make use of it as hee shall direct them, they shall be able, (like saint George,) to terrifie the greate Dragon, error; and defend truth, which error with her wide chaps would devoure: whose mouth shall be filled with the shredds and parings, which hee continually gapes for under the cutting bourd.

A third, hee supplies the rome: and in the exercise of his guifts begins with a text that is drawne out of a *A Tapster.* fountaine that has in it no dreggs of popery. This shall proove unto you, (says hee,) the Cup of repentance: it is not like unto the Cup of the Whore of Babilon, who will make men drunk with the dreggs thereof: It is filled up to the brim with comfortable joyce, and will proove a comfortable cordiall to a sick soule, sayes hee. And so hee handles the matter as if hee dealt by the pinte and the quarte, with Nic and Froth.

A Cobler. An other, (a very learned man indeed,) goes another way to worke with his auditory; and exhorts them to walke upright, in the way of their calling, and not, (like carnall men,) tread awry. And if they should fayle in the performance of that duety, yet they should seeke for amendement whiles it was time; and tells them it would bee to late to seek for help when the shop windowes were shutt up: and pricks them forward with a freindly admonition not to place theire delight in worldly pleasures, which will not last, but in time will come to an end; but so to handle the matter that they may be found to wax better and better, and then they shall be doublely rewarded for theire worke: and so closes up the matter in a comfortable manner.

But stay: Here is one stept up in haste, and, (being not minded to hold his auditory in expectation of any long discourse,) hee takes a text; and, (for brevities sake,) divides it into one part: and then runnes so fast a fore with the matter, that his auditory cannot follow him. Doubtles his Father was some Irish foote-man; by his speede it seemes so. And it may be at *A very patorick.* the howre of death, the sonne, being present, did participat of his Fathers nature, (according to Pithagoras,) and so the vertue of his Fathers nimble feete being infused into his braines, might make his tongue outrunne his wit.

Well, if you marke it, these are speciall gifts indeede: which the vulgar people are so taken with, that there is no perswading them that it is so ridiculous.

This is the meanes, (O the meanes,) that they pursue: This that comes without premeditation; This is the Suparlative: and hee that does not approove of this, they say is a very reprobate.

Many unwarrantable Tenents they have likewise: some of which being come to my knowledge I wil here set downe: one wherof, being in publicke practise maintained, is more notorious then the rest. I will therefore beginne with that, and convince them of manifest error by the maintenance of it, which is this:

Tenent I. That it is the Magistrates office absolutely, (and not the Minsters,) to joyne the people in lawfull matrimony. And for this they vouch the History of Ruth, saying Boas was married to Ruth in presence of the Elders of the people. Herein they mistake the scope of the text.

2. That it is a relique of popery to make use of a ring in marriage: and that it is a diabolicall circle for the Divell to daunce in.

3. That the purification used for weomen after delivery is not to be used.

4. That no child shall be baptised whose parents are not receaved into their Church first.

5. That no person shall be admitted to the Sacrament of the Lords supper that is without.

6. That the booke of Common prayer is an idoll: and all that use it, Idolaters.

7. That every man is bound to beleeve a professor upon his bare affirmation onely, before a Protestant upon oath.

8. That no person hath any right to Gods creatures, but Gods children onely, who are themselves: and that all others are but usurpers of the Creatures.

9. And that, for the generall good of their Church and commonwealth, they are to neglect father, mother and all freindship.

10. Much a doe they keepe about their Church discipline, as if that were the most essentiall part of their Religion. Tythes are banished from thence, all except the tyth of Mint and Commin.

11. They differ from us something in the creede too, for if they get the goods of one, that is without, into their hands, hee shall be kept without remedy for any satisfaction: and they beleeve that this is not cosenage.

12. And lastly they differ from us in the manner of praying; for they winke when they pray, because they thinke themselves so perfect in the highe way to heaven that they can find it blindfould: so doe not I.

CHAP. XXVIII.
Of their Policy in publik Justice.

Now that I have anottomized the two extreame parts of this Politique Commonwealth, the head and the inferior members, I will shew you the hart, and reade a short lecture over that too; which is Justice.

I have a petition to exhibit to the highe and mighty Mr. Temperwell; and I have my choise whether I shall make my plaint in a case of conscience, or bring it with in the Compas of a point in law. And because I will goe the surest way to worke, at first, I will see how others are answered in the like kinde, whether it be with hab or nab, as the Judge did the Countryman.

Here comes Mr. Hopewell: his petition is in a case of conscience, (as hee sayes.) But, see, great Josua allowes conscience to be of his side: yet cuts him off with this answere; Law is flat against him. Well let me see another. I marry: Here comes one Master Doubtnot: his matter depends, (I am sure,) upon a point in Law: alas, what will it not doe, looke ye it is affirmed that Law is on his side: but Conscience, like a blanket, over spreades it. This passage is like to the Procustes of Roome, mee thinks; and therefore I may very well say of them,

Even so, by racking out the joynts & chopping of the head,
Procustes fitted all his guests unto his Iron bedd.

And, if these speede no better, with whome they are freinds, that neither finde Law nor Conscience to helpe them, I doe not wonder to see mine Host of Ma-re-Mount speede so ill, that has bin proclaimed an enemy so many yeares in New Canaan to their Church and State.

CHAP. XXIX.
How mine Host was put into a whales belly.

THE Seperatists, (after they had burned Ma-re-Mount they could not get any shipp to undertake the carriage of mine Host from thence, either by faire meanes or fowle,) they were inforced, (contrary to their expectation,) to be troubled with his company: and by that meanes had time to consider more of the man, then they had done of the matter: wherein at length it was discovered that they, (by meanes of their credulity of the intelligence given them in England of the matter, and the false Carecter of the man,) had runne themselves headlonge into an error, and had done that on a sodaine which they repented at leasure, but could not tell which way to help it as it stood now. They could debate upon it and especially upon two difficult points, whereof one must be concluded upon: If they sent mine Host away by banishment, hee is in possibility to survive, to their disgrace for the injury done: if they suffer him to stay, and put him in *statu quo prius*, all the vulgar people will conclude they have bin too rashe in burning a howse that was usefull, and count them men unadvised.

So that it seemes, (by theire discourse about the matter,) they stood betwixt Hawke and Bussard: and could not tell which hand to incline unto. They had sounded him secretly: hee was content with it, goe which way it would. Nay Shackles himselfe, (who was imployed in the burning of the howse, and therefore feared to be caught in England,) and others were so forward in putting mine Host *in statu quo prius*, after they had found their error, (which was so apparent that Luceus eies would have served to have found it out in lesse time,) that they would contribute 40. shillings a peece towards it; and affirmed, that every man according to his ability that had a hand in this black designe should be taxed to a Contribution in like nature: it would be done exactly.

Now, (whiles this was in agitation, and was well urged by some of those partys to have bin the upshot,) unexpected, (in the depth of winter, when all shipps were gone out of the land,) in comes Mr. Wethercock, a proper Mariner; and, they said, he could observe the winde: blow it high, blow it low, hee was resolved to lye at Hull rather than incounter such a storme as mine Host had met with: and this was a man for their turne.

Hee would doe any office for the brethren, if they (who hee knew had a strong purse, and his conscience waited on the strings of it, if all the zeale hee had) would beare him out in it: which they professed they would. Hee undertakes to ridd them of mine Host by one meanes or another. They gave him the best meanes they could, according to the present condition of the worke, and letters of credence to the favoures of that Sect in England; with which, (his busines there being done, and his shipp cleared,) hee hoyst the Sayles and put to Sea: since which time mine Host has not troubled the brethren, but onely at the Counsell table: where now Sub judice lis est.

CHAP. XXX.
Of Sir Christopher Gardiner Knight, and
how hee spedd amongst the Seperatists.

Sir Christopher Gardiner, (a Knight, that had bin a traveller both by Sea and Land; a good judicious gentleman in the
Mathematticke and other Sciences usefull for Plantations,
Kimistry, &c. and also being a practicall Enginer,) came into
those parts, intending discovery.

But the Seperatists love not those good parts, when they
proceede from a carnall man, (as they call every good Prottes-
tant); in shorte time they had found the meanes to pick a quarrell with him. The meanes is that they pursue to obtaine what
they aime at: the word is there, the meanes.

So that, when they finde any man like to proove an enemy to
their Church and state, then straight the meanes must be used
for defence. The first precept in their Politiques is to defame
the man at whom they aime, and then hee is a holy Israelite in
their opinions who can spread that fame brodest, like butter
upon a loafe: no matter how thin, it will serve for a vaile: and
then this man, (who they have thus depraved,) is a spotted
uncleane leaper: hee must out, least hee pollute the Land, and
them that are cleane.

If this be one of their guifts, then Machevill had as good
gifts as they. Let them raise a scandall on any, though never so
innocent, yet they know it is never wiped cleane out: the staind
marks remaines; which hath bin well observed by one in these
words of his,

> Stick Candles gainst a Virgin walls white back;
> If they'l not burne yet, at the least, they'l black.

And thus they dealt with Sir Christopher: and plotted by all the
wayes and meanes they could, to overthrow his undertakings
in those parts.

And therefore I cannot chuse but conclude that these Seperatists have speciall gifts: for they are given to envy and mallice
extremely.

The knowledge of their defamacion could not please the
gentleman well, when it came to his eare; which would cause

him to make some reply, as they supposed, to take exceptions at, as they did against Faire cloath: and this would be a meanes, they thought, to blow the coale, and so to kindle a brand that might fire him out of the Country too, and send him after mine Host of Ma-re-Mount.

They take occasion, (some of them,) to come to his howse when hee was gone up into the Country, and (finding hee was from home,) so went to worke that they left him neither howse nor habitation nor servant, nor any thing to help him, if hee should retorne: but of that they had noe hope, (as they gave it out,) for hee was gone, (as they affirmed,) to leade a Salvage life, and for that cause tooke no company with him: and they having considered of the matter, thought it not fit that any such man should live in so remoate a place, within the Compas of their patent. So they fired the place, and carried away the persons and goods.

Sir Christopher was gone with a guide, (a Salvage,) into the inland parts for discovery: but, before hee was returned, hee met with a Salvage that told the guide, Sir Christopher would be killed: Master Temperwell, (who had now found out matter against him,) would have him dead or alive. This hee related; and would have the gentleman not to goe to the place appointed, because of the danger that was supposed.

But Sir Christopher was nothing dismaid; hee would on, whatsoever come of it; and so met with the Salvages: and betweene them was a terrible skermish: But they had the worst of it, and hee scaped well enough.

The guide was glad of it, and learnd of his fellowes that they were promised a great reward for what they should doe in this imployment.

Which thing, (when Sir Christopher understood,) hee gave thanks to God; and after, (upon this occasion to sollace him-selfe,) in his table booke hee composed this sonnet, which I have here inserted for a memoriall.

THE SONNET.

Wolfes in Sheeps clothing, why will ye
Think to deceave God that doth see
Your simulated sanctity?
For my part, I doe wish you could
Your owne infirmities behold,
For then you would not be so bold.
Like Sophists, why will you dispute
With wisdome so?   You doe confute
None but yourselves.   For shame, be mute,
    Least great Jehovah, with his powre,
Do come upon you in a howre
When you least think, and you devoure.

This Sonnet the Gentleman composed as a testimony of his love towards them, that were so ill-affected towards him; from whome they might have receaved much good, if they had bin so wise to have imbraced him in a loving fashion.

But they despise the helpe that shall come from a carnall man, (as they termed him,) who, after his retorne from those designes, finding how they had used him with such disrespect, tooke shipping, and disposed of himselfe for England; and discovered their practises in those parts towards his Majesties true harted Subjects, which they made wery of their aboade in those parts.

CHAP. XXXI.
Of mine Host of Ma-re-Mount how hee played Jonas
after hee had bin in the Whales belly for a time.

MINE Host of Ma-re-Mount, being put to Sea, had delivered him, for his releese by the way, (because the shipp was unvitteled, and the Seamen put to straight allowance, which could hold out but to the Canaries,) a part of his owne provision, being two moneths proportion; in all but 3. small peeces of porke, which made him expect to be famished before the voyage should be ended, by all likelyhood. Yet hee thought hee would make one good meale, before hee died: like the Colony servant in Virginea, that, before hee should goe to the gallowes, called to his wife to set on the loblolly pot, and let him have one good meale before hee went; who had committed a petty crime, that in those dayes was made a cappitall offence.

And now, mine Host being merrily disposed, on went the peeces of porke, wherewith hee feasted his body, and cherished the poore Sailers; and got out of them what Mr. Wethercock, their Master, purposed to doe with him that hee had no more provision: and along they sailed from place to place, from Iland to Iland, in a pittifull wether beaten ship, where mine Host was in more dainger, (without all question,) then Jonas, when hee was in the Whales belly; and it was the great mercy of God that they had not all perished. Vittelled they were but for a moneth, when they wayd Ancor and left the first port.

They were a pray for the enemy for want of powther, if they had met them: besides the vessell was a very slugg, and so unserviceable that the Master called a counsell of all the company in generall, to have theire opinions which way to goe and how to beare the helme, who all under their hand affirmed the shipp to be unserviceable: so that, in fine, the Master and men and all were at their wits end about it: yet they imployed the Carpenters to search and caulke her sides, and doe theire best whiles they were in her. Nine moneths they made a shifte to use her, and shifted for supply of vittells at all the Islands they touched at: though it were so poorely, that all those helpes, and the short allowance of a bisket a day, and a few Lymons taken in at the Canaries, served but to bring the vessell in view of the lands end.

They were in such a desperat case, that, (if God in his greate mercy had not favoured them, and disposed the windes faire untill the vessell was in Plimmouth roade,) they had without question perished; for when they let drop an Anchor, neere the Island of S. Michaels, not one bit of foode left, for all that starving allowance of this wretched Wethercock, that, if hee would have lanched out his beaver, might have bought more vittells in New England then he, and the whole ship with the Cargazoun, was worth, (as the passingers hee carried who vittelled themselves affirmed). But hee played the miserable wretch, and had possessed his men with the contrary; who repented them of waying anchor before they knew so much.

Mine Host of Ma-re-Mount, (after hee had bin in the Whales belly,) was set a shore, to see if hee would now play Jonas, so metamorphosed with a longe voyage that hee looked like Lazarus in the painted cloath.

But mine Host, (after due consideration of the premisses,) thought it fitter for him to play Jonas in this kinde, then for the Seperatists to play Jonas in that kinde as they doe. Hee therefore bid Wethercock tell the Seperatists, that they would be made in due time to repent those malitious practises, and so would hee too; for hee was a Seperatist amongst the Seperatists, as farre as his wit would give him leave; though when hee came in Company of basket makers, hee would doe his indevoure to make them pinne the basket, if hee could, as I have seene him. And now mine Host, being merrily disposed, haveing past many perillous adventures in that desperat Whales belly, beganne in a posture like Jonas, and cryed, Repent you cruell Seperatists, repent; there are as yet but 40. dayes, if Jove vouchsafe to thunder, Charter and the Kingdome of the Seperatists will fall asunder: Repent you cruell Schismaticks, repent. And in that posture hee greeted them by letters retorned into new Canaan; and ever, (as opportunity was fitted for the purpose,) he was both heard and seene in the posture of Jonas against them, crying, repent you cruel Seperatists, repent; there are as yet but 40. dayes; if Jove vouchsafe to thunder, the Charter and the Kingdome of the Seperatists will fall a sunder: Repent, you cruell Schismaticks, repent. If you will heare any more of this proclamation meete him at the next markettowne, for *Cynthius aurem vellet.*

A TABLE OF THE CONTENTS
OF THE THREE BOOKES:

THE TENENTS OF THE THIRD BOOKE.

FINIS.

THE EDITORS' COMMENT

Perhaps best known as the target of William Bradford's ire in *Of Plimoth Plantation*, Thomas Morton established a small trading post at Passonagessit (now Quincy), where he allied with Massachusett traders and English indentured servants. Morton's witty rhetorical style and membership in the Church of England, including his celebration of religious festivals, put him at odds with the Plymouth settlers' repudiation of the Church of England. Additionally, the Plymouth colonists accused him of supplying Massachusett and Wampanoag people with guns. Plymouth eventually sent armed men led by Miles Standish to halt Morton's celebrations and his trade with Indigenous people. Morton used praise for Native communities to amplify his criticism of the Plymouth settlers. Along the way, he described Indigenous diplomacy and traditional ecological knowledge he had observed as he traded with Indigenous people and relied on their hospitality to provision him. For example, he described the aftermath of the epidemics that spread from European traders through Native communities and Indigenous practices of meeting at springs to celebrate seasonal changes.

Experience Mayhew:
from *Indian Converts*

EXAMPLE XVII.
Mr. JAPHETH HANNIT, *the third Pastor of the Indian Church on* Martha's Vineyard, *who died* July 29, 1712.

JApheth hannit was born in or about the Year 1638, in the Place now called *Chilmark*, on *Martha's Vineyard*. His Father was an *Indian* of prime Quality there, named *Pamchannit*; which Name being contracted into *Hannit* only, by leaving out the two first Syllables of it, became afterward the Sirname of his Son *Japheth*, and others of his Offspring: a thing very common among our *Indians*.

This *Pamchannit* and his Wife having buried their first five Children successively, every one of them within ten Days of their Birth, notwithstanding all their Use of the *Pawwaws* and Medicines to preserve them, had a sixth (a Son) born to them, the same whom I am here speaking of, a few Years before the *English* first settled on the said *Vineyard*.

The Mother being then greatly distressed with fear that she should lose this Child as she had done the former, and utterly despairing of any Help from such Means had been formerly try'd without any Success, as soon as she was able, which was within ten Days after his Birth, she with a sorrowful Heart took him up and went out into the Field, that she might there weep out her Sorrow. But while she was there musing on the Insufficiency of human Help, she found it powerfully suggested to her Mind, that there is one *Almighty God* who is to be prayed to; that *this God* hath created all things that we see; and that the *God* who had given Being to herself and all other People, and had given her Child to her, was able to preserve and continue his Life.

On this she resolved that she would seek to God for that Mercy, and did accordingly; the Issue was that her Child lived,

and her Faith (such as it was) in him who had thus answered her
Prayer, was wonderfully strengthened; and the Consideration
of *God's Goodness* herein manifested to her, caused her to dedicate this Son of hers to the Service of that God who had thus
preserved his Life: Of her doing of which she early informed
him, and did, as far as she could, educate him accordingly.
But this she did yet more vigorously, and to better Purpose
prosecute, when a few Years after she was by the preaching of
the Gospel, instructed in the way of Salvation by a Redeemer,
and by the Grace of God enabled truly to believe in *Jesus Christ*
our only Saviour.

Japheth's Father being also about this time converted, and
so becoming a serious and godly Man, this his Son had the
Advantage of a Christian Education, while he was but a Child,
not only living in a Family where *God* was daily worshipped,
but was himself taught to call on the Name of that God to
whose Service he had been devoted: and when there was a
School set up for the *Indians* on the Island in the Year 1651,
his Father sent him to it, and he then learned to read both in
the *English* and *Indian* Tongue, and also to write a very legible
Hand, and was then also well instructed in his Catechism.

How he behaved himself while he was a Youth, I have no
particular Account; however I never understood that he was
viciously inclined.

After he was grown up, he marry'd a Daughter of a very
godly Man, named *Keestumin*, whom I shall afterwards mention; and she prov'd a very pious Person, and did *him Good and
not Evil all the Days of her Life.*

When the first *Indian* Church was here gathered in the
Year 1670, our *Japheth* was, as he himself told me, in a most
distressed Condition for not being of the number of them
who first confederated to walk together as a Church of Christ,
according to the Order of the Gospel: he on the *one hand*
greatly lamented his not being of that happy number, as he
esteemed them; and on the *other*, at the same time fear'd to
offer himself to the Society of God's People, lest he should be
unqualified for the Privileges to which they were admitted.

But tho *Japheth* could not at this time enter into a solemn
Covenant to serve the Lord, in an Attendance on all the
Duties incumbent on particular Churches; yet it was not long

after this, before he made a publick Profession of Repentance towards God, and Faith towards our Lord *Jesus Christ*, and join'd as a Member in full Communion to the Church which he before long'd to be one of: in which Relation he from time to time behaved himself as became a good Christian.

He was not after this presently called to the Work of the Ministry, but was for a considerable time imployed in Offices civil and military, being first made a *Captain* over a Company of his own *Nation*, and also a *Magistrate* among them; in both which Places of Trust he behaved himself well, and to the Acceptation of both the *English* and *Indians*: and in the time of that War betwixt them, which began in the Year 1675, and was commonly call'd *Philip's War*, good *Japheth* was very serviceable to both those of his *own Nation* and *ours* on this Island: for being firmly set, if possible, to maintain and preserve Peace betwixt the *English* and *Indians* here; and, being an *Indian* Captain, as has been already said, he was imployed by the *English* to observe and report how things went among the *Indians*: and to his Faithfulness in the Discharge of this Trust, I conceive that the Preservation of the Peace of our Island was very much owing, when the People on the Main were all in *War* and *Blood*.

Japheth's Fidelity to the *English* in this Affair gained him a high Esteem, and kind Treatment among them, he being generally look'd on as a godly and discreet Man by them; and being well accounted of among the *Indians* also, they not long after this called him to the Work of the Ministry among them. His Office of a Captain he now laid down, but that of a Magistrate he still sustain'd for some Years after he began to preach, none else being thought so fit for that Trust. The Place he preached at was that wherein he liv'd and dy'd, being join'd in that Work with his Uncle *Janawonit*, before mentioned in Example the fifth.

Being called to the Work of the Ministry, he was very faithful and diligent in it, and was esteemed the best qualified of any *Indian* on the Island not yet in the Pastoral Office. He was therefore by *John Tackanash* Pastor of the *Indian* Church here, in the time of his last Sickness, nominated as a fit Person to succeed him in the Office which he then expected a Discharge from; and the said *Tackanash* dying in *January* 1683–4, and being interred on the 23*d* of the same Month, the pious *Japheth*, who much lamented his Death, made a grave Speech at his Funeral, some of the Heads whereof being by my Father, who heard part of it, preserved in Writing, and now before me, I shall here insert them, and they are as followeth.

We ought, *said he*, to be very thankful to God for sending the Gospel to us, who were in utter Blindness and Ignorance, both we and our Fathers. Our Fathers Fathers, and their Fathers, and we, were at that time utterly without any means whereby we might attain the Knowledge of the only true *God*. That People also which knew the Ways of God, were some thousands of Miles distant from us; some of whom, by reason of Difference among themselves about their Way, removed into this Land; but it was God that sent them, that they might bring the Gospel to us. Therefore, I say, we have great reason to be thankful to God; and we have reason to be thankful to them also, for that they brought the Gospel to us: but most especially we ought to thank God for this, for tho they taught us, it was God that sent them, and made choice of them for this Work, of instructing us in the Ways of the Lord.

Before we knew God, when any Man dy'd, we said the Man is *dead*; neither thought we any thing further, but said he is *dead*, and mourned for him, and buried him: but now it is far otherwise; for now this good Man being dead, we have Hope towards God concerning him, believing that God hath received him into everlasting Rest.

Now therefore we ought to improve the Benefit which we have by the Gospel. And first, such of us as had like not to have received this Kindness, I mean such of us as were grown up when the Gospel came to us, so that it only found us in being, such are strongly obliged to improve the same, since they scarcely received it, or were in danger not to have enjoyed it.

Secondly, There are others of us that have been born under the Gospel; and we that were so, ought duly to improve the same, inasmuch as we have received so wonderful a Benefit.

And now tho this Man that went before us, leading us in the Way of God according to the Gospel, be deceased, and helps us no more, yet his Doctrine remaineth still for us to improve; nor ought we to forget him, but should remember him by his Wife and Children, whom he hath left among us.

Thus far *Japheth's* Speech, which savoureth of the Piety of the Man by whom it was uttered.

Good *John Takanash* being thus laid in his Grave, Mr. *Japheth* was the next *Spring* called to succeed him in the same Place and Office; and in the Fulfilment of the Ministry thus committed to him, he continued about 28 Years, *viz.* till the Year 1712. He was faithful and diligent in the Work of God, unto which he was called, preaching the Word in season and out of season, reproving, rebuking, and exhorting, with all Long-suffering and Doctrine, and used frequently to catechise the Children of his Flock in publick.

He maintained a good Discipline in the Church over which the Holy Ghost had made him Overseer, knew, how to *have Compassion* on those whose Case called for it, and how *to save others with Fear.* In difficult Cases that occurred, he was careful to take the best Advice he could get. He was not at all inclined to *lord it over his Flock*, but willing in Meekness to instruct them. And when there was danger of Discord among his Brethren, he would not side with any Party of them, but would in such Case make most winning and obliging Speeches to them all, tending to accommodate the Matters about which they were ready to fall out; and so wonderful an Ability had he this way, that he seldom failed of the End he aimed at.

He frequently visited the Families under his Care and Charge, especially when they were under Affliction by Sickness, or otherwise; and in the Visits he made them, he usually entertained them with serious and profitable Discourses, and I have heard him tell how very advantageous that kind of Visits had proved to some of his People.

He very often performed the Work of an Evangelist, in carrying of the Gospel into other Places, and endeavouring to promote the Kingdom of Christ in those of his own Nation; and God gave considerable Success to his Endeavours to do Good in this Way.

Tho his sermons were not very accurate, yet were they very serious, and had a great deal of good Matter in them, and he seem'd to me to do best when he did not try to oblige himself to any strict Method in them.

In Prayer he was very fervent, frequently praying with much Enlargement and Affection. On Sacrament Days I have more especially observed that he has done so; and God did sometimes shew a gracious regard to the Petitions by this his Servant put up to him. One Instance whereof has been formerly published in Dr. *Mather's* History of *New-England*, *Book* VI. *pag.* 63. But in nothing was he this way more highly favoured than in God's helping of him against a Temptation, with which for some time conflicting, and crying earnestly to God for Deliverance from it, he obtained the Mercy he sought to him for.

He was fully resolved that he and his House should serve the Lord; with them therefore he constantly prayed, and frequently sang Praises to God: he also read the Holy Scriptures in his House, and often gave serious Exhortations to all that were about him.

He was much given to Hospitality: for being frequently visited, both by Neighbours and Strangers, they were always kindly and generously entertained in his House with the best he had, or could readily procure.

He well understood, and steadily adhered to the Truths of our holy Religion in which he had been instructed, and would not be *driven about by every Wind of Doctrine.*

One Instance of his Stability in the Truth, I think it may not be amiss here to give my Reader: A godly *Englishman*, who had formerly been a School-master to the *Indians* here, and had taught *Japheth* and many others to read and write, and had also learned them their Catechisms, and instructed them in the Principles of Religion, having unhappily imbibed the Errors of the *Antipedobaptists*, thought himself obliged to endeavour to bring Mr. *Japheth* over to his Persuasion: To this End he therefore visited him at his House, took much Pains to convince him that theirs was the right Way, and that ours of baptizing Infants, and sprinkling in Baptism, was very wrong: But none of the Arguments used by the Man, could convince *Japheth* of what they were brought to prove; at length being just about to go away, *Japheth* told him he would only say one thing more to him before he went.

You know, Sir, *said he*, that we *Indians* were all in Darkness and Ignorance before the *English* came among us, and instructed us, and that your self are one of those *English* Men by whom we have been taught and illuminated. You taught us to read, and instructed us in the Doctrines of the Christian Religion, which we now believe, and endeavour to conform our Practices to. And when, Sir, you thus instructed us, you told us, that it may be there would shortly false Teachers come among us, and endeavour to pervert us, or lead us off from our Belief of the things wherein we had been instructed; but you then advised us to take heed to our selves, and beware that we were not turned aside by such Teachers, so as to fall into the Errors into which they would lead us. And now, Sir, I find your Prediction true; for you your self are become one of these Teachers you cautioned us against: I am therefore fully resolved to take your good Counsel, and not believe you, but will continue stedfast in the Truths wherein you formerly instructed me.

This Speech of *Japheth's* put an End to the Disputation.

As for *Japheth's* Morals, he was generally and justly esteemed, as well by the *English* as *Indians*, a Person of a good Conversation: nor did he discover any such Infirmity in his Life, or Deportment in the World, as was inconsistent with such an Esteem; or which thro' Prayer, and the Supply of the Spirit of Jesus Christ, he did not obtain a compleat Victory over, being only privately admonished of a Failure, which some began to be offended at.

As he was generally by the *English* esteemed a truly godly Man, so being a Person of a very genteel and obliging Conversation, and one who went clean and neat in his Apparel, he was every where courteously received and entertained by them, the best Gentleman on the Island not scrupling to invite him to sit at their Tables with them; and speaking *English* considerably well, Strangers that came to the Place took Delight in conversing with him. And once a Master of a Vessel discoursing with him, on the Morrow after the *Sabbath*, facetiously asking him, whether he prayed for him yesterday or not? *Japheth* readily reply'd, *Sir, I prayed for all God's People, and if you be one of them, I consequently prayed for you.*

Persons have sometimes had Premonitions of their own Death, and something of this Nature our *Japheth* did experience, as he did in the time of his last Sickness declare, together with the Influence the same had on his Life; an Account of which, with some of his dying Speeches, &c. his honest Son in law, *Job Soomannah*, who was frequently with him in his

Sickness, having written in *Indian*, communicated to me soon after *Japheth's* Death: An Extract of which Account I shall here in *English* insert, and it is as followeth.

He said, that about a Year before he was taken sick, he went out of his House, and walked alone in the Woods, and there it was by God revealed to him, that he had but a little time to live in this World; and that being thereupon much concerned in his Mind, he did immediately set himself on doing all that he could to prepare for his approaching End, as taking it for a Truth that his End was now very near, an looking Day and Night for it: but he said, he still misliked himself, or reckoned that he came short.

Thus it was with him till *April* the 2*d*, 1712, which being a Day of Thanksgiving, he went and preached thereon; but as with his Wife he returned home in the Evening, before they had gotten to their House he felt a Pain in his Side, and was never able after this to go to God's House of Prayer, his Sickness gradually encreasing on him from that time forward.

And having been sick about ten Weeks, he sent for the Brethren of the Church, and said to them as followeth, *viz. That it did often distress him in his Heart, and cause him to weep, when he saw the miserable Estate of all the People by reason of their Sins; but especially how unapt the generality of the Church were to the Duties incumbent on them, and how often they did fall by reason of one kind of Infirmity or another, to which they were subject, tho he had very often instructed them in their Duty.*

I have, said he, *often wished for your sakes, that you might still enjoy me; but now I am willing to die: however, as to this, let the Will of God be done. But do you go on to pray to God, and worship him both stedfastly and fervently.*

To his own Family, and such others as attended on him, he afterwards, not long before his Death, said, *Be not feeble in your Minds, I'm hitherto stedfastly resolved that I will love the Lord my God. I shall,* said he, *now quickly go my last Journey, as others have done before me. Now I shall quickly set out. Thus it has been wont to be, when a Thing has here no further Use to be made of it. But Oh, what sweet Melody is there now in Heaven!* To his Son in law, the Writer hereof, he then said, *My Son, be thou of good Courage, and fail not to lay hold of the heavenly Salvation, for the sake of the things of this World But as for me,* said he, *I need to have my Mind further strengthened, and encouraged; for I think I shall now quickly leave you.*

The 28*th* of *July* 1712, was the last Day he lived in the World; for the Night following it, a little after Midnight, having desired those that were with him to praise God, by singing the 13*th* Psalm, and then by Prayer to commit both him and themselves to God, his Breath failed, and he resigned up his Spirit to God who gave it.

Thus far *Job Soomannah's* Memoirs of his good Father in law. As I was well acquainted with *Japheth* in his Life, so I frequently visited him in the time of his last Sickness; and on the whole of my Acquaintance with him, I cannot but think, that he was a very serious and godly Man, and a Man of great Moderation and Prudence. His Discourse in the time of his last Sickness, when I was with him, was very pious and savoury. He then expressed a humble Sense of the Sin of his Nature and Life, and yet his Hopes of eternal Salvation thro' the infinite Mercy of God, and Merits of his Son Jesus Christ. He then also expressed a Readiness and Willingness to resign himself and all that the had into the Hands of God, his faithful Creator, and merciful Redeemer. I remember also that he told me, that God had in the latter Part of his Life given him a more effectual Sense of the Evil of Sin, than formerly he had had; and that he had also enabled him with more Vigilance and Industry, to endeavour the Mortification of the Corruptions of his Heart.

Among other *Evidences* of the *real Piety* of this good Man, the Grief of his Heart for the Sins of his Countrymen, especially those who had been under his own Care and Charge, together with his Care and Concern for their Reformation, may justly be reckoned as *one*; for besides what of this Nature was discovered by him, in what is above-said, he a few Days before his Death, with his feeble and dying Hand wrote an affectionate Address to the People of his own Charge, which he desired might be communicated to them: which Writing of his being now by me, I shall render into *English*, and here insert, and with that conclude my Account of the Person that penned it. It is then as followeth:

> Is it not a most desirable thing for Persons in this Life certainly to know, that they shall go to Heaven when they leave this World?

Therefore now take heed, and consider well what you do, and do not cast away such Hopes as these for nothing, nor for a little of the Pleasure of this World: for it is certain, that your carnal and worldly Actions can't give you Rest. Moreover, by these you do bring all sorts of Misery on your selves; yea, and not only so, but you do thereby trouble others also, so long as you remain unconverted.

Thus you trouble such as are Magistrates to rule and govern you, and by their penal Laws to punish you.

Next, you trouble such as are *Pastors* or *Ministers*, while you hate to hear, believe, and practice their Doctrine. While your Sin and Misery is great, their Trouble and Sorrow is so too here in this World.

You do also trouble the common People by your Sins, by bringing on them various Sicknesses and pestilential Diseases, and all other divine Chastisements.

You do also hereby hinder and disturb the holy Peace of God's praying People among the Churches, and make those ashamed that are religious; and you who are still ungodly laugh at it.

Alas! Oh Lord, how very heavy is my Grief on the account hereof? seeing we now hear the Gospel preached to us, and have the Light of God's Word shining on us, and he in Peace giveth his *Sabbaths* to us.

God is constantly calling of us to Repentance, and has often repeated his Chastisements on us, by grievous Sicknesses; but, this notwithstanding, how full of Wickedness has he seen all our Towns? for both Men and Women, young Men and Maids, do all delight in Sin, and do things therein greatly grievous.

People should all of them now forsake their Sins, and turn to God; and they should come to their Ministers, and make penitential Confessions of their Transgressions to them, and entreat them to pray to God for them: then would God forgive their Iniquities, and teach them to do that which is right all the Days of their Lives.

Then also would God teach them to know Jesus Christ, and believe in him: and then they should receive Remission of all their Sins, and should be caused to walk according to the Word of God to the End of their Lives. Whoso heareth this, Oh let it put him on Consideration! These are my last Words to you. Now fare you all well. *Amen.*

EXAMPLE III.
HANNAH AHHUNNUT, *who died at* Nashouohkamuk, *alias* Chilmark, *in or about the Year* 1704.

HANNAH Ahhunnut, commonly called by the *Indians Pah-kehtau*, was a Daughter of an *Indian* who formerly liv'd in *Tokame*, now *Tisbury*, of whom I know nothing remarkable.

Her first Husband's Name was *John Momonequem*, a Son of that *Momonequem* mention'd *Chap.* II. *Examp.* II. The said *John* being a very worthy Man, a Preacher of the Word of God, and a *Ruling Elder* of the Church whereof Master *Japheth Hannit* was the *Pastor*; he was sent to preach the Gospel to the *Indians* at *Dartmouth*, and there died many Years since.

The *Hannah* of whom I am speaking, being there left a Widow, return'd again to *Martha's Vineyard*, the Place of her Nativity: She was a Member of the Church whereof her Husband was a *Ruling Elder* while he lived; and so far as I can understand, lived very blamelesly from the time she first join'd to it, to the end of her Life.

She was a Person of good Knowledge in the things of God, was able and willing to read the *Scriptures*, and other good Books translated into the *Indian* Tongue. And I have heard her discourse very understandingly and seriously in matters of Religion, and about the State of her own Soul; tho I cannot not particularly remember what she said.

She constantly attended God's publick Worship and Ordinances, and appeared very serious therein; was often much affected while she was waiting on God in the Duties of his House, wherein she drew nigh to him.

She was observed, by such as were acquainted with her, to make conscience of retiring for secret Prayer: I have heard an *English* Woman, worthy of Credit, with whom she labour'd some time, give her this Testimony.

Her second Husband, *Job Ahhunnut*, whom I look upon as a godly Man, affirms, that she gave her self much to Prayer while she was his Wife. He says she encourag'd him in his Duty towards God, and used to pray constantly in the Family when he was abroad.

She very frequently instructed and exhorted those of her own Sex, who stood in need of such Admonitions as she was able to give them: And young People especially, she in this way spake often to.

She was very merciful to the Poor, tho she was not her self rich; and would very often extend her Charity towards them, by bestowing on them such things as she had, and as she thought their Needs called for.

She was remarkable for her Willingness and Ability to be helpful to the Sick; such she very often visited, carrying such things to them as she thought they needed, and doing such things for them, while with them, as she saw needful to be done. And being looked upon as a Woman of Prayer, and one who had an Interest in Heaven, Persons of her own Sex used to desire her to pray with and for them, when in their Sickness she visited them, and there were no Men present for whom it might be more proper to perform that Office. She used to perform the same Duty at Womens Travails also, when in difficult Cases there were special Occasions for it; and it has been reported, that she had sometimes very remarkable Answers.

She seemed to have a great Veneration for the *Ministers* of God, shewing by her Practice, that she *accounted them worthy of double Honour, esteeming them highly for their Work's sake*; and communicating to them in all such temporal good things as God had bestowed on her. And when there were Days of Thanksgiving among our *Indians*, she was a most diligent Provider and Dresser of the Food wherewith the Poor as well as the Rich were then to be entertain'd; and usually order'd the setting of it on the Tables, at which People were to sit and eat it.

She died very suddenly of, as I suppose, an Apoplexy; but I trust Death did not find her unprepared for it.

EXAMPLE VI.
ABIGAIL, *called by the* Indians AMMAPOO, *who died at* Sanchecantacket *in* Edgartown, *in the Year* 1710.

THIS *Abigail* was the Daughter of a petty *Sachim* of *Homes's Hole*, called *Cheshchaamog*, and a Sister of that *Caleb Cheshchaamog*, who took a Degree in *Harvard* College in the

Year 1665. When she became a Woman, she was married to
Wunnannauhkomun a godly Minister, mentioned *Chapter* I.
Example 5. And, tho she was esteemed worthy to be a Wife
to such a Husband, yet she made not a publick Profession of
Religion until after the gathering of the first *Indian* Church
on *Martha's Vineyard*, in the Year 1670.

She was taught to read while young, and made a good
Improvement of that Advantage, till by a Scald in her Face,
she in a great measure lost her Sight, within a few Years after
she was first marry'd.

She used, while her Husband lived, to pray in the Family
in his Absence, and frequently gave good Counsel to her
Children.

After she had lived so long with her Husband that the eldest
of the three Daughters which she had by him, was become a
Mother, he dy'd and left her a Widow; but just as he was going
out of the World, desiring his Wife and Daughters to tell him
what Petitions he should put up to God for them, before he
took his leave of them, the Mother, her Daughters joining with
her in it, requested him to pray for spiritual Blessings for her
and them, which he did accordingly, as is related in his Life.

Being thus left a Widow, she lived in that Estate the greatest
part of her time after; for tho she after some Years marry'd
again, yet her Husband soon dying, she chose not to marry
after this, but lived with her Children, and used to pray with
them, and frequently gave many good Instructions to them, as
two of them yet living do testify.

As she prayed much at other times, so she made God her
Refuge in an evil Day, calling on him without fainting until
he had Mercy on her; and experiencing the Mercy of God her
self, she was very merciful to the Poor, being, according to
her Capacity, *ready to distribute, and willing to communicate
to them.*

She delighted much in going to the House of God, and
would scarce ever stay from Meeting, unless there were some
very necessary Occasion for it.

She was a diligent Instructor of her Grandchildren, as well
as of her own, earnestly exhorting them to love and fear God,
and believe in Jesus Christ their only Saviour; and lived to see

some good Effects of her pious Endeavours in this Way: nor did she neglect to instruct and exhort other ignorant Persons.

When she prayed, she was careful not to forget her Enemies, and would seldom fail of putting up some good Petitions for them: and as she prayed for them, so she sought Oportunities to do good to them, and would sometimes say, that that was the way in which People should *heap Coals of Fire on the Heads of them that hated them.*

She often spake of this World as none of our resting Place, and of her self and others as Strangers and Pilgrims in it. But of Heaven she used to talk as a Place of excellent Glory, where God the Father, Son, and Holy Spirit dwell, and from whence the holy Angels come to minister to the Saints on the Earth, and to which they would at their Death convey them. And of Death she would sometimes speak as the Hand of God, by which his People were removed into a better Place than this World is: and would also call it a *Ferryman*, by which we have our Passage out of this Life into the next.

As she was her self careful to abstain from Sin, so she was also a serieus and sharp Reprover of it, and used to call it the Way to Hell and Damnation.

She was long sick before she dy'd, and tho she underwent much Pain in that time, yet she bare it with Patience and Resignation, being full of heavenly Discourses, and calling often on God her Saviour.

One of her Daughters, who, I hope, is a pious Woman, affirms, that being much broken of her Rest, by tending her Mother Night and Day in her Sickness, and being her self not well, her Mother desired her to lie down and try to get a little Sleep, before it was well light, on the Morning of the Day on which she dy'd, but that telling her she was afraid she would suffer for want of Help if she did so, her Mother told her, that *God would take Care of her*: but this Argument not prevailing with her to lie down, she, as she sat in the Room drowsy, with her Eyes well nigh shut, suddenly saw a Light which seemed to her brighter than that of Noonday; when looking up, she saw two bright shining Persons, standing in white Raiment at her Mother's Bed-side, who, on her Sight of them, with the Light attending them, immediately disappeared; and that hereupon saying something to her Mother of what she had seen, she replied, *This is what I said to you, God taketh Care of me.* She also, as I am informed, told another Person before she dy'd, that her Guardians were already come for her.

She, just before she departed this Life, prayed earnestly to God for all her Children and Offspring, as her first Husband did before he dy'd; nor did she now forget to pray for others also, and even for her Enemies. And having thus called on the Lord, she presently after committed her Soul into the Hands of her Redeemer, and so expired.

I was long acquainted with the Person of whom these things are related, and always esteemed her a very godly Woman.

The Account given by her Daughter of what she saw before her Mother dy'd, being alone with her, she related soon after her Death, and still maintains the Truth of it.

THE EDITORS' COMMENT

Indian Converts relays the experiences of four generations of Wampanoag men, women, and children from Noepe (currently Martha's Vineyard). Transcribed and published by the missionary Experience Mayhew, the book gathers the biographies of Christian Wampanoags, drawing on stories from the Mayhew family's multigenerational relationships with Wampanoag families, going back to the 1640s. Mayhew wrote as a settler who grew up on Noepe, learning both Wôpanâak and English languages as a child. He offers a detailed glimpse of Wampanoag people who had experienced decades of contact with colonists, negotiated settlers' presence on their lands, and survived epidemics in 1616–19, 1633, 1643, and 1645. *Indian Converts* attests to the ways that Wampanoag people on Noepe brought Christianity and English-language literacy into existing practices and highlights the island's difference from the mainland "Praying Towns" that John Eliot established to try to create separate Christian Native communities. On Noepe, Wampanoag people used their knowledge of Christianity to comfort neighbors who were ill or who had lost children in the epidemics of the 1630s and 1640s. The missionary project thus did not produce simply "Indian converts" but also generations of leaders, some of whom went on to attend the Harvard Indian College, and others who played important roles on Noepe, including those like Japheth Hannit, who worked to maintain peace during King Philip's War. Moreover, Mayhew's depictions of Wampanoag women illuminated the roles they played in their communities, often as teachers and caretakers for the sick, even as English missionaries imposed European gender roles that shifted women's positions within their communities and as King Philip's War uprooted families. For example, in one of the excerpts included here, Mayhew discusses the life of Hannah Ahhunnut, whose first husband, John Momonequem, was sent to preach to the Native community at Dartmouth, a town built on the Wampanoag lands of Acushnet, Acoaxet, and Aponeganset, where Wampanoag people gathered after King Philip's War. Hannah remained on Noepe after Momonequem's death, where she was known for her care for the ill and needy.

Caleb Cheeshateaumuck to
"Honoratissimi Benefactores"

Honoratissimi Benefactores

Referunt historici de Orpheo musico et insigni Poeta quod
ab Appolline Lyram acceperit eaque tantum valuerit, ut illius
Cantu sylvas saxumque moverit et Arbores ingentes post se
traxerit, ferasque ferocissimas mitiores rediderit imo, quod
accepta Lyrâ ad inferos descenderit et Plutonem et Proserpi-
nam suo carmine demulserit, et Eurydicen uxorem ab inferis
ad superos evexerit: Hoc symbolum esse statuunt Philosophi
Antiquissimi, ut ostendant quod tanta et vis et virtus doctrinae
et politioris literaturae ad mutandum Barborum Ingenium: qui
sunt tanquam arbores, saxa, et bruta animantia: et eorum quasi
matephorisin efficiendam, eosque tanquam Tigres Cicurandos
et post se trahendos.

Deus vos delegit esse patronos nostros, et cum omni sapi-
entiâ intimâque Commiseratione vos ornavit, ut nobis paganis
salutiferam opem feratis, qui vitam progeniemque a majoribus
nostris ducebamus, tam animo quam corporeque nudi fuimus,
et ab omni humanitate alieni fuimus, in deserto huc et illuc
variisque erroribus ducti fuimus.

O terque quaterque ornatissimi, amantissimique viri, quas
quantasque quam maximas, immensasque gratias vobis tribua-
mus: eo quod onmium rerum Copiam nobis suppetitaveritis
propter educationem nostram, et ad sustentationem corporum
nostrorum: immensas maximasque expensas effudistis.

Et praecipuè quas quantasque, Gratias Deo Optimo Maximo
dabimus qui sanctas scripturas nobis revelavit, Dominumque
Jesum Christum nobis demonstravit, qui est via veritatis et
vitae. Praeter haec omnia, per viscera miserecordiae divinae,
aliqua spes relicta sit, ut instrumenta fiamus, ad declarandum et
propogandum evangelium Cognatis nostris Conterraneisque:
ut illi etiam Deum Cognoscant: et Christum.

Quamvis non posumus par pari redere vobis, reliquisque
Benefactoribus nostris, veruntamen speramus. nos non defu-

turos aped Deum supplicationibus importunis exorare pro illis
pijs miserecordibus viris, qui supersunt in vetere Angliâ, qui
pro nobis tantam vim auri, argentique effuderunt ad salutem
animarum nostrarum procurandam et pro vobis etiam, qui
instrumenta, et quasi aquae ductus fuistis omnia ista benefi-
centia nobis Conferendi.

Vestre Dignitati devotissimus: Caleb Cheeshateaumauk

Honored benefactors,

Historians tell about Orpheus the musician and remarkable
poet, that he received a lyre from Apollo, and that he was so
excellent upon it that the forests and the rocks were moved
by his song. The song's power was so great that he made the
great trees follow behind him, and made the wild animals
tame. Indeed the lyre was so powerful that, having received
it, he descended into the underworld, softened even Pluto and
Proserpina with his song, and led Eurydice, his wife, out of
the underworld into the upper world. The most ancient phi-
losophers make this a symbol in order that they might show
how strong the power and virtue of education and of refined
literature are in the transformation of the barbarians' nature.
They are like the trees, the rocks, and the unthinking animals,
and a metamorphosis, as it were, of them must be brought
about. They have to be tamed like tigers and must be drawn
to follow behind.

The Lord delegated you to be our patrons, and he endowed
you with all wisdom and intimate compassion, so that you may
perform the work of bringing blessing to us pagans, who derive
our life and origin from our forebears. We were naked in our
souls as well as in our bodies, we were aliens from all humanity,
and we were led around in the desert by various errors.

Oh threefold and fourfold most illustrious and most
loving men, what kind of thanks, if not the greatest and most
immense, should we give to you, for that you have supported
us with an abundance of all things for our education and for
the sustenance of our bodies. You have poured forth immense,
the greatest, resources.

And we will especially give great thanks to God the most
excellent and highest, who has revealed the sacred scriptures

to us, and who has shown to us our Lord Jesus Christ, who is the way of truth and of life. Besides all this, another hope has been left us through the depths of divine mercy: that we may be instruments to spread and propagate the gospel among our kin and neighbours, so that they also may know the Lord and Christ.

Even though we cannot commensurately reciprocate your kindness and that of our other benefactors, we do hope, however. We are not left alone praying before the Lord with importunate supplications for those pious and merciful men who are still in the old England, who disbursed so much gold and silver for us to obtain the salvation of our souls, and for you as well, who were instruments like aquaeducts in bestowing all these benefits on us.

Most devoted to your dignity: Caleb Cheeshateaumauk

1663

THE EDITORS' COMMENT

Caleb Cheeshateaumuck was a Wampanoag scholar from the island of Noepe (Martha's Vineyard), the son of the sachem Cheeschumuck of Nobnocket. He was one of many young Indigenous men who were recruited to attend colonial schools by missionaries like Thomas Mayhew, Jr., and John Eliot, where they mastered Latin, Greek, Hebrew, and English alongside English students. The scholars were also encouraged to learn to read and write in their Indigenous languages, in preparation for teaching their kin. Native communities saw this as an opportunity to gain skills that would facilitate communication with the newcomers. Caleb was the first Native graduate of Harvard College (class of 1665), and lived in the Indian College, Harvard's first brick building, which housed the Massachusetts Bay colony's printing press. Here, Native scholars helped to produce a library of Indigenous language texts, including the first Bible printed in North America, also known as the Wôpanâak Bible. Caleb's 1663 letter to his "honored benefactors" in England is one of the only surviving texts written by Harvard's early Native students. He was a fluent writer of Latin, as this letter demonstrates, and a scholar of both "pagan" (Latin and Greek) literature and Protestant scripture. This letter combines his knowledge of Latin poetry (the Orpheus myth), Puritan interpretation (application of the Orpheus myth), and Wampanoag traditional knowledge (which had parallels to Roman concepts). Although this letter was intended to demonstrate the success of missionary endeavors with Native students, it also stands as a testament to the intelligence and achievements of this first generation of Wampanoag scholars. As the writings of Caleb's relations on Noepe demonstrate, literacy quickly spread through Wampanoag communities and Wampanoag people were quick to question missionaries, based on their own interpretation of the Bible. The Wôpanâak Bible is now used by Wampanoag people in the revitalization of their language.

Thomas Cooper: Traditional Story from Martha's Vineyard

and

Helen Attaquin: How Martha's Vineyard Came to Be

*The following fabulous Traditions and Customs of the Indians
of Martha's Vineyard, were communicated to BENJAMIN
BASSET, Esq. of Chilmark, by THOMAS COOPER, a half
blooded Indian, of Gay Head, aged about sixty years; and
which, he says, he obtained of his grandmother, who, to use
his own expression, was a stout girl, when the English came
to the island.*

THE first Indian who came to the Vineyard, was brought
thither with his dog on a cake of ice. When he came to Gay
Head, he found a very large man, whose name was Moshup. He
had a wife and five children, four sons and one daughter; and
lived in the Den. He used to catch whales, and then pluck up
trees, and make a fire, and roast them. The coals of the trees,
and the bones of the whales, are now to be seen. After he was
tired of staying here, he told his children to go and play ball
on a beach that joined Noman's Land to Gay Head. He then
made a mark with his toe across the beach at each end, and so
deep, that the water followed, and cut away the beach; so that
his children were in fear of drowning. They took their sister
up, and held her out of the water. He told them to act as if they
were going to kill whales; and they were all turned into killers,
(a fish so called.) The sister was dressed in large stripes. He gave
them a strict charge always to be kind to her. His wife mourned
the loss of her children so exceedingly, that he threw her away.
She fell upon Seconet, near the rocks, where she lived some
time, exacting contribution of all who passed by water. After a
while she was changed into a stone. The entire shape remained

for many years. But after the English came, some of them broke off the arms, head, &c. but the most of the body remains to this day. Moshup went away nobody knows whither. He had no conversation with the Indians, but was kind to them, by sending whales, &c. ashore to them to eat. But after they grew thick around him he left them.

WHENEVER the Indians worshipped, they always sang and danced, and then begged of the sun and moon, as they thought most likely to hear them, to send them the desired favour; most generally rain or fair weather, or freedom from their enemies or sickness.

BEFORE the English came among the Indians, there were two disorders of which they most generally died, viz. the consumption and the yellow fever. The latter they could always *lay* in the following manner. After it had raged and swept off a number, those who were well, met to lay it. The rich, that is, such as had a canoe, skins, axes, &c. brought them. They took their seat in a circle; and all the poor sat around, without. The richest then proposed to begin to lay the sickness: and having in his hand something in shape resembling his canoe, skin, or whatever his riches were, he threw it up in the air; and whoever of the poor without could take it, the property it was intended to resemble became forever transferred to him or her. After the rich had thus given away all their moveable property to the poor, they looked out the handsomest and most sprightly young man in the assembly, and put him into an entire new wigwam, built of every thing new for that purpose. They then formed into two files at a small distance from each other. One standing in the space at each end, put fire to the bottom of the wigwam on all parts, and fell to singing and dancing. Presently the youth would leap out of the flames, and fall down to appearance dead. Him they committed to the care of five virgins, prepared for that purpose, to restore to life again. The term required for this would be uncertain, from six to forty-eight hours; during which time the dance must be kept up. When he was restored, he would tell, that he had been carried in a large thing high up in the air, where he came to a great company of white people, with whom he had interceded hard to have the distemper layed; and generally after much persuasion, would obtain a promise, or answer of peace, which never failed of laying the distemper.

How Martha's Vineyard Came to Be

Moshop was a man of peace who first lived on the elbow of Cape Cod. He loved to contemplate the beauty about him and would sit long hours tranquilly smoking his big Peudelee, or pipe, while he watched the clouds or stared out at the ever-changing sea. He was known as a just man and a kindly philosopher whose wisdom was unquestioned. He excelled in feasts of strength and bravery, which the envious attributed to magic. This caused malice and dissension to arise among some of his neighbors. After long consideration, Moshop decided he was weary of strife and discord. He would search out a new place where he and his followers might live in peace.

Along the marshes of Nauset on Cape Cod, over the dunes and through the forests, Moshop and his wife Squant and their people walked with the rising sun and the sun guided them toward land which was new to them. The shore birds flew up ahead of them. Pheasant and deer looked on with wonder, then scurried into hiding behind bayberry, sumac, viburnum, and wind-swept oaks.

At last, spent with walking, Moshop paused to look about him. As he slowly dragged one huge foot, water rushed in and a pool formed behind him. The pool deepened and became a channel and the tide swept in to separate a portion of land. That land became an island separated from Cape Cod by blue water. Soon his footsteps were marked by a chain of small islands, but it was the land that lay ahead which fulfilled Moshop's desire and became the beautiful island of all. Moshop named this largest island Capawack, or "Refuge Place."

From the westernmost high clay cliffs of Capawack, Moshop could see whales playing close to shore. There were forests edged by ponds of fresh water; sheltered fields for planting, and beauty wherever he looked. Never before had he gazed on such perfection. Truly the Great Spirit had led him here. This was the Refuge Place he had been seeking.

With housewifely concern, Squant set about preparing their first meal. Moshop pointed to nearby young trees and she pulled some of them up for firewood. Today there are no sizable trees on Gay Head, for Moshop's wife and children burned constant fires in their lodges. Smoke from these fires settled in a haze over the hills and today Old People sagely nod their heads and say the haze that often is seen comes from Old Squant's fire, or if the fog is unusually thick, then Moshop is smoking his pipe, or Peudelee.

Moshop provided the food for Squant to cook by wading out into the sea and catching a whale by the tail. Quickly he dashed it against the cliff so the blood ran down in a crimson stain. It ran down into the sea and stained the water red, as the water sometimes is stained today when the surf washes against the cliffs, which have red clay deposits.

As the family of Moshop and Squant grew in size, they continued to eat their meals at the edge of their cliff home, where they discarded the whale bones as well as bones of other animals. There were many bones and sometimes teeth of animals unknown in present times. These are still found today by sharp-eyed visitors who recognize them embedded in the cliffs or washed down on the beach.

Scientists say that the rise of the land ceased at that time, but it still continues today and the sea is constantly nibbling away at Moshop's land.

THOMAS COOPER: TRADITIONAL STORY
FROM MARTHA'S VINEYARD

and

HELEN ATTAQUIN: HOW MARTHA'S
VINEYARD CAME TO BE

THE EDITORS' COMMENT

Founded in 1791, the Massachusetts Historical Society was initially dedicated to collecting records and objects related to the colonies' early history, which its founders defined as beginning with the Plymouth settlers' arrival. Yet the historical society also collected and published accounts from Wampanoag people who remembered their families' first interactions with English settlers. These accounts include Wampanoag stories about how the islands like Noepe were formed. Printed amongst other documents the members of the Massachusetts Historical Society deemed crucial to narrating the region's history, these Wampanoag accounts are part of a vast Indigenous history that includes, even as it extends far beyond, colonial memories and written histories.

Following the account conveyed by Benjamin Basset to Thomas Cooper is a more contemporary oral tradition about the creation of Noepe, written in the late twentieth century by Helen Attaquin, a Wampanoag author and educator from Aquinnah. The deep time story, featuring the creative shapers and transformers Moshup and Old Squant (also known as Granny Squannit), contains vital cultural and ecological knowledge and is rooted in the cliffs of Aquinnah, where Wampanoag people continue to tell this story today. Helen Attaquin wrote this piece to impact public education, as she worked for the Wampanoag Indigenous Program at Plimoth plantation and the Boston Children's Museum. Helen Attaquin was from an influential leadership family and earned her doctorate in education.

Daniel Gookin: from *Historical Collections of the Indians in New England*

CHAP. II.
Of the principal Indians that inhabit New England.

§. 1. THE principal nations of the Indians, that did, or do, inhabit within the confines of New England, are five: 1. Pequots; 2. Narragansitts; 3. Pawkunnawkuts; 4. Massachusetts; and, 5. Pawtucketts.

§. 2. The Pequots, or Pequods, were a people seated in the most southerly bounds of New England; whose country the English of Connecticut jurisdiction doth now, for the most part, possess. This nation were a very warlike and potent people, about forty years since; at which time they were in their meridian. Their chief sachem held dominion over divers petty sagamores; as over part of Long Island, over the Mohegans, and over the sagamores of Quinapeake, yea over all the people that dwelt upon Connecticut river, and over some of the most southerly inhabitants of the Nipmuck county, about Quinabaag. The principal sachem lived at, or about, Pequot, now called New London. These Pequots, as old Indians relate, could in former times, raise four thousand men, fit for war; and held hostility with their neighbours, that lived bordering upon them to the east and north, called the Narragansitts, or Nechegansitts; but now they are few, not above three hundred men; being made subject unto the English, who conquered and destroyed most of them, upon their insolent deportment and just provocation, Anno 1638: of which we shall have occasion to speak more particularly in the sequel of our history.☞

§. 3. The Narragansitts were a great people heretofore; and the territory of these sachem extended about thirty or forty miles from Sekunk river and Narragansitt bay, including Rhode

☞ See the Postcript.

Island and other islands in that bay, being their east and north bounds or border, and so running westerly and southerly unto a place called Wekapage, four or five miles to the eastward of Pawcutuk river, which was reckoned for their south and west border, and the eastermost limits of the Pequots. This sachem held dominion over divers petty governours; as part of Long Island, Block Island, Cawesitt, Niantick, and others; and had tribute from some of the Nipmuck Indians, that lived remote from the sea. The chief seat of this sachem was about Narragansitt bay and Cannonicut island. The Narragansitts were reckoned, in former times, able to arm for war more than five thousand men as ancient Indians say. All do agree they were a great people, and oftentimes waged war with the Pawkunnawkutts and Massachusetts, as well as with the Pequots. The jurisdiction of Rhode Island and Providence plantations, and part of Connecticut people, possess their country. These Indians are now but few comparatively: all that people cannot make above one thousand able men.

§. 4. The Pawkunnawkutts were a great people heretofore. They lived to the east and northeast of the Narragansitts; and their chief sachem held dominion over divers other petty sagamores; as the sagamores upon the island of Nantuckett, and Nope, or Martha's Vineyard, of Nawsett, of Mannamoyk, of Sawkattukett, Nobsquasitt, Matakees, and several others, and some of the Nipmucks. Their country, for the most part, falls within the jurisdiction of New Plymouth colony. This people were a potent nation in former times; and could raise, as the most credible and ancient Indians affirm, about three thousand men. They held war with the Narragansitts; and often joined with the Massachusetts, as friends and confederates against the Narragansitts. This nation, a very great number of them, were swept away by an epidemical and unwonted sickness, An. 1612 and 1613, about seven or eight years before the English first arrived in those parts, to settle the colony of New Plymouth. Thereby divine providence made way for the quiet and peaceable settlement of the English in those nations. What this disease was, that so generally and mortally swept away, not only these, but other Indians, their neighbours, I cannot well learn. Doubtless it was some pestilential disease. I have discoursed with some old Indians, that were then youths; who say, that the bodies all over were exceeding yellow, describing it by a yellow garment they showed me, both before they died, and afterward.

§. 5. The Massachusetts, being the next great people north-ward, inhabited principally about that place in Massachusetts bay, where the body of the English now dwell. These were a numerous and great people. Their chief sachem held dominion over many other petty governours; as those of Weechagaskas, Neponsitt, Punkapaog, Nonantum, Nashaway, some of the Nipmuck people, as far as Pokomtacuke, as the old men of Massachusetts affirmed. This people could, in former times, arm for war, about three thousand men, as the old Indians declare. They were in hostility very often with the Narragansitts; but held amity, for the most part, with the Pawkunnawkutts, who lived on the south border, and with the Pawtucketts, who inhabited on their north and northeast limits, In An. 1612 and 1613, these people were also sorely smitten by the hand of God with the same disease, before mentioned in the last section; which destroyed the most of them, and made room for the English people of Massachusets colony, which people this country, and the next called Pawtuckett. There are not of this people left at this day above three hundred men, besides women and children.

§. 6. Pawtuckett is the fifth and last great sachemship of Indians. Their country lieth north and northeast from the Massachusets, whose dominion reacheth so far as the English jurisdiction, or colony of the Massachusetts, doth now extend, and had under them several other smaller sagamores; as the Pennakooks, Agawomes, Naamkeeks, Pascatawayes, Accomintas, and others. They were also a considerable people heretofore, about three thousand men; and held amity with the people of Massachusetts. But these also were almost totally destroyed by the great sickness before mentioned; so that at this day, they are not above two hundred and fifty men, besides women and children. This country is now inhabited by the English under the government of Massachusets.

CHAP. III.
Of the Language, Customs, Manners,
and Religion of the Indians.

§. 1. THE Indians of the parts of New England, especially upon
the sea coasts, use the same sort of speech and language, only
with some difference in the expressions, as they differ in several
countries in England, yet so as they can well understand one
another. Their speech is a distinct speech from any of those
used in Europe, Asia, or Africa, that I ever heard of. And some
of the inland Indians, particularly the Mawhawks, or Maquas,
use such a language, that our Indians upon the coast do not
understand: So the Indians to the southward, upon the sea
coast about Virginia, use a speech much different from those
in New England.

§. 2. The customs and manners of these Indians were, and
yet are, in many places, very brutish and barbarous in several
respects, like unto several savage people of America. They take
many wives; yet one of them is the principal or chief in their
esteem and affection. They also put away their wives; and the
wives also leave their husbands frequently, upon grounds of
displeasure or disaffection. They are very revengeful, and will
not be unmindful to take vengeance upon such as have injured
them or their kindred, when they have opportunity, though it
be a long time after the offence was committed. If any murther,
or other great wrong upon any of their relations or kindred,
be committed, all of that stock and consanguinity look upon
themselves concerned to revenge that wrong, or murder, unless
the business be taken up by the payment of wompompeague,
or other satisfaction, which their custom admits, to satisfy for
all wrongs, yea for life itself.

§. 3. They are much addicted to idleness, especially the men,
who are disposed to hunting, fishing, and the war, when there
is cause. That little tillage or planting used among them, was
principally done by the women. Also in their removals from
place to place, which they are inclined to, for their fishing and
hunting at the several seasons, the women carry the greatest
burthen: they also prepare all the diet. They are naturally much
addicted to lying and speaking untruth; and unto stealing,

especially from the English. The men and women are very loving and indulgent to their children.

§. 4. Their houses, or wigwams, are built with small poles fixed in the ground, bent and fastened together with barks of trees oval or arbour-wise on the top. The best sort of their houses are covered very neatly, tight, and warm, with barks of trees, slipped from their bodies, at such seasons when the sap is up; and made into great flakes with pressures of weighty timber, when they are green; and so becoming dry, they will retain a form suitable for the use they prepare them for. The meaner sort of wigwams are covered with mats, they make of a kind of bulrush, which are also indifferent tight and warm, but not so good as the former. These houses they make of several sizes, according to their activity and ability; some twenty, some forty feet long, and broad. Some I have seen of sixty or a hundred feet long, and thirty feet broad. In the smaller sort they make a fire in the centre of the house; and have a lower hole on the top of the house, to let out the smoke. They keep the door into the wigwams always shut, by a mat falling thereon, as people go in and out. This they do to prevent air coming in, which will cause much smoke in every windy weather. If the smoke beat down at the lower hole, they hang a little mat, in the way of a skreen, on the top of the house, which they can with a cord turn to the windward side, which prevents the smoke. In the greater houses they make two, three, or four fires, at a distance one from another, for the better accommodation of the people belonging to it. I have often lodged in their wigwams; and have found them as warm as the best English houses. In their wigwams, they make a kind of couch or mattresses, firm and strong, raised about a foot high from the earth; first covered with boards that they split out of trees; and upon the boards they spread mats generally, and sometimes bear skins and deer skins. These are large enough for three or four persons to lodge upon; and one may either draw nearer, or keep at a more distance from the heat of the fire, as they please; for their mattresses are six or eight feet broad.

§. 5. Their food is generally boiled maize, or Indian corn, mixed with kidney-beans, or sometimes without. Also they frequently boil in this pottage fish and flesh of all sorts, either new taken or dried, as shads, eels, alewives or a kind of herring, or any other sort of fish. But they dry mostly those sorts before mentioned. These they cut in pieces, bones and all, and boil them in the aforesaid pottage. I have wondered many times that they were not in danger of being choked with fish bones; but they are so dexterous to separate the bones from the fish in their eating thereof, that they are in no hazard. Also they boil in this furmenty all sorts of flesh, they take in hunting; as venison, beaver, bear's flesh, moose, otters, rackoons, or any kind that they take in hunting; cutting this flesh in small pieces, and boiling it as aforesaid. Also they mix with the said pottage several sorts of roots; as Jerusalem artichokes, and ground nuts, and other roots, and pompions, and squashes and also several sorts of nuts or masts, as oak-acorns, chesnuts, walnuts: these husked and dried, and powdered, they thicken their pottage therewith. Also sometimes they beat their maize into meal, and sift it through a basket, made for that purpose. With this meal they make bread, baking it in the ashes, covering the dough with leaves. Sometimes they make of their meal a small sort of cakes, and boil them. They make also a certain sort of meal of parched maize. This meal they call nokake. It is so sweet, toothsome, and hearty, that an Indian will travel many days with no other food but this meal, which he eateth as he needs, and after it drinketh water. And for this end, when they travel a journey, or go a hunting, they carry this nokake in a basket, or bag, for their use.

§. 6. Their household stuff is but little and mean. The pots they seeth their food in, which were heretofore, and yet are, in use among some of them, are made of clay or earth, almost in the form of an egg, the top taken off, but now they generally get kettles of brass, copper, or iron. These they find more lasting than those made of clay, which were subject to be broken; and the clay or earth they were made of, was very scarce and dear. Their dishes, and spoons, and ladles, are made of wood, very smooth and artificial, and of a sort of wood not subject to split. These they make of several sizes. Their pails to fetch their water in, are made of birch barks, artificially doubled up, that it hath four corners and a handle in the midst. Some of these will hold two or three gallons; and they will make one of them in an hour's time. From the tree where the bark grows, they make several sorts of baskets, great and small. Some will hold four bushels, or more; and so downward, to a pint. In their baskets they put their provisions. Some of their baskets are made of rushes; some, of bents; others, of maize husks; others, of a kind of silk grass; others, of a kind of wild hemp; and some, of barks of trees; many of them, very neat and artificial, with the portraitures of birds, beasts, fishes and flowers, upon them in colours. Also they make mats of several sorts, for covering their houses and doors, and to sleep and sit upon. The baskets and mats are always made by their women; their dishes, pots, and spoons, are the manufacture of the men. They have no other considerable household stuff except these; only of latter years, since the English came among them, some of them get tin cups and little pails, chests of wood, glass bottles, and such things they affect.

§. 7. Their drink was formerly no other but water, and yet it doth continue, for their general and common drink. But of late years some of them planted orchards of apples, and make cider: which some of the worst of them are too prone to abuse unto drunkenness; though others of them that are christians, use it or any other strong drink with great sobriety. Many of the Indians are great lovers of strong drink, as aqua vitæ, rum, brandy, or the like, and are very greedy to buy it of the English: and though all strong drink is strickly prohibited to be sold to any Indian in the Massachusetts colony, upon the penalty of forty shillings a pint; yet some ill-disposed people, for filthy lucre's sake, do sell unto the Indians secretly, though the Indians will rarely discover these evil merchants—they do rather suffer whipping or fine than tell. Hereby they are made drunk very often; and being drunk, are many times outrageous and mad, fighting with and killing one another, yea sometimes their own relations. This beastly sin of drunkenness could not be charged upon the Indians before the English and other christian nations, as Dutch, French, and Spaniards, came to dwell in America; which nations especially the English in New England, have cause to be greatly humbled before God, that they have been, and are, instrumental to cause these Indians to commit this great evil and beastly sin of drunkenness.

§. 8. The Indians' clothing in former times was of the same matter as Adam's was, viz. skins of beasts, as deer, moose, beaver, otters, rackoons, foxes, and other wild creatures. Also some had mantles of the feathers of birds, quilled artificially; and sundry of them continue to this day their old kind of clothing. But, for the most part, they sell the skins and furs to the English, Dutch and French, and buy of them for clothing a kind of cloth, called duffils, or trucking cloth, about a yard and a half wide, and for matter, made of coarse wool, in that form as our ordinary bed blankets are made, only it is put into colours, as blue, red, purple, and some use them white. Of this sort of cloth two yards make a mantle, or coat, for men and women, and less for children. This is all the garment they generally use, with this addition of some little piece of the same, or of ordinary cotton, to cover their secret parts. It is rare to see any among them of the most barbarious, that are remiss or negligent in hiding those parts. But the christian and civilized Indians do endeavour, many of them, to follow the English mode in their habit. Their ornaments are, especially the women's, bracelets, necklaces, and head bands, of several sorts of beads, especially of black and white wompom, which is of most esteem among them, and is accounted their chief treasure.

§. 9. The wompompeague is made artificially of a part of the wilk's shell. The black is of double value to the white. It is made principally by the Narragansitt black islanders* and Long Island Indians. Upon the sandy flats and shores of those coasts the wilk shells are found. With this wompompeague they pay tribute, redeem captives, satisfy for murders and other wrongs, purchase peace with their potent neighbours, as occasion requires; in a word, it answers all occasions with them, as gold and silver doth with us. They delight much in having and using knives, combs, scissors, hatchets, hoes, guns, needles, awls, looking glasses, and such like necessaries, which they purchase of the English and Dutch with their peague, and then sell them their peltry for their wompeague.

Their weapons heretofore were bows and arrows, clubs, and tomahawks, made of wood like a pole axe, with a sharpened stone fastened therein; and for defence, they had targets made of barks of trees. But of latter years, since the English, Dutch,

*So written in the M. S. probably by mistake for Block Island.

and French have trafficked with them, they generally disuse their former weapons, and instead thereof have guns, pistols, swords, rapier blades, fastened unto a staff of the length of a half pike, hatchets, and axes.

§. 10. For their water passage, travels, and fishing, they make boats, or canoes, either of great trees, pine or chesnut, made hollow and artificially; which they do by burning them; and after with tools, scraping, smoothing, shaping them. Of these they make greater or lesser. Some I have seen will carry twenty persons, being forty or fifty feet in length, and as broad as the tree will bear. They make another sort of canoes of birchen bark, which they close together, sewing them with a kind of bark; and then smearing the places with turpentine, of the pine tree. These kinds of canoes are very neatly and artificially made, being strengthened in the inside with some few thin timbers and ribs; yet are they so light, that one man will, and doth, ordinarily carry one of them upon his back several miles, that will transport five or six people. When in their huntings or wars, they are to pass falls of rivers, or necks of land, into other rivers or streams, they take up their canoes upon their backs, and others carry their arms or provisions; and so embark again, when their difficulty is past, and proceed in their journey or voyage. But these kind of canoes are much more ticklish and apt to overset, than the former. But the Indians are so used to them, and sit so steady, that they seldom overturn with them; and if they should, they can all swim well and save their lives, though sometimes they may lose their peltry, arms, and provisions.

§. 11. They used to oil their skins and hair with bear's grease heretofore, but now with swine's fat, and then paint their faces with vermilion, or other red, and powder their heads. Also they use black and white paints; and make one part of their face of one colour; and another, of another, very deformedly. The women especially do thus; and some men also, especially when they are marching to their wars; and hereby, as they think, are more terrible to their enemies. The women, in the times of their mourning, after the death of their husbands or kindred, do paint their faces all over black, like a negro; and so con-tinue in this posture many days. But the civilized and christian

Indians do leave these customs. The men, in their wars, do use turkey or eagle's feathers, stuck in their hair, as is traced up in a roll. Others wear deer shuts, made in the fashion of a cock's comb died red, crossing their heads like a half moon.

They are addicted to gaming; and will, in that vein, play away all they have. And also they delight much in their dancings and revellings; at which time he that danceth (for they dance singly, the men, and not the women, the rest singing, which is their chief musick) will give away in his frolick, all that ever he hath, gradually, some to one, and some to another, according to his fancy and affection. And then, when he hath stripped himself of all he hath, and is weary, another succeeds and doth the like: so successively, one after another, night after night, resting and sleeping in the days; and so continue sometimes a week together. And at such dancings, and feastings, and revellings, which are used mostly after the ingathering of their havests, all their neighbours, kindred, and friends, meet together; and much impiety is committed at such times. They use great vehemency in the motion of their bodies, in their dances; and sometimes the men dance in greater numbers in their war dances.

They are much given to hospitality in their way. If any strangers come to their houses, they will give him the best lodging and diet they have; and the strangers must be first served, by themselves. The wife makes ready; and by her husband's direction, delivers to the strangers, according to their quality, or his affection.

§. 12. Their government is generally monarchical, their chief sachem or sagamore's will being their law; but yet the sachem hath some chief men, that he consults with as his special counsellors. Among some of the Indians their government is mixed, partly monarchical, and partly aristocratical; their sagamore doing not any weighty matter without the consent of his great men, or petty saggamores. Their sachems have not their men in such subjection, but that very frequently their men will leave them upon distaste or harsh dealing, and go and live under other sachems that can protect them: so that their princes endeavour to carry it obligingly and lovingly unto their people, lest they should desert them, and thereby their strength, power, and tribute would be diminished.

§. 13. Their religion is as other gentiles are. Some for their God, adore the sun; others the moon; some the earth; others, the fire; and like vanities. Yet generally they acknowledge one great supreme doer of good; and him they call Woonand, or Mannitt: another that is the great doer of evil or mischief; and him they call Mattand, which is the devil; and him they dread and fear, more than they love and honour the former chief good which is God.

There are among them certain men and women, whom they call powows. These are partly wizards and witches, holding familiarity with Satan, that evil one; and partly are physicians, and make use, at least in show, of herbs and roots, for curing the sick and diseased. These are sent for by the sick and wounded; and by their diabolical spells, mutterings, exorcisms, they seem to do wonders. They use extraordinary strange motions of their bodies, insomuch that they will sweat until they foam; and thus continue for some hours together, stroking and hovering over the sick. Sometimes broken bones have been set, wounds healed, sick recovered; but together therewith they sometimes use external applications of herbs, roots, splintering and binding up the wounds. These powows are reputed, and I conceive justly, to hold familiarity with the devil; and therefore are by the English laws, prohibited the exercise of their diabolical practices within the English jurisdiction, under the penalty of five pounds,—and the procurer, five pounds,—and every person present, twenty pence. Satan doth strongly endeavour to keep up this practice among the Indians: and these powows are factors for the devil, and great hinderers of the Indians embracing the gospel. It is no small discouragement unto the Indians in yielding obedience unto the gospel, for then, say they, if we once pray to God, we must abandon our powows; and then, when we are sick and wounded, who shall heal our maladies?

Upon this occasion I shall relate a true history, that happened about five and twenty years since, at their first beginning to pray to God.

§. 14. At the island of Nope, or Martha's Vineyard, about the year 1649, one of the first Indians that embraced the christian religion on that island, named Hiacoomes who is living at this day, and a principal teacher among them, and is a grave and serious christian, and hath had a great blessing since upon his posterity; for his sons and his daughters are pious, and one, if not more of his sons, teachers to them; and his eldest son, called Joel, of whom we shall speak afterwards, was bred a scholar at Cambridge in New England, and was not only a good and diligent student, but a pious man,—though he was taken away by death, before he came to maturity:—This Hiacoomes, as I said before, not long after he had embraced the gospel; his wife also being a good woman and a believer; she, being great with child, fell into travail of child birth and had great pains and sorrowful throws for sundry days, and could not be delivered;—which is a thing unusual with the Indian women, who are ordinarily quickly and easily delivered; and many times are so strong, that within a few hours after the child's birth, they will go about their ordinary occasions:—But this woman, the wife of Hiacoomes, was, as I said, in sore labour and travail in child birth several days, and could not be delivered; insomuch than nothing less than death was expected by herself and husband. In this strait, several of their carnal and unconverted kindred and relations applied themselves unto Hiacoomes and his wife, pressing them to send for a powow, and use that help for relief. But both husband and wife utterly refused their temptation; the man being willing to submit to God's disposal, and lose his wife, though he loved her dearly, rather than take assistance from the devil and his instruments, whom he had renounced; and the woman, who was the sufferer, yet, through the grace of God, was endowed with such christian fortitude, that she also utterly refused this method for her deliverance, and would rather lose her life than seek help that way. In this exigence, they earnestly cried to God in prayer, to show mercy to them for Jesus Christ's sake; imploring also the prayers of Mr. Thomas Mayhew junior, their teacher, and other English christians, living nigh them. Mr. Mayhew, being affected with the case, got together some godly christians to meet together; and those kept a day of fasting and prayer, to implore the help of God for these poor, distressed, christian Indians. And the Lord was graciously pleased to hear and answer their prayers, and shortly after gave the woman safe deliverance of a daughter; which the father named by a word in the Indian language, which signified in English, Return. When Mr. Mayhew, the minister, understood this, he demanded of Hiacoomes the reason, why he gave his daughter that name; whose answer was to this effect: Sir, said he, a little while since, you know, I, and my wife and children, were travelling on a pace in the broad way to hell and all misery, and going from God; but now, since you preached to us, I, and my wife and children, are, through God's grace, *returning* back the contrary way, with our faces set towards God, heaven, and happiness. Secondly, you know, before my wife was delivered of this child, how great peril of life she was in, and God seemed to be very angry with us; but he was intreated and heard our prayers, and is *returned* to us with mercies, in my wife's safe deliverance of this daughter. And for these two reasons, I call this child Return. This story is most certainly true; and was told me distinctly by Mr. Thomas Mayhew junior, their minister, Hiacoomes being present, in travelling on foot between Watertown lecture and Cambridge, the Indian that was the principal person concerned being with him; and this he related not long after the thing was done: and although it be a digression, yet the example being so instructive, I thought it might be of good use to insert it here; there being apparently much faith and love to God, great christian fortitude, prudence, and thankfulness, resisting of Satan, overcoming temptation, encouragement to prayer, and hope and reliance on God in cases of difficulty and distress; and all this wonderfully exemplified in poor Indians, newly come to the faith, out of the depth of ignorance and barbarism: all which doth greatly tend to magnify and illustrate the free and powerful virtue of God's grace in Christ Jesus.

CHAP. V.
Of the Instruments and Means that God hath used, for the Civilizing and Conversion of some of the New England Indians.

§. 1. HAVING, in the former chapters, declared some short hints concerning the Indians in general, I shall now, by God's assistance, speak more particularly of the civilized and religious Indians, which I shall denominate by the name of Praying

Indians, a title generally understood; and in this chapter, begin first to speak of the instruments, that the blessed God hath raised up and used in this matter. In the first place, we are to ascribe all glory, honour, and praise, unto God in Jesus Christ, who was, and is, the first mover and efficient in this work, wherein he hath remembered, and begun to fulfil, unto this forlorn and outcast people, those gracious promises made unto his son, our Lord Jesus Christ: Ps. ii. 8. *Ask of me and I will give thee, the heathen for thine inheritance, and the uttermost parts of the earth for thy possession.* And in Ps. lxxii. 8. *He shall have dominion from sea to sea, and from the river unto the ends of the earth.*

§. 2. For second causes, that which, in the first place, is deservedly to be mentioned, is the Lord's gracious inclining, disposing, and fitting, that pious servant of God, Mr. John Eliot, the only teacher of the church of Christ at Roxbury in New England; for his colleague, Mr. Thomas Weld, was a little before removed for England. Yet notwithstanding the weight of the work, incumbent upon him in that church, was sufficient to take up the time and strength of one man; but that God who is the God of the spirits of all flesh did endow him with an extraordinary spirit suitable for the work. This reverend, learned, and worthy man, in the year of our Lord 1646, as I take it, and about the forty second year of his age, did intensely set upon the work of preaching Christ to the Indians in New England; and was so divinely assisted by the spirit of God, that it was not long after he set upon the work of learning the Indian language: but he attained such a measure thereof, that he adventured to make beginning to preach the glad tidings of salvation unto their competent understanding. The first place he began to preach at, was Nonantum,* near Watertown mill, upon the south side of Charles river, about four or five miles from his own house; where lived at that time Waban, one of their principal men, and some Indians with him.

§. 3. His manner of teaching them was, first to begin with prayer, and then to preach briefly upon a suitable portion of scripture; afterwards to admit the Indians to propound questions;—and divers of them had a faculty to frame hard and

The east part of Newton.

difficult questions, touching something then spoken, or some other matter in religion, tending to their illumination;—which questions Mr. Eliot, in a grave and christian manner, did endeavour to resolve and answer to their satisfaction.

Within a short time after this first attempt, finding the Indians, at least some of them, inclined to meet together to hear him, and that God was pleased graciously to assist him, and increase his knowledge of their language; he set up another lecture at a place, called Neponsitt,* within the bounds of Dorchester, about four miles from his house southward; where another company of Indians lived, belonging unto the sachem Kuchamakin. Among these Indians there were sundry grave and intelligent persons. But at Nonantum especially, one of most remark was named Waban, a grave and sober person, of whom we shall have occasion to speak more hereafter. God was pleased to open the understanding, and affect the heart, of this man, that he became, by his example and activity, a leader and encourager to many others. And thus Mr. Eliot continued to preach these two lectures at Nonantum and Neponsitt, for several years with good success.

Besides his preaching to them, he framed two catechisms in the Indian tongue, containing the principles of the christian religion; a lesser for children, and a larger for older persons. These also he communicated unto the Indians gradually, a few questions at a time, according unto their capacity to receive them. The questions he propounded one lecture day, were answered the next lecture day. His manner was, after he had begun the meeting with prayer, then first to catechise the children; and they would readily answer well for the generality. Then would he encourage them with some small gift, as an apple, or a small biscuit, which he caused to be bought for that purpose. And by this prudence and winning practice, the children were induced with delight, to get into their memories the principles of the christian religion. After he had done the children, then would he take the answers of the catechetical questions of the elder persons; and they did generally answer judiciously. When the catechising was past, he would preach to them upon some portion of scripture, for about three quarters

*Neponsitt river separates Dorchester from Milton.

of an hour; and then give liberty to the Indians to propound questions, as I intimated before; and in the close, finish all with prayer.

This worthy man hath been all along to this day, exceeding diligent and careful to instruct the Indians in the sound principles of the christian religion: so that there is none of the praying Indians, young or old, but can readily answer any question of the catechism; which, I believe, is more than can be said of many thousands of English people; the more cause of mourning! Besides, the praying Indians have been so instructed and learned, that they generally pray in their families morning and evening, and that with much affection and reverence. This is a practice, which, I fear, is neglected in many English, as well in New England, as in Old England.

§. 4. In this work did this good man industriously travail sundry years, without any external encouragement, from men I mean, as to the receiving any salary or reward. Indeed verbal encouragements, and the presence of divers persons at his lectures, he wanted not. The truth is, Mr. Eliot engaged in this great work of preaching unto the Indians upon a very pure and sincere account: for I being his neighbour and intimate friend, at the time when he first attempted this enterprise, he was pleased to communicate unto me his design, and the motives that induced him thereunto; which, as I remember, were principally these three.

First, the glory of God, in the conversion of some of these poor, desolate souls.

Secondly, his compassion and ardent affection to them, as of mankind in their great blindness and ignorance.

Thirdly, and not the least, to endeavour, so far as in him lay, the accomplishment and fulfilling the covenant and promise, that New England people had made unto their king, when he granted them their patent or charter, viz. that one principal end of their going to plant these countries, was, to communicate the gospel unto the native Indians; which in truth is a clause in the charter, as will in the following book appear. ☞

☞ The III. Book of the History of New England. See the Postscript.

By that which hath been said in this particular, it doth evidently appear, that they were heroick, noble, and christian principles, that induced this precious servant of Christ to enter upon this work, and not any carnal or by-ends: for in those times nothing of outward encouragement did appear. Indeed it must be acknowledged to the praise of God, that he hath made good that gracious promise, *First seek the kingdom of heaven and the righteousness thereof, and all other things shall be added unto thee.* The truth is, that God is so good a master, that never any man did lose by his service; and although not always paying them with things of this life,—for the promise of those things is conditional, so far as shall be for our good and his glory— but in the inward consolations and communications of spiritual good things (the least whereof is worth the whole world) whilst we are in this life, and abundant recompense in heaven is most sure and certain. But sometimes it pleaseth God to bestow his beneficence in both kinds, as he did unto this good man. For after some years' travail in this work, the Lord was pleased to stir up divers worthy and pious persons in Old England (and if I knew their names, I would here record them, for their eternal honour, and for example to posterity,—though, I believe, many of them had such a measure of the spirit of Christ, not willing to let their left hand know what their right did, and would be offended, if I should mention them) to be benefactors unto this good work: and from that beneficence this blessed instrument had some annual encouragement; which, I have heard him say, he never expected, but yet with abundant acknowledgment and thankfulness to God and men for it.

Hereby he was enabled to educate his five sons then living, viz. John, Joseph, Samuel, Aaron, and Benjamin, in learning, both at the schools, and after in the college at Cambridge. But Aaron died soon after his entering the college; and all lived to take their degrees of bachelors and masters of art. And also it was his great desire and earnest prayer to God, that he would incline and sit them all to engage with him in teaching the Indians; to which he was willing, as much as in them lay, to dedicate them to God for that work. And although God saw not meet to grant him his full desire in that respect, yet his prayers and endeavours were very graciously answered: for all his sons have given demonstrations, not only of their sufficiency in learning, but of their true piety. All of them became preachers of the gospel.

His eldest son, John, was not only pastor of an English church at Cambridge village,* and a very excellent preacher in the English tongue; but also, for sundry years, he preached the gospel unto the Indians, once a fortnight constantly at Pakemitt,† and sometimes at Natick and other places: and the most judicious christian Indians esteemed very highly of him, as a most excellent preacher in their language, as I have often heard them say. But God was pleased to put an end to his work and life, October 11, 1668, and to carry him with full sail to heaven, there to receive his crown: of whom I shall say no more in this place; for he well deserves a station among the worthies in New England, which is designed in the sequel of this our history. ☞

His second son, Joseph, is now pastor of a church of Christ at Guildford in New-England: a preacher inferiour to few in this country, for his age and time.

His third son, Samuel, before his death, gave abundant demonstration of his piety, ability, gravity, and excellent temper. He was a fellow of Harvard college in Cambridge in New England. He left this world and ascended to glory, after he had taken his second degree in the college. He hath undoubtedly arrived to his highest degree in the empyreal heaven. He was a person of whom the world was not worthy.

His fourth and youngest son, Benjamin, is a person approved for piety and ability. He hath divers times been invited to places that wanted a minister; but yet is not settled, but lives at home with his parents.§

I have been the larger in mentioning God's blessing upon this good man and his posterity, to set forth the gracious goodness and loving kindness of God extended to him thereby, making good what he hath said: *Them that honour me, I will*

---

*Now Newton.

†In Stoughton.

☞ The VI. Book of the History of New England. See the Postscript.

§*Benjamin was afterwards settled at Roxbury, and was, during many years, his father's assistant. The venerable apostle Eliot outlived all his sons, and died at the advanced age of eighty-six, A.D. 1690. For the particulars of his life and character, see Mather's Magnalia, Book III. page 170.*

honour, 1 Sam. ii. 30. *Behold, that thus shall the man be blessed, that feareth the Lord, and walketh in his ways. The Lord shall bless thee out of Zion; and thou shalt see the good of Jerusalem all the days of thy life. Yea, thou shalt see thy childrens' children, and peace upon Israel.* Ps. cxxviii. 1, 4, 5, 6. And again, *Trust in the Lord, and do good, so shalt thou dwell in the land, and verily thou shalt be fed. Delight thyself also in the Lord; and he shall give thee the desires of thine heart.* Ps. xxxvii. 3, 4.

§. 5. This worthy and active instrument, Mr. Eliot, who was, and is, and, I believe, will be, to his dying day unwearied in his endeavours to promote the salvation of the poor Indians, contented not himself with preaching to those people at the places before mentioned; but went further into the country divers ways, far and near, preaching the gospel to the wild and barbarous Indians; and sometimes reaped fruit of his labour.

Moreover he stirred up divers other ministers and scholars, in our own and other colonies, by his words and letters, to fit themselves to labour in this Indian harvest, and that not without some good success. For in Plymouth colony, one Mr. Bourne, having some skill in the Indian language, entered upon this service, and hath had a great blessing upon his endeavours, as will be declared in the sequel. Also Mr. John Cotton, now pastor at Plymouth, hath gained the Indian language, and did sometime at Martha's Vineyard, and now at Plymouth and places adjacent, labour herein Also at Martha's Vineyard and Nantucket, Messrs. Thomas Mayhew, father and son, attempted this enterprise, which God hath greatly blessed, as will be declared hereafter. Again Mr. Pierson heretofore, and Mr. Fitch at present, did and doth preach to some Indians in Connecticut colony; of whom afterwards.

But besides his industry to provoke others, and his frequent travels and preaching among the Indians, he set up that great work of translating the bible into the Indian language; which the Honourable Corporation for propagating the gospel in New England, residing in London, did greatly encourage, and out of the revenues belonging to that flock, which then was more considerable than now it is, did pay for the printing thereof.* Besides, he framed and translated into the Indian

---

* *There are several copies of Eliot's Indian Bible in the library of Harvard College.*

language divers other books; as Indian catechisms, a grammar, primer, singing psalms, the Practice of Piety, Baxter's Call to the Unconverted, and other things; all which are printed at the charge of the Corporation stock.

§. 6. Moreover he took great care, that schools should be planted among the praying Indians; and he taught some himself to read, that they might be capable to teach others; and by his procurement, some of the choice Indian youth were put to school with English shoolmasters, to learn both the English, Latin, and Greek tongues.

There was much cost out of the Corporation stock expended in this work, for fitting and preparing the Indian youth to be learned and able preachers unto their countrymen. Their diet, apparel, books, and schooling, was chargeable. In truth the design was prudent, noble, and good; but it proved ineffectual to the ends proposed. For several of the said youth died, after they had been sundry years at learning, and made good proficiency therein. Others were disheartened and left learning, after they were almost ready for the college. And some returned to live among their countrymen; where some of them are improved for schoolmasters and teachers, unto which they are advantaged by their education. Some others of them have entered upon other callings: as one is a mariner; another, a carpenter; another went for England with a gentleman, that lived sometimes at Cambridge in New England, named Mr. Drake, which Indian, as I heard, died there not many months after his arrival.

I remember but only two of them all, that lived in the college at Cambridge; the one named Joel,* the other, Caleb; both, natives of Martha's Vineyard. These two were hopeful young men, especially Joel, being so ripe in learning, that he should, within a few months, have taken his first degree of bachelor of art in the college. He took a voyage to Martha's Vineyard to visit his father and kindred, a little before the commencement; but upon his return back in a vessel, with other passengers and mariners, suffered shipwreck upon the island of Nantucket; where the bark was found put on shore; and in all probability the people in it came on shore alive, but afterwards were

*Son of Hiacoomes, mentioned chap. iii. §. 14.

murthered by some wicked Indians of that place; who, for lucre of the spoil in the vessel, which was laden with goods, thus cruelly destroyed the people in it; for which fault some of those Indians was convicted and executed afterwards. Thus perished our hopeful young prophet Joel. He was a good scholar and a pious man, as I judge. I knew him well for he lived and was taught in the same town where I dwell. I observed him for several years, after he was grown to years of discretion, to be not only a diligent student, but an attentive hearer of God's word; diligently writing the sermons, and frequenting lectures; grave and sober in his conversation.

The other called Caleb, not long after he took his degree of bachelor of art* at Cambridge in New England, died of a consumption at Charlestown, where he was placed by Mr. Thomas Danforth, who had inspection over him, under the care of a physician in order to his health; where he wanted not for the best means the country could afford, both of food and physick; but God denied the blessing, and put a period to his days.

Of this disease of the consumption sundry of those Indian youths died, that were bred up to school among the English. The truth is, this disease is frequent among the Indians; and sundry die of it, that live not with the English. A hectick fever, issuing in a consumption, is a common and mortal disease among them. I know some have apprehended other causes of the mortality of these Indian scholars. Some have attributed it unto the great change upon their bodies, in respect of their diet, lodging, apparel, studies; so much different from what they were inured to among their own countrymen.

These awful providences of God, in frustrating the hopeful expectations concerning the learned Indian youth, who were designed to be for teachers unto their countrymen, concurring with some other severe dispensations of God obstructive to this work,—some whereof may be hereafter mentioned,—caused great thoughts of heart unto the well willers and promoters thereof. Some conceived, God was not pleased yet to make use of any of the Indians to preach the gospel; and that the time of the great harvest of their ingathering is not yet come, but will follow after the calling of the Jews. Others thought that this

---

*Caleb Cheeschaumuch took his degree of bachelor of arts, A.D. 1665.

honour of their instruction and conversion shall be continued with Englishmen. Others were of opinion, that Satan, the great enemy and opposer of men's salvation, who had for many years held these poor barbarians under his dominion, did use all his stratagems and endeavours to impede the spreading of the christian faith, that he might the better keep possession of his kingdom among them. But others, whose faith I hope in God was active and vigorous, did conclude that there was nothing more in these providences and remoras, than did usually attend and accompany all good designs, tending to the glory of God and salvation of souls; whereof plentiful examples are recorded in holy scriptures, especially in the primitive times; which in several chapters of the Acts of the Apostles may be demonstrated. Therefore it is our duty to persist and go on in a good work, locking by the eye of faith unto our Lord Jesus Christ, the great captain and conductor of all affairs, and especially those of this kind. He is the king, priest, and prophet of his church; who hath commanded and encouraged his servants, that he calleth to engage under him, in the wars of the Lord, against sin and Satan, &c. *to be strong and very courageous,* &c. *for I will be with thee; I will not fail thee, nor forsake thee.* Josh. i. 5, 6, 7. Heb. xiii. 5. Yea Christ hath promised all his servants and embassadors, that he employs in this work, *that he will be with them always, and unto the end of the world.* Mat. xxviii. 19, 20.

§. 7. In the former part of this chapter, I briefly touched the godly care, zeal, and industry of Mr. Eliot, in setting upon the translating of the scriptures into the Indian tongue. This work being a considerable time in hand, it pleased God in his divine providence so to order it, that the new testament, being first printed, was finished about the time of his Majesty's return to his crown in peace; for whom God had reserved the honour of the dedication thereof; as may appear by the Epistle Dedicatory, to him presented by the Commissioners of the united colonies in New England; which here follows.

"To the High and Mighty Prince, Charles the second, by the grace of God, King of England, Scotland, France, and Ireland, Defender of the faith, &c.

The Commissioners of the United Colonies in New England with increase of all happiness.

Most dread Sovereign,

If our weak apprehensions have not misled us, this work will be no unacceptable present to your Majesty, as having a greater interest therein, than we believe is generally understood, which upon this occasion we conceive it our duty to declare.

The people of these four colonies* (confederate for mutual defence, in the times of the late distractions of our dear native country) your Majesty's natural born subjects, by the favour and grace of your royal father and grandfather of famous memory, put themselves upon this great and hazardous undertaking, of planting themselves at their own charge in these remote ends of the earth; that without offence or provocation to our dear brethren and countrymen, we might enjoy that liberty to worship God, which our own conscience informed us was not only our right but duty; as also that we, if it so pleased God, might be instrumental to spread the light of the gospel, the knowledge of the son of God, our saviour, to the poor, barbarous heathen; which by his late Majesty, in some of our patents, is declared to be the principal aim.

These honest and pious intentions have, through the grace of God and our kings, been seconded with proportionable success. For, omitting the immunities indulged by your Highness's royal predecessors, we have been greatly encouraged by your Majesty's gracious expressions of favour and approbation, signified unto the address made by the principal of our colonies; to which the rest do most cordially subscribe; though wanting the like seasonable opportunity, they have been till now deprived of the means to congratulate your Majesty's happy restitution, after your long sufferings; which we implore may yet be graciously accepted, that we may be equal partakers of your royal favour and moderation; which hath been so illustrious, that to admiration, the animosities of different persuasions of men have been so soon composed, and so much cause of hope, that, unless the sins of the nation prevent, a blessed calm will succeed the late horrid confusions of church and state. And shall not we, dread sovereign, your subjects of these colonies, of the same faith and belief in all points of doctrine with our countrymen and other reformed churches, though perhaps not alike persuaded in some matters of order, which in outward respects hath been unhappy for us;—promise and assure ourselves of all just favour and indulgence from a prince so graciously and happily endowed?

*Massachusetts, Plymouth, Connecticut, and New Haven.

The other part of our errand hither hath been attended with endeavours and blessing; many of the wild Indians being taught, and understanding, the doctrine of the christian religion, and with much affection attending such preachers as are sent to teach them. Many of their children are instructed to write and read; and some of them have proceeded further to attain the knowledge of the Latin and the Greek tongues, and are brought up with our English youth in university learning. There are divers of them that can and do read some parts of the scripture, and some catechisms which formerly have been translated into their own language: which hath occasioned the undertaking of a great work, viz. the printing the whole bible: which, being translated by a painful labourer among them, who was desirous to see the work accomplished in his days, hath already proceeded to the finishing of the new testament; which we here humbly present to your Majesty, as the first fruit and accomplishment of the pious design of your royal ancestors. The old testament is now under the press, wanting and craving your royal favour and assistance for the perfecting thereof.

We may not conceal, though this work hath been begun and prosecuted by such instruments as God hath raised up here; yet the chief charge and cost, which hath supported and carried it thus far, hath been from the charity and piety of divers of our well affected countrymen in England; who, being sensible of our inability in that respect, and studious to promote so good a work, contributed large sums of money, which were to be improved according to the direction and order of the then prevailing powers; which hath been faithfully and religiously attended, both there and here, according to the pious intentions of the benefactors. And we most humbly beseech your Majesty, that a matter of so much devotion and piety, tending so much to the honour of God, may suffer no disappointment through any legal defect, without the fault of the donors, or poor Indians, who only receive the benefit; but that your Majesty be graciously pleased to establish and confirm the same; being contrived and done, as we conceive, in that first year of your Majesty's reign, as this book was begun and now finished the first year of your establishment: which doth not only presage the happy success of your Highness's government, but will be a perpetual monument, that by your Majesty's favour, the gospel of our Lord Jesus Christ was made known to the Indians; an honour whereof, we are assured, your Majesty will not a little esteem.

Sir, the shine of your royal favour upon these undertakings will make these tender plants to flourish, notwithstanding any malevolent aspect from those that bear evil will to this Sion; and render your Majesty more illustrious and glorious to after generations.

The God of heaven long preserve and bless your Majesty with many happy days, to his glory, the good and comfort of his church and people. Amen."

This epistle was framed, and the Indian translation of the new testament finished, printed, and set forth, in September 5th, 1661; from whence we may infer, that as it was a credit to this work to have so great a prince to offer it unto; so it was no less an honour to his Majesty, that one of his subjects should put the holy scriptures into the Indian language; and that himself should be the first christian prince, unto whom a work of this nature should be presented and dedicated.

One thing falls in here fitly to be spoken of, as a means intended for the good of the Indians; which was the erecting a house of brick at Cambridge in New-England, which passeth under the name of the Indian college. It is a structure strong and substantial, though not very capacious. It cost between three or four hundred pounds. It is large enough to receive and accommodate about twenty scholars with convenient lodgings and studies; but not hitherto hath been much improved for the ends intended, by reason of the death and failing of Indian scholars. It hath hitherto been principally improved for to accomodate English scholars, and for placing and using a printing press belonging to the college. This house was built and finished at the charge, and by the appointment, of the Honourable Corporation for propagating the gospel in New England.

CHAP. VII.

Of the Number, Names, and Situation of the Indian praying towns, within the Colony of Massachusetts, with the Churches gathered in some of them, the Quantities of Land belonging to them, a Conjecture at the Number of Families and People that inhabit in them, with other matters thereunto appertaining.

*§. I. THE *first town of praying Indians in Massachusetts is Natick. The name signifieth a place of hills.*† *It lieth upon Charles river, eighteen miles south west from Boston, and ten miles north west from Dedham. It hath twenty nine families, which, computing five persons to a family, amount to one hundred and forty five persons.*‡ *The town contains about six thousand acres. The soil is good and well watered, and produceth plenty of grain and fruit. The land was granted to the Indians, at the motion of Mr. Eliot, by the general court of Massachusetts;*§ *and in the year* 1651, *a number of them combined together, and formed a town, which is the place of the greatest name among the Indians,*¶ *and where their principal courts are held.***

As soon as the Indians had fixed their settlement, they applied to Mr. Eliot for a form of civil government; and he advised them to adopt that which Jethro proposed to Moses for the Israelites in the wilderness, Exod. xviii. 21. *Accordingly, on the sixth of August, about one hundred of them met together, and chose one ruler of a hundred, two rulers of fifties, and ten rulers of tens. After this they entered into the following covenant.*

"We are the sons of Adam. We and our fathers have a long time been lost in our sins; but now the mercy of the Lord beginneth to

---

**A leaf of the M. S. equal to about three fifths of a page of this printed edition, is here torn out, and we fear, irrecoverably lost. We have filled up the chasm with some particulars collected from other authors, and from tradition.*

†*Our authority for this was Deacon Ephraim, a Natick Indian lately deceased. The Indian name for hills, in the Massachusetts Psalter, is* wadchuash. *In Roger Williams's Key into the language of America, we find the word* nittauke, *which signifies,* my land.

‡*See the note* * *at the end of the* 17*th* §.

§*Hubbard's M. S. Hist. chap.* lviii.

¶*Mather's Magnalia. Book* iii. *page* 197.

***Huth. Hist. vol.* I. *page* 167, *note.*

find us out again. Therefore, the grace of Christ helping us, we do give ourselves and our children to God, to be his people. He shall rule us in all our affairs, not only in our religion and affairs of the church, but also in all our works and affairs in this world. God shall rule over us. The Lord is our judge; the Lord is our lawgiver; the Lord is our king: he will save us. The wisdom which God hath taught us in his book, that shall guide us, and direct us in the way. O Jehovah, teach us wisdom to find out thy wisdom in the scriptures. Let the grace of Christ help us, because Christ is the wisdom of God. Send thy spirit into our hearts and let it teach us. Lord, take us to be thy people, and let us take thee to be our God."*

§. 2. *This town consisteth of three long streets; two on the north side of the river; and one, on the south; with house lots to every family. There is a handsome large fort, of a round figure, palisaded with trees; and a foot bridge over the river, in form of an arch, the foundation of which is secured with stone. There is also one large house built after the English manner. The lower room is a large hall, which serves for a meeting house, on the Lord's day, and a school house, on the week days. The upper room is a kind of wardrobe, where the Indians hang up their skins, and other things of value. In a corner of this room Mr. Eliot has an apartment partitioned off, with a bed and bedstead in it.*† Their other houses in this town are generally after their old mode before described; though some they have built in this and other of the praying villages, after the English form. But these being more chargeable to build and not so warm, and cannot be removed so easily as their wigwams, wherein there is not a nail used, to avoid annoyance by fleas, and themselves being generally artists in building and finishing their own wigwams: for these and like reasons, they do incline to keep their old fashioned houses.

§. 3. In this town was the first church of Indians imbodied, in the year of our Lord 1660. Unto this church some pious Indians of other places, both men and women, are since joined. The number of men and women, that are in full communion in this church, are about‡ and baptized,

---

*Neal's Hist. of N. Eng. chap. vi. page 235.
†Ibid. page 234.
‡In the year 1670 there were between forty and fifty communicants belonging to the church of Natick. Hutch. vol. 1. page 167.

Here we are to consider, that all those we call praying Indians are not all visible church members, or baptized persons: which ordinance of baptism is not to be administered unto any that are out of the visible church, until they profess their faith in Christ and obedience to him, but the infants of such as are members of the visible church are to be baptized: this being sound doctrine, as we believe, asserted in that excellent letter catechism of the assembly of divines, in their answer to the 95th question; and according to this doctrine it is practised among the Indians.

Here I shall take the liberty, though it be a digression, to relate a story of remark concerning a child at Natick, a youth of about eleven years of age, who was of a sober and grave carriage, and an attentive hearer of the word, considering his age and capacity, but he had a weak body and was consumptive. This child hearing Mr. Eliot preach upon a time at Natick, when the ordinance of baptism was to be administered unto some children, whose parents had made profession of their faith and were joined to the church; upon which occasion Mr. Eliot said, that baptism was Christ's mark, which he ordered to be set upon his lambs, and that it was a manifest token of Christ's love to the offspring of his people to set this mark upon them; this child taking special notice of this passage, did often solicit his father and mother, that one or both of them would endeavour to join to the church, that he might be marked for one of Christ's lambs before he died. The parents who were well inclined, especially the mother, and being also very affectionate to their child, as the Indians generally are, did seriously ponder the child's reiterated intreaties; and not long after, first the mother, and then the father of the child, joined to the church. Soon after the lad was baptized; in which he did greatly rejoice and triumph, that now he was marked for one of Christ's lambs; and now said he to his father and mother, I am willing to die; which shortly after came to pass; and I doubt not, but as the child had Christ's name set upon him in baptism and by faith, so his immortal soul is now in glory, rejoicing in communion with Christ.

This relation, which is a most true and certain thing, should methinks be argumentative to persuade the Antipædobaptists of our age to so much affection and humanity unto their offspring, as the poor Indians had to their child, to offer them up to God, that his mark and name in baptism might be set upon them.

There are many Indians that live among those that have subjected to the gospel, that are catechised, do attend publick worship, read the scriptures, pray in their family morning and evening; but being not yet come so far, as to be able or willing to profess their faith in Christ, and yield obedience and subjection unto him in his church, are not admitted to partake in the ordinances of God, proper and peculiar to the church of Christ; which is a garden enclosed, as the scripture faith.

§. 4. The manner practised by these Indians in the worship of God, is thus. Upon the Lord's days, fast days, and lecture days, the people assemble together at the sound of a drum,—for bells they yet have not,—twice a day, in the morning and afternoon, on Lord's days, but only once upon lecture days; where one of their teachers, if they have more than one, begins with solemn and affectionate prayer. Then, after a short pause, either himself or some other thereunto appointed, readeth a chapter distinctly out of the old or new testament. At the conclusion thereof a psalm, or part of a psalm, is appointed, rehearsed, and solemnly sung. Then the minister catechises and prays before his sermon; and so preacheth from some text of scripture. Then concludeth with prayer, and a psalm, and a blessing pronounced. Sometime, instead of reading the chapter, some persons do answer some part of the catechism.

In all these acts of worship, for I have been often present with them, they demean themselves visibly with reverence, attention, modesty, and solemnity; the menkind sitting by themselves and the womenkind by themselves, according to their age, quality, and degree, in a comely manner. And for my own part, I have no doubt, but am fully satisfied, according to the judgment of charity, that divers of them do fear God and are true believers; but yet I will not deny but that there may be some of them hypocrites, that profess religion, and yet are not sound hearted. But things that are secret belong to God; and things that are revealed, unto us and our children.

§. 5. Their teachers are generally chosen from among themselves,—except some few English teachers,—of the most pious and able men among them. If these did not supply, they would generally be destitute: for the learned English young men do not hitherto incline or endeavour to fit themselves for that service, by learning the Indian language. Possibly the reasons may be: First, the difficulty to attain that speech. Secondly, little encouragement, while they prepare for it. Thirdly, the difficulty in the practice of such a calling among them, by reason of the poverty and barbarity, which cannot be grappled with, unless the person be very much mortified, self denying, and of a publick spirit, seeking greatly God's glory; and these are rare qualifications in young men. It is but one of an hundred that is so endowed.

Mr. Eliot hath of late years fallen into a practice among the Indians, the better to prepare and furnish them with abilities to explicate and apply the scriptures, by setting up a lecture among them in logick and theology, once every fortnight, all the summer, at Natick; whereat he is present and ready, and reads and explains to them the principles of those arts. And God hath been pleased graciously so to bless these means, that several of them, especially young men of acute parts, have gained much knowledge, and are able to speak methodically and profitably unto any plain text of scripture, yea as well as you can imagine such little means of learning can advantage them unto. From this church and town of Natick hath issued forth, as from a seminary of virtue and piety, divers teachers that are employed in several new praying towns; of which we shall hear more, God willing, hereafter,

In this town they have residing some of their principal rulers, the chief whereof is named Waban, who is now above seventy years of age. He is a person of great prudence and piety. I do not know any Indian that excels him. Other rulers there are living there, as Nattous and Piam Boohan, and others. These are good men and prudent, but inferiour to the first. The teachers of this town are Anthony and John Speen, which are grave and pious men. They have two constables belonging to this place, chosen yearly; and there is a marshal general belonging to all the praying Indian towns, called Captain Josiah, or Pennahannit. He doth attend the chief courts kept here, but he dwells at another place, called Nashobah.

I have been the larger in speaking of this place, because it is the chiefest town and eldest church; and what is said of this doth agree to all the rest in divers things.*

§. 6. The next town is Pakemitt, or Punkapaog.† The signification of the name is taken from a spring, that ariseth out of red earth. This town is situated south from Boston, about fourteen miles. There is a great mountain, called the Blue Hill, lieth north east from it about two miles: and the town of Dedham, about three miles north west from it. This is a small town, and hath not above twelve families in it; and so about sixty souls. This is the second praying town. The Indians that settled here, removed from Neponsitt mill. The quantity of land belonging to this village, is about six thousand acres; and some of it is fertile, but not generally so good as in other towns. Here they worship God, and keep the sabbath, in the same manner as is done at Natick, before declared. They have a ruler, a constable, and a schoolmaster. Their ruler's name is Ahawton; an old and faithful friend to the English. Their teacher is William Ahawton, his son; an ingenious person and pious man, and of good parts. Here was a very able teacher, who died about three years since. His name was William Awinian. He was a very knowing person, and of great ability, and of genteel deportment, and spoke very good English. His death was a very great rebuke to this place. This town hath within this ten years, lost by death several honest and able men; and some have turned apostates, and removed from them: which dispensations of God have greatly damped the flourishing condition of this place. Here it was that Mr. John Eliot, junior, before mentioned, preached a lecture once a fortnight, for sundry years, until his decease. In this village, besides their planting and keeping cattle and swine, and fishing in good ponds, and upon Neponsitt river which lieth near them; they are also advantaged by a large cedar swamp; wherein such as are laborious and diligent, do get many a pound, by cutting and preparing cedar shingles

---

*Natick was incorporated into an English district in the year 1761; and into a town, in the year 1781. It still retains its Indian name.
†Within the limits of Stoughton.

and clapboards, which sell well at Boston and other English towns adjacent.

§. 7. Hassanamesitt* is the third town of praying Indians. The name signifieth a place of small stones. This place lieth about thirty-eight miles from Boston, west southerly; and is about two miles to the eastward of Nipmuck river;† and near unto the old road way to Connecticut. It hath not above twelve families; and so, according to our computation, about sixty souls; but is capable to receive some hundreds, as generally the other villages are, if it shall please God to multiply them. The dimensions of this town is four miles square; and so about eight thousand acres of land. This village is not inferiour unto any of the Indian plantations for rich land and plenty of meadow, being well tempered and watered. It produceth plenty of corn, grain, and fruit; for there are several good orchards in this place. It is an apt place for keeping of cattle and swine; in which respect this people are the best stored of any Indian town of their size. Their ruler is named Anaweakin; a sober and discreet man. Their teacher's name is Tackuppa-willin, his brother; a pious and able man, and apt to teach. Their aged father, whose name I remember not, is a grave and sober christian, and deacon of the church. They have a brother that lives in the town, called James, that was bred among the English, and employed as a press man in printing the Indian bible; who can read well, and, as I take it, write also. The father, mother, brothers, and their wives, are all reputed pious persons, and the principal studs of the town. Here they have a meeting house for the worship of God after the English fashion of building, and two or three other houses after the same mode; but they fancy not greatly to live in them. Their way of living is by husbandry, and keeping cattle and swine; wherein they do as well, or rather better, than any other Indians, but yet are very far short of the English both in diligence and providence. In this town was the second Indian church gathered, about three years since, in summer, 1671. The pastor of this church is Tackuppa-willin; the ruling elder, Piambow; the deacon, father to the pastor. There are in full communion in this church, and living in the town,

---

Now generally pronounced Hassanamisco. Grafton.
†Blackstone river.

about sixteen men and women; and about thirty baptised persons, but there are several others, members of this church, that live in other places. This is a hopeful plantation. The Lord give his blessing to it. The way of their worship and civil order, is here as in other Indian towns before mentioned.

§. 8. Okommakamesit, alias Marlborough, is situated about twelve miles north north east from Hassanamesitt, about thirty miles from Boston westerly. This village contains about ten families, and consequently about fifty souls. The quantity of land appertaining to it is six thousand acres. It is much of it good land, and yieldeth plenty of corn, being well husbanded. It is sufficiently stored with meadow, and is well wooded and watered. It hath several good orchards upon it, planted by the Indians; and is in itself a very good plantation. This town doth join so near to the English of Marlborough, that it was spoken of David in type, and our Lord Jesus Christ, the antitype, *Under his shadow ye shall rejoice*: but the Indians here do not much rejoice under the English men's shadow; who do so overtop them in their number of people, stocks of cattle, &c. that the Indians do not greatly flourish, or delight in their station at present. Their ruler here was Onomog, who is lately deceased, about two months since; which is a great blow to that place. He was a pious and discreet man, and the very soul, as it were, of that place. Their teacher name is* [   ] Here they observe the same decorum for religion and civil order, as is done in other towns. They have a constable and other officers, as the rest have. The Lord sanctify the present affliction they are under by reason of their bereavements; and raise up others, and give them grace to promote religion and good order among them.

§. 9. Wamesit† is the fifth praying town; and this place is situate upon Merrimak river, being a neck of land, where Concord river falleth into Merrimak river. It is about twenty miles from Boston, north north west, and within five miles of Billerica, and as much from Chelmsford: so that it hath Concord river upon the west north west; and Merrimak river, upon the north north east. It hath about fifteen families; and consequently, as we compute, about seventy-five souls. The

---

*Hutchinson says his name was Solomon. Vol. I. page 167.
†Tewksbury.

quantity of land belonging to it is about twenty five hundred acres. The land is fertile, and yieldeth plenty of corn. It is excellently accommodated with a fishing place; and there is taken variety of fish in their seasons, as salmon, shads, lamprey eels, sturgeon, bass, and divers others. There is a great confluence of Indians, that usually resort to this place in the fishing seasons. Of these strange Indians divers are vitious and wicked men and women; which Satan makes use of to obstruct the prosperity of religion here. The ruler of this people is called Numphow. He is one of the blood of their chief sachems. Their teacher is called Samuel; son to the ruler, a young man of good parts, and can speak, read, and write, English and Indian competently. He is one of those that was bred up at school, at the charge of the Corporation for the Indians. These Indians, if they were diligent and industrious,—to which they have been frequently excited,—might get much by their fish, especially fresh salmon, which are of esteem and good price at Boston in the season; and the Indians being stored with horses of a low price, might furnish the market fully, being at so small a distance. And divers other sort of fish they might salt or pickle, as sturgeon and bass; which would be much to their profit. But notwithstanding divers arguments used to persuade them, and some orders made to encourage them; yet their idleness and improvidence doth hitherto prevail.

At this place, once a year, at the beginning of May, the English magistrate keeps his court, accompanied with Mr. Eliot, the minister; who at this time takes his opportunity to preach, not only to the inhabitants, but to as many of the strange Indians, that can be persuaded to hear him; of which sort, usually in times of peace, there are considerable numbers at that season. And this place being an ancient and capital seat of Indians, they come to fish; and this good man takes this opportunity to spread the net of the gospel, to fish for their souls. Here it may not be impertinent to give you the relation following.

May 5th, 1674, according to our usual custom, Mr. Eliot and myself took our journey to Wamesit, or Pawtuckett; and arriving there that evening, Mr. Eliot preached to as many of them as could be got together, out of Mat. xxii. 1–14. the parable of the marriage of the king's son. We met at the wigwam of one called Wannalancet, about two miles from the town, near Pawtuckett falls, and bordering upon Merrimak river. This person, Wannalancet, is the eldest son of old Pasaconaway, the chiefest sachem of Pawtuckett. He is a sober and grave person, and of years, between fifty and sixty. He hath been always loving and friendly to the English. Many endeavours have been used several years to gain this sachem to embrace the christian religion: but he hath stood off from time to time, and not yielded up himself personally, though for four years past he hath been willing to hear the word of God preached, and to keep the sabbath.—A great reason that hath kept him off, I conceive, hath been the indisposition and averseness of sundry of his chief men and relations to pray to God; which he foresaw would desert him, in case he turned christian.—But at this time, May 6th, 1674, it pleased God so to influence and overcome his heart, that it being proposed to him to give his answer concerning praying to God, after some deliberation and serious pause, he stood up, and made a speech to this effect:

Sirs, you have been pleased for four years last past, in your abundant love, to apply yourselves particularly unto me and my people, to exhort, press, and persuade us to pray to God. I am very thankful to you for your pains. I must acknowledge, said he, I have, all my days, used to pass in an old canoe (alluding to his frequent custom to pass in a canoe upon the river) and now you exhort me to change and leave my old canoe, and embark in a new canoe, to which I have hitherto been unwilling: but now I yield up myself to your advice, and enter into a new canoe, and do engage to pray to God hereafter.

This his professed subjection was well pleasing to all that were present, of which there were some English persons of quality; as Mr. Richard Daniel, a gentleman that lived in Billerica, about six miles off; and Lieutenant Henchman, a neighbour at Chelmsford; besides brother Eliot and myself, with sundry others, English and Indians. Mr. Daniel before named desired brother Eliot to tell this sachem from him, that it may be, while he went in his old canoe, he passed in a quiet stream; but the end thereof was death and destruction to soul and body: But now he went into a new canoe, perhaps he would meet with storms and trials; but yet he should be encouraged to persevere, for the end of his voyage would be everlasting rest.

Moreover he and his people were exhorted by brother Eliot and myself, to go on and sanctify the sabbath, to hear the word, and use the means that God hath appointed, and encourage their hearts in the Lord their God. Since that time, I hear this sachem doth persevere, and is a constant and diligent hearer of God's word, and sanctifieth the sabbath, though he doth travel to Wamesit meeting every sabbath, which is above two miles; and though sundry of his people have deserted him, since he subjected to the gospel, yet he continues and persists.

In this town they observe the same civil and religious orders, as in other towns, and have a constable and other officers. This people of Wamesit suffered more in the late war with the Mawhawks, than any other praying town of Indians: for divers of their people were slain; others, wounded; and some, carried into captivity; which providence hath much hindered the prosperous estate of this place.

§. 10. Nashobah* is the sixth praying Indian town. This village is situated in a manner in the centre between Chelmsford, Lancaster, Groton, and Concord. It lieth from Boston about twenty five miles, west north west. The inhabitants are about ten families, and consequently about fifty souls. The dimensions of this village is four miles square. The land is fertile, and well stored with meadows and woods. It hath good ponds for fish adjoining to it. The people live here, as in other Indian villages, upon planting corn, fishing, hunting, and sometimes labouring with the English. Their ruler of late years was John Ahatawance, a pious man. Since his decease, Pennakennit† is the chief. Their teacher is named John Thomas, a sober and pious man. His father was murthered by the Maquas in a secret manner, as he was fishing for eels at his wear, some years since, during the war. He was a pious and useful person; and that place sustained a great loss in him. In this village, as well in other old Indian plantations, they have orchards of apples, whereof they make cider; which some of them have not the wisdom and grace to use for their comfort, but are prone to abuse unto drunkenness. And although the laws be strict to suppress this sin, and some of their own rulers are very careful

*Littleton.
†Or Pennahannit. See §. 5.

and zealous in the execution of them; yet such is the madness and folly of man naturally, that he doth eagerly pursue after that which tendeth to his own destruction. I have often seriously considered what course to take, to restrain this beastly sin of drunkenness among them; but hitherto cannot reach it. For if it were possible, as it is not, to prevent the English selling them strong drink; yet they having a native liberty to plant orchards and sow grain, as barley and the like, of which they may and do make strong drink that doth inebriate them: so that nothing can overcome and conquer this exorbitancy, but the sovereign grace of God in Christ; which is the only antidote to prevent and mortify the poison of sin.

Near unto this town is a pond, wherein at some seasons there is a strange rumbling noise, as the Indians affirm; the reason whereof is not yet known. Some have conceived the hills adjacent are hollow, wherin the wind being pent, is the cause of this rumbling, as in earthquakes.

At this place they attend civil and religious order, as in the other praying towns: and they have a constable and other officers.

This town was deserted during the Maquas' war, but is now again repeopled, and in a hopeful way to prosper.

§. 11. Magunkaquog* is the seventh town where praying Indians inhabit. The signification of the place's name is a place of great trees. It is situated partly within the bounds of Natick, and partly upon land granted by the country. It lieth west southerly from Boston, about twenty four miles, near the midway between Natick and Hassanamesitt. The number of its inhabitants are about eleven families, and about fifty five souls. There are, men and women, eight members of the church at Natick, and about fifteen baptized persons. The quantity of land belonging to it is about three thousand acres. The Indians plant upon a great hill, which is very fertile. These people worship God, and keep the sabbath, and observe civil order, as do the other towns. They have a constable and other officers. Their ruler's name is Pomhaman; a sober and active man, and pious. Their teacher is named Job; a person well accepted for piety and ability among them. This town was the last setting of

*Pronounced at present Magunkook.—Hopkinton.

the old towns. They have plenty of corn, and keep some cattle, horses, and swine, for which the place is well accommodated.

§. 12. Having now spoken briefly of the seven old towns of praying Indians, I shall endeavour more briefly to give an account of seven towns more of praying Indians, within the jurisdiction of Massachusetts; which for distinction sake we call, the new praying towns in the Nipmuck country. The Indians of some of these towns began to hearken unto the gospel about three years since, or thereabouts. In July, 1673, Mr. Eliot and myself made a journey to visit some of them, and to encourage and exhort them to proceed in the ways of God.

This year again, on the 14th of September last, 1674, we both took another journey. Our design was to travel further among them, and to confirm their souls in the christian religion, and to settle teachers in every town, and to establish civil government among them, as in other praying towns. We took with us five or six godly persons, who we intended to present unto them for ministers.

The first of these new praying towns is Manchage,* which lieth to the westward of Nipmuck river, about eight miles; and is from Hassanamesitt, west and by south, about ten miles; and it is from Boston about fifty miles, on the same rhumb. It is seated in a fertile country for good land. To it belongeth about twelve families, and about sixty souls: but the people were generally from home, though we spoke with some of them afterward. For this place we appointed Waabesktamin, a hopeful young man, for their minister, whom the people, with whom we spake afterward, accepted. There is no land yet granted by the general court to this place, nor to any other of the new praying towns. But the court intendeth shortly, upon the application and professed subjection of these Indians unto the yoke of Christ, to do for them as they have done for other praying Indians.

§. 13. About five miles distant from hence is a second town called Chabanakongkomun.† It hath its denomination from a very great pond, about five or six miles long, that borders upon the south end of it. This village is fifty five miles, west

*Oxford.
†Dudley.

and by south, from Boston. There are in it about nine families, and about forty five fouls. The people are of a sober deportment, and better instructed in the worship of God, than any of the new praying towns. Their teacher's name is Joseph, who is one of the church of Hassanamesitt; a sober, pious, and ingenious person, and speaks English well, and is well read in the scriptures. He was the first that settled this town, and got the people to him about two years since. It is a new plantation, and is well accommodated with upland and meadows. At this place dwells an Indian called Black James, who about a year since was constituted constable of all these new praying towns. He is a person that hath approved himself diligent and courageous, faithful and zealous to suppress sin; and so he was confirmed in his office another year. Mr. Eliot preached unto this people, and we prayed and sung psalms with them, and they were exhorted by us to stand steadfast in the faith. A part of one night we spent in discoursing with them, and resolving variety of questions propounded by them, touching matters of religion and civil order. The teacher Joseph and the constable James went with us unto the next town, which is called

§. 14. Maanexit,* which is a third village, and lieth about seven miles westerly from Chabanakongkomun. It is situated in a fertile country, and near unto a fresh river, upon the west of it, called Mohegan river.† It is distant from Boston about sixty miles, west and by south. The inhabitants are about twenty families, and, as we compute, one hundred souls. Mr. Eliot preached unto this people out of the xxivth Ps. 7. to the end: *Lift up your heads, O ye gates, and be ye lift up, ye everlasting doors, and the king of glory shall come in,* &c. After sermon was ended, we presented unto them John Moqua, a pious and sober person there present, for their present minister, which they thankfully accepted. Then their teacher named, and set, and rehearsed, a suitable psalm, which being sung, and a conclusion with prayer, they were exhorted, both the teacher to be diligent and faithful, and to take care of the flock, whereof the

---

The north-east part of Woodstock.
†*Now called Quinabaug river, which falls into Shetucket river, four miles above Norwich Landing.*

holy Ghost had made him overseer, and the people also to give obedience and subjection to him in the Lord.

§. 15. Quantisset* is a fourth village, which lieth about six miles to the south of Maanexit, and within four miles of the south line of Massachusetts colony. This place hath about twenty families, and one hundred souls. We went not to it, being straitened for time; but we spake with some of the principal people at Wabquissit. For them we appointed a sober and pious young man of Natick, called Daniel, to be minister, whom they accepted in the Lord.

§. 16. Wabquissit† is a fifth town, which lieth about nine or ten miles from Maanexit, upon the west side, six miles, of Mohegan river; and is distant from Boston west and by south, about seventy two miles. It lieth about four miles within the Massachusetts south line. It hath about thirty families, and one hundred and fifty souls. It is situated in a very rich soil, manifested by the goodly crop of Indian corn then newly ingathered, not less than forty bushels upon an acre. We came thither late in the evening, upon the 15th of September, and took up our quarters at the sagamore's wigwam, who was not at home: but his squaw courteously admitted us, and provided liberally, in their way, for the Indians that accompanied us. This sagamore inclines to religion, and keeps the meeting on sabbath days at his house, which is spacious, about sixty feet in length, and twenty feet in width.

The teacher of this place is named Sampson; an active and ingenious person. He speaks good English, and reads well. He is brother unto Joseph, before named, teacher at Chabanakongkomun; being both the only sons of one Petavit, alias Robin, one of the late rulers of Hassanamesitt, who died not above three days before our coming thither, after about a year's sickness of the stone. He was in his time a courageous and stout man for God and religion; and was one that stood in the gap against the pride and insolency of wicked Indians,

*The south-east part of Woodstock.
†The south-west corner of Woodstock. Woodstock is in Connecticut; but it was formerly considered as within the limits of Massachusetts. See Huth. Hist. vol, II. page 202–206.

although sagamores, who sometimes would ruffle against religion and good order in his presence. He would venture him to oppose them, to good success. I remember sundry years since, a sagamore that lived up in the inland country, came to Hassanamesitt, and brought with him a rundlet of strong liquors; and lodging in his house, Petavit in the morn sent for the constable, and ordered him, and according to law, seized the rundlet of liquors. At which act the sagamore drew a long knife, and stood with his foot at the rundlet, daring any to seize it. But Petavit thereupon rose up and drew his knife, and set his foot also to the rundlet, and commanded the constable to do his office. And the sagamore [   ] Some other actions of the like kind he did. In truth God hath magnified his grace to his two sons; being both hopeful, pious, and active men; especially the younger before named Sampson, teacher at Wabquissit, who was, a few years since, a dissolute person, and I have been forced to be severe in punishing him for his misdemeanors formerly. But now he is, through grace, changed and become sober and pious; and he is now very thankful to me for the discipline formerly excercised towards him. And besides his flagitious life heretofore, he lived very uncomfortably with his wife; but now they live very well together. I confess this story is a digression. But because it tendeth to magnify grace, and that to a prodigal, and to declare how God remembers his covenant unto the children of such, as are faithful and zealous for him in their time and generation, I have mentioned it.

We being at Wabquissit, at the sagamore's wigwam, divers of the principal people that were at home came to us, with whom we spent a good part of the night in prayer, singing psalms, and exhortations. There was a person among them, who sitting mute a great space, at last spake to this effect: That he was agent for Unkas, sachem of Mohegan, who challenged right to, and dominion over, this people of Wabquissit. And said he, Unkas is not well pleased, that the English should pass over Mohegan river, to call his Indians to pray to God.

Unto which speech Mr. Eliot first answered, that it was his work to call upon all men every where, as he had opportunity, especially the Indians, to repent and embrace the gospel; but he did not meddle with civil right or jurisdiction.

When he had done speaking, then I declared to him, and
desired him to inform Unkas what I said, that Wabquissit was
within the jurisdiction of Massachusetts, and that the government of that people did belong to them; and that they do look
upon themselves concerned to promote the good of all people
within their limits, especially if they embraced christianity.
Yet it was not hereby intended to abridge the Indian sachems
of their just and ancient right over the Indians, in respect of
paying tribute or any other dues. But the main design of the
English was to bring them to the good knowledge of God in
Christ Jesus; and to suppress among them those sins of drunkenness, idolatry, powowing or witchcraft, whoredom, murder,
and like sins. As for the English, they had taken no tribute from
them, nor taxed them with any thing of that kind.

Upon the 16th day of September, being at Wabquissit, as
soon as the people were come together, Mr. Eliot first prayed,
and then preached to them in their own language, out of Mat.
vi. 33. *First seek the kingdom of heaven, and the righteousness
thereof, and all other things shall be added unto you.* Their
teacher Sampson first reading and setting the cxix. Ps. 1st part,
which was sung. The exercise was concluded with prayer.

Then I began a court among the Indians. And first I
approved their teacher Sampson, and their constable Black
James; giving each of them a charge to be diligent and faithful
in their places. Also I exhorted the people to yield obedience
to the gospel of Christ and to those set in order there. Then
published a warrant or order, that I had prepared, empower-
ing the constable to suppress drunkenness, sabbath breaking,
especially powowing and idolatry. And after warning given, to
apprehend all delinquents, and bring them before authority, to
answer for their misdoings; the smaller faults to bring before
Wattasacompanum, ruler of the Nipmuck country; for idolatry
and powowing to bring them before me: So we took leave of
this people of Wabquissit, and about eleven o'clock, returned
back to Maanexit and Chabanakongkomun, where we lodged
this night.

§. 17. We took leave of the christian Indians at Chabanakongkomun, and took our journey, 17th of the seventh month,
by Manchage, to Pakachoog; which lieth from Manchage,
north west, about twelve miles. We arrived there about noon.

This village lieth about three miles south from the new road way that leadeth from Boston to Connecticut; about eighteen miles, west southerly, from Marlborough; and from Boston about forty four miles. It consists of about twenty families, and hath about one hundred souls therein. This town is seated upon a fertile hill;* and is denominated from a delicate spring of water that is there.

We repaired to the sagamore's house, called John, alias Horowanninit, who kindly entertained us. There is another sagamore belonging to this place, of kindred to the former, whose name is Solomon, alias Wooanaskochu. This man was also present, who courteously welcomed us. As soon as the people could be got together, Mr. Eliot preached unto them; and they attended reverently. Their teacher, named James Speen, being present, read and set the tune of a psalm, that was sung affectionately. Then was the whole duty concluded with prayer.

After some short respite, a court was kept among them. My chief assistant was Wattasacompanum, ruler of the Nipmuck Indians, a grave and pious man, of the chief sachem's blood of the Nipmuck country. He resides at Hassanamesitt; but by former appointment, calleth here, together with some others. The principal matter done at this court, was, first to constitute John and Solomon to be rulers of this people and co-ordinate in power, clothed with the authority of the English government, which they accepted: also to allow and approve James Speen for their minister. This man is of good parts, and pious. He hath preached to this people almost two years; but he yet resides at Hassanamesitt, about seven miles distant. Also they chose, and the court confirmed, a new constable, a grave and sober Indian, called Mattoonus. Then I gave both the rulers, teacher, constable, and people, their respective charges; to be diligent and faithful for God zealous against sin, and careful in sanctifying the sabbath.

Moreover at this court it was agreed to send a grave and pious Indian there present, called Jethro, belonging to Natick,

*This seems to be the same hill, which in the description of Worcester, page 113, is called Boggachoag. It is situated partly in Worcester, and partly in Ward. Boggachoag brook runs on the west side of it.

to be a teacher unto a people living about ten miles more to the northward, at a place called Weshakim, alias Nashaway, near unto an English town called Lancaster. These have been a great people in former times; but of late years, have been consumed by the Maquas' wars and other ways; and are not above fifteen or sixteen families. I gave this Jethro a letter or order of the purport following.

> For the sagamore Shoshanim and the Indian people that live with him at Weshakim,
>
> Grace, mercy, and peace be multiplied.
>
> Whereas the Honourable General Court of the Massachusetts, hath appointed and authorized me to rule and govern the Indians within this jurisdiction; and in a special manner to endeavour the promoting of religion and civility among them; I have thought it expedient, with the concurrence of Mr. John Eliot, principal teacher unto the Indians, and approbation of several of the rulers and teachers belonging to the churches of Natick and Hassanamesitt, to send unto you Jethro, a man approved in the church of Natick, to be a minister and teacher among you, and to instruct you in the good knowledge of the Lord God, and in the gospel of his son, our Lord Jesus Christ. We pray you therefore to receive him in the Lord, and yield ready obedience to the word of the Lord dispensed by him. And in a special manner, we exhort you, to keep the sabbath carefully, and abstain from drunkenness, whoredom, and powowing, and all other evils. In ready compliance herewith you will promote your own temporal and eternal happiness. So committing you to the Lord, and the word of his grace; praying for a blessing upon the means, for God's glory and your good; I remain your loving and affectionate friend, for promoting your everlasting welfare,
>
> DANIEL GOOKIN.
>
> Dated at Pakachoog, the 17th September, 1674.

Letters of the same import are intended to be given to the teachers of the other new praying Indian towns.

After this business was over, it being night before we had finished the court, there was an Indian present, which came into the wigwam about an hour before. He was belonging to

Weshakim, or Nashaway. This Indian desired liberty to speak; which being admitted, he made a speech with much affection and gravity to this effect: To declare that he belonged to Weshakim near Nashaway; and that he was desirously willing, as well as some others of his people, to pray to God; but that there were sundry of that people very wicked and much addicted to drunkenness, and thereby many disorders were committed among them: and therefore he earnestly importuned me, that I would put forth power to help in that case, to suppress the sin of drunkenness. Then I asked him, whether he would take upon him the office of a constable, and I would give him power to apprehend drunkards, and take away their strong drink from them, and bring the delinquents before me to receive punishment. His answer was, that he would first speak with his friends, and if they chose him, and strengthened his hand in the work, then he would come to me for a black staff and power. I asked him, whether he were willing to have Jethro to go and preach to them; to which he readily complied, and seemed joyful thereat. After this discourse, we concluded with singing a psalm and prayer; and so retired to rest. And the next morning early, being September the 18th, we took our leave of these Indians, and passed to Marlborough; and from thence returned to our own habitations.

There is yet another praying town in the Nipmuck country called Waeuntug.* This place lieth to the westward of Nipmuck river, against an English town called Mendon, which is on the east side of the river. It lieth about ten miles from Hassanamesitt, to the south of this place. There are two teachers; the one named James, brother to the pastor of Hassanamesitt; the other, called Sasomet. They both live at Hassanamesitt, and are of the church there, and both preach to that people. I never was at the place; and therefore cannot give a particular account thereof at present.

There are two other Indian towns, viz. Weshakim and Quabaug,† which are coming on to receive the gospel: and reckoning these, there are nine in the Nipmuck country. But they being not fully settled, I omit them.

*Uxbridge.
†The south-east part of Brookfield.

Thus I have endeavoured particularly to describe these Indian praying villages within the jurisdiction of Massachusetts; which are

Towns	14	Souls yielding obedience	⎫	1100*
Churches	2	to the gospel about	⎭	

That is, in

Natick [*supposed*	145
Punkapaog	60
Hassanamesitt	60
Okommakamesit	50
Wamesit	75
Nashobah	50
Magunkaquog	55
Manchage	60
Chabanakongkomun	45
Maanexit	100
Quantisset	100
Wabquissit	150
Packachoog	100
Waeuntug [*supposed*	50
Total	1100

*Tradition says, that a hundred and twenty years ago the Indians in Natick were comparatively numerous. See note * to §. 3. A large proportion of the communicants were probably inhabitants of Natick.*

It may perhaps afford satisfaction to some persons to know the number of Indians in Massachusetts, at different periods since the year 1674. *The following is the only account which we have had time and opportunity to collect. We regret that it is not in our power to make it more complete; but we hope that some of our readers, who possess better information, will supply our deficiences.—The war with Philip greatly interrupted the progress of christianity among the Indians.* [*Hubbard's M. S. Hist. chap.* lxxiv.] *Many praying towns in Massachusetts were broken up. Mr. Eliot says, that in the year* 1684, *they were reduced to four.* [*Appendix to the Life of Boyle, page* 445.] *They seem however to have increased soon after; for in the year* 1687, *Dr. Increase Mather mentions five churches.* [*Lett. to Leusden.*] *They have gradually diminished since that period. In the year* 1753, *there were in Natick, the principal town of Indians in the colony, twenty five families, beside several individuals. Some of the males were soldiers in the war against the French, which took place soon after. Returning from the lakes, they brought home a mortal disease, of which twenty three died in the year* 1759. *In the year* 1763, *according to a census then taken, there were thirty seven Indians only in Natick; but in this return, probably the wandering Indians were not included. The Indians in Natick are now reduced to one family of five persons, and two single women. There are besides, belonging to this place, ten adults, some of whom have children. They lead a wandering life, seldom residing long in one place.—The Indians of Grafton have not wasted so fast. In* 1764 *there were eight*

The harvest is ripe for many more, if God please to thrust forth labourers. The pious reader, whose heart desires the honour of God, and the salvation of these poor heathen, may here see some small beginnings that God hath wrought, and what foundations, through grace, are laid for the future good, and increasing their numbers: for every one of these towns are able to entertain considerable number of Indians, and it pleaseth God now and then to call in some wild Indians to settle among them.

Now we shall proceed to inform you, according to the best intelligence I can obtain, of the progress of the gospel among the Indians, in or near the other English colonies and plantations of New England.

---

or ten families. [*Hutch. vol.* I. *page* 167.] *And there are still about thirty persons, who retain a portion of their lands, and receive their annual quit rent from the white inhabitants.—These Indians, with a few in Stoughton, are, we believe, all the remains of the numerous tribes who formerly inhabited the old colony of Massachusetts.—The Mukkekaneew, or Stockbridge Indians, who migrated from Hudson's river, about the year* 1734, *no longer reside in the state, having, between the years* 1785 *and* 1787, *removed to Oneida. Whilst they remained, they wasted away, like all other Indians. Forty years ago, there were about a hundred and fifty families; but in the year* 1763, *they were reduced to two hundred and twenty one persons, and in* 1786, *to about one third of that number.*

THE EDITORS' COMMENT

Daniel Gookin was a settler first in Virginia and then in Massachusetts Bay, where he assisted the minister John Eliot in the effort to convert Wampanoag, Nipmuc, Massachusett, and Patucket/Pennacook people to Christianity. He also served as an Assistant on the Massachusetts Bay General Court from 1652 to 1675 and again from 1677 to 1687. Gookin participated in the organization and administration of Praying Towns, the villages where Native converts, called "Praying Indians," were expected to adopt English-styled houses, clothing, gender roles, and agriculture—even if, as Gookin notes, they continued to employ their own ways of living, especially when it meant a warmer house and a more fertile field. Gookin described fourteen Praying Towns in *Historical Collections*, noting that there were several others but omitting them because they were not "fully settled." Praying Towns were most often established within long-standing Native communities and homelands, and Native people continued to maintain leadership roles in these mission communities, even as colonists like Gookin and other officials increasingly intervened in the towns' selection of leaders and sought to oversee and direct Native peoples' governance and behavior. Gookin wrote *Historical Collections* just before King Philip's War, and he provides a view of the Native nations in the region and careful descriptions of the Praying Towns, as well as those Nipmuc towns, like Nashaway, where there was tension among the missionaries, converts, and those who rejected colonial rule. He described the childhood and education of youth like Joel Iacoomes and Caleb Cheeshateaumuck, who studied at Harvard Indian College, and detailed the Native leaders in various Praying Towns, men who went on to face difficult decisions during the war about how to keep their communities safe as anti-Indian sentiment among colonists rose. Some Massachusett and Nipmuc men made the decision, based on their relationship with Massachusetts Bay Colony, to aid colonial forces during the war, serving as scouts in Wampanoag country when the conflict first arose. Others remained neutral or were sheltered in inland sanctuaries. During the war, Praying Town inhabitants also faced increasingly severe colonial laws that restricted their movements, including internment on deforested islands in Boston harbor, where many people died in the winter of 1675–76. Men whose families were interned were compelled to serve as scouts for colonial forces in 1676, enabling English military leaders to access Native spaces that had previously been impossible to locate. After the war, many of the men who had served as scouts led the effort to protect the communal lands of the Praying Towns in order to sustain the families who survived the war.

KING PHILIP'S WAR
OR
THE FIRST INDIAN WAR

John Easton:
A Relacion of the Indyan Warre

*a true relation of wt I kno and of reports, and my understanding
Conserning the begining and progres of the war now betwen
the English and the indians.*

IN the winter in the year 1674 an indian was found dead,
and by a Corener iquest of Plimoth Coleny judged murdered.
he was found dead in a hole thro ies broken in a pond with
his gun and sum foulle by him. sum English suposed him
throne in sum indians that I judged intelegabell and impartiall
in that Case did think he fell in and was so drouned and that
the ies did hurt his throat as the English saied it was cut, but
acnoledged that sumtimes naty indians wold kill others but,
not as ever thay herd to obscuer as if the dead indian was not
murdered. the dead indian was caled Sausimun and a Christian
that could read and write. report was he was a bad man that
king Philop got him to write his will and he made the writing
for a gret part of the land to be his but read as if it had bine
as Philop wold, but it Came to be knone and then he run
away from him. now one indian informed that 3 indians had
murdered him, and shewed a Coat that he said thay gave him to
Conseall them, the indians report that the informer had played
away his Coate, and these men sent him that coate, and after
demanded pay and he not to pay so acused them, and knoing
it wold pleas the English so to think him a beter Christian,
and the reporte Came, that the 3 indians had confesed and
acused Philop so to imploy them, and that the English wold
hang Philop, so the indians wear afraid, and reported that the
English had flatred them (or by threts) to bely Philop that thay
might kill him to have his Land and that if Philop had dun it
it was ther Law so to execute home ther kings judged deserved
it that he had no Case to hide it.

so Philop kept his men in arems. Plimoth Governer, required
him to disband his men, and informed him his jelosy was falce.

Philop ansered he wold do no harem, and thanked the Governer for his information. the 3 indians wer hunge, to the last
denied the fact, but one broke the halter as it is reported then
desiere to be saved and so was a litell while then confesed thay
3 had dun the fact and then he was hanged and it was reported
Sausimun before his death had informed of the indian plot and
that if the indians knew it thay wold kill him, and that the
hethen might destroy the English for ther wickedness as god
had permited the heathen to destroy the iserallits of olde, so
the English wear afraid and Philop was afraid and both incresed
in arems but for 40 years time reports and jelosys of war had
bine veri frequent that we did not think that now a war was
breking forth, but about a wecke before it did we had Case to
think it wold, then to indever to prevent it, we sent a man to
Philop that if he wold Cum to the fery we wold Cum over to
speke with him. about 4 mile we had to Cum thether. our
mesenger Come to them, thay not awar of it behaved themselefs as furious but sudingly apesed when thay understood
who he was and what he came for. he Called his counsell and
agreed to Cum to us came himsrlef unarmed and about 40 of
his men armed. then 5 of us went over. 3 wear magestrats. we
sate veri frindly together. we told him our bisnes was to indever
that thay might not reseve or do rong. thay said that was well
thay had dun no rong, the English ronged them, we saied we
knew the English saied the indians ronged them and the indians saied the english ronged them but our desier was the quarell might rightly be desided in the best way, and not as dogs
desided ther quarells. the indians owned that fighting was the
worst way then thay propounded how right might take plase,
we saied by arbetration. thay saied all English agred against
them, and so by arbetration thay had had much rong, mani
miles square of land so taken from them for English wold have
English Arbetrators, and once thay wer perswaided to give in
ther arems, that therby Jelosy might be removed and the
English having ther arems wold not deliver them as thay had
promised, untill thay consented to pay a 100^{po}, and now thay
had not so much land or muny, that thay wear as good be kiled
as leave all ther liveflyhode. we saied thay might Choose a
indian king, and the English might Choose the Governer of
new yorke that nether had Case to say ether weare parties in

the diferans. thay saied thay had not herd of that way and saied
we onestly spoke so we wear perswaided if that way had bine
tendered thay wold have acsepted. we did indever not to here
ther Cumplaints, saied it was not Convenient for us now to
Consider of, but to indever to prevent war, saied to them when
in war against English blud was spilt that ingadged all Englishmen for we wear to be all under one king. we knew what ther
Cumplaints wold be, and in our Colony had removed sum of
them in sending for indian rulers in what the Crime Conserned
indians lives which thay veri lovingly acsepted and agreed with
us to ther execution and saied so thay wear abell to satesfie ther
subjects when thay knew an indian sufered duly, but saied in
what was only betwen ther indians and not in towneshipes that
we had purchased, thay wold not have us prosecute and that
thay had a great fear to have ani of ther indians should be Caled
or forsed to be Christian indians. thay saied that such wer in
everi thing more mischivous, only disemblers, and then the
English made them not subject to ther kings, and by ther lying
to rong their kings. we knew it to be true, and we promising
them that how ever in government to indians all should be
alicke and that we knew it was our kings will it should be so,
that altho we wear wecker then other Colonies, thay having
submited to our king to protect them others dared not otherwise to molest them, so thay expresed thay tooke that to be
well, that we had litell Case to doute but that to us under the
king thay wold have yelded to our determenations in what ani
should have Cumplained to us against them, but Philop
Charged it to be disonesty in us to put of the hering the complaints therfore we Consented to here them. thay saied thay
had bine the first in doing good to the English, and the English
the first in doing rong, saied when the English first Came their
kings father was as a great man and the English as a litell Child,
he Constraened other indians from ronging the English and
gave them Coren and shewed them how to plant and was free
to do them ani good and had let them have a 100 times more
land, then now the king had for his own peopell, but ther kings
brother when he was king Came miserabely to dy by being
forsed to Court as thay judged poysoned, and another greavanc
was if 20 of there onest indians testefied that a Englishman had
dun them rong, it was as nothing, and if but one of ther worst

indians testefied against ani indian or ther king when it plesed
the English that was sufitiant. a nother grivanc was when ther
kings sold land the English wold say it was more than thay
agred to and a writing must be prove against all them, and sum
of ther kings had dun rong to sell so much he left his peopell
none and sum being given to drunknes the English made them
drunk and then cheted them in bargens, but now ther kings
wear forewarned not for to part with land for nothing in Cum-
pareson to the valew therof. now home the English had owned
for king or queen thay wold disinheret, and make a nother king
that wold give or seell them there land, that now thay had no
hopes left to kepe ani land. a nother grivanc the English Catell
and horses still incresed that when thay removed 30 mill from
wher English had anithing to do, thay Could not kepe ther
coren from being spoyled, thay never being iused to fence, and
thoft when the English boft land of them that thay wold have
kept ther Catell upone ther owne land. a nother grevanc the
English wear so eger to sell the indians lickers that most of the
indians spent all in drunknes and then ravened upone the sober
indians and thay did belive often did hurt the English Catell,
and ther kings Could not prevent it. we knew before these were
ther grand Cumplaints, but then we only indevered to perswaid
that all Cumplaints might be righted without war, but Could
have no other answer but that thay had not herd of that way for
the Governer of yorke and a indian king to have the hering of
it. we had Case to thinke in that had bine tendred it wold have
bine acsepted. we indevered that however thay should lay
doune ther arems for the English wear to strong for them. thay
saied then the English should do to them as thay did when thay
wear to strong for the english. so we departed without ani
discurtiousnes, and sudingly had leter from Plimoth Governer
thay intended in arems to Conforem philop, but no information what that was thay required or what termes he refused to
have ther quarell desided, and in a weckes time after we had
bine with the indians the war thus begun. Plimoth soldiers
were Cum to have ther head quarters within 10 mile of philop.
then most of the English therabout left ther houses and we had
leter from Plimoth governer to desier our help with sum boats
if thay had such ocation and for us to looke to our selefs and
from the genarall at the quarters we had leter of the day thay

intended to Cum upon the Indians and desier for sum of our bots to atend, so we tooke it to be of nesesety for our Ieslanders one halef one day and night to atend and the other halef the next, so by turens for our oune safty. in this time sum indians fell a pilfering sum houses that the English had left, and a old man and a lad going to one of those houses did see 3 indians run out therof. the old man bid the young man shoote so he did and a indian fell doune but got away againe. it is reported that then sum indians Came to the gareson asked why thay shot the indian. thay asked whether he was dead. the indians saied yea. a English lad saied it was no mater. the men inde-vered to inforem them it was but an idell lads words but the indians in hast went away and did not harken to them. the next day the lad that shot the indian and his father and fief English more wear killed so the war begun with philop. but ther was a queen that i knew was not a party with philop and Plimoth Governer recumended her that if shee wold cum to our Iesland it wold be well and shee desiered shee might if it wear but with six of hir men. I Can sufitiantly prove, but it is to large here to relate, that shee had practised much the quarell might be desided without war, but sum of our English allso in fury against all indians wold not Consent shee should be reseved to our Iesland alltho I profered to be at all the Charg to secuer hir and those shee desiered to Cum with hir, so at length pre-vailed we might send for hir, but one day acsedentaly we wear prevented, and then our men had seased sum Cannos on hir side suposing they wear Philops and the next day a English house was there burned and mischif of ether side indevered to the other and much dun, hir houses burned, so we wear pre-vented of ani menes to atain hir. the English army Cam not doune as informed thay wold so Philop got over and thay could not find him. 3 days after thay came doune had a veri stormy night, that in the morning the foote wear disabled to returen before thay had refreshment. thay wear free to acsept as we wear willing to relive them, but boston trupers Sayed by thear Captaine thay despised it and so left the foote. after the foote had refreshed themselefs thay allso returned to ther head quar-ters, and after hunting Philop from all sea shors that thay Could not tell what was becum of him, the naroganset kings informed us that the queen aforesaied must be in a thicket a

starving or conformed to Philop, but thay knew shee wold be
glad to be from them, so from us had incuredgment to get hir
and as mani as thay Could from Philop. after the English army
with out our Consent or informing us came into our coleny,
broft the naroganset indians to artickels of agreement to them
philop being flead about a 150 indians Came in to a Plimoth
gareson volentarely. Plimoth authority sould all for slafes (but
about six of them) to be Caried out of the Cuntry.—it is true
the indians genaraly ar very barbarus peopell but in this war I
have not herd of ther tormenting ani but that the English army
Cote an old indian and tormented him. he was well knone to
have bine a long time a veri decreped and haremless indian of
the queens. as Philop flead the fore said queen got to the narogansets and as mani of hir men as shee could get, but one part
of the narogansets agreement to bostun was to kill or deliver
as mani as they Could of philops peopell, therfore bostun men
demanded the fore said queene and others that thay had so
reseved for which the indians wear unfree and made mani
excuses as that the queen was none of them and sum others
wear but sudieners with philop becase removed by the English
having got ther land and wear of ther kindred which we kno is
true. not but we think thay did shelter mani thay should not,
and that thay did kno sum of ther men did asist Philop, but
acording to ther barbarus ruells thay acounted so was no rong
or thay could not help it, but sum enemis heds thay did send
in and told us thay wear informed that however when winter
Came thay might be suer the English wold be ther enemies,
and so thay stood doutful for about 5 months. the English wear
jelous that ther was a genarall plot of all indians against English
and the indians wear in like maner jelous of the english. I think
it was genarall that thay wear unwilling to be ronged and that
the indians do judg the English partiall against them and
among all a philthy Crue that did desier and indever for war
and those of ani solidety wear against it and indevered to prevent the war, for conserning Philop we have good intelegenc
that he advised sum English to be gon from ther out plases
wher thay lived or thay wear in danger to be killed, but whether
it wear to prevent a war, or by ther prests informed if thay
begun thay should be beaten and otherwise not so we have
good intelegenc for I do think most of them had a desier the

English wold begin, and if the English be not carefull to manefest the indians mai expect equity from them, thay mai have
more enemies then thay wold and more Case of Jelosy. the
report is that to the estward the war thus began, by suposing
that sum of those indians wear at a fight in thes parts and that
thear thay sa a man wonded, so authority sent sum forth to
discufer, having before disarmed those indians and confined
them to a place, which the indians wear not ofended at, but
those men Coming upon them in a warlike postuer thay fled
that the men Cote but 3 of them. those in authority sent out
againe to excuse them selefs, but thay could only cum to the
spech with one man as he kept out of ther reach. thay excused
them selefs and saied his father was not hurt, one of them thay
had taken. he saied he could not belive them, for if it wer so
thay wold have broft him, thay had bin desaitfull to disarem
them and so wold have killed them all, and so he run away, and
then English wear killed, and the report is that up in the cuntri
here away thay had demanded the indians arems and went
againe to parell with them and the indians by ambushcade
tretcherously killed 8 that wear going to treat with them. when
winter was Cum we had leter from bostun of the iunited Comi-
tioners that thay wear resolved to reduce the narogansets to
Conformity not to be trubled with them ani more and desiered
sum help of botes and otherwise if we sa Case and that we
should kepe secret conserning it. our governer sent them word
we wear satesfied naragansets wear tretcherous, and had ayded
Philop, and as we had asisted to relive ther army before so we
should be redy to asist them still, and advised that terems
might be tendered that such might expect Cumpation that
wold acsept not to ingag in war and that ther might be a seperation betwene the gilty and the inosent which in war Could not
be expected, we not in the lest expecting thay wold have begun
the war and not before proclaimed it or not give them Defianc,
I having often informed the indians that English men wold not
begin a war otherwise it was brutish so to do. i am sory so the
indians have Case to think me desaitfull for the English thus
began the war with the narogansets we having sent ofe our
Iesland mani indians and informed them if thay kept by the
water sides and did not medell that how ever the English wold
do them no harem alltho it was not save for us to let them live

here. the army first take all those prisoners then fell upone Indian houses burned them and killed sum men. the war began without proclemation and sum of our peopell did not kno the English had begun mischif to the indians and being Confedent and had Case therfore, that the indians wold not hurt them before the English begun, so did not kepe ther gareson exactly, but the indians having reseved that mischif Came unexpected upone them destroyed 145 of them beside other gret lose, but the English army say thay suposed coneticot forses had bine there. thay solde the indians that thay had taken as aforesaied, for slafes, but one old man that was Caried of our Iesland upone his suns back. he was so decriped Could not go and when the army tooke them upone his back Caried him to the garison, sum wold have had him devouered by doges but the tendernes of sum of them prevailed to Cut ofe his head, and after Came sudingly upone the indians whear the indians had prepared to defend themselfs and so reseved and did much mischif and for aboute six weeks sinc hath bine spent as for both parties to recruet, and now the English army is out to seecke after the indians but it is most lickly that such most abell to do mischif will escape and women and children and impotent mai be destroyed and so the most abell will have the les incumbranc to do mischif.

but I am confident it wold be best for English and indians that a peas wear made upone onest terems for each to have a dew propriety and to injoy it without opretion or iusurpation by one to the other. but the English dear not trust the indians promises nether the indians to the Englishes promises and each have gret Case therfore. I see no way lickly but if a sesation from arems might be procured untill it might be knone what terems King Charels wold propound, for we have gret Case to think the naroganset kings wold trust our king and that thay wold have acsepted him to be umpier if it had bine tendered about ani diferanc, for we do kno the English have had much contention against those indians to invaled the kings determenation for naroganset to be in our colony, and we have Case to think it was the greatest Case of the war against them. I see no menes lickly to procuer a sesation from arems exept the governer of new york can find a way so to intersete and so it will be lickly a pease mai be made without trubling our king. not but it allwais hath bine a prinsipell in our Colony that ther should be but one supreme to English men and in our natief Cuntry wher ever English have jurisdiction and so we know no English should begin a war and not first tender for the king to be umpier and not persecute such that will not Conforem to ther worship, and ther worship be what is not owned by the king. the king not to mind to have such things redresed, sum mai take it that he hath not pouer, and that ther mai be a wai for them to take pouer in oposition to him. I am so perswaided of new England prists thay ar so blinded by the spiret of persecution and to maintaine to have hyer, and to have rume to be mere hyerlings that thay have bine the Case that the law of nations and the law of arems have bine voiolated in this war, and that the war had not bine if ther had not bine a hyerling that for his maneging what he Caleth the gospell, by voiolenc to have it Chargabell for his gaine from his quarters and if ani in magestrasy be not so as ther pack horses thay will be trumpating for inovation or war.

5th: 12m: 1675. *Roadiesland.*

JOHN EASTON

THE EDITORS' COMMENT

John Easton, a Quaker, was the deputy governor of Rhode Island. His *Relacion* was one of the first full narratives of King Philip's War to circulate in the colonies. Unlike later narratives published by Puritan ministers Increase Mather (1676) and William Hubbard (1677), Easton's narrative was written with the aim of halting the conflict, and he advocated for diplomatic solutions. Easton's narrative is one of the only accounts of the war that included and acknowledged Wampanoag motivations and reasonings. He recounted a council he had had with Metacom (Philip) and his counselors on the eve of war, in which the Wampanoag leaders emphasized the dire conditions they faced in regard to dispossession and displacement from their lands and decried the deceitful ways in which colonial leaders from Plymouth and Massachusetts Bay sought to disempower their leaders. Easton was sympathetic to his neighbors on all sides, and believed the violence of war could have been avoided through fair diplomacy. In contrast, Puritan accounts, such as those written by Nathaniel Saltonstall, Mather, and Hubbard, described the war, from its beginning, as an inevitable and necessary defense against "insolent" Indians "skulking" on the edges of Plymouth Colony settlements, in a planned conspiracy against the English. Easton's account, which allowed for multiple points of view and described a more complex political environment, may be the most accurate English-authored assessment of the origins of the war. It is also an important testimonial that arose in the midst of the chaos of violence. The original manuscript of Easton's *Relacion* is held by the New York State Library. It was first published in Albany in 1858, edited by Franklin B. Bough.

John Easton to Josiah Winslow

Frind Josiah Winslow Governor of Plimoth Colony—

Weetomuw the quene of Pocaset and hir husband, showd mee a leter Constant Southworth and others names to it dated aprell 30: 75 by which thay have great feare of opretion from the English, that thay could not tell how to trust mee, but that I wold to pleas—English joyne to do them rong therfore did not shew mee the leter untill the 24: of may alltho I had informed theme that I take my self as much ingadged that thay should not be ronged as if thay wer my Cuntry men, and I of ther nation and ingadged on of ther counsell to his ruler or landlord and I so understood that I did not take that to be good to my self or English which was by hurte to any and thay had purchased of mee so to promise them,—when I herd what thay informed me of ther Case I saied if it were true ther Case was good but I could no otherwise be absolute without I had heard both partys thay and Plimoth men wold defer them selfs as you thoft was for yourselefs and that later told [   ] judgmentes allredy I saied in such Cases I thoft you wold be willing to have it [   ] and here what Indians could say and so do as for what was [   ] and for that to take place—I earnestly desier you may so deall with them for acording to right I wold have them in submition to you the Case why thay so much stand upon for what thay wold now have ther bounds north and south is to maintaine a river at each end by which thay have gret dependanc for fish, but ar free to acomodat thee or home they shall admit with thee of fouer mile square of land at least at the hed of dartmoth bounds and of the lotes on the other side of the fales river and dout not but by having ther other bounds confirmed in your records thay shall agree to what more they will give them thay prefer so faier and as it apereth to mee desier only of you what is ther resonabell dew that I have larg hope you will not deny it and to have the diferanc desided as to them it may apere not to be by such as determen in ther own Case I am perswaided both mai be so satesfied, I am largly ingadged in my self to manefest to them that I am not falce, but to indever thay may have right acording to English Law and hope it will not be in ani oposition to your desires or to your ruell in your Colony I know about 60 have confirmrd to the quens right to be to a far greter tract of land beside what now shee and thay would be contented with—if you will proseed to try the Case at your Court I having a gret desier that thay may not be scared to do rong, alltho I desier as much as any thay mai fear for having dun rong. I will be hir bayle if you will order it so as I may have a opertunity and if I can atend to maneg hir Case or send an aturny if thou canst be an instrument for ther peasabell setellment and by a way of peace thay promis not to be ungratfull so I am thy true frind as it mai not be hurt to ani willing to serve thee.

John Easton

26: 3m: 1675

THE EDITORS' COMMENT

Although Easton's *Relacion* is fairly well-known, this letter existed only in manuscript within a Boston archive, receiving little to no attention until the twenty-first century. However, Easton's letter is one of the most vital statements regarding the "great fear of oppression from the English" that Wampanoag leaders like Weetamoo and Metacom faced. Easton composed the letter to Plymouth governor Josiah Winslow on May 26, 1675, one month before the outbreak of King Philip's War. According to the document, the Wampanoag Sôkusgâ Weetamoo asked Easton to write the letter on her behalf, requesting that the "bounds" of Pocasset be set by her and recorded by the Plymouth Court. This document is among several that shows that Weetamoo had begun to adopt the form of the English deed to protect the land on which her community depended. It is also important to note that Easton and several other settlers were ready to testify to Weetamoo's authority and her rightful claim. In the letter he referred to Weetamoo as a "Queen," an English interpretation of Sôkushgâ, although that title is not entirely accurate. Still, with this English title Easton conveyed the respect he held for Weetamoo and for her position. Moreover, understanding the ways in which the colonial legal system operated, Easton offered to serve as her "attorney" if necessary. Both the letter to Winslow and the *Relacion* convey the primacy of land in Wampanoag complaints about settler encroachment, particularly from Plymouth Colony. Together, they also demonstrate that both Weetamoo and Metacom were trying to pursue diplomatic solutions and the protection of their communities' rights in the months leading up to the war, which broke out in Wampanoag country and Plymouth Colony in late June 1676.

John Brown
to
Josiah Winslow

Swansey June 11: 1675

Sir some lines of mine I understand came to your hand Unexpected to you and not intended by me the hast & Rudenes
whereof I did intend to excuse to the person to whom I did
direct it. the matter where of I still beleve for they have bin
and are in arms to this day as appears by the witness of Inglish
of Credit yea this day there is above 60 double armed men
and they stand upon ther gard on reason say they is because
they heare you intend to send for phillip but they have sent
there wifes to Narrogansent all or some and an Indian told
me this day That he saw 20 men came to phillip from Coweset
side and they flock to him from Narroganset Coweset pocasset showomet Assowomset from whence ther Came 3 men the
Last nigh well armed after there Coming to phillips town &
ower within night they gave us an Alarm by 2 guns & 1 in
the morning before day and the continued warninge of the
drum and the above said Indian told me that he heard that
the passages betwixt tanton & us were garded by Indians and
that the younger sort were much set Againts the Inglish and
this day one Indian Leift both work and wages saying he wase
sent for to fight with the Inglish within 2 dayes the truth is
they are in a posture of war there has bin sene above 150 toge-
athere at once how many in private there be we know not but
for further intelligence the bearer is able to informe Sir I reit
onely this by my Commision I have not power to set awash the
Lawes are unserten the providence of god hath prevented me
from Weighting uppoun you for enlargement here in. theres

not appointed a councell of war in our town I thought good
to aquaint you here with I am in hast And Reit youres to serve

John Brown

Narragansett.
Cowesett between the Narragansett Country (properly so
called) and Pawcatuck River
Pocasset—Tiverton
Shawomet—Warwick
Assawomsett—Middleboro

THE EDITORS' COMMENT

This oft cited letter from the Massachusetts Historical Society provides a snapshot of a colony on the precipice of war. Following the execution in early June of three Wampanoag counselors for the purported murder of Massachusett interpreter and informant John Sassamon, the fear from oppression of which Weetamoo had spoken increased dramatically. Rumors circulated that Plymouth was amassing an army to move on the Montaup, the peninsula in Pokanoket territory, with the goal of apprehending Metacom. On June 11, 1675, Plymouth Colony magistrate and Swansea resident John Brown reported to Josiah Winslow on the rising tensions. He described the arrival in Pokanoket territory of men from Narragansett country as well as from neighboring Wampanoag homelands like Coweset and Pocasset, stirring rumors of an Indian uprising. Brown likewise noted that Wampanoag families were traveling from Montaup to Narragansett in fear of an assault by Plymouth. As Easton related, "the English were afraid and Philip was afraid, and both increased in Arms." In writing to Winslow, John Brown sought clarification of the governor's intentions and his own capacity to act. Brown noted his uncertainty about the powers of war that he might possess "by" his "commission," most likely referring to his role as a captain, and his concern about the lack of a council of war or clarity in the law. This man was the grandson of the "John Brown" who participated with Edward Winslow and Ousamequin in the original Seekonk agreement.

Thomas Church and Benjamin Church: from *Entertaining Passages Relating to Philip's War (I)*

IN the Year 1674, Mr. *Benjamin Church* of *Duxbury* being providentially at *Plymouth* in the time of the Court, fell into acquaintance with Capt. *John Almy* of *Rhode-Island*. Capt. *Almy* with great importunity invited him to ride with him, and view that part of *Plymouth* Colony that lay next to *Rhode-Island*, known then by their Indian Names of *Pocasset* & *Sogkonate*. Among other arguments to perswade him, he told him, the Soil was very rich, and the Situation pleasant. Perswades him by all means, to purchase of the Company some of the Court grant rights. He accepted his invitation, views the Country, & was pleased with it; makes a purchase, settled a Farm, found the Gentlemen of the Island very Civil & obliging. And being himself a Person of uncommon Activity and Industry, he soon erected two buildings upon his Farm, and gain'd a good acquaintance with the Natives: got much into their favour, and was in a little time in great esteem among them.

The next Spring advancing, while Mr. *Church* was diligently Settling his new Farm, stocking, leasing & disposing of his Affairs, and had a fine prospect of doing no small things; and hoping that his good success would be inviting unto other good Men to become his Neighbours; Behold! the rumour of a War between the *English* and the Natives gave check to his projects. People began to be very jealous of the *Indians*, and indeed they had no small reason to suspect that they had form'd a design of War upon the *English*. Mr. *Church* had it daily suggested to him that the Indians were plotting a bloody design. That *Philip* the great *Mount-hope* Sachem was Leader therein: and so it prov'd, he was sending his Messengers to all the Neighbouring Sachems, to ingage them in a Confederacy with him in the War.

Among the rest he sent Six Men to *Awashonks* Squaw-Sachem of the *Sogkonate* Indians, to engage her in his Interests: *Awashonks* so far listened unto them as to call her Subjects together, to make a great Dance, which is the custom of that Nation when they advise about Momentous Affairs. But what does *Awashonks* do, but sends away two of her Men that well understood the *English* Language (*Sassamon* and *George* by Name) to invite Mr. *Church* to the Dance. Mr. *Church* upon the Invitation, immediately takes with him *Charles Hazelton* his Tennants Son, who well understood the *Indian* Language, and rid down to the Place appointed: Where they found hundreds of *Indians* gathered together from all Parts of her Dominion. *Awashonks* her self in a foaming Sweat was leading the Dance. But she was no sooner sensible of Mr. *Churches* arrival, but she broke off, sat down, calls her Nobles round her, orders Mr. *Church* to be invited into her presence. Complements being past, and each one taking Seats. She told him, King *Philip* had sent Six Men of his with two of her People that had been over at *Mount-hope*, to draw her into a confederacy with him in a War with the *English*. Desiring him to give her his advice in the case, and to tell her the Truth whether the *Umpame* Men (as *Philip* had told her) were gathering a great Army to invade *Philips* Country. He assured her he would tell her the Truth, and give her his best advice. Then he told her twas but a few days since he came from *Plymouth*, and the *English* were then making no Preparations for War; That he was in Company with the Principal Gentlemen of the Government, who had no Discourse at all about War; and he believ'd no tho'ts about it. He ask'd her whether she tho't he would have brought up his Goods to Settle in that Place, if he apprehended an entering into War with so near a Neighbour. She seem'd to be somewhat convin'd by his talk, and said she believ'd he spoke the Truth.

Then she called for the *Mount-hope* Men: Who made a formidable appearance, with their Faces Painted, and their Hair Trim'd up in Comb-fashion, with their Powder-horns, and Shot-bags at their backs; which among that Nation is the posture and figure of preparedness for War. She told Mr. *Church*, these were the Persons that had brought her the Report of the

English preparation for War: And then told them what Mr. *Church* had said in answer to it.

Upon this began a warm talk among the Indians, but 'twas soon quash'd, and *Awashonks* proceeded to tell Mr. *Church*, that *Philips* Message to her was, that unless she would forthwith enter into a confederacy with him in a War against the *English*, he would send his Men over privately, to kill the *English* Cattel, and burn their Houses on that side the River, which would provoke the *English* to fall upon her, whom they would without doubt suppose the author of the Mischief. Mr. *Church* told her he was sorry to see so threatning an aspect of Affairs; and steping to the *Mount-hopes*, he felt of their bags, and finding them filled with Bullets, ask'd them what those Bullets were for: They scoffingly reply'd to shoot *Pigeons* with.

Then Mr. *Church* turn'd to *Awashonks*, and told her, if *Philip* were resolv'd to make War, her best way would be to knock those Six *Mount-hopes* on the head, and shelter her self under the Protection of the *English*: upon which the *Mount-hopes* were for the present Dumb. But those two of *Awashonks* Men who had been at *Mount-hope* express'd themselves in a furious manner against his advice. And *Little Eyes* one of the Queens Council joyn'd with them, and urged Mr. *Church* to go aside with him among the bushes that he might have some private Discourse with him, which other Indians immediately forbid being sensible of his ill design: but the Indians began to side and grow very warm. Mr. *Church* with undaunted Courage told the *Mount-hopes* they were bloody wretches, and thirsted after the blood of their *English* Neighbours, who had never injur'd them, but had always abounded in their kindness to them. That for his own part, tho' he desired nothing more than Peace, yet if nothing but War would satisfie them, he believed he should prove a sharp thorne in their sides; Bid the Company observe those Men that were of such bloody dispositions, whether Providence would suffer them to Live to see the event of the War, which others more Peaceably disposed might do.

Then he told *Awashonks* he thought it might be most advisable for her to send to the Governour of *Plymouth*, and shelter her self, and People under his Protection. She lik'd his advice, and desired him to go on her behalf to the *Plymouth* Government, which he consented to: And at parting advised her what ever she did, not to desert the *English* Interest, to joyn with her Neighbours in a Rebellion which would certainly prove fatal to her. [He mov'd none of his Goods from his House that there might not be the least umbrage from such an Action.] She thank'd him for his advice, and sent two of her Men to guard him, to his House, which when they came there, urged him to take care to secure his Goods, which he refused for the reasons before mentioned. But desired the *Indians*, that if what they feared, should happen, they would take care of what he left, and directed them to a Place in the woods where they should dispose them; which they faithfully observed.

He took his leave of his guard, and bid them tell their Mistress, if she continued steady in her dependence on the *English*, and kept within her own limits of *Sogkonate*, he would see her again quickly; and then hastned away to *Pocasset*, where he met with *Peter Nunnuit*, the Husband of the Queen of *Pocasset*, who was just then come over in a Canoo from *Mount-hope*. *Peter* told him that there would certainly be War; for *Philip* had held a Dance of several Weeks continuance, and had entertain'd the Young Men from all Parts of the Country: And added that *Philip* expected to be sent for to *Plymouth* to be examined about *Sasamon*'s death, who was Murder'd at *Assawomset*-Ponds; knowing himself guilty of contriving that Murder. The same *Peter* told him that he saw Mr. *James Brown* of *Swanzey*, and Mr. *Samuel Gorton* who was an Interpreter, and two other Men who brought a Letter from the Governour of *Plymouth* to *Philip*. He observ'd to him further, that the Young Men were very eager to begin the War, and would fain have kill'd Mr. *Brown*, but *Philip* prevented it; telling them, that his Father had charged him to shew kindness to Mr. *Brown*. In short, *Philip* was forc'd to promise them that on the next Lords-Day when the *English* were gone to Meeting they should rifle their Houses, and from that time forward kill their Cattel.

Peter desir'd Mr. *Church* to go and see his Wife, who was but up the hill; he went and found but few of her People with her. She said they were all gone, against her Will to the Dances; and she much fear'd there would be a War. Mr. *Church* advis'd her to go to the Island and secure her self, and those that were with her; and send to the Governour of *Plymouth* who she knew was her friend; and so left her, resolving to hasten to *Plymouth*, and wait on the Governour: and he was so expeditious that he was with the Governour early next Morning, tho' he waited on some of the Magistrates by the way, who were of the Council of War, and also met him at the Governours. He gave them an account of his observations and discoveries, which confirmed their former intelligences, and hastned their preparation for Defence.

THE EDITORS' COMMENT

Entertaining Passages Relating to Philip's War was published in 1716, by Benjamin Church's son, Thomas, who based the narrative on his father's oral accounts and notes. The narrative portrays the elder Church as a chivalrous hero who performed a difficult but necessary role to protect the colony during the "Indian wars." The book was first published in 1716 by Boston printer Bartholomew Green and a second edition was published in 1772 by Solomon Southwick in Providence, Rhode Island. Nineteenth-century antiquarians Samuel Gardner Drake and Henry Dexter published subsequent editions in 1825 and 1865. Dexter noted that Church's account was more "materials toward a memoir" than "such a Memoir itself." Among the "first born sons," Benjamin Church was born in Plymouth/Patuxet in 1639. Like his father Thomas, he was a carpenter. However, after he married Constant Southworth's daughter Alice, Benjamin's fortune changed. In the narrative, Church portrays his acquisition of fertile lands in Sakonnet as happenstance. However, deeds and court records reveal that Church played a leading role in acquiring deeds for Wampanoag lands at Sakonnet, Pocasset, and Nemasket on behalf of Plymouth, including lots he secured for himself and for the colony. Church also portrays King Philip's War as a conflict instigated by Indigenous people that arose amid his peaceful settlement, rather than the result of ongoing land disputes. In the narrative, Church appears effective both in chivalrous protection of female Wampanoag leaders and in manly defense of English settlements. In contrast, the documents show that Church led military expeditions into both Awashonks's and Weetamoo's territories early in the war. The narrative includes an account of Church's pursuit of Metacom in August 1676, following his capture of Metacom's wife and son (see pp. 988–992 in this volume). Although Church led the forces that captured the Wampanoag leader, he attributed Metacom's death to Alderman, a Wampanoag scout from Pocasset. William Apess highlighted Alderman's act in his frontispiece to the *Eulogy on King Philip* (included in this volume), to call attention to colonial "divide-and-conquer" strategies.

Josiah Winslow to Weetamoo and Ben

To Weetamoo, and Ben her husband
Satchems of pocasset
Freinds and Neighbors
I am informed that phillip the sachem of Mount hope contrary to his many promises and ingagements; and that upon no provocation nor unfairness in the least from us, but meerly from his owne base groundles feare is Creating new trobles to himself & us; And hath indeavored to ingage you & your people with him, by intimations of notoriouse falshoods as if wee were secretly designeing mischeef to him, and you, such unmanly treacherouse practices as wee abhor to thinke of, and that hee hath also [   ] against you if you shall deny to help him; I am [   ] hath prevayled very little with you, except it bee to some few of your giddy inconsiderate young men; if it bee fact, as I am willing to believe it may; you shall finde us allwayes redy to acknowledge & incourage your faith fullness, and protect you also so farr as in us lyeth from his pride & tirany; And if you Contynew faithfull, you shall assuredly reape the fruite of it to your Comfort, when hee by his pride & treachery hath wrought his owne ruine. As a testimony of your contynued friendship I desire you will give us what intelligence you may have, or shall gather up, that is of concernment, and you shall not finde mee ungratefull, who am and desire to contynew

your reall freind
Jos: Winslow

Marshfeild
June 15 · 75

THE EDITORS' COMMENT

This document, written by Plymouth governor Josiah Winslow to Wampanoag Sôkushgâ Weetamoo and her husband Petono-wowet, or Ben, was delivered to Weetamoo on the eve of war, after Benjamin Church was sent to negotiate with her at Pocasset on June 7. The letter demonstrates Weetamoo's importance; Winslow sought her neutrality even as he was building a force and a case for the invasion of Montaup and capture of Metacom. This letter, along with other documents, provides a contrast to Church's portrayal of Weetamoo, in accordance with English gender norms, as a worried, uncertain woman torn between two sides. Winslow sent this letter to Weetamoo, as a neighboring leader, at the same time he sent letters to the neighboring governors of Rhode Island and Massachusetts Bay, seeking their assistance. Weetamoo subsequently gave shelter to Metacom, her sister Wootonakanuske, and their Wampanoag kin following the outbreak of war in Wampanoag country. When the combined colonial troops of Plymouth and Massachusetts Bay arrived at Montaup on June 30, 1675, Metacom and the Wampanoag families had already crossed the Taunton River and taken shelter in the cedar swamps of Pocasset. After this failed attempt to capture Metacom, colonial troops divided to attempt to track him and his warriors in the wider Wampanoag homeland. As families gathered at Pocasset, Wampanoag warriors struck key towns in Plymouth Colony, creating vital diversions and inspiring fear, drawing attention away from this sanctuary.

Roger Williams to John Winthrop, Jr.

To my much honored kind friend Mr. John
Winthrop, Governor of Connecticut, present.

From Mr. SMITH'S AT NAHIGONSIK, June 25, 1675.

SIR,—This inclosed of a former date comes to my hand again at Mr. Smith's. Mr. Smith is now absent at Long Island. Mrs. Smith, though too much favoring the Foxians (called Quakers) yet she is a notable spirit for courtesy toward strangers, and prays me to present her great thanks for your constant remembrance of her, and of late by Capt. Atherton.

Sir, this morning are departed from this house Capt. Hutchinson and two more of Boston Commissioners from the Governor and Council of Boston to the Narragansett and Cowesit Indians. They came (three days since) to my house at Providence, with a letter to myself from the Governor and Council at Boston, praying my advice to their Commissioners and my assistance, &c., in their negotiations with the Narragansett Indians. I, within an half hour's warning) departed with them toward the Narragansett. We had one meeting that night with Quaunoncku, Miantunnomu's youngest son, and upon the opening of the Governor's letters, he readily and gladly assented to all the Governor's desires, and sent post to Mausup, (now called Canonicus), to the Old Queen, Ninicraft and Quawnipund, to give us a meeting at Mr. Smith's. They being uncivil and barbarous, and the Old Queen (especially timorous, we condescended to meet them all near the great pond, at least ten miles from Mr. Smith's house. We laid open the Governor's letter: and accordingly they professed to hold no agreement with Philip, in this his rising against the English. They professed (though Uncas had sent twenty to Philip, yet) they had not sent one nor would: that they had prohibited all their people from going on that side, that those of their people who had made marriages with them, should return or perish there: that if Philip or his men fled to them, yet they would not receive them, but deliver them up unto the English.

They questioned us why Plymouth pursued Philip. We answered: he broke all laws, and was in arms of rebellion against that Colony, his ancient friends and protectors, though it is believed that he was the author of murdering John Sossiman, for revealing his plots to the Governor of Plymouth, and for which three actors were two weeks since executed at Plymouth, (though one broke the rope, and is kept in prison until their Court in October.)

2. They demanded of us why the Massachusetts and Rhode Island rose, and joined with Plymouth against Philip, and left not Philip and Plymouth to fight it out. We answered that all the Colonies were subject to one King Charles, and it was his pleasure, and our duty and engagement, for one English man to stand to the death by each other, in all parts of the world.

Sir, two particulars the Most Holy and Only Wise made use of to engage (I hope and so do the Commissioners) in earnest to enter into those aforesaid engagements.

First, the sense of their own danger if they separate not from Plymouth Indians, and Philip their desperate head. This argument we set home upon them, and the Bay's resolution to pursue Philip (if need be) and his partakers with thousands of horse and foot, beside the other Colonies, &c.

3. Their great and vehement desire of justice upon Tatuphosuit, for the late killing of a Narragansett young man of account with them, which point while we were discoursing of, and their instance with me to write to the Governor and Council of Massachusetts about it (which I have this morning done by their Commissioners) in comes (as from Heaven) your dear son Major Winthrop to our assistance, who affirmed that he saw Tatuphosuit sent bound to Hartford jail, and his father Uncas, taking boat with him. The Sachems said they knew it, and had written about it (by my letter inclosed) to yourself: but they were informed that he was set free, and was keeping his Nicommo, or dance in triumph, &c. Your son replied that either it was not so, or if it were, it was according to your law of leaving Indians to Indian justice, which if neglected you would then act, &c. In fine, their earnest request was that either Tatuphosuit might have impartial justice, (for many reasons,

or else they might be permitted to right themselves, which the Commissioners thought might be great prudence (in this juncture of affairs) that these two nations, the Narragansetts and Mohegans might be taken off from assisting Philip (which passionately he endeavors), and the English may more securely and effectually prosecute the quenching of this Philippian fire in the beginning of it. The last night they have (as is this morning said) slain five English of Swansey, and brought their heads to Philip, and mortally wounded two more, with the death of one Indian. By letters from the Governor of Plymouth to Mr. Coddington, Governor of Rhode Island, we hear that the Plymouth forces (about two hundred) with Swansey and Rehoboth men, were this day to give battle to Philip. Sir, my old bones and eyes are weary with travel and writing to the Governors of Massachusetts and Rhode Island, and now to yourselves. I end with humble cries to the Father of Mercies to extend his ancient and wonted mercies to New England, and am, Sir,

Your most unworthy Servant,
ROGER WILLIAMS.

Mrs. Smith earnestly desires your loving advice to her husband, to lay by his voyage to England: partly by reason of his inward grief, and also that his business may be transacted by delegation. She prays you also to consider your own age and weakness, and not to lay your precious bones in England.

Sir, my humble respects to your honored Council.

ROGER WILLIAMS.

From MR. SMITH'S, 27 June, 75, (so called.)

SIR,—Since my last (enclosed) the next day after the departure of Capt. Hutchinson and the messengers from Boston, a party of one hundred Narragansett Indians, armed, marched to Warwick, which, as it frightened Warwick, so did it also the inhabitants here; though since we hear that the party departed from Warwick without blood shedding: however, it occasioned the English here (and myself) to suspect that all the fine words from the Indian Sachems to us were but words of policy, falsehood and treachery: especially since now the English testify, that for divers weeks (if not months) canoes passed to and again (day and night between Philip and the Narragansetts) and the Narragansett Indians have committed many robberies on the English houses. Also, it is thought that Philip durst not have proceeded so far, had he not been assured to have been seconded and assisted by the Mohegans and Narragansetts.

Two days since, the Governor and Council of Rhode Island sent letters and messengers to Mausup (Canonicus) inviting him to come to them to Newport, and assuring him of safe conduct to come and depart in safety. His answer was, that he could not depart from his child which lay sick: but (as he had assured the Boston messengers) so he professed to these from Newport, that his heart affected and sorrowed for the English, that he could not rule the youth and common people, nor persuade others, chief amongst them, except his brother Miantunnomu's son, Nananautunu. He advised the English at Narragansett to stand upon their guard, to keep strict watch, and, if they could, to fortify one or more houses strongly, which if they could not do, then to fly. Yesterday, Mrs. Smith (after more, yea, most of the women and children gone) departed in a great shower, by land, for Newport, to take boat in a vessel four miles from her house. Sir, just now comes in Sam. Dier in a catch from Newport, to fetch over Jireh Bull's wife and children, and others of Puttaquomscutt He brings word that last night Caleb Carr's boat (sent on purpose to Swansey for tidings) brought word that Philip had killed twelve English at Swansey, (the same Canonicus told us,) and that Philip sent three heads to them, but he advised a refusal of them, which some say was done, only the old Queen rewarded the bringers for their travel. Caleb Carr saith also, that one English sentinel was shot in the face and slain by an Indian that crept near unto him: that they have burnt about twelve houses, one new great one (Anthony Loes): that Philip had left his place, being a neck, and three hundred of Plymouth English, Swansey and others know not where he is, and therefore Capt. Oliver (being at Mr. Brown's) rode post to Boston for some hundreds of horse: that some hurt they did about Providence, and some say John Scot, at Pawtucket ferry, is slain. Indeed, Canonicus advised the English to take heed of remaining in lone out places, and of travelling in the common roads.

Sir, many wish that Plymouth had left the Indians alone, at least not to put to death the three Indians upon one Indian's testmony, a thing which Philip fears; and that yourselves (at this juncture) could leave the Mohegans and Narragansetts to themselves as to Tatuphusoit, if there could be any just way by your General Court found out for the preventing of their conjunction with Philip, which so much concerneth the peace of New England. Upon request of the Government of Plymouth, Rhode Island hath set out some sloops to attend Philip's motions by water and his canoes: it is thought he bends for an escape to the Islands. Sir, I fear the enclosed and this will be grievous to those visible spirits, which look out at your windows: mine, I am sure to complain, &c., yet I press them for your and the public sake, for why is our candle, yet burning, but to glorify our dreadful former, and in making our own calling and election sure, and serving God in serving the public in our generation.

Your unworthy servant,
ROGER WILLIAMS.

THE EDITORS' COMMENT

In 1643, Roger Williams published his *Key into the Language of America*, a bilingual text that translates biblical concepts into Narragansett and imagines dialogues among English- and Narragansett-speaking people. He was expelled from Massachusetts Bay Colony in 1635 for his radical religious beliefs and established a trading post on Narragansett lands in 1636, where he relied on diplomacy with Narragansett leaders for access to trade routes and permission to settle on their lands. Because of his linguistic knowledge and his relationships with Narragansett leaders, Williams frequently served in the role of translator and diplomatic intermediary for Plymouth and Massachusetts Bay colonies. In 1675, as Plymouth settlers continued to encroach on Wampanoag lands and Plymouth executed several of Philip's men, Williams continued to translate messages between settlers and Narragansetts, while also urging Massachusetts Bay and Rhode Island settlers to distance themselves from Plymouth and affirm their trustworthiness to the Narragansetts. The three letters included in this volume, to Connecticut Colony governor John Winthrop, Jr. and Massachusetts Bay governor John Leverett (see pp. 921–23), reflect information Williams was receiving from his Narragansett contacts. Williams relayed messages from meetings with Narragansett leaders, including Canonicus, Canonchet, and the Saunkskwa Quaiapin (whom Williams calls the "Old Queen"), including their queries as to why Plymouth insisted on pursuing Philip, and he relayed information about Philip's supposed plan of attack. He also recalled his conversation with Canonchet, following the Narragansett leader's diplomatic council with Leverett in October 1675. Williams's letters reflect the perspective of someone who knew Narragansett and other Indigenous leaders well and who, while allied with other settlers, conveyed the messages of Indigenous leaders hoping to see peace continue in their homelands. Narragansett leaders only fully entered the war as a result of the Great Swamp massacre in December 1675, when troops from the United Colonies (Massachusetts Bay, Plymouth, and Connecticut), led by Josiah Winslow, killed and imprisoned hundreds of Narragansett and Wampanoag families.

John Freeman to Josiah Winslow, July 3, 1675

HONOURED GOVERNOR,

WE are a distressed people. We hear nothing since from the army. We find the enemy is dispersed through the wilderness; they are, as we judge, round about us. This morning, three of our men are slain, close by one of our courts of guard; houses burnt in our fight; our men being so picked off out of every bush and so few of them, dare not issue out, I have sent to governor Leverett for forty or fifty men and arms. We are forced to keep our courts of guard, and we are not capable to withstand the enemy, though we see houses burning before our eyes. I pray send some arms to us, if you can, and some to our southern towns. *Eastham* hath, as I think, not twenty good arms in it. I pray give them instruction how to manage things for their security, for they much want help. We expect this night to be further surprised by the enemy. We see their design is not to face the army; but to keep a flying army about the woods, to fall on us and our army, as they have advantage. I judge there should be what Indians may be engaged in the quarrel for us, which must hunt them out for us, or else our English will be disheartened to travel about in the woods, and get nothing but a clap with a bullet out of every bush. The Lord humble us for our sins, which are the procuring causes of God's judgments, and remember mercy, and bestow it on us, is the prayer of your unworthy servant,

JOHN FREEMAN.

Taunton, the 3d of the 4th month, 1675.

P. S. I have received yours this instant, with much thankfulness, hoping we shall improve your instructions.

The men that were slain, were John Tisdill, senior, of Taunton, John Knolles, and Samuel Atkins, of Eastham. John Tisdill's house burned, and James Walker's, as we judge.

THE EDITORS' COMMENT

This document is held by the Massachusetts Historical Society and was published in their *Collections* in 1798. John Freeman offered a firsthand account of the outbreak of King Philip's War from Taunton, a Plymouth Colony settlement at the crossroads of Wampanoag trails, which became a military hub at the beginning of the war. The letter provides an effective and evocative portrait of the settler experience of Wampanoag tactics, more reflective of guerilla or woodland warfare than the organized drills for open-field battle that English colonists had been trained to perform. These tactics included the strategy of quick strikes and elusive dispersal, which Freeman described as "a flying army" that they could neither identify nor anticipate. The letter also evokes the chaos of war, in contrast to the orderly march on Montaup that Josiah Winslow envisioned. The letter lists the names of the English men who were killed in a Wampanoag strike on John Tisdall's house, which was located at the edge of Weetamoo's territory of Pocasset and had been built as part of the recent encroachments on Wampanoag homelands. Freeman also noted that the house of James Walker was burned during this strike. Walker was the chairman of the Council of War in 1675 and had also held that position in 1671, during an earlier attempt at military containment. Tisdall's "farm" was the rendezvous point for the planned strike on Awashonks's village in 1671 and Walker was one of the lead planners. (This letter was dated according to the "Old Style" Julian calendar. The "fourth month" is the month of June, and the letter must have been written after the strike on Tisdall's and Walker's houses on June 27, 1675, probably on July 3.)

Thomas Church and Benjamin Church: from *Entertaining Passages Relating to Philip's War (II)*

Mr. *Church* after their slender breakfast proposed to Capt. *Fuller*, That he would March in quest of the Enemy, with such of the Company as would be willing to March with him; which he complyed with, tho' with a great deal of scruple, because of his small Number, & the extream hazard he foresaw must attend them.

But some of the Company had reflected upon Mr. *Church*, that notwithstanding his talk on the other side of the River, he had not shown them any *Indians* since they came over. Which now mov'd him to tell them, That if it was their desire to see *Indians*, he believ'd he should now soon shew them what they should say was enough.

The Number allow'd him soon drew off to him, which could not be many, because their whole Company consisted of no more than Thirty Six. They mov'd towards *Sogkonate*, until they came to the brook that runs into *Nunnaquohqut* Neck, where they discovered a fresh and plain Track, which they concluded to be from the great Pine Swamp about a Mile from the Road that leads to *Sogkonet*. Now says Mr. *Church* to his Men, If we follow this Track no doubt but we shall soon see *Indians* enough; they express'd their willingness to follow the Track, and mov'd in it, but had not gone far before one of them narrowly escaped being bit with a *Rattle-snake*: And the Woods that the Track lead them through was haunted much with those Snakes, which the little Company seem'd more to be afraid of than the black Serpents they were in quest of, and therefore bent their course another way; to a Place where they thought it probable to find some of the Enemy. Had they kept the Track to the Pine Swamp they had been certain of meeting

Indians enough; but not so certain that any of them should have return'd to give account how many.

Now they pass'd down into *Punkatees* Neck; and in their March discocovered a large Wigwam full of *Indian* Truck, which the Souldiers were for loading themselves with; until Mr. *Church* forbid it; telling them they might expect soon to have their hands full, and business without caring for Plunder. Then crossing the head of the Creek into the Neck, they again discovered fresh, Indian Tracks, very lately pass'd before them into the Neck. They then got privately and undiscovered, unto the Fence of Capt. *Almy*'s Pease-field, and divided into two Parties, Mr. *Church* keeping the one Party with himself, sent the other with *Lake* that was acquainted with the ground, on the other side. Two *Indians* were soon discovered coming out of the Pease-field towards them: When Mr. *Church* & those that were with him concealed themselves from them, by falling flat on the ground: but the other division not using the same caution were seen by the Enemy, which occasioned them to run; which when Mr. *Church* perceiv'd, he shew'd himself to them, and call'd, telling them he desired but to speak with them, and would not hurt them. But they run, and *Church* pursued. The *Indians* clim'd over a Fence and one of them facing about discharged his Piece, but without effect on the *English*: One of the *English* Souldiers ran up to the Fence and fir'd upon him that had discharged his Piece; and they concluded by the yelling they heard that the *Indian* was wounded; but the *Indians* soon got into the thickets, whence they saw them no more for the present.

Mr. *Church* then Marching over a plain piece of Ground where the Woods were very thick on one side; order'd his little Company to March at double distance, to make as big a show (if they should be discovered) as might be. But before they saw any body, they were Saluted with a Volly of fifty or sixty Guns; some Bullets came very surprizingly near Mr. *Church*, who starting, look'd behind him, to see what was become of his Men, expecting to have seen half of them dead, but seeing them all upon their Leggs and briskly firing at the Smokes of the Enemies Guns, (for that was all that was then to be seen) *He Bless'd God, and called to his Men not to discharge all their*

Guns at once, lest the Enemy should take the advantage of such an opportunity to run upon them with their Hatches.

Their next Motion was immediately into the Pease-field. When they came to the Fence Mr. *Church* bid as many as had not discharg'd their Guns, to clap under the Fence, and lye close, while the other at some distance in the Field stood to charge; hoping that if the Enemy should creep to the Fence to gain a shot at those that were charging their Guns, they might be surprized by those that lay under the Fence. But casting his Eyes to the side of the Hill above them; the hill seem'd to move, being covered over with *Indians*, with their bright Guns glittering in the Sun, and running in a circumference with a design to surround them.

Seeing such Multitudes surrounding him and his little Company; it put him upon thinking what was become of the Boats that were ordered to attend him: And looking up, he spy'd them a shore at *Sandy-point* on the Island side of the River, with a number of Horse and Foot by them, and wondred what should be the occasion; until he was afterwards informed, That the Boats had been over that Morning from the Island, and had landed a Party of Men at *Fogland*, that were design'd in *Punkatees* Neck to fetch off some Cattel and Horses, but were Ambuscado'd, and many of them wounded by the Enemy.

Now our Gentlemans Courage and Conduct were both put to the Test, he incourages his Men; and orders some to run and take a Wall to shelter before the Enemy gain'd it. Twas time for them now to think of escaping if they knew which way. Mr. *Church* orders his Men to strip to their white Shirts, that the *Islanders* might discover them to be English Men; & then orders Three Guns to be fired distinct, hoping it might be observ'd by their friends on the opposite Shore. The Men that were ordered to take the Wall, being very hungry, stop'd a while among the Pease to gather a few, being about four Rod from the Wall; the Enemy from behind it hail'd them with a Shower of Bullets; but soon all but one came tumbling over an old hedge down the bank where Mr. *Church* and the rest were, and told him that his Brother *B. Southworth*, who was the Man that was missing, was kill'd, that they saw him fall; and so they did indeed see him fall, but 'twas without a Shot, and lay no longer than till he had opportunity to clap a Bullet into one of the Enemies Forehead, and then came running to his Company. The meanness of the *English*'s Powder was now their greatest misfortune; when they were immediately upon this beset with Multitudes of *Indians*, who possessed themselves of every Rock, Stump, Tree, or Fence that was in sight, firing upon them without ceasing; while they had no other shelter but a small bank & bit of a water Fence. And yet to add to the disadvantage of this little handful of distressed Men; The *Indians* also possessed themselves of the Ruines of a Stone-house that over look'd them, and of the black Rocks to the Southward of them; so that now they had no way to prevent lying quite open to some, or other of the Enemy, but to heap up Stones before them, as they did, and still bravely and wonderfully defended themselves, against all the numbers of the Enemy. At length came over one of the Boats from the Island Shore, but the Enemy ply'd their Shot so warmly to her as made her keep at some distance; Mr. *Church* desired them to send their Canoo a-shore to fetch them on board; but no perswasions, nor arguments could prevail with them to bring their Canoo to shore. Which some of Mr. *Churches* Men perceiving, began to cry out, *For God's sake to take them off, for their Ammunition was spent*, &c. Mr. *Church* being sensible of the danger of the Enemies hearing their Complaints, and being made acquainted with the weakness and scantiness of their Ammunition, fiercely called to the Boatsmaster, and bid either send his Canoo a-shore, or else begone presently, or he would fire upon him.

Away goes the Boat and leaves them still to shift for themselves. But then another difficulty arose; the Enemy seeing the Boat leave them, were reanimated & fired thicker & faster than ever; Upon which some of the Men that were lightest of foot, began to talk of attempting an escape by flight: until Mr. *Church* sollidly convinc'd them of the impracticableness of it; and incouraged them yet, told them, *That he had observ'd so much of the remarkable and wonderful Providence of God hitherto preserving them, that incouraged him to believe with much confidence that God would yet preserve them; that not a hair of their head should fall to the ground; bid them be Patient, Couragious and Prudently sparing of their Ammunition, and*

he made no doubt but they should come well off yet, &c. until his
little Army, again resolve one and all to stay with, and stick by
him. One of them by Mr. *Churches* order was pitching a flat
Stone up an end before him in the Sand, when a Bullet from
the Enemy with a full force stroke the Stone while he was
pitching it an end; which put the poor fellow to a miserable
start, till Mr. *Church* call'd upon him to observe, *How God
directed the Bullets that the Enemy could not hit him when in the
same place, yet could hit the Stone as it was erected.*

While they were thus making the best defence they could
against their numerous Enemies that made the Woods ring
with their constant yelling and shouting: And Night coming
on, some body told Mr. *Church*, they spy'd a Sloop up the
River as far as *Gold-Island*, that seemed to be coming down
towards them: He look'd up and told them *Succour was now
coming, for he believ'd it was Capt.* Golding, *whom he knew to
be a Man for business; and would certainly fetch them off, if he
came*: the Wind being fair, the Vessel was soon with them;
and Capt. *Golding* it was. Mr. *Church* (as soon as they came to
Speak one with another) desired him *to come to Anchor at such
a distance from the Shore that he might veer out his Cable and
ride a float, and let slip his Canoo that it might drive ashore*;
which directions Capt. *Golding* observ'd; but the Enemy gave
him such a warm Salute, that his Sails, Colour, and Stern were
full of Bullet holes.

The Canoo came ashore, but was so small that she would not
bare above two Men at a time; and when two were got aboard,
they turn'd her loose to drive ashore for two more: and the
Sloops company kept the *Indians* in play the while. But when
at last it came to Mr. *Churches* turn to go aboard, he had left
his Hat and Cutlash at the Well where he went to drink, when
he first came down; he told his Company, *He would never go off
and leave his Hat and Cutlash for the* Indians; *they should never
have that to reflect upon him.* Tho' he was much disswaded from
it, yet he would go fetch them. He put all the Powder he had
left into his Gun (and a poor charge it was) and went presenting his Gun at the Enemy, until he took up what he went for;
at his return he discharged his Gun at the Enemy to bid them
farewel, for that time; but had not Powder enough to carry the
Bullet half way to them.

Two Bullets from the Enemy stuck the Canoo as he went on Board, one grazed the hair of his Head a little before; another struck in a small Stake that stood right against the middle of his Breast.

Now this Gentleman with his Army, making in all 20 Men, himself, and his Pilot being numbred with them, got all safe aboard after Six hours ingagement with 300 *Indians*; whose Number we were told afterwards by some of themselves. *A deliverance which that good Gentleman often mentions to the Glory of God, and His Protecting Providence.* The next day meeting with the rest of their little Company, whom he had left at *Pocasset*, (that had also a small skirmish with the *Indians*, and had two Men Wounded) they return'd to the *Mount-hope* Garrison; which Mr. *Church* us'd to call the loosing Fort. Mr. *Church* then returning to the Island to seek Provision for the Army, meets with *Alderman*, a noted *Indian* that was just come over from the *Squaw Sachem's* Cape of *Pocasset*, having deserted from her, and had brought over his Family: Who gave him an account of the State of the *Indians*, and where each of the *Sagamores* head quarters were. Mr. *Church* then discours'd with some who knew the Spot well where the *Indians* said *Weetamores* head quarters were, and offered their Service to Pilot him. With this News he hastned to the *Mount-hope* Garrison. The Army express'd their readiness to imbrace such an opportunity.

All the ablest Souldiers were now immediately drawn off equip'd & dispatch'd upon this design, under the Command of a certain Officer: and having March'd about two Miles, *viz.* until they came to the Cove that lyes *S.W.* from the Mount, where orders was given for an halt. The Commander in Chief told them he thought it proper to take advice before he went any further; called Mr. *Church* and the Pilot, and ask'd them, *How they knew that* Philip *and all his Men were not by that time got to* Weetamores *Camp; or that all her own Men were not by that time return'd to her again?* With many more frightful questions. Mr. *Church* told him, *they had acquainted him with as much as they knew, and that for his part he could discover nothing that need to discourage them from Proceeding, that he thought it so practicable, that he with the Pilot would willingly lead the way to the Spot and hazard the brunt.* But the Chief

Commander insisted on this, *That the Enemies number were so great, and he did not know what numbers more might be added unto them by that time: And his Company so small, that he could not think it practicable to attack them.* Added moreover, *That if he was sure of killing all the Enemy, and knew that he must lose the Life of one of his Men in the action, he would not attempt it.* Pray Sir, then (Reply'd Mr. *Church*) *Please to lead your Company to yonder Windmill on* Rhode-Island, *and there they will be out of danger of being kill'd by the Enemy, and we shall have less trouble to supply them with Provisions.* But return he would, and did, unto the Garrison until more strength came to them: And a Sloop to transport them to the Fall River, in order to visit *Weetamores* Camp. Mr. *Church*, one *Baxter* and Capt. *Hunter* an Indian, profer'd to go out on the discovery on the left Wing; which was accepted; they had not March'd above a quarter of a Mile before they started Three of the Enemy. Capt. *Hunter* wounded one of them in his knee, whom when he came up he discovered to be his near kinsman; the Captive desired favour for his *Squaw*, if she should fall into their hands, but ask'd none for himself, excepting the liberty of taking a Whiff of Tobacco, and while he was taking his Whiff, his kinsman with one blow of his Hatchet dispatch'd him. Proceeding to *Weetamores* Camp, they were discover'd by one of the Enemy, who ran in and gave Information; upon which a lusty Young Fellow left his Meat upon his Spit, running hastily out told his companions, *he would kill an English man before he eat his dinner*: but fail'd of his design, being no sooner out but shot down. The Enemies fires, and what shelter they had was by the Edge of a thick Cedar Swamp, into which on this Alarm they betook themselves; and the English as nimbly pursued; but were soon commanded back by their Chieftain after they were come within hearing of the Crys of their Women, and Children, and so ended that Exploit. But returning to their Sloop the Enemy pursued them and wounded two of their Men. The next day return'd to the *Mount-hope* Garrison.

Soon after this, was *Philips* head Quarters visited by some other *English* Forces; but *Philip* and his gang had the very fortune to escape that *Weetamore* and hers (but now mentioned) had: they took into a Swamp and their pursuers were commanded back. After this *Dartmouths* distresses required

Succour, great Part of the Town being laid desolate, and many of the Inhabitants kill'd; the most of *Plymouth* Forces were order'd thither: And coming to *Russels* Garrison at *Poneganset*, they met with a Number of the Enemy that had surrendred themselves Prisoners on terms promised by Capt. *Eels* of the Garrison; and *Ralph Earl* that perswaded them (by a friend *Indian* he had employed) to come in. And had their promises to the *Indians* been kept, and the *Indians* farely treated, 'tis probable that most if not all the *Indians* in those Parts, had soon followed the Example of those that had now surrendred themselves; which would have been a good step towards finishing the War. But in spite of all that Capt. *Eels, Church*, or *Earl* could say, argue, plead, or beg, some body else that had more Power in their hands improv'd it; and without any regard to the promises made them on their surrendring themselves, they were carry'd away to *Plymouth*, there sold, and transported out of the Country; being about Eight-score Persons. An action so hateful to Mr. *Church*, that he oppos'd it to the loss of the good Will and Respects of some that before were his good Friends. But while these things were acting at *Dartmouth, Philip* made his escape, leaving his Country, fled over *Taunton*-River, and *Rehoboth*-Plain, and *Petuxet*-River, where Capt. *Edmunds* of *Providence* made some spoil upon; and had probably done more, but was prevented by the coming up of a Superiour Officer, that put him by. And now another Fort was built at *Pocasset*, that prov'd as troublesome and chargeable as that at *Mount-hope*; and the remainder of the Summer was improv'd in providing for the Forts and Forces there maintained, while our Enemies were fled some hundreds of Miles into the Country, near as far as *Albany*.

THE EDITORS' COMMENT

Entertaining Passages Relating to Philip's War was published in 1716, by Benjamin Church's son, Thomas, who based the narrative on his father's oral accounts and notes. The narrative portrays the elder Church as a chivalrous hero who performed a difficult but necessary role to protect the colony during the "Indian wars." The book was first published in 1716 by Boston printer Bartholomew Green and a second edition was published in 1772 by Solomon Southwick in Providence, Rhode Island. Nineteenth-century antiquarians Samuel Gardner Drake and Henry Dexter published subsequent editions in 1825 and 1865. Dexter noted that Church's account was more "materials toward a memoir" than "such a Memoir itself." Among the "first born sons," Benjamin Church was born in Plymouth/Patuxet in 1639. Like his father Thomas, he was a carpenter. However, after he married Constant Southworth's daughter Alice, Benjamin's fortune changed. In the narrative, Church portrays his acquisition of fertile lands in Sakonnet as happenstance. However, deeds and court records reveal that Church played a leading role in acquiring deeds for Wampanoag lands at Sakonnet, Pocasset, and Nemasket on behalf of Plymouth, including lots he secured for himself and for the colony. Church also portrays King Philip's War as a conflict instigated by Indigenous people that arose amid his peaceful settlement, rather than the result of ongoing land disputes. In the narrative, Church appears effective both in chivalrous protection of female Wampanoag leaders and in manly defense of English settlements. In contrast, the documents show that Church led military expeditions into both Awashonks's and Weetamoo's territories early in the war. The narrative includes an account of Church's pursuit of Metacom in August 1676, following his capture of Metacom's wife and son (see pp. 988–992 in this volume). Although Church led the forces that captured the Wampanoag leader, he attributed Metacom's death to Alderman, a Wampanoag scout from Pocasset. William Apess highlighted Alderman's act in his frontispiece to the *Eulogy on King Philip* (included in this volume), to call attention to colonial "divide-and-conquer" strategies.

William Bradford to John Cotton

Honoured Sir

After my Best respects p'sented to your selfe & Mrs Cotton this is to Certify of my health, (Blessed be god) though i may say wonderfully p'served by especiall providence, we ralled forth from roade iland the last weke with our one peopell on the maine as far as Cokset & att our returne we found the tracke of the enimi we follow it to a great Swampe entered it but they oute rane us, onli fond thire habitations which we burned and tow old men whome we dispaced. tow dayes after we marched againe and found them hid in an hidious swame, we entred had a hard dispute with them they shot on all sides att us, we followd home to them beate them of thire place, fired thire wigwams slew aboute seven of them, they wounded foure of ours and one of our owne men lost by accidentall providence by one of our owne peopell, here we found thire lugage gote divers pots & kittles of thires, then we returned to mount hope to refresh our selfs met with the bay forces come from Naraganset, then together the last munday marched up into the cuntry, after halfe a days march met with the enimi, who charged upon our Forelorne, kiled tow of ours we followed on and in a great swampe we found thire body we entred in, the bay forces first, the enmi seing it, betooke them selfs to trees & thickets fired thicke upon us we drafe them from thire first station, but sudine the hand of god seemed to be against us we had many slaine and wounded, fife slaine and six wounded & some of them i feare mortall & of these most were Capt Mosles, men & tow of Capt Hinchmams men so we retreated to the water side with our wounded men we toke an old indian in the swame, who told us that philipe & the squa shachem were both thire with thire men

Sir this is the substance of things that hath happenned and what the lord calls us furder to do we are weighting upon hime, desiring to lay our selfs low before hime who will exalt us in his due time, i am a fraid we[   ]ow much in our owne strenght, thirefore th[   ]e of providence upon us, we are now gowing to make another garison on pocasset side towards Roade iland to keepe the enmi from thire corne & the watter side which Capt Hinchman hath undertaken, we & the Bay have written home for furder advice, for we are at a stand, the good lord direct us, all our plimoth men are well. I pray remember me to all my frids especalli to my deare deare wife & childen to home i shall not have now time to write pase by my spelling for i write in great hast your

your sarvant & loving frind
WILL' BRADFORD

from mount hope
  21 July 75

THE EDITORS' COMMENT

William Bradford, Jr., was the eldest son of Governor William Bradford and an officer in the Plymouth company. This letter is a report on the first expeditions on the east side of the Taunton River, Mount Hope Bay, and the Sakonnet River, as colonial forces sought to contain Wampanoag people and locate Metacom, who had evaded capture. Bradford described the troops' scouting in Acoaxet and Sakonnet, Awashonks's territory, and their two attempts to infiltrate the vast cedar swamp at Pocasset to engage and capture Wampanoag people who had taken sanctuary there. On July 18, the Massachusetts Bay and Plymouth forces combined with the intent to invade Pocasset. They were informed by intelligence provided by Benjamin Church and his company of forty men, who had made an earlier expedition to Acoaxet, Sakonnet, and Pocasset, where they were ambushed while scouting the edge of the cedar swamp. On July 19, the Plymouth men, joined by Massachusetts Bay troops, including a company of Native scouts from the Praying Towns, entered the cedar swamp and experienced a barrage of shot from the "trees and thickets," as Wampanoag warriors used camouflage to hide themselves among the foliage. While warriors engaged English troops, Wampanoag families moved northward. Although the combined colonial army failed in their mission to find or capture Wampanoag leaders, Bradford believed that if they remained nearby, establishing a garrison at Pocasset, they could starve them out of the swamp. However, they failed to account for Wampanoag plant knowledge, which enabled them to harvest food within the swamps, or navigational knowledge, which enabled them to move toward shelter within neighboring communities.

Testimony of Peter, George, and David

The 28th of June, 1676, three Indians—the first named Peter, (Awashunckes, the squa sachems son,) the 2cond Gorge, the third David, allies Chowahunna—appeered before the councell, in the behalfe of themselves and other Indians of Saconett to the number of about thirty men, with theire wives and children, and tendered to renew theire peace with the English, and requested libertie to sitt downe in quietnes on theire lands att Saconett.

The Examination of the said Indians before the Councell in Reference to the Premises.

Peter, (Awashuncks son,) being asked the reason of theire coming hither, answered, because hee and the Indians of Saconett desired to settle there againe; unto which was replyed as followeth: What reason have you to expect that youer request heerin should be graunted, since you have broken youer engagements with us by joyning with the sachem Phillip att Mount Hope and other Indians, our professed enimies, and have bin copartenors with them in all assaults and enterprises against us, in which said hostile attemptes many of ours have lost theire lives, habitations, and estates? And you must not thinke that wee can passe over matters of such a high nature soe shighly. Wee are not willing to vallue the blood of our English frinds att soe low a rate. You are never able to make satisfaction for the wronge, nor make good the damage you have don us by youer perfiduous dealings in this respect. Youer way had bine, when you saw the said Phillip and other our enimies to rise up in rebellion against us, to have declined them and repaired to the English, and placed your selves under our protection, &c.

Then Peter said they had not bin active in fighting with the English, but fled away for feare.

Ques. Why did you feare the English?

Ans. When the English army went out, wee were afraid, and desired to go over to Rhode Iland; but the younge men there kept such a strict watch that wee could not get over in saftey.

Then wee were forced to hyde ourselves in swampes; and the English army came and burnt our houses; and wee understanding that the Narragansetts were frinds to the English, wee went to them.

Qustion. Did the Indians burne the English houses before the army came?

Answar. Yee, they burned theire forsaken houses.

Quest. Did the English doe you any wrong att any time, or speak high or threating words to you that scared you? Speake freely, without feare.

Answ. The English never did us any hurt or wronge to this day; if they had, wee would speake of it.

Gorge, another of the three Indians, said, that att the first breakeing forth of the warr, divers of them satt still and minded theire worke att home; but some of theire Indians did then goe to Phillip, and fight with him against the English.

Peter and Gorge againe desired the goverment heer to give them leave to live somewhere within our liberties, and they would be subject to the English, and desired that the English would propound tearmes, and they and all theire companie would consent to them; for they had noe cause to be angry with the English, who had don them noe wronge.

To which wee answered, Wee have found you soe perfiduous, that wee must have some good cecurity for youer fidelitie before wee can graunt youer desires.

Chowohumma, allies David, said, Wee cannot make satisfaction for the wronge don; but if our weemen and children can be cecured, wee will doe any service wee can by fighting against the enimie. They further said, that Succanowassucke was the first man that stired up the Indians to joyne with Philip to fight against the English, and that hee now is att Saconett; and they promise to surprise him if they can, as soon as they returne home; they owned, alsoe, that divers of the Saconett Indians were killed in the fight att Narragansett.

After some time of consideration of the foregoing debate, the councell came to this conclusion, that they would returne the answare:—

Wee take notice of youer tender soe farr as to waite for further probation of youer fidellitie; and in order unto further experience and knowlidge therof, doe appoint you to returne to youer associates againe, and to procure them to our army now abroad; and that you all personally ingage with our commander incheiffe respecting the premises, and to be att his dispose in reference unto improveing any of you in the present expedition against the enimie; and that such as are not improved shall surrender up theire armes to Major Bradford, our commander in cheiffe aforsaid; and, alsoe, that such murdering Indians amongst you that have bin active in crewelty and hostillitie upon any of our English in the takeing away of theire lives and destroying theire estates in a murderous way shalbe delivered up unto the English; and, likewise, that you shall not harbour or retain any strangers of our enimies that may or shall endeavor to shelter themselves amongst you.

The councell alsoe proposed, that if the said Peter, Awashunckes son, were willing, that hee should stay as a hostage; to which hee replyed, hee was willing to stay untill further and matture knowlidge can be taken of theire fidelitie.

In fine, they subjecting themselves and theire estates to his majestie the Kinge of England, &c., our dread sovereign, and to this collonie, it was promised and engaged unto them by the councell, that they shall have a place assigned them for theire present residence in peace; and incase the warr doe sease, and that they approve themselves in faithfulness, peace, and quietnes, and reall to theire ingagements to the English, they shall have a place assigned them for theire improvement and subsistence for longer time and continewance, or otherwise to be disposed of as the councell shall see meet.

THE EDITORS' COMMENT

Peter was the son of Awashonks of Sakonnet. He remained loyal to her even as his brother Mammanuah collaborated with Plymouth Colony to dispossess his mother of her leadership role and land rights before the war. Peter's testimony corresponds with Bradford's account, which alongside other documents provides a more complex narrative of the beginning of the war in Sakonnet than Church's memoir. Peter and his kin testified that many Wampanoags sought to "stay still," that is, remain in their homes in a state of peace, when war first broke out, although some did "go to Philip." Although Peter stood accused of joining with Philip, he testified that he, his mother, and his kin "had not been active in fighting" against the colonists, but "fled away for fear." They sought to steer clear of the conflict, but could not find a safe space to take shelter. He described the fear they faced when the colonial army "went out" to Montaup, then Sakonnet and Pocasset, and their attempt to travel over the Sakonnet River to Rhode Island, which was prevented by English patrols. Thus, Peter testified, they were forced to hide in the swamps at Sakonnet, where Church and Bradford's men "burnt our houses." Eventually they made their way to Narragansett country, where neighboring leaders provided shelter to Wampanoag families, including Weetamoo and her kin. Peter testified during a time when some Native leaders, including Awashonks, were attempting to return to their homelands and broker peace with their former English neighbors, even as the combined Plymouth and Massachusetts Bay forces, including Church, were pursuing the capture and execution of Native people, including both combatants and noncombatants, throughout southern New England. The colonial troops were aided by Native scouts, many of whom were compelled to serve in the campaign by military leaders such as Church, rather than face execution or enslavement, for themselves or their families. The stakes of Peter's testimony were thus quite high. Through their testimony, Peter and his kin sought to return to their places in peace and avoid execution, enslavement, or imprisonment. At the end of this council, the English required that they surrender their arms to William Bradford, Jr., deliver their kin who were active in the war, and that Peter remain as a "hostage" among them.

Josiah Winslow and Thomas Hinckley: "A Brief Narrative of the Beginning and Progress of the Present Trouble"

Plymouth Comissioners Presented this following

NARRATIVE shewing the manor of the begining of the present Warr with the Indians of Mount hope and Pocassett;

A BREIFF Narrative of the begining and progresse of the present trouble between us and the Indians; takeing its Rise in the Collonie of New Plymouth

Anno Domini 1675

NOT to Looke backe further then the troubles that were between the Collonie of New Plymouth and Phillip Sachem of mount hope In the yeer 1671 It may be Remembred that the settlement and Issue of that controversye obtained and made principally by the mediation and Interposed advice and councell of the other two confeaderate Collonies, whoe upon a carefull Inquiry and serch into the grounds of that trouble found that the said Sachems pretence of wronges and Injuries, from that Collonie were Groundles and falce; and that hee (although first in Armes) was the Pecant and offending party; And that Plymouth had Just cause to take up armes against him; And it was then agreed that hee should pay that Collonie a certaine sume of money, in parte of theire damage and charge by him occationed; and hee then not onely renewed his ancient covenant of frendship with them; but made himselfe and his people absolute subjects to our Sovereign: Lord Kinge Charles the second; and to that his Collonie of New Plymouth since which time wee know not that the English of that or any other of the Collonies have bin Injurious to him or his, that might Justly provoake them to take up armes against us;

But somtime the Last winter the Governor of Plymouth was Informed by Sassamon a faithfull Indian that the said Phillip was undoubtedly Indeavoring to Raise new troubles; and was Indeavoring to engage all the Sachems round about in a warr against us some of the English alsoe that lived neare the said Sachem, comunicated theire feares and Jealousyes concurrant with what the Indian had Informed; about a weeke after John Sassamon had given his Information; hee was barbarously murdered by some Indians for his faithfulnes (as wee have cause to beleive) To the Interest of God and of the English; somtime after Sassamons Death Phillip haveing heard that the Governor of Plymouth had received some Information against him and purposed to send for or to him to appeer att theire Next Court that they might Inquire into those Reports, came downe of his own accord to Plymouth a little before theire Court, in the begining of March last; att which time the Councell of that Collonie upon a large debate with him; had great Reason to beleive, that the Information against him might be in substance true, but not haveing full proffe therof and hopeing that the descovery of it soe farr would cause him to desist they dismised him frindly; giveing him onely to understand that if they heare further concerning that matter they might see reason to demaund his Armes to be delivered up for theire securitie; which was according to former agreement between him and them; and hee Ingaged on theire demaund they should be surrendered unto them or theire order; Att that court wee had many Indians in examination concerning the Murder of John Sassamon but had not then testimony in the case but not longe after, an Indian appearing to testify; wee apprehended three by him charged to be the murderers of Sassamon; and cecured them to a triall att our next Court (holden in June) att which time a little before the Court Phillip began to Keep his men in Armes about him and to gather strangers unto him and to march about in Armes towards the uper end of the Necke on which hee lived and neare to the English houses; whoe began therby to be somwhat disquieted, but tooke as yett noe further Notice but onely to sett a milletary watch in the next Townes; as Swansey and Rehoboth some hints wee had that Indians were in Armes whiles our Court was siting but wee hoped it might arise from a guilty feare in Phillip; that wee would send for him and bring him to tryall with the other Murderers; and that if hee saw the Court broken up and hee not sent for; the cloud might blow over; and indeed our Innosensy made us very secure and confident it would not have broken out into a warr But noe sooner was our Court desolved but wee had Intelligence from Leift: John Browne of Swansey that Phillip and his men continewed constantly in Armes, many strang Indians from severall places flocked in to him & that they sent away theire wives to Narragansett; and were giveing our people frequent alarums by drums and guns in the night and Invaded theire passage towards Plymouth; and that theire younge Indians were earnest for a warr; on the 7th of June Mr Benjamine Church being on Rhod Island; Weetamo and some of her cheiffe men told him that Phillip Intended a warr speedily with the English some of them saying that they would healp him; and that hee had alreddy given them leave to kill English mens Cattle and Robb theire houses; about the 14th and 15th of June Mr James Browne went twise to Phillip to perswade him to be quiett but att both times found his men in armes and Phillip very high and not perswadable to peace; on the 14th June our Councell wrot an amicable frindly letter to Phillip therin shewing our dislike of his practices; and adviseing him to dismise his strange Indians and comand his owne men to fall quietly to theire busines that our people might alsoe bee quiett; and not to suffer himselfe to be abused by Reports concerning us, whoe Intended him noe wronge; nor hurt towards him; but Mr Browne could not obtaine an answare from him; on the 17th June Mr Paine of Rehoboth and severall others of the English goeing unarmed to Mount hope to seeke theire horses att Phillips request; the Indians came and presented theire guns att them and carried it very Insolently tho noe way provoaked by them; on the 18th or 19th Job Winslow his house was broken up and Rifled by Phillips men; June the 20th being the sabbath the people att Swansey were alarumed by the Indians two of our Inhabitants burned out of theire houses and theire houses Rifled; and the Indians were marching up as they Judged to assault the Towne; and therfore Intreated speedy healp from us; Wee heerupon the 2i of June sent up some forces to releive that towne and dispached more with speed; on weddensday the 23 of June a dozen more of theire houses att Swansey were

Rifled; on the 24th Thomas layton was slaine att the fall River; on the 25th of June divers of the people att Swansey slaine; and many houses burned untill which time, and for severall daies tho wee had a considerable force there both of our owne and of the Massachusetts (To our Greiffe and shame) they tooke Noe Revenge of the enimie; thus slow were wee and unwilling to engage ourselves and Naighbours in a warr; haveing many Insolencyes almost Intollerable from them, of whose hands wee had deserved better;

The substance of what is heer declared doth clearly more particularly appeer in the Records and letters Related · unto of the severall dates above mensioned;

JOSIAH WINSLOW
THOMAS HINCKLEY

THE EDITORS' COMMENT

This is the official narrative of the Plymouth Colony Commissioners, Winslow and Hinckley, in which they put forth the colony's account of events and their case for a just and necessary war. While Winslow was governor, Hinckley was an Assistant of the Plymouth General Court. Born in England, Hinckley lived in Barnstable, and became the last governor of Plymouth Colony following Winslow's death in 1680. The Plymouth Commissioners delivered this narrative to the other Commissioners of the United Colonies in September 1675. The Commissioners included representatives from Plymouth (Winslow and Hinckley), Massachusetts Bay (Thomas Danforth and William Stoughton), and Connecticut (Governor John Winthrop, Jr., and James Richards, who was by November replaced by Wait Winthrop). With this narrative, Plymouth sought to secure their alliance with Massachusetts Bay and Connecticut and regain control over the discourse, as rumors spread about a conflict that was rapidly spiraling beyond their control.

Statement by the Commissioners of the United Colonies

Wee haveing received from the Comissioners of Plymouth a Narrative shewing the rise and severall stepps of the proceedinge of that Collonie as to the present warr with the Indians; which had its begininge there; and its progresse into the Massachusetts; by theire Insolencyes outrages; murdering many persons and burning theire houses in sundry plantations in both Collonies; and haveing duely considered the same doe declare that the said warr doth appeer to be both Just and Nessesarie; in its first Rise a defensive warr; and therfore wee doe agree and conclude that it ought now to be Joyntly prosecuted by all the united Collonies; and the charges therof to be bourne and payed as is agreed in the articles of Confederation

	THOMAS DANFORTH
JOHN WINTHORPE	WILLAM STAUGHTON
JAMES RICHARDS	JOSIAH WINSLOW
	THOMAS HINCKLEY

The Comissioners of the Collonies haveing fully concurred in the Righteousnes of the present warr with the Barbarous Natives for the better Management therof doe agree and conclude that there be forthwith Raised a Thousand souldiers wherof 500 to be Dragoones or troopers with longe Armes out of the severall Collonies in such proportions as the Articles of Confeaderation doe appoint;

The Massachusetts	527	⎫	
Plymouth -	158	⎬	1000
Conecticot -	315	⎭	

September 9, 1675

THE EDITORS' COMMENT

At their September 1675 meeting, the Commissioners of the United Colonies responded to the narrative presented by Winslow and Hinckley by jointly declaring that the conflict was "a defensive war" that was "both just and necessary," and committing 1,000 soldiers, the majority from Massachusetts Bay. The Commissioners included the narrative in their records for their November 1675 meeting as part of the body of evidence that justified the United Colonies' expedition against the Narragansetts, led by Winslow in December 1675. Many Wampanoags, including Weetamoo, had taken shelter with their Narragansett kin, and the Narragansetts had not complied with the Commissioners' orders to deliver them to the English. Even as the United Colonies issued their declaration of war in November 1675, the Narragansetts were utilizing both Indigenous and English methods to construct a defensive fort in the midst of the Great Swamp, where they gathered the families under their protection. (The fort was located in what is now South Kingston, Rhode Island.)

Roger Williams to John Leverett

PROVIDENCE, 11, 8, 75, so accounted.

SIR,—Yours of the 7th I gladly and thankfully received, and humbly desire to praise that Most High and Holy Hand, invisible and only wise, who casts you down, by so many public and personal trials, and lifts you up again with any (*lucida intervalla*) mitigations and refreshments. *Ab inferno nulla redemptio*: from the grave and hell no return. Here, like Noah's dove, we have our checker work, blacks and whites come out and go into the ark, out and in again till the last, whom we never see back again.

The business of the day in New England is not only to keep ourselves from murdering, our houses, barns, &c., from firing, to destroy and cut off the barbarians, or subdue and reduce them, but our main and principal *opus diei* is, to listen to what the Eternal speaketh to the whole ship, (the country, colonies, towns, &c) and each private cabin, family, person, &c. He will speak peace to his people; therefore, saith David, "I will listen to what Jehovah speaketh." Oliver, in straits and defeats, especially at Hispaniola, desired all to speak and declare freely what they thought the mind of God was. H. Vane (then lain by) wrote his discourse, entitled "A Healing Question," but for touching upon (that *noli me tangere*) State sins, H. Vane went prisoner to Carisbrook Castle, in the Isle of Wight. Oh, Sir, I humbly subscribe (*ex animo*) to your short and long prayer, in your letter. The Lord keep us from our own deceivings. I know there have been, and are, many precious and excellent spirits amongst you, (if you take flight before me, I will then say you are one of them, without daubing,) but *rebus sic stantibus*, as the wind blows, the united colonies dare not permit, *candida et bona fide*, two dangerous (supposed) enemies: 1. dissenting and non-conforming worshippers, and 2. liberty of free (really free) disputes, debates, writing, printing, &c.; the Most High hath begun and given some taste of these two dainties in some parts, and will more and more advance them when (as Luther and Erasmus to the Emperor, Charles V., and the Duke of

Saxony,) those two gods are famished, the Pope's crown and the Monks' bellies. The same Luther was wont to say, that every man had a pope in his belly, and Calvin expressly wrote to Melancthon, that Luther made himself another Pope; yet, which of us will not say, Jeremiah, thou liest, when he tells us (and from God) we must not go down to Egypt?

Sir, I use a bolder pen to your noble spirit than to many, because the Father of Lights hath shown your soul more of the mysteries of iniquity than other excellent heads and hearts dream of, and because, whatever you or I be in other respects, yet in this you will act a pope, and grant me your love, pardon and indulgence.

Sir, since the doleful news from Springfield, here it is said that Philip with a strong body of many hundred cutthroats, steers for Providence and Seekonk, some say for Norwich and Stonington, and some say your forces have had a loss by their cutting off some of your men, in their passing over a river. *Fiat voluntas Dei*, there I humbly rest, and let all go but himself. Yet, Sir, I am requested by our Capt. Fenner to give you notice, that at his farm, in the woods, he had it from a native, that Philip's great design is among all other possible advantages and treacheries) to draw Capt. Mosely and others, your forces, by training and drilling, and seeming flights, into such places as are full of long grass, flags, sedge, &c., and then environ them round with fire, smoke and bullets. Some say no wise soldier will so be caught; but as I told the young prince, on his return lately from you, all their war is commootin; they have commootined our houses, our cattle, our heads, &c., and that not by their artillery, but our weapons; that yet they were so cowardly, that they have not taken one poor fort from us in all the country, nor won, nor scarce fought, one battle since the beginning. I told him and his men, being then in my canoe, with his men with him, that Philip was his cawkakin-namuck, that is, looking glass. He was deaf to all advice, and now was overset, Cooshkowwawy, and catched at every part of the country to save himself, but he shall never get ashore, &c. He answered me in a consenting, considering kind of way, Philip Cooshkowwawy. I went with my great canoe to help him over from Seekonk (for to Providence no Indian comes) to Pawtuxet side. I told him I would not ask him news, for I knew matters were private; only I told him that if he were false to his engagements, we would pursue them with a winter's war, when they should not, as musketoes and rattlesnakes in warm weather, bite us, &c.

Sir, I carried him and Mr. Smith a glass of wine, but Mr. Smith not coming, I gave wine and glass to himself, and a bushel of apples to his men, and being therewith (as beasts are) caught, they gave me leave to say anything, acknowledged loudly your great kindness in Boston, and mine, and yet Capt. Fenner told me yesterday, that he thinks they will prove our worst enemies at last. I am between fear and hope, and humbly wait, making sure, as Haselrig's motto was, sure of my anchor in heaven, *Tantum in Coelis*, only in heaven. Sir, there I long to meet you.

Your most unworthy,
ROGER WILLIAMS.

To Mrs. Leverett, and other honored and beloved friends, humble respects, &c.

Sir, I hope your men fire all the woods before them, &c.

Sir, I pray not a line to me, except on necessary business; only give me leave (as you do) to use my foolish boldness to visit yourself, as I have occasion. I would not add to your troubles.

THE EDITORS' COMMENT

In 1643, Roger Williams published his *Key into the Language of America*, a bilingual text that translates biblical concepts into Narragansett and imagines dialogues among English- and Narragansett-speaking people. He was expelled from Massachusetts Bay Colony in 1635 for his radical religious beliefs and established a trading post on Narragansett lands in 1636, where he relied on diplomacy with Narragansett leaders for access to trade routes and permission to settle on their lands. Because of his linguistic knowledge and his relationships with Narragansett leaders, Williams frequently served in the role of translator and diplomatic intermediary for Plymouth and Massachusetts Bay colonies. In 1675, as Plymouth settlers continued to encroach on Wampanoag lands and Plymouth executed several of Philip's men, Williams continued to translate messages between settlers and Narragansetts, while also urging Massachusetts Bay and Rhode Island settlers to distance themselves from Plymouth and affirm their trustworthiness to the Narragansetts. The three letters included in this volume, to Connecticut Colony governor John Winthrop, Jr. and Massachusetts Bay governor John Leverett (see pp. 921–23), reflect information Williams was receiving from his Narragansett contacts. Williams relayed messages from meetings with Narragansett leaders, including Canonicus, Canonchet, and the Saunkskwa Quaiapin (whom Williams calls the "Old Queen"), including their queries as to why Plymouth insisted on pursuing Philip, and he relayed information about Philip's supposed plan of attack. He also recalled his conversation with Canonchet, following the Narragansett leader's diplomatic council with Leverett in October 1675. Williams's letters reflect the perspective of someone who knew Narragansett and other Indigenous leaders well and who, while allied with other settlers, conveyed the messages of Indigenous leaders hoping to see peace continue in their homelands. Narragansett leaders only fully entered the war as a result of the Great Swamp massacre in December 1675, when troops from the United Colonies (Massachusetts Bay, Plymouth, and Connecticut), led by Josiah Winslow, killed and imprisoned hundreds of Narragansett and Wampanoag families.

Examination and Relation of James Quananopohit

T HE examination & relation of James Quannapaquait, allias
James Rumny-Marsh beeing one of the christian Indians
belonging to Natick; taken the 24th day of Janry 1675–6, on
which day hee returned from his jorney, [for this man and
another called Job of Magungoog, a christian man also] were
sent forth by order of the councill of Massachusetts upon the
last of December, [as spyes], to discover the enemyes quarters
& motions & his state & condition, & to gaine what intelegence they could; for which end they had particuler instruction. Though when first they were moved to goe this jorny,
they saw it would bee a hazardous undertaking, & that they
should runne the hazard of their lives in it, yet they were willing to venture upon these & like considerations (1, that they
might declare their readines to serve the English). 2ly one of
them namly Job had 3 children [even all he had] that were carried away with the Hassanameshe indians &, as he conceived
were with the enemy, & he was willing to know their state as
wel as the condition of the praying indians of Hassameske &
Magunkoog that were hee thought in the power of the enemy.
3d They hoped to sugest somthing in order to the enemies
submission to the English & making peace if they found the
enimy in a temper fit for it & if that could bee effected then
they hoped the poor christian Indians at the Deer Island & in
other places posibly might bee restored to their places againe,
& bee freed from much suffering they are now in by this warre,
& therby the jelosyes that the English have now of them might
bee removed, these & other reasons induced them to runne
this adventure for which also if they returned in safty they had
a promise of a reward.

They doubted the indian enimy would mistrust them for
spyes, & that they would move them [to] fight for them against
the English, unto which doubts they were advised to tell the

925

Indian enemy a lamentable story [& that agreable to truth] of
their deepe sufferings by the English; that Job was imprisoned
severall daies [as hee was] where hee suffered much, though hee
had served the English faithfully as an interprter & in actull
armes being with the Mohegins at the fight neare Secunke
with Philip, the begining of August last, but imprisonment &
suspitions the English had of him was part of his reward for
that service to the English. And as for the other, James, he &
his brother went out with Captian Prentis with their horses &
armes at the first going out against Philipp in June & had done
faithfull service for the English as his captains had testified by
their certificate & continued in their service many weekes &
was in severall fights, & that his bro: Thomas had kild one of
Philip's cheefe men & brought in his head to the Governor
of Boston, & had also in the service by accident lost the use
of his left hand, & that both James and his brother Thomas
had since in November last [beeing called to it] was out with
Captain Syll in the Nipmuck contry & [as his captaine had
certified] had performed faithfull service; & was instrumentall
to recover an English captive Peter Bentt's servant from the
enimey, & his brother savd the lives of two English men at a
wigwam at Pakachooge, vizt Mr Mackarty, servant, a surgeon
to Captian Henchman, & one Goodwin, a soldier of Charles-
towne, as they both could & would testify. Yet after all these
services both they & their wives & children & all their country
men that lived at Naticke were mistrusted by the English &
thereupon [at a few houres warning] brought away from their
place & fort & houses at Naticke & carried down in boats to
Deare Island, leaving & loosing much of their substance, catle,
swine, horse & corn, & at the Hand were exposed to great
sufferings haveing litle wood for fuell, a bleak place & poore
wigwams such as they could make a shift to make themselves
with a few matts, & here at the iland had very little provision,
many of them, & divers other sorrowes & troubles they were
exposed to, & were about 350 soules, men women & children;
& that now haveing an opperfuny to get off the iland they
came to see how things were with the indians in the woods;
& if they preferred them to fight with & for them they were
advised to manifest all readines & forwardnes & not shew any
aversenes. Things being thus prepared these 2 spyes were sent

away without armes excepting hatchetts & with a little parcht
meal for provision, & they tooke their jorny from Cambridge
the 30th of December, & from Natick they set forth the 31th
of December being Friday early in the morning. That day
they past through the woods directly to Hassomesed where
they lodged that night; on Saterday morn, being the first of
Janury they past over Nipmuck River & lodged at Manchage
that night. On the 2 Janury they went forward to Maanexit
which is about 10 miles & there they met with seaven Indians
of the enimy: some of them had armes; having confered with
these indians they were conducted by those indians next day
to Quabaage old fort where they met severall other Indians of
their company's; & by them the next day were conducted to
the enemies quarters which is about twenty miles northward
of Quabauge old fort at a place called Menemesseg, which is
about 8 miles north of where Captain Hutchison & Captain
Wheeler was woonded & several men with them slayn (in the
begining of August last) as these indians informed them. At
this place among these Indians they found all the christian
Indians belonging to Hassannmiske & Magunhooge wich are
about forty men & about 80 women & children. These praying
indians were carried away by the enemy somewhat willingly,
others of them unwillingly, as they told him. For before they
went away they were in a great strait, for if they came to the
English they knew they shold be sent to Deere Iland, as others
were, & their corne beeing at such a distance about 40 miles
from Boston it could not bee caried to susteyne their lives &
so they should bee in danger to famish, & others feard they
should bee sent away to Barbados, or other places. And to
stay at Hassanamesho these indians our enemies would not
permit them, but said they must have the corne, but promised
them if they would goe with them they should not die but bee
preserved; these being in this condition most of them thought
it best to go with them though they feared death every way:
only Tukuppawillin [the minister] he lamented much & his
aged father the deacon & son and som others & would faine
have come back to the English after they were gone as far as
Manchange but the enimy mockt him, for crying & drew him
[   ] the rest that were unwilling along with them: These
things our spies understood from the p[raying] indians here.

The enimys that hee was among & live at the afforesaid places
are in [   ] small townes about 20 wigwams at a place & they
are all within 3 miles com [pass], and to consist of about 300
fighting men besides duble as many women & children [   ]
they have no fort, but wigwams only, some covred with barks
& som with matts. The Indians that are heare are the Nipmuck
indians, the Quabaag indians, the Paca-[choog] indians, the
Weshakum & Nashaway indians. The cheef sagomeres & captains are Mawtaamp, John with one eye & Sam [of Weshukum
or Nashaway] Sagamore John [having one leg bigger than the
other] of Pakachooge. Here also is Matoonus & his sons. Of
the Hassanamesho & christian Indians, he saw here Captain
Tom allias Wattasakomponin & his son Nehimiah. They say
that the enimy have solic[it]ed them to take armes & fight
against the English but they told James they would not fight
against the English, they will rather die. Here he also saw
Tukuppawillin their pastor & his aged father their deacon,
whome he saith mourn greatly & daily read the bible which is
their greatest comfort. Also he there saw James Printer brother
to the minister, & Joseph & Sa[   ] two brethern [sons to
Robin of Hassameshe deceased]. Hee also saw Pumhamun &
Jacob of Magunkoog with divers others that he could have
mentioned but those are the principal.

Some of the Indians [our enimies] mistrusted that these two
men were spies, especially Matoonus & his sonnes & some
others: these solicited James to borrow his hatchet & his knife
[when he saw they needed none] which made him cautious
of himselfe & suspitious of their evill intention to him, but
James [at the second towne] he came to meet with John with
one eye, of Weshakum [a stout captaine among them] this man
knew James & said thou hast been with me in the warr with
the Mauhaks & I know thou art a valiant man & therefore
none shall wrong thee nor kill thee here, but they shall first
kill me. Therefore abide at my wigwam & I will protect thee.
So this man entertained him kindly, & protected him. Job his
companion stayd at Pumhams wigwame wher his 3 children
were kept: hee and Job aboad with these indians severall daies
& sometimes went forth to hunt deere not farr off & returnd
againe. Hee laboured to gaine what information hee could of
their affayres, & was informed by Capt John [with one eye]
his host & others said things, viz. That Philip was quartered

this winter within halfe a dayes jorny [   ] fort Albany [The same thing is certifyed by a letter from Major Andros Governor of New York sent Mr Leet deputy Governor of Connecticut dated 5th January which letter being sent to Governor Winthrop by Mr Leet was read in our Councill on Thursday last 23 instant. This also may tend to confirme the truth of James his intelegence, as wel as divers other passages both before & aftermentioned]. Moreover they informed our spy that the Hadly Northampton & Spinkfield Indians had their winter quarters between them & Philip & som quartered at Squakeake. They told him also that a cheefe captaine named——of Hadley & Northampton indians, who was a valiant man, had been a chiefe captaine in the Mawhak warre had attempted to kill Philip & intended to do it; alleaging that Philip had begun a warr with the English that had brought great trouble upon them. Hee saieth that these Indians told him that it was som of their number that were in the Nipmuck country to get the corn & that the English came upon them in the wigwam at Hassunnamesuke & there they killed two Englishmen, & that they had got & caried away all the corne at Pakuahooge & in the Nipmuck country unto their quarters, upon which they had lived this winter, & upon beef & pork they had killed about Quaboage, & venison [of which there is great store in those parts & by reason of the deep snow there beeing mid thigh deep] it is easy to kill deare without gunns. He saieth that ere long, when their beefe & porke & deare is spent & gon, that they wilbe in want of corne, but they intend then to com down upon the English townes, of Lancaster Marlborow Grotaon, & particulely they intend first to cut off Lancaster bridge, & then say they there can be no releef com to them from Boston, the people cannot escape & there they hope to have corne enough. Hee saieth they have store of armes, & have a gunsmith among them, a lame man that is a good workman & keeps their gunns well fixt. They have some armes among them that they tooke in the 2 fights when Captain Beeares & Captain Lothrop was slayne. As for amunition they have some but not great store that he saw: Captian John with one eye shewed him a small kettle full of powder about half a peck & 2 hornes full besides. Hee asked them where they got their ammuntion, hee answered some we had from the English were kild, & som from Fort Albany, but (said he) the Dutch wil not sell us powder; but

wee give our bever & wompon to the Mawhakes & they buy
it & let us have it of them. They told him that they had sent
to the Wompeages & Mawquas to aid them in the spring, that
the Wampeages promised them help, but the Maquaws said
they were not willing to fight with English, but they would
fight with the Mohegins & Pequots that were brethern to the
English. Further hee saieth that they told him that the Frenchman that was at Boston this sumer [viz. Monsieur Norman-
vile] was with Philip & his company as hee went back at their
quarter about Pokomtuck, after he returnd from Boston. And
that in their sight hee burned certene papers that hee said were
letters from Boston to the French, saying what shall I doe with
these papers any longer. Hee said to the Indians I would not
have you burne the English mill, nor the meeting houses, nor
the best houses for we [ie the French] intend to be with you in
the spring before planting time & I will bring three hundred
of your countrymen that are hunters & have been three years at
the French. And we will bring armes & ammunition enough,
for wee intend to helpe you against the English & posses our
selves of Keneckticut river & other English plantations, and our
King [ie the French King] will send shipps to stopp supplyes
from coming by sea [from their King] to Boston.

Hee saieth that they told him that the Pennakooge indians
were quartered about the head of the Keneticut river, & had
not at all ingaged in any fight with the English, & would not,
their sagamors Wannalancet & others restrayned the young
men (who had an opptunity to have destroyd many of Capt
Moselys men when he was at Pennakooge last sumer but their
sagamores would not suffer them to shoot a gunne).

Further he saieth that he understood by the cheefe men &
old men that they were inclinable to have peace againe with the
English, but the young men [who are their principal soldiers]
say we wil have no peace wee are all or most of us alive yet &
the English have kild very few of us last summer; why shall wee
have peace to bee made slaves, & either be kild or sent away to
sea to Barbadoes &c. Let us live as long as wee can & die like
men, & not live to bee enslaved. Hee saieth there is an English
man a young man amongst them alive named Robert Pepper
who, being woonded in the legg in the fight when Captain
Beares was kild, hid himselfe in the crotch of a great tree that

lay on the ground, where an Indian called Sam Sagamore of Nashaway found him alive & tooke him prisoner & hee became his master. Hee lay lame severll weekes but beeing well used by his master & means used hee is now wel recovered. Hee saieth that once since hee was wel his master [carring him abroad with him] left him at Squakeake neare where hee was taken prisoner, his Master wishing him to goe to the English [whither there was a cart way led]. But Robert Pepper told James hee was afrayd his master did it but to try his fidelity to him to intrap him, & that if he should have gon away towards the English they would have intercepted him & so his life had beene in danger, so he went after his master & enquired after him & at last found him out, he saith Rob Peper would be glad to escape home and hopes hee shall meet with an oppertunity, when the Indians march nearer the English. James said his master told him hee would send him home when hee had convenient opptunety. Also hee was informed that there are two more English men prisoners with Philip & Hadly Indians, one is of Boston servant to a ship carpenter Grenhough, and the other he remembers not his name.

Hee saieth, that before hee & Job came among those indians they told them the Narragants had sent in one or 2 English scalps, but these indians would not receive them, but shot at their messenger & said they were English mens friends all last summer & would not creditt their first messangers. After there came other messengers from Narragansetts & brought more heads [he saw twelve scalpes of English hangd upon trees], that then these Indians beeleved the Narragansset & receved the scalps & paid them [as their manner is], & now they beeleved that the Naragansitts & English are at warre, of which they are glad. The Narragansets told these indians that the English had had fight with them, & killed about forty fighting men & one Sachem, & about 300 old men women & children were kild & burnt in the wigwams, most of which were destroyd. They told him that the Narragansetts said the Mohegins & Pequitts Indians killed & woonded of them, as many as the English had kild. Being questioned by Mr. Danforth whether hee could learne whether the Narragansetts had ayded & assisted Philip & his companey in the summer against the English, hee answered that hee understood by those indians that they had not, but

lookt on them as freinds to the English all along til now &
their enemies. Hee saieth that hee was informed that the Nar-
gansets said that an Inglish man one Joshua Tift was among
them when they had their fight at the English, & that he did
them good service & kild & woonded 5 or 6 English in that
fight, & that before they wold trust him he had kild a miller
an English man at Narragansit, & brought his scalpe to them.
Also hee said that the Naragansits told these indians that one
William that lives in those parts brought them some powder &
offered them all his catle for provisions desiring only that his
life might bee spared & his children & grandchildren. These
Narragansits solicited these indians to send them som help
[   ] they knew them to be stout soldiers], they promised to
send with them 20 men to goe with them to see how things
were, & they determined to begin their jorny last Saturday [ie
22th January] and they also resolved to take Job with them to
Narraganset indians; and upon the same day Mawtaamp the
sagamor said hee would goe with another company up to Phillip, to informe him & those Indians of the breach betwene the
English & Narragansitts & he said that James [our spy] should
goe along with him to Philipp to acquaint him of the state of
affayres among the English & praying indians. James said to
Mataamp I am willing to goe to Philip but not at this present
because Philip knowes that I fought against him on the English
side at Mount Hope & other places, & hee will not beeleve that
I am realy turned to his party, unies I first do some exployt
& kill some English men & carry their heads to him. Let me
have opportunity to doe somthing of this nature before I goe
to Philip. This answer of James seemed to satisfy the sagamore
Mawtaump. But James doubting notwithstanding, that he
might change his mind and take him with him when hee went,
hee was resolved to endevor an escape before the time they
intended the jorny, especially considering what Tachupawillin
told him in secret that Philip had given order to his men that if
they met with these John Hunter, James Speen, this James &
Thomas Quannupaquit [brethren & Andrew Pitamee & Peter
Ephraim they bring them to him or put them to death].

   Accordingly James moved Job [his companion] to contrive a
way for an escape. Job concealed his purpose, and upon Wens-
day the 19th of this instant they 2 early in the morne went out

as if they would goe a hunting for deare, as they had don at other times & returnd againe [James having goten about a pint of nokake of Symon Squa one of the praying indians]. They beeing in the woods hunted for deere & killd 4 deare & as they traveld to & fro they percevd that by som footing of indians that some did watch their motions, so towards night they being neare a pond they drew the deer at the pond & tooke up their quarters in thicke swampe & there made a fire & dresd some of the venison, but no other indians came to them; so about 3 oclock before day, James said to Job now let us escape away if wee can. But Job said I am not willing to goe now, because my children are here and I will stay longer. If God please hee can preserve my life; if not I am willing to die. I will therfore goe backe againe to the indians & goe along with the company to the Naragansitt, & if I returne I will use what policy I can to get away my children. If I live, about [   ] weeks hence I will com back & I will com to Naticke & therfore if you can, take 4 or 5 indians to meet me there. I shall if I live by that time get more intelligence of affayres. Then James said to him, I must now goe away for I am not like to have a better opptunity, & if they should carry mee to Philip I shall die. But I am sorry for you Job, lest when I am gon they will kill you for my sake; but you may tel them I runne away from you & was afrayd to goe to Philip before I had don some exployt. So they parted—& James our spy came homeward travilling through the woods night & day untill he came to Naticke to James Spene wigwam, who lives their to looke to som aged & sick folks that were not in capacity to be brought downe to Deare Hand, & on Lord's day came to Serjant Williams at the village & by him was conducted to & so to Boston before the Councel the same day which was the 24th day of this instnt Janury 1675 where his examination & relation was written by 2 scribes: & though this may a little differ from others in some particulars yet for substance it is the same.

Moreover hee said that hee heard that the Narragansit were marched upp into the woods toward Quantesit & they were in company & the first company of above 200 among them were several woonded werre come before the Narragansit come up to these Indians:—being omitted beefore it is put in heare.

THE EDITORS' COMMENT

James Quanapohit was from a Massachusett family, a Christian convert and a scout who served with the Massachusetts Bay troops alongside his brother Thomas from the beginning of the war. He was originally from Winisimet, or Rumney Marsh, which had been struck hard by epidemics, and was sometimes called James Rumneymarsh; he was also identified with the praying town of Natick. Fluent in both English and Massachusett, James was also skilled in Indigenous warfare tactics, having joined with other Massachusett and Nipmuc men in defending Natick and other Native towns against Mohawk raids. His Relation is an account of a spy mission he undertook in late December 1675 for Massachusetts Bay Colony, along with Job Kattenanit, to locate the Nipmuc stronghold of Menimesit and report intelligence on the multifaceted alliance of Indigenous people gathered there. Both Job and James were released from internment at Deer Island, in Boston harbor, to carry out the mission. Their mission also enabled Job to discern the condition of his own family, who remained at Menimesit, and perhaps persuade them to leave. James gave this report to Daniel Gookin, in Cambridge, on his return from Menimesit in late January, conveying, among other news, intelligence about the planned raid on Lancaster. Job Kattenanit also returned in February 1676, traveling eighty miles on snowshoes to report that the raid on Lancaster was imminent. James and Job both served with a company of scouts (drawn from Deer Island and the Praying Towns) who were instrumental to Massachusetts Bay colony's success in tracking and capturing Native people and places in the spring and summer of 1676. At the same time, they also used their positions as scouts in order to advocate for and protect their kin as colonial campaigns to capture Native people intensified.

Mary Rowlandson:
The Sovereignty and Goodness of God

The Preface to the Reader

IT was on Tuesday, Feb. 1, 1675, in the afternoon, when the *Narrhagansets* quarters (in or toward the *Nipmug* Country, whither they are now retyred for fear of the *English* Army lying in their own Country) were the second time beaten up by the Forces of the united Colonies, who thereupon soon betook themselves to flight, and were all the next day pursued by the *English*, some overtaken and destroyed. But on *Thursday*, Feb. 3d, the *English* having now been six dayes on their march, from their head quarters, at *Wickford*, in the *Narrhaganset* Country, toward, and after the Enemy, and provision grown exceeding short, insomuch that they were fain to kill some Horses for the supply, especially of their *Indian* friends, they were necessitated to consider what was best to be done: And about noon (having hitherto followed the chase as hard as they might) a Councill was called, and though some few were of another mind, yet it was concluded by far the greater part of the Councill of War, that the Army should desist the pursuit, and retire: the Forces of *Plimoth* and the *Bay* to the next Town of the *Bay*, and *Connecticut* Forces to their own next Towns; which determination was immediately put in execution. The consequent whereof, as it was not difficult to be foreseen by those that knew the causless enmity of these *Barbarians*, against the *English*, and the malicious and revengefull spirit of these Heathen: so it soon proved dismall.

The *Narrhagansets* were now driven quite from their own Country, and all their provisions there hoarded up, to which they durst not at present return, and being so numerous as they were, soon devoured those to whom they went, whereby both the one and other were now reduced to extream straits, and so necessitated to take the first and best opportunity for supply, and very glad, no doubt of such an opportunity as this, to provide for themselves, and make spoil of the *English* at once; and seeing themselves thus discharged of their pursuers, and a little refreshed after their flight, the very next week upon *Thurseday*, Feb. 10, they fell with mighty force and fury upon *Lancaster*: which small Town, remote from aid of others, and not being Gerisoned as it might, the Army being now come in, and as the time indeed required (the design of the *Indians* against that place being known to the *English* some time before), was not able to make effectual resistance: but notwithstanding utmost endeavor of the Inhabitants, most of the buildings were turned into ashes; many People (Men, Women and Children) slain, and others captivated. The most solemn and remarkable part of this Trajedy, may that justly be reputed, which fell upon the Family of that reverend Servant of God, Mr. *Joseph Rolandson*, the faithfull Pastor of Christ in that place, who being gone down to the Councill of the *Massachusets* to seek aid for the defence of the place, at his return found the Town in flames, or smoke, his own house being set on fire by the Enemy, through the disadvantage of a defective Fortification, and all in it consumed: his precious yokefellow, and dear Children, wounded and captivated (as the issue evidenced, and following Narrative declares) by these cruel and barbarous Salvages. A sad Catestrophe! Thus all things come alike to all: None knows either love or hatred by all that is before him. It is no new thing for Gods precious ones to drink as deep as others, of the Cup of common Calamity: Take just Lot (yet captivated) for instance beside others. But it is not my business to dilate on these things, but only in few words introductively to preface to the following script, which is a Narrative of the wonderfully awfull, wise, holy, powerfull, and gracious providence of God, towards that worthy and precious Gentlewoman, the dear Consort of the said Reverend Mr. *Rowlandson*, and her Children with her, as in casting of her into such a waterless pit, so in preserving, supporting, and carrying through so many such extream hazards, unspeakable difficulties and disconsolateness, and at last delivering her out of them all, and her Surviving Children also. It was a strange and amazing dispensation, that the Lord should so afflict his precious Servant, and Hand maid. It was a strange, if not more, that he should so bear up the spirits of his Servant under such bereavements and of his handmaid under such captivity, travels and hardships (much too hard for flesh and blood) as he did, and at length deliver and restore. But he was their Saviour, who hath said, *When thou passest through the Waters, I will be with thee, and through the Rivers, they shall not overflow thee: When thou walkest through the fire thou shalt not be burnt, nor shall the flame kindle upon thee,* Isa. 43, ver. 2, and again, *He woundeth and his hands make whole. He shall deliver thee in six troubles, yea in seven there shall no evil touch thee. In Famine he shall redeem thee from Death, and in War from the power of the sword.* Job 5.18, 19, 20. Methinks this dispensation doth bear some resemblance to those of *Joseph, David* and *Daniel;* yea, and of the three Children too, the Stories whereof do represent us with the excellent textures of divine providence, curious pieces of divine work: and truly so doth this, and therefore not to be forgotten, but worthy to be exhibited to, and viewed, and pondered by all, that disdain not to consider the operation of his hands.

The works of the Lord (not only of Creation, but of Providence also, especially those that do more peculiarly concern his dear ones, that are as the Apple of his Eye, as the Signet upon His Hand, the Delight of his Eyes, and the Object of his tenderest Care) are great, sought out of all those that have pleasure therein. And of these verily this is none of the least.

This Narrative was penned by the Gentlewoman her self, to be to her a memorandum of Gods dealing with her, that she might never forget, but remember the same, and the severall circumstances thereof, all the dayes of her life. A pious scope which deserves both commendation and imitation: Some friends having obtained a sight of it, could not but be so much affected with the many passages of working providence discovered therein as to judge it worthy of publick view, and altogether unmeet that such works of God should be hid from present and future Generations: And therefore though this Gentlewomans modesty would not thrust it into the Press, yet her gratitude unto God made her not hardly perswadable to let it pass, that God might have his due glory and others benefit by it as well as herself. I hope by this time none will cast any reflection upon this Gentlewoman, on the score of this publication of her affliction and deliverance. If any should, doubtless they may be reckoned with the nine lepers, of whom it is said, *Were there not ten cleansed, where are the nine?* but one *returning to give God thanks.* Let such further know that this was a dispensation of publick note, and of universall concernment, and so much the more, by how much the nearer this Gentlewoman stood related to that faithfull Servant of God, whose capacity and employment was publick in the house of God, and his name on that account of a very sweet savour in the Churches of Christ. Who is there of a true Christian spirit, that did not look upon himself much concerned in this bereavement, this Captivity in the time thereof, and in this deliverance when it came, yea more than in many others; and how many are there, to whom so concerned, it will doubtless be a very acceptable thing to see the way of God with this Gentlewoman in the aforesaid dispensation, thus laid out and portrayed before their eyes.

To conclude, whatever any coy phantasies may deem, yet it highly concerns those that have so deeply tasted, how good the Lord is, to enquire with *David, What shall I render to the Lord for all his benefits to me? Psal.* 116. 12. He thinks nothing too great; yea, being sensible of his own disproportion to the due praises of God he calls in help. *Oh, magnifie the Lord with me, let us exalt his Name together,* Psal. 34. 3. And it is but reason, that our praises should hold proportion with our prayers: and that as many hath helped together by prayer for the obtaining of this Mercy, so praises should be returned by many on this behalf; And forasmuch as not the generall but particular knowledge of things make deepest impression upon the affections, this Narrative particularizing the several passages of this providence will not a little conduce thereunto. And therefore holy *David* in order to the attainment of that end, accounts himself concerned to declare what God has done for his soul, *Psal.* 66.16. *Come and hear, all ye that fear God, and I will declare what God hath done for my soul,* i.e. *for his life,* see v. 9, 10. *He holdeth our soul in life, and suffers not our feet to be moved, for thou our God hast proved us, thou hast tried us, as silver is tried.* Life-mercies, are heart-affecting mercies, of great impression and force, to enlarge pious hearts in the praises of God, so that such know not how but to talk of Gods acts, and to speak of and publish his wonderfull works. Deep troubles, when the waters come in unto thy soul, are wont to produce vowes: vowes must be paid. *It is better not vow, than vow and not to pay.* I may say, that as none knows what it is to fight and pursue such an enemy as this, but they that have fought and pursued them: so none can imagine what it is to be captivated, and enslaved to such atheistical, proud, wild, cruel, barbarous, brutish (in one word) diabolicall creatures as these, the worst of the heathen; nor what difficulties, hardships, hazards, sorrows, anxieties and perplexities do unavoidably wait upon such a condition, but those that have tryed it. No serious spirit then (especially knowing anything of this Gentlewomans piety) can imagine but that the vows of God are upon her. Excuse her then if she come thus into publick, to pay those vows. Come and hear what she hath to say.

I am confident that no Friend of divine Providence will ever repent his time and pains spent in reading over these sheets, but will judg them worth perusing again and again.

Here *Reader*, you may see an instance of the Soveraignty of God, who doth what he will with his own as well as others; and who may say to him, *What dost Thou?* Here you may see an instance of the faith and patience of the Saints, under the most heart-sinking tryals; here you may see, the promises are breasts full of consolation, when all the world besides is empty, and gives nothing but sorrow. That God is indeed the supream Lord of the world, ruling the most unruly, weakening the most cruel and salvage, granting his People mercy in the sight of the unmercifull, curbing the lusts of the most filthy, holding the hands of the violent, delivering the prey from the mighty, *and gathering together the out casts of* Israel. Once and again you have heard, but here you may see, *that power belongeth unto God*; that our God is the God of Salvation, and to him belong the issues from Death. That our God is in the Heavens, and doth whatever pleases him. Here you have *Sampsons* Riddle exemplified, and that great promise, *Rom.* 8. 28. verified, *Out of the Eater comes forth meat, and sweetness out of the strong,* The worst of evils working together for the best good. How evident is it that the Lord hath made this Gentlewoman a gainer by all this affliction, that she can say, *'tis good for her, yea better that she hath been, than that she should not have been thus afflicted.*

Oh how doth God shine forth in such things as these!

Reader, if thou gettest no good by such a Declaration as this, the fault must needs be thine own. Read therefore, Peruse, Ponder, and from hence lay up something from the experience of another, against thine own turn comes, that so thou also through patience and consolation of the Scripture mayest have hope.

PER AMICAM

A Narrative of the Captivity and Restauration of Mrs. Mary Rowlandson

O<small>N</small> the tenth of February 1675, Came the *Indians* with great numbers upon *Lancaster*: Their first coming was about Sun-rising; hearing the noise of some Guns, we looked out; several Houses were burning, and the Smoke ascending to Heaven. There were five persons taken in one house, the Father, and the Mother and a sucking Child, they knockt on the head; the other two they took and carried away alive. There were two others, who being out of their Garison upon some occasion were set upon; one was knockt on the head, the other escaped: Another there was who running along was shot and wounded, and fell down; he begged of them his life, promising them Money (as they told me) but they would not hearken to him but knockt him in head, and stript him naked, and split open his Bowels. Another seeing many of the *Indians* about his Barn, ventured and went out, but was quickly shot down. There were three others belonging to the same Garison who were killed; the *Indians* getting up upon the roof of the Barn, had advantage to shoot down upon them over their Fortification. Thus these murtherous wretches went on, burning, and destroying before them.

At length they came and beset our own house, and quickly it was the dolefullest day that ever mine eyes saw. The House stood upon the edge of a hill; some of the *Indians* got behind the hill, others into the Barn, and others behind any thing that could shelter them; from all which places they shot against the House, so that the Bullets seemed to fly like hail; and quickly they wounded one man among us, then another, and then a third. About two hours (according to my observation, in

that amazing time) they had been about the house before they
prevailed to fire it (which they did with Flax and Hemp, which
they brought out of the Barn, and there being no defence about
the House, only two Flankers at two opposite corners, and one
of them not finished) they fired it once and one ventured out
and quenched it, but they quickly fired again, and that took.
Now is that dreadfull hour come, that I have often heard of
(in time of War, as it was the case of others) but now mine eyes
see it. Some in our house were fighting for their lives, others
wallowing in their blood, the House on fire over our heads,
and the bloody Heathen ready to knock us on the head, if we
stirred out. Now might we hear Mothers & Children crying
out for themselves, and one another, *Lord, What shall we do?*
Then I took my Children (and one of my sisters, hers) to go
forth and leave the house: but as soon as we came to the door
and appeared, the *Indians* shot so thick that the bullets rattled
against the House, as if one had taken an handfull of stones
and threw them, so that we were fain to give back. We had
six stout Dogs belonging to our Garrison, but none of them
wou'd stir, though another time, if any *Indian* had come to
the door, they were ready to fly upon him and tear him down.
The Lord hereby would make us the more to acknowledge
his hand, and to see that our help is alwayes in him. But out
we must go, the fire increasing, and coming along behind us,
roaring, and the *Indians* gaping before us with their Guns,
Spears and Hatchets to devour us. No sooner were we out of
the House, but my Brother in Law (being before wounded,
in defending the house, in or near the throat) fell down dead,
whereat the *Indians* scornfully shouted, and hallowed, and
were presently upon him, stripping off his cloaths, the bulletts flying thick, one went through my side, and the same (as
would seem) through the bowels and hand of my dear Child
in my arms. One of my elder Sisters Children, named *William*, had then his Leg broken, which the *Indians* perceiving,
they knockt him on head. Thus were we butchered by those
merciless Heathen, standing amazed, with the blood running
down to our heels. My eldest Sister being yet in the House,
and seeing those wofull sights, the Infidels haling Mothers
one way, and Children another, and some wallowing in their

blood: and her elder Son telling her that her Son *William* was dead, and my self was wounded, she said, And, *Lord, let me dy with them*; which was no sooner said, but she was struck with a Bullet, and fell down dead over the threshold. I hope she is reaping the fruit of her good labours, being faithfull to the service of God in her place. In her younger years she lay under much trouble upon spiritual accounts, till it pleased God to make that precious scripture take hold of her heart, 2 *Cor.* 12. 9. *And he said unto me, my grace is sufficient for thee.* More than twenty years after I have heard her tell how sweet and comfortable that place was to her. But to return: the *Indians* laid hold of us, pulling me one way, and the Children another, and said, *Come go along with us*; I told them they would kill me: they answered, *If I were willing to go along with them, they would not hurt me.*

Oh the dolefull sight that now was to behold at this House! *Come, behold the works of the Lord, what desolations he has made in the Earth.* Of thirty seven persons who were in this one House, none escaped either present death, or a bitter captivity, save only one, who might say as he, *Job* 1. 15. *And I only am escaped alone to tell the News.* There were twelve killed, some shot, some stab'd with their Spears, some knock'd down with their Hatchets. When we are in prosperity, Oh the little that we think of such dreadfull sights, and to see our dear Friends, and Relations ly bleeding out their heart-blood upon the ground. There was one who was chopt into the head with a Hatchet, and stripped naked, and yet was crawling up and down. It is a solemn sight to see so many Christians lying in their blood, some here, and some there, like a company of Sheep torn by Wolves. All of them stript naked by a company of hellhounds, roaring, singing, ranting and insulting, as if they would have torn our very hearts out; yet the Lord by his Almighty power preserved a number of us from death, for there were twenty-four of us taken alive and carried captive.

I had often before this said, that if the *Indians* should come, I should chuse rather to be killed by them than be taken alive, but when it came to the tryal my mind changed; their glittering weapons so daunted my spirit, that I chose rather to go along with those (as I may say) ravenous Beasts, than that moment to end my dayes; and that I may the better declare what happened to me during that grievous Captivity, I shall particularly speak of the severall Removes we had up and down the Wilderness.

THE FIRST REMOVE

Now away we must go with those Barbarous Creatures, with our bodies wounded and bleeding, and our hearts no less than our bodies. About a mile we went that night, up upon a hill within sight of the Town, where they intended to lodge. There was hard by a vacant house (deserted by the English before, for fear of the *Indians*). I asked them whither I might not lodge in the house that night to which they answered, what will you love *English men* still? This was the dolefullest night that ever my eyes saw. Oh the roaring, and singing and danceing, and yelling of those black creatures in the night, which made the place a lively resemblance of hell. And as miserable was the waste that was there made, of Horses, Cattle, Sheep, Swine, Calves, Lambs, Roasting Pigs, and Fowls (which they had plundered in the Town) some roasting, some lying and burning, and some boyling to feed our merciless Enemies; who were joyfull enough though we were disconsolate. To add to the dolefulness of the former day, and the dismalness of the present night: my thoughts ran upon my losses and sad bereaved condition. All was gone, my Husband gone (at least separated from me, he being in the Bay; and to add to my grief, the *Indians* told me they would kill him as he came homeward) my Children gone, my Relations and Friends gone, our House and home and all our comforts within door, and without, all was gone, (except my life) and I knew not but the next moment that might go too. There remained nothing to me but one poor wounded Babe, and it seemed at present worse than death that it was in such a pitiful condition, bespeaking Compassion, and I had no refreshing for it, nor suitable things to revive it. Little do many think what is the savageness and brutishness of this barbarous Enemy, aye even those that seem to profess more than others among them, when the *English* have fallen into their hands.

Those seven that were killed at *Lancaster* the summer before upon a Sabbath day, and the one that was afterward killed upon a week day, were slain and mangled in a barbarous manner, by One-ey'd *John*, and *Marlborough's* Praying *Indians*, which Capt. *Mosely* brought to *Boston*, as the *Indians* told me.

THE SECOND REMOVE

But now, the next morning, I must turn my back upon the Town, and travel with them into the vast and desolate Wilderness, I knew not whither. It is not my tongue, or pen can express the sorrows of my heart, and bitterness of my spirit, that I had at this departure: but God was with me, in a wonderfull manner, carrying me along, and bearing up my spirit, that it did not quite fail. One of the *Indians* carried my poor wounded Babe upon a horse, it went moaning all along, I shall dy, I shall dy. I went on foot after it, with sorrow that cannot be exprest. At length I took it off the horse, and carried it in my arms till my strength failed, and I fell down with it: Then they set me upon a horse with my wounded Child in my lap, and there being no furniture upon the horse back, as we were going down a steep hill, we both fell over the horses head, at which they like inhumane creatures laught, and rejoyced to see it, though I thought we should there have ended our dayes, as overcome with so many difficulties. But the Lord renewed my strength still, and carried me along, that I might see more of his Power; yea, so much that I could never have thought of, had I not experienced it.

After this it quickly began to snow, and when night came on, they stopt: and now down I must sit in the snow, by a little fire, and a few boughs behind me, with my sick Child in my lap; and calling much for water, being now (through the wound) fallen into a violent Fever. My own wound also growing so stiff, that I could scarce sit down or rise up; yet so it must be, that I must sit all this cold winter night upon the cold snowy ground, with my sick Child in my armes, looking that every hour would be the last of its life; and having no Christian friend near me, either to comfort or help me. Oh, I may see the wonderfull power of God, that my Spirit did not utterly sink under my affliction: still the Lord upheld me with his gracious and mercifull Spirit, and we were both alive to see the light of the next morning.

THE THIRD REMOVE

The morning being come, they prepared to go on their way: One of the Indians *got up upon a horse, and they set me up behind him, with my poor sick Babe in my lap.* A very wearisome and tedious day I had of it; what with my own wound, and my Childs being so exceeding sick, and in a lamentable condition with her wound. It may be easily judged what a poor feeble condition we were in, there being not the least crumb of refreshing that came within either of our mouths, from *Wednesday* night to *Saturday* night, except only a little cold water. This day in the afternoon, about an hour by Sun, we came to the place where they intended, *viz.* an Indian town called *Wenimesset*, northward of *Quabaug*. When we were come, Oh the number of Pagans (now merciless enemies) that there came about me, that I may say as *David*, Psal 27. 13, *I had fainted, unless I had believed, &c.* The next day was the Sabbath: I then remembered how careless I had been of Gods holy time: how many Sabbaths I had lost and misspent, and how evilly I had walked in Gods sight; which lay so close unto my spirit, that it was easie for me to see how righteous it was with God to cut off the thread of my life, and cast me out of his presence forever. Yet the Lord still shewed mercy to me, and upheld me; and as he wounded me with one hand, so he healed me with the other. This day there came to me one *Robert Pepper* (a man belonging to *Roxbury*) who was taken in Captain *Beers* his fight, and had been now a considerable time with the *Indians*; and up with them almost as far as *Albany* to see king *Philip*, as he told me, and was now very lately come into these parts. Hearing, I say, that I was in this *Indian* Town, he obtained leave to come and see me. He told me, he himself was wounded in the leg at Captain *Beers* his Fight; and was not able some time to go, but as they carried him, and as he took Oaken leaves and laid to his wound, and through the blessing of God he was able to travel again. Then I took Oaken leaves and laid to my side, and with the blessing of God it cured me also; yet before the cure was wrought, I may say, as it is in *Psal.* 38. 5, 6. *My wounds stink and are corrupt, I am troubled, I am bowed down greatly, I go mourning all the day long.* I sat much alone with a poor wounded Child in my lap, which moaned night and day, having nothing to revive the body, or cheer the spirits of her, but in stead of that, sometimes one *Indian* would come and tell me in one hour, that your *Master* will knock your Child in the head, and then a second, and then a third, your *Master* will quickly knock your Child in the head.

This was the comfort I had from them, miserable comforters are ye all, as he said. Thus nine days I sat upon my knees, with my Babe in my lap, till my flesh was raw again; my Child being even ready to depart this sorrowful world, they bade me carry it out to another Wigwam (I suppose because they would not be troubled with such spectacles) Whither I went with a very heavy heart, and down I sat with the picture of death in my lap. About two houres in the night, my sweet Babe, like a lamb departed this life, on *Feb. 18. 1675,* It being about six *yeares,* and *five months* old. It was *nine dayes* from the first wounding, in this miserable condition, without any refreshing of one nature or other, except a little cold water. I cannot but take notice, how at another time I could not bear to be in the room where any dead person was, but now the case is changed; I must and could ly down by my dead Babe, side by side all the night after. I have thought since of the wonderfull goodness of God to me, in preserving me in the use of my reason and senses, in that distressed time, that I did not use wicked and violent means to end my own miserable life. In the morning, when they understood that my child was dead they sent for me home to my Masters Wigwam: (by my Master in this writing, must be understood *Quanopin,* who was a *Saggamore,* and married King *Philips* wives Sister; not that he first took me, but I was sold to him by another *Narhaganset Indian,* who took me when first I came out of the Garison). I went to take up my dead child in my arms to carry it with me, but they bid me let it alone: there was no resisting, but goe I must and leave it. When I had been at my masters *wigwam,* I took the first opportunity I could get, to go look after my dead child: when I came I askt them what they had done with it? then they told me it was upon the hill: then they went and shewed me where it was, where I saw the ground was newly digged, and there they told me they had buried it: *There I left that Child in the Wilderness, and must commit it, and my self also in this Wilderness-condition, to him who is above all.* God having taken away this dear Child, I went to see my daughter *Mary,* who was at this same *Indian Town,* at a *Wigwam* not very far off, though we had little liberty or opportunity to see one another: she was about ten years old, & taken from the door at first by a *Praying Indian* & afterward sold for a gun. When I came in sight, she would fall a weeping;

at which they were provoked, and would not let me come near her, but bade me be gone; which was a heart-cutting word to me. I had one Child dead, another in the Wilderness, I knew not where, the third they would not let me come near to: *Me* (as he said) *have ye bereaved of my children*, Joseph *is not, and* Simeon *is not, and ye will take* Benjamin *also, all these things are against me.* I could not sit still in this condition, but kept, walking from *one* place to another. And as I was going along, my heart was even overwhelm'd with the thoughts of my condition, and that I should have Children, *and a Nation which I knew not ruled over them.* Whereupon I earnestly entreated the Lord, that he would consider my low estate, and shew me a token for good, and if it were his blessed will, some sign and hope of some relief. And indeed quickly the Lord answered, in some measure, my poor prayers: for as I was going up and down mourning and lamenting my condition, my Son came to me, and asked me how I did; I had not seen him before, since the destruction of the Town, and I knew not where he was, till I was informed by himself, that he was amongst a smaller parcel of *Indians*, whose place was about six miles off; with tears in his eyes, he asked me whether his sister *Sarah* was dead; and told me he had seen his sister *Mary*; and prayed me, that I would not be troubled in reference to himself. The occasion of his coming to see me at this time, was this: There was, as I said, about six miles from us, a smal Plantation of *Indians*, where it seems he had been during his Captivity: and at this time, there were some Forces of the *Indians* gathered out of our company, and some also from them (among whom was my Sons master) to go to assault and burn *Medfield*: In this time of the absence of his master, his dame brought him to see me. I took this to be some gracious answer to my earnest and unfeigned desire. The next day, *viz.* to this, the *Indians* returned from *Medfield*, all the company, for those that belonged to the other smal company, came through the Town that now we were at. But before they came to us, Oh! the outragious roaring and hooping that there was: They began their din about a mile before they came to us. By their noise and hooping they signified how many they had destroyed (which was at that time twenty three). Those that were with us at home, were gathered together as soon as they heard the hooping, and every time that the other went over their number, these at home gave a shout, that the very Earth rung again: And thus they continued till those that had been upon the expedition were come up to the *Sagamores Wigwam*; and then, Oh, the hideous insulting and triumphing that there was over some *Englishmens* scalps that they had taken (as their manner) and brought with them. I cannot but take notice of the wonderfull mercy of God to me in those afflictions, in sending me a Bible. One of the *Indians* that came from *Medfield* fight, had brought some plunder, came to me, and asked me, if I wou'd have a Bible, he had got one in his basket. I was glad of it, and asked him, whether he thought the *Indians* would let me read? He answered, yes: So I took the Bible, and in that melancholy time, it came into my mind to read first the 28. *Chap.* of *Deut.* which I did, and when I had read it, my dark heart wrought on this manner, *That there was no mercy for me, that the blessings were gone, and the curses come in their room, and that I had lost my opportunity.* But the Lord helped me still to go on reading till I came to *Chap.* 30 the seven first verses, where I found, *There was mercy promised again, if we would return to him by repentance; and though we were scattered from one end of the Earth to the other, yet the Lord would gather us together, and turn all those curses upon our Enemies.* I do not desire to live to forget this Scripture, and what comfort it was to me.

Now the *Indians* began to talk of removing from this place, some one way, and some another. There were now besides my self nine *English* Captives in this place (all of them Children, except one Woman). I got an opportunity to go and take my leave of them; they being to go one way, and I another, *I asked them whether they were earnest with God for deliverance*; they told me, they did as they were able, and it was some comfort to me, that the Lord stirred up *Children to look to him.* The Woman *viz.* Goodwife *Joslin* told me, she should never see me again, and that she could find in her heart to run away; I wisht her not to run away by any means, for we were near *thirty miles* from any *English* Town, and she very big with Child, and had but one week to reckon; and another Child in her Arms, two years old, and bad Rivers there were to go over, and we were feeble, with our poor and coarse entertainment. I had my Bible with me, I pulled it out, and asked her whether she would read;

we opened the Bible and lighted on *Psal.* 27. in which Psalm we especially took notice of that, *ver ult.*, *Wait on the Lord, Be of good courage, and he shall strengthen thine heart, wait I say on the Lord.*

THE FOURTH REMOVE

And now I must part with that little company I had. Here I parted from my daughter *Mary*, (whom I never saw again till I saw her in *Dorchester*, returned from Captivity), and from four little Cousins and Neighbours, some of which I never saw afterward: the Lord only knows the end of them. Amongst them also was that poor Woman before mentioned, who came to a sad end, as some of the company told me in my travel: She having much grief upon her Spirit, about her miserable condition, being so near her time, she would be often asking the *Indians* to let her go home; they not being willing to that, and yet vexed with her importunity, gathered a great company together about her, and stript her naked, and set her in the midst of them; and when they had sung and danced about her (in their hellish manner) as long as they pleased, they knockt her on head, and the child in her arms with her: when they had done that, they made a fire and put them both into it, and told the other Children that were with them, that if they attempted to go home, they would serve them in like manner: The Children said, she did not shed one tear, but prayed all the while. But to return to my own Journey; we travelled about half a day or little more, and came to a desolate place in the Wilderness, where there were no *Wigwams* or *Inhabitants* before; we came about the middle of the afternoon to this place; cold and wet, and snowy, and hungry, and weary, and no refreshing, for man, but the cold ground to sit on, and our poor *Indian cheer.*

Heart-aking thoughts here I had about my poor Children, who were scattered up and down among the wild beasts of the forrest: My head was light and dizzy (either through hunger or hard lodging, or trouble or all together) my knees feeble, my body raw by sitting double night and day, that I cannot express to man the affliction that lay upon my Spirit, but the Lord helped me at that time to express it to himself. I opened my Bible to read, and the Lord brought that precious scripture to me, *Jer.* 31. 16. *Thus saith the Lord, refrain thy voice from weeping, and thine eyes from tears, for thy work shall be rewarded, and they shall come again from the land of the Enemy.* This was a sweet Cordial to me, when I was ready to faint, many and many a time have I sat down, and wept sweetly over this Scripture. At this place we continued about four dayes.

THE FIFTH REMOVE

The occasion (as I thought) of their moving at this time, was, the English *Army, it being near and following them*: For they went, as if they had gone for their lives, for some considerable way, and then they made a stop, and chose some of their stoutest men, and sent them back to hold the *English* army in play whilst the rest escaped: And then, *like Jehu, they marched on furiously,* with their old, and with their young: some carried their old decrepit mothers, some carried one, and some another. Four of them carried a great *Indian* upon a Bier; but going through a thick Wood with him, they were hindered, and could make no haste; whereupon they took him upon their backs, and carried him, one at a time, till they came to *Bacquaug* River. Upon a *Friday,* a little after noon we came to this River. When all the company was come up, and were gathered together, I thought to count the number of them, but they were so many, and being somewhat in motion, it was beyond my skil. In this travel, because of my wound, I was somewhat favored in my load; I carried only my knitting work and two quarts of parched meal: Being very faint I asked my mistriss to give me one spoonfull of the meal, but she would not give me a taste. They quickly fell to cutting dry trees, to make Rafts to carry them over the river: and soon my turn came to go over: By the advantage of some brush which they had laid upon the Raft to sit upon, I did not wet my foot (which many of themselves at the other end were mid-leg deep) which cannot but be acknowledged as a favour of God to my weakened body, it being a very cold time. I was not before acquainted with such kind of doings or dangers. *When thou passeth through the waters I will be with thee, and through the rivers they shall not overflow thee,* Isai. 43. 2. A certain number of us got over the River that night, but it was the night after the Sabbath before all the company was got over. On the *Saturday* they boyled an old Horses leg which they had got, and so we drank of the broth, as soon as they thought it was ready, and when it was almost all gone, they filled it up again.

The first week of my being among them, I hardly ate any thing; the second week, I found my stomach grow very faint for want of something; and yet it was very hard to get down their filthy trash: but the third week, though I could think how formerly my stomach would turn against this or that, and I could starve and die before I could eat such things, yet they were sweet and savory to my taste. I was at this time knitting a pair of white cotton stockins for my mistriss: and had not yet wrought upon a Sabbath day; when the Sabbath came they bade me go to work; I told them it was the Sabbath-day, and desired them to let me rest, and told them I would do as much more tomorrow; to which they answered me, they would break my face. And here I cannot but take notice of the strange providence of God in preserving the heathen: They were many hundreds, old and young, some sick, and some lame, many had *Papooses* at their backs, the greatest number at this time with us, were *Squaws*, and they travelled with all they had, bag and baggage, and yet they got over this River aforesaid; and on *Munday* they set their *Wigwams* on fire, and away they went: On that very day came the *English* Army after them to this River, and saw the smoak of their *Wigwams*, and yet this River put a stop to them. God did not give them courage or activity to go over after us; we were not ready for so great a mercy as victory and deliverance; if we had been, God would have found out a way for the *English* to have passed this River, as well as for the *Indians* with their *Squaws* and *Children*, and all their Luggage: *Oh, that my People had hearkened to me, and* Israel *had walked in my ways, I should soon have subdued their Enemies, and turned my hand against their Adversaries,* Psal. 81. 13, 14.

THE SIXTH REMOVE

On Munday *(as I said) they set their* Wigwams *on fire, and went away.* It was a cold morning, and before us there was a great Brook with ice on it; some waded through it, up to the knees & higher, but others went till they came to a Beaver dam, and I amongst them, where through the good providence of God, I did not wet my foot. I went along that day mourning and lamenting, leaving farther my own Country, and travelling into the vast and howling *Wilderness*, and I understood something of *Lot's*, Wife's Temptation, *when she looked back*: we came that day to a great Swamp, by the side of which we took up our lodging that night. When I came to the brow of the hill, that looked toward the Swamp, I thought we had been come to a great *Indian* Town (though there were none but our own Company). The *Indians* were as thick as the trees: it seemed as if there had been a thousand Hatchets going at once: if one looked before one, there was nothing but *Indians*, and behind one, nothing but *Indians*, and so on either hand, I my self in the midst, and no Christian soul near me, *and yet how hath the Lord preserved me in safety! Oh the experience that I have had of the goodness of God, to me and mine!*

THE SEVENTH REMOVE

After a restless and hungry night there, we had a wearisome time of it the next day. The Swamp by which we lay, was, as it were, a deep Dungeon, and an exceeding high and steep hill before it. Before I got to the top of the hill, I thought my heart and legs, and all would have broken, and failed me. What through faintness, and soreness of body, it was a grievous day of travel to me. As we went along, I saw a place where *English* cattle had been: that was comfort to me, such as it was: quickly after that we came to an *English* Path, which so took with me, that I thought I could have freely lyin down and dyed. That day, a little after noon, we came to *Squakheag*, where the *Indians* quickly spread themselves over the deserted *English* fields, gleaning what they could find; some pickt up ears of Wheat that were crickled down, some found ears of *Indian* Corn, some found Ground-nuts, and others sheaves of Wheat that were frozen together in the shock, and went to threshing of them out. My self got two ears of *Indian* Corn, and whilst I did but turn my back, one of them was stolen from me, which much troubled me. There came an *Indian* to them at that time, with a basket of Horse-liver. I asked him to give me a piece: *What*, sayes he *can you eat Horse-liver*? I told him, I would try, if he would give a piece, which he did, and I laid it on the coals to roast; but before it was half ready they got half of it away from me, so that I was fain to take the rest and eat it as it was, with the blood about my mouth, and yet a savory bit it was to me: *For to the hungry Soul, every bitter thing is sweet.* A solemn sight me thought it was, to see Fields of wheat and *Indian* Corn forsaken and spoiled: and the remainders of them to be food for our merciless Enemies. That night we had a mess of wheat for our Supper.

THE EIGHTH REMOVE

On the morrow morning we must go over the River, *i.e.* Connecticot, to meet with King *Philip*, two *Cannoos* full, they had carried over, the next Turn I myself was to go; but as my foot was upon the *Cannoo* to step in, there was a sudden out-cry among them, and I must step back; and instead of going over the River, I must go four or five miles up the River farther Northward. Some of the *Indians* ran one way, and some another. The cause of this rout was, as I thought, their espying some *English Scouts*, who were thereabout. In this travel up the river, about noon the Company made a stop, and sat down; some to eat, and others to rest them. As I sate amongst them, musing of things past, my Son *Joseph* unexpectedly came to me: we asked of each others welfare, bemoaning our dolefull condition, and the change that had come upon us. We had Husband and Father, and Children, and Sisters, and Friends, and Relations, and House, and Home, and many Comforts of this Life: but now we may say, as Job, *Naked came I out of my Mothers Womb, and naked shall I return: The Lord gave, and the Lord hath taken away, Blessed be the Name of the Lord.* I asked him whither he would read; he told me, he earnestly desired it. I gave him my Bible, and he lighted upon that comfortable scripture, Psal. 118. 17, 18. *I shall not dy but live, and declare the works of the Lord: the Lord hath chastened me sore, yet he hath not given me over to death.* Look here, *Mother* (sayes he), did you read this? And here I may take occasion to mention one principall ground of my setting forth these Lines: even as the Psalmist sayes, *To declare the Works of the Lord,* and His wonderfull Power in carrying us along, preserving us in the *Wilderness,* while under the Enemies hand, and returning of us in safety again. And His goodness in bringing to my hand so many comfortable and suitable Scriptures in my distress. But to Return, We travelled on till night; and in the morning, we must go over the River to *Philip's* crew. When I was in the

Cannoo, I could not but be amazed at the numerous crew of Pagans that were on the Bank on the other side. When I came ashore, they gathered all about me, I sitting alone in the midst: I observed they asked one another questions, and laughed, and rejoyced over their Gains and Victories. Then my heart began to fail: and I fell a weeping which was the first time to my remembrance, that I wept before them. Although I had met with so much Affliction, and my heart was many times ready to break, yet could I not shed one tear in their sight: but rather had been all this while in a maze, and like one astonished: but now I may say as, Psal. 137. 1. *By the rivers of* Babylon, *there we sat down: yea, we wept when we remembered Zion.* There one of them asked me, why I wept, I could hardly tell what to say: yet I answered, they would kill me: No, said he, none will hurt you. Then came one of them and gave me two spoon-fulls of Meal to comfort me, and another gave me half a pint of Pease; which was more worth than many Bushels at another time. Then I went to see King *Philip,* he bade me come in and sit down, and asked me whether I would smoke (a usual Complement now adayes amongst Saints and Sinners) but this no way suited me. For though I had formerly used Tobacco, yet I had left it ever since I was first taken. *It seems to be a bait, the devil lays to make men loose their precious time*: I remember with shame, how formerly, when I had taken two or three pipes, I was presently ready for another, such a bewitching thing it is: But I thank God, he has now given me power over it; surely there are many who may be better imployed than to ly sucking a stinking Tobacco-pipe.

Now the *Indians* gather their Forces to go against *North-Hampton*: over-night one went about yelling and hooting to give notice of the design. Whereupon they fell to boyling of Ground-nuts, and parching of Corn (as many as had it) for their Provision: and in the morning away they went. *During my abode in this place*, Philip *spake to me to make a shirt for his boy, which* I *did, for which he gave me a shilling*: I *offered the money to my master, but he bade me keep it: and with it* I *bought a piece of Horse flesh.* Afterwards he asked me to make a Cap for his boy, for which he invited me to Dinner. I went, and he gave me a Pancake, about as big as two fingers; it was made of parched wheat, beaten, and fryed in Bears grease, but I thought I never tasted pleasanter meat in my life. There was a *Squaw* who spake to me to make a shirt for her *Sannup*, for which she gave me a piece of Bear. Another asked me to knit a pair of Stockins, for which she gave me a quart of Pease: I boyled my Pease and Bear together, and invited my master and mistriss to dinner, but the proud Gossip, because I served them both in one Dish, would eat nothing, except one bit that he gave her upon the point of his knife. Hearing that my son was come to this place, I went to see him, and found him lying flat upon the ground: I asked him how he could sleep so? He answered me, *That he was not asleep, but at Prayer*; and lay so, that they might not observe what he was doing. I pray God he may remember these things now he is returned in safety. At this Place (the Sun now getting higher) what with the beams and heat of the Sun, and the smoak of the *Wigwams*, I thought I should have been blind, I could scarce discern one *Wigwam* from another. There was here one *Mary Thurston* of *Medfield*, who seeing how it was with me, lent me a Hat to wear: but as soon as I was gone, the *Squaw* (who owned that *Mary Thurston*) came running after me, and got it away again. *Here was the* Squaw *that gave me one Spoonfull of Meal.* I put it in my Pocket to keep it safe: yet notwithstanding somebody stole it, but put five *Indian* Corns in the room of it: which Corns were the greatest Provisions I had in my travel for one day.

The *Indians* returning from *North-Hampton*, brought with them some Horses, and Sheep, and other things which they had taken: I desired them, that they would carry me to *Albany*, upon one of those horses, and sell me for powder: for so they had sometimes discoursed. I was utterly hopless of getting home on foot, the way that I came. I could hardly bear to think of the many weary steps I had taken, to come to this place.

THE NINTH REMOVE

But instead of going either to *Albany* or homeward, we must go five miles up the River, and then go over it. Here we abode a while. Here lived a sorry *Indian*, who spoke to me to make him a shirt, when I had done it, he would pay me nothing. But he living by the River side, where I often went to fetch water, I would often be putting of him in mind, and calling for my pay: at last he told me if I would make another shirt, for a *Papoos* not yet born, he would give me a knife, which he did when I had done it. I carried the knife in, and my master asked me to give it him, and I was not a little glad that I had any thing that they would accept of, and be pleased with. When we were at this place, my Masters maid came home, she had been gone *three weeks* into the *Narrhaganset Country*, to fetch Corn, where they had stored up some in the ground: she brought home about a peck and half of corn. This was about the time that their great captain, *Naananto*, was killed in the *Narrhaganset Country. My Son being now about a mile from me*, I *asked liberty to go and see him, they bade me go, and away I went: but quickly lost my self, travelling over Hills and through Swamps, and could not find the way to him.* And I cannot but admire at the wonderfull power and goodness of God to me, in that, though I was gone from home, and met with all sorts of *Indians*, and those I had no knowledge of, and there being no Christian soul near me; yet not one of them offered the least imaginable miscarriage to me. I turned homeward again, and met with my master, he shewed me the way to my Son: When I came to him I found him not well: and withall he had a boyl on his side, which much troubled him: We bemoaned one another a while, as the Lord helped us, and then I returned again. When I was returned, I found myself as unsatisfied as I was before. I went up and down mourning and lamenting: and my spirit was ready to sink, with the thoughts of my poor Children: my Son was ill, and I could not but think of his mournfull looks, and no Christian Friend was near him, to do any office of love for him, either for Soul or Body. And my poor Girl, I knew not where she was, nor whither she was sick, or well, or alive, or dead. I repaired under these thoughts to my Bible (my great comfort in that time) and that Scripture came to my hand, *Cast thy burden upon the Lord, and He shall sustain thee*, Psal. 55. 22.

But I was fain to go and look after something to satisfie my hunger, and going among the *Wigwams*, I went into one, and there found a *Squaw* who shewed herself very kind to me, and gave me a piece of Bear. I put it into my pocket, and came home, but could not find an opportunity to broil it, for fear they would get it from me, and there it lay all that day and night in my stinking pocket. In the morning I went to the same *Squaw*, who had a Kettle of Ground-nuts boyling: I asked her to let me boyle my piece of Bear in her Kettle, which she did, and gave me some Groundnuts to eat with it: and I cannot but think how pleasant it was to me. I have sometimes seen Bear baked very handsomely among the *English*, and some like it, but the thought that it was Bear, made me tremble: but now that was savoury to me that one would think was enough to turn the stomach of a bruit Creature.

One bitter cold day, I could find no room to sit down before the fire: I went out, and could not tell what to do, but I went into another Wigwam, *where they were also sitting round the fire, but the* Squaw *laid a skin for me, and bid me sit down, and gave me some Ground-nuts, and bade me come again: and told me they would buy me, if they were able, and yet these were strangers to me that I never saw before.*

THE TENTH REMOVE

That day a small part of the Company removed about three quarters of a mile, intending further the next day. When they came to the place where they intended to lodge, and had pitched their *Wigwams*, being hungry I went again back to the place we were before at, to get something to eat: being encouraged by the *Squaws* kindness, who bade me come again; when I was there, there came an *Indian* to look after me, who when he had found me, kicked me all along: I went home and found Venison roasting that night, but they would not give me one bit of it. Sometimes I met with favour, and sometimes with nothing but frowns.

THE ELEVENTH REMOVE

The next day in the morning they took their Travel, intending a dayes journey up the River. I took my load at my back, and quickly we came to wade over the River: and passed over tiresome and wearisome hills. One hill was so steep that I was fain to creep up upon my knees, and to hold by the twiggs and bushes to keep myself from falling backward. My head also was so light, that I usually reeled as I went; but I hope all these wearisome steps that I have taken, are but a forewarning to me of the heavenly rest. *I know, O Lord, that thy Judgements are right, and that thou in faithfulness hast afflicted me*, Psal. 119. 75.

THE TWELFTH REMOVE

It was upon a Sabbath-day morning, that they prepared for their Travel. This morning I asked my master whither he would sell me to my husband; he answered me *Nux*, which did much rejoyce my spirit. My mistriss, before we went, was gone to the burial of a *Papoos*, and returning, she found me sitting and reading in my Bible; she snatched it hastily out of my hand, and threw it out of doors; I ran out and catch it up, and put it into my pocket, and never let her see it afterward. Then they packed up their things to be gone, and gave me my load: I complained it was too heavy, whereupon she gave me a slap in the face, and bade me go; I lifted up my heart to God, hoping the Redemption was not far off: and the rather because their insolency grew worse and worse.

But the thoughts of my going homeward (for so we bent our course) much cheared my Spirit, and made my burden seem light, and almost nothing at all. But (to my amazement and great perplexity) the scale was soon turned: for when we had gone a little way, on a sudden my mistress gives out, she would go no further, but turn back again, and said, I must go back again with her, and she called her *Sannup*, and would have had him gone back also, but he would not, but said, *He would go on, and come to us again in three dayes.* My Spirit was upon this, I confess, very impatient, and almost outragious. I thought I could as well have dyed as went back: I cannot declare the trouble that I was in about it; but yet back again I must go. As soon as I had an opportunity, I took my Bible to read, and that quieting Scripture came to my hand, *Psal.* 46. 10. *Be still, and know that I am God.* Which stilled my spirit for the present: But a sore time of tryal, I concluded, I had to go through. My master being gone, who seemed to me the best friend that I had of an *Indian*, both in cold and hunger, and quickly so it proved. Down I sat, with my heart as full as it could hold, and yet so hungry that I could not sit neither: but going out to see what I could find, and walking among the Trees, I found six *Acorns*, and two *Ches-nuts*, which were some refreshment to me. Towards Night I gathered me some sticks for my own comfort, that I might not lie a-cold: but when we came to ly down they bade me go out, and ly somewhere else, for they had company (they said) come in more than their own: I told them, I could not tell where to go, they bade me go look; I told them, if I went to another *Wigwam* they would be angry, and send me home again. Then one of the Company drew his sword, and told me he would run me through if I did not go presently. Then was I fain to stoop to this rude fellow, and to go out in the night, I knew not whither. *Mine eyes have seen that fellow afterwards walking up and down* Boston, *under the appearance of a* Friend-Indian, *and severall others of the like Cut.* I went to one *Wigwam*, and they told me they had no room. Then I went to another, and they said the same; at last an old *Indian* bade me come to him, and his *Squaw* gave me some Ground-nuts; she gave me also something to lay under my head, and a good fire we had: and through the good providence of God, I had a comfortable lodging that night. In the morning, another *Indian* bade me come at night, and he would give me six Groundnuts, which I did. We were at this place and time about two miles from *Connecticut River.* We went in the morning to gather Ground-nuts, to the River, and went back again that night. I went with a good load at my back (for they when they went, though but a little way, would carry all their trumpery with them) I told them the skin was off my back, but I had no other comforting answer from them than this, *That it would be no matter if my head were off too.*

THE THIRTEENTH REMOVE

Instead of going toward the Bay, *which was that I desired, I must go with them five or six miles down the River into a mighty Thicket of Brush: where we abode almost a fortnight.* Here one asked me to make a shirt for her *Papoos* for which she gave me a mess of Broth, which was thickened with meal made of the Bark of a Tree, and to make it the better, she had put into it about a handfull of Pease, and a few roasted Ground-nuts. I had not seen my son a pritty while, and here was an *Indian* of whom I made inquiry after him, and asked him when he saw him: he answered me, that such a time his master roasted him, and that himself did eat a piece of him, as big as his two fingers, and that he was very good meat: *But the Lord upheld my Spirit, under this discouragement; and I considered their horrible addictedness to lying, and that there is not one of them that makes the least conscience of speaking of truth.* In this place, on a cold night, as I lay by the fire, I removed a stick that kept the heat from me, a *Squaw* moved it down again, at which I lookt up, and she threw a handfull of ashes in mine eyes: I thought I should have been quite blinded, and have never seen more: but lying down, the water run out of my eyes, and carried the dirt with it, that by the morning, I recovered my sight again. Yet upon this, and the like occasions, I hope it is not too much to say with Job, *Have pitty upon me, have pitty upon me, O ye my friends, for the Hand of the Lord has touched me.* And here I cannot but remember how many times sitting in their *Wigwams*, and musing on things past, I should suddenly leap up and run out, as if I had been at home, forgetting where I was, and what my condition was: But when I was without, and saw nothing but *Wilderness*, and *Woods*, and a company of barbarous heathens: my mind quickly returned to me, which made me think of that, spoken concerning *Sampson*, who said, *I will go out and shake myself as at other times, but he wist not that the Lord was departed from him.* About this time I began to think that all my hopes of Restoration would come to nothing. I thought of the *English* Army, and hoped for their coming, and being taken by them, but that failed also. I hoped to be carried to *Albany*, as the *Indians* had discoursed before, but that failed also. I thought of being sold to my Husband, as my master spake, but in stead of that, my master himself was gone, and I left behind, so that my Spirit was now quite ready to sink. I asked them to let me go out and pick up some sticks, that I might get alone, *And poure out my heart unto the Lord.* Then also I took my Bible to read, but I found no comfort here neither, which many times I was wont to find: *So easie a thing it is with God to dry up the Streames of Scripture-comfort from us.* Yet I can say, that in all my sorrows and afflictions, God did not leave me to have my impatience work towards himself, as if his wayes were unrighteous. *But I knew that he laid upon me less than I deserved.* Afterward, before this dolefull time ended with me, I was turning the leaves of my Bible, and the Lord brought to me some Scriptures, which did a little revive me, as that Isai. 55.8. *For my thoughts are not your thoughts, neither are your wayes my ways, saith the Lord.* And also that, *Psal. 37. 5. Commit thy way unto the Lord, trust also in him, and he shall bring it to pass.* About this time they came yelping from

Hadly, where they had killed three *English men*, and brought one Captive with them, *viz. Thomas Read*. They all gathered about the poor Man, asking him many Questions. I desired also to go and see him; and when I came, he was crying bitterly, supposing they would quickly kill him. Whereupon I asked one of them, whether they intended to kill him; he answered me, they would not: He being a little cheared with that, I asked him about the wel-fare of my *Husband*, he told me he saw him such a time in the *Bay*, and he was well, but very melancholly. By which I certainly understood (though I suspected it before) that whatsoever the *Indians* told me respecting him was vanity and lies. Some of them told me, he was dead, and they had killed him: some said he was Married again, and that the Governour wished him to marry; and told him he should have his choice, and that all perswaded I was dead. So like were these barbarous creatures to him who was a lyar from the beginning.

As I was sitting once in the *Wigwam* here, *Philips* Maid came in with the Child in her arms, and asked me to give her a piece of my Apron, to make a flap for it, I told her I would not: then my Mistress bade me give it, but still I said no: the maid told me if I would not give her a piece, she would tear a piece off it: I told her I would tear her Coat then, with that my Mistriss rises up, and takes up a stick big enough to have killed me, and struck at me with it, but I stepped out, and she struck the stick into the Mat of the Wigwam. But while she was pulling of it out, I ran to the Maid and gave her all my Apron, and so that storm went over.

Hearing that my Son was come to this place, I went to see him, and told him his Father was well, but very melancholly: he told me he was as much grieved for his Father as for himself; I wondred at his speech, for I thought I had enough upon my spirit in reference to my self, to make me mindless of my Husband and every one else: they being safe among their Friends. He told me also, that a while before, his Master (together with other *Indians*) were going to the *French* for *Powder*; but by the way the *Mohawks* met with them, and killed four of their Company which made the rest turn back again, for which I desired that my self and he may bless the Lord; for it might have been worse with him, had he been sold to the *French*, than it proved to be in his remaining with the *Indians*.

I went to see an *English* Youth in this place, one *John Gilberd* of *Springfield*. I found him lying without dores, upon the ground; I asked him how he did? He told me he was very sick of a flux, with eating so much blood: They had turned him out of the *Wigwam*, and with him an *Indian Papoos*, almost dead, (whose Parents had been killed) in a bitter cold day, without fire or clothes: the young man himself had nothing on, but his shirt and wast-coat. This sight was enough to melt a heart of flint. There they lay quivering in the Cold, the youth round like a dog, the *Papoos* stretcht out, with his eyes and nose and mouth full of dirt, and yet alive, and groaning. I advised John to go and get to some fire: he told me he cou'd not stand, but I perswaded him still, lest he should ly there and die: and with much adoe I got him to a fire, and went my self home. As soon as I was got home, his Masters Daughter came after me, to know what I had done with the *English man*, I told her I had got him to a fire in such a place. Now had I need to pray *Pauls* prayer, 2 Thess. 3. 2. *That we may be delivered from unreasonable and wicked men.* For her satisfaction I went along with her, and brought her to him; but before I got home again, it was noised about, that I was running away and getting the *English* youth, along with me; that as soon as I came in, they began to rant and domineer: asking me where I had been, and what I had been doing? and saying they would knock him on the head: I told them, I had been seeing the *English Youth*, and that I would not run away, they told me I lyed, and taking up a Hatchet, they came to me, and said they would knock me down if I stirred out again; and so confined me to the *Wigwam*. Now may I say with *David*, 2 Sam. 24. 14. *I am in a great strait.* If I keep in, I must dy with hunger, and if I go out, I must be knockt in head. This distressed condition held that day, and half the next; *And then the Lord remembered me, whose mercyes are great.* Then came an *Indian* to me with a pair of stockings that were too big for him, and he would have me ravel them out, and knit them fit for him. I shewed my self willing, and bade him ask my mistriss if I might go along with him a little way; she said yes, I might, but I was not a little refresht with that news, that I had my liberty again. Then I went along with him, and he gave me some roasted Ground-nuts, which did again revive my feeble stomach.

Being got out of her sight, I had time and liberty again to look into my Bible: *Which was my Guid by day, and my Pillow by night.* Now that comfortable Scripture presented itself to me, *Isa.* 54. 7. *For a small moment have I forsaken thee, but with great mercies will I gather thee.* Thus the Lord carried me along from one time to another, and made good to me this precious promise, and many others. Then my Son came to see me, and I asked his master to let him stay a while with me, that I might comb his head, and look over him, for he was almost overcome with lice. He told me, when I had done, that he was very hungry, but I had nothing to relieve him; but bid him go into the Wigwams as he went along, and see if he could get any thing among them. Which he did, and it seems tarried a little too long; for his Master was angry with him, and beat him, and then sold him. Then he came running to tell me he had a new Master, and that he had given him some Ground-nuts already. Then I went along with him to his new Master who told me he loved him: and he should not want. So his master carried him away, & I never saw him afterward, till I saw him at *Pascataqua* in *Portsmouth.*

That night they bade me go out of the *Wigwam* again: my Mistrisses Papoos was sick, and it died that night, and there was one benefit in it, that there was more room. I went to a *Wigwam,* and they bade me come in, and gave me a skin to ly upon, and a mess of Venison and Ground-nuts, which was a choice Dish among them. On the morrow they buried the *Papoos,* and afterward, both morning and evening, there came a company to mourn and howle with her: though I confess, I could not much condole with them. Many sorrowfull dayes I had in this place: often getting alone; *like a Crane, or a Swallow, so did I chatter: I did mourn as a Dove, mine eyes fail with looking upward. Oh, Lord, I am oppressed; undertake for me,* Isa. 38. 14. I could tell the Lord as *Hezekiah,* ver. 3. *Remember now O Lord, I beseech thee, how I have walked before thee in truth.* Now had I time to examine all my wayes: my Conscience did not accuse me, of un-righteousness toward one or other: yet I saw how in my walk with God, I had been a careless creature. As *David* said, *Against thee, thee only have I sinned:* & I might say with the poor Publican, *God be merciful unto me a sinner.* On the Sabbath-dayes, I could look upon the Sun and think

how People were going to the house of God, to have their
Souls refresht; & then home, and their bodies also: but I was
destitute of both; & might say as the poor Prodigal, *he would
fain have filled his belly with the husks that the Swine did eat, and
no man gave unto him*, Luke 15. 16. For I must say with him,
Father I have sinned against heaven, and in thy sight, ver. 21.
I remembered how on the night before & after the Sabbath,
when my Family was about me, and Relations and Neighbours
with us, we could pray and sing, and then refresh our bodies
with the good creatures of God; and then have a comfortable
Bed to ly down on: but in stead of all this, I had only a little
Swill for the body, and then like a Swine, must ly down on the
ground. I cannot express to man the sorrow that lay upon my
Spirit, the Lord knows it. Yet that comfortable Scripture would
often come to my mind, *For a small moment have I forsaken
thee, but with great mercies will I gather thee.*

THE FOURTEENTH REMOVE

Now must we pack up and be gone from this Thicket, bending
our course toward the Bay-towns, I haveing nothing to eat by
the way this day, but a few crumbs of Cake, that an *Indian*
gave my girle the same day we were taken. She gave it me, and
I put it in my pocket; there it lay, till it was so mouldy (for want
of good baking) that one could not tell what it was made of;
it fell all to crumbs, & grew so dry and hard, that it was like
little flints; & this refreshed me many times, when I was ready
to faint. It was in my thoughts when I put it into my mouth;
that if ever I returned, I would tell the World what a blessing
the Lord gave to such mean food. As we went along, they
killed a *Deer*, with a young one in her, they gave me a piece of
the *Fawn*, and it was so young and tender, that one might eat
the bones as well as the flesh, and yet I thought it very good.
When night came on we sate down; it rained, but they quickly
got up a Bark Wigwam, where I lay dry that night. I looked
out in the morning, and many of them had lain in the rain all
night, I saw by their Reaking. Thus the Lord dealt mercifully
with me many times, and I fared better than many of them.
In the morning they took the blood of the *Deer*, and put it
into the Paunch, and so boyled it; I could eat nothing of that,
though they ate it sweetly. And yet they were so nice in other

things, that when I had fetcht Water, and had put the Dish I dipt the water with, into the Kettle of water which I brought, they would say, they would knock me down; for they said, it was a sluttish trick.

THE FIFTEENTH REMOVE

We went on our Travel. I having got one handfull of Ground-nuts, for my support that day, they gave me my load, and I went on cheerfully (with the thoughts of going homeward) haveing my burden more on my back than my spirit: we came to *Baquaug River* again that day, near which we abode a few dayes. Sometimes one of them would give me a Pipe, another a little Tobacco, another a little Salt: which I would change for a little Victuals. I cannot but think what a Wolvish appetite persons have in a starving condition: for many times when they gave me that which was hot, I was so greedy, that I shou'd burn my mouth, that it would trouble me hours after, and yet I should quickly do the same again. And after I was thoroughly hungry, I was never again satisfied. For though sometimes it fell out, that I got enough, and did eat till I could eat no more, yet I was as unsatisfied as I was when I began. And now could I see that Scripture verified (there being many Scriptures which we do not take notice of, or understand till we are afflicted) *Mic.* 6. 14. *Thou shalt eat and not be satisfied.* Now I might see more than ever before, the miseries that sin hath brought upon us: Many times I should be ready to run out against the Heathen, but the Scripture would quiet me again, *Amos,* 3.6, *Shal there be evil in the City, and the Lord hath not done it?* The Lord help me to make a right improvement of His Word, and that I might learn that great lesson, *Mic.* 6. 8, 9. *He hath showed thee (Oh Man) what is good, and what doth the Lord require of thee, but to do justly, and love mercy, and walk humbly with thy God? Hear ye the rod, and who hath appointed it.*

THE SIXTEENTH REMOVE

We began this Remove with wading over Baquag *River: the water was up to the knees, and the stream very swift, and so cold that I thought it would have cut me in sunder.* I was so weak and feeble, that I reeled as I went along, and thought there I must end my dayes at last, after my bearing and getting through so many difficulties; the *Indians* stood laughing to see me staggering along: but in my distress the Lord gave me experience of the truth, and goodness of that promise, *Isai.* 43. 2. *When thou passest through the Waters, I will be with thee, and through the Rivers, they shall not overflow thee.* Then I sat down to put on my stockins and shoes, with the teares running down mine eyes, and many sorrowfull thoughts in my heart, but I gat up to go along with them. Quickly there came up to us an *Indian*, who informed them, that I must go to *Wachusett* to my master, for there was a Letter come from the Council to the *Sagamores*, about redeeming the Captives, and that there would be another in fourteen dayes, and that I must be there ready. My heart was so heavy before that I could scarce speak or go in the path; and yet now so light, that I could run. My strength seemed to come again, and recruit my feeble knees, and aking heart: yet it pleased them to go but one mile that night, and there we stayed two dayes. In that time came a company of *Indians* to us, near thirty, all on horse-back. My heart skipt within me, thinking they had been *English men* at the first sight of them, for they were dressed in *English* Apparel, with Hats, white Neckcloths, and Sashes about their waists, and Ribbonds upon their shoulders: but when they came near, there was a vast difference between the lovely faces of Christians, and the foul looks of these Heathens, which much damped my spirit again.

THE SEVENTEENTH REMOVE

A comfortable Remove it was to me, because of my hopes. They gave me a pack, and along we went chearfully; but quickly my will proved more than my strength; having little or no refreshing my strength failed me, and my spirit were almost quite gone. Now may I say with *David*, Psalm 109. 22, 23, 24. *I am poor and needy, and my heart is wounded within me. I am gone like the shadow when it declineth: I am tossed up and down like the locusts; my knees are weak through fasting, and my flesh faileth of fatness.* At night we came to an *Indian Town*, and the *Indians* sate down by a *Wigwam* discoursing, but I was almost spent, and could scarce speak. I laid down my load, and went into the *Wigwam*, and there sat an *Indian* boyling of *Horses feet* (they being wont to eat the flesh first, and when the feet were old and dried, and they had nothing else, they would cut off the feet and use them). I asked him to give me a little of his Broth, or Water they were boiling in; he took a dish, and gave me one spoonful of Samp, and bid me take as much of the Broth as I would. Then I put some of the hot water to the Samp, and drank it up, and my spirit came again. He gave me also a piece of the Ruff or Ridding of the small Guts, and I broiled it on the coals; and now may I say with *Jonathan, See, I pray you, how mine eyes have been enlightened, because I tasted a little of this honey*, 1 Sam. 14. 29. Now is my Spirit revived again, though means be never so inconsiderable, yet if the Lord bestow his blessing upon them, they shall refresh both Soul and Body.

THE EIGHTEENTH REMOVE

We took up our packs and along we went, but a wearisome day I had of it. As we went along I saw an *English-man* stript naked, and lying dead upon the ground, but knew not who it was. Then we came to another *Indian Town*, where we stayed all night. In this Town there were four *English Children*, Captives; and one of them my own Sisters. I went to see how she did, and she was well, considering her Captive-condition. I would have tarried that night with her, but they that owned her would not suffer it. Then I went into another *Wigwam*, where they were boyling Corn and Beans, which was a lovely sight to see, but I could not get a taste thereof. Then I went to another *Wigwam*, where there were two of the *English Children*; the *Squaw* was boyling *Horses feet*, then she cut me off a little piece, and gave one of the *English Children* a piece also. Being very hungry I had quickly eat up mine, but the Child could not bite it, it was so tough and sinewy, but lay sucking, gnawing, chewing and slobbering of it in the mouth and hand, then I took it of the Child, and ate it myself, and savoury it was to my taste. Then I may say as *Job Chap.* 6. 7. *The things that my soul refused to touch, are as my sorrowful meat.* Thus the Lord made that pleasant refreshing, which another time would have been an abomination. Then I went home to my mistresses *Wigwam*; and they told me I disgraced my master with begging, and if I did so any more, they would knock me in the head: I told them, they had as good knock me in the head as starve me to death.

THE NINETEENTH REMOVE

They said, when we went out, that we must travel to Wachuset *this day.* But a bitter weary day I had of it, travelling now three dayes together, without resting any day between. At last, after many weary steps, I saw *Wachuset* hills, but many miles off. Then we came to a great *Swamp*, through which we travelled, up to the knees, in mud and water, which was heavy going to one tyred before. Being almost spent, I thought I should have sunk down at last, and never gat out; but I may say, as in Psal. 94. 18. *When my foot slipped, thy mercy, O Lord, held me up.* Going along, having indeed my life, but little spirit, *Philip,* who was in the Company, came up and took me by the hand, and said, *Two weeks more and you shal be Mistress again.* I asked him, if he spake true? He answered, Yes, *and quickly you shall come to your master again*; who had been gone from us three weeks. After many weary steps we came to *Wachuset*, where he was: and glad I was to see him. He asked me, *When I washt me?* I told him not this month, then he fetcht me some water himself, and bid me wash, and gave me the Glass to see how I lookt; and bid his *Squaw* give me something to eat: so she gave me a mess of Beans and meat, and a little Ground-nut Cake. I was wonderfully revived with this favour shewed me, *Psal.* 106. 46, *He made them also to be pittied, of all those that carried them Captives.*

My master had three *Squaws*, living sometimes with one, and sometimes with another one, this old Squaw, at whose *Wigwam* I was, and with whom my master had been those three weeks. Another was *Wettimore*, with whom I had lived and served all this while: A severe and proud Dame she was, bestowing every day in dressing herself neat as much time as any of the Gentry of the land: powdering her hair, and painting her face, going with Neck-laces, with Jewels in her ears, and Bracelets upon her hands: When she had dressed her self, her work was to make Girdles of *Wampom* and *Beads.* The third *Squaw* was a younger one, by whom he had two *Papooses.* By that time I was refresht by the old *Squaw*, with whom my master was, *Wettimores* Maid came to call me home, at which I fell a weeping. Then the old *Squaw* told me, to encourage me, that if I wanted victuals, I should come to her, and that I should ly there in her *Wigwam.* Then I went with the maid, and quickly came again and lodged there. The *Squaw* laid a Mat under me, and a good Rugg over me; the first time I had any such kindness shewed me. I understood that *Wettimore* thought, that if she should let me go and serve with the old *Squaw*, she would be in danger to loose, not only my service, but the redemption-pay also. And I was not a little glad to hear this; being by it raised in my hopes, that in Gods due time there would be an end of this sorrowfull hour. Then in came an *Indian*, and asked me to knit him three pair of Stockins, for which I had a Hat, and a silk Handkerchief. Then another asked me to make her a shift, for which she gave me an Apron.

Then came *Tom* and *Peter*, with the second Letter from the Council, about the Captives. Though they were *Indians*, I gat them by the hand, and burst out into tears; my heart was so full that I could not speak to them; but recovering my self, I asked them how my husband did, and all my friends and acquaintance? they said, *They are all very well, but melancholy.* They brought me two Biskets, and a pound of Tobacco. The Tobacco I quickly gave away; when it was all gone, one asked me to give him a pipe of Tobacco, I told him it was all gone; then began he to rant and threaten. I told him when my Husband came I would give him some: *Hang him Rogue (sayes he) I will knock out his brains, if he comes here.* And then again, in the same breath they would say, *That if there should come an hundred without Guns, they would do them no hurt.* So unstable and like mad men they were. So that fearing the worst, I durst not send to my Husband, though there were some thoughts of his coming to Redeem and fetch me, not knowing what might follow; *For there was little more trust to them than to the master they served.* When the Letter was come, the *Saggamores* met to consult about the Captives, and called me to them to enquire how much my husband would give to redeem me, when I came I sate down among them, as I was wont to do, as their manner is: Then they bade me stand up, and said, *they were the General Court.* They bid me speak what I thought he would give. Now knowing that all we had was destroyed by the *Indians*, I was in a great strait: I thought if I should speak of but a little, it would be slighted, and hinder the matter; if of a great sum, I knew not where it would be procured: yet at a venture, I said *Twenty pounds*, yet desired them to take less; but they would not hear

of that, but sent that message to *Boston*, that for *Twenty pounds*
I should be redeemed. It was a Praying-*Indian* that wrote their
Letter for them. There was another Praying *Indian*, who told
me, that he had a brother, that would not eat Horse; his conscience was so tender and scrupulous (though as large as hell,
for the destruction of poor *Christians*). Then he said, he read
that Scripture to him, 2 Kings, 6. 25. *There was a famine in*
Samaria, *and behold they besieged it, until an Asses head was
sold for fourscore pieces of silver, and the fourth part of a Kab of
Doves dung, for five pieces of silver.* He expounded this place to
his brother, and shewed him that it was lawfull to eat that in
a Famine which is not at another time. And now, says he, he
will eat horse with any *Indian* of them all. There was another
Praying-*Indian*, who when he had done all the mischief that he
could, betrayed his own Father into the *English* hands, thereby
to purchase his own life. Another Praying-*Indian* was at *Sudbury-fight*, though, as he deserved, he was afterward hanged for
it. There was another Praying *Indian*, so wicked and cruel, as
to wear a string about his neck, strung with *Christians* fingers.
Another Praying-*Indian*, when they went to *Sudbury-fight*,
went with them, and his *Squaw* also with him, with her *Papoos*
at her back. Before they went to that fight, they got a company
together to *Powaw*; the manner was as followeth. There was
one that kneeled upon a *Deer-skin*, with the company round
him in a ring who kneeled, and striking upon the ground with
their hands, and with sticks, and muttering or humming with
their mouths, besides him who kneeled in the ring, there also
stood one with a Gun in his hand: Then he on the *Deer-skin*
made a speech, and all manifested assent to it: and so they
did many times together. Then they bade him with the Gun
go out of the ring, which he did, but when he was out, they
called him in again; but he seemed to make a stand, then they
called the more earnestly, till he returned again: Then they all
sang. Then they gave him two Guns, in either hand one: And
so he on the *Deer-skin* began again; and at the end of every
sentence in his speaking, they all assented, humming or muttering with their mouthes, and striking upon the ground with
their hands. Then they bade him with the two Guns go out of
the ring again; which he did, a little way. Then they called him
in again, but he made a stand; so they called him with greater

earnestness; but he stood reeling and wavering as if he knew not whither he should stand or fall, or which way to go. Then they called him with exceeding great vehemency, all of them, one and another: after a little while he turned in, staggering as he went, with his Armes stretched out, in either hand a Gun. As soon as he came in, they all sang and rejoyced exceedingly a while. And then he upon the *Deer-skin*, made another speech unto which they all assented in a rejoicing manner: and so they ended their business, and forthwith went to *Sudbury-fight*. To my thinking they went without any scruple, but that they should prosper, and gain the victory: And they went out not so rejoycing, but they came home with as great a Victory. For they said they had killed two Captains, and almost an hundred men. One *English-man* they brought along with them: and he said, it was too true, for they had made sad work at *Sudbury*, as indeed it proved. Yet they came home without that rejoycing and triumphing over their victory, which they were wont to shew at other times, but rather like Dogs (as they say) which have lost their ears. Yet I could not perceive that it was for their own loss of men: They said, they had not lost above five or six: and I missed none, except in one *Wigwam*. When they went, they acted as if the Devil had told them that they should gain the victory: and now they acted, as if the Devil had told them they should have a fall. Whither it were so or no, I cannot tell, but so it proved, for quickly they began to fall, and so held on that Summer, till they came to utter ruine. They came home on a Sabbath day, and the *Powaw* that kneeled upon the *Deer-skin* came home (I may say, without abuse) as black as the Devil. When my master came home, he came to me and bid me make a shirt for his *Papoos*, of a hollandlaced Pillowbeer. About that time there came an *Indian* to me and bid me come to his *Wigwam*, at night, and he would give me some Pork & Ground-nuts. Which I did, and as I was eating, another *Indian* said to me, he seems to be your good Friend, but he killed two *Englishmen* at *Sudbury*, and there lie their Cloaths behind you: I looked behind me, and there I saw bloody Cloaths, with Bullet holes in them; yet the Lord suffered not this wretch to do me any hurt; Yea, instead of that, he many times refresht me: five or six times did he and his *Squaw* refresh my feeble carcass. If I went to their *Wigwam* at any time, they would alwayes give me something, and yet they were strangers that I never saw before. Another *Squaw* gave me a piece of fresh Pork, and a little Salt with it, and lent me her Pan to Fry it in; and I cannot but remember what a sweet, pleasant and delightfull relish that bit had to me, to this day. So little do we prize common mercies when we have them to the full.

THE TWENTIETH REMOVE

It was their usual manner to remove, when they had done any mischief, lest they should be found out: and so they did at this time. We went about three or four miles, and there they built a great *Wigwam*, big enough to hold an hundred *Indians*, which they did in preparation to a great day of Dancing. They would say now amongst themselves, that the *Governour* would be so angry for his loss at Sudbury, that he would send no more about the Captives, which made me grieve and tremble. My Sister being not far from the place where we now were, and hearing that I was here, desired her master to let her come and see me, and he was willing to it, and would go with her: but she being ready before him, told him she would go before, and was come within a Mile or two of the place; Then he overtook her, and began to rant as if he had been mad; and made her go back again in the Rain; so that I never saw her till I saw her in *Charlestown*. But the Lord requited many of their ill doings, for this *Indian* her master, was hanged afterward at *Boston*. The *Indians* now began to come from all quarters, against their merry dancing day. Among some of them came one *Goodwife Kettle*: I told her my heart was so heavy that it was ready to break: so is mine too, said she, but yet said, I hope we shall hear some good news shortly. I could hear how earnestly my Sister desired to see me, and I as earnestly desired to see her: and yet neither of us could get an opportunity. My Daughter was also now about a mile off, and I had not seen her in nine or ten weeks, as I had not seen my Sister since our first taking. I earnestly desired them to let me go and see them: yea, I intreated, begged, and perswaded them, but to let me see my Daughter; and yet so hard hearted were they, that they would not suffer it. They made use of their tyrannical power whilst they had it: but through the Lord's wonderful mercy, their time was now but short.

On a Sabbath day, the Sun being about an hour high in the afternoon, came Mr. John Hoar *(the Council permitting him, and his own foreward spirit inclining him) together with the two forementioned Indians,* Tom *and* Peter, *with their third Letter from the Council.* When they came near, I was abroad: though I saw them not, they presently called me in, and bade me sit down and not stir. Then they catched up their Guns, and away they ran, as if an Enemy had been at hand; and the Guns went off apace. I manifested some great trouble, and they asked me what was the matter? I told them, I *thought they had killed the* English-man (for they had in the mean time informed me that an *English-man* was come), they said, *No*; They shot over his Horse, and under, and before his Horse; and they pusht him this way and that way, at their pleasure, shewing what they could do: Then they let them come to their *Wigwams.* I begged of them to let me see the *English man,* but they would not. But there was I fain to sit their pleasure. When they had talked their fill with him, they suffered me to go to him. We asked each other of our welfare, and how my Husband did, and all my Friends? He told me they were all well, and would be glad to see me. Amongst other things which my Husband sent me, there came a pound of *Tobacco*: which I sold for nine shillings in Money: for many of the *Indians* for want of *Tobacco,* smoaked *Hemlock,* and *Ground Ivy.* It was a great mistake in any, who thought I sent for *Tobacco*: for through the favour of God, that desire was overcome. I now asked them, whither I should go home with Mr. *Hoar*? They answered *No,* one and another of them: and it being night, we lay down with that answer; in the morning, Mr. *Hoar* invited the *Saggamores* to Dinner; but when we went to get it ready, we found that they had stollen the greatest part of the Provision Mr. *Hoar* had brought, out of his Bags, in the night: *And we may see the wonderfull power of God, in that one passage, in that when there was such a great number of the* Indians *together, and so greedy of a little good food; and no* English *there, but Mr. Hoar and my self: that there they did not knock us in the head, and take what we had: there being not only some Provision, but also Trading-cloth, a part of the twenty pounds agreed upon: But instead of doing us any mischief, they seemed to be ashamed of the fact, and said, it were some* Matchit Indian *that did it.* Oh, that we could believe that there is nothing too hard for God! God shewed his Power over the Heathen in this, *as he did over the hungry Lyons when* Daniel *was cast into the Den.* Mr. *Hoar* called them betime to Dinner, but they ate very little, they being so busie in dressing themselves, and getting ready for their Dance: which was carried on by eight of them, four *Men* and four *Squaws*; My master and mistriss being two. He was dressed in his Holland shirt, with great Laces sewed at the tail of it, he had his silver Buttons, his white Stockins, his Garters were hung round with Shillings, and he had Girdles of *Wampom upon his head and shoulders.* She had a Kersey Coat, and covered with Girdles of *Wampom* from the Loins upward: her armes from her elbows to her hands were covered with Bracelets; there were handfulls of Neck-laces about her neck, and severall sorts of Jewels in her ears. She had fine red Stockins, and white Shoos, her hair powdered and face painted Red, that was alwayes before Black. And all the Dancers were after the same manner. There were two other singing and knocking on a Kettle for their musick. They keept hopping up and down one after another, with a Kettle of water in the midst, standing warm upon some Embers, to drink of when they were dry. They held on till it was almost night, throwing out *Wampom* to the standers by. At night I asked them again, if I should go home? They all as one said No, except my Husband would come for me. When we were lain down, my Master went out of the *Wigwam*, and by and by sent in an *Indian* called *James the Printer*, who told Mr. *Hoar*, that my Master would let me go home tomorrow, if he would let him have one pint of Liquors. Then Mr. *Hoar* called his own *Indians*, *Tom* and *Peter*, and bid them go and see whither he would promise before them three: and if he would, he should have it; which he did, and he had it. Then *Philip* smelling the business cal'd me to him, and asked me what I would give him, to tell me some good news, and speak a good word for me. *I told him, I could not tell what to give him, I would anything I had, and asked him what he would have?* He said, two Coats and twenty shillings in Mony, and half a bushel of seed Corn, and some Tobacco. I thanked him for his love: but I knew the good news as well as the crafty *Fox*. My Master after he had had his drink, quickly came ranting into the *Wigwam* again, and called for Mr. *Hoar*, drinking to him, and saying, *He was a good man*:

and then again he would say, *Hang him, Rogue*: Being almost drunk, he would drink to him, and yet presently say he should be hanged. Then he called for me, I trembled to hear him, yet I was fain to go to him, and he drank to me, shewing no incivility. He was the first *Indian* I saw drunk all the while that I was amongst them. At last his *Squaw* ran out, and he after her, round the *Wigwam*, with his money jingling at his knees: But she escaped him: But having an old *Squaw* he ran to her: and so through the Lords mercy, we were no more troubled that night. *Yet I had not a comfortable nights rest: for I think I can say, I did not sleep for three nights together.* The night before the Letter came from the Council, I could not rest, I was so full of feares and troubles, God many times leaving us most in the dark, when deliverance is nearest: yea, at this time I could not rest, night nor day. The next night I was overjoyed, Mr. *Hoar* being come, and that with such good tidings. The third night I was even swallowed up with all thoughts of things, *viz.* that ever I should go home again; and that I must go, leaving my Children behind me in the *Wilderness*; so that sleep was now almost departed from mine eyes.

On *Tuesday morning* they called their *General Court* (as they call it) to consult and determine, whether I should go home or no: And they all as one man did seemingly consent to it, that I should go home; except *Philip*, who would not come among them.

But before I go any further, I would take leave to mention a few remarkable passages of providence, which I took special notice of in my afflicted time.

1. *Of the fair opportunity lost in the long March, a little after the* Fort-fight, *when our* English Army *was so numerous, and in pursuit of the* Enemy, *and so near as to take several and destroy them: and the* Enemy *in such distress for food, that our men might track them by their rooting in the earth for Ground-nuts whilest they were flying for their lives.* I say, that then our Army should want Provision, and be forced to leave their pursuit and return homeward: and the very next week the *Enemy* came upon our *Town*, like Bears bereft of their whelps, or so many ravenous Wolves, rending us and our Lambs to death. But what shall I say? God seemed to leave His People to themselves, and order all things for His own holy ends. *Shall there be evil in the*

City and the Lord hath not done it? They are not grieved for the affliction of Joseph, *therefore shal they go Captive, with the first that go Captive. It is the Lords doing, and it should be marvelous in our eyes.*

2. *I cannot but remember how the* Indians *derided the slowness, and dulness of the* English *Army, in its setting out.* For after the desolations at *Lancaster* and *Medfield,* as I went along with them, they asked me when I thought the *English* Army would come after them? I told them I could not tell: It may be they will come in *May,* said they. Thus did they scoffe at us, as if the *English* would be a quarter of a year getting ready.

3. *Which also I have hinted before, when the* English *Army with new supplies were sent forth to pursue after the enemy, and they understanding it, fled before them till they came to* Baquaug *River, where they forthwith went over safely: that that River should be impassable to the* English. I can but admire to see the wonderfull providence of God in preserving the heathen for farther affliction to our poor Countrey. They could go in great numbers over, but the *English* must stop: God had an over-ruling hand in all those things.

4. *It was thought, if their corn were cut down, they would starve and dy with hunger: and all their Corn that could be found, was destroyed, and they driven from that little they had in store, into the Woods in the midst of Winter;* and yet how to admiration did the Lord preserve them for his Holy ends, and the destruction of many still amongst the *English!* Strangely did the Lord provide for them; that I did not see (all the time I was among them) one Man, Woman, or Child, die with hunger.

Though many times they would eat that, that a Hog or a Dog would hardly touch; yet by that God strengthened them to be a scourge to His People.

The chief and commonest food was Ground-nuts: They eat also Nuts and Acorns, Harty-choaks, Lilly roots, Ground-beans, and several other weeds and roots, that I know not.

They would pick up old bones, and cut them to pieces at the joynts, and if they were full of wormes and magots, they would scald them over the fire to make the vermine come out, and then boile them, and drink up the Liquor, and then beat the great ends of them in a Morter, and so eat them. They would eat Horses guts, and ears, and all sorts of wild Birds which they could catch: also Bear, Venison, Beaver, Tortois, Frogs, Squirrels, Dogs, Skunks, Rattle-snakes; yea, the very Bark of Trees; besides all sorts of creatures, and provision which they plundered from the *English*. I can but stand in admiration to see the wonderful power of God, in providing for such a vast number of our Enemies in the *Wilderness*, where there was nothing to be seen, but from hand to mouth. Many times in a morning, the generality of them would eat up all they had, and yet have some further supply against what they wanted. It is said, *Psal.* 81. 13, 14. *Oh, that my People had hearkened to me, and* Israel *had walked in my wayes, I should soon have subdued their Enemies, and turned my hand against their Adversaries.* But now our perverse and evil carriages in the sight of the Lord, have so offended Him, that instead of turning His hand against them, the Lord feeds and nourishes them up to be a scourge to the whole Land.

5. *Another thing that I would observe is, the strange providence of God, in turning things about when the* Indians *were at the highest, and the* English *at the lowest.* I was with the Enemy eleven weeks and five dayes, and not one Week passed without the fury of the Enemy, and some desolation by fire and sword upon one place or other. They mourned (with their black faces) for their own losses, yet triumphed and rejoyced in their inhumane, and many times devilish cruelty to the *English*. They would boast much of their Victories; saying, that in two hours time they had destroyed such a *Captain*, and his *Company* at such a place; and such a *Captain* and his *Company* in such a place; and such a *Captain* and his *Company* in such a place; and boast how many *Towns* they had destroyed, and then scoffe, and say, *They had done them a good turn, to send them to Heaven so soon.* Again, they would say, *This summer that they would knock all the Rogues in the head, or drive them into the Sea, or make them flie the Countrey*: thinking surely, *Agag*-like, *The bitterness of Death is past.* Now the Heathen begins to think all is their own, and the poor Christians hopes to fail (as to man) and now their eyes are more to God, and their hearts sigh heaven-ward: and to say in good earnest, *Help Lord, or we perish*: When the Lord had brought his people to this, that they saw no help in any thing but himself: then he takes the quarrel into his own hand: and though they had made a pit, in

their own imaginations, as deep as hell for the Christians that Summer, yet the Lord hurll'd themselves into it. And the Lord had not so many wayes before to preserve them, but now he hath as many to destroy them.

But to return again to my going home, where we may see a remarkable change of Providence: At first they were all against it, except my Husband would come for me; but afterwards they assented to it, and seemed much to rejoyce in it; some askt me to send them some Bread, others some Tobacco, others shaking me by the hand, offering me a Hood and Scarfe to ride in; not one moving hand or tongue against it. Thus hath the Lord answered my poor desire, and the many earnest requests of others put up unto God for me. In my travels an *Indian* came to me, and told me, if I were willing, he and his *Squaw* would run away, and go home along with me: I told him *No*: I was not willing to run away, but desired to wait Gods time, that I might go home quietly, and without fear. And now God hath granted me my desire. O the wonderfull power of God that I have seen, and the experience that I have had: *I have been in the midst of those roaring Lyons, and Salvage Bears, that feared neither God, nor Man, nor the Devil, by night and day, alone and in company: sleeping all sorts together, and yet not one of them ever offered me the least abuse of unchastity to me, in word or action.* Though some are ready to say, I speak it for my own credit; *But I speak it in the presence of God, and to His glory.* Gods power is as great now, and as sufficient to save, as when he preserved *Daniel* in the Lions den; or the three *Children* in the fiery Furnace. I may well say as his *Psal.* 107. 1, 2, *Oh give thanks unto the Lord for He is good, for his mercy endureth for ever.* Let the Redeemed of the Lord say so, whom He hath redeemed from the hand of the Enemy, especially that I should come away in the midst of so many hundreds of Enemies quietly and peacably, and not a Dog moving his tongue. So I took my leave of them, and in coming along my heart melted into tears, more then all the while I was with them, and I was almost swallowed up with the thoughts that ever I should go home again. About the Sun going down, Mr. *Hoar*, and my self, and the two *Indians* came to *Lancaster*, and a solemn sight it was to me. There had I lived many comfortable years amongst my Relations and Neighbours, and now not one *Christian* to be seen, nor one house left standing. We went on to a Farm house that was yet standing, where we lay all night: and a comfortable lodging we had, though nothing but straw to ly on. The Lord preserved us in safety that night, and raised us up again in the morning, and carried us along, that before noon, we came to *Concord*. Now was I full of joy, and yet not without sorrow: joy to see such a lovely sight, so many *Christians* together, and some of them my Neighbours: There I met with my Brother, and my Brother in Law, who asked me, if I knew where his Wife was? Poor heart! he had helped to bury her, and knew it not; she being shot down by the house was partly burnt: so that those who were at *Boston* at the desolation of the *Town*, and came back afterward, and buried the dead, did not know her. Yet I was not without sorrow, to think how many were looking and longing, and my own Children amongst the rest, to enjoy that deliverance that I had now received, and I did not know whither ever I should see them again. Being recruited with food and raiment we went to *Boston* that day, where I met with my dear Husband, but the thoughts of our dear Children, one being dead, and the other we could not tell where, abated our comfort each to other. I was not before so much hem'd in with the merciless and cruel Heathen, but now as much with pittiful, tender-hearted and compassionate Christians. In that poor, and destressed, and beggerly condition I was received in, I was kindly entertained in severall Houses: so much love I received from several (some of whom I knew, and others I knew not) that I am not capable to declare it. But the Lord knows them all by name: *The Lord reward them seven fold into their bosoms of his spirituals, for their temporals!* The *twenty pounds* the price of my redemption was raised by some *Boston* Gentlemen, and Ms. *Usher*, whose bounty and religious charity, I would not forget to make mention of. Then Mr. *Thomas Shepard* of *Charlestown* received us into his House, where we continued eleven weeks; and a Father and Mother they were to us. And many more tender-hearted Friends we met with in that place. We were now in the midst of love, yet not without much and frequent heaviness of heart for our poor Children, and other Relations, who were still in affliction. The week following, after my coming in, the Governour and Council sent forth to the *Indians* again; and that not without success; for they brought in my Sister, and Good-wife Kettle: Their not knowing where our Children were, was a sore tryal to us still, and yet we were not without secret hopes that we should see them again. That which was dead lay heavier upon my spirit, than those which were alive and amongst the Heathen; thinking how it suffered with its wounds, and I was in no way able to relieve it; and how it was buried by the Heathen in the *Wilderness* from among all Christians. We were hurried up and down in our thoughts, sometimes we should hear a report that they were gone this way, and sometimes that; and that they were come in, in this place or that: We kept enquiring and listening to hear concerning them, but no certain news as yet. About this time the Council had ordered a day of publick *Thanks-giving*: though I thought I had still cause of mourning, and being unsettled in our minds, we thought we would ride toward the *Eastward*, to see if we could hear anything concerning our Children. And as we were riding along, (God is the wise disposer of all things) between *Ipswich* and *Rowley* we met with Mr. *William Hubbard*, who told us that our Son *Joseph* was come in to Major *Waldrens*, and another with him, which was my Sisters Son. I asked him how he knew it? He said, the Major himself told him so. So along we went till we came to *Newbury*; and their Minister being absent, they desired my Husband to preach the *Thanks-giving* for them; but he was not willing to stay there that night, but would go over to *Salisbury*, to hear further, and come again in the morning; which he did, and Preached there that day. At night, when he had done, one came and told him that his Daughter was come in at *Providence*: Here was mercy on both hands: Now hath God fulfilled that precious Scripture which was such a comfort to me in my distressed condition. When my heart was ready to sink into the Earth (my Children being gone I could not tell whither) and my knees trembled under me, *And I was walking through the valley of the shadow of Death*: Then the Lord brought, and now has fulfilled that reviving word unto me: Thus saith the Lord, *Refrain thy voice from weeping, and thine eyes from tears, for thy work shall be rewarded*, saith the Lord, *and they shall come again from the Land of the Enemy*. Now we were between them, the one on the *East*, and the other on the *West*: Our Son being nearest, we went to him first, to *Portsmouth*, where we met with him, and with the Major also: who told us he had done what he could, but could not redeem him under *seven pounds*; which the good People thereabouts were pleased to pay. The Lord reward the Major, and all the rest, though unknown to me, for their labour of Love. My Sisters Son was redeemed for *four pounds*, which the Council gave order for the payment of. Having now received one of our Children, we hastened toward the other: going back through *Newbury*, my Husband Preached there on the *Sabbath-day*: for which they rewarded him many fold.

On *Munday* we came to Charlestown, where we heard that the Governour of *Road-Island* had sent over for our Daughter, to take care of her, being now within his Jurisdiction: which should not pass without our acknowledgments. But she being nearer *Rehoboth* than *Road-Island*, Mr. *Newman* went over, and took care of her, and brought her to his own House. And the goodness of God was admirable to us in our low estate, in that he raised up passionate Friends on every side to us, when we had nothing to recompance any for their love. The *Indians* were now gone that way, that it was apprehended dangerous to go to her: But the Carts which carried Provision to the *English* Army, being guarded, brought her with them to *Dorchester*, where we received her safe: blessed be the Lord for it, *For great is his Power, and he can do whatsoever seemeth him good.* Her coming in was after this manner: She was travelling one day with the *Indians*, with her basket at her back; the company of *Indians* were got before her, and gone out of sight, all except one *Squaw*; she followed the *Squaw* till night, and then both of them lay down, having nothing over them but the heavens, and under them but the earth. Thus she travelled three dayes together, not knowing whither she was going: having nothing to eat or drink but water, and green *Hirtle-berries*. At last they came into *Providence*, where she was kindly entertained by several of that *Town*. The *Indians* often said, that I should never have her under *twenty pounds*: But now the Lord hath brought her in upon free-cost, and given her to me the second time. The Lord make us a blessing indeed, each to others. Now have I seen that Scripture also fulfilled, *Deut.* 30. 4, 7. *If any of thine be driven out to the outmost parts of heaven, from thence will the Lord thy God gather thee, and from thence will he fetch thee. And the Lord thy God will put all these curses upon thine enemies, and on them which hate thee, which persecuted thee.* Thus hath the Lord brought me and mine out of that horrible pit, and hath set us in the midst of tender-hearted and compassionate Christians. It is the desire of my soul, that we may walk worthy of the mercies received, and which we are receiving.

Our family being now gathered together (those of us that were living) the South Church *in* Boston *hired an House for us: Then we removed from Mr.* Shepards, *those cordial Friends, and went to* Boston, *where we continued about three quarters of a year: Still the Lord went along with us, and provided graciously for us.* I thought it somewhat strange to set up Housekeeping with bare walls; but as *Solomon* says, *Mony answers all things*; and that we had through the benevolence of Christian-friends, some in this *Town*, and some in that, and others: And some from *England*, that in a little time we might look, and see the House furnished with love. The Lord hath been exceeding good to us in our low estate, in that when we had neither house nor home, nor other necessaries, the Lord so moved the hearts of these and those towards us, that we wanted neither food, nor raiment for our selves or ours, *Prov.* 18. 24. *There is a Friend which sticketh closer than a Brother.* And how many such Friends have we found, and now living amongst? And truly such a Friend have we found him to be unto us, in whose house we lived, *viz.* Mr. *James Whitcomb*, a Friend unto us near hand, and afar off.

I can remember the time, when I used to sleep quietly without workings in my thoughts, whole nights together, but now it is other wayes with me. When all are fast about me, and no eye open, but his who ever waketh, my thoughts are upon things past, upon the awfull dispensation of the Lord towards us; upon his wonderfull power and might, in carrying of us through so many difficulties, in returning us in safety, and suffering none to hurt us. I remember in the night season, how the other day I was in the midst of thousands of enemies, & nothing but death before me: It is then hard work to perswade myself, that ever I should be satisfied with bread again. But now we are fed *with the finest of the Wheat*, and, as I may say, *with honey out of the rock*: In stead of the Husk, we have the fatted Calf: The thoughts of these things in the particulars of them, and of the love and goodness of God towards us, make it true of me, what David said of himself, *Psal.* 6. 6. *I watered my couch with my tears.* Oh! the wonder-full power of God that mine eyes have seen, affording matter enough for my thoughts to run in, that when others are sleeping mine are weeping.

I have seen the extrem vanity of this World: One hour I have been in health, and wealth, wanting nothing: But the next hour in sickness and wounds, and death, having nothing but sorrow and affliction.

Before I knew what affliction meant, I was ready sometimes to wish for it. When I lived in prosperity, having the comforts of the World about me, my relations by me, my Heart chearfull: and taking little care for any thing; and yet seeing many, whom I preferred before my self, under many tryals and afflictions, in sickness, weakness, poverty, losses, crosses, and cares of the World, I should be sometimes jealous least I should have my portion in this life, and that Scripture would come to my mind, *Heb.* 12. 6. *For whom the Lord loveth he chasteneth, and scourgeth every Son whom he receiveth.* But now I see the Lord had his time to scourge and chasten me. The portion of some is to have their afflictions by drops, now one drop and then another; but the dregs of the Cup, the Wine of astonishment: like a sweeping rain that leaveth no food, did the Lord prepare to be my portion. Affliction I wanted, and affliction I had, full measure (I thought) pressed down and running over; yet I see, when God calls a Person to any thing, and through never so many difficulties, yet he is fully able to carry them through and make them see, and say they have been gainers thereby. And I hope I can say in some measure, As *David* did, *It is good for me that I have been afflicted.* The Lord hath shewed me the vanity of these outward things. That they are the *Vanity of vanities, and vexation of spirit*; that they are but a shadow, a blast, a bubble, and things of no continuance. That we must rely on God himself, and our whole dependance must be upon him. If trouble from smaller matters begin to arise in me, I have something at hand to check my self with, and say, why am I troubled? It was but the other day that if I had had the world, I would have given it for my freedom, or to have been a Servant to a Christian. I have learned to look beyond present and smaller troubles, and to be quieted under them, as *Moses* said, *Exod.* 14. 13. *Stand still and see the Salvation of the Lord.*

FINIS.

THE EDITORS' COMMENT

Mary Rowlandson's *Narrative* is the most popular and best-known settler account from King Philip's War, due in part to its publication in both Boston and London in 1682 and its frequent reprintings. The narrative describes Rowlandson's experience as a captive held for eleven weeks among Nipmuc, Narragansett, and Wampanoag families as they traveled through the Nipmuc homeland and the Connecticut River Valley. In February 1676, the Nashaway Nipmuc leader Monoco led a raid on Rowlandson's town of Lancaster, located in the center of the Nashaway homeland, to reclaim Nashaway, to replenish their corn, and to take English captives and firearms. Rowlandson's home was in one of the most fertile fields and she was a high-status captive, the wife of town minister Joseph Rowlandson and daughter of John White, a significant landholder. Rowlandson, her children, and other settler women and children were taken captive at Lancaster, in the wake of the Great Swamp massacre, in part to protect Indigenous people and places from attacks by colonial armies, who did not hesitate to set fire to Native towns when women and children were present. Rowlandson made sense of her captivity by drawing on Puritan practices of interpretation, including reading remarkable or unusual events as signs of divine providence, or special interventions of God, and framing her experiences as a spiritual test she must endure and then convey, in this case, through publication. Although Rowlandson was often assisted by Native people in her travels, she attributed her survival and redemption to the hand of God; her narrative was published as a testament to the triumph of Puritan faith over savagery. It is instructive to compare Rowlandson's and Edward Winslow's narratives of their experiences: while Winslow produced a narrative attuned to the details of Native life important in his role as a diplomat, Rowlandson used Puritan theology to write about her captivity, giving Native warriors and families roles to play within a spiritual drama. Even as she sought to convey her experiences through this lens, Rowlandson sometimes provided insights into the experiences of Indigenous leaders and families living through a war. Throughout most of her captivity, she lived with the Wampanoag Sôkushqâ Weetamoo. While Rowlandson deferred to the authority of male leaders like Metacom and the Narragansett sachem Quinnapin, with whom Weetamoo had recently formed a marriage alliance, she resisted Weetamoo's authority as a female leader, in line with her own cultural norms. Weetamoo and Quinnapin were among the survivors of the Great Swamp massacre, and many people had traveled with them from Narragansett country to seek sanctuary among the Nipmucs. Despite the spiritual trials and Christian redemption that drive the narrative, Rowlandson gives a sustained account of the travels of Weetamoo, and the families who moved with her, from the Nipmuc sanctuary of Menimesit to Sokoki country on the Connecticut River, and down to Mount Wachusett, where Rowlandson participated in the councils where her release was negotiated as part of a peace process.

Note attributed to James Printer

The enemy as Mr Wilson told me he thought was something suprizd, wth their great Guns & such a Number of men wch they percieved was amongst them & therefore gave their watchwords to draw off, their passage away was over Brigstreet bridge wch they fyred, & for awhile encamped on the other side, & from thence past away a writing was found at ye foot of the Bridge wth this impost & Quakere Language

Thou Englishman hath provoked us to anger & wrath & we care not though we have war wth thee this 21 years for there are many of us 300 of wch hath fought wth thee at this time, we have nothing but our lives to loose but thou hast many faire houses cattell & much Good things.

THE EDITORS' COMMENT

The original note, posted on the remains of a bridge in the English settlement of Medfield, does not survive, but it was transcribed by minister Noah Newman in his letter to John Cotton, in which he reported the raid. Newman's letter is held by the American Antiquarian Society, and this note has been reprinted in histories of King Philip's War. The note, which critiques the greed of English settlers as a primary cause of war, has been attributed to Nipmuc scholar James Printer, who was living at Menimesit, among his Nipmuc relations, at the time of the raid. James had attended preparatory schools in Cambridge and operated the Harvard printing press, which was housed in the Indian College. This was the first printing press in New England, and James's skill was rare in the colonies. He worked at the press before and after the war, in addition to serving as a teacher in Nipmuc Praying Towns, along with his brothers. James was fluent in English and Nipmuc, with scholarly training in Latin, Greek, and Hebrew. He would have been familiar with the troops from Cambridge and Boston who were stationed at Medfield at the time of the raid. James was highly capable of analyzing from multiple perspectives the chaos that had torn apart and dispersed his family. His brother Job Kattenanit served as a scout for the Massachusetts Bay troops and his brother Annaweekin was killed in the war. James served as a scribe for Nipmuc leaders during peace negotiations in the spring of 1676 and protected Nipmuc people and lands for decades after the war. In the note, James may have been writing from his point of view, having suffered both imprisonment by the English and a form of captivity among his own relations, or on behalf of the Nipmuc company that raided Medfield, a site located within the Nipmuc homeland, along the path between Cambridge and James's hometown of Hassanamesit.

Thomas Church and Benjamin Church: from *Entertaining Passages Relating to Philip's War (III)*

Now Capt. *Church* being arrived at *Plymouth*, received thanks from the Government for his good Service, *&c.* many of his Souldiers were disbanded; and he tho't to rest himself awhile, being much fategued and his health impared, by excessive heats and colds, and wading thro' Rivers, *&c.* But it was not long before he was call'd upon to Rally, upon advice that some of the Enemy were discovered in *Dartmouth* woods. He took his *Indians*, and as many *English* Volunteers as presented, to go with him, and scattering into small parcels. Mr. *Jabez Howland* (who was now, and often his Lieutenant and a worthy good Souldiers) had the fortune to discover and imprison a parcel of the Enemy. In the Evening they met together at an appointed place, and by examining the Prisoners, they gain'd intelligence of *Totosons* haunt; and being brisk in the Morning, they soon gain'd an advantage of *Totosons* company, tho' he himself with his Son of about Eight Years old made their escape, and one old Squaw with them, to *Agawom* his own Country. But *Sam Barrow*, as noted a Rogue as any among the Enemy, fell into the hands of the *English*, at this time. Capt. *Church* told him, *That because of his inhumane Murders and Barbarities, the Court had allow'd him no quarter, but was to be forthwith put to Death, and therefore he was to prepare for it.* Barrow reply'd, *That the Sentence of Death against him was just, and that indeed he was ashamed to live any longer, and desired no more favour than to Smoke a Whiff of Tobacco before his Execution.* When he had taken a few Whiffs, he said, *He was ready;* upon which one of Capt. *Churches* Indians sunk his Hatchet into his Brains. The famous *Totoson* arriving at *Agawom,* his Son which was the last which was left of his Family (Capt. *Church* having destroyed all the rest) fell sick: The wretch reflecting upon the miserable condition he had bro't himself into, his heart became as a stone within him, and he dy'd. The old Squaw flung a few leaves and brush over him, and came into *Sandwich*, and gave this account of his death, and offered to shew them where she left his body; but never had the opportunity, for she immediately fell sick and dy'd also.

Capt. *Church* being now at *Plymouth* again weary and worn, would have gone home to his Wife and Family, but the Government being Solicitous to ingage him in the Service until *Philip* was slain, and promising him satisfaction and redress for some mistreatment that he had met with: He fixes for another Expedition; he had soon Volunteers enough to make up the Company he desired and Marched thro' the Woods, until he came to *Pocasset*. And not seeing nor hearing of any of the Enemy, they went over the Ferry to *Rhode-Island*, to refresh themselves. The Captain with about half a dozen in his company took Horse & rid about eight Miles down the *Island*, to Mr. *Sanfords* where he had left his Wife; who no sooner saw him but fainted with the surprize; and by that time she was a little revived, they spy'd two Horsemen coming a great pace. Capt. *Church* told his company that those men (by their riding) came with Tydings. When they came up they prov'd to be Maj. *Sanford* and Capt. *Golding*; who immediately ask'd Capt. *Church, What he would give to hear some News of* Philip? He reply'd, *That was what he wanted.* They told him, *They had rid hard with some hopes of overtaking of him, and were now come on purpose to inform him, That there was just now Tydings from* Mount-hope; *An* Indian *came down from thence (where* Philips *Camp now was) on to* Sandpoint *over against* Trips, *and hollow'd, and made signs to be fetch'd over; and being fetch'd over, he reported, That he was fled from* Philip, *who* (said he) *has kill'd my Brother just before I came away, for giving some advice that displeased him.* And said, *he was fled for fear of meeting with the same his Brother had met with.* Told them also, *That* Philip *was now in* Mount-hope *Neck.* Capt. *Church* thank'd them for their good News, and said, he hop'd by to Morrow Morning to have the Rogues head. The Horses that he and his company came on standing at the door, (for they had not been unsaddled) his Wife must content her self with a short visit, when such game was a-head; they immediately Mounted, set Spurs to their

Horses, and away. The two Gentlemen that bro't him the Tydings, told him, *They would gladly wait upon him to see the event
of this Expedition.* He thank'd them, and told them, he should
be as fond of their company as any Mens; and (in short) they
went with him. And they were soon as *Trips* Ferry (with Capt
Churches company) where the deserter was; who was a fellow
of good sense, and told his story handsomely: he offered Capt.
Church to Pilot him to *Philip*, and to help to kill him, that he
might revenge his Brothers death. Told him, That *Philip* was
now upon a little spot of Upland that was in the South end of
the miery Swamp just at the foot of the Mount, which was a
spot of ground that Capt. *Church* was well acquainted with. By
that time they were got over the Ferry, and came near the
ground half the Night was spent, the Capt. commands a halt,
and bringing the company together, he asked Maj *Sanford* &
Capt. *Goldings* advice, what method was best to take in making
the onset, but they declining giving any advice, telling him,
*That his great Experience & Success forbid their taking upon
them to give advice.* Then Capt. *Church* offered Capt. *Golding*,
that he should have the honour (if he would please accept of it)
to beat up *Philips* headquarters. He accepted the offer and had
his alotted number drawn out to him, and the Pilot. Capt
Churches instructions to him were to be very careful in his
approach to the Enemy, and be sure not to shew himself until
by day light they might see and discern their own men from
the Enemy. Told him also, That his custom in the like cases was
to creep with his company on their bellies, until they came as
near as they could; and that as soon as the Enemy discovered
them they would cry out; and that was the word for his Men
to fire and fall on. Directed him when the Enemy should start
and take into the Swamp, they should pursue with speed, every
man shouting and making what noise they could; for he would
give orders to his Ambuscade to fire on any that should come
silently. Capt. *Church* knowing it was *Philips* custom to be foremost in the flight, went down to the Swamp and gave Capt.
Williams of *Situate* the command of the right wing of the
Ambush, and placed an *English-man* and an *Indian* together
behind such shelters of Trees, &c. that he could find, and took
care to place them at such distance as none might pass undiscovered between them, charg'd 'em to be careful of themselves,

and of hurting their friends: And to fire at any that should come silently thro' the Swamp: But it being some-what further thro' the Swamp than he was aware of, he wanted men to make up his Ambuscade; having placed what men he had, he took Maj. *Sanford* by the hand, said, *Sir, I have so placed them that 'tis scarce possible* Philip *should escape them.* The same moment a Shot whistled over their heads, and then the noise of a Gun towards *Philips* camp. Capt. *Church* at first tho't it might be some Gun fired by accident: but before he could speak, a whole Volley followed, which was earlier than he expected. One of *Philips* gang going forth to ease himself, when he had done, look'd round him, & Capt. *Golding* thought the *Indian* looked right at him (tho' probably 'twas but his conceit) so fired at him, and upon his firing, the whole company that were with him fired upon the Enemies shelter, before the *Indians* had time to rise from their sleep, and so over-shot them. But their shelter was open on that side next the Swamp, built so on purpose for the convenience of flight on occasion. They were soon in the Swamp and *Philip* the foremost, who starting at the first Gun threw his Petunk and Powder-horn over his head, catch'd up his Gun, and ran as fast as he could scamper, without any more clothes than his small breeches and stockings, and ran directly upon two of Capt. *Churches* Ambush; they let him come fair within shot, and the *English* mans Gun missing fire, he bid the *Indian* fire away, and he did so to purpose, sent one Musket Bullet thro' hls heart, and another not above two inches from it; he fell upon his face in the Mud & Water with his Gun under him. By this time the Enemy perceived they were way laid on the east side of the *Swamp*, tack'd short about. One of the Enemy who seem'd to be a great surly old fellow, hollow'd with a loud voice, & often called out, *iootash, iootash,* Capt. *Church* called to his *Indian Peter* and ask'd him, *Who that was that called so?* He answered, It was old *Annowon Philips* great Captain, calling on his Souldiers to stand to it and fight stoutly. Now the Enemy finding that place of the *Swamp* which was not Ambush'd, many of them made their escape in the *English* Tracks. The Man that had shot down *Philip*, ran with all speed to Capt *Church*, and informed him of his exploit, who commanded him to be Silent about it, & let no man more know it, until they had drove the *Swamp* clean; but when they had drove the *Swamp* thro' & found the Enemy had escaped, or at least the most of them; and the Sun now up, and so the dew gone, that they could not so easily Track them, the whole Company met together at the place where the Enemies Night shelter was; and then Capt. *Church* gave them the news of *Philips* death; upon which the whole Army gave Three loud *Huzza*'s. Capt *Church* ordered his body to be pull'd out of the mire on to the Upland, so some of Capt. *Churches Indians* took hold of him by his Stockings, and some by his small Breeches, (being otherwise naked) and drew him thro' the Mud unto the Upland, and a doleful, great, naked, dirty beast, he look'd like. Capt. *Church* then said, *That forasmuch as he had caused many an* English-mans *body to lye unburied and rot above ground, that not one of his bones should be buried.* And calling his old *Indian* Executioner, bid him behead and quarter him. Accordingly, he came with his Hatchet and stood over him, but before he struck he made a small Speech directing it to *Philip*; and said, *He had been a very great Man, and had made many a man afraid of him, but so big as he was he would now chop his Ass for him*; and so went to work, and did as he was ordered. *Philip* having one very remarkable hand being much scarr'd, occasioned by the splitting of a Pistol in it formerly. Capt. *Church* gave the head and that hand to *Alderman*, the *Indian* who shot him, to show to such Gentlemen as would bestow gratuities upon him; and accordingly he got many a Peny by it. This being on the last day of the Week, the Captain with his Company returned to the Island, tarryed there until Tuesday; and then went off and ranged thro' all the Woods to *Plymouth*, and received their *Pramium*, which was *Thirty Shillings per* head, for the Enemies which they had killed or taken, instead of all Wages; and *Philips* head went at the same price. Methinks it's scanty reward, and poor incouragement; tho' it was better than what had been some time before. For this March they received *Four Shillings* and *Six Pence* a Man, which was all the Reward they had, except the honour of killing *Philip*. This was in the latter end of *August*, 1676.

THOMAS CHURCH AND BENJAMIN CHURCH: FROM
Entertaining Passages Relating to Philip's War (III)

THE EDITORS' COMMENT

Entertaining Passages Relating to Philip's War was published in 1716, by Benjamin Church's son, Thomas, who based the narrative on his father's oral accounts and notes. The narrative portrays the elder Church as a chivalrous hero who performed a difficult but necessary role to protect the colony during the "Indian wars." The book was first published in 1716 by Boston printer Bartholomew Green and a second edition was published in 1772 by Solomon Southwick in Providence, Rhode Island. Nineteenth-century antiquarians Samuel Gardner Drake and Henry Dexter published subsequent editions in 1825 and 1865. Dexter noted that Church's account was more "materials toward a memoir" than "such a Memoir itself." Among the "first born sons," Benjamin Church was born in Plymouth/Patuxet in 1639. Like his father Thomas, he was a carpenter. However, after he married Constant Southworth's daughter Alice, Benjamin's fortune changed. In the narrative, Church portrays his acquisition of fertile lands in Sakonnet as happenstance. However, deeds and court records reveal that Church played a leading role in acquiring deeds for Wampanoag lands at Sakonnet, Pocasset, and Nemasket on behalf of Plymouth, including lots he secured for himself and for the colony. Church also portrays King Philip's War as a conflict instigated by Indigenous people that arose amid his peaceful settlement, rather than the result of ongoing land disputes. In the narrative, Church appears effective both in chivalrous protection of female Wampanoag leaders and in manly defense of English settlements. In contrast, the documents show that Church led military expeditions into both Awashonks's and Weetamoo's territories early in the war. The narrative includes an account of Church's pursuit of Metacom in August 1676, following his capture of Metacom's wife and son (see pp. 988–992 in this volume). Although Church led the forces that captured the Wampanoag leader, he attributed Metacom's death to Alderman, a Wampanoag scout from Pocasset. William Apess highlighted Alderman's act in his frontispiece to the *Eulogy on King Philip* (included in this volume), to call attention to colonial "divide-and-conquer" strategies.

Edward Rawson to Josiah Winslow

Honored Sir

Your letter by Capt Church his information & the paws of that monster that hath caused us so much mischief were welcome to us which is yet attended with the soe awfull news of the losses of near one hundred souls at Casco Bay & Kinnibeck & now whither we are hastning help as we are able, though attended with great difficulty of an unpassable country, would have been glad of Capt Church his help, but perceive his businesse is yet before him of joynt benefit, which we pray God prosper; Touching your motion of demand of the Rhoad Islanders of our enemys harboured by them; the Council now present concurrs therewith and advise the same, and desire you would prosecute into effect in our name as well as your owne; as for considerations in your letters referring to charge & division of spoyle will admit of more time; and a Commissione & meeting which wee judge needfull speedily to be called wee hope will procure an equall & satisfactory settlement herein. I am sending our very hearty respects unto you & both you & our affayres to our good God for such faith & Guidance & blessing as yet wee may stand in need.

Boston August 28, 1676

Your Humble Servant
Edward Rawson, Secretary by
Order of the Council

THE EDITORS' COMMENT

In this document, the governor and council of Massachusetts
Bay Colony acknowledged receipt of Josiah Winslow's letter
and sent news of Wabanaki raids on the northern front of the
war. (The letter was sent on behalf of Governor Leverett by
Edward Rawson, the colony's secretary.) Although Winslow's
letter did not survive, this document demonstrates several key
facts related to the end of King Philip's War in southern New
England. Benjamin Church delivered Winslow's letter, with
his report of Metacom's death, along with Metacom's hands,
to Governor Leverett, symbolizing a trophy of war and a gift
between allies. In response to Winslow's motion, Massachusetts Bay joined with Plymouth in demanding that Rhode
Island turn over the Native prisoners they held. The letter also
confirms that the war continued, after Metacom's death, in
Wabanaki territory to the north, with reports of nearly one
hundred settlers lost to the ongoing conflict. Although Plymouth Colony would soon begin to pull back its own forces,
Massachusetts Bay took the lead in pursuing the war in the
north, including the capture of Wampanoag, Narragansett,
Penacook, and Nipmuc people who had sought shelter in
Wabanaki territory.

Petition of William Wannukhow, Joseph Wannukhow, and John Appamatahqeen

To the Hon. Court of Assistants sitting in Boston,
September the 5th 1676.

The humble Petition of William Wannuckhow, Joseph Wannuckhow and John Appamatahqeen, all prisoners at the barr: Humbly imploreth your favor to hear and consider our application. We know that your Honours are men of truth, fearing God, and will faithfully perform your promises especially when it concerns so great a matter as the lives of men. You were pleased (of your own benignity) not for any desert of ours, to give forth your declaration dated the 19th of June, wherein you were pleased to promise life and liberty unto such of your enemies as did come in and submit themselves to your mercy and order and disposal within a time limited which afterwards was enlarged to a longer time, and tidings thereof sent by James Prentice unto us, which offers of grace, as soon as we heard of it, we readily embraced it, and came in accordingly ourselves wives and children, as Capt. Prentice and his son, with others, to whose house we were directed to come, are ready to testify; and those orders of yours are upon record, the copies whereof we are ready to present. If it should be said that we are known to be notorious in doing mischief to the English, we answer, none can so say in truth, or prove any such thing against us. Indeed we do acknowledge that we were in company of those that burnt Goodman Eames his house. But we did not act in it. It was done by others, who were slain in the war, and so have answered God's justice for their demerits; as for our part we came along with that company upon a necessary and just occasion, to get our corn which we had planted gathered and put up at Magunquog. But finding our corn taken away, we intended to return. But Netus and another man that were our leaders earnestly moved to go to Goodman Eames's farm for to get corn, and they said they did believe he had taken our corn. But we were unwilling to go. But they by their persuasion and threatening carried us with them. But as we said before, we neither killed nor burnt nor took away any thing there. But were instrumental to save Goodman Eames his children alive, one of us carried one boy upon our backs rather then let them be killed. This is the truth of things, so that we cannot be reckoned among such as have been notorious in doing mischief. Indeed we were enemies, being tempted to go among them by the example of our choice men Capt. Tom and others. But we had no arms and did not hurt the English as many others have done, that upon their submission to your mercy are pardoned. Besides it was a time of war, when this mischief was done; and though it was our unhappy portion to be with those enemies yet we conceive that depredations and slaughters in war are not chargeable upon particular persons, especially such as have submitted themselves to your Honours upon promise of life, &c. as we have done.

Therefore we desire again to insist upon that plea, that we may receive the benefit of your declarations before mentioned. Our lives will not be at all beneficial to Goodman Eames. Those that slew his wife and relations and burnt his house have already suffered death, and the satisfaction of Goodman Eames in our death will not countervail the honour and justice or authority of the country that may be blemished thereby.

THE EDITORS' COMMENT

William Wannukhow and his family were from the Nipmuc
praying town of Magunkaquog, where they had lived before
the war. After James Quanapohit, Job Kattenanit, and their
company of Native scouts secured amnesty for their kin who
were displaced by war, the Wannukhows traveled to settler
Thomas Prentice's house in Cambridge, seeking to return
peacefully to their homes. However, William Wannukhow,
his son Joseph Wannukhow, and John Appamatahqeen were
charged with burning the house of Thomas Eames, who had a
farm near Magunkaquog, and attacking his family. In the petition, the men described the incident, stated their innocence,
and advocated for amnesty. They specifically mentioned their
protection of Eames's children. The petition may have been
written by the Wannukhows, or recorded by some of their
relations, including James Printer, who had advocated for the
Wannukhows, or his brother, the scout Job Kattenanit, who
had co-authored the earlier petition for amnesty. The petition
demonstrates the authors' knowledge of English law, particularly regarding acts committed in a "time of war." Despite their
petition, William Wannukhow, Joseph Wannukhow, and John
Appamatahqeen were convicted and hanged in Boston. This
petition is a rare example of Native authors' own accounts of
the complex, chaotic violence of the war, as well as the narrowing channels for justice as colonial forces sought to capture
and execute Native people in Massachusetts Bay and Plymouth
colonies during the summer and fall of 1676.

Record of a Court Martial
Held at Newport

Newport, August 24th, 1676.

THE Names of the Members of the Court Martiall.

Mr. Walter Clarke, Governour,
Major John Crayton, Dept. Governour,
Mr. John Coggeshall, Assistant,
Mr. James Barker, Assistant,
Mr. John Easton, Assistant,
Mr. William Harris, Assistant.
Capt. Arthur Fenner, Assistant,
Mr. Thomas Borden, Assistant,
Mr. Joshua Coggeshall, Assistant,
Mr. William Cadman, Assistant,
Capt. Randall Houlden, Assistant,
Mr. Samuell Gorton, Jun., Assistant,
Edward Richmond, Secretary,
Capt. Edmund Calverly, Attorney General,
James Rogers, Gen. Sergeant,
Henry Lilly, Marshall and Cryer.

Military Officers.

Capt. Peleg Sanford,
Capt. Roger Williams,
Capt. Samuell Wilbore,
Capt. John Albro,
Capt. Edmund Calverly.
Capt. John Foanes,
Left. Edward Richmond.
Left. John Green,
Left. William Correy,

Left. Latham Clarke,
Left. Francis Gisborn,
Left. Ireh Bull,
Ensn. Weston Clarke,
Ensn. James Barker,
Ensn. Caleb Arnold,
Ensn. Hugh Mosher,
Ensn. John Potter.

I Edmund Calverly, Attorney Generall, in the Behalfe of our soveraigne Lord the King Charles the second, of England, Scotland, France and Ireland, King, &c. Doe impeach the Quanpen otherwise Sowagonish, an Indian Sachim, relating to the Narragansett Country in the Collony of Rhode Island, and Providence Plantations in New England, for these sundry Crimes following, namely: for being disloyall to his said Majesty sundry Ways.

Videleset. for that thou hast not faithfully adheared to the Government established in this said Collony by his said Majesty, but hast rebelliously adheared to Indians of another Collony called Plymoth, namely, Philip chiefe Sachem of the Indians in that said Collony, whoe with his Indians did within sixteen Months past trayterously, rebelliously, royetously and routously arm, weapon, and array themselves with Swords, Guns and Staves, &c., and have killed and bloodely muthered many of his said Majestys good Subjects, who lived peaceably under the sundry Governments to which they did belong.

Butt more partikularly thou hast through thy wicked bloody Minde and trayterous, rebellious, roietous and routous Acts, with Swords, Guns, Staves, &c., in thy owne Person, within this his Majesties Collony, and many great Companys of Indians with the, some of them yett unknowne, armed and arrayed as aforesaid, didst doe great Damage to our soveraigne Lord the King, by killing his Subjects, burning their Houses, killing and driving away their Cattell, and many more Outrages of that Nature, have been by the and thy Confederats done and committed, all against the Peace of our soveraigne Lord the King, his Crowne and Dignity, for all which Acts of thine, I doe on the Behalfe of his said Majesty, impeatch the as a Rebell in the Face of this Court, and pray Justice against thee the said Quanapen, otherwise Sowagonish, &c.

EDWARD CALVERLY,
Attorney Generall.

Dated at a Court Martiall held in Newport,
   the 24th of August, 1676.

Quanopen owned, that he among the Rest was in Armes against the English Nation, and that he was at the swamp Fight, and that he had nothing to say against the Indians burning and distroying Pettacomscutt, and that he was at the Assaulting of Mr. William Carpenters Garisson at Pawtuxet, and that he was in Armes at Nashaway, and did asist in distroyinge and burninge the Towne, and takeinge and carrying away the English Captives to the Number of about 20.

Voted. Guilty of the Charge, and that he shall be shott to death in this Towne on the 26th Instant, at about one of the Clock in the Afternoone.

An Indian with one Eye, Quanopens Brother saith his Brother Quanopen was a Comander in the Warr, but he was not, he being soe defective in his eye Sight, that he was incapable.

Voted, that at present Judgment is suspended.

August 25th.

Sunkeecunasuck upon his Examination owneth, that he was at the burning and destroying of Warwick, and that Wenunaquabin, an Indian that is now in Prison, was at the burning and distroying Warwick with him, at the same Time, and that his Brother Quanopin, was the second Man in Comand in the Narragansett Cuntry, that he was the next to Nenanantenentt.

And Nechett, an Indian, owned that he saw Sunkeecunasuck at Warwick, and that he was instrumentall in chief in saveing his Life.

Voted guilty of the Charge, and to suffer Death, the same Time and Place with his Brother.

Ashamattan, upon his Examination, owneth that his Brother Quanapin, had some of the Wampanooage with him, and that his Brother Quanapin had many Indians under his Comand, but Nenanantenentt was counted the chiefest of the two, and that they had recrute of Powder latly from the Dutch.

Voted that present Judgement is suspended.

Wenanaquabin of Pawtuxett saith, that he was not at the wounding of John Scott, but was at that Time living at Abiah Carpenters, and he could cleer him. Abiah Carpenters being sent for, before his Face saith, that he went away from their House some Time in May, 1675, and did not see him againe, nor could heare of him till towards Winter, which he saith is true. The said Wenanaquabin further saith, that he did not come to Warwick till Night after the Towne was burned, and after owned that he saw Nechett an Indian there. The said Nechett, to his Face afirmed that he saw him at Warwick at the burning the Towne with his Gun, about Noone. The said Wenanaquabin also confesseth, that he was at the Fight with Capt. Turner, and there lost his Gun, and swam over a River to save his Life.

Voted guilty of the Charge, and that he shall be putt to Death after the same Manner, and Time and Place as Quanopin.

John Wecopeak, on his Examination saith, that he was never out against the English, but one Time with other Narragansett Indians about the Month of March last, against a Towne upon Conecticutt River called in Indian Pewanasuck, and at that Time their Company burned a Barne and two dwelling Houses, and killed two Englishmen, and that he was not at the burninge of Pettacomscutt, but was at that Time with Indian John, William Heiffermans Man, removeinge their Wigwams, but shortly after he was sent downe by the Sachems to fetch off two dead Indians from thence, and saith that Georg Crafts Wife was shott with a Slugg, and chopt in some Parts of her Body with a Hatchett, and saith she did not crye hoe. Also saith, that he was at the Fight with Capt. Turner, and run away by Reason the Shott came as thick as Raine, but said alsoe, that he was at a great Distance. Butt John Godfree and William Heifferman saith, that he the said Wecopeak told them, that he saw Capt. Turner, and that he was shott in the Thigh, and that he knew it was him, for the said Turner said that was his Name.

Voted guilty of the Charge, and to dye as the others.

Anashawin of Narragansett denyeth, that he layed Hands on John Green of Narragansett, occasioned about the Death of a dumb Boy, although afirmed by three Witnesses to his Face, to wit: Mr. Thomas Gould, John Andra and Daniel Green.

The Court adjourned till Thursday next at ten of the Clock in the Morning, being the 31st of this Instant.

Before the Court Martiall the 31st of August, 1676.

Quonaehewacout saith, that he was informed that all the Sachims was at the takeing and burning of Jreh Bulls Garrison.

Manasses Molasses, called and answered to the Name, being examined concerning Low Howland, kild at Pocassett Side (being an Englishman) and slaine or murdered by the Indians, and this Mollasses being charged or suspected to have a Hand in the Crime, answers, that he did not kill him, but being in the Woods, the Indians came and said such a one was kild, and offered to sell the Coate of the Person soe murdered or slaine, and that he the said Mollasses bought the Coate (of the said dead Man) for ground Nuts, and further saith, that it was one Quasquomack kild the said Howland.

This Deponent, John Cook, aged about forty-five Yeares, testefyeth, being at Punckatest, in the Midle of July, or thereabout, did ask of severall Indians, named as followeth: Woodcock, Matowat, and Job, whome they were, that kild Low Howland, the foresaid Indians' Answer was, that there was six of them in Company, and Manasses was the Indian that fetcht him out of the Water. Further this Deponent saith not.

This Deponant, John Brigs, aged thirty-five Yeares or thereabout, testefyeth to the above written Testamony, and alsoe, that the said Manasses shot at Joseph Russell, as the Indians, first above named re'ate, and further this Deponent saith not.

Taken before me this 25th of August, 1676.

Wm. CADMAN, Assist.

This Deponant William Manchester, aged twenty and two Yeares, or thereabout, being at Pocasset, asked of Peter Nonoet, the Husband of Wetamoe, whoe it was that killed Low Howland, his Answer was, that Manasses fetcht him out of the Water, and further saith not.

Taken before me, Wm. CADMAN, Asist., August 25th, 1676.

Court adjourned until to-morrow Morning, eight of the Clock.

September 1st, 1676. The Court called.

Awetamoes Sister being examined, what she could say concerning the killing of Low Howland, she saith, she was informed by one of those that was at his killing, called Ohom, that this abovsaid Molasses was the Person that fetcht Low Howland out of the Water, at the Time he was kild, although the Indians that were with them perswaded him not to persue him, and alsoe further saith, that she knoweth him the said

Mollases to be one of the 12, that was of that Company, that took and kild the said Howland.

Mumuxuack alias Toby, being charged for Suspition of killing or assisting, or being in the Company of them that killed John Archer. Upon his Examination saith that he was one of four at the killing of John Archer and his Sonn, but he was with one more, that was about tenn Rod Distance, and that the other called whether they should shoot, or not, but did shoot; but after, the said Mamuxack said, being over-perswaded, and threatned by his Brother to carry away John Archers Head, he did doe it to Awetamoe by Reason his Brother threatened him, if he refused to take off his Head, and that he carryed the Head to Awetamoe, and that his Brother gave him a Shirt for soe doeing, for carrying the Head.

Jack Havens saith that he heard the Indians say, that John Archer had like to have escaped, by takeing hold of Mamuxuats Brother called Whaweapunet his Hatchett: but that he, the said Mamuxuat came behind the said Archer, and struck him on the Head with his Hatchitt, and soe they kild him.

Wechuncksum, alias Abram, saith, that he well knoweth the above said Molasses, and that he heard at the Spring of the Yeare last, being then at Wachusett, there was then Information given, what Execution had lately been done against the English, amongst which was afirmed, that the above said Malasses had latly killed an Englishman at Pocasset.

Suckats Squa, that lives with Daniel Wilcocks, saith, that she heard the above said Malasses say, being askt, or examined by the Indians at the Spring of the Yeare last, towards Wachusett, whether he had latly killed an Englishman at Pocassett, he answered that he had done it.

Whawinuckshin, Serjeant Roger's Man, being examined saith that he was at Thomas Gould's Garrison, and the Occasion of his cominge was to bury his Father, or help bury him, and there found severall Indians upon their Gard, but stayed not long there, but emediatly came away.

Voted that Serjeant Rogers shall have his Indian Man home with him, provided that the said Indian shall be brought forth, if required, which the said Serjeant Rogers doe in the Face of the Court, engage to doe.

The Court adjourned till tomorrow Morning at eight of the Clock.

The following Record is, probably, a Copy of a Letter, addressed by the Court Martial to Walter Clarke, of Newport, the Governour.

(Place and Date, probably)

Newport, R. I., August 31, 1676.

"SIR:

The Court adjourned till tomorrow Morning at eight of the C'ck. The Letter sent by the Governour of Plymouth to your-selfe, and by yourselfe to us bearing Date August 28, last past, purporating the Massachusetts and New Plymoths Demand of Indians on this Island, &c., an Answer to which Concerne in a speciall Manner your selfe, and need of all Expedition for divers Reasons, besides Safety and Charge. Wee therefore pray your Presence at the usiall Place of Meeting this Day to consider what Answer, or to require a full Apearance of the Councell, or otherwise, as you please; with Speed doe what seems best to you; we are redy to doe our Service to the publick Peace and Safety."

The Letter of the Governor of Plymouth to the Governor of Rhode Island is as follows:

"These are to certefy all whome it may Concerne that Capt. Benjamin Church is authorized and fully empowered by the Authority of this Collony of New Plymoth, in the Name of the said Collony, and for their Use and Benefitt, to demand and receive of the Governor and Authority of Rhode Island, all such of our Indian Enemys, whether Men, Women, or Children, as whilst our forces were abroad ranging, the adjacent Parts of our Collony, in Pursute of the said Enemyes, were received by, and are entertained upon the said Island. And having received them, he is ordered to guard and conduct them to Plymoth aforesaid and alsoe impowred to sell and dispose of such of them, and soe many as he shall see Cause for, there: to the Inhabitants, or others, for Term of Life, or for shorter Time, as there may be Reasons. And his actinge, herein, shall at all Times be owned and justefyed by the said Collony.

August 28, '76.

Pr. JOSIAH WINSLOW, Governor.

Voted, That Malasses and Mamuxuat and Quanachuagat are ordered to be delivered out of the Prison to Capt. Benjamin Church, and seven more to be delivered to Capt. Anthony Low, whoe have engaged to transport them out of the Collony, and that they shall not returne here againe, and one more to be at the Dispose of Henry Lilly, which he receives in full Satisfaction for his Attendance at this Court, and to be transported, as the other to Capt. Low; and that, at or before the Delivery of these the Mashall shall take all their Names, and give Returne thereof to the Clerk of this present Court.

Whereas it is reported that divers Indians are now brought to Newport, and severall upon the main Land, neer Shores of Rhode Island, wee doe therefore declare, and in his Majesty's Name require, that noe Indian, either great or small, be landed on any Part of Rhode Island aforesaid, or any Island in the Narragansett Bay, upon the Penalty, as formerly imposed upon such Offenders; and they shall be taken as being contemney of the Authorety of this Collony; Always, provided that bee, or may bee, upon just Cause detected, he, or they, at all Times, shall be lyable to be brought forth to answer the same, by Warrant from the Governor or Dept. Governor, or any two Assistants.

Dated at a Court Martiall held in Newport,
on Rhode Island, August 24th, 1676.
Pr. EDWARD RICHMOND, Secretary
to the Court.

THE EDITORS' COMMENT

This document demonstrates how Rhode Island Colony worked alongside Plymouth and Massachusetts Bay colonies during the military campaigns in the summer of 1676. John Easton and Roger Williams were among the English men on the court. Although the testimony of the Native prisoners was coerced, it still offers important firsthand accounts by some of the Indigenous actors in the war, with references to both obscure and well-known events. The document focuses on the prosecution of the Narragansett leader Quinnapin and his brothers. Quinnapin was a prominent leader of resistance, breaking out of the Newport jail before the war, and joining in a marriage alliance with Weetamoo during the war, providing protection in Narragansett country for her kin. This document also mentions a sister of Weetamoo, who was likely captured with Quinnapin and his brothers. The Rhode Island leaders, following the lead of Massachusetts Bay and Plymouth, framed Indigenous resistance as "rebellion" not only against the colonies but also against "the King," and they accused Quinnapin and his kin of violence against the King's "subjects." Thus, even as the New England colonies sought to capture and execute leaders like Quinnapin, Weetamoo, and Philip through military expeditions and court proceedings, they also sought through legal documents to impose sovereignty and jurisdiction within Narragansett and Wampanoag homelands. The record of the court-martial was published in 1858 by Albany publisher Joel Musnell, a New Englander with strong interests in both print history and colonial history, and a member of the American Antiquarian Society.

Deeds for Conquered Wampanoag Lands, 1676–1680

1676　:60:　Winslow Governor

To all people whom this doth or may Concerne the subscribers to these presents sendeth Greeting &c:

Wheras there are divers Neckes tracts and persells of upland swamps and meddowes scittuate lying and being on the southerly syde of the Towne of Rehobothes bounds; bordering upon the westerly syde of the Great River now Called and knowne by the name of Swansey River; and extending to some parte of the Narragansett Bay; as alsoe within the presincts of Swansey aforsaid; which Tracts of land aforsaid, were longe since bought and purchased of Osamequin, and Wamsutta his son; By the honorable Thomas Prence Esquire Captaine Thomas Willett Capt: Myles Standish; and the Now honorable Governor Josiah Winslow Esqr: as agents for and in the behalfe of themselves and severall of the Inhabitants of the Jurisdiction of New Plymouth; as by a Certaine deed of feofement under the hands and seales of the said Sachems Osamequin and Wamsutta his son bearing date March the twentyninth day Anno: 1653 may more att Large appeer; most parte of which Lands aforsaid have bin since sold and allianated by some of the said Purchasers to divers of the Inhabitants of the Jurisdiction aforsaid; and wheras it is Credably Reported That parte of the lands aforsaid; are or have been; exposed to sale in behalfe of the publicke, under the Notion or denomination of lands Conquered from the Late bloodey and Barbarous Indians; Wee the subscribers, either for ourselves, or as Comittees, in the behalfe of them that are particular propriators and sole owners of the land aforsaid; doe by these presents enter this our Lawfull Claime and publicke signification of our Just Right; and title of in and unto; all and singulare the premises according to our Respective shares and proportions, well knowne to each other and doe in all humillitie desire that this our Caviott and signification may be entered; and Remaine on the file with the Records of the honorable Court of Plymouth aforsaid; In testimony wherof wee have heerunto sett our hands this twentysixt day of October, one thousand six hundred seaventy and six;

Samuell Newman
Samuell Pecke
Israell Pecke
John Browne
James Browne
John Saffin
Nathaniell Paine
John Allin
Stephen Paine Junior
Thomas Chaffey
Peter Huntt
Phillip Walker

Att the Court of his Majestie held att Plymouth the 22cond of November 1676 It was ordered by the Court that the men of Swansey whose names are Subscribed to this Instrument above written; shall appeer att the Court of his Majestie to be holden att Plymouth aforsaid the first Tusday in June next ensueing the date heerof; further to Cleare up theire title unto the lands above specifyed

October 26–November 22, 1676

———————————

Wheras the late warr hath bine very chargable to the severall townes of this goverment, and many debts occationed therby are still due, this Court, considering that, by the good providence of God, there are severall tracts of conquered lands, doe therfore order, that Showmett lands and Assonett shalbe sold to defray the present debts, and that all other such lands shalbe either sold, if chapmen appeer to buy them, within a yeer or two, soe as to settle plantations theron in an orderly way, to promote the publicke worship of God, and our owne common good; and the produce therof shalbe devided to the severall townes in this goverment, according to thiere different disbursments towards the aforsaid warr, and what of the aforsaid lands shall then remaine unsold shalbe divided to every of our townes, theire parte according to the rate foremensioned; alsoe the committee to make sale as aforsaid shall give accoumpt of any theire actings therin, to the next Generall Court after such theire actings.

In reference unto one hundred acrees of land formerly graunted by the Court unto Capt. John Gorum, deceased, which land lyeth att Papasquash Necke. This Court doth give unto his heires and successors the Indians purchase of the said hundred acrees of land, and upon consideration that it was graunted unto him formerly by the Court as aforsaid, and forasmuch as hee hath performed good service for the country in the late warr, and ended his life in the said service, this Court sees reason, and doe heerby rattify, establish, settle, and confeirme, the aforsaid hundred acrees of land, formerly graunted unto the aforsaid Capt. John Gorum, lying on Papasquash Necke aforsaid, to his heires and successors for ever.

July 13, 1677

Wheras the Generall Court held the 10th of July, 1677, appointed and impowered the Treasurer, with the assistance of Cornett Studson and Mr Nathaniel Thomas, to make sale of the lands att Shawamett, &c, to defray the countryes debts, this Court doth declare, that the said words, "the lands att Shawamett," are to be interpretted to containe the lands called the out lett, as well as the necke itselfe, called Shawamett, and therfore doe heerby allow and confeirme the sale of the said out lett lands, as well as the necke itselfe, to all those to whom the said Treasurer hath made sale therof, according to the boundaries of the said out lett heerby mensioned, viz.: bounded on the east by Taunton River, on the north by Taunton lands, on the west, partely by Swansey lands which were purchased of the Indians by Capt. Thomas Willett and Mr Stephen Paine, Senior, and partely by the lands of Rehoboth, if the countreys lands extend soe farr westwards, and on the south by the said necke.

And forasmuch as the towne of Swansey conceive themselves to have right to the aforsaid outlett lands, which although this Court att present are otherwise minded, yett being willing for the quiett settleing and satisfaction of Swansey, soe farr as to appoint a committee to view a stripp of land att the enterance of Mount Hope Necke, with some of Swansey, and some of the present puchasers of Mount Hope, which said committee, after the hearing of both parties, shal have power to determine that stripp of land soe farr to belonge to Swansey as they shall judge most commodious, and least prejudiciall to either place, provided theire graunt and determination extend not above 50 or 60 rodd from the said fence downward into the necke, except the committee shall see cause to extend it soe farr as Kekamenest Springe, and provided that incase Swansey accept therof, then to relinquish all theire claime to the said outlett, and all theire claime of jurisdiction to the said Mount Hope; and Mr Hinckley and Major Cudworth are appointed by the Court to determine as abovesaid, in the behalfe of the collonie.

The committee appointed by the Court to treate with the agents of Swansey in reference to a settlement of the matters now in controversy between the collonie and them about the claime made by Swansey men upon theire borders, were—

Mr Constant Southworth,	Mr Barnabas Laythorpe,
Mr Daniell Smith,	Mr William Paybody,
Mr Thomas Huckens,	Mr Nathaniell Thomas,
and Cornett Robert Studson.	

November 1, 1677

1677   143   Winslow Governor

To all to whom these presents shall Come Constant South-worth Esqr: Treasurer of his Majesties Collonie of New Plymouth in New England in America sendeth Greeting &c:

Wheras the Generall Court held att Plymouth in the Collonie aforsaid the tenth day of July one thousand six hundred seaventy and seaven appointed and Impowered the aforsaid Treasurer with the Assistance of Cornett Studson and Mr Nathaniel: Thomas to make sale of the lands of Showamett &c; To defray the said Collonies debts; and att an other Generall Court held att Plymouth aforsaid; the first day of November one thousand six hundred seaventy and seaven the said Court did declare that the said words (the lands of Showamett) are to be Interpretted to containe the Lands Called the outlett as well as the Necke it selfe Called Showamett, and therfore did allow and Confeirme the sale of the said outlett land as well as the necke ittselfe, To all those to whom the said Treasurer hath made sale therof according to the boundaries of the said outlett therby mensioned :viz, bounded on the East by Taunton River and on the North by Taunton lands; and on the west, partely by Swansey lands which were purchased of the Indians by Captaine Thomas Willett and Mr Stephen Paine senior; and partely by the Lands of Rehoboth if the said Collonies Lands extend soe farr westward; and on the south by the said Necke; as doth and may appeer more fully upon Record, in the said Courts Records; Now Know yee that I the said Constant Southworth as Treasuere, by vertue of the above Resighted orders in the said Collonies behalfe for and in consideration of the full and Just sume of eight hundred pounds; That is to say for every Share or thirtieth parte of the abovesaid Necke and outlett the sume of twentysix pounds thirteen shillings and four pence in lawfull mony of New England, to mee the said Treasurer in hand well and truely payed before the Insealing and delivery of these presents; By Josiah Winslow Esqr: Nathaniel: Winslow Isacke Little Ephraim Little Samuell Little John Mendall; of the Towne of Marshfeild, in the aforsaid Collonie and Walter Briggs Capt: John Williams Richard Dwelley John James William Hatch William Peakes Jonathan Jackson Richard Proutey Leiftenant Isack Buck Zacheriah Damon and Daniell Daman; of the Towne of Scituate in the said Collonie; And Capt: Benjamine Church, Ensigne Jonathan Aldin of the Towne of Duxburrow in the Collonie aforsaid; and Edward Gray of the Towne of Plymouth in the Collonie aforsaid; and Captaine Mathew Fuller of the Towne of Barnestable in the Collonie aforsaid and Encrease Robinson Mallachy Halloway Thomas Linkhorne John Smith Joseph Wood and David Wood of the Towne of Taunton in the Collonie aforsaid and Thomas Paine of the Towne of Eastham in the Collonie of New Plymouth aforsaid and Samuell Prince of Hull in the Collonie of the Massachusetts in New England aforsaid, aforsaid; and which said sume of eight hundred pounds; That is to say, the sume of twenty six pounds thirteen and four pence; for every share or thirtieth parte of all the said Necke and outlett I the said Treasurer; doe acknowlidg to have Received from all the

aboveNamed barganees; according to each mans Interest quantity share or shares of and into all the said Necke and outletts;
which hee holdeth by these presents and is Mensioned in the
same That is to say; from him that holdeth more then one share
proportionably more; and from him that holdeth lesse then one
share proportionably Lesse, and therof doe acquitt and discharge all the abovenamed barganees, them and every of theire
heires executors and administrators for ever; By these presents
have Given Graunted bargained sold enfeoffed and Confeirmed
and by these presents doe freely fully and absolutely Give
Graunte bargaine sell enfeoffe and Confeirme unto all the
above Named bargainees; all the abovesaid Neck of land Called
Showamett; which is sittuated lying and being in the collonie
aforsaid; and is bounded Easterly by the Bay or mouth of
Taunton River aforsaid and southerly by the said Bay; and
westerly by a River or cove of the said Bay which parteth the
said Necke from a Necke of Land Comon Called Mr Brentons
Necke; and Northerly partely by the lands Purchased of the
Indians by Capt: Thomas Willett and Mr Stephen Paine Before
Mensioned and partely adjoyned to the outlett land and alsoe
all the abovemensioned outlett Land; according to the abovemensioned boundaryes of the same; with all and singulare the
wayes waters benifitts proffitts privilidges and heredittements
whatsoever to the said outlett belonging, or any wayes appertaining or to any parte or persell Therof; To have and to hold,
all the said Neck and outlett land with all and singulare the
heerby Graunted and bargained and Intended to be Graunted
premises; unto them the said Bargainees them and every of
them, theire and every of theire heires and assignes for ever;
That is to say to the said Josiah Winslow one share; To him his
heires and assignes for ever; and to the said Nathaniel Winslow
two shares; To him his heires and assignes for ever; and to the
said Isacke Little two shares To him his heires and assignes for
ever, and to the said Ephraim Little halfe a share, to him and
his heires and assignes for ever; and to the said Samuell Little
halfe a share, To him and his heires and assignes for ever; and
to the said John Mendall one share, To him and his heires and
assignes for ever; and to the said Walter Briggs five shares To
him and his heires and assignes for ever; And to the said John
Williams two shares To him and his heires and assignes for ever

and to the said Richard Dwelley one share to him and his heires and assigns for ever; and to the said John James one share to him and his heires and assignes for ever; and to the said William Hatch halfe a share to him and his heires and assignes forever; ever; And to the said William Peakes halfe a share to him and his heires and assignes for ever; And to the said Jonathan Jackson threequarters of a share To him and his heires and assignes for ever To the said Richard Proutey one quarter of a share To him and his heires and assignes for ever; and To the said Isacke Buck Zacheriah Daman and Daniell Daman one share To them their severall heires and severall assignes for ever; And to the said Bejamine Church one share To him his heires and assignes for ever; To him the said Jonathan Aldin one share To him and his heires and assignes for ever; And to the said Mathew Fuller one share to him and his heires and assignes for ever; And to the said Encrease Robinson one share To him and his heires and assignes for ever; And to the said Mallachy Holloway one share and To him and his heires and assignes for ever; And to the said Thomas Linkhorn halfe a share to him and his heires and assignes for ever; To the said John Smith halfe a share To him and his heires and assignes for ever; and To the said Joseph Wood halfe a share To him and his heires and assignes forever; and To the said David Wood halfe a share To him his heires and Assignes for ever; And To the said Thomas Paine one share To him and his heires and assignes for ever; And to the said Edward Gray two shares To him and his heires and assignes for ever; And to the said Samuell Prince one share To him and his heires and assignes for ever; And I the said Constant Southworth Treasurer, for mee and my Successors To and with the abovenamed Bargainees, and every of them theire and every of theire heires executors and adminnestrators, doe promise Covenant and Graunt, in manor and forme following that is to say That I the said Treasurer have full power and lawfull Authoritie To make sale of all and singulare the above Named Showamett and outlett according to the boundaries of the same above mensioned; and therof to make a pure ane perfeict estate of Inheritance in fee simple in Mannor and forme above expressed and that the said land and every parte therof is free and Cleare and Clearly acquited off and from all other and former Gifts bargaines sales titles

Charges & Incomberances whatsoever; Att the time of the Insealing and delivery of these presents and that I the said Treasurer and my successors To the said Bargainees and every of them theire and every of theire heires executors and assignes; shall and will warrant; and for ever defend the same, by these presents; In Witnes wherof I the said Constant Southworth Treasurer have heerunto sett my hand and the publick seale of the said Collonie or New Plymouth the 12th day of November in the yeer of our Lord one Thousand six hundred seaventy and seaven; And in the nine and twentieth yeer of the Raigne of our Sovereign Lord Charles the second of England Scotland France and Ireland Kinge, defender of the faith &c:

Constant Southworth Treasurer The seale of the Goverment

Signed sealed and delivered in the presence of us,

The Marke of John Berry

Nathaniell Thomas

This deed was Acknowlidged by Mr Constant Southworth Treasurer this 12th day of November 1677 Before mee John Alden Assistant;

To all to whom these presents shall Come Know yee that I the within named Constant Southworth Treasurer on the 28th day of November 1677 entered into the within mensioned and bounded land Called Showamett and outlett of the same, and then and there by turff and twigg delivered Zeisen and posession together with these presents, with all the within mensioned and bounded land unto the within Named Edward Gray and John Williams as agents for all the within Named Bargainees To have and to hold according to the forme and effect of the within written deed; excepting and Reserving all the meddowes within the same Showamett Necke and outlett of the same which were formerly purchased of the Indians by the old freemen together with the bounds on the east syde of Taunton River; between the fall River and Taunton Towne bounds neare Stacyes Creek; as by a deed Recorded in the Court Roles of New Plymouth Collonie doth and may appeer In the presence of us

James Walker   John Richmond   Nathaniel Thomas

November 12, 1677

———————

The Commissones of the united Collonies haveing Carefully
perused the severall accounts and Claimes of debt, presented
from the severall Collonies Refering to the late Indian Warrs,
and finding therin many difficulties not easey Rectifyed to such
axactnes as from theme to draw up ballence to mutuall satisfaction; for a full acommodation & finall settlement; of all Claimes
from any of the severall Collonies now made, or heerafter to be
made ther[   ] as alsoe for the division of Conquest lands &
proffitts of prisoners acrewing by the late warr; doe agree that
the severall Collonies shall fully posesse and freely dispose to
theire owne advantage all such lands as lye within their owne
precints Respectively; and such prisoners with other proffits; as
have been brought to them; and are now possessed by them;
without lett disturbance of Claime of from or by each othere;
and that the Collonie of Newe Plymouth shall pay unto the
Massachusetts the Just sume of one thousand pound law full
mony of New England

March 20, 1679

———————

Hinckley Governor
To all to whom these presents shall come Josiah Winslow Esqr:
Govr: of the Collonie of New Plymouth Major William Brad-
ford Treasurer of the said collonie Mr Thomas Hinckley and
Major James Cudworth Assistants to the said Govr: sendeth
Greeting &c:
Wheras wee the said Govr: Treasurer Thomas Hinckley and
James Cudworth; or any two of us, By vertue of an order of the
Generall Court of the Collonie aforsaid, bearing date Novem-
ber 1676) are Impowered in the said Collonies behalfe; To
make sale of Certaine lands belonging to the collonie aforsaid;
and to make and seale deeds for the confeirmation of the same;
as by the said order Remaining on Record in the said Court
Roles more att Large appeereth; Now Know yee That wee the
said Govr: Treasurer Thomas Hinckley and James Cudworth as
Agents and in the behalfe of the said collonie, for and in consideration off the full and Just sume of one Thousand and one
hundred pounds: lawfull mony of New England; To us in hand

before the ensealling and delivery of these presents; well and truely payed by Edward Gray of Plymouth in the collonie afor-said Nathaniel: Thomas of Marshfeild in the Collonie aforsaid; Benjamine Church of Punckateesett in the collonie aforsaid Christopher Almey Job Almey Thomas Waite of Portsmouth in the Collonie of Rhode Iland and Providence Plantations; Daniel Wilcockes of Punckateesett; And William Manchester of Punckateesett; in the collonie of New Plymouth aforsaid; with which said sume wee the said agents doe acknowlidge to be fully satisfyed & contented and payed; and therof doe acquitt and discharge the said Edward Gray Nathaniel: Thomas Ben-jamine Church Christopher Almey Job Almey Thomas Waite Daniell Wilcockes and William Manchester; Theire, either and every of theire heires Executors Adminnestrators and Assignes for ever: By these presents have Given Graunted bargained sold alliened enfeoffed and Confeirmed And by these presents for us and the said Collonie of New Plymouth; doe freely fully and absolutely: Give Graunt bargaine sell allien Infeoffe and confeirm; unto the said Edward Gray Nathaniel Thomas Ben-jamine Church; Christopher Almey Job Almey Thomas Waite Daniel: Wilcockes and William Manchesther; All these Lands sitteate lying and being att Pocasset and places Adjacent in the Collonie of New Plymouth aforsaid; and is bounded as followeth (viz) Northward and westward by the freemens lotts neare the fall River; And westward by the Bay or sound That Runeth between the said Land and Rhode Iland; Southward partly by Saconett bounds; and partely by Dartmouth bounds; and Northward and Eastward up into the woods untill it meets with the Lands formerly Graunted by the Court To other men and legally obtained by them from the Natives Not extending further then Middleberry Towne bounds; and Quitquesett ponds (onely excepting and Reserveing out of this bargaine and sale on hundred Acrees of Land Graunted and layed out; to Captaine Roger Goulding, and one hundred acrees of Land Graunted and Layed out To David and Thomas Lake; and the Land of Right appertaining to Punckateesett Purchase; And the Lands formerly Graunted by the Court of Plymouth to Captain Richard Morris) To have and to hold all the above mensioned and bounded Lands, with all and singular the woods waters coves Creekes Ponds brookes benifitts proffitts privilidges and heredittiments whatsoever, in before ariseing accruing belonging or therunto any wayes appertaining or to any parte or persell therof; To them the said Edward Gray Nathaniel Thomas Benjamine Church Christopher Almey Job Almey Thomas Waite Daniel Wilcockes and William Manchester; them and every of them theire and every of theire heires And Assignes forever; (except as before excepted; and alsoe excepting fourscore acrees of land exchanged between Punckatessett and Saconett Propriators posessed by Capt: Church) To the onely proper use and behoofe of them the said Edward Gray Nathaniel Thomas Benjamine Church Christopher Almey Job Almey Thomas Waite Daniell Wilcockes and William Manchester Them and every of them; theire and every of theire heires and Assignes for ever; That is to say, To the said Edward Gray Nine Shares or thirtyeth partes of the said land To him his heires or Assignes forever; And To the said Nathaniel: Thomas five Shares or thirtyeth partes of all the said Lands, To him his heires and Assignes for ever; And to the said Benjamine Church one Share To him his heires and Assignes for ever; And to the said Christopher Almey three Shares and three quarters of one Share; To him his heires and Assignes forever; And to the said Job Almey And to the said Job Almey three Shares and one quarter of one Share, To him his heires and Assignes for ever; And to the said Thomas Waite one Share To him his heires and Assignes for ever; And to the said Daniel Wilcockes two Shares To him and his heires and Assignes for ever; And to the said William Manchester five Shares To him and his heires and assignes for ever; And wee the said Governor Treasurer Thomas Hinckley And James Cudworth; for us as agents of the said Collonie of New Plymouth; and for the successive Governor and Treasurer Therof To and with the said Edward Gray Nathaniel: Thomas Benjamine Church Christopher Almey Job Almey Thomas Waite Daniel Wilcockes and William Manchester and every of them theire and every of theire heires Executors Adminnestrators and assignes doe promsie covenant and Graunt in Manor and forme following; That is to say That wee the said agents have full power and Lawfull Authoritie to bargaine sell and Confeirme all and singular the above Graunted and bargained premises; and therof to make a pure and perfect estate of Inheritance in

fee simple in manor and forme above expressed; And that the
said Lands and every parte and persell therof att the time of
the Insealing and delivery, of these presents is free and cleare
and Clearely acquitted of and from all other and former gifts
Graunts bargaines sales titles troubles Charges and Incomber-
ances whatsoever; And that wee the said Governor Treasurer
Thomas Hinckley and James Cudworth; And the successive
Governor Goverment and Treasurer of the Collonie of New
Plymouth aforsaid To the said Edward Gray Nathaniel Thomas
Benjamine Church Christopher Almey Job Almey Thomas
Waite Daniell Wilcockes and William Manchester them and
every of them theire and every of theire heires and assignes
Shall and Will Warrant; all and singulare the above Graunted
& bargained premises and every parte and persell therof from
all lawfull Claimes; and for ever Confeirm the same by threse
presents In Witnes wherof wee the said Governor Treasurer
Thomas Hinckley And James Cudworth have heerunto sett
our hands; and the publicke Seale of the said Collonie of New
Plymouth the fift day of March in the yeer of our Lord one
Thousand six hundred and seaventy nine eighty; And in the
thirty second yeer of the Raigne of our Sovereign Lord Charles
the second By the Grace of God of England Scotland France
and Ireland Kinge defender of the faith &c:
Josiah Winslow Governor
William Bradford Treasurer
Thomas Hinckley Assistant
James Cudworth Assistant
The publick seale of the Collonie of New Plymouth
Signed sealed and delivered in the presence of us John Freeman
Daniell Smith
This Instrument was owned and Acknowlidged by Josiah
Winslow Esqr: Govr: William Bradford Thomas Hinckley And
James Cudworth this sixt of March 1679/80 Before mee John
Aldin Assistant;
The Indorsement on the Backside of the deed abovewritten;
On the 20th day of May 1680, I Joseph Church of Sacon-
ett; in the Collonie of New Plymouth By vertue of a letter
of Attorney from the within Named Josiah Winslow William
Bradford Thomas Hinckley and James Cudworth sealed with
the publicke seale of the said Collonie did enter into the within

mensioned land by this within written deed sold to the within Named feofees and heerof quiett and peacable posesseion did take and after quiett and peacable posession had and taken together with this deed did deliver quiett and peacable posession of the land contained and mensioned to be sold by this within written Instrument; unto the within Named Edward Gray Nathaniel Thomas Benjamine Church Christopher Almey Job Almey Thomas Waite Daniell Wilcockes and William Manchester; To have and to hold Acording to the form and effect of this within written Instrument In Witnes wherof I the said Joseph Church have heerunto sett my hand

Joseph Church

This within mensioned and bounded Land; was delivered and the abovewritten Indorsment signed in the presence of us

John Briggs his marke

Thomas Pardaine his Marke

Ephraim Allin

Samuell Briggs his marke

The abovewritten deed and Indorsment were entered and Recorded per me Nathaniel Morton Secretary to the Court for the Jurisdiction of New Plymouth. for the abovemensioned Letter of Attorney to Joseph Church see second booke of evidence of lands Inroled folio *362*)

March 5–May 20, 1680

THE EDITORS' COMMENT

Following the military campaigns that led to the capture and deaths of Metacom, Weetamoo, and many of their kin, Plymouth Colony sought through the legal language of conquest to claim and secure the Wampanoag lands they had protected. These deeds are among those written documents that solidified Plymouth's claims to land. Among the beneficiaries were the Plymouth men whose names were also prominent in the prosecution of the war. Ironically, these claims for Plymouth Colony were short-lived. The lands within these deeds were later absorbed by the colonies of Rhode Island and Massachusetts Bay, although individual colonists retained title to their allotted tracts. Thus some of these documents also demonstrate Massachusetts Bay's growing dominance in the United Colonies. Importantly, Wampanoag people continued to live in many of these places in small enclaves and in protected reserves in towns like Fall River and Dartmouth, as well as on Cape Cod and the islands.

Moxus and Other Wabanaki Leaders to John Leverett

Having English friends I have sent Mrs Hamons to tell you that we have been careful of our prisners this is 3 times we have sent to you & have allways mised of you govenour of boston we would find your mind you find us all way for peace you allways broke the peace I would entreat you to send us a Answer of this letter by Mr. garner or Mr. Oliver If they be not at home send Mr wesell but send non of them that have been here already we think that them men that you sent before were minded to shoot us Mrs Hamons and the rest of the prisners can tell that we have drove Away all the damrallscogon engins from us for they will fight and we are not willing of their company we are willing to trade with you as we have done for many years we pray you send us such things as we name powder cloth tobacko liker corn bread and send the captives you toke at Pemaquid

governor of boston we do understand that Squando is minded to cheat you he is mind to get as many prisners as he can and so bring them to you & so make you believe that it is Kenebeck men that have don all this spoul

govenour of boston we have bin cheted so often & drove off from time to time about powder that this time we would willingly se it furst & you shall have your prisners we can fight as well as others but we are willing to live pesabel we will not fight without they fight with us first

here is 20 men women and children that is prisners most of them was bought we have not don as the damrellscoging engons did they kiled all their prisners at the spring we would have you com with your vessell to Abonnegog Mr Garner can tell that last somer that we did Agree and it was Squando Angons that did all the hurt

William Woum Wood
   hen nwedloked
     his   mark

winakeermit	tasset
moxes	john
essomonosko	shyrot
deogenes	mr thomas
pebemoworet	

[   ] gov of boston this is to let you understand, how we have been abused. we love yo but when we are dronk you will take away our cot & throw us out of dore if the wolf kill any of your catell you take away our gons for it & arrows and if you see a engon dog you will shoot him if we should do so to you cut down your houses kill your dogs take away your things we must pay a 100 skins if we brek a tobarko pip they will prisson us becaus there was war at naragans you com here when we were quiet & took away our gons & mad prisners of our chief sagamore & that winter for want of our gons there was severall starved we count it kild with us whenever we are bound and thrown in the siler this doings is not like to mans hart it is more like womon hart now we hear that you say you will not leave war as long as on engon is in the country we are owners of the country & it is wide and full of engons & we can drive you out but our desire is to be quiet as for exsampl a hors was kiled by som yung boys & we are were to pay 40 skins

governor of boston this is to let you to understand how major walldin served us we cared 4 prisners abord we would fain know whither you did give such order to kill us for bring-ing your prisners is that your fashing to com & mke pese & then kill us we are afraid you will do so agen Major Waldin do ly we were not minded to kill no body Major Waldin did wrong to give cloth & powder but he gave us drink & when we were drunk killed us if it had not a bin for this falt you had your prisners long ago [   ] Major Waldin have bin the cause of killing all that have bin kiled this sommer you may see how honest we have bin we have kiled non of your English prisners if you had any of ours prisners you wold a knocked them on the hed do you think all this is nothing

deogenes madoasquarbet

c. July 1, 1677

THE EDITORS' COMMENT

Even as the war was contained in southern New England, it continued until 1677–78 in Wabanaki country to the north. This document represents a rare and significant statement by Wabanaki leaders on the Kennebec River attesting to the causes of the war and its continuance on the northern front. They conveyed that, at the beginning of the conflict, they were in a state of peace, when settlers under the authority of Massachusetts Bay Colony attempted to confiscate Wabanaki men's guns, which were used primarily for hunting, causing starvation in winter. They also testified to numerous deceits by trader and military leader Richard Waldron, of Dover, who captured hundreds of people and sent them to Boston and into the transatlantic slave trade, in collaboration with local settlers in Wabanaki territory and the governors of Massachusetts Bay. The Kennebec leaders' testimony was recorded, at their request, by a captive, Elizabeth Hammond, the widow of Kennebec River trader Richard Hammond. The Wabanaki leaders called on Massachusetts Bay to end the war by ending duplicity and violence, and offered to use their influence either toward diplomacy, which was their preference, or if necessary, toward war, with more raids against English settlements in Wabanaki territory. Wabanaki people and their allies had nearly cleared the settlements, in what is now Maine, by this time. One Kennebec leader, Mogg, had even threatened to take Boston. The Kennebec leaders later joined with New York governor Andros, who operated under the authority of the English king, to broker a treaty with Massachusetts Bay in August 1677, which finally brought the war to a close, with equal terms on both sides. Those terms included the return of Wabanaki captives, some of whom Massachusetts Bay had to locate as far away as the Azores. This document is one of many that was published in the *Documentary History of the State of Maine, containing the Baxter Manuscripts* by antiquarian James Phinney Baxter, who was a president of the Maine Historical Society.

WAMPANOAG CONTINUANCE

William Apess: from
Indian Nullification of the Unconstitutional Laws of Massachusetts

TO THE WHITE PEOPLE OF MASSACHUSETTS.

THE red children of the soil of America address themselves to the descendants of the pale men who came across the big waters to seek among them a refuge from tyranny and persecution.

We say to each and every one of you that the Great Spirit who is the friend of the Indian as well as of the white man, has raised up among you a brother of our own and has sent him to us that he might show us all the secret contrivances of the pale faces to deceive and defraud us. For this, many of our white brethren hate him, and revile him, and say all manner of evil of him; falsely calling him an impostor. Know, all men, that our brother APES is not such a man as they say. White men are the only persons who have imposed on us, and we say that we love our red brother, the REV. WILLIAM APES, who preaches to us, and have all the confidence in him that we can put in any man, knowing him to be a devout Christian, of sound mind, of firm purpose, and worthy to be trusted by reason of his truth. We have never seen any reason to think otherwise.

We send this forth to the world in love and friendship with all men, and especially with our brother APES, for whose benefit it is intended.

Signed by the three Selectmen of the Marshpee Tribe, at the Council House, in Marshpee.

ISRAEL AMOS,
ISAAC COOMBS,
EZRA ATTAQUIN.

March, 19, 1835.

BOSTON, OCTOBER 2, 1834.

To whom it may concern.

THE undersigned was a native of the County of Barnstable, and was brought up near the Marshpee Indians. He always regarded them as a people grievously oppressed by the whites, and borne down by laws which made them poor and enriched other men upon their property. In fact the Marshpee Indians, to whom our laws have denied all rights of property, have a higher title to their lands than the whites have, for our forefathers claimed the soil of this State by the *consent of the Indians*, whose title they thus admitted was better than their own.

For a long time the Indians had been disaffected, but no one was energetic enough among them to combine them in taking measures for their rights. Every time they had petitioned the Legislature, the laws, by the management of the interested whites, had been made more severe against them. DANIEL AMOS, I believe, was the first one among them, who conceived the plan of freeing his tribe from slavery. WILLIAM APES, an Indian preacher, of the Pequod tribe, regularly ordained as a minister, came among these Indians, to preach. They invited him to assist them in getting their liberty. He had the talent they most stood in need of. He accordingly went forward, and the Indians declared that no man should take their wood off their plantation. APES and a number of other Indians quietly unloaded a load of wood, which a Mr. SAMPSON was carting off. For this, he and some others were indicted for a riot, upon grounds extremely doubtful in law, to say the least. Every person on the jury, who said he thought the Indians ought to have their liberty, was set aside. The three Indians were convicted, and APES was imprisoned thirty days.

It was in this stage of the business, after the conviction, that I became the counsel of the Indians, and carried their claims to the Legislature, were they finally prevailed.

The persons concerned in the riot, as it was called, and imprisoned for it, I think were as justifiable in what they did, as our fathers were, who threw the tea overboard; and to the energetic movements of WILLIAM APES, DANIEL AMOS and others, it was owing that an impression was made on the Legislature, which induced them to do partial justice toward this long oppressed race. The imprisonment of those men, in such a cause, I consider an honour to them, and no disgrace; no more than the confinement of our fathers, in the Jersey prison-ship.

BENJAMIN F. HALLETT,
Counsel for the Marshpee Indians.

INTRODUCTION.

THE writer hopes that the public will give him credit for an intention to adhere rigidly to the truth, in presenting his views of the late difficulties of the Marshpee Tribe, as it is as much his wish as his intention to do justice to all his brethren, without distinction of colour. Yet he is sensible that he cannot write truly on this subject without attracting the worst wishes of those who are enemies to liberty, or would reserve it exclusively to themselves. Could he speak without incurring such enmity, he would be most happy to do so; but he is fully aware that he cannot even touch this matter without exposing himself to certain calumny. This has been his portion whenever he has attempted to plead the cause of his ignorant and ever-oppressed red brethren. Nevertheless, he will endeavour to speak independently, as if all men were his friends, and ready to greet him with thundering applause; and he would do so if their voices were to pronounce on him a sentence of everlasting disgrace. He writes not in the expectation of gathering wealth, or augmenting the number of his friends. But he has not the least doubt that all men who have regard to truth and integrity, will do justice to the uprightness of his intentions. (Heaven be praised! there are some such men in the world.) He is equally sure that the evidence contained in this little work will be satisfactory, as to all the points he wishes to establish, to all who are open to conviction.

It is true that the author of this book is a member of the Marshpee Tribe, not by birth, but by adoption. How he has become one of that unfortunate people, and why he concerns himself about their affairs, will now be explained to the satisfaction of the reader. He wishes to say in the first place, that the causes of the prevalent prejudice against his race have been his study from his childhood upwards. That their colour should be a reason to treat one portion of the human race with insult and abuse has always seemed to him strange; believing that God has given to all men an equal right to possess and occupy the earth, and to enjoy the fruits thereof, without any such distinction. He has seen the beasts of the field drive each other out of their pastures, because they had the power to do so; and he knew that the white man had that power over the Indian which knowledge and superior strength give; but it has also occurred to him that Indians are men, not brutes, as the treatment they usually receive would lead us to think. Nevertheless, being bred to look upon Indians with dislike and detestation, it is not to be wondered that the whites regard them as on a footing with the brutes that perish. Doubtless there are many who think it granting us poor natives a great privilege to treat us with equal humanity. The author has often been told seriously, by sober persons, that his fellows were a link between the whites and the brute creation, an inferior race of men to whom the Almighty had less regard than to their neighbours, and whom he had driven from their possessions to make room for a race more favoured. Some have gone so far as to bid him remove and give place to that pure and excellent people who have ever despised his brethren and evil entreated them, both by precept and example.

Assumption of this kind never convinced WILLIAM APES of its own justice. He is still the same unbelieving Indian that he ever was. Nay, more, he is not satisfied that the learned and professedly religious men who have thus addressed him, were more exclusively the favourites of his Creator than himself, though two of them at least have been hailed as among the first orators of the day, and spoke with an eloquence that might have moved stocks and stones. One of them dwells in New York and the other in Boston. As it would avail him little to bespeak the favour of the world in behalf of their opinions by mentioning their names, he will proceed with the matter in hand, viz. the troubles of the Marshpee people, and his own trial.

INDIAN NULLIFICATION, &C.

IT being my desire, as well as my duty as a preacher of the gospel, to do as much good as in me lay to my red brethren, I occasionally paid them a visit, announcing and explaining to them the word of life, when opportunity offered. I knew that no people on earth were more neglected; yet whenever I attempted to supply their spiritual wants, I was opposed and obstructed by the whites around them, as was the practice of those who dwelt about my native tribe, (the Pequods,) in Groton, Conn. of which more will be said in another place.

Being on a tour among my brethren in May, 1833, I was often asked why I did not visit my brethren of Marshpee, of whom I had often heard. Some said that they were well provided, and had a missionary, named FISH, who took care of their lands and protected them against the fraud of such of their neighbours as were devoid of principle. Others asserted that they were much abused. These things I heard in and about Scituate and Kingston, where I had preached. Some of those who spoke thus, were connected with the missionary. The light thus obtained upon the subject being uncertain, I resolved to visit the people of Marshpee, and judge for myself. Accordingly I repaired to Plymouth, where I held forth on the civil and religious rights of the Indians, in Dr. KENDALL's church, and was treated with Christian kindness by the worthy pastor and his people. Dr. KENDALL gave me a letter of introduction to Mr. FISH, at Marshpee. Being unacquainted with the way, I strayed a little from it, and found a number of good Congregationalists of the old school, who invited me to tarry and preach to them in the evening, which I did, to their acceptance; for they and their pastor desired me to remain and preach on the Sabbath, which, however, I could not consistently do. I proceeded thence to Sandwich, where I made my mission known to Mr. COBB, the Orthodox preacher, who appeared to be pleased.

Mr. COBB said that he had agreed to exchange with Mr. FISH, on the Sabbath following, but as it was inconvenient for him to do so, he would give me a line to him. With this furtherance I set forward, and arrived at Mr. FISH's house before sunset, informing those I met on the way that I intended to preach on the next day, and desiring them to advise others accordingly. When I made my business known to Mr. FISH, he treated me with proper kindness, and invited me to preach for him. When I awoke in the morning, I did not forget to return thanks to God for his fatherly protection during the night, and for preserving me in health and strength, to go through the duties of the day. I expected to meet some hundreds of the tribe, and to hear from their lips the sweet song of salvation which should prepare their minds for the words of life, to be delivered by one of the humblest servants of God. I hoped that grace might be given to me to say something to my poor brethren that might be for their advantage in time and eternity; after which I thought I should see their faces no more. I looked to see them thronging around their missionary in crowds, and waited for this agreeable sight with great anxiety.

The time appointed for the service was half past ten. When it arrived, we got into our carriages and proceeded to the Meeting-house, which was about two miles and a half distant. The sacred edifice stood in the midst of a noble forest, and seemed to be about a hundred years old; circumstances which did not render its appearance less interesting. Hard by was an Indian burial ground, overgrown with pines, in which the graves were all ranged North and South. A delightful brook, fed by some of the sweetest springs in Massachusetts, murmured beside it. After pleasing my eyes with this charming landscape, I turned to meet my Indian brethren and give them the hand of friendship; but I was greatly disappointed in the appearance of those who advanced. All the Indians I had ever seen were of a reddish color, sometimes approaching a yellow; but now, look to what quarter I would, most of those who were coming were pale faces, and, in my disappointment, it seemed to me that the hue of death sat upon their countenances. It seemed very strange to me that my brethren should have changed their natural color, and become in every respect like white men. Recovering a little from my astonishment, I entered the house with the missionary. It had the appearance of some ancient monument set upon a hill-top, for a landmark to generations yet unborn. Could Solomon's temple have been set beside it, I think no one would have drawn an architectural comparison. Beautiful as this place was, we had little time to admire it; something more solemn demanded our attention. We were to prepare ourselves for a temple more splendid than ever was built by hands. When the congregation were seated, I arose and gave out the psalm. I now cast my eyes at the gallery, that I might see how the songsters who were tuning their harps appeared; but, with one exception, paleness was upon all their faces. I must do these *Indians* the justice to say that they performed their parts very well. Looking below, something new caught my attention. Upon two seats, reserved along the sides of the temple for some of the privileged, were seated a few of those to whom the words of the Saviour, as well as his scourge of small cords, might be properly applied, "It is written that my house shall be called the house of prayer, but ye have made it a den of thieves;" for these pale men were certainly stealing from the Indians their portion in the gospel, by leaving their own houses of worship and crowding them out of theirs. The law, perhaps, allowed them to do so. After singing and prayer, I preached one of my humble sermons, after which I attended a Sabbath School, in which a solitary red child might he seen here and there. By what I saw, I judged that the whites were much favored, while the little red children were virtually bidden to stand aside. I understood that the books that were sent to them had been given to the white scholars.

After a slight refreshment, the duty of worship was resumed; and I discovered that plain dealing was disagreeable to my white auditory. I inquired where *the Indians* were; to which Mr. FISH replied, that they were at a place called Marshpee, and that there was a person called *Blind Joe*, who tried to preach to them, which was the cause of their absence. Though the said Joe was one of them, he had done them more harm than good. I asked why he did not imitate Blind Joe, and get him to preach for him a part of the time. He answered, that that could not be; that Joe was not qualified to preach and instruct. I replied that he could not, perhaps, be sure of that, and that if he had followed the course I had mentioned, it would at least have been the means of uniting the people, which would of itself have been great good. It was then concluded to have a meeting at Marshpee; and, in the afternoon of the next day, I paid the people of that place a visit in their Meeting-house.

I addressed them upon temperance and education, subjects which I thought very needful to be discussed, and plainly told them what I had heard from their missionary, viz: That it was their general disposition to be idle, not to hoe the corn-fields they had planted, to take no care of their hay after mowing it, and to lie drunken under their fences. I admonished them of the evil of these their ways, and advised them to consider any white man who sold them rum their enemy, and to place no confidence in him. I told them that such a person deserved to have his own rum thrown into his face. I endeavored to show them how much more useful they might be to themselves and the world if they would but try to educate themselves, and of the respect they would gain by it. Then, addressing the throne of grace, I besought the Lord to have mercy on them and relieve them from the oppressions under which they laboured. Here Mr. FISH cautioned me not to say any thing about oppression, that being, he said, the very thing that made them discontented. They thought themselves oppressed, he observed, but such was not the case. They had already quite liberty enough. I suggested to him the propriety of granting them the privileges enjoyed by the whites about them; but he said that that would never do, as they would immediately part with all their lands. I told him that, if their improvement was his aim, he ought to go among them and inquire into their affairs; to which he replied that he did go at times, but did not say much to them about their worldly concerns. He asked me if I thought it proper to preach about such things. I answered that I thought it proper to do good in any way; that a variety was not amiss, and that such a course would convince his flock that he had their welfare at heart.

I had now appointed to meet my brethren on Wednesday evening following, when I expected to bid them farewell forever; and in the mean while I had obtained a letter of introduction to Mr. PRATT, of Great Marshes. There I gave the audience a word in season, upon the subject of Indian degradation, which did not appear to please them much. I then visited Barnstable, and finding no resting place there for the sole of my foot, I journeyed as far as Hyannis, where I was entertained with hospitality and kindness. On the evening of the fourteenth day, I again preached on the soul-harrowing theme of Indian degradation; and my discourse was generally well received; though it gave much offence to some illiberal minds, as truth always will, when it speaks in condemnation. I now turned my face toward Marshpee, to preach the word there.

I had made up my mind to depart early on the morrow, and therefore, that I might hear of their concerns, and how they fared from their own mouths, I intended to commence my labours early in the day. I had not the least intention of staying with my brethren, because I saw that they had been taught to be sectarians, rather than Christians, to love their own sect and to hate others, which was contrary to the convictions of my own experience as well as to the doctrine of Jesus Christ. What ensued led me to look farther into their case. The lecture I had delivered in the Meetinghouse, had wrought well, and a small pamphlet that contained a sketch of the history of the Indians of New England had had a good effect. As I was reading from it, an individual among the assembly took occasion to clap his hands, and with a loud shout, to cry, "Truth, truth!" This gave rise to a general conversation, and it was truly heart-rending to me to hear what my kindred people had suffered at the hands of the whites.

Having partook of some refreshment, we again met to worship God in the School-house; where I believe that the Spirit of the Lord was revealed to us. Then, wishing to know more of their grievances, real or supposed, and upon their invitation, I appointed several meetings; for I was requested to hear their whole story, and to help them. I therefore appointed the twenty-first of May, 1833, to attend a council to be called by my brethren. In the mean while I went to Falmouth, nine miles distant, where I held forth upon the civil and religious rights of the Indians. Some, who apparently thought that charity was due to themselves, but not to the red men, did not relish the discourse; but such as knew that all men have rights and feelings, and wished those of others to be respected as well as their own, spoke favourably of it. Of this number was Mr. Woodbury, the minister, who thought it would do good. I then returned to Marshpee, to attend the council.

The meeting was held in the school-room. Business commenced at about nine in the morning, and continued through the day. The first that arose to speak was an Indian, Ebenezer Attaquin by name. Tears flowed freely down his time-furrowed cheeks, while he addressed us in a manner alike candid and affectionate. The house was well filled.

After listening patiently to the tale of their distresses, I counselled them to apply for redress to the Governor and Council. They answered, that they had done so; but *had never been able to obtain a hearing.* The white agents had always thrown every obstacle in their way. I then addressed them in a speech which they all listened to with profound attention.

I began by saying that, though I was a stranger among them, I did not doubt but that I might do them some good, and be instrumental in procuring the discharge of the overseers, and an alteration of the existing laws. As, however, I was not a son of their particular tribe, if they wished me to assist them, it would be necessary for them to give me a right to act in their behalf, by adopting me; as then our rights and interests would become identical. They must be aware that all the evil reports calumny could invent, would be put in circulation against me by the whites interested, and that no means to set them against me would be neglected. (Had the inspiration of Isaiah spoken these words, they could not have been more fully accomplished, as is known to the whites of Barnstable County, as well as the Indians.)

Mr. Ebenezer Attaquin, being one of the prayer leaders, replied first, and said, "If we get this man to stand by us, we must stand by him, and if we forsake him after he undertakes for us, God will forsake us also."

Mr. Ezra Attaquin wished to know if I could not come and dwell with them, as so I could do them more good than if abiding at a distance. Mr. Ebenezer Attaquin said in reply, that if such a chance should be offered to a white man, he would be very glad to accept it.

I now inquired what provision could be made for me, if I should consent to their wishes. They answered that their means were small, but that they would provide a house for me to live in, and do what they could for my support. I said that, knowing their poverty, I did not expect much, and gave them to understand that I could dig, and fish, and chop wood, and was willing to do what I could for myself. The subject of religious instruction was then discussed, and the inquiry was made, what should be done with their poor, blind brother, (who was then absent among another sect.) I answered that I was very willing to unite my labours with his, as there was plenty of work for both of us; and that had I but half a loaf of bread, I would gladly divide it with him. It was then agreed that we should unite, and journey together on the road toward heaven.

The case of Mr. Fish was next laid before the council, and complaints were made, that he had neglected his duty; that he did not appear to care for the welfare of the tribe, temporal or spiritual; that he had never visited some of the brethren at all, and others only once in five or seven years; that but eight or ten attended his preaching; that his congregation was composed of white people, to whom his visits were mostly confined, and that it seemed that all he appeared to care for was to get a living, and make as much as he could out of the Indians, who could not see any reason to think him their friend. It was, therefore, agreed to discharge him, and three papers were draughted accordingly. One was a petition to the Governor and Council, a second to the Corporation of Harvard College; the first complaining against the Overseers, and the laws relating to the tribe; and the second against the missionary set over them by Harvard College and the Overseers. The third document was a statement of my adoption into the tribe, and was signed by all present, and subsequently by others, who were not present, but were equally desirious of securing their rights. It was as follows.

To all whom it may concern, from the beginning of the world up to this time, and forever more.

Be it known, that we, the Marshpees, now assembled in the presence of God, do hereby agree to adopt the Rev. William Apes, of the Pequod tribe, as one of ours. He, and his wife, and his two children, and those of his descendants, forever, are to be considered as belonging to the Marshpee tribe of Indians. And we solemly avow this, in the presence of God, and of one another, and do hereby attach our names to the same, that he may take his seat with us and aid us in our affairs. Done at the Council House in Marshpee, and by the authority of the same, May 21st, 1833.

EBENEZER ATTAQUIN, *President.*
ISRAEL AMOS, *Secretary.*

To this instrument there are about a hundred signatures, which were affixed to the other papers above mentioned also. The resolutions which were sent to the two bodies were these:

Resolved, That we, as a tribe, will rule ourselves, and have the right to do so; for all men are born free and equal, says the Constitution of the country.

Resolved, That we will not permit any white man to come upon our plantation, to cut or carry off wood or hay, or any other article, without our permission, after the 1st of July next.

Resolved, That we will put said resolutions in force after that date, (July next,) with the penalty of binding and throwing them from the plantation, if they will not stay away without.

These resolutions were adopted by the tribe, and put in force, as will be seen hereafter. It was hoped that, though the whites had done all they could to extinguish all sense of right among the Indians, they would now see that they had feelings as well as other men.

The petition to the corporation of Harvard set forth the general dissatisfaction of the tribe with the missionary sent them by that honorable body, according to the intended application of the Williams Fund. The money was no more intended for Mr. Fish than for any other clergyman; neither had the Indians given him a call. They thought it right to let his employers know that he had not done his duty, because he not only received between five and six hundred dollars from the college, but had possession of five or six hundred acres of the tribe's best woodland, without their consent or approbation, and converted them to his own exclusive use, pretending that his claim and right to the same was better than that of the owners themselves. Not liking this, the Indians solicted his discharge. The document runs thus:

To our white brethren at Harvard College and trustees of the Williams fund, that is under the care of that body, for the important use of converting the poor heathen in New England, and who, we understand, by means of that fund, have placed among us the Rev. Phineas Fish.

We thought it very likely that you would like to know if we, as a people, respected his person and labors, and whether the money was benefiting the Indians or not. We think it our duty to let you know all about it, and we do say, as the voice of one, with but few exceptions, that we as a tribe, for a long time, have had no desire to hear Mr. Fish preach, (which is about ten years) and do say sincerely that we, as a body, wish to have him discharged, not because we have anything against his moral character, but we believe his labors would be more useful somewhere else, and for these reasons,

1st. We, as a people, have not been benefited by his preaching; for our moral character has not been built up, and there has been no improvement in our intellectual powers, and we know of no Indian that has been converted by his preaching.

2d. We seldom see him upon our plantation to visit us, as a people. His visits are as follows—To one house, one visit in one year—to another, two visits in five years—to another one in seven—and to many, none at all. (We would here remark that Mr. Fish has not improved, but rather lost ground; for history informs us that such was the anxiety of the whites, that it was thought best to visit the Indians twice in one year, and preach to them, so as to save them.)

3d. We think that twenty years are long enough for one trial. Another reason is that you and the people think that we are benefited by that fund, or money paid to him for preaching to the Indians—and we are not. White people are his visitors and hearers. We would remark here that we have no objection to worship with our white neighbors, provided they come as they ought to come, and not as thieves and robbers, and we would ask all the world if the Marshpee Indians have not been robbed of their rights. We wonder how the good citizens of Boston, or any town would like to have the Indians send them a preacher and force him into the pulpit and then send other Indians to crowd the whites out of their own meeting house, and not pay one cent for it. Do you think the white men would like it? We trow, not; and we hope others will consider, while they read our distressing tale. It will be perceived that we have no objection if hundreds of other nations visit our meeting house. We only want fair play; for we have had foul play enough.

4th. We do not believe but that we have as good a right to the table of the Lord as others. We are kept back to the last, merely because our skins are not so white as the whites', and we know of no scriptures that justify him in so doing. (The writer would here observe, that he wonders any person guilty of a dark skin will submit to such unchristian usage, especially as the minister is as willing to shear his black sheep as his white ones. This being the case, ought he not to pay as much regard to them? Should he turn them loose to shift for themselves, at the risk of losing them?)

5th. We never were consulted as to his settlement over us, as a people. We never gave our vote or voice, as a tribe, and we fully believe that we are capable of choosing for ourselves, and have the right to do so, and we would now say to you, that we have made choice of the Rev. Wm. Apes, of the Pequod tribe, and have adopted him as one of ours, and shall hear him preach, in preference to the missionary, and we should like to have him aided, if you can do it. If not, we cannot help it—he is ours—he is ours.

Perhaps you have heard of the oppression of the Cherokees and lamented over them much, and thought the Georgians were hard and cruel creatures; but did you ever hear of the poor, oppressed and degraded Marshpee Indians in Massachusetts, and lament over them? If not, you hear now, and we have made choice of the Rev. Wm. Apes to relieve us, and we hope that you will assist him. And if the above complaints and reasons, and the following resolutions, will be satisfactory, we shall be glad, and rejoice that you comply with our request.

Resolved, That we will rule our own tribe and make choice of whom we please for our preacher.

Resolved, That we will have our own meeting house, and place in the pulpit whom we please to preach to us.

Resolved, That we will publish this to the world; if the above reasons and resolutions are not adhered to, and the Rev. Mr. Fish discharged.

The foregoing addresses and resolutions were adopted by a vote of the tribe, almost unanimous. Done at the Council House at Marshpee, May the 21st, 1833.

EBENEZER ATTAQUIN, *President.*
ISRAEL AMOS, *Secretary.*

MARSHPEE INDIANS.

MESSRS. EDITORS,

We observed in one of your late papers, some editorial remarks which breathed a spirit of candor and good will towards us, and not of ridicule and sarcasm, like that of your neighbor, the Patriot. Now Messrs. Editors, as our situation is but little understood, and the minds of the people much agitated, we feel a desire to lay before them some of the causes of the late excitement. We have long been under guardians, placed in authority over us, without our having any voice in the selection, and, as we believe, not constitutional. Will the good people of Massachusetts revert back to the days of their fathers, when they were under the galling yoke of the mother country? when they petitioned the government for a redress of grievances, but in vain? At length they were determined to try some other method; and when some English ships came to Boston, laden with tea, they mustered their forces, unloaded and threw it into the dock, and thereby laid the foundation of their future independence, although it was in a terrible war, that your fathers sealed with their blood a covenant made with liberty. And now we ask the good people of Massachusetts, the boasted cradle of independence, whom we have petitioned for a redress of wrongs, more grievous than what your fathers had to bear, and our petitioning was as fruitless as theirs, and there was no other alternative but like theirs, to take our stand, and as we have on our plantation but one harbor, and no English ships of tea, for a substitute, we unloaded two wagons loaded with our wood, without a wish to injure the owners of the wagons. And now, good people of Massachusetts, when your fathers dared to unfurl the banners of freedom amidst the hostile fleets and armies of Great Britain, it was then that Marshpee furnished them with some of her bravest men to fight your battles. Yes, by the side of your fathers they fought and bled, and now their blood cries to you from the ground to restore that liberty so unjustly taken from us by their sons.

MARSHPEE.

AN INDIAN'S APPEAL TO THE WHITE MEN OF MASSACHUSETTS.

As our brethren, the white men of Massachusetts, have recently manifested much sympathy for the red men of the Cherokee nation, who have suffered much from their white brethren; as it is contended in this State, that our red brethren, the Cherokees, should be an independent people, having the privileges of the white men; we, the red men of the Marshpee tribe, consider it a favorable time to speak. We are not free. We wish to be so, as much as the red men of Georgia. How will the white man of Massachusetts ask favor for the red men of the South, while the poor Marshpee red men, his near neighbors, sigh in bondage? Will not your white brothers of Georgia tell you to look at home, and clear your own borders of oppression, before you trouble them? Will you think of this? What would be benevolence in Georgia, the red man thinks would be so in Massachusetts. You plead for the Cherokees, will you not raise your voice for the red man of Marshpee? Our overseers are not kind; they speak, you hear them. When we speak for ourselves, our voice is so feeble it is not heard.

You think the men you give us do us good, and that all is right. Brothers, you are deceived; they do us no good. We do them good.

They like the place where you have put them. Brothers, our fathers of this State meet soon to make laws; will you help us to enable them to hear the voice of the red man?

Marshpee, Dec. 19, 1833.

The next is from the Liberator of Jan. 25, 1834.

THE MARSHPEE INDIANS.

This is a small tribe, comprising four or five hundred persons, residing at the head of Cape Cod, in Barnstable County. They have long been under the guardianship of the State, treated as paupers, and subjected to the control of a Board of Overseers. A memorial from them was presented to the Legislature last week, (written entirely by one of their number,) in which they set forth the grievances which are imposed upon them, the injustice and impolicy of the laws affecting their tribe, the arbitrary and capricious conduct of the Overseers, and the manner in which they are defrauded of the fruits of their labor; and earnestly beseech the Legislature to grant them the same liberty of action as is enjoyed by their white brethren, that they may manage their own concerns, and be directly amenable to the laws of the State, and not to their present Overseers.

A delegation from this tribe is now in this city, consisting of Deacon Coombs, Daniel Amos, and William Apes. The use of the Hall of the House of Representatives having been granted to them, they made a public statement of their situation and wants to a crowded audience on Friday evening last, principally composed of members of the House; and were listened to most respectfully and attentively.

Deacon Coombs first addressed the assembly, in a brief but somewhat indefinite speech; the purport of which was, that, although by taking side with the Overseers, he might have advanced his own interests, he nevertheless chose to suffer with his people, and to plead in their behalf. Their condition was growing more and more intolerable; excessive exactions were imposed upon them; their industry was crippled by taxation; they wished to have the Overseers discharged.

Daniel Amos next addressed the meeting. He said he was aware of his ignorance; but although his words might be few, and his language broken, he as deeply sympathized with his suffering constituents, as any of his tribe. He gave a short sketch of his life, by which it appeared that he went at an early period on a whaling voyage, and received some bodily injury which incapacitated him from hard labor for a long time. He sought his native home, and soon experienced the severity of those laws, which, though enacted seemingly to protect the tribe, are retarding their improvement, and oppressing their spirits. The present difficulties were not of recent origin. He stated, with commendable pride, that he had never been struck for ill-behaviour, nor imprisoned for crime or debt; nor was he ashamed to show his face again in any place he had visited; and he had been round a large portion of the globe. The memorial before the Legislature had been read to the tribe; some parts had been omitted at their request; and nothing had been sent but by their unanimous consent. After vindicating the character of Mr. Apes, and enumerating some of the complaints of the tribe,

He was followed by William Apes, who, in a fearless, comprehensive and eloquent speech, endeavored to prove that, under such laws and such Overseers, no people could rise from their degradation. He illustrated the manner in which extortions were made from the poor Indians, and plainly declared that they wanted their rights as men and as freemen. Although comparatively ignorant, yet they knew enough to manage their own concerns more equitably and economically than they were then managed; and notwithstanding the difficulties under which they labored, their moral condition was improving. There was not so much intemperance among them as formerly; many of the tribe were shrewd, intelligent and respectable men; and all that was necessary to raise up the entire mass from their low estate, was the removal of those fetters and restrictions which now bind them to the dust. Mr. Apes described the cause and the extent of the disturbance which took place last summer, and which resulted in his imprisonment. The head and front of their offending was in going into the woods, and unloading a cart, and causing it to be sent away empty. The reason for that procedure was, that they wished no more wood to be cut until an investigation of their rights had been made. They used no violence; uttered no oaths; made no threats; and took no weapons of defence. Every thing was done quietly, but firmly. Mr. Apes wished to know from whence the right to tax them without their consent, and at pleasure, and subject them to the arbitrary control of a Board of Overseers, was derived? He knew not himself; but he feared it was from the color of their skin. He concluded by making a forcible appeal to the justice and humanity of the Legislature, and expressing his confidence that the prayer of the memorialists would not be made in vain.

In several instances, the speakers made some dextrous and pointed thrusts at the whites, for their treatment of the sons of the forest since the time of the pilgrims, which were received with applause by the audience. They were all careful in their references to the conduct of the Overseers; they wished to say as little about them as possible; but they wanted their removal forthwith.

This is the first time our attention has been seriously called to the situation of this tribe. It is a case not to be treated with contempt, or disposed of hastily. It involves the rights, the interests, and the happiness of a large number of that race which has been nearly exterminated by the neglect, the oppression, and the cruelty of a superior number of foreign invaders.

In the enslavement of two millions of American people in the Southern States, the tyranny of this nation assumes a gigantic form. The magnitude of the crime elevates the indignation of the soul. Such august villainy and stupendous iniquity soar above disgust, and mount up to astonishment. A conflagration like that of Moscow, is full of sublimity, though dreadful in its effects; but the burning of a solitary hut makes the incendiary despicable by the meanness of the act.

In the present case, this State is guilty of a series of petty impositions upon a feeble band, which excite not so much indignation as disgust. They may be, and doubtless are, the blunders of legislation; the philanthropy of proscriptive ignorance; the atoning injuries of prejudice, rather than deliberate oppression. No matter who are the Overseers, (we know them not,) nor how faithfully they have executed the laws. The complaint is principally against the State; incidentally against them. They may succeed, perhaps, in vindicating their own conduct; but the State is to be judged out of the Statute Book, by the laws now in force for the regulation of the tribe. Fearing, in the plenitude of its benevolence, that the Indians would never rise to be men, the Commonwealth has, in the perfection of its wisdom, given them over to absolute pauperism. Believing they were incapable of self-government as free citizens, it has placed them under a guardianship which is sure to keep them in the chains of a servile dependance. Deprecating partial and occasional injustice to them on the part of individuals, it has shrewdly deemed it lawful to plunder them by wholesale, continually. Lamenting that the current of vitality is not strong enough to give them muscular vigor and robust health, it has fastened upon them leeches to fatten on their blood. Assuming that they would be too indolent to labor if they had all the fruits of their industry, it has taken away all motives for superior exertions, by keeping back a portion of their wages. Dreading lest they should run too fast, and too far, in an unfettered state, it has loaded them with chains so effectually as to prevent their running at all. These are some of the excellencies of that paternal guardianship, under which they now groan, and from which they desire the Legislature to grant them deliverance.

We are proud to see this spontaneous, earnest, upward movement of our red brethren. It is not to be stigmatized as turbulent, but applauded as meritorious. It is sedition, it is true; but only the sedition of freedom against oppression; of justice against fraud; of humanity against cruelty. It is the intellect opposed to darkness; the soul opposed to degradation. It is an earnest of better things to come, provided the struggling spirit be set free. Let this tribe have at least a fair trial. While they remain as paupers, they will feel like paupers; be regarded like paupers; be degraded like paupers. We protest against this unnatural order of things; and now that the case has come under our cognizance, we shall not abandon it hastily.

We are aware that another, and probably an opposite view of this case is to be laid before the public, on the part of a commissioner delegated by the Governor and Council, to inquire into the difficulties which have arisen between the tribe and the Overseers. We shall wait to get a glimpse of it before we pass judgment upon it. Whatever may be alleged either against the Indians or against those who hold a supervision over them, or whatever may be said in favor of them both; we have felt authorized to make the foregoing remarks, upon an examination of the laws enacted for the government of these discordant parties. An augmentation, diminution, or change of the Board of Overseers, will not remedy the evil. It lies elsewhere; in the absolute prostration of the petitioners by a blind legislation. They are not, and do not aspire to be an independent government, but citizens of Massachusetts.

Fortunately, there is a soul for freedom in the present Legislature. A more independent House of Representatives has never been elected by the people. The cries of the Indians have reached their ears, and we trust affected their hearts. They will abolish a needless and unjust protectorate. The limb, which is now disjointed and bleeding, will be united to the body politic. What belongs to the red man shall hereafter in truth be his; and, thirsting for knowledge and aspiring to be free, every fetter shall be broken and his soul made glad.

WILLIAM APESS: FROM *Indian Nullification of the Unconstitutional Laws of Massachusetts*

THE EDITORS' COMMENT

When Pequot minister and writer William Apess traveled to Mashpee (then also spelled Marshpee), on Cape Cod, in the summer of 1833, he found settlers holding church services in the Mashpee Wampanoag meetinghouse. Constructed in 1684, the meetinghouse became a hub for Indigenous ministers who preached in Wôpanâak and advocated for Wampanoag rights against settlers who sought to claim resources from their lands, which were held exclusively and in common by the Mashpee women and their families. Their efforts ensured that the meetinghouse and community at Mashpee remained, in spite of settler claims about Indigenous people vanishing. Apess used irony on the page and in public speeches to disrupt settlers' expectations for Indigenous vanishing and to criticize colonists, primarily the Mashpees' appointed minister Phineas Fish, for occupying the meetinghouse, diverting funds promised for the community to his own use, and, along with guardians appointed as overseers to Mashpee people, illegally selling timber from Mashpee lands. *Indian Nullification* describes how Apess and the Mashpees confronted Fish and other settlers for these actions, and how Apess was imprisoned and accused of inciting a riot for his willingness to assert Mashpee rights to self-determination and resource management alongside his Mashpee brethren. *Indian Nullification* is a book that brings together multiple voices and texts, including newspaper articles and collectively authored petitions, to critique the measures by which Massachusetts settlers sought to use and usurp Mashpee lands. The state legislature eventually affirmed the Mashpees' rights to their land, meetinghouse, trees, and town governance with the Mashpee Act of 1834. Apess sought to use the publication of *Indian Nullification* to galvanize public action in support of Mashpee. In the twenty-first century the Mashpee Wampanoag community continues to draw upon centuries of political action and diplomacy to secure reaffirmation of their lands in an ongoing fight for federal recognition.

KING PHILIP DYING FOR HIS COUNTRY.

EULOGY
ON
KING PHILIP,

AS PRONOUNCED AT
THE ODEON,
IN FEDERAL STREET, BOSTON,

BY THE REV. WILLIAM
APES, AN INDIAN.

Who shall stand in after years in this famous temple, and declare that Indians are not men? if men, then heirs to the same inheritance.

BOSTON:
PUBLISHED BY THE AUTHOR.
1836.

William Apess: *Eulogy on King Philip*

I DO not arise to spread before you the fame of a noted warrior, whose natural abilities shone like those of the great and mighty PHILLIP of Greece, or of ALEXANDER the Great, or like those of WASHINGTON,—whose virtues and patriotism are engraven on the hearts of my audience. Neither do I approve of war as being the best method of bowing the haughty tyrant, MAN, and civilizing the world. No, far from me be such a thought. But it is to bring before you beings, made by the GOD of Nature, and in whose hearts and heads he has planted sympathies that shall live forever in the memory of the world, whose brilliant talents shone in the display of natural things, so that the most cultivated, whose powers shone with equal lustre, were not able to prepare mantles to cover the burning elements of an uncivilized world. What, then, shall we cease to mention the mighty of the earth, the noble work of GOD?

Yet those purer virtues remain untold. Those noble traits that marked the wild man's course lie buried in the shades of night; and who shall stand? I appeal to the lovers of liberty. But those few remaining descendants who now remain as the monument of the cruelty of those who came to improve our race, and correct our errors; and as the immortal Washington lives endeared and engraven on the hearts of every white in America, never to be forgotten in time,—even such is the immortal PHILIP honored, as held in memory by the degraded, but yet grateful descendants, who appreciate his character; so will every patriot, especially in this enlightened age, respect the rude yet all-accomplished son of the forest, that died a martyr to his cause, though unsuccessful, yet as glorious as the *American* Revolution. Where, then, shall we place the hero of the wilderness?

Justice and humanity for the remaining few prompt me to vindicate the character of him who yet lives in their hearts, and, if possible, melt the prejudice that exists in the hearts of those who are in the possession of his soil, and only by the right of conquest—is the aim of him who proudly tells you, the blood of a denominated savage runs in his veins. It is, however, true, that there are many who are said to be honorable warriors, who, in the wisdom of their civilized legislation, think it no crime to reek their vengeance upon whole nations and communities, until the fields are covered with blood, and the rivers turned into purple fountains, while groans, like distant thunder, are heard from the wounded, and the tens of thousands of the dying, leaving helpless families depending on their cares and sympathies for life; while a loud response is heard floating through the air from the ten thousand Indian children and orphans, who are left to mourn the honorable acts of a few—civilized men.

Now, if we have common sense and ability to allow the difference between the civilized and the uncivilized, we cannot but see that one mode of warfare is as just as the other; for, while one is sanctioned by authority of the enlightened and cultivated men, the other is an agreement according to the pure laws of nature, growing out of natural consequences; for nature always has her defence for every beast of the field; even the reptiles of the earth and the fishes of the sea have their weapons of war. But though frail man was made for a nobler purpose,—to live, to love and adore his God, and do good to his brother; for this reason, and this alone, the GOD of heaven prepared ways and means to blast anger, man's destroyer, and cause the Prince of Peace to rule, that man might swell those blessed notes, My image is of God, I am not a beast.

But as all men are governed by animal passions who are void of the true principles of GOD, whether cultivated or uncultivated, we shall now lay before you the true character of PHILIP, in relation to those hostilities between himself and the whites, and in so doing permit me to be plain and candid.

The first inquiry is, Who is PHILIP? He was the descendant of one of the most celebrated chiefs in the known world, for peace and universal benevolence towards all men; for injuries upon injuries, and the most daring robberies and barbarous deeds of death that were ever committed by the American Pilgrims, were with patience and resignation borne, in a manner that would do justice to any Christian nation or being in the world,—especially when we realize that it was voluntary suffering on the part of the good old chief. His country extensive—his men numerous, so as the wilderness was enlivened by them, say a thousand to one of the white men, and they, also, sick and feeble—where, then, shall we find one nation submitting so tamely to another, with such a host at their command? For injuries of much less magnitude have the people called Christians slain their brethren, till they could sing, like Sampson, With a jaw bone of an ass have we slain our thousands, and laid them in heaps. It will be well for us to lay those deeds and depredations committed by whites upon Indians, before the civilized world, and then they can judge for themselves.

It appears from history that in 1614, "There came one Henry Harley unto me, bringing with him a native of the Island of Capawick, a place at the south of Cape Cod, whose name was Epenuel. This man was taken upon the main by force, with some twenty-nine others," very probably good old Massasoit's men—see Harlow's Voyage, 1611, "by a ship, and carried to London, and from thence to be sold for slaves among the Spaniards; but the Indians being too shrewd, or, as they say, unapt for their use, they refused to traffic in Indians' blood and bones." This inhuman act of the whites caused the Indians to be jealous forever afterwards, which the white man acknowledges upon the first pages of the history of his country. (See Drake's Hist. of the Indians, page 7.)

How inhuman it was in those wretches, to come into a country where nature shone in beauty, spreading her wings over the vast continent, sheltering beneath her shades those natural sons of an Almighty Being, that shone in grandeur and lustre like stars of the first magnitude in the heavenly world; whose virtues far surpassed their more enlightened foes, notwithstanding their pretended zeal for religion and virtue. How they could go to work to enslave a free people, and call it religion, is beyond the power of my imagination, and out-strips the revelation of God's word. Oh, thou pretended hypocritical Christian, whoever thou art, to say it was the design of God, that we should murder and slay one another, because we have the power. Power was not given us to abuse each other, but a mere power delegated to us by the King of heaven, a weapon of defence against error and evil; and when abused, it will turn to our destruction. Mark, then, the history of nations throughout the world.

But notwithstanding the transgression of this power to destroy the Indians at their first discovery, yet it does appear that the Indians had a wish to be friendly. When the pilgrims came among them, (IYANOUGH's men,) there appeared an old woman, breaking out in solemn lamentations, declaring one Capt. Hunt had carried off three of her children, and they would never return here. The pilgrims replied, that they were bad and wicked men, but they were going to do better, and would never injure them at all. And to pay the poor mother, gave her a few brass trinkets, to atone for her three sons, and appease her present feelings, a woman nearly one hundred years of age. Oh, white woman! what would you think, if some foreign nation, unknown to you, should come and carry away from you three lovely children, whom you had dandled on the knee, and at some future time you should behold them, and break forth in sorrow, with your heart broken, and merely ask, sirs, where are my little ones, and some one should reply, it was passion, great passion; what would you think of them? Should you not think they were beings made more like rocks than men. Yet these same men came to these Indians for support, and acknowledge themselves, that no people could be used better than they were; that their treatment would do honor to any nation; that their provisions were in abundance; that they gave them venison, and sold them many hogsheads of corn to fill their stores, besides beans. This was in the year 1622. Had it not been for this humane act of the Indians, every white man would have been swept from the New England colonies. In their sickness too, the Indians were as tender to them as to their own children; and for all this, they were denounced as savages by those who had received all the acts of kindness they possibly could show them. After these social acts of the Indians towards those who were suffering, and those of their countrymen, who well knew the care their brethren had received by them: how were the Indians treated before that? Oh, hear! In the following manner, and their own words, we presume, they will not deny.

December, (O. S.) 1620, the pilgrims landed at Plymouth, and without asking liberty from any one, they possessed themselves of a portion of the country, and built themselves houses, and then made a treaty, and commanded them to accede to it. This, if now done, would be called an insult, and every white man would be called to go out and act the part of a patriot, to defend their country's rights; and if every intruder were butchered, it would be sung upon every hill-top in the Union, that victory and patriotism was the order of the day. And yet the Indians, (though many were dissatisfied,) without the shedding of blood, or imprisoning any one, bore it. And yet for their kindness and resignation towards the whites, they were called savages, and made by God on purpose for them to destroy. We might say, God understood his work better than this. But to proceed, it appears that a treaty was made by the pilgrims and the Indians, which treaty was kept during forty years; the young chiefs during this time, was showing the pilgrims how to live in their country, and find support for their wives and little ones; and for all this, they were receiving the applauses of being savages. The two gentlemen chiefs were Squanto and Samoset, that were so good to the pilgrims.

The next we present before you are things very appalling. We turn our attention to dates, 1623, January and March, when Mr. Weston's Colony, came very near starving to death; some of them were obliged to hire themselves to the Indians, to become their servants, in order that they might live. Their principal work was to bring wood and water; but not being contented with this, many of the whites sought to steal the Indian's corn; and because the Indians complained of it, and through their complaint, some one of their number being punished, as they say, to appease the savages. Now let us see who the greatest savages were; the person that stole the corn was a stout athletic man, and because of this, they wished to spare him, and take an old man who was lame and sickly, and that used to get his living by weaving, and because they thought he would not be of so much use to them, he was, although innocent of any crime, hung in his stead. Oh, savage, where art thou, to weep over the Christian's crimes. Another act of humanity for Christians, as they call themselves, that one Capt. Standish, gathering some fruit and provisions, goes forward with a black and hypocritical heart, and pretends to prepare a feast for the Indians; and when they sit down to eat, they seize the Indian's knives hanging about their necks, and stab them to the heart. The white people call this stabbing, feasting the savages. We suppose it might well mean themselves, their conduct being more like savages than Christians. They took one Wittumumet, the Chief's head, and put it upon a pole in their fort; and for aught we know, gave praise to their God for success in murdering a poor Indian; for we know it was their usual course to give praise to God for this kind of victory, believing it was God's will and command, for them to do so. We wonder if these same Christians did not think it the command of God, that they should lie, steal, and get drunk, commit fornication and adultery. The one is as consistent as the other. What say you, judges, is it not so, and was it not according as they did? Indians think it is.

But we will proceed to show another inhuman act. The whites robbed the Indian graves, and their corn, about the year 1632, which caused CHICATAUBUT to be displeased, who was chief, and also a son to the woman that was dead. And according to the Indian custom it was a righteous act to be avenged of the dead. Accordingly he called all his men together, and addressed them thus: "When last the glorious light of the sky was underneath this globe, and birds grew silent, I began to settle, as is my custom, to take repose. Before my eyes were fast closed, methought I saw a vision, at which my spirit was much troubled. A spirit cried aloud, Behold, my son, whom I have cherished, see the paps that gave thee suck, the hands that clasped thee warm, and fed thee oft. Can thou forget to take revenge of those wild people that have my monument defaced in a despiteful manner, disdaining our ancient antiquities and honorable customs? See, now, the Sachem's grave lies, like unto the common people of ignoble race, defaced. Thy mother doth complain, and implores thy aid against these thievish people, now come hither. If this be suffered, I shall not rest quiet within my everlasting habitation." War was the result. And where is there a people in the world that would see their friends robbed of their common property, their nearest and dearest friends; robbed, after their last respects to them? I appeal to you, who value your friends, and affectionate mothers, if you would have them robbed of their fine marble, and your storehouses broken open, without calling those to account, who did it? I trow not;

and if another nation should come to these regions, and begin to rob and plunder all that came in their way, would not the orators of the day be called to address the people, and arouse them to war, for such insults? and, for all this, would they not be called Christians and patriots? Yes, it would be rung from Georgia to Maine, from the Ocean to the lakes, what fine men and Christians there were in the land. But when a few red children attempt to defend their rights, they are condemned as savages, by those, if possible, who have indulged in wrongs more cruel than the Indians.

But there is still more. In 1619 a number of Indians went on board of a ship, by order of their chief, and the whites set upon them, and murdered them without mercy; says Mr. Dermer, "without the Indians giving them the least provocation whatever." Is this insult to be borne, and not a word to be said? Truly, Christians would never bear it; why, then, think it strange that the denominated savages do not? Oh, thou white Christian, look at acts that honored your countrymen, to the destruction of thousands, for much less insults than that. And who, my dear sirs, were wanting of the name of savages—whites, or Indians? Let justice answer.

But we have more to present; and that is, the violation of a treaty that the Pilgrims proposed for the Indians to subscribe to, and they the first to break it. The Pilgrims promised to deliver up every transgressor of the Indian treaty, to them, to be punished according to their laws, and the Indians were to do likewise. Now it appears that an Indian had committed treason, by conspiring against the king's life, which is punishable with death; and MASSASOIT makes demand for the transgressor, and the Pilgrims refuse to give him up, although by their oath of alliance they had promised to do so. Their reasons were, he was beneficial to them. This shows how grateful they were to their former safeguard, and ancient protector. Now, who would have blamed this venerable old chief if he had declared war at once, and swept the whole colonies away? It was certainly in his power to do it, if he pleased; but no, he forbore, and forgave the whites. But where is there a people, called civilized, that would do it? we presume, none; and we doubt not but the Pilgrims would have exerted all their powers to be avenged, and to appease their ungodly passions. But it will be seen that this good old chief exercised more Christian forbearance than any of the governors of that age, or since. It might well be said he was a pattern for the Christians themselves; but by the Pilgrims he is denounced, as being a savage.

It does not appear that MASSASOIT or his sons were respected because they were human beings, but because they feared him; and we are led to believe that if it had been in the power of the Pilgrims, they would have butchered them out and out notwithstanding all the piety they professed. Only look for a few moments at the abuses the son of MASSASOIT received. ALEXANDER being sent for with armed men, and while he and his men were breaking their fast in the morning, they were taken immediately away, by order of the governor, without the least provocation, but merely through suspicion. ALEXANDER and his men saw them, and might have prevented it, but did not, saying the governor had no occasion to treat him in this manner; and the heartless wretch informed him that he would murder him upon the spot, if he did not go with him, presenting a sword at his breast; and had it not been for one of his men he would have yielded himself up upon the spot. ALEXANDER was a man of strong passion, and of a firm mind; and this insulting treatment of him caused him to fall sick of a fever, so that he never recovered. Some of the Indians were suspicious that he was poisoned to death. He died in the year 1662. "After him," says that eminent divine, Dr. Mather, "there rose up one PHILIP, of cursed memory." Perhaps if the Dr. was present, he would find that the memory of PHILIP was as far before his, in the view of sound, judicious men, as the sun is before the stars, at noonday. But we might suppose that men like Dr. Mather, so well versed in Scripture, would have known his work better than to have spoken evil of any one, or have cursed any of GOD's works. He ought to have known that GOD did not make his red children for him to curse; but if he wanted them cursed, he could have done it himself. But, on the contrary, his suffering Master commanded him to love his enemies, and to pray for his persecutors, and to do unto others as he would that men should do unto him. Now, we wonder if the sons of the Pilgrims would like to have us, poor Indians, come out and curse the Doctor, and all their sons, as we have been, by many of them. And suppose that, in some future day, our children should repay all these wrongs, would it not be doing as we, poor Indians, have been done to? But we sincerely hope there is more humanity in us, than that.

In the history of MASSASOIT we find that his own head men were not satisfied with the Pilgrims; that they looked upon them to be intruders, and had a wish to expel those intruders out of their coast; and no wonder that from the least reports the Pilgrims were ready to take it up. A false report was made respecting one TISQUANTUM, that he was murdered by an Indian, one of COUBANTANT's men. Upon this news, one Standish, a vile and malicious fellow, took fourteen of his lewd Pilgrims with him, and at midnight, when a deathless silence reigned throughout the wilderness; not even a bird is heard to send forth her sweet songs to charm and comfort those children of the woods; but all had taken their rest, to commence anew on the rising of the glorious sun. But to their sad surprise there was no rest for them, but they were surrounded by ruffians and assassins; yes, assassins; what better name can be given them? At that late hour of the night, meeting a house in the wilderness, whose inmates were nothing but a few helpless females and children; soon a voice is heard—Move not, upon the peril of your life. I appeal to this audience if there was any righteousness in their proceedings? Justice would say no. At the same time some of the females were so frightened, that some of them undertook to make their escape, upon which they were fired upon. Now it is doubtless the case that these females never saw a white man before, or ever heard a gun fired. It must have sounded to them like the rumbling of thunder, and terror must certainly have filled all their hearts. And can it be supposed that these innocent Indians could have looked upon them as good and trusty men? Do you look upon the midnight robber and assassin as being a Christian, and trusty man? These Indians had not done one single wrong act to the whites, but were as innocent of any crime, as any beings in the world. And do you believe that Indians cannot feel and see, as well as white people? If you think so, you are mistaken. Their power of feeling and knowing is as quick as yours. Now this is to be borne, as the pilgrims did as their Master told them to; but what color he was I leave it. But if the real sufferers say one word, they are denounced, as being wild and savage beasts.

But let us look a little further. It appears that in 1630, a benevolent Chief bid the pilgrims welcome to his shores; and in June 28, 1630, ceded his land to them for the small sum of eighty dollars, now Ipswich, Rowley, and a part of Essex. The following year, at the July term, 1631, these pilgrims of the new world, passed an act in court, that the friendly chief should not come into their houses short of paying fifty dollars, or an equivalent, that is ten beaver skins. Who could have supposed that the meek and lowly followers of virtue would have taken such methods to rob honest men of the woods. But for this insult, the pilgrims had well nigh lost their lives and their all, had it not been prevented by ROBBIN, an Indian, who apprized them of their danger. And now let it be understood, notwithstanding all the bitter feelings the whites have generally shown towards Indians, yet they have been the only instrument in preserving their lives.

The history of New England writers say, that our tribes were large and respectable. How then, could it be otherwise, but their safety rested in the hands of friendly Indians. In 1647, the pilgrims speak of large and respectable tribes. But let us trace them for a few moments. How have they been destroyed, is it by fair means? No. How then? By hypocritical proceedings, by being duped and flattered; flattered by informing the Indians that their God was a going to speak to them, and then place them before the cannon's mouth in a line, and then putting the match to it and kill thousands of them. We might suppose that meek Christians had better gods and weapons than cannon; weapons that were not carnal, but mighty through God, to the pulling down of strong holds. These are the weapons that modern Christians profess to have; and if the pilgrims did not have them, they ought not to be honored as such. But let us again review their weapons, to civilize the nations of this soil. What were they: rum and powder, and ball, together with all the diseases, such as the small pox, and every other disease imaginable; and in this way sweep off thousands and tens of thousands. And then it has been said, that these men who were free from these things, that they could not live among civilized people. We wonder how a virtuous people could live in a sink of diseases, a people who had never been used to them.

And who is to account for those destructions upon innocent families and helpless children. It was said by some of the New England writers, that living babes were found at the breast of their dead mothers. What an awful sight! and to think too, that these diseases were carried among them on purpose to destroy them. Let the children of the pilgrims blush, while the son of the forest drops a tear, and groans over the fate of his murdered and departed fathers. He would say to the sons of the pilgrims, (as Job said about his birth day,) let the day be dark, the 22d of December, 1620; let it be forgotten in your celebration, in your speeches, and by the burying of the Rock that your fathers first put their foot upon. For be it remembered, although the gospel is said to be glad tidings to all people, yet we poor Indians never have found those who brought it as messengers of mercy, but contrawise. We say, therefore, let every man of color wrap himself in mourning, for the 22d of December and the 4th of July are days of mourning and not of joy. (I would here say, there is an error in my book; it speaks of the 25th of December, but it should be the 22d. See Indian Nullification.) Let them rather fast and pray to the great Spirit, the Indian's God, who deals out mercy to his red children, and not destruction.

Oh, Christians, can you answer for those beings that have been destroyed by your hostilities, and beings too that lies endeared to God as yourselves? his Son being their Saviour as well as yours, and alike to all men? And will you presume to say that you are executing the judgments of God by so doing, or as many really are approving the works of their fathers to be genuine, as it is certain that every time they celebrate the day of the pilgrims they do? Although in words they deny it, yet in works they approve of the iniquities of their fathers. And as the seed of iniquity and prejudice was sown in that day, so it still remains; and there is a deep rooted popular opinion in the hearts of many, that Indians were made, &c. on purpose for destruction, to be driven out by white Christians, and they to take their places; and that God had decreed it from all eternity. If such theologians would only study the works of nature more, they would understand the purposes of good better than they do. That the favor of the Almighty was good and holy, and all his nobler works were made to adorn his image, by being his grateful servants, and admiring each other as angels;

and not as they say, to drive and devour each other. And that you may know the spirit of the pilgrims yet remain, we will present before you the words of a humble divine of the far West. He says, "the desert becomes an Eden." Rev. NAHUM GOLD, of Union Grove, Putnam, writes under date June 12, 1835, says he, "let any man look at this settlement, and reflect what it was three years ago, and his heart can but kindle up while he exclaims, 'what has God wrought!' the savage has left the ground for civilized man; the rich prairie, from bringing forth all its strengths to be burned, is now receiving numerous enclosures, and brings a harvest of corn and wheat to feed the church. Yes, sir, this is now God's vineyard; he has gathered the vine, the choice vine, and brought it from a far country, and has planted it on a goodly soil. He expects fruit now. He gathered out the stones thereof, and drove the red Canaanites from trampling it down, or in any way hindering its increase."—*N. Y. Evangelist, August* 1.

But what next should we hear from this very pious man. Why, my brethren, the poor missionaries want money to go and convert the poor heathen, as if God could not convert them where they were; but must first drive them out. If God wants the red man converted, we should think he could do it as well in one place as in another. But must I say, and shall I say it, that missionaries have injured us more than they have done us good, by degrading us as a people, in breaking up our governments, and leaving us without any suffrages whatever, or a legal right among men. Oh, what cursed doctrine is this, it most certainly is not fit to civilize men with, much more to save their souls; and we poor Indians want no such missionaries around us. But I would suggest one thing, and that is, let the ministers and people use the colored people they have already around them, like human beings, before they go to convert any more; and let them show it in their churches; and let them proclaim it upon the house tops, and I would say to the benevolent, withhold your hard earnings from them, unless they do do it; until they can stop laying their own wickedness to God, which is blasphemy.

But if God was like his subjects, we should all have been swept off before now; for we find that of late, pilgrims' children have got to killing and mobbing each other, as they have got rid of most all the Indians. This is worse than my countrymen ever did; for they never mobbed one another, and I was in hopes that the sons of the pilgrims had improved a little. But the more honorable may thank their fathers for such a spirit in this age. And remember that their walls of prejudice was built with untempered mortar, contrary to God's command; and be assured, it will fall upon their children, though I sincerely hope they will not be seriously injured by it. Although I myself, now and then feel a little of its pressure, as though I should not be able to sustain the shock; but I trust the great Spirit will stand by me, as also good and honorable men will, being as it were the last, still lingering upon the shores of time, standing as it were upon the graves of his much injured race, to plead their cause, and speak for the rights of the remaining few. Although it is said by many, that Indians had no rights, neither do they regard their rights; nor can they look a white man in the face, and ask him for them. If the white man did but know it, the Indians knows it would do no good to spend his breath for nought. But if we can trust to ROGER WILLIAMS' word, in regard to Indian rights: he says, no people were more so; that the cause of all their wars were about their hunting grounds. And it is certain their boundaries were set to their respective tribes; so that each one knew his own range. The poet speaks thus of CANONICUS, in 1803:

> A mighty Prince, of venerable age,
> A fearless warrior, but of peace the friend;
> His breast a treasury of maxims sage,
> His arm a host, to punish or defend.

It was said he was eighty-four years of age when he died, an able defender of his rights. Thus it does appear that Indians had rights, and those rights were near and dear to them, as your stores and farms, and firesides are to the whites, and their wives and children also. And how the pilgrims could rejoice at their distresses, I know not; what divinity men were made of in those days, rather puzzles me now and then. Now, for example, we will lay before you the conduct of an Indian and the whites, and leave you, dear sirs, to judge.

History informs us that in Kennebunk there lived an Indian, remarkable for his good conduct, and who received a grant of land from the State, and fixed himself in a new township, where a number of white families were settled. Though not ill-treated, yet the common prejudices against Indians prevented any sympathy with him, though he himself did all that lay in his power to comfort his white neighbors, in case of sickness and death. But now let us see the scene reversed. This poor Indian, that had nourished, and waited to aid the Pilgrims in their trouble, now vainly looks for help, when sickness and death comes into his family. Hear his own words. He speaks to the inhabitants thus: "When white man's child die, Indian man he sorry; he help bury him. When my child die, no one speak to me; I make his grave alone. I can no live here." He gave up his farm, dug up the body of his child, and carried it 200 miles, through the wilderness, to join the Canadian Indians. What dignity there was in this man; and we do not wonder that he felt so indignant at the proceedings of the then called Christians. But this was as they were taught by their haughty divines and orators of the day. But, nevertheless, the people were to blame, for they might have read for themselves; and they doubtless would have found that we were not made to be vessels of wrath, as they say we were. And had the whites found it out, perhaps they would not have rejoiced at a poor Indian's death; or when they were swept off, would not have called it the Lord killing the Indians to make room for them upon their lands. This is something like many people wishing for their friends to die, that they might get their property. I am astonished when I look at peoples' absurd blindness—when all are liable to die, and all subject to all kinds of diseases. For example; why is it that epidemics have raged so much among the more civilized? in London, 1660, the plague; and in 1830 and 1831, the cholera, in the old and new world, when the inhabitants were lain in heaps by that epidemic. Should I hear of an Indian rejoicing over the inhabitants, I would no longer own him as a brother. But, dear friends, you know that no Indian knew by the Bible it was wrong to kill, because he knew not the Bible, and its sacred laws. But it is certain the Pilgrims knew better than to break the commands of their Lord and Master; they knew that it was written, "thou shalt not kill."

But having laid a mass of history and exposition before you, the purpose of which is to show that PHILIP and all the Indians generally, felt indignantly towards whites, whereby they were more easily allied together by PHILIP, their King and Emperor, we come to notice more particularly his history. As to his Majesty, King PHILIP, it was certain that his honor was put to the test, and it was certainly to be tried, even at the loss of his life and country. It is a matter of uncertainty about his age; but his birth-place was at Mount Hope, Rhode Island, where MASSASOIT, his father lived, till 1656, and died, as also his brother, ALEXANDER, by the governor's ill-treating him, (that is, Winthrop,) which caused his death, as before mentioned, in 1662; after which, the kingdom fell into the hands of PHILIP, the greatest man that ever lived upon the American shores. Soon after his coming to the throne, it appears he began to be noticed, though, prior to this, it appears that he was not forward in the councils of war or peace. When he came into office it appears that he knew there was great responsibility resting upon himself and country; that it was likely to be ruined by those rude intruders around him; though he appears friendly, and is willing to sell them lands for almost nothing, as we shall learn from dates of the Plymouth Colony, which commence June 23, 1664. William Benton, of Rhode Island, a merchant, buys Matapoisett of PHILIP and wife, but no sum is set, which he gave for it. To this deed, his counsellors, and wife, and two of the Pilgrims, were witnesses. In 1665 he sold New Bedford and Compton for forty dollars. In 1667 he sells to Constant Southworth and others all the meadow lands from Dartmouth to Matapoisett, for which he received sixty dollars. The same year he sells to Thomas Willet a tract of land two miles in length, and perhaps the same in width, for which he received forty dollars. In 1668 he sold a tract of some square miles, now called Swanzey. The next year he sells five hundred acres in Swanzey, for which he received eighty dollars. His counsellors and interpreters, with the Pilgrims, were witnesses to these deeds.

OSAMEQUAN, for valuable considerations, in the year 1641 sold to John Brown and Edward Winslow a tract of land eight miles square, situated on both sides of Palmer's River. PHILIP, in 1668 was required to sign a quit-claim of the same, which we understand he did in the presence of his counsellors. In the same year PHILIP laid claim to a portion of land called New Meadows, alleging that it was not intended to be conveyed in a former deed, for which Mr. Brown paid him forty-four dollars, in goods; so it was settled without difficulty. Also, in 1669, for forty dollars he sold to one John Cook, a whole island, called Nokatay, near Dartmouth. The same year PHILIP sells a tract of land in Middleborough for fifty-two dollars. In 1671 he sold to Hugh Cole a large tract of land, lying near Swanzey, for sixteen dollars. In 1672 he sold sixteen square miles to William Breton and others, of Taunton, for which he and his chief received five hundred and seventy-two dollars. This contract, signed by himself and chiefs, ends the sales of lands with PHILIP, for all which he received nine hundred and seventy-four dollars, as far as we can learn by the records.

Here PHILIP meets with a most bitter insult, in 1673, from one Peter Talmon, of Rhode Island, who complained to the Plymouth Court against PHILIP, of Mount Hope, predecessor, heir, and administrator of his brother ALEXANDER, deceased, in an action on the case, to the damage of three thousand and two hundred dollars, for which the Court gave verdict in favor of Talmon, the young Pilgrim; for which PHILIP had to make good to the said Talmon a large tract of land at Sapamet and other places adjacent; and for the want thereof, that is, more land that was not taken up, the complainant is greatly damnified. This is the language in the Pilgrims' Court. Now let us review this a little. The man who bought this land made the contract, as he says, with Alexander, ten or twelve years before; then why did he not bring forward his contract before the Court? It is easy to understand why he did not. Their object was to cheat, or get the whole back again in this way. Only look at the sum demanded, and it is enough to satisfy the critical observer. This course of proceedings caused the Chief and his people to entertain strong jealousies of the whites.

In the year 1668 Philip made a complaint against one Weston, who had wronged one of his men of a gun and some swine; and we have no account that he got any justice for his injured brethren. And, indeed, it would be a strange thing for poor unfortunate Indians to find justice in those Courts of the pretended pious, in those days, or even since; and for a proof of my assertion I will refer the reader or hearer to the records of Legislatures and Courts throughout New England; and also to my book, Indian Nullification.

We would remark still further; who stood up in those days, and since, to plead Indian rights? Was it the friend of the Indian? No; it was his enemies who rose; his enemies, to judge and pass sentence. And we know that such kind of characters as the Pilgrims were, in regard to the Indians' rights, who, as they say, had none, must certainly always give verdict against them, as, generally speaking, they always have. Prior to this insult it appears that Philip had met with great difficulty with the Pilgrims; that they appeared to be suspicious of him in 1671; and the Pilgrims sent for him, but he did not appear to move as though he cared much for their messenger, which caused them to be still more suspicious. What grounds the Pilgrims had is not ascertained, unless it is attributed to a guilty conscience for wrongs done to Indians. It appears that Philip, when he got ready, goes near to them, and sends messengers to Taunton, to invite the Pilgrims to come and treat with him; but the governor being either too proud, or afraid, sends messengers to him to come to their residence at Taunton, to which he complied. Among these messengers was the Honorable Roger Williams, a Christian and a patriot, and a friend to the Indians, for which we rejoice. Philip, not liking to trust the Pilgrims, left some of the whites in his stead, to warrant his safe return. When Philip and his men had come near the place, some of the Plymouth people were ready to attack him; this rashness was, however, prevented by the Commissioner of Massachusetts, who met there with the Governor, to treat with Philip; and it was agreed upon to meet in the meetinghouse. Philip's complaint was, that the Pilgrims had injured the planting grounds of his people. The Pilgrims acting as umpires say the charges against them were not sustained; and because it was not, to their satisfaction, the whites wanted that Philip should order all his men to bring in his arms and ammunition; and the Court was to dispose of them as they pleased. The next thing was, that Philip must pay the cost of the treaty, which was four hundred dollars. The Pious Dr. Mather says, that Philip was appointed to pay a sum of money to defray the charges that his insolent clamors had put the Colony to. We wonder if the Pilgrims were as ready to pay the Indians for the trouble they put them to. If they were, it was with the instruments of death. It appears that Philip did not wish to make war with them, but compromised with them; and in order to appease the Pilgrims he actually did order his men, whom he could not trust, to deliver them up; but his own men withheld, with the exception of a very few.

Now what an unrighteous act this was in the people, who professed to be friendly and humane, and peaceable to all men. It could not be that they were so devoid of sense as to think these illiberal acts would produce peace; but contrawise, continual broils. And in fact it does appear that they courted war instead of peace, as it appears from a second council that was held by order of the Governor, at Plymouth, September 13, 1671. It appears that they sent again for PHILIP; but he did not attend, but went himself and made complaint to the governor, which made him write to the council, and ordered them to desist, to be more mild, and not to take such rash measures. But it appears that on the 24th, the scene changed; that they held another council, and the disturbers of the peace, the intruders upon a peaceable people, say they find PHILIP guilty of the following charges:

1. That he had neglected to bring in his arms, although competent time had been given him.

2. That he had carried insolently and proudly towards us on several occasions, in refusing to come down to our courts, (when sent for,) to procure a right understanding betwixt us.

What an insult this was to his Majesty, and independent Chief of a powerful nation, should come at the beck and call of his neighbors whenever they pleased to have him do it. Besides, did not PHILIP do as he agreed, at Taunton, that is in case there was more difficulty they were to leave it to Massachusetts, to be settled there in the high council, and both parties were to abide by their decision; but did the Pilgrims wait? No. But being infallible, of course they could not err.

The third charge was, harboring divers Indians not his own men; but vagabond Indians.

Now what a charge this was to bring against a King, calling his company vagabonds, because it did not happen to please them; and what right had they to find fault with his company. I do not believe that PHILIP ever troubled himself about the white people's company, and prefer charges against them for keeping company with whom they pleased. Neither do I believe he called their company vagabonds, for he was more noble than that.

The fourth charge is, that he went to Massachusetts with his council, and complained against them, and turned their brethren against them.

This was more a complaint against themselves than Philip, inasmuch it represents that Philip's story was so correct, that they were blameable.

5. That he had not been quite so civil as they wished him to be.

We presume that Philip felt himself much troubled by these intruders, and of course put them off from time to time, or did not take much notice of their proposals. Now such charges as those, we think are to no credit of the pilgrims. However, this council ended much as the other did, in regard to disarming the Indians, which they never were able to do. Thus ended the events of 1671.

But it appears that the pilgrims could not be contented with what they had done, but they must send an Indian, and a traitor, to preach to Philip and his men, in order to convert him and his people to Christianity. The preacher's name was Sassamon. I would appeal to this audience, is it not certain that the Plymouth people strove to pick a quarrel with Philip and his men. What could have been more insulting than to send a man to them who was false, and looked upon as such; for it is most certain that a traitor was above all others, the more to be detested than any other. And not only so, it was the laws of the Indians, that such a man must die; that he had forfeited his life; and when he made his appearance among them, Philip would have killed him upon the spot, if his council had not persuaded him not to. But it appears that in March, 1674, one of Philip's men killed him, and placed him beneath the ice in a certain pond near Plymouth; doubtless by the order of Philip. After this, search was made for him, and he found there a certain Indian, by the name of Patuckson; Tobias, also, his son were apprehended and tried. Tobias was one of Philip's counsellors, as it appears from the records that the trial did not end here, that it was put over, and that two of the Indians entered into bonds for $400, for the appearance of Tobias at the June term; for which a mortgage of land was taken to that amount, for his safe return. June having arrived, three instead of one are arraigned. There was no one but Tobias suspected at the previous Court. Now two others are arraigned, tried, condemned and executed, (making three in all,) in June the 8th, 1675, by hanging and shooting. It does not appear that any more than one was guilty, and it was said that he was known to acknowledge it; but the other two persisted in their innocency to the last.

This murder of the preacher brought on the war a year sooner than it was anticipated by Philip. But this so exasperated King Philip, that from that day he studied to be revenged of the pilgrims; judging that his white intruders had nothing to do in punishing his people for any crime, and that it was in violation of treaties of ancient date. But when we look at this, how bold and how daring it was to Philip, as though they would bid defiance to him, and all his authority, we do not wonder at his exasperation. When the Governor finds that his Majesty was displeased, he then sends messengers to him, and wishes to know why he would make war upon him, (as if he had done all right,) and wished to enter into a new treaty with him. The King answered them thus: Your Governor is but a subject of King Charles of England, I shall not treat with a subject; I shall treat of peace only with a King, my brother; when he comes, I am ready.

This answer of Philip's to the messengers, is worthy of note throughout the world. And never could a prince answer with more dignity in regard to his official authority than he did; disdaining the idea of placing himself upon a par with the minor subjects of a King; letting them know at the same time, that he felt his independence more than they thought he did. And indeed it was time for him to wake up, for now the subjects of King Charles had taken one of his counsellors and killed him, and he could no longer trust them. Until the execution of these three Indians, supposed to be the murderers of Sassamon, no hostility was committed by Philip or his warriors. About the time of their trial, he was said to be marching his men up and down the country in arms; but when it was known, he could no longer restrain his young men, who, upon the 24th of June, provoked the people of Swansey, by killing their cattle and other injuries, which was a signal to commence the war, and what they had desired, as a superstitious notion prevailed among the Indians, that whoever fired the first gun of either party, would be conquered. Doubtless a notion they had received from the pilgrims. It was upon a fast day too, when the first gun was fired; and as the people were returning from church, they were fired upon by the Indians, when several of them were killed. It is not supposed that Philip directed this attack, but was opposed to it. Though it is not doubted that he meant to be revenged upon his enemies; for during some time he had been cementing his countrymen together, as it appears that he had sent to all the disaffected tribes, who also had watched the movements of the comers from the new world, and were as dissatisfied as Philip himself was with their proceedings.

> Now around the council fires they meet,
>   The young nobles for to greet;
> Their tales of wo and sorrows to relate,
>   About the pilgrims, their wretched foes.
>
> And while their fires were blazing high,
>   Their King and Emperor to greet;
> His voice like lightning fires their hearts,
>   To stand the test or die.
>
> See those pilgrims from the world unknown,
>   No love for Indians do know:
> Although our fathers fed them well
>   With venison rich, of precious kinds.
>
> No gratitude to Indians now is shown,
>   From people saved by them alone;
> All gratitude that poor Indians do know,
>   Is, we are robbed of all our rights.

At this council it appears that Philip made the following speech to his chiefs, counsellors and warriors:

BROTHERS,—You see this vast country before us, which the great Spirit gave to our fathers and us; you see the buffalo and deer that now are our support.—Brothers, you see these little ones, our wives and children, who are looking to us for food and raiment; and you now see the foe before you, that they have grown insolent and bold; that all our ancient customs are disregarded; the treaties made by our fathers and us are broken, and all of us insulted; our council fires disregarded, and all the ancient customs of our fathers; our brothers murdered before our eyes, and their spirits cry to us for revenge. Brothers, these people from the unknown world will cut down our groves, spoil our hunting and planting grounds, and drive us and our children from the graves of our fathers, and our council fires, and enslave our women and children.

This famous speech of Philip was calculated to arouse them to arms, to do the best they could in protecting and defending their rights. The blow had now been struck, the die was cast, and nothing but blood and carnage was before them. And we find Philip as active as the wind, as dextrous as a giant, firm as the pillows of heaven, and as fierce as a lion, a powerful foe to contend with indeed: and as swift as an eagle, gathering together his forces, to prepare them for the battle. And as it would swell our address too full, to mention all the tribes in Philip's train of warriors, suffice it to say that from six to seven were with him at different times. When he begins the war, he goes forward and musters about 500 of his men, and arms them complete, and about 900 of the other, making in all about fourteen hundred warriors when he commenced. It must be recollected that this war was legally declared by Philip, so that the colonies had a fair warning. It was no savage war of surprise as some suppose, but one sorely provoked by the pilgrims themselves. But when Philip and his men fought, as they were accustomed to do, and according to their mode of war, it was no more than what could be expected. But we hear no particular acts of cruelty committed by Philip during the seige. But we find more manly nobility in him, than we do in all the head pilgrims put together, as we shall see during this quarrel between them. Philip's young men were eager to do exploits, and to lead captive their haughty lords. It does appear that every Indian heart had been lighted up at the council fires, at Philip's speech, and that the forest was literally alive with this injured race. And now town after town fell before them.

The pilgrims with their forces were ever marching in one direction, while Philip and his forces were marching in another, burning all before them, until Middleborough, Taunton and Dartmouth were laid in ruins, and forsaken by its inhabitants.

At the great fight at Pocasset, Philip commanded in person, where he also was discovered with his host in a dismal swamp. He had retired here with his army to secure a safe retreat from the pilgrims, who were in close pursuit of him, and their numbers were so powerful they thought the fate of Philip was sealed. They surrounded the swamp, in hopes to destroy him and his army. At the edge of the swamp Philip had secreted a few of his men to draw them into ambush, upon which the pilgrims showed fight; Philip's men retreating and the whites pursuing them till they were surrounded by Philip, and nearly all cut off. This was a sorry time to them; the pilgrims, however, reinforced, but ordered a retreat, supposing it impossible for Philip to escape, and knowing his forces to be great, it was conjectured by some to build a fort to starve him out, as he had lost but few men in the fight. The situation of Philip was rather peculiar, as there was but one outlet to the swamp, and a river before him nearly seven miles to descend. The pilgrims placed a guard around the swamp for 13 days, which gave Philip and his men time to prepare canoes to make good his retreat; in which he did, to the Connecticut river, and in his retreat lost but fourteen men. We may look upon this move of Philip's to be equal, if not superior to that of Washington crossing the Delaware. For while Washington was assisted by all the knowledge that art and science could give, together with all the instruments of defence, and edged tools to prepare rafts, and the like helps for safety across the river, Philip was naked as to any of these things, possessing only what nature, his mother had bestowed upon him; and yet makes his escape with equal praise. But he would not even lost a man, had it not been for Indians who were hired to fight against Indians, with promise of their enjoying equal rights with their white brethren; but not one of those promises have as yet been fulfilled by the pilgrims or their children, though they must acknowledge, that without the aid of Indians and their guides, they must inevitably been swept off. It was only then by deception that the pilgrims gained the country, as their word has never been fulfilled in regard to Indian rights.

Philip having now taken possession of the back settlements of Massachusetts, one town after another was swept off. A garrison being established at Northfield by the pilgrims, and while endeavoring to reinforce it with thirty-six armed, twenty out of their number was killed, and one taken prisoner. At the same time Philip so managed it as to cut off their retreat, and take their ammunition from them.

About the month of August, they took a young lad about fourteen years of age, whom they intended to make merry with the next day; but the pilgrims said God touched the Indians' heart, and they let him go. About the same time, the whites took an old man of Philip's, whom they found alone; and because he would not turn traitor, and inform them where Philip was, they pronounced him worthy of death; and by them was executed, cutting off first his arms and then his head. We wonder why God did not touch the pilgrims' heart, and save them from cruelty, as well as the Indians.

We would now notice an act in King Philip, that outweighs all the other princes and emperors in the world. That is, when his men began to be in want of money, having a coat neatly wrought with mampampeag, (*i. e.* Indian money,) he cut it to pieces, and distributed it among all his chiefs and warriors; it being better than the old continental money of the revolution, in Washington's day, as not one Indian soldier found fault with it, as we could ever learn; so that it cheered their hearts still to persevere to maintain their rights and expel their enemies.

On the 18th of September, the pilgrims made a tour from Hadley to Deerfield, with about eighty men, to bring their valuable articles of clothing and provisions. Having loaded their teams and returning, Philip and his men attacked them, and nearly slew them all. The attack was made near Sugar-loaf Hill. It was said that in this fight, the pilgrims lost their best men of Essex, and all their goods; upon which there were many made widows and orphans in one day. Philip now having done what he could upon the Western frontiers of Massachusetts, and believing his presence was wanted among his allies, the

Narragansetts, to keep them from being duped by the pilgrims, he is next known to be in their country.

The pilgrims determined to break down Philip's power, if possible, with the Narragansetts: thus they raised an army of 1500 strong, to go against them and destroy them if possible. In this, Massachusetts, Plymouth and Connecticut all join in severally, to crush Philip. Accordingly in December, in 1675, the pilgrims set forward to destroy them. Preceding their march, Philip had made all arrangements for the winter, and had fortified himself beyond what was common for his countrymen to do, upon a small island near South Kingston, R. I. Here he intended to pass the winter with his warriors, and their wives and children. About 500 Indian houses was erected of a superior kind, in which was deposited all their stores, tubs of corn, and other things, piled up to a great height, which rendered it bullet proof. It was supposed that about 3000 persons had taken up their residence in it. (I would remark, that Indians took better care of themselves in those days than they have been able to since.) Accordingly on the 19th day of December, after the pilgrims had been out in the extreme cold, for nearly one month, lodging in tents, and their provision being short, and the air full of snow, they had no other alternative than to attack Philip in the fort. Treachery however, hastened his ruin; one of his men by hope of reward from the deceptive pilgrims, betrayed his country into their hands. The traitor's name was Peter. No white man was acquainted with the way, and it would have been almost impossible for them to have found it, much less to have captured it. There was but one point where it could have been entered or assailed with any success, and this was fortified much like a block house, directly in front of the entrance, and also flankers to cover a cross fire. Besides high palisides, an immense hedge of fallen trees of nearly a rod in thickness. Thus surrounded by trees and water, there was but one place that the pilgrims could pass. Nevertheless, they made the attempt. Philip now had directed his men to fire, and every platoon of the Indians swept every white man from the path one after another, until six captains, with a great many of the men had fallen. In the mean time, one Captain Moseley, with some of his men had some how or other gotten into the fort in another way, and surprised them; by which the pilgrims were enabled to capture the fort, at the same time setting fire to it, and hewing down men, women and children indiscriminately. Philip, however, was enabled to escape with many of his warriors. It is said at this battle eighty whites were killed, and one hundred and fifty wounded; many of whom died of their wounds afterwards, not being able to dress them till they had marched 18 miles; also leaving many of their dead in the fort. It is said that 700 of the Narragansetts perished. The greater part of them being women and children.

It appears that God did not prosper them much after all. It is believed that the sufferings of the pilgrims were without a parallel in history; and it is supposed that the horrors and burning elements of Moscow, will bear but a faint resemblance of that scene. The thousands and tens of thousands assembled there with their well disciplined forces, bear but little comparison to that of modern Europe, when the inhabitants, science, manners and customs are taken into consideration. We might well admit the above fact, and say, the like was never known among any heathen nation in the world; for none but those worse than heathens, would have suffered so much, for the sake of being revenged upon those of their enemies. Philip had repaired to his quarters to take care of his people and not to have them exposed. We should not have wondered quite so much if Philip had gone forward and acted thus. But when a people, calling themselves Christians, conduct in this manner, we think they are censurable, and no pity at all ought to be had for them.

It appears that one of the whites had married one of Philip's countrymen; and they, the pilgrims, said he was a traitor, and therefore they said he must die. So they quartered him; and as history informs us, they said, he being a heathen, but a few tears was shed at his funeral. Here, then, because a man would not turn and fight against his own wife and family, or leave them, he was condemned as an heathen. We presume that no honest man will commend those ancient fathers, for such absurd conduct. Soon after this, Philip and his men left that part of the country, and retired farther back, near the Mohawks; where, in July 1676, some of his men were slain by the Mohawks. Notwithstanding this, he strove to get them to join him; and here it is said that Philip did not do that which was right; that he killed some of the Mohawks and laid it to the whites, in

order that he might get them to join him. If so, we cannot
consistently believe he did right. But he was so exasperated
that nothing but revenge would satisfy him. All this act was
no worse than our political men do in our days, of their strife
to wrong each other, who profess to be enlightened; and all for
the sake of carrying their points. Heathen-like, either by the
sword, calumny or deception of every kind; and the late duels
among the called high men of honor, is sufficient to warrant my
statements. But while we pursue our history in regard to Philip,
we find that he made many successful attempts against the pilgrims, in surprising and driving them from their posts, during
the year 1676, in February, and through till August, in which
time many of the Christian Indians joined him. It is thought
by many, that all would have joined him, if they had been
left to their choice, as it appears they did not like their white
brethren very well. It appears that Philip treated his prisoners
with a great deal more Christian-like spirit than the pilgrims
did; even Mrs. Rolandson, although speaking with bitterness
sometimes of the Indians, yet in her journal she speaks not a
word against him. Philip even hires her to work for him, and
pays her for her work, and then invites her to dine with him
and to smoke with him. And we have many testimonies that
he was kind to his prisoners; and when the English wanted to
redeem Philip's prisoners, they had the privilege.

Now did Governor Winthrop, or any of those ancient divines
use any of his men so? No. Was it known that they received any
of their female captives into their houses and fed them? No; it
cannot be found upon history. Were not the females completely
safe, and none of them were violated, as they acknowledge
themselves? But was it so when the Indian women fell into the
hands of the pilgrims? No. Did the Indians get a chance to
redeem their prisoners? No. But when they were taken, they
were either compelled to turn traitors and join their enemies,
or be butchered upon the spot. And this is the dishonest
method that the famous Capt. Church used in doing his great
exploits; and in no other way could he ever gained one battle.
So after all, Church only owes his exploits to the honesty of the
Indians, who told the truth, and to his own deceptive heart in
duping them. Here it is to be understood, that the whites have
always imposed upon the credulity of the Indians. It is with

shame, I acknowledge, that I have to notice so much corruption of a people calling themselves Christians. If they were like
my people, professing no purity at all, then their crimes would
not appear to have such magnitude. But while they appear to
be by profession more virtuous, their crimes still blacken. It
makes them truly to appear to be like mountains filled with
smoke; and thick darkness covering them all around.

But we have another dark and corrupt deed for the sons of
the pilgrims to look at, and that is the fight and capture of
Philip's son and wife, and many of his warriors, in which Philip
lost about 130 men killed and wounded; this was in August
1676. But the most horrid act was in taking Philip's son, about
ten years of age, and selling him to be a slave away from his
father and mother. While I am writing, I can hardly restrain
my feelings, to think a people calling themselves Christians,
should conduct so scandalous, so outrageous, making themselves appear so despicable in the eyes of the Indians; and even
now in this audience, I doubt not but there is men honorable
enough to despise the conduct of those pretended Christians.
And surely none but such as believe they did right, will ever go
and undertake to celebrate that day of their landing, the 22d
of December. Only look at it, then stop and pause. My fathers
came here for liberty themselves, and then they must go and
chain that mind, that image they professed to serve; not content to rob and cheat the poor ignorant Indians, but must take
one of the King's sons, and make a slave of him. Gentlemen
and ladies, I blush at these tales, if you do not, especially when
they professed to be a free and humane people. Yes, they did;
they took a part of my tribe, and sold them to the Spaniards in
Bermuda, and many others; and then on the Sabbath day, these
people would gather themselves together, and say that God is
no respecter of persons; while the divines would pour forth,
"he that says he loves God and hates his brother, is a liar, and
the truth is not in him." And at the same time they hating and
selling their fellow men in bondage. And there is no manner of
doubt but that all my countrymen would have been enslaved if
they had tamely submitted. But no sooner would they butcher
every white man that come in their way, and even put an end
to their own wives and children, and that was all that prevented
them from being slaves; yes, *all*. It was not the good will of

those holy pilgrims that prevented, no. But I would speak, and I could wish it might be like the voice of thunder, that it might be heard afar off, even to the ends of the earth. He that will advocate slavery, is worse than a beast, is a being devoid of shame; and has gathered around him the most corrupt and debasing principles in the world; and I care not whether he be a minister or member of any church in the world; no, not excepting the head men of the nation. And he that will not set his face against its corrupt principles, is a coward, and not worthy of being numbered among men and Christians. And conduct too that libels the laws of the country, and the word of God, that men profess to believe in.

After Philip had his wife and son taken, sorrow filled his heart; but notwithstanding, as determined as ever to be revenged, though was pursued by the duped Indians and Church, into a swamp; one of the men proposing to Philip that he had better make peace with the enemy, upon which he slew him upon the spot. And the pilgrims being also repulsed by Philip, were forced to retreat with the loss of one man in particular, whose name was Thomas Lucas, of Plymouth. We rather suspect that he was some related to Lucas and Hedge, who made their famous speeches against the poor Marshpees, in 1834, in the Legislature, in Boston, against freeing them from slavery, that their fathers, the pilgrims, had made of them for years.

Philip's forces had now become very small, so many having been duped away by the whites, and killed, that it was now easy surrounding him. Therefore, upon the 12th of August, Captain Church surrounded the swamp where Philip and his men had encamped, early in the morning, before they had risen, doubtless led on by an Indian who was either compelled or hired to turn traitor. Church had now placed his guard so that it was impossible for Philip to escape without being shot. It is doubtful, however, whether they would have taken him if he had not been surprised. Suffice it to say, however, this was the case. A sorrowful morning to the poor Indians, to lose such a valuable man. When coming out of the swamp, he was fired upon by an Indian, and killed dead upon the spot.

I rejoice that it was even so, that the Pilgrims did not have the pleasure of tormenting him. The white man's gun missing fire lost the honor of killing the truly great man, Philip. The place where Philip fell was very muddy. Upon this news, the Pilgrims gave three cheers; then Church ordering his body to be pulled out of the mud, while one of those tender-hearted Christians exclaims, what a dirty creature he looks like. And we have also Church's speech upon that subject, as follows: For as much as he has caused many a pilgrim to lie above ground unburied, to rot, not one of his bones shall be buried. With him fell five of his best and most trusty men; one the son of a chief, who fired the first gun in the war.

Captain Church now orders him to be cut up. Accordingly, he was quartered and hung up upon four trees; his head and one hand given to the Indian who shot him, to carry about to show. At which sight it so overjoyed the pilgrims, that they would give him money for it; and in this way obtained a considerable sum. After which, his head was sent to Plymouth, and exposed upon a gibbet for twenty years; and his hand to Boston, where it was exhibited in savage triumph; and his mangled body denied a resting place in the tomb, as thus adds the poet,

> "Cold with the beast he slew, he sleeps,
> O'er him no filial spirit weeps."

I think that as a matter of honor, that I can rejoice that no such evil conduct is recorded of the Indians; that they never hung up any of the white warriors, who were head men. And we add the famous speech of Dr. Increase Mather; he says, during the bloody contest, the pious fathers wrestled hard and long with their God, in prayer, that he would prosper their arms, and deliver their enemies into their hands. And when upon stated days of prayer, the Indians got the advantage, it was considered as a rebuke of divine providence, (we suppose the Indian prayed best then,) which stimulated them to more ardor. And on the contrary, when they prevailed, they considered it as an immediate interposition in their favor. The Doctor closes thus: Nor could they, the pilgrims, cease crying to the Lord against Philip, until they had prayed the bullet through his heart. And in speaking of the slaughter of Philip's people at Narraganset, he says, We have heard of two and twenty Indian captains slain, all of them, and brought down to hell in one

day. Again, in speaking of a Chief who had sneered at the
pilgrims' religion, and who had withal, added a most hideous
blasphemy, Immediately upon which a bullet took him in the
head, and dashed out his brains, sending his cursed soul in a
moment among the devils and blasphemers in hell forever. It
is true that this language is sickening, and is as true as the sun
is in the heavens, that such language was made use of, and it
was a common thing for all the pilgrims to curse the Indians,
according to the order of their priests. It is also wonderful
how they prayed, that they should pray the bullet through the
Indian's heart, and their souls down into hell. If I had any
faith in such prayers, I should begin to think that soon we
should all be gone. However, if this is the way they pray, that
is bullets through people's hearts, I hope they will not pray for
me; I should rather be excused. But to say the least, there is
no excuse for their ignorance how to treat their enemies, and
pray for them. If the Dr. and his people had only turned to
the 23d of Luke, and 34th verse, and heard the words of their
Master, whom they pretended to follow, they would see that
their course did utterly condemn them; or the 7th of Acts, and
60th verse, and heard the language of the pious Stephen, we
think it vastly different from the pilgrims; he prayed, Lord, lay
not this sin to their charge. No curses were heard from these
pious martyrs.

I do not hesitate to say, that through the prayers, preaching,
and examples of those pretended pious, has been the foundation of all the slavery and degradation in the American Colonies, towards colored people. Experience has taught me that
this has been a most sorry and wretched doctrine to us poor
ignorant Indians. I will mention two or three things to amuse
you a little; that is, as I was passing through Connecticut,
about 15 years ago, where they are so pious that they kill the
cats for killing rats, and whip the beer barrels for working upon
the Sabbath, that in a severe cold night, when the face of the
earth was one glare of ice, dark and stormy, I called at a man's
house to know if I could not stay with him, it being about nine
miles to the house where I then lived, and knowing him to be
a rich man, and with all very pious, knowing if he had a mind
he could do it comfortably, and with all we were both members
of one church. My reception, however, was almost as cold as

the weather, only he did not turn me out of doors; if he had I know not but I should have frozen to death. My situation was a little better than being out, for he allowed a little wood, but no bed, because I was an Indian. Another Christian asked me to dine with him, and put my dinner behind the door; I thought this a queer compliment indeed.

About two years ago, I called at an inn in Lexington; and a gentleman present, not spying me to be an Indian, began to say they ought to be exterminated. I took it up in our defence, though not boisterous, but coolly; and when we came to retire, finding that I was an Indian, he was unwilling to sleep opposite my room, for fear of being murdered before morning. We presume his conscience plead guilty. These things I mention to show that the doctrines of the pilgrims has grown up with the people.

But not to forget Philip and his lady, and his prophecy: it is, (that is 1671,) when Philip went to Boston, his clothing was worth nearly one hundred dollars. It is said by some of the writers in those days, that their money being so curiously wrought, that neither Jew nor devil could counterfeit it. A high encomium upon Indian arts; and with it they used to adorn their Sagamores, in a curious manner. It was said that Philip's wife was neatly attired in the Indian style; some of the white females used to call her a proud woman, because she would not bow down to them, and was so particular in adorning herself. Perhaps while these ladies were so careful to review the Queen, they had forgot that she was truly one of the greatest women there was among them, although not quite so white. But while we censure others for their faults, in spending so much time to view their fair and handsome features, whether colored or white, we would remind all the fair sex it is what they all love, that is jewels and feathers. It was what the Indian women used to love, and still love. And customs, we presume, that the whites brought from their original savage fathers, 1000 years ago. Every white that knows their own history, knows there was not a whit difference between them and the Indians of their days.

But who was Philip, that made all this display in the world; that put an enlightened nation to flight, and won so many battles? It was a son of nature; with nature's talent alone. And who did he have to contend with? With all the combined arts of cultivated talents of the old and new world. It was like putting one talent against a thousand. And yet Philip with that, accomplished more than all of them. Yea, he out-did the well-disciplined forces of Greece, under the command of Philip, the Grecian Emperor; for he never was enabled to lay such plans of allying the tribes of the earth together, as Philip of Mount Hope did. And even Napoleon patterned after him, in collecting his forces and surprising the enemy. Washington, too, pursued many of his plans in attacking the enemy, and thereby enabled him to defeat his antagonists and conquer them. What, then, shall we say; shall we not do right to say that Philip, with his one talent, out-strips them all with their ten thousand? No warrior of any age, was ever known to pursue such plans as Philip did. And it is well known that Church and nobody else could have conquered, if his people had not used treachery, which was owing to their ignorance; and after all, it is a fact, that it was not the pilgrims that conquered him, it was Indians. And as to his benevolence, it was very great; no one in history can accuse Philip of being cruel to his conquered foes; that he used them with more hospitality than they, the pilgrims did, cannot be denied; and that he had knowledge and forethought, cannot be denied. As Mr. Gooking, in speaking of Philip says, that he was a man of good understanding and knowledge in the best things. Mr. Gooking it appears was a benevolent man, and a friend to Indians.

How deep then was the thought of Philip, when he could look from Maine to Georgia, and from the ocean to the lakes, and view with one look all his brethren withering before the more enlightened to come; and how true his prophesy, that the white people would not only cut down their groves, but would enslave them. Had the inspiration of Isaiah been there, he could not have been more correct. Our groves and hunting grounds are gone, our dead are dug up, our council-fires are put out, and a foundation was laid in the first Legislature, to enslave our people, by taking from them all rights which has been strictly adhered to ever since. Look at the disgraceful laws, disfranchising us as citizens. Look at the treaties made by Congress, all broken. Look at the deep-rooted plans laid, when a territory becomes a State, that after so many years, the laws shall be extended over the Indians that live within their boundaries. Yea, every charter that has been given, was given with the view of driving the Indians out of the States, or dooming them to become chained under desperate laws, that would make them drag out a miserable life as one chained to the galley; and this is the course that has been pursued for nearly two hundred years. A fire, a canker, created by the pilgrims from across the Atlantic, to burn and destroy my poor unfortunate brethren, and it cannot be denied. What then shall we do, shall we cease crying, and say it is all wrong, or shall we bury the hatchet and those unjust laws, and Plymouth Rock together, and become friends. And will the sons of the pilgrims aid in putting out the fire and destroying the canker that will ruin all that their fathers left behind them to destroy? (by this we see how true Philip spake.) If so, we hope we shall not hear it said from ministers and church members, that we are so good no other people can live with us, as you know it is a common thing for them to say, Indians cannot live among Christian people; no, even the President of the United States tells the Indians they cannot live among civilized people, and we want your lands, and must have them, and will have them. As if he had said to them, we want your lands for our use to speculate upon, it aids us in paying off our national debt and supporting us in Congress, to drive you off.

You see, my red children, that our fathers carried on this scheme of getting your lands for our use, and we have now become rich and powerful; and we have a right to do with you just as we please; we claim to be your fathers. And we think we shall do you a great favor, my dear sons and daughters, to drive you out, to get you away out of the reach of our civilized people, who are cheating you, for we have no law to reach them, we cannot protect you although you be our children. So it is no use, you need not cry, you must go, even if the lions devour you, for we promised the land you have to somebody else long ago, perhaps twenty or thirty years; and we did it without your consent, it is true. But this has been the way our fathers first brought us up, and it is hard to depart from it; therefore you shall have no protection from us. Now while we sum up this subject. Does it not appear that the cause of all wars from beginning to end, was and is for the want of good usage? That the whites have always been the aggressors, and the wars, cruelties and blood shed is a job of their own seeking, and not the Indians? Did you ever know of Indians' hurting those who was kind to them? No. We have a thousand witnesses to the contrary. Yea, every male and female declare it to be the fact. We often hear of the wars breaking out upon the frontiers, and it is because the same spirit reigns there that reigned here in New England; and wherever there are any Indians, that spirit still reigns; and at present, there is no law to stop it. What, then, is to be done; let every friend of the Indians now seize the mantle of Liberty and throw it over those burning elements that has spread with such fearful rapidity, and at once extinguish them forever. It is true, that now and then a feeble voice has been raised in our favor. Yes, we might speak of distinguished men, but they fall so far short in the minority, that it is heard but at a small distance. We want trumpets that sound like thunder, and men to act as though they were going at war with those corrupt and degrading principles that robs one of all rights, merely because he is ignorant, and of a little different color. Let us have principles that will give every one his due; and then shall wars cease, and the weary find rest. Give the Indian his rights, and you may be assured war will cease.

But, by this time you have been enabled to see that Philip's prophesy has come to pass; therefore, as a man of natural abilities, I shall pronounce him the greatest man that was ever in America; and so it will stand, until he is proved to the contrary, to the everlasting disgrace of the pilgrims' fathers.

We will now give you his language in the Lord's Prayer.

Noo-chun kes-uk-qut-tiam-at-am unch koo-we-su-onk, kuk-ket-as-soo-tam-oonk pey-au-moo-utch, keet-te-nan-tam-oo-onk ne nai; ne-ya-ne ke-suk-qutkah oh-ke-it; aos-sa-ma-i-in-ne-an ko-ko-ke-suk-o-da-e nut-as-e-suk-ok-ke fu-tuk-qun-neg; kah ah-quo-an-tam-a-i-in-ne-an num–match-e-se-ong–an-on-ash, ne-match-ene-na-mun wonk neet-ah-quo-antam-au-o-un-non-og nish-noh pasuk noo-na-mortuk-quoh-who-nan, kah chaque sag-kom-pa-ginne-an en qutch-e-het-tu-ong-a-nit, qut poh-qud-wus-sin-ne-an watch match-i-tut.

Having now given historical facts, and an exposition in relation to ancient times, by which we have been enabled to discover
the foundation which destroyed our common fathers, in their
struggle together; it was indeed nothing more than the spirit
of avarice and usurpation of power, that has brought people in
all ages to hate and devour each other. And I cannot for one
moment look back upon what is past, and call it religion. No,
it has not the least appearance like it. Do not then wonder, my
dear friends, at my bold and unpolished statements; though I
do not believe that truth wants any polishing whatever. And
I can assure you, that I have no design to tell an untruth, but
facts alone. Oft have I been surprised at the conduct of those
who pretend to be Christians, to see how they were affected
towards those who were of a different cast, professing one faith.
Yes, the spirit of degradation has always been exercised towards
us poor and untaught people. If we cannot read, we can see
and feel; and we find no excuse in the Bible for Christians
conducting towards us as they do.

It is said that in the Christian's guide, that God is merciful,
and they that are his followers are like him. How much mercy
do you think has been shown towards Indians, their wives
and their children? Not much, we think. No. And ye fathers,
I will appeal to you that are white. Have you any regard for
your wives and children, for those delicate sons and daughters?
Would you like to see them slain and laid in heaps, and their
bodies devoured by the vultures and wild beasts of prey? and
their bones bleaching in the sun and air, till they moulder
away, or were covered by the falling leaves of the forest, and
not resist? No. Your hearts would break with grief, and with
all the religion and knowledge you have, it would not impede
your force to take vengeance upon your foe, that had so cruelly
conducted thus, although God has forbid you in so doing. For
he has said, vengeance is mine, and I will repay. What, then,
my dear affectionate friends, can you think of those who have
been so often betrayed, routed and stripped of all they possess,
of all their kindred in the flesh? Can, or do you think we have
no feeling? The speech of Logan, the white man's friend, is no
doubt fresh in your memory, that he intended to live and die
the friend of the white man; that he always fed them and gave

them the best his cabin afforded; and he appealed to them
if they had not been well used; to which they never denied.
After which, they murdered all of his family in cool blood;
which roused his passions to be revenged upon the whites. This
circumstance is but one in a thousand.

Upon the banks of Ohio, a party of two hundred white warriors, in 1757, or about that time, came across a settlement of
Christian Indians, and falsely accused them of being warriors;
to which they denied, but all to no purpose; they were determined to massacre them all. They, the Indians, then asked
liberty to prepare for the fatal hour. The white savages then
gave them one hour, as the historian said. They then prayed
together; and in tears and cries, upon their knees, begged
pardon of each other, of all they had done. After which, they
informed the white savages that they were now ready. One
white man then begun with a mallet, and knocked them down,
and continued his work until he had killed fifteen, with his own
hand; then saying it ached, he gave his commission to another.
And thus they continued till they had massacred nearly ninety
men, women and children, all these innocent of any crime.
What sad tales are these for us to look upon the massacre of our
dear fathers, mothers, brothers and sisters; and if we speak, we
are then called savages for complaining. Our affections for each
other, are the same as yours; we think as much of ourselves as
you do of yourselves. When our children are sick, we do all we
can for them; they lie buried deep in our affections; if they die,
we remember it long, and mourn in after years. Children also
cleave to their parents; they look to them for aid, they do the
best they know how to do for each other; and when strangers
come among us, we use them as well as we know how; we feel
honest in whatever we do, we have no desire to offend any one.
But when we are so deceived, it spoils all our confidence in our
visitors. And although I can say that I have some dear, good
friends among white people, yet I eye them with a jealous eye,
for fear they will betray me. Having been deceived so much by
them, how can I help it; being brought up to look upon white
people as being enemies and not friends, and by the whites
treated as such, who can wonder? Yes, in vain have I looked for
the Christian to take me by the hand and bid me welcome to
his cabin, as my fathers did them, before we were born; and if

they did, it was only to satisfy curiosity, and not to look upon me as a man and a Christian. And so all of my people have been treated, whether Christians or not. I say then, a different course must be pursued, and different laws must be enacted, and all men must operate under one general law. And while you ask yourselves, what do they, the Indians, want? you have only to look at the unjust laws made for them, and say they want what I want, in order to make men of them, good and wholesome citizens. And this plan ought to be pursued by all missionaries, or not pursued at all. That is not only to make Christians of us, but men; which plan as yet has never been pursued. And when it is, I will then throw my might upon the side of missions, and do what I can to favor it. But this work must begin here first, in New England.

Having now closed, I would say that many thanks is due from me to you, though an unworthy speaker, for your kind attention; and I wish you to understand that we are thankful for every favor; and you and I have to rejoice that we have not to answer for our fathers' crimes, neither shall we do right to charge them one to another. We can only regret it, and flee from it, and from henceforth, let peace and righteousness be written upon our hearts and hands forever, is the wish of a poor Indian.

ERRATA.

In the Frontispiece, the man at the head of PHILIP, should be an Indian.

THE EDITORS' COMMENT

In the 1830s, Philip (or Metacom) was once again a person much discussed in New England, thanks to the popular play *Metamora: Or The Last of the Wampanoags* (1829), written by John Augustus Stone and starring the popular actor Edwin Forrest. Well-known American writers, from Washington Irving to the poet Lydia Huntley Sigourney, wrote highly romanticized sketches of Philip, casting the Wampanoag leader as a figure both tragic and safely vanished, contained by the past. As he often did throughout his career, William Apess engaged this popular interest and completely upended it by centering Indigenous perspectives and lives. His *Eulogy on King Philip* tells the history of the Plymouth settlers' arrival and Ousamequin's hospitality and diplomacy, before re-creating the history of King Philip's War as a conflict in which Wampanoag and other Indigenous people sought to protect their lands from settler greed. Apess performed the *Eulogy* on multiple occasions along the eastern seaboard, selling tickets to large crowds and offering copies of the *Eulogy* and his autobiography *Son of the Forest* for sale. If crowds attended his performance out of curiosity to see yet another account of Philip, they heard an Indigenous history of Plymouth Colony and Wampanoag homelands that reminded U.S. settlers of their "founding" on homelands generously shared and then defended by Wampanoag people. They also heard a minister call them to account for contemporary policies that continued to oppress their Indigenous neighbors and "brethren."

Wamsutta Frank James: Speech at the First National Day of Mourning

I speak to you as a man—a Wampanoag man. I am a proud man, proud of my ancestry, my accomplishments won by a strict parental direction ("You must succeed—your face is a different color in this small Cape Cod community!"). I am a product of poverty and discrimination, two social and economic diseases. I, and my brothers and sisters, have painfully overcome, and to some extent we have earned the respect of our community. We are Indians first—but we are termed "good citizens." Sometimes we are arrogant but only because society has pressured us to be so.

It is with mixed emotion that I stand here to share my thoughts. This is a time of celebration for you—celebrating an anniversary of a beginning for the white man in America. A time of looking back, of reflection. It is with a heavy heart that I look back upon what happened to my People.

Even before the Pilgrims landed it was common practice for explorers to capture Indians, take them to Europe, and sell them as slaves for 220 shillings apiece. The Pilgrims had hardly explored the shores of Cape Cod for four days before they had robbed the graves of my ancestors and stolen their corn and beans. *Mourt's Relation* describes a searching party of sixteen men. Mourt goes on to say that this party took as much of the Indians' winter provisions as they were able to carry.

Massasoit, the great Sachem of the Wampanoag, knew these facts, yet he and his People welcomed and befriended the settlers of the Plymouth Plantation. Perhaps he did this because his tribe had been depleted by an epidemic. Or his knowledge of the harsh oncoming winter was the reason for his peaceful acceptance of these acts. This action by Massasoit was perhaps our biggest mistake. We, the Wampanoag, welcomed you, the white man, with open arms, little knowing that it was the beginning of the end; that before 50 years were to pass, the Wampanoag would no longer be a free people.

What happened in those short 50 years? What has happened in the last 300 years? History gives us facts and there were atrocities; there were broken promises—and most of these centered around land ownership. Among ourselves we understood that there were boundaries, but never before had we had to deal with fences and stone walls. But the white man had a need to prove his worth by the amount of land that he owned. Only 10 years later, when the Puritans came, they treated the Wampanoag with even less kindness in converting the souls of the so-called "savages." Although the Puritans were harsh to members of their own society, the Indian was pressed between stone slabs and hanged as quickly as any other "witch."

And so down through the years there is record after record of Indian lands taken and, in token, reservations set up for him upon which to live. The Indian, having been stripped of his power, could only stand by and watch while the white man took his land and used it for his personal gain. This the Indian could not understand; for to him, land was survival, to farm, to hunt, to be enjoyed. It was not to be abused. We see incident after incident where the white man sought to tame the "savage" and convert him to the Christian ways of life. The early Pilgrim settlers led the Indian to believe that if he did not behave, they would dig up the ground and unleash the great epidemic again.

The white man used the Indian's nautical skills and abilities. They let him be only a seaman—but never a captain. Time and time again, in the white man's society, we Indians have been termed "low man on the totem pole."

Has the Wampanoag really disappeared? There is still an aura of mystery. We know there was an epidemic that took many Indian lives; some Wampanoags moved west and joined the Cherokee and Cheyenne. They were forced to move. Some even went north to Canada! Many Wampanoag put aside their Indian heritage and accepted the white man's way for their own survival. There are some Wampanoag who do not wish it known they are Indian for social or economic reasons.

What happened to those Wampanoags who chose to remain and live among the early settlers? What kind of existence did they live as "civilized" people? True, living was not as complex as life today, but they dealt with the confusion and the change.

Honesty, trust, concern, pride, and politics wove themselves in and out of their daily living. Hence, he was termed crafty, cunning, rapacious, and dirty.

History wants us to believe that the Indian was a savage, illiterate, uncivilized animal. A history that was written by an organized, disciplined people, to expose us as an unorganized and undisciplined entity. Two distinctly different cultures met. One thought they must control life; the other believed life was to be enjoyed, because nature decreed it. Let us remember, the Indian is and was just as human as the white man. The Indian feels pain, gets hurt, and becomes defensive, has dreams, bears tragedy and failure, suffers from loneliness, needs to cry as well as laugh. He, too, is often misunderstood.

The white man in the presence of the Indian is still mystified by his uncanny ability to make him feel uncomfortable. This may be the image the white man has created of the Indian; his "savageness" has boomeranged and isn't a mystery; it is fear; fear of the Indian's temperament!

High on a hill, overlooking the famed Plymouth Rock, stands the statue of our great Sachem, Massasoit. Massasoit has stood there many years in silence. We, the descendants of this great Sachem, have been a silent people. The necessity of making a living in this materialistic society of the white man caused us to be silent. Today, I and many of my people are choosing to face the truth. We ARE Indians!

Although time has drained our culture, and our language is almost extinct, we the Wampanoags still walk the lands of Massachusetts. We may be fragmented, we may be confused. Many years have passed since we have been a people together. Our lands were invaded. We fought as hard to keep our land as you the whites did to take our land away from us. We were conquered, we became the American prisoners of war in many cases, and wards of the United States government, until only recently.

Our spirit refuses to die. Yesterday we walked the woodland paths and sandy trails. Today we must walk the macadam highways and roads. We are uniting. We're standing not in our wigwams but in your concrete tent. We stand tall and proud, and before too many moons pass we'll right the wrongs we have allowed to happen to us.

We forfeited our country. Our lands have fallen into the hands of the aggressor. We have allowed the white man to keep us on our knees. What has happened cannot be changed, but today we must work towards a more humane America, a more Indian America, where men and nature once again are important; where the Indian values of honor, truth, and brotherhood prevail.

You the white man are celebrating an anniversary. We the Wampanoags will help you celebrate in the concept of a beginning. It was the beginning of a new life for the Pilgrims. Now, 350 years later, it is a beginning of a new determination for the original American: the American Indian.

There are some factors concerning the Wampanoags and other Indians across this vast nation. We now have 350 years of experience living amongst the white man. We can now speak his language. We can now think as a white man thinks. We can now compete with him for the top jobs. We're being heard; we are now being listened to. The important point is that along with these necessities of everyday living, we still have the spirit, we still have the unique culture, we still have the will and, most important of all, the determination to remain as Indians. We are determined, and our presence here this evening is living testimony that this is only the beginning of the American Indian, particularly the Wampanoag, to regain the position in this country that is rightfully ours.

THE EDITORS' COMMENT

Amid pan-Indian "Red Power" political movements and cultural revitalization, Wampanoag people, their kin, and their allies organized the first National Day of Mourning in November 1970, on Cole's Hill at Plymouth. The Day of Mourning was a powerful protest of the popularization of the Thanksgiving holiday and its associated national mythologies. The recent silencing of Wamsutta Frank James's speech had been a galvanizing moment. In September 1970, Wamsutta Frank James, of the Aquinnah Wampanoag Tribe, was asked to give a speech at a state dinner to commemorate the 350th anniversary of the *Mayflower*'s landing at Patuxet. Although the organizers imagined an Indian celebration and commemoration of the landing, James instead presented a critique, offering an alternative history, a narrative of resilience and continuance, and a call for a more just future. The organizers of the commemoration asked to see his written speech before he presented it and, after reading it, did not allow him to give the address. James did read his speech at the first National Day of Mourning, an event that continues today. Wamsutta Frank James's repressed speech has since been circulated and reproduced countless times, in regional and national newspapers, in print anthologies, and online. Most recently, his speech was featured in the *Wampanoag World* exhibit at Pilgrim Hall in Plymouth. A talented musician as well as a respected activist, Frank James was a graduate of the New England Conservatory of Music and one of the founders of the United American Indians of New England.

Linda Coombs: The Audacity of Assumption

Over the last 400 years, Native Americans have been portrayed in a multitude of ways—basically every way imaginable but the right one: that which communicates the reality of the people, their histories, and cultures. All of the misinformation that is put forward also promotes disrespect and disregard for Native people as human beings.

These countless misrepresentations have generally gone unquestioned; and have been used to accomplish the objectives of authors, film makers, teachers, among others. This whole "genre" of misrepresentation includes stereotype, misconception and marginalization, as well as outright false information and complete omission. Everyone has experienced each of these erroneous representations of Native Americans, whether they recognize them for what they are or not. People will accept, or not think to question, a whole host of ludicrous things about Native people that they would not even begin to consider in application to themselves.

I worked for many years in the Wampanoag Indigenous Program at Plimoth Plantation, where Wampanoag and other Native people staff the "Wampanoag Homesite." We talk to visitors about everything from our origins on the continent to the 17th century contact period to present day life, while demonstrating "material culture," or traditional life. Our purpose was to provide visitors with the experience of speaking directly with Native people to hear our perspectives on history. This included addressing the stereotypes or misconceptions visitors came in with, and hopefully bringing them to a new awareness.

On one occasion, some folks actually became angry because they did not see tipis or buffalo on the site of old Patuxet in what is now Massachusetts! The stereotype that all Indians are, or should be, like the people of the Plains tribal nations was fully embedded in their minds. Some very persistent beliefs still exist: that Native Americans were few in number, lived in "scattered villages," had very short life spans due to our ways of life, and struggled and scrambled to find food, when we weren't stricken with famine. These misunderstandings reveal the complete lack of awareness about our traditional cultures and how they functioned; what our populations were (and are), etc. The belief that we were "all wiped out" by disease or war still persists. Children still ask if the Native person standing in front of them is really 350 years old because they cannot grasp that we are still here today. Personally, I have been informed by total strangers that I am not a "real" Indian; and conversely told I am "not a person, you're an Indian." History books are still being written as if Native people are some incidental phenomenon that settlers had to contend with, as opposed to groups of human beings with long-established, legitimate, viable, sustainable ways of life with the God-given right to be as we were created, as well as where we were created. Some history books still leave Native people out completely, putting forth the misguided idea that we are not relevant to history or to modern life in this country.

These few examples are like a speck of dust on the surface of the moon. Many books have been written about all of these problems, addressing what stereotypes are, where they originate from; why they exist or what purpose they serve; the damage they do to Native peoples; and to the fact that there is damage done to those who believe as fact such false things about other people. This is especially true as these beliefs get passed down the generations, and as they do, become more embedded and made more "real" with their repetition over time.

There is one major element that underlies each of the examples above, and is foundational to their existence and their perpetuation. That element is assumption. Assumption has been the basis of every instance of erroneous thinking about Native peoples since Europeans began to come over here.

WHY did the visitor to the Wampanoag Homesite *assume* he would see tipis and buffalo?

Where did that thinking come from? Why was it upsetting for him to realize that his understanding of Native people was wrong? From where, and how, and why is this information still being perpetuated if it is wrong?

Why would a child make the *assumption* that the Native person in front of him is 350 years old?

Why would a total stranger *assume* that it was appropriate to inform me as to whom he thought I was?

Why would another person *assume* it was acceptable to tell me I am not a person because I am "an Indian?"

Why would authors continue to misrepresent and misinform; or continue to put forth their own theories or ideas about Native people as if they are truth? Some go forward seemingly thinking no comprehensive research or documentation is necessary, other than that which will support their own thoughts. The concept of consultation with Native people does not even occur to some authors, never mind be done as a matter of course.

For 400 years, a host of theories has been bandied about as if Native peoples are merely objects of study or discussion, rather than human beings with real knowledge of their own histories. One of the biggest and most primary *assumptions* is the Doctrine of Discovery. This is actually a collection of edicts or "papal bulls" issued by the Vatican in the 15th century. In 1452, Pope Nicholas issued a bull that stated that Christians can go into the lands of non-Christians, extract any or all of their "riches" or resources, and enslave or even kill them, as people who were not Christian were not considered human. And as non-humans, or sub-humans, they were not entitled to the same rights and privileges afforded Christians.

What is it that makes the Pope—the world Christian leader—decide that it is right for Christians to treat non-Christians in such a fashion? The papal bull of 1452 is in total contradiction to Christian philosophy, and is certainly not what Jesus would have done.

Actually, the Doctrine of Discovery twists its *assumption* into a declaration: if (whomever or whatever Christian entity) declares that something is so, then it IS so, and thus can be acted upon in any way seen fit. Certain Native authors and educators today have written about how the themes, concepts, and even wording within the Doctrine of Discovery have been incorporated into the body of U.S. law.

A mere 40 years after its issuance, Columbus acted on the message of the Doctrine of Discovery as he made his way around the world in his quest to prove the earth was round. During the process of the sum total of his voyages, he and his crews were responsible for the deaths of some 60 million Native people, not to mention the impacts on their cultures and environments of their homelands.

In his quest for gold or other riches, Columbus *assumed* that since the people of the Caribbean into whose lands he entered were not human (per the Vatican) then it was permissible to rape, torture, enslave and murder them, and to plunder and destroy their countries in the process.

Over the next 100+ years, the Age of Discovery sailed into full swing. For a century before the landing of the Pilgrims in Patuxet in 1620, ships were regularly crossing the Atlantic to trade with Native peoples on this continent, or to "explore" the country here. There is rarely any further question as to the nature of the "explorations" or "discoveries," or the reasons for them. There is the *assumption* that these are acceptable, normal processes to enter the countries of other nations, and "explore" them for riches, resources, slaves, and/or land for settlement.

The Native peoples of those territories are *assumed* to have not had any objections to others coming into their homelands in the manner they did. It is often a shock to some to learn that Native people did have objections to these actions, and were not happily waiting at the door or at the shore to welcome them in.

Native people did have protocols for others entering their territories, whether from another village, another nation, or another country or continent. They included approaching leadership—our sachems, councils and clan mothers—and stating the reasons for entering these homelands. Every nation has such protocols—but it was *assumed* that we did not.

1620 brings the arrival of the English Pilgrims into Patuxet in Wampanoag territory. They were having their religious troubles in England; made their escape and lived in Holland for 12 years; and then made the decision to move to "America."

They made the *assumption* that "America" was there for them to come in and settle, and establish a colony. They knew there were Native peoples here, whom the English considered to have a natural right, but not a legal one to the land. The English had clear intent to take the land and total control over it, as evidenced by the land patents of the 1620's. The King of England had already claimed a huge portion of this continent as belonging to the British Empire. It did not however, include north of what is now the state of Virginia. That is the area that the Pilgrims were heading for, but were blown off course and ended up off of what is now Cape Cod. In other words, they were here illegally by their own laws. Not to mention those of Native people. . . .

So before leaving the ship to "explore" this (to them) new place, they wrote the Mayflower Compact. Some people today *assume* that the Compact is the basis or impetus for the Declaration of Independence. It only addressed, however, how the group of people aboard the Mayflower would govern and conduct themselves "in a civil body politic" until such time as they received a proper patent from the King.

They had previously received the (first) Peirce Patent, for the territory in Virginia, and which did not apply to the area when they landed at Cape Cod. By 1621, they had received the second Peirce Patent, giving them claim to what became Plymouth.

There is also the Charter of New England of 1620, issued by the King of England, both the second Peirce or Plymouth Patent and the Charter are documents that *assume* that the portions of this continent outlined in them belonged to, or were *assumed* by the King as British possessions.

Who is the King of England to *assume* that it is his right to create a document declaring that certain parts of the world belong to him or his empire? Because he is the monarch of one country, that entitles him to claim the lands of other nations?

As one reads the Patents and Charter, they describe in great detail all of the territory that they claim, from certain latitudes and longitudes to various bodies of water or land forms. Even with the diseases that had already taken a great toll prior to the landing of the Pilgrims, there were still large numbers of Wampanoag and other Indigenous people of what is now southern New England: Nipmuc, Narragansett, Niantic, Mohegan, Pequot, among many others. The authors of the patents nor the King ever set foot on this continent to confer or consult with our leaders to grant the allowance for the Pilgrims to establish their colony.

No one asked us, nor even thought that they should have to. They *assumed* that this country was theirs to come in to settle, extract resources, and treat the people of the land in whatever fashion was convenient to their objectives. Who rightfully goes into the country of another nation to settle and *assumes* that there is no need to consult with the leaders of that nation? That was not deemed necessary, as Wampanoag people were considered less than human.

The *assumptions* of the English stem from the Doctrine of Discovery, and were solidly entrenched in their minds some 130 years after it was issued. They wrote that the land was "full of wild beasts and wild men" who were "like the foxes and do but run over the land."

The English also had *assumptions* about the land itself. They perceived that it was "vast," "empty," "unused," "unpeopled" "wilderness." To them, and even still today, there is a negative connotation to that word—as opposed to the "wild" being the natural state of the Earth, or the way in which it was created. The English perceived that the land suffered for not being "manured" or "ordered" (used in an orderly way, by their definition). They *assumed* that we did not use it because it was in a natural state. They didn't ask and didn't understand that we lived with the Earth in this natural state in a purposefully designed manner. The *assumption* here is that we didn't know any better way to build houses, obtain food, dress ourselves, etc. and that our life ways were inferior to those of the Europeans. Many non-Native people still hold those *assumptions* today.

There are *assumptions* embedded in *assumptions*. If a land is empty, unused, etc., etc., then it is permissible to take possession of it. If the land is not being used in a manner acceptable to English definitions and sensibilities, then it is permissible to take possession of it. If the people are like wild beasts just running over the land (however foxy), then it is permissible to take possession of it.

The English gave no real thought to the concept of learning from us how they might live on this land in a way that would have worked for all. It was offered. They chose instead to focus on Native people as less than human and our ways of life those of savages, which they as "civilized" people could not adopt. Dealing with Native people didn't mean living cooperatively. It meant forced conformity to English ways; myriad manipulative and coercive methods to obtain land; people being shipped out of the country and sold into indenture or slavery simply to get rid of them. These are a few of the aspects of colonization utilized against Native people. Not all.

It never ceases to astound me that people don't/can't/won't make the connection between the natural, beautiful, abundant Earth that the Pilgrims entered and our ways of life. There is still the *assumption* that the way Native peoples lived with the Earth was random, happenstance or by mere chance because we were backward and primitive, etc., etc. This attitude prevents people from understanding that our ways of life were purposefully developed to keep the Earth as it was created. That concept was embedded in our hearts and minds, and informed everything we did—the way we developed our nations, societies, clans, families and individuals, including our relationship with Earth and the natural world.

So—isn't it time now, after 400 years, that we question the mythologies put forward as history, which have been so misleading and so damaging? Will we continue to carry attitudes, assumptions, or perceptions of other people that relegate them as non-human? Would you accept that for you and yours? WHY wouldn't you? Then why should anyone?

Earlier I mentioned Columbus traveling around the world to prove it was round. As Wampanoag people continue to reclaim our language, the language itself teaches us about the depth of knowledge that our ancestors had. They fully understood that the Earth is round, that the Moon travels around the Earth, and the Earth around the Sun. That knowledge is many, many thousands of years old. Not a mere 500. Imagine what the natural world would look like if the Pilgrims had thought us worthy of listening to, let go the assumptions, and viewed us as equal human beings. Maybe an MOU rather than a patent.

Linda Coombs
Aquinnah Wampanoag

THE EDITORS' COMMENT

Linda Coombs is a tribal historian and author from the Wampanoag Tribe of Aquinnah. This essay draws on her long experience at Plimoth plantation, where she worked for nearly thirty years and served as the associate director of the Wampanoag Indigenous Program. She was also program director of the Aquinnah Cultural Center and has served as a consultant and exhibit curator for many museums and historical institutions, including the Boston Children's Museum and Pilgrim Hall Museum. She is a board member of Plymouth 400 and the chair of the Plymouth 400 Wampanoag Advisory Committee. This essay was written in 2020 and includes a Wampanoag analysis of the founding legal documents of Plymouth Colony and New England, as well as a reflection on the faulty assumptions made both then, and now, about Indigenous people and the concepts of discovery and settlement. It also presents a counternarrative to those assumptions, based in long-standing Indigenous knowledge grounded in Wampanoag homelands.

Chronology, 1524–1970

1524–25   Italian explorer Giovanni da Verrazzano, outfitted with ships from France, travels up the northeast coast of North America in 1524, probably stopping at Noepe (Martha's Vineyard) and in Narragansett Bay. Verrazano takes several Indigenous captives, extending a practice that Christopher Columbus had initiated in the Caribbean. Estêvão Gomes, a Portuguese explorer in the Spanish service, sails to the northeast in 1524–25 and takes more than fifty Wabanaki captives, whom he intends to sell as slaves. (Charles V of Spain reportedly requires Gomes to free the captives.)

1534   Jacques Cartier, a French explorer, travels to the Gulf of Ktsitekw (the Gulf of St. Lawrence), including Mi'kmaq territory at Kespek (Gaspé), where he engages in trade.

1602   English navigator Bartholomew Gosnold and his chronicler John Brereton travel to Wabanaki territory and observe Wabanaki people holding items acquired in trade with Europeans and conversing in English. (It is likely that they had traded with English ships fishing off the northeast coast.)

1603   Englishman Martin Pring sails to Cape Cod, where he trades with Wampanoag people. When his crew wishes to be "rid" of Native company, they let loose mastiff dogs.

1604   French colonists establish a fortified settlement and trading post on an island in the St. Croix River in Wabanaki territory. Many of the settlers die during the winter, and the fort is abandoned in 1605.

1605   George Waymouth and James Rosier sail to Wabanaki territory, trading with the Penobscot leader Bashabes and taking several Wabanaki men captive to England. Frenchmen Samuel de Champlain and Pierre du Gua, Sieur de Monts, sail from the St. Croix River along the coast of Wabanaki and Wampanoag lands, giving the name Port St. Louis to Patuxet, which John Smith will later name Plymouth.

1606   King James I grants charters to two joint-stock compa-
            nies, the London Company, which is granted the right
            to establish North American colonies between latitudes
            34° and 41° North, and the Plymouth Company, which
            is granted settlement rights between latitudes 38° and
            45° North.

1607   London Company establishes Jamestown Colony in
            Powhatan territory near the mouth of Chesapeake
            Bay. English investors Ferdinando Gorges and John
            Popham send ships captained by George Popham
            and Raleigh Gilbert to Wabanaki territory, looking to
            establish a settlement under the Plymouth Company
            charter. Skidwarres, one of the Wabanaki men captured
            by Waymouth in 1605, returns with Gilbert, serving
            as a guide. Tahanedo, another Wabanaki man taken
            captive in 1605 who had returned home the previous
            year, meets Gilbert with a force of armed men. George
            Popham establishes a fort and settlement at Sagadahoc,
            near the mouth of the Kennebec River, in August.

1608   Popham and many other colonists die during the
            winter, and the survivors abandon the Sagadahoc
            settlement in the fall.

1609   English Separatists begin settling in Leiden in the
            Netherlands.

1611   Five Wabanaki and Wampanoag men, including
            Epenow from Noepe, are kidnapped and taken to
            England by ship captain Edward Harlow. Epenow is
            sent to live with Ferdinando Gorges.

1614   John Smith sails along the Wabanaki, Massachusett,
            and Wampanoag coasts, observing the large numbers
            of Native people living there. He gives the name "New
            England" to the region and "Plymouth" to Patuxet.
            Thomas Hunt, a shipmaster in Smith's expedition,
            kidnaps almost thirty Wampanoag men from Patuxet
            and Nauset and takes them to Spain to be sold as slaves.
            Spanish priests intervene, and Tisquantum, one of the
            men from Patuxet, is transported to London. Epenow
            returns to Noepe on ship commanded by Nicholas
            Hobson and escapes. Dutch explorer Adriaen Block
            leads an expedition to Narragansett, Wampanoag,

Pequot, and Mohegan territories and establishes trade along the Connecticut River.

1616–19   A major wave of epidemics spreads through Wampanoag, Massachusett, and Wabanaki coastal communities, including Patuxet. (The disease, or diseases, involved are still unidentified, but are believed to have been of European origin.) Tisquantum returns to Wampanoag territory in 1619 on English ship commanded by Thomas Dermer.

1620   Members of the Separatist congregation in Leiden make an agreement with London merchant Thomas Weston and other English investors to form a joint-stock company for the purpose of establishing a colony in North America. The *Mayflower* sails from Plymouth on September 6 with 102 colonists on board and anchors on November 11 in Wampanoag territory at the tip of Cape Cod. Lacking a patent that would allow them to form a government, and knowing they were beyond the northern bounds of the London Company's charter, male colonists compose and sign the Mayflower Compact, establishing a government for the colony, and elect John Carver as governor. Colonists begin exploring Cape Cod on foot and by boat looking for possible settlement sites. Wampanoag families keep their distance and observe as settlers dig up corn stores and desecrate graves. A group of Wampanoag men attack an exploring party with arrows on December 8; the colonists shoot off muskets before returning to their boat, and no one is killed. Colonists begin exploring Patuxet on December 12 and decide on December 20 to settle there, choosing the site for its harbor, cleared fields, and prominent hill; they name their settlement Plymouth.

1621   During the winter many colonists remain on the *Mayflower* as the settlement is built. About half of the settlers die by spring, suffering from exposure, malnutrition, and disease, and lacking knowledge of indigenous plants that could cure them of scurvy. Ousamequin, the sôtyum of Pokanoket and paramount leader of the Wampanoag, decides to establish contact with the colonists. He sends the Wabanaki diplomat Samoset to Patuxet, where Samoset greets the settlers in English on March 16. Samoset returns, accompanied by Tisquantum (known to the English as Squanto), on March 22 and initiates a meeting between Ousamequin and Plymouth governor John Carver. Ousamequin and Carver make an agreement of mutual aid, with both parties pledging not to bring weapons to their meetings. The *Mayflower* sails for England on April 5. Governor John Carver dies in April and William Bradford is chosen as his successor (Bradford will serve almost continually as governor until his death in 1657). In the summer, the Plymouth colonists send Stephen Hopkins and Edward Winslow with gifts to visit Ousamequin at Sowams, his village in Pokanoket. The ship *Fortune* arrives at Plymouth in late November, carrying more than thirty new settlers and bringing a charter for the colony granted by the Council for New England, a successor to the Plymouth Company led by Ferdinando Gorges. One of its passengers, Robert Cushman, returns to England when the *Fortune* sails in December, carrying with him a journal of the colony's first year. (It is published in London in 1622 as *A Relation or Journall of the beginning and proceedings of the English Plantation settled at Plimoth in New England*, later known as *Mourt's Relation*.)

1622   In the spring a member of Tisquantum's family warns the Plymouth colonists that the Narragansetts, Ousamequin, and Conbitant, the Wampanoag sôtyum of Pocasset, are planning to attack them. The Wampanoag guide and translator Hobbomock, who is living at Plymouth, rejects this report as false and accuses Tisquantum of plotting against the colonists with Narragansett and Massachusett leaders. Ousamequin seeks to have Tisquantum executed for spreading false rumors, but the Plymouth colonists refuse. News arrives of violence at Jamestown, where Powhatans resisting colonial expansion killed more than three hundred settlers in March. Two ships arrive at Plymouth in the summer carrying sixty men sent by Thomas Weston to found a new colony. They settle in Massachusett territory at Wessagusset (present-day Weymouth) but rely on corn from Plymouth, causing the colonists there to worry they will run out of food. The Wessagusset settlers also steal food from Massachusett people, and their leaders refuse to punish the thieves. Tisquantum falls ill and dies during a trading expedition to Cape Cod in November.

1623 Wituwamet, a Massachusett counselor-warrior, threatens the Wessagussett settlement. In March Plymouth receives word that Ousamequin is seriously ill. Edward Winslow, John Hamden, and Hobbomock travel to Pokanoket, observing Wampanoag practices of paying respect to an ailing leader. After Winslow gives Ousamequin the gift of a healing broth, the Wampanoag leader relays through Hobbomock news of a Massachusett plot against the Wessagussett settlement. According to Winslow, Ousamequin advises Plymouth to kill the Massachusett men who are planning the attack. On March 23 Bradford orders Miles Standish, Plymouth's military commander, and eight other men to inform Wessagussett colonists of the plot and to kill Wituwamet. Before Standish departs, Phenehas Pratt arrives at Plymouth from Wessagussett to warn of a plot against both colonies. Standish and his company go to Wessagusset, kill seven Massachusett men, and return to Plymouth with Wituwamet's head. Wessagusset Colony is abandoned, and its settlers either return to England or join Plymouth. Two ships from England arrive at Plymouth during the summer, bringing almost one hundred new colonists. Plymouth ends the practice of sharing labor and harvests in common, assigning each household a plot of land.

1625 Plymouth colonists struggle to provide the returns of fish and furs they owe their London investors, producing a surplus of corn to trade for furs with Indigenous peoples. Captain Richard Wollaston and his partners, including Thomas Morton, and about thirty indentured servants establish a settlement two miles from Wessagusset, which they name Mount Wollaston.

1627 Plymouth renegotiates their agreement with London investors, with William Bradford and other colony leaders purchasing control of the enterprise in return for obtaining more of the profits. Thomas Morton invites the indentured servants at Mount Wollaston to join him as equal partners and leaders of the settlement, which they rename Ma-re Mount.

1628   Plymouth arrests Thomas Morton and banishes him
            from the region. Bradford writes to Ferdinando Gorges,
            alleging that Morton sold guns to Massachusett people
            in defiance of a royal edict banning such sales. The
            Plymouth Separatists are also offended by Morton's
            celebration of Anglican feast days and other festivities.
            To control and pursue trade in the region, Plymouth
            colonists obtain a patent from the Council for New
            England for a monopoly (ultimately unsuccessful) on
            the Kennebec fur trade and establish a trading post at
            the mouth of the Kennebec River, in Wabanaki terri-
            tory. John White establishes the New England Com-
            pany, a joint-stock enterprise of London merchants.
            The company moves a fishing venture on Cape Ann to
            Naumkeag, later renamed Salem, and expands it into a
            small settlement, with aspirations to grow larger than
            Plymouth.

1629   New England Company is reorganized as the Mas-
            sachusetts Bay Company. The company sends more
            colonists to Naumkeag/Salem, beginning the "Great
            Migration," which will bring fifteen thousand English
            settlers, most of them Puritans, to Massachusetts Bay
            Colony by 1640.

1630   John Winthrop preaches his sermon "A Model of
            Christian Charity" while en route to Massachusetts
            Bay. Masconomo, a Patucket leader, formally welcomes
            Winthrop and other colonists to his territory. Bradford
            begins writing *Of Plimoth Plantation*.

1631   Puritan minister Roger Williams arrives in Boston,
            then moves to Plymouth after religious disagreements
            with other Massachusetts Bay settlers.

1632   Conflicts between Narragansetts and Wampanoags ease,
            as both Wampanoags and Narragansetts build trade and
            diplomatic relations with neighboring colonies.

1633   Plymouth leaders attempt to expand their fur trade
            to the west, including Narragansett territory and the
            Connecticut River, fostering conflict with Dutch set-
            tlers. Roger Williams composes a tract on the invalidity
            of English patents and the necessity of purchasing land
            from Native people that he shares with Bradford before
            leaving Plymouth and returning to Massachusetts Bay.

1633–34   A smallpox epidemic, probably carried by newly arrived
           colonists, causes much death among Native com-
           munities on the coast and inland, including on the
           Connecticut River, where Plymouth settlers seek to
           trade. Patucket and Massachusett communities, near
           Massachusetts Bay Colony settlements, are devastated;
           among the dead are Wonohaquaham (also known as
           Sagamore John of Winisimet) and Montowampate (also
           known as Sagamore James of Saugus), two sons of a
           powerful Massachusett saunkskwa whose given name is
           unrecorded. Settlers remove some Native orphans into
           colonial homes, where they are made servants, learn the
           English language, and adopt Christian beliefs.

1634–35   Narragansett sachems Canonicus and Miantonomi
           give Roger Williams permission to establish a trading
           post on Narragansett land, a diplomatic agreement that
           leads to the settlement of Providence and Rhode Island
           Colony in 1636.

1636   Williams is banished from Massachusetts Bay for his
           radical religious and political views. He uses his exist-
           ing diplomatic relations with Narragansett people
           to found Providence, which later merges with other
           settlements to form the colony of Rhode Island. Wil-
           liams advises both Narragansett leaders and Plymouth
           colonists when conflict arises from a trading post at
           Pokanoket, built by Plymouth near Narragansett Bay.
           The Plymouth General Court revises the colony's laws,
           solidifying the agreement that all freemen who had
           held a share in the joint-stock company that established
           the colony would hold the right and requirement to
           attend the annual Court, where they would vote for the
           governor and Assistants and make laws. As the original
           settlers included some Adventurers (non-Separatists),
           church membership is not a requirement. Not all men
           who arrived in the colony are recognized as freemen
           with the right to vote, and this helps the early settlers
           maintain power as newcomers arrive.

1636–37   After years of rising tensions over trade and land, Con-
           necticut Colony, supported by Massachusetts Bay and
           Plymouth, leads a war against the Pequot, seeking to
           end the powerful Pequot-Dutch trade and drawing on

Mohegan and Narragansett allies who seek to rein in the Pequots' power.

1638   Treaty of Hartford, signed in September by Connecticut colonists, the Narragansett sachems Miantonomi and Canonicus, and the Mohegan sachem Uncas, pledges lasting peace among the signatories and attempts to eliminate the Pequots as a separate people. Ousamequin grants permission to Plymouth colonists to build a settlement at Cohannet, in the Pokanoket homeland, which will become the town of Taunton.

1638–41   Governor Bradford and other leaders of Plymouth Colony seek to solidify their claims to land in Wampanoag territory through a series of deeds, known as the Old Comers grants.

1641   In council at Sowams, Ousamequin gives Edward Winslow and John Brown permission to build a settlement at Seekonk, in the Pokanoket homeland, on the boundary of Narragansett territory.

1642   Massachusetts Bay Colony circumvents the authority of Miantonomi and Rhode Island colonists, making an agreement with a local Narragansett leader to acquire land for settlement at Shawomet, in Narragansett territory. Thomas Lechford, a Boston settler who had returned to England, accuses Massachusetts Bay Colony of failing to fulfill the charge in its charter to send missionaries to Indigenous people, as no missionary efforts then existed. Civil war begins in England between parliamentary and royalist forces (war continues until 1651).

1642–43   Narragansett sachem Miantonomi travels to various Indigenous communities in the northeast, seeking to build an alliance against English expansion.

1643   Leaders of Massachusetts Bay, New Haven, Connecticut, and Plymouth colonies form the United Colonies of New England. (New Haven will become part of Connecticut Colony in 1665.) Colonial forces capture Miantonomi and insist that his rival, the Mohegan sachem Uncas, execute him. *New Englands First Fruits* is published anonymously in London to raise funds for Harvard College and for missionary work in Massachusetts Bay. (The pamphlet was probably written by Thomas Weld and Hugh Peter, two Puritan ministers who had returned to England, and by Henry Dunster, the first president of Harvard.)

1643–45   Wampanoag communities on Noepe suffer from epidemics. Hiacoomes, a Wampanoag survivor, begins preaching about Christianity and engages in language exchange with English settler Thomas Mayhew, Jr.

1644   Six sachems, including Ousamequin (representing Quaboag, a Nipmuc community), Cutshamequin (Neponset), Mascanomet (Agawam), Showanon (Nashaway), and the Saunkskwa of Massachusett (Mystic River), enter into a treaty with Massachusetts Bay Colony, which the colonists regard as a form of submission.

1645   The Nipmuc sachem at Nashaway, Showanon, deeds a tract of land to Massachusetts Bay settlers, seeking to promote trade. (Settlers rename the town Lancaster in 1653.)

1646   The minister John Eliot preaches at Neponset, in Massachusett territory. Eliot reports that the sachem Cutshamequin "despised" his sermon. He turns instead to another Massachusett man, Waban, who becomes his interpreter and a "ruler" at Natick.

1649   Charles I is executed and the Commonwealth of England is established, drawing some Puritan colonists back to England. The Rump Parliament passes "An Act for the Propagating and Promoting of the Gospel of Jesus Christ in New England," which includes funding for the conversion of Native people.

1650   Massachusetts Bay grants charter to Harvard College, which includes the mission of educating both English and Indigenous students.

1651   The first of fourteen "praying towns" (towns for "praying Indians," Native people practicing Christianity) is established at Natick, on land belonging to Nipmuc leader Qualalanset (John Speen). Eliot and other ministers establish codes for governing the behavior of Natick's inhabitants and attempt to mandate English ways. Wampanoag communities cement an alliance through a dual marriage of the sôkushqâ Weetamoo, of Pocasset, and her sister Wootonakunske, daughters of Conbitant, to Wamsutta (Alexander) and Metacom (Philip), the sons of Ousamequin.

1652–59   Plymouth leaders pursue deeds for land in Pocasset territory, under Weetamoo's jurisdiction.

1652   Thomas Mayhew establishes a school on Noepe, with permission of Wampanoag leaders. Hiacoomes sends his son Joel to the school, which is also attended by Caleb, son of the sôtyum Cheeschumuck.

1653   Ousamequin and Wamsutta authorize the "Sowams and Parts Adjacent" deed, which allows further expansion of Plymouth Colony at Pokanoket; the land deeded becomes the town of Swansea.

1655   Harvard Indian College built in Cambridge.

1656   Caleb Cheeshateaumuck and Joel Iacoomes of Noepe, Wawaus and his brother Job Kattenanit of Hassanamesit, and other Native students begin studies at the Roxbury grammar school in Massachusetts Bay Colony.

1657   William Bradford dies. Thomas Prence is elected governor of Plymouth Colony.

1660   Restoration of the Stuart monarchy in England as Charles II returns from exile. Population of Plymouth Colony triples between 1640 and the 1660s, increasing demands for Wampanoag lands.

1661   Ousamequin dies. Wamsutta becomes the primary sôtyum of Pokanoket as Plymouth leaders seek to consolidate authority over Wampanoag lands. Caleb Cheeshateaumuck and Joel Iacoomes begin studies at Harvard, living at the Indian College, where Wawaus works for printer Samuel Green and becomes known as James Printer. The New Testament is published in Wôpanâak by Green's press in a printing of 1,500 copies.

1662   Wamsutta comes into conflict with Plymouth by selling land to Rhode Island settlers. He is captured in June by armed men led by Josiah Winslow and taken to Plymouth to appear before the Court, then suddenly sickens and dies en route home. Metacom, the next sôtyum, later conveys his belief that his brother had been poisoned.

1663   James Printer, Samuel Green, and Marmaduke Johnson print *Mamusse Wunneetupanatamwe Up-Biblum God*, a translation of the Christian Bible into Wôpanâak by Wampanoag and Massachusett scholars. John Eliot, who himself is not fluent in the language, oversees the project. Rhode Island is granted charter by Charles II.

1664–65   Royal Commission visits New England and asserts sovereignty of the crown over Narragansett country. Commission resolves competing claims between two colonial companies, one representing Rhode Island settlers and the other settlers from Massachusetts Bay, Connecticut, and Plymouth. The crown authorizes Rhode Island's colonial jurisdiction in Narragansett territory, an act that recognizes, but also attempts to limit, the authority of Narragansett leaders.

1665   Caleb Cheeshateaumuck and Joel Iacoomes complete their final year at Harvard. Joel dies in a shipwreck on a visit to his family on Noepe just before commencement. Caleb becomes the first Native graduate of Harvard College. Mashpee is recognized by Plymouth Court as an Indian town, governed by Mashpee people, with the missionary Richard Bourne in an advisory role.

1665–70   Plymouth Colony calls on Metacom to sign a series of deeds and to confirm Plymouth's preemptive rights to Wampanoag land against other colonies. At some point after signing these deeds, Metacom pledges to sell no more land.

1666   The Pequots reassert their presence in their ancestral homeland as a reservation is established for them at Mashantucket.

1668   Weetamoo orchestrates a deed to protect her land from settlement and maintains strongholds at Quequechand and Assonet. Metacom maintains a stronghold at Montaup, even as Plymouth settlements expand toward the peninsula.

1671   Plymouth leaders become alarmed by rumors that Metacom is preparing for war. At a tense council held at Taunton in April, Metacom surrenders some of his firearms. Plymouth Colony forms a Council of War and raises a force, led by Josiah Winslow, to march on the sôkushqâ Awashonks at Sakonnet, which Plymouth leaders desire to settle. Under this threat, they compel her to sign Articles of Agreement, including submission of her lands to the authority of Plymouth Colony. The Council of War also authorizes the "reducement of Philip by force," and attempts to compel Metacom to attend a meeting at Plymouth in August. Metacom refuses and travels instead to Boston, seeking mediation by Massachusetts Bay leaders. At council held in late September commissioners from Massachusetts Bay and Connecticut side with Plymouth and force Metacom to sign an agreement acknowledging himself and his people to be subjects of the king of England and the government of Plymouth Colony.

1673–74   Daniel Gookin, Massachusetts Bay's Superintendent of Indians, and John Eliot tour Nipmuc territory. Gookin reports on established "praying towns" and plans for new towns in the Nipmuc interior, including the homeland of Nashaway.

1673   Thomas Prence dies in March. Josiah Winslow is elected as the new governor of Plymouth Colony. Settlers from Plymouth seek to expand the town of Swansea, extending to the east into Pocasset (including Assonet) and to the south toward Montaup. After Plymouth Court recognizes Mammanuah, Awashonks's son, as the "Chief Sachem" and "true proprietor and disposer of all lands" at Sakonnet, he authorizes a grant of nearly all Sakonnet land. As plans are made to divide the land for settlement, a tract is reserved for Awashonks. Plymouth Court acquires consent from Mammanuah and other Wampanoag men to relinquish their rights to land within the town of Dartmouth, whose bounds are expanded through a survey conducted by John Sassamon, a Massachusett convert to Christianity who served as interpreter for multiple deeds.

1674   Awashonks and other Wampanoags at Sakonnet forcibly confront Mammanuah about land he granted to Plymouth settlers. Plymouth Court authorizes Constant Southworth and John Thompson to purchase

land on their behalf in Nemasket, for the town of
Middleboro, hoping to extend a grant Thompson
and Benjamin Church had acquired from the sôtyum
Tuspaquin in 1673, one of several Middleboro deeds.
The new grant includes tracts of land at Assomawet,
Tuspaquin's principal residence, and where John Sas-
samon claimed Tuspaquin had recently granted a deed
to him that included Assomawet Pond. In the summer
Mammanuah lodges his complaint against Awashonks
at Plymouth Court, which decides the conflict in his
favor, benefitting the claims of Plymouth settlers.
Benjamin Church builds his house on a lot granted
by Plymouth Court, part of the "new plantation" of
Sakonnet.

1675   In February, the body of John Sassamon is found under
the ice in Assomawet Pond. Although it is uncertain
whether Sassamon's death was accidental or intentional,
the Plymouth Court arrests two of Metacom's counselors, Tobias and Mattashunannamo, and Tobias's son,
Wampapaquan, for his murder. The court grants Tobias
a bond that is dependent on the sale of the remaining
Nemasket lands at Assawomet. Mammanuah, Awashonks's son, signs a deed in April granting all of Sakonnet to Plymouth settlers, including Josiah Winslow and
Constant Southworth. In May, Weetamoo meets with
John Easton, the deputy governor of Rhode Island, and
expresses her concerns regarding "oppression" by Plymouth men and her desire to protect her community's
land by setting the bounds of Pocasset through a deed;
Easton conveys her message to Josiah Winslow.

Trial of Tobias, Mattashunannamo, and Wampapaquan for Sassamon's murder begins in Plymouth
Colony on June 1. All three men are found guilty, and
Tobias and Mattashunannamo are hanged on June
8; Wampapaquan is later shot. Rumors circulate that
Metacom is gathering men at Montaup and that Winslow is raising a force to bring Metacom to Plymouth.
Winslow writes to Weetamoo, requesting her neutrality, and sends Benjamin Church to meet with her and
Awashonks. John Easton meets with Metacom and
his counselors at Montaup, hoping to prevent war.
When Easton proposes resolving the Wampanoag
conflict with Plymouth through arbitration, Metacom

reminds him that English colonists have used arbitration to obtain land. Easton then proposes mediation between a Native leader of the Wampanoags' choice and Sir Edmund Andros, the royal governor of New York Colony. Easton believes Metacom will accept this proposal if Plymouth agrees. However, when he returns home, Easton learns that Governor Winslow is planning to send an armed force to compel Metacom into subjection. Winslow sends Metacom a letter on June 19 requiring him and his counselors to relinquish their arms and report to Plymouth Court. Metacom does not comply, instead sending a letter relaying "his great desire of concluding of peace with neighboring English." Plymouth forces march toward Sowams and Montaup, establishing garrisons at Swansea and Rehoboth. Edward Hutchinson and other representatives of Massachusetts Bay Colony meet in Narragansett territory with the saunkskwa Quaiapin and sachems Quinnapin, Canonchet, Ninigret, and Quissuequnash (also known as Canonicus), with Roger Williams serving as interpreter. The colonists carry a message from Massachusetts Bay governor John Leverett, asking them not to join with Metacom. The Narragansett sachems say they "had no agreement with Metacom" and would not send men to him, asking why Massachusetts Bay and Rhode Island men were allied with Plymouth. Ephraim Curtis travels to Nipmuc territory, carrying a similar message from Leverett. Many Nipmuc leaders and their families take shelter and council at Menimesit. Nipmuc converts in praying towns pledge not to join Metacom, some volunteering to serve as scouts. Wampanoag warriors begin ransacking and burning empty settler houses and killing cattle in Swansea. On June 23 John Salisbury of Swansea kills a Wampanoag man who is leaving an abandoned house. Wampanoag warriors then kill several Swansea colonists at Mattapoisett on June 24, a raid colonists take as marking the war's beginning. Massachusetts Bay sends troops to join with Plymouth at Rehoboth. Wampanoag warriors ambush colonial troops that attempt to cross into Montaup, shoot Englishmen who venture outside their fortified garrisons, and attack houses in Rehoboth and Taunton, June 26–29. Metacom leads

Wampanoag families to Pocasset, where Weetamoo shelters them. When Massachusetts Bay and Plymouth troops reach Montaup on June 30, they find it empty.

Church leads scouting expeditions to Sakonnet and Pocasset in early July. Wampanoag warriors strike English settlements at Swansea, Taunton, Middleboro, and Dartmouth, causing many colonists to abandon their homes, and diverting colonial forces from Pocasset. Nipmuc leader Matoonas leads a raid on Mendon on July 14 as the war spreads to Massachusetts Bay Colony. Plymouth and Massachusetts Bay forces march to Pocasset Swamp, recruiting scouts from Natick, including James and Thomas Quananophit, to guide them. Colonial forces enter the cedar swamp on July 19 but become disoriented as hidden warriors fire upon them. The chaos allows Wampanoag people sheltering in the swamp to escape. Colonial troops build forts in Montaup and Pocasset. On July 29 Metacom, Weetamoo, and the families under their protection escape to the north and cross the Taunton River.

Colonial forces and their Mohegan allies attack the Wampanoags at Nipsachuck (present-day Smithfield, Rhode Island), in northern Narragansett territory, on August 1, but are unable to stop their flight. Weetamoo and her company seek shelter with Narragansett leaders while Metacom leads his company to Nipmuc territory. Massachusetts Bay forces march toward the Nipmuc gathering place of Menimesit but are ambushed en route, leading to the siege at the English settlement in Quabaug (later Brookfield), August 2–5. Nipmuc leaders accept Metacom and his people at Menimesit, where they remain sheltered, and Metacom distributes wampum among them. Nipmuc leader Monoco leads a raid on Lancaster, in his homeland of Nashaway, on August 22. Massachusetts Bay forces hold a council of war in Hadley, in the Connecticut River Valley, and decide to preemptively disarm the local Nonotuck community, fearing they will join with their relations from Quabaug. Nonotuck people escape north to Pocumtuck on August 25, pursued by Richard Beers, Thomas Lathrop, and about one hundred Massachusetts Bay soldiers, launching the war in the Connecticut River Valley. Unable to locate Nipmuc or Wampanoag warriors, Massachusetts Bay commander Samuel Mosely and his men take James Printer and ten other Christian Native men captive at Okkanamesit (a praying town near Marlboro), August 30, accusing them of the murder of Lancaster settlers, and march them to Cambridge. Massachusetts Bay Council orders all Native converts in their colony confined to five mission communities, Natick, Punkapoag, Nashobah, Wamesit, and Hassanamesit.

Pocumtuck, Sokoki, and Nonotuck warriors raid Pocumtuck (Deerfield) and Squakeag (Northfield), September 1–2. Captain Richard Beers and about twenty of his men are killed near Squakeag on September 4. Massachusetts Bay Company destroys corn and burns houses at Hassanamesit, James Printer's home. John Eliot and Daniel Gookin seek the release of Printer and the ten other Christian Native men imprisoned in Cambridge, where their lives are threatened by a mob. Wabanaki people living along the coast from Newichiwannock (now South Berwick, Maine) to the Kennebec River face starvation in the coming winter as Massachusetts Bay demands that they surrender their weapons. Violence breaks out in coastal territory in mid-September as Wabanaki forces raid mills, trading posts, and houses built on Indigenous planting grounds in Piscataqua, Saco, Owascoag (Scarborough), and Casco Bay. Pocumtuck and Nipmuc warriors kill Captain Thomas Lathrop and sixty of his men in ambush near Deerfield on September 18. The survivors are rescued by Connecticut troops and their Mohegan allies. After Mohegan leaders intercede on their behalf, James Printer and his fellow prisoners are brought to trial, and almost all of them are acquitted. Penacook sachem Wannalancet leads families north to the headwaters of the Connecticut River, far from the conflict.

Pocumtuck and Wampanoag warriors burn Springfield, October 5, as several English settlements in the Connecticut River Valley are abandoned. Colonists repel attack on Hatfield, October 19. During the fall Weetamoo marries the Narragansett sachem Quinnapin, forging an alliance. Narragansett sachem Canonchet travels to Boston for council, where Massachusetts Bay leaders demand the surrender of the Wampanoags living among the Narragansetts including Weetamoo. The Narragansetts maintain a neutral stance as they build a large, fortified settlement in the Great Swamp (present-day South Kingston, Rhode Island). As colonists become increasingly fearful of the Native people of the praying towns, Massachusetts Bay authorities intern converts from Natick on Deer Island in Boston Harbor, where they suffer from hunger, cold, and sickness during the winter. By March 1676, more than four hundred men, women, and children are confined on the island.

Nipmuc warriors take the remaining harvest from Hassanamesit to Menimesit in early November. They are accompanied by almost all the town's inhabitants, including James Printer, his family, and his kinsman Tom Wuttascomponom (also known as Captain Tom), the town's leader, who fear that the English will intern them on Deer Island or sell them into slavery. Nathaniel Saltonstall, a Boston merchant, sends an account of the war to London, where it is printed as *The Present State of New-England with Respect to the Indian War*, one of the first narratives of the conflict to circulate in England. The pamphlet advocates attacking the Narragansett and describes Weetamoo as "as Potent a Prince as any around her." Plymouth convinces the United Colonies to launch a major strike on the Narragansetts, arguing that Metacom is among them (which proves false), and that the Narragansett will soon join the anticolonial alliance. Josiah Winslow is named to lead the expedition as the colonies begin recruiting men with promises of land bounties.

Massachusetts Bay and Plymouth forces rendezvous at Rehoboth on December 10. Rhode Island provides ships to transport men and supplies across Narragansett Bay to Wickford on its western shore. Colonial patrols kill and capture Narragansett people and burn two villages. Quinnapin leads a strike on English garrison house at Pettaquamscut on December 15, killing fifteen colonists. Connecticut troops arrive in Narragansett territory, forming a colonial army of one thousand men accompanied by 150 Mohegan and Pequot allies. Led by a captive forced to reveal its location, the United Colonies army attacks the fortified Narragansett settlement in the Great Swamp on December 19. After being initially repulsed in fierce fighting, the colonial forces breach the settlement's palisade, set fire to its dwellings, and slay people trying to flee. While some Narragansett and Wampanoag people escape, hundreds of men, women, and children are killed; the colonial forces lose about seventy men killed or fatally wounded. Daniel Gookin recruits two Native scouts from Deer Island, James Quanapohit and Job Kattananit, to pursue a spying mission to Menimesit, where Job's family had been taken by Nipmuc relations.

1676   Metacom travels to Mohican territory, in the Hudson Valley north of Albany, where he seeks additional Native allies. United Colonies forces patrol Narragansett territory to capture survivors from the Great Swamp and seize food supplies. James Quanapohit returns from his mission and warns Gookin on January 24 that Nipmucs are planning raid on Lancaster and several other Massachusetts Bay towns. Narragansett warriors led by Canonchet burn Rhode Island settlement at Pawtuxet on January 27. Weetamoo and Quinnapin travel with other Narragansett and Wampanoag survivors north to Menemesit in Nipmuc territory.

Job Kattananit warns Gookin on February 9 that a raid on Lancaster is imminent, but Massachusetts Bay forces reach the town too late. Narragansett, Nipmuc, and Wampanoag warriors attack Lancaster, February 10, killing at least fourteen colonists and capturing twenty-three, including Mary Rowlandson, the wife of the town's minister. Rowlandson is taken to Menimesit and placed in the household of Quinnapin and Weetamoo. Nipmucs lead raids on Medfield, February 21, and on Weymouth, south of Boston, February 24. New York governor Andros supplies Mohawk warriors with arms, which they use to attack the Wampanoag camp in the Hudson Valley and drive Metacom from the colony.

Weetamoo and other Native leaders at Menimesit gather their people after learning that Massachusetts Bay forces are planning a raid on the Nipmuc stronghold. They travel northward through Nipmuc territory into Sokoki country on the upper Connecticut River, beyond the reach of English troops. Metacom reunites with his relations, including Weetamoo, in Sokoki territory. Raid on Clark's Garrison, two miles south of

Plymouth, kills eleven colonists on March 12; Native coalition also attacks Groton, Northampton, Warwick, and Marlborough, March 13–26. Coalition warriors led by Canonchet virtually annihilate Plymouth company in battle along the Pawtucket (Blackstone) River, March 26, then burn Rehoboth and Providence, March 28–29. Narragansett women retrieve seed corn from hidden stores in their territory and bring it back to the Connecticut River Valley.

Canonchet is captured near Pawtucket on April 3 by Connecticut forces and their Niantic, Mohegan, and Pequot allies. He is taken to Stonington, Connecticut, and executed. Massachusetts Bay governor John Leverett begins negotiations with Shoshanim and other Nipmuc leaders for the release of captives. Nipmuc scribes, including James Printer, transcribe messages for Native leaders, while other Nipmuc men deliver messages for the English. Weetamoo, Quinnapin, Metacom, and many other Native allies travel to Wachusett in Nipmuc territory to hold council. Narragansett and Nipmuc forces, led by Quinnapin and Monoco, raid Sudbury, seventeen miles west of Boston, on April 21, and kill about forty English militiamen in battle. By this time Native forces have succeeded in pushing English settlers from the westernmost settlements around Boston and Plymouth and the northernmost settlements in the Connecticut River Valley. Massachusetts Bay sends John Hoar to Nipmuc country to negotiate for Mary Rowlandson's release and explore possibilities for peace.

Rowlandson is released on May 2 in return for £20 worth of goods. (Other English captives will be freed in May and June.) Rowlandson and Hoar return to Boston on May 3 carrying a collective letter from the Native leaders gathered at Wachusett calling for peace so that Native families can return to their homelands and plant their fields. As negotiations continue, colonial forces from Hatfield, Northampton, and Hadley launch a surprise assault on Native families gathered at the fishing falls of Peskeompscut, on the Connecticut River north of Pocumtuck (Deerfield). As many as two hundred Native people, mostly women, children, and old men, are killed in the attack on May 19, which upends peace negotiations and helps convince the United Colonies to pursue a military victory.

Plymouth, Massachusetts Bay, and Connecticut forces go on the offensive, tracking down Wampanoag, Nipmuc, and Narragansett people as they return to their homelands, either killing them or taking them prisoner, and sending many of the captives into slavery. Colonial forces are aided by Native scouts, including many recruited from families held on Deer Island. Job Kattananit, James Quanapohit, and other scouts petition Massachusetts Bay authorities for amnesty for their relations to prevent their execution and enslavement. The Massachusetts Bay Council pardons and grants protection to some families and issues proclamation on June 19 offering possible amnesty to "enemys" who "come in" and submit to colonial authority. No clemency is given to Tom Wuttascomponom, the leader at Hassanamesit who left the town with Nipmuc warriors in November 1675; he is hanged for treason on June 22. Benjamin Church leads a force of English soldiers and Native scouts for Plymouth, capturing Native men and holding their families as hostages for their participation in his expeditions.

James Printer, who left Hassanamesit with Tom Wuttascomponom in 1675, receives amnesty in Cambridge on July 2, then returns to Natick and Magunkaquog (present-day Ashland) to bring in Nipmuc people seeking protection from reprisals. On July 3 several Native leaders, including the Penacook sachem Wannalancet, sign treaty with Massachusetts Bay representatives at Cocheco (present-day Dover, New Hampshire) that seeks to protect those who had remained neutral in the conflict and those who had sought refuge in the north. Native attack on Taunton is repulsed on July 11 as colonial forces continue to sweep through Narragansett and Wampanoag homelands. Nipmuc leader Matoonas is executed in Boston on July 27.

Weetamoo dies in early August, reportedly drowned while trying to escape across the Taunton River, although she may have been killed by English soldiers. Her body is dismembered, and her head is displayed in Taunton. Metacom is pursued by a company led by Benjamin Church and killed on the Montaup peninsula on August 12. His head is displayed in Plymouth and his hands are sent to Governor Leverett as a trophy. Plymouth Colony claims Weetamoo's and Metacom's lands by right of conquest. Quinnapin is executed in Newport, Rhode Island, on August 25. Raids on English settlements continue in Wabanaki territory. Some Indigenous refugees take shelter in the north, but those who remain below the Piscataqua River face a continuing threat from colonial forces.

In September, Richard Waldron, a trader and militia commander at Cocheco, captures hundreds of Native people by tricking them into thinking he was hosting a feast. The captives, who are mostly women and children and include both Wabanaki people and people who had sought refuge in Wabanaki territory, are sent to Boston, where almost all of them are executed or sold into slavery. Ten men are spared to serve as scouts on military expeditions into Wabanaki country, most of which prove fruitless. Nipmuc leaders Shoshanim and Monoco are hanged in Boston on September 26. Captured Native people are sent to the West Indies, Bermuda, Virginia, the Iberian Peninsula, and North Africa; some Native children, including James Printer's nephews, are kept in colonial homes as indentured servants. Many residents of the praying towns are forced to live in servitude under guard in Boston and Cambridge. Massachusett converts are allowed to return to the praying town of Punkapoag (present-day Canton) where many of them work for nearby settlers.

1677   James Printer and other Nipmuc people begin to regather at Hassanamesit as Native converts and their surviving kin gradually return to the praying towns. Leaders in the towns, many of whom served as scouts, will petition to protect Nipmuc lands for many years after the war. Wampanoag and Narragansett people regather in their homelands, and places such as Mashpee on Cape Cod, Dartmouth, and Niantic become refuges for survivors. A regional network of Native people forms, including both those held as captive servants in colonial centers and those who reside far from these centers. In places like Noepe and Cape Cod, Wampanoag people continue to practice traditional subsistence and culture while adopting and adapting structures such as churches and schools that make them appear safe to settlers.

Escaped captive Francis Card reports to colonial leaders on the strength of Wabanaki forces in January. He communicates the proclamation by the Saco River leader Squando "that god doth speak to him and doth tell him that god hath left our nacion [i.e., the English] to them to destroy." Card also reports the Wabanaki leader Mogg's claim that he had "found the way to burn Boston," a message likely intended to circulate among Massachusetts Bay leaders.

Wabanaki forces led by Squando defeat expedition from Massachusetts Bay near the abandoned settlement of Scarborough on June 29. In July Wabanaki leaders on the Kennebec River send a letter to Governor Leverett, denouncing Richard Waldron for his deceits and suggesting terms for renewing trade and peaceful relations. They affirm their desire for peace while noting that Wabanaki leaders like Squando are reluctant to pursue diplomacy and fully capable of raiding colonial settlements. New York governor Edmund Andros sends commissioners to negotiate terms of peace between Wabanaki leaders and Massachusetts Bay, representing the United Colonies. (At the time, the colony of New York claimed the eastern part of present-day Maine.)

Treaty of Pemaquid, concluded in August, ends warfare in Wabanaki lands, with equal terms negotiated through the mediation of Kennebec Wabanaki leaders and Andros's representatives. Although the treaty terms apply to all English settlers in the region, Plymouth leaders do not directly participate in the councils at Pemaquid.

1678   Treaty of Casco signed in April requires English colonists resettling lands in Wabanaki territory to give annual tribute to Wabanaki people.

1682   Mary Rowlandson's account of her captivity, *The Sovereignty and Goodness of God*, is published in Boston. James Printer had returned to work for the elder Samuel Green, a printer in Cambridge who published the second and third editions of Rowlandson's narrative, and it is likely that Printer set the type for those editions.

1684   The Mashpee meetinghouse is built on traditional Wampanoag lands on Cape Cod, solidifying Mashpee's status as an Indian town, protected under colonial law.

1691   Plymouth Colony is absorbed into Massachusetts Bay Colony in a new charter granted by King William III and Queen Mary II.

1833   Mashpee leaders Jo Amos, Ebenezer Attaquin, Israel Amos, and Isaac Coombs and the Pequot minister William Apess lead the "Mashpee Revolt," a protest movement that seeks to end control of Mashpee affairs by overseers appointed by the state government, halt the theft of timber from Mashpee lands by Cape Cod settlers, and remove from office Phineas Fish, a minister appointed by Harvard who had usurped the Mashpee meetinghouse. The Mashpee send a petition to the Massachusetts legislature declaring their right to rule themselves, and Apess is jailed for thirty days for leading a nonviolent action blocking the removal of cut timber from Mashpee lands.

1834   Massachusetts legislature recognizes and grants local self-rule to Wampanoag people living at Mashpee.

1835   William Apess publishes *Indian Nullification of the Unconstitutional Laws of Massachusetts's Relative to the Marshpee Tribe; or, the Pretended Riot Explained*, a pamphlet documenting how the Mashpee Wampanoag defended their sovereignty.

1836   William Apess twice delivers a public lecture in Boston on Metacom and the legacy of violence in New England and publishes it as *Eulogy on King Philip*.

1863   President Abraham Lincoln declares a National Day of Thanksgiving, one of the predecessors of today's federal Thanksgiving holiday.

1970   Wamsutta Frank James delivers a speech about the legacies of colonial violence at the first National Day of Mourning, held in Plymouth on the Thanksgiving holiday. The speech had originally been written for an event commemorating the 350th anniversary of the colonists' arrival at Patuxet but had been suppressed by the event's organizers.

Note on the Texts

This volume collects seventeenth- and early eighteenth-century writing about Plymouth Colony and the Native peoples of the Northeast, as well as nineteenth-, twentieth-, and twenty-first-century writing about the continuance of Wampanoag people in their homelands. It brings together narratives, traditional stories, letters, speeches, testimony, and court documents, some of which were not written for publication and existed only in manuscript form during the lifetimes of the persons who wrote them. With five exceptions, the texts presented in this volume are taken from printed sources. In cases where there is only one printed source for a document, the text offered here comes from that source. Where the choice is between a first edition (or other early printings) and a later scholarly edition, the text printed in this volume is taken from the scholarly edition (and where more than one scholarly edition exists, from the one that makes the fewest textual alterations). In five instances where no printed sources were available, the texts in this volume are printed from manuscripts.

VOYAGES AND CAPTIVITIES

James Rosier (1573–1609) made his first transatlantic voyage with Bartholomew Gosnold in 1602 and his second with George Weymouth (or Waymouth) three years later. Rosier's *A True Relation of the most prosperous voyage made the present yeere 1605, by Captaine George Waymouth, in the Discovery of the land of Virginia* was printed in London by George Bishop in 1605. The text printed here is taken from *Early English and French Voyages, chiefly from Hakluyt, 1534–1608*, ed. Henry S. Burrage (New York: Charles Scribner's Sons, 1906), 357–94, and is based on the copy of the pamphlet in the John Carter Brown Library, Providence, Rhode Island.

Samuel de Champlain (1567–1635) visited Port Saint Louis (Patuxet) in 1605. He published his chart of the harbor in *Les Voyages du Sieur de Champlain*, printed in Paris in 1613 for sale by Jean Berjon. The text printed here of the key to the chart is taken from *Voyages of Samuel de Champlain, Vol. II: 1604–1610*, ed. Edmund F. Slafter (Boston: The Prince Society, 1878), 78.

Captain John Smith (1580–1631) sailed along the coast of Wabanaki and Wampanoag homelands in 1614 and made two unsuccessful attempts to return the following year. *A Description of New England*, printed in London by Humfrey Lownes for sale by Robert Clerke, was entered in the Stationers' Register on June 3, 1616. The text printed here is taken from *The Complete Works of Captain John Smith*, volume I, ed. Philip L. Barbour (Chapel Hill: The University of North Carolina Press, 1986), 305–61.

Thomas Dermer (d. 1620) wrote about his recent visit to Patuxet to the English clergyman and historian Samuel Purchas on December 27, 1619. Purchas published the letter in the fourth volume of *Purchas his Pilgrimes*, printed in London in 1625 by William Stansby for sale by Henry Featherstone. The text printed here is taken from *Sir Ferdinando Gorges and his Province of Maine, Vol. I*, ed. James Phinney Baxter (Boston: The Prince Society, 1890), 219n–22n.

Sometime after 1635 Ferdinando Gorges (c. 1566–1647) wrote a memoir of his efforts to promote colonization in New England. It was published posthumously by his grandson as *A Briefe Narration of the Originall Undertakings of the Advancement of Plantations into the parts of America*, printed in London in 1658 by E. Brudenell for sale by Nathaniel Brook. The text of the excerpt printed here is taken from *Sir Ferdinando Gorges and his Province of Maine, Vol. II*, ed. James Phinney Baxter (Boston: The Prince Society, 1890), 7–30.

PLYMOUTH PLANTATION IN PATUXET

A Relation or Journall of the beginnings and proceedings of the English Plantation settled at Plimoth in New England, by certaine English Adventurers both Merchants and Others, sometimes referred to as *Mourt's Relation*, was printed in London in 1622 for sale by John Bellamie. *A Relation* included unsigned narratives of the first year of the Plymouth Colony that are attributed to William Bradford (1590–1657) and Edward Winslow (1595–1655), Separatist Puritans who were passengers on the *Mayflower*. The work also included a dedicatory epistle signed by "R.C." that is attributed to Robert Cushman (1577–1625), the agent for the colony's investors who visited Plymouth in December 1621 and brought the journals of the first year back to England; a preface signed by "G. Mourt," probably George Morton (c. 1585–1624), a Separatist living in London; and a letter addressed to the "Planters in *New England*," signed by "J.R." and attributed to John Robinson (1576–1625), the pastor of the Separatist congregation in Leiden. The text printed here is taken from *Mourt's Relation, or Journal of the Plantation at Plymouth*, ed. Henry Martyn Dexter (Boston: John Kimball Wiggin, 1865).

Good Newes from New England: or, A True Relation of things very remarkable at the Plantation of Plimoth in New-England was printed in London in 1624 by John Dawson for sale by William Bladen and John Bellamie. Edward Winslow, its author, who had traveled to England to meet with Plymouth colony's financial backers, was identified on the title page as "*E.W.*" A second edition, also printed in 1624, omitted the postscript (240.29–37 in this volume) and added a "brief Relation" concerning events in the Virginia Colony. The text printed here is taken from *"Good News from New England" by Edward Winslow: A Scholarly Edition*, ed. Kelly Wisecup (Amherst and Boston: University of Massachusetts Press, 2014), 53–117. In her edition, Wisecup uses the 1624 first edition as her copytext, and prints the text of the "brief Relation" following the postscript to the first edition.

Phenehas Pratt (c. 1593–1680) arrived at Plymouth in 1622 and became one of the settlers of the short-lived English colony at Wessagusset (modern-day Weymouth, Massachusetts). Pratt submitted his narrative of the Wessagusset Colony, "A Declaration of the Affairs of the English People that First Inhabited New England," as part of a petition seeking a land grant from the Massachusetts Bay General Court in 1662. The "Declaration" was first printed in *Collections of the Massachusetts Historical Society*, Fourth Series, Volume IV (Boston: Little, Brown and Company, 1858), 476–89 in a text edited by Richard Frothingham, Jr., and the text printed here is taken from that source.

In the spring of 1621 William Bradford was elected governor of Plymouth Colony, a position he held almost continuously for thirty-five years. Bradford began writing *Of Plimoth Plantation*, his history of the colony, in 1630 and completed the first ten chapters that year. He then set the manuscript aside and did not complete his annal for 1620 until 1644. Bradford continued working on *Of Plimoth Plantation* until about 1652, composing new annals and making alterations and additions to the existing manuscript. After Bradford's death Nathaniel Morton, his nephew and secretary, drew heavily on *Of Plimoth Plantation* while writing *New-Englands Memoriall* (1669), the first work of history published in the English North American colonies. Morton also copied most of the first nine chapters of Bradford's work into the Plymouth church records. *Of Plimoth Plantation* was also used as a source by the seventeenth-century colonial historians Increase Mather, William Hubbard, and Cotton Mather. In the early eighteenth century the manuscript came into the possession of Thomas Prince, minister of Old South Church in Boston, and was used by him in writing *A Chronological History of New-England* (1736). It remained in the library of Old South Church after Prince's death and was also used by Governor Thomas Hutchinson as a source for his *History of Massachusetts-Bay* (1767).

After the British army withdrew from Boston in 1776 the Bradford manuscript was discovered to be missing from Old South Church, which the garrison had used as an indoor riding arena. It is not known how the manuscript made its way to England, but in 1844 Samuel Wilberforce, the Bishop of Oxford, quoted from *Of Plimoth Plantation* in his *History of the Protestant Episcopal Church in America*, citing as his source a manuscript in Fulham Palace, the residence of the Bishop of London. In 1855 Wilberforce's book came to the attention of Charles Deane of the Massachusetts Historical Society, who arranged for a transcription of the manuscript to be made in England. Edited by Deane, the transcribed text, which contained errors and omissions, was published in 1856 as *History of Plymouth Plantation* in *Collections of the Massachusetts Historical Society*, Fourth Series, Volume III, and in book form the same year by Little, Brown and Company. (The nine chapters from *Of Plimoth Plantation* that Nathaniel Morton had copied into the Plymouth church records were first published in 1841 by Alexander Young in *Chronicles of the Pilgrim Fathers*.)

Thomas F. Bayard, the American ambassador to Great Britain, secured the return of Bradford's manuscript to the United States in 1897, when it was placed in the State Library of Massachusetts in Boston. The next year saw the publication of a new edition, *Bradford's History "Of Plimoth Plantation,"* edited by William M. Olin, that corrected some, but not all, of the errors made by the original English copyist. Another edition, *Bradford's History of Plymouth Plantation, 1606–1646*, published in 1908 and edited by William T. Davis, also reproduced copying errors while omitting material from the 1642 annal concerning the punishment of sexual offenses in the colony.

History of Plymouth Plantation 1620–1647, edited by Worthington Chauncey Ford and published in two volumes by the Massachusetts Historical Society in 1912, was based on a new transcription that corrected errors and omissions found in previous editions. Ford expanded the abbreviations Bradford used in his manuscript while retaining his spelling, capitalization, and punctuation. A more recent edition, *Of Plymouth Plantation 1620–1647*, edited by Samuel Eliot Morison and published in 1952, modernized Bradford's spelling and placed in appendices letters and documents that Bradford had incorporated in his manuscript. *Of Plimoth Plantation: The 400th Anniversary Edition*, edited by Kenneth P. Minkema, Francis J. Bremer, and Jeremy D. Bangs, was published in 2020 by the Colonial Society of Massachusetts and the New England Historic Genealogical Society. The editors used a high-resolution color scan of the manuscript to prepare a "born-digital" verbatim transcription that has been posted at the websites of the State Library of Massachusetts (mass.gov/orgs /state-library-of-massachusetts), the Colonial Society of Massachusetts (colonialsociety.org) and the New England Historic Genealogical Society (americanancestors.org). In their print edition, the editors

regularized Bradford's spelling and used the modern accepted spell-
ings for Native names and geographic features. This volume prints
the text of the 1912 Ford edition.

TRANSNATIONAL DIPLOMACY

The following is a list of the documents included in this section, in
the order of their appearance, giving the source of each text:

Seekonk Deed, 1642. *Records of the Colony of New Plymouth in
    New England: Court Orders, Vol. II, 1641–1651*, ed. Nathaniel B.
    Shurtleff (Boston: William White, 1855), 49–50.

Bridgewater Deed, 1649. Ebenezer Peirce, *Indian History, Biog-
    raphy and Genealogy: Pertaining to the Good Sachem Massasoit
    of the Wampanoag Tribe, and his descendants* (North Abington,
    MA: Zerviah Gould Mitchell, 1878), 229–30.

Nonaquaket Deed, 1651. *Proceedings of the Massachusetts Historical
    Society*, vol. XLVIII (May 1915), 492–93.

"Oldcomers" Deeds, 1652. Jeremy Dupertuis Bangs, *Indian Deeds:
    Land Transactions in Plymouth Colony, 1620–1691* (Boston: New
    England Historic Genealogical Society, 2008), 238–39, 247–50,
    263. Copyright © 2002 by the New England Historic Genea-
    logical Society. Reprinted by permission of New England His-
    toric Genealogical Society and American Ancestors. (Hereafter,
    Bangs.)

Old Dartmouth Deed, 1652. *Bangs*, 263–64.

Sowams Deed, 1653. *Bangs*, 269–70.

Wamsutta's Mortgage, 1657. *Bangs*, 286–87.

Freemen's Deeds, 1659. *Bangs*, 291–93.

Wamsutta's Protests Over Cattle, 1659–60. *Records of the Colony of
    New Plymouth in New England: Court Orders, Vol. III, 1651–1661*,
    ed. Nathaniel B. Shurtleff (Boston: William White, 1855), 167,
    192.

Metacom to Governor Prence. *Collections of the Massachusetts
    Historical Society*, First Series, Volume II (Boston: Belknap and
    Hall, 1793), 40.

Exchange Between Awashonks and Governor Prence, 1671. *Collec-
    tions of the Massachusetts Historical Society*, First Series, Volume
    V (Boston: Samuel Hall, 1798), 195–97.

THE BROADER WAMPANOAG
AND MASSACHUSETT HOMELANDS

William Wood is believed to have arrived in Massachusetts Bay in 1629 and to have returned to England four years later. *New Englands Prospect, a true, lively, and experimentall description of that part of America commonly called New England* was printed in London in 1634 by Thomas Cotes for sale by John Bellamie. The text of the excerpts printed here is taken from *Wood's New-England's Prospect* (Boston: Printed for the [Prince] Society, 1865), 15–20, 77–84, 105–10.

Thomas Morton (1580–1647) arrived in New England in 1624 and soon became the leader of the Ma-re Mount Colony, located in present-day Quincy, Massachusetts. His conduct angered the leaders of Plymouth and Massachusetts Bay, and he was expelled back to England in 1630. Morton's book about New England, *New English Canaan*, was first printed in 1637 in Amsterdam by Jacob Frederick Stam. The text printed here is taken from *The New English Canaan*, ed. Charles Francis Adams, Jr. (Boston: Printed for the [Prince] Society, 1883).

Experience Mayhew (1673–1758) was, like his father John Mayhew, a missionary who ministered to Wampanoag people on Noepe (Martha's Vineyard). His book *Indian Converts, or Some account of the lives and dying speeches of a considerable number of the Christianized Indians of Martha's Vineyard, in New-England* was first printed in London in 1727 for sale by Samuel Gerrish in Boston and by John Osborn and Thomas Longman in London. The text of the excerpts printed here is taken from *Experience Mayhew's Indian Converts: A Cultural Edition*, ed. Laura Arnold Leibman (Amherst: University of Massachusetts Press, 2008), 139–49, 232–33, 239–42.

Caleb Cheeshateaumuck (c. 1644–c. 1666), a Wampanoag man from Noepe, was the first Native scholar to graduate from the Harvard Indian College. In 1663 the younger John Winthrop wrote to the English scientist Robert Boyle, a supporter of the Indian College, and enclosed a Latin text Cheeshateaumuck had written in honor of his benefactors. The Latin text printed here is based on the manuscript in the Archive of the Royal Society, London, and is taken from Wolfgang Hochbruck and Beatrix Dudensing Reichel, "'Honoratissimi Benefactores': Native American students and two seventeenth-century texts in the university tradition," in *Early Native American Writing: New Critical Essays*, ed. Helen Jaskoski (Cambridge: Cambridge University Press, 1996), 3–6. Copyright © Cambridge University Press 1996. Used by permission of Cambridge University Press. The Hochbruck and Reichel essay is also the source for the English translation, except for the first paragraph (805.10–25). The translation of the first paragraph printed here is by Cassandra

Hradil and Lisa Brooks, and is taken from Lisa Brooks, *Our Beloved Kin: A New History of King Philip's War* (New Haven: Yale University Press, 2018), 90–91. Copyright © 2018 by Lisa Brooks.

The traditional story told by Thomas Cooper was first published in "Fabulous Traditions and Customs of the Indians of Martha's Vineyard," *Collections of the Massachusetts Historical Society*, First Series, Volume I (Boston: Belknap and Hall, 1792), 139–40, the source of the text printed here.

Helen Attaquin (1923–1993), an Aquinnah Wampanoag educator, wrote "How Martha's Vineyard Came to Be," her modern retelling of a traditional Native story, while working at the Children's Museum of Boston. The text printed here is taken from *Dawnland Voices: An Anthology of Indigenous Writing from New England*, ed. Siobhan Senier (Lincoln: University of Nebraska Press, 2014), 459–60. Copyright © 2014 by the Board of Regents of the University of Nebraska.

Daniel Gookin (1612–1687) was appointed Superintendent of the Christian Indians by the Massachusetts Bay General Court in 1657. Gookin completed his manuscript on the Indians of New England in 1674, but it remained unpublished until 1792, when it was printed in *Collections of the Massachusetts Historical Society*, First Series, Volume I, and in book form. The text of the excerpts printed here is taken from Daniel Gookin, *Historical Collections of the Indians in New England, of their several nations, numbers, customs, manners, religion and government, before the English planted there* (Boston: Belknap and Hall, 1792), 7–16, 28–36, 40–56.

KING PHILIP'S WAR OR THE FIRST INDIAN WAR

John Easton (1624–1705), the deputy governor of Rhode Island, wrote his narrative of the outbreak of King Philip's War in February 1676. The text printed here is taken from "A Relacion of the Indyan Warre," *Narratives of the Indian Wars, 1675–1699*, ed. Charles H. Lincoln (New York: Charles Scribner's Sons, 1913), 7–17, and is based on the manuscript in the New York State Library, Albany.

The text printed here of the letter sent by John Easton to Josiah Winslow, May 26, 1675, is taken from the manuscript, Mss C 357, R. Stanton Avery Special Collections, New England Historic Genealogical Society, and is reprinted by permission of New England Historic Genealogical Society and American Ancestors.

The text printed in this volume of the letter John Brown (1650–1709) sent to Josiah Winslow, June 11, 1675, is taken from the manuscript, Winslow Family Papers II, N-487, Massachusetts Historical Society, and is reprinted by permission of the Massachusetts Historical Society.

Benjamin Church (1639–1718) fought in King Philip's War as a colonial commander. His son Thomas Church (1674–1746) used his father's recollections to write a narrative of Benjamin Church's experiences in the war. *Entertaining Passages Relating to Philip's War, Which Began in the Month of June, 1675* was printed in Boston in 1716 by Bartholomew Green, with its author identified as "T.C." The text of the first selection from *Entertaining Passages Relating to Philip's War* printed in this volume is taken from *The History of King Philip's War by Benjamin Church*, ed. Henry Martyn Dexter (Boston: John Kimball Wiggin, 1865), 1–15. (Hereafter, *Church*.)

The text printed here of the letter from Josiah Winslow (1629–1680) to Weetamoo and Ben, June 15, 1675, is taken from the manuscript, Winslow Family Papers II, N-487, Massachusetts Historical Society. Reprinted by permission of the Massachusetts Historical Society.

The text of the letters from Roger Williams (1603–1683) to John Winthrop, Jr., June 25 and 27, 1675, printed in this volume is from *The Letters of Roger Williams, 1632–1682*, ed. John Russell Bartlett (Providence, RI: Printed for the Narragansett Club, 1874), 366–72. (Hereafter, *Williams*.)

The text of the letter from John Freeman to Josiah Winslow, July 3, 1675, printed in this volume is taken from *Collections of the Massachusetts Historical Society*, First Series, Volume VII (Boston: Belknap and Hall, 1800), 91.

The text of the second excerpt from *Entertaining Passages Relating to Philip's War* printed in this volume is taken from *Church*, 29–48.

The text printed here of the letter from the younger William Bradford (1624–1703) to John Cotton, July 21, 1675, is taken from *A Letter from Major William Bradford to the Reverend John Cotton, written at Mount Hope on July 21, 1675* (Providence, RI: Society of Colonial Wars, 1914), 15–16.

The testimony printed here of the Wampanoag men Peter, George, and David regarding the outbreak of the war is taken from *Bangs*, 485–87.

The text printed here of "A Brief Narrative of the Beginning and Progress of the Present Trouble," written by Josiah Winslow and Thomas Hinckley (1618–1706), is taken from *Records of the Colony of New Plymouth in New England: Acts of the Commissioners of the United Colonies of New England, Vol. II, 1653–1679*, ed. David Pulsifer (Boston: William White, 1859), 362–64. (Hereafter, *Pulsifer*.)

The text of the statement by the commissioners of the United Colonies, September 9, 1675, printed in this volume is taken from *Pulsifer*, 364–65.

The text printed here of the letter from Roger Williams to John Leverett, October 11, 1675, is taken from *Williams*, 373–76.

James Quananopohit (c. 1636–1712) was a Nipmuc man who served as a scout for Massachusetts Bay during King Philip's War. The text printed here of his "Examination and Relation" recorded on January 24, 1676, is based on the manuscript in the Connecticut Archives and is taken from *The Sovereignty and Goodness of God by Mary Rowlandson, with Related Documents*, ed. Neal Salisbury, 2nd edition (Boston: Bedford/St. Martin's, 2018), 130–39. Copyright © 2018, 1997 by Bedford/St. Martin's.

Mary Rowlandson (c. 1637–1711) was taken prisoner by Native warriors in February 1676 and held in captivity for three months. After her release she drafted a narrative of captivity, possibly in 1677–78, that was privately circulated before being published in 1682 as *The Sovereignty and Goodness of God, together, With the Faithfulness of His Promises Displayed, Being a Narrative of the Captivity and Restoration of Mrs. Mary Rowlandson*. It appeared with an unsigned preface attributed to Increase Mather (1639–1723). Only four pages are known to be extant of the first edition, which was printed in Boston by the younger Samuel Green. A second edition was also published in 1682, printed in Cambridge by the elder Samuel Green. The text printed here is based on the 1682 2nd edition and is taken from *The Sovereignty and Goodness of God by Mary Rowlandson, with Related Documents*, ed. Neal Salisbury, 2nd edition (Boston: Bedford/St. Martin's, 2018), 69–118. Copyright © 2018, 1997 by Bedford/St. Martin's.

The text of the excerpt printed here from a letter from Noah Newman to John Cotton, March 14, 1676, containing a note attributed to James Printer (1640–1709), is taken from the manuscript in the Curwen Family Papers, American Antiquarian Society, and is reprinted courtesy of the American Antiquarian Society.

The text of the third excerpt printed in this volume from *Entertaining Passages Relating to Philip's War* is taken from *Church*, 138–53.

The text of the letter from Edward Rawson (1615–1693) to Josiah Winslow, August 28, 1676, printed in this volume is taken from the manuscript in the Winslow Family Papers II, 103, Massachusetts Historical Society, and is reprinted by permission of the Massachusetts Historical Society.

The text printed here of the petition submitted by William Wannukhow, Joseph Wannukhow, and John Appamatahqeen in September 1676 is taken from J. H. Temple, *History of Framingham, Massachusetts, early known as Danforth's Farms, 1640–1880* (Framingham, MA: 1887), 77–78.

The text printed here of the record of the court-martial of Native prisoners held at Newport, Rhode Island, in the late summer of 1676 is taken from *A Narrative Of the Causes which led to Philip's Indian War, of 1675 and 1676, by John Easton, of Rhode Island, With other Documents concerning this Event in the Office of the Secretary of State of New York*, ed. Franklin B. Hough (Albany, NY: J. Munsell, 1858), 173–90.

The text printed in this volume of the deeds submitted for conquered Wampanoag lands, 1676–80, is taken from *Bangs*, 488–89, 495–500, 506–7, 517–20.

The text printed here of the message sent by Moxus and other Wabanaki leaders to John Leverett, c. July 1, 1677, is taken from *Documentary History of the State of Maine*, volume VI, ed. James Phinney Baxter (Portland: Maine Historical Society, 1900), 177–79.

WAMPANOAG CONTINUANCE

William Apess (1798–1839), a Methodist minister of Pequot descent, was an active participant in the struggle of the Mashpee Wampanoag for self-rule in 1833–34. Apess gathered documents and newspaper articles about the "Marshpee Revolt" and incorporated them into a narrative published in 1835. The text of the excerpts printed in this volume is taken from *Indian Nullification of the Unconstitutional Laws of Massachusetts, Relative to the Marshpee Tribe: or, the Pretended Riot Explained* (Boston: Jonathan Howe, 1835), 5, 7–55, 69–70, 89–93.

Apess delivered his eulogy on King Philip for the first time in Boston on January 8, 1836. The text printed here is taken from the unabridged first edition, *Eulogy on King Philip, as pronounced at the Odeon, in Federal Street, Boston, by the Rev. William Apess, an Indian* (Boston: Belknap and Hall, 1836).

Wamsutta Frank James (1923–2001), an Aquinnah Wampanoag man, was invited to give a speech at an official event held in September 1970 to commemorate the 350th anniversary of Plymouth Colony. When the event organizers rejected his speech, Wamsutta James delivered it at the first National Day of Mourning, held on the federal Thanksgiving holiday in 1970. The text printed here is taken from the website of the United American Indians of New England, http://www.uaine.org/suppressed_speech.htm, accessed July 30, 2021, and is reprinted by permission of Moonanum James.

The essay "The Audacity of Assumption" by Linda Coombs is published here for the first time. Copyright © 2021 by Linda Coombs.

Texts are printed here as they appeared in the sources from which they were taken, with a few alterations. Errata that were listed in the original sources have now been incorporated into the texts, and some marginalia, including biblical citations, in the source texts have been printed in this volume in "windows" (indented spaces within the texts). In cases where the source texts print contractions using superscript letters, the present volume expands the contractions, so that "w^{ch}" becomes "which," "wth" becomes "with," "y^e" becomes "the," and "y^t" becomes "that." Contractions that are expanded in the source texts using bracketed or italic letters are printed in this volume in their expanded form without brackets or italics. Bracketed editorial emendations used to supply letters or words omitted from the source texts by an obvious slip of the pen or printer's error are accepted in this volume and printed without brackets, but bracketed editorial insertions used to clarify meaning have been deleted. Passages in the source texts that are illegible or damaged are indicated in this volume by a bracketed two-em space, i.e., [   ]. Some of the source texts printed in this volume use bracketed numerals to record the page or leaf numbers of earlier printings or manuscripts; these numbers are deleted in the present volume, as are the symbols used in some source texts to mark page and paragraph breaks.

This volume presents the texts of the original printings and manuscripts chosen for inclusion here without change, except for the alterations previously discussed and for the correction of typographical errors. It does not attempt to reproduce nontextual features of their typographical design or features of seventeenth- and eighteenth-century typography such as the long "s" and the use of "u" for "v" (for example, "sauage" for "savage"), "v" for "u" (for example, "vtterly" for "utterly"), "i" for "j" (for example, "adioyning" for "adjoyning"), or "j" for "i" ("xviij" for "xviii"). Spelling, punctuation, and capitalization are often expressive features, and they are not altered, even when inconsistent or irregular. The following is a list of typographical errors corrected, cited by page and line number: 42.30, may he; 115.23, exawple; 115.24, distasters; 117.3, associciates; 153.30, Instrument,; 247.11, see ships? Thay; 248.5,] This; 250.20, me. Then; 275.9, cartaine; 377.5, one the; 518.35, bever; 632.21, dewlling; 830.8, Pakemitt††; 912.12, i675; 957.37–38, Psal. 199. 71; 966.30, Psalm 119; 1055.10, do not; 1060.10, 1622; 1062.25, Almighty.

Notes

In the notes below, the reference numbers denote page and line of this volume (the line count includes headings, but not rule lines). No note is made for material included in the eleventh edition of *Merriam-Webster's Collegiate Dictionary*. Biblical references are keyed to the King James Version. Footnotes and bracketed editorial notes within the text were in the originals. For further historical and biographical background, references to other studies, and more detailed notes, see *Sailors Narratives of Voyages along the New England Coast, 1524–1624*, ed. George Parker Winship (Boston: Houghton, Mifflin & Company, 1905); Coll Thrush, *Indigenous London: Native Travelers at the Heart of Empire* (New Haven: Yale University Press, 2016); Andrew Lipman, *The Saltwater Frontier: Indians and the Contest for the American Coast* (New Haven: Yale University Press, 2015); Neal Salisbury, *Manitou and Providence: Indians, Europeans and the Making of New England, 1500–1643* (New York: Oxford University Press, 1982); John G. Turner, *They Knew They Were Pilgrims: Plymouth Colony and the Contest for American Liberty* (New Haven: Yale University Press, 2020); Kelly Wisecup, ed., *"Good News from New England" by Edward Winslow: A Scholarly Edition* (Amherst: University of Massachusetts Press, 2014); Betty Booth Donohue, *Bradford's Indian Book: Being the True Roote & Rise of American Letters as Revealed by the Native Text Embedded in* Of Plimoth Plantation (Gainesville: University Press of Florida, 2011); *Dawnland Voices: An Anthology of Indigenous Writing from New England*, ed. Siobhan Senier (Lincoln: University of Nebraska Press, 2014); Lisa Brooks, *Our Beloved Kin: A New History of King Philip's War* (New Haven: Yale University Press, 2018); Christine M. DeLucia, *Memory Lands: King Philip's War and the Place of Violence* (New Haven: Yale University Press, 2018); *The Sovereignty and Goodness of God by Mary Rowlandson, with Related Documents*, ed. Neal Salisbury, 2nd edition (Boston: Bedford/St. Martin's, 2018); Eric B. Schulz and Michael J. Tougias, *King Philip's War: The History and Legacy of America's Forgotten Conflict* (Woodstock, VT: The Countryman Press, 1999); *On Our Own Ground: The Complete Writings of William Apess, a Pequot*, ed. Barry O'Connell (Amherst: University of Massachusetts Press, 1992); Drew Lopenzina, *Through an Indian's Looking-Glass: A Cultural Biography of William Apess, Pequot* (Amherst: University of Massachusetts Press, 2017); and Jean M. O'Brien, *Firsting and Lasting: Writing Indians out of Existence in New England* (Minneapolis: University of Minnesota Press, 2010).

64.17   the harbor of Quonahassit] Probably Cohasset Harbor.

64.20   an excellent good harbor] Probably Plymouth Harbor, at Patuxet.

64.38   Ile of Nausit] Probably referring to Nantucket, an island in Wampanoag territory.

64.39   Capawack] Noepe, now also Martha's Vineyard, an island in Wampanoag territory.

65.20   highest Ile is Sorico] Mount Desert Island, in the Penobscot homeland.

65.22   Matinnack] Metinic, now also Matinicus Island, in the Penobscot homeland.

65.23   Monahigan] Moniekek, now also Allen Island, in the Penobscot homeland.

65.24   Monanis] Mənəhanis, now also Monhegin Island, in the Penobscot homeland.

65.25   Damerils Iles] Damariscove Islands, south of the Damariscotta River and west of Monhegan] Island, in Wabanaki territory.

65.32   them of Penobscot] Mount Katahdin, and other mountains at the headwaters of the Penobscot River, in the Penobscot homeland, Wabanaki territory.

65.32–33   twinkling mountaine of Aucocisco] Wobiadenak, the White Mountains in Wabanaki territory, now in New Hampshire and Maine.

65.34   the high mountaine of Massachusit] Massachusett, now Great Blue Hill, Milton, Massachusetts.

65.40   pumpions] Pumpkins.

66.19   Aroughconds] Raccoons.

66.19   Wild-cats] Bobcats and cougars.

66.20   Fitches, Musquassus] Polecats, probably referring to fishers; muskrats.

66.25   Clampes] Clams.

76.17   Dohannida] Tahanedo, also sometimes referred to as "Nahanda," "Dehamda," or "Tahanda" by English writers, was one of the Wabanaki men taken by George Waymouth from Pemaquid in 1605. He returned to his home with Martin Pring in 1606 and later served as an interpreter for John Smith, who referred to him as Dohanidda, during Smith's expedition to Wabanaki homelands. Smith's description of Wabanaki place-names is much more precise than his description of place-names to the south, including in Wampanoag territory; this is likely because of Tahanedo's knowledge of Wabanaki territory.

77.24 Thomas Smith] A London merchant who was treasurer of the Virginia Company.

77.30 betrayed twenty seaven . . . soules] Hunt captured twenty Wampanoag men at Patuxet and another seven at Nauset.

77.36 Ferdinando Gorge] Sir Ferdinando Gorges (c. 1566–1647) was an investor in colonial settlements in New England, especially Wabanaki lands in what is now Maine, and president of the Council for New England.

83.2 cutchanell] Cochineal, a red dye made from insects found in Mexico, Central America, and South America.

90.8 antient Plantations] Native towns along the coast, including Wampanoag homelands.

90.10 the Plague] The disease that devastated Native communities in the northeast in 1616–19 remains unknown, although scholars agree that it was not bubonic plague, and believe the epidemics were caused by a disease common in Europe but not in the Americas.

90.13 my savages native country] Dermer was accompanied by Tisquantum (d. 1622), also called Squanto by the English, one of the Wampanoag men seized by Thomas Hunt in 1614. His homeland, Patuxet, was hard hit by the epidemics.

90.14 Nummastaquyt] Nemasket, a Wampanoag homeland east of Patuxet and a gathering place for Wampanoag people during spring fishing, now also Middleboro, Massachusetts.

90.16 Poconackit] Pokanoket, a Wampanoag homeland, led by Ousamequin.

90.17 two Kings] Two Wampanoag leaders, perhaps including Ousamequin.

90.22 Mastachusit] Massachusett homeland, to the north.

91.34 Sawahquatooke] Probably Msoakwtok, on the Saco River, in Wabanaki homelands.

91.35 Manamock] Manomet, a Wampanoag homeland, south of Patuxet, on Cape Cod.

92.12 Epinew] Epenow, a Wampanoag man from Noepe who had been taken captive by Captain Edward Harlow in 1611. After spending time in England with Sir Ferdinando Gorges, he escaped from his captors on a return voyage to Noepe in 1614 commanded by Nicholas Hobson.

93.17 Kecoughtan] In Virginia, near what is now Hampton Roads.

96.12–13 *Manida*, *Skettwarroes*, and *Tasquantum*] Wabanaki men taken captive by Weymouth in 1605 and given to Gorges. Tasquantum is not to be confused with the Patuxet Wampanoag man Tisquantum (Gorges may be conflating the two men here).

98.5   Lord Chief Justice *Popham*] Sir John Popham (1531–1607) was Speaker of the House of Commons, 1580–83, attorney-general, 1581–92, and the lord chief justice, 1592–1607. He was a principal member of the Plymouth Company, along with Ferdinando Gorges, and his nephew, George Popham.

98.9   *Captaine* Prin] Martin Pring (c. 1580–1626), an English explorer who led an expedition to Wabanaki and Wampanoag homelands in 1603. He returned to Wabanaki territory in 1606, to explore prospects for colonial settlement, following on Weymouth's report and guided by Dehanda and Skettawares, who had been taken captive by Weymouth.

99.3   Sir *Thomas Gates*, Sir *George Summers*] Sir Thomas Gates (d. 1622) and Sir George Somers (1554–1610) were shipwrecked in Bermuda while sailing on the *Sea Venture* to the Jamestown Colony in July 1609. After spending ten months on the island, they arrived at Jamestown in May 1610 at the end of the "starving time" in which hundreds of colonists died of hunger and disease or were killed by Powhatan warriors, as part of a strategy to expel the English colonists after initial attempts by the Powhatan leader Wahunsonacock to incorporate the English into his paramount chieftaincy were rejected. Gates decided to abandon the colony, but as the surviving settlers sailed down the James River, they met three ships carrying Lord De La Warr, the new governor, and 150 new colonists. Gates served as the lieutenant governor of Jamestown, 1611–14, while Somers died during a return voyage to Bermuda.

99.20–22   Captain *Popham* . . . *Rawley Gilbert*] George Popham (c. 1550–1608), nephew of Sir John Popham and member of the Plymouth Company. Raleigh Gilbert (c. 1580–1634), nephew of Sir Walter Ralegh and son of Humphrey Gilbert (1539–1583), who was lost at sea after leading an expedition to Newfoundland.

99.26   their Rendezvouz] Sagadahoc, at the mouth of the Kennebec River, in Wabanaki territory.

99.37   *Sassenow, Aberemet*] Sasanoa, a Wabanaki sôgamô of the Kennebec River. Champlain referred to him as Sasinou and said that following his death, he was succeeded by his son, Pememem. He is also mentioned in *A Relation of a Voyage to Sagadahoc, 1607–8*, attributed to James Davies, as "the Chief Commander to the westward." The Sasanoa River, which connects the Kennebec and Sheepscot Rivers, was likely named for him. Aberemet, a Wabanaki sôgamô, probably from the Kennebec River or nearby.

100.1   *Bashabas*] See note 15.40.

101.6   heard of the Sir *John Gilbert*] Possibly a setting error for "heard of the death of Sir John Gilbert." John Gilbert (c. 1572–1608), older brother of Raleigh Gilbert, died in London on July 5, 1608.

101.12   Sir *Francis Popham*] See note 48.30.

102.18   *Vines*] Richard Vines (c. 1597–1651), an English explorer and colonist. Ferdinando Gorges sent Vines to explore land Gorges had claimed in New England.

102.27   the War] Penobscot author Joseph Nicolar (1827–1894) wrote in *The
Life and Traditions of the Red Man* (1893) that an unusual conflict among
Wabanaki spiritual leaders led to a war that coincided with the arrival of
European ships and disease, part of the "fog" which overcame the land
during this time. The violence was also exacerbated by the fur trade and the
introduction of guns, as well as by disruptions in trade and diplomacy. For
example, Mi'kmaq raiders, coming from a climate where planting was not
possible, took corn by force from Patucket and Massachusett communities
to the south.

104.18   *Assacumet*] Assacomet, or Sassacomoit, a Wabanaki man from the
Kennebec River region, one of those taken captive by Weymouth in 1605
and held by Gorges. He sailed with the expedition led by Henry Challoung
in 1606, survived capture by the Spanish, and was "recovered" by Gorges.
The language difference between Epenow and Sassacomoit was significant;
Sassacomoit would have spoken what linguists classify as Eastern Abenaki,
which is related to Wôpanâak but distinct from it.

107.22   *Captain* Dormer] Thomas Dermer (d. 1620), the explorer with
whom Tisquantum returned to his homeland, and who observed the effects
of epidemics in Native communities. He led expeditions in 1619 and 1620,
sponsored by Ferdinando Gorges, and recounted the capture of Tisquantum
and others in a 1619 letter.

108.4–5   from *Sagadahock* . . . to *Capawike*] The Plymouth Company had
initially set its sights on Sagadahoc, the Kennebec River and surrounding
coast, for a settlement, but knowledge gained from Epenow's captivity and
Dermer's voyage helped turn its gaze toward Wampanoag territory.

108.12   *Nautican*] Probably Nauset, Wampanoag homeland on Cape Cod.

PLYMOUTH PLANTATION IN PATUXET

114.2   Mr. *J. P.*] John Peirce, one of the stockholders or investors in Plymouth Colony. He obtained a patent in 1621 giving the Plymouth settlers permission from King James I to settle in what the patent called the "Country
of New England."

114.36   *R.C.*] Robert Cushman (1577–1625), a member of the Separatist congregation in Leiden, became the chief agent for the Plymouth settlers in their
dealings with the Adventurers (investors) who financed the colony. Cushman
arrived at Plymouth on the *Fortune* in November 1621 and left for England a
few weeks later, carrying with him the manuscript of *A Relation*.

115.38   G. Mourt] Probably a reference to George Morton (c. 1585–1624),
William Bradford's brother-in-law, who arrived in Plymouth in 1623 and died
there the following year. Nathaniel Morton (c. 1613–1685), his son, was raised
by Bradford and later served as secretary of the Plymouth Court and wrote a
history of the colony, *New-Englands Memoriall* (1669).

119.20   J. R.] John Robinson (c. 1575–1625), a clergyman in the Church of England who became a Separatist. He moved to the Netherlands in 1609 and served as pastor to the Separatist congregation in Leiden that contained many of the Plymouth settlers. Robinson remained in the Netherlands during the settlement of Plymouth Colony and died in Leiden.

122.35   *Miles Standish*] Standish (c. 1584–1656), a resident of the colonial settlement of Duxbury in Wampanoag territory, was military advisor for Plymouth Colony, leader of its militia, and, in 1653, deputy governor. He had previously fought against the Spanish in the Netherlands.

122.36–37   *Stephen Hopkins*, and *Edward Tilley*] Hopkins (1581–1644), a London merchant believed to be the same Stephen Hopkins who was a colonist bound for Jamestown on the *Sea Venture* when it wrecked in Bermuda in 1609 (see note 99.3) and who spent several years in the Jamestown Colony before returning to England; Tilley (1588–1621), a *Mayflower* passenger and a member of the Leiden congregation, who served as an advisor to Myles Standish, died in the first winter at Plymouth.

123.29   a deepe Valley] East Harbor, on Wampanoag lands on Cape Cod.

123.30   wood-gaile] Bog myrtle or sweet gale.

124.21   Vines] Grapevines.

124.23   new gotten] Recently harvested.

125.32   Spritt] Sapling.

126.28   scurvey] Scurvy, a disease caused by vitamin C deficiency. The settlers did not know that some of the trees found in the region could supply the needed nutrient.

127.9   *Cold Harbour*] Some scholars identify this river as the Pamet River, on Wampanoag lands on Cape Cod.

127.40   Wheat-eares] Ears of corn.

128.34   resolved to digge it up] Although the writer treats this act casually, disturbing a grave was a major violation of Wampanoag spiritual values and common Indigenous culture.

129.3   fine yellow haire] The body the colonists found may have been that of one of the Frenchmen known to have traded with Wampanoag peoples in the early seventeenth century.

129.11–12   fine white Beads] Probably wampumpeag or wampum, the ceremonial beads made of quahog and whelk shells that Wampanoag and other Native people wove into strings and belts and used for diplomacy and collective history. For the Wampanoag and other Indigenous nations, wampum symbolized alliance, bonds, and words pledged in council. The English also used wampum as currency.

131.28–29 *Anguum* or *Angoum*] Probably Agawam, now also Ipswich, Massachusetts.

131.40–132.1 good harbour . . . this Bay] Patuxet, or Plymouth Harbor.

132.8 Mistris *White*] Susanna White (c. 1592–after 1654) married Edward Winslow in May 1621 after the deaths of William White in February and Elizabeth Winslow in March.

132.11 one of *Francis Billingtons Sonnes*] Francis Billington (c. 1606–1684) was the younger son of John Billington (c. 1580–1630), who was later hanged at Plymouth for the murder of John Newcomen.

132.25 Maister *Carver*] John Carver (d. 1621), first governor of Plymouth Colony.

132.26 *John Tilley, Edward Tilley, John Houland*] John Tilley (c. 1571–1620/1621) was a member of the Separatist community in Leiden; his brother Edward Tilley, see note 122.36–37; John Howland (c. 1592–1672/3) traveled to Plymouth as an indentured servant in John Carver's household, later became a freeman, established a trading post in Wabanaki lands on the Kennebec River, and served as a deputy in the Plymouth General Court.

132.27–30 *Richard Warren* . . . Master *Clarke*] Richard Warren (c. 1578–1628), a financial backer of the Plymouth Colony; Stephen Hopkins, see note 122.36–37; Edward Doty (c. 1599–1655), a servant to Hopkins who later became a landowner in the colony. John Alderton, Thomas English, and Richard Clarke all died in the winter of 1620–21.

133.8 a Bay] Wellfleet Bay, in the Nauset homeland.

135.24–25 *Indians, Indians*] Wampanoag men from Nauset. Samoset later relayed that the defensive reaction to the English settlers at Nauset arose from Thomas Hunt's earlier capture of their kin.

135.28 snaphance] An early type of flintlock musket or pistol.

137.8 the Harbour] Patuxet, Plymouth Harbor.

138.7 Skote] Skate.

138.24 Carvell] Chervil.

140.11–12 Good wife *Alderton*] Mary Allerton (c. 1590–1621), a member of the Leiden congregation and the wife of Isaac Allerton (c. 1586–1659).

141.39 Master *Marten*] Christopher Martin (c. 1582–1620), one of the Plymouth settlers who died during the first winter.

142.35 huckle-bone] Hip bone.

147.20–21 presented himself a *Savage*] Samoset (d. 1653), a Wabanaki leader from Pemaquid who interacted with European fishing crews in the early seventeenth century and welcomed the Plymouth settlers in their own language, playing a diplomatic role.

147.26 *Monchiggon*] See note 48.5.

148.17 the *Masasoits*] That is, Samoset returned to the homeland of Ousamequin, the Wampanoag sôtyum at Pokanoket. Massasoit is a title meaning great or supreme leader, but the settlers clearly misunderstood this as a name of a neighboring people. Patuxet and Pokanoket were part of the greater Wampanoag territory.

148.19 *Nausites*] Wampanoag people at Nauset.

148.30 *Hunt*] Thomas Hunt, the explorer and captain with John Smith's expedition who in 1614 captured Tisquantum and twenty-six other Wampanoag men to sell as slaves.

150.26 *Squanto*] Tisquantum (d. 1622), a Patuxet Wampanoag man called Squanto by the English, who was taken captive by Thomas Hunt in 1614 and lived in England for a few years before returning to his homelands and finding that his community had been hard hit by diseases likely transmitted by colonists. Tisquantum was one of the men Ousamequin appointed as a translator for the Plymouth colonists.

150.29 *John Slanie*] Also spelled Slaney, a London merchant who was treasurer of the Newfoundland Company.

150.33 *Quadequina*] A Wampanoag counselor, Ousamequin's brother.

152.16 white bone Beades] See note 129.11–12.

153.13–14 ground Nuts] A tuber or small potato, commonly harvested in the spring.

154.20 coat, of red Cotton] A symbolic gift that recognized leadership.

155.9 *Paomet*] See note 52.22–23.

155.25 *Namaschet*] See note 90.14.

156.9 *Namascheucks*] People of Nemasket. The suffix, ending in -k, denotes the people of a place in the plural. The writers of *A Relation* add an "-s" to match English spelling conventions.

156.14–15 houses they had none] The English visitors may not have seen houses in this particular location, and some Wampanoag people may have enjoyed sleeping outdoors, but the people at Nemasket certainly had houses available for sleeping during the summer.

159.32 *Tokamahamon*] A Wampanoag man whom Ousamequin appointed as a messenger and diplomat to the Plymouth settlers.

161.3 seeke a Boy] John Billington (c. 1604–between 1627 and 1630), the son of an elder John Billington, who was also one of the Plymouth settlers.

161.13   *Cummaquid*] Wampanoag homeland on Cape Cod.

161.26–27   Iyanough] Also Ianough, Wampanoag sôtyum of Cummaquid, on Cape Cod.

162.26   *Maramoick*] See note 52.22–23.

164.12   *Coubatant*] Conbitant, also spelled Corbitant, Wampanoag sôtyum of Pocasset and the father of Weetamoo. His primary residence was at Mattapoisett in Pocasset territory (now Gardner's Neck, Swansea, Massachusetts).

165.33   *Neensquaes*] This is an Anglicized spelling of a Wôpanâak word referring to a young woman or girl. The boys were likely talking about the young women in the house, not saying they were women. "Squa" or "-skwa" was not the Wôpanâak word for woman, but rather a suffix denoting female. As a noun used to describe an Indian woman, it became a derogatory word in the English language, and a racial slur.

165.35   *Towam*] Neetôp would be the Wôpanâak word for "my friend," Neetôpâak for "my friends."

167.5   Massachusets] The people of the Massachusett homeland, in Massachusetts Bay. Winslow correctly identifies the relationships between the names of people and the names of places, by identifying both Massachusett and Narragansett people as "the people of that place." Winslow adds the English "s" to make "Massachusett" plural in his language.

167.28–29   *Obbatinewat*] Probably the Massachusett sôtyum known as Obtakiest or Chickataubut.

167.32   *Tarentines*] See note 62.30. In conflicts that arose in the wake of European trade and epidemics, Mi'kmaq people raided Massachusett communities for corn.

167.32   *Squa Sachim*, or *Massachusets* Queene] The sôkushqâ of Massachusett, whose primary residence was on the Missitekw or Mystic River, was also the mother of several neighboring sôtyumâak. She was part of a network of alliances formed after the epidemics of 1616–19. Her name was not recorded by English writers. "Squa Sachim" or "Sachim-squa" is an English adaptation of sôkushqâ, female leader. This was not a term that referred to Native "queens" or to the wives of male leaders. The English misused and misunderstood the word in Wôpanâak and other Algonquian languages, in which the suffix "skwa" denotes female. It is not a suffix that conveys less power. For example, awassoskwa means "bear woman" in the Western Abenaki language, a word that conveys the great power of female bears. The English later adopted "squa" as a derogatory word for Native women, and in the United States, this word is used as a racial slur.

167.38   the Bay] Massachusetts Bay.

168.10   *Nanepashemet*] Patucket leader (d. 1619) and husband to the Massachusett sôkushqâ. He was killed by Mi'kmaq raiders.

169.17   two Rivers] Missitekw, or Mystic River, and Charles River. This was the territory of the sôkushqâ of Massachusett.

171.39   Othus] An apparent setting error in the 1622 first printing of *A Relation.*

172.5   Damsen] Raspberries.

173.31   E. W.] Edward Winslow (1595–1655).

180.7–8   *Take thou . . . the left*] Cf. Genesis 13:9.

180.26   *Paul* and *Barnabas*] Cf. Acts 15:36–41.

183.26   *John Bellamie*] Bellamie (c. 1596–1653) was printer for several works on English colonization, including the 1622 *A Relation or Journal of the Beginning and Proceedings of the English Plantation Settled at Plimoth in New England.*

186.21   *my private friends*] Probably John Robinson (see note 119.20), as well as investors in the colony.

186.23   *disorderly Colony*] Thomas Weston's colony at Wessagusset on Massachusett lands near what is now Weymouth, Massachusetts.

187.24   *Conanacus*] Canonicus (d. 1647), Narragansett sachem who allowed Roger Williams to establish the settlement of Providence in Narragansett territory.

187.25   *Tokamahamon*] See note 159.32.

187.26   *Tisquantum*] See note 150.26.

187.30   Governours] William Bradford (c. 1590–1657) was governor; Isaac Allerton (c. 1586–1658) was his assistant.

188.8   his Master] Canonicus, see note 187.24.

190.8   *Hobbamock*] A trusted Wampanoag advisor whom Ousamequin sent to live with the Plymouth colonists. He translated in meetings between the colonists and Native emissaries and brought information to and from Ousamequin.

191.11   *Gurnets nose*] Now Gurnet Point, Massachusetts, in Plymouth Harbor.

191.19   *Massassowat*] Ousamequin (d. 1661), sôtyum of Pokanoket, and Metacom's father. Massassoit is a term referring to the Wampanoag great leader's title.

191.20   *Conbatant* our feared enemy] Conbatant, see note 164.12. The Plymouth colonists suspected that Conbatant was making plans to ally with the Narragansetts against them, although their suspicions were largely based on hearsay and their own fears.

192.9   *Puckanokick*] See note 90.16.

194.17   brabbles] A noisy dispute or quarrel.

197.3   their Masters] Thomas Weston (1584–c. 1647) was a London merchant who helped finance Plymouth Colony and organized the Plymouth colonists' voyage to Wampanoag lands, including hiring the *Mayflower* and organizing additional settlers to accompany the thirty-five Separatists from Leiden. Weston later financed a second colony at Wessagussett, on Massachusett lands near what is now Weymouth, Massachusetts.

197.17   our Surgeon] Samuel Fuller (1580–1633), one of the members of the Leiden congregation and Plymouth colonists. Fuller served as a lay physician to the Plymouth settlers during their first years, although he apparently had no medical training.

197.29   Captain *Jones*] Possibly Christopher Jones (c. 1570–c. 1622), the pilot of the *Mayflower*.

197.40   trucking stuff] Goods for trading.

199.1   *Manamoycke*] See note 52.22–23.

200.11   the *Sachim*] The Wampanoag sôtyum Aspinet.

200.13   *Mattachiest*] Wampanoag homeland, between what are now Barnstable and Yarmouth harbors on Cape Cod.

202.6   *Namasket . . . Manomet*] Nemasket, see note 90.14. Winslow engaged in trade there, including corn grown by Wampanoag women; Manomet, see note 91.35.

202.23   *Canacum*] Also Cawnacome, Wampanoag sôtyum at Manomet.

203.5   *Powah*] As Winslow notes, powahs were of "special note" among Wampanoag and other Native nations; they were advisors, sometimes healers and spiritual leaders. The colonists' description of powahs as people who communicated with the devil was a projection of their own beliefs.

203.35–36   the *Sachims* house] Since Standish was at Mattachiest, this may be the sôtyum Ianough.

204.27   *Wituwamat*] Wituwamat was a Massachusett pniese, a warrior-counselor.

205.8   *Ianough*] See note 161.26–27.

205.19   *Paomet*] See note 52.22–23.

206.37   *Mattapuyst*] Mattapoisett, Conbitant's community, now also Gardner's Neck in Swansea, Massachusetts.

207.29–30   *Squa-sachim*] This is a mistranslation for sôkushqâ, a female leader. The woman referred to is the wife of Conbitant and the mother of

Weetamoo and Wootonakanuske. Weetamoo succeeded Conbitant as the primary leader of Pocasset.

208.11 *Winsnow*] Wampanoags pronounced Winslow's name with an "n" as there is no "l" in the Wôpanâak language, and neighboring languages used "l" in place of "n" in their dialects.

211.23–24 *Nauset . . . Agowaywam*] Wampanoag towns along Cape Cod.

211.24 Ile of *Capawack*] Noepe (Martha's Vineyard).

212.5 *Sawaams*] Sowams, Wampanoag homeland within Pokanoket territory, residence of Ousamequin and Wamsutta.

214.9 *Ferdi: Gorges*] See note 77.36.

217.4 one of Mr. *Westons* Company] Phenehas Pratt.

219.29 *Pecksuot*] A Massachusett pniese; his name is also spelled Peckworth, Pexworth, and Pexsouth in colonial documents.

222.35 *Obtakiest*] See note 167.28–29.

227.4 *David Tomson*] Tomson (1593–1628) worked for Ferdinando Gorges; he settled in 1623 at Piscataqua, on Wabanaki lands.

228.33 therein I erred] In *A Relation* Winslow had claimed that Native people had no religion.

229.15 they call *Hobbamock*] Not to be confused with the Wampanoag advisor named Hobbomock. Note that Winslow is simplifying complex spiritual figures and dualities. Hobbamock was a transformative being, and not equivalent to the Christian "devil."

230.35–36 kill children] No evidence exists that northeastern Native people killed children as part of their ceremonies. Winslow may be drawing on earlier colonial reports that made unsubstantiated claims about Native people.

231.36 Sentry] Centaury, a bitter herb.

233.33 slavish life] This stereotype is common in settler reports of Native women, from the seventeenth to the nineteenth century. Since planting was the work of men in English society and they generally believed women were weaker than men, Winslow portrays Wampanoag women's planting as "slavish" labor and portrays their ability to carry their own loads as burdensome. Indigenous oral narratives, in contrast, associate women's ability to grow and harvest corn with strength, motherhood, and birth.

234.24 adultery] It is unclear from where Winslow derives this belief, as Wampanoag women, like men, could take multiple partners.

236.26 *Mohegon*] Muhhekunnutuk, Mohican River, or Hudson River.

236.31 *Powhatan*] Name used by the colonists in Virginia for Wahunsenacawh

(d. c. 1618), the werowance (leader) of the Powhatans when Jamestown was established.

240.32 *two former printed books*] *A briefe Relation of the Discovery and Plantation of New England: and of sundry accidents therein occuring, from the yeere of our Lord M. D.C. VII. To this present M. D.C. XXII., Together with the state thereof as now it standeth the generall forme of government intended; and the division of the whole Territorie into Counties, Baronries, &c.* (London: 1622), printed with a dedicatory epistle signed by the "President and Council for New England"; the book has been attributed to Ferdinando Gorges. *A Relation or Journall of the beginnings and proceedings of the English Plantation settled at Plimoth in New England* (London: 1622), see pp. 113–81.

241.14 that bloody slaughter] The March 1622 attack of Powhatan people on Jamestown that killed more than 300 colonists.

241.21 *Opachancano*] Opachancano (d. 1646), also spelled Opechanca-nough, was the brother of Wahunsenacawh and succeeded him as werowance of the Powhatans.

245.11–12 Indescret men ... writ Letters] Pratt may be referring to *A Relation*.

245.18 Thomas Westorne] See note 197.3.

245.22 Damoralls Cove] Probably the Damariscove Islands. See note 65.25.

245.25–29 Mr. Rodgers ... Gibbs] Rogers and Gibbs were sailors on the *Sparrow*, the ship that brought Weston's men to Plymouth, but they do not appear to have remained as settlers.

245.34 Capt Mason] John Mason (1586–1635), a settler and explorer of Wabanaki lands in Mi'kmaq territory, or Newfoundland, where he served as the appointed governor, 1615–21. He received, along with Ferdinando Gorges, a Council of New England patent for Abenaki lands, which became New Hampshire Colony.

246.21 Pennesses] Pnieseoak, the Wôpanâak word for the people, often war-riors, who advised sôtyumâak and sôkushqâak.

247.28 thayr Sacham] Probably Chickataubut (see note 167.28–29.).

247.35 Matchet] An Algonquian word meaning "bad."

251.6 James Ryver] Jones River, in Patuxet, now Kingston, Massachusetts.

252.6 10 or 11 men] This group of men was led by Myles Standish.

252.10 Wittiwomitt] Wituwamat, see note 204.27.

252.16 Hobermack] Hobbamock, see note 190.8. Pratt errs here in saying that Hobbomock fled for his life.

253.7   Capt. Wooliston] Richard Wollaston (d. 1626) established a settlement and trading post on Massachusett lands, naming it Mount Wollaston. Most of the settlers were indentured servants.

256.12–13   As witneseth Socrates] The Greek ecclesiastical historian Socrates (c. 380–c. 450), whose history of the Christian church from 305 to 439 was one of three works translated into English by Meredith Hanmer (1543–1604) as *The Auncient Ecclesiastical Histories of the First Six Hundred Years After Christ* (1577).

256.28   queene Mary] Mary I (1516–1558), queen of England, 1553–58, who attempted to restore the Roman Catholic Church in England.

257.1   Mr. Foxe] John Foxe (1516/17–1587), author of *Actes and Monuments of these Latter and Perillous Days, Touching Matters of the Church* (1563), popularly known as *Foxe's Book of Martyrs.*

259.3   *Mr. Perkins*] William Perkins (1558–1602), a theologian and clergyman in the Church of England. Bradford quotes here from Perkins's *A Faithfull and Plaine Exposition upon the 2. chapter of* Zephaniah (1605).

260.11   Jebusites] A Canaanite tribe.

260.15   Anakimes] In the Hebrew Bible, warriors who inhabited the mountains of Judea before being driven out by Joshua.

262.8   John Smith] John Smyth (d. 1612), a Baptist minister who established a church in Amsterdam in 1608 and was known to the Separatists led by John Robinson.

267.24   Mr. Robinson] See note 119.20.

267.24   Mr. Brewster] William Brewster (1566/57–1644), the Plymouth settlers' ruling (lay) church elder in Leiden who later fulfilled many ministerial duties in Plymouth.

269.22   Taborits to find another Ziska] Jan Žižka (1376–1424) was a military commander who led the Hussites in Bohemia against the Holy Roman Empire. The Taborites were a militant Hussite sect who fought under Žižka until his death from the plague in 1424.

270.38   Episcopius] Simon Bisschop (1583–1643), a Dutch theologian who was professor at Leiden, 1612–19.

272.13–14   As Orpah did her mother-in-law Naomie] In the book of Ruth, Orpah, the daughter-in-law of Naomi, returns to her people after the death of her husband, unlike her sister-in-law Ruth, who remains with Naomi.

274.29   other cruelties] It is not clear exactly which travel narrative Bradford is drawing from here, but he is probably relying on stories about the Americas circulated by Spanish explorers and the English translators who brought their works into print. These accounts often relied on existing stories about non-European people and places, rather than on firsthand experience, to describe Indigenous people.

276.1   Guiana] See note 24.16–17.

276.2   some parts of Virginia] In the early seventeenth century, the English colony of Virginia was defined by patents as extending over unceded Indigenous lands from the Chesapeake Bay north to the Great Lakes.

277.11   one of his cheefe secretaries] Robert Naunton (1563–1635), an English politician who served as a secretary of state under James I, 1618–23.

278.13   *Edwin Sands*] Sir Edwin Sandys (1561–1629), a member of the Virginia Company starting in 1607 and an investor in the East India Company.

278.16   Robert Cushman] See note 114.36.

278.16   John Carver] See note 132.25.

280.27   *John Worssenham*] John Wolstenholme (1562–1639), a merchant who was one of the directors of the East India Company and a member of the Virginia Council starting in 1624.

283.7   Mr. B.] Probably William Brewster. See note 267.24.

283.33   Captaine Argoll] Samuel Argall (d. 1626), a merchant who served as governor of the Virginia colony, 1617–19. Argall made many voyages between London and Virginia, and it was on one of these voyages in 1613 that he kidnapped the Powhatan girl Matoaka, also called Pocahontas, and brought her back to Jamestown.

283.34   George Yeardley] Sir George Yeardley (1588–1627), governor of the Virginia colony from 1619 until 1621.

283.36   Mr. Blackwell] Francis Blackwell (d. 1618/19), an exiled English separatist who sailed for the Virginia colony in 1618 but died at sea during the journey.

285.26–27   brother Maistersone] Richard Masterson.

285.31   Lord Cooke] Sir Edward Coke (1552–1634), a jurist and politician.

286.16   SABIN STARESMORE] A London Separatist who joined Robinson's Leiden congregation.

288.1   Thomas Weston] See note 197.3.

289.28   adventurers] Those who financially invested in Plymouth Colony.

291.4   Mr. Pickering] Edward Pickering, a merchant and member of the Leiden congregation.

291.28   Georg Morton] See note 115.38.

292.32   Mr. Nash] Thomas Nash, a member of the Leiden congregation.

293.36   S.F. E.W. W.B. I.A.] Samuel Fuller (c. 1580–1633), see note 197.17; Edward Winslow (1595–1655); William Bradford (1590–1657); Isaac Allerton (c. 1586–1659). Allerton was assistant to John Carver during his governorship and traveled to London throughout the 1620s to negotiate with and make payments to the Plymouth investors.

294.11   Georg Farrer and his brother] It is possible that Cushman was referring to John Ferrar (c. 1588–1657) and his brother Nicholas Ferrar (1593–1637), both merchants involved with the Virginia Company.

295.24   like Jonas to Tarshis] See Jonah 1:1–3.

296.25   John Turner] Turner (c. 1590–1620) was a merchant and Plymouth colonist who died in the winter of 1620.

297.12   Mr. *Reinholds*] Reynolds, the master of the *Speedwell*.

298.4   Mr. Martin] See note 141.39.

300.25   they knew they were pilgrimes] Cf. Hebrews 11.13.

302.34   Mr. Peirce] See note 114.2.

302.37   Mr. Mullins] William Mullins (d. 1621) was one of the Plymouth colonists who died in the first winter.

309.5   Gedions armie] See Judges 7.

310.2   Ed: S] Edward Southworth, a member of the Leiden congregation who died in 1621. Alice Carpenter Southworth, his widow, married William Bradford in 1623, and his sons Constant and Thomas Southworth were among the Plymouth settlers.

311.35   Nehemiah] Cf. Nehemiah 1.

311.37   Rehoboams braggs] See I Kings 1–12.

314.5   John Howland] See note 132.26.

314.34   Capten Gosnole] Bartholomew Gosnold (c. 1572–1607), a colonial promoter and explorer. Gosnold traveled to Wampanoag lands on what is now Cape Cod and Wabanaki lands in what is now Maine in the early seventeenth century. He died at Jamestown.

314.35   Cape James] Now Cape Cod, in Wampanoag homelands.

315.8–10   wise Seneca . . . affirmed] Lucius Annaeus Seneca (4 BCE–65 CE), the Roman Stoic philosopher, in his Epistle 53.

315.21–22   apostle and his shipwraked company] Cf. Acts 27–28.

315.33   Pisgah] The mountain from which Moses viewed the Promised Land in Deuteronomy 34:1–4.

317.21   espied ·5· or ·6· persons] Cape Cod is on Wampanoag lands, so the colonists likely saw Wampanoag people.

318.25   like the men from Eshcoll] See Numbers 13:23–26.

321.21   Mr. Coppin] Robert Coppin, pilot and one of the master's mates aboard the *Mayflower*.

323.14–15   patente they had being for Virginia] The Plymouth settlers landed outside the jurisdiction of the Virginia Company and in the area falling under the jurisdiction of the newly formed Council for New England. The company's claims to Wampanoag lands were fictional, for Wampanoag leaders retained sovereignty over their lands.

326.8   the Indians came skulking] These "Indians" were probably Wampanoag or Massachusett men investigating the arrival of the settlers.

326.12   certaine Indian] Samoset, see note 147.26.

326.31–32   *Massasoyt*] See note 191.19.

327.20   *Hunt*] See note 148.30.

327.24   *Dermer*] See note 107.22.

327.25   Sir Ferdinando Gorges] See note 77.36.

327.28   Counsell for New-England] The Council for New England was formed in 1620 with a royal charter to colonize the northern parts of what had previously been referred to as Virginia.

328.6   *Pocanawkits*] The Wampanoag people of Pokanoket (see note 90.16). Here, Bradford may have been erroneously conflating Pokanoket with Wampanoag.

328.8   Penobscote] Penobscot territory, in Wabanaki homelands.

328.19   *Saughtughtett*] Satucket, a fishing place within Wampanoag territory, west of Patuxet/Plymouth and Duxbury. This town was later named Bridgewater by English colonists. Satucket is also the name of a river that flows into the Matfield River, which then joins with the Town River to form the Taunton River.

328.23   *Massachusets*] The homeland of Massachusett people, not Massachusetts Bay Colony, which did not exist in 1620.

328.28   *Manamoiak*] Monamoit, a Wampanoag homeland. Now also Chatham, Massachusetts.

328.35–36   Ile of *Capawack*] See note 64.39.

329.20   *Powachs*] See note 203.5.

331.36   Mr. Hopkins] See note 122.36–37.

332.15 John Billington] See note 161.3.

332.36 Corbitant] See note 164.12.

333.34 to the Massachusets] The Massachusett people lived to the north of Plymouth/Patuxet and Pokanoket. Massachusett is a place-name within the larger Dawnland, and its people had kinship ties to Wampanoag homelands.

338.22–23 put forth in printe . . . Mr. Winslow] In *Good News from New England* (1624).

341.13–14 *Mr. Beachamp*] John Beauchamp (1592–1655), a key sponsor and investor of Plymouth Colony.

341.37 St. James speaks of] Cf. James 2:15–16.

347.44 William Trevore] William Trevor, a man who accompanied the Plymouth colonists as a hired laborer, most likely a seaman.

349.39 JOHN HUDLESTON] John Huddleston (d. c. 1624), a ship's captain who supplied the Virginia colony.

351.17 John Poory] John Pory (1572–1636), an assistant to Richard Hakluyt, the collector and publisher of colonial travel narratives in the early seventeenth century, served as the secretary of the Jamestown Colony under Governor George Yeardly, 1619–21. Pory visited Plymouth in 1622 while returning to England from Virginia.

351.24 Ainsworths] Henry Ainsworth (1569–1622), a Separatist minister in Amsterdam who published an annotated translation of the five books of Moses in 1619.

351.37 Mr. Westons people] The colonists funded by Weston established a small settlement at Wessagusset, in the Massachusett homeland.

354.24 one of them] Phenehas Pratt (c. 1593–1680), one of the Wessagusset colonists. See pp. 244–54 in this volume.

355.27 Pascataquack] See note 52.22–23.

358.4 Peter Martire] Peter Martyr d'Anghiera (1457–1526), an Italian historian of Spanish voyages to the Americas. His collections of narratives and letters related to these travels, published in Latin from 1511 to 1530, were translated into English as *The Decades of the newe worlde or west India* (1555) by Richard Eden (c. 1520–1576).

361.15–16 Captaine Francis West] Francis West (1586–1634), who served as commander at Jamestown, 1612–17, and as governor of the Virginia colony, 1627–29.

367.14–15 Robart Gorges] Robert Gorges (b. 1595), a son of the colonial investor Ferdinando Gorges, was appointed governor-general of New

England by the Council for New England in 1623. He is believed to have died in the late 1620s.

367.21   Christopher Levite] Christopher Levett (1586–1630), author of *A Voyage into New England* (1624). Levett was hosted by Wabanaki leaders and formed a settlement at their invitation, according to his narrative, in what is now Maine. He was a member of the Council for New England and was named governor of Plymouth by the council in 1623.

371.9   Mr. Morell] William Morrell (fl. 1611–1625) was a poet and clergyman who accompanied Robert Gorges with a commission to administer the churches in Gorges's colony. After his return to England Morrell published a poem based on his observations, *New-England, or, A briefe narration of the eyre, earth, water, fish, and fowles of that country, with a description of the natures, orders, habits and religion of the natives; in Latine and English verse* (1625).

371.18   David Thomson] David Thompson (c. 1587–1627) was an associate of John Mason and Ferdinando Gorges, who established a small colony on the Piscataqua River in Wabanaki territory.

375.10   JAMES SHERLEY] Sherley was treasurer and business agent for the Plymouth Colony in London, where he managed the colony's financial affairs.

379.7   killing of those poor Indeans] Standish's killing of seven Massachusett men in spring 1623, in response to rumors that they were planning to attack Plymouth and Wessagusset.

381.7   *Consilium capere in arena*] Latin: Make a plan in the arena. The saying is taken from Seneca, epistle 22, describing how a gladiator must respond to the immediate situation facing him.

383.35–36   John Lyford] Lyford (c. 1574–1629) was a minister sent to Plymouth Colony by its investors.

384.26   Mr. John Oldom] John Oldham (1592–1636), a trader who joined with John Lyford in disagreement with some of the Plymouth Separatists' policies. He also proved a key figure in the events leading up to the Pequot War.

392.9   Billington] Probably the elder John Billington (c. 1579–1630), not his sons John and Francis.

396.16   Jaacob and Laban] See Genesis 29.

400.24   Pequente warr] Colonial histories claimed that the main cause of the Pequot War (1636–38) was the killing of the English merchants John Oldham in 1636 and John Stone in 1634, obfuscating the fact that Stone was killed in retaliation for the execution by the Dutch of the Pequot sachem Tatobem, and that the Pequots had attempted to use diplomacy to resolve their conflicts with the English colonists.

403.19–21 Natasco . . . Namkeke] Coastal areas in Massachusett territory, now Hull and Salem, Massachusetts, respectively.

404.17 Brownists] Followers of Robert Brown (c. 1550–1633), who led a Separatist movement in Norwich in the 1580s.

407.25 Methusala] Cf. Genesis 5:21–27, where Methuselah is said to have lived 969 years.

407.30 J.S. W.C. T.F. R.H.] James Sherley, see note 375.10; William Collier (c. 1585–1670); Thomas Fletcher; and Robert Holland (1557–1622). Collier was another financial backer of Plymouth Colony in England. Holland was an Anglican clergyman and religious writer.

408.11 Sabastians] San Sebastian, in Spain.

411.29 new-king Charles] See note 41.2.

413.16 Sacadahock] See note 52.18–21.

422.8 Manamet] See note 91.35.

424.12 ISAAK DE RASIERE] Rasiers (b. 1595) was a trading agent for the Dutch East Indies Company and secretary of the New Netherland Colony.

428.1–2 Mr. *Goffe*] Thomas Goffe was a London merchant and investor in Plymouth Colony.

428.22 Mr. Andrews] Either Thomas or Richard Andrews, both merchant investors in Plymouth Colony.

432.23 Manonscussett] Also known as Scusset, a place within the Wampanoag homeland of Manomet, also now part of Sandwich, Massachusetts. Scusset Creek flowed into Cape Cod Bay and was separated by a short portage from the Manomet River, which flowed into Buzzards Bay. Plymouth settlers sometimes used this route to avoid having to navigate around Cape Cod, and in the twentieth century the two rivers were widened and joined to form the Cape Cod Canal.

432.33 Wampampeake] See note 129.11–12.

432.35 forte Orania] Fort Orange, built in the Mohican homeland on the site where Albany, New York, would later be established.

433.37 Captaine Wolastone] See note 253.7.

434.4–5 Mr. Morton] Thomas Morton (1580–1647), the author of *New English Canaan* (1637).

434.20 Furneffells Inne] One of the Inns of Chancery in London, buildings that contained residences, offices, and dining clubs for attorneys.

435.18 John Indecott] John Endecott (d. 1665) settled on Massachusett lands near what is now Salem, Massachusetts, just prior to the arrival of colonists who formed Massachusetts Bay Colony in 1630.

441.7 it was the Lords doing] Cf. Psalm 118:23.

441.28 Mr. Hatherley] Timothy Hatherly (1588–1666), one of the merchant adventurers, settled in Scituate in 1634 and served as an Assistant in the Plymouth General Court, 1651–58.

442.30 karsey] A coarse woolen cloth.

444.12 *Earle of Warwick*] Robert Rich, Earl of Warwick (1587–1658), president of the Council for New England.

444.20 Festus said to Paule] Cf. Acts 22:28. The speaker is not Porcius Festus, the procurator of Judea, but Claudius Lysias, the commander of the Roman garrison in Jerusalem.

448.20 Edward Ashley] Ashley (d. c. 1632) made several trips to North America, where he sometimes traded with Wabanaki people at Penobscot.

454.33 A bishop must be blamles] Cf. I Timothy 3:2.

454.35 What should let from being baptised] Cf. Acts 8:6.

454.38–39 Skelton] Samuel Skelton (1592–1634), the first pastor of the First Church of Salem, Massachusetts.

454.39 Higginson] Francis Higginson (1586–1630) served as the assistant to Skelton in the First Church of Salem. He is the author of *New-Englands plantation* (1630).

462.29 Mr. Winthrop] John Winthrop (1588–1649), first governor of Massachusetts Bay Colony.

463.4 Mr. Johnson] Isaac Johnson (1601–1630), a member of the group of settlers who traveled with Winthrop on the *Arbella*.

463.37 Mr. Dudley] Thomas Dudley (1576–1653), father of the poet Anne Bradstreet (1612–1672).

463.37 Mr. Willson] John Wilson (1588–1667), a minister in Boston who traveled to the colony in 1630.

463.40–41 Mr. Cottington] William Coddington (1601–1678), a 1630 settler and merchant who was elected an assistant (magistrate) of Massachusetts Bay Colony and later served as governor of Rhode Island, 1674–76.

476.29 *Josias Winslow*] Josiah Winslow (1628–1680), Assistant and deputy from Marshfield, son of Edward Winslow, and governor of Plymouth Colony, 1673–1680, including the duration of King Philip's War.

476.32–33 Christopher Gardener . . . Bishop of Winchester] Gardener (1596–1662), also spelled Gardiner, was an agent of Ferdinando Gorges. He claimed to be a relative of Stephen Gardiner (1483–1555), Bishop of Winchester, 1531–51 and 1553–55, and lord chancellor under Queen Mary, 1553–55.

478.32   Captaine Masson] See note 245.34.

482.9   Mr. *Mahue*] Thomas Mayhew (1593–1682), a merchant who came to the Massachusetts Bay Colony in 1631. Mayhew later settled on Wampanoag lands on Noepe (Martha's Vineyard) after receiving a title to the lands in 1641. His sons were missionaries to Wampanoag people, learning Wôpanâak in the process.

483.36–37   Greens Harbor] Currently Marshfield, Massachusetts.

488.10   Roger Williams] Williams (c. 1603–1683) later established Rhode Island Colony in 1636 on Narragansett lands, with Wampanoag and Narragansett permission. He also learned the Narragansett and Wôpanâak languages well enough to serve as a translator.

489.3   banishte Indeans] The Mohegan nation, who made the decision to split from the Pequots over the question of how to interact with English settlers. The Mohegan sachem Uncas argued for alliances with the English, a course that future Mohegan sachems followed as a strategy for maintaining their lands in the northeast.

491.5   Thomas Blossome, Richard Masterson] Both men had traveled from Leiden to Plymouth in the late 1620s.

491.33   Thomas Prence] Thomas Prence (c. 1600–1673), assistant governor of Plymouth Colony, 1632–33, 1635–37, and 1639–1656; governor of Plymouth Colony, 1657–1673.

492.15–16   patente as gives them right . . . Kenebeck] This patent is from January 1630.

493.1   cheefe of the place] John Howland, see note 132.26.

494.4   Mr. Alden] John Alden (c. 1599–1687), a cooper and one of the Plymouth colonists in 1620. Alden served as a Plymouth Colony Assistant, settler of Duxbury, and father of Jonathan Alden.

501.22   Captaine Stone] John Stone (c. 1580–1634), a trader in New England, Virginia, and the West Indies.

501.32   *Als't u beleeft*] Dutch: As you please.

502.19   the Indeans knoct him] Massachusetts Bay colonists claimed that Pequots had killed Stone and his crew and used the event to justify starting the Pequot War. Some scholars argue that Stone was killed by Niantics, not Pequots, while others contend that Pequot men killed Stone in response to the Tatobem, one of their sachems, by the Dutch.

508.2   Monsier de Aulnay] Charles de Menou d'Aunay Charnisay (c. 1604–1650), who fished in Abenaki waters and in 1635 settled on Abenaki lands in an attempt to secure French claims to the region.

523.14   Mr. Vane] Sir Henry Vane (1613–1662) was governor of Massachusetts Bay Colony, 1636–37. He supported Roger Williams's creation of Rhode
Island Colony. After his return to England Vane became a Parliamentary
leader during the Civil War and Commonwealth and was executed for treason
early in the reign of Charles II.

529.36   the wife . . . Mononotto] Mononotto was a Pequot sachem.

530.27–28   Monhiggs] Mohegans, formerly united with the Pequots.

535.32   Sityate] Scituate, Massachusetts.

539.23   Old comers] Those people in the first group of colonists at Plymouth.

542.25–26   John Atwode] Atwood (1576–1644) was treasurer of Plymouth
Colony, 1641–44.

547.24   Charles Chansey] Charles Chauncy (1592–1672), who later served as
the second president of Harvard College, 1654–72.

547.27   John Reinor] John Reyner (c. 1605–1669), minister at Plymouth,
1636–54.

551.6   The note inclosed . . . other side] The note from Richard Bellingham
is missing from the extant manuscript of *Of Plimoth Plantation*. It referred to
the case of Dorcas Humfrey, a nine-year-old girl living in Salem. In October
1641 Dorcas accused Daniel Fairfield, Jenkin Davis, and John Hudson of
repeatedly sexually assaulting her. The three men confessed to abusing Dorcas
but denied "entrance of her body." Because there was no civil law in Massachusetts Bay specifically addressing the offenses the men had admitted to,
the colonial authorities consulted with ministers regarding the appropriate
biblical punishment. In June 1642 the three men were fined and sentenced to
be "severely whipped" in Boston and Salem. Daniel Fairfield, who had also
been found guilty of sexually abusing Sarah Humfrey, Dorcas's younger sister,
was also punished by having his nostrils "slit and seared."

552.17   cum penetratione corporis] Latin: with bodily penetration.

552.20–21   contactus . . . effusionem seminis] Latin: contact and friction with
effusion of seed.

553.8–9   Nemo tenetur prodere seipsum] Latin: No one is bound to accuse
himself.

554.7–8   per modum concubitus] Latin: by lying together.

554.12   similitudo concubitus muliebris] Latin: like lying with a woman.

554.41   subesse falsum] Latin: be falsehoods.

555.5–6   An contactus et . . . morte plectenda?] Latin: Should contact and
friction to the point of emitting seed, without bodily penetration, constitute
sodomy punishable by death?

555.18–24 Luther, Tom. 1 . . . Piscat:] Chauncey cites writings by Protestant theologians Martin Luther (1483–1546), Philip Melanchthon (1497–1560), Jean Calvin (1509–1564), Francis Junius (1545–1602), Heinrich Bullinger (1504–1575), Wolfgang Musculus (1497–1563), Martin Bucer (1491–1551), Theodore de Beza (1519–1605), Girolamo Zanchi (1516–1590), Zacharias Ursnus (1534–1583), and Johann Piscator (1497–1560).

555.36 P. Martire] Italian-born Protestant theologian Peter Martyr Vermigli (1488–1562).

556.23 retegere pudenda . . . per euphemismum] Latin: to reveal one's shame; by euphemism.

556.24 detegere ad cubandum] Probably a copying error for "detergere ad concumbendum." Latin: to uncover nakedness for carnal purposes.

556.30 ἀρσενοκοῖται] Greek: those who burn, i.e., sodomites.

556.34–35 omnes modos . . . abutatur] Latin: all the ways in which a man can improperly use a man.

556.36 arogare sibi cubare] Latin: to arrogate sexual intercourse for oneself.

556.38–39 ob solum contiē] Latin: only by undertaking.

556.41–43 In crimine adulterii . . . de jure attenditur] Latin: In the crime of adultery, desire, regardless of its fulfillment, is what legally matters.

556.43–557.5 Solicitations alienum . . . et horum similibus] Latin: Those who make attempts on marriages and seduce wives, even when they do not succeed at their crime, are still given an exceptional punishment because of their destructive lust. For while desire without result generally is not punished, the opposite is done in the most terrible sort of crimes.

557.8 paribus similibus, minore ad majus] Latin: things being equal, the lesser to the greater.

557.18–21 beluina crudelitas quam . . . occisus est] Latin: bestial cruelty God regards the same as parricide. For to corrupt one's seed, what is that but killing the man the seed should have generated? Therefore, it was just that God slew him.

557.21–23 Discamus quantopere . . . et corruptionem] Latin: Let us learn how God abhors all corruption, illicit effusion, and wasting of seed.

557.33 contra naturam] Latin: against nature.

557.36 a pari] Latin: by parity.

557.38 Circumstantiæ variant vis e actuines] Possibly a copying error for the Latin phrase "circumstantiæ variant res et actiones": circumstances alter cases and actions.

558.6 perditio seminis] Latin: wasted discharge.

573.30   Daniell . . . liking with pulse] See Daniel 1:5–16. Pulse here refers to legumes such as peas, beans, and lentils.

573.31   Jaacob . . . one nation] See Psalm 105.

580.8   Uncass] Uncas (1598–1683), a Mohegan sachem.

580.16   Myantinomo] Miantonomo (d. 1643), a Narragansett sachem, who led an effort to unite Native peoples living around the Long Island Sound.

582.37   Uncaway] A town later known as Fairfield, Connecticut.

585.24   Mowacks] Mohawks, or Kanienkehaka, one of the nations of the Haudenosaunee (Iroquois) Confederacy.

590.1   Pessecuss] Pessicus (1623–1676), a Narragansett leader and the younger brother of Miantonimo, later known as Sucquansh and Canonicus.

590.1   Innemo] Also spelled Janemo, and also called Ninigret (c. 1610–1677), a Niantic and Narragansett sachem and brother of Quaiapin.

591.14   Ossamequine, Pumham, Sokananoke, Cutshamakin] Ousamequin, see note 191.19; Pumham (d. 1676) was a Narragansett sachem at Shawomet; Sokananoke was sachem at Pawtuxet; Cutshamakin (d. 1654) was sachem of Neponset.

594.40–595.1   Samuell Gorton] was a minister who settled at Shawomet (Warwick, in Rhode Island Colony) after being tried for heterodoxy in Massachusetts Bay. He obtained Narragansett lands through means the sachem Pumham claimed were dishonest.

596.1   ANNO ·1647· . . . ·1648·] Bradford wrote this heading on page 270 of the manuscript; the remainder of the page is blank.

596.2   *The names of those which came over first*] It is believed that Bradford wrote this list of the passengers on the *Mayflower* in 1650.

TRANSNATIONAL DIPLOMACY:
COUNCILS AND DEEDS BETWEEN INDIGENOUS LEADERS
AND SETTLERS FROM PLYMOUTH COLONY

607.2   *Court of Assistances*] A group of freemen elected to govern the colony. The Court included William Bradford, the governor, as well as Edward Winslow (1595–1655) and John Brown (1584–1662), Assistants, who represented Plymouth in the Seekonk council.

607.11   John Hassell] John Hazell (d. 1651), a settler who was living at Seekonk in 1642. Here he gave testimony as a witness to the original verbal council and agreement at Seekonk. Hazell was allowed to remain at Seekonk, with permission of the Plymouth Court, if he formally pledged his allegiance to the government of Plymouth Colony and to the King of England. Hazell represented a number of settlers living in Wampanoag territory who did not necessarily regard themselves as members of the Separatist faction at Plymouth, or under their jurisdiction. It is useful to recall that the government of Plymouth was relatively new and precarious at this time.

607.11–12   x fathome of beads] Ten fathoms (units) of wampum strings, representing the diplomatic agreement made at Seekonk, and the Plymouth settlers' acknowledgment of Ousamequin's leadership in Wampanoag homelands, including his own territory of Pokanoket. Although wampum had diplomatic and ceremonial symbolism and significance for Native communities, for the English wampum also served as a local currency.

607.12   Mr Williams] Roger Williams served as a host and interpreter for this council. See note 488.10.

607.14   Seacunck] Seekonk, a Wampanoag homeland within Pokanoket territory, under Ousamequin's jurisdiction. Seekonk is just east of the Seekonk River, a waterway that joins (or divides) Wampanoag and Narragansett territories. Plymouth colonists who settled in Seekonk, under this agreement, later named their town Rehoboth, which expanded through a series of deeds.

607.17   Redstone Hill] A place within Seekonk and a distinctive marker for the bounds of the agreement.

607.17   viii miles] Eight miles, referring to the eight miles square that was supposed to be the original size of the English settlement within Seekonk, and specifically the imagined line from the Seekonk River inland.

607.18   Annawamscoate] Annawomscutt, a Wampanoag planting peninsula within the Pokanoket homeland, east of the Seekonk River and south of the Seekonk/Rehoboth settlement of Wannamoisett, now part of Barrington, Rhode Island.

607.18   vii miles] Seven miles down Seekonk River, referring to the eastern bounds.

609.6–7   Miles Standish . . . Constant Southworth] Myles Standish (1584–1656), see note 122.35; Samuel Nash (c. 1602–1682), Plymouth settler and military officer, resident of the colonial settlement of Duxbury, in Wampanoag territory; Constant Southworth (c. 1614–1679), Plymouth Colony treasurer and Assistant, deputy from Duxbury in Wampanoag territory, stepson of the elder William Bradford and brother of Thomas Southworth and the younger William Bradford.

609.9   Satucket] See note 328.19.

609.10   wear] A fishing weir.

609.25   John Bradford] John Bradford (c. 1617–1678), Plymouth settler, son of William Bradford.

609.26   Wm. Otway (alias) Parker] William Parker, alias Otway (1599–1662), Plymouth Colony settler.

610.6   Moose Skins] The Plymouth men would have acquired moose hides through trade with Wabanaki people to the north, probably on the Kennebec River. William Bradford had obtained for Plymouth from England a patent for land on the Kennebec River, in Wabanaki territory, for the purpose of the fur trade.

612.4   Nabor Sachims] Neighboring sôtyumâak (sachems, in Anglicized spelling), male leaders who are related by kinship and in neighboring homelands within Wampanoag territory.

612.5   wequequinequa] A relative of Namumpum (Weetamoo), in Pocasset. Some have suggested this could be Weetamoo's first husband, but it also could be another male relative.

612.6   Nummampaum] Namumpum, later Weetamoo (c. 1630–1676), Wampanoag sôkushqâ of Pocasset, a Wampanoag homeland.

612.6   Squa Sachim] See note 167.32.

612.8   Rood Eyland] Rhode Island, referring here to Aquidneck Island, where the English town of Pocasset, renamed Portsmouth, was located. This settlement was established, with permission of the Narragansetts and Wampanoags, when Anne Hutchinson and her adherents were banished from Massachusetts Bay Colony.

612.9   Richard morris] Richard Morris (c. 1595–1672), a Rhode Island settler to whom Wequequinequa and Namumpum gave permission to use land on Nonaquaket for grazing his cattle. Morris was later called before the Plymouth Court to submit to Plymouth Colony's authority in order to uphold the "purchase" he made "of the Indians" at Nonaquaket. Morris also served as captain of the military company at Portsmouth in Rhode Island Colony.

612.11   Nunequoquit or Pogasek Neck] Nonaquaket, a Wampanoag peninsula within the Pocasset homeland, including coastal marsh and planting grounds. The English called this area Pocasset Neck. This area later became part of Tiverton, Rhode Island.

612.25   my brothars dafter] My brother's daughter. Ousamequin is referring to his kinship relationship with Namumpum (Weetamoo) and her father Conbitant. He does not mean that Conbitant is his biological brother (sons of same mother and father) but his relation in the same generation.

612.31   porchmoth] Portsmouth was an English town in Rhode Island Colony, in Narragansett territory.

613.5   WAMSUTTA] Wamsutta, or Alexander (d. 1662), Wampanoag sôtyum of Pokanoket, son of Ousamequin and husband to Weetamoo, sôkushqâ of Pocasset.

613.6   TASOMOCKON] Tuspaquin (d. 1676), sôtyum of Nemasket, a neighboring Wampanoag homeland, and kin to Ousamequin and Weetamoo. He was married to Ousamequin's daughter, Amie.

615.14   Mr Bradford] William Bradford (c. 1590–1657), governor of Plymouth Colony.

615.14–15   Mr Prence] See note 491.33.

615.32   two or three places] Two or three tracts of land within Wampanoag territory, which were later selected.

616.8   No more Plantacions erected] The Governor and Assistants were declaring that no more settlements or land grants should be made in Plymouth Colony until the Old Comers selected their two or three tracts.

616.25   Yarmouth] An English town on Cape Cod, in Wampanoag territory.

616.26   Naemskeckett] Namskaket (Orleans), a Wampanoag fishing place on Cape Cod, within the Nauset homeland.

616.27–28   Acconquesse, alias Acokcus] Acoaxet, a Wampanoag homeland east of Sakonnet, now Westport, Massachusetts. Includes Acoaxet River (Westport River), which flows into what is now Westport Harbor.

616.29   Pynt Perrill] Point Peril, a peninsula near the mouth of Acoaxet River, now Gooseberry Neck in Westport.

616.30   Acquissent River] Acushnet River, in the Wampanoag homeland. Also referred to as Cusheningg.

616.33–34   Sowamset River . . . Causumpsit Neck] Sowams River, now Warren River, with the east and west branches now called Palmer River and Barrington River; Patucket River, a waterway that formed a boundary between Wampanoag and Narragansett territories, now Blackstone River in Patucket, Rhode Island; Causumpsit Neck, a large peninsula in Pokanoket Wampanoag territory, which included Montaup.

619.4   Nathaniell Sowther] Nathaniel Souther (1607–1655), first secretary of Plymouth Colony.

619.16   Atquiod, alias, Aquiatt] A peninsula within Wampanoag territory, on Cape Cod.

619.22   Massatanpaine] A Wampanoag sôtyum.

619.28   Barnestable] Barnstable, an English town on Cape Cod, in Wampanoag territory.

621.35   Thomas Southworth John Winslow John Cooke] Thomas Southworth (c. 1617–1669), Plymouth Colony Assistant, stepson of William Bradford, and brother to Constant Southworth; John Winslow (1597–1674), deputy to Court from town of Plymouth, brother to Edward Winslow; John

Cooke or Cook (c. 1607–1695), deputy and selectman from the town of Plymouth. Cook was one of the original grantees for the settlement of Dartmouth, and later a deputy to Plymouth Court from Dartmouth.

622.23   Wampam] See note 129.11–12.

622.32   Sowams] See note 212.5.

623.4   Thomas Willett] Thomas Willett (c. 1608–1674), Assistant, captain of Plymouth Colony military company, resident of Rehoboth, son-in-law of John Brown, settled Wannamoisett (in Pokanoket territory) with John Brown, part of Rehoboth's expansion.

623.5   Josiah Winslow] See note 476.29.

623.15–16   Thomas Clarke . . . Experience Mitchell] Thomas Clark (c. 1599–1697), deputy to Court from the town of Plymouth, 1651 and 1655; William White (1642–1695), the son of Resolved White (c. 1615–c. 1687), who was Josiah Winslow's half-brother and an Old Comer, the son of William White (1587–1621) and Susanna (nee Jackson) Winslow. William White later lived with Josiah Winslow in Marshfield; John Adams (1627–1704), Plymouth Colony settler and son of John Adams (d. 1633), an Old Comer; Experience Mitchell (c. 1603–1689), Plymouth Colony settler and resident of Duxbury.

623.20   Sinckuncke alias Rehoboth] See note 607.14.

623.21   Mosskituash] A brook, leading into Providence River and Bullocks Cove.

623.24   the great River] Sowams River, see note 616.33–34.

623.29   Chachacust] A planting peninsula, also known as New Meadow Neck, now part of Barrington, Rhode Island. Land, by the "Sowams and Parts Adjacent" deed of 1653, that was reserved to Wampanoags, unless they "removed" from it. By the 1660s, Rehoboth settlers, and their cattle, were encroaching upon the reserved lands.

623.30   Papasquash Necke] A small peninsula extending from Montaup, now known as Poppasquash Neck or Point in Bristol, Rhode Island.

623.31   Keecomewett] Kickemuit, a Wampanoag planting peninsula within Pokanoket territory, now part of Warren, Rhode Island.

624.12–13   John Browne James Browne Richard Garrett] John Brown (1584–1662), an Assistant and Rehoboth resident, father-in-law of Thomas Willett; James Brown (c. 1619–1710), a colonist who lived in Rehoboth, in Wampanoag territory, and served Plymouth Colony as an Assistant, a deputy, and, on the eve of war, a messenger to Metacom. He was the son of John Brown, Sr., who participated in the original Seekonk agreement; Richard Garrett (1611–c. 1662), Plymouth Colony settler, resident of Scituate.

624.19 Thomas Hinkley] Thomas Hinckley (1618–1706), Plymouth Colony settler and Assistant, who held an interest in Sakonnet land; last governor of Plymouth Colony, 1680–92.

626.6 Capt: James Cudworth] Major James Cudworth (c. 1612–1682), Plymouth Colony military officer and Assistant, commander of Plymouth forces during King Philip's War.

626.7–8 John Barnes] John Barnes (d. c. 1671), tavern keeper and trader in Plymouth.

626.9 graunted by the Court of Plymouth] The court granted the land, but the grantees had to acquire consent from the Wampanoag leader whose jurisdiction the land was in. They sought Wamsutta's consent, but the land was in Weetamoo's territory of Pocasset. The Court in December 1657 included Governor Thomas Prence, and Josiah Winslow, James Cudworth, Thomas Southworth, John Alden, Thomas Willet, William Collyar, and Timothy Hatherley, Assistants.

626.17–20 Quequetham . . . Wepoisett River] Quequequachand, the river of falls that was at the center of Pocasset, known also as Falls River; Assonet Neck, an ancient planting peninsula in Pocasset territory and Wampanoag stronghold that Plymouth Colony claimed by conquest in 1676; Sebadecauson or Tabadacauson (also Tabadacanson or Tebadecauson), a Wampanoag man who represented a group of people who lived on Assonet Neck and kept a canoe ferry, for the crossing of Kteticut or Taunton River; Taunton, a Plymouth Colony town in Wampanoag territory that became a military center during King Philip's War; Weyposet, a river in Pocasset territory, in the Showamet homeland.

627.10 John Tisdall] A Plymouth Colony settler, constable, and selectman in Taunton, Freemen's deed grantee.

627.11 John Sasamon] John Sassamon (d. 1675), a Massachusett man who was raised as a servant in an English colonist's home and became a translator for the Massachusetts Bay colonists. Sassamon's name appeared on multiple deeds, as witness or interpreter, in Plymouth, Massachusetts Bay, and Rhode Island colonies. Colonists and later historians cited his death early in 1675 (see Chronology) as a primary cause of King Philip's War, although other factors played a role, such as the increasingly expansive land claims Plymouth and Massachusetts Bay colonists were making on Wampanoag lands.

627.17 Tatapanum] Weetamoo, see note 612.6.

627.20–27 James Cudworth . . . John Waterman] James Cudworth, see note 626.6; Josiah Winslow, see note 476.29; Constant Southworth, see note 609.6–7; John Barnes (d. c. 1671), tavern keeper and trader in Plymouth; John Tisdall, see note 627.10; Humphrey Turner (d. c. 1673), Plymouth Colony

settler, a former deputy to Plymouth Court from the town of Scituate whose
lot was sold by his son to Benjamin Church after King Philip's War; Walter
Hatch (1625–1699), Plymouth Colony settler who resided in Scituate, son
of William Hatch; Samuel House, Jr. (1610–1661), Plymouth Colony settler,
resided in Scituate, his share of the Freemen's grant was inherited by his sons,
Samuel III and Joseph House; Samuel Jackson (d. 1682), Plymouth Colony
settler, resided in Scituate; John Damon or Daman (c. 1621–c. 1677), Plymouth Colony settler, resided in Scituate; Timothy Hatherly, see note 441.28;
Timothy Foster (1640–1688), Plymouth Colony settler, resided in Scituate,
son of Edward Foster; Thomas Southworth, see note 621.35; George Watson
(c. 1602–1689), Plymouth Colony settler, resided in the town of Plymouth;
Nathaniel Morton, see note 115.38; Richard Moore, Plymouth Colony settler,
resided in the town of Duxbury; Edmund Chandler (d. 1662), Plymouth
Colony settler, resided in Duxbury; Samuel Nash, see note 609.6–7; Henry
Howland (c. 1599–1673), Plymouth Colony settler, resided in Duxbury, former
servant of Governor John Carver; Ralph Partridge (c. 1579–1658), Plymouth
Colony settler, first minister of Duxbury; Love Brewster (c. 1611–1650) was a
Plymouth Colony settler who resided in Duxbury and whose lot was inherited
by his son, Wrestling Brewster; William Peabody (c. 1620–1707), deputy to
Plymouth Court from Duxbury; Christopher Wadsworth (c. 1609–1677),
Plymouth Colony settler, resided in Duxbury; Kenelm Winslow (1599–1672),
Plymouth Colony settler, resided in the town of Marshfield and was brother
of Edward Winslow; Thomas Bourne (1581–1664), Plymouth Colony settler,
resided in Marshfield; John Waterman (1642–1718), Plymouth Colony settler,
resided in Marshfield. Almost none of the freemen listed in this deed ever
lived on the lots allotted to them by the deed.

627.35   Stacyes Creeke] Mastucksett brook or Stacey's creek, a brook that
flows into the Assonet River from the north side of Assonet Bay.

629.12   Thomas Cooke Jonathan Briggs] Thomas Cook (c. 1600–1677),
Rhode Island settler, resided in Portsmouth; Jonathan Briggs (1635–1689),
Plymouth Colony settler, resided in Taunton.

630.4   Annawamscutt] See note 607.18.

632.7   King Philip] Metacom or Philip (d. 1676), the Wampanoag sôtyum of
Pokanoket, whose main residence was at Montaup, or Mount Hope.

632.8   Tom] A Native man who served as an interpreter for Metacom, perhaps the scribe for this letter.

632.9   Philip sister] Perhaps Philip's sister, Amie, who lived at Nemasket.

632.12   Engians] Indians.

632.18–19   mount hope nek] Montaup, or Mount Hope, a peninsula and
stronghold in Pokanoket territory where Metacom, or Philip, resided before
King Philip's War. Now in Bristol and (partially) Warren, Rhode Island.

632.24   Awashonks] Awashonks, leader of Sakonnet, a Wampanoag homeland.

633.13   Mr. Almy] John Almy (d. c. 1676), a colonist who lived in Plymouth and Rhode Island colonies. He was a witness to the agreements made between the Plymouth leaders and Awashonks, the Sakonnet leader, in 1671. Almy had a house and field in Weetamoo's territory of Pocasset, the site of the "pease field" battle at Pocasset in the summer of 1675.

633.28   Mr. H.] Thomas Hinckley, see note 624.19.

633.28   Mr. Southworth] Constant Southworth (see note 609.6–7), who held an interest in Sakonnet land, was commissary for the planned military expedition on Awashonks and her land. The threat of this expedition prompted Awashonks to come into Plymouth Court and sign "tenders of peace" on July 24, 1671.

634.1–2   your two sons] Awashonks's sons, Mammanuah and Peter Awashonks. Mammanuah undermined Awashonks's leadership, seeking the title of sôtyum for himself, and conspired with Plymouth settlers, including Southworth, to sell Sakonnet lands to Plymouth Colony. Peter remained loyal to her and testified on behalf of Sakonnet people at the end of the war.

634.3   your brother] Awashonks's brother, Tatacomuncah, of Sakonnet, who supported her leadership.

WRITINGS ABOUT THE BROADER WAMPANOAG AND MASSACHUSETT HOMELANDS

639.8   Isquouterquashes] Askootasquash, a variation on an Algonquian word for squash, also asquash, of which there were multiple varieties.

639.14   Peneriall] Pennyroyal.

639.17   Bilberies] Although "bilberries" grew in Europe, Wood is likely referring to blueberries, which are similar.

639.18   Hurtleberries] Likely referring to huckleberries.

639.30   *Spaniards* blisse] Gold.

640.36   Osiers] Osier, a tree, probably a willow tree, or perhaps red osier dogwood.

643.2–3   Horne-bound tree] American hornbeam, also known as blue beech or musclewood.

647.33   *Spanish* progge] A pole weapon with straight and curved blades.

648.3   *Aramouse*] Aremos or alemos, word for "dog" in "r" or "l" dialects of Eastern Algonquian languages (see note 208.11).

649.7   malepart] Probably malapert, a saucy person.

649.17   *Democrite . . . Heraclite*] Democritus, the Greek philosopher from the fifth century B.C.E. known as "the laughing philosopher," and Heraclitus, also a fifth century B.C.E. Greek philosopher, known as "the weeping philosopher."

650.16   tectonists] Builders.

651.21   flagges] Reeds or rushes, including cattails.

651.24   protractures] Designs, shapes.

651.25   quarter] One fourth of a peck, i.e., about 2.4 quarts.

651.39   passeboard] Navel.

652.12–13   milde carriage and obedience] Wood's description of Indigenous women as obedient and subservient reflects English stereotypes. Indigenous women were responsible for planting, labor that in English was gendered as male, leading English colonists to portray Indigenous women as doing service and labor (assuming it was for their husbands), as Wood does here. Likewise, his description of Indigenous men as characterized by "savage inhumanity" reflects stereotypes of Indigenous people as not fully human.

652.26   *pares cum paribus congregatæ*] Latin: equals gathered with equals.

652.33   love to the *English*] Wood may be mistaking trade and diplomatic protocols for "love."

655.5   *Canaan*] In the Hebrew Bible, the promised land for the children of Israel.

655.21   Cliffords Inne] One of the Inns of Chancery; see note 434.20.

656.2–3   his Majesties] See note 41.2.

659.1   Christoffer Gardiner] See note 476.32–33.

659.10   *mint and Cummin*] See Matthew 23:23.

660.16   *Cyrus*] Cyrus II (c. 600–530 BCE), king of Persia, also known as Cyrus the Great.

660.21   *sacrifice of Kain*] See Genesis 4:2–5.

662.20–21   proud like Nebuchadnezar] See Daniel 4:29–33.

662.21   despaire like Jobs wife] See Job 2:9.

662.24   venenum] Latin: poison.

662.27   *Inimica naturæ*] Latin: Natural enemy.

663.21   Tornathees] Hurricanes.

663.35–36   Grashoppers . . . Ant and Bee] In Aesop's fables the ant and the bee store up food for the winter, while the grasshopper goes hungry because it fails to prepare.

663.37–38   Captaine Davis] Morton confused John Davis with Henry Hudson (c. 1565–1611), who in 1610 spent a winter near the bay to which he gave his name, Hudson Bay.

664.13–15   *Impiger . . . per ignes*] Latin: Ardent trader that you are, you rush to the furthest Indies, fleeing poverty through sea, through rocks, through flame. Horace, *Satires, Epistles, and Ars Poetica*, I.1.45–46, trans. H. Rushton Fairclough (1929).

664.16   as Salomon saith] Cf. Ecclesiastes 2:18–19.

665.2–3   *Sol & Homo . . . hominem*] Latin: The sun shapes a man.

666.28–29   use very many wordes . . . Latine] Morton's interest in Indigenous languages in this section participates in a broader European project to investigate the origins of Indigenous people. Believing that all people originated from one creation located in "Old World," seventeenth-century Europeans struggled to explain Indigenous peoples' origins. Native people have their own origin stories placing their emergence in the Americas.

669.1   gould of Ophir] Cf. 1 Kings 9:28.

669.20   David Tompson] Thompson (d. 1628), an English associate of John Mason and Ferdinando Gorges, who established a small colony in Wabanaki territory on the Piscataqua River.

670.1   Anckies] Probably auks, a diving bird.

671.4   wild Irish] English writers and travelers frequently compared Native and Irish people, drawing on English conceptions of cultural difference to describe Native people.

672.21–23   Cicero . . . Tully] Roman philosopher and politician Marcus Tullius Cicero (106–43 B.C.E.).

672.33–34   *sine fide, sine lege, & sine rege*] Latin: without trust, without law, without king.

673.4   Thomas May] May (c. 1596–1650) was an English poet and dramatist.

676.11–12   *nan weeto . . . squaa*] Morton's translations of these phrases are incorrect, attributing crude meanings to the words.

676.34   Powahs] See note 203.5.

677.13   Papasiquineo] Passaconaway, great sachem and spiritual leader of the Pennacook, who collaborated with other Native leaders to renew kinship networks through intermarriage among leadership families in the wake of epidemics.

679.36–38   Sagus . . . Daughter to Papasiquineo] Saugus, part of Winisimet, now also Chelsea, Massachusetts. Montowampate, or "Sagamore James" (d. 1633), son of the Patucket leader Nanepashemet and the Massachusett saunk-skwa, became the sachem of Saugus, and married a daughter of Passaconaway, the Pennacook leader. This marriage was one of many between the sons and daughters of leaders in the region, part of a network of reparative alliances in the wake of the epidemics. Montowampate was brother to Wenepoykin or "Sagamore George," who married Joane Ahawayet, daughter of a Saugus leader, and Wonohaquahan or "Sagamore John," who married a daughter of the Agawam leader, Masconomet. The story relayed by Morton in this chapter is a romanticized fable that reflects English literary genres.

679.38–680.1   territories neare Merrimack River] Patucket and Pennacook homelands, on the river Molôdemak, or Merrimack River.

680.3   Nigromancer] Necromancer, perhaps referencing colonists' belief that the man could communicate with the dead.

683.26   Cheecatawback] See note 167.28–29.

683.37   Wassaguscus] See note 197.3.

684.13–14   not being of power to resist them] Chickataubut's community had recently been decimated by an epidemic.

684.38   furmety] A dish of hulled wheat boiled in milk.

686.29   pricking] Wounding.

687.5   Sir William Alexander] Sir William Alexander (1577–1640), a Scottish poet and politician who received a royal charter to lands that are now Nova Scotia, New Brunswick, and parts of the northern United States.

687.18   Kytan] Although Morton's account of Massachusett beliefs and origin stories is not reliable, he does name Kiehtan, the creator and transfor-mative spiritual figure who is central to Wampanoag and Narragansett oral traditions and ceremonial life, associated with the sun, the upper world, and the arrival of corn from the southwest.

691.21   gallouses] Gallows.

691.27   flowre-de-luce] Fleur-de-lis, a representation of a lily used to indicate north on a compass.

691.34   carking] Worry.

692.2   *sic transit gloria Mundi*] Latin: thus passes the glory of the world.

692.24   Platoes Commonwealth] The ideal society described in Plato's *Republic*.

692.36   *Natura paucis contentat*] Latin: Nature is content with a few things.

694.10   Anno Salutis] Latin: In the year of salvation, dating an event from the birth of Jesus.

694.34   Daphnean-tree] In Greek mythology, Daphne was a daughter of the river. Her father turned her into a laurel tree to keep her safe from Apollo, who was in love with her.

695.16–18   *Non nobis . . . amici vindicant*] Latin: We are born not for ourselves alone; our country, our parents, our friends lay claim to us.

697.21   Garrets herball] Probably John Gerard, *Herbal, or General Historie of Plants* (1597).

704.36   busse] Possibly buff-skin, leather.

705.39   the humbles] The entrails of a deer.

705.40   wesell] Windpipe.

706.19   cunny] Coney, i.e., a rabbit.

707.13–14   Angels of gold] A gold coin issued in England, inscribed with the figure of the Archangel Michael.

707.18   Luseran] Lynx.

709.7   Muskewashe] Muskrat.

709.23   Hedgehoggs] A mistaken identification, as there are no hedgehogs in North America.

710.33   malkin] A cat.

711.39   *Duris in Cotibus illum*] From Virgil's Eclogue VIII: *Nunc scio quid sit Amor: duris in cotibus illum*: "Now I know what love is, amid savage rocks."

713.5   one Harboure] Casco Bay, in Wabanaki territory.

713.27   Marybones] Possibly marrowbones.

714.12   *regalis piscis*] Royal fish.

715.31   Pilchers] Possibly pilchards.

715.31   Michelmas] The season around the feast of St. Michael (September 29).

717.21   Abrahams and Lots] See Genesis 13:5–11.

717.28   Weenasemute] Winisimet, now also Chelsea, Massachusetts.

717.32   Squantos Chappell] Squantum, a peninsula in what is now Quincy, Massachusetts.

718.16   flowes with Milke and Hony] The description of Canaan in Exodus 3:17.

720.8–9   a very spacious Lake] Betobagw, the lake between Wabanaki territory and Haudenosaunee (Iroquois) territory; also known as Lake Champlain. It was sometimes described as the Lake of the Iroquois.

720.10   Lake of Genezereth] The Sea of Galilee.

720.32–33   River of Canada] Morton's understanding of northeastern geography beyond the coast of Massachusetts was limited. He may be referring to the Richelieu River, which flows north from Lake Champlain, or Ktsitekw (St. Lawrence River), the great river, which some English referred to as the Canada River. The association with de Caen is a misnomer.

721.2   Patomack] Morton confuses the Potomac with the Muhhekunnutuk, or Hudson River, which he correctly references later in his text.

721.33   Henry Joseline] Probably Henry Josselyn (1606–1683), a settler at Owascoag in Wabanaki territory and brother to John Josselyn (1608–1675), the author of *New England's Rareties* (1671) and *An Account of Two Voyages to New England* (1674).

722.5   River of Mohegan] See note 236.26.

724.26   *Anastomases*] Possibly a reference to links between two channels.

724.31   *Colcos*] In Greek mythology, the place from where Jason retrieved the Golden Fleece.

725.11   *Sachem of those Territories*] Ousamequin, see note 191.19.

725.20   one that had beene in England] Tisquantum, see note 150.26.

726.6   great mortality] The epidemics of 1616–19.

727.12   defaced the monument of the ded at Pasonagessit] See the account in *A Relation* where the authors describe how Plymouth settlers dug up a grave. Pasonagessit, a Massachusett homeland, now also known as Quincy, Massachusetts, north of Wessagusset. The area was attractive to English settlers because it had long been cleared for planting. Chickataubut was sachem here, but he and other survivors had left this location for another in their homeland after epidemics devastated their families.

727.15   Chuatawbacks mother] Mother of Chickataubut, Massachusett sachem of Neponset, also known as Obtakiest.

728.28   an Indian barne] Corn storage cache, usually underground and covered by woven mats.

728.37   Edward Johnson] This may be an error, as Edward Johnson (1598–1672) is thought to have traveled to Massachusetts Bay Colony in the 1630s.

729.8   Embrion] Embryo.

730.14   Will Sommers] William Sommers (d. 1560), court jester for Henry VIII of England.

731.24   THIS Merchant] Thomas Weston, see note 197.3.

731.37   of their neighbours] Morton probably refers to Phenehas Pratt, who warned the Plymouth settlers of the supposed plot against them.

734.10   *Facilis descensus averni*] Latin: The descent to Avernus [the under-world] is easy.

734.39–40   sparkling neate] Elegant.

735.5   kellecke] A stone used for an anchor.

735.21   MASTER Layford] See note 383.35–36.

735.29   John Oldam] See note 384.26.

736.8   Hanniball . . . Fabius] In the Second Punic War the Roman military commander Quintus Fabius Maximus Verrucosus (c. 280–203 BCE) fought a prolonged campaign of delay and attrition against the Carthaginian army led by Hannibal Barca (247–c. 181).

736.16   Luscus] Latin: One-eyed.

736.32   CHILDREN, and the fruit] See Psalm 127:3.

737.20–21   Bussardes bay] Wampanoag lands on the western side of what is now Cape Cod.

738.13   Master Bubble] Scholars have not identified this person.

738.16–17   Mercuries pipes . . . Argus eyes] In Greek mythology, Hermes (Mercury in Roman mythology) used the music of his pipes to lull the hun-dred-eyed giant Argos to sleep, and then slew him with his sword.

739.6   mine host] Morton himself.

739.11–12   *brevis oratio penetrat Coelum*] Latin: a short prayer reaches heaven.

739.12   Canaw] Possibly canoe.

739.13   Nut Island] A small island in Massachusetts Bay.

739.21   *Sachem*] Probably Chickataubut, see note 167.28–29.

740.26   *Neepenett*] Nipmuc territory, the people of the inland "freshwater" country, now also central Massachusetts. There are many freshwater wetlands in Nipmuc territory, many of which were (and are) made and maintained by beavers.

740.37   Milo] Possibly Milo of Croton, a sixth-century BCE Greek wrestler, said to have carried an ox on his shoulders.

742.28–31   Phillis . . . Demopheon] In Greek mythology, Phillis, a Thracian princess, and Demopheon, the king of Athens, marry, only for Demopheon to leave her to return to Greece.

742.38 Cony katchers] Rabbit catchers.

743.12 Caron] Charon, who ferries souls to Hades.

743.25 *CARMEN ELEGIACUM*] Latin: Verses on Mortality.

743.26 *Melpomene*] The Greek muse of tragedy.

743.32 *Alecto*] One of the Greek Furies.

743.36 *Great Squa Sachem*] Morton is playing on the title of Native female leaders, sôkushqâ, following other English writers who used the term "squa sachem" interchangeably with "Queen." See note 167.32.

744.7 *Satyres whelp*] The offspring of a woodland god.

744.14 fountaine at Ma-re Mount] Morton details Native knowledge of springs and rivers throughout *New English Canaan*, so he may refer to one of those springs here.

744.30–31 festivall day of Philip and Jacob] In early May.

745.20 *Amphitrites Darling*] Aphrodite.

745.22 *Triton*] The merman son of Poseidon and Amphitrite.

745.33 *Esculapius*] God of medicine.

745.36 *Cithareas*] Another name for Venus.

746.3–4 Calfe of Horeb] See Exodus 32:4.

746.5 Mount Dagon] See Judges 16:23.

747.18 tyth of Muit and Cummin] See note 659.10.

747.23 Phaos box] Morton draws from an English translation of Ovid's *Heroides*, in which Venus gives Phaon, an elderly boatman, a box of ointment in payment for ferrying her from Lesbos to Asia Minor. The ointment made Phaon an object of great desire.

748.16 Maja] Maia, in Greek and Roman mythology, one of the Pleiades (daughters of Atlas and Pleione).

750.1 Hippeus] Possibly a pun on Epeus, the name of the Greek soldier who built the wooden horse the Trojans brought into their city.

750.5–6 Geese kept in the Roman Cappitall] In 390 BCE honking geese warned the Romans under siege on the Capitoline Hill of a night attack by the invading Senone Gauls.

750.19 Captaine Shrimp] Morton's name for the Plymouth colonist Myles Standish (c. 1584–1656).

751.5–6 nine Worthies] Medieval art and pageantry often depicted the deeds of a group of nine heroes, generally made up of three Jews from the Bible, three figures from classical antiquity, and three Christian kings.

751.11 Diogenes tubb] The Greek philosopher Diogenes the Cynic (c. 404–323 BCE) was said to have lived in a large ceramic storage jar.

752.35 Eacus] Some scholars have suggested that this is a reference to Samuel Fuller. See note 197.17.

753.16 Sachem of Passonagessit] Chickataubut, see note 167.28–29.

754.1 THE POEM] This poem is modeled on "On the Famous Voyage" (1616) by Ben Jonson (1572–1637).

754.18 *Alcides*] An alternate name for Hercules.

754.35 *Per fas aut nefas*] Latin: By what is proper or improper, i.e., by any means.

754.39 *Lerna Lake to Plutos court*] Lake Lerna in Greece was the legendary home of the Hydra; Pluto is the ruler of the underworld.

755.8 *Cecrops*] The mythical founder of Athens, depicted as having a human upper body and a serpent-like lower body.

755.11 *Minos . . . Radamand*] The judges of the dead in Hades.

755.22–23 *Phaeton . . . Phebus*] In Ovid's *Metamorphoses*, Phaeton asks his father Phoebus, the sun god, for permission to drive the chariot of the sun to prove his divine origin. When Phaeton loses control of the chariot and burns much of Africa, Jupiter intervenes and kills him with a thunderbolt.

756.23 Kynyback] Kennebec River, see note 50.1.

758.10 stile him Doctor] Likely referring to Samuel Fuller. See note 197.17.

759.6 Richard the seconds time] Richard II (1367–1400), king of England, 1377–99.

759.10 silenced Minister] Possibly the Rev. Francis Bright (b. 1602), one of the Massachusetts Company ministers who went to New England in 1629.

759.17 Josua] Morton uses this name to refer to John Winthrop (1588–1649), governor of Massachusetts Bay Colony, 1630–34, 1637–40, 1642–44, and 1646–49.

759.21 Caiphas] Caiaphas (c. 14 BCE–c. 46 CE), a Jewish high priest who, according to the gospels of Matthew and John, charged Jesus with blasphemy and sent him to Pontius Pilate, the Roman governor of Judea, for final judgment.

761.27 Littleworth] Later "Captain Littleworth," Morton's name for John Endicott (c. 1588–1665), governor of the Massachusetts Bay Colony, 1629–30, 1644–45, 1649–50, 1651–54, and 1655–64.

761.31 Master Charter] Matthew Craddock (c. 1590–1641), first governor of Massachusetts Bay Company, 1628–29. Morton also calls him Mathias Charterparty.

762.19   Pastor Master Eager] Samuel Skelton, see note 454.38–39.

765.10   Issacar] Issachar, a son of Jacob and Leah in the Hebrew Bible.

765.15   Israelites . . . Jordan drishod] See Joshua 3.

766.21   Sacrifice of Kain] See note 660.21.

766.24   Epictetus] A Greek Stoic philosopher (c. 50–c. 135 CE).

766.25–26   *ludibria fortunæ*] Latin: the plaything of fortune.

767.5–6   second commandement] The prohibition against making graven images; see Exodus 20:4–6.

767.9   Judas] The disciple who hanged himself after betraying Jesus to the Romans; see Matthew 27:3–5.

769.4   Innocence Fairecloath] Philip Ratcliff, a servant of Matthew Craddock.

770.21   Shackles] This may be either Robert Hale (1606/7–1636) or Ralph Monsall (d. 1657), both deacons.

770.23   Doctor Faustus] Possibly a reference to the play *The Tragical History of the Life and Death of Doctor Faustus* by Christopher Marlowe (1564–1593).

773.23   Lewes the Eleventh] Louis XI (1423–1483), king of France, 1461–83.

773.34   *loquere ut te videam*] Latin: speak so that I may see you.

774.2   Jonas taske] See Jonah 1:1–2, 3:1–10.

774.27   saint George . . . Dragon] According to legend, St. George, the patron saint of England, slew a dragon in North Africa and converted thousands of people to Christianity before being martyred in 303 CE.

775.21   Pithagoras] The Greek philosopher Pythagoras (c. 580–c. 500 BCE) held that the souls of the dying transmigrated into the bodies of the living.

775.38–39   History of Ruth . . . the Elders] See Ruth 4:9–13.

778.4   *statu quo prius*] Latin: the state of things previously.

778.14   Luceus eies] See note 736.16.

778.37   Sub judice lis est] Latin: The case is before the court.

779.23   Machevill] Niccolò Machiavelli (1469–1527), author of *The Prince* (1532).

782.31   S. Michaels] Probably São Miguel in the Azores.

783.25–26   *Cynthius aurem vellet*] Latin: The Cynthian plucked my ear, from Virgil's Eclogue VI.

788.15–16 buried their first five Children] Pamchannit and his wife may have lost their children to the epidemics of European diseases, particularly small-pox, that were devastating to Native communities in the 1630s.

788.21 The Mother] Wuttunnohkomkooh.

789.18 School set up] The school established by Thomas Mayhew, an associ-ate of John Eliot, who worked with Wampanoag men who translated the Bible into Wôpanâak.

789.25 marry'd a Daughter] Sarah Mensoo.

792.14–15 *save others with Fear*] Jude 1:23.

792.17 *lord it over his Flock*] 1 Peter 5:3.

793.20 *every Wind of Doctrine*] Ephesians 4:14.

793.22 godly *Englishman*] Peter Folger (1617–1690), the maternal grandfa-ther of Benjamin Franklin.

795.28 *enjoy me*] To have use of.

798.6 *Tokame*] Also known as Takemmy.

798.12 *Indians* at *Dartmouth*] Dartmouth was an English town established by Plymouth colonists in the Wampanoag territories of Acoaxet, Acushnet, and Apponaganset, and was one of the places to which Native people went for safety after King Philip's War.

799.34–35 *Caleb Cheshchaamog*] Caleb Cheeshateaumuck (d. 1666) was a Wampanoag Harvard Indian College student and the first Native person to graduate from Harvard. He was the son of the sôtyum Cheeschumuck of Nobnocket, also known as Holmes Hole and Vineyard Haven.

799.35 *Harvard* College] The Indian College at Harvard, established in 1655.

800.32–33 *ready to . . . communicate to them*] 1 Timothy 6:18.

801.7–8 *heap Coals . . . that hated them*] See Romans 12:20.

805.8 benefactors] Men in England who provided funding for the mission to the Indians in New England, including funding for the education of Native scholars at Harvard College.

806.13 aquaeducts] Conduits.

808.11 *Gay Head*] Aquinnah, a Wampanoag homeland on Noepe (Martha's Vineyard).

808.17 Moshup] Moshup is a transformative being with great power who is a central figure in Wampanoag oral tradition, including the creation story of Noepe (Martha's Vineyard). See www.wampanoagtribe.org/ancientways, accessed July 8, 2021.

808.32   Seconet] Sakonnet, see note 881.11.

813.3–4   Daniel Gookin ... *New England*] Gookin completed the manuscript of *Historical Collections of the Indians in New England* in 1674, but the work was not published until 1792. The footnotes added by the editor of the 1792 edition appear in italic.

813.34   See the Postscript] In the postscript Gookin outlined his plans for a "History of New England" in eight books. The work was never completed.

816.16   brutish and barbarous] Like other English colonists, Gookin uses European categories for describing difference when discussing Native peoples' marriage practices, divisions of labor, agricultural practices, and more. His descriptions are oriented by large cultural categories rather than individual people and experiences.

818.7   furmenty] See note 684.38.

819.21   great lovers of strong drink] Gookin is generalizing here, transforming observations of a few people into a general characteristic.

823.10   wizards and witches] Like other English colonial writers, Gookin describes non-Christian religious practices in terms of witchcraft.

823.39   Hiacoomes] Hiacoomes (d. 1690) was a Wampanoag man from Nunnepog (Edgartown) on Noepe (Martha's Vineyard) who converted to Christianity and became proficient in English literacy.

824.4   Joel] Joel Hiacoomes (d. 1665) was Hiacoomes's son and, with Caleb Cheeshateaumuck, was one of the Wampanoag scholars at the Harvard Indian College. Joel died in a shipwreck just before his graduation from Harvard.

824.32   Thomas Mayhew junior] Mayhew (1618–1657) grew up on Noepe, learning English and Wôpanâak as a child. Mayhew established a school on the island and carried on the missionary projects his father began.

826.15–16   John Eliot] Eliot (1604–1690) settled in Massachusetts Bay Colony in 1631. He established missions to Native people, creating what colonists called "Praying Towns" for Native converts. With the work of Wampanoag, Massachusett, and Nipmuc scholars, Eliot oversaw a translation of the Bible into Wôpanâak that was printed in 1663 as *Mamusse Wunneetupanatamwe Up-Biblum God*.

826.17   Thomas Weld] Weld (1595–1661) was a minister at Roxbury, Massachusetts Bay Colony, where Eliot was also minister.

827.12   Kuchamakin] Cutshamekin (d. 1654), a Massachusett sachem.

827.14   Waban] Waban (d. 1685), a Nipmuc man and an early convert to Christianity. He was not a traditional leader, but rather rose to an influential position through his relationship to missionaries, his role as an advocate for conversion, and his marriage into a leadership family. Waban lived at Nonantum, now also known as Newton, Massachusetts.

829.30   John . . . Benjamin] John Eliot, Jr. (1635–1668), Joseph Eliot (1638–1694), Samuel Eliot (b. 1641), and Benjamin Eliot (1646–1687) were all sons of John Eliot.

831.20   Bourne] Richard Bourne (1609–1682) was one of the missionaries who joined Eliot in preaching to Native people.

831.22–23   John Cotton] Gookin seems to refer to John Cotton, Jr. (1639–1699), who, like Thomas Mayhew, Jr., learned Wôpanâak as a young man and worked for a time as a minister on Noepe.

831.26–27   Thomas Mayhew, father and son] See notes 482.9 and 824.32.

831.28–29   Mr. Pierson . . . Fitch] Abraham Pierson (1614–1678), minister and author of the pamphlet *Some Helps for the Indians* (1659); James Fitch (1622–1702) preached to the Mohegans.

832.2   Practice of Piety, Baxter's Call] Devotional texts, first printed in England, that Wampanoag men translated as part of Eliot's missionary project.

832.4   Corporation] The Company for Propagation of the Gospel in New England and the parts adjacent in America, the primary funding body for Eliot's missions.

832.29   Caleb] Caleb Cheeshateaumuck, see note 799.34–35.

833.14–15   Thomas Danforth] Danforth (1623–1699) served as treasurer of Harvard College and oversaw Native students during the time Caleb was in Cambridge. He also served as an Assistant in Massachusetts Bay Colony, 1659–79, and as commissioner from Massachusetts Bay in the United Colonies, 1662–78.

840.39–40   Antipædobaptists] The Puritans considered Anabaptists to be a radical religious group and attempted to banish them from New England.

842.32   Nattous . . . Piam Boohan] Netus (d. 1676), a Nipmuc man who lived at Natick and who sold a large tract of Nipmuc land to Elijah Corlett in 1661 to satisfy a debt. The land was then sold to Thomas Danforth and later became the town of Framingham, Massachusetts. Piambow or Piambouhou was a Nipmuc man who became a convert after losing his family to the epidemics. He lived at Nonantum, then Natick, and was among the men whose spiritual confessions Eliot published. Piambow later became a convert leader at Hassanamesit and was interned on Deer Island during King Philip's War.

842.34   Anthony and John Speen] Anthony Speen was from a prominent family of Native converts, who lived at Natick. His confession, in which he "prayed" to "go with his brother," was among those published by Eliot. He was interned on Deer Island during King Philip's War. John Speen, or

Qualalanset, was Anthony's brother, and was granted land at Natick on behalf of his family. Of his conversion, he testified, according to Eliot, "And because I saw the English took much ground, and I thought if I prayed, the English would not take away my ground, for these causes I prayed."

842.37   Captain Josiah, or Pennahannit] A Nipmuc convert and ruler at Nashoba, a mission community, now Littleton, Massachusetts.

843.4   Pakemitt, or Punkapoag] A mission community in Massachusett territory, on the Neponset River

843.7   the Blue Hill] See note 52.33–23.

843.12   Neponsitt mill] Neponset was the location of a large Massachusett community when the Massachusetts Bay Colony settlers arrived.

843.17   Ahawton] William Ahaton (d. 1717) or Nahaton, son of the sachem Tahattawan of Nashoba and Musketaquid. His sister married Waban (see note 827.14). William Ahaton was incarcerated on Deer Island during King Philip's War and then, along with other converts whose families remained on the island, served as a scout for the English.

844.3   Hassanamesitt] A Nipmuc homeland and mission community also known as Hassanamisco, now also Grafton, Massachusetts.

844.6   Nipmuck river] Upper Blackstone River, in central Massachusetts.

844.18   Anaweakin] Annaweekin (d. 1676), son of Naoas and brother to Wawaus or James Printer, Joseph Tupukawillin, and Job Kattenanit, was a Nipmuc leader from the praying town of Hassanamesit who died during King Philip's War.

844.19   Tackuppa-willin] Joseph Tukuppawillin, a Nipmuc teacher and preacher at Hassanamesit, son of Naoas, brother to James Printer, Job Kattenanit, and Annaweekin.

845.17   *Under his shadow ye shall rejoice*] Psalm 63:7.

845.21   Onomog] Owannamug, ruler at Okkanamesit, a mission community adjacent to Marlborough, a Massachusetts Bay Colony town.

846.9   Numphow] Sachem at the Patucket fishing falls and homeland. Wamesit was the location of the mission community in the Patucket homeland and was a major gathering place for Patucket and Pennacook families, especially during spring fishing. It continued to host Native people who practiced traditional ceremonies as well as converts.

846.11   Samuel] Samuel Numphow, son of the Patucket sachem Numphow, and a scholar trained in preparatory schools. During King Philip's War Samuel penned a letter to the Massachusetts Bay Colony on his expedition to locate or gain news of the Pennacook sachem Wannalancet. The letter reported on Native raids on English settlements on the Wabanaki coast.

847.1 Wannalancet] A Pennacook leader who was also affiliated with Patucket, son of the Pennacook great sachem Passaconaway. Wannalancet pursued neutrality during King Philip's War by taking his people to Wabanaki territory at the head of the Connecticut River, far from English settlements.

847.2 Merrimak river] River Molôdemak, or Merrimack River. Patucket communities lived on the lower part of the river, centered at the falls, while related Pennacook communities lived on the upper part of the river, centered at Amoskeag (now Manchester, New Hampshire) and "Pennacook" (now Concord, New Hampshire), while traveling among kin in multiple locations. One of the goals of the missionaries who supported "praying towns" was to encourage Native converts to live in a more settled, contained manner.

847.3 Pasaconaway] See note 677.13.

847.32 Lieutenant Henchman] Thomas Henchman (c. 1629–1703), a trader who lived in Concord, then Chelmsford, in the Massachusetts Bay Colony, one of the few settlers granted an exclusive right to trade with Native people on the Merrimack River.

848.26–27 John Ahatawance] John Ahatawan or Tahattawan was a son of Tahattawn, the sachem of Nashoba and Musketaquid. He married Sarah, a daughter (or granddaughter) of Nanapashemet and the saunkskwa of Massachusett, one of the intertribal marriage alliances forged in the wake of the epidemics.

848.29 Maquas] Mohawks, see note 585.24. Gookin is referring to the raids Kanienkehaka warriors carried out on Massachusett and Nipmuc towns in the 1660s. Gookin and others encouraged their converts to directly attack in English fashion the Mohawks at their town of Kahnawake on the Mohawk River, but failed to provide any military support themselves. The strategy resulted in a failed raid and further conflicts. An English missionary among the Mohawks characterized the Nipmuc and Massachusett raiders in a similar manner to the way Gookin described the Mohawks.

849.23 Magunkaquog] A Nipmuc homeland, now also Ashland, Massachusetts.

849.36 Pomhaman] Nipmuc ruler at Magunkaquog. Also known as Pomham, not to be confused with the Narragansett leader of the same, or similar, name.

849.37 Job] Job Kattenanit, a Nipmuc teacher at Magunkaquog (now Ashland, Massachusetts) and brother of James Printer, Annaweekin, and Joseph Tukupawillin, and son of Naoas. He was originally from Hassanamesit, a praying town. During King Philip's War, Job served as a scout and warned Massachusetts Bay colonists of the imminent attack on Lancaster the allied Native forces were planning. He also advocated for the protection of the extended families of Native scouts.

850.19   Manchage] Manchaug, a Nipmuc homeland, now also Sutton, Massachusetts.

850.35   Chabanakongkomun] Chabonagonkamug, a Nipmuc homeland, now also Webster, Massachusetts.

851.4   Joseph] Joseph Petavit, the son of Nipmuc leader Robin Petavit, of Hassanamesit, and brother to Sampson Petavit, also a teacher. Both brothers served as scouts for Massachusetts Bay Colony during King Philip's War.

851.10   Black James] Also known as Walamachin, he was appointed constable for five to seven of the newly established mission communities, starting in 1673.

851.21   Maanexit] A Nipmuc homeland, now also Oxford, Massachusetts.

851.24   Mohegan River] Quinebaug River, which leads from Nipmuc territory to Mohegan territory.

852.3   Quantisset] A Nipmuc homeland, now also Thompson, Connecticut.

852.8   Wabquissit] Webquasset, a Nipmuc homeland, now also Woodstock, Connecticut.

852.26   Sampson] Sampson Petavit, the son of Nipmuc leader Robin Petavit, from Hassanamesit, and brother to Joseph Petavit. Both brothers served as scouts for Massachusetts Bay Colony during King Philip's War, including scouting for the expedition to Menimesit led by Edward Hutchinson and Thomas Wheeler in the summer of 1675. Sampson had taught with Job Kattenanit at the Nipmuc town of Okkanamesit (near Marlboro) and at the Nipmuc town of Webquasset. Joseph taught at the Nipmuc town of Chabanakongkomun.

853.32   Unkas] See note 580.8.

854.39   Pakachoog] Pakachoag, a Nipmuc homeland, now also Auburn, Massachusetts.

855.8   John, alias Horowanninit] Hoorawannonit, known also as Sagamore John, Nipmuc sachem from Pakachoag.

855.14–15   James Speen] Nipmuc teacher and leader from Natick who served as a scout; brother of Qualalanset or John Speen.

855.19   Wattasacompanum] Tom Wuttasacomponom (d. 1676), Nipmuc convert and leader from Hassanamesit, relative of Job Kattenanit.

855.31   Mattoonus] Matoonus (d. 1676), Nipmuc sachem from Pakachoag.

855.36   Jethro] Probably Peter Jethro (c. 1614–d. after 1688), a Nipmuc convert who served as a scout in King Philip's War and as a scribe for the Nipmuc leaders in their peace negotiations with Massachusetts Bay Colony. He was the son of Tantamous, or "Old Jethro," a convert who lived at Natick. Jethro betrayed his father and the Nipmuc leader Shoshanim to the English during King Philip's War.

856.2–3 Weshakim, alias Nashaway . . . Lancaster] Weshawkim, the Nipmuc town near Lancaster, Massachusetts, within the larger Nashaway homeland. Lancaster, a Massachusetts Bay Colony town built at the confluence of the Nashua and North Nashua Rivers, was raided by combined Nipmuc, Narragansett, and Wampanoag forces in February 1676. The English mistress Mary Rowlandson was taken captive in the raid and given to Quinnapin and Weetamoo.

856.9 Shoshanim] Shoshanim (d. 1676), also known as Sagamore Sam, Nipmuc from Weshawkim and Nashaway. Gookin and Eliot had opposed his being elected as sachem, following the death of Nashaway sachem Showanon, as they preferred a convert named Matthew who was sachem during the Mohawk raids. Shoshanim had assumed leadership by the time of Gookin's visit in 1674.

857.25 Waeuntug] Waentuk, a Nipmuc homeland, now known as Uxbridge, Massachusetts.

857.29 James] Wawaus (d. 1717), also called James the Printer and James Printer, a Nipmuc scholar from the praying town of Hassanamesit (now Grafton, Massachusetts) who worked as a teacher and as an apprentice at the colonies' only printing press, which was housed in the Harvard Indian College. Wawaus played a key role in producing the Wôpanâak Bible, and he sought throughout King Philip's War to keep his family safe, despite being imprisoned on charges of conspiring against the English forces. He was the brother of Job Kattenanit.

857.35 Quabaug] A Nipmuc homeland, also called Quaboag. It was the location of a Massachusetts Bay Colony town later known as Brookfield that was raided by Nipmuc forces in August 1676 as Metacom made his way to the sanctuary of Menimesit, north of Quaboag.

KING PHILIP'S WAR OR THE FIRST INDIAN WAR

865.8 indian was found dead] John Sassamon, see note 627.11.

865.10 a pond] Assawompset Pond, in the Wampanoag territory of Nemasket.

865.19 king Philop] See note 632.7.

865.33 home] Whom.

865.33 ther kings] Sôtyumâak, Wampanoag leaders.

865.35 Plimoth Governor] Josiah Winslow, see note 476.29.

866.2 indians wer hunge] See Chronology, February–June 1675.

866.9   iserallits] Israelites.

866.15   fery] The ferry from Portsmouth in Rhode Island Colony to the south end of Montaup.

866.34–35   the English having ther arems] A reference to the council held at Taunton in 1671 where Plymouth men forced Metacom and his men to disarm. The Wampanoags believed this to be a temporary laying down of arms at the meeting place, but the colony later argued that it was a permanent surrender and applied to all Wampanoags.

866.39–40   Governer of new yorke] Edmund Andros (1637–1714), appointed governor of the colony of New York in 1675.

867.22–23   thay having submited to our king] Easton refers here to the agreement made between Plymouth and OusAmequin to provide mutual protection. Plymouth colonists frequently interpreted this agreement as one that indicated submission to the English king.

867.31–32   their kings father] Ousamequin, see note 191.19.

867.36–37   kings brother] Wamsutta, see note 613.5.

868.15   spoyled] Destroyed by livestock.

868.16   thoft] Thought.

868.16   boft] Bought.

868.26   in] If.

868.32   Conforem] To bring into conformity or obedience, subdue.

868.36   ther head quarters] Miles Garrison, in Rehoboth, a Plymouth Colony town within Pokanoket territory, just north of the entrance to Montaup.

868.40   the genarall] James Cudworth, see note 626.6.

869.2   our Ieslanders] Rhode Islanders. "We" and "our" refers here to the leaders and settlers of Rhode Island Colony.

869.7   the old man bid the young man shoote] The young man was John Salisbury of Swansea.

869.15–16   ther was a queen] Weetamoo, see note 612.6.

869.30   the English army] The combined forces of Plymouth and Massachusetts Bay.

870.5   naroganset indians to artickels of agreement] Edward Hutchinson led an expedition in June 1675 to meet with Narragansett leaders. He delivered a message from Massachusetts Bay governor John Leverett and sought to compel them to restrain their young men from joining Metacom. Hutchinson returned to Narragansett territory in July with a large military force seeking to compel a treaty of submission, but the Narragansett leaders did not show up for council. Instead, he had a group of ordinary Narragansett men sign the document.

870.6–7   indians Came in to a Plimoth gareson] The house of settler John Russell, in the Wampanoag territory of Apponaganset, where a large group of Wampanoags sought shelter. As Easton notes, they were taken to Plymouth and sold into slavery, contrary to the promises of protection given to them.

870.13–14   queen got to the narogansets] After the Plymouth and Massachusetts Bay forces invaded Weetamoo's sanctuary in Pocasset Swamp, she and the Wampanoag families under her protection traveled to Narragansett territory and received sanctuary with Narragansett leaders, to whom she had ties of kinship. During the fall of 1675 she also forged a marriage alliance with the Narragansett sachem Quinnapin, affording herself and her kin further protection. At the same time, Metacom traveled with other Wampanoag families to Nipmuc territory.

870.20   sudieners] Sojourners.

871.4   to the estward] To the eastward, referring to the outbreak of the northern front of the war in Wabanaki territory. Massachusetts Bay instituted a policy of disarming Wabanaki people near settlements on the coast of what is now Maine, suspecting that they might join with Native people to the south. See the statement of Moxus et al., pp. 1022–23 in this volume.

871.19   parell] Parley.

871.21–22   iunited Comitioners] Commissioners of the United Colonies. In November 1675 the Commissioners voted to raise a force under Josiah Winslow to subdue the Narragansetts and force them to surrender the Wampanoags under their protection.

871.25   our governer] William Coddington, see note 463.40–41.

871.29   Cumpation] Compensation.

872.12   decriped] Decrepit.

872.25   peas] Peace.

872.31   King Charels] Charles II (1630–1685) ruled England, Scotland, and Ireland, 1660–85.

872.36   kings determenation for naroganet to be in our colony] Following the visit of the Royal Commission to the New England colonies in 1664–65, Charles II delivered his decision that Rhode Island Colony should have governance over Narragansett country, which he claimed for England. There had been ongoing disputes between multiple colonial proprietary companies over large tracts of land in the Narragansett country. Easton suggests here that the United Colonies' expedition into Narragansett country was motivated by their desire to claim that land versus Rhode Island. The United Colonies (Massachusetts Bay, Plymouth, and Connecticut) continued to pursue these claims to the Narragansett country after the war.

873.15 hyerling] Hireling, mercenary.

873.18 inovation] Political revolution or rebellion, insurrection.

873.20 JOHN EASTON] Easton (1617–1705) was deputy governor of Rhode Island, 1674–76, and later governor, 1690–95.

875.5 hir husband] Petonowowet, also called Ben or Peter Nunnit, one of the sôkushqâ Weetamoo's husbands, a Wampanoag man who was not a sôtyum. Weetamoo dissolved her relationship with him shortly after the beginning of the war.

875.30 hed of dartmoth bounds] The northern boundary of Dartmouth, a settlement in Plymouth Colony. Weetamoo and Easton refer to the head of the Acoaxet (Westport) River.

875.31 the fales river] The river Quequequachand (see note 626.17–20).

876.6 the quens right] Weetamoo's land rights at Pocasset, or the land over which she had jurisdiction as sôkushqâ.

878.2 John Brown] Captain John Brown III (1650–1709), Plymouth Colony settler who resided in Swansea, grandson of the John Brown who participated in the original Seekonk agreement with Edward Winslow and Ousamequin.

878.11 double armed men] Wampanoag men who carried two guns, likely flintlock muskets.

878.13–14 sent there wifes to Narrogansent] Brown is reporting a rumor that Wampanoag men at Montaup had sent their families to take shelter in Narragansett territory, believing that Plymouth forces were coming to Montaup to hunt Metacom.

878.15 Coweset] A Wampanoag homeland, now part of Norton, Massachusetts, also the name of a neighboring Narragansett homeland.

878.16–17 pocasset showomet Assowomset] Weetamoo's territory of Pocasset, which she did not regard as part of Plymouth Colony. Shawomet, a Wampanoag homeland and planting peninsula in Pocasset territory, near Swansea (now Somerset, Massachusetts), claimed by conquest by Plymouth Colony in 1676. (It should not be confused with a place of the same name in Narragansett territory, near Warwick, Rhode Island.) Assawomset pond, in Nemasket territory, under the leadership of Wampanoag sôtyum Tuspaquin and Amie, Philip's sister.

881.7 *John Almy*] See note 633.13.

881.10 *Pocasset*] Benjamin Church held the grant to an unimproved tract of land in Weetamoo's territory.

881.11 *Sogkonate*] Sakonnet, the Wampanoag sôkushqâ Awashonks's territory, also the English settlement by the same name, later Little Compton, Rhode Island.

881.16   the Island] Rhode Island Colony. See note 612.8.

881.23   his new Farm] Church's settlement in Sakonnet. His claim arose from deeds that Church helped to orchestrate as a representative of Plymouth Colony.

882.21   *Umpame*] Plymouth Colony.

884.24–25   *Assawomset*-Ponds] See note 878.16–17. Sassamon had claimed land at Assawomset under a false deed, as Plymouth Colony sought to expand their own claims at Nemasket with his assistance. Benjamin Church helped to orchestrate deeds in Nemasket, including acquiring land for himself in what became the town of Middleboro, or Middlebury.

884.26–27   *James Brown . . . Mr. Samuel Gorton*] James Brown, see note 623.13; Samuel Gorton, see note 594.40–595.1.

884.37   up the hill] The hill above Quequequachand, the river of falls that was at the center of Pocasset. This was the location of Weetamoo's main home within her territory, now also called Tiverton Heights.

884.40   the Island] Aquidneck Island, in Rhode Island Colony, across the river from Pocasset.

887.16   some few of your giddy inconsiderate young men] Winslow's observation in June 1675 that few of Weetamoo's men had joined with Philip stands in stark contrast to Church's retrospective account that "they were all gone against her will to the dances." Church served as Winslow's intermediary and informant, having met with Weetamoo on June 7, 1675.

887.21   fruite] Both the political and material benefits that would be accrued from siding with Plymouth Colony, which Winslow assumes would prevail, and the fruits of Philip's fields.

887.29   Marshfield] See note 483.36–37.

889.2   *John Winthrop Jr.*] John Winthrop the Younger (1606–1676) served as governor of Connecticut Colony, 1657 and 1659–76, and as Connecticut commissioner to the United Colonies.

889.5   AT NAHIGONSIK] At Narragansett, in Narragansett territory.

889.5   Mr. SMITH'S] Richard Smith, Jr. (1630–1692), had a trading post at Cocumcosuck (Wickford, Rhode Island), which United Colonies soldiers used as a garrison and base during King Philip's War.

889.11   Capt. Atherton] Humphrey Atherton (1608–1661), one of the proprietors of the Atherton Company, which continued in 1675–76 to claim large tracts of land in Narragansett territory against the claims of the Rhode Island Company. Increase Atherton, his son, inherited his claims.

889.12–13   Capt. Hutchinson] Edward Hutchinson (1613–1675), the son of the Puritan dissident Anne Hutchinson, was a land speculator and leader of

Massachusetts Bay Colony militia during King Philip's War. He was ambushed and fatally wounded by Nipmuc warriors in August 1675 while leading a force from Massachusetts Bay Colony toward Menimesit. The Nipmucs then raided the English settlement in Quaboag.

889.21 Quaunoncku, Miantunnomu's youngest son] Canonchet, also called variations of the name Naananto (d. 1676), a Narragansett sachem and son of the sachem Miantonomo (d. 1643).

889.22 the Governor's letters] The statement sent by John Leverett (1616–1679), governor of Massachusetts Bay Colony, to the Narragansett leaders in June 1676.

889.24–25 Mausup ... Quawnipund] Mausup, also known as Quissucquansh, or Canonicus (c. 1623–1676), a Narragansett sachem, brother to Miantonomo, also known as Mosump and Pessicus; the "Old Queen" Quaiapin (d. 1676), a Narragansett saunkskwa; Ninicraft, see note 590.1; Quinnapin (d. 1676), Narragansett sachem who married Weetamoo in fall 1675.

889.31 Uncas] The claim here is that Uncas sent twenty men to Philip, but a company of Mohegan scouts joined with Connecticut forces to track him in July 1675 and there is little evidence that any Mohegans joined with Philip.

890.6–7 John Sossiman] John Sassamon, see note 627.11. No evidence exists that Philip called for Sassamon's death.

890.7 Governor of Plymouth] Josiah Winslow, see note 476.29.

890.8 three actors] See Chronology, February–June 1675.

890.18 the Commissioners] Commissioners of the United Colonies.

890.21 Plymouth Indians] Wampanoags.

890.25–26 Tatuphosuit] Uncas's son, also called Owaneco (1642–1712). The Narragansett sachems inquired why the United Colonies were not pursuing this case of Tatuphosuit killing a Narragansett man, on behalf of their Narragansett allies, if they had taken to prosecuting the killing of one Indian by another Indian, as was the case with Sassamon.

890.31 Major Winthrop] Wait Winthrop (1642–1717), son of John Winthrop, Jr., governor of Connecticut Colony.

890.36 Nicommo] A gathering or festival.

891.8 Swansey] A Plymouth Colony town within Pokanoket Wampanoag territory, including much of Sowams.

891.11 Mr. Coddington] William Coddingon (1601–1678).

891.34 Warwick] A Rhode Island Colony town, in the Narragansett homeland of Shawomet, raided by combined Native forces in March 1676.

892.6   Governor] William Coddington, see note 463.40–41.

892.21   Sam. Dier] Samuel Dyer (1635–1678), son of William Dyer, Jr., one of the original settlers of Portsmouth in Rhode Island Colony.

892.22   Newport] An English town in Rhode Island Colony, on Aquidneck Island, in Narragansett territory.

892.22–23   Jireh Bull . . . Puttaquomscutt] Jereh Bull (1638–1684), a trader and son of Rhode Island Assistant (and later governor) Henry Bull, built a stone block house garrison at Pettaquamscut, a Narragansett peninsula and planting field that was claimed by competing companies of settlers from Rhode Island Colony and the United Colonies. On December 15, 1675, as Plymouth and Massachusetts Bay troops were moving through Narragansett country, Narragansett warriors destroyed Bull's block house and killed more than a dozen of its defenders.

892.24   Caleb Carr] Carr (1616–1695), an English settler who resided in Newport. He served as deputy governor and Assistant, 1664–90, and was governor of Rhode Island Colony for a short period in 1695.

892.28   old Queen] Quaiapin (see note 889.24–25) offered the young men who killed the Englishmen refuge.

892.32   that Philip had left his place] Philip had left Montaup and traveled to Pocasset, the territory of Weetamoo, but the Plymouth and Massachusetts Bay forces were not yet aware of his location.

892.34–35   Capt. Oliver . . . Mr. Brown's] James Oliver (1617–1682), military officer from Massachusetts Bay Colony who commanded a Boston company, including in the expedition to Narragansett territory in December 1675; Captain John Brown III, see note 878.2.

892.35   hundreds of horse] Hundreds of cavalry soldiers, to search the country for Metacom and the Wampanoags.

892.36–37   John Scot] John Scott (d. 1677), an English settler who resided in Moshasuck, now part of Providence, Rhode Island, in Narragansett territory, and a soldier during King Philip's War. He lived at Patucket ferry, where he was wounded but not killed in 1675, as the rumor recorded in this letter suggests.

895.1   TAUNTON] See note 626.17–20.

895.2   John Freeman] Captain John Freeman, Plymouth Colony settler, Assistant, and military officer, a resident of Eastham.

895.11   governor Leverett] John Leverett (1616–1679), governor of Massachusetts Bay Colony.

895.15   Eastham] A town in Plymouth Colony, in Wampanoag territory, on Cape Cod.

895.32–34 John Tisdill . . . Walker] John Tisdale (d. 1675) was a Plymouth Colony settler and representative to the General Court for Taunton. His residence was within contested Assonet land in Wampanoag territory, on the path to Weetamoo's homeland of Pocasset, and his house was the mustering point for the planned expedition against the saunkskwa Awashonks in 1671. Captain John Knowles (1640–1675) was a Plymouth Colony settler and military officer who resided in Eastham but was with the colony's forces stationed at Taunton at the beginning of King Philip's War. Samuel Atkins (1651–1675) was a Plymouth settler and soldier who resided in Eastham. James Walker, Tisdale's brother-in-law, was a Plymouth settler who served as chairman of Taunton's Council of War.

897.6–7 Capt. *Fuller*] Matthew Fuller (bap. 1603–1678), son of Samuel Fuller, was a military officer who assisted Church in scouting Sakonnet and Pocasset at the beginning of King Philip's War. A Plymouth settler with interest in Sakonnet lands, Fuller had also served with the force that sought Awashonks's submission in 1671.

897.13 on the other side of the River] Referring to Pocasset and Sakonnet, on the east side of the Kteticut (Taunton) and Sakonnet Rivers.

897.21–22 *Nunnaquohqut* Neck] See note 612.11. Also referred to in this account as "Punkatees Neck." Benjamin Church had a claim on the Pocasset Neck lands.

898.4 *Indian* Truck] Trading goods, in this case plunder from a Wampanoag home.

898.11 Capt. *Almy*'s Pease-field] Job Almy's pea (or bean) field, one of the few English settlements in Pocasset territory, located on Pocasset Neck. This was the site of the battle recounted by Church. In James Cudworth's account, in a letter to Winslow from the field, he relayed that "40 men under Capt. Fuller and Benjamin Church have been on Pocasset side and had a hot dispute." He said they "skirmished" for "two hours" until the Plymouth men "spent all their ammunition," but that Church could not say how many men they had killed.

898.13 *Lake*] David Lake (c. 1646–c. 1709), son of Henry Lake (d. 1673), a Dartmouth settler. David Lake was a soldier and Plymouth Colony settler who had interest in Pocasset lands. He later settled at Nonaquaket, after those lands were claimed by conquest at the end of King Philip's War.

898.22 The *Indians*] Wampanoag men who were lying in ambush, awaiting Church's company. They diverted Church from Weetamoo, Metacom, and the Wampanoag families who were sheltered in the Pocasset cedar swamp.

899.21 *Fogland*] Fogland point, south of Nonaquaket, a round peninsula that juts out into the Sakonnet River.

899.29 the *Islanders*] Men from Rhode Island Colony.

899.37   *B. Southworth*] This seems to refer to Benjamin Church's brother-in-law, one of the sons of Constant Southworth. There may be an error in the printing, as Constant's sons were named Edward, Nathaniel, and William. Church was married to Alice Southworth.

900.3   meanness] Meager supply.

901.16   *Capt.* Golding] Roger Goulding (d. 1695), Rhode Island settler and soldier, granted one hundred acres of land at Pocasset for his assistance to Plymouth Colony in King Philip's War, including assisting Benjamin Church's company at Pocasset by providing rescue boats.

902.13–14   *Mount-hope* Garrison] The fort the English army had set up at Montaup after they failed to find Metacom there.

902.16   *Alderman*] Alderman, a Pocasset Wampanoag man who, according to Church, killed Philip in August 1676 while serving as an English scout.

902.17   *the Squaw Sachem*] Weetamoo, see note 612.6. For the origin of the phrase "squaw sachem," see note 167.32.

902.22   *Weetamores* head quarters] The Pocasset cedar swamp where Weetamoo and the Wampanoag families under her protection were sheltered. Church also referred to this place as "Weetamore's camp."

903.13   *Baxter* and Capt. *Hunter*] Thomas Baxter, a Plymouth Colony settler and soldier, who lived in Yarmouth; Thomas Hunter, a Wampanoag man from Nemasket, who served as a scout for Church.

903.36   *Philips* head Quarters] The location within the Pocasset cedar swamp where Philip and his kin were sheltered.

903.40   *Dartmouths*] See note 798.12. The Wampanoag leader Totoson led a raid on the dispersed settlement on the east side of the cedar swamps, blocking access to Pocasset via the Dartmouth path and drawing Plymouth forces away from families who were escaping via trails that led north and west.

904.3   *Russels* Garrison at *Poneganset*] The house of settler John Russell, in the Wampanoag territory of Apponaganset, where a large group of Wampanoags sought shelter. As Church acknowledges, they were taken to Plymouth and sold into slavery, contrary to the promises of protection given to them.

904.21   *Taunton*-River] Also Kteticut, a central river in Wampanoag territory, which Metacom, Weetamoo, and the families who traveled with them crossed as they evaded the colonial troops at Pocasset Swamp.

904.22   *Rehoboth*-Plain] An area on the north side of Rehoboth (see note 607.14). Metacom, Weetamoo, and their company traveled through Rehoboth Plain, north of the garrisons, undetected.

904.22   *Petuxet*-River] Patucket River (see note 616.33–34), which Metacom, Weetamoo, and their company crossed en route to Narragansett territory.

904.22 Capt. *Edmunds*] Captain Andrew Edmunds, a settler who lived in Providence, Rhode Island Colony.

904.30 *Albany*] Albany, the center of New York Colony's government, formerly the central Mohican village and council fire. Metacom traveled to Mohican territory near Albany on a diplomatic expedition to forge alliances in the winter of 1675–76.

906.2 William Bradford . . . John Cotton] William Bradford, Jr. (1624–1703), Plymouth Colony military commander and Assistant, son of Governor William Bradford; John Cotton, Jr. (1640–1699), minister at Plymouth Colony from 1669 to 1698. The son of the Massachusetts Bay Colony minister John Cotton, he had previously been a missionary at Noepe (Martha's Vineyard).

906.4 Mrs Cotton] Joanna Rossiter Cotton (1642–1702).

906.8 Cokset] Acoaxet, see note 616.27–28.

906.9 a great Swampe] Cedar swamp in Awashonks's territory of Sakonnet. See Peter Awashonk's testimony, pp. 909–11 in this volume.

906.12 found them in an hidious swame] Pocasset cedar swamp, in Weetamoo's territory. Although Bradford conflates them as the "enemy," these were two distinct groups of Wampanoag people, who took shelter in dense cedar swamps in Sakonnet and in Pocasset.

906.13 hard dispute] Bradford, Benjamin Church, and James Cudworth arrived at Pocasset on July 16 with more than one hundred men and were ambushed as they marched into the Pocasset cedar swamp.

906.17 lugage] The baggage of an army, or goods in general.

906.18–19 mount hope] The fort the English army had set up at Montaup, after they failed to find Metacom there.

906.20 the last munday] July 19, 1675. This was the second expedition to Pocasset Swamp, with a combined army of Massachusetts Bay and Plymouth troops, including several Native scouts.

906.22 Forelorne] The scouts and soldiers on the front line.

906.28–29 Capt Mosles] The notorious Samuel Mosely (1641–1680), a Massachusetts Bay settler who led a company during King Philip's War that was largely composed of privateers, servants, and released prisoners.

906.29 Capt Hinchmam] Captain Daniel Henchman (1623–1685), Massachusetts Bay settler and military commander of a company from Boston and Cambridge during King Philip's War.

906.31 the squa shachem] Weetamoo.

907.1 garison on pocasset side] This referred to the plan to build a garrison at Pocasset, on the east side of the Taunton and Sakonnet Rivers.

909.3–5   Peter . . . allies Chowahunna] Peter was the son of the sôkushqâ Awashonks, from the Wampanoag homeland of Sakonnet; George, a Wampanoag man from Sakonnet, who Benjamin Church reported was fluent in English; Chowohumma, or David, a Wampanoag man from Sakonnet, who had reported John Sassamon's death to settlers at Taunton before the war.

910.14   satt still] Kept the peace, strove to remain in a peaceful state.

910.34   the fight att Narragansett] The expedition, led by Josiah Winslow, of United Colonies forces against the Narragansetts, and the Wampanoag people they sheltered, at Great Swamp in December 1675.

911.6   Major Bradford] William Bradford, Jr., see note 906.2.

914.14–15   Phillip Sachem of mount hope] Winslow and Hinckley's narrative portrayed Philip as both a colonial subject who had rebelled and an insolent heathen who required containment. The commissioners sought to place the blame for the war squarely on Philip, constructing a narrative that he had planned and organized a conspiracy to which Plymouth Colony leaders had rationally responded in defense. This enabled them to portray a much more orderly political and military structure on both sides of the conflict than actually existed.

914.18   two confeaderate Collonies] Massachusetts Bay and Connecticut.

915.29–30   three by him charged] See Chronology, February–June 1675.

915.38   Swansey and Rehoboth] See note 607.14. Swansea's settlement arose from the "Sowams and Parts Adjacent" deed, with Wamsutta and Ousamequin.

916.12–13   Mr Benjamine Church] Benjamin Church (1639–1718), Plymouth Colony settler, who was involved in the orchestration of deeds for Plymouth Colony. He was the son-in-law of Constant Southworth and lived in the Wampanoag territory of Sakonnet at the beginning of the war. Church later settled in Bristol, Rhode Island, on Montaup lands claimed by conquest.

916.28   Mr Paine] Stephen Paine, Jr. (1629–1678), Plymouth Colony settler and resident of Rehoboth, brother of Nathaniel Paine, and son of Stephen Paine, Sr., an original Rehoboth grantee.

916.32   Job Winslow his house] Job Winslow (1641–1720), Plymouth Colony settler and Swansea resident, had built a house in Kickemuit, a Wampanoag planting peninsula, close to Montaup, eight or nine years before the war.

917.1   Thomas layton] Winslow and Hinckley seem to be referring to John Lawton, who was living at Pocasset and may have been killed at the beginning of King Philip's War. His date of death is not recorded, but his wife remarried in 1678. His father, George Lawton (1607–1693), and his uncle, Thomas Lawton (1614–1681), lived nearby in Portsmouth, Rhode Island. Like other colonial narrators, Winslow and Hinckley may have further confused Lawton with his neighbor, John Archer (d. 1675), who was killed by Wampanoag men at Pocasset in June 1675. Archer had previously tried to defraud Weetamoo of land at Pocasset through a false deed. Both Lawton and Archer, along with Matthew Boomer, Lawton's brother-in-law, had been called into Plymouth Court earlier in June 1675, for living "in a heathenish way from good society" at Pocasset and not attending church.

919.17–20 Thomas Danforth John Winthorpe ... Thomas Hinckley] Thomas Danforth, see note 833.14–15; John Winthrop, Jr., see note 889.2; William Stoughton (1631–1681), commissioner from Massachusetts Bay Colony, later famous for his role as chief justice in the Salem witch trials; James Richards (1631–1680), commissioner from Connecticut Colony; Josiah Winslow, see note 476.29; Thomas Hinckley, see note 624.19.

921.7–8 *lucida intervalla*] Latin: lucid intervals.

921.8–9 *Ab inferno nulla redemptio*] Latin: In hell there is no redemption.

921.9–10 Noah's dove] See Genesis 8:6–12.

921.16 *opus diei*] Latin: the day's work.

921.20–21 Oliver ... Hispaniola] An expedition sent by Oliver Cromwell (1599–1658), Lord Protector of England, to seize Hispaniola was defeated by Spanish colonists in 1655.

921.22–23 H. Vane ... "A Healing Question"] Pamphlet (1656) by Sir Henry Vane (see note 523.14) proposing that the Protectorate be replaced by a republican government based on a written constitution.

921.24 *noli me tangere*] Latin: touch me not.

921.26 *ex amino*] Latin: from the heart.

921.30 *rebus sic stantibus*] Latin: in these circumstances.

921.31–32 *candida et bona fide*] Latin: always honest and in good faith.

922.5 Jeremiah, thou liest] See Jeremiah 42:7–22.

922.13 Springfield] An English town within Agawam and Woronoco territory, on the Connecticut River.

922.15–16 Norwich and Stonington] English towns in Connecticut Colony and in Mohegan and Pequot territories, respectively.

922.17–18 *Fiat voluntas Dei*] Latin: Let God's will be done.

922.19 Capt. Fenner] Arthur Fenner (1619–1703), a Rhode Island settler, who served as an Assistant and as a military officer in King Philip's War. He resided in Providence.

922.26 the young prince] Canonchet, see note 889.21. He had traveled to Boston to engage in council with the commissioners of the United Colonies in early October 1675, and Williams ferried Canonchet and his counselors over the Seekonk River on their return.

923.12–13 Haselrig's motto ... *Tantum in Coelis*] Sir Arthur Haselrig (1601–1661), a Parliamentarian in the English Civil War, led a cavalry regiment known as Haselrig's Lobsters after the full body armor worn by its men. *Tantum in Coelis*, "Only in Heaven," was the regimental motto.

925.3–4 Examination and Relation of James Quananopohit] The bracketed words in the text are present in the original manuscript and were inserted by the original recorder of James Quananopohit's testimony.

925.5–6 James Quannapaquait, allias James Rumny-Marsh] James Quananopohit (c. 1636–1712), or James Rumney Marsh, and his brother Thomas (b. c. 1642) were originally from Winisimet, with ties to Massachusett and Patucket communities. The English renamed a coastal marsh in their homeland Rumney Marsh, after Romney Marsh in southeast England. The brothers served as scouts for Massachusetts Bay during King Philip's War, and advocated for the protection of Native scouts and their families. They lived at Natick, a praying town, before and after the war.

925.9 Job of Magungoog] Job Kattenanit, see note 849.37.

925.11 the enemyes quarters] Referring to the sanctuary maintained by the Nipmuc leaders during the fall and winter of 1675–76, at Menimesit, on the Ware River in central Massachusetts. Metacom and Weetamoo had sought refuge there, with the Wampanoag families under their protection, in August and December 1675, respectively.

925.20 Hassanameshe indians] Nipmuc people of Hassanamesit (see note 843.1), Job Kattenanit's town. Nipmuc forces had gathered up their relations from the praying town of Hassanamesit in November 1675, after the Massachusetts Bay Colony began enforcing an order to intern "praying Indians" on Deer Island in Boston Harbor. Most of Job's family, including his children, had been taken by the Nipmuc forces to Menimesit, where they were living in the winter of 1675–76.

925.27 poor christian Indians at the Deer Island] Native people from the praying towns were forcibly interned on Deer Island in Boston Harbor with no shelter and few supplies. Many people perished on the deforested island in the winter of 1675–76.

925.30 jelosyes] Suspicions. Despite the fact that few converts participated in violence against the English, many settlers were highly suspicious and fearful of Christian Indians, believing they were inherently savage and would join with other Native people against the English. The scouts believed their service to the English might convince them otherwise.

926.2 Job was imprisoned] Although he served as a scout, Job Kattenanit was mistakenly captured and imprisoned in Boston in November 1675 by the notorious Samuel Moseley; see note 906.28–29.

926.5 Mohegins] Mohegans, referring to the Mohegan scouts who were allied with Connecticut Colony, and were recruited at the beginning of the war.

926.5–6 the fight neare Secunke with Philip] Massachusett, Nipmuc, and Mohegan scouts were with the United Colonies troops at Seekonk, in Wampanoag territory, in late July and early August 1676. The scouts discerned the trail of Metacom as he and his relations moved across the north side of their territory, through Seekonk, above the settlements of Rehoboth, and across the Patucket River to the Narragansett territory of Nipsachuck. There the colonial forces killed several people in Metacom's and Weetamoo's camps but failed to capture the Wampanoag leaders.

926.9 Captian Prentis] Captain Thomas Prentiss (1620–1710), military commander, with Daniel Henchman, of the Massachusetts Bay Colony troops that went out from Boston and Cambridge to Wampanoag territory in June 1676. This company included the Quananopohit brothers and Job Kattenanit.

926.18 Captain Syll] Captain Joseph Syll, or Sill (c. 1639–1696), Massachusetts Bay settler and commander of a company from Cambridge, Watertown, and Charlestown during King Philip's War.

926.22 Pakachooge] Pakachoag, see note 854.39. Thomas Quananopohit served with Syll's company in an expedition to Pakachoag, where Nipmuc people had stores of corn.

927.7 Nipmuck River] See note 844.6.

927.12 Quabaage old fort] See note 857.35.

927.16 Captain Hutchison] See note 889.12–13.

927.16–17 Captain Wheeler] Thomas Wheeler (c. 1620–1686), Massachusetts Bay military officer and trader. He was ambushed and wounded while leading a Massachusetts Bay Colony company toward Menimesit with Hutchinson. The ambush became known as "Wheeler's Surprise."

927.20 Magunhooge] Magunkaquog, the Nipmuc town where Job Kattenanit lived and served as a teacher before the war.

927.29 sent away to Barbados] During King Philip's War, many Native people, including peaceful converts, were enslaved and shipped to Barbados and other islands in the West Indies, as well as Bermuda and islands off the coast of Iberia and North Africa.

927.30 these indians our enemies] The Nipmuc, Wampanoag, and other people who were living at Menimesit, regarded as enemies to the English. Job Kattenanit sought to distinguish between his relatives, from the praying towns, and those who engaged in resistance, insisting that his relations went to Menimesit, under the persuasion of other Nipmuc leaders, with great reluctance.

927.31 the corne] The harvest of Hassanamesit, needed by the many people who took refuge at Menimesit.

927.35 Tukuppawillin] Joseph Tukuppawillin, see note 844.19.

927.35–36 his aged father] Naoas, a Nipmuc deacon at Hassanamesit, father to Job Kattenanit, James Printer, and Joseph Tukuppawillin.

927.38 Manchange] Manchaug, a Nipmuc town.

928.8 Nashaway] See note 856.2–3.

928.9 Mawtaamp] Muttaump (d. 1676), Nipmuc sachem from Quaboag.

928.9 John with one eye] Monoco (d. 1676), a Nipmuc leader from Weshawkim and Nashaway, who led raids on Lancaster in August 1675 and February 1676.

928.9 Sam] Shoshanim or Sagamore Sam, see note 856.9.

928.10 Sagamore John of Pakachooge] See note 855.8.

928.12–13 Captain Tom allias Wattasakomponin] Tom Wuttasacomponom, see note 855.19. James Quananopohit advocated for Tom's release when he was tried as a prisoner of war in Boston in June 1676, testifying that he had not fought against the English. Despite his testimony, Tom was executed.

928.13 Nehimiah] Nehemia, eldest son of Tom Wuttasacomponom, also from Hassanamesit.

928.15 James] James Quananopohit.

928.19 James Printer] See note 857.29.

928.20 Joseph & . . . Two brethern] Joseph and Sampson Petavit, see note 852.26.

928.21 Pumhamun] Pumham, the elder in whose home Job Kattenanit's children lived while at Menimesit.

928.32 Mauhaks] Mohawks, see note 585.24. Monoco knew and trusted James Quananopohit because they had fought against the Mohawks together in the 1660s, including during a Mohawk raid on Nashaway, where James had also lived. James's value to the English army was in his tactical skills, as well as his linguistic ability.

928.40 Capt John] See note 928.9.

929.1 fort Albany] See note 904.30. James's report was important because the United Colonies had believed Metacom was at Narragansett, in the Great Swamp, and at various other places in New England.

929.2 Major Andros] See note 866.39–40.

929.3 Mr Leet] William Leete (c. 1613–1683), deputy governor of Connecticut Colony.

929.5   our Councill] The governor and assistants of Massachusetts Bay Colony.

929.8–9   Hadly Northampton & Spinkfield Indians] Native people of Nonotuck, who lived near the colonial towns of Hadley and Northampton, and Agawam and Woronoco, near the English town of Springfield, in the Connecticut River Valley. They sought shelter with their relations upriver in the fall and winter of 1675–76. Many of the Native inhabitants of the Connecticut River Valley were also kin to Nipmuc people.

929.10   Squakeake] Squakeag, also Sokwakik, a large area in the Connecticut River Valley and the southernmost Abenaki territory; it included the northernmost English settlement of Northfield, and the Sokoki towns above. Sokoki people were kin to Pocumtuck, Nonotuck, and other Connecticut River Valley people, as well as other Wabanaki people, including Pennacooks, to the north and east. Thousands of displaced Wampanoag, Nipmuc, and Narragansett people joined Connecticut River Valley families in this northern territory during the winter of 1675–76.

929.28   Lancaster] See note 856.2–3. James and Job traveled through snow to Cambridge to report the planned raid on Lancaster, which occurred on February 10, 1676, but their warning was not heeded quickly enough. Monoco led a combined force to strike the town, taking Mary Rowlandson and other captives to Menimesit.

929.35   Captain Beeares & Captain Lothrop] Richard Beers and Thomas Lathrop (d. 1675) were commanders of a Massachusetts Bay company sent to the Connecticut River Valley in August 1675. The first "fight" occurred when a company of one hundred men under the command of Beers and Lathrop pursued Nonotuck noncombatants to their relations' territory in Pocumtuck on August 26, 1675. Beers was ambushed and killed in Sokwakik territory (Northfield, Massachusetts) as he led a company upriver on September 4, 1675. Lathrop was ambushed and killed on September 18, 1675, in Pocumtuck territory (South Deerfield, Massachusetts).

930.1–4   Mawhakes . . . Maquaws] Mohawks, see note 585.24.

930.3–4   Wompeages . . . Wampeages] Most likely referring to Wabanaki people to the north, who joined with the Nipmucs, Narragansetts, and Wampanoags to raid settlements in the Connecticut River Valley, alongside their relations from those places, and provide sanctuary for displaced persons. May also refer to Wappingers, who lived on the Hudson River, but they did not assist the allied Native forces.

930.6   Mohegins & Pequots] Some Mohegans and Pequots served as scouts for Connecticut Colony.

930.8–9   Monsieur Normanvile] Jean de Godefroy de Lintot (c. 1607–1681), sieur de Normanville, a French diplomat and interpreter sent by Governor-General Frontenac, of New France, to Boston in May 1675 to seek the release of French seigneurs who had been captured by buccaneers and held by Massachusetts Bay Colony in Boston. The plan described here was not carried out.

930.24   the head of the Keneticut river] The headwaters of the Connecticut River, where the Pennacook leader Wannalancet and his kin spent the winter of 1675–76.

930.26   Wannalancet] See note 847.1.

930.38   Robert Pepper] Pepper (d. 1684), an English settler from Roxbury, in Massachusetts Bay, was captured in Sokwakik territory when Captain Beers was ambushed in September 1675.

931.22   Narragants] Narragansetts. The "fight" they describe was the offensive by United Colonies forces, led by Josiah Winslow, against the Narragansetts, and the Wampanoag people they sheltered, at Great Swamp in December 1675. The attack turned the Narragansetts against the English.

932.3   Joshua Tift] Joshua Tefft, or Tift (d. 1676), was an English settler who was found living among the Narragansetts during the expedition against the fortified village at Great Swamp. He was accused of fighting against the English and executed.

932.17–23   Mawtaamp . . . Mataamp] See note 928.9.

932.35–37   John Hunter . . . Ephraim] John Hunter, a scout for the English; James Speen, see note 855.14–15; Peter Ephraim (d. 1685), a Native man from Natick who served as a scout.

933.3   nokake] Corn meal or bread, used as food while traveling.

935.2   Mary Rowlandson] Mary White Rowlandson (c. 1637–1711), a settler of Lancaster, in the Nashaway homeland, who, as wife of Joseph Rowlandson, held the title of mistress instead of the more common goodwife. She was the daughter of John White, a large landowner in Lancaster.

935.4   *Preface*] Written by Increase Mather (1639–1723), Boston minister, who composed several accounts of King Philip's War to demonstrate that it was a just war against a heathen people. He is also credited with editing and encouraging the publication of Rowlandson's narrative.

935.5–6   the Narrhagansets quarters (in or toward the Nipmug Country] Many Narragansett people had taken refuge in Nipmuc territory (first at Menimesit, later at Wachusett) and in the Connecticut River Valley after the United Colonies invaded their sanctuary and stronghold at Great Swamp.

936.13   Mr. *Joseph Rolandson*] Joseph Rowlandson, settler and minister who resided in Lancaster, on one of the most fertile lots in Nashaway, at the confluence of rivers. As a minister, he held the title of "Mr."

936.25   Take just Lot] See Genesis 14.

937.10–11   *Joseph, David* and *Daniel*] See Daniel 3.

937.39   nine lepers] See Luke 17:8–19.

939.1   *better not vow*] Ecclesiastes 5:5.

939.19   *What dost Thou?*] Job 9:2.

939.32   Sampsons Riddle] See Judges 14:4.

940.10   the *Indians*] The raid on Lancaster was led by Monoco, a Nipmuc Nashaway leader who lived at the neighboring town of Weshawkim.

941.4   Flankers] Projecting fortifications.

941.14   my Children] Rowlandson's children were Joseph, Jr. (b. 1661), Mary (b. 1665), and Sarah (b. 1669).

942.17   *Come, behold*] Psalm 46:8.

943.6   up upon a hill] George Hill, in Lancaster.

943.8   a vacant house] Likely the former trading post of Thomas King. The town of Lancaster had its origins in an agreement between King and the Nipmuc leader Showanon to foster trade at his homeland of Nashaway.

943.23   in the Bay] At Boston, on Massachusetts Bay.

943.35–38   killed at *Lancaster* . . . Praying *Indians*] The first raid on Lancaster was led by Monoco on August 22, 1675. For Samuel Mosely's arrest of James Printer and ten other men, see Chronology, August–September 1675.

944.3   *vast and desolate Wilderness*] Although Rowlandson described the landscape as uncultivated and ungoverned, the party traveled along established trails in the Nipmuc homelands of Weshawkim and Wachusett.

945.8   *Wenimesset*] The Nipmuc sanctuary of Menimesit, where leaders and families gathered from the beginning of the war. There were three towns within Menimesit, which was located on the Ware River.

945.20   *Robert Pepper*] See note 930.38.

945.21   Captain *Beers* his fight] See note 929.35.

945.25   this *Indian* Town] One of the three towns at Menimesit.

945.28   Oaken leaves] Oak leaves were recommended to treat inflammation and prevent infection by Nicholas Culpeper's *English Physician and Complete Herbal* (1653).

946.1–2   *This was the comfort . . . as he said*] Job 16:2.

946.22   *Quanopin*] Quinnapin, see note 889.24–25. Rowlandson refers to the home where she stayed as "my Masters Wigwam," but this would have been Weetamoo's house, their temporary shelter at Menimesit.

946.23   King *Philips* wives Sister] Metacom was married to Wootonakanuske, Weetamoo's sister.

946.24   sold to him] Mary Rowlandson was given to Quinnapin and Weet-amoo, as part of Native exchange networks at Menimesit and in recognition of their leadership. As the wife of the town minister, Rowlandson was a high-value English captive.

947.5   Joseph *is not*] Genesis 42:36.

947.20   whose place was about six miles off] One of the other towns at Menimesit.

947.29   *Medfield*] A Massachusetts Bay town in Nipmuc territory.

948.3–4   the *Sagamores Wigwam*] The council house.

948.33   Goodwife *Joslin*] Ann Joslin (d. c. 1676), a Lancaster settler, wife of Abraham Joslin.

949.26   a desolate place in the Wilderness] Nichewaug, a Nipmuc homeland at a trail crossroads, now Petersham, Massachusetts.

950.12   *like Jehu*] 2 Kings 9:20.

950.18–19   *Bacquaug* River] Paquaug, a Nipmuc homeland and river, now Millers River.

950.25   my mistriss] Weetamoo, who was conserving corn meal for the journey.

951.18   *Papooses*] A derogatory word for a baby or small child.

951.19   *Squaws*] See note 167.32 for information on the suffix "skwa." By Rowlandson's time, colonists were using the word to distinguish between English/civilized women and Native/savage women.

951.36   a Beaver dam] Weetamoo and a company that consisted largely of Native women, children, and elders used a beaver dam to cross a tributary of the Paquaug River, in the Paquaug homeland (at or near present-day Orange, Massachusetts).

952.2   *Lot's*, Wife's Temptation] Genesis 19:26.

952.3   a great Swamp] A large swamp within Sokoki territory, now in North-field State Forest.

952.21–22   place where *English* cattle had been] A trail leading toward the Connecticut River, near what is now Northfield.

952.25   *Squakheag*] See note 929.10.

953.1   *For to the hungry Soul . . . sweet.*] Proverbs 27:7.

953.7–8   the River, *i.e.* Connecticot] The Connecticut River, or Kwinitekw. During this remove, the company was within Sokoki territory at Coasset (now Vernon, Vermont, and Hinsdale, New Hampshire), where there were several encampments.

953.8   to meet with King *Philip*] Weetamoo and her kin were receiving or meeting Metacom as he returned from Mohican territory.

953.23   *Naked came I*] Job 1:21.

954.28   a stinking Tobacco-pipe] Metacom was inviting Rowlandson to participate in ceremonial use of tobacco, but the English had adopted tobacco as a common stimulant, and some of them already considered it a vice.

954.29–30   *North-Hampton*] Northampton, a Massachusetts Bay Colony town in Nonotuck territory, was raided in March 1676.

954.32   Ground-nuts] A tuber, or small potato, commonly gathered in early spring.

955.2   *Sannup*] Husband, married man.

955.17   *Mary Thurston*] Mary Thurston Smith (1643–1696), a settler in Medfield, a Massachusetts Bay town in Nipmuc territory.

955.34   five miles up the River] In Sokoki territory, on the Connecticut River, near its confluence with the Ashuelot River.

957.16   *a small part of the Company*] Weetamoo and Quinnapin set off on an expedition northward, encamping just below the Ashuelot River crossing.

957.29   *the River*] Ashuelot River.

958.4   *Nux*] Yes.

958.19–20   she would go no further] Weetamoo turned back at this point to return to the large encampments to the south, most likely because her child was so ill.

958.21   her *Sannup*] Her husband, Quinnapin.

959.26–27   *a mighty Thicket of Brush*] Rowlandson is vague about the location, but other documents place this camp at Pocumtuck, near the English town of Deerfield.

960.8–10   *Have pitty . . . touched me.*] Job 19:21.

960.17–18   *I will go out . . . departed from him*] Judges 16:20.

961.2   *Thomas Read*] Thomas Reed was captured in April 1676 at Hockanum, in Hadley, a Massachusetts Bay Colony town in Nonotuck territory. He escaped and was a soldier on Captain Turner's raid at the Great Falls of the Connecticut River in May 1676.

961.13–14   the Governour] John Leverett, see note 895.11.

961.17   *Philips* Maid] A kinswoman of Metacom.

962.1–2   *John Gilberd*] John Gilbert (b. 1657), Massachusetts Bay settler and soldier who resided at Springfield, where he was captured in October 1675.

963.20   *Pascataqua* in *Portsmouth*] See note 612.31.

963.33   *Remember now*] Isaiah 38:3.

963.38–39   *Against thee . . . God be merciful*] Psalm 51:4 and Luke 18:13.

964.3   the poor Prodigal] See Luke 15.

964.15   *For a small moment*] Isaiah 54:7.

964.20   Cake] Cornbread, or journey cake.

965.10   *Baquaug River*] Weetamoo's company crossed the Paquaug River again, as they reversed their course to travel to Wachusett, in Nipmuc territory, for councils.

966.9   *Wachusett*] A Nipmuc homeland and stronghold where many Native leaders gathered in the spring of 1676, including Quinnapin and Weetamoo.

966.10   Letter come from the Council] This is a letter from Massachusetts governor John Leverett asking Native leaders for the redemption of English captives as part of the opening of peace negotiations.

968.31–32   painting her face] This refers to ceremonial paint, although Rowlandson's depiction makes it appear that Weetamoo was using cosmetics.

968.34   Girdles of *Wampom* and *Beads*] Weetamoo wove and wore wampum belts, which symbolized her leadership and her community's agreements and alliances with other nations. The necklaces, jewels, and bracelets are also likely wampum, the sacred shell bead worn by leaders. See note 129.11–12.

969.6   redemption-pay] The items of trade goods or money that Massachusetts settlers would deliver in exchange for Rowlandson, a high-status captive.

969.12   *Tom* and *Peter*] Tom Nepanet, one of the Nipmucs who had been imprisoned on Deer Island, and Peter Tatatoqinea (or Peter Conway), another Nipmuc man.

970.2   a Praying-*Indian*] Wawaus, or James Printer (see note 850.18), served as a scribe for the Nipmuc leaders.

970.13–15   another Praying-*Indian* . . . into the *English* hands] Probably Peter Jethro, see note 855.36.

970.16–17   *Sudbury-fight*] See Chronology, April 1676.

970.23   *Powaw*] Traditional ceremony, dance.

971.27   the *Powaw*] See note 203.5.

971.28–29   black as the Devil] The leader's face was painted black in mourning.

971.30   hollandlaced Pillowbeer] A pillowcase made from cloth from the Netherlands.

972.11 great *Wigwam*] Longhouse, large council house, built at Wachusett.

972.26–27 *Goodwife Kettle*] Elizabeth Kettle, another Lancaster settler.

973.2 John Hoar] John Hoar (d. 1704), a settler who resided in Concord or Musketaquid, and served as overseer of Native converts at Nashoba, was sent to negotiate with the leaders gathered at Wachusett. When he returned to Boston with Rowlandson, he delivered a collective letter from the leaders regarding a possible treaty with Massachusetts Bay Colony, in response to the "third letter" mentioned by Rowlandson.

973.40 Matchit] Bad.

975.30 Fort-fight] The English attack on the Narragansett Great Swamp fortress, December 19, 1675.

975.40–976.3 *Shall there be evil . . . that go Captive.*] Amos 3:6, Amos 6:6–7.

976.3–4 *It is the Lords doing . . . in our eyes.*] Psalm 118:23.

977.33 *Agag*-like] I Samuel 15:32.

977.37 *Help Lord*] Matthew 8:25.

979.32 *Thomas Shepard*] Thomas Shepard, Jr. (1635–1677), Massachusetts Bay Colony minister and settler of Charlestown.

980.18–19 Mr. *William Hubbard*] Hubbard (1621–1704), Massachusetts Bay Colony minister who wrote a narrative of King Philip's War published in 1677.

980.19–20 Major *Waldrens*] Richard Waldron (1615–1689), English trader and military commander at Dover, New Hampshire, in Cocheco, a Wabanaki homeland.

980.33–34 *valley of the shadow of Death*] Psalm 23:4.

980.35 *Refrain thy voice*] Jeremiah 31:16.

981.10 Governour of *Road-Island*] William Coddington, see note 463.40–41.

981.13 Mr. *Newman*] Noah Newman (1631–1678), minister at Rehoboth in Plymouth Colony, in Wampanoag territory.

982.10 Mony answers] Ecclesiastes 10:19.

982.22 *James Whitcomb*] Whitcomb (1626–1686), a Boston merchant who housed Rowlandson and her family. He traded in enslaved Native people during and after the war.

982.35–36 *honey out of the rock*] Psalm 81:16.

982.36 fatted Calf] Luke 15:11–32.

983.26–27 *It is good for me*] Psalm 119:71.

983.28–29 *Vanity of vanities*] Ecclesiastes 1:2 and 1:14.

986.7 Brigstreet bridge] A bridge in Medfield, a town in Massachusetts Bay Colony, within Nipmuc territory, that was later known as "Death Bridge."

987.5–6 John Cotton] See note 906.2.

989.17 Mr. *Sanfords* . . . his Wife] Captain John Sanford, Jr. (1633–1686), colonial leader in Portsmouth, Rhode Island, had tried to create a false deed to "deceive" Weetamoo "of her land," according to testimony in Plymouth Court, and who also had conflicts with Metacom over the free-range hogs Metacom raised on Chesawanocke, known also as Hog-Island. Alice Southworth Church (1648–1719) was the wife of Benjamin Church and daughter of Constant Southworth.

989.22 Capt. *Golding*] Roger Goulding, see note 901.16.

989.28 Sandpoint] Sandy Point in Bristol, Rhode Island, a name that settlers gave to the feature after Montaup was claimed by conquest.

990.5 *Trips* Ferry] Bristol Ferry, run by Abial Trip, a settler in Portsmouth, Rhode Island.

990.35–36 Capt. *Williams*] John Williams, Jr. (d. 1694), a settler of Scituate in Plymouth Colony, who was granted payment in land for service as a military officer in King Philip's War.

991.20 Petunk] Pouch.

991.25 the *Indian*] Alderman, see note 902.16.

991.31 *iootash*] Missionaries, including John Eliot and Roger Williams, translated this as "fight."

991.32 his *Indian Peter*] Probably Peter, son of Awashonks, sôkushqâ of Sakonnet.

991.33 *Annowon*] Annawon, a Wampanoag counselor and elder who had a close relationship with Metacom.

992.17 a small Speech] This speech is likely fictional.

992.23 that hand] Metacom's hands were delivered by Church to the Massachusetts governor and council, on behalf of Josiah Winslow, the Plymouth governor. The story Church tells of giving Philip's hand to Alderman is likely apocryphal.

996.2 William Wannukhow, Joseph Wannukhow, and John Appamatahqeen] William Wannukhow, a Nipmuc man who lived at Magunkaquog, a praying town (now Ashland, Massachusetts); Joseph Wannukhow, the son of William Wannukhow, who also lived at Magunkoag; John Appamatahqeen, a Nipmuc man who lived at Magunkoag.

996.14 your declaration dated the 19th of June] Massachusetts Bay Colony's declaration, June 19, 1676, allowing amnesty to those Native people who came in and surrendered, which was prompted by a petition of the Native scouts who served with the troops, including James Quananopohit and Job Kattenanit. The scouts pleaded for "the lives and libertyes of those few of our poor friends and kindred, that, in this time of temptation and affliction, have been in the enemy's quarters" and asked Massachusetts Bay Colony leaders "to shew mercy, and especially to such who have (as we conceive) done no wrong to the English." The Wannukhows and John Appamatahqeen came in under this declaration.

996.21 Capt. Prentice] See note 926.9. Prentiss's farm was on the Connecticut Path, relatively close to Natick and Magunkoag, and he received some of those who came in under the amnesty declaration at his house, including James Printer and the Wannukhow family.

996.28 Goodman Eames] Thomas Eames (1618–1680), a Massachusetts Bay Colony settler who had built a house near Magunkaquog on land leased from Thomas Danforth.

996.34 Netus] Netus had previously sold the land upon which the Eames farm was built. See note 842.32.

996.34 another man] Annaweekin, see note 844.18.

998.19 James Printer] James Printer (see note 857.29) had come in under the declaration and encouraged the Wannukhow family to come in, believing they would be granted amnesty. He may have helped to author the petition to the Massachusetts Bay Council.

1000.4 Quanpen, otherwise Sowagonish, an Indian sachem] Quinnapin, see note 889.24–25.

1000.38–39 the swamp Fight] The United Colonies attack on the Narragansetts, and the Wampanoag people they sheltered, at the Great Swamp in December 1675.

1001.1 Pettacomscutt] See note 892.22–23.

1001.2 William Carpenters Garisson at Pawtuxet] William Carpenter (c. 1610–1685), a Rhode Island settler and land speculator, built a fortified block house in the Narragansett territory of Pawtuxet, which was raided by a large Native force after the Great Swamp battle. Pawtuxet is at the confluence of the Pawtuxet and Providence Rivers.

1001.3 Nashaway] See note 856.2–3.

1001.15 Sunkeecunasuck] Sunkeejunasuc (d. 1676), a Narragansett man, brother to Quinnapin.

1001.16 Warwick] See note 891.34.

1001.16–17 Wenunaquabin] Wenanaquabbin (d. 1676), a Narragansett man, who resided at Pawtuxet, at the home of Abiah Carpenter (1643–c. 1689), William Carpenter's son.

1001.26 Ashamattan] A Narragansett man, brother to Quinnapin.

1001.30 the Dutch] Dutch settlers in New York Colony.

1001.33 John Scott] See note 892.36–37.

1002.4–5 the Fight with Capt. Turner] Captain William Turner (d. 1676) led a deadly assault on Peskeompscut, the fishing falls on the Connecticut River, in Pocumtuck territory on May 19, 1676, where many Native families were gathered for spring fishing.

1002.9 John Wecopeak] A Narragansett man.

1002.29 Anashawin] A Narragansett man.

1002.30 John Green] John Greene, Jr. (1620–1708), English settler who held a large estate in Warwick, in Pawtuxet Narragansett territory, and later served as deputy governor of Rhode Island Colony.

1002.36 Quonaehewacout] A Narragansett man.

1002.37 Jreh Bulls Garrison] See note 892.22–23.

1002.38 Manasses Molasses] A Wampanoag man, at Pocasset in the summer of 1676.

1002.39 Low Howland] Zoeth or Zoar Howland (c. 1636–1676), a settler who was killed at Howland's Ferry in Pocasset territory (Stone Bridge in Tiverton, Rhode Island).

1002.39 Pocasset Side] On the east or "Pocasset" side of the Sakonnet River, in Pocasset territory.

1003.9 John Cook] See note 621.35.

1003.10 Punckatest] See note 612.11.

1003.18 Joseph Russell] Joseph Russell, Sr. (1650–1739), the son of Dartmouth settler John Russell (1608–1694), whose house became a garrison in the Wampanoag homeland of Apponagansett.

1003.21 Wm. Cadman] William Cadman (c. 1625–1684) deputy to the General Assembly and settler who resided in Portsmouth, Rhode Island Colony, in Narragansett territory.

1003.22 William Manchester] William Manchester (1654–1718), Rhode Island settler, resident of Portsmouth, held a claim on the Pocasset Neck lands.

1003.31 Awetamoes Sister] An unnamed sister of Weetamoo.

1004.3 Mumuxuack alias Toby] A Wampanoag man.

1004.5 John Archer] See note 917.1.

1004.15 Jack Havens] A Wampanoag man who was with the saunkskwa Awashonks of Sakonnet in the summer of 1676, who Benjamin Church said had "never been in the war."

1004.17 Whaweapunet] A Wampanoag man, brother to Mumuxuack alias Toby.

1004.26 Suckats Squa . . . Daniel Wilcocks] "Suckats Squa" probably refers to the wife of a Native man named Suckats, who was likely a servant of Daniel Wilcox (1632–1702), a settler who resided in Dartmouth and had a claim on the Pocasset Neck lands.

1004.31 Serjeant Roger's] James Rogers (d. 1676), keeper of the colonial prison in Newport.

1005.4 Walter Clarke] Walter Clarke (c. 1638–1714), governor of Rhode Island Colony, 1676–77, and a resident of Newport.

1006.2 WINSLOW] Josiah Winslow, see note 476.29.

1008.10 the Great River] Sowams River.

1008.15 Captaine Thomas Willett] See note 623.4.

1008.19 a Certaine deed] The "Sowams and Parts Adjacent" deed of 1653. Settlers of Swansea and Rehoboth claimed land under the 1653 deed that Plymouth Colony sought to distribute by right of conquest.

1008.35 Caviott] Caveat.

1009.4–15 Samuell Newman . . . Phillip Walker] Samuel Newman, Jr. (1625–1711), son of Samuel Newman (1602–1663), original grantee and Rehoboth's first minister, who renamed Seekonk in biblical fashion. Newman and all the men listed below held long-standing interest in large tracts of land in Rehoboth and Swansea, and all but one resided in those towns. They all held land through the Sowams and Parts Adjacent deed, either as original proprietors, by inheritance, or by sale. Samuel Peck (1638–1708), son of Joseph Peck, an original Rehoboth grantee; Israel Peck (1644–1723), brother of Samuel Peck and son of Joseph Peck; Captain John Brown III, see note 878.2; James Brown (c. 1624–1710), son of John Brown, see note 624.12–13; John Saffin (1632–1710), a judge who resided in Boston but held land at Rehoboth and Swansea, son-in-law of Thomas Willett; Nathaniel Paine (1631–1678), son of Stephen Paine, Sr., an original Rehoboth grantee; John Allen, an original Rehoboth grantee; Stephen Paine, Jr., see note 916.28; Thomas Chaffee (c. 1610–1683), Plymouth Colony settler who held land in Rehoboth and Swansea; Peter Hunt (1619–1692), an original Rehoboth grantee; Phillip Walker (c. 1625–1679), an original Rehoboth grantee.

1009.28 Showmett] See note 878.16–17.

1009.28 Assonett] See note 626.17–20.

1010.7 Capt. John Gorum] Captain John Gorham (1620–1676), Plymouth Colony military officer who was granted land on Papasquash neck by the Plymouth Court in 1673, with the condition that it be purchased "of the Indians." Papasquash neck was included in the Sowams and Parts Adjacent deed of 1653, but it was also part of the larger peninsula of Montaup.

1010.8 Papasquash Necke] See note 1010.7.

1010.20 the Treasurer] Constant Southworth, see note 609.6–7.

1010.21 Cornett Studson and Mr Nathaniel Thomas] Robert Studson (1615–1703), military officer during King Philip's War, deputy to Plymouth Court from Scituate; Nathaniel Thomas, Jr. (1643–1718), military officer, deputy to Plymouth Court from Marshfield, son of Captain Nathaniel Thomas, Sr.

1010.31 Swansey lands] Land belonging to the town of Swansea via deeds from Tatamomock, a Wampanoag man, in May 1673.

1011.3 Mount Hope Necke] Montaup, or Mount Hope. Plymouth Colony claimed this peninsular land by conquest in 1676 but their claim was not confirmed by Charles II until 1680. Swansea also claimed a tract at the north end of the peninsula, based on previous deeds, and with this document Plymouth Colony sought to resolve the conflict by settling a boundary within "a strip of land at the entrance of Mount Hope neck."

1011.11 Kekamenest Springe] Kickemuit springs, a vital water source within the Wampanoag homeland and planting place of Kickemuit, northeast of Montaup, now in Warren, Rhode Island.

1011.14 Mr Hinckley] Thomas Hinckley, see note 624.19.

1011.20–22 Barnabas Laythorpe . . . Huckens] Barnabus Laythorpe (1636–1715), deputy to Plymouth court from Barnstable; Daniel Smith (1635–1692) deputy to Plymouth Court from Rehoboth; William Peabody, see note 627.20–27; Thomas Huckins or Huckens (1618–1679), deputy to Plymouth Court from Barnstable, commissary general during King Philip's War.

1012.20–21 Nathaniel: Winslow . . . John Mendall] Nathaniel Winslow (1639–1719), cousin of Josiah Winslow and son of Kenelm Winslow (1599–1672), settler of Marshfield in Plymouth Colony; Isaac Little (1646–1699), settler of Marshfield in Plymouth Colony, son of Thomas Little; Ephraim Little (1650–1717), brother of Isaac and Samuel Little, settler of Marshfield and Scituate in Plymouth Colony; Samuel Little (c. 1656–c.1707), brother of Isaac and Ephraim Little, settler of Marshfield in Plymouth Colony; John Mendall (c. 1738–c.1711), settler of Marshfield in Plymouth Colony.

1012.22–25 Walter Briggs . . . Daniell Daman] Walter Briggs (d. c. 1684), settler of Scituate in Plymouth Colony, granted payment in land for service in King Philip's War; John Williams, Jr., see note 990.35–36; Richard Dwelley (d. 1692), settler of Scituate in Plymouth Colony, granted payment in land for service in King Philip's War; John James (c. 1646–c. 1678), settler of Scituate in Plymouth Colony, wounded in King Philip's War; William Hatch (c. 1624–c. 1702), settler of Scituate and Swansea in Plymouth Colony, granted payment in land for service in King Philip's War; William Peakes (d. c. 1682), settler of Scituate in Plymouth Colony; Jonathan Jackson (1647–1725), settler of Scituate in Plymouth Colony, granted payment in land for service in King Philip's War; Richard Prouty (1652–1708), settler of Scituate in Plymouth Colony, granted payment in land for service in King Philip's War; Isaac Buck (d. c. 1695), selectman and town clerk of Scituate in Plymouth Colony, granted payment in land for service as a lieutenant in King Philip's War; Zacharia (also Zachary) Damon (1655–1730), settler of Scituate in Plymouth Colony, granted payment in land for service as a lieutenant in King Philip's War; Daniel Damon (1651–1696), settler of Scituate in Plymouth Colony, brother of Zacharia. Their brother John was also granted payment in land for service in King Philip's War, but died in October 1677.

1012.26–27   Capt: Benjamine Church . . . Jonathan Aldin] Benjamin Church, see note 916.12–13; Jonathan Alden (c. 1632–1687), settler of Duxbury in Plymouth Colony, son of John Alden (c. 1599–1687), served as a soldier and officer in King Philip's War.

1012.28–30   Edward Gray . . . Mathew Fuller] Edward Gray (1623–1681), settler of Plymouth, son-in-law of John Winslow; Matthew Fuller, see note 897.6–7.

1012.31–35   Encrease Robinson . . . Samuell Prince] Increase Robinson, Sr. (1642–1699), one of the original purchasers of Taunton lands; Malachi Holloway (c. 1647–c. 1725), settler of Taunton, son of William Holloway of Marshfield; Thomas Lincoln (c. 1601–1683), settler of Taunton; John Smith (1618–1692), settler of Taunton; Joseph Wood (1653–1697), settler of Taunton; David Wood (1651–1717), settler of Taunton, brother of Joseph; Thomas Paine, Jr. (1610–1706), settler of Eastham; Samuel Prince (1649–1728), settler of Hull, in Massachusetts Bay Colony.

1013.17   Mr Brentons] William Brenton or Brinton (1610–1674), governor of Rhode Island Colony, 1666–69, landholder in Taunton and Mattapoisett (Pocasset territory).

1015.18–19   John Alden Assistant] See note 494.4.

1016.1   Commissones of the united Collonies] The commissioners of the United Colonies in March 1679 included Thomas Danforth (1623–1699) and Joseph Dudley (1647–1720) for Massachusetts Bay, Thomas Hinckley (1618–1706) and Josiah Winslow (c. 1629–1680) for Plymouth, and John Allyn (1631–1696) and James Richards (1631–1680) for Connecticut.

1016.9   proffitts of prisoners] Native prisoners taken during and after the war, some of whom were sold as slaves. Plymouth had previously demanded that Rhode Island turn over the "enemies" that were in their colony, authorizing

Benjamin Church to bring the prisoners to Plymouth and "sell and dispose of them."

1016.21–22   Major William Bradford] See note 906.2.

1017.4   Punckateeset] See note 612.11.

1017.5   Christopher Almey . . . Waite] Christopher Almy (1632–1714/13), Rhode Island settler, resident of Portsmouth, brother of Captain John Almy, who had one of the few houses on Pocasset Neck before the war; Job Almy (1639–1684), Rhode Island settler, resident of Portsmouth, brother of Captain John Almy and Christopher Almy; Thomas Waite, Jr. (1648–1733), Rhode Island settler, resident of Portsmouth.

1017.7   Daniel Wilcockes] Daniel Wilcox, see note 1004.26.

1017.7   William Manchester] See note 1003.22.

1017.22   Pocasset] Plymouth Colony claimed the area by conquest after the war. This deed is known as the Pocasset purchase, and most of the lots, which were south of the river Quequachand or Fall River, were later incorporated as the town of Tiverton, Rhode Island.

1017.24–25   freemens lotts neare the fall River] Lots surveyed in association with the Freemens' deed of 1659. These lots, on the north side of the river Quequechand or Fall River, in Weetamoo's territory of Pocasset, were not settled until after the war.

1017.25   the Bay or sound] Mount Hope Bay and the Sakonnet River.

1017.31   Middleberry] Middleboro, an English town within the Wampanoag territory of Nemasket.

1017.31–32   Quitquesett ponds] Quitacass Ponds, in Nemasket and Middleboro.

1017.35   David and Thomas Lake] Thomas Lake (c. 1644–c. 1687) and his brother David Lake (see note 898.13) were granted one hundred acres of land at Pocasset for their service under Benjamin Church in King Philip's War. They were sons of Henry Lake (d. 1673), a Dartmouth settler.

1017.38   Captain Richard Morris] See note 612.9.

1019.36   Joseph Church] Joseph Church (1637–1711), brother to Benjamin Church, settler at Sakonnet.

1020.20   Nathaniel Morton] See note 115.38.

1022.4   Mrs Hamons] Elizabeth Hammond (d. 1684), wife of trader Richard Hammond (d. 1676), was a captive taken from the Hammond trading post on the Kennebec River at Arrowsic, south of Taconnic, where Wabanaki leaders were gathered. This statement was transcribed for the Wabanaki leaders whose names are listed below, either by Elizabeth Hammond or William Wormwood.

1022.6 govenour of boston] John Leverett, see note 895.11.

1022.9 Mr. garner] Thomas Gardner, a trader at Pemaquid, who advocated for Wabanaki people on the Kennebec.

1022.13 damrallscogon engins] Ameriscoggin Indians, Wabanaki people on the Androscoggin River.

1022.17 Pemaquid] Pemaquid, a peninsula at the mouth of the Kennebec River, in Sagadahoc, in the Wabanaki homeland.

1022.18 Squando] Squando (d. c. 1682), a Wabanaki leader on the Saco River, who led raids on English settlements in the northern front of King Philip's War, 1675–78.

1022.25 pesabel] Peaceable.

1022.31–32 Squando Angons] Squando's Indians.

1022.33–1023.2 William Woum Wood . . . john] William Wormwood (1620–1690), an English settler who lived in Wabanaki territory, taken captive in the war; Winekemet or Winawermet, Wabanaki leader from the Kennebec River; Moxus, Wabanaki leader from the Kennebec River, a party to multiple treaties, including the Treaty of Casco Bay in 1701, a renewal of the treaty of 1678 that ended the northern front of King Philip's War. In 1677, the Wabanaki leaders of the Kennebec were gathered at Taconnic, but Moxus later represented the Wabanaki community at Narantsoak, or Norridgewock, upriver; Essemenosque or Assiminsqua, Wabanaki leader from Taconnic, on the Kennebec River; Madoasquarbet, a Wabanaki spiritual leader from the Kennebec River, known to the English as Deogenes; tasset probably refers to Toxus, a Wabanaki leader from the Kennebec River; john probably refers to Sheepscot John, a Wabanaki leader with ties to the Saco River, Sheepscot River, and Kennebec River.

1023.8 cot] Coat.

1023.10 engon dog] Indian dog.

1023.12 skins] Beaver pelts or moose hides, both common in trade.

1023.13 war at naragans] The Wabanaki leaders referred to the beginning of King Philip's War as the war at Narragansett, although it broke out in neighboring Wampanoag territory. From their perspective, the war began far to the south, beyond Wabanaki territory.

1023.14 took away our gons] Confiscated our guns, used primarily for hunting.

1023.15 sagamore] Wabanaki leader.

1023.17 siler] Cellar, storeroom.

1023.19 on engon] One Indian.

1023.26   fashing] Fashion, way, manner.

1023.27   Major Waldin] Richard Waldron, see note 980.19–20. Waldron had engaged in several deceits that facilitated the capture of Wabanaki people and was renowned for his nefarious trading practices.

1023.36   deogenes madoasquarbet] See note 1022.33–1023.2.

WAMPANOAG CONTINUANCE

1027.29–31   Israel Amos, Isaac Coombs, Ezra Attaquin] Israel Amos was tribal secretary for the Mashpee; Coombs and Attaquin were also Mashpee Wampanoag leaders (Apess later calls them selectmen).

1029.4   BENJAMIN F. HALLETT] Hallett (1797–1862) was the attorney for the Mashpees and editor of the *Boston Advocate*.

1032.14   FISH] Phineas Fish (1785–1854), the minister appointed by Harvard College as the minister to Mashpee in 1811, as part of the college's oversight of the reservation.

1033.38   Solomon's temple] Cf. 1 Kings 6.

1034.13   It is written that my house] Matthew 21:13.

1034.29   *Blind Joe*] Blind Joe Amos (1805–1869) was a Mashpee minister who preached to Native people while Fish used the Mashpee meetinghouse to preach to settlers.

1037.1–2   Ebenezer Attaquin] Tribal president at Mashpee.

1038.21   Corporation of Harvard College] The corporation held Mashpee lands in trust and appointed a minister to serve the community.

1039.21   Williams Fund] A fund established in 1711 by Daniel Williams (c. 1643–1716), Presbyterian minister, for Native people of New England.

1041.9   oppression of the Cherokees] The Cherokees faced political pressure and violence from the state of Georgia, which sought jurisdiction of Cherokee lands and resources.

1043.21   Daniel Amos] Amos owned an oyster concern and served as a Mashpee leader during and after the revolt.

1050.5   PHILLIP of Greece] Philip II (382–336 BCE), king of Macedonia and father of Alexander the Great.

1051.34   one of the most celebrated chiefs] Ousamequin, see note 191.19.

1052.8   like Sampson] See note 852.26.

1052.13–14   Henry Harley] Edward Harlow, who led an expedition to capture slaves on the Wabanaki and Wampanoag coast and took Epenow captive. Apess is quoting Ferdinando Gorges (from Drake's *Book of the Indians*), who referred to him as Henry Harley. Harlow's expedition was in 1611, but Epenow returned to Noepe, with Captain Hobson's expedition for Gorges in 1614, escaping the ship.

1052.15 Capawick] Capawick or Capoge, which Samuel Drake identifies as Martha's Vineyard, or Noepe.

1052.16 Epenuel] See note 92.12.

1052.25 Drake's Hist. of the Indians] Samuel Gardner Drake (1798–1875), *Book of the Indians, Or, Biography and History of the Indians of North America: From Its First Discovery to the Year 1841* (1833), Book II, pp. 7–8.

1053.6 IYANOUGH] See note 161.26–27.

1053.8 Capt. Hunt] See note 148.30.

1054.19 Squanto and Samoset] Tisquantum, see note 150.26; and Samoset, see 147.20–21.

1054.22 Mr. Weston's Colony] See note 197.3.

1055.5 Wittumumet] See note 204.27.

1055.17 CHICATAUBUT] Chickatawbut, see note 167.28–29.

1056.6 Georgia to Maine] Many New Englanders were aware of and vocal in opposition to the removal of the Cherokees from Georgia, and they criticized Georgia settlers who advocated for removal.

1056.13–14 Mr. Dermer] See note 107.22.

1056.29 MASSASOIT] See note 191.19.

1057.11 ALEXANDER] Wamsutta, see note 613.5.

1057.25 Dr. Mather] Increase Mather (1639–1723), Massachusetts Bay Colony minister and author of the *Brief History of the Warr with the Indians in New-England* (1676) and other texts (see note 935.4). Mather's account was one of three conflicting narratives of Wamsutta's capture and death, all written after King Philip's War. It was republished in Drake's *Book of the Indians*, Book III, pp. 7–8.

1058.10 COUBANTANT] See note 164.12.

1059.1–2 a benevolent Chief] Masconomet or Masconomo, sôtyum of Agawam, who had formally welcomed John Winthrop and his company when they arrived in 1630.

1060.10–11 forgotten . . . in your speeches] Apess alludes to the famous oration given by Daniel Webster at Plymouth on December 22, 1820.

1060.11 the Rock] Plymouth Rock, where the Plymouth colonists supposedly landed, despite the absence of any such account in colonial narratives;

a myth developed in the early nineteenth century with the celebration of Plymouth Colony as the foundation of the future United States.

1061.4–5   NAHUM GOLD] A minister in Union Grove, Putnam County, Illinois.

1062.19   ROGER WILLIAMS] See note 488.10.

1062.24   CANONICUS] See note 187.24.

1064.10   Winthrop] Apess identified Winthrop as the governor, but he must have meant Josiah Winslow, who led the expedition to capture Wamsutta and was governor of Plymouth Colony during King Philip's War.

1064.21–1065.8   William Benton . . . Hugh Cole] Apess lists here men, from Rhode Island and Plymouth colonies, who were beneficiaries of deeds in which Metacom and his kin purportedly sold land or consented to extend the bounds of earlier deeds to encompass more land. Some, like Constant Southworth, a Plymouth Colony Assistant, were central to Plymouth's attempts to increase the colony's land base and profits, including the use of debt and force to compel Native people to sell or confirm lands.

1064.22   Matapoisett] This was Conbitant's central village, part of Pocasset territory, which may be why Metacom's wife, Wootenakanuske (Conbitant's daughter), was required to sign. Legally, Plymouth Colony should have sought consent from Weetamoo, who was the leader of Pocasset at that time. Mattapoisett was later absorbed by Swansea, Massachusetts.

1064.26–27   Dartmouth to Matapoisett] This was an extension of the earlier deed for land that became the town of Dartmouth, from Acoaxet to Acushnet. This extended Dartmouth's bounds easterly, to Mattapoisett (now Mattapoisett, Massachusetts), a different location from Conbitant's village (now Swansea, Massachusetts), but with a similar place-name.

1064.36   John Brown and Edward Winslow] Plymouth Colony leaders who negotiated with Ousamequin in 1641 for land in Seekonk, in Pokanoket territory, which became the town of Rehoboth. In 1668, Plymouth Colony leaders required that Metacom sign a quitclaim or confirmation deed, as the original agreement did not exist.

1065.1–2   New Meadows] See note 623.29.

1065.6   Nokatay] An island within Wampanoag territory, south of Mattapoisett, now West Island, Fairhaven, Massachusetts. John Cook was one of the original settlers of the town of Dartmouth and this deed was an extension of the town bounds.

1065.7   Middleborough] Middleboro, see note 1017.31. The sôtyum of Nemasket was Tuspaquin, who was married to Metacom's sister, Amie.

1065.16   Peter Talmon] Peter Tallman (1623–1708), a Rhode Island colonist who in 1674 brought to the Plymouth Court a deed claiming that Wamsutta gave him a large tract of land in 1661. Weetamoo had made a complaint to the Plymouth Court against Tallman's deed in 1662, ultimately compelling Plymouth to recognize her jurisdiction. In 1674, the Plymouth Court forced Tallman to surrender the deed, which they declared null and void, as he had acted without the approval of the Plymouth Court, claiming land which they insisted was within their jurisdiction versus Rhode Island's.

1066.19–20 the governor] Thomas Prence, see note 491.33. Prence was governor in 1671, but Josiah Winslow, who succeeded him in 1673, led the effort to try to contain Metacom, in both 1671 and 1675–76.

1066.28 Massachusetts] The governor and council of Massachusetts Bay Colony. Metacom and his counselors traveled to Boston in September 1671 to make a complaint against Plymouth Colony's encroachment on Wampanoag lands and liberty to the other commissioners of the United Colonies, insisting that Plymouth was violating the Articles of Confederation and that Governor Prence was "a subject of King Charles of England" and he, Metacom, "would treat of peace only with the King."

1068.37 Patuckson; Tobias] Patuckson, the Native convert who accused Philip's counselors Tobias and Mattashunannamo, as well as Tobias's son, Wampapaquan, of killing John Sassamon, which relieved him of the debt he owed one of them; Tobias, Wampanoag leader (d. 1675), tried and executed by Plymouth Colony for the murder of John Sassamon, along with his son, Wampapaquan (d. 1675) and the Wampanoag leader Mattashunannamo (d. 1675). Plymouth Court offered bail to Tobias in exchange for a deed to Assowamsett, in Nemasket, making the sôtyum Tuspaquin, Tobias, and Tuspaquin's son "bind over all their lands" to the Court for the price of his bond. See Chronology, February–June 1675.

1070.33–34 the following speech] This was not an actual speech of Metacom. Apess does not identify his source, or the preceding poem. The style reflects nineteenth-century American literary practices.

1072.5 great fight at Pocasset] The battle at Pocasset cedar swamp, in Weetamoo's homeland. A combined army of Massachusetts and Plymouth troops, including several Native scouts, entered the cedar swamp on July 19, 1675.

1072.6 his host] Weetamoo, the leader of Pocasset, had given Metacom (her brother-in-law) shelter, along with their kin. Neither Metacom nor Weetamoo was taken by the troops, and most of their kin escaped with them to Narragansett and Nipmuc territories.

1073.5 Northfield] See note 929.10.

1073.23 mampampeag] See note 129.11–12. George Memecho reported that Metacom divided his wampum among the Nipmuc leaders at Menimesit, a symbol of their alliance, after he arrived with his kin in August 1675 during the siege at Quaboag.

1073.34–35   Sugar-loaf Hill] The mountain known also as the Great Beaver (South Deerfield, Massachusetts). Captain Thomas Lathrop and his Massachusetts Colony troops were ambushed on the west side of the mountain on September 18, 1675.

1074.1   Narragansetts] Although many settlers believed Metacom went to Narragansett at this time, it was later demonstrated that he was not there. He was with Nipmuc leaders in August and at least part of fall 1675, and later pursued a diplomatic expedition in Mohican country, in winter 1675–76. The United Colonies did raise one thousand men to march to Narragansett country, in part because Narragansett leaders did not release the Wampanoag people who took sanctuary among them, including Weetamoo and her kin. However, Metacom was not at Great Swamp when the United Colonies troops invaded in December 1675, as Apess suggested here.

1074.26   Peter] "Indian Peter" was taken captive by the English and when threatened with hanging, told colonial forces the location of the Narragansett fortress at Great Swamp and guided them there.

1074.38   Captain Moseley] See note 906.28–29.

1075.27   one of the whites had married] Joshua Tefft, or Tift, see note 932.3.

1075.36   Mohawks] Kanienkehaka people of the Haudenosaunee (Iroquois) Confederacy. While Metacom was pursuing a possible alliance with Mohicans, New York Colony used its diplomatic relationship with Kaniekehaka people to encourage them to expel Metacom from their colony and Mohawk-Mohican territory. Governor Edmund Andros did not want to see what he regarded as New England's war spread into his colony. Mohawk warriors continued to strike Native people in New England periodically, but sometimes attacked Christian Indian allies of the colonies as well, pursuing their own goals.

1076.18   Mrs. Rolandson] See note 935.2.

1076.35   Capt. Church] See note 916.12–13.

1077.10   Philip's son and wife] Metacom was married to Wootonakanuske of Pocasset, Weetamoo's sister. The name of his son is not recorded.

1078.20   Thomas Lucas] Lucas (c. 1614–1675), a Plymouth settler.

1078.21   Lucas and Hedge] In *Indian Nullification*, Apess lists Lucas of Plymouth as one of the members of the Massachusetts House of Representatives who argued against hearing a petition drawn up by the Mashpee Wampanoags in defense of the right to retain and manage their woods and in protest of the colonial overseers who misused their position. Apess identified Hedge as a state senator from Plymouth who tried to remove Apess's name from a resolution.

1079.21   "Cold with the beast] Charles Sprague (1791–1875), "An Ode: pronounced before the Inhabitants of Boston," to celebrate the "centennial settlement of the city," September 17, 1830. Apess may also be drawing from Samuel Drake's *The Book of the Indians of North America*, which includes a slightly longer selection from Sprague's ode.

1082.23   Mr. Gooking] Daniel Gookin (1612–1687) helped establish the "praying towns" and served in the Massachusetts Bay Colony militia, as a deputy to the General Court, and as superintendent of the Christian Indians.

1090.11–12   pressed between stone slabs] Giles Corey (1611–1692), a farmer in Salem, was accused during the 1692 witchcraft prosecutions. When Corey refused to enter a plea, he was placed under a wooden board loaded with heavy stones to force him to plead either guilty or not guilty to the charges. Corey continued to resist and was eventually crushed to death.

1090.14   reservations set up] Connecticut Colony established reservations for Pequot people in the 1650s and 1680s, as part of its efforts to contain the tribe.

1090.23–24   dig up the ground . . . unleash the great epidemic] Cf. *A Relation*, where Tisquantum says that the colonists "had the plague buried in our store-house; which, at our pleasure, we could send forth to what place or people we would, and destroy them therewith, though we stirred not from home."

1091.20   statue of our great Sachem] A statue of Massasoit stands on Cole's Hill, in Plymouth. James helped to found the United American Indians of New England, a group that worked with the town of Plymouth to erect several plaques near this statue, one about Philip and one about the National Day of Mourning that the UAINE observes on the fourth Thursday in November.

1091.33   wards of the United States government] The U.S. Supreme Court's 1831 decision in *Cherokee Nation v. Georgia* defined Native nations as "domestic dependent nations" whose relationship to the United States was that of a "ward to his guardian."

1096.18   "papal bulls"] A formal, official letter or proclamation of the pope, which is marked by the "bulla," a metal seal. In 1493, Pope Alexander VI issued the first papal bull, which authorized Spanish (Catholic) colonization of the Americas.

1096.19   Pope Nicholas] Nicholas V (1397–1455), born as Tommaso Parentucelli in the Republic of Genoa, was elected pope of the Roman Catholic Church in 1447. Two papal bulls issued by Nicholas V, in 1652 ("Dum Diversas") and 1655 ("Romanus Pontifex"), authorized and encouraged the conquest and enslavement of non-Christian peoples in the lands that Catholic Europeans sought to colonize, including Africa and the Americas, and claimed dominion for Catholic nations over those lands, authorizing the seizure of lands from Indigenous peoples. Together, the papal bulls of Nicholas V and Alexander VI form the basis for the Doctrine of Discovery.

1098.14   (first) Peirce Patent] The first "Peirce Patent" was issued to John Peirce in February 1620 by the Virginia Company of London, authorizing a particular plantation within the bounds of the Virginia Company, in the jurisdiction of Jamestown.

1098.16–17   second Peirce Patent] This Patent, granted by the Council for New England in 1621, authorized the development of a plantation in that "country of New England," within the limited time of seven years. This patent also authorized the formation of a local government among the settlers at Patuxet/Plymouth.

1098.18   Charter of New England] King James I issued the Charter of New England in 1620 to the Council for New England, a joint-stock company led by Ferdinando Gorges and other merchant-speculators in England. The Council issued both the second Peirce Patent (in 1621) and the Warwick/Bradford Patent in 1629 to William Bradford and other Plymouth Colony settlers. The council held the royal patent and granted the right to continue to settle their particular plantation to Bradford and his associates.

1099.17   "manured"] Cultivated.

Index

This book is set in 10 point ITC Galliard, a face designed
for digital composition by Matthew Carter and based
on the sixteenth-century face Granjon. The paper is acid-free
lightweight opaque that will not turn yellow or brittle with age.
The binding is sewn, which allows the book to open easily and lie flat.
The binding board is covered in Brillianta, a woven rayon cloth
made by Van Heek–Scholco Textielfabrieken, Holland.
Composition by Publishers' Design and Production Services, Inc.
Printing by Sheridan Grand Rapids, Grand Rapids, MI.
Binding by Dekker Bookbinding, Wyoming, MI.
Designed by Bruce Campbell.

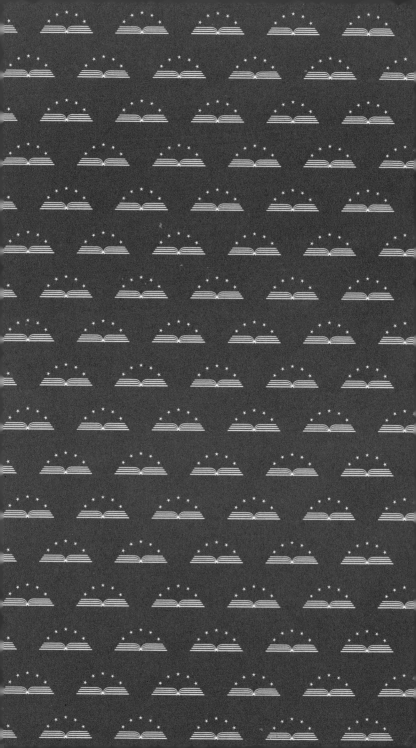